THE CAMBRIDGE HANDBOOK OF SHAREHOLDER ENGAGEMENT AND VOTING

The global economy is driven by companies that create wealth. Of the various stakeholders that influence the fortunes of a company, the role played by shareholders is pivotal. In return for financing a company's activities, shareholders have a say on how it should be organized and how its activities should be structured. They do this primarily through voting and engagement. The mechanisms governing their participation allow shareholders to decide significant aspects of a company's structure, ranging from who governs it to how much its directors are paid. However, different countries take different approaches to how shareholders vote and engage, and how far their rights stretch. This pioneering book examines the voting and engagement of shareholders in nineteen different jurisdictions (including the United States and China), and discusses how the shareholders of companies participate in corporate life through voting and engagement. Comparative and international in scope, it illustrates with vivid examples how the approaches taken by jurisdictions around the world align and differ.

Harpreet Kaur is Professor of Law and Director of the Centre for Corporate Law and Governance at National Law University Delhi. She teaches corporate law, securities and antitrust laws. She has been a Fulbright Scholar in Residence at MDC, Miami, and Fulbright Nehru Academic and Professional Excellence Scholar at Emory Law School, USA. She has co-authored and edited many law books and has conducted research in her areas of expertise.

Chao Xi is Professor and Associate Dean (Research), and chairs the CCTL Corporate Law and Governance Cluster at the Chinese University of Hong Kong Faculty of Law. He is author of *Corporate Governance and Legal Reform in China* (Willy, Simmons & Hill, 2009) and co-authors *Doing Business in China* (Routledge, 3rd ed. 2009; 4th ed. 2016). His empirical research on shareholder voting and engagement has attracted significant funding support from funding agencies and regulatory bodies.

Christoph Van der Elst was among the first scholars studying shareholder voting and engagement (see 'Attendance of Shareholders' in *European Business Organization Law Review*, 2004) and has built a long track record in this research field. He is Professor of Business Law and Economics at Tilburg University and Ghent University, and as an independent director and member of an audit committee he is also familiar with how corporate voting and governance work in action.

Anne Lafarre is Associate Professor at Tilburg University, the Netherlands and programme director of the Joint Bachelor's Program in Data Science (with the Technical University of Eindhoven, the Netherlands). She received a personal research grant from the Dutch organization NWO to study the role of shareholders in sustainability from June 2021 onwards (four-year project). Her research interests are sustainable finance, corporate governance, corporate law and the application of (new and classical) empirical methods in legal research.

The Cambridge Handbook of Shareholder Engagement and Voting

Edited by

HARPREET KAUR

National Law University Delhi

CHAO XI

The Chinese University of Hong Kong

CHRISTOPH VAN DER ELST

Tilburg University and Ghent University

ANNE LAFARRE

Tilburg University

CAMBRIDGE UNIVERSITY PRESS

CAMBRIDGE
UNIVERSITY PRESS

Shaftesbury Road, Cambridge CB2 8EA, United Kingdom

One Liberty Plaza, 20th Floor, New York, NY 10006, USA

477 Williamstown Road, Port Melbourne, VIC 3207, Australia

314–321, 3rd Floor, Plot 3, Splendor Forum, Jasola District Centre, New Delhi – 110025, India

103 Penang Road, #05–06/07, Visioncrest Commercial, Singapore 238467

Cambridge University Press is part of Cambridge University Press & Assessment, a department of the University of Cambridge.

We share the University's mission to contribute to society through the pursuit of education, learning and research at the highest international levels of excellence.

www.cambridge.org
Information on this title: www.cambridge.org/9781108823708

DOI: 10.1017/9781108914383

First published 2022
First paperback edition 2024

A catalogue record for this publication is available from the British Library

ISBN 978-1-108-83088-1 Hardback
ISBN 978-1-108-82370-8 Paperback

Contents

Figures

Tables

Contributors

Gaia Balp is Associate Professor of Business Law and a member of the Faculty of the PhD in Legal Studies at Bocconi University, Milan. She has authored a book on proxy advisors and many law journal articles and book chapters, mainly in the fields of corporate law and securities regulation.

Hanne S. Birkmose is Professor at the Department of Law, Aarhus University. Her research areas include company law and corporate governance. In recent years, she has worked in the fields of shareholder activism and the role of institutional shareholders. She is also the author of books on Undertakings for the Collective Investment in Transferable Securities (UCITS) and alternative investment funds.

Rigas G. Giovannopoulos is Assistant Professor of Law at the Law School, Aristotle University of Thessaloniki, Greece, and practises as a qualified lawyer and an accredited mediator. He is a company law expert, member of various expert groups and author of the leading book in Greek on voidable general meeting (GM) resolutions.

Suren Gomtsian is Associate Professor at the School of Law, University of Leeds. His research, which focuses on corporate law and private ordering, has been published in leading academic journals and cited in the *Financial Times*, by the US Court of Appeals (4th Circuit) and the Delaware Court of Chancery.

Gen Goto is Professor of Law at the Graduate Schools for Law and Politics, University of Tokyo. His main field of research is comparative corporate governance, with recent focus on the role of shareholders in Japanese context. His articles in English can be found at http://ssrn.com/author=608493.

Ankita Gupta (JD Osgoode Hall Law School, BBA University of Toronto) is a lawyer licensed to practise law in Ontario and former judicial law clerk for Chief Justice Wagner of the Supreme Court of Canada and Justices Pepall, Brown and Zarnett of the Court of Appeal for Ontario.

Anil Hargovan is Associate Professor in the School of Management and Governance, Australian School of Business at the University of New South Wales, Sydney. He is the former President of the Corporate Law Teachers Association of Australia. He is the foundational author, and co-author, of *Australian Corporate Law* (7th ed., LexisNexis, 2021).

Chao-Tsung Huang is Partner of Chen & Lin Attorneys-at-Law. His practice focuses on commercial matters. In addition to acting as a practitioner, he is also Adjunct Professor at

National Tsing Hua University, with multiple academic papers on corporate and securities regulation.

Harpreet Kaur is Professor of Law and Director of the Center for Corporate Law and Governance at National Law University Delhi. She has been a Fulbright Nehru Scholar at Emory Law School and Fulbright Scholar in Residence at Miami Dade College, USA. Her research interests include corporate law, corporate governance, securities market and antitrust laws.

Vikramaditya S. Khanna is Professor of Law at the University of Michigan Law School. His interests include corporate and securities laws, corporate crime, law in India and law and economics. He is co-author of a leading text on the law of business organizations and has published papers in the *Harvard Law Review*, *Journal of Finance* and *Michigan Law Review* amongst others.

Berte-Elen Konow is Professor of Law at the University of Bergen (Vice Dean 2013–17). Her publications cover various areas of commercial law such as the law of obligation, secured transactions, comparative law and private international law. She took part in preparing DCFR IV B on Lease of Goods and was a member of the editorial board of Restatement of Nordic Contract Law.

Anne Lafarre is Associate Professor at Tilburg University, the Netherlands and programme director of the Joint Bachelor's Program in Data Science (with the Technical University of Eindhoven, the Netherlands). She received a personal research grant from the Dutch organization NWO to study the role of shareholders in sustainability from June 2021 onwards (four-year project). Her research interests are sustainable finance, corporate governance, corporate law and the application of (new and classical) empirical methods in legal research.

Lauren Yu-Hsin Lin is Associate Professor of Law at City University of Hong Kong and holds a JSD degree from Stanford University. Her research focuses on corporate law and governance and relies on empirical data and economic theories to dissect and understand the effect of different governance and regulatory measures on corporations.

Florian Möslein is Director of the Institute for Law and Regulation of Digitalization and Professor of Law at the Philipps-University Marburg. He has published three monographs and over eighty articles and book contributions, and has edited seven books. His current research focus is on regulatory theory, corporate sustainability and the legal challenges of the digital age.

Kartika Paramita is Assistant Professor in the International Business Law Program, Universitas Prasetiya Mulya, Indonesia. She is a member of the Indonesian Bar Association and graduated from the Master of Commercial Law Program of Erasmus University Rotterdam, the Netherlands, with a specialization in Maritime and Transport Law.

Ulya Yasmine Prisandani is Assistant Professor in the International Business Law Program, Universitas Prasetiya Mulya, Indonesia and a member of the Indonesian Bar Association. She holds an Advanced LLM degree from Leiden University, and has published several books and articles on the topic of corporate and commercial law.

Poonam Puri (LLB University of Toronto, LLM Harvard) is Full Professor of Law at Osgoode Hall Law School and former Associate Dean and Associate Dean Research. She is an internationally recognized scholar in corporate governance, corporate law and securities law. She is the Co-Founder and Director of Osgoode Investor Protection Clinic and Founder and Director of the Business Law LLM at Osgoode Professional Development.

Christopher Rennig is Postdoctoral Researcher at the Institute for Law and Regulation of Digitalization, Philipps-University Marburg. He wrote his dissertation on FinTech in supervisory law (Marburg, 2021). He passed the second state exam (Darmstadt, 2021) and first state exam (Marburg, 2015), and is editor-in-chief of *Recht Digital*.

Karsten Engsig Sørensen is Professor at the Department of Law, Aarhus University, Denmark. He holds a Danish law degree, an LLM (from Exeter), a PhD (on EU company law) and a Danish Dr Jur (on joint ventures). His research is mainly focused on EU law and company law, and within these areas he has published several books and articles in both Danish and English.

Giovanni Strampelli is Full Professor of Business Law and Director of the PhD in Legal Studies at Bocconi University, Milan. He teaches and writes in the areas of corporate law, accounting law, bankruptcy law and securities regulation. He is author of two books and more than 100 law journal articles and book chapters.

Roman Tomasic is Professor of Law in Justice and Society at the University of South Australia and a Visiting Professor at Durham Law School. He is a Fellow of the Australian Academy of Law and has published widely on corporate law and insolvency topics both in Australia and internationally.

Vassilios D. Tountopoulos is Full Professor of Law at the University of the Aegean and a member of the scientific committee of various legal journals. He is an active lawyer at the Greek Supreme Court. He has served as a member of various expert groups. He has also served as a non/executive member of the board of directors of various companies.

Chang-Hsien Tsai (LLB, LLM, National Taiwan University; LLM in Corporate Law, New York University School of Law; JSD, University of Illinois College of Law) is Professor of Law and Business at National Tsing Hua University, Taiwan. His research interests focus on comparative corporate law and comparative financial regulation.

Christoph Van der Elst is Professor of Business Law and Economics at Tilburg University, the Netherlands, Professor at Ghent University, Belgium and is a European Corporate Governance Institute research associate. His current research interests are corporate governance, corporate voting, company law and DLT, all topics on which he has published widely in academic and professional journals.

Wai Yee Wan is Associate Dean and Professor at the School of Law, City University of Hong Kong. Her main areas of research are in global restructuring and insolvency, corporate law, mergers and acquisitions and securities regulation. Her publications have appeared in books and in several international peer-reviewed legal journals and she has received several external grants for research projects in Hong Kong and Singapore.

Chao Xi is Professor and Outstanding Fellow at the Faculty of Law, the Chinese University of Hong Kong (CUHK), where he concurrently serves as Associate Dean (Research) and Head of

Graduate Division of Law. He also chairs the CUHK LAW's CCTL Corporate Law and Governance Cluster.

Seung Young Yoon is Associate Professor at the Law School, Hankuk University of Foreign Studies. He served as Vice Dean of the Law School from 2019–20. Professor Yoon received an LLB from the Hankuk University of Foreign Studies and LLM and JSD from the Washington University in St Louis School of Law. He is admitted to the DC Bar.

Preface

Shareholder engagement and voting are considered pivotal features of corporate governance across nations. Relationships between shareholders and companies are broadly governed by corporate laws and corporate governance codes. The decision-making in a company is generally left to the wisdom of directors and managers of companies by shareholders. The problem relating to shareholder engagement and voting gets acknowledged when corporate governance standards are framed and, therefore, efforts are made to improve shareholder engagement and voting to ensure that shareholders can participate in decision-making and take informed decisions. Different means and methods for engagement and voting are provided by corporate laws and corporate governance codes to shareholders to protect their interests and add value to decision-making. Against this background, the *Handbook* re-examines shareholders' position and role and presents readers with a comparative view regarding the exercise of voting rights by different classes of shareholders through a variety of instruments. The *Handbook* employs a fully comparative approach for which the chapter authors were provided with guidelines containing a specific set of theoretical and practical questions. It seeks to provide a broader understanding of current issues and provides information about practices adopted for improving shareholder engagement in companies in select jurisdictions covered in the book.

The *Handbook* is divided into four Parts. Part I covers eight Asian jurisdictions, including China (Mainland), Hong Kong, India, Indonesia, Japan, Singapore, South Korea and Taiwan. Part II addresses Australia and North America including the jurisdictions of Australia, Canada and the United States. Part III contains jurisdiction-specific studies on eight European economies, namely Denmark, France, Germany, Greece, Italy, Norway, the Netherlands and the United Kingdom. Each of the chapters in Parts I, II and III focuses only on one jurisdiction. Part IV covers three comparative chapters which provide answers to the main central question of the *Handbook* along with the concluding chapter.

The writing process of the *Handbook* involved two international conferences held in 2019 and 2020, respectively, at National Law University Delhi and virtually at the Chinese University of Hong Kong's Faculty of Law, in collaboration with Tilburg University, the Netherlands. The process also coincided with the Covid-19 pandemic, which presented our contributors with great difficulties and challenges. The editors acknowledge the hard work of all chapter contributors and would like to express their gratitude to them.

The editors want to give their formal acknowledgements to the Scheme for Promotion of Academic and Research Collaboration (SPARC), Ministry of Human Resource and Development, Government of India, the Hong Kong SAR Research Grants Council (General Research Fund CUHK-14613616), the Chinese University of Hong Kong's Faculty of Law,

Tilburg Law School (Tilburg University) and the National Law University Delhi for their support in completing this work. They are also thankful to Yurong Huang and Sirui Han for their excellent editorial assistance, and to all other research associates and support colleagues. The editors would also like to express their profound gratitude to Joe Ng at Cambridge University Press for his unwavering support.

The editors have consistently worked for almost two years presenting the *Handbook* to a wider readership. Each of the four co-editors has contributed equally to the editorial work. The editorial team is happy to present to you *The Cambridge Handbook of Shareholder Engagement and Voting.*

In Memoriam

The corporate and insolvency law community of scholars are saddened by the news of Roman's passing in July 2022, succumbing to illness shortly after completion of his contribution to this book. Roman was an intellectual giant, successfully combining his sociological and legal background to present ground-breaking work in comparative and international aspects of corporate and insolvency law. His empirical scholarship, with a special interest in the Chinese and East Asian legal systems, remains highly influential. Roman's contribution to Australian corporate law was invaluable. He was the founding editor of the Australian Journal of Corporate Law (1991–2007) and a foundational member of the Society of Corporate Law Scholars (formerly the Corporate Law Teachers Association). A quietly kind man and an independent thinker, colleagues learned a great deal from Roman, who will be sorely missed.

It was a privilege to work with Roman on this book chapter. I am grateful for his intellectual insights, which have made our book chapter much better than it might otherwise have been.

Anil Hargovan
Also on behalf of the Editorial Team
20 July 2022

Abbreviations

ACCR	Australian Centre for Corporate Responsibility
ACSI	Australian Council of Superannuation Investors
AFEP	Association française des entreprises privées (French Association of Private Enterprises)
AG	Aktiengesellschaft
AGM	annual general meeting
ASEAN	Association of South East Asian Nations
ASIC	Australian Securities and Investments Commission
ASX	Australian Stock Exchange
AoA	articles of association
AoI	articles of incorporation
AUM	assets under management
BCIMC	British Columbia Investment Management Corporation
BGB	Bürgerliches Gesetzbuch (German Civil Code)
BGH	Bundesgerichtshof (Federal Court of Germany)
BMAA	Business Mergers and Acquisitions Act
BoC	board of commissioners
BoD	board of directors
CAHL	China Assets Holdings Ltd
CAIML	China Assets Investment Management Ltd
CBCA	Canada Business Corporations Act
CCASS	Central Clearing and Automated Settlement System
CDP	Central Depository
CEO	chief executive officer
CGFC	Corporate Governance of Financial Companies Act
CII	Council of Institutional Investors
CKI	Cheung Kong Infrastructure Holdings Ltd
CLF	Consolidated Law on Finance
CLFRC	Company Legislation and Framework Committee
CMS	controlling minority structure
CPA	Chartered Professional Accountants (Canada)
CPPIB	Canadian Pension Plan Investment Board
CSA	Canadian Securities Administrators
CSR	corporate social responsibility

CSISC	China Securities Investor Services Centre
CSRC	China Securities Regulatory Commission
DCC	Dutch Civil Code
DCGC	Dutch Corporate Governance Code 2016
DCGK	German Corporate Governance Code
DCS	dual-class shares
DGCL	Delaware General Corporation Law
DVR	differential voting rights
EDF	Électricité de France
EFAMA	European Fund and Asset Management Association
EGM	extraordinary general meeting
ESG	environmental, social and governance
ESP	environmental, social and political
EU	European Union
FDI	foreign direct investment
FII	foreign institutional investor
FISCMA	Financial Investment Services and Capital Markets Act
FSC	Financial Services Commission / Financial Supervisory Commission
FSCMA-E	Enforcement Decree of the FSCMA
FY	financial year
GCA	Greek Company Act
GL	Glass, Lewis & Co.
GM	general meeting
GmbH	Gesellschaft mit beschränkter Haftung
GMS	general meeting of shareholders
HCGE	High Committee of Corporate Governance
HCMC	Hellenic Capital Market Commission
HKET	Hong Kong Economic Times Holdings Ltd
HKSCC	Hong Kong Securities Clearing Company
HKSCCN	Hong Kong Securities Clearing Company Nominees
HKSE	Hong Kong Stock Exchange
ICL	Indonesian Company Law
ICSA	Institute of Chartered Secretaries and Administrators
IDX	Indonesia Stock Exchange
IFA	independent financial adviser
IGOPP	Institute for Governance of Public and Private Organizations
INED	independent non-executive director
IPO	initial public offering
IPT	interested party transaction
ISS	Institutional Shareholder Services
JPY	Japanese yen
KCC	Korean Commercial Code
KCGI	Korea Corporate Governance Improvement Fund
KGaA	Kommanditgesellschaft auf Aktien
KLCA	Korea Listed Companies Association
KMP	key managerial personnel
KOSDAQ	Korea Securities Dealers Automated Quotations

KOSPI	Korean Composite Stock Price Index
KRW	Korean won
KRX	Korea Exchange
KSD	Korea Securities Depository
KSEI	Kustodian Sentral Efek Indonesia
KT&G	Korea Tobacco & Ginseng Corporation
LLC	limited liability company
LLSV	La Porta, Lopez-de-Silanes, Shleifer and Vishny
M&A	merger and acquisition
MBO	management buy-outs
MCA	Ministry of Corporate Affairs (India)
MEDEF	Movement of the Enterprises of France
METI	Ministry of Economy, Trade and Industry (Japan)
MOEA	Ministry of Economic Affairs (Taiwan)
MOF	Ministry of Finance (Taiwan)
MOJ	Ministry of Justice (Japan)
MoM	majority of the minority
NBIM	Norway Government Pension Fund Global
NCLT	National Company Law Tribunal
NGO	non-governmental organization
NOK	Norwegian kronor
NPC	National People's Congress
NPCSC	National People's Congress Standing Committee
NPS	National Pension Service (Korea)
NSSF	National Social Security Fund
NTD	New Taiwan dollar
OECD	Organisation for Economic Cooperation and Development
OJK	*Otoritas Jasa Keuangan* (Indonesian Financial Services Authority)
OSOV	one-share-one-vote
OTE	Hellenic Telecommunications Organisation
OTPP	Ontario Teachers' Pension Plan
P&PG	promoter and promoter group
PAF	proxy advisory firm
PDG	President-directeur-général
PDPD	People's Solidarity for Participatory Democracy
PRC	People's Republic of China
Q&A	question and answer
QFII	Qualified Foreign Institutional Investor
RMB	Chinese renminbi
RPT	related-party transaction
SA	Société Anonyme
SCA	Sociétés en commandite par actions
SE	Societas Europaea
SEA	Securities and Exchange Act (Taiwan)
SEB	Securities and Exchange Board of India
SEC	US Securities and Exchange Commission
SEHK	Stock Exchange of Hong Kong

SFC	Securities and Futures Commission
SFIPC	Securities and Futures Investors Protection Center
SGX	Singapore Exchange
SHSE	Shanghai Stock Exchange
SIAS	Securities Investors Association (Singapore)
SOEL	Law No. 19 of 2003 Concerning State-Owned Enterprises
SRD	Shareholder Rights Directive
SRD II	Revised Shareholder Rights Directive
SRI	socially responsible investment
SSGA	State Street Global Advisors
SVR	superior voting rights
SZSE	Shenzhen Stock Exchange
TSX	Toronto Stock Exchange
TSX-V	TSX Venture Exchange
TWSE	Taiwan Stock Exchange
UCITS	undertakings for collective investment in transferable securities
UG	Unternehmergesellschaft
UK	United Kingdom
USA	United States of America
USD	United States dollar
VEB	Association for Securities Holders
VBDO	Shareholder Association for Sustainable Development (Dutch)
WpÜG	Wertpapierübertragungsgesetz

Introduction

1

Shareholder Voting and Engagement

An Introduction

Chao Xi and Anne Lafarre

1.1 INTRODUCTION

Few topics have received greater attention in the current corporate law and governance discourse than shareholder voting and shareholder engagement, especially concerning institutional investors. Institutional investors have become an important shareholder class in many jurisdictions, and the shares of many companies are aggregated in the portfolios of large asset managers. Therefore, emphasis is increasingly being placed on institutional shareholder stewardship and accountability.[1] In particular, the spectacular increase in assets under the management of large US institutional investors has forced these investors to expand their portfolios into foreign markets, creating large ownership stakes in many markets around the globe.[2] Economic globalization and capital market internationalization have thus served as a key driving force for the adoption of common principles, rules and practice in respect of shareholder engagement in many jurisdictions around the globe.[3] In addition, retail shareholders have also been called upon to depart from their traditional passive role and to exercise proactively their rights to vote.[4] It is no exaggeration to say that shareholder engagement and voting are generally considered to be a pivotal feature of good and effective corporate governance.[5] Despite the broad convergence towards an increasing role for shareholders in governance, however, considerable national differences remain, as this Handbook demonstrates, depending on nation-specific and path-dependent settings such as the division of powers between the corporate boards, shareholders and other corporate constituencies (e.g. worker unions), and also on differences in shareholder and ownership structures and types.

This research was partially supported by a General Research Fund (CUHK-14613616) from the Hong Kong SAR Research Grants Council.

1 See e.g. Jennifer G. Hill, 'Good Activist/Bad Activist: The Rise of International Stewardship Codes' (2018) 41 Seattle University Law Review 497; Lucian Bebchuk and Scott Hirst, 'Index Funds and the Future of Corporate Governance: Theory, Evidence, and Policy' (2019) 119 Columbia Law Review 2029.

2 Edward B. Rock and Marcel Kahan, 'Index Funds and Corporate Governance: Let Shareholders Be Shareholders' (2020) 100 Boston University Law Review 1771.

3 Reena Aggarwal et al., 'Does Governance Travel Around the World? Evidence from Institutional Investors' (2011) 100 Journal of Financial Economics 154; Peter Iliev et al., 'Shareholder Voting and Corporate Governance Around the World' (2015) 28 The Review of Financial Studies 2167.

4 Jill E. Fisch, 'Standing Voting Instructions: Empowering the Excluded Retail Investor' (2018) 102 Minnesota Law Review 11.

5 OECD, *G20/OECD Principles of Corporate Governance* (OECD Publishing 2015) 29. See also Directive 2007/36/EC of the European Parliament and of the Council of 11 July 2007 on the Exercise of Certain Rights of Shareholders in Listed Companies [2007] OJ L184/17 (SRD I), preamble (3); Directive (EU) 2017/828 of the European Parliament and of the Council of 17 May 2017 amending Directive 2007/36/EC as regards the Encouragement of Long-Term Shareholder Engagement [2017] OJ L132/1 (SRD II).

The Handbook seeks to re-examine corporate law and corporate governance from the viewpoint of the position and role of shareholders, taking a comparative and global perspective. More specifically, it examines how different types of shareholders make use of their voting rights and other engagement instruments within their own jurisdictions' legal, regulatory and broader institutional contexts. The Handbook aims to contribute to current academic and policy debates by providing a broad, comparative, evidence-based understanding of current issues in major jurisdictions around the world.

In general, non-controlling shareholders in publicly traded companies, when dissatisfied with the ways in which their invested companies are run, can consider three courses of action.[6] They can either (1) take the 'Wall Street Walk' and sell; (2) remain (rationally) passive; or (3) exercise their voice and seek greater engagement. Traditionally, small public shareholders have tended to choose either the first or second option.[7] However, the rise of institutional investors and a greater consciousness among shareholders of their rights have recently made engagement and voting an increasingly attractive option, or even a duty.[8]

The term 'shareholder engagement' covers the third situation where shareholders become actively involved with their investee companies, using their shareholder rights and powers, both formal and informal, to influence corporate affairs. Perhaps the most important form of shareholder engagement is shareholder voting, which takes place at the general meetings of shareholders. As Easterbrook and Fischel put it, 'if limited liability is the most distinctive feature of corporate law, voting is second'.[9] In virtually every jurisdiction, shareholders have voting rights.[10] Besides voting, shareholders can also potentially make use of a wide range of non-litigious engagement instruments. These methods range from submitting shareholder proposals to initiating or supporting a proxy contest; from private on-site visits to a threat to exit; from direct, behind-the-scene meetings and communications with the board and the management to openly questioning and criticizing the management (e.g. at general meetings or by mounting media campaigns).[11] The choice between a collaborative and confrontational tactic varies from case to case, and is usually determined at firm level by the relationship between the shareholders and their engagement targets.

1.2 METHODOLOGICAL CONSIDERATIONS

The Handbook conscientiously embraces a sophisticated functionalist approach. First and foremost, the comparative methodology of the Handbook consists mostly of a functionalist

6 Borrowing the frame of Albert O. Hirschman, *Exit, Voice, and Loyalty: Responses to Decline in Firms, Organizations, and States* (Harvard University Press 1970). Exit refers to an economic market-based response where the unsatisfied shareholder leaves the company. In comparison, voice represents a political response using communication in an attempt to rectify performance lapses.

7 Adolf Augustus Berle and Gardiner Coit Means, *The Modern Corporation and Private Property* (rev. ed., Harcourt, Brace & World 1968).

8 See e.g. Hanne S. Birkmose and Konstantinos Sergakis, *Enforcing Shareholders' Duties* (Edgward Elgar 2019); Directive (EU) 2017/828 (n. 5).

9 Frank H. Easterbrook and Daniel R. Fischel, *The Economic Structure of Corporate Law* (Harvard University Press 1996) 63.

10 A major exception is the non-voting share arrangement. See Dorothy S. Lund, 'Nonvoting Shares and Efficient Corporate Governance' (2019) 71 Stanford Law Review 687.

11 Willard T. Carleton, James M. Nelson and Michael S. Weisbach, 'The Influence of Institutions on Corporate Governance through Private Negotiations: Evidence from TIAA-CREF' (1998) 53 Journal of Finance 1335; Marco Becht et al., 'Returns to Shareholder Activism: Evidence from a Clinical Study of the Hermes UK Focus Fund' (2010) 23 The Review of Financial Studies 3093; Joseph A. McCahery, Zacharias Sautner and Laura T. Starks, 'Behind the Scenes: The Corporate Governance Preferences of Institutional Investors' (2016) 71 Journal of Finance 2905.

approach.[12] The central functional question of this Handbook concerns the shareholders' (shifting) position and role in corporate law and corporate governance. More specifically, it is about how shareholders make use of their voting rights and other engagement instruments to influence the conduct of affairs in their investee companies. It is this functional inquiry that guides the formulation of the Handbook's analytical framework (Section 1.3 of the present Chapter), which in turn intellectually drives the assessment of shareholder voting and engagement in the Handbook's jurisdiction-based studies, as well as its comparative analysis (Chapters 2–23). To be sure, opinions differ markedly on whether shareholders in public companies should be empowered to effect major corporate changes.[13] However, there seems to be a trend in many jurisdictions around the world favouring the enhancement of shareholder rights, both generally in respect of their invested public companies, and particularly in terms of greater institutional investor stewardship of their portfolio companies. More fundamentally, modern corporate law jurisprudence assumes that shareholders are generally entitled to have some say on how (at least certain fundamental) affairs of their investee companies are managed. Virtually all modern corporate law regimes are faced with the problem of resolving how engaged shareholders *can* vote and otherwise engage with the companies in which they invest. The chapter contributions to the Handbook have therefore all sought to address this functional problem, enabling a 'deep' comparative analysis of convergences and divergences in Chapters 21–23 in the Handbook. By focusing strongly on the central functional problem, the Handbook ensures that it does not become bogged down prematurely in ideological debates.

The Handbook aims to provide generally useful perspectives, while also being sensitive to significant local differences, in light of the starkly divergent legal systems and traditions, capital market structures and share ownership patterns around the globe. As such, while the nineteen jurisdiction-based reports all set out to address the common framework of research questions (Section 1.3 of the present Chapter), they also examine at length the legal traditions, ownership structures, dominant shareholder types and other jurisdiction-specific conditions in their respective jurisdictions. This results in rich descriptions of a wide variety of legal (and extralegal) doctrines, principles, approaches, techniques and tactics developed in different jurisdictions, as summarized in the comparative Chapters 21–22. Importantly, these jurisdiction-specific approaches are placed in the economic, ideological, historical, cultural and political contexts which shaped them. These broader institutional idiosyncrasies also inform the Handbook's discussions of how legal (and extralegal) rules, techniques and tactics are actually used by shareholders to engage their investee companies. Overall, the Handbook takes a holistic methodological approach, looking not only at what the rules governing shareholder voting and engagement are in the nineteen jurisdictions it studies, but also how these rules have been shaped and are used in practice.

The Handbook's use of doctrinal and empirical methods is also mixed. While nuanced doctrinal analysis of the jurisdictions' legal rules and techniques is central to its contents, the nineteen expert reports and the comparative analysis either draw on the findings of prior empirical research or conduct original empirical research of their own. The Handbook takes the position that some research questions can best be answered with reference to empirical

[12] '[I]ncomparables cannot be usefully compared and in the law the only things which are comparable are those which fulfil the same function'. Following Mathias Siems, *Comparative Law* (Cambridge University Press 2018) 33. See, more generally, Konrad Zweigert and Hein Kötz, *Introduction to Comparative Law* (Tony Weir tr., 3rd rev. ed., Clarendon Press 1998).

[13] Lucian Arye Bebchuk, 'The Case for Increasing Shareholder Power' (2005) 118 Harvard Law Review 833. Cf. Stephen M. Bainbridge, 'Director Primacy and Shareholder Disempowerment' (2006) 119 Harvard Law Review 1735.

evidence. For instance, an evaluation of the effectiveness of the legal rules on shareholders' initiation rights (e.g. the right to make shareholder proposals) would ideally consider evidence for the turnout of minority shareholders at the general meetings, insofar as these data are readily available. Clearly, the shareholder right to initiate a proposal can be meaningless in practice if a jurisdiction sets the threshold for proposing a shareholder resolution at 10 per cent of the company's shares, while the average minority voter turnout is typically far lower than that figure.

The Handbook's nineteen jurisdiction reports therefore follow a common analytical framework with specific topical categories. As will be discussed at greater length in the comparative Chapters 21–23, this collaborative endeavour by the jurisdiction experts yields fresh insights on substantial convergences and divergences among nineteen major jurisdictions in four continents. Together they offer a truly global perspective on some of the most debated current issues in comparative corporate law and governance.

1.3 FRAMEWORK OF RESEARCH QUESTIONS

The Handbook's focus on the position and role of shareholders in corporate law and corporate governance is reflected in the way we have divided our research questions, and related research topics for our contributors, into three parts. Part I addresses the particular characteristics of these jurisdictions, including their capital market structures, ownership and corporate governance model. Part II relates to the legal framework of shareholder voting and engagement, with a special focus on general meetings. Part III concerns the law in action, and considers the use of shareholder voting rights, voting modes and other engagement mechanisms. The specific research questions addressed in the three Parts are described below.

1.3.1 *General Jurisdictional Features (Part I)*

This Part sets the contextual stage for the discussions of specific laws, regulations and practices in respect of shareholder voting and engagement. It also discusses broader topics, including the pattern of ownership concentration in different jurisdictions, shareholder types, attributes of the company's board and the demarcation of power between the board and the shareholders.

1.3.1.1 Ownership Concentration

Most previous studies of corporate governance have tended to assume that the dispersed ownership of American public companies, as described by Berle and Means in their seminal work in 1932, is the model behind most modern corporations.[14] Comparative corporate governance studies in the past three decades have, however, repeatedly called that assumption into question. For instance, drawing upon their case studies of corporate ownership in the UK, France and Germany, Franks and Mayer in 1995 made an important distinction between two types of ownership structures: the 'outsider system' seen in the USA and the UK, where share ownership is dispersed, and the 'insider system' in many other jurisdictions, where ownership concentration is remarkably higher.[15] Franks and Mayer's insights have been extended in the seminal works of La Porta, Lopez-de-Silanes, Shleiffer and Vishny, which find that, in global terms, state- and family-controlled firms are far more common than Berle-and-Means

[14] See n. 7.

[15] Julian Franks and Colin Mayer, 'Ownership and Control' in Horst Siebert (ed.), *Trends In Business Organization: Do Participation and Cooperation Increase Competitiveness?* (University of Michigan Press 1995).

corporations, and that a jurisdiction's legal origin (civil law versus common law) is strongly correlated with its prevailing ownership structure.[16] Further studies have since shown that ownership patterns in continental Europe[17] and Asian countries[18] are generally more concentrated than in Anglo-Saxon countries.[19] Recent empirical research has also highlighted the pervasive role of government and family control, notably in civil law jurisdictions.[20] It is also interesting to note the recent institutionalization of securities markets and the reconcentration of ownership in institutional investors, particularly in the US markets, which has given rise to the phenomenon known as 'the agency costs of agency capitalism'.[21]

The existence of national differences in respect of ownership structures has important implications for corporate governance. Agency problems of conflicting goals and opportunistic behaviour exist not only between managers and shareholders, but also in the relationships between small shareholders and controlling blockholders.[22] The types of legal strategies for controlling the principal-agent conflicts can therefore differ fundamentally across jurisdictions, depending heavily on their prevailing structures of shareholder ownership.[23] For instance, blockholders may be tempted to use their majority stake to maximize their own private benefits rather than acting in the interests of the welfare of the shareholders as a whole,[24] or, to put it another way, to extract the private benefits of control.[25] Thus, in a jurisdiction where blockholder ownership (either by a government or a family) is prevalent, the legal system may concern itself less with the opportunistic behaviour of management (vis-à-vis the shareholders) than with that of the blockholder (vis-à-vis the minority or outsider shareholders).

Given these important differences between jurisdictions in terms of ownership structures, we asked the contributors to this Handbook to provide information, and, if possible, data about the typical ownership structure (widely dispersed or concentrated) of listed companies in their jurisdiction.

16 Rafael La Porta et al., 'Legal Determinants of External Finance' (1997) 52 Journal of Finance 1131; Rafael La Porta et al., 'Law and Finance' (1998) 106 Journal of Political Economy 1113; Rafael La Porta, Florencio Lopez-de-Silanes and Andrei Shleifer, 'Corporate Ownership Around the World' (1999) 54 Journal of Finance 471. For critiques of the legal origin theory, see Holger Spamann, 'The "Antidirector Rights Index" Revisited' (2010) 23 The Review of Financial Studies 467.

17 Christoph Van der Elst, 'Shareholder Mobility in Five European Countries' (2008) ECGI – Law Working Paper No. 104/2008 https://papers.ssrn.com/sol3/papers.cfm?abstract_id=1123108 accessed 5 May 2021.

18 Stijn Claessens, Simeon Djankov and Larry H. P. Lang, 'The Separation of Ownership and Control in East Asian Corporations' (2000) 58 Journal of Financial Economics 81; Richard W. Carney and Travers Barclay Child, 'Changes to the Ownership and Control of East Asian Corporations Between 1996 and 2008: The Primacy of Politics' (2013) 107 Journal of Financial Economics 494.

19 Cf. Clifford G. Holderness, 'The Myth of Diffuse Ownership in the United States' (2009) 22 The Review of Financial Studies 1377. See also Brian R. Cheffins, *Corporate Ownership and Control: British Business Transformed* (Oxford University Press 2008).

20 Adriana De La Cruz, Alejandra Medina, and Yun Tang, 'Owners of the World's Listed Companies' (2019) OECD Capital Market Series www.oecd.org/corporate/Owners-of-the-Worlds-Listed-Companies.htm accessed 3 May 2021. See also Gur Aminadav and Elias Papaioannou, 'Corporate Control around the World' (2020) 75 Journal of Finance 1191.

21 Ronald J. Gilson and Jeffrey N. Gordon, 'The Agency Costs of Agency Capitalism: Activist Investors and the Revaluation of Governance Rights' (2013) 113 Columbia Law Review 863; Scott Hirst and Lucian Bebchuk, 'The Specter of the Giant Three' (2019) 99 Boston University Law Review 721.

22 There is a third type of agency problems between the firm's shareholders and its stakeholders.

23 John Armour, Henry Hansmann and Reinier Kraakman, 'Agency Problems and Legal Strategies' in Reinier Kraakman et al., *The Anatomy of Corporate Law* (3rd ed., Oxford University Press 2017).

24 The trade-off here is that the presence of a controlling shareholder may reduce the managerial agency problem. See Ronald J. Gilson and Jeffrey N. Gordon, 'Controlling Controlling Shareholders' (2003) 152 University of Pennsylvania Law Review 785.

25 Alexander Dyck and Luigi Zingales, 'Private Benefits of Control: An International Comparison' (2004) 59 Journal of Finance 537.

1.3.1.2 Shareholder Types

Ownership concentration is not the only important factor here. Different shareholder types can also have varying levels and kinds of impact on shareholder voting and engagement. Take institutional investors for instance. Public pension funds can be sensitive to incentives and pressures (such as local economy and employment) to which other types of institutional investors may be indifferent.[26] Hedge funds are known to have played a more activist role than index funds, for example.[27] A particular contextual consideration is the stewardship requirement that holds certain types of institutional investors accountable for their ultimate investors, to which they own a fiduciary duty. In the USA, the SEC has required US-registered investment advisers to adopt policies and procedures to ensure that proxies vote in the best interests of ultimate beneficiaries, and to also provide beneficiaries with information about how these proxies have voted.[28] In the European Union too, the Revised Shareholder Rights Directive (SRD II) requires institutional investors and asset managers to disclose their engagement policies and the implementation of these policies on a comply-or-explain basis.[29] Similarly, the UK Stewardship Code establishes a framework to determine the monitoring role for institutional investors, namely asset owners and asset managers.[30] Principle 6 of the Stewardship Code states that 'institutional investors should seek to vote all shares held'.[31] The role of proxy advisors, which exert much greater influence over votes cast by institutional investors in some jurisdictions (in particular, the US) than in other jurisdictions, is also directly relevant.[32]

Similarly, the motivations for controlling families may not be the same as those for state owners, and they may behave differently in the face of shareholder activism. The government as controlling shareholder may be prone to placing its own (short-term) non-commercial, political agenda (such as political stability, employment and the government's own financial interests) ahead of long-term shareholder welfare.[33] In family-controlled firms, by contrast, family controllers may be motivated to extract value from their controlled firm (by using complex pyramids or cross-shareholding structures),[34] and to reduce managerial agency costs.[35]

To conclude, taking into account the ownership model including different shareholder types is important for a comparative study on shareholder voting and engagement. Therefore, the

[26] Roberta Romano, 'Public Pension Fund Activism in Corporate Governance Reconsidered' (1993) 93 Columbia Law Review 795; Marcel Kahan and Edward B. Rock, 'Hedge Funds in Corporate Governance and Corporate Control' (2007) 155 University of Pennsylvania Law Review 1021. See also David Webber, *The Rise of the Working-Class Shareholder: Labor's Last Best Weapon* (Harvard University Press 2018).

[27] Alon Brav et al., 'Hedge Fund Activism, Corporate Governance, and Firm Performance' (2008) 63 The Journal of Finance 1729. See also Lucian A. Bebchuk et al., 'Dancing with Activists' (2020) 137 Journal of Financial Economics 1.

[28] Securities and Exchange Committees, Final Rule: Proxy Voting by Investment Advisers (2003), 17 CFR Part 275 www.sec.gov/rules/final/ia-2106.htm accessed 6 May 2021. See also Alan R. Palmiter, 'Mutual Fund Voting of Portfolio Shares: Why Not Disclose?' (2002) 23 Cardozo Law Review 1419.

[29] Directive (EU) 2017/828 of the European Parliament and of the Council of 17 May 2017 amending Directive 2007/36/EC as Regards the Encouragement of Long-Term Shareholder Engagement [2017] OJ L 132/1.

[30] The UK Stewardship Code 2012, 2.

[31] See n. 9.

[32] Andrew F. Tuch, 'Proxy Advisor Influence in a Comparative Light' (2019) 99 Boston University Law Review 1459. Cf. Stephen Choi, Jill Fisch and Marcel Kahan, 'The Power of Proxy Advisors: Myth or Reality?' (2010) 59 Emory Law Journal 869.

[33] Victor Nee, Sonja Opper and Sonia Wong, 'Developmental State and Corporate Governance in China' (2007) 3 Management and Organization Review 19. See also Marcel Kahan and Edward Rock, 'When the Government is the Controlling Shareholder' (2011) 89 Texas Law Review 1293.

[34] Claessens, Djankov and Lang (n. 18).

[35] Belen Villalonga and Raphael Amit, 'How Do Family Ownership, Control and Management Affect Firm Value?' (2006) 80 Journal of Financial Economics 385.

contributors provide valuable information in their chapters about the shareholder types typically present in companies in their jurisdictions, including institutional investors, families, pyramid structures and the government.

1.3.1.3 Board Characteristics

The board serves as a focal point for shareholder engagement. It plays an important monitoring role of hiring, firing and assessing the performance of the management. It is also typically tasked with various advisory and managerial functions, such as the setting of the company's strategies and the selection of projects.[36] Hence, if shareholders are dissatisfied with their investee companies' state of affairs or with the direction the companies are taking, the board will act as the interface between shareholders and the management or controlling shareholder. Indeed, board members themselves stand for election at the shareholders' meeting and, in that sense, are held accountable to the shareholders who elect them.

The board-shareholder engagement process is sensitive to various board characteristics, which may differ across jurisdictions. Board structure can potentially affect that process. The one-tier board, two-tier board and some hybrid board structure forms found in different jurisdictions[37] – in tandem with the representation of stakeholders (in particular, employees)[38] – can impact on the way in which shareholder engagement feeds into corporate decision-making. Board composition is also an important consideration. The presence of independent, outside directors on the board and its committees, particularly if they hold leading positions, can help to bridge the gap between shareholders and management,[39] and their monitoring role may also be beneficial to shareholder value.[40] The method of board appointment is a significant variable that determines the strength of shareholder rights. Staggered board[41] and plurality voting,[42] for instance, can help to insulate board members from market and shareholder pressures. By contrast, cumulative voting can help to empower minority shareholders by electing their representatives onto the board and increasing their say in the conduct of the company's affairs.[43]

36 Renée B. Adams, Benjamin E. Hermalin and Michael S. Weisbach, 'The Role of Boards of Directors in Corporate Governance: A Conceptual Framework and Survey' (2010) 48 Journal of Economic Literature 58. See also Miriam Schwartz-Ziv and Michael S. Weisbach, 'What Do Boards Really Do? Evidence from Minutes of Board Meetings' (2013) 108 Journal of Financial Economics 349.

37 Paul L. Davies and Klaus J. Hopt, 'Corporate Boards in Europe – Accountability and Convergence' (2013) 61 American Journal of Comparative Law 301.

38 Larry Fauver and Michael E. Fuerst, 'Does Good Corporate Governance Include Employee Representation? Evidence from German Corporate Boards' (2006) 82 Journal of Financial Economics 673.

39 Amy Freedman, Wes Hall, and Ian Robertson, 'The Director-Shareholder Engagement Guidebook', The Harvard Law School Forum on Corporate Governance (2 March 2019) https://corpgov.law.harvard.edu/2019/03/02/the-director-shareholder-engagement-guidebook/ accessed 7 May 2021.

40 Bang Dang Nguyen and Kasper Meisner Nielsen, 'The Value of Independent Directors: Evidence from Sudden Deaths' (2010) 98 Journal of Financial Economics 550; Reena Aggarwal et al., 'Differences in Governance Practices between U.S. and Foreign Firms: Measurement, Causes, and Consequences' (2009) 22 The Review of Financial Studies 3131; Larry Fauver et al., 'Board Reforms and Firm Value: Worldwide Evidence' (2017) 125 Journal of Financial Economics 120.

41 Lucian Bebchuk, John Coates IV and Guhan Subramanian, 'The Powerful Anti-Takeover Force of Staggered Boards: Theory, Evidence and Policy' (2002) 54 Stanford Law Review 887. Cf. K. J. Martijn Cremers, 'The Shareholder Value of Empowered Boards' (2006) 68 Stanford Law Review 67.

42 Stephen J. Choi et al., 'Does Majority Voting Improve Board Accountability?' (2016) 83 University of Chicago Law Review (2016) 1119.

43 Sanjai Bhagat and James A. Brickley, 'Cumulative Voting: The Value of Minority Shareholder Voting Rights' (1984) 27 The Journal of Law and Economics 339. Cf. Jeffrey N. Gordon, 'Institutions As Relational Investors: A New Look at Cumulative Voting' (1994) 94 Columbia Law Review 124.

Given the differences in the board's role, structure and composition in many jurisdictions, which has amongst others an impact on shareholder voting and engagement, the contributors also address (albeit briefly) the board structure of companies in their jurisdiction, including the board's characteristics and duties.

1.3.1.4 Demarcation of Powers

A closely related issue is the balance of power between the shareholders and the board in respect of corporate decision-making. Shareholders are the residual claimants of the corporation, and naturally wish to maximize the value of their residual claim,[44] albeit research also shows that shareholder preferences can be very heterogenous.[45] In corporate law theory, shareholders are generally assumed to have appropriate incentives to engage in corporate decision-making. Yet, concentrating all corporate powers in the hands of shareholders would be unworkable in (public) companies with numerous and constantly changing shareholders. Moreover, in many jurisdictions, the interest of the company is not defined as the aggregate interests of the shareholders, but considered as a separate interest, often mediating between the differing partial interests of the different stakeholders.[46] This, and the function of representation, create a need to delegate most of the decision-making powers to a centralized board of directors and also to full-time, professional managers. It then becomes necessary to decide which fundamental decisions should be reserved for the shareholders and which should be delegated to the board or its professional managers.[47] Corporate laws in different jurisdictions offer varying solutions to this conundrum. Presumably, shareholders will find it more difficult to have a say on matters reserved for the board under corporate law and, even if they are successful, their voice may not be binding. Say-on-pay serves as a prominent example of this constraint on shareholder engagement in many jurisdictions.[48] Moreover, shareholders often have the ratification or approval rights of a management board proposal (such as the election of board candidates and the aforementioned say-on-pay rights), instead of initiation rights.

The appropriate demarcation of powers between shareholders and the board has been the subject of constant debate between policymakers, academics and other stakeholders, and it is interesting to note that the balance seems to have shifted recently.[49] The USA serves as an important example. There, there is an increasing use of 'private ordering' to expand shareholders' right to participate. So, shareholders, particularly institutional investors, take into their own hands governance rights that are traditionally assigned to the board, thereby shifting the allocation of power between the board and shareholders.[50] Once again, jurisdictions vary in their approaches in this respect.

44 Frank H. Easterbrook and Daniel R. Fischel, 'Voting in Corporate Law' (1983) 26 Journal of Law and Economics 395.

45 See e.g. Patrick Bolton et al., 'Investor Ideology' (2020) 137 Journal of Financial Economics 320.

46 For instance, in Germany, this is called *Unternehmensinteresse* (Andreas Cahn and David C. Donald, *Comparative Company Law* (2nd ed., Cambridge University Press 2018) 396). In the Netherlands, this is referred to as the '*vennootschappelijk belang*'.

47 Klaus J. Hopt, 'Modern Company and Capital Market Problems: Improving European Corporate Governance after Enron' (2003) 3 Journal of Corporate Law Studies 221.

48 Randall S. Thomas and Christoph Van der Elst, 'Say on Pay around the World' (2015) 92 Washington University Law Review 653.

49 Edward B. Rock, 'Adapting to the New Shareholder-Centric Reality' (2013) 161 University of Pennsylvania Law Review 1907.

50 Jennifer G. Hill, 'The Trajectory of American Corporate Governance: Shareholder Empowerment and Private Ordering Combat' (2019) University of Illinois Law Review 507.

To conclude, the balance between shareholder decision-making rights and boards' powers sets the stage for discussions of jurisdiction-specific voting and engagement rules. The contributors therefore individually identify which matters fall within the purview of the shareholders, and which matters are the responsibility of the board. They also outline whether there is a clear demarcation of powers between boards and shareholders in their jurisdiction.

1.3.1.5 Other Jurisdiction-Specific Aspects

There might also be other important aspects which vary between jurisdictions. The contributors therefore address whether the corporate law and corporate governance framework in their particular jurisdiction has any such distinctive features.

1.3.2 *Legal Means of Shareholder Voting and Engagement (Part II)*

This Part describes the legal means by which shareholders, in particular minority shareholders, in public companies exercise their rights to vote and engage.

1.3.2.1 Procedures for General Meetings

Shareholders' meetings are the venue at which shareholders exercise their rights to vote. These meetings are also a primary channel for shareholders to engage the management, acquire information and make their voices heard. Procedural rules pertaining to general meetings therefore have an important impact on shareholder voting and engagement. They can, for instance, affect the ability of shareholders to engage, and thus limit or stimulate shareholder participation in governance.

General meetings typically include annual general meetings (AGMs), usually held shortly after the end of each financial year, and extraordinary general meetings (EGMs). As their name implies, EGMs are usually convened only in exceptional circumstances, to consider proposed fundamental changes to the company. Shareholder voting rights are arguably collective in nature, as the (special or qualified) majority of the shareholders – sometimes subject to a quorum – determines whether a proposal is adopted. The majority and quorum rules can therefore all prominently influence shareholders' ability to vote and engage.

The ease with which shareholders can call a shareholders meeting is also an important procedural aspect of shareholder engagement. La Porta and his associates considered the percentage of share capital needed to call an EGM to be an important part of their shareholders' right matrix.[51] It follows that the lower the percentage, the greater the opportunity for minority shareholders to bring matters that concern them to the attention of a broader audience (i.e. the shareholders' meeting, and potentially the media and the general public), and the better their chance of pressurizing the management to address their concerns. Also of relevance are the cost rules of convening an EGM, that is, whether the shareholders calling the EGM are liable for all the costs.[52] Overall, the procedural rules governing the requisitioning of EGMs by shareholders impact on their ability to use this engagement tool.

Other less-studied procedural aspects may also be relevant. The minimum notice period rules serve an important informational function, affecting shareholders' ability to acquire the

[51] La Porta et al., 'Law and Finance' (n. 16).

[52] Priya P. Lele and Mathias M. Siems, 'Shareholder Protection: A Leximetric Approach' (2007) 7 Journal of Corporate Law Studies 17.

information they need to cast an informed vote.[53] The record date[54] and share blocking rules[55] can also affect activist shareholders' ability to amass shares in a proxy contest. There is also evidence that even routine procedural matters, such as the choice of venue for general meetings, can influence shareholders' ability to scrutinize their investee companies.[56]

All these aspects have an important impact on the exercise of shareholder voting rights and engagements. The contributors therefore consider the regular procedure for holding an AGM or EGM in their jurisdiction, quorum and majority rules, and the conditions under which shareholders can call a general meeting (assuming they can), and the regular terms involved.

1.3.2.2 Voting Rules

The traditional principle of one-share-one-vote (OSOV) promises to align the shareholder's cash flow rights with voting rights. Separation between cash flow and voting rights is, however, commonplace among public corporations around the world.[57] This misalignment is particularly acute in economies with concentrated share ownership and weak governance institutions, where pyramidal and cross-holding structures can be used by an opportunistic controller to extract value from the controlled firms at the expense of the public investors.[58] It has also been an issue of intense debate as to whether dual-share structures[59] and loyalty shares[60] serve to institutionalize and formalize the wedge between cash flow and voting rights, and expose minority shareholders to the risks of majority overreach and expropriation.

Deviations from the OSOV principle, however, do not always place minority shareholders at a disadvantage. Indeed, they can often be empowering, as the majority-of-the-minority (MoM) voting practice demonstrates. The MoM mechanism excludes those shareholders with a conflict of interest (typically, the controller) from voting, thereby effectively vesting in the disinterested shareholders (often minority shareholders) a power of veto. Therefore, as a 'property rule', MoM voting prevents the controlling shareholder from pushing through a controversial transaction against the wishes of the minority, as this transaction simply cannot be performed without the consent of the minority.[61] Other useful empowering tools that also deviate from OSOV include

53 Christoph Van der Elst and Anne Lafarre, 'Bringing the AGM to the 21st century: Blockchain and Smart Contracting Tech for Shareholder Involvement' (2017) European Corporate Governance Institute (ECGI)-Law Working Paper 358/2017 https://ssrn.com/abstract=2992804 assessed 1 May 2021.

54 John Pound, 'Proxy Contests and the Efficiency of Shareholder Oversight' (1988) 20 Journal of Financial Economics 237.

55 Luc Renneboog and Peter Szilagyi, 'Shareholder Engagement at European General Meetings' in Massimo Belcredi and Guido Ferrarini (eds.), *Boards and Shareholders in European Listed Companies: Facts, Context and Post-Crisis Reforms* (Cambridge University Press 2013).

56 Yuanzhi Li and David Yermack, 'Evasive Shareholder Meetings' (2016) 38 Journal of Corporate Finance 318.

57 La Porta et al., 'Corporate Ownership Around the World' (n. 16).

58 Joseph P. H. Fan and T. J. Wong, 'Corporate Ownership Structure and the Informativeness of Accounting Earnings in East Asia' (2002) 33 Journal of Accounting and Economics 401.

59 Jennifer Francis et al., 'The Market Pricing of Accruals Quality' (2005) 39 Journal of Accounting and Economics, 295. Cf. Zohar Goshen and Assaf Hamdani, 'Corporate Control and Idiosyncratic Vision' (2016) 125 Yale Law Journal 588.

60 Paul H. Edelman, Wei Jiang and Randall S. Thomas, 'Will Tenure Voting Give Corporate Managers Lifetime Tenure?' (2019) 97 Texas Law Review 991; Marco Becht, Yuliya Kamisarenka and Anete Pajuste, 'Loyalty Shares with Tenure Voting: Does the Default Rule Matter? Evidence from the *Loi Florange* Experiment' (2020) 63 Journal of Law and Economics 473.

61 Zohar Goshen, 'The Efficiency of Controlling Corporate Self-Dealing: Theory Meets Reality' (2003) 91 California Law Review 393. See also Luca Enriques, 'Related Party Transactions: Policy Options and Real-World Challenges with a Critique of the European Commission Proposal' (2015) 16 European Business Organization Law Review 1.

cumulative voting and slate voting, which has been deployed in jurisdictions such as Mainland China,[62] Taiwan[63] and Italy.[64]

Given the importance of different voting rights and actual voting arrangements in companies, the contributors address how far the OSOV principle holds in their jurisdiction, whether any deviations are allowed, and if so, whether they are frequently used. Special attention is given to voting mechanisms that promise to empower minority shareholders, such as the MoM, cumulative voting or slate voting.

1.3.2.3 Shareholder Proposals

The shareholder's right to propose is also a potentially effective tool to constrain agency problems of different types. This particular right has been fiercely debated in recent years by academics and policymakers. Its vocal advocates believe that vesting in shareholders greater power to propose and intervene can improve corporate governance and enhance shareholder value.[65] However, their opponents have argued that giving shareholders such power is inefficient,[66] and can indeed reduce shareholder wealth.[67] Empirical evidence on the effects of shareholder proposals is also mixed. Some work suggests that shareholder proposals on governance topics that pass with a small margin can be value-enhancing,[68] and ESG proposals may (sometimes) lead to higher corporate sustainability and performance.[69] Uninformed shareholders submitting shareholder proposals may destroy shareholder value, but particularly informed proposals can be value-enhancing.[70] Hence, it is perhaps fair to say that shareholder proposals, on balance, are a useful device of external constraint on shareholder–manager agency problems[71] and, under the right conditions, can

62 Chao Xi and Yugang Chen, 'Does Cumulative Voting Matter? The Case of China: An Empirical Assessment' (2014) 15 European Business Organization Law Review 585. See also Yinghui Chen and Julan Du, 'Does Regulatory Reform of Cumulative Voting Promote a More Balanced Power Distribution in the Boardroom?' (2020) 64 Journal of Corporate Finance 101655.

63 Yu-Hsin Lin and Yun-chien Chang, 'An Empirical Study of Corporate Default Rules and Menus in China, Hong Kong, and Taiwan' (2018) 15 Journal of Empirical Legal Studies 875.

64 Massimo Belcredi and Luca Enriques, 'Institutional Investor Activism in a Context of Concentrated Ownership and High Private Benefits of Control: The Case of Italy' in Jennifer G. Hill and Randall S. Thomas (eds.) *Research Handbook on Shareholder Power* (Edward Elgar Publishing 2015).

65 Lucian A. Bebchuk, 'Letting Shareholders Set the Rules' (2005) 119 Harvard Law Review 1784. See also Milton Harris and Artur Raviv, 'Control of Corporate Decisions: Shareholders vs. Management' (2010) 23 The Review of Financial Studies 4115.

66 Stephen M. Bainbridge, 'The Case for Limited Shareholder Voting Rights' (2006) 53 UCLA Law Review 601.

67 John G. Matsusaka and Oguzhan Ozbas, 'A Theory of Shareholder Approval and Proposal Rights' (2017) 33 Journal of Law, Economics, and Organization 377.

68 Vicente Cuñat, Mireia Gine, Maria Guadalupe, 'The Vote is Cast: The Effect of Corporate Governance on Shareholder Value' (2012) 67 Journal of Finance 1943.

69 Cynthia E. Clark, Andrew P. Bryant and Jennifer J. Griffin, 'Firm Engagement and Social Issue Salience, Consensus, and Contestation' (2017) 56 Business & Society 1136; Jody Grewal, George Serafeim and Aaron Yoon, 'Shareholder Activism on Sustainability Issues' (2016) Harvard Business School Working Paper No. 17-003 https://dash.harvard.edu/bitstream/handle/1/27864360/17-003.pdf?sequence=1 accessed 15 July 2020; Min-Dong Paul Lee and Michael Lounsbury, 'Domesticating Radical Rant and Rage: An Exploration of the Consequences of Environmental Shareholder Resolutions on Corporate Environmental Performance' (2011) 50 Business & Society 155.

70 When shareholders are more informed, they are able 'to weed out ill-informed proposals'. See Nickolay Gantchev and Mariassunta Giannetti, 'The Costs and Benefits of Shareholder Democracy: Gadflies and Low-Cost Activism' (2021) 34 The Review of Financial Studies 5629.

71 Randall S. Thomas and James F. Cotter, 'Shareholder Proposals in the New Millennium: Shareholder Support, Board Reponse and Market Reaction' (2007) 13 Journal of Corporate Finance 368; Yonca Ertimur, Fabrizio Ferri and Stephen R. Stubben, 'Board of Directors' Responsiveness to Shareholders: Evidence from Shareholder Proposals'

create value for shareholders.[72] As we will see in Section 1.3.3.3 of this chapter, existing evidence shows a very mixed picture on the actual use of shareholder proposals in practice across jurisdictions. This may be caused by the various ownership requirements and other procedural and material requirements, which are addressed by the contributors in this Handbook.

1.3.2.4 Shareholder Information Rights

Information rights are generally regarded as the fundamental rights of the shareholder.[73] Ready and easy access to information about the companies they invest in is crucial to shareholders' role as monitors.[74] Much corporate governance debate on access to information has focused on disclosure rules under securities laws. Legal rules requiring issuers to make disclosures in prescribed manners and at prescribed frequencies help to provide shareholders with reliable, low-cost information which enable them to monitor their invested firms. It has been shown that more extensive mandatory disclosure requirements (in tandem with effective private enforcement) are positively associated with more robust national stock markets.[75] Of course, it has not always been possible to find the right balance between a sufficiency of information and information overload.[76]

However, the shareholder's right to request information beyond what is required in the mandatory disclosure regime has not so far been adequately studied. One particularly important venue for shareholders' information acquisition is the general meeting, where shareholders generally have the opportunities to ask the management questions. Asking questions can also be a powerful form of shareholder engagement, influencing the way in which the management thinks and acts.[77] Therefore, the contributors to this Handbook outline whether and to what extent shareholders have the right to ask questions or request information in and outside the general meeting.

1.3.2.5 Other Jurisdiction-Specific Aspects

While we seek to clarify the legal means of shareholder voting and engagement, we recognize that other, less formal, channels may also be important. The contributors will therefore address channels specific to their jurisdiction which complement the legal means for shareholder engagement. Here it is worth noting that while the Handbook mainly focuses on shareholder voting as a primary form of shareholder engagement, it also addresses other forms of (informal) shareholder engagement, such as engagements behind the scenes, other stewardship activities by institutional investors and, to a lesser degree, private actions.

The impact of the Covid-19 pandemic on shareholder voting and engagement has naturally attracted attention recently. Corporate and securities law responses to the pandemic have varied

(2010) 16 Journal of Corporate Finance 53. See also Luc Renneboog and Peter G. Szilagyi, 'The Role of Shareholder Proposals in Corporate Governance' (2011) 17 Journal of Corporate Finance 167.

72 Vicente Cuñat et al., 'The Vote is Cast: The Effect of Corporate Governance on Shareholder Value' (2012) 67 The Journal of Finance 1943.

73 Julian Velasco, 'The Fundamental Rights of the Shareholder' (2006) 40 U.C. Davis Law Review 407.

74 Randall S. Thomas, 'Improving Shareholder Monitoring of Corporate Management by Expanding Statutory Access to Information' (1996) 38 Arizona Law Review 331.

75 Rafael La Porta et al., 'What Works in Securities Laws?' (2006) 61 The Journal of Finance 1.

76 Troy A. Paredes, 'Blinded by the Light: Information Overload and its Consequences for Securities Regulation' (2003) 81 Washington University Law Quarterly 417.

77 Lisa A. Fontenot, 'Public Company Virtual-Only Annual Meetings' (2018) 73 The Business Lawyer 35.

from country to country around the globe, and have ranged from doing nothing to the wholesale adoption of virtual-only general meetings (though perhaps only temporarily). While it may be premature to draw any definitive conclusions in respect of the Covid-19 pandemic, we have taken this opportunity to reflect on the conventional approaches to shareholder voting and engagement in each jurisdiction, when facing challenges posed by this and similar once-in -a-century crises.

1.3.3 *Shareholder Voting and Engagement in Practice (Part III)*

In Part III, shareholder engagement is considered in practice. The third set of questions covered in this Part address shareholder voting and engagement in practice, using empirical methodology where appropriate and to the extent that data is readily accessible. The availability of the data determines whether these questions can be answered in a quantitative, qualitative or illustrative way.

1.3.3.1 Voting Modes and Turnout

Shareholders' turnout decisions are assumed to depend on a rational, costs and benefits calculation of voting.[78] Acquiring and analyzing firm-specific information in order to cast an informed vote is likely to account for the bulk of the costs involved, but other costs may also be important. Voting in person at the shareholders' meeting will probably cost more (in terms of travel and accommodation expenses) than voting electronically. Voting modes can therefore influence shareholders' decisions as to whether to vote. Contributors are, therefore, asked to consider how votes are cast; the type of voting mode (vote in person, by proxy, remote voting) available to shareholders; and whether technology-enabled virtual-only or hybrid meetings are permissible.

The conventional theory of shareholder rational passivity dictates that shareholders owning a tiny fraction of the company's shares are likely to be passive or to vote with their feet.[79] In other words, it is not economically justifiable for small investors to participate in the voting process. Recent empirical scholarship has suggested, however, that low (retail) shareholder turnout can have profound governance consequences. It can distort vote outcomes, limit shareholders' ability to initiate governance changes[80] and impair a firm's ability to amend corporate charters for the improvement of governance.[81] Calls have repeatedly been made to incentivize retail shareholders to cast votes,[82] and recommendations have been made to combat shareholder 'absenteeism'.[83] Contributors will therefore also consider who votes, how regularly retail (small)

78 Konstantinos E. Zachariadis, Dragana Cvijanovic and Moqi Groen-Xu, 'Free-Riders and Underdogs: Participation in Corporate Voting' (2020) European Corporate Governance Institute – Finance Working Paper No. 649/2020 https://ssrn.com/abstract=2939744 accessed 1 May 2021.

79 Alon Brav, Matthew D. Cain and Jonathon Zytnick, 'Retail Shareholder Participation in the Proxy Process: Monitoring, Engagement, and Voting' (2019) European Corporate Governance Institute – Finance Working Paper 637/2019 https://papers.ssrn.com/sol3/papers.cfm?abstract_id=3387659 accessed 1 May 2021.

80 Kobi Kastiel and Yaron Nili, 'In Search of the Absent Shareholders: A New Solution to Retail Investors' Apathy' (2016) 41 Delaware Journal of Corporate Law 55.

81 Scott Hirst, 'Frozen Charters' (2017) 34 Yale Journal on Regulation 91.

82 Jill E. Fisch, 'Standing Voting Instructions: Empowering the Excluded Retail Investor' (2018) 102 Minnesota Law Review 11.

83 European Parliament, 'Rights and Obligations of Shareholders: National Regimes and Proposed Instruments at EU Level for Improving Legal Efficiency' (May 2012) www.europarl.europa.eu/thinktank/en/document.html?reference=IPOL-JURI_ET(2012)462463 accessed 1 May 2021.

shareholders exercise their voting rights and how large the shareholder turnouts are at general meetings.

1.3.3.2 Voting Items and Outcomes

A jurisdiction's demarcation between shareholders and management powers can be empirically understood by examining the range of matters laid before shareholders' meetings for a vote. These matters can be mandated by a jurisdiction's corporate and securities rules and are therefore 'routine'. Board elections are a primary example. There can also be ad hoc matters that, insofar as law allows, shareholders decide to take into their own hands and have a say on. These matters can be wide-ranging and vary greatly across jurisdictions and at different times in the same jurisdiction. Contributors will therefore consider the type of mandatory and routine resolutions that shareholders vote on, the type of resolutions that are non-mandatory yet commonplace and the type of less regular or less common resolutions.

Previous research has shown that shareholder approval/dissent can be sensitive to resolution types[84] (and the proponent of the resolution, which is an issue to be addressed in Section 1.3.3.3). Some resolutions such as the listed company transacting with its controlling shareholder (or its close-knit associates) are more susceptible to conflicts of interest and therefore attract greater shareholder scrutiny. Shareholder dissent is likely to be high if the terms of the related-party transaction are perceived to be unfairly set. On the other hand, shareholder approval is likely to be higher for resolutions that are more routine and uncontroversial. Contributors are asked to consider, where jurisdiction-specific data is available, the types of resolution which are likely targets of activist shareholders, and the types which usually face little shareholder resistance.

1.3.3.3 Shareholder Proposals

As we have seen in Section 1.3.2.3, putting a shareholder proposal on the agenda is considered an important shareholder initiation right. Empirical evidence on the role of shareholder-initiated proposals in corporate governance is mixed, and moreover, highly jurisdiction-specific. Shareholder proposals have played a crucial role in the growth of shareholder activism in the USA, though their prevalence has showed a modest decline in recent years.[85] The practice of shareholders initiating proposals intervening the conduct of affairs in their investee companies has also gained some momentum around the globe, including in economies where concentrated ownership is the norm, such as in continental European countries,[86] Japan[87] and Hong Kong.[88] Contributors will address the issue of the prominence of shareholder-initiated proposals to the corporate governance landscape in general. Where jurisdiction-specific information is available, they will consider the typical topics of shareholder proposals (such as ESG); whether shareholder proposals often make it to the general meeting agenda; whether they usually receive the

[84] Renneboog and Peter Szilagyi (n. 55); Chao Xi, 'Shareholder Voting and Corporate Sustainability in China' in Beate Sjåfjell and Christopher Bruner (eds.) *Cambridge Handbook of Corporate Law, Corporate Governance and Sustainability* (Cambridge University Press 2019).

[85] Gibson, Dunn & Crutcher LLP, 'Shareholder Proposal Developments During the 2020 Proxy Season' www.gibsondunn.com/shareholder-proposal-developments-during-the-2020-proxy-season/ assessed 1 May 2021.

[86] Peter Cziraki, Luc Renneboog and Peter G. Szilagyi, 'Shareholder Activism through Proxy Proposals: The European Perspective' (2010) 16 European Financial Management 738. See also Renneboog and Szilagyi (n. 55).

[87] Tsung-ming Yeh, 'Large Shareholders, Shareholder Proposals, and Firm Performance: Evidence from Japan' (2014) 22 Corporate Governance: An International Review 312.

[88] Yu-Hsin Lin, 'When Activists Meet Controlling Shareholders in the Shadow of the Law: A Case Study of Hong Kong' (2019) 14 Asian Journal of Comparative Law 1.

necessary shareholder support to pass; and how often shareholder proposals are associated with proxy fights.

1.3.3.4 Other Forms of Shareholder Voice

Shareholder voice can manifest in various forms that are enabled by a jurisdiction's economic structure, market conditions, historical and cultural conditions and, of course, the characteristics of its corporate sector. Private actions brought by shareholders to enforce their rights are of great importance in certain jurisdictions (such as the USA), but are much less relevant to many other jurisdictions.[89] Jurisdictions in which the securities markets are 'institutionalized' are more likely to witness institutional investors wielding their influence over invested companies via private, behind-the-scene engagement than jurisdictions with a relatively weak institutional presence in their stock markets. Similarly, proxy advisors might be powerful corporate governance players in some jurisdictions, but practically irrelevant in others. In some jurisdictional settings, pension funds have been able to effect striking corporate governance changes such as board diversity and managerial remuneration.[90] Publicly funded institutions or shareholders backed by or closely linked to the state have been able to force governance improvements in the listed sector in some jurisdictions, whereas in other jurisdictions such a role would be unthinkable.

Contributors will therefore consider the additional channels through which shareholders have made their voice heard. In particular, they will explore the importance of private, behind-the-scene engagement; how often such engagement is used; and whether there are any practical examples or anecdotal evidence related to the engagement types special to a particular jurisdiction.

1.3.3.5 Other Jurisdiction-Specific Aspects

Other aspects not already covered in the preceding sections may also be important. The contributors will therefore also address other jurisdiction-specific aspects of shareholder voting and engagement in practice.

1.4 BRIEF OUTLINE OF THE HANDBOOK

The rest of the Handbook consists of four Parts. Part I covers eight Asian jurisdictions, including China (Mainland) (Chapter 2), Hong Kong (Chapter 3), India (Chapter 4), Indonesia (Chapter 5), Japan (Chapter 6), Singapore (Chapter 7), South Korea (Chapter 8) and Taiwan (Chapter 9). Part II addresses three other important jurisdictions: Australia (Chapter 10), Canada (Chapter 11) and the United States (Chapter 12). Part III contains jurisdiction-specific studies on eight European economies: Denmark (Chapter 13), France (Chapter 14), Germany (Chapter 15), Greece (Chapter 16), Italy (Chapter 17), Norway (Chapter 18), the Netherlands (Chapter 19) and the United Kingdom (Chapter 20). Each of the chapters in Parts I, II and III focuses on one jurisdiction, guided by the general analytical framework and specific research questions as described above.

89 John Armour et al., 'Private Enforcement of Corporate Law: An Empirical Comparison of the United Kingdom and the United States' (2009) 6 Journal of Empirical Legal Studies 687.

90 David Webber, *The Rise of the Working Class Shareholder: Labor's Last Best Weapon* (Harvard University Press 2018).

Part IV of the Handbook takes stock of the jurisdiction-based studies comprising the preceding Parts, and develops an evidence-based, reflective account of what the Handbook has to offer to advance the extant scholarship on shareholder voting and engagement from a comparative perspective. Chapters 21 and 22 approach our central research question, as laid out at the outset of this Introduction, by looking at how the law functions both in theory and in practice. Chapter 23 concludes the Handbook with discussions on the implications, both theoretical and policy-wise, of the Handbook to the enterprise of shareholder voting and engagement around the world.

PART I

Asia

2

Shareholder Voting and Engagement in China

Chao Xi

2.1 INTRODUCTION

2.1.1 *Corporate Law Framework*

The legal system in the mainland People's Republic of China (PRC), as a jurisdiction that is distinct from the jurisdictions of Hong Kong (Chapter 3) and Taiwan (Chapter 9), falls broadly into the civil law tradition.. The primary source of corporate law is the PRC Company Law, a codified statute enacted by the PRC's national legislature, the National People's Congress Standing Committee (NPCSC). The Company Law was first enacted in 1993, and came into effect in 1994. The 1993 Company Law was subsequently repealed and replaced by the current Company Law, which was promulgated in 2005 and has been in effect since 2006, with important amendments in 2013 and 2018.[1] Another important source of primary legislation on the corporate governance of listed companies is the PRC Securities Law, enacted in 1998 and since revised. The current Securities Law has been in effect since March 2020.[2]

The Company Law and Securities Law lay out a broad framework for corporate law and governance. However, as with many other pieces of PRC national legislation, their provisions are often expressed in general terms and are lacking in specificity.[3] They are supplemented by important subsidiary provisions in the form of PRC regulations, rules and norms. The most important form of subsidiary backing is the regulations enacted by the State Council, the Chinese Cabinet. These regulations often take the form of policy pronouncements issued by the State Council in regard to, among other things, the direction of corporate governance reforms. They are therefore typically general in nature, but herald specific reform measures to be introduced by the ministerial-level, sector-based securities regulatory authority, the China Securities Regulatory Commission (CSRC).

Below the State Council's regulations, but also an important source of law in respect of corporate law and governance in China, are the rules enacted by the CSRC. Of particular relevance to this chapter are three CSRC-made sets of rules. First, the Code of Corporate Governance. The current Code has been in effect since 2018, and repealed and replaced the original Code promulgated in 2002. The Code is applicable to all companies listed on China's

This research was supported by a General Research Fund (CUHK-14613616) from the Hong Kong SAR Research Grants Council. I am grateful for the excellent research assistance of Ning Cao and Yurong Huang.

1 For the purpose of this chapter, references to the Company Law are made to the current 2018 Company Law, unless otherwise specified.

2 For the purpose of this chapter, references to the Securities Law are made to the current 2020 Securities Law, unless otherwise specified.

3 For a general critique of this characteristic of PRC law, see, e.g., Randall Peerenboom, *China's Long March toward Rule of Law* (Cambridge University Press 2002).

two official stock exchanges, the Shanghai and Shenzhen Stock Exchanges.[4] The Code is semi-mandatory; any significant non-compliance with the Code can lead to enforcement or disciplinary action brought by the CSRC, its local offices, the Exchanges or other self-regulatory organizations.[5] Second, the Guidance on the Articles of Association of Listed Companies (Model AoA).[6] The Guidance is in effect a model set of articles of association that Chinese listed companies are generally expected to follow. Deviations from the Model AoA are generally discouraged by way of, for instance, additional regulatory requirements for reporting and approval.[7] Third, the Rules on the General Meeting of Listed Companies (GM Rules).[8] The GM Rules set out the rules for the conduct of meetings of general shareholders. The Rules are legally binding on Chinese listed companies, and the CSRC, its local offices and the Exchanges can take enforcement or disciplinary actions against the listed company, the board of directors or responsible individuals for violations.[9]

Finally, we should mention the self-regulatory rules made by the Shanghai and Shenzhen Stock Exchanges and other self-regulatory organizations. Of particular importance are the Exchanges' listing rules, which specify detailed procedures for the conduct of the shareholders' meeting and set out the circumstances where the majority of the minority rule applies.

2.1.2 *Allocation of Corporate Decision-Making*

Under Chinese company law, there are two types of companies: limited liability companies and joint stock companies.[10] The former is broadly the Chinese equivalent of the closed company, and the latter the equivalent of the public company. The listed company is a subcategory of the joint stock company. The Chinese company in general, and the Chinese listed company in particular, are generally required by law to have three governance organs: the shareholders' meeting, the board of directors and the supervisory board.[11] Both boards are elected by a meeting of the shareholders, and are held to account by the shareholders.[12] The board of directors of a listed company should consist of no less than five and no more than nineteen members,[13] of whom no less than one-third should be independent.[14] The supervisory board should contain at least three members, of whom at least one-third should be representatives of the employees.[15]

4 Article 2, Code of Corporate Governance.

5 Article 6, Code of Corporate Governance. For an empirical assessment of the enforcement regime, see, e.g., Ning Cao, Paul B. McGuinness and Chao Xi, 'Does Securities Enforcement Improve Disclosure Quality? An Examination of Chinese Listed Companies' Restatement Activities' (2021) 67 *Journal of Corporate Finance* 101877.

6 The Model AoA was first promulgated in 1997, and amended in 2006, 2014, 2016 and 2019. For the purpose of this chapter, 'the Model AoA' refers to the current 2019 Model AoA, unless otherwise specified.

7 Lauren Yu-Hsin Lin and Yun-chien Chang, 'An Empirical Study of Corporate Default Rules and Menus in China, Hong Kong, and Taiwan' (2018) 15 *Journal of Empirical Legal Studies* 875.

8 The GM Rules were first promulgated in 2000, and amended in 2006, 2014 and 2016. For the purpose of this chapter, 'the GM Rules' refer to the current 2016 GM Rules, unless otherwise specified.

9 Chapter V, GM Rules.

10 Article 8, Company Law.

11 There are notable exceptions, such as a one-member company which is not required to hold a shareholders' meeting, see Articles 61 and 66, Company Law.

12 Under PRC law, board accountability is owed to the shareholders in meeting, rather than to the company. This is derived from the requirement for the dual-boards to submit reports to the shareholders' meeting for its approval. See Article 37, Company Law.

13 Article 108, Company Law.

14 On the requirement for independent directors in Chinese listed companies, see in general Chao Xi, 'In Search of an Effective Monitoring Board Model: Board Reforms and the Political Economy of Corporate Law in China' (2006) 12 *Connecticut Journal of International Law* 1.

15 Article 117, Company Law.

The PRC legal framework for corporate decision-making is characteristically shareholder-centric. The Company Law vests the shareholders' meeting with decision-making over a wide array of corporate matters, leaving the board of directors a role that is broadly managerial in nature.[16] The demarcation of decision-making between the shareholders' meeting and the board of directors is succinctly stated in an official explanatory note accompanying the original 1993 Company Law:[17]

> The shareholders' meeting . . . is the organ of power of a company, and it determines all material matters of the company. The board of directors is the decision-making organ of the company, and it is accountable to the general meeting. Within the power vested by the law and the authority delegated by the shareholders' meeting, it makes business and managerial decisions, appoints and dismisses senior executives including the manager, and represents the company.

More specifically, the shareholders' meeting has a wide array of authority prescribed by the Company Law:[18] determining the company's business policies and investment plans; electing members of the board of directors and the supervisory board and determining their remuneration; approving the reports of the board of directors and the supervisory board; approving the company's annual budget and accounts; approving the company's profit distribution and loss recovery plans; approving resolutions on the increase or decrease of capital; approving resolutions on the issuance of bonds; approving resolutions on the merger, split, dissolution or liquidation of the company; and amending the articles of association. While some of these powers fall conveniently into the business of the shareholders' meeting in other jurisdictions (such as director election and charter amendments), others (such as business planning and bond issuance) do not.

It should be noted that the Company Law authorizes the company's articles of association to grant its shareholders' meeting further powers in addition to the prescribed lines of statutory authority.[19] The Model AoA significantly widens the broad range of decision-making powers that the shareholders' meeting already enjoys under the law. These matters include: passing resolutions on the appointment and removal of the accounting firm; approving the giving of certain types of guarantee; approving substantial acquisition or disposal of assets; approving of any changes to the purposes of funds raised; and approving share incentive schemes.[20] These transactions either involve a potential conflict of interest (such as share incentive schemes, and the provision of guarantee in favour of the controlling shareholder or its affiliates) or are of fundamental significance to the company (such as acquisition or disposal of substantial assets, the size of which is equivalent to 30 per cent or more of the company's assets). It should be borne in mind that the Model AoA prohibits the delegation to the board of any of the powers conferred upon the shareholders' meeting by the Company Law and by the Model AoA. In other words, shareholder approval is mandatory in respect of those matters reserved for the shareholders.

The board of directors, on the other hand, mainly plays a managerial role. It is authorized by the Company Law to implement any resolutions of the shareholders' meeting; to propose resolutions for approval by the shareholders' meeting; to convene the shareholders' meeting; to set out the company's internal systems; to appoint senior executives and determine their remuneration; and perhaps most importantly, to make business plans and investment

[16] The role of the supervisory board is largely one of oversight. See in general Xi (n. 14).

[17] Chao Xi, *Corporate Governance and Legal Reform in China* (Wildy, Simmonds & Hill 2009) 36–7.

[18] Article 37(1)(1)–(1)(10), Company Law.

[19] Article 37(1)(11), Company Law.

[20] Articles 40 and 41, Model AoA.

proposals.[21] The board of directors is also allowed by law to exercise any powers that the company's articles of association confers upon it.[22]

It is evident that there remains considerable ambiguity under the Company Law regarding the apportionment of authority between shareholders and directors in respect of business and investment matters. Both organs are entitled to make decisions on those matters, and the wording in the statutory provisions regulating their respective authority is at best vague. As far as listed companies are concerned, the Chinese law approach to addressing this statutory ambiguity is to allow the shareholders to define in the company's articles of association the parameters within which authority is delegated to the board of directors to make business decisions. This approach is manifested in the Model AoA. The board of directors is entitled to decide on such matters as investment, acquisition and disposal of assets, mortgage of the company's assets, provision of guarantee, related-party transactions, so long as they act within the authority delegated by the shareholders' meeting.[23] Any residual powers belong to the shareholders, and any matters that go beyond the board's delegated authority should be taken to the shareholders for approval.[24]

The Company Law, the Model AoA and the company's articles of association, together, demarcate the respective spheres of authority for both shareholders and directors. The PRC jurisprudence is not yet settled in regards to whether the board is 'supreme in its own sphere',[25] that is, whether the shareholders in meeting can interfere in the board's exercising of the power that is conferred upon it either by law or delegation by the articles.[26] The Company Law seems to approach this question from a shareholder right perspective. It provides that where the content of a resolution passed by the shareholders' meeting violates the company's articles of association, shareholders are entitled to apply to the court to rescind the resolution in breach.[27] This seems to mean that the shareholders acting in violation of the articles and passing a resolution on a matter within the board's delegated authority run the risk of being challenged by dissenting shareholders, but not by the board. The shareholders in meeting can of course either revoke the delegation or alter it ex ante, but this would require the approval of two-thirds of the votes present at the meeting by way of a special resolution.[28]

Overall, the PRC approach to corporate decision-making strongly emphasizes shareholder primacy. The shareholders in meeting are given authority both by law and by virtue of the Model AoA over a wide range of matters. In these areas, shareholder approval is mandatory, and may not be delegated. In respect of matters that can be delegated to the directors, the shareholders enjoy 'residual' authority. In other words, such matters are presumed to be reserved for the shareholders unless they have been explicitly assigned to the board by the articles of association. This shareholder-centric position has been shaped by a confluence of factors, both conventional and contemporary.

Conventionally, the shareholder-oriented model fits well with the state's predominant concern to retain control over companies that were partially privatized from former state-owned enterprises. The notion of the modern corporation was not accepted by the Chinese state until

21 Article 46(1)–(10), Company Law.
22 Article 46(11), Company Law.
23 Article 107(1)(8), Model AoA.
24 Article 107(3), Model AoA.
25 Paul Davies, *Introduction to Company Law* (3rd ed., Oxford University Press 2020) 35.
26 Jennifer G. Hill, 'The Trajectory of American Corporate Governance' (2019) *University of Illinois Law Review* 507; Junhai Liu, *Xian Dai Gong Si Fa [Modern Corporation Law]* (Law Press 2015) 585–6.
27 Article 22(2), Company Law. Any such application must be made within sixty days of passing the resolution.
28 Article 103(2), Company Law.

the early 1990s. It was seen as a means to salvage China's then ailing state-owned sector. Its attraction to the state lays in the fact that it offers a way of organizing businesses whereby private capital (in particular, the massive body of household savings) can be channelled into the state-owned sector and, typically, is allowed to take only a minority interest.[29] The state was particularly concerned with holding its agents, that is, the directors and senior managers, to account. A legal strategy adopted was to leave decision-making on 'major' matters in the state's own hands, and to delegate management powers to the agent/directors only in relation to relatively 'minor' issues. Moreover, this approach to corporate governance also mimics China's broader political governance arrangements,[30] under which all powers of the state are vested on principle in the National People's Congress (NPC), and the State Council (China's Cabinet) derives its authority by way of delegation from the NPC. Formally, at least, the NPC takes all decisions perceived to be of fundamental importance, and the State Council plays largely an executive and implementing role. This NPC–State Council relationship can be seen imitated in the setting of corporate governance, or more specifically, in how decision-making is apportioned between the shareholders and the directors.

A more contemporary consideration is China's broader corporate governance reforms of the past two decades aimed at reducing agency conflicts between the controlling shareholders and the minority shareholders. The Model AoA requirement – deriving from a statutory requirement (Article 16, Company Law) – for mandatory shareholder approval of certain types of guarantee provision offers a good example.[31] The provision of guarantee has been a uniquely popular form of the controlling shareholder benefitting at the expense of the minority shareholders. The listed company, typically at the direction of its controlling shareholder, guarantees debts on behalf of the controller or parties related to the controller, thereby exposing the listed company to a heightened risk of default.[32] The requirement for shareholder approval of these transactions, a manifestation of the majority of the minority rule,[33] effectively requires that these transactions be performed only with the approval of minority shareholders.

2.1.3 *Ownership Structure*

There were 1,980 firms listed on the main boards of one of the two official Exchanges at the end of 2019. Concentrated ownership is a common feature of Chinese listed firms. Their ownership information was sourced from the WIND database, a leading data source for corporate governance research on Chinese firms. The single largest shareholders of the Chinese firms owned on average 35.93 per cent (median 33.53 per cent) of the outstanding shares. Out of 1,980 sample firms, 59.95 per cent or 1,175 firms had a largest shareholder possessing 30 per cent or more of the company's shares. This figure of 30 per cent is an important threshold of shareholding under PRC law.[34] Crossing the 30 per cent mark generally triggers a legal obligation to make a general offer to all other shareholders so that the control premium is shared among shareholders in

[29] Xi (n. 17).

[30] Feng Deng, 'Zhong Guo Fa Shang Dong Shi Hui De Jue Se, Zhi Neng Ji Si Xiang Su Yuan [The Roles, Functions and Ideological Origin of the Board of Directors in Chinese Law: An Investigation from Empirical Perspective]' (2013) 3 *China Legal Science* 98.

[31] Article 41, Model AoA.

[32] Xi (n. 17).

[33] See n. 98 and n. 99, and accompanying text.

[34] It is the 30 per cent of the company's outstanding shares, rather than its voting shares. Articles 24 and 47, Shang Shi Gong Si Shou Gou Guan Li Ban Fa [Administrative Measures on Takeovers of Listed Companies], issued by the CSRC on 20 March 2020.

a change of control premium. This mandatory bid rule (first introduced back in 1993 under PRC law), in tandem with China's corporate finance regime which has remained hostile to the notion of bank-loan-financed acquisition, is generally perceived to make any attempt of crossing the 30 per cent mark prohibitively expensive.[35]

The data on the share ownership of the largest shareholder can, however, understate the degree of control that the controlling shareholders have over the Chinese listed sector. It is well known that some other large shareholders are related to the largest shareholder, and that they often act in concert with the largest shareholder. No systematically organized data on these related shareholders (such as their identities and shareholdings) is available. Nevertheless, the shareholdings of the ten largest shareholders give an indication: the largest ten shareholders of the sample firms[36] possessed on average 60.54 per cent (median 61.65 per cent) of the shares. It follows that the next nine largest shareholders (some of them are related to the largest shareholder) held on average 24.61 per cent of the shares. It would thus be fair to state that it is the norm for a Chinese listed company to be under the control (defined as an interest of 30 per cent or more) of a controlling shareholder.[37]

The largest shareholders fall conveniently into four categories. First, the PRC central government and its agencies[38] as the ultimate owners. These are typically listed companies affiliated to the national champions.[39] Of the sample firms,[40] 16.98 per cent belonged to this cohort. Second, local governments at various levels and their agencies. Of the sample firms, 31.47 per cent fell into this category. The first and second groups are collectively known as the state-controlled firms. The third category consists of private individuals, contributing 49.54 per cent of the sample firms. Most of the private individuals are Chinese nationals, and some are foreign. These are privately owned companies. The remaining 2.01 per cent of the sample firms had the largest shareholders that do not fall into any of the afore-mentioned categories. These include the village 'collective' (a form of rural economic organization), employee shareholding schemes (trade unions) and charities. Earlier studies have shown that state-owned listed firms tend to be disproportionately larger than non-state-owned firms, measured by market capitalization. State-owned firms remain dominant in the Chinese stock markets.[41]

Institutional investors are an important group in China's A-share markets.[42] For the purpose of this study, China-domiciled institutional investors are distinguished from foreign institutional investors investing in the Chinese A-share markets. As will be discussed in the rest of this section, domestic institutional investors include securities investment funds, insurance companies, pension funds and so on. At the end of March 2020, they collectively owned 17.04 per cent of A-shares in value. Chinese retail shareholders, on the other hand, owned 28.64 per cent of

35 Chao Xi, 'The Political Economy of Takeover Regulation: What Does the Mandatory Bid Rule in China Tell Us?' (2015) 58 *Journal of Business Law* 142.

36 N=1,959. Data was missing on the ten largest shareholders' holdings in respect of twenty-one firms.

37 Indeed, our data shows that, among the 805 firms with no shareholder holding greater than 30 per cent of the shares, 703 firms were controlled by shareholders possessing less than the 30 per cent mark.

38 These include, notably, the State-owned Assets Supervision and Administration Commission.

39 Curtis J. Milhaupt and Li-Wen Lin, 'We Are the (National) Champions: Understanding the Mechanisms of State Capitalism in China' (2013) 65 *Stanford Law Review* 697.

40 N=1,844. Data was missing on the identities of the largest shareholders in respect of 136 firms.

41 T. J. Wong, *Corporate Governance Research on Listed Firms in China: Institutions, Governance and Accountability*, vol. 9 (Foundations and Trends in Accounting 2014) 259, 271–2.

42 A-shares are shares denominated in Renminbi, China's official currency, and traded on the Shanghai and Shenzhen Stock Exchanges. They stand in contrast to B-shares, which are also traded on the same Exchanges but are denominated in foreign currencies. The B-share markets have largely been marginalized.

A-shares.[43] Foreign institutional investors owned a mere 2 per cent of A-shares, but can nevertheless play an important role in the governance of the Chinese firms in which they invested, as will be elaborated in this section. Overall, institutional investors, both domestic and foreign, held shares in 1,865 (out of 1,980) sample firms. They aggregately hold, on average, 4.88 per cent (median 1.89 per cent) of the shares in their portfolio companies.

The largest category of institutional investors in the Chinese stock markets consists of the securities investment funds. Broadly speaking, securities investment funds are the Chinese equivalents of mutual funds. They are governed by the Law on Securities Investment Funds,[44] and are closely regulated and supervised by the CSRC. They typically invest in stocks, bonds and monetary market instruments. By the end of 2018, there were 135 licensed securities investment fund managers licensed, managing 5,625 securities investment funds with total assets under management of RMB13.05 trillion (approximately USD1.86 trillion).[45] By 31 March 2020, securities investment funds owned 4.18 per cent of A-shares, measured by market capitalization.[46] At the end of 2019, these funds held stakes, large or small, in over 97 per cent of the sample firms, with an average of 2.75 per cent (median 0.80 per cent) of the shares in their portfolio companies.

Insurance companies are the second largest institutional investors in A-shares. Chinese insurers have been allowed to hold equity shares for their own account since 2004. Chinese portfolio regulations have allowed insurance companies and their asset management arms to invest up to 30 per cent of their total assets into A-shares. By 31 March 2020, insurance companies owned 4.10 per cent of the A-shares, measured by market capitalization.[47] At the end of 2019, Chinese insurers were present in 228 (out of 1,980) sample firms, with an average of 4.80 per cent (median 2.06 per cent) of the shares in their invested companies.

Pension funds are another important type of institutional investor. The principal player is the National Social Security Fund (NSSF), established in 2000 by the Chinese central government to fund the country's social security system. The NSSF may invest in stocks, fixed-income products and unlisted equity. At 31 March 2020, the NSSF owned 2.08 per cent of A-shares.[48] At the end of 2019, the NSSF was counted as a shareholder of 308 (out of 1,980) sample firms, with an average of 2.58 per cent (median 1.68 per cent) of the shares in their invested companies. Enterprise annuities, the Chinese equivalents of corporate pension plans, remain a modest presence in the Chinese stock markets. They were seen in only 3 (out of 1,980) sample firms.

Other important categories of China-domiciled institutional investors include securities companies (owning 0.59 per cent of A-shares by 31 March 2020)[49] and their investment arms, trust companies, finance companies, banking institutions and private equity firms.

Of particular importance to our research is a unique type of institutional investor in the Chinese A-share markets, the Qualified Foreign Institutional Investor (QFII). The QFIIs are a selected cohort of foreign institutional investors authorized to invest in A-share stocks, typically on behalf of their ultimate beneficiaries. At the end of 2018, 309 QFIIs were licensed.[50] Until recently, QFIIs were the main, if not the only, formal channel through which foreign capital

43 Guo Jin Zheng Quan Yan Jiu Bao Gao [Sinolink Securities Analyst Report], 'Qi Di A Gu Tou Zi Zhe Chou Ma – A Gu Tou Zi Zhe Jie Gou [Structure of A-Share Investors] (2020 Q1)' https://pdf.dfcfw.com/pdf/H3_AP202011251432611764_1.pdf?1606301375000.pdf accessed 15 July 2020.

44 The Law was first enacted in 2003. It was substantially revised in 2012 and 2015.

45 2019 Zhong Guo Zheng Quan Tou Zi Ji Jin Ye Nian Bao [2019 China Securities Investment Fund Fact Book], 4–5.

46 n. 43.

47 Ibid.

48 Ibid.

49 Ibid.

50 2018 CSRC Annual Report, Appendix 5.

could invest in China's stock markets. The recent stock market open-up initiatives, such as the Shanghai–Hong Kong Stock Connect (introduced in 2014) and Shenzhen–Hong Kong Stock Connect (introduced in 2016), have enabled international investors to bypass the QFIIs and invest directly in the A-share markets. However, the QFIIs have remained important players and, as discussed in Section 2.3.2.1, some of them are particularly activist shareholders.[51] Official statistics show that, in August 2019, QFIIs owned 1.5 per cent of A-shares, amounting to just over 40 per cent of all foreign portfolio investments in the A-shares.[52] At the end of 2019, QFIIs held investments in 194 (out of 1,980) sample firms, with an average of 1.51 per cent (median 0.95 per cent) of the shares in their portfolio firms.

2.2 LEGAL MEANS OF SHAREHOLDER ENGAGEMENT

2.2.1 *Shareholders' Right to Call a Meeting*

There are two types of shareholders' meeting for the listed company: the annual meeting (AGM) and extraordinary general meeting (EGM).[53] In general, the shareholder meeting is convened by the board of directors.[54] The annual meeting, of course, is held once a year, and normally within the first six months of the calendar year. The extraordinary meeting is required to be held within two months of the occurrence of certain events prescribed by law.[55] One such event is where shareholders owning, either individually or collectively, 10 per cent or more of the company's voting shares request in writing that an extraordinary general meeting be held.[56] The request should be made in the first instance to the board of directors, which shall take a decision within ten days upon receiving the written request as to whether to convene the requested meeting.[57] Where the board of directors decides in favour of the request, it should give notice of the shareholders' meeting within five days of taking the decision.[58] The board of directors can decide against the request,[59] but its decision is not final. The requesting shareholders are entitled to then take their request further, in writing, to the supervisory board which, if it agrees to the request, should give notice within five days of receiving it.[60] If the supervisory board fails to give notice within this prescribed period, it is deemed to have refused to call the requested meeting, in which case the requesting shareholders are entitled to call the requested meeting and convene it on their own.[61]

In the case that the requesting shareholders proceed to convene the shareholders' meeting, they are required to notify the board of directors in writing.[62] The requesting shareholders should also give notice fifteen days in advance of the meeting.[63] Chinese law requires a degree of

[51] See infra Section 2.3.2.

[52] Wensi Zhang, 'QFII Tou Zi E Du Qu Xiao Wai Zi Jia Su Liu Ru A Gu [Investment Quota of QFIIs is Revoked: Foreign Investment Inflows in A-share Accelerated]' *Xin Lang Cai Jing [Sina Finance]* https://finance.sina.com.cn/money/fund/jjyj/2019-09-23/doc-iicezueu7695643.shtml accessed 15 July 2020.

[53] Article 100, Company Law.

[54] Article 101, Company Law.

[55] Article 4, GM Rules. See n. 83 and accompanying text.

[56] Article 100(3), Company Law.

[57] Article 9(1), GM Rules. That decision should be based upon laws, regulations and the articles.

[58] Article 9(2), GM Rules.

[59] It is also envisaged that the board of directors can opt not to react at all to the request within ten days, which is deemed to have the same effect as rejecting the request. Article 9(3), GM Rules.

[60] Article 9(3) and (4), GM Rules.

[61] Article 9(5), GM Rules.

[62] Article 10(1), GM Rules. The requesting shareholders must have held 10 per cent or more of the company's voting shares for ninety consecutive days or more, see Article 9(5), GM rules.

[63] Article 102(1), Company Law.

regulatory oversight over these procedural issues, though it is generally applied with a light touch. So, both the notification served to the board of directors in respect of the meeting and the notice of the meeting are required to be filed with the CSRC's local office of the company's domicile and the Exchange on which the company is listed.[64] No approval or endorsement is, however, required from the regulator and the Exchange.

The board of directors must assist the requesting shareholders in the convening of the meeting. The board is required to provide the requesting shareholders with the list of shareholders at the record day.[65] The necessary costs of the meeting convened by the shareholders shall be borne by the company,[66] removing an important financial hurdle for activist shareholders to call and convene a general meeting.

2.2.2 *Shareholder Proposal Right*

Shareholders holding, either individually or collectively, 3 per cent or more of the shares are entitled to initiate a proposal no less than ten days before the meeting.[67] The proposal must be in writing and should be submitted to the board of the directors. The board must notify all shareholders of the proposal within two days of receiving it.[68]

The questions of whether the shareholder proposal is excludable, and if so by whom, are not well settled under PRC law. The relevant statutory provision[69] in the Company Law appears, on the one hand, to suggest that the convener of the meeting (typically the board of directors) is obliged to include in the meeting agenda any shareholder proposal received. It seems to follow that the shareholder proposal is not excludable. On the other hand, however, the same provision also stipulates that the shareholder proposal should meet certain criteria. It should concern matters falling under the authority of the shareholders' meeting, and it must carry particular topic(s) and specific issues to vote on.[70] It can be inferred that a proposal failing to meet these criteria may well be excludable. The Shanghai Stock Exchange has attempted to reconcile the seeming inconsistencies in law. In a regulatory guidance, it makes the following statement:[71]

> The convener of the general meeting is not vested with the formal authority to vet the merit of the shareholder proposal. Where the convener is the board of directors, there is in principle no need for it to hold a meeting to vet the proposal. Where the board receives a proposal, it is obliged to verify the identity of the initiating shareholder, and [ensure] the proposal's compliance with [the prescribed criteria], subject to which the proposal should be put to vote at the meeting. The board can request further information from the proposing shareholder should it decide that the proposal fails to meet [the prescribed criteria], but should not [unreasonably] delay or reject the proposal.

Under the Shanghai Stock Exchange's approach, the board's decision in respect of excludability of the proposal does not constitute a board resolution per se, which under the PRC law is judicially challengeable. Thus the board's discretion is generally insulated from judicial

64 Article 10(1) and (3), GM Rules.
65 Article 50, Model AoA.
66 Article 51, Model AoA.
67 Article 102(2), Company Law.
68 Ibid.
69 Ibid.
70 Ibid. Under the GM Rules, there is an additional requirement that the proposal must be in keeping with laws, regulations and the articles of association. Article 13, GM Rules.
71 Regulatory Q&As on Information Disclosure of Listed Companies (Issue 2), dated 16 June 2017, available at http://roadshow.sseinfo.com/resources/uploadfile/documents/201707/1499751511943.pdf accessed 15 July 2020.

scrutiny. However, the board may find its decision closely scrutinized by the Exchanges. Anecdotal evidence suggests that both the Shanghai and Shenzhen Stock Exchanges have intervened in respect of the board's determinations about the excludability of shareholder proposals. The Exchanges have publicly questioned the boards for excluding shareholder proposals.[72]

2.2.3 *Shareholder's Informational Right at the Meeting*

The shareholders are entitled to an annual work report from the board of directors and the supervisory board, respectively, at the annual shareholders' meeting.[73] The annual reports are routine agenda items for the annual meeting, on which shareholders cast their votes. Shareholders are also provided with detailed information on candidates standing for election. Such information includes candidates' personal profiles, their relationship with the company or its controlling shareholder, their holdings in the company and the record of any disciplinary or enforcement actions taken against the candidate.[74]

To obtain further information about the agenda items and more generally about the company, shareholders have the right to make queries at the shareholders' meeting.[75] Members of both boards and senior executives present at the meeting should respond to those queries, providing shareholders with 'explanations',[76] presumably, on given courses of action the company has taken that have come to shareholders' attention. Shareholders are also entitled to make 'suggestions' at the meeting, to which the board members and executives present are to respond and reply.[77] The shareholders' queries and suggestions are required to be recorded in the meeting minutes; so are the explanations and replies given.[78] However, the minutes are not publicly accessible.[79]

The shareholder meeting theoretically offers shareholders an important avenue to access information and voice their concerns. There is, however, little legal guarantee that their questions and suggestions will be taken seriously by the management. Anecdotal evidence suggests that sometimes those queries have been brushed aside by the management as unwanted 'disruptions' to the conduct of the meeting, or have simply been ignored.[80]

72 For instance, 'Jia Tong Lun Tai Gu Fen You Xian Gong Si Guan Yu Shou Dao Shang Hai Zheng Quan Jiao Yi Suo Jian Guan Gong Zuo Han De Gong Gao [Announcement of Giti Tire Corporation on Receiving the Supervisory Work Letter from the Shanghai Stock Exchange]' (10 October 2019) http://static.sse.com.cn/disclosure/listedinfo/announcement/c/2019-10-10/600182_20191010_2.pdf accessed 15 July 2020; 'Shen Zhen Shi Zhao Xin Neng Yuan Gu Fen You Xian Gong Si Guan Yu Dui Shen Zhen Zheng Quan Jiao Yi Suo Guan Zhu Han Hui Fu De Gong Gao [Announcement of Shenzhen Sunrise New Energy Co., Ltd. on Reply to Shenzhen Stock Exchange's Letter of Concern]' (5 December 2019) http://xinpi.stcn.com/finalpage/2020-06/08/1207900907.PDF accessed 15 July 2020.

73 Article 28, GM Rules.

74 Article 17, GM Rules.

75 Article 97, Company Law.

76 Article 29, GM Rules.

77 Article 97, Company Law and Article 29, GM Rules.

78 Article 41(1)(5), GM Rules.

79 Shareholders are however granted the power to inspect and presumably access such minutes. Article 97, Company Law.

80 Qing Pan, 'Bu Fen Shang Shi Qi Ye Mo Shi Zhong Xiao Gu Dong, Gu Dong Da Hui Lun Wei Shao Shu Ren You Xi [Due to Listed Companies' Ignorance of Small and Medium Shareholders, Shareholders' Meetings Have Become a Game of Majority Shareholders]' *Jing Ji Can Kao [Economic Information Daily]* (Shanghai, 21 May 2018) http://finance.china.com.cn/stock/zqyw/20180521/4643278.shtml.

2.2.4 *Voting, Cumulative Voting and the Majority of the Minority Rule*

Votes are cast by shareholders in Chinese listed firms at both AGMs and EGMs. As indicated above, the listed company is required to hold its AGM on an annual basis.[81] The EGMs are required to be held within two months where any of the circumstances prescribed by the PRC Company Law and the company's articles of association occur.[82] These include: where the number of directors falls below two-thirds of the number stipulated by the Company Law or the company's articles of association; where the uncovered loss exceeds one-third of the company's paid-up capital; where shareholders owning, either individually or collectively, no less than 10 per cent of the company's shares so require; where it is deemed necessary by the board of directors; where it is proposed by the supervisory board; and in any other circumstances prescribed by the company's articles of association.[83]

Shareholders can cast votes in person and by proxy at the meeting.[84] The shareholder is entitled to authorize an agent (or proxy) to attend the general meeting, and the authorization must be in writing.[85] The proxy votes in the name of the shareholder within the scope of the shareholder's authorization.[86] Proxy solicitation has been permitted since the early 1990s under PRC law.[87] It has been codified as part of China's recent overhaul of its Securities Law, which came into effect in March 2020. A shareholder owning 1 per cent or more of the shares is entitled to publicly solicit proxies,[88] provided that the proxy materials provide accurate and sufficient information and that shareholders are not remunerated for granting proxies.[89] According to recent studies, 415 proxy solicitations were recorded during the period from 2004 to 2017.[90] Of these, 83 per cent were initiated by independent directors, 17 per cent by the board of directors and 1 per cent by the majority shareholder. None of the recorded proxy solicitations was initiated by minority shareholders. Of these proxy solicitations, 71 per cent concerned the share option scheme, 23 per cent concerned an ad hoc reform initiative imposed by the CSRC in 2006 and the remaining 6 per cent concerned other matters. Out of the 415 instances of shareholders' solicitations, 412 were successful.[91]

In theory, a Chinese listed company must hold physical shareholder meetings.[92] In other words, virtual-only meetings are not permitted. However, shareholder participation in the meeting by Internet or other electronic means has been strongly encouraged in recent years, and shareholders participating online are deemed as being present at the meeting.[93] The regulatory emphasis has been on shareholder voting via the internet, which has been allowed since 2004 and was made mandatory for Chinese listed companies in 2014. The time window for,

81 Article 100, Company Law.
82 Article 100, Company Law.
83 Ibid.
84 Article 106, Company Law.
85 Ibid. See also Article 55(1)(3), Model AoA.
86 Article 106, Company Law.
87 Article 65 of 1993 Gu Piao Fa Xing Yu Jiao Yi Guan Li Zan Xing Tiao Li [Provisional Regulations on the Administration of Share Issuance and Trading] (promulgated by the CSRC, 22 April 1993, effective 22 April 1993).
88 Article 90, Securities Law. Also entitled to solicit proxies are the board of directors, individual directors and the China Securities Investor Service Centre.
89 Article 31(4), GM Rules.
90 Qinyu Zhang, 'Wo Guo Gong Kai Zheng Ji Tou Piao Quan Gui Fan Xing Yan Jiu [Normative Research on China's Public Solicitation of Voting Rights]' (2018) 3 *The Investor* 84.
91 Proxy solicitations are typically linked to specific items (such as resolutions on share option scheme) listed in the agenda of the shareholder meeting.
92 Articles 20(1) and (2), GM Rules.
93 Article 20(2), GM Rules.

and methods of, online voting must be stated in the meeting notice.[94] Online voting is conducted through the platforms hosted by the Exchanges.

As a matter of general principle, each share is entitled to one vote on each matter voted on at the shareholders' meeting.[95] The one share–one vote rule is, however, subject to important exceptions, one of which is cumulative voting.[96] Cumulative voting has become mandatory since 2002 in China for blockholder firms (i.e., firms where the blockholder owns more than 30 per cent of the company's outstanding shares), though it remains elective for non-blockholder firms. Empirical studies have shown that cumulative voting has been widely adopted both by blockholder firms (for which cumulative voting is mandatory) and by non-blockholder firms (for which cumulative voting is only optional).[97] Cumulative voting is generally understood to give (large) minority shareholders some representation on the board, and therefore a greater voice.

Another important deviation from the one share–one vote principle is the majority of the minority (MOM) rule. The MOM rule is widely perceived as a device to limit controlling shareholder conflicts of interest, by requiring disinterested shareholder approval of transactions where the conflicts are acute. A prime example of such transactions is the related-party transaction, where the controlling shareholder engages in a transaction with its controlled company. The MOM rule is expressed in Chinese law as a rule that excludes the interested shareholder from voting on an interested agenda item at the meeting.[98] Where a shareholder is interested in a transaction voted on at the shareholder meeting, insofar as that transaction is concerned, the votes that related shareholder holds do not count toward the total number of votes cast on the transaction.[99]

2.2.5 *Stewardship Code*

The notion of institutional investor stewardship has gained some traction in China's recent overhaul of its Code of Corporate Governance.[100] The Code adopts a "soft" approach; stewardship is encouraged for institutional investors, but is not mandatory. The Code envisages two ways in which institutional investors engage their portfolio firms. First, the shareholder right. Institutional investors are encouraged to exercise their shareholder rights, such as the right to vote, the right to make queries and the right to make suggestions.[101] The second way centres on the board. Institutional investors are encouraged to recommend candidates for the board of directors and the supervisory board, and to monitor the performance of board members.[102] However, the Code stops short of suggesting that institutional investors, subject to their holdings in the invested firms, initiate shareholder proposals for, among other things, director nomination. The Code also encourages transparency. The institutional investor is encouraged to

94 Article 21, GM Rules.
95 Article 103(1), Company Law.
96 Article 105, Company Law. Another important exception is the dual-class structure, which is permissible for companies listed at China's fledging STAR market (China's technology stock board, unveiled in late 2018), but not yet for China's other stock markets.
97 Chao Xi and Yugang Chen, 'Does Cumulative Voting Matter? The Case of China: An Empirical Assessment' (2014) 15 *European Business Organization Law Review*.
98 Article 79, Model AoA.
99 Article 31(1), GM Rules. Interestingly, the primary company legislation does not contain a general MoM rule pertaining to shareholder approval. It does include a rule that excludes conflicted directors from voting at the board meeting. Article 124, Company Law.
100 There exists no separate stewardship code under PRC law.
101 Article 78, Code of Corporate Governance.
102 Article 79, Code of Corporate Governance.

disclose publicly its objectives and principles of engagement, its strategies on shareholder voting, its engagement activities and the extent of their effectiveness.[103]

Several types of institutional investors are named specifically in the Code for the stewardship role: social security funds, corporate annuities, insurance companies and securities investment funds.[104] The Code also highlights a unique institution: the China Securities Investor Services Centre (CSISC). The CSISC claims to be a non-profit, shareholder-protection organization, and it is officially affiliated to the CSRC. Of particular note is the CSISC's initiative coined as 'holding shares, exercising rights', under which it holds, though open market acquisition, 100 shares in each of the companies listed on the Shanghai and Shenzhen Stock Exchanges. Though almost negligible, CSISC's shareholding serves, however, an important purpose: it gives the CSISC the necessary standing required under Chinese law to act in the capacity of a shareholder, thereby entitling it to all rights conferred upon the shareholder. The CSISC claims that it avails itself of the wide array of shareholder rights vested in it as a shareholder[105] in order to serve a public good, namely the safeguarding of the legal rights and interests of minority shareholders.[106] It may do so on its own or, where appropriate, acting in concert with other shareholders.[107]

The CSISC has in recent years emerged as an activist shareholder, wielding considerable influence on the Chinese listed sector. By August 2019, the CSISC had participated in 2,471 shareholder meetings, exercised shareholder rights on 3,210 occasions and brought one lawsuit against a listed company.[108]

2.3 SHAREHOLDER VOTING AND ENGAGEMENT IN PRACTICE

2.3.1 *Voting in Practice*

Chinese listed companies have since 2006 been required to disclose, after each shareholders' meeting, information on shareholder turnout and voting outcomes. Such disclosures include the number of shareholders (and proxies) attending the shareholders' meeting, the number and percentage of shares held by them and the voting outcomes of each of the resolutions.[109] An additional disclosure requirement was introduced in 2014 for minority votes. As well as disclosing the votes cast by all of the shareholders, listed companies are now also required to disclose separately the votes cast by minority shareholders, as a group, on the resolutions that are deemed to have a significant impact on their interests. Minority shareholders are defined as shareholders holding 5 per cent or less of the company's shares. The purpose of the reform was to amplify the 'voice' of minority shareholders, thereby incentivizing their participation in the governance of

103 Article 80, Code of Corporate Governance.

104 Article 78, Code of Corporate Governance.

105 Article 2, Zhong Zheng Zhong Xiao Tou Zi Zhe Fu Wu Zhong Xin Chi Gu Xing Quan Gong Zuo Gui Ze (Shi Xing) [CSISC Rules For Shareholding and Exercising the Rights of Shareholders (for Trial Implementation)], promulgated by CSISC, 15 May 2019.

106 Ibid., Article 1.

107 Ibid., Articles 2 and 3.

108 Doudou Qi, 'Tou Fu Zhong Xin: Ji Xu Tui Chu Tou Bao Xin Fang Fa Xin Ju Cuo Ji Zhi [Investment Service Center: Continue to Introduce New Measures and Mechanisms for Insuring]' *Shang Hai Zheng Quan Bao [Shanghai Securities News]* (Shanghai, 9 September 2019) http://company.cnstock.com/company/scp_gsxw/201909/4428212.htm accessed 15 July 2020. These figures, although significant, need of course to be understood in the context of the size of the Chinese listed sector, which at the end of 2018 boasted a total of 3,583 listed companies. See 2018 CSRC Annual Report, 79.

109 Article 39(1), GM Rules.

their invested firms.[110] The disclosure requirement for minority votes, per se, does not confer upon disinterested, minority shareholders the power to veto a resolution.

Data on shareholder voting was manually and systematically collected from the company disclosure documents released after each and every shareholders' meeting of all Chinese companies listed on the main board of the Shanghai Stock Exchange (SHSE) during the four-year period from 2015 to 2018. The period of investigation commenced in 2015 because this was the first year in which the disclosure requirement for minority votes was universally observed.[111] The sample firms were all drawn from those listed on the SSE, and did not include those listed on its sibling Shenzhen Stock Exchange (SZSE). This was because new initial public offerings (IPOs) on the SZSE were halted in 2000. All Chinese IPOs since then have been floated only on the SHSE. The SHSE samples thus present a considerably fuller and less biased picture of the A-share listed sector.

The source of the sample firms' disclosure documents is CNInfo,[112] a website officially designated by the Chinese regulatory authorities for online release of disclosure documents. These documents are in PDF format, and are mostly machine readable. Data has subsequently been extracted from them by using advanced data mining programmes that have been developed for the special purposes of this study.

Our dataset thus includes 1,041 SHSE-listed firms in 2015, 1,117 firms in 2016, 1,341 firms in 2017 and 1,434 firms in 2018, respectively.[113] These firms held 14,959 annual and extraordinary shareholders' meetings during the period 2015 to 2018. In other words, each Chinese listed company held, on average, 3.03 meetings per year. In total over 124,652 resolutions (or, on average, 8.33 resolution per shareholders' meeting) with voting outcomes were recorded in our dataset. To the best of our knowledge, this is by far the most comprehensive and inclusive dataset on shareholder voting in China's A-share markets.

As Figure 2.1 shows, there was a marked variation in shareholders' turnout, ranging from close to 0 per cent to close to 100 per cent. The close to 0 per cent attendance occurred in rare circumstances where a shareholders' meeting was not attended by the largest shareholder (or indeed any large shareholders) but by only small, minority shareholders. A closer look at the data shows that attendance differed significantly from one company to another, and often differed within the same company from one meeting to another. However, there appears, overall, to have been a general uptick of shareholders turnout during the 2015–18 period. The median (and average) ratios of shares held by the shareholders participating in the shareholders' meeting increased from below 50 per cent in 2015 to slightly over 50 per cent in 2018. To place the turnout ratios in context, it is worth noting that the single largest shareholders of the Chinese firms owned on average 35.93 per cent of the shares, as indicated above.

Counterintuitively, the general upward trend in respect of shareholders' participation as measured by shares they represented did not translate into a similar increase in the headcounts of attending shareholders. On the contrary, the average (and median) numbers of shareholders

110 'Jie Du Zhong Xiao Tou Zi Zhe Bao Hu Yi Jian De Liu Da Liang Dian [Interpretation of the Six Improvements on the Protection of Small and Medium Investors]' *Xinhua News Agency* (China, 27 December 2013) www.gov.cn/jrzg/2013-12/27/content_2555926.htm accessed 15 July 2020.

111 In 2014, 64 per cent of Chinese listed companies had complied with the requirement. See, '2015 Nian Quan Guo Zheng Quan Qi Huo Jian Guan Gong Zuo Hui Yi Zai Jing Zhao Kai [The 2015 National Securities and Futures Regulatory Work Conference was Held in Beijing]', CSRC (16 January 2015) www.csrc.gov.cn/pub/newsite/zjhxwfb/xwdd/201501/t20150116_266708.html accessed 15 July 2020.

112 See www.cninfo.com.cn accessed 15 July 2020.

113 A small number of SHSE-listed firms do not appear in our dataset, for two main reasons. Either their company disclosure documents are not machine-readable, or they were firms which listed in the latter part of the year and did not hold a shareholders' meeting before the end of the year.

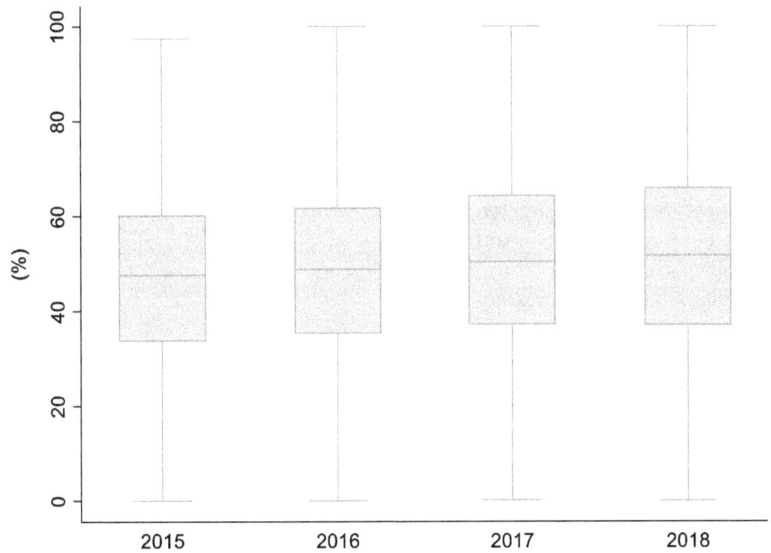

FIGURE 2.1 Shareholder turnouts at the Shanghai Stock Exchange, 2015–18
Note: Turnouts are defined as the shares held by the participating shareholders relative to the company's total outstanding shares, expressed in percentage terms.

participating in the meeting, either in person, by proxy or online, decreased sharply from 46 (21) in 2015 to 36.19 (15) in 2016, as shown in Figure 2.2. The numbers have generally stabilized since. The sharp drop seen in 2015–16 seems perplexing. It may have resulted from the turmoil in the securities market in the summer of 2015, when the SSE Composite Index fell by as much as 43 per cent in the three months of June, July and August. The market boom in 2015 seems to have propelled the yearly number of active share trading accounts to a historical high of 58.8 million in 2015, up from 33.8 million in 2014. The number dropped sharply by over 55 per cent to 26.2 million in 2016.[114] The marked decline in the headcounts of shareholders in 2015–16 may have mirrored a broader drop in the number of active investors in the A-share markets. Taking the modest increase in shareholder turnouts and sharp decline in shareholder headcounts together, the drop seems largely to have been attributable to investors holding insignificant equity stake. It may also have resulted from growing interest, albeit modest, among large shareholders in participating in shareholders' meetings.[115]

Consisting of over 120,000 resolutions, our dataset sheds fresh light on the types of resolutions on which Chinese shareholders in the sample firms voted. The parameters for the resolution types are defined broadly by the Model AoA, as indicated above. Table 2.1 shows that, among the fifteen types of resolutions prescribed by the Model AoA,[116] the largest cohort of resolutions consists of election of directors/supervisors and their remuneration, accounting for 21.48 per cent. It is followed by business policies and investment plans (15.61 per cent) and capital increase/decrease (14.11 per cent). The least common types of resolutions are merger, split, dissolution or liquidation (0.64 per cent) and share-option scheme (2.01 per cent). It should

[114] The 2014 and 2015 data is drawn from the annual reports of the China Securities Depository and Clearing Corporation Limited (CSDC). The 2016 data is drawn from the CSDC monthly reports in 2016. No comparable data has been released by the CSDC since 2017.

[115] I thank Christoph van der Elst for this observation.

[116] Among these fifteen types, one type, that is, use of the funds raised for other purposes, recorded almost negligible percentage of resolutions and, therefore, it grouped into the Others category.

TABLE 2.1 *Resolutions at the shareholders meetings at the Shanghai Stock Exchange, 2015–18*

Resolution Type	Percentage	Approval Rate
Business polies and investment plans	15.61%	97.96%
Director/supervisor election and remuneration	21.48%	N.A.[117]
Work report of the board of directors	3.88%	99.43%
Work report of the supervisory board	3.81%	99.38%
Annual budget and accounts	4.29%	99.45%
Profit distribution and loss coverage	3.95%	99.26%
Capital increase or decrease	14.11%	97.56%
Bond issuance	4.50%	99.43%
Merger, split, dissolution, or liquidation	0.64%	99.10%
Charter amendments	3.30%	99.26%
Appointment of accountants	4.50%	99.11%
Guarantees	4.83%	98.85%
Substantial acquisition or disposal of assets	2.94%	97.50%
Share-option scheme	2.01%	98.62%
Others	10.15%	98.94%

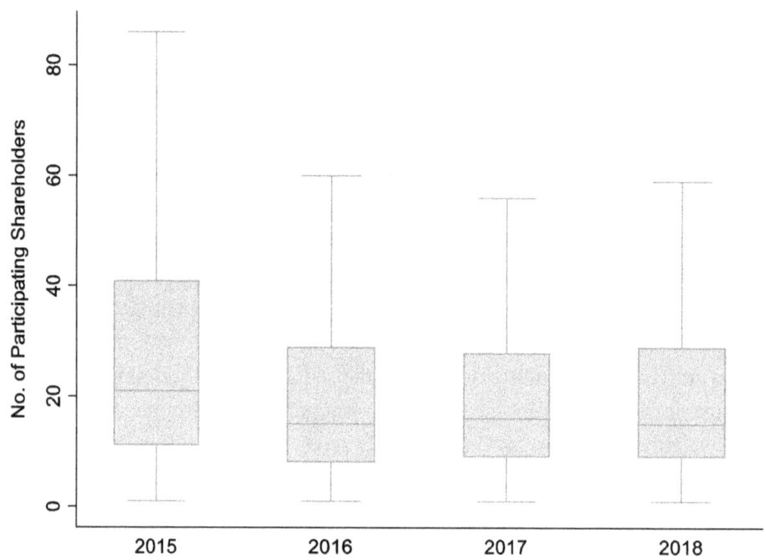

FIGURE 2.2 The numbers of shareholders participating in the shareholders meetings at the Shanghai Stock Exchange, 2015–18
Note: Outliers have been removed.

be noted that 10.15 per cent of the resolutions did not fall conveniently into the resolution types preset by the Model AoA, and have been classified by us as 'Others'.

Formal shareholder dissent was infrequent in the sample firms, as our data shows in Figure 2.3. Of sample resolutions (ex-director/supervisor elections), 22.73 per cent were approved unanimously, and a further 49.10 per cent were approved by between 99.9 per cent and 100 per cent of the participating shareholders. Another 16.56 per cent of the sample resolutions

[117] Due to the use of cumulative voting, approval rates for director/supervisor elections can go beyond the 0–100 per cent range and are therefore not comparable.

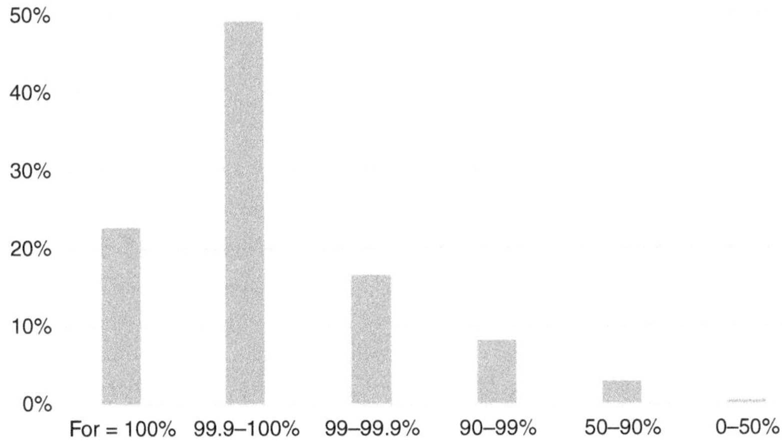

FIGURE 2.3 Resolution-level approval ratios at the Shanghai Stock Exchange, 2015–18

were supported by over 99 per cent but less than 99.9 per cent of shareholders who cast votes. Together, close to 90 per cent of the sample resolutions had approval rates higher than 99 per cent. Clearly, formal shareholder dissent is almost unknown in the Chinese listed sector. It is notable that 0.50 per cent of the sample resolutions were not supported by a majority of the shareholders.[118] Among these resolutions, 34 per cent fall into the category of 'business policies and investment plans', and 22 per cent into the group of 'capital increase or decrease'.

Having said this, the levels of shareholder approval differed across various types of resolutions, as shown in Table 2.1. Shareholder approval was the highest in the more routine and mundane types of resolutions considered at the annual shareholders' meeting. These include the work report of the board of directors (99.43 per cent on average), the work report of the supervisory board (99.38 per cent on average) and the annual budget and accounts (99.45 per cent on average). Bond issuance was another resolution type that received high levels of shareholder support (99.43 per cent on average). Shareholder dissent was most common in two types of resolutions known for their potential conflicts of interest in China's institutional settings: (1) capital increase, typically via rights issues or private placements (97.56 per cent on average); and (2) substantial acquisition (or disposal) of assets (97.50 per cent on average). Surprisingly, the provision of a guarantee (typically in favour of the listed company's controlling shareholder or its affiliates), a once-popular method of 'tunnelling' in the Chinese markets, did not record particularly high levels of shareholder disapproval (such resolutions, on average, were supported by 98.85 per cent of the shareholders).

2.3.2 *Shareholder Activism: Case Studies*

Our dataset offers a new window through which the role of institutional investors can be examined more empirically. Importantly, they offer a way of more directly identifying companies that were targets of activist investors, by pinning down the resolutions that were either voted down (typically receiving less than 50 per cent of the votes cast) or faced high levels of

[118] Certain types of resolutions require the approval of a super-majority. These include charter amendments; capital increase or decrease; and merger, split, dissolution or liquidation. See Article 103(2), Company Law. For the ease of reporting the findings, a universal line of 50 per cent is drawn for all types of resolutions.

shareholder disapproval. This enabled us to focus our inquiry on a relatively small pool of target companies.

Having identified these target companies, we arranged semi-structured elite interviews, to the extent that access could be secured, in which we met face-to-face with activist investors and, where possible, management of the sample companies. The circumstances surrounding the activist events were discussed with interviewees. In keeping with standard practices, interviewees were promised total anonymity and confidentiality. Importantly, because of the highly sensitive nature of the matters involved, interviewees' identities are anonymized to the best of our ability.[119] Interview data were verified against, and supplemented by, news media coverage of the activist events.

Two activist scenarios have emerged: activist investors voting down resolutions initiated by the management or the controlling shareholder; and activist investors initiating their own proposals. Each of the scenarios are illustrated in reference to specific activist cases.

2.3.2.1 Shareholder Voting on Management Resolutions

An overwhelming majority of the resolutions put to the vote at the shareholder's meetings in Chinese listed companies are initiated either by the board of directors or by the company's controlling shareholder (which in effect appoints the board). For ease of reference, these resolutions are referred to generally as management resolutions. By contrast, proposals initiated by non-controlling shareholders were rare, and will be dealt with at greater length in the succeeding Section 2.3.2.2.

Company A

Company A is one of the national leaders in its own sector. Its 2016 AGM was otherwise uneventful but for the shareholder disapproval of one resolution. The resolution concerned was a related-party transaction, more specifically, a proposed transaction between Company A and a finance company controlled by Company A's controlling shareholder, under which the latter was to provide financial services to Company A. By way of background, it has become common for each Chinese central state-owned enterprise (SOE) to set up an in-house finance company, which in many cases takes the place of external banking institutions to provide financial services to its members, including its controlled listed companies.[120] The resolution had the unanimous support of Company A's board of directors.

As the interested shareholder, Company A's controlling shareholder was excluded from voting on the related-party transaction in question, by way of the operation of the MoM rule. The controller owned close to two thirds of Company A's outstanding shares, giving any large minority shareholder the opportunity to leverage on the MoM rule and swing the voting outcomes. The voting results showed that close to 10 per cent of Company A's eligible votes were cast, presumably all by minority shareholders, on the resolution concerned, and close to 90 per cent of the shares cast were against it. Among the dissenting shareholders, a non-controlling shareholder owning well over 5 per cent (but less than 10 per cent) of Company A's outstanding shares was almost single-handedly responsible for the defeat of the resolution concerned.

The activist shareholder concerned is part of one of the world's largest mutual fund groups (Group), operating primarily outside Mainland China at the time of the AGM. The Group as

119 Mark N. K. Saunders, Philip Lewis and Adrian Thornhill, *Research Methods for Business Students* (7th ed., Pearson 2015).

120 Milhaupt and Lin (n. 39).

a whole, and a subsidiary of the Group in particular, have gained the reputation of being active owners in their invested portfolio companies. For over a decade, Company A had been a portfolio company, at different times, of at least six of the Group's emerging markets or Asian-focused mutual funds, among which one Asian-focused fund (Fund) was at the very centre of the activist situation under discussion. In the Fund's highly diversified portfolios, Company A was not an insignificant investment. At the time of the 2016 AGM, Company A represented just under 2 per cent of the Fund's assets under management (with many other portfolio companies weighing less than 1 per cent). The Group, as indicated above, was a significant minority shareholder of Company A. Its funds constantly appeared in Company A's list of top ten shareholders and were, indeed, collectively the largest shareholder outside of the controlling shareholder at various times. The Group's holding in Company A climbed, over time, from below the threshold of 5 per cent (which triggers a disclosure obligation on the part of the Group under PRC law) of its outstanding shares to over 5 per cent and, in more recent years, gradually stabilized.

Company A's management was aware that the resolution was likely to be contentious with minority shareholders. The Group's significant holding in Company A meant that the Group's support for the resolution was crucial for its safe passage.[121] After the AGM notice was released, the management used standard communication methods, such as emails and telephone calls, to reach out to the Fund manager in relation to the resolution in question. The management indeed went the extra mile to engage with the Fund manager prior to the AGM: they enlisted the help of a leading global investment bank that at the time was advising the Company on a separate business matter to arrange a visit for them to an overseas office of the Fund manager.

The positions of the management and the Fund manager were far apart. The management emphasized that the resolution concerned was an arrangement commonly seen among their peers, that is, listed companies controlled by central SOEs. From a pragmatic point of view, it would not be in a position to resist such a top-down, centralized arrangement made by the parent central SOE. The Fund manager counterclaimed that, though they understood the resolution to be a commonality, there was not much they could do either. Their hands were also tied, the Fund manager explained, as their voting decisions were informed, if not dictated, by recommendations from a third-party proxy advisory firm, which advised that the resolution concerned should not be supported. Neither party felt that it was possible to change their prior positions.

Despite the impasse, the resolution proceeded to a vote at the 2016 AGM, only to be rejected, principally because of the Fund's opposition. The management had to subsequently reduce the aggregate size of the related-party transactions involved to a level that fell below the threshold that triggers the requirement for the approval of the minority shareholders. As a result, only board-level endorsement would be required, and this was successfully secured for what was essentially a toned-down version of the rejected resolution.

This was not the end of the saga. The management made a second attempt to push through the proposed related-party transaction voted down at the 2016 AGM at an EGM in 2018. Neither the management nor the Fund was prepared to move from the positions which they had held in 2016, and in the run-up to the EGM did little more than restate these positions. Unsurprisingly, therefore the second resolution met the same fate as the first, with the Fund, once again, casting votes decisively against it.

121 Abstaining from voting does not count as a form of 'support' under PRC law. This is because abstentions are counted toward the total number of votes cast on a resolution.

Company B

Company B is one of the many listed companies controlled by its parent conglomerate. At its 2016 AGM, two resolutions received less than 50 per cent of the votes cast to pass. Both resolutions were concerned with related-party transactions with other firms under the control of Company B's parent firm. One of these resolutions sought an *en bloc* ratification of a number of related-party transactions which had taken place earlier in the year, while the other sought blanket shareholder approval of a related-party transaction planned for 2017. While transactions of this nature may seem dubious to outside observers, they are far from uncommon in the A-share market. They both had the support of all independent members of the board (non-independent directors excused themselves from the board deliberation on the resolutions concerned, as required under PRC law).

Company B's parent company controlled just over 50 per cent of its outstanding shares at the time of its 2016 AGM. When it comes to holdings of minority shareholders, Company B differed from Company A in an important way: it did not count institutional investors as its large minority shareholders; nor did it have individual shareholders who had significant holdings. Perhaps as a result of Company B's dispersed minority shareholder base, attendance by non-controlling shareholders of its AGMs and EGMs was historically low (in many cases, lower than 0.2 per cent of the shares)

For related-party resolutions, the low attendance rate of non-controlling shareholders poses a significant risk that the resolution will fail because of opposition from relatively insignificant shareholders. This was indeed what happened with the two resolutions in question. Minority shareholders holding just less than 0.9 per cent of Company B's outstanding shares took part in its 2016 AGM. Among their number, shareholders holding just over 0.5 per cent of outstanding shares voted against the resolutions, sealing their fate. None of these dissenting shareholders were among Company B's list of top ten shareholders, and many of them were retail, individual shareholders, disgruntled at their personal financial losses because of the sharp drop in Company B's shares.

The voting outcomes delivered a severe shock to the management, which promptly entered negotiations with around a dozen activist shareholders, mostly individual shareholders with relatively large holdings. The management's position was that the related-party transactions involved were indispensable for the company's conduct of business. Shareholder disapproval would only thrust the transactions into a state of legal uncertainty and hamper the company's operations, thereby threatening to reduce the company's share price even further. The shareholders' discontent, on the other hand, was apparently more with Company B's sub-par share price performance than with the shareholder wealth effect of the resolutions concerned. As a result, an improvement in Company B's share price performance took the sting out of the issue and enabled a consensus to be reached. A number of dissenting shareholders were approached by the management, and agreed not to oppose the resolutions concerned if they were again put to the vote at a further EGM.

The following EGM was attended by minority shareholders holding 2.5 per cent of Company B's outstanding shares (compared to 0.9 per cent at the 2016 AGM). On this occasion, the shareholders who voted against the resolutions represented slightly less than 0.2 per cent of the shares (compared to just over 0.5 per cent at the 2016 AGM). With over 90 per cent approval rates, both resolutions passed without further ado.

2.3.2.2 Shareholder-Initiated Proposals

As noted in the previous Section, resolutions of A-share listed companies are predominantly management or controlling-shareholder initiated. There were, however, cases where minority shareholders proposed resolutions ('shareholder proposals') of their own, resulting in proxy contests in certain circumstances. It remains a technically daunting task to discern with any precision the frequency and level of shareholder proposals in the Chinese securities markets. It is safe to state, however, that shareholder proposals are far from common.

Shareholder proposals were submitted in both of the following activist cases, succeeding in one case and largely failing in the other. Both of the companies involved were household names in Mainland China. Activist interventions in both cases unfolded in dramatic ways and drew considerable media attention.

Company C

Company C used to be a leading player in its own market, but in recent years its financial performance has been in decline. The parent SOE's holding in Company C was unusually low; by the time the activists intervened, it held just over 20 per cent of Company C's outstanding shares. On the other hand, there was a strong presence of large minority shareholders, each owning not insignificant percentages (over 2 per cent) of its shares.

Minority shareholders were dissatisfied with Company C' s financial performance. They attributed it to what they perceived as the parent company's predatory behaviour. Among the most dramatic was the parent company's claim for title over a valuable piece of land that had been thought to belong solely to Company C, a disagreement resulting dramatically in an arbitration initiated by Company C against its parent company.

The tension between the controlling shareholder and minority shareholders culminated in confrontations during board elections at Company C's 2014 AGM. Both of Company C's dual boards were subject to elections. Our focus here is, however, on the election of the board of directors, since it was the key to the contest for corporate control. Company C's seven-member board reserves four seats for non-independent directors and three for independent directors. Rather than holding one single election for all seven seats, two 'tranche' elections were held separately, one for independent directors and the other for non-independent directors. The practical effect of the arrangement was to blunt the full force of cumulative voting, from the controlling shareholder's point of view.

For the four board seats reserved for non-independent directors, seven candidates stood for election, of whom four were nominees of the controlling shareholders and three were proposed by minority shareholders. In this unusually contested election, the importance of an effective voting strategy loomed large. The controlling shareholder spread its votes evenly and cast the same number of votes for each of its four candidates. By contrast, the dissenting minority shareholders voted more strategically. In what appeared to be a coordinated effort, they pooled their multiplied votes between two of the three candidates they nominated. The voting strategy turned out to be a success. The two minority-shareholder nominees were both elected, receiving far more votes than the candidates nominated by the controlling shareholder. Hence, two out of the four management nominees were defeated.

The elections to the three board seats earmarked for independent directors were equally dramatic. Once again, the controlling shareholders nominated three candidates,[122] and cast their votes evenly among their three nominees.[123] The minority shareholders, on the other hands, concentrated their votes on the two candidates they nominated. As a result, the two minority-shareholder nominees defeated two of the three management nominees.

[122] In practice, the controlling shareholder is entitled to nominate, typically via its controlled board, independent directors, insofar as the nominees meet the requirements for independence prescribed by law.

[123] The MoM rule does not apply to cumulative voting.

The voting outcomes dealt a heavy blow to the controlling parent SOE. It lost its control over Company C's board to a coalition of effectively organized minority shareholders that strategically used cumulative voting to their advantage. Out of the seven board seats, four seats went to the nominees representing the minority shareholders. Even more worrying for the controlling shareholder was the election at a subsequent board meeting of one of the minority-shareholder nominees to the board chairmanship.

The activist shareholders' success in winning a contest for corporate control over a central SOE-controlled listed company was unprecedented, and thrust Company C into media spotlight. The controlling shareholder came under considerable pressure, and was forced to negotiate with the dissenting minority shareholders with a view to regaining control over the board. The shareholder activists, on the other hand, seemed to be more interested in changing the direction of the company's businesses in ways that better aligned with their interests than in taking the control of Company C into their own hands. After all, their victory was precarious. The controlling shareholder could call a re-election, use the same strategic voting tactics previously used by the activists, and win back board control. The parent SOE also enhanced its position by significantly increasing its shareholding in Company C to just below 30 per cent, presumably to avoid triggering the mandatory bid rule.

Negotiations soon resolved the disagreements between the parent SOE and shareholder activists. Within a few months, two activist-shareholder nominees resigned from the board and were replaced by two directors nominated by the controlling shareholder, resulting in a resumption of control by the parent company.

Company D

Company D's parent company has been a national champion. It controlled Company D and another listed company. It owned over 50 per cent of Company D's outstanding shares. Company D was popular among institutional investors, with many mutual funds and hedge funds reportedly building not insignificant stakes in Company D.

The issue at the centre of Company D's shareholder discontent was a corporate governance problem that has long plagued the Chinese listed sector, that is, the parent company putting itself in direct competition with its own controlled subsidiaries. This represents a typical instance of a majority-minority conflict and, in the case of Company D, its parent company was perceived have exploited the conflict at the expense of the minority shareholders. The Chinese regulatory authorities had taken active steps to push the controlling shareholders in conflict to mitigate the corporate governance concern. As with many other SOE groups, Company D's parent company promised in the early 2010s to resolve within a five-year period the parent-subsidiary competition, widely speculated to be by way of a listing of the whole SOE group that promised to eradicate the conflict and boost Company D's performance.

Just before the five-year period elapsed in mid-2016, however, Company D's controlling company announced its intention to extend this period by three years. The announcement resulted in a plunge in Company D's share price (which fell by a stunning 13.5 per cent in the two trading days immediately following the announcement), triggering an unprecedented public campaign levelled by activist investors against Company D.

At the centre of the campaign was a medium-sized, activist investment fund manager (hereafter 'the Fund'). Its investment portfolios in Company D were relatively modest and below the 3 per cent threshold necessary for it to submit a shareholder proposal on its own. Thus, soon after Company D's announcement was made, the Fund released a series of widely reported public letters on its official website, seeking proxies to vote against the parent company's proposal and to back the Fund's own proposals. In very little time, proxies from over 100 shareholders, mostly individual shareholders and some institutional investors, had been acquired by the Fund, allowing it to meet the 3 per cent eligibility requirement for shareholder proposals. The Fund brought forward three proposals, all contesting the controlling shareholder's period extension proposal. One of these proposals was particularly noteworthy, namely that Company D's parent company should fulfil its pledge as originally scheduled, failing which it should be held liable for compensating investors for any losses arising from their reliance on the company's earlier promise.

The Fund's many attempts to table its proposals, however, met considerable resistance from Company D's management. It was only with the securities regulatory agency's intervention that the proposals were successfully delivered to Company D. Subsequently, it took the intervention of the stock exchange on which Company D is listed and traded for the company to acknowledge the deposit of the proposals. However, the management went on to reject the Fund's proposals on narrow procedural grounds (the signed authorisation forms were not original copies), and excluded its supporters from the 2015 AGM altogether.

Having failed to have its proposals included in the AGM agenda, the Fund proceeded to intensify its efforts to level a proxy contest. About one week ahead of the 2015 AGM, the Fund issued another public letter, which again attracted keen media interest, calling for institutional investors to join forces. It also publicized its own proxy form, opposing most of the management proposals, particularly the period-extension proposal.

The dispute had been widely and enthusiastically reported in the media, with the result that the company's 2015 AGM attracted unprecedented shareholder interest. Over 4,000 minority shareholders cast votes, representing over 15 per cent of Company D's outstanding shares. As it was categorized as a related-party proposal, the parent company was excluded from voting on its own period-extension proposal. Over 97 per cent of the minority shareholders casting votes opposed the proposal, and it was decisively defeated.

2.4 CONCLUDING REMARKS

Empowerment of minority shareholders has been a central theme of China's corporate governance movements in the past two decades. Cumulative voting and the majority of the minority rule are exemplary of Chinese reformers' efforts to strengthen shareholders' rights to vote. Other shareholders' rights, such as the right to call a meeting, the right to propose and the right to information, are also in place and, at least in theory, enable public shareholders to engage the controlling shareholders of their investee companies. The practical effect of these legal rights needs to be evaluated in the context of China's path-dependent conditions, notably the prevalence of concentrated share ownership, the relatively weaker presence of institutional investors and the approach to allocating corporate power which centres on the shareholders' meeting.

The shareholder turnouts at shareholders' meetings stood at around 50 per cent during the 2015–19 period at the Shanghai Stock Exchange, placing China among the jurisdictions with the lowest levels of shareholder participation in the nineteen jurisdictions surveyed in the Handbook. Overall, shareholder dissent was infrequent, with a large percentage (over 20 per cent) of the resolutions winning the unanimous support of the shareholders who attended. Shareholders seem to have differentiated among different resolution types when casting their votes, lending some support to an observation made elsewhere that Chinese shareholders are not invariably passive and indifferent.[124] Anecdotes of institutional (and individual) shareholders opposing management proposals and initiating shareholder proposals, sometimes with success, highlight the potential of shareholder activism and engagement in China.[125]

[124] Chao Xi, 'Shareholder Voting and Corporate Sustainability in China' in Beate Sjåfjell and Christopher Bruner (eds.), *Cambridge Handbook of Corporate Law, Corporate Governance and Sustainability* (Cambridge University Press 2019) 431.

[125] For an earlier assessment of shareholder activism in China, see Chao Xi, 'Institutional Shareholder Activism in China: Law and Practice' (2006) 17 International Company and Commercial Law Review 251 and 287.

3

Shareholder Engagement and Voting in Hong Kong

Lauren Yu-Hsin Lin

3.1 OVERVIEW OF CORPORATE GOVERNANCE IN HONG KONG

Hong Kong has a mature capital market and well-developed corporate governance system. The Hong Kong Stock Exchange (HKSE) is the fourth-largest exchange in Asia and the seventh largest in the world.[1] As of December 2021, the HKSE had 2,572 listed companies with a combined market capitalization of US$5.4 trillion.[2] According to the corporate governance ranking published by the Asian Corporate Governance Association in 2020, Hong Kong ranked second amongst the twelve jurisdictions in the Asia-Pacific region.[3] Hong Kong is a common law jurisdiction, and the source of company law in Hong Kong comprises both statutory and common law.[4] Hong Kong has been improving its corporate law and corporate governance standards; the main statutory law, the Companies Ordinance (Cap. 622), underwent a major rewrite in 2014 to enhance Hong Kong's competitiveness and attractiveness as a major international financial centre.[5] With the rewrite, new sets of model articles of association were implemented as the default rules for companies that do not write their own articles.[6] The Companies (Model Articles) Notice (Cap. 622 H) stipulates various sets of model articles for both public and private companies. For companies listed on the main board of HKSE, the Main Board Listing Rules (Listing Rules) and the Appendix 14, 'Corporate Governance Code and Corporate Governance Report' (the 'Corporate Governance Code' hereafter), also govern the corporate governance of listed companies. The Corporate Governance Code sets out the principles of good corporate governance, and issuers must state whether they have complied with its provisions and supply reasons for any deviations from them in their interim and annual reports.

In general, minority shareholders in Hong Kong do not actively engage with companies or vote on company affairs. Given the presence of controlling shareholders, individual shareholders in Hong Kong usually support family controllers rather than the company when investing, and they vote with their feet to avoid poor corporate governance. Hedge funds were not active in the past simply because there was little opportunity to profit. Institutional shareholders, such as index funds and mutual funds, have been investing in Hong Kong for some time

1 Statista, 'Largest Stock Exchange Operators Worldwide as of March 2022' https://www.statista.com/statistics/270126/largest-stock-exchange-operators-by-market-capitalization-of-listed-companies/ accessed 24 May 2022.
2 HKEX Statistics, 'HKEX Annual Market Statistics' https://www.hkex.com.hk/Market-Data/Statistics/Consolidated-Reports/Annual-Market-Statistics?sc_lang=en accessed 24 May 2022.
3 ACGA, 'CG Watch 2020: Future Promise' https://www.acga-asia.org/cgwatch.php accessed 24 May 2022.
4 Stefan H. C. Lo and Zhen Charles Qu, *Law of Companies in Hong Kong* (3rd ed., Sweet & Maxwell 2018) 12.
5 Companies Ordinance Rewrite www.fstb.gov.hk/fsb/co_rewrite/eng/home/home.htm accessed 23 June 2020.
6 Cap. 622, s. 80.

but are also generally passive.[7] Activist campaigns, however, have increased steadily in recent years following promulgation of the 'Principles of Responsible Ownership' in March 2016. The Principles encourage investors to communicate with companies regularly about their expectations and voting policies. Whilst Asian controlling shareholders are generally hostile to outsiders, the Principles nevertheless provide institutional shareholders with a lever to engage company management, and some asset-management firms have made shareholder engagement part of their regular routines. For example, BlackRock has an investment-stewardship team dedicated to shareholder engagement and communication. There are also signs of change on the company side, with companies increasingly recognizing the virtues of engaging with their key stakeholders and carrying out crisis training and scenario planning to prepare for greater investor scrutiny.[8]

This chapter starts by introducing the basic corporate governance structure of Hong Kong companies in Section 3.1. It then discusses the legal means of shareholder engagement under Hong Kong company law and their pros and cons in Section 3.2. Finally, the practical application of each legal means is discussed and analyzed in Section 3.3. Section 3.4 concludes.

3.1.1 *The Role of the Board and Directors' Duties*

The board structure of Hong Kong companies follows the UK and US model, with a unitary board in charge of managing corporate affairs. General management power is usually vested in the board of directors by the company's constitution.[9] In general, directors owe a duty of care and fiduciary duties to the company. They must consider the interests of the company, meaning the interests of shareholders as a general body, when making business decisions.[10] Even though directors do not owe duties to creditors directly, they have a duty to consider the interests of creditors when the company is in the vicinity of insolvency.[11]

In the past, Hong Kong followed English common law in regulating director duties. The UK codified director duties in the Company Act of 2006. Following the UK, Hong Kong codified directors' duty of care in the Companies Ordinance in 2014. However, fiduciary duties are still largely governed by general law. Directors' equitable duties include a duty to act in good faith in the interests of the company; exercise power for a proper purpose; avoid conflicts of interest; not make secret profits; and not misappropriate company assets.[12] In addition to these equitable duties, statutory law strengthens the regulation of conflict-of-interest transactions that are of significance to the company's business by requiring the disclosure of material interests by directors and additional approval by boards of directors.[13] The HKSE's Listing Rules set out additional disclosure and procedural requirements for entering into 'connected transactions'

7 Yu-Hsin Lin, 'When Activists Meet Controlling Shareholders in the Shadow of the Law: A Case Study of Hong Kong' (2019) 14 Asian Journal of Comparative Law 1, 8.

8 Ibid.

9 Companies (Model Articles) Notice (Cap. 622H), Model Articles for Public Companies Limited by Shares, art. 2: 'Subject to the Ordinance and these articles, the business and affairs of the company are managed by the directors, who may exercise all the powers of the company'.

10 *Parke* v. *Daily News Ltd (No. 2)* [1962] ch. 927.

11 *Kinsela* v. *Russell Kinsela Pty Ltd (in liq)* (1986) 4 NSWLR 722; *Chingtung Futures Ltd (in liq)* v. *Lai Cheuk Kwan Arthur* [1992] 2 HKC 637.

12 *Moulin Global Eyecare Holdings Ltd* v. *Olivia Lee Sin Mei* 2014 WL 7153(CFA); [2014] HKEC 1175; *Wong Kam San* v. *Yeung Wing Keung* [2007] 2 HKLRD 267; *Man Luen Corp* v. *Sun King Electronic Printed Circuit Board Factory Ltd* [1981] HKC 407; *Kishimoto Sangyo Co Ltd* v. *Akio Oba* [1996] 2 HKC 260.

13 Cap. 622, ss. 536–8; Model Articles art. 15 (public companies) and Model Articles art. 16 (private companies): Companies (Model Articles) Notice (Cap. 622H) schs. 1 and 2.

with connected persons by listed companies.[14] In general, connected transactions require the approval of shareholders advised by an independent board committee solely comprising independent non-executive directors (INEDs).[15] Continuing connected transactions also require an annual review by INEDs and auditors.

INEDs play an important role on boards. The Listing Rules require at least one-third of the boards of listed companies to consist of INEDs.[16] To maintain their independence, the Corporate Governance Code stipulates a nine-year maximum period of service for INEDs. If an INED serves for more than nine years, any further appointment must be subject to a separate resolution approved by shareholders.[17] However, the effectiveness of independent directors has been widely questioned. The challenge in Hong Kong lies in the fact that boards are typically controlled by founding families or close-knit shareholding groups.[18] It is thus difficult for INEDs, who make up only one-third of boards, to effect changes or voice contrary opinions. A number of suggestions have been made for improving the professionalism of INEDs, including enhancing their training and education, limiting the number of directorships and reserving seats for minority shareholders.[19]

3.1.2 *Division of Corporate Powers*

The division of corporate powers between the board and general meeting is generally decided by company's articles of association (AoA). As noted, management power is generally vested in the board of directors. However, in cases where the articles are not clear about the division of powers, the courts must decide whether and how shareholders can override directors on management decisions. Before 2003, the division of corporate power was an unresolved, and even controversial, issue in Hong Kong. There are two views under general law: one allows shareholders to take over the management power of directors by a resolution, the threshold of which depends on the relevant regulation in the AoA, whilst the other treats directors' management power as exclusive – that is, shareholders can remove directors only if they do not agree with them.[20]

The issue was resolved in 2003 by adopting provisions in the Model Articles allowing shareholders to give directions to the board via a special resolution passed with the approval of 75 per cent of the total voting rights of the shareholders presented.[21] According to the Model Articles, management powers are vested in directors but are subject to control by shareholders through a special resolution of the general meeting.[22] However, to protect the third parties

14 Hong Kong Stock Exchange (HKSE) Main Board Listing Rules (Listing Rules), LR 13.68, ch. 14A.

15 Listing Rules, r. 14A.36–14A.43.

16 Listing Rules, r. 3.10A.

17 Listing Rules, Appendix 14 Corporate Governance Code and Corporate Governance Report, Part 2, r B.2.3.

18 Hong Kong Institute of Directors, 'Guide for Independent Non-executive Directors', July 2012.

19 Douglas W. Arner and others, 'Assessing Hong Kong as an International Financial Centre' (2014) University of Hong Kong Faculty of Law Research Paper No. 2014/012, 123–7.

20 The first view was illustrated in *Marshall's Valve Gear Co Ltd* v. *Manning Wardle & Co Ltd* [1909] 1 ch. 267 and arguably followed by the Hong Kong court in *Tam Kam-yip* v. *Yau Kung School* [1986] 1 HKLR 448. The latter view was led by *Automatic Self-Cleansing Filter Syndicate Co Ltd* v. *Cuninghame* [1906] 2 ch. 34 and followed in the later cases of *Quinn and Axtens Ltd* v. *Salmon* [1909] AC 442 (HL) and *John Shaw & Sons (Salford) Ltd* v. *Shaw* [1935] 2 KB 113.

21 Cap. 622, s. 564.

22 Regs. 2(1) and 3(1) of the 'Model Articles for Public Companies Limited by Shares' in Companies (Model Articles) Notice (Cap. 622H). Reg. 2(1): 'Subject to the Ordinance and these articles, the business and affairs of the company are managed by the directors, who may exercise all the powers of the company'. Reg. 3(1): 'The members may, by special resolution, direct the directors to take, or refrain from taking, specified action'. Similar provisions for private

involved in a given transaction, shareholders cannot invalidate a prior act of directors.[23] In addition to the general power-allocation provision, certain powers are vested specifically in directors or the general meeting pursuant to the Companies Ordinance or Model Articles.[24]

3.1.3 *Ownership Structure*

There are two main features of the ownership structure of Hong Kong-listed companies: share concentration and foreign incorporation. Around 85 per cent of the listed companies on the HKSE are foreign incorporated companies.[25] A study on the shareholding structure of fifteen major Hong Kong corporate groups found that more than 60 per cent of them were controlled by families or the state, whilst less than 10 per cent had a dispersed ownership structure.[26] In addition, a survey on the changes in controlling shareholdings from 2003 to 2012 found that the distribution of shareholdings moved towards concentration rather than dispersion in that period.[27] Family ownership is more common amongst listed companies in Hong Kong than it is in Indonesia, Korea, Japan or Singapore. A study published in 2000 revealed that the fifteen families in Hong Kong controlled 84 per cent of the listed assets of Hong Kong companies and that 72.5 per cent of the largest companies in Hong Kong were family-owned.[28]

Recent statistics show that mainland China concept firms, incorporated in the mainland or elsewhere, dominate the listing market in Hong Kong. There are three main types of mainland concept firms: H-Share, red chip and mainland private enterprises.[29] In 2004, mainland enterprises comprised only 16.6 per cent of HKSE listed companies and 27.7 per cent of HKSE market capitalization.[30] By the end of 2021, however, mainland enterprises accounted for 53 per cent of all Hong Kong listed companies and more than 79 per cent of HKSE market capitalization.[31] The composition of listed companies poses challenges for the HKSE and relevant government

companies are provided in regs. 3(1) and 4(1) of the 'Model Articles for Public Companies Limited by Shares' in Companies (Model Articles) Notice (Cap. 622H).

23 Reg. 4(2) of the 'Model Articles for Public Companies Limited by Shares' in Companies (Model Articles) Notice (Cap. 622H) states 'The special resolution does not invalidate anything that the directors have done before the passing of the resolution'.

24 For the board, some examples of its exclusive powers include (1) the power to appoint the company's first auditors, (2) the power to appoint an auditor to fill a casual vacancy in the office of the auditor and (3) the power on the part of the holding company's directors to decide whether the financial year of each subsidiary should coincide with the holding company's own financial year. The powers specifically reserved to the general meeting include the power to (1) alter the articles by special resolution, (2) alter the company's objects in the articles, (3) remove directors and (4) alter share capital. See Lo and Qu (n. 4) 198.

25 David C. Donald, *A Financial Centre for Two Empires: Hong Kong's Corporate, Securities and Tax Laws in Its Transition from Britain to China* (International Corporate Law and Financial Market Regulation, Cambridge University Press 2014) 54–6.

26 Ibid.

27 Ibid.

28 Stijn Claessens, Simeon Djankov and Larry H. P. Lang, 'The Separation of Ownership and Control in East Asian Corporations' (2000) 58 Journal of Financial Economics 81, 106.

29 H-share companies are enterprises that are incorporated in mainland China that are controlled by either mainland government entities or individuals; red chip companies are enterprises that are incorporated outside the mainland and are controlled by mainland government entities; and mainland private enterprises are companies that are incorporated outside the mainland and controlled by mainland individuals. HKSE, 'Annual Market Statistics 2021' https://www.hkex.com.hk/-/media/HKEX-Market/Market-Data/Statistics/Consolidated-Reports/Annual-Market-Statistics/2021-Market-Statistics_e.pdf accessed 26 May 2022.

30 Joseph Lee and Joanna Poon, 'The Listing of Mainland Companies on HKEx and the Implications for Hong Kong', SFC Research Paper (September 2004) www.sfc.hk/web/doc/EN/research/research/rs%20paper%2017.pdf accessed 10 July 2020.

31 HKSE (n. 29).

agencies in monitoring corporate governance and enforcing the Listing Rules and securities regulations. They must reconcile the differences in corporate governance standards in different jurisdictions and enhance cross-border cooperation in securities law enforcement, especially because 11 per cent of listed companies are Chinese state-owned enterprises, in which the Chinese government is the controlling shareholder.[32]

3.2 LEGAL MEANS OF SHAREHOLDER ENGAGEMENT AND VOTING

3.2.1 *Right to Attend the General Meeting*

In Hong Kong, shareholders have the right to attend general meetings. That right is fundamental because it affords shareholders an opportunity to meet and discuss corporate affairs, inspect annual financial statements, consider the reports of directors and auditors and elect directors.[33] Shareholders attending a general meeting are also entitled to raise questions with management concerning the company's affairs.[34] A hybrid meeting (online and in person) is generally allowed, meaning that a company can use relevant technology to hold a general meeting at more than one place unless its AoA state otherwise.[35] Shareholders can vote and speak even if they attend meetings online. In general, purely virtual meetings are not supported by the Companies Ordinance; listed companies are required to convene either physical or hybrid shareholder meetings.[36]

In light of the COVID-19 pandemic, the Hong Kong government has put social distancing measures in place to prohibit group gatherings in public places, including any place that the public or a section of the public can access or is permitted to access from time to time.[37] Following the prohibition on group gatherings, the Securities and Futures Commission (SFC) and HKSE released a joint statement on 1 April 2020 to instruct public companies on how to properly conduct general meetings during the pandemic.[38] By and large, annual general meetings (AGMs), which are required under the Companies Ordinance, are exempt from the group-gathering prohibition. Although extraordinary general meetings (EGMs) also fall within the exemption, they must be held within the prohibition's effective period to comply with the law or another regulatory instrument. The aforementioned joint statement also encourages listed companies to consider longer adjournments or delays and to ensure that necessary precautions are in place to ensure the safety of attendees.[39]

3.2.2 *Right to Vote*

In the general meeting, shareholders vote to make decisions collectively by resolution. The Companies Ordinance requires a quorum of two members for a general meeting.[40] As a general

32 Donald (n. 25) 56.
33 Lo and Qu (n. 4) 344–5.
34 Ibid.; see also *Standard Bank Offshore Trust Co Jersey Ltd* v. *Belgravia Properties Ltd* [2013] HKEC 1429, [14].
35 Cap. 622, s. 584(1): 'A company may hold a general meeting at 2 or more places using any technology that enables the members of the company who are not together at the same place to listen, speak and vote at the meeting'.
36 HKSE, 'Hybrid Virtual Meeting in HK' (2019) https://aecsd.org/upload/iblock/64e/GM_24_354.pdf accessed 10 July 2020.
37 The Prevention and Control of Disease (Prohibition on Group Gathering) Regulation (Cap. 599G).
38 Joint Statement in relation to General Meetings in light of the Prevention and Control of Disease (Prohibition on Group Gathering) Regulation (1 April 2020) www.sfc.hk/edistributionWeb/gateway/EN/news-and-announcements/news/doc?refNo=20PR30 accessed 8 July 2020.
39 Ibid.
40 Cap. 622, s. 585(3).

rule, there are two types of resolution in Hong Kong: ordinary resolutions and special resolutions. Pursuant to section 563 of the Companies Ordinance, ordinary resolutions are passed by a simple majority. All resolutions stipulated in the Ordinance and companies' AoA are ordinary resolutions unless otherwise specified.[41] Special resolutions, in contrast, are passed by a majority of at least 75 per cent.[42] Certain affairs must be decided by special resolutions, such as an alteration in the company's AoA,[43] a change of the company name,[44] a reduction in the company's share capital[45] or members' voluntary winding-up.[46]

Every shareholder has a right to vote in the general meeting subject to the company's AoA.[47] In principle, one share is entitled to one vote unless the company issues dual-class shares and defines relevant rights in its AoA.[48] In the past, the HKSE followed the one-share-one-vote principle, and consequently rejected Alibaba's initial public offering (IPO) request.[49] Because Alibaba is a benchmark enterprise and its 2014 IPO on the New York Stock Exchange was the largest IPO in the world at the time, the HKSE experienced immense pressure from market participants in Hong Kong to lift the ban on dual-class shares and other similar governance structures.[50] After three public consultations, the HKSE finally decided to allow the dual-class share structure in firms listed in or after April 2018.[51] To protect minority shareholders, the Listing Rules require that firms that issue so-called 'weighted-voting rights' shares must cap these super-voting shares at ten votes per share and decide certain issues, such as article alterations, on a one-share-one-vote basis.[52]

Shareholders can vote for or against a resolution. In general, voting is conducted by a show of hands unless a poll is demanded.[53] However, for listed companies, the HKSE requires that all votes at the general meeting be taken by poll except for those concerning procedural or administrative matters decided by the chairperson of the meeting.[54] Shareholders can attend the meeting either in person or online. They also have the option not to attend the meeting but to submit a proxy to appoint nominees to attend, speak and vote on their behalf.[55] Normally,

41 Cap. 622, s. 562(3).
42 Cap. 622, s. 564.
43 Cap. 622, s. 88(2).
44 Cap. 622, s. 107.
45 Cap. 622, s. 218.
46 Companies (Winding Up and Miscellaneous Provisions) Ordinance (Cap. 32), s. 228.
47 Cap. 622, s. 588(1), (4).
48 Cap. 622 s. 588 (3)(a)(i), ss. 176–84; Model Articles (public companies) art. 61.
49 Paul J. Davies and Arash Massoudi, 'Alibaba Abandons $60bn Hong Kong Listing' *Financial Times* (London, 26 September 2013) www.ft.com/content/525f4bc2-25ae-11e3-aee8-00144feab7de accessed 22 July 2020.
50 Reuters, 'Loss of Alibaba IPO Spurs Calls for Reforms of Hong Kong Listing Rules' *South China Morning Post* (Hong Kong, 27 September 2013) www.scmp.com/business/companies/article/1318917/loss-alibaba-ipo-spurs-calls-reforms-hong-kong-listing-rules accessed 22 July 2020.
51 The consultation started in August 2014. After three rounds of public consultation, in April 2018, the HKSE finally proposed an amendment to its listing rules to allow newly listed companies to issue dual-class shares. See HKSE, 'Concept Paper – Weighted Voting Rights' (August 2014); HKSE, 'Consultation Conclusions – To Concept Paper on Weighted Voting Right' (June 2015); HKSE, 'Concept Paper – New Board' (June 2017); HKSE, 'Consultation Conclusions – New Board Concept Paper' (December 2017); HKSE, 'Consultation Paper-A Listing Regime for Companies from Emerging and Innovative Sectors' (February 2018); HKSE, 'Consultation Conclusion – A Listing Regime for Companies from Emerging and Innovative Sectors' (April 2018) www.hkex.com.hk/News/Market-Consultations/2016-to-Present?sc_lang=en accessed 22 July 2020.
52 Main Board Listing Rules, r. 8A.10, 8A.24, 8A.25.
53 Model Articles (public companies) art. 47(1); Model Articles (private companies) art. 43(1).
54 Main Board Listing Rules, r. 13.39 (4): 'Any vote of shareholders at a general meeting must be taken by poll except where the chairman, in good faith, decides to allow a resolution which relates purely to a procedural or administrative matter to be voted on by a show of hands'.
55 Cap. 622, s. 596.

such appointments are made in the form of a signed hard copy of a written proxy document with the member's name and address and the nominee's name on it unless the company provides an online submission alternative.[56] As a general protection for shareholder interests, companies are obliged to endeavour to ensure that all shareholders are aware of their right to appoint nominees under the Companies Ordinance.[57] The HKSE further mandates that listed companies send their registered shareholders proxy forms with voting options on each resolution and notice of the general meeting.[58]

However, to attend the meeting in person or online or submit a proxy, investors must first be registered with the company concerned. Under the current regime, registered shareholders are usually not public investors who buy shares through a broker, bank or custodian. Accordingly, shares are either held by intermediaries through the Central Clearing and Automated Settlement System (CCASS), which is run by the Hong Kong Securities Clearing Company (HKSCC), or registered in the name of the intermediary's own nominee. Currently, most shares are held through CCASS because they must be in the system to be traded.[59] Shares so held are registered in the name of Hong Kong Securities Clearing Company Nominees (HKSCCN), which is the nominee subsidiary of HKSCC. Therefore, in reality, HKSCCN is the true legal owner, whilst investors are only the beneficial owners of their shares.[60]

Shareholders are eligible to attend, speak and vote at the general meeting only if they are the shareholders whose names are entered into the company's register of members.[61] Therefore, public investors who wish to attend the meeting can either try to register with the company as registered shareholders or, if the shares are held by intermediaries or CCASS, instruct them to appoint investors to attend the meeting in respect of their shares. Even if investors do not wish to attend the meeting, they can still instruct the intermediaries or CCASS, depending on how the shares are registered, how to vote their shares. The HKSE maintains an investor participant system by which shareholders can instruct the HKSCC on how to vote on corporate actions and activities.[62] Investors can send their instructions to CCASS either by phone or via the internet, and CCASS then sends its nominee or nominates the chairperson of the meeting to vote upon the investor's demand with a proxy form in the name of the HKSCC.[63] No vote is made if the investors concerned do not make such a demand.

However, when it comes to shares held by institutional investors, such as mutual funds and pension funds, those investors are expected to seek to vote all shares held for their clients according to the Principles of Responsible Ownership published in March 2016. The investors referred to in the Principles are those 'who invest money, or hold shares, on behalf of clients and other stakeholders and are accountable to such clients and other stakeholders', including but not

[56] Cap. 622, ss. 598, 599.

[57] Cap. 622, s. 597.

[58] Main Board Listing Rule, rr. 13.38, 2.07C(3).

[59] David Webb, 'How to Vote' (16 December 2010) at https://webb-site.com/pages/howtovote.asp accessed 2 July 2020.

[60] Hong Kong Stock Exchange, 'Guide to Eligibility and Admission of Securities to the Central Clearing and Settlement System' www.hkex.com.hk/-/media/HKEX-Market/Services/Settlement-and-Depository/Securities-Admission-into-CCASS/CCASS-Guide-July-2018.pdf?la=en accessed 2 November 2019.

[61] Cap. 622, s. 112(3).

[62] Investors, whether individuals, joint individuals or corporations, may apply to become Investor Participants of the HKSCC to enjoy the investor account services provided by the HKSCC. Investor Participants may vote on corporate actions and activities by giving voting instructions to HKSCC. See HKSE, 'Investor Account Services' www.hkex.com.hk/Services/Settlement-and-Depository/Investor-Account-Services?sc_lang=en accessed 2 November 2019.

[63] CCASS Operation Procedure Rule 8.6.2. See HKSE, CCASS Operation Procedure, www.hkex.com.hk/Services/Rules-and-Forms-and-Fees/Rules/HKSCC/Operational-Procedures?sc_lang=en accessed 2 November 2019.

limited to institutional shareholders.[64] The Principles are not intended to apply to retail and individual investors. If it is inappropriate to vote all of the shares held, institutional investors should disclose the reasons to their stakeholders. They should also not automatically support the board.[65] Having said that, the stewardship code in Hong Kong is entirely voluntary and non-binding.

3.2.3 *Right to Call a Meeting*

A company must call an AGM at least once a year. Under the Companies Ordinance and Model Articles, the board of directors has the power to call a general meeting.[66] Such power must be exercised by the board as a corporate organ, not by an individual director, unless otherwise authorized by statutory law or the company's AoA.[67] Companies must give proper notice to all parties eligible to attend the general meeting,[68] including notice of the place and time of the meeting, the issues to be discussed at the meeting, whether the meeting is an AGM and the content of any resolutions.[69] A company and its officers commit an offence if they fail to hold an AGM within the specified period.[70]

In general, shareholders do not have the power to call a general meeting if the board is capable of and willing to convene the meeting.[71] Shareholders who wish to have a meeting called must first demand that the board do so. Under the Companies Ordinance, shareholders who hold at least 5 per cent of total shares are entitled to demand that the board call an EGM.[72] Upon receiving a shareholder's demand, the board of directors is required to call the meeting within a specified period; otherwise, the shareholder who made the demand or any shareholders representing more than one-half of shareholders' total voting rights can call a meeting at the company's expense.[73] If a company lacks a director or sufficient directors capable of acting to form a quorum, two or more shareholders representing at least 10 per cent of the total voting rights can directly call a meeting without first demanding that the board do so.[74]

3.2.4 *Shareholder Proposal Right*

Shareholders have a right to make proposals at both the AGM and EGM. In an AGM, shareholders with at least 2.5 per cent of the voting rights of the total shares eligible to vote on the proposed resolution, or at least fifty shareholders entitled to vote on the resolution, can request in writing that the company include the resolution for discussion in the AGM's agenda.[75] Pursuant to section 616(1) of the Companies Ordinance, companies must also send a notice of the resolution proposed by shareholders to each member at the AGM.[76] For an EGM, the

[64] Securities and Futures Commission (SFC), 'Consultation Conclusions on the Principles of Responsible Ownership' (7 March 2016) 9.
[65] SFC, 'Principles of Responsible Ownership' (March 2016), principle 4, rule 25.
[66] Cap. 622, ss. 565, 610(1); Model Articles (public companies) art. 38(2); Model Articles (private companies) art. 34(2).
[67] Lo and Qu (n. 4) 347–8.
[68] Cap. 622, ss. 571–4.
[69] Cap. 622, s. 576(1).
[70] Cap. 622, s. 610(9).
[71] Cap. 622, s. 565.
[72] Cap. 622, s. 566(2).
[73] Cap. 622, ss. 567–8.
[74] Cap. 622, s. 569.
[75] Cap. 622, s. 615.
[76] Cap. 622, s. 616(1).

shareholders who demanded that the board convene the EGM can simultaneously propose a resolution intended to be moved at that meeting.[77] Also, according to the Corporate Governance Code, listed companies must provide their shareholders with the information they need to add a proposal to the meeting agenda.[78]

3.3 SHAREHOLDER ENGAGEMENT AND VOTING IN PRACTICE

As noted, most of the shares of Hong Kong-listed companies are controlled by families or the state. This concentration of corporate ownership poses a challenge to shareholder engagement and voting. Despite the passage of an investor stewardship code, via the Principles of Responsible Ownership, encouraging investors to communicate and engage with companies, engagement is generally ineffective in the absence of a strong voting position or a legal tool that can leverage the relatively weak voting position of outside shareholders. In situations in which Hong Kong company shares are concentrated in the hands of a few, legal mechanisms that protect minority shareholders could be decisive in campaigns against controlling shareholders. This section discusses shareholder voting in practice and the main legal tools that could be effective in engaging controlled firms in Hong Kong.

3.3.1 *Shareholder Voting in Practice*

The HKSE maintains a disclosure website on which investors can search and obtain information on voting in general meetings.[79] However, no single consolidated report exists on the aggregate level of shareholder voting and attendance in Hong Kong. Computershare, a proxy management firm, published a report on the voting statistics of the 377 Hong Kong-listed companies they managed from April to June 2017. It observed an increasing trend in retail shareholder attendance in recent years. The overall voting rate reached 70.10 per cent of total issued share capital in 2017. However, that high percentage was not the result of retail shareholder attendance, as only 26 per cent of those present actually voted. It was chiefly the result of votes cast by the HKSCC and majority shareholders.[80] According to Computershare, most retail shareholders attend general meetings to collect the gifts or souvenirs distributed by the companies concerned. More than 55 per cent of the questions asked at AGMs are related to gifts and souvenirs rather than to business or governance.[81]

Institutional Shareholder Services (ISS) also gathered general meeting voting data on the fifty largest companies in the HKSE, which represented around 60 per cent of its market capitalization from 2010 to 2013. The ISS report shows that the average voter turnout rate for AGMs and EGMs in Hong Kong increased from 68.8 per cent in 2010 to 74.4 per cent in 2013.[82] Based on the 2013 data, the voter turnout rate in Hong Kong in that year was higher than that in mainland China (54.7 per cent), France (69.6 per cent) or the UK (73.5 per cent) but lower than that in the

77 Cap. 622, s. 566 3(b).
78 Corporate Governance Code, para. O (c).
79 HKEx News www1.hkexnews.hk/search/titlesearch.xhtml?lang=en accessed 20 July 2020.
80 Lucy Newcombe, 'AGM Review 2017' (13 December 2017) http://csj.hkics.org.hk/site/2017/12/13/agm-review-2017/ accessed 18 July 18 2020.
81 Ibid.
82 Voter turnout is defined as the proportion of a company's issued shares that are actually voted at a shareholder meeting. Institutional Shareholder Services (ISS), 'China: Investor Stewardship. An Examination of Voting and Engagement Activities in China' 5–7 www.issgovernance.com/library/china-investor-stewardship/ accessed 18 July 2020.

USA (86.5 per cent).[83] As for the voting results, the average approval rate for Hong Kong-listed companies declined from 95.9 per cent in 2010 to 93.3 per cent in 2013.[84] Compared to the four other jurisdictions, the average approval rate of Hong Kong companies in 2013 was the lowest, meaning that shareholders in Hong Kong had a lower degree of consensus with the board than their counterparts in the other jurisdictions.[85] Closer study of the type of proposals that receive low approval rates shows that Hong Kong shareholders disagree with management most often on share issuance without pre-emptive rights (80.4 per cent), commonly known as 'general mandates' in Hong Kong.[86] Such disagreement probably stems from the law granting boards broad power to issue shares with general mandates authorized by the general meeting. Once shareholders approve general mandates, boards have the power to issue up to 20 per cent of outstanding shares with a maximum discount of 20 per cent, which common shareholders may find excessive.[87]

Table 3.1 shows the voting items and approval rates of the types of proposals discussed at the general meetings of the fifty sampled Hong Kong-listed companies from 2010 to 2013. Of the 1,863 agenda items, the most commonly discussed were director elections (762), share issuance without pre-emptive rights (290), audit-related issues (155), share repurchases (155) and statutory reports (147). The proposals that received the lowest approval rates were share issuance without pre-emptive rights (80.39 per cent), equity-based compensation plans (85.39 per cent), a share capital increase (86.75 per cent), related-party transactions (RPTs; 91.58 per cent) and board-related proposals (93.35 per cent).[88]

3.3.2 *Shareholder Engagement in Practice*

Shareholders in Hong Kong, like their counterparts in other jurisdictions, generally communicate with firms through both informal and private engagement.[89] Overall, private engagement is the dominant and preferred mode of communication between activists and companies in Hong Kong, which is consistent with the situation in other parts of the world.[90] In practice, unobservable, undocumented private engagement occurs behind the scenes. Public communication or intervention is typically considered only after the failure of private engagement because of the costs and risks involved.[91] The goal of private engagement is to inform investors about voting decisions and to bring about changes that benefit both firms and their investors. If private engagement is ineffective, shareholders may escalate by making their interventions public. Almost all public interventions by shareholders involve the public announcement of their demands. However, if those demands are made against the interest of the controllers, they are likely to be ignored by controllers.

83 Ibid.

84 Ibid. The average approval rate is the average percentage of shares voted in favour of a management proposal over the shares voted at the meeting.

85 Ibid.

86 Ibid. Proposals concerning share issuance without pre-emptive rights accounted for 15.6 per cent of all resolutions sampled at Hong Kong-listed companies.

87 ISS (n. 82) 15.

88 Ibid.

89 Joseph A. McCahery, Zacharias Sautner and Laura T. Starks, 'Behind the Scenes: The Corporate Governance Preferences of Institutional Investors' (2016) 71 Journal of Finance 2905, 2907.

90 Marco Becht, Julian R. Franks and Jeremy Grant, 'Hedge Fund Activism in Europe: Does Privacy Matter?' in Jennifer G. Hill and Randall S. Thomas (eds.), *Research Handbook on Shareholder Power* (Edward Elgar 2015) 116.

91 Davis Polk & Wardwell LLP, *Getting the Deal through – Shareholder Activism & Engagement 2017* (2nd ed., Law Business Research 2017) 77.

TABLE 3.1 *Voting items and approval rates in a sample of Hong Kong-listed companies*

	Share Issuance w/o Pre-emptive Rights	Equity Comp.	Share Capital Increase	RPTs	Board-related	M&A	Director Election	Bylaw amend	Audit	Other	Board & Executive Rem.	Share Repurchase	Statutory Report	Dividend	Total
2010															
n	71	1	3	15		8	173	2	38	2	24	38	36	35	446
Mean	85.46%	74.19%	88.84%	88.63%		99.36%	97.26%	70.27%	99.68%	99.76%	99.97%	99.88%	99.91%	99.98%	95.91%
2011															
n	74	13	4	6	1	3	199	14	39	5	29	39	37	35	498
Mean	80.58%	84.30%	85.19%	83.90%	99.99%	98.28%	96.17%	99.69%	99.26%	99.97%	99.95%	99.92%	99.96%	99.92%	94.77%
2012															
n	74	5		8		2	197	7	39	1	25	39	37	32	466
Mean	78.68%	89.15%		99.82%		100.00%	96.26%	99.85%	99.64%	99.99%	99.75%	99.92%	99.97%	99.98%	94.86%
2013															
n	71	1		3	2	4	193	2	39	5	25	39	37	32	453
Mean	76.90%	91.91%		99.77%	90.03%	83.80%	93.48%	94.41%	99.78%	99.06%	99.83%	99.94%	99.93%	99.96%	93.32%
Total	290	20	7	32	3	17	762	25	155	13	103	155	147	134	1863
	80.39%	85.39%	86.75%	91.58%	93.35%	95.58%	95.76%	96.96%	99.59%	99.59%	99.87%	99.91%	99.94%	99.96%	94.71%

Source: ISS, 'China: Investor Stewardship an Examination of Voting and Engagement Activities in China', Appendix 2. The sample comprised 50 HSI index companies that represent about 60 per cent of HKSE market capitalization.

In 2019, the author collected data on activist initiatives against companies listed in Hong Kong from April 2003 to April 2017. The study identified twenty-four cases and investigated how the law influenced strategy planning and activism outcomes in practice.[92] It focused on activist activities initiated by institutions because institutions have more financial resources and professional knowledge than individuals and are more capable of employing legal tools to exert influence on controlling shareholders.[93] The study found initiatives involving formal legal mechanisms to have the highest success rate compared with those involving only non-legal mechanisms. Amongst the legal tools available, minority veto rights were the most popular mechanism used by activists in Hong Kong, who are quite effective at leveraging their positions in controlled firms. The following subsections summarize the study's key findings on the legal tools utilized by activists.

3.3.2.1 Shareholder Proposals and the Calling of an EGM

Controlling shareholders hold majority shares in listed companies in Hong Kong. Therefore, activist shareholders rarely engage in shareholder meetings. The aforementioned ISS survey on the fifty largest Hong Kong-listed companies from 2010 to 2013 reported that no shareholder proposal emerged in a general meeting during that period.[94] Similarly, of the twenty-four cases in my study of activist initiatives, only one sought a shareholder proposal. It concerned a US hedge fund, H Partners Management LLC, that was a shareholder in Hong Kong Economic Times Holdings Ltd (HKET). On 16 June 2011, the fund proposed an ordinary resolution in an AGM to increase dividends and later published a letter in various newspapers seeking support. However, the proposal was unsuccessful. As a result, HKET refused to declare special dividends, and H Partners sold its stake.

Similarly, the only case involving the use of an EGM also failed. On 19 March 2012, QVT Financial LP (QVT) sent a letter to China Assets Holdings Ltd (CAHL) calling for an EGM. Beforehand, CAHL had breached the Listing Rules in renewing its investment-management agreement with China Assets Investment Management Ltd (CAIML). QVT called for an EGM to reject the agreement. It also sought to publicly intervene and sent an open letter calling for compliance by CAHL and criticizing CAIML. However, an amended agreement was passed by the controlling shareholder. It seems that shareholders are unlikely to achieve their purpose in shareholder meetings in Hong Kong.

3.3.2.2 Board Representation

Shareholders can seek to appoint a board director to influence a firm's corporate choices. In most controlled firms, shareholder activists cannot win a full or even a majority slate because of the presence of controlling shareholders. Whilst seeking board representation appears to be a popular form of activism in other jurisdictions, it is rare in Hong Kong.[95] Hong Kong law does

[92] Lin (n. 7).

[93] David Webb has been identified as an individual shareholder activist who initiated several public demands against Hong Kong-listed companies. He maintains a website, Webb-site.com, to publicize his demands, very few of which are effective. See Frank M. K. Wong, 'Shareholder Engagement and Activism under the Radar: Empirical Evidence from Hong Kong (2003–15) – Rethinking Disclosure of Interests Regime' (Hong Kong Shareholder Engagement and Activism Conference 2016) 68. Webb has also engaged in lobbying activities to improve corporate governance-related legislation and regulations. However, for the purpose of this study, Webb's actions were not included in the sample.

[94] ISS (n. 82) 19.

[95] Kobi Kastiel, 'Against All Odds: Hedge Fund Activism in Controlled Companies' (2016) 2016 *Columbia Business Law Review* 60; Massimo Belcredi and Luca Enriques, 'Institutional Investor Activism in a Context of Concentrated

not offer minimum board representation to minority shareholders. Because dual-class shares were not allowed in Hong Kong-listed companies until April 2018, there is no practice of granting outside shareholders the right to nominate and elect minority board representatives, as would be the case in certain US dual-class companies.[96] In addition, cumulative voting, which favours minority shareholders, is not mandatory under Hong Kong law and is rarely adopted by Hong Kong-listed companies.[97] Therefore, the odds of obtaining minority seats on the boards of Hong Kong-listed companies are slim. For example, of the twenty-four activist initiatives in my study, only one sought board representation. Seeking board representation is thus a weaker activist strategy than either commencing litigation or exercising minority veto rights given the institutional setting in Hong Kong.

3.3.2.3 Court Proceedings

In Hong Kong, as in other Asian jurisdictions, shareholders can resort to court proceedings as a lever to pressure controlling shareholders. For example, they can apply for a court order to inspect company records or documents.[98] Such rights can be exercised by shareholders to challenge a specific transaction if a firm does not disclose sufficient information about that transaction to the public, although their exercise must satisfy the good faith and proper purpose tests.[99] The Companies Ordinance requires plaintiff shareholders to hold at least 2.5 per cent of the voting rights or comprise a group of at least five shareholders in order to apply for an inspection order.[100] However, a court inspection order cannot stop a transaction, and so it is not as effective as an 'interim injunction', which restrains controlling shareholders from engaging in transactions that would harm shareholders' interests, pending litigation. Under sections 728–30 of the Companies Ordinance, any shareholder can apply for a statutory injunction if any person engages in conduct contravening that ordinance, including a breach of the fiduciary duties of directors or a breach of the company's AoA.

The timing of inspection orders can also be an issue. As Hong Kong lacks a specialized business court, a transaction may have been completed by the time a court grants an inspection order. The intervention of Elliott Management (Elliott), a US hedge fund, against the Bank of East Asia's (BEA) private-placement arrangement is a case in point. On 5 September 2014, BEA announced a proposed placement of shares to a substantial shareholder, Sumitomo Mitsui Banking Corporation, which would support the Li family's control over management.[101] Elliott applied for an inspection order on 16 January 2015 requesting the disclosure of documents related to the private placement at issue.[102] Shortly after this activist initiative, BEA held a board

Ownership and High Private Benefits of Control: The Case of Italy' in Jennifer G. Hill and Randall S. Thomas (eds.), *Research Handbook on Shareholder Power* (Edward Elgar Publishing 2015); Matteo Erede, 'Governing Corporations with Concentrated Ownership Structure: An Empirical Analysis of Hedge Fund Activism in Italy and Germany, and Its Evolution' (2013) 10 European Company & Financial Law Review 328.

96 The HKSE has amended its listing rules to lift the ban on dual-class shares; the new rule took effect on 30 April 2018. See HKSE, 'Amendments to the Main Board Listing Rules' (HKSE, April 2018) http://en-rules.hkex.com.hk/en/display/display_main.html?rbid=4476&element_id= 5243 accessed 28 February 2019.

97 Section 23 Companies (Model Articles) Notice (Cap. 622H), Schedule 1 Model Articles for Public Companies Limited by Shares (2018); Yu-Hsin Lin and Yun-Chien Chang, 'An Empirical Study of Corporate Default Rules and Menus in China, Hong Kong, and Taiwan' (2018) 15 *Journal of Empirical Legal Studies* 875.

98 Cap. 622, s. 740.

99 Cap. 622, s. 740(2).

100 Cap. 622, s. 740(6).

101 *Artan Investments Ltd* v. *Bank of East Asia Ltd* [2015] HKEC 1055 [3], [5] (Court of First Instance).

102 Ibid. [1], [8], [9].

meeting, and it approved the placement on 12 February 2015, completing the subscription on 27 March 2015. The court did not issue its order until 5 June 2015.[103] Elliott, of course, failed to stop the transaction and was thus unsuccessful in its intervention.

An interim injunction, in contrast, proved effective in a private-placement case involving Passport Special Opportunities Master Fund LP (Passport) and eSun Holdings Ltd (eSun). Passport, a US hedge fund and major shareholder holding roughly 28 per cent of eSun's issued shares, was unhappy about a private-placement transaction with Chung Name Securities Ltd that had been authorized by eSun's board on 10 December 2008.[104] After private engagement and communication with the board failed, Passport applied for an ex parte injunction to restrain eSun from proceeding with the placement on 22 December 2008 – shortly before the scheduled completion date.[105] Passport alleged that eSun's directors were acting for an improper purpose in entering into the placement agreement, and the injunction was granted by the court, thereby postponing the placement.[106] Unlike the BEA case, in which Elliott applied only for an inspection order and ultimately failed to stop the transaction, Passport utilized a more effective legal tool – a statutory injunction – to successfully postpone the proposed transaction and eventually force eSun to terminate the agreement.[107] This example demonstrates that activist minority shareholders can use court orders to stop controlling shareholders from engaging in impugned conduct pending the court's final verdict.

3.3.2.4 Litigation

An activist can also exert pressure on a controlling shareholder by filing a lawsuit, although this is the most time-consuming and expensive approach amongst the various legal means available. Minority shareholders can bring derivative actions under the Companies Ordinance.[108] For listed firms incorporated overseas, Hong Kong shareholders who wish to bring derivative actions in Hong Kong still need to meet the substantive requirement for derivative action under the law of the jurisdiction of incorporation. In *Wong Ming Bun* v. *Wang Ming Fan*,[109] the Hong Kong Court of First Instance held that whether shareholders can bring a derivative action depends on the law where the company is incorporated. Alternatively, shareholders can seek relief under the unfair prejudice remedy if the company or its controllers have engaged in oppressive behaviour against them, and the court may make any order it thinks fit.[110]

Although private enforcement is rare in Hong Kong, shareholder litigation was effective in the Passport case.[111] In addition to the interlocutory injunction, Passport also filed a petition under the unfair prejudice remedy, seeking injunctive and declaratory relief to prevent the completion of the proposed placement and to declare the transaction invalid.[112] Soon after the interlocutory injunction was granted pursuant to the petition for unfair prejudice, eSun terminated the placement agreement.[113] Passport thus effectively forced eSun to terminate the placement by

103 Ibid. [6].
104 *Passport Special Opportunities Master Fund LP* v. *Esun Holdings Ltd* [2011] 4 HKC 62 [3] (Court of First Instance).
105 Ibid. [3], [5].
106 Ibid. [5].
107 Ibid. [6]–[7].
108 Cap. 622, ss. 732–3.
109 [2014] 1 HKLRD 1108.
110 Cap. 622, ss. 724–5.
111 David C. Donald and Paul W. H. Cheuk, 'Hong Kong's Public Enforcement Model of Investor Protection' (2017) 4 Asian Journal of Law and Society 349, 369–72.
112 *Passport Special Opportunities Master Fund LP* v. *Esun Holdings Ltd* [2011] 4 HKC 62 [6].
113 Ibid. [7].

resorting to formal legal recourse. In this case, shareholder litigation played only a supplementary role by justifying the interlocutory injunction order, which stopped the transaction immediately. The court eventually dismissed Passport's claims for relief after two and a half years and decided not to set aside or void the placement agreement on the grounds of protecting third-party placees.[114] Nevertheless, Passport still succeeded in terminating the placement.

However, litigation and court orders remain rare. Only three of the actions in my 2019 study involved formal court proceedings, and only one succeeded, which is unsurprising given the general reliance in Hong Kong on public rather than private enforcement. Shareholder litigation is rare because class action is not available in Hong Kong and the procedural rules for shareholder derivative actions do not favour plaintiff shareholders.[115] The SFC is the driving force in the enforcement of corporate and securities law.[116]

3.3.2.5 Minority Veto Rights

Finally, shareholders can block a transaction if the law requires special approval by independent shareholders. In Hong Kong, RPTs, which fall within the stated definition, must be disclosed and submitted to the general meeting for approval by a majority of the minority shareholders (MoM approval). This minority veto power is designed to protect the interests of minority shareholders in conflict-of-interest transactions, and it could be an effective legal tool for activists seeking to intervene in transactions in which a controlling shareholder is interested. Before submitting a transaction for shareholder approval, listed companies must set up an independent board committee to advise minority shareholders based on the opinion of an independent financial adviser.[117] Aside from the more stringent rule on RPTs, the HKSE also requires any shareholder who has a material interest in a transaction or arrangement to abstain from voting on a resolution to approve that transaction or arrangement at the general meeting.[118] As long as the controlling shareholder is a party to the contract or the contract confers a benefit upon the controlling shareholder or a close associate (economic or otherwise) that is not available to the other shareholders, the controlling shareholder cannot vote on the resolution.[119] In effect, all conflict-of-interest transactions that require shareholder approval under the Listing Rules require MoM approval. This requirement for an independent minority shareholder vote can mitigate expropriation by controlling shareholders.[120] In this case, controlling shareholders have an incentive to engage with minority shareholders who have a say in the transaction. Another example of MoM approval is mergers proposed by controlling shareholders through schemes of arrangement, which must be approved by at least 75 per cent of disinterested votes, and the votes cast against cannot exceed 10 per cent of disinterested votes.[121]

[114] Ibid. [156]–[157].

[115] Raymond Siu Yeung Chan and John Kong Shan Ho, 'Should Listed Companies Be Allowed to Adopt Dual-Class Share Structure in Hong Kong?' (2014) 43 Common Law World Review 155, 177–9; Félix E. Mezzanotte, 'The Unconvincing Rise of the Statutory Derivative Action in Hong Kong: Evidence from Its First 10 Years of Enforcement' (2017) 17 Journal of Corporate Law Studies 469.

[116] Donald and Cheuk (n. 111) 372–5.

[117] MLR, r. 14A.39–14A.45.

[118] MLR, r. 2.15.

[119] MLR, r. 2.16.

[120] Roger Barker and Iris H. Y. Chiu, 'Protecting Minority Shareholders in Blockholder-Controlled Companies: Evaluating the UK's Enhanced Listing Regime in Comparison with Investor Protection Regimes in New York and Hong Kong' (2015) 10 Capital Markets Law Journal 98, 129.

[121] Takeovers Code, r. 2.10.

The Listing Rules provide additional minority protection for the shareholders of listed companies. The specific transactions that require minority shareholder approval under the Listing Rules are (1) connected transactions;[122] (2) a voluntary withdrawal of listing from the HKSE if the issuer has no alternative listing;[123] (3) rights issues or open offers that would increase the number of issued shares or the market capitalization of the issuer by more than 50 per cent;[124] (4) rights issues or open offers within twelve months of the commencement of securities dealings on the HKSE;[125] (5) refreshment of the general mandate (to allot, issue or grant securities) obtained from shareholders before the next AGM;[126] (6) any material transaction or substantial disposal or acquisition of assets, as determined by the various ratios set by the HKSE;[127] (7) a reverse takeover with a change in control resulting from an acquisition or series of acquisitions of assets by a listed issuer used as an attempt to avoid the requirements for new listing applicants;[128] (8) acquisitions, disposals, transactions or arrangements that would result in material changes within twelve months of the commencement of securities dealings on the HKSE;[129] and (9) spin-off proposals.[130]

Of all the legal mechanisms discussed, the most effective against controlling shareholders is the use of minority veto rights. Of the twenty-four cases I examined, four required MoM approval, all of which involved transactions with parent companies, including HIL's asset sale to its parent company (2007), PCPD's privatization offer by its parent company (2008), Power Assets' proposed merger with its parent company (2015) and GOME Electrical's asset purchase from its parent company (2015). In all these events, the activists' demands were met regardless of whether they had made the demand publicly or privately. The activists forced the controllers to sweeten the offer in an asset sale transaction, reduce the price for an asset purchase transaction and allow them to vote down a privatization or merger proposal. The Power Assets case in 2015 is a good example of proxy advisers, who were not shareholders themselves, persuading minority shareholders to vote down a merger proposal. On 20 October 2015, the company announced a merger proposal by its controlling shareholder, Cheung Kong Infrastructure Holdings Ltd (CKI), which held 38.87 per cent of Power Assets' shares at the time.[131] The proxy advisory firms ISS and Glass Lewis considered the offer price too low and advised institutional shareholders to vote against the proposal.[132] As noted above, the votes cast against such a proposal cannot exceed 10 per cent of the total voting rights attached to all disinterested shares of the company.[133] In the Power Assets case, 50.8 per cent of the minority shareholders approved the proposal, and 49.2 per cent voted against it.[134] The merger failed because

122 MLR, r. 14A.36.

123 MLR, r. 6.12(1).

124 MLR, r. 7.19(6)(a), 7.24(5)(a).

125 MLR, r. 7.19(7), 7.24(6).

126 MLR, r. 13.36(4)(a).

127 MLR, r. 14.06(3), (4), (5), 14.33.

128 MLR, r. 14.06(6), 14.55.

129 MLR, r. 14.90(2).

130 MLR, Practice Note 15, para. 3(e)(2).

131 Power Assets Holdings Limited, 'Notices, Announcements & Circulars' Power Assets (10 October 2015) www.powerassets.com/en/InvestorRelations/InvestorRelations_GLNCS/Documents/E2_Scheme%20Doc.pdf accessed 28 February 2019.

132 Eric Ng, 'Tough Decision for Minority Shareholders of Li Ka-Shing-Controlled CKI and Power Assets' *South China Morning Post* (Hong Kong, 22 November 2015) www.scmp.com/business/companies/article/ 1880801/tough-decision-minority-shareholders-li-ka-shing-controlled-cki accessed 29 February 2019.

133 Takeovers Code, s. 674.

134 Timmy Sung, 'Minority Shareholders Block Power Assets Buy-Out' *RTHK.hk* (Hong Kong, 24 November 2015) http://gbcode.rthk.org.hk/TuniS/news.rthk.hk/rthk/en/component/k2/1225674-20151124.htm?share= twitter accessed 29 February 2019.

the opposition from minority shareholders exceeded 10 per cent. Minority veto rights can indeed be powerful.

3.4 CONCLUDING REMARKS

This chapter has reviewed the rights of shareholders to participate in corporate affairs and engage with companies in Hong Kong. Because the ownership of most Hong Kong-listed companies is concentrated in the hands of families or the state, it is unlikely that shareholders can change or influence corporate decisions through voting or engagement. In addition, there is no single consolidated voting platform that can facilitate retail shareholder voting in Hong Kong. Retail and minority shareholders rarely vote in general meetings. The promulgation in March 2016 of the Principles of Responsible Ownership, which constitutes the investor stewardship code in Hong Kong, raised awareness of shareholder participation amongst large institutional shareholders. Legal means of protecting minority shareholders can help institutional shareholders to leverage their weak voting position when demanding changes in controlled firms. The foregoing review of past activist initiatives conducted by institutional shareholders in Hong Kong reveals that shareholders can truly be empowered in approving transactions that require a majority of minority votes. Filing a lawsuit or statutory injunction can also be effective in curbing transactions harmful to shareholder welfare, but litigation requires substantial human and financial resources, which only institutional shareholders can afford. Hence, facilitating the online voting of retail shareholders and encouraging participation by institutional shareholders might be the best direction for future shareholder engagement in Hong Kong.

4

Shareholder Engagement and Voting in India

Harpreet Kaur

4.1 INTRODUCTION

The history of Indian company law dates to 1850, when India enacted its first Joint Stock Companies Act based on the corresponding English Joint Stock Companies Act.[1] Being a British colony, India's company law followed the developments in English law, and the Companies Act 1956 although frequently amended remained in force for more than fifty years. It was only after the enforcement of the English Companies Act 2006 that India, in 2008, initiated discussions on enacting a new company law that would repeal the 1956 Act. Finally, after the proposal of numerous bills, India passed the new Companies Act 2013 (CA 2013 hereafter). Amongst the new Act's objectives improving transparency, corporate governance, compliance and the protection of minority shareholders were noticeable. CA 2013 is not exhaustive of the whole of company law, as common law still plays an important role in India. The Securities Contracts (Regulation) Act 1956 and Securities and Exchange Board of India Act 1992 are important legislations for dealings in securities and the regulation of the securities market in India.

Concentrated ownership structures and company affiliations with business groups are common features of Asian economies,[2] with the prevalence of family ownership and relationship-based transactions the most important commonality across economies.[3] Indian companies are no exception,[4] with ownership and control aligned traditionally. Five major forms of control were identified by Berle and Means, namely, control through almost complete ownership, majority control, control through a legal device without majority ownership, minority control

The author has been supported by the Scheme for Promotion of Academic and Research Collaboration (SPARC) project team comprising Dr Aparajita Bhatt (Asst Prof, National Law University Delhi (NLUD)), Dr Anant Vijay Maria (Adv), Ankita Sangwan (PhD Scholar, NLUD), and Ipsita Pallavi Sahoo, Nikhitha Tadigoppula and Anushka Pandey (students, NLUD). Mr Devashish Yadav (PhD Scholar, NLUD), who worked on the empirical component of the research unfortunately passed away during the project work. His contribution will never be forgotten.

1 Avtar Singh, *Company Law* (17th ed., Eastern Book Company 2018) 3.

2 Stijn Claessens and Joseph P. H. Fan, 'Corporate Governance in Asia: A Survey' [2002] International Review of Finance 105; Pursey P. M. A. R. Heugens, Marc van Essen and J. (Hans) van Oosterhout, 'Meta-analyzing Ownership Concentration and Firm Performance in Asia: Towards a More Fine-grained Understanding' (2009) 26 Asia Pacific Journal of Management 481.

3 Raghuram G. Rajan and Luig Zingales, 'Which Capitalism? Lessons from the East Asian Crisis' (1998) 11 Journal of Applied Corporate Finance 40, cited in Stijn Claessens and Joseph P. H. Fan, 'Po Hung Joseph P. H. in Corporate Governance in Asia: A Survey' (January 2003). Available at SSRN https://ssrn.com/abstract=386481 or http://dx.doi.org/10.2139/ssrn.386481 accessed 15 July 2020.

4 India ranks third globally in terms of the number of family-owned businesses, with 111 companies with US$839 billion in total market capitalization, according to a report published in 2018.

and management control.[5] In the case of Indian companies, control through almost complete ownership, although presumed to be applicable to private companies alone, was previously observed in public listed companies too. In 2010, however, such control was regulated through the stipulation that listed companies must maintain 25 per cent mandatory public shareholdings in an amendment to the Securities Contracts (Regulation) Rules 1957.[6] Accordingly, promoters' shareholding was mandated to be brought down to 75 per cent by the Securities and Exchange Board of India (SEBI).[7] Special provisions relating to subsidiary companies were introduced by CA 2013 to reduce vertical cross shareholdings.[8] With a view to reducing the complexity of cross shareholdings, the Act imposed a restriction beyond two layers of subsidiaries. The relevant rules have been enforced since 2017, meaning that no companies other than banking, insurance, government-owned and non-banking financial companies are permitted to have more than two layers of subsidiaries.[9]

Identification of the real owners of shares has long been an issue in India. To identify individuals holding the beneficial ownership of shares, to elucidate the layering of intermediate entities and to identify the ultimate individual owners, a number of provisions and rules were inserted into CA 2013.[10] Every significant beneficial owner is required, under section 90 of that Act, to declare his or her beneficial interest, rights and/or any change thereto to the company.[11]

Foreign direct investment (FDI) in Indian companies has increased in recent years owing to the open FDI policy of the Indian government. Manufacturing sector companies received the bulk of such investments in 2018–19.[12] However, the FDI Policy 2017 has been revised to curb opportunistic takeovers and acquisitions of Indian companies in view of the unpredictable circumstances arising out of the COVID-19 pandemic.[13]

A pilot study of Nifty-50 companies was conducted in support of this country-specific chapter on Indian listed companies.[14] The study was based on data collected from the annual reports of

5 The first three are forms of control resting on a legal base and revolve about the right to vote a majority of the voting stock. The last two, minority control and management control, are extralegal, resting on a factual rather than legal base. See Adolf A. Berle and Gardiner C. Means, *The Modern Corporation and Private Property* (2nd ed., Routledge 1991) 70.

6 Rule 19A – Continuous Listing Requirements inserted by Securities Contracts Regulation (Amendment), 2010 made by amending Securities Contracts (Regulation) Rules, 1957; also mandated for public sector undertakings by the 2018 Securities Contracts Regulation (Amendment).

7 The term 'Promoter' is defined by s. 2(69), CA 2013; Harpreet Kaur, 'Securities Market in India: Regulation of Undesirable Practices by the Securities and Exchange Board of India' in Jing Bian and Kiymet Caliyurt (eds.), *Regulations and Applications of Ethics in Business Practice* (Springer 2018); Amit Mudgil, 'FM Nirmala Sitharaman Pushes SEBI to Raise Public Stake Limit to 35%, Analysts Cagey' *The Economic Times* (New Delhi, 5 July 2019) https://economictimes.indiatimes.com/markets/stocks/news/fm-nirmala-sitharaman-pushes-sebi-to-raise-public-stake-limit-to-35-analysts-cagey/articleshow/70085955.cms?from=mdr accessed 27 April 2020; more discussion has been provided in Section 4.1.4.

8 Provisions relating to the holding of shares by a subsidiary in a holding company and voting are discussed in the section on voting later in the chapter.

9 Companies (Restriction on number of layers) Rules 2017.

10 CA 2013, s. 89.

11 CA 2013, ss. 2(27) and 90.

12 Reserve Bank of India, *Foreign Direct Investment Flows to India: Country-wise and Industry-wise* https://m.rbi.org.in/Scripts/AnnualReportPublications.aspx?Id=1278 accessed 19 April 2020.

13 Between January and March 2020, the People's Bank of China purchased shares in HDFC Bank; see 'People's Bank of China Picks up 1.75 Crore Shares in HDFC' *Money Control* (12 April 2020) www.moneycontrol.com/news/business/peoples-bank-of-china-picks-up-1–75-crore-shares-in-hdfc-5135931.html?fbclid=IwAR1ctrPnoRpBfmphgpm44qNTwnqzMECmXhoZaCOPsCtb5XJBjgZNmo1uMa8 accessed 12 April 2010.

14 The NIFTY-50 is the flagship index of the National Stock Exchange (NSE) that tracks the behaviour of a portfolio of blue-chip companies, the largest and most liquid Indian securities. It includes 50 of the approximately 1,600 companies traded (both listed and traded companies as well as not listed but permitted to trade) on the NSE and

Nifty-50 companies.[15] Five companies on the Nifty-50 Index were found to have more than 50 subsidiary companies, and one company had 148.

4.1.1 *The Board of Directors*

India follows a one-tier board structure, and boards are central to the decision-making and governance processes.[16] The board of directors is collectively responsible for supervising the management of the company. The legislative intent to make the board liable for any kind of malfunctioning within the company is evident from the provisions of the Companies Act. Over the years, many structural reforms have been implemented for boards to improve corporate governance. CA 2013 provides for the composition of the board along with other requirements for an effective board.[17] It also introduced the terms 'key managerial personnel' (KMP) and 'senior management' to distinguish boards from the management of companies.

4.1.1.1 Board Composition

The Indian legislative framework allows for the constitution of a diverse board comprising executive and non-executive directors, including independent directors and female directors.[18] It is mandatory for one-third of the boards of listed public companies to be made up of independent directors.[19] CA 2013 allows companies to appoint additional directors, alternate directors, nominee directors and a director appointed by small shareholders to represent their concerns in front of the board.[20] Adequate parameters for the appointment, removal and resignation of directors, along with the manner in which the board shall function, are laid down in the Act in order to ensure the integrity of board members and their functioning. The decisive responsibility to appoint or remove any director rests with the company through its general meeting. If the directors themselves are legally disqualified from holding directorships, then they have an equal responsibility for disclosing that fact and the reasons for their disqualification.

Under the erstwhile CA 1956, common law duties were imposed on directors. However, CA 2013 codifies the duties of directors and lays down their liability in section 166. Directors are required to act in accordance with the articles of the company. They have to act in good faith to promote the objects of the company for the benefit of its members as a whole and in the best interests of the company, its employees and shareholders, the community and the environment.[21] Therefore, directors' scope of duties seems to be broader than that stipulated by the

captures approximately 65 per cent of the total float-adjusted market capitalization of the NSE. The companies are domiciled in India and traded on the NSE. The index is based on liquidity, float-adjusted market capitalization, listing history and trading frequency as per NIFTY-50 – Index Methodology, August 2019. Details of the index are available at www1.nseindia.com/products/content/equities/indices/nifty_50.htm accessed 15 July 2020.

15 Securities Exchange Board of India (Listing Obligations and Disclosure Requirement) Regulations 2015 (LODR Regulations 2015), reg. 46 requires index-listed companies to maintain a website, and clause 2 specifies the necessary information to be provided; Companies began uploading data from 2016 onwards.

16 www.mca.gov.in/MinistryV2/management+and+board+governance.html accessed 22 October 2019.

17 CA 2013, s. 149; certain exemptions have been granted under s. 149 for IFSC (International Financial Services Centres) public companies.

18 CA 2013, s. 149. It has been found that 25 per cent of companies have appointed women from promoter families as board members. Further, at the recommendation of the Kotak Committee, SEBI mandated that the top 1,000 Indian companies by market capitalization have one female independent director on their boards by 1 April 2020.

19 CA 2013, s. 149.

20 CA 2013, s. 151.

21 CA 2013, s. 166(2).

enlightened shareholder value approach under section 172 of the English Companies Act 2006. The other duties of directors include the duty to exercise reasonable care and skill, make independent judgements and avoid conflicts of interest and undue advantage for themselves or their relatives, partners or associates. Directors are also not authorized to delegate their duties. It is interesting to note here that 309,619 directors have been disqualified under section 164(2)(a), read with section 167 of CA 2013, for the non-filing of financial statements or annual returns for a continuous period of the immediately preceding financial years (FYs) (2013–14, 2014–15 and 2015–16). Of these disqualified directors, 210,116 were directors on the boards of struck-off shell companies.[22]

4.1.1.2 Presence of Independent Directors

The presence and effect of independent directors in listed companies is overemphasized by CA 2013. To ensure the independence of directors, an extensive definition of 'independent director' is given in section 149(6) of the Act. An independent director has to make a self-declaration of his or her independence at the first board meeting and at the first meeting of every FY and also declare whether there has been any change in his or her status as an independent director. The liability of independent and non-executive directors is limited to acts of omission or commission by the company that occurred with their knowledge, are attributable to board processes and that took place with their consent or connivance or to instances in which they did not act diligently.

It was observed in the aforementioned pilot study that in the ten-year period from 2008–18, board compositions have exhibited a trend towards having more independent directors (up to 45 per cent of the board), whereas the percentage of executive and non-executive directors ranged from 25–28 per cent. In FY 2017–18, 51 per cent of directors in Nifty-50 companies were independent directors, with executive and non-executive directors constituting 26 per cent and 20 per cent, respectively.

The role played by independent directors was questioned in India in the wake of a scam by Satyam Computers Services Ltd, as the company had permitted its chairman-promoter to take independent decisions leading to account manipulation and inflated revenues.[23] The case highlighted the need to re-examine the then existing legal and regulatory framework. In the wake of the Satyam case, the landscape for corporate governance in India underwent a change with the passage of CA 2013 and the more vigilant role played by SEBI.[24] Also important to mention here is that comparatively more independent directors than non-independent directors reportedly resigned in 2019.[25] The reduction in numbers of independent directors may have been the result of the increased stringency of liability, accountability and personal conflict-of-interest requirements.

[22] Shell companies after demonetization, Response to the Unstarred question no. 359, answered on Tuesday, 6 February 2018 in Rajya Sabha, Ministry of Corporate Affairs, Government of India www.mca.gov.in/Ministry/pdf/ru359_07022018.pdf available on www.mca.gov.in accessed 18 April 2020.

[23] Harpreet Kaur, 'Corporate Fraud: Auditors' and Managerial Liability' in Kiymet Caliyurt Tunca (ed.), *Emerging Fraud* (online ed., Springer 2012) 115.

[24] Rica Bhattcharyya and Sachin Dave, 'Lesson from Satyam: Corporate Governance Evolves, Not Execution' *The Economic Times* (Mumbai, 7 January 2016) https://economictimes.indiatimes.com/news/company/corporate-trends/lesson-from-satyam-corporate-governance-evolves-not-execution/articleshow/50476372.cms?from=mdr accessed 18 April 2020.

[25] Kala Vijayraghavan and Lijee Phillip, 'Worried Independent Directors No Longer Keen to Hold Board Seats' *The Economic Times* (Mumbai, 20 November 2019) https://economictimes.indiatimes.com/news/company/corporate-trends/worried-independent-directors-no-longer-keen-to-hold-board-seats/articleshow/72135108.cms accessed 21 November 2019.

4.1.2 *Shareholder versus Board Supremacy*

CA 2013 allocates powers to shareholders and company boards. The board of directors is entitled to exercise all such powers and to do all such acts and things that the company is authorized to exercise and do.[26] However, the board's powers are not absolute. There are two major limitations on the powers of boards. First, the board can exercise its powers subject to any provisions contained in CA 2013 or in the company's memorandum, articles or regulations, including regulations made by the company in a general meeting. Second, the board cannot exercise any power that is directed to be exercised by the company in the general meeting. No regulation made by the company in the general meeting can invalidate any prior act of the board that would have been valid had the regulation not been made.[27] The board of directors functions as the 'brain' of the company, and directors' powers are thus co-extensive with those of the company itself. The board of directors, after a resolution passed at board meetings, is vested with a range of powers, namely, powers to make calls on shareholders in respect of money unpaid on their shares, to authorize the buyback of securities, to issue securities, including debentures, to borrow monies, to invest the funds of the company, to grant loans or to give a guarantee or provide security in respect of loans, to approve the company's financial statement and the board's report, to diversify the business of the company, to approve an amalgamation, merger or reconstruction and to take over a company or acquire a controlling or substantial stake in another company, as well as powers concerning any other matter that may be prescribed.[28] The board of directors may also, subject to a resolution passed at a meeting, delegate the power to borrow money, to invest the funds of the company and to grant loans or give a guarantee or provide security in respect of loans. Such delegation may be made to any committee of directors, the managing director, the manager or any other principal officer of the company.[29]

Shareholders' supremacy is reflected in the general meetings of the company, wherein directors are appointed by the company and the board cannot exercise some of its powers without the consent of shareholders.[30] The board cannot exercise its discretion in matters that can be decided only with the consent of the company by a special resolution.[31] Such powers include the power to sell, lease or otherwise dispose of the whole or substantially the whole of the undertaking of the company; to invest otherwise in trust securities the amount of compensation received by it as a result of any merger or amalgamation; to borrow money where the money to be borrowed, together with the money already borrowed by the company, exceeds the aggregate of its paid-up share capital; to free reserves and securities premiums; and to remit or allow additional time for the repayment of any debt due from a director. However, shareholders are not authorized to affect any reduction in the share capital of the company except in accordance with the provisions of CA 2013.

Thus, the inherent and ultimate powers lie with the general meeting of shareholders, and they exercise those powers through the passing of an ordinary or special resolution. The approach of CA 2013 is to a large extent aligned with the English Companies Act 2006, which is shareholder-centric with enabling provisions. The only difference is that CA 2013 provides for the allocation

26 CA 2013, s. 179(1).
27 CA 2013, s. 179(2).
28 CA 2013, s. 179.
29 CA 2013, s. 179(3).
30 CA 2013, s. 152(2) provides that save as otherwise expressly provided in the Act, every director shall be appointed by the company in a general meeting.
31 CA 2013, s. 180.

of powers, whereas the English Act does not dictate how corporate power is to be allocated, leaving it as a matter for the constitution of the company.

There have been occasions on which shareholders have displayed their supremacy over the board. The Supreme Court of India had held that

> it is a very strong thing to indeed to prevent shareholders from holding a meeting of the company, when such a meeting is the only way in which they can interfere if the majority of them think that the course taken by the director, in a matter *intra vires* of the director, is not for the benefit of the company.[32]

CA 2013 also takes care of the interests of small shareholders in a listed company by empowering them to elect their own representative on the company's board.[33] The company may appoint a director elected by small shareholders if it receives a notice by at least 1,000 small shareholders or one-tenth of the total number of small shareholders, whichever is lower.[34] A listed company may also opt to have a director representing small shareholders *suo motu*.[35] The appointment of such a small shareholders' director is subject to the same qualifications as those prescribed for other directors under section 152 of CA 2013.[36] However, to date no such appointments have been made owing to the combined effects of entrenched promoters and regulatory provisions.[37]

4.1.3 *Ownership Structure*

Majority control, which is the first step towards the separation of ownership from control, is the ownership form most prevalent amongst listed companies in India through majority shareholdings lying with promoters and promoter groups. Control through a legal device without major ownership, namely, pyramiding, is also observed in listed companies and takes place through networks of group companies, including subsidiary and associate companies. Cross shareholdings have created complex webs, and steps to reduce them have been taken even in public sector undertakings, as well as in listed companies.[38] Minority control is not commonly observed in Indian companies. Management control is exercised through control over the appointments of directors, KMP and senior management.

Family businesses are prominent in India.[39] From the common law understanding of the term 'promoter' as the person who promotes a company to the first definition of the term provided by

32 *LIC* v. *Escorts Ltd.* [1986] 1 SCC 264.

33 CA 2013, s. 151(explanation). The explanation to s. 151 defines a small shareholder as a shareholder holding shares of a nominal value of no more than 20,000 rupees or such other sum as may be prescribed.

34 Companies (Appointment and Qualification of Directors) Rules 2014, r. 7.

35 Companies (Appointment and Qualification of Directors) Rules 2014, r. 7(1) proviso.

36 Companies (Appointment and Qualification of Directors) Rules 2014, r. 7(5).

37 Sachin P. Mampatta, 'Five Years on, Sec 151 on Small-shareholder Directors Makes Little Headway' *Business Standard* (29 June 2019) www.business-standard.com/article/companies/five-years-on-sec-151-on-small-shareholder-directors-makes-little-headway-119062900156_1.html accessed 15 July 2020.

38 The government wants to end cross-holdings in the oil sector and go for consolidation; see 'Govt Plans to End Anti-competitive, Complex Cross-holding in Oil PSUs' *Financial Chronicle* (15 October 2018) www.deccanchronicle.com/business/companies/151018/govt-plans-to-end-anti-competitive-complex-cross-holding-in-oil-psus.html accessed 10 April 2020.

39 Family-owned Indian companies have delivered an average 13.9 per cent annual return since 2006 compared with 6 per cent returns generated by their non-family-owned peers; see Amit Mudgill, 'India's Family-owned Firms Making More Money for Investors than Others' *The Economic Times* (New Delhi, 14 September 2018) https://economictimes.indiatimes.com/markets/stocks/news/indias-family-owned-firms-making-more-money-for-investors-than-others/articleshow/65806161.cms?from=mdr accessed 20 April 2020;.

the erstwhile SEBI (Issue of Capital and Disclosure Requirements) Regulations 2009, effort has been made to make promoters accountable within the companies they promote. CA 2013 introduced a definition that is in line with SEBI regulations.[40] It is also important to understand who is included in the 'promoter group' because control within companies is exercised through the shareholdings of such groups.[41]

The promoter's role does not end with the formation of the company. The legislative intent behind the CA 2013 definition is to make promoters liable and responsible for other company matters that may arise during the company's lifetime. In the pilot study of Nifty-50 companies, the pattern of shareholdings depicted in Table 4.1 amongst the promoter and promoter group (P&PG) for the year 2017–18 was observed.

Seven companies had more than 50 per cent foreign holdings in their P&PG shares, as shown in Table 4.2.

The average shareholding pattern for the categories of Indian and foreign P&PG and institutional and non-institutional public shareholdings, along with depository receipts, has been calculated to afford a picture of the true concentration of power in various categories of shareholders.[42] The results are reported in Table 4.3.

TABLE 4.1 *P&PG shareholdings in Nifty-50 companies*

Year	No of Companies	Percentage of P&PG shareholding
2017–18	4	75–100%
2017–18	24	50–75%
2017–18	10	25–50%
2017–18	4	0–25%
2017–18	8	Nil

TABLE 4.2 *Foreign P&PG holdings in Nifty-50 companies in 2017–18*

S. No	Name of the company	Percentage of foreign holding in P & PG shares
1.	ABB India Ltd	75%
2.	Siemens Ltd	75%
3.	Oracle Financial Services Software Ltd	74%
4.	Proctor and Gamble Hygiene & Health Care Ltd	69%
5.	Bosch Ltd	69%
6.	Ambuja Cements Ltd	63%
7.	United Spirits Ltd	55%
8.	Colgate Palmolive (India) Ltd	51%

40 CA 2013, s. 2(69), SEBI (Issue of Capital and Disclosure Requirements) Regulations 2018, Regulation 2(oo).

41 'Promoter Group' is defined by reg. 2(1) (pp), SEBI (ICDR) Regulations, 2018.

42 Reg. 2(1)(jj), ICDR Regulations, 2018. A 'non-institutional investor' is defined as an investor other than a retail individual investor of qualified institutional buyer. The different types of shareholders are defined by the ICDR Regulations, 2018.

TABLE 4.3 *Shareholding pattern in Nifty-50 companies (FY 2017–18)*

P&PG	44.97%
Public shareholding	23.49%
Non-institutional	13.63%
Foreign shareholding (outside P&PG)	17.88%
ADR-GDR (American and Global Depository Receipts)	0.043%

TABLE 4.4 *Shareholding pattern of FIIs and non-institutional investors in Nifty-50 companies in FY 2017–18*

Percentage of FII shareholdings	No of companies	No of companies	Percentage of Shareholding- NIIs under P&PG
0%-10%	24	5	More than 50%
10%-20%	14	10	15–50%
20%-30%	10	35	Less than 15%
30%-40%	2		

Foreign institutional investors (FIIs) are a major category of shareholders in Indian listed companies owing to the government's liberal FDI policy. However, data collected for FY 2017–18 on the shareholdings of FIIs reveal an interesting pattern: no FIIs had a major shareholding in a Nifty-50 company in that FY, with non-institutional investors appearing to be a more important stakeholder in Indian listed companies. These results are presented in Table 4.4.

Public shareholdings in Indian listed companies are regulated by SEBI (Issue of Capital and Disclosure Requirements) Regulations 2018. As stated earlier, SEBI mandates that listed companies maintain a minimum public shareholding level of 25 per cent.[43] However, the data collected from Nifty-50 companies indicates that in FY 2017–18, only twenty-three companies maintained that level, with the remaining twenty-seven companies failing to do so.[44]

4.1.4 *Role of Promoters As Shareholders and Directors*

The changed role of the promoter highlights the fact that a shareholder, director or other party who has direct or indirect control of a company can be the company's promoter. Moreover, a person can be a promoter without being a shareholder or director by way of being someone in accordance with whose directions the board of directors is accustomed to act.[45] By holding the majority block of shares in the company, promoters are able to control the affairs of the company, dominate and influence the management of the company, and get resolutions in general meetings passed with an adequate majority.[46] Retail, institutional and non-institutional shareholders do not make strategic investments in these companies and are unwilling to participate in their internal affairs. Owing to P&PG dominance, it seems that these shareholders are interested only in receiving returns on their investments by way of capital appreciation.

43 Compliance with minimum public shareholding, LODR Regulations 2015, reg. 38 of the SEBI (LODR); refer to n. 7.

44 Public shareholdings include the shareholdings of persons other than promoters and the promoter group.

45 Harpreet Kaur, 'Promoters and Corporate Governance under the Companies Act, 2013' (2015–16) 3 Journal of National Law University Delhi 53.

46 See CA 2013, s. 2(27).

It is pertinent to note here that vide the amendment of SEBI (Listing Obligations and Disclosure Requirements) Regulations 2015,[47] the recommendations of the Kotak Committee regarding the reclassification of promoters have been implemented, and the promoters of listed companies are now allowed to reclassify as public shareholders to reduce their shareholding to 75 per cent.[48] To reduce their shareholdings, promoters have been given many options, such as the facility of a single window for selling shares by auction, in addition to the options already available, such as offering shares for sale, institutional private placements and further public offers.[49] At that time, because promoters had also reclassified themselves without supplying information to SEBI, it had to come up with a mechanism to permit reclassification.

Reclassification of the promoters of existing listed companies as public shareholders can be done only after obtaining the permission of the stock exchange(s) on which the company's shares are listed, subject to satisfaction of the conditions stipulated in the regulations.[50] The main conditions for the reclassification of an outgoing promoter include the relinquishment of special rights and control over the affairs of the listed firm and maintaining a shareholding exceeding no more than 10 per cent.[51] After board approval, such a reclassification request must be approved by the general meeting by way of an ordinary resolution on which persons related to the promoter seeking reclassification are prohibited from voting.[52] Hence, shareholder approval is significant when promoters seek to change and reclassify their status to public shareholder.[53] Similarly, a public shareholder can also seek to reclassify as a promoter.[54] It is important to mention here that SEBI is examining the possibility of changing the terminology from 'promoters' to 'controlling shareholders' on the ground that the latter is more prevalent globally.[55]

4.2 LEGAL MEANS OF SHAREHOLDER ENGAGEMENT

CA 2013 has expanded the rights of shareholders by adding new rights and extending the scope of rights that existed under the erstwhile CA 1956. In addition to the exercise of ownership rights by all shareholders in the form of voting rights and the receipt of dividends, pre-emptive rights are protected in the form of a rights issue under section 62 of CA 2013. Shareholders have the right to participate in and be sufficiently informed of decisions concerning fundamental corporate changes, as well as the right to timely information and equitable treatment.[56] For a variation in shareholder rights, a three-quarters majority of the class in question is required or a special resolution passed by that class, subject to the existence of a provision in the constitution

47 SEBI (Listing Obligations and Disclosure Requirements) (Sixth Amendment) Regulations, 2018.
48 LODR Regulations 2015, reg. 31A.
49 Supra note 7.
50 ibid.
51 LODR Regulations 2015, reg. 31A (3)(b).
52 LODR Regulations 2015, reg. 31A (3) (ii) and (iii).
53 The promoters of Mindtree requested that its board of directors remove the tag of promoter from them after 60 per cent of the shareholding was acquired by L&T in July 2019 and applied to the BSE and NSE for reclassification; see Ayushman Barauh, 'Mindtree Submits Applications for Reclassification of Promoters to Public' *Livemint* (28 July 2019) www.livemint.com/companies/news/mindtree-submits-applications-for-reclassification-of-promoters-to-public-11595930698513.html accessed 15 July 2020.
54 LODR Regulations 2015, reg. 31A (5).
55 'SEBI to Soon Take a View on Rights Issue; Examines Promoter Concept' *The Economic Times* (26 September 2019) https://economictimes.indiatimes.com/markets/stocks/news/sebi-to-soon-take-a-view-on-rights-issue-examines-promoter-concept/articleshow/71312745.cms?from=mdr accessed 23 March 2020.
56 LODR Regulations 2015, reg, 4 (2) (a) (b) (c).

documents or variation not being prohibited by the terms of issue of shares of that class. If holders of no less than 10 per cent of issued shares of the class do not consent, they can apply to the National Company Law Tribunal (NCLT) for cancellation within twenty-one days of consent being given or a special resolution being passed.[57] The right to transfer shares, debentures or another interest in the company is subject to the company's constitution and CA 2013. Shareholders have the right to appoint directors and auditors on the recommendations of the board. Other shareholder rights are discussed in the following paragraphs.

4.2.1 *Calling a Meeting*

A forum for self-protection is provided to shareholders in the form of general meetings, and every company in India except for one-person companies is statutorily mandated under section 96, CA 2013 to hold one general meeting as its annual general meeting (AGM). An AGM can be called only on the authority of a resolution by the company's board of directors.[58] The board also has the power to postpone the meeting after it has been called. However, that power can be exercised only for bona fide and proper reasons.[59] In the case of a default to hold the AGM, the NCLT, upon the application of any member, may call or direct the calling of the meeting to consider the agenda outlined in the application.[60] The board's power is restricted to calling the meeting; it cannot decide upon the validity of a meeting that has already been held.[61] Only a member can apply for the calling of an AGM; a company cannot do so because a company cannot seek a direction against itself.[62] A meeting held by order of the NCLT is deemed to be an AGM.[63] A maximum gap of fifteen months is permissible between two consecutive AGMs, although the Registrar of Companies permits extensions of up to three months in certain circumstances.[64] The company does not have *suo motu* authority to hold an AGM beyond the prescribed time period because the holding of an AGM is an obligation of the company rather than a right. In a 2011 court case, it was held that an AGM convened by a company itself beyond the prescribed time period would not be considered a validly convened meeting.[65] However, this judgment was held not to be correct in law later by courts. A delay in holding a meeting leads only to the

[57] The National Company Law Tribunal (NCLT) is constituted under s. 408, CA 2013 as a quasi-judicial authority to adjudicate on company law, insolvency and bankruptcy matters. Appeals to NCLT decisions are made to the National Company Law Appellate Tribunal (NCLAT).

[58] Any general meeting called with such authority by a managing director, manager, etc., will not be effectual unless the board ratifies it before the meeting; see *Re, Haycraft Gold Reduction and Mining Co* [1900] 2 Ch 230. The congregation of shareholders after the decision of directors to abandon the AGM cannot be legitimately characterized as an AGM, see *Selvaraj (V)* v. *Mylapore Hindu Permanent Fund Ltd* AIR [1968] Mad 378.

[59] *Rajpal Singh* v. *State of U.P.* [1968] 1 Comp LJ 21.

[60] CA 2013, s. 97. The NCLT can give necessary and consequential directions relating to a meeting; it can also give a direction that one member of the company present in person or by proxy shall be deemed to constitute a meeting under that section.

[61] *Gracy Thomas* v. *Four Square Estates Pvt Ltd* [2008] 141 Com Cases 770.

[62] *Cannanore Whole Body CT scan and Research Center Pvt Ltd* v. *Saibunnisa S V* [1998] 93 Com Cases 99.

[63] If the meeting so held does not fall within the year in which the default in holding the AGM occurs, the company in the meeting will have to resolve that it should be treated as an AGM. If appropriate notice is given, then the meeting may be treated as an AGM for both years; see A. Ramaiya, *Guide to the Companies Act* (18th ed., vol. 1, LexisNexis 2014) 1643.

[64] CA 2103, s. 96(1). The registrar should consider the grant of extension of time only in cases where the application for extension is made before the expiry of the period laid down in s. 96(1); a delay in completion of the company's audit of accounts or accounts that have not yet been compiled or submitted to auditors do not constitute a special reason for extension.

[65] *Sadhan Kumar Ghosh* v. *Bengal Brick Field Owners Association* [2011] 102 CLA 347.

imposition of a fine.[66] If an AGM is adjourned, the adjourned meeting should be held within the prescribed maximum time limit.[67]

The first AGM must be held within nine months of the date of the company's FY-end, and in other cases it should be held within six months of that date.[68] A notice of the AGM should be given in writing or electronic mode no less than a clear twenty-one days in advance of the meeting, although shorter notice may be given if 95 per cent of members entitled to vote at the AGM consent in writing or by electronic mode.[69] Because of the difficulties arising from the COVID-19 pandemic, the rules were relaxed to allow companies whose FY (other than first FY) ended on 31 December 2019 to hold their AGM for that FY within nine months of the FY-end (i.e. by 30 September 2020). Doing so would not be viewed as a violation. The references to the AGM due date or the date by which the AGM should have been held under CA 2013, or rules made thereunder, would be construed accordingly.[70]

The AGM agenda is generally divided into two categories: general business and special business. The general business agenda is set as per the provisions of CA 2013 and includes the presentation by the board of directors of financial statements, accounts and the directors' report to shareholders.[71] The declaration of dividends for the FY, appointment of directors and auditors and the fixation of their remuneration also fall within the general business agenda.[72] Any business other than general business is deemed to be special business. Adequate information is required to be provided to shareholders in advance to allow them to make informed decisions on the agenda items. A statement containing the material facts of each item of special business to be transacted is to be annexed to the notice calling the meeting in question. The nature of the concerns or interests of each director, manager, KMP and their relatives should be disclosed in the statement. Where any special business affects any other company, that should also be mentioned in the statement if the shareholding of each promoter, director, manager and KMP of the company conducting the AGM is more than 2 per cent in the second company.[73]

The right to call a shareholder meeting is granted to shareholders by CA 2013. Under section 100, such a meeting is known as an extraordinary general meeting (EGM).[74] An EGM can also be called by the board if it deems fit. The NCLT also has the power to call a meeting of a company other than the AGM under section 98 if it is impracticable to call or hold and conduct the meeting under the provisions of CA 2013 or the company's articles of association (AoA).[75] The NCLT may, either *suo motu* or upon the application of any director or member of the company entitled to vote at the meeting, order a meeting and give necessary ancillary or

66 Ramaiya (n. 63) 96.

67 The power of directors to call a meeting is not exhausted after the issue of the notice; it continues to enable them to postpone the meeting, and such power can be exercised only for bona fide and proper reasons. The proper course is to hold the convened meeting, and the board should not abrogate to itself such power. See *Rajpal Singh* (n. 59).

68 When the first AGM is held within nine months of the date of the FY-end, no AGM is required to be held for the second year.

69 CA 2013, s. 101.

70 Ministry of Corporate Affairs, Government of India, 'Holding of Annual General Meetings by Companies Whose Financial Year has Ended on 31st December, 2019' General Circular No. 18/2020, dated 21 April 2020) www.mca.gov.in/Ministry/pdf/Circular18_21042020.pdf accessed 27 April 2020.

71 CA 2013, s. 129. If the balance sheet laid before the AGM is not adopted or if the meeting is adjourned before adoption or if the AGM is not held, a statement of that fact and its reasons are required to be annexed to the balance sheet as per s. 137, CA 2013.

72 Singh (n. 1) 377; CA 2013, s. 102(2).

73 CA 2013, s. 102.

74 According to clause 42, Table F, Schedule I dealing with the articles of association for a company limited by shares, all general meetings other than annual general meetings shall be known as extraordinary general meetings.

75 Only the power to call or convene a meeting can be exercised. The NCLT does not have the power of postponement.

consequential directions.[76] Holders of one-tenth of paid-up share capital having the right to vote or as many members having one-tenth of voting power can requisition a meeting in case of need. The board should move for the meeting on requisition within twenty-one days, and the actual meeting must be held within forty-five days from the date of the requisition; otherwise, the requisitionists themselves may call the meeting within three months of the requisition date. The requisition must set out the matters for consideration of which the meeting has been requisitioned. No other matter can be dealt with in the meeting. The agenda of an EGM falls within the category of special business.[77] Shareholders must provide the agenda for the EGM that they have requisitioned. Failure of the board to hold the meeting is not punishable. However, companies' reimbursement of expenses to the requisitionists holding the EGM is deducted from the fee or remuneration paid to the directors in default.[78]

The results of the pilot study suggest that the right to call an EGM is not frequently exercised by shareholders in Indian companies (see Table 4.5). Within the decade from 2009–18, forty-three companies called for EGMs less than twice. The data include both the EGMs called by shareholders and those called under the direction of the NCLT. Only three companies, namely, the Bank of Baroda, United Spirits and Vodafone Idea Ltd, called EGMs more than five times. Vodafone was restructuring after the merger of Vodafone and Idea Ltd, the Bank of Baroda had to issue preference shares to the government of India and the Life Insurance Corp of India and United Spirits had to call EGMs to discuss the erosion of its net worth, as well as distribution agreements and rehabilitation.

CA 2013 contains no provision allowing the conduct of meetings through video conferencing or other audiovisual means. All meetings are required to be held physically. In view of the pandemic, however, companies have been allowed to request members' approval on urgent matters through a postal ballot or e-voting without holding a general meeting requiring the physical presence of members, although this is not permitted for ordinary business or business involving any member's right to be heard. In the event that holding an EGM became unavoidable before 30 June 2020, it could be held by video conferencing or other audiovisual means. Recordings of meetings are required to be kept in safe custody and, in the case of public companies, should be uploaded to their websites as soon as possible after the meeting.[79]

4.2.2 *Shareholders' Right to Add a Proposal to the Agenda*

Holders of one-tenth of paid-up share capital having the right to vote or as many members as have one-tenth of voting power can move any resolution in an AGM or EGM or insist that the company include such a matter in the meeting agenda[80] and can ask to serve notice to members.[81] They may also requisition the circulation of any statement with respect to matters on the proposed resolution or business that is to be dealt with in the general meeting after complying with other requirements. Two or more copies of the requisition signed by all of them should be deposited at the registered office of the company. If a notice of a resolution is required,

[76] The power to order a meeting under CA 2013, s. 98(1)(a) and to give ancillary or consequential directions under s. 98(1)(b) are independent powers.

[77] CA 2013, s. 102(2)(b).

[78] CA 2013, s. 100(6).

[79] For a clarification on the passing of ordinary and special resolutions, see General Circular No 14/2020 No. 2/1/2020-CL-V Ministry of Corporate Affairs, Government of India.

[80] *Pedley v. Inland Waterways Association Ltd* [1977] 1 All ER 209.

[81] CA 2013, s. 111.

TABLE 4.5 *Virtual AGMs and resolutions*

Company	Number of Resolutions	Vote Percentage	Dissent Rate
Tech Mahindra	5 resolutions	82–84% votes polled – e-voting	4% dissent in reappointment of a director by public institutions (diluted to 2.4% in total shares polled)
TCS	3 resolutions	92–93% votes polled – e-voting	Public institution – 10.5% dissent in reappointment of a director (diluted to 2.33% in total shares polled)
SBI	5 resolutions	99.8% votes polled	Negligible dissent in appointment of 4 directors; annual financial statement adoption – 99.9%
RIL	8 resolutions	83–84.5% votes polled	10.9–13.2% dissent in 3 resolutions for reappointment of 3 directors; less than 1% dissent in remaining resolutions
Tata Motors	7 resolutions	75% votes polled	Negligible dissent
Tata Steel	6 resolutions	70% votes polled	18% dissent in commission to non-executive directors of the company
ITC	12 Resolutions	83% votes polled	Negligible dissent
Larsen and Turbo	12 Resolutions	68% votes polled	4 Resolutions – 18.9% dissent in appointment of whole time director 4 Resolutions – 4.85% dissent in appointment of director
Wipro	5 resolutions	89.6% votes polled	31.5% and 58.3% dissent in appointment of CEO
Bajaj Auto	7 resolutions	79% votes polled	40% dissent in appointment of company's managing director and CEO; 41% dissent in reappointment of director; 4.5% dissent in appointment of independent director

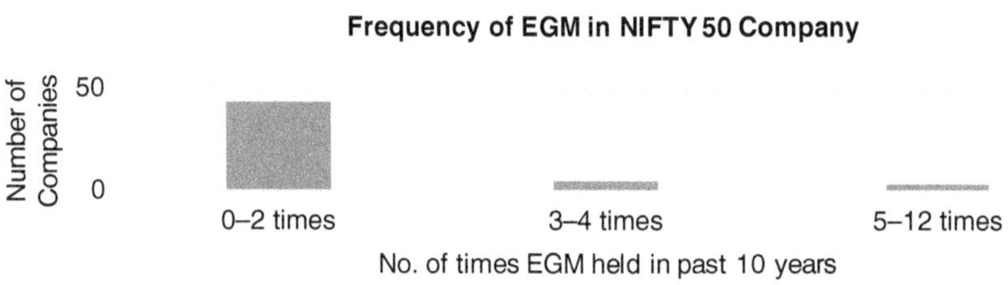

FIGURE 4.1 Frequency of EGMs in Nifty-50 companies (2009–18)

it should be deposited six weeks before the meeting; otherwise, two weeks is sufficient. When requirements are complied with, the company becomes bound to notify members of the intended resolution.[82] If the company receives notice of any resolution or statement to be circulated by fewer than the specified number of members, directors may, under their ordinary power of resolution notification, circulate it, but not under section 111 of CA 2013. Nominations for directorship and resolutions for the removal of a director can be proposed under sections 160 and 169, respectively.

[82] The company can be relieved of this obligation if the central government is satisfied that the right is being abused to secure needless publicity for a defamatory matter.

4.2.3 *Voting*

Before discussing voting procedures, it is important to reiterate that promoters with a controlling block of shares maintain cross holdings in their group companies to retain control.[83] CA 2013 introduced a few provisions to regulate such cross shareholdings. In addition to bringing related entities or associations of individuals into the 'promoter group', restrictions have been placed on subsidiary companies holding shares in their holding company. A subsidiary company cannot have shares in its holding company, and the transfer of shares in a company to its subsidiary is void.[84] A new type of company called the 'associate company' was introduced by CA 2013 in which the relationship between an associate company and another company is established through significant influence being exercised over the associate company by the other company.[85] Joint venture companies fall within this category.

It is also important to mention here that the term 'group companies' is defined by SEBI (Issue of Capital and Disclosures) Regulations 2018. Regulation 2(1)(t) provides that 'group companies' include companies (other than the promoter and subsidiary/subsidiaries) with which there were related-party transactions (RPTs) during the period for which financial information is disclosed, as covered under the applicable accounting standards, as well as other companies considered material by the issuer's board.[86] A 'material subsidiary' is defined in regulation 3(f) of SEBI (Listing Obligations and Disclosure Requirements) Regulations 2015.[87]

4.2.3.1 One Share-One Vote

A company limited by shares can have equity and preference share capital. Equity shares can simply have voting rights or differential voting rights (DVRs) as to dividends, voting or otherwise.[88] Therefore, the 'one share-one vote' rule is subject to the provisions of section 43, CA 2013 relating to DVRs. Every member holding equity share capital has a right to vote on every resolution, whereas preference shareholders have rights to vote only on matters affecting their rights, resolutions for winding up or the repayment or reduction of share capital.[89] However, if a company defaults on the payment of dividends to preference shareholders for two years or more, such shareholders become entitled to vote on all resolutions.[90]

DVRs are not popular with Indian companies. As of 2012, only three Indian companies had issued such shares, and investors were unwilling to subscribe to them because of the fewer voting rights attached even though they offered higher dividends.[91] However, start-up companies have

83 All entities falling under the promoter and promoter group are required to be shown separately in the shareholding pattern in any listed company on all national stock exchanges where the securities of said company are listed; see Reg. 31, SEBI (LODR) Regulations, 2015.

84 CA 2013, s. 19.

85 CA 2013, s. 2(6). 'Significant influence' means control of at least 20 per cent of total voting power or control of or participation in business decisions under an agreement.

86 'Group company' was defined earlier in 2013 by FDI policy through Circular No 68 [AP (DIR series)] as two or more enterprises that, directly or indirectly, are in a position to exercise 26 per cent or more of voting rights in the other enterprise or appoint more than 50 per cent of the members of the board of directors in the other enterprise; see Reserve Bank of India, 'Foreign Direct Investment (FDI) in India – Definition of "group company"' (1 November 2013) www.rbi.org.in/Scripts/NotificationUser.aspx?Id=8551&Mode=0 accessed 19 April 2020.

87 'Material subsidiary' means a subsidiary whose income or net worth exceeds 20 per cent of the consolidated income or net worth, respectively, of the listed entity and its subsidiaries in the immediately preceding accounting year.

88 CA 2013, s. 43.

89 CA 2013, s. 47; if the shares held by the minor are fully paid, the minor is entitled to vote at the meeting.

90 Ibid.

91 Vijay Gurav, 'Investor Snub Makes DVRs Issued by Tata Motors, Pantaloon Retail and Gujrat NRE Coke a Losing Proposition' *The Economic Times* (Mumbai, 21 February 2012) https://economictimes.indiatimes.com/markets/

begun to exhibit a preference for issuing DVRs with more voting rights to protect the promoter voting powers needed to increase the cap on the maximum that can be raised under DVRs. Doing so is considered necessary to enable the promoters of Indian companies to retain control of their companies in their pursuit of growth and the creation of long-term value for shareholders even as they raise equity capital from global investors. SEBI has permitted the issuance of shares with superior voting rights (SVR) for new technology companies since August 2019.[92] The holders of such shares are at par with other shareholders in all respects except for voting on resolutions.[93] The Companies (Share Capital & Debentures) Rules 2014 were amended to raise the existing cap of 26 per cent of total post-issue paid-up equity share capital to a revised cap of 74 per cent of total voting power for DVRs and to remove the earlier requirement of distributable profits for three years for a company to be eligible to issue shares with DVRs.[94] SVR equity shares are treated as ordinary equity shares with one share-one vote in the appointment or removal of independent directors and/or auditors, a promoter's wilful transfer of control to another entity, RPTs involving an SVR shareholder, the voluntary winding up of the listed entity, changes to the AoA or memorandum of association of the listed entity, any change affecting the SVR equity share, the initiation of a voluntary resolution process under the Insolvency and Bankruptcy Code, the utilization of funds for purposes other than business, substantial value transactions based on a materially specified threshold, the passing of a special resolution in respect of delisting or the buyback of shares and other circumstances or subject matter to be specified by SEBI.

SVR equity shares convert into ordinary equity shares under the one share-one vote rule after five years of their listing. The conversion period may be extended if a resolution to that effect is passed by shareholders other than SVR equity shareholders. However, they can be converted at any time before the end of the extended period. SVR equity shares compulsorily convert into equity shares having similar voting rights to those of ordinary shares upon the demise of the promoter or founder holding such shares. If an SVR shareholder resigns from an executive position in the listed entity or in the event of a merger or acquisition of a listed entity having an SVR shareholder, where control would no longer remain with the SVR shareholder, the SVR equity shares are sold by an SVR shareholder who continues to hold such shares after the lock-in period but prior to the lapse of the shares' validity.[95]

4.2.3.2 Cumulative and Slate Voting

CA 2013 does not specifically define cumulative voting. It defines a voting right as the right of a member of a company to vote in any meeting of the company or by means of a postal ballot.[96]

stocks/news/investor-snub-makes-dvrs-issued-by-tata-motors-pantaloon-retail-and-gujarat-nre-coke-a-losing-proposition/articleshow/11969515.cms accessed 19 April 2020.

92 ICDR Regulations 2018, reg. 2(eeea). 'SVR equity shares' are the equity shares of an issuer with superior voting rights relative to all other equity shares issued by the issuer in question.

93 LODR Regulations 2015, reg. 41(3).

94 Ministry of Corporate Affairs, 'MCA Amends Provisions Related to Differential Voting Rights under Companies Act' (16 August 2019) https://pib.gov.in/newsite/PrintRelease.aspx?relid=192676 accessed 19 April 2020. Shares with superior rights can be issued up to 74 per cent of the total voting power in such companies.

95 SEBI (LODR) Regulations 2015, reg. 41.

96 CA 2013, s. 2(93); a voting right can be exercised only in respect to the amount called up and paid up by the member under s. 50.

Voting by postal ballot means voting by post or through an electronic mode.[97] The Act provides an option to adopt the principle of proportional representation for the appointment of directors under section 163 if the company's AoA allow for it.[98] Two-thirds of directors may be appointed by proportional representation by a single transferable vote, cumulative voting or otherwise under section 163. That section begins with the phrase 'notwithstanding anything contained in this Act', and thus excludes the appointment of directors to be voted on individually, as provided under section 162, CA 2013.

CA 2013 also does not define or specifically provide for slate voting, which is seen only in the context of the appointment of directors at an AGM. Section 162 provides that the appointment of every director must be put to the vote at the AGM. Each candidate has to be voted for individually because candidates cannot be put to the vote *en bloc*. If two or more persons are appointed as directors by a single resolution, their appointment would be void unless the meeting had unanimously resolved that more than one person could be elected by a single resolution.[99]

4.2.3.3 Majority of Minority Approval

It is difficult to say whether the principle of majority of minority rights exists in CA 2013. Analysis suggests that few of its provisions recognize the existence of such rights for minority shareholders. The Act does, however, provide for the compulsory squeeze-out of minority shareholders under a few provisions. In the case of mergers and acquisitions, the transferee company has the power to acquire the shares of dissenting shareholders if the transfer of shares is approved by the majority. The Act also empowers acquirer companies to purchase minority shareholdings if the acquirer and a person acting in concert have already become the registered holders of 90 per cent or more of equity shares in the company.[100]

In the case of RPTs, section 188, CA 2013 provides that contracts or arrangements with related parties by companies with prescribed share capital or transactions exceeding a prescribed turnover require prior approval via a resolution. Minority shareholders get veto power here because related parties are prohibited from voting on such resolutions. If a member of the company is a related party, he or she cannot vote on such a resolution unless 90 per cent or more of the members of that company are relatives of the promoters or related parties. This was an interesting third proviso added to the Act in 2018 in respect of promoter-driven companies to provide a respite from having no voting rights in RPTs.[101]

In the case of the delisting of shares from any stock exchange, a company has to pass a special resolution through a postal ballot with an explanatory statement. Such special resolutions are acted upon if and only if the number of votes cast by public shareholders in favour of the proposal amount to at least two times the number of votes cast against.[102]

97 CA 2013, ss. 2(65) and 110. Section 110 provides that for the passing of a resolution through a postal ballot items of business will be provided by the central government. Any special business and business where directors or auditors do not have a right to be heard may also be transacted though a postal ballot by the company. A postal ballot is comparable to a poll except that it cannot be demanded.

98 CA 2013, s. 152.

99 CA 2013, s. 162. A proposal to move a motion for the appointment of two or more directors by a single resolution has first been agreed to at the meeting without any vote being cast against it.

100 CA 2013, s. 235.

101 CA 2013, s. 188.

102 SEBI (Delisting of Equity Shares) Regulations 2009, reg. 9.

Provisions relating to oppression and mismanagement give shareholders the right to file a motion with the NCLT pertaining to such matters. The scope of the term 'oppression' has been broadened by CA 2013. The conduct of affairs by a company in a way prejudicial to the public interest also gives shareholders a ground to petition for a finding of oppression. This ground is in addition to prejudice or the oppression of a shareholder or any other member and prejudice to the company.[103] The right is granted to a minimum of 100 members of the company or not less than one-tenth of the total number of members, whichever is less, or to any member or members holding not less than one-tenth of the issued share capital of the company if the company has share capital. However, it is subject to the condition that the applicant or applicants has/have paid all calls and other sums due on his or her/their shares. In the event that the company has no share capital, the right can be exercised by not less than one-fifth of the total number of members.[104] The NCLT has the discretion to waive this requirement, discretion that was exercised by the National Company Law Appellate Tribunal in the case of *Cyrus Mistry* v. *Tata Sons*.[105] In the pilot study, effort was made to locate any litigation relating to oppression or mismanagement undertaken by shareholders against Nifty-50 companies, but no such litigation was observed between 2016 and 2020 (as of March 2020) apart from the aforementioned case.[106]

The right to file class action suits was also added to the powers of members and depositors by CA 2013. If they are of the opinion that the management or conduct of the affairs of the company is being conducted in a manner prejudicial to the interests of the company or its members or depositors, they can file an application with the NCLT on behalf of the members or depositors.[107]

4.2.4 *Question and Information Request Rights of Shareholders*

Shareholders have the right to discuss all proposed resolutions and move amendments. If an amendment is reasonably germane to a proposed resolution, it must be admitted.[108] CA 2013 does not contain any direct provision providing shareholders with a right to question or seek information but such rights occur on the basis of their power to pass resolutions in general meetings of the company. Such rights are also indirectly provided under the Secretarial Standards (SS) with respect to general and board meetings, which are required to be observed by every company under section 118(10), CA 2013. As per SS-2, the chair of a general meeting is required to explain the objective and implications of each resolution even though resolutions forming part of special business are accompanied by a special note. The chair is also required to provide a fair opportunity to members who are entitled to vote to seek clarifications and/or offer comments related to any item of business and to address the same, as warranted. He or she is further required to provide a fair opportunity to members to raise questions relating to agenda items and to ensure that members who have sought clarifications, information or explanations are given an effective and timely reply.[109] Members have the right to speak on a motion even if

103 CA, 2013, s. 241 (3), additional powers are given to the Central Government by the amendment in 2019.
104 CA 2013, s. 244.
105 2017 SCC OnLine NCLT 1508.
106 Orders filed with the Principal Bench, New Delhi along with New Delhi Bench II, III, IV, V and VI and Mumbai Bench of NCLT were studied thoroughly. There were 1000+ orders from 2016–20 relating to oppression and mismanagement. However, no case was related to a Nifty-50 company.
107 CA 2013, s. 245.
108 Singh (n. 1) 385.
109 ICSI, 5.2 of guidance note on general meetings.

there is a clear majority on the agenda item concerned.[110] The company may invite members to submit questions in advance to limit the time of debate on each resolution and restrict repetitive questions. In addition, it may select common questions to provide a comprehensive answer at the general meeting.

4.3 SHAREHOLDER ENGAGEMENT AND VOTING IN PRACTICE

4.3.1 *Voting in Practice*

4.3.1.1 Voting by a Show of Hand or Poll

At a general meeting, a resolution put to a vote is decided based on the result of voting by a show of hands unless a poll is demanded or voting is carried out electronically.[111] Voting rights on a poll are in proportion to the shares of shareholders in paid-up equity or preference share capital, whereas in voting by a show of hands each member has one vote.[112] A member may split his or her votes both for and against the same resolution on a poll, which is permissible even if a proxy is voting. As the owner of the specific property in each specific share, a shareholder can distribute his or her votes in any manner on the shares he or she holds. Under no doctrine of inconvenience, convenience or propriety, it has been held that a shareholder can be precluded from voting both 'yes' and 'no' on the same resolution because the way in which he or she votes cannot take away the legal right on each share carrying the right to vote.[113] In the case of joint holders, the vote of the senior party who tenders the vote, whether in person or by proxy, is accepted to the exclusion of the votes of the other joint holders.[114]

A member may be prohibited from exercising his or her voting rights only if he or she does not pay calls or any other sum due on his or her shares or the company exercises its right of lien on the shares. However, such a prohibition applies only if it is specified in the company's AoA.[115] No rights attached to any shares can be exercised by the beneficial owner of the shares or any person claiming through him or her if a declaration of a beneficial interest in such shares has not been made.[116]

4.3.1.2 Voting in Person or Proxy

A member may vote either in person or by proxy.[117] A proxy is not allowed to speak at the meeting and is not entitled to vote except on a poll. The proxy system may not be available in companies

110 The chairperson of a general meeting has no right to prevent discussion of a matter included in the notice convening the meeting.

111 Voting by a show of hands, voting by electronic means and a demand for a poll are dealt with, respectively, by ss. 107, 108 and 109, CA 2013. A poll may be taken up by the chair *suo motu* or demanded by members before or upon the declaration of the result by a show of hands. Members having 10 per cent of the total voting power or having 5 lakh rupees as the paid-up value of shares can demand a poll. Such a demand may be withdrawn at any time by the person(s) who it.

112 CA 2013, ss. 47 and 107.

113 *Mahaliram Santhalia* v. *Gloster Jute Manufacturing Co. Ltd.* [1954] 24 Com Cases 311.

114 Seniority is determined by the order in which the names stand in the register of members under art. 52, Table F, Schedule I, CA 2013; joint holders have a right to instruct the company as to the order in which their names should appear in the register of members; see *T. H. Saunders & Co Ltd, Re* [1908] 1 Ch 415.

115 CA 2013, s. 106; a member is restricted from voting in related part transactions that require approval by a resolution under s. 188, CA 2013.

116 CA 2013, s. 89.

117 CA 2013, s. 195.

specified by the central government. A single proxy may act for fifty members at a time holding no more than 10 per cent of the company's total share capital carrying voting rights. If a member holding more than 10 per cent of total share capital appoints a single person as his or her proxy, that person is not permitted to act as the proxy of any other person or shareholder.[118] If a shareholder personally attends and votes in the meeting after issuing a proxy, the proxy stands as cancelled. A proxy can at any time be revoked by a written notice of revocation. A proxy of a member of any section 8 company can only be another member of the same company.[119]

4.3.1.3 Postal Ballot

The postal ballot system can be used by listed companies to pass resolutions only in respect of businesses notified by the central government. It can be used for special business in respect of which directors or auditors do not have a right of hearing.[120] Earlier, items specified for a postal ballot could be transacted only through the postal ballot and not at the general meeting.[121] However, the rule was amended, and such matters may now be transacted at the general meeting of a company required to facilitate the vote by electronic means.[122] It has been held that all provisions for compulsory voting by postal ballot and by electronic voting to the exclusion of an actual meeting cannot and do not apply to court-convened meetings.[123] One-person companies and other companies with 200 or fewer members are not required to transact any business through a postal ballot.

4.3.1.4 E-Voting

The central government prescribes the class of companies and the manner of exercising voting by electronic means.[124] All listed companies with at least 1,000 shareholders have to provide for e-voting.[125] An e-voting system is a secure system based on the display of electronic ballots. The recording of members' votes and number of votes polled in favour of or against a proposition, such that the entire voting process is registered and counted in an electronic registry in a centralized server, is deemed to have adequate 'cyber security'. A resolution proposed to be considered through e-voting is not allowed to be withdrawn.[126] A member who has e-voted is permitted to attend the general meeting in person, but is not allowed to vote at the meeting. His or her e-vote is treated as final. A show of hands is not allowed in e-voting. In the case of companies having share capital, e-voting takes into account the 'proportion principle', that is, one share-one vote, unlike the one person-one vote principle under a show of hands.[127]

[118] Ibid.

[119] Companies (Management and Administration) Rules, 2014, r. 19; s. 8 companies are companies with charitable objects.

[120] Section 110, CA 2013.

[121] General Circular No. 20 in pursuance of CA 2013, s. 108 read with Companies (Management and Administration) Rules 2014, r. 20 and 22(16).

[122] Companies (Management and Administration) Rules 2014, r. 22(16) as amended in 2018.

[123] See *Companies Act* v. *Unknown (Bom)* decision dated 8 May 2014 concerning the scheme of amalgamation of Wadala Commodities Ltd with Godrej Industries Ltd.

[124] CA 2013, s. 108.

[125] E-voting was not considered mandatory until 31 December 2014, as per General Circular No. 20 in pursuance of s. 108, CA 2013 read with Companies (Management and Administration) Rules 2014, r. 20.

[126] Companies (Management and Administration) Rules, 2014, r. 20.

[127] For clarification with regard to voting by electronic means, see General Circular No. 20/2014 No 1/34l2013-CL-V Ministry of Corporate Affairs, Government of India www.mca.gov.in/Ministry/pdf/General_Circular_20_2014.pdf accessed 15 July 2020.

4.3.2 *Resolutions for Shareholding Voting and Quorum for General Meetings*

Shareholder resolutions may be passed as ordinary or special resolutions. An ordinary resolution is a resolution passed by a simple majority of members present and voting, whereas a special resolution requires the support of a three-fourths majority of shareholders present and entitled to vote at the meeting.[128] The intention to propose a resolution as a special resolution should be declared in the notice calling the general meeting. A special notice may be required for certain resolutions by the provisions of CA 2013 or the company's articles.[129] In such a case, notice of the intention should be given by members holding a minimum of 1 per cent of total voting power or shares on which an aggregate sum not exceeding 5 lakh rupees (US$0.5 million) has been paid up. The company is also required to give notice of the meeting and inform shareholders that the resolution concerned is an ordinary resolution with special notice. Companies are given the flexibility for the entrenchment of articles, which means that specified provisions in the articles may be altered only if conditions or procedures stricter than a special resolution are met or complied with.[130]

Ordinary resolutions are required to be passed for the general business of an AGM, whereas special resolutions are required for alteration of the articles and/or memorandum of the company, a variation in shareholder rights, the issue of sweat equity shares, the further issue of capital through employee stock options, the conversion of debentures or loans into company shares, a reduction in share capital, the purchase of the company's own shares and/or the buy-back of shares, the reappointment or removal of a retiring auditor, the reappointment of an independent director, restrictions on the powers of the board, loans to directors, the remuneration of directors in the event of inadequate profits, investigations of the company's affairs, removal of the company's name from the register of companies and winding up by the NCLT and arrangements relating to such winding up.

Unless the company's AoA provide otherwise, the quorum for meetings is five members personally present in the case of a public company with 1,000 or fewer members. If the number of members is between 1,000 and 5,000, the quorum is 15 members personally present, and if the number exceeds 5,000, then 30 members personally present make a quorum.[131] Along with the e-voting facility provided in companies with 1,000 shareholders, hybrid meetings are allowed in Indian listed companies, although fully virtual meetings are not. On the basis of the aforementioned quorum requirements, one might assume that shareholder engagement is minimal in Indian companies. However, generally high levels of voting by institutional investors are seen when it comes to such important matters as the issue of employee stock options at par or at a huge discount on the current market price.[132]

128 CA 2013, s. 114; a special resolution is required, inter alia, for the purposes of altering the constituent documents of a company, changing the name of the company, a reduction in capital and winding up.

129 CA 2013, s. 115; a special notice is required when a retiring auditor is not appointed under s. 140, CA 2013 and when a director is removed before the end of his or her term and a new director is appointed under s. 169, CA 2013.

130 CA 2013, s. 5(3).

131 A quorum should be present when the questions before the meeting are being decided. The mere presence of a quorum at the beginning of the meeting is not sufficient; see Secretarial Standards on General Meetings SS-2 revised standards applicable from 1 October 2017.

132 Rajesh Mascarenhas, 'ESOP Issue a Pain for Companies with Big Institutional Holdings' *The Economic Times* (28 August 2018) https://economictimes.indiatimes.com/markets/stocks/news/esop-issue-a-pain-for-companies-with-big-institutional-holdings/articleshow/65575812.cms?from=mdr accessed 19 April 2020.

4.3.3 *Observations on Voting Patterns*

Some interesting observations on voting are offered here before discussing the voting patterns identified in the pilot study. These observations are based on reported incidents.

One of the earliest examples of shareholder engagement through e-voting was seen in Tata Motors Ltd when a resolution to ratify the salaries of three executives was voted against by nearly 64 per cent of institutional investors and 41 per cent of the company's public shareholders in 2014. Such large-scale participation by institutional and public shareholders is rare in Indian companies, as few shareholders turn up at AGMs, where such proposals are usually put to the vote.[133] A comparatively higher participation rate of institutional investors in companies listed on the National Stock Exchange was observed in 2018 relative to 2017, with more than 20 per cent of institutional shareholders voting against 716 resolutions in the latter year compared to voting against 629 resolutions in the former. Proxy advisors played an important role in increasing the voting rate. There was a 14 per cent increase in resolutions over the two years, with most of them relating to the appointment of directors or their remuneration and stock options.[134] Around 700 votes were cast owing to the higher shareholdings of promoters. The increase can be credited to the facility to engage in e-voting, as well as to the applicability of the stewardship code to institutional investors.[135] Forty-five dissenting votes were cast in 2018, compared with thirty-four and twenty-eight in 2017 and 2016, respectively.

A resolution to approve the continuation of Deepak Parekh's directorship of HDFC Ltd when he came up for reappointment as a non-executive director upon attaining the age of seventy-five on 18 October 2019 exemplifies the role of proxy advisory firms in India. Two US-based proxy advisory firms advised their investors not to vote in favour of his reappointment because, in their view, the HDFC board was not sufficiently independent. The disclosed voting pattern reveals that 24.86 per cent of shareholders in the public institution category voted against the resolution, with the remaining 75.14 per cent voting for it.[136] Because proxy advisory firms are playing an increasingly prominent role in listed companies, they are now required to disclose any conflicts of interest in giving recommendations and to make adequate disclosures regarding their business model and ancillary business activities.[137]

In another example, a proposal to appoint an independent director representing small shareholders in Alembic Ltd was made in 2017 by an institutional investor in a company called Unifi Capital Pvt Ltd. However, Alembic's board did not accept the proposal on the ground of the close nexus observed between Unifi and its group of companies, which were found to have a large shareholding in Alembic. Out of 914, 320 shareholders, who had made the proposal,

[133] Lijee Philip, 'Mandatory e-Voting Gives Shareholders Upper Hand' *The Economic Times* (12 July 2014) https://economictimes.indiatimes.com/news/company/corporate-trends/mandatory-e-voting-gives-shareholders-upper-hand/articleshow/38249628.cms?from=mdr accessed 19 April 2020.

[134] PTI, '2018 Saw Greater Advocacy by Institutional Shareholders' *The Business Standard* (14 February 2019) www.business-standard.com/article/pti-stories/2018-saw-greater-advocacy-by-institutional-shareholders-report-119021400408_1.html accessed 28 April 2020.

[135] Principles on voting by mutual funds were implemented by SEBI in 2010 and 2014; SEBI Circular on Stewardship Code to be applicable to all Mutual Funds and Alternative Investment Funds, CIR/CFD/CMD1/ 168 /2019 issued on 24 December 2019 and Code to be applicable from 1 April 2020.

[136] 'Two U.S. Advisory Firms Asked Investors to Vote Against Parekh's Reappointment' *Bloomberg Quint* (31 July 2018) www.bloombergquint.com/business/agm-voting-pattern-against-deepak-parekh-a-surprise-says-proxy-advisory-firm accessed 27 April 2020.

[137] 'SEBI to Issue Special Guidelines for Proxy Advisory Firms' *The Hindu Business Line* (Mumbai, 29 July 2019) www.thehindubusinessline.com/money-and-banking/sebi-to-issue-special-guidelines-for-proxy-advisory-firms/article28749627.ece accessed 20 April 2020.

become shareholders in Alembic just five days before the proposal and were discovered to be clients of Unifi.[138]

As stated earlier, the conduct of AGMs was relaxed by the Ministry of Corporate Affairs (MCA) in view of COVID-19, with companies afforded the flexibility to hold AGMs virtually.[139] Four big-cap companies, that is, TCS, SBI, RIL and Tech Mahindra, duly held their AGMs by means of a virtual conference or other audio-visual means pursuant to the MCA's relaxation and SEBI Guidelines[140] until Unlock 3.[141] A total of twenty-one resolutions were passed in the four companies' AGMs, as seen in Table 4.6 below. The preferred mode of voting was e-voting. Public institutions registered dissent rates of 13.2 per cent in resolutions for the reappointment of directors. It can be observed that the dissent rate was diluted in comparison to the total votes polled on the various resolutions.

4.3.3.1 Observations on Voting Pattern in the Pilot Study

In the pilot study, the number of resolutions passed during AGMs were noted, along with the percentage of votes cast for FYs 2016–17, 2017–18 and 2018–19. Data analysis revealed the maximum number of resolutions to fall into the committee and reporting category, whereas the board of directors' category had the most tabled resolutions. From 2016–19, the preferred method of voting was e-voting, followed by polling. The results are reported in Table 4.7.

Table 4.7 reports the voting pattern for annual financial statement adoption in Nifty-50 companies for FY 2018. The voting pattern was divided into three categories of shareholders, namely, P&PG, public institutions and non-public institutions. The following observations are made.

(1) P&PG shareholders voted 100 per cent in favour of adoption.
(2) Public non-institutional shareholders dissented overall as a category, although the rate of dissent was less than 2 per cent.
(3) A case study of Steel Authority of India Ltd revealed a dissent rate of 10.25 per cent amongst public shareholders for the adoption of the 2018 annual financial statement. The maximum rate of dissent in all three categories was 2.96 per cent.

In forty-nine companies, voting by shareholders in person and through proxy for adoption of the annual financial statement in 2018 ranged from 0.01–4.69 per cent. In only four companies did voting take place in person by more than 1 per cent of shareholders present and voting. For forty-nine companies, the three top modes of voting were e-voting, polling and postal ballots. In thirty-six companies, P&PG shareholders utilized the e-voting option, whilst the e-voting trend was more prominent amongst public institutional shareholders and public non-institutional shareholders. The figures for postal ballots for all three categories were meagre, accounting for less than 6 per cent.

[138] Jayshree P. Upadhyay, 'Alembic Minority Shareholders Seek Seat on Company Board, Jayashree Upadhyay' *Live Mint* (25 July 2017) www.livemint.com/Companies/Q8MoZXurHinigWBcSd7t8H/Alembic-minority-shareholders-seek-seat-on-company-board.html accessed 15 July 2020.

[139] Refer to n. 70.

[140] Clarification on holding of Annual General Meeting (AGM) through video conferencing (VC) or other audio visual means (OAVM) www.mca.gov.in/Ministry/pdf/Circular20_05052020.pdf accessed 15 July 2020; additional relaxation in relation to compliance with certain provisions of SEBI (Listing Obligations and Disclosure Requirements) Regulations 2015 – Covid-19 pandemic www.sebi.gov.in/legal/circulars/may-2020/additional-relaxation-in-relation-to-compliance-with-certain-provisions-of-sebi-listing-obligations-and-disclosure-requirements-regulations-2015-covid-19-pandemic_46661.html accessed 15 July 2020.

[141] After complete lockdown due to Covid-19, unlocking was done in four phases, MHA, Unlock 3 order www.mha.gov.in/sites/default/files/DOLrDt_29072020.pdf accessed 15 July 2020.

TABLE 4.6 *Voting pattern in pilot study*

Resolutions (FY 2016–17)	Number of Resolutions	Voting percentage	Mode of voting: e-voting	Poll	Postal ballot
Remuneration of Directors[142]	28	7%	85%	11%	4%
Governance	1	0%			
Corporate Structure[143]	50	12%			
Committee and Reporting[144]	165	39%			
Board of Directors[145]	151	36%			
Miscellaneous[146]	25	6%			
Resolutions (FY 2017–18)	**Number of Resolutions**	**Voting percentage**	**Mode of Voting: e-voting**	**Polling**	**Postal Ballot**
Remuneration of Directors	20	5%	94%	05%	01%
Corporate Structure	50	14%			
Committee and Reporting	145	39%			
Board of Directors	139	38%			
Miscellaneous	14	4%			
Resolutions (FY 2018–2019)	**Number of Resolutions**	**Voting percentage**	**Mode of Voting: e -voting**	**Polling**	**Postal Ballot**
Remuneration of Directors	31	5%	88%	8%	4%
Governance	6	1%			
Corporate Structure	69	11%			
Committee and Reporting	167	27%			
Board of Directors	279	44%			
Miscellaneous	75	12%			

4.4 CONCLUDING REMARKS

CA 2013 brought about several changes with respect to ownership, shareholder engagement and the remedies in place for minority shareholders, which attests to the fact that CA 2013 operates on the fundamental principles of transparency and compliance. The legal framework has kept abreast of all relevant changes with respect to the corporate governance of companies, and those changes have been observed. The core philosophy underpinning both the Act and legal framework is the need to improve investor protection and enhance shareholder engagement. The duties of directors have been codified and are broadly in line with the duties accepted internationally, whilst the concept of KMP has been identified to ascertain and assign responsibility. New shareholder rights have been introduced and strengthened. The purpose of improving shareholders' rights is to provide them with more opportunities to engage with companies. Shareholder engagement is a method for shareholders to communicate their views, concerns,

142 Commission remuneration for non-executive directors, remuneration under employee stock ownership plan, etc.

143 Amendment to articles, issue of non-convertible debenture, pledging of assets for debts in a corporate structure.

144 Committee and reporting include approving auditors, financial statements, dividends, etc.

145 Board of director election and re-election-related resolutions.

146 Resolutions related to threshold increases and the redesignation of officials fall into the miscellaneous category.

TABLE 4.7 *Voting for adoption of annual financial statement*

Types of voting	P&PG	Public Institutional Shareholders	Public Non-institutional shareholders
E-voting	36	49	49
Poll	16	6	48
Postal Ballot	2	0	3

ideas and opinions to companies' boards of directors and managers.[147] Under the present scheme, shareholders can either voice their concerns or exit the company.

Family-owned companies are common in India, with shareholdings largely concentrated in the hands of promoters and promoter groups. Further, a promoter who is a controlling shareholder can appoint him or herself as a director or control the appointment of other directors. On the one hand, efforts have been made to reduce the shareholdings of promoters. On the other hand, the promoters of start-up companies are allowed to have shares with SVR to protect their control over their companies.

The right to call an EGM is afforded to shareholders by the Companies Act. However, in Nifty-50 companies, no such meeting has been called by shareholders within the last ten years. Further, with one exception, no case of oppression or mismanagement has been observed in those companies on the NCLT benches of Delhi and Bombay, which are the major commercial hubs of India. Stakeholder engagement through whistle blower activity and grievance redressal ranges from 84–98 per cent. Shareholder engagement has also been encouraged through improved methods of voting, including e-voting. As seen in the pilot study, e-voting was the preferred method of voting for the adoption of companies' annual financial statements in FY2018. The voting pattern for other resolutions in that year is not available.

The real test lies post-COVID-19. Although companies' shareholdings have been affected, many important deals have been closed during the COVID period.[148] It thus remains an open question whether shareholder engagement will be improved by the greater use of audiovisual modes of voting, as well as whether shareholder engagement will increase in India, where retail and institutional shareholders do not have the majority votes to defeat resolutions. Finally, it remains to be seen how corporate governance can be improved to make Indian companies and in turn society more sustainable.

[147] Nicholas J. Price, 'Shareholder Engagement Policy in Corporate Governance' *Diligent Insights* (15 March 2019) https://insights.diligent.com/shareholder-engagement/shareholder-engagement-policy-corporate-governance/ accessed 19 September 2019.

[148] 'Despite Covid-19, M&A and PE Deal Value Rose by 7% to $80 billion in 2020' *The Business Standard* www.business-standard.com/article/companies/despite-covid-19-m-a-and-pe-deal-value-rose-by-7-to-80-billion-in-2020–120122300296_1.html accessed 15 July 2020.

5

Corporate Governance and Shareholder Engagement Practices in Indonesia: A Shifting Paradigm

Ulya Yasmine Prisandani and Kartika Paramita

5.1 INTRODUCTION

The origins of Indonesian company history lie in the development of private family businesses. More than 95 per cent of businesses in Indonesia today were created as family firms[1] with a small number of shareholders who were acquainted with or related to one another. The family nature of the businesses, however, tends to make it difficult to separate the interests of the family from those of the company.[2] Research conducted by Carney and Child in 2008 found that 68.1 per cent of the 200 participating Indonesian companies had no second owner holding at least 10 per cent of the company's stock.[3] In addition, in 58.2 per cent of the companies, the CEO, board chair or vice chair was a member of the controlling family.[4] On the whole, Indonesia is known to have a concentrated ownership structure wherein controlling shareholders often assume both supervisory and management roles.[5]

The corporate governance of Indonesian limited liability companies (LLCs) is subject primarily to Law No. 40 of 2007 Concerning Limited Liability Companies as amended by Law No. 11 of 2020 Concerning Job Creation, which is commonly known as the Indonesian Company Law (ICL).[6] The ICL acknowledges three general company organs: the general meeting of shareholders (GMS), the board of directors (BoD) and the board of commissioners (BoC). Indonesia's corporate board structure is a dual-board system with distinct authorities given to the BoC and BoD. The BoD is authorized to conduct and is fully responsible for the overall management of day-to-day operations and is required to serve the company's interests in accordance with the company's purpose and objectives, whereas the BoC is tasked with supervising and advising the BoD on management policy in accordance with laws and regulations and the company's articles of association (AoA).

1 Fitri Oktaviani et al., 'Family, Feudalism and Selfishness: Looking at Indonesian Leadership through a Wisdom Lens' (2015) 12 *Leadership* 538, 540.

2 Benny Simon Tabalujan, 'Family Capitalism and Corporate Governance of Family-Controlled Listed Companies in Indonesia' (2002) 25 *UNSW Law Journal* 486, 510 https://dx.doi.org/10.2139/ssrn.323948 accessed 15 July 2020.

3 Richard W. Carney and Travers Barclay Child, 'Changes to the Ownership and Control of East Asian Corporations between 1996 and 2008: The Primacy of Politics' (2013) 107 *Journal of Financial Economics* 494.

4 Ibid.

5 Asian Development Bank, 'ASEAN Corporate Governance Scorecard Country Reports and Assessments 2015: Joint Initiative of the ASEAN Capital Markets Forum and the Asian Development Bank' (Asian Development Bank 2017) 26 www.adb.org/publications/asean-corporate-governance-scorecard-country-reports-assessments-2015 accessed 26 April 2020.

6 Foreign investment companies have additional obligations to fulfil under Law No. 25 of 2007 concerning Investment Law.

5.1.1 *Indonesian Corporate Law Framework*

The ICL classifies companies into three types: private companies, non-listed public companies and publicly listed companies. State-owned enterprises (SOEs) are regulated separately outside the ICL. This section elaborates on each company type under Indonesia's existing legal framework.

5.1.1.1 Private Companies

Private companies are entities that have a rather small number of shares and whose shareholders are acquainted with one another and whose roles are explicitly outlined in the company's AoA. In most private companies, registered shares (*aandelen op naam* shares) are assigned to each shareholder and are difficult to transfer to another party.

The ICL provides no explicit rules on the share composition within a company. However, it does stipulate that an LLC be founded by at least two persons.[7] It was previously the case that to establish a private company, the authorized capital had to be at least fifty million rupiah,[8] 25 per cent of which had to be issued and paid up.[9] However, this stipulation was changed in 2016 to give small- and medium-sized enterprises a boost. Accordingly, the minimum amount of authorized capital is now based solely on the agreement amongst the founders,[10] although, in practice, public notaries still refer to the requirement in the ICL with respect to company establishment.

5.1.1.2 Public Companies

Both non-listed public companies and publicly listed companies deal with a larger number of shareholders than private companies. To be a public company, a company's shares must be owned by at least 300 shareholders, and the company must have at least 3 billion rupiah[11] of paid-up capital. Both types of companies are identified by the suffix *terbuka*, abbreviated as *Tbk*, and they have an obligation to disclose information on their financial position, operations and governance to the public. Publicly listed companies are companies that conduct a public offering in the stock exchange market.[12] They are bound to comply with the laws and regulations of the capital market, OJK regulations and the listing rules of the Indonesia Stock Exchange (IDX) and other capital market self-regulatory organizations such as the Indonesian Central Securities Depository, or *Kustodian Sentral Efek Indonesia* (KSEI), and the Indonesian Clearing and Guarantee Corporation.[13] When a company intends to list on the IDX, it must first register itself with OJK. To change its status from a private to a public entity, or vice versa, a company must follow the procedures set out under Indonesia's Capital Market Law, which include

[7] Art. 7, para. 1 of ICL.

[8] Equivalent to US$3,401 based on an exchange rate of US$1 = 14,700 Indonesian rupiah.

[9] Arts. 32 and 33 of ICL.

[10] Government Regulation of the Republic of Indonesia No. 29 of 2016 Concerning Changes to Authorized Capital of Limited Liability Companies. This stipulation is not applicable to all business sectors, however. Several high-risk sectors such as banking, insurance and construction services still require a higher minimum of authorized capital, particularly during the business permit application period.

[11] Equivalent to US$204,082 based on exchange rate in n. 8.

[12] Art. 1, para. 7 of ICL.

[13] Over the course of a company's business operations, it will generally be subjected to the regulations of OJK, the Ministry of Trade, the Investment Coordination Board and other related ministries depending on the scope of its business activities. However, an additional set of regulations is imposed on publicly listed companies.

amending the company's AoA and business registration certificate. Such conversions do not affect the company's legal identity.

There are no restrictions on the transferability of shares (with the exception of voting preference shares and the shares held by founding shareholders) for either public or publicly listed companies,[14] although a company's AoA may contain specific requirements for share transfers. However, as a general rule, the consent of neither other shareholders nor the company is needed during the process of transferring shares. A specific percentage of shares is assigned to the public at the initial public offering (IPO), whereas non-public shareholders usually retain their shares in the event of IPO.

5.1.1.3 State-Owned Enterprises

In addition to the aforementioned company categorizations, SOEs in Indonesia are subject to additional regulations under Law No. 19 of 2003 Concerning State-Owned Enterprises (SOEL) as amended by Law No. 11 of 2020 Concerning Job Creation. SOEs are companies whose shares are wholly or dominantly[15] owned by the state. Although the majority of SOEs in Indonesia are formed as LLCs, and are hence subject to the provisions of the ICL, the SOEL further distinguishes between limited liability SOEs and public SOEs. As a result of this arrangement, the state's asset ownership in SOEs is limited proportional to its ownership of shares, and thus a company's assets cannot be automatically regarded as state assets. The state's shares in an SOE can be obtained only through direct investment, not through the market.[16]

In a company whose shares are wholly owned by the state, the GMS function is carried out by an appointed minister, whilst in companies whose shares are partially owned by the state the appointed minister merely acts as a shareholder.[17] Special authority, such as the authority to appoint and dismiss members of the BoD and BoC, is granted to the minister in the event that he or she serves the GMS function.[18] In general, the appointed minister in a public SOE serves as one of the company organs together with the BoD and a supervisory council.[19]

The state plays a major role in the operation of SOEs, for example, in determining increases and decreases in its equity participation. State plans to increase the state's capital participation must be proposed by the Minister of Finance to the President of Republic of Indonesia based on a prior study or research conducted by ministers in relevant fields.[20] Although a decrease in the state's equity participation requires the approval of the GMS, it must also be finalized through a government regulation based on the appointed minister's decision in relation to the shareholder role in limited liability SOEs.[21]

14 International Finance Corporation, 'Indonesia Corporate Governance Manual, Second Edition' (International Finance Corporation 2018) 58 www.ifc.org/wps/wcm/connect/e66bacdc-07c6-40f3-b094-8d3ca96a77a0/Indonesia_CG+Manual_2nd_Edition.pdf?MOD=AJPERES&CVID=mf8483z accessed 27 April 2020.

15 Dominant ownership refers to at least 51 per cent state ownership in a company, as provided in art. 1, para. 2 of SOEL.

16 Art. 1, paras. 1–2 of SOEL; arts. 52–53 of ICL.

17 Art. 14, para. 1 of SOEL.

18 Art. 15, para. 2 and art. 27, para. 2 of SOEL.

19 Art. 38 of SOEL.

20 Art. 14 of Government Regulation No. 44 of 2005 as amended by Government Regulation No. 77 of 2016 Concerning the Procedure of the State's Capital Participation and Management in State-Owned Enterprises and Limited Liability Companies.

21 Ibid., art. 22.

5.1.2 *Indonesian Corporate Board Structure*

The ICL bestows upon the GMS authority beyond that afforded the BoD and BoC, as long as it remains within the limits provided under regulations and/or the company's AoA.[22] It grants the GMS the authority[23] to approve changes to the company's AoA, approve company plans for share buy-backs or the further transfer of shares, approve additions or reductions of the company's capital, approve the BoC's supervisory reports and the company's annual and financial reports, decide on the utilization of the company's net profits, appoint and dismiss members of the BoD and BoC,[24] approve merger and acquisition transactions, approve the salaries, honoraria and incentives of BoD and BoC members and authorize decisions on the company's dissolution.

The ICL and relevant laws[25] also outline the duties of the BoD, which has the authority to hold a GMS, create the company's annual reports and financial documents, declare and distribute interim dividends after obtaining BoC approval, record transfers of shares and maintain all company documents. All companies in Indonesia must have at least one member on their BoD. If a company's BoD consists of two or more members, the allocation of duties and authority amongst the directors must be determined by a GMS resolution. If the GMS does pass such a resolution, then it must be determined by a BoD resolution.[26] No term limits for BoD members are specified in the ICL, but the Indonesian Financial Services Authority – *Otoritas Jasa Keuangan* (OJK) – stipulates that the terms of office for elected BoD and BoC members must not exceed five years for issuers and public companies.[27] BoD members may be dismissed at any time through a GMS resolution provided that they have been given a chance to submit a defence.[28]

The BoC acts as the supervisory organ in a company and reports its supervisory duties for each financial year during the annual GMS. BoC members may assist and/or approve BoD legal actions, as well as perform management tasks at certain times or in specific situations, as allowed under the company's AoA or by a GMS resolution.[29] Publicly listed companies are required to have at least two members on their BoCs, one of whom serves as the chair.[30]

Indonesia only recently eliminated the requirement for public companies to have independent directors, and affiliated directors and commissioners constitute a de facto longstanding practice. OJK's stance also reflects a focus on independent supervision by the BoC instead of independent directorship. The matter is addressed in the OJK Corporate Governance Roadmap of 2014 and OJK Regulation No. 33/POJK.04/2014 Concerning the Board of Directors and Board of Commissioners of Issuers or Public Companies.[31]

22 Art. 75, para 1 of ICL.

23 Arts. 19, 38, 41, 44, 66, 71, 94, 111, 113, 116, 127 and 142 of ICL.

24 Additional requirements are sometimes imposed by the government to tighten control in certain sectors. For example, in the banking sector, members of the BoC and BoD appointed by the GMS can exercise their duties only after obtaining OJK approval. See art. 2(4) of OJK Regulation No. 27/POJK.03/2016 Concerning Fit and Proper Test for Principal Parties of Financial Institutions.

25 For example, in arts. 50, 66, 72 and 79 of ICL and art. 9 of Law No. 8 of 1997 Concerning Companies' Documents.

26 Art. 92 of ICL.

27 Arts. 3 and 23 of OJK Regulation No. 33/POJK.04/2014 Concerning the Board of Directors and Board of Commissioners of Public Companies.

28 Art. 105 of ICL.

29 Arts. 116, 117 and 118 of ICL.

30 Art. 20 of OJK Regulation No. 33/POJK.04/2014 Concerning the Board of Directors and Board of Commissioners of Public Companies. The BoCs of banks in Indonesia are required to have at least three members. See art. 23(1) of OJK Regulation No. 55/POJK.03/2016 Concerning the Implementation of Corporate Governance in Commercial Banks.

31 In the event that the BoC of a publicly listed company has two members, one member must be an independent commissioner. If it has more than two members, 30 per cent of them must be independent commissioners.

5.1.3 *Shareholding Structure*

The shareholding structure under Indonesian law takes into account the different types of shares regulated under the ICL, as such differences may give rise to different shareholder rights. The following paragraphs thus discuss both share types and differing shareholder rights. The share ownership structure and corporate control in the Indonesian listed sector are discussed at greater length in Section 5.3.1 of the present chapter.

5.1.3.1 Types of Shares under ICL

The ICL gives Indonesian companies the facility to determine one or more share classifications to be written into their AoA. As provided for in the elucidation[32] of article 53 paragraph (4) of the ICL, in the event that there is more than one class of shares, those classes do not necessarily stand alone, but may be combined. However, one class must be designated as common shares, and the other as preferred shares.[33]

Common shares give rise to the right to vote at the GMS for the adoption of resolutions on points related to the company's management, the right to receive dividends and the right to receive the company's remaining assets in the event of liquidation. In addition to common shares, the ICL also allows companies in Indonesia to issue various classes of preferred shares according to the rights they confer, including shares without voting rights, shares with a special right to nominate members of the BoD and/or members of the BoC and shares with certain priority rights. All shares within the same class, however, must contain the same shareholder rights and obligations. The GMS of a publicly listed company must approve the rights and obligations attached to each class of preferred shares and disclose that information to all of its shareholders. The implementation of class share options is further elaborated upon in Section 5.3 of this chapter, which covers shareholder engagement and voting in practice, but current practice denotes that special shares exist only in state-owned public LLCs in the form of golden shares.

5.1.3.2 Shareholder Rights

In addition to collective rights in the form of GMS authority, the ICL also recognizes individual shareholder rights, namely, the right to attend and vote in the GMS;[34] the right to file a lawsuit against the company in the event of losses resulting from unfair action on the company's part;[35] the right to freely transfer and demand the redemption of shares;[36] the right to receive information on the company;[37] the right to receive dividends; and the right to receive the company's remaining assets in the event of liquidation.[38] Shareholders who individually or jointly represent

[32] Elucidation of a law or regulation is the formal elaboration of each article contained within that law or regulation. It is presented as an attachment to the law (or regulation) itself, and serves as an official interpretation for certain words, phrases or sentences used in each article.

[33] Common and preferred shares are regulated under arts. 52 and 53 of ICL.

[34] Except where otherwise stipulated by the company's AoA, each issued share confers one voting right, as stipulated in art. 84 of the ICL, with the following exception: (1) a company's own shares; (2) shares owned by subsidiaries; and (3) shares in a cross-holding structure. See M. Yahya Harahap, *Hukum Perseroan Terbatas* (Jakarta: Sinar Grafika 2015) 327.

[35] Art. 61 of ICL.

[36] Art. 62 of ICL.

[37] Art. 100, para. 3 of ICL, which also states that shareholders' right to receive information about the company extends to requesting company documents, financial information and other information in and outside the GMS context.

[38] Art. 52, para. 1b of ICL.

one-tenth or more of the total shares with voting rights are granted additional rights, including the right to initiate a GMS; the right to file a claim with the district court on behalf of the company against members of the BoD who cause a loss to the company owing to fault or negligence; and the right to submit an application to the district court calling for an inspection of the company to obtain data or an explanation if suspicions arise concerning illegal action by the company, the BoD or the BoC.[39]

Shareholders are permitted to exercise their voting rights by proxy through power of attorney. Listed companies[40] must facilitate the ability of all shareholders to participate in the GMS and attach a standard proxy-authorization form/letter in the notice of a GMS. However, members of the BoD and BoC and other company employees are prohibited from acting as proxies.[41]

Furthermore, shareholders can also freely transfer shares subject to exceptions in the company's AoA, which generally apply to special voting preferred shares or founder shares. This freedom is not always subject to pre-emptive rights, but if the AoA so stipulate, then selling shareholders must first offer the shares in question to other shareholders in the company. The ICL specifies a period of thirty days for this offer to other shareholders, after which the selling shareholder is free to withdraw the offer and offer the shares to external third parties. Shareholders in a public company who own a minimum of 5 per cent of the company's total shares are required to report any changes in their shareholding in the increment of 0.5 per cent to OJK within ten days.[42]

5.2 GMS AND VOTING MECHANISM

The GMS under Indonesian law comprises the annual GMS and extraordinary GMS. During an annual GMS, the company's annual report must be submitted, as specified by article 66 of the ICL. The annual GMS usually focuses on a fixed agenda, whereas an extraordinary GMS can involve a discussion of matters outside that agenda. The ICL and OJK regulations applicable to public companies stipulate the GMS mechanism and voting procedure, which are discussed in turn below, followed by a brief explanation of the requirements for GMS minutes.

5.2.1 *GMS Mechanism*

The ICL specifies that an annual GMS must be held no later than six months after the fiscal year end,[43] whereas an extraordinary GMS can be held at any time depending on the needs of the company. A GMS is generally initiated by the BoD, although a shareholder representative[44] or the BoC can also request the organization of a GMS. The ICL also specifies the required timeline for holding a GMS. In the event that a GMS has been held but did not fulfil the

39 See also arts. 79, 97 and 138 of ICL.

40 If a public company wants to amend the rights attached to one class of shares, the regulations stipulate that only the shareholders of that particular class may vote on the amendment. If the shares in that class do not carry voting rights, OJK grants the shareholders concerned voting rights with respect to the GMS resolution relating to the proposed amendment. See art. 29B of OJK Regulation No. 10/POJK.04/2017 on Amendment to OJK Regulation No. 32/POJK.04/2014 Concerning the Planning and Holding of General Meeting of Shareholders of Public Companies.

41 Art. 85, para. 4 of ICL.

42 Art. 2(2)(3) of OJK Regulation No. 11/POJK.04/2017 Concerning Report on Shareholding or Any Changes in Shareholding in Listed Companies.

43 Art. 78, para. 2 of ICL.

44 The term 'shareholder representative(s)' here refers to one or more shareholders who jointly represent at least one-tenth of the total number of shares with voting rights, unless otherwise specified in the company's AoA. Such a request should be submitted to the BoD by registered mail with the reasons for the request attached.

attendance quorum requirement, then a second GMS can be held. Invitations for the second GMS must be distributed at least seven days before the second GMS is held and must state that the first GMS has been held but failed to fulfil the attendance quorum requirement. The second GMS must be held within ten to twenty-one days of the first. If the second GMS also fails to fulfil the attendance quorum requirement, then a third GMS can be held, although doing so requires authorization from OJK. The invitation for the third GMS must also state that the second GMS failed to fulfil the requirement. OJK determines the timing and quorum for the third GMS.

If the BoD does not make a GMS announcement, then shareholders have the right to submit a request for a GMA to the BoC, which should then make the announcement no later than fifteen days from the date of the request's receipt. If neither the BoD nor BoC makes a GMS announcement within fifteen days, then it is required to provide an explanation for why it has not done so within fifteen days. If the BoC still does not make a GMS announcement, then shareholders can file a request with the district court for permission to hold a GMS.

A certain set of information and documents must be distributed to shareholders at the GMS. Further, in addition to specifying the date of the meeting, the GMS announcement must declare that shareholders have the right to attend the meeting and propose a meeting agenda. The ICL also lists the information that must be presented to the GMS by the BoD, most notably the annual company report, which must have been produced no later than six months after the fiscal year end. A company is also bound by other requirements, including, inter alia, an obligation to determine the salaries and remuneration of BoD and BoC members through the GMS. The list of mandatory GMS agenda items is usually regulated by the company's AoA, but commonly includes approval of the annual report, a determination of net profit utilization, changes in management structure, a determination of BoD and/or BoC salaries and incentives for the next financial year and public accountant appointments for the subsequent year's audit.

Article 77 of the ICL specifies that a GMS can be held via a teleconference, video conference or other electronic means as long as all participants can directly see and hear one another and participate in the meeting. Shareholders can attend the GMS in person, appoint a proxy and/or vote online. In the event that a GMS is conducted by electronic means, the GMS minutes must be signed by all shareholders, a considerably more onerous requirement than is the case for a conventional GMS, where only the head of the meeting and one shareholder representative are required to sign the minutes. This requirement is the likely explanation for the general reluctance of public companies to conduct an electronic GMS.

After the GMS has been held, publicly listed companies need to publish a summary of the meeting minutes in at least one national newspaper in the Indonesian language, on the IDX website and on the company's official website in both Indonesian and another language (generally English).[45] Non-listed public companies are obliged only to publish the summary in a national Indonesian-language newspaper and on their official website.

5.2.2 *Modes of Participation and Voting*

According to the ICL, GMS resolutions must be adopted through 'deliberation to reach a consensus', meaning the consensus of all shareholders who are present or represented at the GMS.[46] If consensus is not achieved, then deliberation must be conducted by way of voting in

[45] These requirements are imposed through enactment of OJK Regulation No. 32/POJK.04/2014 Concerning the Planning and Holding of General Meetings of Shareholders of Public Limited Companies.

[46] Art. 87 of ICL.

accordance with the 'one vote one share' principle unless the company's AoA provide otherwise. Some companies' AoA allow for the possibility of issuing shares without voting rights.

Voting takes place after the GMS chair has invited each shareholder or his or her proxy to vote subsequent to the discussion of a certain agenda item. There is no ICL requirement pertaining to the format of voting ballots, but the ballot must offer three voting options for each agenda item: 'agree', 'disagree' or 'abstain'. Public companies are required to announce the result of each vote before moving on to the next agenda item. A decision is generally considered valid if it is approved by a qualified majority (more than one-half) of the total votes cast unless the law or the company's AoA require a greater number of affirmative votes. For example, the ICL mandates a higher number of affirmative votes for the passage of AoA amendments. The requirements for AoA amendments vary for different GMS stages and agenda items, as summarized in Table 5.1.[47]

TABLE 5.1 *GMS agenda quorum under Indonesian law*

GMS Agenda Items	GMS Sequence	Attendance Quorum	Decision Quorum
General GMS decision based on agenda determined by GMS	GMS 1	More than half of all shares with voting rights present at the GMS	More than half of the votes cast
	GMS 2*	At least one-third of all shares with voting rights present at the GMS	
	GMS 3**	Determined by OJK based upon the request of a public company	
Amendment of AoA, which requires approval from the Minister of Law and Human Rights (an exception applies for the extension of a public company's establishment period)	GMS 1	At least two-thirds of all shares with valid voting rights present at the GMS	More than two-thirds of the votes cast
	GMS 2*	At least three-fifths of all shares with valid voting rights present at the GMS	More than two-thirds of the votes cast
	GMS 3**	Determined by OJK based upon the request of a public company	
• Transfer of assets > 50% of the company's net worth • Creation of a debt guarantee with assets >50% of the company's net worth • Merger, acquisition, consolidation or spin-off • Bankruptcy declaration request • Extension of company's establishment period	GMS 1	At least three-quarters of all shares with valid voting rights present at the GMS	More than three-quarters of the votes cast
	GMS 2*	At least two-thirds of all shares with valid voting rights present at the GMS	More than three-quarters of the votes cast
	GMS 3**	Determined by OJK based upon the request of a public company	

[47] The ICL allows voting by way of proxy, and hence the attendance and decision quorum also takes into account voting by and the presence of shareholder representatives. The quorum set out in this table serves as the minimum requirement under the ICL. More specific laws and/or the company's AoA may stipulate a higher quorum requirement for both attendance and decision-making.

TABLE 5.1 *(continued)*

GMS Agenda Items	GMS Sequence	Attendance Quorum	Decision Quorum
Transaction with a conflict of interest[48]	GMS 1	More than half of all shares with valid voting rights owned by independent shareholders present at the GMS	More than half of the votes cast by independent shareholders present at GMS
	GMS 2*	More than half of all shares with valid voting rights owned by independent shareholders present at the GMS	More than half of the votes cast by independent shareholders present at GMS
	GMS 3**	Determined by OJK based upon the request of a public company	More than 50% of shares owned by independent shareholders present at GMS
Change of rights attached to a certain share classification in the event that the public company has more than one such classification[49]	GMS 1	At least three-quarters of all affected shares present at the GMS	More than three-quarters of the votes cast
	GMS 2*	At least 2/3 of all affected shares present in the GMS	
	GMS 3**	Determined by OJK based upon the request of a public company	

* GMS 2 is held if the quorum requirement is not fulfilled at GMS 1.
** GMS 3 is held if the quorum requirement is not fulfilled at GMS 2.

If the group of shareholders affected by a change in the rights attached to shares holds only non-voting shares, then OJK Regulation No. 10/POJK.04/2017 Concerning the Amendment of OJK Regulation No. 32/POJK.04/2014 Concerning [the] Planning and Holding of General Meetings of Shareholders of Public Limited Companies grants them rights to attend the GMS and be involved in the decision-making process pertaining to those rights.

5.2.3 *GMS Minutes*

For every GMS held, GMS minutes must be drawn up and signed by the GMS chair and at least one shareholder appointed from amongst and by the GMS participants.[50] GMS minutes are mandatory and imperative. If they are not provided after the GMS, then the GMS will be considered not to have been held, which gives rise to legal consequence because all of the matters decided and agreed upon at the GMS will be unenforceable and non-executable. The published summary of the GMS minutes must contain at least the following information.

48 This agenda item is not provided for under the ICL, but is regulated by OJK through art. 29 of OJK Regulation No. 32/POJK.04/2014 Concerning the Planning and Holding of General Meetings of Shareholders of Public Limited Companies.

49 This GMS should be attended only by shareholders holding the class of shares affected. If those shares do not incur voting rights, the affected shareholders have the right to attend and take a decision in the GMS based on a Financial Services Authority regulation.

50 Art. 90, para. 1 of ICL.

(1) The date, place, time and agenda items of the GMS;
(2) the BoD and BoC members present at the GMS;
(3) the number of shares with valid voting rights present at the GMS and the percentage of all shares with valid voting rights;
(4) whether or not shareholders had an opportunity to submit questions and/or provide opinions related to the meeting agenda;
(5) the number of shareholders who submitted questions and/or provided opinions regarding the meeting agenda if shareholders were given an opportunity for such submission/provision;
(6) the GMS decision-making mechanism;
(7) the voting results for each agenda item, including the number of 'agree' and 'disagree' votes and number of abstentions, if the decision-making was performed by voting;
(8) the GMS decision; and
(9) the implementation of cash dividend payments to entitled shareholders, if applicable.

In the event that the GMS minutes are drawn up in a notarial deed, then the signatures of the GMS chair and shareholder representative are not required.[51] Because the minutes are presented in the form of a notarial deed, they are considered to constitute an authentic deed and, as a result, are regarded as a conclusive document regarding the content therein, as stipulated in article 1875 of the Indonesian Civil Code.

Public companies must submit their GMS minutes no more than thirty days after the GMS has taken place, and the deadline for publishing a summary of the minutes in a national newspaper is no more than two working days after the GMS date. There is no requirement to disseminate the full meeting minutes to the public, but they must be submitted to OJK together with the company's annual report.

5.3 SHAREHOLDER ENGAGEMENT AND VOTING IN PRACTICE

The ownership structure and control practices discussed in this section pertain largely to the non-state-owned public companies listed in the LQ45 index of the IDX. The data presented are for LQ45 companies during the February–July period of 2020. Where applicable, the analysis herein also reflects the general trend amongst all 687 public companies listed on the IDX. Specific references to a listed company in this section use the company's listing code provided in the IDX database.

Furthermore, the dataset is obtained from analysis of the data in company annual reports, the IDX database and IDX reports, the KSEI (*Kustodian Sentral Efek Indonesia*) database and KSEI reports, and the summaries of companies' annual GMS, including the GMS announcements and summaries published in national newspapers. Interviews have also been conducted with representatives of the IDX, KSEI and Capital Market Legal Consultants Association to confirm the patterns and numbers in the data. The analysis of shareholder engagement and voting in practice is conducted specifically with respect to ownership structure and control, voting practices and various means of shareholder engagement.

We first examine the trend towards more dispersed share ownership and changes in the free float share percentage and number of affiliated directors and commissioners in Indonesia. Analysis of the free float share percentage is performed by looking at company annual reports and reports in the IDX database from 2015 to 2019. Analysis of the degree of affiliation amongst

[51] Art. 90, para. 2 of ICL.

shareholders, BoDs and BoCs draws on a 2008 study, but takes into account 2019 data on affiliated directors and commissioners, as well as the regulatory change implemented through the Decree of the Board of Directors of Indonesian Stock Exchange No. Kep-00183/BEI/12–2018, which eliminated the requirement for public companies to have an independent director and independent commissioners.

Finally, a questionnaire survey was administered to collect shareholder perspectives on share ownership and decision-making through a GMS. Purposive sampling took place from 14–31 July 2020. Eligible respondents were individual shareholders in a publicly listed company who had purchased their shares through a securities company, not in the form of mutual funds.[52] The questionnaires were distributed online in cooperation with several online media outlets.

5.3.1 *Ownership Structure and Control*

The growing interest in Indonesia in buying shares and investing in the capital market needs to be understood in the context of the historical background of the country's capital market, which is thus the subject of Section 5.3.1.1 below. The discussion then turns to the free float shares of LQ45 companies to consider whether Indonesian publicly listed companies are genuinely moving towards public-driven profiles or whether public ownership is still of minor importance owing to the immense control exhibited by certain corporate groups. Finally, the protection of minority shareholders in practice is also examined to determine whether there has been any shift away from Indonesia's tradition of concentrated corporate ownership to offer a better balance of non-controlling shareholders.

5.3.1.1 Trend towards More Dispersed Ownership

The Indonesian capital market was considered in the past to be relatively small, underdeveloped and illiquid, resulting in weak oversight of corporate management control.[53] Furthermore, the Indonesian ownership structure tended to be highly concentrated, with most companies managed and owned by members of their founding families, leaving little room for the separation of ownership and control. The majority of companies belonged to or were affiliated with a business group, which was also owned by related families, and thus were considered family business groups. These family business groups controlled the majority of publicly listed companies either through direct control or through a pyramid of share ownership through other companies or firms.

However, a significant increase in IPOs and stock market activity was seen in the 2017–19 period, with IDX data showing Indonesia to have had the largest average number of newly listed companies per year amongst ASEAN members, with thirty-one, fifty-three and fifty-four in 2017, 2018 and 2019, respectively. As of April 2020, there were 687 companies listed on the IDX, 26 of them newly listed between January and March of 2020. If this pattern of increasing IPOs and interest in shareholding continues, it may lead to a move away from the longstanding tradition of conglomerate ownership amongst Indonesian public companies.

[52] In Indonesia, individual shareholders can purchase shares only through intermediary institutions, namely, securities companies, and their investments can be made in the form of mutual funds that are professionally managed by intermediary institutions. Because investors in mutual funds do not make decisions and do not directly engage with the companies concerned, they were excluded from the survey.

[53] Huge Patrick, 'Corporate Governance and the Indonesian Financial System: A Comparative Perspective' (2001) Discussion Paper Series APEC Study Center, Columbia Business School, 23–5.

5.3.1.2 Free Float Share Percentage

IDX further distinguishes publicly listed companies by three board classifications: Main Board, Development Board and Acceleration Board. The Main Board lists large companies with an established track record, whilst the Development Board lists companies that have not yet fulfilled the listing requirement for the Main Board, including prospective companies that have not yet accrued profits and companies undergoing restructuring. A Main Board listing requires a minimum of 1,000 shareholders, and a Development Board listing at least 500. The Acceleration Board was recently introduced to encourage share listings from small- and medium-scale issuers.

As of March 2020, there were 326 and 362 companies, respectively, listed on the Main Board and Development Board of the IDX. For Main Board companies, the free float minimum share requirement after the IPO but prior to listing is at least 300 million rupiah, with total paid-up capital amounting to at least 20 per cent (if the company's pre-IPO total equity is 500 billion rupiah), 15 per cent (if the company's pre-IPO total equity is between 500 and 2,000 billion rupiah) or 10 per cent (if the company's pre-IPO total equity is more than 2,000 billion rupiah). Companies listed on the Development Board are required to float free shares worth at least 150 million rupiah after the IPO and prior to listing, subject to the same percentage requirements for total paid-up capital proportional to total equity. Finally, the public share requirement for companies on the Acceleration Board is 20 per cent of total shares, with a minimum of 300 shareholders.[54] After listing, companies are required to maintain a free float percentage of 7.50 per cent and at least fifty million shares circulating in public.

As noted, Indonesian companies in general have a very concentrated ownership and control structure, as evidenced by the fact that the average number of free float shares rarely constitutes a controlling percentage. All companies in the LQ45 are listed on the Main Board, and are thus subject to the aforementioned minimum free float requirement. Table 5.2 shows the shareholding structure of public companies listed on the LQ45 index from February–July 2020.

As of the first quarter of 2020, the LQ45 company with the most dispersed ownership structure and highest public ownership of shares was LPPF, which had a free float percentage of more than 80 per cent. LPPF is the only company in the index with a relatively dispersed ownership structure on paper. It is followed by two real-estate companies: ASRI with a 52.61 per cent free

TABLE 5.2 *Free float data in % for LQ45 companies**

Year	Mean	Median	Minimum	Maximum	Standard Deviation
2015	36.63%	37.07%	4.22%	79.52%	0.1595
2016	38.17%	39.70%	4.22%	82.52%	0.1518
2017	36.69%	39.42%	7.50%	82.52%	0.1359
2018	37.04%	39.42%	7.50%	82.52%	0.1365
2019	37.73%	39.89%	7.50%	81.82%	0.1408
Average	37.25%	39.08%	6.19%	81.78%	0.1449

*Excluding the ten SOEs in the LQ45 index.

[54] Additional ownership requirements are applicable to publicly listed companies in certain sectors, including publicly listed companies in the banking industry that are subject to ownership rules under OJK Regulation No. 56/POJK.03/2016 Concerning Public Bank Share Ownership.

float percentage and LPKR with 52.06 per cent. All other companies in the index have less than 50 per cent free float shares, with the most concentrated shareholder structure exhibited by TPIA with 8.60 per cent and HMSP with 7.50 per cent.

When a public company's free float share percentage falls lower than the requirement, the company is obliged to submit an action plan and timeline for fulfilling the free float requirements within two trading days of the company becoming aware of the breach. A free float requirement breach can also be subject to the OJK Takeover Rule, in which case the company is given a two-year deadline to comply with the requirement.

In practice, even in the event that public ownership exceeds 51 per cent, control measures are still wielded by controlling shareholders by way of driving or directing certain decisions reached by the majority owners. A common practice is for controlling shareholder to nominate all candidates for the BoD and BoC, meaning that public shareholders can vote only for select candidates. Furthermore, control by certain groups of companies or families can still be observed even when the free float percentage is high, as seen, for example, in the ownership structures of LPPF, which has an 82.52 per cent free float, and LPKR, which has a 52.06 per cent free float. Each public shareholder in LPPF and LPKR holds fewer than 5 per cent of shares. In contrast, the sole non-public shareholder in LPPF is MLPL, which is controlled by PT, and Inti Anugerah Pratama holds the largest shareholding in LPKR.

5.3.1.3 Protection of Independent and/or Minority Shareholders in Practice

The concentrated ownership and control structure in Indonesia results in low levels of disclosure and transparency. Concentrated control by a group of shareholders also results in lax supervision and a high probability of insider trading, as external shareholders often refuse to participate. Given the immense power of controlling shareholders, corporate governance remains an urgent issue in Indonesian corporate law,[55] with minority shareholder rights a particular concern.

Public participation in the decision-making processes of companies remains low because individual shareholders hold only a small percentage of shares. This pattern has remained constant in the past few years, and the decision-making process is thus still dominated by controlling shareholders. To address the level of power that controlling shareholders wield in most public companies, the government has taken a few measures to afford greater protection to independent and minority shareholders in practice. For example, OJK recently issued OJK Regulation No. 14/POJK.04/2019 Concerning the Increase of Public Company Capital through Rights Issue, which changed the shareholder approval requirement for a capital increase without a rights issue in publicly listed companies that are not in financial distress. The new regulation requires the GMS that approves a capital increase plan that is exempted from the rights issue requirement to be attended by shareholders representing more than 50 per cent of the total shares owned by independent and unaffiliated shareholders,[56] and the plan must also be approved by independent and unaffiliated shareholders holding more than half of total shares. The regulation thus places a more stringent requirement on the existing GMS quorum and voting requirements imposed by the ICL, which does not distinguish between independent and unaffiliated shareholders.

55 Yetty Komalasari Dewi, 'In Search of Legal Foundation for Indonesian Family Firms' (2016) 6 *Indonesia Law Review* 246 http://ilrev.ui.ac.id/index.php/home/article/view/228 accessed 15 July 2020.

56 OJK Regulation No. 14/POJK.04/2019 stipulates that such shareholders must not be an affiliated party to the publicly listed company, a member of the BoD or BoC, or a majority or controlling shareholder.

In addition, if these publicly listed companies want to issue new shares, with or without pre-emptive rights, they must issue a circular disclosing that information to their shareholders and obtain GMS approval. In the event that a given party owns 5 per cent or more of a public company's issued shares, the company is required to submit a report on such ownership or any change thereto to OJK within ten days of the date on which the transaction takes place. The report should contain the identity of the shareholders concerned, the number of shares acquired or sold, the purchase or sale price per share, and the date and purpose of the transaction. OJK has been observed[57] in recent years to have taken a position that leans towards favouring minority shareholders, which is in line with its aim to change Indonesia from a 'saving society' to an 'investing society'.

Publicly listed companies must also perform certain notification procedures before undertaking material corporate actions. Depending on the value of the proposed actions, they must either issue a circular disclosing information on the actions to their shareholders and obtain GMS approval or make a public announcement. In the case of affiliated party transactions, the company must either issue a similar circular disclosing information on the transaction or obtain approval from independent shareholders in the GMS. The requirement to obtain approval from independent shareholders also depends on whether the affiliated party transaction constitutes a conflict of interest.

Shareholder activism remains relatively unknown in Indonesia, and relevant case law is scarce. Article 61 of the ICL stipulates that shareholders have a right to instigate legal proceedings against a company in the district court of the company's domicile in the event that they suffer losses deemed to have been caused by unjust and unreasonable acts of the company resulting from a GMS resolution or a decision of the BoD or BoC. The most recent implementation of a shareholder derivative action was the legal proceeding initiated by KIJA shareholders in July 2019 that sought the annulment of the 2019 GMS decision on the appointment of BoD and BoC members. The lawsuit was later withdrawn by the shareholders,[58] which may indicate the existence of an out-of-court dispute settlement mechanism between the company and the disputing shareholders. Another shareholder derivative action was initiated in 2018 against BCIC[59] by a Singaporean shareholder in respect of share pricing measures taken by the Indonesian Deposit Insurance Corporation during the Bank Century bailout process in 2008, as well as the bank's related corporate actions. In January 2021, the Central Jakarta District Court issued a decision stating that it does not have jurisdiction over the matter. As one of the defendants in the lawsuit is a government agency, the court determined that the matter should be filed with the State Administrative Court.

Furthermore, Indonesia is not yet familiar with the practice of proxy fights. Hence, even changes in control mechanisms that may disadvantage minority shareholders, such as hostile takeovers, are not yet recognized under Indonesian laws and regulations.

57 In practice, aside from changing the regulatory requirement on a capital increase without a rights issue, OJK has also been known to give warnings to capital market players that carry out actions that exert detrimental effects on minority shareholders, for example, an order to remove clauses that negatively affect public shareholders from agreements or the commitments of prospective listed companies.

58 The withdrawal was granted by Central Jakarta District Court Stipulation No. 413/Pdt.G/2019/PN Jkt.Pst.

59 The Indonesian Deposit Insurance Corporation is an independent governmental agency that is directly responsible to the president and was a co-defendant in the lawsuit. The acquisition related to the Bank Century bailout decision following the bank's declaration of insolvency in 2008. The lawsuit was registered under case number 488/Pdt.G/2018/PN Jkt.Pst.

5.3.2 *Voting in Practice*

Agenda voting is the essence of the GMS, and voting is one mechanism whereby shareholders can pilot the company's future development and express opinions on BoD and BoC actions. The validity of decisions made through voting depends on several factors, one of which is the GMS quorum. The number of shareholders who participate in a GMS may affect the validity of a decision. This subsection thus begins with analysis of GMS participation in relation to total attendance and the questions asked by shareholders. It also elaborates on the percentage of votes cast per agenda item and the availability of e-voting and e-proxy mechanisms.

5.3.2.1 Total Participation in Annual GMS

In 2015, the Asian Development Bank recommended that engagement with institutional shareholders in Indonesia be improved to promote active shareholder involvement, as shareholder participation has been cited as one of the areas in need of improvement in terms of corporate governance.[60] To gauge shareholder participation, the percentage of shareholders attending the annual GMS of LQ45 companies from 2017 to 2019 was analyzed, with the results reported in Table 5.3.

It can be seen from Table 5.3 that although the vast majority of shareholders in LQ45 companies attended the companies' annual GMS in the three years in question, the average attendance percentage never reached 100 per cent. The published summaries of the meeting minutes provide no information on the percentage of public and non-public shareholders in attendance. Full notarized GMS minutes are seldom made public, as their disclosure is not required under Indonesian law.

Shareholders can also put forward questions with respect to the reports presented or agenda items discussed during the GMS. Table 5.4 presents data on the total number of questions asked by shareholders during the annual GMS of LQ45 companies from 2017 to 2019.

TABLE 5.3 *Shareholder attendance (in %) in the annual GMS of LQ45 companies*

Year	Mean	Median	Minimum	Maximum	Standard Deviation
2017	80.96%	82.38%	59.41%	99.09%	0.09
2018	82.72%	83.84%	65.25%	95.00%	0.07
2019	81.92%	82.86%	62.65%	94.90%	0.08

TABLE 5.4 *Total number of questions asked by shareholders during annual GMS of LQ45 companies*

Year	Mean	Minimum	Maximum
2017	1.3	0	7
2018	1.44	0	9
2019	1.48	0	9

60 Asian Development Bank (n. 5) 29.

Because independent individual shareholders usually hold only a very small percentage of a company's shares, they rarely request company information and are generally rather passive throughout the GMS process, as shown by the low average number of questions indicated in Table 5.4 (fewer than two for the 2017–19 period). Most of the few questions asked concerned the annual report presented by the BoD or net profit utilization, which was the case at the annual GMS of INKP in 2017, WSBP in 2018 and 2019 and ADRO in 2018.

The questions asked and comments made by shareholders are usually very technical and specific in nature. For example, the questions raised in the UNVR GMS of 2019 concerned the use of certain accounting standards and their effect on the calculation of the company's profit and the benchmarking standard for the remuneration percentage in contrast with the annual net profit percentage.

5.3.2.2 Voting Agenda

The percentage of votes cast per agenda item in LQ45 companies from 2017 to 2019 is presented in Table 5.5.

Companies report the percentage of votes for each agenda item in their summaries of annual GMS minutes. These summaries are available in the IDX database, and also are published by the companies in national newspapers no more than two working days after the GMS date. It can be seen from Table 5.5 that the lowest percentage of approval was obtained for a change in the company's management structure, followed by the appointment of a public accountant. Interestingly, even though most of the questions raised at the companies' GMS concerned the annual and financial report or allocation of net profits, these two agenda items attracted the highest approval percentages, at 99.81 per cent and 99.80 per cent, respectively.

5.3.2.3 Implementation of e-Proxy and e-Voting Platforms during COVID-19 Mitigation Period

The majority of GMS sessions in Indonesia are held in Jakarta to accommodate the 78.86 per cent of shareholders who are located on Java Island. The remainder are spread across

TABLE 5.5 *Voting percentages for GMS agenda items in LQ45 companies (2017–19)*

Agenda Item	Agree	Disagree	Abstain
Approval of annual and financial report	2017 99.87%	2017 0.01%	2017 0.12%
	2018 99.74%	2018 0.01%	2018 0.26%
	2019 99.83%	2019 0.009%	2019 0.159%
Allocation of net profits	2017 99.81%	2017 0.12%	2017 0.07%
	2018 99.74%	2018 0.09%	2018 0.17%
	2019 99.86%	2019 0.10%	2019 0.04%
Determination of salaries and incentives for BoD and BoC members	2017 98.17%	2017 1.57%	2017 0.26%
	2018 94.17%	2018 1.39%	2018 4.44%
	2019 99.31%	2019 0.57%	2019 0.12%
Appointment of public accountant	2017 97.41%	2017 2.18%	2017 0.41%
	2018 91.54%	2018 5.18%	2018 3.28%
	2019 97.99%	2019 1.84%	2019 0.17%
Change in company's management structure	2017 95.32%	2017 4.25%	2017 0.38%
	2018 93.87%	2018 5.59%	2018 0.55%
	2019 92.58%	2019 7.05%	2019 0.38%

the country: in Sumatra (12.12 per cent), Sulawesi (2.94 per cent), Kalimantan (3.75 per cent), Bali and Nusa Tenggara (2.32 per cent) and Maluku and Papua (0.61 per cent).[61] As mandated by OJK, publicly listed companies are obliged to hold their annual GMS and submit their annual report by 30 June at the latest,[62] which results in a busy GMS season from May to June, when most publicly listed companies hold their annual GMS. During the 2016 GMS season, the average number of GMS held per day was six, with one day recording twenty-six meetings.[63] The record for the number of meetings held on a single day during the 2018 season was forty. The average number of shareholders invited to concurrent GMS has also increased, rising from 12,660 shareholders per day in 2016 to around 18,000 in 2018.[64]

Despite the potential of e-Proxy and e-Voting platforms to increase shareholder participation, most Indonesian companies prefer in-person GMS, and online GMS remain rare. Nevertheless, electronic GMS mechanisms offer a solution to the geographic and time constraints that arise when a shareholder has to attend simultaneous GMS sessions. KSEI has developed an online e-Voting and e-Proxy system (the e-GMS system) to resolve the concurrent GMS issue, and the system was recently implemented as a COVID-19 mitigation measure in Indonesia to reduce the number of physical meetings and avoid large gatherings of people. OJK Letter No. S-92/D.04/2020 of 2020 Concerning the Relaxation of Obligations for Submission of Reports and Implementation of General Meetings of Shareholders states that the holding of a GMS by a public company can be accomplished by means of an electronic power-of-attorney mechanism using the e-GMS system developed by KSEI[65] as long as the GMS is conducted as efficiently as possible without affecting its validity in accordance with OJK Regulation No. 32 of 2014 and the ICL.

As of April 2020, seventeen companies (3 per cent) had announced that they would use KSEI's e-GMS system for their next annual GMS. They include such major companies as ADRO, EXCL, GOOD and HMSP. Two companies, BJTM and EPMT, announced that they would use a live-streaming teleconferencing mechanism for their upcoming annual GMS rather than the KSEI system.

5.3.3 *Shareholder Engagement in Practice*

This section draws on the results of the aforementioned survey questionnaire to elucidate the common perspectives on engagement and voting of Indonesian individual shareholders. Shareholder engagement in SOEs is then discussed as a contrast, as the Indonesian government exerts considerable influence on shareholder engagement and voting procedures in these firms. Finally, the section concludes with a look at other means of shareholder engagement such as decision-making through circular resolutions.

5.3.3.1 Individual Shareholder Engagement

No empirical study of shareholder engagement in Indonesia has yet been carried out. To inform this subsection on Indonesian shareholder engagement in practice, we thus distributed online

61 Interview with KSEI representative (Jakarta, 19 February 2020).
62 This deadline was extended to 31 August 2020 owing to COVID-19 mitigation measures.
63 Interview with KSEI representative (n. 61).
64 Ibid.
65 KSEI subsequently announced that it would provide an e-Proxy option in the KSEI system for issuers whose GMS date was after 3 April 2020 and GMS notification date after 20 April 2020.

questionnaires on shareholder motives for ownership and engagement to illustrate the general perspective of individual shareholders on these issues.

Questionnaire distribution adhered to the purposive sampling method, with the criterion that the individual shareholder respondents invest through securities companies rather than being mutual fund investors. We received 312 responses, 310 of which were valid. Nearly half (47.7 per cent) of the respondents resided in the greater Jakarta area, and most were between the ages of eighteen and thirty.[66] The responses revealed the majority of respondents to hold an investor point of view, displaying a lack of willingness or desire to participate in companies' decision-making processes as shareholders. Figure 5.1 illustrates the respondents' answers to a question concerning the purpose of their share ownership.

The majority of respondents cited a financial motive for their share purchase,[67] with 92.5 per cent (288) stating that their purpose for buying shares had been to make a profit from the margin between the purchase price and sale price, whilst 63.7 per cent (198) claimed that their purpose had been to periodically attain additional income through dividend distribution. A small percentage (5.5 per cent or seventeen) acknowledged a company control purpose, and 4.2 per cent (thirteen) said their purpose had been to act in accordance with the latest shareholding trend.

Further, 223 respondents (71.9 per cent) were absolutely certain that share purchases constitute an investment method, but only 60 (19.4 per cent) expressed certainty about a share purchase being a method of owning and controlling a company. Sixty respondents (19.4 per cent) were long-term investors who had held their shares for more than five years, 88 (28.4 per cent) were medium-term investors who had held their shares for between one and five years and 162 (52.3 per cent) were short-term investors who had held their shares for less than a year.

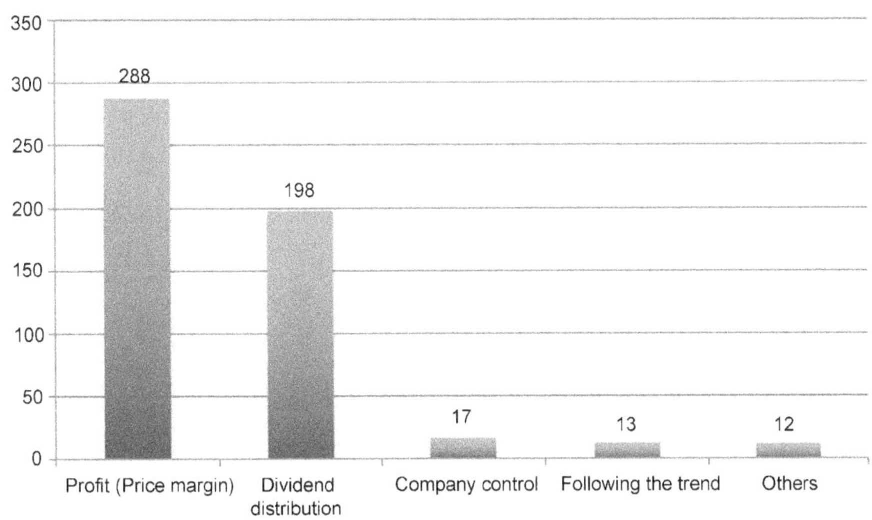

FIGURE 5.1 Purpose of share ownership by individual shareholders in Indonesia

66 Nearly half (49.7 per cent) were between the ages of eighteen and twenty-four, and 31 per cent were between the ages of twenty-five and thirty. These age ranges are in line with a 2019 IDX press release reporting a significant increase in young shareholders (aged eighteen to thirty).

67 The respondents were allowed to select more than one answer for this question.

On the question of whether they had ever attended and/or participated in a GMS, 242 respondents (78.1 per cent) said they had not been able to attend a GMS,[68] and 51 (16.5 per cent) said that they had attended a GMS either directly or through a proxy. Seventeen respondents (5.5 per cent) answered that they were not even aware of the existence of GMS.

With regard to the source of GMS invitations and information,[69] 225 respondents (72.3 per cent) said they received an invitation directly from securities companies, and 116 (37.3 per cent) that they had received it directly from the issuers. Thirty (9.6 per cent) reported that they found information concerning a GMS through the announcement made in national newspapers, and seven (2.3 per cent) that they received such information from emails sent by KSEI. Other sources of GMS information included shareholder forums, social media and financial and news apps.

With respect to raising questions during a GMA, only seven respondents (4.2 per cent) said they had done so, whilst sixteen (9.6 per cent) indicated that they would have liked to ask a question but were hesitant about doing so. Such passivity is in line with the respondents' answers to the question of what motivated them to attend a GMS, as indicated in Figure 5.2.

The purpose of this question was to identify the factors motivating individual shareholders to attend and participate in a GMS.[70] One hundred and eighty respondents (58.1 per cent) cited an opportunity to monitor the company's progress as the greatest motivation for GMS attendance. One hundred and forty-one (45.5 per cent) stated that GMS attendance informs their future investment decisions. Other GMS attendance benefits cited included the receipt of souvenirs or goodie bags (the response of 123 respondent (39.7 per cent)), the enjoyment of banquet facilities (92/29.7 per cent) and an opportunity to network with fellow shareholders and/or board members (172/55.5 per cent). Thirty-eight respondents (12.3 per cent) mentioned shareholders acting as proxies for other shareholders, and twenty-three (7.4 per cent) viewed attending a GMS as an

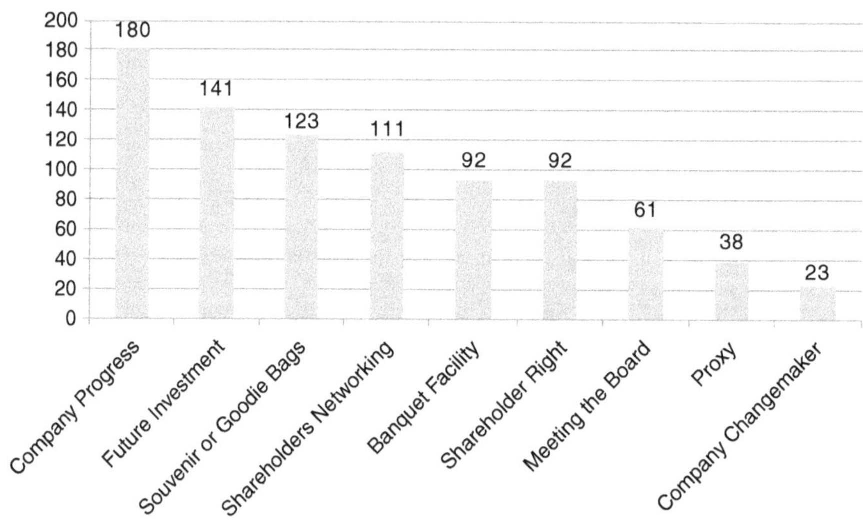

FIGURE 5.2 Motivations for Indonesian shareholders' GMS attendance

68 193 respondents (62.1 per cent) cited a lack of time as the reason for their absence from a GMS, with 49 (15.8 per cent) citing a personal unwillingness to attend.

69 The respondents were allowed to select more than one answer for this question.

70 The respondents were allowed to select more than one answer for this question.

opportunity to bring about change in the company. In conclusion, it seems that GMS attendance is seen by individual shareholders in Indonesia not as an opportunity to speak up and provide input to the company, but rather as an opportunity to listen and enjoy the festivities.

5.3.3.2 Shareholder Engagement in State-Owned Companies

As of March 2020, there were a total of 142 Indonesian SOEs, just 25 of which were publicly listed companies. Because the government is the majority shareholder in SOEs, the shareholder engagement regime for SOEs is significantly different owing to the difference in power between the government and other shareholders. One of the most noteworthy differences is the possibility of the government being a golden shareholder, as regulated in a company's AoA.[71] The golden share provision allows the government to control all shareholder votes for the sake of a public interest that may have a significant impact on the company.

Take BMRI as an example. The golden share owned by the government grants special rights to, inter alia, nominate BoD and BoC members who will be appointed by the GMS. As the golden shareholder in BMRI, the government is also granted the right to request a BoD report and/or obtain a BoD explanation at any time in accordance with the prevailing laws and regulations. In the event of BoC positions in BMRI being completely vacant, the government, as the golden shareholder, is authorized to appoint temporary members to carry out the BoC function.

In practice, such significant differences in rights between different classes of shares exists only in SOEs, as non-state-owned publicly listed companies usually grant the same rights to all shares. In the majority of IPO prospectuses, the wording 'The new shares offered consist of shares issued from portfolio shares which give the holders equal rights and equal degree in all respects to other shares of the Company that have been issued and fully paid' can be found as a required standard template. Its aim is to assure the public that all shareholders receive the same rights, which can be inferred to be the preferred stance of the Indonesian capital market authorities with regard to maintaining the same rights for all share classes. Further analysis of the practices of shareholder engagement in SOEs reveals that even a small percentage of government-owned shares affects the decision-making processes in a GMS because other shareholders tend to agree with government decisions.

5.3.3.3 Other Means of Shareholder Engagement

The basic terms concerning the interests of shareholders are regulated under shareholder agreements, and the limits of shareholder engagement thus depend on the provisions of such agreements. Shareholders can also resort to circular resolutions to the extent that all shareholders with voting rights have given signed, written approval.[72] In practice, many decisions in private companies are passed through circular resolutions because holding a GMS requires the fulfilment of certain procedures. Circular resolutions can also replace a GMS, as AirAsia Indonesia demonstrated towards the end of 2019 when it changed the structure of its BoD and BoC by such means. As a side note, circular resolutions also prevail in the decision-making processes of SOEs.

[71] In the Minister of State-Owned Enterprises Letter No. S-163/MBU/03/2017 of 10 March 2017 Concerning the Non-Banking Sector Public State-Owned Companies Articles of Association Draft Submission, the golden share series (*Saham Seri A Dwiwarna*) is defined as a special share series owned by the Republic of Indonesia that grants its shareholders special rights as the owner of golden share series.

[72] Art. 91 of ICL.

For instance, in 2019, shareholders in Pertamina revised the company's corporate budget and workplan without holding a GMS to speed up the acquisition of Tuban Petro.

In practice, shareholder engagement is also supported by corporate secretaries, especially in terms of keeping the company in line with good corporate governance principles and other corporate governance rules. Publicly listed companies often have a designated corporate secretary who deals with shareholder or investor relations. Corporate secretaries can also be involved in the GMS process, particularly in terms of dealing with communications and publications for all stakeholders, including shareholders, the BoD and the BoC.

In certain cases, public companies have a higher threshold for shareholder approval, for example in a transaction with conflict of interest that may require independent or minority shareholder approval. There is no regulatory limitation on shareholder engagement as long as it is in accordance with the principles of good corporate governance. Nevertheless, the government's golden shares bestow higher overall control amongst shareholders in SOEs.

5.4 CONCLUDING REMARKS

This chapter on shareholder engagement and voting practices in Indonesia provides a detailed account of developments and practices in the capital market, specifically with respect to shareholder engagement, a seldom discussed issue in Indonesia. Public interest in the capital market sector is on the rise, and the country's highly concentrated shareholding structure is slowly shifting towards a more dispersed shareholder structure with increased participation. Further, the degree of affiliation and control has lessened despite the policy change eliminating the independent director requirement for public companies. State control of publicly listed SOEs remains very much in existence, and such control also applies to certain group corporations that control a number of publicly listed companies through share ownership. Moreover, shareholder participation has been quite high in recent years, although the shareholder profile in Indonesia can be considered amicable and rather passive, as demonstrated by the very low number of questions asked or comments made in the course of a GMS. With the increasing percentage of foreign ownership in the country, it remains to be seen whether there will be any substantial changes in terms of shareholder engagement.

The ICL is a very thorough regulation that provides a comprehensive set of rules on company operations. However, there remains a gap between regulation and practice, a gap that can perhaps be reduced through improved compliance and continuous education for capital market industry actors and the public, particularly with regard to technological innovations. The application of KSEI's e-GMS system serves as a starting point for better accommodating Indonesia's shareholder needs, despite companies' longstanding general hesitation to 'go digital'.

6

Shareholder Engagement and Voting in Japan

Gen Goto

6.1 INTRODUCTION

Japanese companies have long been known for their stakeholder-oriented corporate governance system,[1] which arguably supported Japan's rapid recovery from the devastation of World War II. However, after suffering from stagnation of over two decades from 1991 onwards, the Japanese government turned to shareholder-oriented corporate governance in the 2010s as one of the solutions to revive its economy and implemented several reforms.[2] Most notably, the 2014 Japanese Stewardship Code (revised in 2017 and 2020) emphasizes the role of shareholder engagement by institutional investors in promoting the mid- to long-term growth of listed companies, and the 2015 Japanese Corporate Governance Code (revised in 2018 and 2021) instructs corporate management to take shareholders' interests seriously.

As a consequence, shareholder engagement and voting have attracted considerable attention in the corporate governance scene in Japan in recent years. For example, it has been reported that domestic institutional investors played a decisive role in the victory of a shareholder group over incumbent management during a proxy fight in June 2019 at LIXIL, the leading housing equipment manufacturer in Japan.[3] Also, the recent resurgence of hedge fund activism in Japan can be explained, at least in part, by activists' expectations that they would receive more support from domestic institutional investors than they had in the past.[4]

After describing the transition of the Japanese corporate governance system (Section 6.2) and the legal measures granted to shareholders (Section 6.3), this chapter analyzes the current state of the shareholder meeting and shareholder voting and engagement in Japan (Section 6.4). Section 6.5 offers concluding remarks.

The author would like to thank the editors of and contributors to this volume for their valuable comments and the Japan Society for Promotion of Science for its financial support (JSPS Kakenhi 20H01436) for this research.

[1] Gregory Jackson and Hideaki Miyajima, 'Introduction: The Diversity and Change of Corporate Governance in Japan' in Masahiko Aoki, Gregory Jackson and Hideaki Miyajima (eds.), *Corporate Governance in Japan: Institutional Change and Organizational Diversity* (Oxford University Press 2007) 1, 3.

[2] See Hideaki Miyajima and Takuji Saito, 'Corporate Governance Reforms under the Abenomics: The Economic Consequences of Two Codes' in Takeo Hoshi and Phillip Y. Lipscy (eds.), *The Political Economy of the Abe Government and Abenomics Reforms* (Cambridge University Press 2021) 357.

[3] Akihiro Ota, 'Shareholders Prevail in LIXIL Showdown, Restoring Ousted CEO' *Nikkei Asia* (26 June 2019, 4:18 JST) https://asia.nikkei.com/Business/Companies/Shareholders-prevail-in-Lixil-showdown-restoring-ousted-CEO (last visited 9 July 2021).

[4] Takenori Miyamoto, Tomohiro Noguchi and Yoshinaru Sakabe, 'Activist Investors Regain their Appetite for Japanese Stocks' *Nikkei Asia* (26 January 2020, 3:50 JST) https://asia.nikkei.com/Spotlight/Datawatch/Activist-investors-regain-their-appetite-for-Japanese-stocks (last visited 9 July 2021).

6.2 BASIC STRUCTURE OF JAPANESE CORPORATE LAW AND GOVERNANCE

6.2.1 *Japanese Corporate Governance in Transition*

The legal framework for shareholder engagement and voting is set by the Companies Act,[5] which is the corporate law in Japan applicable to all types of companies,[6] and by the Financial Instruments and Exchange Act,[7] which provides securities regulation, including rules on disclosure by listed companies, tender offers, the solicitation of proxies and insider trading. Of the four types of companies covered by the Companies Act, listed companies must take the form of a stock corporation (*kabushiki kaisha*).[8] Whilst this chapter focuses on shareholder engagement and corporate governance in listed companies, it is noteworthy that the stock corporation form is often used by non-listed, closely held companies in Japan.[9]

Although the Japanese Companies Act itself, which grants strong powers to shareholders, as described in detail in subsections 6.3.1, 6.3.2 and 6.3.3, follows the shareholder-primacy model as it does not mandate co-determination and makes no explicit reference to the interests of employees, the environment or society,[10] Japanese companies after World War II established a unique system of corporate governance focusing on the interests of employees and other stakeholders, which are often referred to as the 'corporate community' or 'company as a family'.[11] First, under the so-called 'lifetime employment system', Japanese companies refrained from layoffs as much as possible, semi-guaranteeing a job at the company to employees until their retirement age. Second, directors were predominantly selected from employees of the company as an extension of the internal promotion system. The number of directors was often large, sometimes more than thirty, to accommodate the promotion of senior employees. Third, a large proportion of shares, often the majority, was held by the company's banks and friendly business partners.[12] The incumbent management teams of listed companies relied upon these shareholders as 'stable shareholders' (*antei kabunushi*), as they tended to support the incumbents and not sell their shares even at a premium in order to

[5] *Kaisha-ho*, Law No. 86 of *Heisei* 17 (2005), last revised by Law No. 70 of *Reiwa* 1 (2019).

[6] Japan does not have a special court for corporate law issues. Whilst the first instance courts in Tokyo and Osaka, the two largest cities in Japan, have divisions specializing in corporate law cases amongst other commercial cases (Tokyo District Court Civil Division No. 8 and Osaka District Court Civil Division No. 4), there is no such division in other district courts or higher instance courts. For information, on court procedure in Japan, see www.courts.go.jp/english/index.html (last visited 9 July 2021).

[7] *Kinyushohin-torihiki-ho*, Law No. 25 of *Showa* 23 (1948), last revised by Law No. 37 of *Reiwa* 1 (2019).

[8] The three other types are the limited liability company (*godo kaisha*), limited partnership company (*goshi kaisha*) and general partnership company (*gomei kaisha*), which together are classified as membership companies (*mochibun kaisha*). See Japanese Companies Act, art. 2, item 1 and art. 575.

[9] As of 9 July 2021, 3,787 companies are listed on the Tokyo Stock Exchange, which is the main exchange of Japan, whereas there are 2,554,582 stock corporations (as of 31 July 2019). See Japan Exchange Group, 'Number of Listed Companies/Shares' www.jpx.co.jp/english/listing/co/index.html (last visited 9 July 2021); Kokuzeicho Chokan-kanbo Kikaku-ka [National Tax Agency, Commissioner's Secretariat, Planning Division], *Heisei 30-nendo Zeimu Tokei kara Mita Hojin Kigyo no Jittai* [*The Actual Conditions of Incorporated Businesses for FY 2018*] (May 2020) 14 www.nta.go.jp/publication/statistics/kokuzeicho/kaishahyohon2018/pdf/h30.pdf (last visited 9 July 2021).

[10] Although art. 355 of the Japanese Companies Act imposes on directors a duty to comply with laws and regulations, they are not obliged to consider the interests of employees, the environment or society beyond the extent required by law.

[11] For a more detailed description of the traditional Japanese corporate governance system, see Zenichi Shishido, 'Japanese Corporate Governance: The Hidden Problems of Corporate Law and Their Solutions' (2000) 25 Delaware Journal of Corporate Law 189; Jackson and Miyajima (n. 1) 3–6.

[12] For the formation process of webs of stable shareholders, see Julian Franks, Colin Mayer and Hideaki Miyajima, 'The Ownership of Japanese Companies in the 20th Century' (2014) 27(9) Review of Financial Studies 2580.

maintain their business relationships.[13] In addition, because each 'stable shareholder' held only a very small percentage of shares, sometimes as little as 1 per cent, there was no single controlling shareholder.[14] This ownership structure effectively insulated managers from shareholder pressure, and especially from the capital market. Fourth, companies were financed mostly by bank loans, and the main bank, that is, the bank that lent the largest amount to the company, played an important role in the borrower's governance. This traditional system seems to have worked quite well until the mid-1980s, supporting Japan's rapid economic recovery after World War II, as it arguably enabled management to focus on growth in the long term and incentivized employees to make firm-specific human capital investments.

With the bursting of the so-called Bubble Economy in 1991, however, Japan's high-growth period finally came to an end, and some aspects of the traditional model were forced to change. Most notably, the share-ownership structure has changed dramatically, as shown in Figure 6.1 below.

The three categories of investors on the left-hand side of each row in Figure 6.1, namely, non-financial business corporations, banks and insurers, are 'stable shareholders' that tend to support the incumbent management. The percentage of shareholdings held by such stable shareholders fell from 61.8 per cent in 1986 to 29 per cent in 2018. The decline was primarily the result of the sale of shares held by banks and insurance companies in the late 1990s when they were in financial distress.[15] Correspondingly, trust banks[16] and foreign investors[17] increased their holdings during this period, reaching 50.6 per cent in 2018. Because these shareholders, as well as individual investors, often have no business ties with the companies in which they invest, they cannot be relied upon by incumbent management as loyal supporters.[18] This change in share-ownership structure, which has occurred most often in larger listed companies,[19] means that

[13] As companies often hold shares in their stable shareholders, making it reciprocal, such shareholding relationships are also dubbed 'cross-shareholdings' (*kabushiki mochiai*).

[14] Although the share-ownership structure of Japanese listed companies in general is dispersed (albeit with 'stable shareholders'), some listed companies do have controlling shareholders. The peculiarity of Japan is that such controlling shareholders are often listed companies themselves. See Tokyo Stock Exchange, 'TSE-Listed Companies White Paper on Corporate Governance 2019' 9–10, chart 12 www.jpx.co.jp/english/equities/listing/cg/tvdivq0000008jb0-att/b5b4pj000002xyj7.pdf (last visited 9 July 2021).

[15] See Gen Goto, 'Legally "Strong" Shareholders of Japan' (2014) 3(2) Michigan Journal of Private Equity & Venture Capital Law 125, 145.

[16] Shareholdings by trust banks consist of shareholdings for the banks' own account and shareholdings as trustees for beneficiaries, such as investment trusts (mutual funds), private pension trusts and other domestic investment funds, including public pension funds. These include investments by the Government Pension Investment Fund and the Bank of Japan (through its purchase of exchange traded funds as a form of quantitative easing). In contrast, shareholdings by the government, which are nominal, consist of shares directly held by the government, prefectures and municipalities. See Kenjiro Egashira, 'Jyojyo gaisha no kabunushi' ['Shareholders of Listed Companies'] in Kenjiro Egashira (ed.), *Kabushiki gaisha ho taikei* [*A Treatise on Stock Corporation Law*] (Yuhikaku 2013) 3, 6–7.

[17] Investments by foreign investors are held in accounts at trust banks, but are identified as such through the submission of documents regarding tax treaties to enjoy a lower rate on tax withholding for dividends. See Egashira (n. 16) 8.

[18] With a view to garnering the support of domestic retail investors, the management teams of Japanese listed companies have introduced so-called 'shareholders' reward programmes' (*kabunushi yutai*), which basically involve a gift from the company to shareholders. The size of the gift is roughly based on their number of shares, subject to an upper limit, and in some cases also on the length of ownership. The gifts provided in such programmes often consist of the company's products, for example free flight tickets in case of airlines, but companies that do not have products attractive to individuals generally purchase gifts from outside. This practice has been welcomed by domestic retail investors, but criticized by institutional investors preferring an increase in dividends to such gifts. See Tsuyoshi Maruki and Satoru Matsuhashi, 'Kinji no kabunushi yutai seido no henka to mondai' ['The Transition and Problem of Recent shareholders' reward program'] (2019) 2211 *Shoji Homu* [*Commercial Law Review*] 102.

[19] Cross-shareholding has been unwound to a greater extent in larger listed companies, as banks that were forced to sell shares of other corporations began doing so from those of companies with a larger market capitalization and higher market valuation. See Goto (n. 15) 145–6. The prevalence of cross-shareholding in smaller listed companies can also

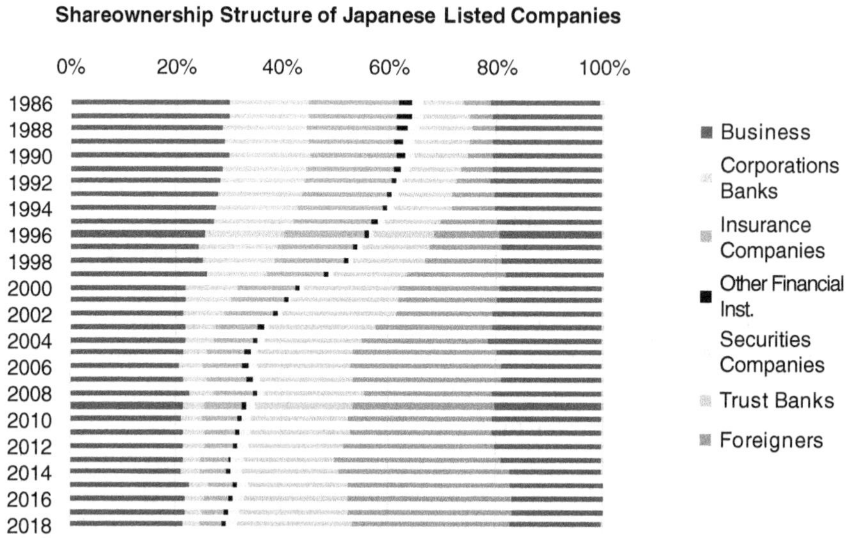

FIGURE 6.1 Transition of share-ownership of Japanese listed companies (1986–2018)
Note to figure: Data are from the Tokyo Stock Exchange, '2019 Share-ownership Survey: Transition in Share Holding Ratio at Market Value by Investor Category'.

large Japanese listed companies now face stronger pressure from the capital market.[20] Also, as the ratio of foreign investors in transaction volumes in the Tokyo market has increased,[21] the Japanese government has become more interested in listening to the voices of foreign investors, as their disappointment could lead to a drop in stock prices.

At the same time, the view that the employee-oriented governance system has been one of the main causes of Japan's structural stagnation has gained popularity amongst Japanese policy-makers. Allegedly, Japanese companies featuring a lifetime-employment system and an insider-dominated board of directors have been risk-averse, accumulating large cash reserves as a hedge against insolvency rather than investing in research and development or mergers and acquisitions, and have also been slow to concentrate on their core competencies, as doing so might lead to the sale of business units and layoff of excess workers.[22]

These developments resulted in a series of corporate governance reforms in the 2010s that sparked more shareholder-oriented viewpoints in Japanese listed companies.[23] In particular, the

be inferred from a questionnaire on the recognition of listed companies on the ratio of their shares held by 'stable shareholders', which shows that the ratio grows higher as the size of the company grows smaller. See Shojihomu Kenkyukai [Japan Institute of Business Law] (ed.), 'Kabunushi Sokai Hakusho 2019-nen-ban' ['White Paper on Shareholders' Meetings 2019'] (2019) 2216 *Shojihomu* [Commercial Law Review] 92, table 76.

20 Suppose that 30 per cent of the shares of a listed company are held by stable shareholders, with the remaining 70 per cent held by institutional investors and individuals. In times of no trouble, support from 30 per cent of shareholders would be enough for management to run the company without difficulty. However, managers would still face a risk of being voted out of office if a proxy fight were to be launched, as the remaining 70 per cent might vote in favour of the challenging shareholder.

21 In 2019, transactions by foreign investors accounted for 60 per cent of transactions on the Tokyo Stock Exchange in terms of value. Data on transaction volumes are available at www.jpx.co.jp/english/markets/statistics-equities/investor-type/00-02.html (last visited 9 July 2021).

22 For a detailed description and citations of this view, see Gen Goto, Alan K. Koh and Dan W. Puchniak, 'Diversity of Shareholder Stewardship in Asia: Faux Convergence' (2019) 53(3) Vanderbilt Journal of Transnational Law 829, 852–8; Miyajima and Saito (n. 2).

23 See Curtis J. Milhaupt, 'Evaluating Abe's Third Arrow: How Significant are Japan's Recent Corporate Governance Reforms?' in Hiroshi Oda (ed.), *Comparative Corporate Governance: The Case of Japan* (Journal of Japanese Law Special Issue 12, Carl Heymanns Verlag 2018) 65; Miyajima and Saito (n. 2).

2014 revision of the Companies Act and the adoption of the 2015 Japanese Corporate Governance Code were aimed at promoting the appointment of outside/independent directors.[24] The aim of the 2018 revision of the Corporate Governance Code was also to exert further pressure on cross-shareholdings,[25] which seem to be still prevalent in small- and medium-sized listed companies,[26] whereas the Japanese Stewardship Code, introduced in 2014 and revised in 2017 and 2020, sought to encourage engagement by institutional investors.[27]

6.2.2 *Board Structures*

Before delving into shareholders' powers, it is worthwhile to take a brief look at boards of directors, with whom shareholders engage.[28] Currently, the Companies Act provides three types of board structure as alternatives for Japanese listed companies: 'company with a board of statutory auditors' (*kansayaku-kai secchi kaisha*),[29] which is the traditional structure; 'company with three committees' (*shimei i'inkai-tō secchi kaisha*), which was introduced in 2002 as a modified version of US practice; and 'company with an audit-plus committee' (*kansa-tō i'inkai secchi kaisha*), which was introduced in 2014 as an intermediate alternative to the other two.

Whilst the traditional 'company with a board of statutory auditors' has two boards – a board of directors and a board of statutory auditors – it differs sharply from the German vertical two-tier system in that the two boards stand horizontally, as their members are appointed directly and separately by the shareholder meeting,[30] meaning that the board of statutory auditors does not have the power to appoint directors. The role of statutory auditors and their board is to audit the accounts of the company and to check whether the company is conducting its business without violating laws and regulations.[31] Although half or more of statutory auditors must be outside statutory auditors,[32] there was traditionally no requirement or recommendation to appoint an

[24] For recent board of director reforms in Japan, see Gen Goto, 'Recent Boardroom Reforms in Japan and the Roles of Outside/Independent Directors' in Hiroshi Oda (ed.), *Comparative Corporate Governance: The Case of Japan* (Journal of Japanese Law Special Issue 12, Carl Heymanns Verlag 2018) 33; Gen Goto, Manabu Matsunaka and Souichirou Kozuka, 'Japan's Gradual Reception of Independent Directors: An Empirical and Political-Economic Analysis' in Dan W. Puchniak, Harald Baum and Luke Nottage (eds.), *Independent Directors in Asia: A Historical, Contextual and Comparative Approach* (Cambridge University Press 2017) 135. It is also noteworthy that the 2019 revision of the Japanese Companies Act makes it mandatory for listed companies to appoint at least one outside director (Japanese Companies Act, art. 327-2 as amended by the 2019 revision). On the meaning of this revision, see Gen Goto and Nobuko Matsumoto, 'The Upcoming Reform of the Japanese Companies Act', Oxford Business Law Blog (28 June 2019) www.law.ox.ac.uk/business-law-blog/blog/2019/06/upcoming-reform-japanese-companies-act (last visited 9 July 2021).

[25] Tokyo Stock Exchange, 'Japan's Corporate Governance Code: Seeking Sustainable Corporate Growth and Increased Corporate Value over the Mid- to Long-Term' (1 June 2018), Principle 1.4 and Supplementary Principles 1.4.1 and 1.4.2 www.jpx.co.jp/english/news/1020/b5b4pj000000jvxr-att/20180601.pdf (last visited 9 July 2021).

[26] See n. 19.

[27] For details of the Japanese Stewardship Code, see Gen Goto, 'The Logic and Limits of Stewardship Codes: The Case of Japan' (2018) 15(2) Berkeley Business Law Journal 365; Goto, Koh and Puchniak (n. 22) 859–61.

[28] This section is largely based on Goto (n. 24) 35–45.

[29] For a brief history of statutory auditors, see Ronald J. Gilson and Curtis J. Milhaupt, 'Choice as Regulatory Reform: The Case of Japanese Corporate Governance' (2005) 53 American Journal of Comparative Law 343, 348.

[30] Japanese Companies Act, art. 329, para. 1.

[31] Ibid., art. 381, para. 1 and art. 390, para. 2.

[32] Ibid., art. 335, para. 3. An 'outside statutory auditor' is basically a statutory auditor who has not been a director or an employee of the company or its subsidiary within ten years before his/her appointment as statutory auditor and who is not a director, a statutory auditor or an employee of the company's parent company. For exact definition, see Japanese Companies Act, art. 2, item 16.

outside director. As a consequence, for a long time it was uncommon for Japanese companies to appoint an outside director.

With the intention of strengthening the monitoring function of the board of directors, the Japanese legislature has introduced the second structure, which abolishes the board of statutory auditors and instead requires companies to form an audit committee, a nomination committee and a compensation committee within the board of directors, each consisting of three or more directors.[33] To match the reality of Japanese companies then, it has been decided that the majority of each committee – albeit not of the whole board –must be constituted by outside directors.[34] However, this structure has remained unpopular, presumably because incumbent managers dislike granting too much power to outside directors, as the decisions of the three committees cannot be overruled by the board of directors.[35]

Partly in response to criticism from foreign investors of the Japanese practice of insider-dominated boards of directors, the 2014 revision of the Companies Act introduced a so-called 'comply or explain' approach requesting listed companies to either appoint at least one outside director or to explain why doing so would be detrimental to the company. Following the 2014 revision, the Japanese Corporate Governance Code adopted in 2015 introduced another 'comply or explain' rule requesting listed companies to appoint two or more independent directors.[36]

The 2014 revision also introduced the 'company with an audit-plus committee' as the third alternative structure to offer a modified version of the company with three committees that may be more acceptable to those accustomed to the traditional Japanese governance system. In particular, nomination and compensation committees, the most unpopular of the three committees, are not required. Instead, companies are required to form within the board of directors an audit-plus committee,[37] which is granted the power to express its opinion on the election, dismissal, resignation and compensation of other directors at shareholder meetings so as to reinforce the bargaining power of the outside directors on the audit-plus committee.[38]

The three board structures also differ in the extent of powers that the board can delegate to management. In a company with a board of statutory auditors, the board of directors is prohibited from delegating decisions on 'important issues regarding [the] execution of its business' to any of its directors.[39] The vagueness of this threshold arguably induces Japanese companies to put up too many agenda items to be decided by the board in order to reduce the legal risk.[40] In contrast, the board of directors of a company with three committees has greater discretion in delegating its decision-making powers to allow the board to focus on its monitoring function.[41] The third structure, a company with an audit-plus committee, takes a middle path by

33 Ibid., art. 2, item 12 and art. 327, para. 4.

34 Ibid., art. 400, paras. 1 and 3.

35 Such a rule is considered necessary because the majority of the board may be constituted by insiders. See Kenjiro Egashira, *Kabushiki gaisha-ho (Dai-8-han)* [*Laws of Stock Corporations*] (8th ed., Yuhikaku 2021) 580.

36 On the difference between an 'outside director' and an 'independent director', see Goto (n. 24) 40–1.

37 An audit-plus committee must consist of at least three directors, and the majority of the committee, but not of the whole board, must be constituted by outside directors. See Japanese Companies Act, art. 331, para. 6.

38 Japanese Companies Act, art. 342-2, para. 4 and art. 361, para. 6. See also S. Iwahara, 'Kaisha hosei no minaoshi ni kansuru yoko-an no kaisetsu (I)' ['Commentaries on the Draft Legislative Outlines for Reform of the Companies Act (1)'] (2012) 1975 *Shoji Homu* [*Commercial Law Review*] 4, 7–8.

39 Japanese Companies Act, art. 362, para. 4.

40 See Maki Saito, 'Kansayaku secchi kaisha ni okeru torishimariyakukai – Kaishaho 362jyo 4ko wo sozai to shite' ['Board of directors in Companies with Statutory Auditors: On Article 362, Paragraph 4 of the Companies Act'] in Noboru Kawahama et al. (eds.), *Morimoto Shigeru sensei kanreki kinen – Kigyoho no kadai to tenbo* [*Festschrift for the 60th birthday of Professor Shigeru Morimoto: Issues and Prospects of Enterprise Law*] (Shojihomu 2009) 161.

41 Japanese Companies Act, art. 416, para. 4. The items that the board of directors of a company with three committees is prohibited from delegating are listed in an exclusive manner.

adopting the restrictive approach taken for companies with a board of statutory auditors as the default rule but at the same time permitting shareholders to grant more discretion to the board of directors, as in companies with three committees, via articles of incorporation.[42]

These recent reforms have turned out to be effective, at least in terms of the raw number of adoptions. Of the 3,639 companies listed on the Tokyo Stock Exchange as of 12 July 2019, although the first (traditional) structure remains the most popular alternative, being chosen by 2,562 companies (70.4 per cent), the third alternative is doing fairly well, being adopted by 1,001 companies (27.5 per cent), in comparison with the second one, which is chosen by only 76 companies (2.1 per cent).[43] Also, the ratio of companies listed in the First Section of the Tokyo Stock Exchange (the top-tier market in Japan consisting of about 2,000 companies) appointing two or more independent directors jumped from 21.5 per cent in 2014 to 93.4 per cent in 2019.[44] As it became substantially the norm for listed companies to appoint at least one outside director, the 2019 revision of the Companies Act finally imposed a legal obligation on listed companies to do so.[45]

It must be noted, however, that the degree of board independence in Japan is still not as high as that in the United States. As of July 2019, the ratio of companies listed in the First Section of the Tokyo Stock Exchange in which independent directors constitute the majority of the board of directors is only 4.3 per cent, whereas the ratio of companies in which independent directors constitute one-third or more of the board is 43.6 per cent.[46]

6.3 LEGAL MEANS OF SHAREHOLDER ENGAGEMENT

6.3.1 *Decision-Making Power of the Shareholder Meeting*

Shareholder engagement is conducted in the shadow of the decision-making power of the shareholder meeting. In this regard, Japanese law mirrors continental European law in its granting of broader power to the shareholder meeting, as compared to that supplied by Delaware law.[47]

First, directors and statutory auditors are appointed and can be dismissed without cause by a simple majority at any shareholder meeting.[48] Second, whilst the power of the shareholder meeting of a stock corporation with a board of directors is, as a default rule, limited to matters delegated to it by the Companies Act, it can be expanded via articles of incorporation.[49] Third, articles of incorporation can be amended solely by the shareholder meeting,[50] which means that a provision in the articles of incorporation of a stock corporation granting the meeting the power to make decisions on ordinary business matters can be introduced without the consent of the board. Fourth, the power to decide whether the corporation will pay dividends, and, if so, the

42 Japanese Companies Act, art. 399-13, paras. 4, 5 and 6.
43 Tokyo Stock Exchange, 'Appointment of Independent Directors and Establishment of Nomination and Remuneration Committees by TSE-Listed Companies' (1 August 2019) 15 www.jpx.co.jp/english/listing/others/ind-executive/tvdivq0000001j9j-att/b5b4pj000002zfp5.pdf (last visited 9 July 2021).
44 Tokyo Stock Exchange (n. 43) 3.
45 Japanese Companies Act, art. 327-2 (as amended by the 2019 revision).
46 Tokyo Stock Exchange (n. 43) 6.
47 For a detailed comparison, see Goto (n. 15) 129–33.
48 Japanese Companies Act, art. 339, para. 1 and art. 341. In the case of a dismissal without cause, the dismissed director is entitled to receive compensation until the end of her term, under art. 339, para. 2 of the Japanese Companies Act.
49 Ibid., art. 295, para. 2.
50 Ibid., art. 466. Approval by a qualified majority of two-thirds is required for an amendment to articles of incorporation. See Section 6.3.4.2 of this chapter.

dividend amount, is allocated to the shareholder meeting as a default rule.[51] By amending the company's articles of incorporation, however, shareholders can either grant this power to the board as well[52] or go even further and divest themselves fully of it, making the board solely responsible for any decisions about dividend payments.[53] Fifth, in companies with a board of statutory auditors and those with an audit-plus committee, the formula for directors' non-fixed compensation and the content of equity-based or non-monetary compensation must be decided by the shareholder meeting unless they are stipulated in the articles of incorporation.[54]

It must be noted, however, that shareholders' decision-making power is limited in some respects. For example, although the Companies Act stipulates that the fixed compensation of directors shall be determined by resolution of a shareholder meeting,[55] case law has limited the scope of this requirement such that these resolutions create only a ceiling on the maximum aggregate fixed compensation for the company's directors; the board may then divide that maximum aggregate at its discretion.[56] In the case of the payment of a retirement bonus to a retiring director, case law has upheld the stipulation that a resolution of the shareholder meeting can delegate to the board of directors the determination of the bonus amount based on an internal formula.[57] Also, a listed company can allot newly issued shares or its treasury shares to a third party by a decision of the board of directors, unless the third party becomes a new parent company of the company via such allotment.[58]

6.3.2 *Convening a Meeting*

There are two types of shareholder meetings: annual meetings and extraordinary meetings.[59] Both are normally convened by a director based on a decision of the board of directors.[60] However, a shareholder or shareholders holding 3 per cent or more of the company's voting rights for six months can demand that directors convene a shareholder meeting.[61] If the directors fail to do so in a timely manner, the shareholder(s) can obtain permission from the court to call the meeting him or herself.[62] As the board of directors is not allowed to propose its own agenda items at a meeting called by a shareholder,[63] directors tend to respond to a shareholder demand to convene a meeting to avoid losing the power to set the meeting agenda.

The convenor of a shareholder meeting must dispatch a notice providing information on the meeting, including its date, venue and agenda, to shareholders at least two weeks in advance of the meeting.[64] If a company allows its shareholders to vote by mail, which is mandatory for

51 Ibid., art. 454, para. 1.
52 Ibid., art. 459, para. 1, item 4.
53 Ibid., art. 460, para. 1.
54 Ibid., art. 361, para. 1, items 2–6 (as amended by the 2019 revision).
55 Ibid., art. 361, para. 1, item 1.
56 Saiko Saibansho [Supreme Court of Japan], 26 March 1985, 1159 *Hanrei Jiho* [*Case Law Times*] 150. Once the maximum amount is set, a resolution of the shareholder meeting is not necessary as long as the actual compensation fits within the specified maximum. See Wataru Tanaka, *Kaishaho (dai 3 han)* [*Corporate Law*] (3rd ed., Yuhikaku 2021) 260.
57 Saiko Saibansho [Supreme Court of Japan], 11 December 1964, *Saiko Saibansho Minji-haanreishu* [*Supreme Court Civil Case Reporter*], vol. 18, no. 10, 2143.
58 Japanese Companies Act, art. 199, para. 2, art. 201, para. 1, art. 206-2.
59 Ibid., art. 296, paras. 1 and 2.
60 Ibid., art. 296, para. 3.
61 Ibid., art. 296, paras. 1 and 2.
62 Ibid., art. 297, para. 4, item 1.
63 The power to set the agenda of a meeting is valuable, as the shareholder meeting of a company with a board of directors cannot vote on issues that are not listed on the agenda. Japanese Companies Act, art. 309, para. 5.
64 Ibid., art. 299, paras. 1 and 4.

companies with 1,000 or more shareholders, the company must also send reference materials, including financial statements, and a ballot together with the notice.[65] It is also worth noting that the 2019 revision of the Companies Act introduced a Japanese version of the so-called 'notice and access' system, which allows companies to omit reference materials from the package sent to shareholders by uploading relevant information to their websites at least three weeks in advance of the meeting and stating the URL of the website on the notice sent to shareholders.[66] This new system will enter into force on September 1, 2022.

6.3.3 *Shareholder Proposals*

A shareholder or shareholders of a company holding 1 per cent or more of its voting rights or 300 voting rights, whichever is lower, for six months can demand that a certain issue(s) be added to the agenda of an upcoming shareholder meeting and that a summary of his or her proposal be included in the notice sent by the company to other shareholders.[67] Companies are also required to include information on the grounds of the proposal and other information on it in the reference materials and to provide an opportunity for shareholders to express their approval or disapproval of the proposal.[68] Such shareholder demands must be made at least eight weeks in advance of the meeting to provide enough time for the company to prepare.[69]

Traditionally, there has been no limit on the number of proposals that a shareholder or group of shareholders can make at a shareholder meeting. However, the 2019 revision of the Companies Act introduced an upper limit of ten proposals per meeting per shareholder (or group of shareholders) in response to a number of abusive cases wherein a shareholder submitted more than fifty proposals, including some that arguably made no sense and were unworthy of discussion at a shareholder meeting.[70]

Restrictions on the content of shareholder proposals are also not as stringent as they are in the USA.[71] Companies can exclude proposals that are in violation of the law or provisions in the company's articles of incorporation, as well as proposals that are virtually identical to those that failed to receive affirmative votes from 10 per cent or more of total voting rights within the previous three years.[72] Aside from these restrictions, access to the corporate ballot is granted to all proposals as long as they comprise matters that can rightfully be decided at a shareholder meeting. For example, a proposal pertaining to specific decisions about a company's ordinary business operations will be permitted if it is conditioned on the approval of accompanying

65 Ibid., art. 301, para. 1. The content of these documents is prescribed by arts. 65–6 and 73–94 of Kaishaho Seko Kisoku [Ministerial Ordinance for Implementation of the Companies Act], Ministerial Ordinance No. 12 of 2006. For more details on modes of voting, see Section 6.3.4.3 of this chapter.

66 Japanese Companies Act (as amended in 2019), arts. 325-2 and 325-4.

67 Ibid., art. 303, paras. 1 and 2, art. 305, para. 1. A shareholder holding one or more shares can also make a proposal at a shareholder meeting on issues included in the agenda, but is not permitted to add a new issue. Japanese Companies Act, art. 304.

68 Ministerial Ordinance for Implementation of the Companies Act, art. 93, para. 1, item 3, art. 66, para. 1, item 1.

69 Japanese Companies Act, art. 303, paras. 1 and 2, art. 305, para. 1.

70 For the reform on shareholder proposals, see Gen Goto, 'Kabunushi teianken (to sono shushi) no minaoshi' ['Revisiting the Shareholders' Proposal Right (and its Purpose)'] (2020) 2231 *Shojihomu* [*Commercial Law Review*] 12. For examples of abusive shareholder proposals, see Minoru Sawaguchi, 'Kabunushi teianken no ima' ['Shareholder's Proposal Right Today'] (2012) 340 *Siryoban Shoji Homu* [*Commercial Law Review: Cases and Data*] 18, 22.

71 For a comparison of Japanese and US law on shareholder proposals, see Goto (n. 15) 133–6.

72 Japanese Companies Act, art. 305, para. 4. Companies are also not required to state the grounds of the proposal in the reference materials when they are clearly false or made with the purpose of defaming or insulting others. Ministerial Ordinance for Implementation of the Companies Act, art. 93, para. 1, item 3.

proposals for amendments to the articles of incorporation to grant the shareholder meeting authority over such matters.[73]

6.3.4 *Voting*

6.3.4.1 Allocation of Voting Rights

The Japanese Companies Act allocates one vote to one share, or to one share unit, which consists of a certain number of shares prescribed in the company's articles of incorporation.[74] Cumulative voting is available for the appointment of directors as a default rule,[75] but is excluded in most, if not all, listed companies by their articles of incorporation.[76]

Although the Companies Act does not explicitly permit the issuance of class shares with multiple voting rights,[77] it is still possible to introduce a dual-class structure by altering between classes the number of shares necessary to compose one share unit.[78] However, dual-class structures are unpopular in Japan, having been utilized by only one listed company since the Tokyo Stock Exchange permitted their use in 2008.[79]

6.3.4.2 Quorum Requirement and Resolution Threshold

The quorum requirement for a shareholder meeting, whether annual or extraordinary or called by the board or a shareholder, is the presence of shareholders holding in aggregate more than half of the total voting rights, unless waived or lowered by the company's articles of incorporation.[80] Resolutions are adopted with the approval of the majority of voting rights present at the meeting unless a higher threshold is set by the articles of incorporation.[81] There is also an exclusive list of items, such as an amendment of the articles of incorporation or a merger, that require the higher threshold of two-thirds of the voting rights present at the meeting.[82]

73 Shoichi Aotake, '303 jyo' ['Article 303'] in Shinsaku Iwahara (ed.), *Kaishaho Konmentaru Dai 7 Kan* [*Commentaries on Companies Act, vol 7*] (Shojihomu 2013) 98, 101.

74 Japanese Companies Act, art. 308, para. 1, art. 188.

75 Japanese Companies Act, art. 342. See also Tanaka (n. 56) 218.

76 Tanaka (n. 56) 219.

77 The Japanese Companies Act permits stock companies to issue class shares whose voting right is limited or denied. Japanese Companies Act, art. 108, para. 1, item 3. The content and maximum number of class shares that can be issued must be stipulated in the articles of incorporation. Japanese Companies Act, art. 108, para. 2. The number of class shares with limited or no voting rights must be kept at one half of the outstanding shares or less. Japanese Companies Act, art. 115.

78 Japanese Companies Act, art. 188, para. 3. For example, by setting the number to compose one share unit of Class A shares at ten and that for Class B shares at one, shareholders of Class B shares can enjoy voting rights that are ten times as high as those of Class A shares.

79 See Nihon Keizai Shinbun, 'Fukusu giketsuken kabu ni kabunushi hanpatsu, donyuzo ni kikikan: Arufabetto nado kabunushi teian' ['Increasing dual-class structures invokes shareholders' oppositions: Shareholder proposals to Alphabet, Inc and other companies'] 8 June 2019 www.nikkei.com/article/DGXMZO45840370X00C19A6DTA000/ (last visited 9 July 2021).

80 Japanese Companies Act, art. 309, para. 1. For the appointment or removal of a director or a statutory auditor, the quorum requirement can be lowered by the articles of incorporation but it must not be lower than one-third of the total voting rights. Japanese Companies Act, art. 341.

81 Japanese Companies Act, art. 309, para. 1.

82 Ibid., para. 2. For items that require approval by a qualified majority, the quorum requirement can be lowered by the articles of incorporation but it must not be lower than-one third of the total voting rights.

6.3.4.3 Modes of Voting

There are several ways that shareholders can cast their votes. Apart from physical attendance, voting by proxy through an agent is possible at any company.[83] In addition, companies that have 1,000 or more shareholders must allow their shareholders to vote by mail.[84] Electronic voting via the internet is optional[85] but is encouraged by the Japanese Corporate Governance Code considering its convenience for overseas investors.[86] Also, the Tokyo Stock Exchange through its joint venture offers an e-voting platform service designed for institutional investors to listed companies.[87] As of 8 July 2021, 2,254 of 3,735 listed companies (60.3 per cent) allow their shareholders to vote electronically,[88] and 1,234 (33.0 per cent) have joined the e-voting platform offered by the Tokyo Stock Exchange.[89]

6.3.5 *Shareholders' Information Right*

Shareholders can obtain information from the company in several ways.[90] First, subject to court approval, a shareholder can request to inspect and copy the minutes of board meetings.[91] Second, a shareholder with 3 per cent or more of the total voting rights can request to inspect and copy the company's accounting books.[92] Third, a shareholder can ask a question at a shareholder meeting, and directors have a duty to provide an answer unless there is a justifiable ground for not doing so.[93]

6.3.6 *Shareholder Remedy against Unlawful Procedures*

If a shareholder meeting has been convened in a manner not in conformity with the legal requirements described above, or in a manner that is not illegal but significantly unfair, shareholders can file a suit to revoke resolutions adopted at that meeting.[94] Similarly, a violation of procedural rules on discussions and voting at a shareholder meeting or significant unfairness with regard to these issues also leads to revocation of the resolutions concerned.[95]

83 Japanese Companies Act, art. 310, para. 1. The solicitation of proxies is regulated by a cabinet office order based on the Financial Instruments and Exchange Act. See Jyojyo kabushiki no giketsuken no dairi koshi ni kansuru naikaku furei [Cabinet Office Order on Solicitation of Proxy Voting for Listed Shares], Cabinet Office Order No. 21 of 28 March 2003.

84 Japanese Companies Act, art. 298, para. 1, item 3 and para. 2.

85 Ibid., art. 298, para. 1, item 4. For the possibility of virtual shareholder meetings, see Section 6.4.1.2 of this chapter.

86 Tokyo Stock Exchange, 'Japan's Corporate Governance Code: Seeking Sustainable Corporate Growth and Increased Corporate Value over the Mid- to Long-Term' (1 June 2018), Supplementary Principle 1.2.4 www.jpx.co.jp/english/news/1020/b5b4pj000000jvxr-att/20180601.pdf (last visited 9 July 2021).

87 See www.icj.co.jp/en/ (last visited 9 July 2021).

88 The data is retrieved from the Japan Exchange Group's Corporate Governance Information Search www.jpx.co.jp/english/listing/cg-search/index.html (last visited 9 July 2021).

89 Kabushikigaisha ICJ [ICJ, Inc], Giketsuken denshi koshi purattofomu sankahakkogaisha ichiran [List of participating companies to the e-voting platform] www.icj.co.jp/pf_list/ (last visited 9 July 2021).

90 For more details on shareholders' information rights in Japan, see Gen Goto, 'Shareholder Inspection Rights in Japan: A Segmented Multiple-track Approach', in Randall Thomas, Paolo Giudici and Umakanth Varottil (eds.), *Research Handbook on Shareholder Inspection Rights: A Comparative Perspective* (Edward Elgar, forthcoming).

91 Japanese Companies Act, art. 371, paras. 2 and 3.

92 Ibid., art. 433, para. 1.

93 Ibid., art. 314.

94 Ibid., art. 831, para. 1, item 1.

95 Ibid.

However, if the violation in question is not a serious one and did not affect the outcome of the resolution, the court has the power to dismiss the suit.[96]

In the case of a shareholder proposal being ignored by the company, with no other agenda item at the shareholder meeting related to the ignored proposal, filing a suit is not effective, as it is considered that there is no resolution to be revoked with regard to the violation.[97] In such a case, the proposing shareholder can file for a preliminary injunction ordering the company not to hold the shareholder meeting unless it includes the ignored proposal in the agenda and repeats the procedure for convening the meeting.[98]

6.4 SHAREHOLDER MEETINGS, VOTING AND ENGAGEMENT IN PRACTICE

6.4.1 *Shareholder Meetings and Voting in Practice*

Let us now take a look at shareholder meetings and voting in practice amongst Japanese listed companies. Data on shareholder meetings are obtained from the White Paper on Shareholders' Meetings (*Kabunushi Sokai Hakusho*), which has been issued annually since 1971 by the private publisher Shojihomu based on a questionnaire sent to all Japanese listed companies (excluding those listed in emerging markets and foreign companies).[99]

6.4.1.1 Dates: The Problem of 'June Shareholder Meetings'

One peculiarity of Japanese shareholder meetings is their heavy concentration in the latter half of June. In the 2018–19 season, 1,896 of 2,702 companies (70.2 per cent) held their annual meeting in June 2019, and the meetings of 1,272 of them (47.1 per cent) were concentrated on the 25, 26 or 27 June.[100] This practice is the combined result of the custom of allocating the voting rights at an annual meeting to shareholders at the end of the previous business year, which is 31 March for most Japanese companies, and the requirement of the Companies Act that the annual meeting be held within three months of the threshold date for the allocation of voting rights.[101]

Whilst the degree of concentration is much lower than it was in the 1990s, when more than 90 per cent of shareholder meetings were held on a single day to avoid the physical attendance of Japanese corporate racketeers (*sokaiya*) as much as possible,[102] it is still problematic, as it imposes severe time constraints on the ability of institutional investors, index funds in particular, to

96 Ibid., art. 831, para. 2.

97 Tanaka (n. 56) 201–2.

98 Tanaka (n. 56) 173. Preliminary injunctions are prescribed in Minji-hozen-ho [Civil Provisional Remedies Act] (Act No. 91 of 22 December 1989), art. 23, para. 2.

99 The latest issue as of May 2020 covers shareholder meetings held during the July 2018 to June 2019 period and is based on 1,694 responses from 2,690 listed companies (63 per cent). Shojihomu Kenkyukai [Japan Institute of Business Law] (ed.), 'Kabunushi Sokai Hakusho 2019-nen-ban' ['White Paper on Shareholders' Meetings 2019'] (2019) 2216 *Shojihomu* [*Commercial Law Review*] 9.

100 Shojihomu Kenkyukai (n. 99) 22, tables 1–2.

101 Wataru Tanaka, '*Teiji kabunushi sokai ha naze rokugatsu kaisai nanoka*' [Why are annual shareholders' meetings held in June?] in Etsuro Kuronuma and Tomotaka Fujita (eds.), *Egashira Kenjiro sensei kanreki kinenn: Kigyoho no riron (jyo-kan)* [*Festschrift for the 60th Birthday of Professor Kenjiro Egashira: Theory of Enterprise Law (vol I)*] (Shojihomu 2007) 415, 434–7.

102 Atsushi Okubo, 'Kabunushi sokai chosa kekka kara mita teiji kabunushi sokai no keiko' ['Trends Regarding Annual Shareholders' Meetings Seen from a Survey on Shareholders' Meetings'] (2019) 2199 *Shojihomu* [*Commercial Law Review*] 20. On Japanese corporate racketeers, see Mark D. West, 'Information, Institutions and Extortion in Japan and the United States: Making Sense of Sokaiya Racketeers' (1999) 93 Northwestern University Law Review 767.

analyze the agenda/proposals and engage with their investee companies.[103] Despite strong criticism, however, the practice of June shareholder meetings seems to remain intact.[104]

6.4.1.2 Possibility of Virtual Meetings

Even before the outbreak of COVID-19, there was widespread interest in applying information communication technology to shareholder meetings to make it easier for institutional investors and retail investors to attend. However, as the Companies Act requires the convenor of a shareholder meeting to decide the meeting venue,[105] holding a shareholder meeting purely virtually with no physical venue has been considered unlawful.[106]

Accordingly, the Ministry of Economy, Trade and Industry (METI) has focused on promoting 'hybrid' measures, such as the live-streaming of a shareholder meeting being physically held, or going a step further and allowing shareholders to participate via the internet in discussions and voting conducted at the physical venue.[107] Whilst the live-streaming of shareholder meetings has been quite popular amongst Japanese listed companies for some time, real-time online participation has only just taken off.[108]

In April 2020, amidst the COVID-19 outbreak, METI and the Ministry of Justice (MOJ) jointly issued guidance to companies stating that it is legal to request that shareholders do not attend meetings physically but instead exercise their voting rights in advance by mail or by electronic voting.[109] Even if no shareholder has shown up, a shareholder meeting will still be considered valid, and resolutions can be adopted solely by voting rights exercised by mail or electronically.[110] Whilst such guidance is a reasonable response to the need to maintain social distancing during a pandemic, it may give rise to a fundamental question about the significance of holding a meeting, be it physical or virtual, if the results are already determined by votes cast in advance.[111]

In June 2021, through a revision of the Industrial Competitiveness Enhancement Act, METI has succeeded in introducing an exception to the requirement of a physical venue for shareholder meetings.[112] This exception allows a listed company to hold shareholder meetings purely

[103] Tanaka (n. 101) 422–6.

[104] The vast majority of listed companies are not even considering changing the practice mentioned in the text by allocating the voting rights at an annual meeting to shareholders on a day different from the final day of the business year. Shojihomu Kenkyukai (n. 98) 168, table 175.

[105] Japanese Companies Act, art. 298, para. 1, item 1.

[106] See Hideyuki Matsui, 'Bacharu-onri-gata kabunushi sokai – Sono rironteki kiso to kanosei ni tsuite' ['Purely virtual shareholders' meeting: On its theoretical foundation and admissibility'] (2020) No. 1548 *Jyurisuto* [*Jurist*] 22, 23.

[107] See METI, 'Guidelines on Approaches to Hybrid Virtual Shareholder Meetings Formulated' (26 February 2020) www.meti.go.jp/english/press/2020/0226_002.html (last visited 9 July 2021).

[108] In March 2020, a listed company called Fuji Soft, Inc reportedly held the first purely virtual shareholder meeting in Japan. See Masumi Koizumi, 'Coronavirus Forces Japanese Firms to Weigh Hybrid Online-offline Shareholders meetings' *Japan Times* (8 April 2020) www.japantimes.co.jp/news/2020/04/08/business/corporate-business/coronavirus-japanese-firms-hybrid-online-offline-shareholders-meetings/#.Xtc8rZ77S80 (last visited 9 July 2021).

[109] Keizaisangyosho and Homusho [METI and MOJ], Kabunushisokai unei ni kakaru Q&A [Q&As on operation of shareholders' meetings] (2 April 2020) https://www.meti.go.jp/covid-19/kabunushi_sokai_qa.html (last visited 9 July 2021).

[110] Ibid.

[111] Wataru Tanaka, 'Kaigitai to shite no kabunushi sokai no yukue – "Kabunushisokai unei ni kakaru Q&A" no hokaishaku to syorai no tenbo' ['Future of shareholders' meetings as a gathering: Interpretation of law by the "Q&As on operation of shareholders' meetings" and future perspectives'] (2020) 72 *Kigyo Kaikei* [*Accounting*] 41, 44–6.

[112] *Sangyo Kyosoryoku Kyoka-ho*, Law No. 98 of *Heisei* 25 (2013), last revised by Law No. 70 of *Reiwa* 3 (2021), art. 66. As of March 1, 2022, three listed companies (Euglena, GREE, and freee) have held purely-virtual shareholders' meeting using the exception under this Act.

virtually by amending its articles of incorporation, provided that METI and MOJ has confirmed that the company has adopted policies on measures against possible interruption of communication and on protection of the interest of shareholders who do not have connection to the internet.[113] Whether this new exception becomes widespread remains to be seen.

6.4.1.3 Typical Agenda

The typical items on the agendas of annual shareholder meetings are, in order of popularity, the election of directors, decisions on dividends and the election of statutory auditors.[114] To a lesser extent, amendments to articles of incorporation and decisions on directors' compensation, including the payment of retirement bonuses to directors and performance-based compensation, also appear frequently.[115] It is noteworthy that decisions on the introduction or renewal of a takeover defence have become less common in recent years owing to increased pressure from institutional investors.[116]

6.4.1.4 Shareholder Proposals

The number of listed companies receiving proposals from shareholders has been steadily increasing since 1986, the year in which the aforementioned White Paper began reporting that number.[117] The 2018–19 season marked a high point, with sixty-five companies.[118] Although the raw number is not very high considering that there are nearly 4,000 listed companies in Japan, the value of shareholder proposals as a measure of engagement should not be underestimated, particularly given that some proposals are withdrawn because the proposing shareholder reaches an agreement with management in preliminary discussions using his or her right to propose as leverage. Furthermore, the number of proposals in the 2018–19 season was double that in the 2008–9 season. The marked increase can be attributed in part to the resurgence of hedge fund activists, who made proposals to 16 companies in the 2018–19 season.[119]

Aside from hedge fund activists, proposals are often sponsored by such shareholders as the members of a company's founding family, retail investors or a group of individuals pursuing an environmental and/or social agenda. The latter two categories benefit from the provision of the Companies Act granting proposal rights to shareholders with 300 or more voting rights.

In the 2018–19 season, thirty-eight companies received proposals concerning an amendment to their articles of incorporation. The topics of the proposed amendments ranged from governance-related issues, such as separation of the CEO and chairperson of the board of directors or disclosure of the CEO's individual compensation,[120] to environmental or social issues, such as

[113] See METI, 'Outline of Rules Concerning a "Shareholders Meeting without a Designated Location"' (June 2021) www.meti.go.jp/policy/economy/keiei_innovation/keizaihousei/virtual-only-shareholders-meeting_explanatory-material-en.pdf (last visited 9 July 2021).

[114] Shojihomu Kenkyukai (n. 99) 24, table 3.

[115] Ibid.

[116] For the decline of takeover defence in Japan, see Alan K. Koh, Masafumi Nakahigashi and Dan W. Puchniak, 'Land of the Falling "Poison" Pill: Understanding Defensive Measures in Japan on Their Own Terms' (2020) 41 *University of Pennsylvania Journal of International Law* 687.

[117] Manabu Matsunaka, 'Kawaru mono to kawaranai mono – "2019nen-ban kabnushi sokai hakusho" wo yonde' ['Things That Change and Do Not Change – An Impression on the White Paper on Shareholders' Meetings 2019'] (2019) 2218 *Shojihomu* [*Commercial Law Review*] 4, 10.

[118] Shojihomu Kenkyukai (n. 99) 23–4.

[119] Ibid., 28.

[120] As of May 2020, there is no mandatory disclosure of individual compensation except for directors of publicly traded corporations receiving compensation of JPY100 million or more. See Kaishaho Seko Kisoku [Ministerial Ordinance

an objection to nuclear power plants or the promotion of diversity within the board of directors.[121] It is noteworthy that, as of July 2021, proposals focusing on climate change have just taken off and are not yet so prevalent in Japan.[122] Other popular subjects for shareholder proposals include the appointment and/or removal of directors (twenty-nine companies in the 2018–19 season), which sometimes involves a serious contest for company control, such as that seen in June 2019 at LIXIL, and an increase in dividends (twenty-two companies in the 2018–19 season), which is a favourite of hedge fund activists.

Although the number of shareholder proposals has been on the rise, the number of adoptions has remained rather low and stable, often totalling fewer than five.[123] Interestingly, most of the proposals that are adopted concern the appointment and/or dismissal of directors and/or statutory auditors.[124] A potential reason for the high rate of rejection is that shareholders with a nominal number of shares may be pursuing their own agendas, which are not in line with the interests of shareholders as a whole. In fact, one empirical study found that of the 201 shareholder proposals made to listed companies from July 2012 to June 2016, 88 were proposed by shareholders owning less than one per cent of voting rights. Further, fifty-four of the eighty-eight proposals received less than 10 per cent support, whereas only seven of the seventy-one proposed by shareholders owning 1 per cent or more received such a low level of support.[125] However, the Japanese government did not take up this academic's proposal to deny proposal rights to shareholders holding less than 1 per cent of voting rights, as such denial would make

for Implementation of the Companies Act], Ministerial Ordinance No. 12 of 2006, art. 121, para. iii (Japan), and Kigyo naiyo to no kaiji ni kansuru naikaku furei [Cabinet Office Ordinance on Disclosure of Corporate Affairs], Cabinet Office Ordinance No. 5 of 1973 (Japan) (Form 2 (Precautions for Recording (57)a(d)) and Form 3-2 (Precautions for Recording (14)).

121 Shojihomu Kenkyukai (n. 99) 28.

122 In March 2020, a non-profit organization made what was allegedly the first climate change-related shareholder proposal in Japan to Mizuho Financial Group, one of the country's largest financial groups. Kiko Nettowaku [Climate Network], Kiko Network, as Mizuho Financial Group shareholder, files first ever climate resolution in Japan (2020/3/16) www.kikonet.org/eng/press-release-en/2020-03-16/mizuho_shareholder_proposal (last visited 9 July 2021). The proposal was rejected, but obtained support from more than one-third of the votes cast in advance. See Aaron Sheldrick and Takashi Umekawa, 'Mizuho Shareholders Reject First Climate Motion Put to a Japanese Company' *Reuters* (25 June 2020) www.reuters.com/article/us-climate-change-mizuho-coal-idUSKBN23WoKU (last visited 9 July 2021). In June 2021, similar proposals were submitted to Mitsubishi UFJ Financial Group and Sumitomo Corporation, receiving support of 23 per cent and 20 per cent of votes respectively. See Yuzo Yamaguchi, 'Japan's Banks Face Rising Climate Activism Despite Vetoed Motions' (29 June 2021) www.spglobal.com/marketintelligence/en/news-insights/latest-news-headlines/japan-s-banks-face-rising-climate-activism-despite-vetoed-motions-65170953 (last visited 9 July 2021). Whether such proposals become more widespread remains to be seen.

123 Matsunaka (n. 117) 10.

124 The numbers of listed companies that had shareholder proposals adopted in various seasons is three (2014–15 season), four (2015–16), three (2016–17), four (2017–18) and three (2018–19). Shareholder proposals on the appointment and/or dismissal of directors and/or statutory auditors were adopted in sixteen out of seventeen companies. The remaining one dealt with the issuance of shares and share options by private placement to the proposing shareholder, which would make the shareholder a parent company of the issuing company. See Shojihomu Kenkyukai [Japan Institute of Business Law] (ed.), 'Kabunushi Sokai Hakusho 2015-nen-ban' ['White Paper on Shareholders' Meetings 2015'] (2015) 2085 *Shojihomu* [*Commercial Law Review*] 16–18; Shojihomu Kenkyukai (ed.), 'Kabunushi Sokai Hakusho 2016-nen-ban' ['White Paper on Shareholders' Meetings 2016'] (2016) 2118 *Shojihomu* 18, 20–2; Shojihomu Kenkyukai (ed.), 'Kabunushi Sokai Hakusho 2017-nen-ban' ['White Paper on Shareholders' Meetings 2017'] (2017) 2151 *Shojihomu* 20–2; Shojihomu Kenkyukai (ed.), 'Kabunushi Sokai Hakusho 2018-nen-ban' [White Paper on Shareholders' Meetings 2018] (2018) 2184 *Shojihomu* 17–19; Shojihomu Kenkyukai (n. 99) 21.

125 Hidefusa Iida, 'Kabunushi teianken no ranyoteki na koshi to Kaishaho kaisei' ['Abuse of Shareholders' Proposal Right and the Companies Act Reform'] in Shihon-shijyo Kenkyukai [Capital Market Research Institute] (ed.), *Kigyo hosei no shorai tenbo – Shihon-shijyo seido no kaikaku heno teigen – 2018nendo-ban* [*Future Prospects on Business Law: Proposals to Reform Capital Market System – 2018 Version*] (Shihon-shijyo Kenkyukai 2017) 227, 254–5.

environmental, social and governance (ESG)-related proposals more difficult to put forward and would likely invite political criticism.[126]

6.4.1.5 Turnout Rate

In the 2018–19 season, the ratio of voting rights exercised by shareholders, including those by proxy, mail or e-voting, exceeded 70 per cent in 1,263 out of 1,694 companies.[127] The ratio of voting rights held by shareholders who physically attended the annual shareholder meeting, in contrast, was 10 per cent or less in almost one-half of the companies (837, or 49.4 per cent).[128] The implication is that the voting rights exercised by proxy, mail or e-voting up to one day before the meeting determined the outcome in most cases.

Amongst the various types of investors, domestic institutional investors seem to be the most enthusiastic about exercising their voting rights, which is unsurprising as they are expected to do so by the Japanese Stewardship Code.[129] Overseas investors also tend to vote, but they lag behind domestic institutional investors.[130] In contrast, the rate of voting in advance is not very high amongst individual retail investors,[131] which is also not very surprising.

6.4.1.6 Voting Results

In 2010, the Financial Services Agency amended its disclosure ordinance to require listed companies to disclose the percentages of votes for and against every proposal.[132] The intent of this reform was arguably to strengthen shareholders' influence even when a management proposal was adopted by bringing their degree of dissatisfaction to light.[133]

Also, in June 2009, a governmental council urged institutional investors to voluntarily disclose how they had voted at the shareholder meetings of their investee companies on an aggregate basis.[134] Trust banks and investment advisors have been doing so since 2010, and life insurance companies followed suit in 2014 following the adoption of the Japanese Stewardship Code.[135] Moreover, since 2017, the Japanese Stewardship Code requires institutional investors – on

126 Goto (n. 70) 13–15.

127 Shojihomu Kenkyukai (n. 99) 119, table 113.

128 Ibid., 117, table 111. Although 355 companies (21.0 per cent) reported the physical attendance of shareholders holding more than 30 per cent of voting rights, 256 of them were rather small in size, with legal capital of less than JPY10 billion.

129 Naoyoshi Ema, 'Kikantoshika ni yoru giketsuken koshi no jyokyo – 2019nen 6gatsu no kabunushi sokai wo furikaette' ['The State of Voting by Institutional Investors: Reflecting upon Shareholders' Meetings in June 2019'] (2019) 2215 *Shojihomu* [*Commercial Law Review*] 44, 46 (reporting that domestic institutional investors exercised almost all of their voting rights in advance). Ema is a practitioner at a major trust bank offering transfer agent services to listed companies, and his report is based on data from 870 companies that are customers of his bank and held annual meetings in June 2019.

130 Ibid. (overseas investors exercised 79 per cent of their voting rights in advance).

131 Ibid. (individuals exercised 37 per cent of their voting rights in advance).

132 Kigyo naiyo to no kaiji ni kansuru naikaku furei [Cabinet Office Order on Disclosure of Corporate Affairs] (Ministry of Finance Order No. 5 of 30 January 1973), art. 19, para. 2, item 9-2.

133 In particular, a relatively low rate of approval for a CEO's reappointment as director in comparison to other directors might affect the company's subsequent policy.

134 See Report by the Financial System Council's Study Group on the Internationalization of Japanese Financial and Capital Markets – Toward Stronger Corporate Governance of Publicly Listed Companies (17 June 2009), 16–17 www.fsa.go.jp/en/news/2009/20090618-1/01.pdf (last visited 9 July 2021).

135 Naoyoshi Ema, 'Kikantoshika ni yoru giketsuken koshi no jyokyo – Nihon-ban suchuwadoshippu kodo wo fumaete' ['The State of Voting by Institutional Investors: The Effects of the Japanese Stewardship Code'] (2014) 2053 *Shojihomu* [*Commercial Law Review*] 46, 48.

a 'comply or explain' basis – to disclose how they have voted on each proposal.[136] This requirement, which exerts pressure on such investors to vote in a manner that will seem to be free from conflicts of interest, is now complied with by most major Japanese trust banks, insurers and asset management companies.[137]

The most unpopular agenda items amongst institutional investors are the introduction or renewal of a takeover defence and the payment of retirement bonuses to directors.[138] The appointment of director candidates proposed by the board of directors is also likely to receive a high number of 'no' votes, albeit to a lesser extent than the two previous items, as some institutions and major proxy advisors have voting standards requiring them to vote against the re-election of the CEO when return on equity is low or the degree of board independence falls below a certain level.[139] In contrast, management proposals on the amount of dividends usually receive a high level of support,[140] as their rejection means no payouts to shareholders unless a shareholder proposal proposing a higher amount is adopted.

6.4.1.7 Using Proxy Advisors

As institutional investors face considerable time constraints owing to the 'June shareholder meeting' problem,[141] it is becoming increasingly popular to consult proxy advisors on how to vote.[142] Such major global players as Institutional Shareholder Services and Glass Lewis now have a strong presence in Japan.

As of May 2020, there was no regulation on proxy advisors in Japan. However, in response to complaints from investee companies alleging that proxy advisors had issued advice based on an inaccurate understanding of the circumstances of individual companies, the 2020 revision of the Japanese Stewardship Code introduces a separate principle for the providers of services to institutional investors. In particular, it asks proxy advisors to 'develop appropriate and sufficient human and operational resources' to provide 'proxy recommendations based on accurate information on individual companies'; not to rely solely on the information disclosed by companies; to actively exchange views with companies as necessary; and to afford listed companies an opportunity to confirm whether the information upon which proxy advisors have relied is accurate and to provide their clients with the companies' opinions together with their own recommendations.[143]

136 The Council of Experts on the Stewardship Code, 'Principles for Responsible Institutional Investors "Japan's Stewardship Code" – To Promote Sustainable Growth of Companies through Investment and Dialogue' (29 May 2017) Guidance 5-3 www.fsa.go.jp/en/refer/councils/stewardship/20170529/01.pdf (last visited 9 July 2021).

137 See Goto, Koh and Puchniak (n. 22) 861–3.

138 Ema (n. 129) 50, 52. The unpopularity of retirement bonuses is due to its non-linkage to corporate performance, as it is usually calculated based on the length of the retiring director's service.

139 Ema (n. 129) 47–8.

140 Ibid., 47.

141 See nn. 101–4 and the accompanying text.

142 According to a 2019 questionnaire survey of its members by the Japan Investment Advisors Association, thirty-eight out of ninety-three (40.9 per cent) investment advisors that have investments in Japanese stocks have utilized proxy advisors to decide how they vote. See Nihon Toshikomongyo Kyokai [Japan Investment Advisors Association], 'Nihon-ban suchuwadoshippu kodo heno taio to ni kansuru anketo (dai 6kai) no kekka ni tsuite (2019nen 10gatsu jisshi bun)' ['Results of the 6th Questionnaire on Responses to the Japanese Stewardship Code Carried Out on October 2019'] 44 www.jiaa.or.jp/osirase/pdf/steward_enq2019.pdf (last visited 9 July 2021).

143 The Council of Experts on the Stewardship Code (FY2019), 'Principles for Responsible Institutional Investors "Japan's Stewardship Code" – To Promote Sustainable Growth of Companies through Investment and Dialogue' (24 March 2020) 10 (Principle 8) and 22 (Guidance 8-2, 8-3) www.fsa.go.jp/en/refer/councils/stewardship/20200324/01.pdf (last visited 9 July 2021). For details, see Gen Goto, 'Japanese Stewardship Code: Its Resemblance and

6.4.2 *Private, Behind-the-Scenes Engagement*

Although it is difficult to verify the reality of private, behind-the-scenes engagement, institutional investors adopting the Japanese Stewardship Code often summarize their engagement activities in their stewardship reports. For example, Nippon Life Insurance reported that from July 2018 to June 2019, it had discussions with 758 investee companies on various topics, ranging from payout policies to ESG issues.[144]

In June 2017, the Government Pension Investment Fund of Japan, one of the largest public pension funds in the world, with assets of more than US$1.5 trillion, announced that, as a long-term universal investor, it would require its asset managers to 'proactively engage with investee companies' on critical ESG issues.[145] Since then, engagement on ESG issues has gained traction amongst Japanese institutional investors.[146] Whether such engagement is merely a pose to show that investors are following the prevailing trend or a sign of serious commitment to the pursuit of ESG remains to be seen.[147]

Collective engagement is also gaining some traction, as the Japanese Stewardship Code acknowledged its benefits in 2017.[148] Since then, several private initiatives have been put forward to facilitate coordination amongst institutional investors.[149]

6.5 CONCLUDING REMARKS

Shareholder engagement gained prominence in Japan in the 2010s owing to changes in the share-ownership structure and corporate governance reforms focusing on shareholder interests as the key to overturning two decades of economic stagnation, as well as to the strong shareholder rights already granted by law. A recent empirical study showed that these changes and reforms have made Japanese listed companies more pro-shareholder by increasing payouts, but have not been successful in inducing company management to make more investments,[150] suggesting

Non-resemblance to the UK Code' in Dionysia Katelouzou and Dan W. Puchniak (eds.), *Global Shareholder Stewardship* (Cambridge University Press forthcoming 2022).

144 Nihon Seimei Hoken Sogo Gaisha [Nippon Life Insurance Mutual Company], 'Suchuwadoshippu katsudo hokokusho (2019nen)' ['Report on Stewardship Activities 2019'] 21 www.nissay.co.jp/kaisha/otsutaeshitai/shisan_unyou/ssc/pdf/stewardship_hokoku2019.pdf (last visited 9 July 2021).

145 See Government Pension Investment Fund of Japan, 'Stewardship Principles' (established on 1 June 2017, revised on 6 February 2020) 2–3 www.gpif.go.jp/en/investment/pdf/stewardship_principles_and_proxy_voting_principles.pdf (last visited 9 July 2021).

146 See eg Nihon Keizai Shinbun, 'Kokunai unyo gaisha, ESG taisei wo kyoka, mane torikumi nerau' ['Domestic Asset Management Companies Strengthen ESG Operations With an Aim to Attract Capital'] (31 March 2020, 22:30JST) www.nikkei.com/article/DGXMZO57462270R30C20A3EE9000/ (last visited 9 July 2021).

147 Some Japanese institutional investors have disclosed that they voted against the shareholder proposal on global climate change submitted to Mizuho Financial Group's 2020 annual shareholder meeting (see n. 122). See eg Dai-ichi Seimei Hoken Kabushiki Kaisha [Dai-ichi Life Insurance, Ltd.], '2020nen 4gatsu ~ 6gatsu kabunushi sokai ni okeru giketsuken koshi kekka' ['Voting results in shareholders' meetings held from April to June 2020'] www.dai-ichi-life.co.jp/dsr/investment/pdf/ssc2_016.pdf 125 (last visited 9 July 2021).

148 The Council of Experts on the Stewardship Code (n. 136) Guidance 4–5.

149 See e.g. Institutional Investors Collective Engagement Forum www.iicef.jp/en/ (last visited 9 July 2021) and Forum of Investors Japan https://investorforum.jp/%e7%9b%ae%e7%9a%84/ (last visited 9 July 2021). The industrial organization of life insurance companies has also announced its intention to promote collective engagement. See Seimei Hoken Kyokai [Life Insurance Association of Japan], 'Suchuwadoshippu katsudo waking gurupu sanka gaisya ni yoru syudanteki engegimento no jissi' ['Collective engagement by member companies of the working group on stewardship activities'] (30 November 2018) www.seiho.or.jp/info/news/2018/20181130.html (last visited 9 July 2021).

150 Miyajima and Saito (n. 2).

that it would be worthwhile to continue pursuing pro-shareholder governance in Japan.[151] Thus, there is still much to do in the arenas of shareholder engagement and voting.

At the same time, ESG investment is experiencing a gradual rise in Japan, and institutional investors are at least claiming to take ESG issues seriously. However, there could be pushback against the pro-shareholder view, as some Japanese companies have arguably been able to survive the COVID-19 crisis thus far thanks to their rich cash reserves.[152] Whether these factors change the course of shareholder engagement and voting in Japan remains to be seen.

[151] Hideaki Miyajima and Takuji Saito, 'Kigyo tochi kaikaku no kiketsu to kongo no kaikaku hoko (ge)' ['The Consequences of Corporate Governance Reforms and the Direction for Future Reforms'] (2020) 2236 *Shojihomu* [*Commercial Law Review*] 31, 33–4. According to this study, the increase in payouts is on average contributing to a reduction in free cash flows but is not damaging research and development at high growth companies.

[152] For a view praising Japanese companies for their large cash reserves as a buffer in times of crisis, see e.g. Jesper Koll, 'Japan's Cash Reserves are Now a Great Source of Advantage' *Financial Times* (15 May 2020) www.ft.com/content/7fdae7b1-9bc4-43d1-8e9f-72ae82cfc927 (last visited 9 July 2021).

7

Shareholder Engagement and Voting in Singapore

Wai Yee Wan

7.1 INTRODUCTION

Singapore's legislative and regulatory framework on shareholder engagement and voting are found in the Singapore Companies Act,[1] as well as in case law. Listed companies have to additionally comply with the Singapore Exchange listing rules (SGX listing rules)[2] and the Singapore Code on Takeovers and Mergers (Takeover Code hereafter),[3] which contain provisions on voting in takeover situations. Further, for reasons explained in Section 7.2.1 below, the Singapore Code on Corporate Governance (Corporate Governance Code hereafter)[4] operates as 'soft law'. The Companies Act was largely inherited from the UK Companies Act of 1948, although the regulatory framework has undergone significant changes.

In this chapter, I will focus on the shareholder voting and engagement of Singapore-incorporated companies, with particular reference to companies listed on the Singapore Exchange (SGX). In discussing different kinds of shareholder activism, I will extend the study to foreign-incorporated companies listed on the SGX. Other kinds of business vehicles that are listed on the SGX, such as registered business trusts and real estate investment trusts, are beyond the scope of this chapter, as the regulatory framework governing them is quite different from that for corporate vehicles. I will also draw upon empirical evidence in the existing literature in support of my findings.

Section 7.2 first outlines the background of Singapore's company law and regulatory framework and explains the relationship between directors and shareholders, and then goes on to discuss the ownership structure of Singapore-listed companies. Section 7.3 deals with the legal means of shareholder engagement, shareholder proposal rights, voting, questions and information rights. Section 7.4 discusses the formal and informal scope of shareholder engagement in Singapore, as well as giving examples of contentious and challenging aspects of its company law, namely, the regulation of related-party transactions (RPTs), the delisting of proposals amounting to the expropriation of minority shareholders, dual-class structures and 'say on pay'. Section 7.5 concludes with the future of shareholder engagement and voting in Singapore.

[1] Cap. 50, 2006 rev. ed.

[2] SGX listing rules, http://rulebook.sgx.com/rulebook/mainboard-rules accessed 23 February 2022. There are two boards on which companies can listed: the Mainboard and the Catalist. Mainboard companies are more established and have more stringent listing requirements, whereas Catalist companies are fast-growing companies with no quantitative criteria. For the purposes of this chapter, references to the SGX listing rules are to the listing rules that are applicable to companies listed on the Mainboard of the SGX, unless otherwise indicated.

[3] The Singapore Code on Takeovers and Mergers, www.mas.gov.sg accessed 23 February 2022.

[4] The current version of the Corporate Governance Code is the 2018 version, www.mas.gov.sg/regulation/codes/code-of-corporate-governance accessed 23 February 2022.

7.2 GENERAL ACCOUNT OF SINGAPORE COMPANY LAW AND CORPORATE GOVERNANCE

7.2.1 *Background*

Singapore is a former British colony, and its legal system is therefore based on the UK system. English common law was received in Singapore via the Second Charter of Justice 1826 and formalized by the Application of English Law Act.[5] The Singapore Companies Act was first enacted in 1967, and was based on the UK Companies Act 1948. Two significant comprehensive reviews of the Singapore Companies Act have taken place since 1967. The first was the review conducted in 1999 that led to publication of the report of the Company Legislation and Framework Committee (CLFRC).[6] Pursuant to the recommendations of the CLFRC review, a number of shareholder protection rights were enhanced, including amending the Companies Act to statutorily impose limits on majority rule in the context of alterations of articles of association and alterations of class rights.[7] Thus, it is possible to have an entrenching provision in a company constitution stipulating that such provision may not be altered except by unanimous approval, or by a majority greater than the 75 per cent needed for a special resolution, or unless other special conditions are met.

The second review, which was far more comprehensive, commenced in 2007[8] and was not completed until 2014 with the enactment of the Companies (Amendment) Act 2014.[9] Owing to its complexity, this legislation came into force over the 2016–17 period. As a result of this second review, the Companies Act was rewritten to ensure that the legislation was conducive to Singapore's position as a global hub for business and fundraising. With respect to the review's impact on shareholder rights, the amendments included the removal of the one-share-one-vote restriction for public companies (paving the way for the issuance of shares with multiple voting rights)[10] and a provision allowing the shareholders of listed companies to bring derivative actions directly.[11] In 2018, the SGX listing rules were amended to allow companies with dual-class shares (DCS) to be listed on the SGX.[12]

As noted, in addition to the Companies Act, the other relevant regulations in Singapore are the Takeover Code and Corporate Governance Code. The former pertains to voting in mergers and acquisitions transactions. Whilst the Takeover Code does not operate by way of subsidiary legislation,[13] market participants regard it as binding.[14] The Corporate Governance Code operates on a 'comply or explain' basis; the SGX listing rules require that listed companies comply with the Corporate Governance Code,[15] and, if they are unable to do so, to explain the basis of any deviations. Hence the Corporate Governance Code is regarded as 'soft' law.

5 Application of English Law Act, Cap. 7A, 1994 rev. ed.

6 See Company Legislation and Regulatory Framework Committee, Report of the Company Legislation and Regulatory Framework Committee (CLRFC, October 2002); copy on file with the author.

7 Companies Act, s. 26A.

8 Ministry of Finance, *Report of the Steering Committee for Review of the Companies Act* (MOF 2011) (*MOF Report*).

9 The review culminated in the Companies (Amendment) Act 2014. For a discussion of the main changes introduced by the legislation, see Hans Tjio et al., *Company Law* (Singapore Academy of Law 2014), ch 1.

10 Companies Act, s. 64A.

11 Ibid., s. 216A.

12 Section 7.3.4.

13 Securities and Futures Act, Cap. 289, 2006 rev. ed., s. 139(3).

14 See, generally, Wai Yee Wan, 'UK-Style Takeover Regulation in Singapore' in Umakanth Varottil and Wai Yee Wan (eds.), *Comparative Takeover Regulation: Global and Asian Perspectives* (Cambridge University Press 2017) ch. 13. Also see Wai Yee Wan and Umakanth Varottil, *Mergers and Acquisitions in Singapore: Law and Practice* (LexisNexis 2013).

15 See e.g. SGX listing rules, ch. 7; see also Introduction to Corporate Governance Code (6 August 2018) para. 2.

In 2016, Singapore adopted the Stewardship Principles for Responsible Investors (Stewardship Code hereafter), which provide that all institutional investors, including domestic investors, are free to adopt the Stewardship Code, whether in whole or part or not at all. In 2018, the Singapore Family Stewardship Code was adopted, which is a version of the Stewardship Code developed specifically for family companies. Both the Stewardship Code and Family Stewardship Code are strictly voluntary in nature. They also differ from the Corporate Governance Code, as there is no regulatory body that monitors compliance, whereas compliance with the Corporate Governance Code is monitored by the SGX.[16] However, as this chapter focuses on the legal framework surrounding shareholder engagement and voting, the Stewardship Code and Family Stewardship Code fall outside its scope.

7.2.2 *Allocation of Corporate Decision-Making and the Role and Structure of the Board*

The Companies Act provides for a one-tier corporate board. Directors are appointed by shareholders.[17] There is no provision for boards to represent any sectoral interests, including employees. Under section 157A Companies Act, managerial decision-making statutorily lies with the board of directors.[18] Section 157A goes on to provide that directors may exercise all powers of the company with the exception of those that the Companies Act or the company's constitution[19] specify must be exercised by the company in the general meeting. Hence, shareholders prima facie hold only those powers that are granted under the Companies Act and the constitution of the company.[20] It thus appears that if shareholders want more extensive rights than those conferred under the Companies Act, they have to vary the company constitution under sections 180 and 183 Companies Act. However, several questions remain unanswered as to the scope of section 157A.[21] In particular, notwithstanding the express wording of that section, is it still possible for a company's constitution to provide that management powers be conferred upon shareholders directly? This issue arose in *TYC Investment Pte Ltd* v. *Tay Yun Chwan Henry*,[22] where the High Court held that section 157A Companies Act is only a default rule that can be varied by the company's constitution.

Not all of the directors on the boards of listed companies are involved in day-to-day management. Instead, boards exercise oversight over the management of the company, with day-to-day management left in the hands of the company's senior executive officers, who may or may not be board members. At least one-third of the boards of listed companies in Singapore comprise independent directors.[23] An independent director is defined in the Corporate Governance Code as

[16] For a general discussion of the Stewardship Code, see Dan W. Puchniak and Samantha Tang, 'Singapore's Puzzling Embrace of Shareholder Stewardship: A Successful Secret' (23 October 2019), SSRN: https://ssrn.com/abstract=3474151 or http://dx.doi.org/10.2139/ssrn.3474151 accessed 23 February 2022.

[17] Companies Act, s. 149B.

[18] Ibid., s. 157A.

[19] A company's constitution is functionally equivalent to the company's memorandum and articles of association, and is adopted by the company at the time of incorporation. The subsidiary legislation provides for a Model Constitution, which may be adopted in whole or in part. Under the Model Constitution, a new default power allocation article, art. 77, provides for the allocation in the same terms as s. 157A Companies Act.

[20] For a discussion of the relationship between directors and shareholders, see Pearlie M. C. Koh, 'Power Allocation and the Role of Shareholders – A Comparative Examination' (2019) 15 Berkeley Business Law Journal 409.

[21] Ibid.

[22] [2014] 4 SLR 1149 (HC).

[23] SGX listing rules (n. 2). The changes to the listing rules take effect on 1 January 2022 and are mandatory. Currently, the one-third independent director rule applies on a comply-or-explain basis.

> one who is independent in conduct, character and judgement, and has no relationship with the company, its related corporations, its substantial shareholders or its officers that could interfere, or be reasonably perceived to interfere, with the exercise of the director's independent business judgement in the best interests of the company.[24]

However, in certain prescribed circumstances, such as where the board chair is not an independent director, the Corporate Governance Code provides that independent directors must constitute a majority of the board.[25]

Shareholders make corporate decisions through general meetings. Apart from statutory meetings (e.g. the meeting required to be convened under section 210 Companies Act for the rearrangement of shareholder rights), there are two kinds of shareholder meetings: the annual general meeting (AGM) and the extraordinary general meeting (EGM). Listed companies are required to hold their AGM within four months of each financial year end,[26] although the period can be extended by the Registrar of Companies in special circumstances.[27] AGMs are held primarily to approve the financial results of the company,[28] the declaration of dividends,[29] the appointment or re-appointment of directors,[30] the payment of directors' fees,[31] the adoption of share option plans and shareholder mandates for directors to issue new shares,[32] although other business can be conducted at an AGM. EGMs are meetings other than AGMs that are called for matters that require shareholder approval. The Corporate Governance Code encourages management to update shareholders at the AGM or EGM on the financial position of the company and its prospects and for the relevant materials to be published on SGXNET (the SGX platform for the public disclosure of information) and the company's website.[33] The Corporate Governance Code further provides that resolutions should not be made inter-conditional to enable shareholders to vote separately.[34] In the event that resolutions have to be made inter-conditional, clear explanations are required.[35]

7.2.3 *Overview of Shareholding Structures in Singapore*

Empirical evidence demonstrates that the shareholding structures of listed companies in Singapore have been highly concentrated since the 1960s[36] and remain concentrated. Shareholdings were previously concentrated primarily in the hands of the state and families. Two of the first comprehensive (published) studies in this area were undertaken by La Porta et

24 Corporate Governance Code 2018, provision 2.1.
25 Ibid., provision 2.3
26 Companies Act, s. 175(1).
27 Ibid., s. 175(2). For example, an extension was granted in 2020 for listed companies to hold their AGMs if the statutory audits for companies whose financial year ended 31 December 2019 were affected by the travel restrictions imposed by COVID-19: www.sgx.com/media-centre/20200207-sgx-regco-gives-issuers-30-june-2020-hold-agms-approve-fy-dec-2019-results accessed 23 February 2022.
28 Companies Act, s. 201.
29 Ibid., s. 403, read with the constitution of the company.
30 Ibid., s. 149B.
31 Ibid., s. 169.
32 Ibid., s. 161.
33 Corporate Governance Code 2018, Practice Guidance 11.
34 Ibid.
35 Ibid.
36 See Watt Moi Tay, *Ownership and Control of the Singapore Public Companies (1940–1962)* (University of Singapore 1963–4), whose study of sixty=six listed companies in 1963 showed that, for 77.3 per cent of those companies, the largest twenty shareholders held, in aggregate, more than 50 per cent of the votes.

al.[37] and Claessens et al.[38] The former, who investigated the control structure of firms in twenty-seven countries in the early 1990s, found that 45 per cent of large publicly traded firms in Singapore were controlled by the state and 45 per cent by families, with 5 per cent widely held based on data obtained from a sample of the top twenty companies by market capitalization as of 1995. In comparison, the respective averages across the twenty-seven countries as a whole were 20 per cent, 35 per cent and 25 per cent. Claessens et al., in their study of shareholding structures in nine East Asian countries (including Singapore), reported that the corresponding percentages for state, family and widely held firms were 21.8 per cent, 53.3 per cent and 2.5 per cent, respectively, as of 1996 (based on a sample size of 200 firms).[39]

In a more recent, larger-scale empirical study of Singapore, my co-author and I found that shareholdings continue to be concentrated. We examined the shareholding structures and other corporate governance features of listed companies over the 2009–15 period. Looking at the shareholding interests of the largest beneficial owners of 721 companies, which represented 25 per cent of companies listed on the SGX during the period in question, we found them to own an average of 40.72 per cent (median: 39.62 per cent).[40] The other corporate governance features are reported in Table 7.1.

The largest beneficial owners of the shareholdings of listed companies in Singapore fall into the category of either families[41] or the Singapore Government through Temasek.[42] Temasek does not publicly provide a list of all of its investments in SGX-listed companies, although it discloses some of its key investments.[43] Institutional investors, whilst important in SGX-listed companies, do not exhibit as significant an ownership stake in listed firms as do families or the state.[44] There are no readily available data on the holdings of retail investors,[45] although the discussion of Magnus Energy and Hyflux in Section 7.4 of this chapter indicates that retail investors are becoming more vocal and important constituents for listed companies to engage with.

37 Rafael La Porta, Florencio Lopez-De-Silanes and Andrei Shleifer, 'Corporate Ownership around the World' (1999) 54 Journal of Finance 471.

38 Stijn Claessens, Simeon Djankov and Larry H. P. Lang, 'The Separation of Ownership and Control in East Asian Corporations' (2000) 58 Journal of Financial Economics 81–112.

39 Ibid.

40 Christopher C. Chen and Wai Yee Wan, 'Transnational Corporate Governance Codes: Lessons from Regulating Related Party Transactions in Hong Kong and Singapore' (2018) 36 Chinese (Taiwan) Yearbook of International Law and Affairs 63.

41 See Marleen Dieleman, Jungwook Shim and Muhammad Ibrahim, 'Success and Succession: A Study of SGX-Listed Family Firms' (2013) DBS Bank Ltd and Centre for Governance, Institutions and Organisations 8, copy on file with author. In this study, based on the annual reports of 692 firms as of 2011, Dieleman et al. classified approximately 60.8 per cent of the firms as family firms. Family firms are defined in the study as those firms where the (co-)founders or their family members are present amongst the twenty largest shareholders or as board members.

42 See Christopher Chen, 'Solving the Puzzle of Corporate Governance of State-Owned Enterprises: The Path of the Temasek Model in Singapore and Lessons for China' (2016) 36 Northwestern Journal of International Law & Business 303.

43 A list of some of the key investments are found in www.temasekreview.com.sg/our-major-investments/financial-services.html accessed 23 February 2022.

44 See e.g. Adriana de la Cruz, A Medina and Y. Tang, 'Owners of the World's Listed Companies' (2019) OECD Capital Market Series, www.oecd.org/corporate/Owners-of-the-Worlds-Listed-Companies.htm accessed 23 February 2022 (Table A.3 shows that institutional investors owned approximately 12 per cent of the listed companies in Singapore at the end of 2017, based on analysis of 195 listed companies representing approximately 83 per cent of market capitalization in Singapore).

45 Whilst de la Cruz, Medina and Tang show the proportion of shares held by 'free float' for Singapore, the free float is not confined to retail investors but also include other institutional shareholders who are not required to report their substantial shareholdings, as they hold less than 5 per cent of shares.

TABLE 7.1 *Shareholding structures of listed companies in Singapore*

Mean (median) of	2009–15
Total number of observations	721
Board size	7.00 (7)
Number of independent directors	3.38 (3)
Proportion of independent directors on the board	48.86% (50%)
Size of audit committee	3.25 (3)
Shareholding interests of largest beneficial owner (%)	40.72% (39.62%)

Source: Data from C. Chen and W. Y. Wan, 'Transnational Corporate Governance Codes: Lessons from Regulating Related Party Transactions in Hong Kong and Singapore' (2018) 36 *Chinese (Taiwan) Yearbook of International Law and Affairs* 56. The numbers in brackets refer to the median.

7.3 LEGAL MEANS OF SHAREHOLDER ENGAGEMENT

7.3.1 *Formal Powers: Calling for and Attending Meetings*

7.3.1.1 How Meetings Are Called

AGMs and EGMs are usually called by boards of directors. Under the SGX listing rules, ordinary resolutions require fourteen clear calendar days' notice, and special resolutions[46] require twenty-one clear calendar days' notice (clear days exclude the date of notice and the date of the meeting). The Companies Act specifies special notice periods in certain situations such as a proposal to remove the director of a public company, which requires twenty-eight calendar days' notice.[47] Practice Guidance 11 of the Corporate Governance Code stipulates that companies should give a longer notice period if the companies concerned have a number of overseas shareholders or if the matters in question are unduly complex.[48] The Companies Act also provides that shareholders may call for meetings (see Section 7.3.2 below).

Shareholders are entitled to attend a company's general meetings and to ask questions or speak on any resolution tabled at those meetings.[49] If they are unable to attend, they can appoint proxies. According to the Companies Act, a proxy need not be a shareholder, and a shareholder can appoint only two proxies (unless he or she is a designated intermediary). If the shareholder is a designated intermediary,[50] he or she may appoint more than two proxies to attend and vote at the general meeting as long as each proxy is appointed to exercise the rights attached to the different shares held by the shareholder. This provision is important for institutional shareholders, who typically appoint custodian firms to hold their shares, as they can request that the custodians designate them as proxies to attend general meetings.[51]

46 SGX listing rules, r. 704(15); Companies Act, s. 184. S. 184 does not have a reference to 'clear' days.
47 Companies Act, s. 185, read with s. 152.
48 Corporate Governance Code, Guidance 11.
49 Companies Act, s. 180(1).
50 Ibid., s. 181. Relevant intermediaries are allowed to appoint more than two proxies: (1) a licensed bank or its wholly owned subsidiary, which provides nominee services and holds shares in that capacity; (2) a capital market service; or (3) the Central Provident Fund Board (which holds the mandatory retirement contributions of Singapore residents).
51 Cf. M. Chan, 'Shareholder Activism Rises in Singapore' *Business Times* (20 May 2014).

7.3.1.2 Remote Meetings

Arising from the COVID-19 pandemic, the COVID 19 (Temporary Measures) 2020 came into force on 7 April 2020.[52] They allow for subsidiary legislation or orders to be made to provide for alternative meeting arrangements for the conduct of meetings where personal attendance is otherwise required under written law or legal instruments. Pursuant to the COVID 19 (Temporary Measures) (Alternative Arrangements for Meetings for Companies, Variable Capital Companies, Business Trusts, Unit Trusts and Debenture Holders) Order 2020, companies can continue to hold physical meetings as long as they do not breach prevailing safety measures. Alternatively, they can hold meetings remotely for a specified period,[53] as long as they comply with the checklist issued by the Accounting and Corporate Regulatory Authority (ACRA), which is the regulator for companies, the Monetary Authority of Singapore (MAS, the securities regulator) and the SGX.[54] The checklist required listed companies to publish notices of general meetings (on SGXNET and the company's website), specify particulars of the electronic means by which the meeting will be conducted (such as by a live webcast), the arrangements for shareholders to participate in the meeting by electronic means (such as a link to access the audio and/or video feed), whether preregistration is required, how questions are to be submitted ahead of the meeting and how votes are to be cast.[55] Shareholders must be given an opportunity to ask questions within a reasonable period of time prior to the general meeting.[56] Unless the listed company's constitution provides otherwise, shareholders must vote by proxy alone, and only the meeting chair may be appointed as proxy.[57] If the constitution allows for remote electronic voting, such voting can take place, although the company must ensure that safeguards are incorporated to ensure that only valid votes are counted.[58] The company must publish the minutes of the meeting, which should record comments or queries relating to the meeting agenda.[59]

At the date of writing, the regulators continue to allow hybrid physical and remote meetings and there is some indication that such arrangements may continue post-COVID 19.[60] Some corporate governance commentators have expressed concerns, however, that virtual meetings do not permit the free flow of discussion amongst management, advisers and shareholders that occurs in physical meetings,[61] and it remains to be seen whether such hybrid arrangements will be allowed to continue.

52 COVID 19 (Temporary Measures) Act 2020.

53 As of the date of writing, companies can hold remote meetings until the 2020 order is revoked by the Ministry of Law.

54 The current checklist is available at www.sgx.com/media-centre/20200413-additional-guidance-conduct-general-meetings-during-safe-management-period accessed 23 February 2022.

55 Ibid.

56 Ibid.

57 Ibid.

58 Ibid.

59 Ibid.

60 See ACRA, 'Updated Guidance on the Conduct of General Meetings Amid Evolving COVID-19 Situation', 4 February 2022, www.acra.gov.sg/announcements/acra's-support-measures-and-guidance-for-businesses-during-covid-19 accessed 23 February 2022. See Rae Wee, 'Virtual, Hybrid Shareholder Meetings Could Be Here to Stay: SGX, MAS' *Business Times* (13 October 2020) www.businesstimes.com.sg/companies-markets/virtual-hybrid-shareholder-meetings-could-be-here-to-stay-sgx-mas accessed 23 February 2022.

61 Ibid. Under the Corporate Governance Code, Practice Guidance 11, the meeting chair 'should facilitate constructive dialogue between shareholders and the Board, Management, external auditors and other relevant professionals. The Chairman should allow specific directors, such as board committee chairs or the lead independent director, to answer queries on matters related to their roles. Directors should take the opportunity to interact with shareholders before and/or after general meetings'.

7.3.2 *Shareholder Proposal Rights*

Beyond the calling of shareholder meetings by directors, the Companies Act also provides for situations in which shareholders can requisition meetings. Shareholders holding in aggregate 10 per cent of the paid-up capital of the company and shares carrying voting rights can requisition directors to call for an EGM.[62] Alternatively, they can directly call for a meeting themselves.[63] In requisitioning a meeting, the shareholders must give directors up to twenty-one days to convene the meeting, but it must take place no later than two months after receipt of the requisition notice.[64] Whilst it might be more expedient for shareholders to directly call a meeting, if they do so they bear the costs, even if the resolution turns out to be successful. In addition, shareholders holding no less than 5 per cent of total voting rights or comprising at least 100 shareholders holding shares on which there is an average paid-up sum per member of at least S$500, can requisition the company to circulate, along with the agenda for the next AGM, notice of resolutions concerning matters that the shareholders intend to table at that meeting.[65]

The effect of these provisions is that, at least in theory, shareholders have a powerful right to include items on the agendas of shareholder meetings. Whilst it might be argued that the right of minority shareholders to requisition a meeting or place items on the agenda may not be meaningful in the presence of a controlling shareholder, Section 7.4 below details cases in which shareholder requisition rights have in fact been exercised, illustrating that shareholders do indeed exercise these rights, most likely because they want to see directors address public criticism of the manner in which they have conducted their actions.

7.3.3 *Voting, Majorities and Special Meetings*

Shareholder approval is required for a number of corporate actions, including the appointment of directors, the disposal of substantially all assets,[66] the issuance of new voting shares (including pursuant to share option schemes),[67] the amendment of the company's constitution,[68] a capital reduction[69] and share buybacks.[70]

Unless otherwise specified, resolutions at shareholder meetings take the form of either ordinary or special resolutions. Ordinary resolutions require approval by only a simple majority of votes of shareholders who vote in person or by proxy, whereas special resolutions require a majority of no less than 75 per cent of shareholders voting in person or by proxy. All resolutions are ordinary resolutions unless the Companies Act specifies that the matter concerned requires a special resolution (such as the amendment of the company's constitution).[71] A company constitution may, although it is rare, specify a different majority for resolution approval. All resolutions at the general meetings of listed companies must be voted on by poll (unless such a requirement is waived by the SGX).[72]

62 Companies Act, s. 176.
63 Ibid., s. 177.
64 Ibid., s. 176(2).
65 Ibid., s. 183.
66 Ibid., s. 160.
67 Ibid., s. 161.
68 Ibid., s. 26.
69 Ibid., s. 78G.
70 Ibid., ss. 76A–76E.
71 Ibid., s. 26.
72 SGX listing rules, r. 730A.

Both the appointment of directors[73] and the removal of directors[74] take place by ordinary resolution. Director appointments must be voted on individually.[75] Company constitutions typically specify that one-third of directors will stand for election at the AGM.[76] It is not possible to contract out of the provisions on the removal of directors by the constitution or by way of an agreement.[77] Accordingly, staggered boards are not permitted because any of their directors can be removed by shareholder resolution.

In certain other special decisions that require shareholder approval, the Companies Act specifies a higher threshold. For instance, in a scheme of arrangement under section 210 Companies Act,[78] the approval required is a majority both in terms of the number of shareholders (by headcount) and in representing 75 per cent in value of shares. In a scheme of arrangement whereby shareholders are asked to approve proposals that rearrange or compromise their rights (such as asking shareholders to transfer their shares to an acquirer in return for payment), such an arrangement is binding on all shareholders, including dissenting shareholders, if the requisite approval is obtained and the court sanctions the scheme. For that reason, a higher threshold is required, including one that requires a majority by shareholder number. Schemes of arrangement also contain other safeguards. For example, if the proposal for a scheme is made in the context of a takeover or merger transaction that is subject to the Takeover Code, the Takeover Code specifically requires that the acquirer and the parties acting in concert with the acquirer who hold shares in the target company abstain from voting at the scheme meeting.[79]

7.3.4 *Controversy over Dual-Class Shares: Investor Choice and Investor Protection*

One recent development has been the allowing of DCS to be listed on the SGX. The SGX is widely seen as having difficulty maintaining its edge in the capital markets when it comes to attracting new listings, not only relative to the Stock Exchange of Hong Kong (SEHK), the SGX's traditional rival, whose market capitalization is considerably deeper than that of the SGX,[80] but also relative to other regional exchanges in Southeast Asia.[81] In 2014, the Companies Act was amended to allow public companies to issue shares with multiple voting rights. However, it was only in 2018 that the SGX amended its listing rules to permit listed companies to issue DCS,[82] although as of the date of writing, no company issuing DCS has yet listed on the exchange.

73 Ibid., s. 149A.
74 Ibid., s. 149B.
75 Ibid., s. 150. It is possible for director appointments to be voted as a single resolution if agreed by the meeting without any vote against.
76 Model Constitution, art. 67.
77 Companies Act, s. 152.
78 Ibid., s. 210.
79 Singapore Code on Takeovers and Mergers, Definitions, para. 12. See, generally, Wan and Varottil, *Mergers and Acquisitions in Singapore: Law and Practice* (n. 13). Parties act in concert with the acquirer if there is an agreement, arrangement or understanding to obtain control of the target company through the acquisition of shares: see Singapore Code on Takeovers and Mergers, Definitions, para. 1.
80 As of the end of 2018, the Stock Exchange of Hong Kong (SEHK) has three times the number of companies listed as the SGX, and the aggregate market capitalization of companies listed on the SEHK is approximately 4.5 times that of SGX's. Source: World Federation of Exchanges, www.world-exchanges.org accessed 23 February 2022.
81 E. Wilson, 'SGX Scrambles for Listings' *Euromoney* (27 February 2019).
82 See, generally, Robin Hui Huang, Wei Zhang and Kelvin Siu Cheung Lee, 'The (<loc>Re)introduction of Dual-class Share Structures in Hong Kong: A Historical and Comparative Analysis' (2020) 20 Journal of Corporate Law Studies 121.

The reason for the delay in the SGX's introduction of the DCS framework is that the framework is highly controversial. DCS are inimical to shareholder empowerment because they allow a minority of shareholders to have disproportionate voting rights, and they run counter to the idea that voting power should be directly correlated with economic rights. The DCS structure allows insider-minorities to entrench themselves and become takeover-proof. However, DCS are not uncommon in the United States (e.g. for such tech giants as Alibaba and Facebook). The justification for them is that there are successful examples of companies with DCS structures, and investors should be allowed to choose the kinds of companies in which they wish to invest as long as the appropriate disclosures are made. In Singapore, the main concern with DCS is that they represent a race to the bottom[83] and allow for an insider-minority to engage in tunnelling, with critics thus arguing that they should not be permitted.

Ultimately, after lengthy debate, it was the SEHK's decision to allow DCS listings, which itself sparked considerable controversy,[84] that prompted the SGX to follow suit. Prior to 2018, the SEHK disallowed DCS amongst its listed companies. However, the stock exchange market for listings is highly competitive. In 2013, Alibaba, which was considering an initial public offering (IPO) and listing on the SEHK, demanded a weighted voting rights structure (similar to the DCS structure). When SEHK denied its application, Alibaba listed on the New York Stock Exchange instead and raised an unprecedented US$25 billion in its IPO. The loss to the Hong Kong market of the Alibaba IPO prompted a review by the SEHK, which, after several rounds of consultation, announced the new DCS listing framework in April 2018.

Singapore quickly followed suit, announcing its DCS framework in June 2018. However, a series of measures were put in place to mitigate some of the disadvantages of DCS.[85] In particular, for investor protection purposes, only new companies listing on the SGX for the first time are permitted to have a DCS structure, and there is a maximum voting differential, that is, a maximum of ten votes per share is permitted.[86] Holders of weighted voting shares are not able to transfer their shares until after a moratorium.[87] Further, non-weighted voting shareholders may requisition a meeting if they hold a minimum of 10 per cent of voting rights on a one-share-one-vote basis,[88] so as not to deprive ordinary shareholders of their right to call management and the board to account at general meetings. For certain resolutions, such as the appointment and removal of independent directors and a variation in class rights, all shares carry one vote per share, irrespective of the DCS structure.[89] There is also a sunset clause requiring weighted voting shares to be converted to ordinary shares in certain instances such as when shares are transferred outside the original group.[90]

The move by the SGX to allow DCS listings was driven largely by a desire to keep pace with the global capital market, attract listings from new technology companies and afford investors greater choice. However, these aims had to be balanced against potential erosion of the rights available to protect minority shareholders. That balance was struck by implementing a framework that allows for DCS but attempts to mitigate some of the worst features of DCS outcomes.

83 See D. Smith, 'Singapore Risks a Race to the Bottom with Dual Class Shares' *Financial Times* (16 March 2017).
84 See discussion in Huang, Zhang and Lee (n. 81).
85 SGX, 'SGX Launches Rules for Listing of Dual Class Companies' (26 June 2018), https://api2.sgx.com/sites/default/files/news-releases/migration/sgx_launches_rules_for_listing_of_dual_class_shares_companies.pdf accessed 23 February 2022.
86 See SGX listing rules, rule 210, http://rulebook.sgx.com/rulebook/210 accessed 23 February 2022.
87 Ibid.
88 Ibid.
89 Ibid.
90 Ibid.

At the time of writing, only one company, AMTD International Inc, which has a dual class structure, is listed on SGX. However, it is still too early to determine whether the move will in fact attract quality listings given the restrictive framework in place.

7.3.5 *Questions and Information Request Rights*

Shareholders enjoy only those information rights that are specified in the company constitution or by the Companies Act. Under the Companies Act, shareholders can access the registers of companies, including the registers of directors, CEOs, secretaries and auditors.[91] They also have access to the register of charges to afford them information on assets that are being mortgaged or otherwise encumbered.[92] Public companies (including listed companies) are required to keep shareholder registers, which shareholders can access upon request and the payment of a fee.[93] Shareholders also have access to the minutes of general meetings.[94] However, their access to financial information is limited. Shareholders have access to audited (or consolidated) financial statements and balance sheets, which are required to be tabled before shareholders at the general meeting,[95] and they can obtain unaudited financial statements that are released pursuant to the requirement of a periodic announcement under the SGX listing rules. Shareholders do not, however, have the right to inspect the company's accounting records or the minutes of board meetings,[96] and generally do not have access to related party transactions (RPTs) entered into unless they are material transactions requiring shareholder approval, as outlined in Section 7.4.1.1.4 below. It should be noted that the Companies Act prohibits Singapore companies from issuing bearer shares and share warrants.[97]

7.4 SHAREHOLDER ENGAGEMENT AND VOTING IN PRACTICE

7.4.1 *Voting in Practice*

7.4.1.1 Who Votes and What Issues Are Voted on?

HOW SHAREHOLDERS VOTE IN PROPOSALS Few empirical data is available on the voting records of shareholders at AGMs and EGMs in Singapore. However, a study led by Mak Yuen Teen and Chew Yi Hong on AGMs in 2016 reported that, for the 415 AGMs that had poll results, the average percentage of shares voted was approximately 58 per cent.[98] For thirty listed companies, less than 20 per cent of shares were voted at the AGM. However, the major limitation of this study was that there was insufficient information to determine whether the shareholders who voted were the existing controlling shareholders or public shareholders, making it difficult to ascertain the level of shareholder engagement in Singapore.

91 Companies Act, s. 173.
92 Ibid., s. 138.
93 Ibid., s. 192.
94 Ibid., s. 189. For listed companies, the Corporate Governance Code, 'Shareholder Rights and Conduct of Meetings', provides for the posting of meeting minutes on the company's website.
95 Companies Act, s. 203.
96 Ibid., s. 199.
97 Ibid., s. 66.
98 Mak Yuen Teen and Chew Yi Hong, 'The Singapore Report on Shareholder Meetings: Dawn of Activism' (March 2017), copy on file with author.

SHARE ISSUANCE MANDATES The aforementioned study[99] found that shareholder proposals relating to a mandate to directors to issue shares received the least shareholder support, with a small number of cases in which shareholder approval of such a mandate was not obtained, which is a rarity in Singapore. Listed companies are permitted under the SGX listing rules to obtain the approval of shareholders for a mandate to issue new shares at directors' discretion for the period until the next AGM (assuming that the resolution is not revoked before then).[100] Until 2020, the limit was that the new shares to be issued did not exceed 50 per cent on a pro rata basis and 20 per cent on a non-pro rata basis. This general mandate is very useful for directors in the event that the company needs to raise funds, as they will not need to obtain shareholder approval again.[101] However, in cases where shares are issued on a non-pro rata basis, existing shareholders are diluted, and thus are likely to be concerned unless good justifications are given. In fact, the influential Institutional Shareholders Services recommends that shareholders vote in favour of a share issuance mandate if the non-pro rata limit is 10 per cent.[102] Mak and Chew pointed out that five of the issuers in their 2016 study did not manage to get their share issuance mandate approved under the pre-2020 limits. In 2005, three of the issuers did not approve the share issue mandate under those limits. Further, forty-six issuers voluntarily reduced their pro-rata and/or non-pro rata limits. Their study thus suggests that blanket mandates to directors by shareholders in excess of 10 per cent are unlikely to be welcome unless there is engagement by directors, who have to give detailed explanations as to the rationale for seeking such a mandate from shareholders. (In view of COVID-19, and in order to support businesses needing to raise funds on an accelerated basis, the SGX announced on 8 April 2020 that the limit would be temporarily increased to 100 per cent for shares issued on a pro rata basis until 31 December 2021.[103])

EXECUTIVE REMUNERATION Singapore has not moved towards affording shareholders a 'say on pay', although shareholders vote on directors' fees and employee share option schemes. With respect to the former, section 169 Companies Act requires that 'emoluments' in respect of a director's office, or enhancements thereto, may be provided to directors only if they have been approved by a resolution that is 'not related to other matters'.[104] The latter is required under the SGX listing rules.[105] However, executive renumeration (as distinct from directors' fees) is not subject to a shareholder vote, and nor is it required to be disclosed mandatorily. Instead, it is subject to voluntary disclosure under the requirements of the Corporate Governance Code. In its review of the Corporate Governance Code, the Corporate Governance Council considered, but ultimately rejected, requiring an advisory vote on 'say on pay' on various grounds, including that it was not necessary for Singapore at that point in time and that executive remuneration would be better dealt with via enhanced disclosure on the remuneration structure and its link to

99 Ibid.

100 SGX listing rules, r. 806.

101 This applies to situations of pro-rata share issuance or issuance to a new investor, where the new investor is unconnected to the company or to the director or his/her associates. If the new investor is a director or his/her associate, specific shareholder approval is required under SGX listing rules, r. 804.

102 Institutional Shareholder Services, 'Singapore Proxy Voting Guidelines', www.issgovernance.com/file/policy/active/asiapacific/Singapore-Voting-Guidelines.pdf accessed 23 February 2022.

103 SGX, 'SGX RegCo Announces Measures to Support Issuers amid Challenging COVID-19 Business Climate', www.sgx.com/media-centre/20200408-sgx-regco-announces-measures-support-issuers-amid-challenging-covid-19 accessed 15 July 2020.

104 'Emoluments' are defined as including fees, allowances for expenses chargeable to income tax, contributions under any pension scheme and non-cash benefits attributable to services as a director: Companies Act, s. 4.

105 SGX listing rules, ch. 8.

value creation at the company.[106] Such enhancement aimed at improving the disclosure of remuneration to allow shareholders to better engage with directors at AGMs.

Would adopting a 'say on pay' policy facilitate more informative disclosures of executive remuneration to shareholders? At first sight, it appears that such a policy would be a blunt tool given that existing controlling shareholders would be incentivized to monitor executive pay and that the evidence on the impact of 'say on pay' is mixed. Burns et al. have shown that the overall compensation in a sample of US firms did not change after the implementation of 'say on pay', although the components did, with a shift towards incentive payments.[107] By way of comparison, early evidence in the UK suggests that advisory 'say on pay' has limited effects on the excessive remuneration of CEOs.[108] Changes introduced in the UK in 2013 included a binding vote on remuneration policy.[109] However, it could be argued that expressly implementing such a policy could at least improve the level of disclosure of executive remuneration and its link to overall value creation at the company.

SHAREHOLDER VOTING IN CONFLICTED SITUATIONS In situations in which directors have proposed transactions that involve the company and its directors or controlling shareholders, the SGX listing rules intervene specifically. In these RPTs, the concern that regulators have is that directors may engage in tunnelling, and yet such transactions can be beneficial to the company. The principles of the Organisation for Economic Co-operation and Development (OECD) stipulate that '[r]elated party transactions should be approved and conducted in a manner that ensures proper management of conflict[s] of interests and protects the interests of the company and the shareholders'.[110]

Singapore's regulatory framework regulates RPTs using a number of measures, including disclosures and audit committee review and approval (in ensuring that the transactions are at arm's length and on normal commercial terms). Further, where the transactions concerned exceed 5 per cent of net tangible assets, the SGX listing rules stipulate that they require an opinion from independent financial advisers (IFAs) and are subject to shareholder approval. Only independent shareholders can vote on RPTs, which are classified as 'interested party transactions' (IPTs) under the listing rules.[111] (The definition of IPTs is slightly different from that of RPTs, which is an accounting term.) These measures are similar to those used in the UK[112] and in Hong Kong.[113] Transactions with interested persons (including controlling shareholders and directors and their respective associates) are subject to these rules. If there are recurring transactions, companies are permitted to obtain annual mandates from shareholders to approve the transactions, subject to such constraints as an overall cap, and the transactions must

106 Monetary Authority of Singapore, *Recommendations of the Corporate Governance Council* (April 2018), www.mas.gov.sg/-/media/MAS/Regulations-and-Financial-Stability/Regulatory-and-Supervisory-Framework/Corporate-Governance-of-Listed-Companies/Consultation-2018-Jan-16/Response-to-consult/Response-paper-on-Councils-recommendations.pdf accessed 23 February 2022.

107 Natasha Burns and Kristina Minnick, 'Does Say-on-Pay Matter? Evidence from Say-on-Pay Proposals in the United States' (2013) 48 The Financial Review 233.

108 Martin Conyon and Graham Sadler, 'Shareholder Voting and Directors' Remuneration Report Legislation: Say on Pay in the UK' (2010) 18 Corporate Governance: An International Review 296.

109 Carsten Gerner-Beuerle and Tom Kirchmaier, 'Say on Pay: Do Shareholders Care?', https://papers.ssrn.com/sol3/papers.cfm?abstract_id=2720481 accessed 23 February 2022.

110 OECD principle II(F).

111 SGX listing rules, ch. 9.

112 See, generally, Luca Enriques et al., ' Related Party Transactions' in Reinier H. Kraakman et al., *The Anatomy of Corporate Law: A Comparative and Functional Approach* (3rd ed., Oxford University Press 2017) ch. 6.

113 See, generally, Chen and Wan (n. 40).

take place in the ordinary course of business.[114] These annual mandates are typically obtained at the company's AGM.

How significant are RPTs in practice in Singapore? A previous study conducted by myself and others involved a random sample of 25 per cent of the companies listed in Singapore during two periods: 2002–4 and 2009–15. (The difference in the length of the two periods was a result of comparability and data availability. Singapore's accounting rules underwent significant changes during the 2005–8 period, thus rendering a comparison of RPTs undertaken prior to 2005 and after 2008 meaningless, and annual reports prior to 2002 could not be reliably obtained. Hence, the comparison was made for 2002–4 and the period after 2008.) We found that RPTs continue to be substantial, and that they increased in volume over the two periods.[115] The mean in 2009–15 (US$111.90 million) was much higher than that in 2002–4 (US$63.31 million), largely owing to some extremely large observations in the later years. However, the data also revealed a large disparity in RPTs, with 19 per cent of the companies reporting no RPTs at all during the 2009–15 period. These results point to the challenges of regulating different types of listed companies. Hence, the solution selected was to mandate that material transactions require the approval of independent shareholders.

However, challenges remain with respect to ensuring that independent shareholders in fact receive relevant information before they vote on proposals to approve RPTs. In theory, IFAs produce a report that is delivered to the independent directors of the company, and then made known to shareholders, which allows the latter to decide how to vote based on both the directors' recommendations and the IFAs' opinion. In practice, independent directors adopt IFA recommendations in full when making their own recommendations.[116] IFAs also face a number of inherent conflicts of interest that tend to favour the issuing of opinions favourable to the existing management. In all but one of the IFA opinions obtained in the aforementioned study (seven in 2002–4 and 123 in 2009–15), independent directors were advised to recommend that shareholders vote in favour of the IPT resolution. In the sole exception, independent directors were advised only to caution shareholders to read and carefully consider the IPT resolution but did not explicitly recommend dissent.[117]

There is little comprehensive empirical evidence available to ascertain how shareholders vote on IPT resolutions. In Mak and Chew's study, none of the resolutions relating to IPTs was rejected by shareholders in 2016. Whether that outcome indicates that the current situation is satisfactory to investors is unclear. One possible explanation is that directors and audit committees are careful in their explanations to independent shareholders about the rationale for such transactions. However, it should be pointed out that a number of fraud cases in recent years relate to the non-disclosure or inadequate disclosure of RPTs and IPTs, which may indicate that disclosure problems persist.[118]

In addition to IPTs, there is another kind of transaction that does not appear to be an IPT (as it does not involve companies transacting with controlling shareholders) but is regulated as if it were, that is, a transaction in which the company is seeking to delist itself from the SGX. Delisting proposals are carefully scrutinized by the SGX, as they may amount to a de facto

114 SGX listing rules, ch. 9.

115 See Chen and Wan (n. 40).

116 See, generally, Wai Yee Wan, 'Independent Financial Advisers' Opinions for Public Takeovers and Related Party Transactions in Singapore' (2012) 30 Company and Securities Law Journal 32.

117 Chen and Wan (n. 40).

118 See, generally, Wai Yee Wan et al., 'Managing the Risks of Corporate Fraud: The Evidence from Hong Kong and Singapore' (2018) 48 Hong Kong Law Journal 125.

compulsory acquisition of shares by controlling shareholders.[119] Prior to July 2019, controlling shareholders seeking a buyout could choose to first propose that the company be delisted and then make an exit offer thereafter.[120] The rationale was that once the company had been delisted, shareholders would be motivated to accept the exit offer. In the delisting proposal put to a vote, the approval threshold, as it then applied, was 75 per cent approval, with no more than 10 per cent of shareholders objecting. In practice, delisting proposals generally passed because controlling shareholders could and often did vote in favour. Whilst the SGX required that the exit offer be reasonable, IFAs in practice readily offered the opinion that offers were reasonable even though the price was at a significant discount to the net asset value of the company.[121] Recent research also suggests that minority shareholders are worse off in terms of the premium that they obtain for their shares compared with other forms of buyout.[122] In 2019, after lengthy consultation,[123] the SGX amended the rules to further strengthen the protection of minority shareholders.[124] Delisting offers are now effectively treated as IPTs, meaning that the delisting proposal must be approved by 75 per cent of the shares held by independent shareholders present and voting. The controlling shareholder making the bid and the parties in concert cannot vote. In addition, the offer must not only be reasonable; it must also be fair.

7.4.1.2 Shareholder Proposals and Proxy Fights

I have outlined the methods that shareholders can use to directly call for directors to convene a shareholder meeting to vote on a proposal. Given the dominance in Singapore of companies with concentrated shareholdings, conventional theory suggests that these methods should be rarely used, as the presence of a controlling shareholder would make it difficult if not impossible for a minority shareholder to succeed. In this section, I present an account of research on shareholder requisitions in practice, which occur despite the largely concentrated shareholdings amongst listed companies. I also argue that extralegal considerations are important in encouraging minority shareholders to act.

In prior work,[125] my co-authors and I examined a database of shareholder requisition filings made during the 2008–15 period for companies listed on the SGX. My analysis focused on complaints linked to governance failures, that is, shareholder complaints that directors were in breach of their duties or involved in fraud investigations. A total of twenty-five requisitions were filed, of which nine were governance related. Table 7.2 provides further details. In unreported results, it was found that the shareholdings of the requisitioning shareholders ranged from 11.1–25 per cent and that in five of the nine cases, the requisitioning shareholders were not the largest

119 See e.g. 'Cheap Buyout Plans in Singapore? Not So Quick, Say Minority Shareholders' *Straits Times* (28 March 2016).

120 See Christopher C. H. Chen, Wei Zhang and Wai Yee Wan, 'Regulating Squeeze-out Techniques by Controlling Shareholders: The Divergence between Hong Kong and Singapore' (2018) 18 Journal of Corporate Law Studies 185.

121 Ibid.

122 Ibid.

123 SGX, 'Consultation Paper on Proposed Voluntary Amendments to Voluntary Delisting Regime' (9 November 2018), www.sgx.com/regulation/public-consultations/20181109-consultation-paper-proposed-amendments-voluntary-delisting accessed 23 February 2022.

124 SGX, 'SGX RegCo Requires Exit Offers to Be Fair and Reasonable, Shareholder Vote to Exclude Offeror and Concert Parties' (11 July 2019), www2.sgx.com/media-centre/20190711-sgx-regco-requires-exit-offers-be-fair-and-reasonable-shareholder-vote accessed 23 February 2022.

125 Wai Yee Wan, Christopher C. H. Chen and Say H. Goo, 'Public and Private Enforcement of Corporate and Securities Laws: An Empirical Comparison of Hong Kong and Singapore' (2019) 20 European Business Organization Law Review 319.

TABLE 7.2 *Shareholder requisitions filed with SGX*

	Number of requisitions	Of which are governance related; i.e. shareholders complained that the directors were in breach of their duties or involved in fraud investigations
2008	3	3
2009	6	1
2010	2	0
2011	4	2
2012	2	0
2013	3	1
2014	1	0
2015	4	2
	25	9

Source: W. Y. Wan, C. Chen and S. H. Goo, 'Public and Private Enforcement of Corporate and Securities Laws: An Empirical Comparison of Hong Kong and Singapore' (2019) 20 *European Business Organization Law Review* 319.

shareholders (suggesting that they would fail). Thus, even though the number is small, there are shareholders who file requisitions even though they are unlikely to succeed, a finding suggesting that shareholders do so in order to criticize the decision-making of directors or highlight their less-than-exemplary behaviour. This finding contrasts with the findings of other scholars suggesting the lack of an activist culture amongst shareholders in Singapore.[126]

A more recent example of a successful shareholder requisition involved the Magnus Energy Group. In 2019, a group of minority shareholders, frustrated with the company's performance and the depressed share price of the company, had gathered enough votes to reject all of the resolutions tabled before the AGM, including resolutions to adopt the company's financial statements, to reappoint three of the directors, to grant a share issuance mandate, to pay the directors' fees and to appoint auditors.[127] Several minority shareholders holding at least 10 per cent of shares in aggregate then proceeded to requisition the shareholder meeting relating to the appointment of their own nominated directors, and they were successful in obtaining enough votes to pass their own resolutions.[128]

7.4.1.3 Who Is Involved in Shareholder Activism?

In this section, I detail several recent cases of high-profile shareholder activism in Singapore. In addition to the foregoing case involving the Magnus Energy Group, two further examples are given here. The first is Noble Group Ltd. Noble was a Bermuda-incorporated company that was listed on the SGX. It was a blue-chip commodity giant in Asia in its heyday. In 2015, a report was issued questioning the company's financial reporting and highlighting a number of

[126] Cf. Y. T. Mak, 'Responsible Shareholder Activism?' *Business Times* (9 October 2012) (arguing that at times, shareholders may exercise the right to requisition for their own ends to the detriment of the company).

[127] Magnus Energy Group Ltd., 'Results of the AGM on 30 October 2019', https://links.sgx.com/FileOpen/Ann%20-%20Magnus%20Results%20AGM%202019%20.ashx?App=Announcement&FileID=583717 accessed 23 February 2022.

[128] Magnus Energy Group, 'Results of the AGM on 9 January 2020', https://links.sgx.com/1.0.0/corporate-announcements/LD6PB5MIKSMDU9ER/93495b565173a2b4f8e84ae021df6b300e2baf636c7d4f98a72828d7635a107e accessed 23 February 2022.

irregularities.[129] Shortly thereafter, Noble ran into severe financial difficulties. In 2018, the company entered into a debt restructuring plan that would dilute the existing shareholders to just 10 per cent while management would receive 20 per cent of the restructured enterprise. In the event that shareholders voted against the plan, Noble would complete the restructuring by selling its assets to a new company, and the shareholders who voted in favour would receive shares in the new restructured enterprise, whereas those who voted against would receive none. Shareholders were outraged, particularly given that management was alleged to have caused the company's failure. The unfairness of the provision that only supportive shareholders would receive shares was singled out for particular criticism.[130]

One of the minority shareholders, Goldilocks Investments Co., filed an application for a declaration that it was entitled to propose directors for election to Noble's board and an injunction to stop the company from holding its AGM.[131] However, at the time of the injunction, Goldilocks held 8.1 per cent of its shares through a nominee company, which in turn held the shares through the Central Depository (CDP).[132] A dispute arose as to whether Goldilocks had standing to file such an application as it did not hold the shares directly with the CDP. The court granted the interim injunction, giving Goldilocks time to register the shares directly.[133] Ultimately, in June 2018, a revised restructuring arrangement was proposed that gave shareholders 20 per cent of the restructured enterprise, with management receiving 10 per cent.[134] In addition, Goldilocks was to have a board seat in the restructured entity.[135] The arrangement was approved, and the restructuring was completed at the end of 2018.[136]

The second example is the case of Hyflux Ltd., a Singapore company which operated water treatment plants around the world. Hyflux ran into severe financial difficulties and entered into a restructuring agreement with Salim Medco, which would have resulted in a deep haircut for preference shareholders and the holders of perpetual capital securities. Accordingly, these two groups protested against the arrangement, prompting Singapore's leading investor group, the Securities Investors Association (Singapore) (SIAS) to become involved. Amongst other things, SIAS questioned the board on its accountability[137] and submitted an alternative proposal. Hyflux responded by agreeing to change the terms to 'balance the competing legal and commercial interests',[138] and eventually declared that it would not go ahead with the agreement with Salim Medco.[139] At the time of writing, the restructuring did not proceed and the company is now in liquidation.

129 A. Soh, 'Noble Saga Offers Lessons for Singapore Capital Markets' *Business Times* (24 May 2018).

130 A. Soh, 'Noble's Board: Restructuring Plan "Fair and Equitable" to All Shareholders' *Business Times* (27 March 2018).

131 A. Soh and R. Mui, 'Goldilocks Sues to Stop Noble AGM and Further Restructuring Work' *Straits Times* (26 April 2018).

132 *Goldilocks Investment Co Ltd* v. *Noble Group Ltd* [2018] SGHC 108. CDP is a central depository system where shareholders hold scripless shares through the system.

133 Ibid.

134 A. Gabriel, 'Noble Group Rescue; Noble Shareholders Back Crucial Rescue Plan but Challenges Still Abound' *Business Times* (28 August 2018).

135 A. Gabriel, 'New Dawn for Noble as Goldilocks Ends Trench Fight over Debt Revamp' *Business Times* (21 June 2018).

136 'Noble Group Sets aside US$800m in New Money Debt for New Noble as Restructuring Takes Effect' *Straits Times* (20 December 2018).

137 Bei Yi Seow, 'Hyflux Queried over CEO's Remuneration' *Straits Times* (11 February 2019).

138 Grace Leong, 'Hyflux Retail Investors Want Fairer Share of Assets: SIAS' *Straits Times* (1 March 2019).

139 Grace Leong, 'Hyflux Calls Off Rescue Plan, Citing "No Confidence" Indonesian White Knight Will Complete Deal' *Straits Times* (4 April 2019).

7.4.2 *Use of Other Means of Engagement*

Retail shareholders in Singapore have historically relied on SIAS, an investor lobby group that represents retail investors, to engage with the management of companies. SIAS acts as a mediator between retail shareholders and management in resolving disputes, and is often resorted to when such shareholders lack the means to pursue litigation. SIAS prides itself on championing many shareholder rights issues behind the scenes in boardrooms.[140] However, there is little empirical evidence demonstrating the effectiveness of such behind-the-scenes activism.

Enforcement by means of litigation is rare amongst shareholders in Singapore. In theory, minority shareholders are entitled to commence derivative actions against directors suspected of wrongdoings in the name of the company under section 216A Companies Act. In recent research comprehensively reviewing private enforcement actions taken during the 2008–15 period, there was only one reported case, and the action was unsuccessful.[141] The rarity of litigation is likely attributable to the lack of a formal class-action procedure or contingency fee system in Singapore.

Shareholders can also bring a claim under section 216 Companies Act for minority oppression or unfair prejudice. Shareholders in companies incorporated in other jurisdictions and listed on the SGX can also rely on the functional equivalents of minority oppression or unfair prejudice in that section. In one case, action was brought by a minority shareholder in Kingboard Copper Foil Holdings Ltd., an SGX-listed company incorporated in Bermuda, which succeeded in the High Court in Bermuda but failed on appeal.[142] Kingboard had an ultimate majority shareholder, Kingboard Laminates Holdings (Laminates). Kingboard's main operation was supplying Laminates with copper foil, which was clearly an RPT. Pursuant to the SGX listing rules, Kingboard obtained an annual mandate from its independent shareholders to sell copper foil to Laminates and other companies within the Laminates group. However, in 2011, the petitioner, a hedge fund and minority shareholder in Kingboard, requisitioned a special general meeting to consider a resolution to appoint an independent auditor to investigate the historical transfer pricing. That resolution was defeated, but the minority shareholders refused to renew the mandate.

To address the problem, the company's wholly owned subsidiary, Hong Kong Copper Foil Limited, entered into a contract with a company called Harvest Resources Management Limited ('Harvest'), granting Harvest the exclusive right to use Kingboard's copper foil-producing business in return for a monthly fee. Harvest then sold copper foil to Kingboard Laminates Holdings Limited ('Laminates'). Harvest's directors had close ties with Kingboard and Laminates. The petitioner argued that the arrangement was a sham to evade the SGX listing rules. At the first instance, the court found against the petitioner on various grounds, including that the petitioner had not made its case that the pricing was unfair. The Supreme Court then ruled that the licence agreement was oppressive, as it constituted an attempt to get round the petitioner's right to veto the transaction. However, on appeal it was found that Kingboard's entry into the licensing fee arrangement was not a sham, but a legitimate way to address the veto and did not constitute oppressive conduct or unfair prejudice.[143]

140 D. Gerald, 'Shareholder Activism is Very Much Alive; "Quiet Engagement" Has Gotten Results but SIAS Also Unafraid to Lock Horns' *Today* (15 October 2010).

141 See Wan, Chen and Goo (n. 124). The one case was *Chua Swee Keng* v. *E3 Holdings* [2015] SGHC 22. (This was a derivative action taken after the company had been delisted from the SGX, but is included as it is a derivative action in respect of the conduct of senior management while the company was listed on the SGX.)

142 *Kingboard Chemical Holdings* v. *Annuity and Life Reassurance* CA 24 of 2015 (Supreme Court, Bermuda).

143 Ibid.

This case illustrates the challenges faced by the minority shareholders of a listed company that is transacting with its parent company. Much of the enforcement against wrongdoing committed by controlling shareholders or directors takes the form of public enforcement, that is, regulatory action taken by the regulators, including the MAS (as the securities regulator) and the SGX, or by prosecution for criminal offences.[144] Public enforcement, however, does not result in direct remedies for shareholders, as there may be instances in which the MAS uses its existing powers to incentivize wrongdoers to negotiate a settlement that would benefit shareholders.[145]

7.5 CONCLUDING REMARKS

In reviewing the extent of shareholder voting and empowerment in the Companies Act, we can see that shareholders have been granted considerable formal powers, including the power to appoint and remove a company's directors and requisition meetings. Whilst Singapore has not adopted a 'say on pay' advisory or binding vote, which is probably unnecessary in controlled companies, an advisory vote (rather than a binding vote) has the merits of improving the disclosure of executive remuneration and allowing shareholders to assess the performance of management relative to its remuneration. The SGX listing rules also ensure that a company can enter into (material) conflicted transactions with its directors or controlling shareholders only with the approval of independent shareholders. Similarly, the Takeover Code ensures that only independent shareholders can vote at the scheme meeting concerning conflicted transactions where the acquirer or parties in concert with it hold shares in the company.

Owing to concentrated voting structures, there are limits to how effectively these rights can be exercised in practice given the presence of controlling shareholders. However, this chapter demonstrates that in the exercise of both formal and informal powers, there are limited pockets of shareholder activism that occur despite the presence of controlling shareholders, some of which has resulted in positive outcomes for minority shareholders. Nevertheless, litigation as a means to enforce shareholder rights is rare.

There are two developments that are likely to prove important in the near future. First, following the introduction of the DCS framework, largely in response to the perceived market need to remain competitive, it remains to be seen whether that framework will weaken the framework for shareholder engagement and voting in practice. Second, the COVID-19 pandemic has resulted in changes to the regulatory framework to permit remote meetings, and it remains to be seen whether these changes will be made permanent and how remote meetings will affect the level of shareholder voting and engagement.

144 Wan, Chen and Goo (n. 124). For the enforcement of the takeover regulation, see Wai Yee Wan, 'Enforcing Public Takeover Regulation: Reconciling Public and Private Interests' (2019) 31 Singapore Academy of Law Journal 285.

145 Wan, Chen and Goo (n. 124) (citing the example of China Sky, where the regulators seized the assets of the wrongdoing controller who had been engaged in disclosure violations and the controller had to negotiate with the MAS to release the assets, and agreed to a settlement that benefitted the minority shareholders).

8

Shareholder Engagement and Voting in South Korea

Seung Young Yoon

8.1 INTRODUCTION: BRIEF HISTORY OF SHAREHOLDER ENGAGEMENT IN KOREA

Shareholder engagement in Korea began in the late 1990s with minority shareholder engagement campaigns driven by non-governmental organizations (NGOs), such as the People's Solidarity for Participatory Democracy (PSPD).[1] The PSPD filed a suit to revoke a shareholder resolution against Cheil Bank in 1997, and a shareholder derivative lawsuit against Samsung Electronics in 1998. Since then, the PSPD has initiated several shareholder campaigns, which included shareholder movements against Samsung Electronics and SK Telecom.[2] These constituted the first generation of shareholder engagement, which was the result of a growing number of activist shareholders in Korea. These efforts of shareholder engagement helped to improve corporate governance and maximize shareholder value.[3]

The second generation of shareholder engagement in Korea was driven by foreign funds. Shareholder engagement became more active, starting with the Tiger Fund against SK Telecom in 1999,[4] followed by the Sovereign Asset Management against SK in 2003, Hermes Investment Management against Samsung C&T in 2004 and Carl Icahn and Steel Partners against Korea Tobacco & Ginseng Corporation (KT&G) in 2006. In 2015, US hedge fund activist Elliott Management opposed the merger of Samsung C&T and Cheil Industries and filed a preliminary lawsuit (*Samsung C&T* v. *Elliot*).[5]

Domestic activist funds and institutional investors have recently been creating cases of shareholder engagement in Korea. The National Pension Service (NPS), one of Korea's largest institutional investors, has played a particularly important role in shareholder engagement in Korea. Following the adoption of its own stewardship code, the Principles on Stewardship of the

[1] The PSPD was founded in 1994 in Seoul by certain activists, scholars and lawyers who were engaged in various democratic movements for participatory democracy and human rights. PSPD's own website explains its purposes to include the promotion of the people's participation in government decision-making processes and socio-economic reforms, by closely monitoring the abuse of power of the state and corporations in an effort to enhance transparency and accountability. Kyung-Hoon Chun, 'Shareholder Activism in Korea: The Cases of PSPD and NPS' (30 April 2019) 8, available at https://ssrn.com/abstract=3432126. accessed 15 July 2020.

[2] Jooyoung Kim and Joongi Kim, 'Shareholder Activism in Korea: A Review of How PSPD Has Used Legal Measures to Strengthen Korean Corporate Governance' (2001) 1 Journal of Korean Law 52.

[3] Jooyoung Kim and Jeong Seo, 'Shareholder Activism & Engagement in Korea' (2019), available at www.lexology.com/library/detail.aspx?g=12814a23-6c6e-4304-a8a6-e2f7a4a8a229 accessed 15 July 2020.

[4] In August 1999, SK Group acquired 9.5 per cent of SK Telecom shares from Tiger Management, a New York-based fund. At an extraordinary general meeting due four days later, a plan for a rights issue proposed by the management was to proceed to a vote. The PSPD and Tiger Management had been in opposition to the plan. The SK Group's purchase of Tiger-held shares, however, made the group hold 36.5 per cent of SK Telecom shares and have the plan approved successfully. The PSPD criticized the decision of Tiger Managements.

[5] Seoul High Court Decision No. 2015Ra20458, rendered on 16 July 2015.

NPS, in July 2018, the NPS created a set of guidelines aimed at promoting active shareholder engagement to ensure responsible corporate management. According to these guidelines, the NPS allows itself to exercise shareholder rights against its investee companies more actively, pushing them to increase dividends and improve their corporate governance. Other domestic private equity funds are also becoming more active in practicing their rights as shareholders. This trend is expected to continue, as private equity funds are deregulated. For instance, domestic activist fund Korea Corporate Governance Improvement Fund (KCGI) acquired 16 per cent shares in Hanjin Kal Corp (the holding company of Hanjin Group) and 10 per cent shares in Hanjin (an affiliate company). KCGI subsequently called for Hanjin Kal to improve corporate governance, by highlighting well-publicized wrongdoings by the Cho family – the largest shareholder of Hanjin Group – including alleged criminal activities and workplace harassment cases.

Currently, the Korean government has been reinforcing laws and regulations to improve transparency in the investment structures of large business groups as well as their corporate management, in an effort to strengthen shareholders' rights in individual companies. Shareholder engagement has been on the rise, demanding improved corporate governance, financial structures, corporate social responsibilities and shareholder returns. In this changing landscape of the regulatory environment and capital market, the notion of maintaining effective communication and constructive relationships with domestic and foreign shareholders, including institutional and private investors in the capital market, is gaining importance.[6]

This chapter aims to review the engagement and voting behaviour of shareholders in Korea and their position in Korean corporate law. Section 8.1 provides general information on the Korean corporate law framework and the role of the board and shareholders. Section 8.2 reviews the legal means of shareholder engagement in Korea. Further, this research focuses on shareholder engagement in the general meeting of shareholders. Section 8.3 reviews the practice of shareholder engagement and voting in Korea on the basis of recent statistics. Finally, Section 8.4 concludes with some closing remarks.

8.1.1 *Korean Corporate Law: An Overview*

Corporate governance is principally regulated by the Korean Commercial Code (KCC) and the Code's primary enforcing authority is the Ministry of Justice. Korean listed companies are also regulated by the Financial Investment Services and Capital Markets Act (FISCMA) that is primarily enforced by the Financial Supervisory Commission and the Financial Supervisory Service.

Under the KCC, five types of corporate entities can be set up under Korean law: general partnership (*hapmyung hoesa*), limited partnership (*hapja hoesa*), limited liability company (*yuhan chaekim hoesa*), joint stock company (*chusik hoesa*) and closed company (*yuhan hoesa*). Among them, the most commonly established corporate entity is the joint stock company (*chusik hoesa*). This chapter deals only with joint stock companies, whether privately held or listed.

The Annual General Meeting (AGM) is the supreme body of the joint stock company. Directors to the board that manages the corporation are appointed at the AGM. The board in turn elects the company's managing director. In addition, auditors are appointed at the AGM. A company may establish an audit committee within its board of directors provided that it has at

6 Francis J. Aquila, *The Shareholder Rights and Activism Review* (4th ed., Law Business Research Ltd 2019) 66.

least two trillion KRW, the official Korean currency, in capital, that outside directors represent at least half the total number of members on the company's committees and that outside directors account for at least two-thirds of its audit committee.[7]

KCC and the Act on Corporate Governance of Financial Companies (CGFC) provide for a shareholder's right to: (1) request copies of company documents for inspection (e.g., the shareholders' register (Article 396 of the KCC)), and shareholder and board meeting minutes (Articles 396 and 391–3 of the KCC); (2) propose agendas for the shareholders' meeting (Articles 363–2(2) and 542–6 of the KCC); (3) call a temporary shareholders' meeting (Articles 366(1) and 542–6(1) of the KCC and Article 33 of the CGFC); (4) inspect and copy accounting books (Articles 466(1) and 542–6(4) of the KCC and Article 33 of the CGFC); (5) file a derivative lawsuit (Articles 403(1) and 542–6(6) of the KCC and Article 33 of the CGFC); (6) request the court to remove managing directors (Articles 385(2) and 542–6(3) of the KCC and Article 33 of the CGFC); (7) request the court to appoint inspectors (Articles 367(2), 467(1) and 542–6(1) of the KCC and Article 33 of the CGFC); (8) request cumulative voting (Articles 382–2(1) and 547–7(2) of the KCC and Article 33 of the Enforcement Decree of the KCC); and (9) file an injunction suit to stop director misconduct (Articles 402(1) and 542–6(1) of the KCC and Article 33 of the CGFC).

8.1.1.1 Korean Corporate Board

Companies must have a board of directors. However, a company with a total capital of less than one billion KRW (a small-scale company) can elect to have one or two directors if there is no board. Although there is no legal limit on the maximum number of seats on a board, the size can be fixed in the company's articles of incorporation (AOI). Vacancies or newly created seats must be filled at the general meeting of shareholders. In the event of a vacancy, the director who previously held the vacant seat continues to have the rights and obligations of a director until a replacement has been elected.

The board's primary legal responsibilities comprise the making of key decisions on issues of corporate governance and company business. These include transactions involving any disposition or transfer of material assets, borrowing of significant amounts of money, appointment or dismissal of managers and the establishment, change or closure of branch offices (Article 392 of the KCC). In addition, the KCC vests certain powers with the board, including calling general meetings of shareholders,[8] approving competition with the company by directors, dealing with unethical or self-dealing transactions, approving transactions between listed companies and their largest shareholders, issuing bonds and paying interim dividends (e.g., Articles 362, 397 and 398 of the KCC) Although company shareholders elect members of the board, the board (and each of its members) represent and owe legal duties solely to the company.

It is mandatory for listed companies whose total assets are more than two trillion KRW at the end of the fiscal year to establish an audit committee led by outside directors who make up at

[7] A committee can be established within the board of directors pursuant to the AOI. Committees, excluding the committee that recommends candidates for outside directors and the audit committee, must appoint at least two directors. The audit committee of a listed company with total assets of at least two trillion KRW must comprise at least one member who is an accountant or a financial professional and the head of the committee must be an outside director (Article 541–11 of the KCC).

[8] A decision to convene AGM shall be made by the board of directors, unless otherwise prescribed by the KCC (Article 362). When a company convenes AGMs, it shall give a written notice or notice in an electronic form to each shareholder by obtaining the consent of each shareholder, at least two weeks prior to the date set for such general meeting (Article 363(1)).

least two-thirds of the audit committee with at least one member who is an accountant or financial professional (Article 542–11 (1) of the KCC). Listed companies are also required to set up a committee responsible for recommending candidates for outside directors with outside directors representing a majority of this committee (Article 542–8 (4) of the KCC). Only candidates who have been recommended by the recommendation committee may be appointed by shareholders at a general meeting of shareholders (Article 542–8 (5) of the KCC).

As for the audit committee, its function is similar to that of a statutory auditor (i.e., supervision of directors and company accounting). Apart from the committees discussed above, a company may (but is not obliged to) establish other board committees consisting of at least two directors varying in terms of their role, authority and function as contemplated in the AOI or any resolution of the board of directors.

The board must appoint one or more of its members to be representative directors unless the AOI gives this right to shareholders. Representative directors execute board decisions and have the authority to represent the company. Boards can appoint one or more executive officers in lieu of chief inside directors if those companies adopt an executive director system. Directors can serve concurrently as executive officers. Subject to board supervision, executive officers are authorized to manage the company's affairs and make decisions on matters mandated by the AOI or the board. If there are two or more executive officers, the board must also appoint a chief executive officer to represent the company.

Auditors must attend board meetings and present their opinions. Executive officers are required to report to the board at least once every quarter or when requested by the board. When deemed necessary, an executive officer may submit a document requesting a board meeting to a director authorized to convene board meetings. The document should state the reason for the meeting, as well as the meeting agenda.

8.1.1.2 Outside Directors

The outside director system was introduced in 1998 in Korea. It was part of the government's broader Corporate Debt Restructuring (a.k.a. 'Work-Out') and corporate governance improvement programmes that aimed at restoring the competitiveness of the Korean corporate sector in the immediate aftermath of the 1997 Asian financial crisis.[9] Because the companies targeted by the mandatory outside director system were initially limited to those listed on the Korean Composite Stock Price Index (KOSPI) market, mandatory requirements for outside directors were originally added to the KOSPI listing rules. In 2001, this mandatory scheme was further expanded to include Korea Securities Dealers Automated Quotations (KOSDAQ) companies and, subsequently, the relevant rules were codified into Korea's securities exchange law. Eventually, the mandatory outside director programme was written into the Commercial Act of 2009. Outside directors are tasked with raising independent voices based on their expertise in the required areas of business operation.

Except for the requirement for outside directors, there are no additional legal requirements relating to the independence of directors unless otherwise provided for in the AOI.[10] For listed companies, a person can be disqualified from acting as an outside director in prescribed circumstances. Such person includes the shareholder who can exercise actual influence over the company's major business affairs. The recently revised enforcement decrees of the KCC and

[9] See Bernard Black et al., 'Corporate Governance in Korea at the Millennium: Enhancing International Competitiveness' (2001) 26 Journal of Corporation Law 537.

[10] Article 34 (5)(7) of the Enforcement Decree of the KCC.

FISCMA have limited the term of an outside director in a listed company to be six years, or nine years when a subsidiary is included (for instance, Article 34 (5)(7) of the Enforcement Decree of the KCC).

8.1.2 *Ownership Structure: Power without Authority*

Korean companies, including the *Chaebols*, are typically controlled by individuals or families.[11] The line between management and share ownership is not always as clear in Korea as it is in the United States or European Union jurisdictions. The chief executive officer (CEO) and chairman of the board are often representatives of the founding families that have retained control over the companies they founded. It is common for the founding families of Korean companies to assume both shareholder and managerial roles. Even if the founding family owns only a small fraction of the company's shares, it often uses its position to retain de facto control.

Indeed, controlling shareholders in Korea usually own less than 5 per cent of a business group's equity stake. However, they often control the voting rights of another 20 per cent to 50 per cent of shares by "circular shareholdings" through affiliates. Circular-ownership is a typical ownership pattern among *Chaebols*, allowing controlling shareholders to retain control with only minimal actual ownership positions. It is well documented that circular-ownership structures are a source of significant agency costs.[12] Therefore, corporate governance issues in Korea are primarily the conflicts between the controlling shareholder and minority public shareholders.

Concentrated and dispersed ownership can each have their own performance advantages and disadvantages.[13] On the positive side, the Korean system – featured with a concentrated ownership structure – promises to improve managerial efficiency and reduce shareholder-manager agency costs. Controlling shareholders either serve in senior managerial positions (CEO or chairman of the board) or have their nominees fill those positions. Controlling shareholders can thus closely and effectively monitor officers and employees, better aligning the interests between shareholders and managers.

The Korean concentrated ownership patterns can also have other important advantages. Compared to other majority shareholders, family owners are more willing to reduce dividends, and they prefer to invest cash flows in long-term projects such as R&D investment.[14] Family ownership also places greater importance on reputation, thereby fostering special long-term relationships with and a sense of responsibility toward employees, suppliers and clients, and ultimately improving the well-being of stakeholders. In other words, family owners value the reputation and legitimacy of their firms in the eyes of the public.

However, controlling shareholders can also be keenly aware that they cannot easily be ousted since their control is largely insulated by circular shareholdings. Thus, the misalignment between cash flow rights and voting rights can give controlling shareholders strong incentives to appropriate company assets for private benefits. More recently, there has been a trend of the

11 See Black et al. (n. 9).

12 Stijn Claessens, Simeon Djankova and Larry H. P Lang, 'The Separation of Ownership and Control in East Asian Corporations' (2000) 58 Journal of Financial Economics 81.

13 See Hwa-Jin Kim, 'Concentrated Ownership and Corporate Control: Wallenberg Sphere and Samsung Group' (2014) 14 Journal of Korean Law 39.

14 See Dong-Wook Kim, Byoung-Gon Kim and Myoung-Kil Youn, 'Family Ownership and Firm Value: Perspective to Related-Party Transaction and Wealth Transfer' (2017) 15 Journal of Distribution Science 5.

large Korean corporate groups transforming themselves into holding companies.[15] The misalignment between ownership and control seems to have been further exacerbated in these holding companies. In the absence of an effective legal environment reining in opportunism of majority shareholders, the misalignment can lead to expropriations of minority shareholders, by ways of accounting frauds, self-dealings, the misappropriations of corporate opportunities and so on. Recent Korean corporate scandals clearly demonstrate the ineffectiveness of Korea's internal, external, ex ante and ex post mechanisms of the corporate monitoring system.[16]

8.2 LEGAL MEANS OF SHAREHOLDER ENGAGEMENT

8.2.1 *Powers of the AGM*

The AGM is empowered to make decisions only on issues stipulated by law or specially provided for in the company's AOI (Article 361 of the KCC). Fundamental matters such as the appointment of directors or auditors; the remuneration of directors, auditors and liquidators; approval of statements of accountants; and decisions on dividends are among the issues considered at the shareholders' meetings. A change in AOI, reduction of capital, dissolution, transfer of business and mergers and acquisitions are also within the authority of the AGM. Companies may add other lines of authority to the mandate of the AGM by specifying them in the AOI.

The AGM must be held at least once a year (Article 365(1) of the KCC). A shareholders' meeting is convened by the board of directors, which determines the date, place and agenda of the meeting. A shareholders meeting convened without the board's decision is unlawful. In practice, Korean AGMs tend to be concentrated in a short time window. In 2017, 913 (or 47.63 per cent) of Korean listed companies[17] held their AGMs on Friday, 4 March, named the Super AGM Day. After the AGM dispersion policy was implemented in 2018, the Super AGM Day phenomenon considerably lessened. So, the concentration gradually decreased to 542 companies (27.28 per cent) in 2018 and 550 companies (26.35 per cent) in 2019.[18] Similarly, 750 AGMs were held in March 2019,[19] representing 84.7 per cent of the KOSPI listed companies. Notably, the listed companies (76 per cent) that formed the same conglomerate tended to hold their AGMs on the same date.[20]

8.2.2 *Shareholders' Statutory Rights*

The KCC is the principal law governing corporate governance of Korean corporations. It stipulates, among other things, a variety of shareholder rights, which mostly form the basis for the activities of shareholder activists. Under the KCC, the following decisions must be reserved for shareholders and resolved at the AGM by a majority of votes of shareholders who represent more than a quarter of the company's total outstanding shares: (1) appointment of a director or statutory auditor (Article 382 (1)); (2) approval of annual financial statements (Article 449 (1)); (3)

[15] See Sang-Il Kim, Won-Wook Choi and Ho-Young Lee, 'Does the Transformation to Holding Company Systems in Korean Chaebol Improve the Valuation Independence of Affiliated Firms' Cost of Debt?' (2016) 13 Corporate Ownership and Control 447 https://doi.org/10.22495/cocv13i4c3p4 accessed 15 July 2020.

[16] See E. Han Kim and Woochan Kim, 'Changes in Korean Corporate Governance: A Response to Crisis' in Donald H. Chew and Stuart L. Gillan (eds.), *Global Corporate Governance* (Cambridge University Press 2009).

[17] This represents the total listed company, including the KOSPI and KOSDAQ markets.

[18] Jung Eun Lee, 'AGM Dispersion Status' (2019) 9 KCGS Report 34.

[19] Korea Listed Companies Association, 2019 *KOSPI AGM White Book* (hereafter KLCA White Book) (2019) 8.

[20] Lee (n. 18) 36.

TABLE 8.1 *Concentration of 2019 AGMs in Korea: number of AGMs (ratio %)*

Month	Week	Monday	Tuesday	Wednesday	Thursday	Friday	Total
February	4th	-	1 (0.1%)	-	-	-	1 (0.1%)
	5th	-	1 (0.1%)	-	4 (0.5%)	-	5 (0.7%)
March	2nd	-	-	-	-	2 (0.3%)	2 (0.3%)
	3rd	-	1 (0.1%)	4 (0.5%)	7 (0.9%)	71 (9.4%)	83 (11%)
	4th	7 (0.9%)	2 (0.3%)	11 (1.5%)	35 (4.6%)	189 (25%)	244 (32.3%)
	5th	24 (3.2%)	56 (7.4%)	115 (15.2%)	55 (7.3%)	171 (22.6%)	421 (55.7%)
Total		31 (4.1%)	61 (8.1%)	130 (17.2%)	101 (13.4%)	433 (57.3%)	756 (100%)

Source: Korean Listed Companies Association 2019 KOSPI AGM White Book (2019).

approval of remuneration of directors and statutory auditors (Article 388); and (4) declaration of dividends (Article 462 (2)).

For the following decisions reserved for shareholders, the KCC requires approval of a special resolution by more than two-thirds of the votes of shareholders present at the AGM who represent more than a third of the company's total outstanding shares: (1) transfer of all or a material portion of the company's business (Article 374 (1)); (2) removal of directors and statutory auditors (Article 385 (1)); (3) amendments to the AOI of the company (Article 434); (4) capital reduction (Article 438); (5) mergers and spinoffs (Article 522 (3) and Article 530–3 (1)); (6) dissolution or continuance of the company (Article 518 and Article 519); and (7) granting stock options (Article 542–3 (3)).

8.2.3 *Important Rights of Minority Shareholders*

8.2.3.1 Reform of the Provisions on Minority Shareholders' Rights

To empower minority public shareholders in listed companies, the KCC has provided for lower shareholding ratio requirements for shareholder rights in the companies listed on the Korea Exchange (the KRX) ('general provisions'), relative to non-listed companies. To prevent abuse of these enabling provisions, the KCC generally attaches to them a minimum holding period requirement (e.g., six months) ('special provisions'). Until recently, ambiguity existed as to whether minority shareholders of a KRX-listed company may exercise their right when they satisfy KCC's general requirements for shareholder rights (particularly in respect of shareholding ratios) but not the special provisions (particularly the holding period) applicable to listed companies. There was a debate as to the proper interpretation of the law and there was also a divergence among the lower courts' decisions on this very issue.[21]

The recent amendment to the KCC, which became effective on 29 December 2020, with respect to minority shareholder rights resolved such ambiguity. The amendment has allowed the minority shareholders' rights to be exercised as long as the requirements of either the general provisions or the special provisions are met, subject to each of such requirements (Article 542–6 (10) of the KCC).[22] The amendment affirmed that one may choose between minority shareholder rights under the special provisions for listed companies and those under the general provisions. In other words, if minority shareholders of listed companies meet the requirements

[21] Jipyong News, 'Passage of a Proposed Amendment to Corporate Governance Provisions of the Commercial Code' (21 December 2020) www.jipyong.com/kr/board/news_view.php?seq=10059 accessed 3 June 2021.

[22] Articles 542–6 (Minority Shareholders' Rights) (10) Notwithstanding the Provisions of Article 542–2(2), Paragraphs (1) through (7) do not affect the exercise of minority shareholders' rights pursuant to other sections of this Chapter.

TABLE 8.2 *2018–19 AGMs and EGMs: by month*

		AGMs		EGMs		Total	
		n	%	n	%	n	%
2018							
	April	-	-	1	0.1	1	0.1
	May	-	-	11	1.2	11	1.2
	June	6	0.7	13	1.5	19	2.1
	July	-	-	17	1.9	17	1.9
	August	-	-	12	1.4	12	1.4
	September	5	0.6	11	1.2	16	1.8
	October	-	-	8	0.9	8	0.9
	November	-	-	10	1.1	10	1.1
	December	2	0.2	18	2.0	20	2.3
	Subtotal	13	1.5	101	11.4	114	12.9
2019							
	January	-	-	7	0.8	7	0.8
	February	7	0.8	5	0.6	12	1.4
	March	750	84.7	2	0.2	752	85.0
	Subtotal	757	85.5	14	1.6	771	87.1
	Total	770	87.0	115	13.0	885	100

Source: KLCA 2019 KOSPI AGM White Book (2019).

under the general provisions, they may exercise their minority shareholder rights even if they do not satisfy the six-month shareholding period requirement, and vice versa, making it easier for them to exercise their rights.[23]

8.2.3.2 Shareholder Right to Call a Meeting

An extraordinary general meeting (EGM) may be convened whenever necessary (Article 365 (3) of the KCC). A minority shareholder holding at least 1.5 per cent of the total number of issued and outstanding shares of a listed company for at least six months (3 per cent or more without a six-month holding period for non-listed companies) may exercise its right to request convocation of a general meeting of shareholders by submitting a written statement or electronic document (Article 542–6 (1) of the KCC). The shareholder(s) must specify in writing the reason for convening the EGM and its purpose. If procedures to convene an EGM are not taken promptly after the request, the shareholder(s) may convene such meetings with the permission of law courts. In such cases, the chairperson of the EGM may be appointed by the court upon request of any interested person or ex officio member (Article 366 (2) of the KCC).

8.2.3.3 Shareholder Proposal Rights

A shareholder holding at least 1 per cent of the total number of issued and outstanding voting shares of a listed company (0.5 per cent if the company's paid-in capital is no less than 100 billion

[23] Hyeon-Deog Cho et al., 'The Corporate Governance Review: South Korea' in Willem Calkoen (ed.) *The Corporate Governance Review* (11th ed., Law Business Research Ltd 2021).

won, and 3 per cent or more without a six-month holding period for non-listed companies) for at least six months may propose agendas for an AGM by submitting a written statement or electronic document at least six weeks prior to the meeting (Article 542–6 (2) of the KCC). When a shareholder proposes an agenda, the board of directors cannot refuse and must present it at the general meeting of shareholders, unless presenting the proposed agenda would violate any applicable laws (including certain cases described in the presidential decrees of the KCC) or the AOI of the company (Article 363–2(3) of the KCC). Furthermore, where an agenda proposed by a shareholder is presented at a general meeting of shareholders, the shareholder must be given an opportunity to explain the agenda during the meeting, if so requested by the shareholder (Article 363–2(3) of the KCC).

8.2.3.4 Right to File a Derivative Suit

If a director violates any applicable laws or the company's AOI, or neglects his or her duties by willful misconduct or negligence, a shareholder holding 0.01 per cent or more of the total outstanding shares of a listed company for at least six months (1 per cent or more without a six-month holding period for non-listed companies) may request, in writing, that the company file a lawsuit against the director for damages caused (Article 542–6 (1) of the KCC). If the company does not file the lawsuit within thirty days of the date of the shareholders' request, the shareholder can file the lawsuit on behalf of the company (Article 403 (2) of the KCC).

It is worth noting that, prior to the recent amendment to the KCC in 2020, the KCC did not provide for legal means by which the parent company's shareholders could hold the subsidiary's director accountable for causing harm to the parent company or its shareholders.[24] The amended KCC establishes a legal means for shareholders of a parent company who own more than a certain percentage of shares to file a shareholder derivative claim against a director of the subsidiary for causing damage to the subsidiary by neglecting his or her duties (Articles 406–2 and 542–6 of the KCC). With the codification of multistep derivative actions, the directors of a subsidiary may be sued by the shareholders of the parent company. It has been suggested that such threat of a multilevel derivative claim in itself could significantly hinder the subsidiary's directors from performing their duties, potentially causing them to become passive or intimidated in performing their duties.[25]

8.2.4 *Stewardship Code Adoption*

The Principles on Stewardship Responsibilities of Institutional Investor was published by the Korea Stewardship Code Council on 16 December 2016. It establishes key principles essential for institutional investors to follow in effectively exercising their stewardship responsibilities, and also stipulates concrete details pertaining to these principles.[26] The Code's seven principles highlight the importance of disclosing a clear stewardship policy, managing conflicts of interests, monitoring companies targeted for investment, formulating internal stewardship guidelines, establishing a proxy voting policy and disclosing votes cast, reporting to clients and beneficiaries and developing the capabilities and expertise to implement stewardship in an 'active and

24 See n. 21.
25 Cho et al. (n. 23).
26 Korea Stewardship Code Council, 'Principles on the Stewardship Responsibilities of Institutional Investors', http://sc.cgs.or.kr/eng/about/sc.jsp accessed 15 July 2020.

effective manner'.[27] The Code expressly recognizes that successful implementation of stewardship responsibilities not only encourages the mid- to long-term development of companies and contributes to enhancing investor returns, but also supports substantial growth and development of capital markets.[28] Stewardship activities are not limited to the exercise of voting rights. Engagement activities include a broad spectrum of shareholder activities focused on 'clear and constructive goal' in conducting a conversation with investee companies.[29]

The Code's principles generally apply to domestic and overseas institutional investors holding shares of publicly listed companies in Korea, including asset owners and asset managers. The principles are not legally binding and apply only to institutional investors who voluntarily affirm participation by accepting and implementing the principles. When participating institutional investors cannot comply, they should explain the reason ('comply or explain' basis).[30] According to the 2019 Korea Listed Companies Association (KLCA) Survey, 53 per cent of KOSPI companies responded that institutional investors held company shares and exercised their voting rights.[31] When institutional investors exercised their voting rights, 39.4 per cent of the respondents said that they opposed the agenda items. Among those negative votes, 'appointment of directors' was the highest at 25.3 per cent, followed by 'appointing auditors or audit committee members' and 'approval of directors' compensation limit'.[32]

8.2.5 *Relaxation of the Restrictions on Shareholder Engagement*

Under the FSCMA, if a shareholder comes to own at least 5 per cent of a listed company, changes its shareholding ratio thereafter by at least 1 per cent or if there are changes in its purpose of shareholding or any other material matters, the shareholder must report its shareholding status and a detailed account of any changes to the Financial Services Commission (FSC) and the KRX within a prescribed period (Article 147 (1) of the FSCMA). In the past, the FSCMA had classified the purpose of shareholding on a binary basis, depending on whether or not the holder(s) of such shareholding intended to influence corporate management.

Nevertheless, the amendment to the Enforcement Decree of the FSCMA (FSCMA-ED), taking effect from January 2020, has enabled institutional investors including pension funds to carry out shareholder engagement activities more aggressively. The purpose of shareholding is now further divided into: (1) management influence (in cases where its purpose is to influence corporate management as described in the FSCMA-ED); (2) general investment (in cases where its purpose is to implement active shareholder engagement without an intent to influence corporate management); and (3) simple investment (in cases where its purpose is to exercise voting and other rights that are irrespective of the shareholding ratio). Disclosure obligations are imposed on a differentiated basis, depending on purpose of shareholders. This reflects the latest trends toward an increase in shareholder engagement by the NPS and other institutional investors (Article 154 (5) of the FSCMA-ED). The amended FSCMA-ED specifically excludes shareholder activities related to, for example, issuance of dividends, amendment to the AOI to

[27] Ibid.
[28] Ibid.
[29] Ibid., 3.
[30] For example, when participating institutional investors cannot adhere to any practice set forth in the principles, they should provide the reason, sufficiently explain alternatives to their clients and beneficiaries and publicly disclose the contents. Participating institutional investors should publicly disclose matters on their website and periodically review and update contents when necessary.
[31] KLCA White Book (n. 19) 34.
[32] Ibid., 35.

improve corporate governance in line with pre-disclosed principles and exercise of the right to request dismissal against a director's unlawful conduct from activities 'to influence corporate management' (Article 154 (1) of the FSCMA-ED).

Since the 2020 amendment to the FSCMA-ED, some institutional investors have changed their investment purpose from 'simple investment' to 'general investment'. More specifically, out of the thirty-five domestic institutional investors which filed summary reports of large equity ownership during the period from 1 February 2020 to 31 March 2020, the NPS, KB Asset Management and Korea Investment Value Asset Management changed their purpose of investing in some of their portfolio firms.[33] The NPS has changed its purpose of shareholding from 'simple investment' to 'general investment' with respect to 56 out of the 113 listed companies constituting its investment portfolio. These included, notably, Samsung Electronics, SK Hynix and Hyundai Motor Company.[34]

8.3 SHAREHOLDER ENGAGEMENT AND VOTING IN PRACTICE

8.3.1 *Voting in Practice*

8.3.1.1 How to Vote

Shareholders have the right to attend general meetings, ask questions, express their opinions and vote. Shareholders have one vote for each share (Article 369 (1) of the KCC). The company does not have a vote for its own shares. Shareholders with more than one share may vote differently for each share (Article 368–2 (1) of the KCC). Shareholders may exercise their rights either by attending the general meeting in person or through an agent. The KCC has no requirement as to who may be an agent. The company may, however, stipulate certain requirements in the AOI (for instance, only company shareholders may act as agents).[35]

Resolutions are adopted if they are supported by a majority of votes of shareholders present at the general meeting who represent more than a quarter of the company's total outstanding shares (Article 368 (1) of the KCC). In cases such as the transfer of all or a material portion of the company's business, removal of directors and statutory auditors, amendments to the AOI, capital reduction, mergers and spinoffs, dissolution or continuance of the company and granting of stock options, more than two-thirds of the votes of the shareholders present representing more than a third of the total outstanding shares are needed.[36] The requirement is mandatory and may not be altered by the AOI. The consent of all shareholders is needed to discharge the liability of directors in cases other than a conflict of interest (Article 400 (1)).

8.3.1.2 Vote by Indirect Means

Under the KCC, shareholders may cast votes in writing or electronically in lieu of attending in person the AGM so as to meet the minimum requirements needed to pass AGM resolutions or to prevent a large number of resignations (Articles 368–3 and 368–4 of the KCC). Write-in voting is permitted provided that it is stipulated in the AOI, and electronic voting may be adopted only by way of a resolution of the board of directors. According to a KLCA report, 80 of the 742 KOSPI-

33 KCGS, '2020 AGM Review: Changes Driven by Legal Amendments' (April 2020), 2.
34 The number of firms specified by the NPS in its Q1 2020 ownership report as having 5 per cent or more ownership.
35 Supreme Court, 23 April 2009, 2005da22701, 22718.
36 For a more detailed discussion of special resolutions, see Section 8.2.2.

indexed companies had write-in voting rights stipulated in their AOIs in 2017.[37] An analysis of 321 respondents further revealed that 21 KOSPI companies had shareholders exercise their write-in voting rights in 2019.[38]

8.3.1.3 Electronic Voting

Electronic voting is one area of corporate governance reforms that Korea has undertaken successfully in recent years. Electronic voting has been allowed since the amendment to the KCC in 2011. The 2011 legislative reform was intended to address the concentration of AGMs in Korean listed companies, as discussed above. As Korean listed companies are required by law to submit their annual reports ninety days after the end of the fiscal year for approval by the shareholders' meeting, companies whose fiscal year ends on 31 December usually hold their meetings in late March, typically in a brief time window of one to two weeks, if not on the same day. Electronic voting allows shareholders to vote in respect of multiple investee companies holding the AGMs on the same day or within a short time span. Few companies, however, voluntarily adopted electronic voting as it could threaten to dilute the voting power of the controlling shareholders and they would potentially have their proposals rejected at the shareholders' meeting. Indeed, by 2014, no Korean listed companies had adopted electronic voting, with the exception of the companies headquartered overseas and special purpose companies.

Interestingly, the Korea Securities Depository (KSD), a public agency, developed an e-voting platform in 2010. The platform was initially intended to enable low-cost exercise of voting rights by domestic retail shareholders, and to incentivize the exercise of their rights. The e-voting platform had, however, a perhaps unintended effect of enabling a voting practice known as 'shadow voting',[39] under which the KSD by default voted on behalf of absent shareholders. The practice had the effect of ensuring a quorum for the meeting, making it easier for management to obtain a majority vote.

In order to curtail the practice of shadow voting, the FSC amended in December 2014 the presidential Decree of Capital Markets Act, granting listed firms a three-year grace period to phase out shadow voting.[40] This led to 101 KOSPI-listed companies to adopt electronic voting in 2015. The growth trend has continued. By February 2018, 57 per cent of all 2,240 companies listed on the KOSPI and KOSDAQ had embraced electronic voting.[41] Interestingly, larger cap companies tended to participate less – only 16 per cent of the top 100 firms by market cap had e-voting systems compared to an average of 45 per cent for all 789 KOSPI companies. The number of companies using electronic voting in 2018 dropped to 483 from 688 in 2017, while the number of shareholders using the electronic voting system increased to 22,569 from 10,938 in 2017 (see Table 8.3).[42] According to an analysis of 321 respondents among KOSPI companies, 89 companies adopted and conducted electronic voting in 2019.[43] However, the share of electronic

37 KLCA White Book (n. 19) 26.

38 Ibid.

39 'Shadow voting' is a form of proxy voting system which prevents the dissolution of the shareholders meeting due to lack of quorum by allowing the exercise of the voting rights in the name of absent shareholders. The KSD exercise voting rights on behalf of an absent shareholder by dividing his or her voting rights according to the proportion of the approval and disapproval votes of the shareholders present.

40 Shadow voting shall not be applied for proposals on the election of audit committee members.

41 KSD Press Release, 'The Number of E-Voting Shareholders Increased' (22 March 2018).

42 Ibid.

43 KLCA White Book (n. 19) 27.

TABLE 8.3 *The use of electronic voting at shareholders' meetings (2017–18)*

	Annual shareholder meeting of firms whose fiscal year end is December			
	2017		2018	
Content	No. of companies	No. of shareholders	No. of companies	No. of shareholders
KOSPI	210	4,737	155	9,887
KOSDAQ	478	6,201	328	12,682
Total	688	10,938	483	22,569

Source: KSD Press Release, 'The Number of E-Voting Shareholders Increased' (22 March 2018).

TABLE 8.4 *The use of shadow voting (2015–16)*

	KOSPI		KOSDAQ		Total	
Fiscal Year	Requesting Companies	Compared to the previous year	Requesting Companies	Compared to the previous year	Requesting Companies	Compared to the previous year
2015	146	-	309	-	455	-
2016	193	32.2	448	45	641	40.9

Source: KSD, 2016 (December Fiscal Year End) Listed Companies' Shadow Voting Requesting Status, Press Release (April 2017).

voting for fifty-two companies was more than 1 per cent but less than 10 per cent, indicating a very low proportion.[44]

On the other hand, Korean listed companies seemed to have been keen to make use of the three-year grace period before shadow voting was formally abolished in 2018. In practice, requests could be made for a continuation of shadow voting practice prior to 2018. Such requests from KOSPI and KOSDAQ listed companies increased from 455 to 641 (40.9 per cent) during the grace period (2015 to 2016) (Table 8.4).[45]

The 2020 amendment to the KCC relaxed requirements by allowing a resolution of general meeting of shareholders via electronic voting by doing away with the requirement of affirmative votes representing a quarter of the total number of issued and outstanding shares and by simply providing that a resolution to appoint auditors and audit committee members can be adopted with a majority of the voting rights of the shareholders present at the general meeting of shareholders (Articles 409 (3) and 542–12 (8) of the KCC).

8.3.2 *What Issues Are Voted on?*

Table 8.5 shows that 'approval of director's compensation' was the most common agenda item (99 per cent) at the 2019 KOSPI AGMs, followed by 'approval of financial statements' (92.9 per cent) and 'article of incorporations amendments' (91.2 per cent).

44 Ibid.

45 KSD Press Release, '2016 (December Fiscal Year End) Listed Companies' Shadow Voting Requesting Status' (26 April 2017).

TABLE 8.5 *Agenda items of the general meetings in 2019*

	AGMs		EGMs		Total	
Agenda	No. of Companies	Ratio	No. of Companies	Ratio	No. of Companies	Ratio
Director Compensation	762	99	3	2.6	765	86.4
Appointing Director	662	86	82	71.3	744	84.1
Amendments to AOI	702	91.2	36	31.3	738	83.4
Financial Statement Approval	715	92.9	1	0.9	716	80.9
Dividend	501	65.1	-	-	501	56.6
Auditor Compensation	388	50.4	-	-	388	43.8
Appointing Audit Committee	278	36.1	22	19.1	300	33.9
Appointing Auditor	139	18.1	11	9.6	150	16.9
Executive Retirement Package	49	6.4	2	1.7	51	5.8
Stock Option	42	5.5	3	2.6	45	5.1
Spinoff	4	0.5	12	10.4	16	1.8
Stock Split	8	1	2	1.7	10	1.1
Reduction of Capital	7	0.9	1	0.9	8	0.9
Decrease of Reserves	5	0.6	2	1.7	7	0.8
Approving Merger Agreement	-	-	4	3.5	4	0.5
Approval for Agreement for Merger after Division	-	-	3	2.6	3	0.3
Approval for Transfer of Business	-	-	2	1.7	2	0.2
Removal of Director	-	-	1	0.9	1	0.1
Others	4	0.5	2	1.7	6	0.7
# of Companies	770	100	115	100	885	100

Source: KLCA 2019 KOSPI AGM White Book (2019).

Except for the appointment of auditors, fifteen resolution agenda items were rejected at 2018 AGMs in Korea because a quorum had not been reached.[46] In these cases, the average majority shareholder holding ratio was approximately 10.73 per cent. The average majority shareholder holding ratio of the seventeen companies requiring special resolutions that were rejected over the most recent three years was 15.33 per cent (Table 8.6).[47]

46 Tae-kyung Ko, 'Analysis of Listed Companies' AGM Agenda in the Most Recent 3 Years' (2018) 8 KCGS Report 17.
47 Ibid.

TABLE 8.6 *Rejected agenda items according to shareholding levels*

Largest Shareholder Holding Ratio	0~10 %	10~20 %	20~30 %	30~40 %	40~50 %	50~60 %	60~70 %	Total
'General Resolution (For Auditor/Audit Committee)'								
Combine 3%	1	11	16	3	21	3	1	56
Individual 3%	0	0	0	0	1	1	0	2
Sub Total	1	11	16	3	22	4	1	58
'Special Resolution (Ex- Auditor/ Audit Committee)'								
Financial Statements Approval	4	0	0	0	0	0	0	4
Appointing Directors	3	3	0	0	0	0	0	6
Appointing Directors	9	3	1	0	0	0	0	13
Appointing Directors	7	3	1	0	0	0	0	11
Others	1	0	1	0	0	0	0	2
Sub Total	24	9	3	0	0	0	0	36
Special Resolution								
AOI Amendments	5	6	3	1	0	0	0	15
Stock Option	0	1	1	0	0	0	0	2
Sub Total	5	7	4	1	0	0	0	17
Total	30	27	23	4	22	4	1	111

Source: KCGS Report, 'Analysis of Listed Companies' AGM Agenda in the Most Recent 3 Years' (2018) vol. 8.

8.3.2.1 Shareholder Proposals

In terms of the 2019 AGMs, eleven companies (3.4 per cent) responded that they had a shareholder proposal on the agenda, among which eight proposals were for appointing directors and three proposals for dividend-related items.[48] In terms of the proponents of the shareholder proposals, eight out of the eleven were initiated by individual investors, while the rest (three) were proposed by domestic and foreign institutional investors.[49] The number of agenda items rejected at AGMs has been increasing[50] with shareholder proposals experiencing a high rate of rejection. Dividend agenda items are all shareholder proposals and have the highest rejection rate.[51]

According to a recent KCGS report, the number of shareholder proposals put forward for voting has risen during the 2018–21 period, while the number of the targeted companies has remained stable (Table 8.7).[52] During this period, there were shareholder proposals that were put forward for four years in a row at two companies, accounting for 1.7 per cent of the total.[53] The same shareholder proposals were submitted three times at three corporations (around 2.5 per cent) and twice at seventeen firms (about 14.4 per cent).[54]

48 KLCA White Book (n. 19) 23.
49 Ibid., 24.
50 Il-Mook Jung, 'Analysis of the Agenda Rejections in the AGM' (2017) 7 KCGS Report 9.
51 Ibid., 11.
52 This report looks into the shareholder proposals submitted for consideration at the locally listed companies from 2018 through the 2021 AGM season. For 2021, the analysis covers the general meetings held until March 2021, when most of the companies already held their annual general meetings.
53 KCGS, '2021 AGM Review: Shareholder Proposals and Company Reponses' (May 2021).
54 Ibid.

TABLE 8.7 *Number of companies receiving shareholder proposals and number of agenda items: AGMs and EGMs combined*

	2021	2020	2019	2018	Total
Number of Companies Involved	30	31	33	34	118
KOSPI Companies	17	8	16	8	49
KOSDAQ Companies	13	23	17	16	69
Number of Agenda Items	107	120	107	89	423

Source: KCGS, 2021 AGM Review: Shareholder Proposals and Company Reponses (May 2021).

TABLE 8.8 *Agenda items in shareholder proposals (2018–21)*

	Types of agenda items (number)	Total
Dividend and treasury shares	Expanded cash dividend (48), higher payout ratio (1), stock dividend (4), unequal dividend (3), dividend in treasury shares (1), repurchase or cancellation of treasury shares (12)	69
Amendment of AOIs	Adoption of interim or quarterly dividend (6), stock split (11), creation of board committees (11), repeal of golden parachute clause (3), deletion of supermajority system (4), reinforcing director qualifications (5), adoption of cumulative voting (6), adoption of electronic voting (4), etc.	78
Election of directors	Election of inside directors (81), election of outside directors (92), election of non-independent non-executive directors (7), election of auditors (audit committee members) (67), dismissal of directors (auditors) (6)	253
Director Remuneration Cap	Reduction in director remuneration cap (10), increasing auditor remuneration ceiling (5), reduction in auditor remuneration cap (1)	16
Others	Capital reduction (4), reduced liability of directors (1), capital reduction with consideration (1), etc.	7

Source: KCGS, 2021 AGM Review: Shareholder Proposals and Company Reponses (May 2021).

The same KCGS report suggests that the majority of the proposals aimed at protecting the rights and interests of shareholders or at enhancing shareholder value (Table 8.8). It was uncommon, however, that the agendas were actually supported at the shareholders' meeting.[55] About 10.9 per cent of shareholder proposals were approved. Only twenty-three agenda items have actually led to meaningful changes except in special cases where voting agendas are passed at once due to management disputes.[56]

8.3.2.2 Proxy Solicitation

A person who intends to solicit a shareholder to exercise voting rights by proxy must deliver the proxy form and reference documents to that shareholder (Article 152 of the FSCMA). Since the abolition of shadow voting, companies have used the proxy solicitation to secure votes. According to a KLCA report, 459 KOSPI companies exercised proxy solicitations during the surveyed period (1 April 2018–31 March 2019)[57] and only 12.5 per cent used proxy agencies.

55 Ibid.
56 Ibid.
57 KLCA White Book (n. 19) 12.

TABLE 8.9 *Proxy solicitations (2017–18)*

Types	FY 2018		FY 2017	
	No. of Companies	Ratio	No. of Companies	Ratio
Companies reporting proxy solicitations	152	47.4	158	46.3
Companies not reporting proxy solicitations	169	52.6	183	53.7
Total	321	100	341	100
No Answer			14	

Source: KCGS Report, 'Analysis of Listed Companies' AGM Agenda Items in the Most Recent 3 Years' (2018) vol. 8.

In terms of the scope, 86.3 per cent of the companies solicited all of its shareholders and 98 per cent of solicitations were initiated to secure management decisions. See Table 8.9.

8.3.3 *Influence of the National Pension Service*

Since the Korean government introduced guidelines to enhance the participatory role of shareholders in December 2016,[58] the number of institutional investors adopting the Korea Stewardship Code has reached 123. The NPS, Korea's largest institutional investor, actively monitors and engages with companies that it has invested in with reference to the Code.[59] The most notable change is that the Code allows the NPS to actively exercise its voting rights.[60] According to a KLCA survey, 44.9 per cent of the respondent companies reported the NPS held shares in them and exercised voting rights at their 2019 AGMs. Prior to the adoption of the Code, the NPS was passive in exercising its voting rights and routinely agreed to proposed agenda items. The proxy vote dissent rate of local institutions has also increased significantly. According to the KCGS data from September 2018, the votes against domestic institutional investor signatories rose from 1.72 per cent in 2015 to 5.72 per cent in 2018.[61] Table 8.10 presents further details of NPS voting records 2015–19 (April).

Critics of the NPS's showing of activism contest that the NPS risks intervening excessively in the day-to-day management of their investee companies and that other asset managers will blindly apply the NPS voting policies to all of their portfolio firms in Korea.[62] However, empirical evidence shows that the adoption of the Stewardship Code has had a positive impact on the NPS's returns. In respect of portfolio firms in which the NPS holds more than 5 per cent ownership, the effect of the engagement was statistically and significantly positive.[63] The effect is stronger when the NPS ownership stake is higher than 10 per cent.[64] To be sure, it remains to be seen if the enhancement in shareholder value is sustainable as the Stewardship Code adoption is at a nascent stage. Nevertheless, many Korean stakeholders, including the government, have

58 According to the KCGS, 123 institutional investors have adopted the code with an additional 31 planning to adopt it. Korea Stewardship Code Participants list, http://sc.cgs.or.kr/eng/participation/investors.jsp accessed 24 February 2020.

59 Ho-Jeong Lee, 'NPS Adopting Stewardship Code' *Korea JoongAng Daily* (31 July 31, 2018) http://mengnews.joins.com/view.aspx?aid=3051262 accessed 24 February 2020.

60 See www.seoul.co.kr/news/newsView.php?id=20190902006008 accessed 24 February 2020.

61 See http://vip.cgs.or.kr/main/main.asp accessed 24 February 2020.

62 See www.hankyung.com/finance/article/2020020667731 accessed 24 February 2020.

63 See http://sc.cgs.or.kr/resources/trends_list.jsp accessed 24 February 2020.

64 Ibid.

TABLE 8.10 *NPS voting records (2015–April 2019)*

Year	No. of Investee Companies	No. of AGMs	No. of Agenda items	For	Against	N/A
2019 (January – April)	997	636	2,987	2,374 (79.5%)	610 (20.4%)	3 (0.1%)
2018	764	768	2,864	2,309 (80.6%)	539 (18.8%)	16 (0.6%)
2017	772	708	2,899	2,519 (86.9%)	373 (12.9%)	7 (0.2%)
2016	753	796	3,010	2,692 (89.4%)	303 (10.1%)	15 (0.5%)
2015	791	749	2,836	2,542 (89.6%)	287 (10.1%)	7 (0.3%)

Source: NPS Official Website.

anticipated an improvement in corporate governance and shareholder value as a consequence of the NPS's active shareholder engagement.

8.3.4 *Recent Shareholder Activism Campaigns*

8.3.4.1 Foreign Activist Funds

In March 2018, Hyundai Mobis and Hyundai Glovis, both companies affiliated to the Hyundai Motor Group, announced their plan for a spin-off merger. Elliott Management Corporation ('Elliott') publicly objected to such plan on the basis that the spin-off merger ratio was not fair for the shareholders of Hyundai Mobis. Elliott proposed an alternative plan to establish a holding company through a different spin-off merger among Hyundai Mobis, Hyundai Motor and Kia Motors. Following the objection from Elliott and a number of proxy advisors (including KCGS, ISS and Glass Lewis), Hyundai Mobis and Hyundai Glovis voluntarily withdrew their planned spin-off merger.

In February 2019, Elliott further submitted a shareholder proposal. The proposal requested (1) an increase in dividend payouts; (2) the establishment of a compensation committee and a transparent management committee under the board; and (3) the appointment of three outside directors and audit committee members with a multinational background.[65] The activist fund also filed a similar proposal targeting the annual meeting of Hyundai Mobis in the same year. On 29 March 2019, except for the establishment of compensation and management transparency committees, which was not opposed by Hyundai Motor Company and Hyundai Mobis, all of these agenda items were voted down at the shareholders' meetings of the two companies.[66] However, in what appears to be a response to this shareholder activism campaign, Hyundai Motor Company adopted a series of shareholder-friendly measures. These included: (1) to allow

65 See www.acceleratehyundai.com accessed 15 July 2020.
Elliott Advisor (HK) Limited, 'Open Letter to the Shareholders of Hyundai Motor Company' (28 February 2019) https://acceleratehyundai.com/wp-content/uploads/2019/02/2019-02-28-Elliott%E2%80%99s-Letter-to-Fellow-Shareholders-of-Hyundai-Motor-Company-ENG.pdf accessed 15 July 2020. See also So-Jung Yoon, '2021 Annual AGM Review (1): Shareholder Proposals and Company Responses', KCGS Report (6 March 2021) 8 www.cgs.kr/eng/common/brddown.jsp?fnm=FBHesF5SBk9RooH6vwVurAiJfGKNym95%2F1doErLw3fLJZqp6PC8CccibaHGGa9F30sdFYiYXb8J3vhSb%40PLUS%40KGDnFfFH2qZ%2F1T5t6p%40PLUS%40SVEQjsU%3D accessed 3 June 2021.

66 Eun-Young Jeong, 'Elliott Management loses Hyundai proxy fight' *MarketWatch* (22 March 2019) www.marketwatch.com/story/elliott-management-loses-hyundai-proxy-fight-2019-03-22 accessed 15 July 2020.

domestic and foreign public shareholders to nominate an outside director responsible for shareholder rights protection with effect from 2019; (2) to expand the size of the board and to increase diversity and competence in the board; and (3) to reallocate the position of the outside director nomination committee chair to an outside director from an insider director.[67]

8.3.4.2 Domestic Activist Funds

At the end of 2018, KCGI, a Korean activist fund, became the second largest shareholder of Hanjin KAL, a holding company of Hanjin Group which owns Korean Air Lines. The KCGI subsequently called for improved corporate governance of Hanjin KAL, highlighting well-publicized wrongdoings by the Cho family, the largest shareholder of Hanjin Group.[68] At the AGM of Hanjin Kal held in March 2019, the KCGI submitted a shareholder proposal to appoint new outside directors and an auditor and to reduce the ceiling for director remuneration, among others.[69] The NPS also sent a public letter and asked for private dialogue, citing the controlling shareholder family's ethics issues and consequent degradation of the firm value. For the March 2019 annual meeting, the NPS proposed that the company amend its AOI and introduce stricter qualifications for directors.[70]

Such proposals, however, were not put forward for consideration at the AGM because the court cited Hanjin Kal's petition for opposition to the provisional injunction request for an AGM proposal filed by the KCGI. Although the NPS's proposal was also voted down, it remained a successful engagement campaign, as it supposedly motivated active shareholder voting, which removed then-chairman of Hanjin Group Yang-Ho Cho from inside directorship at Korea Air amid mounting negative public sentiment.

In the next AGM held in March 2020, a bitterly contested proxy fight was waged between the board and the three-party alliance participated in by the KCGI, Bando E&C and former VP Hyun-Ah Cho over the appointment of directors and a professional manager, the amendment of the AOI and so on.[71] In February 2020, the KCGI proposed to appoint eight inside and outside directors and to amend the AOI, which included the adoption of the electronic voting system and strengthened directorial qualification requirements. In its board of directors' meeting held in March 2020, Hanjin KAL decided to present the agenda items proposed by the KCGI at the 2020 AGM, but they were all voted down.[72]

8.4 CONCLUDING REMARKS

Shareholder engagement has gained traction in Korea. Institutional investors have become more active, and listed companies have started to proactively adopt shareholder-friendly policies, seeking to improve corporate governance. The Korea Stewardship Code seems to have played

67 See Yoon (n. 65).

68 Joo-young Kim and Jeong Seo, 'First Step Analysis: Shareholder Activism & Engagement South Korea' *Lexology* (23 May 2020) www.lexology.com/library/detail.aspx?g=0ee59c08-5a7b-493b-a9a7-38538758e84f accessed 15 July 2020.

69 Jhoo Dong-chan, 'KCGI Opposes Cho's Return to Hanjin' *The Korea Times* (12 June 2019) www.koreatimes.co.kr/www/biz/2021/04/513_270523.html accessed 15 July 2020.

70 So-Jung Yoon, '2020 AGM Review (4): Detailed Analysis of AGM Voting Results – Focused on Outside Shareholders' voting)', KCGS Report (9 July 2020) www.cgs.kr/eng/common/brddown.jsp?fnm=dFAaWws1FHG1IvDB9Cpn%2FIVHP2bfIpexxX12IdVHIqnlj%40PLUS%40UR9%2FkOgoitJP4jYDuhCKovyFtkaiJ4gUNwreEYm8s8wlKoD8GWXnPy3DvOOKI%3D accessed 3 June 2021.

71 Ji-hyoung Son, 'KCGI-Heiress Coalition Ups Ante to Dethrone Hanjin Successor' *The Korea Herald* (13 February 2020) http://news.koreaherald.com/view.php?ud=20200213000873&md=20200216003050_BL. accessed 15 July 2020.

72 Cho et al. (n. 23).

an important part. Institutional investors adopting the Code have demonstrated greater willingness to communicate and engage with their investee companies and to bring about changes in corporate governance. This has in turn helped to enhance shareholder value, as some empirical evidence suggests.

It remains to be seen how shareholder engagement in Korea will continue to evolve in the future. Recently, there has been a rise in the environmental, social and governance (ESG)-related engagement in Korean capital markets. Korean listed companies are expected to face increasing shareholder activism concerning ESG matters, in the long-term and sustainable interests of both the company, shareholders, stakeholders and the like.

9

Shareholder Voting and Engagement in Taiwan

Chang-Hsien Tsai and Chao-Tsung Huang

Taiwan, along with its East Asian counterparts like China and South Korea, has enthusiastically transplanted legal institutions from legally advanced countries such as the United States to improve its legal infrastructure for corporate governance. After transplanting certain Japanese institutions initially, Taiwan has more recently shifted its focus towards US law, which now significantly influences modern Taiwanese corporate and securities laws.[1]

Taiwan has long struggled with the problem of controlling shareholders retaining their control through corporate pyramids. This issue became particularly problematic after the last Asian economic crisis more than two decades ago.[2] Given the conflicts or agency problems arising between the controlling and minority shareholders due to cross-shareholding corporate pyramids, regulations must be implemented in Taiwan. When it comes to regulatory solutions to the aforementioned problems, independent directors have been presented as corporate governance gatekeepers[3] – the magic bullet for minority shareholders – while amendments to the Company Act (CA) and the Securities and Exchange Act (SEA) for more than a decade have been intended to empower shareholders by balancing the power of minority shareholders and management or controlling shareholders. Accordingly, this chapter will discuss the legal toolkit furnished under the CA and SEA regarding shareholder engagement and voting in Taiwan, as well as its related policy implications.

Section 9.1 provides a general overview of Taiwan's corporate law and governance model. Section 9.2 analyzes the legal means of shareholder engagement in Taiwan from a more doctrinal perspective. Section 9.3 illustrates shareholder voting and engagement in practice, highlighting the role played by the Securities and Futures Investors Protection Center (SFIPC)[4] – a quasi-public foundation established and controlled by the securities authority, that is, the Financial Supervisory Commission (FSC) – in safeguarding the interests of minority shareholders

1 See Wen Yeu Wang and Wang Ruu Tseng, 'Taiwan: Corporate Governance of Publicly Held Companies' in Andreas M. Fleckner and Klaus J. Hopt (eds.), *Comparative Corporate Governance: A Functional and International Analysis* (Cambridge University Press 2013) 212; Wang Ruu Tseng and Wallace Wen Yeu Wang, 'Derivative Actions in Taiwan: Legal and Cultural Hurdles with a Glimmer of Hope for the Future' in Dan W. Puchniak, Harald Baum and Michael Ewing-Chow (eds.), *The Derivative Action in Asia: A Comparative and Functional Approach* (Cambridge University Press 2012) 215–16; Hsin-Ti Chang, Yu-Hsin Lin and Ying-Hsin Tsai, 'From Double Board to Unitary Board System: The Corporate Governance Reform in Taiwan' in Harald Baum et al. (eds.), *Independent Directors in Asia: A Historical, Contextual and Comparative Approach* (Cambridge University Press 2016) 241; Ching-Ping Shao, 'The Evolution of Company Law in Taiwan' in Yun-chien Chang, Wei Shen and Wen-yeu Wang (eds.), *Private Law in China and Taiwan: Legal and Economic Analyses* (Cambridge University Press 2016) 276–7.

2 See s. 9.1.3.

3 See s. 9.1.1.

4 Securities and Futures Investors Protection Center (SFIPC), 'About SFIPC: Introduction' www.sfipc.org.tw/MainWeb/Article.aspx?L=2&SNO=I6M+rmmp+ncCQmZoO7Z28g== accessed 14 July 2020.

via shareholder litigation and engagement. It also discusses the policy approach taken by the FSC in shaping and enhancing shareholder activism, focusing on the role performed by institutional investors in Taiwan. Section 9.4 concludes.

9.1 INTRODUCTION: TAIWAN'S CORPORATE LAW AND CORPORATE GOVERNANCE

9.1.1 *Allocation of Corporate Decision-Making: From Two-Tier to One-Tier Corporate Structure*

Taiwan's civil law is firmly based on that of Japan. Since the enactment of the CA in 1929, as summarized in Table 9.1, Taiwan has adopted the traditional binary or dual board model (also known as the 'two-tier system') in which both directors and supervisors are elected by shareholders.[5] Typically composed of executives and a few outside directors, the board of directors is generally tasked with the management of corporate affairs, while supervisors are responsible for monitoring the performance of managers and the board of directors.[6] However, under the two-tier corporate structure, supervisors have often been criticized for their inability to successfully monitor boards, due to their passivity and close ties with the directors and controlling shareholders, who usually determine the elections of both directors and supervisors.[7]

In the first decade of the twenty-first century, Taiwan formally began to transplant a unitary Anglo-American style of board of directors and independent directors (also known as the 'one-tier system') into its corporate governance structures, with audit committees replacing supervisors.[8] According to the FSC,[9] all publicly traded companies listing shares on the Taiwan Stock Exchange (TWSE) and Taipei Exchange are required to establish audit committees consisting of all independent directors (at least three of whom should sit on an audit committee) to replace

TABLE 9.1 *Simplified classification of corporate governance structure*

Type of structure	One-tier system (Anglo-American style): Taiwan's reform trend	Two-tier system (Japanese/ Taiwanese traditional style)
Task of the board of directors	Monitoring managerial performance	Performing management function
Internal oversight	Independent directors/audit committees	Supervisors (*Kansayaku* in Japanese)

Source: Tsai (n. 5) 471.

5 See Chang-hsien Tsai, 'The Failure of Corporate Internal Controls and Internal Information Sharing: A Conceptual Framework for Taiwan' (2015) 45 Hong Kong Law Journal 469, 470–1; Christopher Chen, 'Taiwan' in Bruce Aronson and Joongi Kim (eds.), *Corporate Governance in Asia: A Comparative Approach* (Cambridge University Press 2019) 327.

6 Ibid., 331.

7 Ibid., 331–2.

8 See Lawrence S. Liu, 'The Politics of Corporate Governance in Taiwan' in Hideki Kanda et al. (eds.), *Transforming Corporate Governance in East Asia* (Routledge 2008) 258–9, 275–6; Yu-Hsin Lin, 'Overseeing Controlling Shareholders: Do Independent Directors Constrain Tunneling in Taiwan?' (2011) 12 San Diego International Law Journal 363, 395–7.

9 The FSC is the competent authority generally in charge of all financial markets in Taiwan, including the securities market. Its position in Taiwan is similar to that of the Securities and Exchange Commission in the United States. See FSC's website www.fsc.gov.tw/en/home.jsp?id=9&parentpath=0,1 accessed 30 July 2019.

all supervisors by the end of 2022.[10] This exemplifies a typical regulatory strategy of the FSC based on the widespread belief that independent directors ensure good corporate governance.[11]

9.1.2 *Power Demarcation between Shareholders and Boards*

As far as the demarcation of powers between the board of directors and shareholders in corporations is concerned, the Taiwanese board of directors has the right to decide on general affairs of the corporation – referred to as director primacy.[12] Therefore, in the execution of general business, shareholder opinions are merely recommendations to the board of directors, with which the board is not obliged to comply.[13] Nevertheless, if the matter is specified – by law or regulation – to be decided by shareholders, the board of directors shall, under Article 193 of the CA, act in accordance with the Articles of Incorporation and the resolutions of the shareholders' meetings. Specifically, the demarcation of authority between shareholders' general meetings and board of directors can be reduced to the following three broad categories under the CA:[14] (1) matters exclusively for shareholders' meetings;[15] (2) matters exclusively for the board of directors;[16] and (3) matters in which general meetings and the board of directors share resolution power.[17] Given the concept of director primacy illustrated under Article 202 of the CA, the issues reserved for a general meeting vote are fewer than those reserved for the board of the directors, to whom residual power belongs.

Under Taiwanese law, there are two main types of shareholder resolutions: ordinary resolutions and special resolutions. Ordinary resolutions are those adopted by a majority of the shareholders present at general meetings representing a majority of the shares issued by the company, provided that these shareholders have the right to vote at the general meeting.[18] Unless it is explicitly provided that a special resolution is required, an ordinary resolution is sufficient for the matters reserved for the shareholder meeting to decide under the CA.

Special resolutions refer to those passed by a majority of the votes cast by the shareholders voting either in person or by proxy at a general meeting attended by holders of two-thirds or more of the total outstanding shares of the company or their representatives. For public companies, the CA also allows a special resolution to be adopted via approval by two-thirds or more of the shareholders present at a shareholder meeting, if the total number of shares represented by those

10 See Order of the FSC, Jin Guan Zheng Fa Zi No. 10703452331 (passed on 19 December 2018) (Taiwan). For private companies, the two-tier system remains. For companies listed on the TWSE and Taipei Exchange, the one-tier system is required. Public companies not listed on the TWSE and Taipei Exchange can choose either the one-tier system or a hybrid system where independent directors and supervisors co-exist.

11 See Tsai (n. 5) 471–2.

12 Len-Yu Liu, *Sian Dai Gong Sih Fa [Modern Corporate Law]* 562 (14th ed. New Sharing 2019). Director primacy can be summarized from art. 202 of the CA.

13 Ibid., 562–3.

14 Lian-Shun Chen, *Sin Gong Sih Fa [New Company Law]* (Rui Xing 2018) 275–7.

15 Examples of this category include: lifting the upper limit of 40 per cent of paid-in capital on investment by a public company (art. 13, para. 2 of the CA), discharging directors and supervisors (art. 199, para. 2 and art. 227, para. 4 of the CA), amending the Articles of Incorporation in a company (art. 277 of the CA), etc.

16 Except for those matters exclusively assigned to general meetings in line with laws or corporate charters, most of the corporate affairs are within the authority of the board of directors. An example under the CA is the appointment, discharging and remuneration of high-ranked managers (art. 29, para. 1 of the CA).

17 Under the final category, this power sharing can be exemplified by substantial property transactions (art. 185 of the CA) and company division or merger with other companies (art. 316, para. 1 and art. 317, para. 3 of the CA). Before the resolutions may be submitted to shareholders' meetings, relevant plans and assessments shall be adopted or made through resolutions by the board of directors, who are required to meet their fiduciary duties of professionals as a gatekeeper.

18 Art. 174 of the CA.

present at such a meeting is less than two-thirds but more than half of the total outstanding shares of the company. In general, a special resolution is passed regarding matters that would significantly affect the company's operations or its shareholders' interests, such as mergers and acquisitions,[19] dismissal of directors[20] or amendments to the Articles of Incorporation.[21]

Based on these policies, the board of directors is the core decision-maker for Taiwanese companies.[22] It is therefore important to know in whose interests the board should make decisions. Following the thoroughgoing revision of Taiwan's CA in 2018, the answer to this question has likely changed with the altered ideology and conception of corporate governance in Taiwan. The newly added Article 1, Paragraph 2 of the CA encourages companies to fulfil their corporate social responsibility (CSR) when management makes business decisions. This means that CSR becomes incorporated into internal corporate governance and operational activities through the adoption of so-called constituency statutes[23] and the transformation of the shareholder primacy model into a stakeholder or CSR model.[24] In this way, the board – in its decision-making – will no longer consider the interest of shareholders alone, but also the potential impact of a proposal on other stakeholders (e.g. suppliers, consumers, employees).

9.1.3 *Ownership Structure: Dominance by Controlling Minority Shareholders*

A 'controlling minority structure' (CMS) refers to a situation in which controlling shareholders possess an excessive extent of control power over a firm larger than that of their cash-flow rights – or the shares they own.[25] It is common in Taiwan for the controlling shareholders of a company to exercise control via a pyramid structure or circular/cross shareholding, as discussed later in this section, while not necessarily holding a majority of shares; a large portion of Taiwanese companies are controlled by families as well.[26]

Table 9.2 illustrates how shares of Taiwanese public companies listed on the TWSE are held among individuals, non-financial institutions and financial institutions. According to the statistics furnished by the TWSE, as of December 2019, 35.99 per cent of the capital of the TWSE-listed companies was invested by individuals (35.55 per cent by domestic individuals and 0.44 per cent by foreign individuals); 35.85 per cent by non-financial institutions (25.33 per cent by domestic ones and 10.52 per cent by foreign ones); 6.75 per cent by financial institutions; 16.49

19 Art. 315 of the CA.

20 Art. 199 of the CA.

21 Art. 277 of the CA.

22 This only holds for the decisions the board is able to make, not for those made by shareholders under the laws.

23 See Caroline Flammer and Aleksandra Kacperczyk, 'The Impact of Stakeholder Orientation on Innovation: Evidence from a Natural Experiment' (2016) 62(7) Management Science 1982, 1982 (stating that US state-level constituency statutes 'allow directors to consider stakeholders' interests when making business decisions').

24 See In-Jaw Lai, 'Zheng Quan Jiao Yi Fa Wu Shi Nian' ['50th Anniversary of the Securities and Exchange Act'] (2019) 293 Yue Dan Fa Xue Za Zhi [*Taiwan LR*] 5, 12; Chang-hsien Tsai, 'Cong Gong Si Fa Di Yi Tiao Xiu Zheng Tan Gong Si Zhi Li Zhi Nei Wai Bu Ji Zhi – Jian Lun Qi Ye She Hui Ze Ren De Tui Dong Mo Shi' ['Reflections from the Amendment to Article 1 of Taiwan's Company Act in 2018 on Internal and External Accountability Mechanisms of Corporate Governance: With a Look at How to Promote Corporate Social Responsibility'] (2018) 36 Cheng Da Fa Xue [*Cheng Kung LR*] 89, 139, 146–7.

25 See generally Lucian Aye Bebchuk et al., 'Stock Pyramids, Cross-Ownership and Dual Class Equity: The Mechanisms and Agency Costs of Separating Control From Cash-Flow Rights' in Randall K. Morck (ed.), *Concentrated Corporate Ownership* (University of Chicago Press 2000) 445–60; Lin (n. 8) 368.

26 Ibid., 368. See also Tseng and Wang (n. 1) 230–1; Cheng-Fong Chou, 'Are Independent Directors Effective Monitors in Taiwan? – A Theoretical Analysis' (2013) 8:1 National Taiwan University Law Review 49, 72–4; Chang and others (n. 1) 259 ('The corporate ownership of Taiwan's public companies is characterised by its concentrated, family-dominated nature, as well as by the prevalence of business groups').

TABLE 9.2 *Source of capital invested in listing companies on the TWSE (as of December 2019)*

	Individual	Non-financial Institution	Financial Institution	Securities Investment Trust	Gov't Agency	Share Buy-backs
Domestic	35.55%	25.33%				
Foreign	0.44%	10.52%				
Total	35.99%	35.85%	6.75%	16.49%	4.79%	0.13%

Source: TWSE.

per cent by securities investment trust companies (i.e. mutual funds);[27] 4.79 per cent by government agencies;[28] and 0.13 per cent bought back by the listed companies themselves.[29]

Regarding the data in Table 9.2, although 35.85 per cent of the capital of the TWSE-listed companies is invested by non-financial institutions, commentators have previously maintained that these institutional investors probably included special-purpose investment legal entities established by controlling shareholders to acquire and retain shareholding in their listed companies. These commentators also noted that the more these legal entities invested into a company's capital, the more extensive the control power exerted by these controlling shareholders over the company in excess of their cash-flow rights, and the greater the probability that these controlling shareholders served as directors or supervisors.[30]

CMS-related issues typically involve a vertical cross-shareholding or a circular shareholding, meaning that a subordinate company also holds shares of its controlling company. The percentage of such shareholdings by a subordinate company might or might not cross the threshold of control defined under the CA.[31] Commentators illustrate that a vertical cross-shareholding structure is very common in Taiwan.[32] This structure would possibly allow the controlling shareholder to avoid rules regulating control under Taiwan's CA, especially those which placed restrictions on purchasing and even holding shares by subordinate companies or affiliated enterprises.[33]

As far as the ownership structure in Taiwan is concerned, the statistics in 1997 and 1998 showed that 72 per cent of Taiwanese firms had controlling shareholders and about 83 per cent of companies were controlled by families.[34] One study further demonstrated that according to the

[27] Given their relatively small stakes in Taiwanese securities markets, financial and non-financial institutional investors generally have not played an active role in corporate governance, although there are anecdotal examples of some rising shareholder activism. See s. 9.3.4.2.

[28] Section 9.1.4 illustrates how some Taiwanese listed firms are controlled by the state via a controlling minority shareholder status, and discusses the ramifications of this control.

[29] TWSE, 'Source of Capital Invested in Companies Listing Shares on the TWSE' www.twse.com.tw/zh/statistics/statisticsList?type=07&subType=256 accessed 23 June 2019.

[30] See Yue Zhong Wu and Xiao Ling Shen, 'Ji Gou Tou Zi Ren Gong Si Zhi Li Yu Gong Si Jia Zhi Yan Jiu – Yi Taiwan Dian Zi Ye Wei Li' ['The Study of Institutional Investor, Corporate Governance and Corporate Value– A Case of Electronic Industry in Taiwan'] (Address, Eighth International Conference on Interdisciplinary and Multifunctional Business Management, Soochow University, Taipei, Taiwan, 22 May 2004) (on file with author) 686.

[31] See s. 9.2.3.1.

[32] See, e.g., Yin-Hua Yeh, 'Cong Gong Si Zhi Li Mian Po Xi Tai Dian Cai Wu Kun Jing Shi Mo' ['Profiling the Financial Distress of the Pacific Electric Wire and Cable Co., Ltd. from the Angle of Corporate Governance'] (2003) 218 Kuai Ji Yan Jiu Yue Kan [*Accounting Research Monthly*] 99, 104.

[33] See s. 9.2.3.1.

[34] Yin-Hua Yeh and Tracie Woidtke, 'Commitment or Entrenchment? Controlling Shareholders and Board Composition' (2005) 29 Journal of Banking and Finance 1857, 1874.

data collected from 2003 to 2015 on voting rights and cash-flow rights in Taiwan, even in 2015, CMS and family control are characteristics of Taiwanese public firms – similar to the pattern of ownership in 1997.[35] This fact is highly relevant to the issue of CMS and circular/cross-shareholding, since circular/cross-shareholding contributes to the control power of the controlling minority shareholders or families. The controlling shareholders (or controlling families) often retain their control by establishing a pyramidal structure, circular/cross-shareholding or personal participation in the board of directors, so that a separation of ownership and cash-flow rights is common.[36] This phenomenon has led to numerous issues such as tunnelling, which exemplifies an agency problem between a 'controlling-minority' shareholder and other minority shareholders.[37] If we examine the Rebar Group corporate scandal of 2006–7 as a classic and representative example, the family patriarch Mr Wang siphoned funds from group companies for years by using shell companies to enter into related party transactions (RPTs)[38] approved by seemingly unrelated juridical directors who were actually controlled by the Wang family.[39] Accordingly, strengthening corporate governance and protecting shareholders' rights have emerged as urgent issues.

9.1.4 *Government: A Regulator, a Player, or Both?*

Like its peers in East Asia, Taiwan's government is actively involved in market development and reform.[40] From time to time, the Taiwanese government, typically through the Ministry of Finance (MoF), even participates in the market aggressively as a player, while doubling as a market regulator.[41] The dual role of the government in the context of the contest over corporate control in Taiwan is well illustrated by the Taishin–CH Bank merger saga, discussed later in this section. This case, by no means untypical, exemplifies the government's involvement in the affairs of private business organizations.

In recent years, efforts to reform the Taiwanese financial markets have resulted in a number of mergers between state-controlled banks (either completely or partially owned by the

35 Yin-Hua Yeh, *Gong Si Zhi Li: Quan Qiu Guan Dian, Tai Wan Ti Yan [Corporate Governance: Global Perspective and Taiwanese Experience]* (2nd ed., Tsang Hai 2017) 113.

36 See Wen-Yeu Wang and Yuan-Chi Pang, 'Minority Controlling Shareholders: An Analytical Framework and Its Application to Taiwan' (2007) 2 National Taiwan University Law Review 81, 87; Yeh (n. 35) 106–7.

37 See Lin (n. 8) 369; Taying Liao, 'Lun Jiao Cha Chi Gu Zhi Du – Ling Lei De Cai Wu Cao Zuo Yu Qi Ye Jie He' ['On the System of Cross Shareholding – An Alternative Financial Tool and Business Combination'] (1999) 45 Yue Dan Fa Xue Za Zhi [*Taiwan Law Review*] 89, 89.

38 Both theoretical and empirical studies have concluded that RPTs 'are evident as one of the major ways through which controlling shareholders divert corporate resources to themselves' and that the 'prevalence of abusive RPTs could hamper market integrity and lead to a national discount on the capital market'. Lin (n. 8) 365. For a recent example of such a study, see Christopher Chen and others, 'Board Independence as a Panacea to Tunneling? An Empirical Study of Related-Party Transactions in Hong Kong and Singapore' (2018) 15(4) Journal of Empirical Legal Studies 987, 988.

39 See Liu (n. 8) 258. The problem demonstrated by the Rebar case is still current, and contributed to sweeping changes in the direction of Taiwan's corporate governance reforms in the wake of this case. For example, the SEA was amended in 2006 to allow public companies to choose whether to adopt the one-tier system and independent directors. From 2007 onwards, more and more public companies have gradually been required by the FSC to appoint independent directors and to establish audit committees. Chang, Shen and Wang (n. 1) 244–8.

40 This is the so-called East-Asian developmental-state model, whose characteristics include administrative control of finance. See Y. P. (Alex) Yang, 'Envisaging an East Asian Model of Corporate Governance: A Developmental State Perspective' in Chang-Fa Lo et al. (eds.), *Legal Thoughts between the East and the West in the Multilevel Legal Order: A Liber Amicorum in Honour of Professor Herbert Han-Pao Ma* (Springer 2016) 448–9.

41 Liu (n. 8) 257.

government).[42] In a proposed merger in 2013 between two listed financial institutions, Taishin Financial Holding Co., Ltd. (Taishin) and Chang-hua Bank (CH Bank), the MoF (the second largest shareholder of CH Bank) strongly opposed the merger initiated by Taishin (CH Bank's largest shareholder), and also requested that Taishin[43] recuse itself from the relevant deliberations in the resolution of the general meeting.[44] Interestingly, the MoF initially supported Taishin's merger proposal,[45] but later changed its mind. This shift of position was due largely to public opinion. Interest groups, including CH Bank employees and its labour union, persuaded the MoF to oppose the merger.[46] Specifically, the MoF's opposition to the merger, according to its claims, reflected the need to retain the jobs of CH Bank employees.[47] In Taiwan, labour unions in state-owned entities (SOEs) usually oppose privatisation or mergers by private entities, viewing such mergers as being tantamount to a cheap sale to private businesses.[48] In the 2000s, labour unions pressured politicians and government agencies against full privatization when the government was promoting mergers between banks.[49] However, because the labour unions are strong enough to defeat privatization plans,[50] they have sometimes supported attempts by government agencies, including the MoF, to maintain control over CH Bank and other banks partially owned by the government, especially during relevant deliberations in the resolution of M&A transactions in the general meeting. Therefore, as seen in the Taishin–CH Bank merger, the result of a government agency like the MoF holding voting equity in a private bank may be costly in particular where labour 'is the primary constituent of the corporation that seeks influence over the corporation'.[51] This representative case in Taiwan illustrates that even in a private bank with a government agency as the second largest majority shareholder,[52] pressure from non-shareholder constituencies as interested groups can effectively influence the government agency's decisions,[53] despite the fact that the benefit of other minority shareholders might be sacrificed.[54]

42 Jihtsan Huang, *Huang Ri Can Kan Bing Gou: Tai Wan Qi Ye Tuo Tai Huan Gu De Sai Ju [Huang Jih-tsan on M&A: A Game for the Resurrection of Taiwanese Businesses]* (Economy Daily News 2012) 218.

43 It seems that Taishin had intended to merge with CH Bank using a traditional approach. After becoming the largest shareholder of CH Bank, Taishin would convene a shareholder meeting to approve the merger agreement. This approach was also initially supported by the government shareholder (the MoF). The MoF had agreed to gradually transfer the control of CH Bank to the highest-price private bidder for CH Bank's shares, which eventually turned out to be Taishin. Huang (n. 42) 221.

44 Taying Liao and Chao-Sheng Chiang, 'Jiu Ping Jiu Jiu De Zhang Yin He Bing Zheng Yi' ['Same Old Controversies in the Chan-Hua Bank Merger'] (2013) 230 Tai Wan Ben Tu Fa Xue Za Zhi [*Taiwan Law Journal*] 29, 32.

45 Huang (n. 42) 221.

46 For an example of the application of the 'public choice' or 'interest group' perspective to corporate law, see Marcel Kahan and Edward Rock, 'Symbolic Corporate Governance Politics' (2014) 94 Boston University Law Review 1997, 2027.

47 Liao and Chiang (n. 44) 34; See also Huang (n. 42) 222 (The labour union of CH Bank has, at least twice, opposed the merger initiated by Taishin at different stages).

48 Liu (n. 8) 261–3.

49 Ibid., 261–2.

50 Ibid., 268–9.

51 See J. W. Verret, 'The Bailout Through a Public Choice Lens: Government-Controlled Corporations as a Mechanism for Rent Transfer' (2010) 40 Seton Hall Law Review 1521, 1553.

52 As of 20 April 2021, Taishin remained the largest shareholder with 22.55 per cent of CH Bank, while the MoF held the second largest share with 12.19 per cent. See 'Major Shareholders' Chang Hwa Bank (彰化銀行), 20 April 2021 www.bankchb.com/frontend/mashup_eng.jsp?funcId=35ebfbf315 accessed 20 February 2022.

53 It should be noted that the proviso made within para. 3 of art. 8 of the CA excludes liabilities from government agencies as controlling shareholders.

54 Verret (n. 51) 1553–4.

9.2 LEGAL MEANS OF SHAREHOLDER ENGAGEMENT

9.2.1 *Shareholders' Right to Call a Meeting*

According to paragraph 1 of Article 170 under the CA, companies in Taiwan hold two types of shareholders' meeting – annual general meetings (AGMs), which are held at least once every year, and extraordinary general meetings (EGMs), which are held when necessary. There are a number of purposes for which EGMs are held. As discussed in this section, EGMs can be held voluntarily by those with statutory authority, such as shareholders that cross ownership thresholds and procedural ones illustrated under Articles 173 and 173-1 of the CA. In addition, EGMs can sometimes be a statutory requirement.[55]

Furthermore, Article 171 states that '[a] shareholders meeting shall, unless otherwise provided for in this Act, be convened by the Board of Directors'. Therefore, as a rule, the board of directors has the right to call both AGMs and EGMs. Shareholders have the right to hold a general meeting under circumstances provided by Articles 173 and 173-1 of the CA as well as Article 43-5 of the SEA. Before the amendment to the CA in 2018, shareholders who intended to call a general meeting were required to ask the board of the directors to call it in the first instance and then obtain approval from the competent authority – that is, the Ministry of Economic Affairs (MoEA) – before convening an EGM or AGM on their own.[56] To strengthen shareholder activism, Article 173-1 was added to the CA in 2018. It gives shareholders who possess 50 per cent or more of the total number of outstanding shares of a company for a period of three months or longer the right to hold an EGM on their own, without having to ask the board of directors to facilitate the convening process and without having to obtain approval from the competent authorities beforehand, as required under Article 173 of the CA.[57] This amendment illustrates the long-standing difficulties facing insurgent shareholders when calling general meetings under Article 173 of the CA. For example, the MoEA and the Supreme Court used to have conflicting views on whether outside insurgents might, after obtaining approval from the competent authority, call an EGM to re-elect directors and supervisors in a contest over control.[58] In practice, however, the MoEA rarely grants approval for insurgents to call an AGM or EGM, due to its philosophy of refraining from intervening in a company's internal governance unless there is a complete functional breakdown. Due to the difficulties mentioned above, the invocation of Article 173 of the CA would often fail, and the inclusion of Article 173-1 helped address this issue. Moreover, to protect the interests of an acquiring company during the restructuring of a target company after a tender offer,[59] paragraph 4 of Article 43-5 of the SEA allows insurgent shareholders that possess more than 50 per cent of the total number of shares to ask the board of directors to convene a special meeting of shareholders without meeting other procedural requirements set out in paragraph 1 of Article 173-1 of the CA. Under this provision, however, outside insurgents are still faced with existing hurdles for making such requests of the board of

[55] See arts. 201 and 217-1 of the CA; arts. 26-3, para. 7 and 14-2, para. 6 of the SEA.

[56] See art. 173, paras. 1 and 2 of the CA (only applied in EGMs); art. 173, para. 4 of the CA (applied in both AGMs and EGMs). This provision is still the current law even subsequent to the amendment to the CA in 2018.

[57] Therefore, under the new law, only the majority shareholders, not minority shareholders, can call an EGM without resorting to the board of directors and/or the MoEA. The insurgent majority shareholders have to surmount this formidable initial hurdle before they have the opportunity to win a majority of seats in the board.

[58] Chih-Ming Jau, '2018 Nian Gong Si Fa Xiu Fa Ho – Gu Dong Zhi Gu Dong Hui Zhao Ji Quan' ['After the Amendment to the Company Act in 2018 – Shareholders' Right to Call General Meetings'] (2019) 197 Yue Dan Fa Xue Jiao Shi [*Taiwan Jurist*] 26, 27–8.

[59] Liu (n. 12) 380.

directors or obtaining approval from competent authorities before successfully seizing control of a given listed company from its incumbent management.

As for the regular term for calling a general meeting, under paragraph 3 of Article 172 of the CA, in any public company, a notice to convene an AGM shall be given to each shareholder no later than thirty days prior to the scheduled meeting date. In the event that a public company intends to convene an EGM, a notice shall be given to each shareholder no later than fifteen days prior to the scheduled meeting date. Furthermore, Article 172, paragraph 4 of the CA states that causes or subjects of a general meeting to be convened shall be indicated in the individual notice to be given to shareholders.

9.2.2 *Shareholders' Proposal Right*

Given the concept of director primacy illustrated by Article 202, the agenda in general meetings is normally set by the board of directors.[60] However, in 2005 and 2018, Article 172-1 was added and amended to the CA, giving shareholders the right to add proposals to the agenda of an AGM.

Under Article 172-1 of the CA, eligibility to add shareholder proposals – that is, the ownership requirement – is limited to shareholders 'holding one percent (1%) or more of the total number of outstanding shares of a company'. This provision has been interpreted to include cases of both shareholding by a single shareholder and joint shareholding by multiple shareholders.[61] Although Taiwan's legislation gives shareholders the right to add proposals in AGMs, this right is limited, as only one matter – which must be described in 300 words or less – is permitted in each single shareholder proposal.[62] These procedural requirements are significant. While the Taiwanese government has transplanted the shareholders' proposal right from the United States, it realizes that this right encourages shareholder activism, and has prudently hedged it around with requirements that tend to blunt its effect.[63]

Significantly, the 2018 amendment to Article 172-1 of the CA provides that the board of directors 'may' include a proposal from shareholders in the agenda that urges a company to promote public interests or fulfill its CSR, while both the aforementioned ownership and procedural requirements apply as well. On the one hand, this introduction of statutory authority demonstrates the capacity of shareholders in an AGM to propose advisory resolutions regarding CSR, which are usually non-binding given director primacy.[64] In fact, a leading scholar has argued that shareholders meeting the ownership requirement such as institutional investors should make good use of this device to carry on shareholder engagement with their portfolio

60 Ibid., 401.

61 Ibid., 402.

62 To encourage brevity, Taiwan applies a 300-word restriction, unlike the 500-word maximum in the United States. Ibid., 403.

63 Ibid., 403. The then general manager of the SFIPC, which was established initially in Taiwan to serve the function of US lawyer-driven class actions, collected data on all exercises of shareholder proposal rights in Taiwanese-listed companies up to September 2019, and found eight proposals that had been made but were later excluded from the agenda in the AGMs. These proposals were excluded primarily because the board of directors concluded either that their nature was such that they could not be resolved by a general meeting, or that they contained more than one matter to be addressed in a single proposal. The general manager also added that given directory primacy under the CA, the board of directors, with the statutory authority to review and interpret proposals, would be more likely to exclude shareholder proposals maliciously. Jue-Sheng Lu, 'Zhuan Jia Hui Zhen Gong Si Fa Gu Dong Xing Dong Zhu Yi Zai Jin Hua' ['Experts Consult Together about the Further Evolution of Shareholder Activism in the Company Act'] (16 September 2019) *Jin Zhou Kan [Business Today]* 46.

64 *See* Stephen Bottomley, 'Rethinking the Law on Shareholder-Initiated Resolutions at Company General Meetings' (2019) 43(1) Melbourne University Law Review 93.

companies.[65] On the other hand, as discussed before,[66] in line with paragraph 2 of Article 1 of the CA, adopting non-shareholder constituency statutes, such as the 2018 amendment to shareholders' proposal rights, has expanded the board's authority to include CSR proposals while introducing shareholder 'sustainability' activism. Nowadays, many international institutional investors would, based on socially responsible investment (SRI), urge portfolio companies to pay attention to Environmental, Social and Governance (ESG) issues.[67]

9.2.3 *Voting*

9.2.3.1 One Share–One Vote and Cumulative Voting

Paragraph 1 of Article 179 of the CA is the statutory basis of one share–one vote (OSOV). Examples of exceptions to OSOV embrace, for instance, the upper limits on the voting rights permissible in the case of proxy voting[68] and prohibitions on voting rights if companies possess their own shares directly – as in case of share buybacks – or indirectly – through their subordinate companies.[69]

Under the current CA, public companies must adopt cumulative voting when electing directors and supervisors, without exceptions. Under this regime, each shareholder's vote number is equal to the number of directors to be elected, and all shareholders can freely cast their votes by, for example, giving all their votes to one single candidate.[70] The purpose of cumulative voting is to make it possible for minority shareholders to have their candidates elected as board members or supervisors.[71]

Although mandatory cumulative voting has been adopted in Taiwan for all companies since 1966, the 2001 amendment to the CA allowed companies to exclude it.[72] In December 2011, the legislature reinstated mandatory cumulative voting. An empirical study of the effectiveness of mandatory cumulative voting in Taiwan indicates that by making use of the exogenous legal change taking place under the CA in December 2011 'mandating cumulative voting may not create a long-term effect because controlling shareholders find other means to maintain influence'.[73] All in all, Taiwan stands out as one of the very few Asian jurisdictions mandating cumulative voting for public companies.[74]

65 Liu (n. 12) 404.
66 See s. 9.1.2.
67 See, e.g., George Serafeim, 'Shareholder Activism on Sustainability Issues' (The Harvard Law School Forum on Corporate Governance and Financial Regulation, 25 July 2016) https://corpgov.law.harvard.edu/2016/07/25/shareholder-activism-on-sustainability-issues/ accessed 15 July 2020.
68 See s. 9.3.1.1.
69 See art. 179, para. 2 of the CA.
70 Art. 198 of the CA.
71 It has been questioned whether cumulative voting could have the function initially intended by the legislature. See Chien-Chung Lin, 'Yi Ge Guan Yu Lei Ji Tou Piao Zhi De Yi Huo' ['A Suspicious Case of Cumulative Voting'] (2013) 132 *Zheng Da Fa Xue Ping Lun [Chengchi LR]* 71. In practice, mandatory cumulative voting succeeded in winning the appointment of minority shareholder representatives to the boards in public companies. See, e.g., Ren Kai Ceng, 'Jing Ying Zheng Duo Wei Wan Dai Xu? Tai Feng Gai Xuan Nan Gang Jin Na Yi Xi Dong Shi' ['Control Contest Is Not Over and About to Be Continued? Nankang Rubber Tire Corp. Seized Merely One Board Seat in Federal Corp.'] *Jing Ji Ri Bao [Economics Daily]* (19 June 2020), https://money.udn.com/money/story/5612/4646307 accessed 21 July 2020.
72 Chen (n. 5) 334, 336.
73 Yu-Hsin Lin and Yun-Chien Chang, 'Does Mandating Cumulative Voting Weaken Controlling Shareholders? A Difference-in-Differences Approach' (2017) 52 International Review of Law and Economics 111, 111.
74 See Yu-Hsin Lin, 'When Activists Meet Controlling Shareholders in the Shadow of the Law: A Case Study of Hong Kong' (2019) 14(1) Asian Journal of Comparative Law 1, 13.

9.2.3.2 Majority of Minority Approval

RPTs could serve as one of the main channels through which controlling shareholders siphon off corporate value to benefit themselves while hurting minority shareholders.[75] Article 178 of the CA provides the statutory basis for a primary form of approval for conflict-of-interest (CoI) transactions by a majority of the minority shareholders (usually known as MoM approval). This recusal requirement gives disinterested or independent minority shareholders a certain form of minority veto power to block an interested transaction involving controlling shareholders. Theoretically, if the controlling shareholder is on the other side of a contract either with a company it controls or one of its subsidiaries and 'the contract confers upon the controlling shareholder or a close associate a benefit (economic or otherwise) not available to the other shareholders, that controlling shareholder cannot vote on the resolution'.[76]

At the same time, as maintained by the legislature to encourage M&A, paragraph 6 of Article 18 of the Business Mergers and Acquisitions Act (BMAA) excludes the recusal requirement such as Article 178 of the CA (hereinafter the 'recusal exemption'). However, this recusal exemption applies *mutatis mutandis* in all types of M&A defined under the BMAA.[77] Hence, in CoI M&As, such as going-private transactions or Management Buy-Outs (MBOs), the majority shareholder or interested parties have no need to abstain from voting in board and general meetings and may surely vote on the resolutions.[78] In this case, controlling shareholders have little incentive to engage with outside minority shareholders, who have no say or veto rights to act as a counterbalance to controlling shareholders' clout in approving interested M&A transactions at both levels of board and general meetings.[79] This might be one of the reasons why in Taiwan, going-private transaction or MBO premiums as offered by controlling shareholders are often much lower than those seen elsewhere, for example in Hong Kong and the United States. In particular, as minority shareholders in Taiwan are deprived of an effective legal tool to seek effective intervention in the aforementioned CoI transactions of M&As, controlling shareholders are not forced to increase offers to win any non-existent MoM approval.[80]

9.2.4 *The Right to Request Information*

In Taiwan, shareholders rely mainly on Article 210 of the CA to request information. Under paragraph 2 of this article, shareholders may ask to inspect (including transcribing and making copies of) the Articles of Incorporation, accounting books and records by providing evidentiary

75 See ibid., 17; Luca Enriques and Tobias H. Tröger, 'The Law and (Some) Finance of Related Party Transactions: An Introduction' in Luca Enriques and Tobias H. Tröger (eds.), *The Law and Finance of Related Party Transactions* (Cambridge University Press 2019) 1, 3.

76 Lin (n. 74) 18.

77 See arts. 27, 28, 29, 30 and 35 of the BMAA.

78 See Chang-hsien Tsai, 'Xia Shi Jiao Yi Zhong Li Yi Chong Tu Zhi Jing Hua Ji Zhi: Cong Mei Guo Dell Gong Si Shou Gou An Tan Qi' ['Cleansing Devices for Conflicts of Interest Underlying Going-Private Transactions: A Commentary on the Management Buyout of Dell Inc.'] (2015) 44(2) Tai Da Fa Xue Lun Cong [National Taiwan University Law Journal] 533, 582.

79 See Lin (n. 74) 17.

80 See ibid., 30; Chang-hsien Tsai, 'Zi Si Fa Yuan Shi Zi Di 770 Hao Jie Shi Tan Si You Hua Bing Gou Jiao Yi Zhi Li Yi Chong Tu Hui Bi Zheng Yi: Jian Lun Yu Guo Ju An, Mei Guo Dai Er Dian Nao An De Bi Jiao' ['Reflections from Judicial Yuan Interpretation No. 770 on the Debate about Interested Directors and Shareholders Recusing Themselves from the Board and General Meeting Votes on Take-Private Transactions: With a Commentary on the Comparison with Management Buyouts of the Yageo Corporation and Dell Inc.'] (2019) 224 Wan Guo Fa Lu Shuang Yue Kan [FT Law Review] 12, 23.

documents to establish their interests involved.[81] While this provision grants shareholders the direct right to information, the books and records that shareholders are allowed to inspect remain quite limited. Further restricting this right is the fact that the MoEA, as the competent authority in this case, has taken a very strict and narrow view of 'his/her interest involved' – only legal interests such as claims and obligations arising from contracts and so forth would suffice.[82] In this case, commentators maintain that this interpretation of shareholder interests is too strict and much narrower than the view of 'a proper purpose for inspection' under US state law, and may therefore limit the frequency with which shareholders can invoke the right successfully.[83] To address the conundrum stemming from the aforementioned interpretation under Article 210, Article 210-1 was added to the 2018 amendment to the CA, granting shareholders mentioned in Article 173-1 and therefore qualified as 'other authorized conveners of shareholders' meetings' the right to request a company or its shareholder service agent (i.e. broker) to provide 'the roster of shareholders' (or shareholder list). The Director General of the Department of Commerce under the MoEA (i.e. the competent authority of the CA) commented that the aim of adding Article 210-1 was to complement the aforementioned new right to call an EGM, so as to empower shareholder activists such as insurgent shareholders to challenge the management in a proxy contest or takeover.[84]

When it comes to indirect rights of shareholders to request information, paragraph 1 of Article 245 of the CA and paragraph 2 of Article 38-1 of the SEA (applied in public companies only) grant shareholders that meet ownership and procedural requirements indirect rights to information. These shareholders may request the court to appoint inspectors who may then seek access to related corporate books and records, or the competent authority for public companies (that is, the FSC) may be requested to do so. Nevertheless, there could be some deficiency with the two indirect rights to information mentioned above. On the one hand, the government might be worried that shareholders are likely to abuse direct rights to information and may also be concerned about the angry backlash it may face from corporate management across industries. Therefore, these two provisions merely grant shareholders indirect rights to information, still relying on orders of the court (plus court-appointed inspectors) and the FSC to control the enforcement of the right to request information.[85] On the other hand, with respect to the court-appointed inspectors, even though the provision may make it easier to inspect books and records in an effort to uncover wrongdoing, it remains difficult to deter the incumbent management from evading, impeding or refusing the inspection as fines are imposed only on the company itself, not on individual evaders, and because fines are still too low to constitute a real deterrence.[86]

Figure 9.1 below summarizes the procedural flow of Taiwanese AGMs or EGMs.

[81] Art. 210, para. 2 of the CA.

[82] Chao-Tsong Huang, *Shou Tuo Yi Wu Jhih Li Lun Yu Ying Yong [Theories and Applications of Fiduciary Duties]* (New Sharing 2019) 345.

[83] Ching-Ping Shao, 'Lun Gong Si Zi Xun Quan De Gui Fan: Yi Dong Shi Zi Xun Quan De Zeng Ding Zheng Yi Wei Zhong Xin' ['On the Right to Information in Company Law: A Look into the Controversies Arising out of the Failed Amendment on Director's Right to Information'] (2019) 30(4) Dong Wu Fa Lu Xue Bao [Soochow Law Review] 1, 5.

[84] Lu (n. 63) 45.

[85] Shao (n. 83) 8.

[86] Lu (n .63) 45.

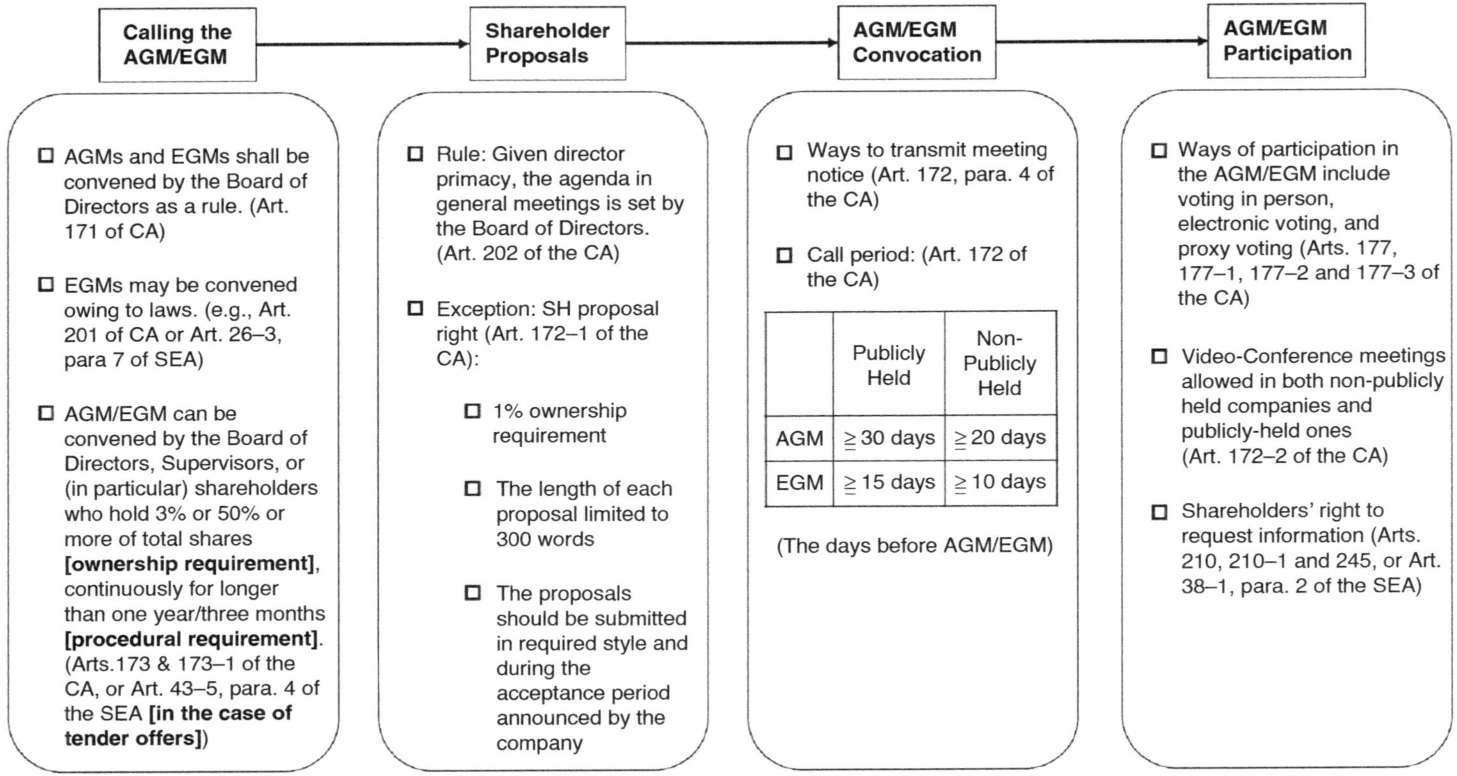

FIGURE 9.1 An overview of the Taiwanese AGM/EGM
Source: The Authors

9.3 SHAREHOLDER ENGAGEMENT AND VOTING IN PRACTICE

9.3.1 *Voting in Practice*

9.3.1.1 Options for Voting

The CA provides that shareholders may vote either in person, or by proxy or electronically.

VOTING IN PERSON Although it is not explicitly provided in the CA, the default method for shareholder voting is to participate and vote in general meetings in person. Shareholders have to report their attendance at the shareholder meeting by demonstrating identity documents to show that they are the exact persons recorded in the shareholder list or ledger,[87] and are only then entitled to participate, pose questions and vote in general meetings. Once the identity of individual shareholders has been verified, the company will provide them with the ballots to be cast for items on the meeting agenda.

PROXY VOTING Proxy voting is the first alternative to in-person voting provided in the CA. A shareholder may authorize a third party to attend a shareholder meeting and vote. According to the CA, a shareholder who desires to adopt proxy voting needs to submit his/her proxy to the company no later than five days before the shareholder meeting.[88] Generally, each shareholder may only appoint one delegate in each shareholder meeting. In the event that more than one proxy is submitted, the proxy that arrives at the company first counts, unless the shareholder explicitly revokes his/her previous authorization in the later proxy.

There are other issues that require attention. First, if any person (other than trust enterprises or stock agencies approved by the securities authority)[89] intends to represent more than one shareholder in a specific shareholder meeting, the CA caps the voting power this person could exercise at 3 per cent of the total voting power.[90] Thus, in practice, it is rare to have one person act as the representative of multiple shareholders in a shareholder meeting.

Second, shareholders have broad discretion in instructing their representatives what items to vote on and how to vote at general meetings. Some shareholders give their representatives wide latitude, and encourage them to use their own judgement; others give them specific instructions on which way they should vote on every single agenda item.

ELECTRONIC VOTING/VOTING IN WRITING Electronic voting and voting in writing were added as additional voting methods in the 2005 amendment to the CA in order to facilitate shareholders' exercise of their voting rights.[91] Nonetheless, neither electronic voting nor voting in

87 In Taiwan, the depository institution will have the name of a beneficial shareholder of each public company while a private company will keep the shareholder list or ledger on their own. This being the case, shareholder-identification should not be an issue. In practice, a shareholder list is important because it determines the individuals to whom the shareholder meeting notice should be served. If a shareholder is not served with the shareholder meeting notice, he/she may ask the court to revoke any shareholder resolution so adopted. See Art. 189 of the CA.

88 Art. 177, para. 3 of the CA.

89 Under Taiwanese law, the CA is enforced by the MoEA, while the securities regulations are enforced by the securities authority or the authority for public companies, that is, the Securities and Futures Bureau under the FSC.

90 Art. 177, para. 2 of the CA. According to the interpretation of the authority, the purpose of the 3 per cent cap is to avoid a concentration of voting power in the hands of minority shareholders who do not own shares but control the company by obtaining proxies. See Interpretation of MoEA, Jing-Shang-No. 2922 (21 December 1966).

91 Shiu-Feng Hung, 'Dian Zi Tou Piao Zhi Du Dui Gu Dong Hui Yun Zuo Zhi Ying Xiang–Bi Jiao Fa Xia De Shi Ye' ['The Impact of the Electronic Voting System on the Performance of Shareholders' Meeting – From the Perspective of Comparative Law'] (2014) 56 Hua Gang Fa Cui [Hwa Kang Law Review] 37, 39.

writing was widely adopted until the Taiwanese legislature further revised the CA to authorize the securities authority (i.e. the FSC) to require public companies to adopt electronic voting in 2011.[92] This resulted in a rapid increase in the popularity of electronic voting in practice.[93] Considering the significant role of electronic voting compared to the voting in writing in practice, this section focuses on the introduction and operation of electronic voting in Taiwan.

Shareholders who vote electronically must cast their votes no later than two days before the shareholder meeting.[94] As with proxy voting, if there is more than one electronic voting decision submitted, the decision that arrives at the company first counts, unless the shareholder explicitly revokes his/her previous decision while submitting the later decision.[95] Shareholders voting by electronic means are deemed to have attended the shareholder meeting.[96] If a shareholder provides the company with both a proxy and an electronic vote, the former shall prevail and thus the vote cast which is based on the proxy counts.[97] If the shareholder who has submitted an electronic vote later decides to attend a general meeting in person, he/she must revoke the vote cast electronically no later than two days before the shareholder meeting, or the electronic vote will prevail.[98]

Since the electronic vote is cast for each item on the agenda as scheduled in general meetings, a shareholder cannot vote on any extemporaneous motion proposed to be added onto the agenda or any existing item proposed to be amended on the spot during the meetings. The CA thus provides that shareholders who have cast their votes electronically are deemed to have waived their votes with respect to any extemporary motions or amendments to the existing item on the agenda, no matter how material the amendment would be.[99] This provision would contribute to the inflexibility of the shareholder's exercise of electronic voting. For example, at the AGM in 2013 of Foxconn, a public company listed on the TWSE, the chairman agreed at this meeting to increase the amount of cash dividend by NTD 0.5 per share in response to a loyal shareholder's request. Such an increase, however, was not legally acceptable, because shareholders with 45.3 per cent of the shares had previously voted electronically and hence could not vote for or against the extemporary motion of increasing the cash dividend.[100]

9.3.1.2 Video-Conference General Meetings

New technological developments have created the opportunity to hold virtual meetings in Taiwan stage by stage. At the first stage, owing to the 2018 amendment to the CA, which became

92 Art. 177-1, para. 1 of the CA.

93 In 2018, the securities authority ordered all companies listed on the TWSE and TPEx to include electronic voting as a voting method at general meetings. See Order of Financial Supervisory Commission, Jin-Guan-Zheng-Jiao-No.1060000381 (24 January 2017).

94 Art. 177-2, para. 1 of the CA.

95 Ibid.

96 Art. 177-1, para. 2 of the CA.

97 Art. 177-2, para. 3 of the CA.

98 Art. 177-2, para. 2 of the CA. If a shareholder votes electronically and does not revoke these votes, the company may in practice allow such a shareholder to attend the general meeting, but he/she could not vote on the spot.

99 Art. 177-1, para. 2 of the CA.

100 Richard Y. Fang, 'Cong Mei Guo Gu Dong Hui Dian Zi Tou Piao Zhi Du Lun Wo Guo Gu Dong Hui Dian Zi Tou Piao Zhi Du Zhi Fa Zhan' ['A Study on the Development of the Taiwan's Electronic Shareholder Voting System from the American Electronic Shareholder Voting System'] (2015) 143 Zheng Da Fa Xue Ping Lun [*Chengchi Law Review*] 303, 354–5. A commentator has argued that this situation could be improved by amending the CA: (1) to deem the electronic votes valid if the extemporaneous motion is to amend an existing item on the agenda and this motion is still covered by the original item; or (2) to prohibit such a motion because it constitutes a new item on the agenda. This proposal, however, has not been adopted by the legislature. Hung (n. 91) 54–5.

effective in 2019, a company was allowed to hold shareholder meetings via video conference or other methods allowed by the competent authority (i.e. the MoEA), as long as the Articles of Incorporation of the company so provided.[101] However, at this stage, the ability to use video conferencing for general meetings applied only to private companies, as public companies were prohibited under the then law from holding their general meetings by video conference.[102] This prohibition was in place to reduce risks associated with identity verification of shareholders, calculation of ballots and Internet outages during the general meeting.[103]

Notably, the recent upsurge of Covid-19 cases in Taiwan from May to July 2021 has likely placed further pressure on the MoEA and FSC to allow flexibility in public companies.[104] At the second stage of allowing companies to convene virtual shareholder meetings, on the one hand, Article 172-2, paragraph 1 of the CA has been amended in December 2021 to add the following proviso: '[u]nder the circumstances of calamities, incidents, or force majeure, the central competent authority may promulgate a ruling that authorizes a company, which has no above provision in its Articles of Incorporation, within a certain period of time can hold its shareholders' meeting by means of visual communication network or other promulgated methods'. Therefore, even though the Articles of Incorporation of the company does not so provide, both public and private companies may hold shareholder meetings via video conference or other methods in line with the ruling by the MoEA under the circumstances of force majeure such as the aforementioned pandemic in 2021. On the other hand, the FSC has been further planning on allowing public companies 'to convene hybrid meetings (i.e. physical shareholder meetings with video conferencing as assistance) and virtual-only meetings (i.e. 100% virtual shareholder meetings with no physical meetings)', aiming at advancing shareholder activism at the same time. [105]

9.3.1.3 Issues for Shareholder Voting

The CA requires a company to hold an AGM at least once a year, as its name implies.[106] During AGMs, several routine matters must be resolved. For example, a company must prepare an

101 Art. 172-2, para. 1 of the CA.

102 See Xiao Jun Yang, 'Xian Shang Gu Dong Hui Jin Guan Hui Ji Yan Yi' ['The Financial Supervisory Commission Is Urgenly Considering the Feasibility of Using Video Conferencing for General Meetings'] *Jing Ji Ri Bao [Economics Daily]* (13 May 2021) https://money.udn.com/money/story/5613/5453573 accessed 7 June 2021.

103 See also Zhen Ling Peng and Qiao Yi Wei, 'Gu Dong Hui Reng Xu Shi Ti Ju Xing' ['Holding Physical Shareholder Meetings Are Still Required'] *Gong Shang Shi Bao [Commercial Times]* (19 May 2021) https://readers.ctee.com.tw/cm/20210519/a03aa3/1125790/share accessed 7 June 2021 (noting FSC officials' concerns about legal and practical difficulties in holding general meetings by video conference for public companies).

104 Financial Supervisory Commission, 'Public Companies Shall Suspend the Convening of Shareholders' Meetings during 24 May to 30 June 2021 for Pandemic Prevention' (20 May 2021), www.sfb.gov.tw/en/home.jsp?id=78&parentpath=0,4&mcustomize=multimessage_view.jsp&dataserno=202105250003&dtable=News accessed 7 June 2021. See also Yi Ru Ye, 'Zheng Qi Ju: Gu Dong Hui Reng Xu Shi Ti Zhao Kai' ['The Securities and Futures Bureau: A Physical Shareholder Meeting Is Still Required'] *Jing Ji Ri Bao [Economics Daily]* (16 May 2021) <https://udn.com/news/story/7239/5460746 accessed 7 June 2021; Financial Supervisory Commission, 'Kai Fang Gong Kai Fa Xing Gong Si Zhao Kai Shi Ti Gu Dong Hui De Yi Shi Xun Fu Zhu, Yi Yin Ying Fang Yi Xu Yao Bing Jian Gu Gu Dong Hui Shun Li Zhao Kai' ['The Financial Supervisory Commission Permits Holding Physical Shareholder Meetings to Be Complemented by Video Conference in Order to Meet Needs of Epidemic Prevention as Well as of the Successful Holding of Shareholders Meetings'] (29 June 2021), www.fsc.gov.tw/ch/home.jsp?id=96&parentpath=0,2&mcustomize=news_view.jsp&dataserno=202106290003&dtable=News accessed 7 July 2021.

105 Financial Supervisory Commission, 'Preannouncement of the Draft Amendments to Some Clauses of Regulations Governing the Administration of Shareholder Services of Public Companies and Regulations Governing Content and Compliance Requirements for Shareholders' Meeting Agenda Handbooks of Public Companies' (21 January 2022), www.sfb.gov.tw/en/home.jsp?id=4&parentpath=0&mcustomize=multimessage_view.jsp&dataserno=202201240001&dtable=News accessed 21 February 2022.

106 Art. 170 of the CA.

operation report, financial statements and a proposal regarding the distribution of surplus or offset of losses for the shareholders' approval. It is also quite common for public companies to revise their internal rules at an AGM in order to update them so that they comply with any recent amendments by the securities authority to the relevant regulations.[107]

Normally, the election of directors and supervisors is a routine agenda item at a shareholder meeting. In the event of a contest over corporate control, however, these elections become controversial, often leading to chaos at general meetings. As discussed above, cumulative voting is mandatory for the election of directors and supervisors across most Taiwanese companies.[108] In the context of contest over corporate control, the issue would be how to effectively allocate the votes in order to win the most board seats as possible. Thus, meticulous calculation is the key to success.

9.3.1.4 Shareholder Proposals and Proxy Fights

SHAREHOLDER PROPOSALS The CA allows a shareholder with 1 per cent or more of the outstanding shares to make proposals at AGMs.[109] However, in practice, it is uncommon for shareholders to make proposals pursuant to the CA; thus, it is rare to see shareholder proposals successfully added to an AGM agenda.

On rare occasions, nevertheless, shareholder proposals may be used in the context of hostile takeovers. For instance, in order to defend against a bid for control launched by Yageo Corporation, the board of the target company, Ta-I Technology Co., Ltd. (Ta-I), using a proposal made by some allied shareholders at its 2007 AGM, proposed a resolution to limit the authority of the Yageo-appointed directors by subjecting any interested transactions between Ta-I and Yageo to shareholder approval during the period when Yageo's assigned representatives were on Ta-I's board.[110] Ultimately, this proposal was withdrawn because Ta-I successfully won all the board seats before this proposal was voted upon at the general meeting.

In addition to defensive tactics, shareholder proposals can also serve as hostile takeover measures to acquire corporate control in the context of proxy contests. The contest over control of CH Bank initiated by Taishin offers a good example. As discussed in Section 9.1.4, before acquiring control over CH Bank from the MoF and becoming its largest majority shareholder, Taishin had been the second largest shareholder of CH Bank and sought to take it over. In order to become the majority on CH Bank's board, Taishin submitted a proposal for CH Bank's AGM in 2008, proposing amending CH Bank's Articles of Incorporation to reduce the number of board members from fifteen seats to nine seats, expecting that Taishin could more easily control the majority of the board in the next re-election. Such a proposal was successfully included on the agenda of CH Bank's 2008 AGM and then adopted by CH Bank's shareholders.[111]

It is generally understood that the introduction of the shareholder proposal mechanism was to strengthen shareholder activism – that is, to encourage small shareholders to actively participate

[107] Two regulations promulgated by the FSC are relevant here: (1) Regulations Governing the Acquisition and Disposal of Assets by Public Companies and (2) Regulations Governing Loaning of Funds and Making of Endorsements/ Guarantees by Public Companies.

[108] See s. 9.2.3.1.

[109] See s. 9.2.2.

[110] Chao-Tsung Huang, 'Gu Dong Hui Fang Yu Cuo Shi Zhi Gui Fan Yu Xing Si' ['Thoughts on Anti-Takeover Measures in Shareholder Meeting'] (2018) 61 Guo Li Zhong Zheng Da Xue Fa Xue Ji Kan [*National Chung Cheng University Law Journal*] 119–20.

[111] Ibid., 19–20.

in the management and oversight of the company.[112] Nevertheless, these examples show that the shareholder proposal mechanism rarely functions in the way the legislature had expected it to do. From a comparative law perspective, this mechanism has been used in connection with ESG issues in the United States,[113] but this has not yet been the case in Taiwan.

PROXY FIGHTS As with shareholder proposals, proxy fights can also be found in the context of hostile takeovers. As we have seen, a shareholder can vote by proxy,[114] so that in the event of a contest over corporate control, another way for the acquirer to prevail is to collect as many proxies as possible, in addition to acquiring as many shares as possible to increase the shareholding in the target company. Proxy fights have therefore become common in corporate control contests.

Unsurprisingly, the solicitation of proxies in public companies is heavily regulated by the securities authority.[115] The Proxy Regulations in Taiwan set different thresholds for the shareholders that are eligible to solicit proxies, depending on different matters involved and whether a trust enterprise or shareholder service agent is retained.[116]

It is not our intention to enter here into the fine details of the Proxy Regulations. Suffice it to say that the common practice in Taiwan is to solicit proxies through trust enterprises and shareholder service agents, because they are also securities firms[117] and have direct access to the shareholders, which means they know who to approach. Another source for acquiring proxies is the so-called 'proxy channel businesses' or groups of people who have their own access to shareholders. These businesses, for example, may have representatives covering almost every listed company during the shareholder meeting season, so that they can approach shareholders not covered by traditional securities firms.[118] Competing to retain competent proxy service providers becomes a key to success in a contest over corporate control.[119]

9.3.2 *Who Owns the Shares: The Unique Case of the SFIPC*

Among Taiwan's various non-financial institutional investors, the SFIPC is unique. Established in 2003, the SFIPC, a quasi-public foundation created and operated by the government, initially served the same function as US lawyer-driven class actions by bringing certain types of securities class action lawsuits as a way of private enforcement to protect minority shareholders. Then, beginning in 2009, the SFIPC was granted the power to bring corporate derivative suits.[120]

112 Kuo-Bin Lin, 'Gu Dong Ti An Quan Zhi Hang Shi Yu Quan Li Bao Zhang Zhi Yan Jiu – Tai Wan Yu Mei Guo Fa Zhi Zhi Bi Jiao' ['The Shareholders' Proposal Right and Its Remedies – The Comparative Study of Taiwan and the U.S. Legal Mechanisms'] (2013) 86 Tai Bei Da Xue Fa Xue Lun Cong [*Taipei University Law Review*] 185, 190.

113 For the overview of the ESG trend in the United States, see Jill E. Fisch, 'From Legitimacy to Logic: Reconstructing Proxy Regulation' (1993) 46 Vanderbilt Law Review 1129, 1152–5. As discussed in s. 9.2.2, the Taiwanese legislature also tries to reposition shareholder proposals as a mechanism to promote CSR activities, which can be found in the revision of art. 172-1 of the CA in 2018.

114 See s. 9.3.1.1.

115 See generally Regulations Governing the Use of Proxies for Attendance at Shareholder Meetings of Public Companies (the 'Proxy Regulations').

116 Arts. 5 and 6 of the Proxy Regulations.

117 Art. 7-1 of the Proxy Regulations.

118 See Yong-Ji Chen, 'Xiao Kan Yi Zhi Wei Tuo Shu Duo Shao Gong Si Tong Shi Jing Ying Quan' ['Ignorance of Proxies Will Cost the Management Corporate Control'] *Zi You Shi Bao [Liberty Times]* (Taiwan, 14 May 2018) https://ec.ltn.com.tw/article/paper/1200239 accessed 10 November 2019.

119 Len-Yu Liu, *Xian Dai Zheng Quan Jiao Yi Fa Shi Li Yan Xi [Modern Securities Regulation: Cases and Explanations]* (16th ed. Angle 2019) 172.

120 See Tseng and Wang (n. 1) 240–1; Andrew Jen-Guang Lin, 'The Challenges and Contemporary Issues of Taiwan's Investor Protection System: A Model to Learn or to Avoid' (2016) 11(1) National Taiwan University Law Review 129, 129–30.

Although not a regulator of the securities market per se, the SFIPC was incorporated, according to the Securities Investor and Futures Trader Protection Act, under the FSC's regulatory design. This nominally private (or quasi-public) organization's mission is to enforce securities law and the CA within public companies by initiating civil lawsuits such as shareholder actions or lawsuits to dismiss directors.[121] The SFIPC is also allowed to use its own funds to purchase shares in each listed company (up to 1,000 shares). Moreover, the underwriting and listing rules also require that companies seeking to list on the TWSE or TPEx and their underwriters must reserve 1,000 shares of each IPO firm for the SFIPC to subscribe.[122] Due to these rules, the SFIPC is formally a shareholder of all listing companies in Taiwan and can enforce the rights under the CA and securities regulations as a shareholder. This scheme – in which the SFIPC acts as a shareholder – is a way to meet the standing requirement under Taiwanese law to initiate civil proceedings. The SFIPC has actively participated in general meetings of listing companies that faced possible legal disputes, and has apparently played a significant role in Taiwan's corporate governance.[123] These roles illustrate how such a peculiar shareholder actively communicates with the firm management in practice.[124]

9.3.3 *Investor Engagement*

Given the recent rise in shareholder activism in many parts of the world, several studies by Western academics have considered how company managers have responded to this trend, in terms of engaging with their investors.[125] In Taiwan, however, shareholder engagement has not received as much attention as it has in Western jurisdictions and in their Asian counterparts such as Hong Kong.[126]

For example, under Taiwanese law, the mechanism most comparable to the Western idea of investor engagement can be found in the institutional investor conference – an arrangement under which management regularly communicates with shareholders outside of shareholder meetings about each other's positions with respect to the company's objectives and strategies forward.[127] The institutional investor conference is described in the rules of both the TWSE[128] and TPEx.[129] For TWSE-listed and TPEx-listed companies to take initiatives in holding or to be

121 For an overview and comment on the use of the SFIPC as the enforcement mechanism, see Guan-Wei Chao, 'Saying is One Thing; Doing is Another? Analyzing the Chinese Nonprofit Organization Model in Investor Protection through the Taiwanese Experience' (2018) 13(1) National Taiwan University Law Review 53, 60–74.

122 Ching-Ping Shao, 'Representative Litigation in Corporate and Securities Laws by Government-Sanctioned Nonprofit Organizations: Lessons from Taiwan' (2013) 15 Asian-Pacific Law and Policy Journal 58, 72.

123 Securities and Futures Investors Protection Center (SFIPC), 'A Report on SFIPC's Attendance at General Meetings in the First Half of 2020' (28 July 2020) www.sfipc.org.tw/MainWeb/Article.aspx?L=1&SNO=7xOHNGge93llt4lwBGrnvg== accessed 19 August 2020.

124 See s. 9.3.4.1.

125 See, e.g., David Shammai and Kiran Vasantham, 'Engaging with Your Investors' (28 April 2019) https://corpgov.law.harvard.edu/2019/04/28/planning-effective-engagement-with-your-investors/ accessed 23 June 2019; Matthew J. Mallow and Jasmin Sethi, 'Engagement: The Missing Middle Approach in the Bebchuk-Strine Debate' (2016) 12 New York University Journal of Law and Business 385. While we understand that 'engagement' and 'activism' sometimes overlap, shareholder 'engagement' is referred to here as interaction initiated by management, while shareholder 'activism' refers to campaigns launched by shareholders themselves. See s. 9.3.4. It is worth noting that an activist campaign does not necessarily lead to management's engagement with shareholders.

126 Lin (n. 74) 1.

127 Mallow and Sethi (n. 125) 392.

128 Art. 8 of the Taiwan Stock Exchange Corporation Procedures for Verification and Disclosure of Material Information of Companies with Listed Securities ('TWSE Information Disclosure Rules').

129 Art. 8 of the Taipei Exchange Procedures for Verification and Disclosure of Material Information of Companies with TPEx Listed Securities.

invited to participate in institutional investor conferences, they must disclose a complete profile of their business and financial information before the conferences, videotape the conference and make the videos available to the public; TWSE Information Disclosure Rules also require all TWSE-listed companies to hold or participate in one institutional investor conference at least once a year. [130]

There exists anecdotal evidence of behind-the-scene engagements between institutional investors or other larger shareholders and corporate management outside general meetings. For instance, Business Today, a major media organization in Taiwan, conducted a survey of eleven leading enterprises in Taiwan to understand the impact of the ESG trend on them. These enterprises included firms in the technology industry (TSMC, Foxconn and MediaTek), traditional industry (Formosa Plastics, Taiwan Cement and President Chain Store), and financial industry (Yuanta Financial Holdings, Fubon Financial Holdings, Cathay Financial Holdings, Chinatrust Financial Holdings and Chailease Finance).[131] It is worth noting that eight of these eleven conglomerates replied: 'In the past year, foreign shareholders or institutional investors asked ESG-related questions more frequently than before'.[132] This means that these leading enterprises were likely to have consulted with professional advisory firms to adapt to the trend of ESG investment.[133] More importantly, ten of these leading enterprises did not wait for inquiries to react; instead, they strengthened 'proactive' communication with foreign shareholders or intuitional investors.[134] This proactive approach can be seen in the private engagement method used by a domestic institutional investor in Taiwan when flight attendants of EVA Air Corporations (EVA), one of Taiwan's two international airlines, came out on strike in June 2019.[135] The new Labor Pension Fund under the Ministry of Labor, which was EVA's sixth largest shareholder at that time, wrote a letter on 24 June to EVA's management, requesting that its board members or other relevant corporate representatives consider shareholders' interests and address the labour dispute with the labour union properly. This demonstrates that the new Labor Pension Fund engaged with EVA as a large shareholder, pressuring the firm's management to settle the dispute quickly in order to mitigate impacts on travellers and losses to shareholders.[136]

9.3.4 *The Prospect of Shareholder Activism in Taiwan*

9.3.4.1 The Policy Direction of the FSC

To date, analysis shows that the shareholder activist tools available under the CA, such as shareholder proposals or proxy solicitation, tend to be applied in the Taiwanese context of corporate control contests. Moreover, the way in which shareholder activism is conceived and utilized in Taiwan differs from the kind of shareholder activism seen in the USA and Europe.

[130] Art. 8, para. 2 of the TWSE Information Disclosure Rules.

[131] Wei Xuan Huang et al., '"Liang Xin Tou Zi" Da Bao Fa Qi Ye Jing Ying Mian Lin Qian Suo Wei Jian Xin Tiao Zhan Zhi Hang Zhang Bi Dong ESG Xue' ['"Responsible Investing on the Rise" Is An Unprecedented Challenge to Business Administration; CEO Must Know ESG'] *Jin Zhou Kan [Business Today]* (Taiwan, 21 October 2019) 94.

[132] Ibid.

[133] Ibid.

[134] Ibid.

[135] Ping Kuan Lo, Op-Ed., 'Gu Dong Xing Dong Zhu Yi De Jue Qi Yu Tiao Zhan' ['The Rise of Shareholder Activism and its Challenges'] *Gong Shang Shi Bao [Commercial Times]* (Taiwan, 30 August 2019) https://view.ctee.com.tw/legal/11250.html accessed 10 November 2019.

[136] Ibid.

From a policy perspective, it should be noted that the enhancement of shareholder activism is constantly encouraged and directed by the securities authority in Taiwan. In the 'Corporate Governance Roadmap (2018–2020)', the FSC lists 'promoting shareholder activism' as one of the action plans to be enforced from 2018 to 2020 via the following objectives: facilitating the exercise of shareholders' rights, urging companies to implement corporate governance and strengthening institutional investors' stewardship responsibilities.[137]

As an example of the FSC's continuous efforts to promote shareholder activism, the SFIPC (which is affiliated to the FSC) has historically been known to participate proactively in communications with the management of Taiwanese listed companies. In the event of corporate governance concerns, the SFIPC would make written inquiries requesting replies or issue press releases to appeal to the company to take necessary measures to protect shareholders. For example, the founder of Yageo, a TWSE-listed company, announced in 2011 that he would ally with the private equity firm KKR to take Yageo private by initiating a tender offer to acquire the outstanding shares of Yageo across the public market. Due to serious CoI concerns, the SFIPC then issued a press release requesting Yageo to set up an independent committee to evaluate the terms of this deal. Although the deal failed because Yageo could not obtain the required governmental approval, this case exemplifies the proactive role the SFIPC plays in shareholder activism.[138]

Accordingly, it seems that the FSC aims for shareholder activism to operate as a measure to enhance the quality of corporate governance in Taiwan, while a careful consideration of potential concerns drawing from comparative experience seems warranted, especially the potential promotion of short-term interest at the expense of a target company's long-term value as sometimes seen in the United States.[139] The activist campaigns in Taiwan further illustrate the discrepancy between the government's stated policy and how things work out in practice.[140]

9.3.4.2 Harbingers of Shareholder Activism in Practice?

Despite their limited presence to date, activist campaigns have been on the rise recently. This recent uptick gives the appearance that the trending type of shareholder activism often seen in the West[141] might have taken hold in Taiwan.

One of the prominent examples of shareholder activism in Taiwan is the acquisition of shares in financial institutions by Bao Jia Institution (BJI). BJI is a conglomerate whose original business focus was construction; nonetheless, from 2011, BJI started to acquire shares in Taichung Bank and then obtained one or two board seats in Taichung Bank following elections in 2011, 2014 and 2017. A news release indicates that BJI sold all the shares in Taichung Bank in

[137] See Financial Supervisory Commission, 'Corporate Governance Roadmap (2018~2020)' (10 May 2018) 20–4, www.fsc.gov.tw/fckdowndoc?file=/CorporateGovernanceRoadmap(2018~2020).doc&flag=doc accessed 19 October 2019 ('CG 2018~2020').

[138] For an overview and comment on the Yageo going-private transaction from the perspective of fiduciary law, see Chao-Tsung Huang, 'Shou Tuo Yi Wu Zhi Qiang Hua Shen Cha Biao Zhun' ['Enhanced Scrutiny of Fiduciary Duty'] (2015) 96 Tai Bei Da Xue Fa Xue Lun Cong [*Taipei University Law Review*] 85, 126–34; Tsai (n. 80) 16–18, 20–6; Tsai (n. 78) 537–8, 585–6.

[139] See, e.g., Martijn Cremers, Saura Masconale and Simone M. Sepe, 'Activist Hedge Funds and the Corporation' (2016) 94 Washington University Law Review 261.

[140] See s. 9.3.4.2.

[141] See, e.g., Alexander I. Platt, 'Index Fund Enforcement' (2020) 53 *UC Davis Law Review* 1453 https://lawreview.law.ucdavis.edu/issues/53/3/53-3_Platt.pdf.

2019 and did not plan to obtain any board seats in the 2020 election,[142] indicating that BJI's strategy here was to participate in the Taichung Bank's operation to improve its share price in the market and then profit by selling its shares. In addition, BJI also acquired shares in COTA Commercial Bank and successfully obtained two board seats therein, for the purpose of urging COTA Commercial Bank to engage in an IPO by coordinating with other minority shareholders (i.e. the 'wolf pack' tactic).[143] According to the above campaigns, it seems that BJI's goal was not to contest the control of those financial institutions but to gain seats on the board so as to participate in the operation of those institutions and reap capital gains.

If the above-mentioned cases can be seen as harbingers of shareholder activism in Taiwan, they show significant differences from their counterparts observed in the United States. Although activist campaigns in both the USA and Taiwan have their own goals to pursue, those in the United States are usually led by financial firms – hedge funds in particular – whose primary goal is to pursue short-term profits.[144] The activists in Taiwan, however, are different; these parties are generally new entrants from a different industry or competitors in the same business, rather than financial firms. To date there has been minimal involvement of financial firms, that is, private equity or hedge funds, in activist campaigns in Taiwan.[145] Therefore, it appears that short-term financial gains may not be the primary aim of the Taiwanese shareholder activists.

Another difference between the USA and Taiwan with respect to shareholder activism is the ownership structure. As mentioned above,[146] financial institutions are not majority shareholders across Taiwanese listed companies. In comparison, in the United States, the three largest index fund groups, Blackrock, Vanguard and State Street, collectively constitute the largest shareholders in 438 of the Fortune 500 companies in 2015.[147] Such a difference reveals that the activists in Taiwan less often appeal for other shareholders' support in the campaigns and may therefore accumulate voting power on their own by acquiring shares. In the USA, the activists may ally with other institutional shareholders as long as they can win support from the proxy advisors, such as Institutional Shareholder Services (ISS) or Glass Lewis (GL).[148]

The final issue related to the difference in the ownership structure is the role proxy advisors play in activist campaigns in Taiwan. Both ISS[149] and GL[150] have their own guidelines for the Taiwan stock market. There appear to be no formal statistics in regard to the influence of their advice on shareholders' voting behaviour; nevertheless, ISS and GL recommendations have

[142] Yueh-Ping Yang, 'Gong Kai Fa Xing Gong Si Zhi Gong Si Zhi Li, Ji Gou Tou Zi Ren Yu Gu Dong Xing Dong Zhu Yi' ['The Corporate Governance of Public Companies, Institutional Investors and Shareholder Activism'] (2020) 2 Tai Wan Cai Jing Fa Xue Lun Cong [*Taiwan Financial and Economic Law Review*] 385, 408.

[143] Ibid., 409–10.

[144] Marcel Kahan and Edward B. Rock, 'Hedge Funds in Corporate Governance and Corporate Control' (2007) 155 University of Pennsylvania Law Review 1021, 1028.

[145] Lo (n. 136).

[146] See s. 9.1.3.

[147] Jan Fichtner, Eelke M. Heemskerk and Javier Garcia-Bernardo, 'Hidden Power of the Big Three? Passive Index Funds, Re-concentration of Corporate Ownership, and New Financial Risk' (2017) 19 Business and Politics 238, 313.

[148] Sharon Hannes, 'Super Hedge Fund' (2015) 40 Delaware Journal of Corporate Law 163, 176–7.

[149] ISS, 'Taiwan Voting Guidelines' (6 December 2018) www.issgovernance.com/file/policy/active/asiapacific/Taiwan-Voting-Guidelines.pdf accessed 3 March 2020.

[150] Glass Lewis, '2020 Guidelines: An Overview of the Glass Lewis Approach to Proxy Advice (Taiwan)' www.glasslewis.com/wp-content/uploads/2016/12/Guidelines_TAIWAN.pdf accessed 3 March 2020.

been reported broadly not only in control contests[151] but also in activist campaigns (including that of BJI in Taishin's 2018 election).[152] Accordingly, this anecdotal evidence demonstrates that the role of proxy firms may be increasing in importance with respect to shareholder activism in Taiwan.[153]

9.4 CONCLUDING REMARKS

The thoroughgoing revision of the CA in 2018 equipped shareholders with more rights, such as the right to convene an EGM without having to making requests to the board of directors or having to obtain approval from competent authorities beforehand. Evidence has shown that these changes have further empowered shareholders, even though the voting regime has been left essentially unchanged. Meanwhile, the FSC has been the primary driver for strengthening corporate governance across Taiwanese public companies, so as to ambitiously keep pace with Western countries in terms of corporate governance indices and rankings.[154] It remains to be seen whether measures taken in the Corporate Governance Roadmap from 2013[155] and its successors, the Corporate Governance Roadmap (2018–2020) and 'Corporate Governance 3.0 – Sustainable Development Roadmap',[156] will serve as the most effective infrastructure for shareholder activism of institutional investors based on the legal toolkit furnished under the CA and SEA for shareholder engagement and voting.

151 See, e.g., Hanlun Chu, 'Wen Ye Gu Dong Hui Yi An Sheng Za Yin Wai Zi Quan Wei GL, ISS Hu Gang' ['Institutional Shareholder Services and Glass Lewis Have Conflicting Advice on How to Vote in the AGM of WT Microelectronics'] *Gong Shang Shi Bao [Commercial Times]* (20 March 2020) www.chinatimes.com/newspapers/20200320000495-260206?chdtv accessed 4 April 2020.

152 For discussions over Taishin, see ss. 9.1.4 and 9.3.1.4.

153 Lo (n. 136).

154 See, e.g., Shao (n. 83) 6–8.

155 'Service: Corporate Governance' Taiwan Stock Exchange www.twse.com.tw/en/page/about/company/service.html accessed 18 October 2019.

156 Financial Supervisory Commission, 'FSC launches Corporate Governance 3.0 – Sustainable Development Roadmap' (25 August 2020), www.sfb.gov.tw/en/home.jsp?id=78&parentpath=0,4&mcustomize=multimessage_view.jsp&dataserno=202008250003&aplistdn=ou=news,ou=multisite,ou=english,ou=ap_root,o=fsc,c=tw&dtable=News accessed 17 October 2020.

PART II

Australia and North America

10

Shareholder Engagement and Voting in Australia

Roman Tomasic and Anil Hargovan

10.1 AUSTRALIA

10.1.1 *Introduction to Australia's Corporate Law and Corporate Governance*

Australia has a national body of corporation law that emerged through negotiations between individual states and the national government via a process of constitutional interpretations and referrals of constitutional power, a process that served to develop a unified national body of corporation law and regulatory structures that have replaced the former regional company law statutes and corporate regulatory agencies of individual Australian states.

A total of 2.7 million companies were registered in Australia in 2018–19, the vast majority of them (approximately 99 per cent) private or proprietary companies. Just 25,445 (roughly 0.9 per cent) were public companies. Of these, only 2,085 (about 8.2 per cent of all public companies) were stock exchange-listed public companies.[1] The number of public companies listed in Australia overall has since been in decline.[2] As of October 2019, the number of companies listed on the Australian Stock Exchange (ASX) included 1,953 domestic public companies and 140 foreign public companies.[3] As of March 2019, Australia's top-100 listed companies were operating in eleven sectors, 33.5 per cent of them in the financial sector,[4] followed by the materials (18.4 per cent), health care (8.6 per cent), industrials (8.6 per cent), real estate (7.0 per cent) and energy (5.9 per cent) sectors. In 2017, the top-200 ASX-listed companies accounted for 82 per cent of share market capitalization.[5]

Foreign and domestic institutional investors in Australian companies held about 80 per cent of all shares in 2010, with individual shareholders holding about 16 per cent of shares in public companies.[6] By 2018, the total capitalization of listed companies in Australia was almost A$2 trillion.[7] Financial corporations (especially banks) and resource companies (especially mining

1 Australian Securities and Investments Commission (ASIC), 'Annual Report 2018–19' 20, 264 https://asic.gov.au/about-asic/corporate-publications/asic-annual-reports/#ar19 accessed 31 July 2020.

2 Also see ASX data from 1989–2019, CEIC, 'Australian ASX Number of Listed Companies: Total' www.ceicdata.com/en/australia/australian-stock-exchange-number-of-listed-company/asx-number-of-listed-companies-total accessed 31 July 2020.

3 Ibid.

4 Also see Australian Securities Exchange, 'ASX Top 100 Companies' (1 June 2020) www.asx100list.com/ accessed 31 July 2020.

5 Australian Stock Exchange, 'ASX 200 List' www.asx.com.au accessed 31 July 2020.

6 See further John Farrar and Pamela Hanrahan, *Corporate Governance* (LexisNexis 2017) 413. These statistics are drawn from Susan Black and Joshua Kirkwood, 'Ownership of Australian Equities and Corporate Bonds' [September 2010] *Reserve Bank of Australia Bulletin* 25, 27.

7 Thomas Matthews, 'The Australian Equity Market over the Past Century' [June 2019] *Reserve Bank of Australia Bulletin*.

firms) accounted for at least half of Australian market capitalization, with manufacturing, consumer goods, and infrastructure companies accounting for about 40 per cent.[8]

10.1.2 *Legal Regulation of Companies in Australia*

Drawing upon British company law precedents and models, Australia has developed a hybrid model of corporate law that supplements its British legal inheritance with home-grown statutory provisions. However, the 2001 Corporations Act does not completely codify pre-existing corporate law principles, meaning that British company law case law remains important in shaping Australian corporate law and practice.

Australian legislative provisions have often been supplemented by more severe and even penal statutory provisions, such as the civil penalty order regime, through the enforcement powers vested in the corporate conduct regulator, the Australian Securities and Investments Commission (ASIC). However, a number of shareholder-related principles have been codified in Australia, such as the proper plaintiff rule in *Foss* v. *Harbottle*, which has been replaced by a new statutory derivative action.[9] The rise of institutional investors has complicated the nature of both shareholding and ownership, leading to calls for such shareholders to play a greater role in the corporate governance of companies. As Farrar and Hanrahan note, institutional shareholders do not have an ultimate economic interest in the shares and interests that they acquire because they invest for the benefit of others and institutional investment tends to involve a long chain of intermediaries or service providers.[10]

10.1.3 *Allocation of Corporate Decision-Making in Australia*

Australian company law provides for a unitary board structure, although larger companies may establish a variety of board subcommittees. The Corporations Act provides that a proprietary company must have at least one director,[11] who must ordinarily be resident in Australia; it must also have at least one member[12] and no more than fifty non-employee members.[13] Proprietary companies are prohibited from seeking to raise capital that would require the issue of a disclosure statement such as a prospectus.[14] In contrast, a public company must also have at least one member and at least three directors, at least two of whom must ordinarily be resident in Australia.[15] Companies may have both executive and non-executive or independent directors. Independent directors are usually expected to bring specific expertise to the board, with the board monitoring management performance and setting a broad policy framework. No statutory provision is made for the appointment of independent directors, although it is expected that public companies will appoint a majority of independent or non-executive directors to their boards. Listed companies are encouraged by the ASX Corporate Governance Council's Principles and Recommendations to appoint independent directors. Larger proprietary companies may also appoint both executive and non-executive directors. Only a small proportion of

8 Ibid.

9 *Foss* v. *Harbottle* [1843] 2 Hare 461; see also Corporations Act 2001, ss. 236 and 237.

10 Farrar and Hanrahan (n. 6) 414–15.

11 Section 201A; if it has crowd-sourced funding shareholders, it must have at least two directors, at least one of whom is resident in Australia: CA s. 201A(1A).

12 Corporations Act 2001, s. 114.

13 Ibid., s. 113.

14 Ibid., s. 113(3); disclosure statements are governed by Chapter 6D of the Corporations Act.

15 Corporations Act 2001, s. 201A(2).

public companies are listed on the ASX. These listed companies tend to be larger companies. Subject to the company's constitution, its board of directors is given broad powers of management and control by section 198A of the Corporations Act. Whilst board members have the power to appoint and remove directors, once appointed, directors have the power to manage the affairs of the company, subject to legislation such as the statutory derivative action procedure. As the members of the board of directors have fiduciary duties to the company as a whole, it would be inappropriate to allow shareholders to displace the management powers held by directors.

In Australia, directors have a paramount duty to protect the interests of the company as a whole. This applies even if they themselves are shareholders or if they have been appointed as a nominee director by a major shareholder to protect the interests of a particular shareholder.[16] The enactment of section 187 has allowed directors sitting on the boards of wholly owned subsidiary companies to pay regard to the policies of the holding company when making decisions on behalf of the subsidiary company board. With regard to directors who are also shareholders, Chief Justice Latham of the High Court of Australia was pragmatic enough to note that the interests of companies are often identical to those of shareholders.[17]

In certain narrow circumstances, at common law, shareholders retain residual powers of management such as when the board is deadlocked or unwilling to act or when the general meeting is called upon to ratify decisions made by directors and officers who act in breach of their duties.[18] Further, under statute, a derivative action procedure allows shareholders to sue in the name of the company when directors are unwilling to take action to protect the rights or interests of the company.

Nevertheless, approval by the general meeting is still necessary in many situations. For example, shareholders retain important powers in regard to such matters as changes to the company's constitution, changes to the company form, the appointment and removal of directors and auditors, variations in class rights, and certain changes to the company's capital structure, such as those made through share buy-backs, capital reductions and the provision of financial assistance in relation to share acquisitions. Securities Exchange Listing Rules also require shareholder approval of certain major transactions, such as the disposal of the company's main undertaking or a change in the nature and scale of its activities.[19]

It is interesting to note that in 2008 the Parliamentary Joint Committee on Corporations and Financial Services focused its attention on improving shareholder engagement and participation in Australian companies.[20] However, tension between shareholders and the board remains a major concern,[21] as evidenced by the large number of successful shareholder-initiated class actions in the country,[22] a situation of concern for many Australian company directors.[23]

16 Walker v. Wimbourne [1976] 137 CLR 1. Regarding the handling of conflicts of interest by directors, the relevant principles are summarized by Owen J. in Bell Group Ltd (in liq) v. Westpac Banking Corp [2008] 39 WAR 1; [2008] WASC 23 [4504–4512].

17 *Mills* v. *Mills* [1938] 60 CLR 150.

18 See also *Baron* v. *Potter* [1914] 1 Ch 895 and Ross Grantham, 'The Reserve Powers of Company Shareholders' (2004) 63 *CLJ* 36.

19 See also ASX Listing Rules 11.1–11.3 and Guidance Note 12 www.asx.com.au/documents/rules/gn12_changes_to_activities.pdf accessed 31 July 2020.

20 Parliamentary Joint Committee on Corporations and Financial Services, 'Better Shareholders – Better Company: Shareholder Engagement and Participation in Australia' (2008) www.aph.gov.au/binaries/senate/committee/corporations_ctte/sharehold/report/report.pdf accessed 31 July 2020.

21 See, generally, Jennifer Hill, 'The Rising Tension between Shareholder and Director Power in the Common Law World' (2010) 18 *Corporate Governance: An International Review* 344.

22 See, generally, Michael Legg, 'Shareholder Class Actions in Australia – the Perfect Storm?' (2008) 31 *University of New South Wales Law Journal* 669.

23 Nicola Berkovic, 'Class Lawsuits "Spooking Directors"', *The Australian* (31 October 2019) 2.

The next sections further discuss the powers of the annual general meeting (AGM) and the relationship between shareholders and the board in Australian corporations.

10.1.4 *Shareholder versus Board/Managerial Supremacy*

The balance of power between shareholders and boards of directors within corporations in Australia has shifted over time, with the board becoming increasingly ascendant, although efforts have been made to more effectively involve shareholders in corporate governance at a time when the role of shareholders in larger companies has also changed. The general meeting of shareholders, particularly the AGM, and the board of directors are the two key organs of the company, and they have distinctive roles, responsibilities and powers. Neither organ is subservient to the other. The differences between the two organs have increased since the nineteenth century, when directors were seen merely as delegates of the members in general meeting.[24] The current division of powers between shareholders in general meeting and the board of directors is justified on the basis that directors are subject to fiduciary duties to act in the best interests of the company as a whole, whilst shareholders are expected only to promote their own best interests and are subject only to a duty to avoid misusing their majority power.[25] In such a situation, it is best for the company as a whole if the board of directors is responsible for making business decisions because directors are constrained by their fiduciary duties.[26]

The legal capacity and powers of companies are provided for in section 124(1) of the Corporations Act, which states that a company has the legal capacity and powers of an individual, including the power to issue and cancel shares in the company (section 124(1)(a)) and the power to 'do anything that it is authorized to do by any other law'. The company's constitution may contain an express restriction on the company's capacity to exercise its powers, although the exercise of a power is not invalid merely because it is limited by the constitution.[27]

The board of directors is given power by section 198A(1) of the Corporations Act to manage the company, and directors are also empowered by section 198A(2) to 'exercise all [of] the powers of the company except any powers that this Act or the company's constitution (if any) requires the company to exercise in general meeting'.[28] In the case of large public companies, however, the board's actual capacity to make business decisions may be limited to the role of merely monitoring or supervising management decisions, as was affirmed in 1992 in *AWA Ltd* v. *Daniels (trading as Deloitte Haskins & Sells)*.[29] The Australian courts have also held that it is not proper for shareholders in a general meeting to express their opinions on the manner in which directors should exercise their management powers or to speak and act on behalf of the corporation.[30]

24 Robert Austin and Ian Ramsay, *Ford, Austin and Ramsay's Principles of Corporations Law* (17th ed., LexisNexis 2018) ch. 7.

25 See also Farrar and Hanrahan (n. 6) 321.

26 Ibid., 125–6.

27 Corporations Act 2001, s. 125.

28 It should be noted that ss. 198A(1) and (2) are listed in s. 141 as 'replaceable rules', which allows the members in a general meeting to incorporate different rules in the company constitution.

29 [1992] 7 ACSR 759 referred to by Austin and Ramsay (n. 24) 243–4.

30 *NRMA* v. *Parker* [1986] 6 NSWLR 517; the decision in *NRMA* v. *Parker* was endorsed by the Full Federal Court in *Australasian Centre for Corporate Responsibility* v. *Commonwealth Bank of Australia* [2016] 113 ACSR 600, which also found that the constitution of the Commonwealth Bank did not have an implied term that would authorize members to make an advisory resolution to the board requiring the bank to report carbon emissions on projects funded by the bank.

It should also be noted that by virtue of section 140(1), a company's constitution has the effect of a 'statutory contract' between the company and its members and amongst the members themselves, which allows the parties to the contract to enforce its terms if a given provision is contravened. However, there is no contract between directors and members, and thus members cannot bring legal action against directors who have breached a provision of the company's constitution. The right to do so is reserved to the company itself, as section 140(1)(b) creates a statutory contract between the company and each director and company secretary. Shareholders may, however, bring such action against directors in the name of the company if the directors have breached the company's constitution by reliance upon the statutory derivative action procedure under section 236.

A shareholder normally acquires the rights of a member either through being a member of the company at the time of its initial registration or through having their name added to the register of members following the acquisition of shares in the company.[31] Shareholders have various important rights such as the power to amend the company constitution. However, the rights attached to their shares may differ widely, and may or may not include the right to vote. If the company is a listed company, ASX Listing Rule 6.8, which specifies the 'one share one vote' principle, applies.[32] A company may issue shares with different terms and rights attached to them.[33] Section 254A(a) of the Corporations Act refers to various types of shares, including 'bonus shares', 'partly paid shares', 'preference shares' and 'redeemable preference shares'. The issue of preference shares does not require the prior issue of ordinary shares, although such issue would intuitively be assumed.[34]

10.1.5 *Powers of the AGM*

The shareholders' general meeting is one of the principal organs of a company, and is not subservient to the other main company organ, namely, the board of directors. Under section 250 N(1), only public companies are required to hold an AGM.[35] The business of the AGM is governed by section 250 R and may include consideration of the company's annual financial report, directors' report and/or auditor's report. The AGM may also deal with the election of directors, appointment of an auditor and/or determination of the auditor's remuneration.

The Corporations Act also provides shareholders in general meeting with a number of other statutory rights that can have important consequences for the company. These rights include the following statutory powers.

(1) *Inspect and copy company registers*: Members have a right to inspect and make a copy of company registers, such as the register of members, and they may do so free of charge (under sections 173(2) and (3)).

(2) *Calling a meeting of members and proposing resolutions:* When at least 5 per cent of members request that a general meeting be called, the directors are required by section 249D to call such a meeting. Under section 249 N, members may also give the company notice of the resolutions that they wish to be put to the general meeting, provided that they represent at least 5 per cent of the votes to be cast or 100 members at the meeting.

31 Corporations Act 2001, s. 231.

32 See also ASX Listing Rules www.asx.com.au/regulation/rules/asx-listing-rules.htm accessed 31 July 2020.

33 Corporations Act 2001, s. 254B.

34 See the discussion of preference shares by the High Court of Australia in *Beck* v. *Weinstock* [2013] HCA 15.

35 Most ASX 200 companies hold their AGM between 1 October and 30 November each calendar year (the AGM season).

Under section 249P, members who satisfy the '5 per cent or 100 member test' may also request that members' statements be distributed at the general meeting. Members are also given the right to inspect the meeting minutes under section 251B.[36]

(3) *Receipt of company financial reports:* Members are entitled under sections 314(1) and (2) to receive company financial information, either in the form of a concise report or the annual financial report, annual directors' report or annual auditor's report.

(4) *Appointment of directors and company auditor:* Shareholders can appoint a director by resolution of the general meeting under section 201 G, and members of a company may also remove a director from office by resolution under section 203 C. In the case of a public company, members are empowered by section 203D to remove a director from office regardless of any constitutional provision or agreement to the contrary. It should be noted that directors also have the power to appoint other directors under section 201 H. Section 329 empowers the general meeting to remove an auditor from office.

(5) *Approval of retirement benefits:* Section 200E requires member approval of any retirement benefits to be paid to employees, managers or executives.

(6) *Approval of a related-party benefit:* Section 208 requires that member approval be obtained before a public company provides a financial benefit to a related company.

(7) *Approval of capital-related transactions:* Shareholder approval is required for financial assistance transactions covered by Chapter 2 J, including capital reductions by the company (under section 256 C), company share buy backs (under sections 257 C and 257D) and the provision of financial assistance by the company (under section 260B).

(8) *Remedies available to members*: Members are empowered to utilize statutory remedies, such as the right to bring action for oppressive or unfairly discriminatory conduct under section 232 and the right under section 236 to initiate a statutory derivative action to enforce the rights of the company. Members are also empowered to seek an injunction under section 1324 where a contravention of the Act is concerned.

(9) *Pre-emption rights of existing members:* Section 254D provides that shareholder pre-emption rights in proprietary companies are a replaceable rule. In some companies, the constitution may provide that existing shareholders are given the right of first refusal to purchase shares that another existing member wishes to sell (or that sellers may be required to follow a special procedure in selling their shares).[37]

(10) *Initiation of insolvency proceedings:* In situations of insolvency, members can initiate the winding up of the company by application to the court under section 459P(1)(a). In situations other than insolvency, shareholders may also apply to the court to wind up the company under section 461(1)(a) after a special resolution to that effect has been passed by the general meeting. An application may also be made through reliance on the just and equitable ground in section 461(1)(k). Where a company is solvent, members may also initiate a voluntary winding up by passing a special resolution under section 491.

Listed public companies may in some circumstances be required by the ASX Listing Rules to seek shareholder approval before a managerial decision can be made. Such circumstances include the sale of the company's main undertaking, the company making a significant change to its activities, a proposal by the company within a twelve-month period to issue new capital

[36] See also Stephen Bottomley, 'Rethinking the Law on Shareholder-Initiated Resolutions at Company General Meetings' (2018) 43 *Melbourne University Law Review* 93.

[37] See, generally, Lion Nathan Australia Pty Ltd v. Coopers Brewery Ltd [2006] 59 ACSR 444.

amounting to more than 15 per cent of existing capital and the proposal of related-party transactions involving more than 5 per cent of the funds contributed by shareholders.[38]

10.1.6 *Ownership Structures*

Approximately 0.5 per cent of businesses in Australia are foreign-owned.[39] Of the large businesses currently operating in the country, 879 are foreign-owned, whilst 3,521 are Australian-owned.[40] Institutional investors have become an increasingly important, if somewhat diverse, component of the body of shareholders in larger Australian companies, especially listed companies. By 2010, domestic institutional investors accounted for about 40 per cent of the market, with foreign institutional investors accounting for another 40 per cent.[41] Institutional investors as a whole comprise a diverse array of firms and actors, including superannuation funds, private equity firms, banks, insurance companies, mutual funds, asset managers and sovereign wealth funds.

Unlike individual shareholders, institutional investors do not hold an ultimate economic interest in the shares they hold, as they invest for the benefit of the members of their respective funds. Furthermore, the interests of institutional investors do not necessarily coincide with those of their fund members or the corporations in which they invest because of the complex chain of intermediaries involved in managing their investments.[42] Nevertheless, institutional investors worldwide have been urged to play a more active role in corporate governance in recent years, as reflected in the stewardship codes introduced in various countries in the past decade.[43]

10.1.7 *Other Developments*

Several other developments relevant to the position of shareholders under Australian corporate law are worthy of mention, including the rise of institutional investors, the protection of other stakeholders such as employees and the power of ASIC to intervene in corporations to enforce provisions of the Corporations Act. Each is briefly discussed below.

Superannuation funds constitute the largest class of institutional investors, and have become increasingly prominent in Australia since 1992 when the government passed the Superannuation Guarantee (Administration) Act, which requires employees to make contributions to one or more superannuation funds that are then invested on their behalf by trustees. The size of such employee contributions has grown considerably over the past three decades, exceeding A$2.7 trillion in assets by 2018, although the performance of superannuation funds has varied widely.[44]

38 See ASX Listing Rules 7.1, 10.2, 11.1–11.2 www.asx.com.au/regulation/rules/asx-listing-rules.htm accessed 31 July 2020.

39 Department of Foreign Affairs and Trade (Commonwealth of Australia), 'Economic Activity of Foreign Owned Businesses in Australia 2014–15' (2018) 3 https://dfat.gov.au/trade/resources/investment-statistics/Documents/economic-activity-of-foreign-owned-businesses-in-australia-2014-15.pdf accessed 31 July 2020.

40 Ibid., 2.

41 Farrar and Hanrahan (n. 6) 413.

42 Ibid., 414–15. Also see Tim Bowley and Jennifer G. Hill, 'Stewardship and Collective Action: The Australian Experience' (30 March 2020) European Corporate Governance Institute Law Working Paper No. 491/2020, Monash University Faculty of Law Legal Studies Research Paper No. 3530402, available at SSRN https://ssrn.com/abstract=3530402 accessed 31 July 2020.

43 See Arad Reisberg, 'The Notion of Stewardship from a Company Law Perspective: Re-defined and Re-assessed in Light of the Recent Financial Crisis?' (2011) 18 *Journal of Financial Crime* 126; Iris H.-Y. Chiu, 'Stewardship As a Force for Governance: Critically Assessing the Aspirations and Weaknesses of the UK Stewardship Code' (2012) 9(1) *European Company Law* 5.

44 See Productivity Commission Inquiry Report No. 91, 'Superannuation: Assessing Efficiency and Competitiveness' (21 December 2018) 2 www.pc.gov.au/inquiries/completed/superannuation/assessment/report accessed 31 July 2020.

It should be noted that some institutional investors tend to adopt short-term horizons, which encourages short-termism on the part of Australian corporate boards.[45] A number of Australian superannuation funds, in contrast, have been criticized for actively seeking to promote broader corporate agendas, such as encouraging boards to be more responsive to climate change issues. Both developments have led to wider debates concerning the shape of the ASX Corporate Governance Council's Principles and Recommendations, although more radical agendas, such as introducing the concept of the 'social licence', have not yet found official favour.[46]

Stakeholder theory suggests that effective corporate governance should pay regard to a wider group of stakeholders than shareholders, including employees.[47] In the UK, this suggestion is encompassed within the concept of enlightened shareholder value.[48] Australian corporation law affords little recognition to employees unless they hold senior managerial positions. A 'senior manager' is defined as a person other than a director or secretary who can make decisions concerning the whole or a substantial part of a corporation's business, and senior managers are subject to the same duties as directors and officers. Australian courts have followed a narrow common law approach to employees, which has meant that benefits can be provided to employees only when it is in the interests of the company to do so.[49]

However, as a result of a number of major corporate collapses and labour disputes in Australia, reforms to the Corporations Act have increasingly sought to protect the position of employees as stakeholders such as through the protection of employee entitlements.[50] The Corporations Act also provides for shareholder approval of financial assistance in connection with employees who purchase shares under an employee share scheme.[51] Employee share buy-back provisions under a share buy-back scheme are referred to in section 257A.

Finally, a distinctive feature of Australian corporate law is the extensive range of powers vested in ASIC, the corporate regulator.[52] Those powers have been widely used in actions against directors for alleged breaches of their duties as directors. ASIC enjoys such broad powers under both the 2001 ASIC Act and Corporations Act.

10.2 LEGAL MEANS OF SHAREHOLDER ENGAGEMENT IN AUSTRALIA

Legal means of shareholder engagement in Australia vary considerably, ranging from reliance on the shareholder rights conferred under the Corporations Act to reliance on class actions seeking the collective enforcement of legal rights arising from corporate conduct involving a breach of

45 John Kehoe, 'Company Directors Admit Boards are Too Short Term', *The Australian Financial Review* (18 September 2019) www.afr.com/technology/company-directors-admit-boards-are-too-short-term-20190917-p52s3t accessed 31 July 2020. Also see, generally, John Kay, 'The Kay Review of UK Equity Markets and Long-Term Decision Making, Final Report' (July 2012) https://assets.publishing.service.gov.uk/government/uploads/system/uploads/attachment_data/file/253454/bis-12-917-kay-review-of-equity-markets-final-report.pdf accessed 31 July 2020.

46 See, for example, the discussion in Pamela Hanrahan, 'Corporate Governance, Financial Institutions and the "Social License"' (2016) 10(3) *Law and Financial Markets Review* 123.

47 See, generally, Roman Tomasic and Florarin Akinbami, 'Trust and Public Companies: Beginning to Reconceptualise Corporate Law in a Networked World' (2013) 27 *Australian Journal of Corporate Law* 233.

48 See also Andrew Keay, *The Enlightened Shareholder Value Principle and Corporate Governance* (Routledge 2014).

49 This was expressed in the UK decision of *Parke* v. *Daily News Ltd* [1962] Ch 927.

50 See, generally, Helen Anderson, *The Protection of Employee Entitlements in Insolvency: An Australian Perspective* (Melbourne University Press 2014).

51 The financial assistance provisions are found in Pt. 2J.3 of the Corporations Act 2001.

52 See, generally, Vicky Comino, *Australia's Company Law Watchdog ASIC and Corporate Regulation* (Thomas Reuters Professional Australia Limited 2015).

disclosure laws or misleading or deceptive conduct.[53] Class actions are further discussed in Section 10.2.4.

10.2.1 *Shareholder Rights to Call a Meeting*

Section 249 F of the 2001 Corporations Act permits an extraordinary general meeting (EGM) to be called by a company's directors or by members themselves if they hold at least 5 per cent of the votes to be cast in the meeting. However, if members call the meeting themselves, they are liable for the costs of holding it, which can be prohibitive. The Australian Institute of Company Directors has estimated that the cost of convening a general meeting can range between A$500,000 and A$1 million or even more.[54] Consequently, EGMs are rarely called by members under this statutory provision. Furthermore, judicial interpretation of section 249 F means that directors can postpone a member-called meeting if they do so for a proper purpose, thereby effectively delaying and undermining the provision's operation.[55]

Alternatively, members may require the company's directors to call an EGM under section 249D of the Corporations Act if members holding at least 5 per cent of the votes in the meeting make a written request to the board. This method of convening an EGM offers many benefits to members. Most notably, the meeting is conducted by the company rather than by members, meaning that the company is responsible for its organization and the considerable costs involved. However, statutory amendments have made it more difficult for a member to rely upon section 249 to convene a meeting. Section 249D, for example, was amended in 2015 to remove the ability of 100 members to requisition a company meeting out of concerns over the potential misuse of the procedure by political and shareholder activists.[56] The Explanatory Memorandum accompanying the repeal of the '100 member rule' stated that the move was necessary to 'better balance the rights of shareholders to raise issues with a company and the costs to companies of being required to call and hold a general meeting'.[57]

The request for a meeting made under section 249D must also contain the proposed resolutions that are to be put to the meeting. Directors are not required to hold such a meeting if the resolutions contained in the written request are invalid or if the meeting is to be held for an improper purpose,[58] defined as any purpose other than having members consider and vote on the resolutions of which the directors have been notified.[59] If it is proven that members are

[53] See also Olivia Dixon and Jennifer Hill, 'Australia: The Protection of Investors and the Compensation for Their Losses' in Pierre-Henri Conac and Martin Gelter (eds.), *Global Securities Litigation and Enforcement* (Cambridge University Press 2019).

[54] Australian Institute of Company Directors, Submission on the *Corporations Legislation Amendment (Deregulatory and Other Measures) Bill 2014* (Cth) (20 January 2015) 2 http://aicd.companydirectors.com.au/-/media/cd2/resources/advocacy/policy/pdf/2014/subm-2014-sencorporations-legislation-amendment-deregulatory-and-other-measures-bill-201420jan2015f.ashx accessed 31 July 2020.

[55] For a critique of the legal authorities seen as undermining the operation of the statutory right in s. 249F, see Neil Pathak and Hugh Lauritsen, 'A Shareholder's Right to Call General Meetings – A Sharp Sword for the Disgruntled Shareholder or Just a Blunt Instrument?' (2005) 23 *Company & Securities Law Journal* 283. For a recent illustration of a lengthy postponement of an EGM by a board, see *Wun* v. *CellOS Software Ltd* [2018] FCA 1947.

[56] For example, see *NRMA Ltd* v. *Snodgrass*; *NRMA Ltd* v. *Dupree* [2002] 42 ACSR 371; *Woolworths Ltd* v. *Getup Ltd* [2012] 90 ACSR 670.

[57] Explanatory Memorandum to the *Corporations Legislation Amendment (Deregulatory and Other Measures) Bill 2014* (Cth) 1.1 For a critical commentary, see Jason Harris, 'Barbarians at the Gate? Activist Investors and S 249N' (2016) 34 *Company and Securities Law Journal* 151.

[58] *NRMA* v. *Parker* [1986] 6 NSWLR 517 (approved in *Australasian Centre for Corporate Responsibility* v. *Commonwealth Bank of Australia* (n. 30).

[59] *NRMA Ltd* v. *Scandrett* [2002] 43 ACSR 401; [2002] NSWSC 1123.

calling a meeting for an improper purpose, the court may grant an order preventing the meeting from taking place.[60]

10.2.2 *Shareholder Proposal Right*

In Australia, the right of shareholders to advance a proposal is permissible but generally constrained, particularly in comparison with countries that encourage shareholder engagement via non-binding resolutions. Shareholder proposals in Australia are generally presented in one of two ways: first, via an amendment to a company's constitution by way of a special resolution and, second (if the first resolution is passed), by a resolution requiring some form of disclosure or action by a company.[61] This process sets the bar very high for successfully converting a proposal into concrete action. The statutory mechanism for shareholder proposals is found in section 249 N of the Corporations Act. It permits at least 100 members who are entitled to vote at a general meeting to give a company written notice of a resolution that they propose to move at a general meeting.[62] The right to advance proposals, together with examples of such proposals, is further discussed in Section 10.3.1.3.

10.2.3 *Voting*

The various ways in which votes can be cast include by a show of hands or via a proxy or poll. The right to vote in a company is given to members by the company's constitution,[63] which may, for example, restrict the voting rights attached to particular classes of shares, as in the case of partly paid shares. It is common, however, for corporate constitutions to have similar provisions to those found in the replaceable rules in section 250E. Subject to their displacement by the company constitution, the 'presumptive rule'[64] in the Corporations Act provides that subject to any rights or restrictions attached to any class of shares, each member in a company with share capital has one vote and, on a poll, each member has one vote for each share held. Each member of a company without share capital has one vote, both on a show of hands and in a poll.[65] This replaceable rule also confers a casting vote on the meeting chair and, if he or she is a member, any vote cast in his or her capacity as a member. The latter provision is significant given that common law does not recognize a chair's casting vote if the outcome of the vote is equal.[66]

Votes are cast in person at a general meeting, or they may be cast by proxy if proxy voting is allowed under the company's constitution. There is no common law right to vote by proxy;[67] therefore, such a right must be conferred by the company's constitution or by statute.[68] The right

60 *Humes Ltd* v. *Unity APA Ltd (in liq)* [1987] VR 467.

61 Governance Institute of Australia/LexisNexis Green Paper, 'Shareholder Resolutions: Is There a Case for Change?' (2018) www.governanceinstitute.com.au/advocacy/thought-leadership/shareholder-resolutions-is-there-a-case-for-change/ accessed 31 July 2020.

62 See, for example, the three alternate shareholder resolutions put forward to the Commonwealth Bank concerning action on greenhouse gas emissions and subsequently litigated in *Australasian Centre for Corporate Responsibility v Commonwealth Bank of Australia* (n. 30).

63 For theoretical analysis of the function of voting rights, see Paul Redmond, *Corporations and Financial Markets Law* (6th ed., Thomson Reuters 2013) [6.75].

64 Ibid.

65 Corporations Act 2001, s. 250E(2).

66 *Bishop of Chichester* v. *Harward* [1787] 1 Term Rep 650.

67 *Harben* v. *Phillips* [1883] 23 Ch D 14, applied in *New South Wales Henry George Foundation Ltd* v. *Booth* [2002] NSWSC 245.

68 These are provided for in pt. 2G.2, div. 6 of the Corporations Act 2001.

to appoint a proxy is a replaceable rule for proprietary companies but is mandatory for public companies.[69] Proxy papers are required to be sent to every member entitled to vote,[70] but a company cannot require proxies to be lodged more than forty-eight hours before the meeting.[71] The requirement for the prior lodgement of proxies is intended to allow for an investigation of their validity prior to commencement of the meeting.[72]

The proxy may either be an individual or a body corporate, and may be a proxy for all or some of a shareholder's votes. The ASX Listing Rules require that all listed companies include a proxy form in any notice of a meeting.[73] The proxy form must enable the shareholder to decide whether to vote for or against each resolution (and it may provide for an abstention on each) or to instead afford the proxy the discretion to decide.[74] The proxy has the same rights as the appointing member, such as the right to speak, vote (subject to the terms of the appointment) and to demand a poll.[75] Proxies can vote on a show of hands, unless forbidden to do so by the company's constitution.[76] Proxy votes can be directed or undirected. The issue of 'cherry picking' (whereby proxy holders choose to exercise proxies that support their position and disregard those that do not) was addressed by statutory amendments in 2011 designed to ensure that all proxies vote as intended.[77] Under these provisions:

- a proxy who is the chair of the meeting must vote on the poll, and must vote as directed;
- a proxy who is not the chair need not vote but, if he or she does vote, must vote as directed;[78] and
- if a nominated proxy does not register as attending the meeting, or attends but does not vote, then any proxies not exercised in the poll vote default to the chair, who has a duty to vote as directed.[79]

The Corporations Act recognizes three types of resolutions: ordinary resolutions, special resolutions and signed resolutions. Many questions requiring a decision at a general meeting are determined by an ordinary resolution,[80] which is passed by a simple majority of the valid votes cast at the meeting. Certain questions, however, must be determined by a special resolution. Special resolutions are required to be passed by a 75 per cent majority of the valid votes cast. The relevant statutory definition under section 9 of the Corporations Act makes it clear that it is 75 per cent of those who vote and not 75 per cent of all members, regardless of whether they vote. Finally, special resolutions are required for significant matters such as the

[69] Corporations Act 2001, s. 249X.

[70] Ibid., s. 249Z. For a discussion on the character of proxy documents, see *Sun Huang Kai Investment Services Ltd* v. *Metals X Ltd* [2019] FCA 1673 [25]–[37].

[71] Corporations Act 2001, s. 250B(1).

[72] *New South Wales Henry George Foundation Ltd* v. *Booth* [2002] NSWSC 245 [19].

[73] ASX Listing Rule 14.2.

[74] ASX Listing Rule 14.2.1, with accompanying note.

[75] Corporations Act 2001, s. 249Y(1).

[76] Ibid., 249Y(2).

[77] Corporations and Markets Advisory Committee (CAMAC), 'The AGM and Shareholder Engagement Discussion Paper' (September 2012) [5.8.10] www.camac.gov.au/camac/camac.nsf/byheadline/pdfdiscussion+papers/$file/agm.pdf accessed 15 July 2020; Explanatory Memorandum to the Corporations Amendment (Improving Accountability on Director and Executive Remuneration) Bill 2011, [6.10].

[78] Corporations Act 2001, s. 250BB. For the duties of a chair when dealing with proxies, see *Whitlam* v. *ASIC* [2003] 57 NSWLR 599; *Re Print Mail Logistics Ltd* [2012] NSWSC 792.

[79] Corporations Act 2001, ss. 250BB and 250BC.

[80] Anthony Lang, *Horsley's Meetings Procedure, Law and Practice* (6th ed., LexisNexis 2010) 141.

alteration of a company's constitution,[81] name[82] or type.[83] They are also required for certain types of approvals such as the approval of financial assistance to buy the company's shares,[84] approval of a capital reorganization[85] or approval of a resolution to wind up the company.[86]

10.2.4 *Questions and Information Request Rights*

Aside from considering annual company reports and the election of directors, the purpose of the AGM is to provide an opportunity for members to put questions to the board regarding the company's performance. The chair of the AGM must provide members with reasonable opportunities to ask questions, as required by sections 250S and 250SA of the Corporations Act. The auditor of a public company may attend the AGM, in which case members are permitted to ask him or her questions (section 250 T), and such attendance and availability for questioning are mandatory for public companies listed on the ASX.[87] Generally speaking, the questions most commonly asked at the AGMs of listed investment companies relate to performance, dividends and investment manager remuneration.[88]

10.2.5 *Class Actions*

The right of shareholders to inspect company registers and obtain copies thereof has become prominent in the past decade, in part because of the increase in shareholder class actions, which some have branded Australia's 'new growth industry'.[89] Class actions, aided by litigation funding, are a regular feature of Australian law. In the 27-year period between their introduction in 1992 and 30 June 2019, there were 634 class actions, representing an annual average of 23.[90] The most common type during that period were shareholder class actions, of which there were 122.[91] Eighty-two (or 67 per cent) of the 122 shareholder class actions were brought against only the relevant companies, as opposed to their directors.[92]

There appears to be very little appetite on the part of ASIC to use class actions to secure monetary relief for shareholders.[93] Research shows that in the class actions generated by the private sector, A$888,605,232 has been paid out to 94,984 shareholders, which equates to individual compensation of A$9,355.[94]

81 Corporations Act 2001, s. 136.
82 Ibid., s. 157.
83 Ibid., s. 162.
84 Ibid., s. 260B.
85 Ibid., s. 411.
86 Ibid., s. 491.
87 Ibid., s. 250RA.
88 Tom Bloomfield, 'LIC Governance Spotlight: AGM Planning and Frequently Asked Questions by Shareholders' (October 2018) https://boardroomlimited.com.au/posts/2018/10/03/lic-governance-spotlight-agm-planning-faqs/ accessed 31 July 2020.
89 Jennifer Hewett, 'The Rise and Rise of Class Actions' AFR (14 October 2019) www.afr.com/companies/professional-services/the-rise-and-rise-of-class-actions-20191010-p52zn4 accessed 31 July 2020. Maurice Blackburn, a law firm specializing in class actions, claims to have obtained more than A$2.6 billion for its clients. See www.mauriceblackburn.com.au/class-actions/ accessed 15 July 2020.
90 Vince Morabito, 'Shareholder Class Actions in Australia – Myths v. Facts' (11 November 2019) https://ssrn.com/abstract=3484660 accessed 31 July 2020.
91 Ibid.
92 ibid.
93 Ibid. See also Michelle Welsh and Vince Morabito, 'Public v. Private Enforcement of Securities Laws: An Australian Empirical Study' (2014) 14 *Journal of Corporate Law Studies* 39.
94 Ibid.

Questions have been raised about the business model used by some litigation funders to fund class actions. Called a common fund order, it allows them to take a share of any payment resulting from a claim paid to anyone in the class action. A recent High Court ruling held that common fund orders were outside the powers of the Federal Court and New South Wales Supreme Court to sanction.[95] The impact of the ruling on the future funding of class actions remains to be seen, as not all litigation funders are reliant on this funding model.

Many of the large companies listed on the ASX have been subjected to class actions in Australia, including Multiplex (a large construction company), Aristocrat Leisure (one of the world's largest poker machine manufacturers), Commonwealth Bank of Australia (one of the country's four largest banks), QBE Insurance, Leighton (now CIMIC, an international construction company), Centro (a large shopping centre owner), BHP Ltd (one of the world's largest mining companies) and AMP Ltd (Australia's oldest mutual fund, which was demutualized in 1988).[96]

Prior to the statutory amendments to the Corporations Act in 2010, unfettered access to a company's share registry gave rise to concerns over improper registry use, particularly for predatory, unsolicited, off-market share offers primarily targeting unsophisticated retail shareholders. Such concerns, together with privacy issues, were addressed by changes introduced under the Corporations Amendment (No. 1) Act 2010. Section 173 was amended to require persons wishing to obtain a copy of a company's Register of Members to disclose their intended use of the information (see section 173(3A)). Any person who makes a profit by contravening section 177 owes a debt to the company to be determined by the profit amount under section 177 (3). Thus, only members retain the right to inspect a register without having to pay a fee.

10.3 SHAREHOLDER ENGAGEMENT AND VOTING IN PRACTICE

There is growing evidence in Australia of apathy on the part of individual shareholders and of the dominance of proxy advisors. Typically, only a small fraction of shareholders attends an AGM, although many absent shareholders may have voted by proxy prior to the meeting.[97]

A study by ASIC into the issues voted on during the 2018 AGM season found sharpened shareholder focus on such matters as a social licence to operate and community expectations.[98] This finding is unsurprising in light of the long shadow cast by the Hayne Royal Commission into Misconduct in the Banking, Superannuation and Financial Services Industry, which drew attention to illegal and unethical conduct in these key sectors of the economy.[99] The 2018 AGM season also continued the trend towards greater shareholder engagement on environmental, social and governance (ESG) issues.[100] Climate change risk and sustainability emerged as the

[95] *BMW Australia Ltd* v. *Brewster*; *Westpac Banking Corporation* v. *Lenthall* [2019] HCA 45.

[96] Stephanie Chalmers, 'AMP Facing Threat of Several Shareholder Class Actions for Misleading ASIC Over "Fee for No Service" Scandal' *ABC News* (24 April 2018) www.abc.net.au/news/2018-04-23/amp-facing-threat-of-several-shareholder-class-actions-banking/9688922 accessed 31 July 2020.

[97] CAMAC, 'The AGM and Shareholder Engagement Discussion Paper' (n. 77) [2.2.2].

[98] Report 609 Annual General Meeting Season 2018, ASIC (January 2019) 3 https://asic.gov.au/regulatory-resources/find-a-document/reports/rep-609-annual-general-meeting-season-2018/ accessed 31 July 2020.

[99] *Final Report of the Royal Commission into Misconduct in the Banking, Superannuation and Financial Services Industry*, vol. 1 (Commonwealth of Australia 2019) [hereinafter Hayne Royal Commission] https://treasury.gov.au/publication/p2019-fsrc-final-report accessed 31 July 2020. Also see Anil Hargovan, 'Banking Royal Commission Final Report – Cultural Issues and Implications' (2019) 71 *Governance Directions* 128; Hayne Royal Commission Interim Report 'Unclogging the Central Artery' (2018) 70 *Governance Directions* 691.

[100] Report 609 Annual General Meeting Season 2018 (n. 98) 3.

most frequently raised ESG issues,[101] with the corporate regulator forecasting that such issues may continue to be raised in the years to come.

The trend towards shareholder-requisitioned resolutions also continued in 2018, with a total of eleven such resolutions received overall.[102] These focused predominantly on climate change (affecting Origin Energy and Whitehaven Coal, for example) and, to a lesser extent, human rights issues (affecting Qantas Airways and the Woolworths Group, for example).[103]

Executive remuneration also proved topical in 2018, which is unsurprising given the introduction of the two-strikes rule in 2011 in response to the egregious behaviour of a number of corporate boards.[104] The number of first strikes on remuneration matters was significantly higher in 2018 than in 2017 (twelve versus five).[105] ASIC attributed the increase to negative shareholder sentiment towards executive pay and accountability arising from the concerns highlighted by the Royal Commission about remuneration amounts (including performance-based payments) and company underperformance.[106]

10.3.1 *Who Votes and How?*

Under the replaceable rule, a resolution put to the vote at a general meeting is decided on a show of hands unless a poll is demanded.[107] Voting by a show of hands is the primary common law method of ascertaining the sense of a meeting.[108] It has long been recognized as a method of voting at AGMs and other shareholder meetings and is seen as an informal method of determining non-contentious matters expeditiously and inexpensively.[109] This method of voting, however, does not allow variations in the size of shareholdings or other entitlements to be taken into account.[110]

Although voting by a show of hands is an option for all types of companies,[111] it is noteworthy that the corporate regulator considers the practice undesirable for listed companies. ASIC instead recommends the use of polls on all resolutions as a matter of course.[112] Changing attitudes towards methods of voting can be seen in the results of an empirical study conducted in 2000, which found that most resolutions at that time were still decided by a show of hands without calling for a poll.[113]

ASIC's recommendation that votes be cast in writing is grounded in the view that polls 'more democratically reflect the principle of one share, one vote and reflect the wishes of shareholders attending the meeting as well as those who have voted by proxy'.[114] In the 2018 AGM season, for example, ASIC was particularly concerned that eleven companies in the ASX 200 were still

101 Ibid.

102 Ibid., 8.

103 Ibid., 9.

104 See Appendix 10.1.

105 Report 609 Annual General Meeting Season 2018 (n. 98) 8–9.

106 Ibid.

107 Corporations Act 2001, s. 250J(1).

108 Lang (n. 80) 195.

109 CAMAC, 'The AGM and Shareholder Engagement Discussion Paper' (n. 77) [5.13.1].

110 Lang (n. 80) 196.

111 Section 250J is a replaceable rule stating that a resolution put to the vote at a meeting of members must be decided on a show of hands unless a poll is demanded.

112 Report 564 Annual General Meeting Season 2017, ASIC (January 2018) 15 https://asic.gov.au/regulatory-resources/find-a-document/reports/rep-564-annual-general-meeting-season-2017/ accessed 31 July 2020.

113 Geof Stapledon et al., *Proxy Voting in Australia's Largest Companies* (Centre for Corporate Law and Securities Regulation and Corporate Governance International 2000) 16.

114 Report 564 Annual General Meeting Season 2017 (n. 112) 15.

deciding resolutions by a show of hands rather than by conducting a poll.[115] Where voting entitlements vary, polls are seen as a safeguard against a minority of persons with large shareholdings being outvoted by a majority with small shareholdings.[116]

A poll can be demanded before a vote on a show of hands is taken or before or immediately after the result of the show of hands is declared.[117] In practice, polls are typically demanded as a means of challenging an incorrect declaration made by the meeting chair based on a show of hands. A poll can be demanded on any resolution[118] by at least five members entitled to vote on the resolution or by members with at least 5 per cent of the votes that may be cast or by the chair.[119] Some company constitutions, however, stipulate that a poll cannot be demanded on any resolution concerning the election of a chair or the adjournment of a meeting.[120]

The use of technology to conduct meetings is becoming commonplace for Australian companies. Live webcasting, electronic voting via handheld devices or smartphone apps and the use of electronic polls rather than voting cards have become frequent features of AGMs in recent years, particularly amongst large listed companies.[121] Meetings can be held at more than one venue with the aid of technology, such as video conferencing, as long as the use of the technology in question gives members as a whole a reasonable opportunity to participate.[122]

The language in section 249S of the Corporations Act, however, does not explicitly reference online participation by shareholders via the internet, although the section is considered sufficiently broad to allow hybrid meetings; that is, shareholders can opt to attend the meeting in person at a physical venue or to attend it online.[123] The general consensus seems to be that hybrid meetings are acceptable under the Corporations Act, although the position on virtual-only meetings (involving the total absence of a physical venue) was less clear[124] prior to the impact of COVID-19 on the conduct of AGMs. Inquiry into reform to reinvigorate the AGM and clarify the permissibility of the online format for the conduct of AGMs remains stalled,[125] although the federal government's response to the coronavirus crisis (discussed below at Section 10.3.5) may be just the catalyst needed to revive the discussion.

10.3.2 *The Two-Strikes Rule in Practice*

The issue of executive remuneration continues to be a hot button issue for shareholders at AGMs,[126] and was for the decade or more preceding the global financial crisis. Supporting the claim that executive pay had 'got out of hand',[127] the Productivity Commission found that in the 1993–2007 period CEO remuneration at the 50–100 largest Australian listed companies had

115 Report 609 Annual General Meeting Season 2018 (n. 98) 13.
116 Lang (n. 80) 190.
117 Corporations Act 2001, s. 250L(3).
118 Ibid., s. 250(k).
119 Ibid., s. 250L, but note that s. 250L(2) allows for fewer members to call a poll if the corporate constitution allows for such a variation.
120 Ibid., s 250(k)(2).
121 Rod Halstead, Rory Moriarty and Lara Solomons, 'Hybrid and Virtual AGMs' (July 2017) Clayton Utz www.claytonutz.com/knowledge/2017/july/hybrid-and-virtual-agms accessed 31 July 2020.
122 Corporations Act 2001, s. 249S.
123 Rod Halstead, Rory Moriarty and Lara Solomons, 'Hybrid and Virtual AGMs', www.claytonutz.com/knowledge/2017/.
124 Ibid.
125 CAMAC (n. 77), the government advisory body, was abolished by the federal government in 2018.
126 See Appendix 10.1.
127 Productivity Commission Report No. 49, Final Inquiry Report 2009, 'Executive Remuneration in Australia', ix.

increased by as much as 300 per cent in real terms.[128] Shareholder attention to executive remuneration issues, including equity-based remuneration, was bolstered by statutory amendments to the Corporations Act in 2011 that introduced the two-strikes rule designed to hold boards accountable for unreasonable levels of executive remuneration and compensation. For listed companies, a resolution to adopt a director's remuneration report must be put to a vote at an AGM.[129]

Shareholders today remain sensitive to executive remuneration levels and entitlements to bonuses. Such long-standing concerns have been fuelled by the governance failures exposed by the Hayne Royal Commission.[130] ASIC shares these concerns and has also set its sights on scrutinizing remuneration practices in Australia.[131] Unsurprisingly, the Commission's findings on misconduct in the Australian financial sector cast a long shadow on the 2018 round of AGMs. Its revelation of poor governance and questionable ethical practices did not sit well with investors.[132] National Australian Bank Ltd bore the brunt of investor dissatisfaction with its dubious financial performance and executive remuneration framework, with a historic 88.43 per cent of shareholders voting against the company's remuneration report. This was the largest vote against a remuneration report recorded against an ASX 300 company since voting was introduced in 2005.[133] At the 2018 AGM of another bank, Westpac Ltd, 64.16 per cent of shareholders voted against its remuneration report.[134] Similarly, at the 2018 AGM of the Australasian and New Zealand Banking Group, there was a 33.76 per cent vote against the bank's remuneration report.[135]

In respect of S&P/ASX 200 listed entities, for the 2018 AGM season, ASIC's report set out some key observations on executive remuneration. It found that:[136]

> the number of remuneration strikes increas[ed] significantly compared to last year's calmer season (12 [strikes in 2018] compared to 5 [strikes] in 2017 [with no second strikes in 2018]). This trend was accompanied by an upsurge in the magnitude of 'against' votes on remuneration reports, with a number of record highs in 2018.

The strikes noted by the regulator appear to have been driven by a number of factors, including negative shareholder sentiment towards executive pay and accountability arising from the concerns highlighted by the Hayne Royal Commission; remuneration amounts (including performance-based payments) and the way in which remuneration is structured (including 'combined' plan incentive structures); and company underperformance.

There was also a significant increase in the number of ASX 300 companies receiving a strike against their remuneration reports in the 2018 AGM season, with nineteen such companies

128 Ibid.

129 Corporations Act 2001, s. 250R(2).

130 The Royal Commission Final Report found that poor conduct in the financial services sector was caused not only by the pursuit of corporate gain, but was also driven by individual gain spurred on by remuneration and other financial incentives that rewarded corporate and individual misconduct.

131 Speech by John Price, Commissioner, 'Australian Securities and Investments Commission at the FINSIA "the Regulators" Panel Event' (Melbourne Australia) 15 November 2018 https://asic.gov.au/about-asic/news-centre/speeches/an-asic-update-by-john-price-commissioner/ accessed 31 July 2020.

132 See Hargovan (n. 99).

133 James Frost, 'NAB Attracts 88 Per Cent No Vote Against Banker Pay at AGM', *Australian Financial Review* (19 December 2018) www.afr.com/business/banking-and-finance/we-got-it-wrong-nab-chairman-ken-henry-tells-shareholders-at-agm-20181218-h198k8 accessed 31 July 2020.

134 Egan Associates, Strikes Against the Remuneration Report – 2018 AGM Season https://eganassociates.com.au/strikes-against-the-remuneration-report-2018-agm-season/ accessed 31 July 2020.

135 Ibid.

136 Report 609 Annual General Meeting Season 2018 (n. 98).

receiving strikes in 2018 compared with just six in 2017.[137] Significantly from a governance perspective, Mineral Resources Ltd received its third strike in a row, with 63.3 per cent of shareholders voting against its executive remuneration report in 2018. The company had received its second strike in 2017, causing a board spill motion. It received a 41.48 per cent vote against its remuneration report in that year, and, in 2016, it was 49.18 per cent. The board spill motion, however, was not carried through, with shareholders voting for the retention of the board and existing management.[138] Similarly, the board of Myer Holdings Ltd also survived the prospect of a spill. During its 2018 AGM, 37.54 per cent of shareholders voted against its remuneration report in a second strike. However, a potential board spill was prevented, as 63 per cent of proxies opposed a spill motion. During the 2017 AGM season, the company received a 29.41 per cent shareholder vote against its remuneration report.[139]

Shareholders are concerned when non-financial market hurdles drive bonuses, particularly when they do not appear to be linked to shareholder value creation. The latter point was evidenced in the historic first strike against Commonwealth Bank Ltd, where 50.9 per cent of the votes and proxies cast at the meeting opposed the remuneration report. Shareholders were sceptical of the bank's use of a 'soft target' to set bonuses and highly critical of its failure to set clear targets and metrics in its report. The 25 per cent non-financial performance hurdle set for 'People and Community' was based on overall progress in diversity and inclusion, sustainability and culture, criteria viewed by shareholders and proxy advisers as unquantifiable performance measures. Moreover, they queried why bonuses were necessary when such progress was seen as a normal performance expectation by the board.[140]

However, it is significant to note, as ASIC observed, that shareholders also use their votes on remuneration reports to demonstrate their discontent with boards more broadly.[141] The regulator's observation is supported by research showing that, from 2011–12, a total of 237 first-strike advisory resolutions in Australian listed companies were aimed more at sustained poor company performance than at excessive executive remuneration.[142] In recent years, the matters that shareholders vote on in AGMs in Australia have broadened considerably beyond 'say on pay' issues. Attention to ESG and human rights issues appears to be gaining momentum at AGMs through reliance on shareholder resolutions,[143] a significant development that is discussed in greater detail in Section 10.3.3.

10.3.3 *Shareholder Proposals and Proxy Fights?*

Non-binding shareholder advisory resolutions can play an important role in improving accountability within companies by providing a formal mechanism for shareholders to give feedback to boards.[144] The framework for shareholder-proposed resolutions in Australia, however, differs

137 Egan Associates (n. 134).

138 Ibid.

139 Ibid.

140 See James Eyers and Julie-Anne Sprague 'CBA Pay Revolt Triggers First Strike at AGM', *Australian Financial Review* (9 November 2016) www.afr.com/business/banking-and-finance/financial-services/cba-pay-revolt-triggers-first-strike-at-agm-20161109-gsl98j accessed 31 July 2020.

141 Report 609 Annual General Meeting Season 2018 (n. 98) 5.

142 Matthew Grosse, Stephen Kean and Tom Scott, 'Shareholder Say on Pay and CEO Compensation: Three Strikes and the Board Is Out' (2017) 57 *Accounting and Finance* 701, 701–2.

143 Report 609 Annual General Meeting Season 2018 (n. 98).

144 For comparative perspectives, see Bottomley (n. 36) 93, 95; Australian Council of Superannuation Investors (ACSI), 'Shareholder Resolutions in Australia – Is There a Better Way?' (October 2017) https://acsi.org.au/wp-content/uploads/2020/02/Shareholder-resolutions-in-Australia.Oct17.pdf accessed 31 July 2020.

from that in many other countries, resulting in few broad-based Australian shareholder resolutions dealing with ESG and human rights issues. Empirical research shows that such resolutions in Australia largely focus on director elections and removals.[145]

Unlike their counterparts in the UK, USA, Canada and New Zealand,[146] shareholders in Australia cannot propose advisory or non-binding resolutions[147] except in very limited circumstances involving the remuneration reports of listed companies.[148] Instead, they can propose constitutional amendments to effect change, although the required threshold is high: a special resolution with a 75 per cent vote in favour. This procedural obstacle presents a real barrier for shareholders looking to successfully effect change through, for example, resolutions on ESG or human rights issues.[149] Noting such difficulties, the Australian Council of Superannuation Investors (ACSI) has called for the introduction of an ordinary non-binding shareholder resolution framework in Australia.[150]

Notwithstanding these practical difficulties, shareholders in Australia often rely on section 249 N of the Corporations Act, which permits at least 100 members who are entitled to vote at a general meeting to give a company written notice of a resolution they propose to move at such a meeting.[151] The prospect of using section 249 N to introduce broad-based advisory resolutions, however, received a setback from the decision of the Full Court of the Federal Court in *Australasian Centre for Corporate Responsibility* v. *Commonwealth Bank of Australia* (2016) 248 FCR 280. The court reasoned that advisory resolutions are permissible only if they have some basis in either legislation or the corporate constitution and that such a basis is not found in section 249 N. Nevertheless, shareholders who are dissatisfied with how a company is managing its environmental risks or human rights obligations can still rely on section 249 N to introduce ordinary resolutions on ESG and human rights issues.

Two recent milestones in shareholder engagement at an AGM via shareholder-proposed resolutions illustrate the current use of statutory machinery to communicate with fellow shareholders on matters of common concern. They concerned engaged shareholders critical of the business practices of Qantas Ltd and Origin Energy Ltd, two companies listed in the ASX 100.

At its November 2019 AGM, 23.56 per cent of Qantas shareholders signalled that the company was not doing enough to respond to their concerns about the rights of asylum seekers affected by Qantas operations.[152] Several shareholders, including US-based asset manager Mercy Investment Services, were concerned about what they perceived to be Qantas's complicity in

145 Xian Chian Hui, 'An Analysis of Shareholder Resolutions Involving Australian Listed Companies from 2004 to 2013' (2016) 34 *Company and Securities Law Journal* 618.

146 Bottomley (n. 36) 93, 122–4.

147 The Companies and Securities Advisory Committee (CASAC) in Australia considered the possibility of introducing a statutory non-binding advisory resolution but decided against such a move fearing that it would blur the distinction between the role of the board and that of the general meeting; see Companies and Securities Advisory Committee, Shareholder Participation in the Modern Listed Public Company (Final Report, June 2000).

148 Corporations Act 2001, s. 250R(3) provides that the vote on a resolution is advisory only and does not bind the directors or company. Note, however, this section is a precursor to, and forms the basis of, the two-strikes rule, which can support a resolution to spill the board. See also ss. 249L, 250V and 250W.

149 Also see ACSI (n. 144).

150 Ibid.

151 See, for example, the three alternate shareholder resolutions put to the Commonwealth Bank concerning action on greenhouse gas emissions and subsequently litigated in *Australasian Centre for Corporate Responsibility* v. *Commonwealth Bank of Australia* (n. 30).

152 Australasian Centre for Corporate Responsibility (ACCR), 'Qantas Asylum Seekers Resolution – Largest Ever Vote Against a Board on Human Rights Issues' (7 November 2019) https://accr.org.au/2019/10/28/qantas-asylum-seekers-resolution-largest-ever-vote-against-a-board-on-human-rights-issues/ accessed 31 July 2020.

the Australian government's refugee policy. A resolution filed by the Australasian Centre for Corporate Responsibility (ACCR)[153] called on Qantas to (1) review its policies and processes relating to involuntary transport, utilizing the UN Guiding Principles on Business and Human Reviews as a basis for review, and (2) to disclose to shareholders the results of that review, outlining any human rights risk that posed a threat to the company's interests in the long term. In 2018, a similar resolution attracted 6.43 per cent of the vote and attracted the support of CalPERS (a California-based pension fund).[154]

Another historic vote was achieved at the 2018 AGM of Origin Energy Ltd on a resolution filed by the ACCR that targeted the company's association with and membership in industry groups on energy and climate change. The resolution sought a review to ensure that the company's relationship with anti-climate lobbying groups was in line with its pledge of support for the Paris Climate Agreement. The subsequent 46 per cent vote against the board has been hailed as a record vote for a shareholder proposal on an ESG issue in Australian corporate history.[155] On the back of its success with Origin Energy, the ACCR filed a similar anti-climate lobbying resolution at the 2019 AGM of BHP Ltd. Almost a third of shareholders (29.58 per cent) voted for the company to suspend its membership in industry associations that advocate issues contrary to the goals of the Paris Agreement.[156]

Recent proxy fights by shareholders and directors over access to proxy information have landed in the courts, with the parties concerned relying upon the statutory provision in section 247A of the Corporations Act, which allows members (or their authorized representatives) to file a court order to inspect a company's books.[157] According to the provision, the court can order such an inspection if it is satisfied that the applicant is acting in good faith (with honesty) and for a proper purpose. If an order is made, the member in question is permitted to make copies of the company's books unless the court orders otherwise.

A critical legal issue in proxy battles goes to the threshold question of whether proxy forms fall within the statutory description 'books of the company'. A recent line of judicial authority suggests that it does not on the basis that proxies are merely received by the company and taken into its possession; they are received for the purpose of the meeting and are not part of the company's records.[158] Shareholders may, however, rely on their common law right to access proxy information, which was the result in a recent case wherein a shareholder in an ASX-listed company and its lawyers were allowed to inspect and make copies of all proxy forms received by the company, as well as its share registry, in order to counter the advantage possessed by the directors to solicit proxy votes.[159]

However, in *Re Cromwell*, a shareholder in another ASX-listed company was denied access to the company's proxy records on the basis that it had no such right under either the Corporations Act or common law.[160] The crucial difference in the facts of this case is that the shareholder in *Re*

[153] The ACCR is a non-profit association that seeks to develop and deploy strategies to improve Australian listed companies' performance on ESG risk indicators https://accr.org.au/ accessed 31 July 2020.

[154] ACCR, 'Qantas Board to Face Shareholders and Experts on Deportations and Transfers to Danger' (24 October 2019) https://accr.org.au/2019/10/24/qantas-board-to-face-shareholders-2019/ accessed 31 July 2020.

[155] ACCR, 'Origin Energy AGM: Record 46% Vote Slams Anti-Climate Lobby' (17 November 2018) https://accr.org.au/2018/10/17/origin-energy-agm-record-46-vote-slams-anti-climate-lobby/ accessed 31 July 2020.

[156] ACCR, 'BHP AGM: Australian Investors Take a Stand on Anti-Climate Lobbying' (7 November 2019) https://accr.org.au/2019/11/07/bhp-agm-australian-investors-take-a-stand-on-anti-climate-lobbying/ accessed 31 July 2020.

[157] For a discussion on the legislative origins of s. 247A, see *Sun Huang Kai Investment Services Ltd* v. *Metals X Ltd* [2019] FCA 1673 [7]–[20].

[158] Ibid., [25]–[42]; Re Cromwell Property Securities Ltd [2019] NSWSC 1608 [30]–[31].

[159] *Sun Huang Kai Investment Services Ltd* v. *Metals X Ltd* [2019] FCA 1673.

[160] Ibid.

Cromwell sought the proxy information in question in order to approach the company's security holders to promote the election of its preferred candidate to the board. In such circumstances, the court queried whether the inspection of proxy forms was necessary with reference to the specific dispute or question in which the shareholder was interested. The key takeaway from these litigated proxy contests is that the Australian courts appear more likely to grant a shareholder access to proxy information if the purpose is to 'level the playing field' in the same way that directors access proxies.

10.3.4 *Who Votes? Individual versus Institutional*

The future of the AGM is under a cloud, as it is seen by some as 'outmoded and ineffectual'.[161] The effectiveness of the AGM as a decision-making body is particularly open to question given the low attendance rates and overall low participation rates of individual shareholders. It has been reported that AGM attendance hovers at 0.16 per cent, and fell 10 per cent in the five-year period from 2011 to 2016,[162] despite personal share ownership in Australian companies remaining high by international standards: 37 per cent of Australian adults, or 6.9 million people, hold investments that are available through a financial exchange, with 31 per cent holding shares.[163] Insight into why this might be the case can be gleaned from an observation made in a report issued by the Productivity Commission:[164] 'Investors will weigh up the costs and benefits associated with monitoring, engaging and voting. For a small retail investor, the benefits associated with voting are likely to be small. Given the size of their investments, institutional investors are more likely to engage with a company'.

It could be argued that the ability of small shareholders in public companies to exert an influential impact on board accountability is minimal. The Commonwealth Parliament's Joint Committee on Corporations and Financial Services produced a report on shareholder engagement in 2008 that reaffirmed the importance of shareholder meetings and recommended a range of ways in which voting rules can be improved to ensure that shareholders are able to express their collective will through such meetings.[165]

Proxy solicitation in Australia is less closely regulated than it is in the USA and Canada, and is thus a major contributor to corporate control through shareholder voting.[166] The growing influence of proxy advisors has been accompanied by the rise of institutional investors in Australia over the past two decades, prompting growing calls for stronger regulation to temper their influence.[167] Many of the resolutions of large public companies are determined by proxy votes, and the results are often known several days before the AGM occurs. A review of the engagement practices and policies of Australia's four main proxy advisors – CGI Glass Lewis, ISS Australia, Ownership Matters and the ASCI – appears to suggest that concerns regarding the

161 Tammy Lim, 'Reinvigorating the AGM: Is Hybrid the Answer' (2017) 69 *Governance Directions* 676.

162 Ibid.; also see Computershare, Intelligence Report (2017) www.computershare.com/SubscriberContent/CIS%20Intel%20Reports/AGM%20Intel%20Report%202017Onscreen.pdf accessed 31 July 2020.

163 Deloitte Access Economics, ASX Australian Investor Study 2017 www.asx.com.au/education/2017-asx-investor-study.htm accessed 30 July 2020.

164 Productivity Commission Report, 'Executive Remuneration in Australia', Report No. 49, Final Inquiry Report, Melbourne, 2009, 303.

165 Parliamentary Joint Committee on Corporations and Financial Services, 'Better Shareholders – Better Company – Shareholder Engagement and Participation in Australia', Commonwealth of Australia, 2008.

166 Redmond (n. 63) [6.85].

167 Ben Power, 'Proxy Music' (Australian Institute of Company Directors, 27 February 2018) https://aicd.companydirectors.com.au/membership/company-director-magazine/2018-back-editions/march/proxy-music accessed 31 July 2020.

extent of the influence of proxy adviser recommendations on the voting outcomes of company resolutions are overstated.[168] A mixed picture therefore emerges on the question of whether there is a need for a code of conduct or self-regulatory mechanism to curb the influence of proxy advisors.[169]

10.3.5 *AGMs in the COVID-19 Environment*

It is trite to observe that COVID-19-induced social distancing requirements, travel restrictions and limits on indoor gatherings are having an adverse impact on companies required to hold their AGMs in the usual manner. In a pragmatic move made to ensure that companies meet their statutory deadline to conduct an AGM, the regulator, ASIC, has adopted a 'no action' position on virtual AGMs, although they are not currently provided for under the Corporations Act.[170] This position, sensibly, is conditional on the technology used to provide members as a whole with a reasonable opportunity to participate, as mandated by section 249S.

The federal government, however, has gone one step further to mitigate the impact of the coronavirus pandemic. By way of a ministerial determination – the Corporations (Coronavirus Economic Response) Determination – the government has temporarily amended the provisions of the Corporations Act concerned with the convening and holding of general meetings.[171] The following is a brief summary of the temporary measures put in place under the determination, which became effective on 6 May 2020:

- companies can convene and hold general meetings by electronic means, ensuring that all persons entitled to attend have a reasonable opportunity to participate;
- all persons participating are taken for all purposes (for example, a quorum requirement) to be present at the meeting;
- a vote taken at the meeting must be taken on a poll, and not a show of hands;
- a proxy may be appointed by using one or more technologies specified in the notice of the meeting; and
- notice of the meeting may be given using one or more technologies, with details of an online location where the contents of the notice can be viewed or from where they can be downloaded.

The conduct of virtual meetings is now a reality, although it is likely to be a short-lived one. The challenge that remains is for the government to exhibit the will to translate these temporary concessions into permanent changes.

10.4 CONCLUDING REMARKS

Engagement is the means by which companies and investors discuss issues of importance to both, although, as one experienced observer has astutely observed, engagement is not an end in

[168] ASIC, 'Report 578, ASIC Review of Proxy Adviser Engagement Practices' (27 June 2018) 4 https://asic.gov.au/regulatory-resources/find-a-document/reports/rep-578-asic-review-of-proxy-adviser-engagement-practices/ accessed 31 July 2020.

[169] Lysarne Pelling, 'Proxy Advisors: Have Your Say' Boardroom Report (April 2017) https://aicd.companydirectors.com.au/membership/the-boardroom-report/volume-15-issue-4/proxy-advisers-have-your-say accessed 31 July 2020.

[170] ASIC, '20-068MR Guidelines for Meeting Upcoming AGM and Financial Reporting Requirements' (20 March 2020) https://asic.gov.au/about-asic/news-centre/find-a-media-release/2020-releases/20-068mr-guidelines-for-meeting-upcoming-agm-and-financial-reporting-requirements/ accessed 31 July 2020.

[171] Corporations (Coronavirus Economic Response) Determination (No. 1) 2020 www.legislation.gov.au/Details/F2020L00553 accessed 31 July 2020.

itself.[172] The tension between shareholders and company boards is an ongoing feature of the corporate governance landscape in Australia, with few shareholders, even large institutions, enjoying sufficient power to exert much influence on boards by themselves. Facilitating enhanced communication and engagement amongst shareholders and between shareholders and the board is one means of seeking to lessen this tension. However, as shareholders are no longer the only stakeholders in larger companies, the views of other stakeholders also need to be considered. The narrow pursuit of profits by Australian banks and financial institutions revealed by the recent Hayne Royal Commission illustrates the consequences of failing to consider wider stakeholder interests, such as those of bank customers and superannuation fund members.

Ongoing communication and engagement between companies and investors is required to better align views and perspectives, especially when dealing with topics often seen as contentious such as climate change and the environment. To a degree, the legal landscape in Australia promotes opportunities for such dialogue to occur by mandating AGMs for public companies and allowing shareholders and directors to call meetings. There is, however, scope to facilitate more effective and meaningful participation by shareholders. The pressing nature of this issue is underscored by the outcome of the litigation in *Australasian Centre for Corporate Responsibility v Commonwealth Bank of Australia* (2016) 248 FCR 280, which limited the extent to which shareholders can speak on behalf of a company. The Full Court of the Federal Court endorsed the statements of Davies J in *Australasian Centre for Corporate Responsibility* v. *Commonwealth Bank of Australia* (2015) FCA 785 at [16]:

> [I]f the company's constitution gives to the board the power to manage the company's business, the directors are exclusively responsible for the management of the company and shareholders cannot control the directors in the exercise of that power or direct the board by resolution to exercise that power in a particular way (save for any matters that are within the power of the company in general meeting).

This judicial statement, together with the absence of any statutory mechanism for broad-based non-binding shareholder resolutions in Australia, presents real challenges for shareholders wishing to express their genuine concerns and offer feedback to the board on a company's policies when these are considered to be misaligned with shareholder values. The current practice, as observed by the CEO of the ACSI, is for shareholders to propose a constitutional amendment or vote against the re-election of directors.[173] This practice is problematic, as it is correctly seen as a blunt instrument for placing ESG resolutions on the agendas of Australian general meetings.[174]

On a positive note, a 2017 initiative by ASIC to actively monitor the AGM season for ASX 200 companies, and to produce annual reports on the results, is a significant development with respect to good governance practices and encouraging greater shareholder engagement. ASIC's annual reports offer transparency and have considerable potential to promote greater board accountability. They not only provide an overview of the AGM season but, more importantly in practice, also provide high-level observations on key governance issues voted on by shareholders and capture the main areas of active shareholder engagement and voting.

172 Governance Institute of Australia and Sandy Easterbrook, 'Improving Engagement Between ASX-listed Entities and Their Institutional Investors: Principles and Guidelines' (2014) 3 www.governanceinstitute.com.au/advocacy/thought-leadership/shareholder-engagement/ accessed 31 July 2020.

173 ACSI (n. 144) 5.

174 Ibid.

In recent years, beyond the typical shareholder focus on executive remuneration issues,[175] corporate Australia has also witnessed a trend towards active shareholder engagement on ESG and human rights issues at AGMs,[176] albeit with varying degrees of success. Climate change risks and sustainability emerged as the most frequently raised ESG issues in the 2018 AGM season,[177] with the country's corporate regulator forecasting that such issues will continue to be raised in the years to come. However, the raising of these issues by shareholders is one thing; the prospect of shareholders effecting real and meaningful change is another. Without legislative change to facilitate advisory or broad-based non-binding shareholder resolutions, that prospect remains doubtful.[178]

APPENDIX 10.1 *Executive remuneration: Two-strikes rule 2007–18*
Largest strikes for S&P/ASX 200 companies

	Year	Against vote (%)
NAB	2018	88
Harvey Norman	2014	76
Valad Property Group	2008	76
Crane Group	2010	71
Challenger	2010	70
PaperlinX	2010	68
Telstra	2007	66
Mineral Resources	2018	64
Westpac	2018	64
OZ Minerals	2009	64
Atlas Iron	2008	63
AGL	2007	63
Telstra	2018	62
Arrium	2015	62
AMP	2018	61
Babcock & Brown Capita	2008	61
St Barbara	2008	61
Transurban	2010	59
Downer EDI	2009	59
Transurban Group	2008	59

Source: Ownership Matters.

175 See Appendix 10.1.
176 Report 609 Annual General Meeting Season 2018 (n. 98).
177 Ibid.
178 The CEO of the ACSI views the absence of an ordinary non-binding shareholder resolution framework in Australia as 'flawed' and has called for reform. See ACSI (n. 144) 3.

11

Shareholder Engagement and Voting in Canada

Poonam Puri and Ankita Gupta

11.1 INTRODUCTION

This chapter examines Canada's corporate governance landscape from the perspective of shareholders and considers both the legal tools that shareholders have available to them under Canadian corporate and securities law and the market mechanisms they can access to protect their financial investment and advocate for change in a corporation. The chapter also critically considers the limitations and effectiveness of these legal and market mechanisms and examines the various market actors who influence shareholder behaviour and can facilitate shareholder engagement.

Under Canadian corporate law, shareholders occupy a preferential role vis-à-vis other stakeholders given that they are the only stakeholder with the statutory right to elect and remove directors, vote on certain fundamental transactions or changes, make shareholder proposals and requisition shareholder meetings. These legal rights are intended to serve a disciplinary purpose. They aim to provide a check on directors and officers to ensure they are acting in the best interests of the corporation, and not their own self-interest. However, shareholders are just one of the many stakeholders whose interests directors and officers must consider in making corporate decisions. Moreover, most of the aforementioned legal tools remain out of reach for ordinary investors because they require a certain degree of sophistication and expertise to exercise, not to mention cost and time. Market mechanisms such as shareholders' ability to 'vote with their feet' and sell their shares at will supplement shareholder's legal rights, providing shareholders with an 'out' for their investment.

Canadian capital markets have undergone significant change in the past few decades. Institutional investors have grown to dominate the ownership of Canadian public companies, and proxy advisory firms have emerged and grown to exert a significant influence on shareholders. As a result, institutional investors and proxy advisory firms have been able to drive changes on important issues such as gender diversity on boards and environmental, social and governance (ESG) disclosure beyond the requirements in corporate statutes or securities laws. We also explore these developments in this chapter.

The chapter proceeds as follows. Section 11.2 provides a snapshot of Canada's capital markets and describes key features of the Canadian corporate governance landscape that provide important background and context to the shareholder rights discussion that follows. Section 11.3 discusses the role of shareholders in Canadian public corporations and their rights vis-à-vis the corporation, directors, officers and other stakeholders. We pay particular attention to the key legal means of engagement available to shareholders under Canadian corporate and securities law, and examine the limitations and effectiveness of these tools. Section 11.4 analyzes three particular trends in shareholder engagement in Canada, namely, institutional investor engagement on ESG issues, the role of proxy advisory firms and the influence they wield over institutional shareholders and the immediate impact of COVID-19 on shareholder engagement. Section 11.5 concludes.

11.2 CANADIAN CAPITAL MARKETS AND CORPORATE GOVERNANCE

11.2.1 *A Snapshot of Canada's Capital Markets*

Canada is a relatively small player in the world's capital markets, with Canadian issuers representing less than 3 per cent of total world market capitalization.[1] Despite being such a small player, the number of Canadian public companies is relatively high compared to other countries, with about 3,270 issuers listed on the Toronto Stock Exchange (TSX) and TSX Venture Exchange (TSX-V) in 2020.[2] Interestingly, of the 1,617 public companies listed on the TSX, Canada's largest capital market, 1,079 (66.7 per cent) are headquartered in Ontario, with Alberta, British Columbia and Quebec trailing far behind, with 150 (9.3 per cent), 136 (8.4 per cent) and 121 (7.5 per cent), respectively.[3] However, when it comes to the TSX-V, of its 1,653 listed public companies, a majority (844 or 51.1 per cent) are headquartered in British Columbia, followed by Ontario and Alberta, which have 373 (22.6 per cent) and 170 (10.3 per cent), respectively.[4] On the whole, Canada's capital markets are well-developed. The market capitalization of Canadian listed issuers is high relative to national GDP, at 112.9 per cent, a sign of healthy capital markets.[5] By comparison, although the United States has a higher market capitalization to GDP ratio of 148.3 per cent, many other countries have a lower ratio, including China with a ratio of 59.4 per cent, the European Union at 54.7 per cent, Germany at 54.3 per cent, India at 75.8 per cent, Brazil at 65.7 per cent and Russia at 34.5 per cent.[6]

Another notable feature of Canada's capital markets is the dominance of mining companies. The TSX's 202 mining companies (out of a total of 1,617) command approximately 16 per cent of its quoted market value, whilst the figure for the TSX-V's 922 mining issuers is over 58 per cent.[7] Trading in mining company shares is almost four times higher on the TSX-V than that in any other sector, and, on the TSX, mining and oil and gas trades account for 50 per cent of trading volume.[8]

Canada's capital markets also comprise a small number of very large issuers and a large number of very small issuers.[9] For example, on the S&P/TSX Composite Index, a market capitalization-weighted index that tracks the performance of the TSX's largest companies, the top-ten public companies account for a staggering 38.6 per cent of the index's market capitalization as a whole.[10]

1 Poonam Puri, 'Legal Origins, Investor Protection, and Canada' [2009] *Brigham Young University Law Review* 1671, 1672.
2 Ibid., 1672; see also TMX, 'The MiG Report' (2020) 3 www.tsx.com/resource/en/2381 accessed 30 August 2020.
3 MiG Report (n. 2) 3.
4 Ibid., 3.
5 CEIC, 'United States Market Capitalization: % of GDP' www.ceicdata.com/en/indicator/united-states/market-capitalization–nominal-gdp#:~:text=United%20States's%20Market%20Capitalization%20accounted,164.8%20%25%20in%20the%20previous%20year accessed 30 August 2020.
6 Ibid.
7 MiG Report (n. 2) 6.
8 Ibid.
9 Puri (n. 1) 1672.
10 Toronto Stock Exchange (TSX), 'S&P/TSX Composite Index' https://web.tmxmoney.com/index_profile.php?qm_symbol=^TSX accessed 30 August 2020.

In addition, a large number of companies listed on the TSX are also dual-listed on US exchanges, and a large number of Canada's largest public companies have controlling or significant shareholders.[11] Over 50 per cent of companies on the S&P/TSX Composite Index have at least one significant shareholder, with over 25 per cent having a single shareholder controlling more than 20 per cent of votes.[12] Moreover, institutional investors dominate the ownership of public companies in Canada, holding 47 per cent of the equity in Canadian listed public companies. Domestic institutional investors hold 25 per cent of market capitalization in the country, followed by US-based institutional investors at 17 per cent and other foreign institutions at 4 per cent.[13] On average, the three largest shareholders in Canadian public companies hold between 25 and 30 per cent of the companies' capital, with the twenty largest shareholders holding between 50 and 60 per cent.[14]

11.2.2 *Overview of Canada's Corporate Governance*

In Canada, the principal sources of corporate governance legal requirements are corporate and securities laws. Canadian corporate law encompasses a federal statute – the Canada Business Corporations Act (CBCA) – and separate provincial and territorial statutes. Companies incorporate under their statute of choice and are subject to its requirements. Securities are regulated wholly at the provincial level.[15] Canada does not have one common or national securities regulator, but provincial securities regulators engage in extensive cooperation and collaboration through the Canadian Securities Administrators (CSA), an umbrella organization of provincial and territorial securities regulators.[16]

Canada is one of the few countries in the world with both common and civil law traditions. Twelve of its thirteen provinces and territories operate under a common law framework, whilst Quebec operates under a civil law system within the larger Canadian common law framework.[17] Interestingly, two of Canada's seminal corporate law cases – *Peoples Department Stores Inc. (Trustee of)* v. *Wise*[18] and *BCE Inc.* v. *1976 Debentureholders*[19] – emerged from the Quebec courts, influencing corporate law at the federal, provincial and territorial levels.

In addition to corporate law statutes and securities regulations, corporations that are listed on a securities exchange such as the TSX are subject to the rules of the exchange,[20] which has its own listing and ongoing listing maintenance requirements. Proxy advisory services, such as

11 Puri (n. 1) 1672.

12 Yvan Allaire, 'Controlled Companies Briefing' (CPA Canada, 2010) 3 www.cpacanada.ca/business-and-accounting-resources/strategy-risk-and-goverance/corporate-governance/publications/controlled-companies-what-directors-should-know accessed 30 August 2020.

13 Adriana De La Cruz, Yung Tang and Alejandra Medina, 'Owners of the World's Listed Companies' (OECD Capital Market Series, 2019) 11, 23 www.oecd.org/corporate/Owners-of-the-Worlds-Listed-Companies.pdf accessed 30 August 2020 (2019 OECD Report).

14 Ibid., 18.

15 Christopher C. Nicholls, *Securities Law* (2nd ed., Irwin Law 2018) 77. Federally incorporated corporations are subject to the provincial securities regulations of the provinces in which they operate: ibid., 77–8. Many Canadian public corporations can also rely on a 'passport system' in certain areas of securities regulation that allows them to deal directly with only their principal regulator and comply with harmonized legislative provisions. See Canadian Securities Administrators (CSA), 'Pan-Canadian' www.securities-administrators.ca/aboutcsa.aspx?id=96 accessed 30 August 2020.

16 CSA, 'Overview' www.securities-administrators.ca/aboutcsa.aspx?id=45 accessed 30 August 2020.

17 Puri (n. 1) 1671–2.

18 2004 SCC 68.

19 2008 SCC 69.

20 TMX Group, 'Company Manual' (*Toronto Stock Exchange*) https://decisia.lexum.com/tsx/m/en/454460/1/document.do accessed 30 August 2020 (TSX Company Manual).

Institutional Shareholder Services (ISS) and Glass, Lewis & Co. ('Glass Lewis' hereafter), also publish policy statements and guidelines that institutional investors rely on for voting and that, as a result, many public corporations follow as corporate governance best practices. These voting guidelines are often more demanding than corporate and securities law requirements, and are highly influential.

11.3 SHAREHOLDER ENGAGEMENT

11.3.1 *The Corporation and the Role of the Shareholder*

Any corporation has a range of stakeholders with different and sometimes competing interests. Shareholders, however, are in a privileged position compared to other stakeholders. Employees, retirees and pensioners, creditors, consumers, governments and the environment have not, until recently, been expressly referenced in Canadian corporate law statutes;[21] generally speaking, these stakeholders must seek legal protection and recourse through other avenues, such as contract law, consumer protection law, employment standards legislation and the like. Canadian corporate law most prominently recognizes the role of the shareholders and provides them with a bundle of rights that they can use to protect their investment.

Shareholders are seen to occupy a preferential role in Canadian corporate law because of their role as 'financiers' of the corporation. Shareholders invest in a corporation in the expectation that they will receive a positive financial return, but in larger corporations they have little direct involvement in, or responsibility for, day-to-day management of the corporation.[22] As a result, one of the fundamental statutory rights shareholders are granted when they invest in a corporation is the right to elect a board of directors with the power and responsibility to manage or supervise the corporation's business and affairs.[23] Directors, in turn, appoint officers and delegate to them a subset of their powers and responsibilities relating to day-to-day management, subject to certain statutory limits.[24] Shareholders, as the residual claimants of the corporation, hold directors and officers to account via the imposition of duties of care and loyalty[25] and the legal rights prescribed by Canadian corporate law as discussed in the remainder of this chapter.

11.3.2 *Means of Shareholder Engagement*

Perhaps most fundamentally, under Canadian corporate law, shareholders have the right to elect directors and the power and ability to remove them. Shareholders also have the ability to vote on certain fundamental transactions or changes that go to the core of a corporation's existence, such as effecting certain amalgamations or reorganizations, selling or leasing all or a substantial proportion of the corporation's assets and creating new classes or shares.

The shareholder voting rights prescribed by Canadian corporate law attempt to strike a balance between the interests of shareholders as financiers and the interests of the corporation's other stakeholders, including employees, retirees, pensioners, creditors, suppliers, consumers, governments and the environment. In addition to voting rights, shareholders also have the legal

21 Canada Business Corporations Act (CBCA), RSC 1985, c. C-44, s. 122(1.1).

22 Poonam Puri et al., *Cases, Materials and Notes on Partnerships and Canadian Business Corporations* (6th ed., Thomson Reuters 2016) 580.

23 CBCA (n. 21), s. 102(1).

24 Ibid., ss. 115, 121(a).

25 Ibid., s. 122(1).

right to make shareholder proposals, requisition shareholder meetings and launch proxy battles. Most of these tools remain out of reach for ordinary retail investors, being accessible primarily to wealthy individual investors and institutional investors. Not only do they require some degree of sophistication and expertise to wield, but they can also require the investment of significant financial costs and time. As a result, the likelihood of an individual retail investor with a small interest in a large corporation requisitioning a shareholder meeting or engaging in a proxy fight is low. However, shareholders also have access to market mechanisms that supplement the rights prescribed by Canadian corporate law. Shareholders can actively reach out to management to advocate for changes they would like to see in the corporation's business affairs, and all shareholders have the power and ability to 'vote with their feet' by selling their shares if they are dissatisfied with a corporation.

In this section, we describe the key legal and market shareholder engagement tools available to shareholders in Canada and analyze their effectiveness and limitations.

11.3.2.1 Legal Rights

SHAREHOLDER VOTING RIGHTS

Electing Directors

Currently, shareholders can elect directors for a term of up to three years, and boards may be staggered such that not all directors are appointed for the same term.[26] There are no statutory limits on the number of terms that a director can serve. Additionally, directors in Canada have historically been elected under a 'plurality' voting system whereby the candidate who receives the most votes is elected even if they do not receive the majority of votes.[27] In uncontested elections, candidates receiving a single vote have been elected, whilst, in contested elections, those receiving the most votes have won irrespective of whether those votes constituted a majority.

One problem posed by the plurality voting system is that a nominee can win a board seat in both uncontested and contested elections without receiving a majority of shareholder votes because, historically, the proxy form in Canada has allowed shareholders only to vote for a nominee or withhold their vote. Theoretically, in either type of election, the plurality system would allow a nominee to win a board seat even if they received only one vote in favour of their election, with all other shareholders withholding their votes. The approach has thus been strongly criticized for preventing shareholders from expressing their views on director nominees and hindering shareholder engagement.

In 2014, the TSX attempted to address some of the issues posed by the plurality system. As of 30 June 2014,[28] not only does the TSX require the annual election of all directors,[29] effectively preventing staggered boards for listed companies, but it has also implemented a majority voting policy for *uncontested* director elections.[30] Under this policy, the directors of all listed

[26] Ibid., ss. 106(3)–(4).

[27] Stephen Erlichman, 'It's Time to Give Shareholders a Real Say in Board Elections' *The Globe and Mail* (Toronto, 29 January 2018) www.theglobeandmail.com/report-on-business/rob-commentary/its-time-to-give-shareholders-a-real-say-in-board-elections/article37776229/ accessed 30 August 2020; see also Edward B. Rock, 'Does Majority Voting Improve Board Accountability?' (27 November 2015) Harvard Law School Forum on Corporate Governance https://corpgov.law.harvard.edu/2015/11/27/does-majority-voting-improve-board-accountability/ accessed 30 August 2020; Laura Levine and Alethea Au, 'Regulations for CBCA's New Diversity, Majority Voting and Notice-for-Access Provisions Released' *Stikeman Elliot* (20 January 2017) www.stikeman.com/en-ca/kh/canadian-securities-law/Regulations-for-CBCAs-New-Diversity accessed 30 August 2020.

[28] TMX Group, 'Toronto Stock Exchange Mandates Majority Voting to Further Enhance Corporate Governance' (13 February 2014) Toronto Stock Exchange www.tsx.com/news?id=110&year=2014 accessed 30 August 2020.

[29] TSX Company Manual (n. 20) s. 461.1.

[30] Ibid., s. 461.3.

companies, with the exception of majority-controlled corporations, must be elected by a majority of votes. In addition, the majority voting policy also requires, amongst other things, that any director immediately tender his or her resignation to the board of directors if they are not elected by at least a majority (50 per cent + one vote) of shares.[31] Although the board is expected to accept the resignation 'absent exceptional circumstances', it can reject it and allow the director to continue to sit on the board. In that case, though, it must promptly issue a news release that 'fully state[s] the reasons for that decision'.[32] For *contested* director elections, a listed company must issue a news release disclosing detailed voting results for the election of each director, although the rules do not mandate a majority voting policy.[33] While this is a significant development, the TSX rules apply only to public companies listed on the TSX, which is a subset of Canadian public companies.

In May 2018, the federal government passed a bill amending the federal corporate statute's director election requirements to require all public companies to implement a 'true' majority voting system for director elections. Shareholders will no longer be restricted to voting in favour of a candidate or withholding their vote. And, unlike under the TSX rules, if a candidate does not receive a majority of favourable shareholder votes, then they will be automatically disqualified from being appointed as a director, subject to two limited exceptions. If a director does not receive a majority of votes, the proposed regulations allow the board to appoint the candidate, if necessary, (1) to satisfy the Canadian residency requirement[34] or (2) to satisfy the requirement that at least two directors not be officers or employees of the company.[35] Although these new CBCA rules have not yet formally come into force, given that TSX companies are required to implement a majority voting policy, both TSX and non-TSX listed federally-incorporated public companies are expected to move towards a 'true' majority voting system as a matter of best practice and to align their director election processes with the approved legislation.

Under Canadian corporate law, directors can also be removed from office during their term by a corporation's shareholders or directors by ordinary resolution at a special meeting.[36] An ordinary resolution is a resolution passed by a majority of the votes cast by shareholders who vote in respect of that resolution.[37] A special meeting of shareholders can be called by directors at any time or by shareholders who hold 5 per cent or more of the corporation's outstanding voting shares.[38]

Fundamental Changes

Canadian corporate law also recognizes certain matters that are considered so fundamental that they must be approved by special resolution,[39] a resolution passed by a majority of no less than two-thirds of the votes cast by shareholders.[40] Fundamental changes to the corporation include

31 Ibid., s. 461.3(a).
32 Ibid., ss. 461.3(b), (c) and (e).
33 Ibid., s. 461.4.
34 Canadian corporate law requires that at least 25 per cent of a corporation's directors be 'resident Canadians': CBCA (n. 21) ss. 105(3)–(4). Not every Canadian jurisdiction has a requirement concerning the residency of a corporation's directors, however. The CBCA and provincial corporate statutes of Alberta, Manitoba, Newfoundland, Ontario and Saskatchewan require that at least 25 per cent of a corporation's directors be 'resident Canadians'. No such requirement is provided for in the provincial corporate statutes of British Columbia, New Brunswick, Nova Scotia, Prince Edward Island and Quebec. This factor can be one of many influencing whether a corporation incorporates under the CBCA or a provincial corporate statute.
35 An Act to amend the Canada Business Corporations Act, the Canada Cooperatives Act, the Canada Not-for-profit Corporations Act and the Competition Act, SC 2018, c. 8, s. 13(2).
36 CBCA (n. 21) s. 109(1)(b).
37 Ibid. s. 2(1).
38 Ibid. ss. 133(2) and 143(1).
39 Ibid. s. 173(1).
40 Ibid. s. 2(1). Certain matters may require approval by the class or series of non-voting classes or series of shares of a corporation: ibid., s. 176(1).

amalgamations and reorganizations; changing the maximum number of shares the corporation is authorized to issue; adding, changing or removing any rights, privileges, restrictions or conditions of shares or the issue, transfer and ownership of shares; and increasing or decreasing the number of directors or the minimum or maximum number of directors.[41] Such changes are considered so fundamental to a corporation that a higher threshold of shareholder approval than a simple majority is required. No other stakeholder group has a right to vote on fundamental corporate changes under corporate law in Canada, although some other stakeholders may have voting or veto rights based on contractual agreements. Further, Canadian corporate law provides shareholders with special 'dissenting' or 'appraisal' rights in certain circumstances. Hence, a shareholder who dissents on a fundamental change that has been approved is entitled to be paid the fair value of the shares in respect of which he or she dissents.[42]

SHAREHOLDER PROPOSALS Under Canadian corporate law, shareholders have the right to make proposals to express their views on issues affecting the corporation, hold management accountable for its actions and influence business decisions by challenging management.[43] Although the shareholder proposal mechanism serves an important governance function in providing shareholders with a 'public forum' mechanism, paid for by the corporation, through which to voice their concerns to both the corporation and other shareholders, it nonetheless may not be the most effective engagement tool for driving corporate change.

A shareholder holding the lesser of 1 per cent of the outstanding voting shares in a corporation or shares with a fair market value of C$2,000 for the six-month period immediately preceding the day on which they submit the proposal is entitled to submit a shareholder proposal.[44] If the proposal involves the nomination of one or more directors, then it must also be signed by one or more shareholders holding at least 5 per cent of the shares and entitled to vote at the meeting at which the proposal is to be presented.[45]

A corporation that receives a valid proposal is required to include it in its management proxy circular, which is circulated in advance of the shareholder meeting. However, there are certain grounds on which a corporation can reject a proposal and exclude it from its proxy circular.[46] It can do so if the proposal does not relate in a significant way to the corporation's business or affairs or if the proposal's primary purpose is to enforce a personal claim or redress a personal grievance.[47] A corporation can also reject a shareholder proposal if substantially the same proposal was submitted in a shareholders' meeting held five years before the current proposal's receipt and failed to attract a certain minimum amount of shareholder support at that meeting.[48] Unlike their counterparts in certain other jurisdictions, securities regulators in Canada do not oversee shareholder proposals or track which proposals corporations reject.[49] Corporations have

[41] Ibid., ss. 173(1), 183(5), 188(5), 189(5), 210(2)–(3) and 211(3).

[42] Ibid., ss. 190(1)–(3).

[43] Aaron Dhir, 'Realigning the Corporate Building Blocks: Shareholder Proposals as a Vehicle for Achieving Corporate Social and Human Rights Accountability' (2006) 43 *American Business Law Journal* 365, 374.

[44] CBCA (n. 21) ss. 137(1)–(1.1); Canadian Business Corporations Regulations, 2001, SOR/2001–512, s. 46 (CBCR).

[45] CBCA (n. 21) s. 137(4).

[46] Ibid., s. 137(2).

[47] Ibid., ss. 137(5)(b) and (b.1).

[48] Ibid., ss. 137(5)(d); CBCR (n. 44) s. 51.

[49] In February 2020, the Ontario government established a Capital Markets Modernization Taskforce ('the Taskforce') to review and modernize the province's capital markets. In July 2020, the Taskforce published forty-seven proposals for comment, including a proposal to empower the Ontario Securities Commission with the ability to provide its views to public companies planning to exclude shareholder proposals in their proxy materials (i.e. a no-action letter). In the United States, the Securities Exchange Commission has a similar procedure whereby a company can seek

the discretion to refuse to include proposals in their management proxy circulars in certain circumstances, and the only recourse for shareholders aggrieved by such refusal is the Canadian courts.[50]

Even if a shareholder proposal is included in a corporation's management proxy circular and receives majority shareholder approval, the corporation's directors are not bound to implement the proposal's recommendations. A shareholder proposal for the nomination of one or more directors, if approved, constitutes a 'nomination' only.[51] Other shareholder proposals, if approved, are advisory in nature. A corporation can choose to implement or reject a proposal's recommendations because, under Canadian corporate law, it is directors, not shareholders, who manage or supervise the management of the business and affairs of the corporation. If a shareholder submits and successfully receives majority support for a proposal to, for example, discontinue the manufacture of a certain product or provision of a certain line of services, it is the prerogative of directors to make the final decision on whether to adopt or reject that proposal.[52]

In 2019, sixty-two shareholder proposals were submitted to companies on the S&P/TSX Composite Index and SmallCap Indices on topics ranging from executive compensation to board diversity, climate change, social and human rights and technology issues.[53] Only one received majority support.[54] Of the thirty-seven shareholder proposals put forward in 2018, only two received majority support.[55] In 2017, forty-six shareholder proposals were submitted, with just three receiving majority support.[56] The five-year average of shareholder support for proposals that did not achieve majority support stands at 12 per cent.[57] Suffice to say, shareholder proposals in Canada generally have little prospect of success.

However, there seem to be competing perspectives on the shareholder proposal mechanism. On the one hand, from a normative perspective, the mechanism is seen as serving important governance and educational functions. It is intended to give shareholders a stronger voice in

a no-action letter from its staff about their informal views on whether there is a basis for excluding a shareholder proposal from a company's proxy materials. In the Taskforce's view, such a process would provide shareholders with an 'efficient means of addressing shareholder proposal disputes while reducing litigation in court'. It is unclear whether this procedure will be adopted in Ontario, but should it be adopted it may provide shareholders with a more accessible recourse for resolving shareholder proposal disputes. The Taskforce closed its comment period in September 2020. See Capital Markets Modernization Taskforce, 'Consultation Report' Government of Ontario (9 July 2020) 27 https://files.ontario.ca/books/mof-capital-markets-modernization-taskforce-report-en-2020–07–09.pdf accessed 30 August 2020.

50 Davies Ward Phillips & Vineberg LLP, 'Davies Governance Insights 2019' 102 www.dwpv.com/en/Insights/Publications/2019/Davies-Governance-Insights-2019 accessed 30 August 2020 (Davies GI 2019). In *Verdun* v. *Toronto-Dominion Bank* [1996] 3 SCR 550 (*Verdun*), the appellant, the beneficial owner of the respondent's common voting shares, Toronto-Dominion Bank ('Bank'), submitted proposals to the Bank for inclusion in its management proxy circular. After the Bank refused to include these proposals in its circular, the appellant applied to restrain the Bank from holdings it annual shareholder meeting until his proposals were included in the Bank's management proxy circular. All levels of the courts found in favour of the Bank. Specifically, the Supreme Court of Canada held that the appellant was not entitled to have his proposals included in the Bank's management proxy circular because the Bank Act permits only 'registered owners' to submit proposals; as the appellant was not a registered owner entitled to vote, he could not submit a shareholder proposal.

51 Puri et al. (n. 22) 644.

52 Ibid.

53 Davies GI 2019 (n. 50) 103.

54 Ibid.

55 Davies Ward Phillips & Vineberg LLP, 'Davies Governance Insights 2018' 6–7 www.dwpv.com/en/Insights/Publications/2018/Governance-Insights-2018?mode=pdf accessed 30 August 2020 (Davies GI 2018).

56 Davies Ward Phillips & Vineberg LLP, 'Davies Governance Insights 2017' 20–1 www.dwpv.com/en/Insights/Publications/2017/What-Canadian-Boards-Need-to-Know-Davies-Governance-Insights-2017 accessed 30 August 2020.

57 Davies GI 2019 (n. 50) 103.

a corporation's affairs.[58] Even if a shareholder proposal is unsuccessful, it can promote dialogue between shareholders and directors, draw public attention to important issues and influence corporate behaviour.[59] The Supreme Court of Canada stated in *Verdun* that the proposal mechanism represents 'a legislative commitment to the promotion of shareholder participation in corporate governance',[60] as it offers shareholders a chance to challenge management decisions.[61] Moreover, the shareholder proposal mechanism is less costly and more accessible than other mechanisms. The requirement that a shareholder hold the lesser of 1 per cent of a corporation's outstanding voting shares or C$2,000 in shares is not onerous for institutional or wealthy investors or prohibitive for ordinary retail investors, who can pool their shares with those of other shareholders.[62] On the other hand, from a practical perspective, some would argue that given the landscape of Canadian capital markets, the shareholder proposal mechanism is in large part ineffective. As mentioned above, a distinctive feature of the Canadian corporate landscape is that a large number of corporations in Canada are closely held, that is, controlled legally or effectively by an individual shareholder or small group of shareholders.[63] The shareholder proposal mechanism is unlikely to prove effective in such companies. The reality is that it is difficult, perhaps even impossible, for minority shareholders to secure enough votes to successfully pass a proposal. And even if a shareholder proposal is passed, it is not legally binding on the corporation.

SHAREHOLDER-REQUISITIONED MEETINGS Another tool shareholders have under Canadian corporate law is the right to requisition a corporation's directors to call a shareholder meeting,[64] although the right is limited to shareholders holding at least 5 per cent of a corporation's outstanding voting shares.[65] When a valid requisition is received, directors must, subject to certain exemptions, call a shareholder meeting as soon as possible.[66] If they do not call a meeting within twenty-one days of receiving the requisition, then any shareholder who signed it can call a meeting.[67]

Similar to the shareholder proposal mechanism, directors are not obligated to call a shareholder meeting if the subject matter of the requisition touches on certain areas.[68] No meeting need be called if it is apparent that its primary purpose is to enforce a personal claim or redress a personal grievance against the corporation or its directors, officers or shareholders; the business of the meeting does not relate in a significant way to the business and affairs of the corporation; the subject matter of the requisition was submitted to shareholders in a shareholder meeting held five years before its receipt and failed to receive a certain minimum amount of support at that meeting; or the right to requisition a meeting is being abused to gain publicity.[69]

In some respects, the right of shareholders to requisition a meeting conflicts with directors' responsibility to manage or supervise the management of the business and affairs of the corporation, which usually extends to the calling and holding of shareholder meetings. However, that right also constitutes an important counterbalance to directors' power to control the business and affairs of the

58 Evaristus Oshionebo, 'Shareholder Proposals and the Passivity of Shareholders in Canada: Electronic Forums to the Rescue?' (2012) 37 *Queen's Law Journal* 619, 620.
59 Puri et al. (n. 21) 654; Oshionebo (n. 58) 620.
60 *Verdun* (n. 50) [32].
61 Oshionebo (n. 58) 620.
62 Ibid., 646.
63 Puri et al. (n. 21) 579, 654 and 699.
64 CBCA (n. 21) s. 143(1).
65 Ibid., s. 143(1).
66 Ibid., s. 143(5).
67 Ibid., s. 143(4).
68 Ibid., s. 143(3)(c).
69 Ibid., ss. 137(5)(b)–(e) and 143(3)(c).

corporation.[70] Notably, the Ontario courts have recognized the right of shareholders to requisition a shareholder meeting as a 'fundamental right' that is 'not lightly to be interfered with'.[71]

PROXY BATTLES Shareholders who are dissatisfied with a corporation's management and performance can also engage in 'activist campaigns' to bring about change in the corporation. Activist campaigns fall along a spectrum based on the primary objective of the shareholder's actions. On the more aggressive end of the spectrum are proxy contests and lawsuits that seek a definitive change in a corporation's board and management and resulting strategy and operations. On the other end of the spectrum are publicity campaigns. Such campaigns may result in change, but the primary focus is to raise awareness of issues in a company's strategy, operations, management or board. Activist campaigns are expensive, time-consuming and laborious. Campaigns may be used to oppose certain transitions or critical business decisions, demand removal or appointment of certain directors or management or advocate for social change. In this section, we will briefly describe the most common form of activist campaigns: proxy battles.

Over the past five years, proxy contests have been the most common form of shareholder campaigns.[72] A 'proxy' is the right to represent a shareholder at a shareholder meeting and to vote the shareholder's shares in accordance with their instructions. In a proxy contest, a shareholder or group of shareholders may persuade other shareholders to delegate their voting power via a proxy vote to represent them at a shareholder meeting and vote their shares to effect certain changes in the corporation. A proxyholder can act at the meeting only in respect of which the proxy is given, in the manner and to the extent authorized by the proxy, and with the authority conferred by the proxy.[73] Shareholders are entitled to withdraw their proxies up to the day of the shareholder meeting.[74]

Although proxy contests are perhaps the most expensive and hostile shareholder engagement tool, they are also one of the most powerful means of bringing about transformative change in a corporation in a short period of time. In the past ten years, proxy contest activity has remained quite consistent in Canada, barring a spike in 2015, with an average of thirty-four proxy battles a year.[75] In the majority of proxy campaigns, the dissident's primary objective has been to replace a minority or majority of a company's directors or replace the entire board, whilst other proxy campaigns have dealt with transactions or other non-board-related matters.[76] In Canada, corporations in the natural resource and energy sectors are the most likely to be subject to proxy battles,[77] and the majority of proxy battles are launched against firms with a market capitalization of at least C$300 million, which is not necessarily surprising given the high cost of a proxy fight.[78]

70 Samuel M. Robinson and Stephen Aylward, 'Requisitioned Meetings of Shareholders: An Uneasy Balance of Powers' (2015) 44 *Advocates' Quarterly* 509, 526.

71 *Koh* v. *Ellipsiz Communications Ltd*, 2017 ONSC 3083 (Div Ct) [15], [44]; *Wells* v. *Bioniche Life Sciences Inc*, 2013 ONSC 4871 [36]–[37] (*Wells*); *Paulson & Co* v. *Algoma Steel Inc* (2006), 79 OR (3d) 191 (Sup Ct) [40]–[41]. See also: *Paulson & Co.* v. *Algoma Steel Inc.* (2006), 79 OR (3d) 191 (Sup Ct) [40]–[41].

72 Kingsdale Advisors, 'Proxy Season Review 2019' https://online.flippingbook.com/view/129112/ accessed 30 August 2020 (Kingsdale 2019).

73 CBCA (n. 21) ss. 148(1) and 148(3).

74 Ibid., s. 148(4).

75 Based on data from Davies GI 2019 (n. 50) 33; Kingsdale 2019 (n. 72) 7.

76 Davies GI 2019 (n. 50) 33; Kingsdale 2019 (n. 72) 12.

77 Davies GI 2019 (n. 50) 33–4.

78 Kingsdale 2019 (n. 72) 3.

11.3.2.2 Market Mechanisms

'VOTING WITH YOUR FEET' In addition to the legal tools described above, shareholders also have several key market mechanisms available to them. One of shareholders' core powers is the ability to sell their shares at will. The alienation and free transferability of shares flows from the fact that shares are a form of personal property.[79] In closely held public corporations, share transferability may be restricted in practice by the absence of purchasers, but, generally speaking, shareholders' ability to sell their shares is a robust mechanism.[80] It is also a tool of great importance to shareholders, 'both because it is a means of obtaining economic benefit from their investment in the corporation and because it is their means of exit should they become dissatisfied with management'.[81]

However, Canadian law does allow for some restrictions on shareholders' ability to sell their shares.[82] If the issue, transfer or ownership of a corporation's shares is restricted, a statement to that effect and the nature of the restrictions must be set out in the corporation's articles of incorporation.[83] A public corporation can also amend its articles to constrain the transfer or ownership of shares, albeit only for certain limited purposes, such as to enable the corporation to obtain licences, permits, grants, payments or other benefits that require attaining or maintaining a specified level of Canadian ownership or control.[84] Additionally, amendments restricting the alienability of shares must be passed by a special resolution requiring no less than two-thirds of the votes cast by shareholders who vote in respect of the resolution.[85] This is a high threshold for most public companies, rendering such amendments infeasible in practice.

The ability of shareholders to sell their shares at will is an important and powerful market mechanism. For smaller shareholders of large, widely held public corporations, it is a non-burdensome and efficient solution to governance, accountability or performance concerns; shareholders are free to sell their shares and protect their interests from poor corporate decision-making.[86] However, the option is not as easily exercisable by shareholders of closely controlled public companies or significant shareholders in public companies. Not only is it difficult to find buyers for large blocks of shares, but, with such transactions, there is a real risk that as unhappy shareholders sell their shares, the company's stock price may decline with a block sale, making it easier for an outside investor to purchase sufficient shares to gain control of the company.[87] Additionally, transactions involving large blocks of shares can also move markets.

Moreover, there is also the question of whether the ability to sell is even effective. Corporate governance issues can be difficult to link directly to a firm's financial performance. If a shareholder has a concern with management, but that concern does not have a direct impact on a company's share price, the shareholder may not have the financial incentive to sell their

79 Julian Velasco, 'The Fundamental Rights of Shareholder' (2006) 40 *UC Davis Law Review* 407, 414–15.

80 Ibid., 415, 425.

81 Ibid., 425.

82 The variations of types of share transfer restrictions that can be employed are infinite, but the main types used are an absolute prohibition on share transferability for a limited time (an absolute prohibition of share transferability for an unlimited time is not permitted); consent restrictions requiring higher director or shareholder approval; a first-option provision or some variation thereof whereby the shareholder must first offer its shares to other shareholders by a specified procedure at a specified price before selling them to an outsider; special time or event buy-out arrangements such as options; and buy-sell agreements contingent on a shareholder's death; see Puri et al. (n. 21) 709–10.

83 CBCA (n. 21) s. 6(1).

84 Ibid., ss 49(9) and 174(1).

85 Ibid., s 174(1).

86 James J. Park, 'The Limits of the Right to Sell and the Rise of Federal Corporate Law' (2017) 70 *Okla. L. Rev.* 159, 162.

87 Ibid., 163.

shares.[88] Where the corporate governance issue is linked directly to a firm's financial performance, it is possible that the corporate governance issue results in a rapid and substantial decline in corporate value such that shareholders do not have sufficient time to sell their shares to protect their interests.[89]

SHAREHOLDER FEEDBACK RIGHTS Shareholders can also actively reach out to a corporation's directors and officers to communicate their views and perspectives. Public corporations are not legally mandated to create a mechanism for this kind of informal shareholder feedback, although they are encouraged to do so under Canada's securities law framework, and such a mechanism can prove beneficial.[90] It can allow corporations to 'gather information regarding potential shareholder concerns and to determine whether and how to respond to inaccurate or objectionable discourse'.[91] More importantly, feedback mechanisms can benefit shareholders. They allow shareholders to communicate their views to management at a minimal cost without having to submit, for example, a formal shareholder proposal, which carries minimum share ownership requirements, or launch an activist campaign, which is expensive, laborious and time-consuming. Moreover, even though a corporation has no obligation to implement or even consider a shareholder's views, the shareholder has other formal mechanisms for advocating those views more vociferously. However, shareholder feedback mechanisms are generally accessible only by institutional investors or wealthy individual investors, not ordinary retail investors.

11.4 EVOLUTION OF SHAREHOLDER ENGAGEMENT IN CANADA

Canadian capital markets have undergone significant change in the past few decades. Institutional investors now dominate the ownership of public companies. Traditionally, institutional investors limited their focus to issues relating directly to a corporation's financial success. However, in the past decade, they have taken a more active stance on ESG issues. As a result, one interesting development in shareholder engagement in Canada has been the prominent role of institutional investors in driving change on issues such as gender diversity on boards and environmental disclosure and in advocating for change to Canadian corporate and securities legal standards.

One effect of the dominance of institutional investor ownership has been the emergence of proxy advisory firms. In any given proxy season, a mid-size or large Canadian public company may receive dozens of shareholder proposals. Proxy advisory firms exert considerable influence on all investors, including institutional investors, many of whom are amongst the most powerful shareholders in Canadian public companies and thus play an important role in Canada's capital markets and in shareholder engagement.

As the COVID-19 pandemic continues to rage across the world, corporations are having to respond to a difficult, constantly evolving business landscape. In the immediate short term, the pandemic has led to the accelerated adoption of virtual general meetings, which Canadian corporations had hitherto been resistant to. Corporations have been forced to consider suitable

88 Ibid., 167–8, 176–9.

89 Ibid., 167–70.

90 CSA, 'National Policy 58–201 Corporate Governance Guidelines' www.osc.gov.on.ca/documents/en/Securities-Category5/rule_20050415_58–201_gov-practices_2.pdf pt. 3.4(g)(i) accessed 30 August 2020.

91 Andrew J. MacDougall and Robert Adamson, 'Directors' Responsibilities in Canada' (October 2014) 11 www.icd.ca/getmedia/581897ca-d69d-4d4f-a2a2-ca6b06ef223b/5467_Osler_Directors_Responsibilities_-Canada-FINAL.pdf.aspx accessed 30 August 2020.

alternatives to in-person shareholder meetings by the physical and social distancing measures in place across Canada. Although it is uncertain at the time of writing this chapter whether the adoption of virtual meetings by Canadian corporations will prove to be a short- or long-term phenomenon, a number of Canadian corporate law statutes have been or are proposed to be amended by regulators to expressly permit virtual shareholding meetings going-forward.[92] However, virtual meetings can pose real concerns for shareholder engagement and the ability of shareholders to effectively exercise their voting rights.

In this section, we analyze these three trends and their effect on shareholder engagement in Canada.

11.4.1 *The Changing Role of Institutional Investors*

As described above, institutional investors dominate the ownership of public companies in Canada. As some of the most powerful shareholders in Canadian public companies, they exert significant influence on these companies' strategies, operations, management and boards. Institutional investors in Canada have become particularly vocal in the past decade, and are increasingly using their influence to drive change on ESG issues, including diversity reporting and climate change disclosure, on the basis that they contribute to the long-term benefit of the corporation concerned.

11.4.1.1 Diversity Requirements

In Canada, unlike many European countries such as Norway, Spain, France, Iceland, Italy, Belgium, the Netherlands and Germany,[93] there are no gender quotas for public company boards in Canada. In 2015, the securities regulators in ten of the country's thirteen provinces and territories adopted 'comply or explain' disclosure requirements on gender diversity for a subset of public companies, requiring those companies to disclose the number and percentage of women on their boards and in senior management positions, policies relating to the identification, nomination and appointment of women directors and officers and targets for women on boards and in senior management positions.[94] Over the last five years, although female representation on public boards has increased, women remain proportionately underrepresented on public boards. In 2018, female directors accounted for 10 per cent of directors on small-cap company boards, 16 per cent on mid-cap company boards and 25 per cent on large-cap company boards.[95] In 2020, the federal government codified the 'comply or explain' diversity disclosure requirements for Canadian boards. Notably, the new regulations go beyond gender by requiring the

[92] See www.osc.ca/en/news-events/news/canadian-securities-regulators-provide-updated-guidance-virtual-shareholder-meetings accessed 20 March 2022.

[93] Aaron Dhir, *Challenging Boardroom Homogeneity: Corporate Law, Governance, and Diversity* (New York: Cambridge University Press, 2015) 11, 72–8; Alison Smale and Claire Cain Miller, 'Germany Set Gender Quota in Boardrooms' The New York Times (New York, 7 March) www.nytimes.com/2015/03/07/world/europe/german-law-requires-more-women-on-corporate-boards.html accessed 30 August 2020; The Guardian, 'Germany Passes Gender Quota Legislation for the Boardroom' *The Guardian* Berlin, 6 March 2015) www.theguardian.com/business/2015/mar/06/germany-gender-quota-legislation-boardroom-law-women accessed 30 August 2020.

[94] CSA, 'CSA Multilateral Staff Notice 58–307 Staff Review of Women on Boards and in Executive Officer Positions – Compliance with NI 58–101 Disclosure of Corporate Governance Practices' www.osc.gov.on.ca/documents/en/Securities-Category5/csa_20150928_58-307_staff-review-women-boards.pdf accessed 30 August 2020.

[95] BMO Capital Markets, '2018 Canadian Board Composition Study' https://womengetonboard.ca/wp-content/uploads/2018/10/2018CanadianBoardCompositionStudy_EN.pdf accessed 30 August 2020.

disclosure of diversity in respect of 'designated groups', which currently include women, Aboriginal peoples, persons with disabilities and members of visible minorities.[96]

Canadian institutional investors have played an active role in diversity reporting and representation requirements, and have incorporated diversity-related guidelines into their voting decisions. In 2017, a group comprising Canada's sixteen largest institutional investors, managing a combined C$2.1 trillion in net assets, called on companies to 'take prompt and considered action' to 'achieve a minimum of 30% women on the boards and at the executive management level of S&P/TSX composite index companies by 2022'.[97] This '30% Club Canada' stated that it would engage in conversations with board chairs and nomination committees to encourage gender diversity, monitor companies' efforts and performance through objective diversity measures, enter into dialogue with investee companies whose nomination process fails to appropriately consider gender diversity and consider using its voting rights against companies whose nomination committees or boards fall short of gender diversity expectations.[98]

Many institutional investors have introduced new requirements in their proxy voting guidelines in support of the 30 per cent club and gender diversity. On 21 December 2018, the Canadian Pension Plan Investment Board (CPPIB), Canada's largest professional pension fund, introduced a policy whereby it will vote against the chair of the board committee responsible for director nominations if that board has no women directors.[99] The CPPIB also requires boards to implement policies designed to ensure that diversity is appropriately considered as part of the director nomination process and to disclose those policies.[100] Similarly, in 2018, RBC Global Asset Management (RBC GAM), a large Canadian investment manager, updated its proxy voting guidelines to require companies lacking female representation on their boards to adopt diversity policies that commit to increasing board diversity and to set clear targets for doing so within a reasonable timeframe.[101] As of February 2019, RBC GAM will also vote against directors who sit on the nominating or corporate governance committees of boards with fewer than two women directors, and it expects companies to disclose their progress on board gender diversity targets and the strategies employed to achieve them.[102] Several other large Canadian institutional investors,

[96] CBCR (n. 44) ss. 72.2(1) and 72.2(4); Employment Equity Act, SC 1995, c. 44, s. 3. Under the new regulations, public companies will have to disclose details of any adopted written policy relating to the identification and nomination of designated groups of directors and, if they do not have such a policy, the reasons for not doing so; how the board, its nominating committee or the corporation considers the level of representation of designated groups in identifying and nominating candidates for election/re-election to the board and/or appointing members of senior management, and if there is no such consideration, the reasons for its absence; whether the corporation has adopted targets for each designated group to hold positions on the board or as members of senior management and progress towards that target, and for each group for which a target has not been adopted, the reasons why; and for each group within the designated groups, the number and proportion of the members of each group who hold positions on the board and are members of senior management, including for all of its 'major subsidiaries'.

[97] 30% Club, '30% Club Canadian Investor Group: Statement of Intent' (2017) https://30percentclub.org/assets/uploads/30_percent_Club_Canadian_Investor_Statement_Updated_May_2019_v2.pdf accessed 30 August 2020.

[98] Ibid.

[99] Canada Pension Plan Investment Board (CCPIB), 'Canada Pension Plan Investment Board to Increase Board Diversity Advocacy' (21 December 2018) www.cppinvestments.com/public-media/headlines/2018/cppib-increase-board-diversity-advocacy accessed 30 August 2020.

[100] CCPIB, 'Proxy Voting Principles and Guidelines' (23 February 2018) 5 www.cppinvestments.com/wp-content/uploads/2019/09/CPPIB_Proxy_Voting_Principles_and_Guidelines_EN_Wz3xvjo.pdf accessed 30 August 2020.

[101] RBC Global Asset Management (RBC GAM), 'The benefits of gender diversity for investors' https://global.rbcgam.com/sitefiles/live/documents/cgri/benefits-of-gender-diversity-for-investors.pdf accessed 30 August 2020.

[102] RBC GAM, 'RBC Global Asset Management Proxy Voting Guidelines' (2019) 10 https://global.rbcgam.com/resources/documents/cgri/rbc-gam-proxy-voting-guidelines.pdf accessed 30 August 2020.

including Ontario Teachers' Pension Plan (OTPP),[103] Fidelity Investments,[104] BlackRock Canada[105] and GLC Asset Management,[106] have adopted similar policies.

It was only in 2019 that investors in Canada voted for the first time in favour of a shareholder proposal on gender diversity, and that proposal could not have succeeded without significant institutional investor support. The British Columbia Teachers Federation, a labour union representing public school teachers in British Columbia, filed a shareholder proposal with Waste Connections Inc. requesting that its board disclose its written diversity policy and file a report outlining the board's plans, timelines, process and activities for increasing the representation of female directors and officers.[107] Waste Connections' directors recommended that shareholders vote against the proposal, claiming that it would 'provide no benefit to the Company or our shareholders and that shareholders are better served by flexible policies that, as demonstrated since our founding in 1997, are effective in retaining and attracting highly effective directors and executive officers and strongly support an environment of continuous improvement and long-term shareholder value creation'.[108] The company's shareholders disagreed, with 64.49 per cent voting in favour of the proposal.[109] Although it was not filed by an institutional investor, the proposal would not have succeeded without significant institutional support given that over 50 per cent of Waste Connections' shares at the time of the proposal were held by twenty institutional investors.[110]

Institutional shareholders play an absolutely critical role in Canadian capital markets, and their adoption of diversity-related voting guidelines is just one example of their increasing interest in corporate governance issues. Recently, in July 2020, in response to the tragic death of George Floyd in the United States and in recognition of the systemic anti-Black racism present in Canada, a number of major banks, asset managers and other institutional investors signed on the BlackNorth Initiative and its pledge to recognize and end anti-Black systemic racism in corporate Canada.[111] It will be important to track whether the pledge leads to a meaningful increase in diversity on boards in Canada.

103 Ontario Teachers' Pension Plan, 'Corporate Governance Principles and Proxy Voting Guidelines' (2020) 29 www.otpp.com/documents/10179/20940/-/bf03be90-a413-433f-bc4a-24a266ae17bb/2020%20Corporat e%20Governance%20Principles%20and%20Proxy%20Voting%20Guidelines.pdf accessed 30 August 2020.

104 Fidelity Investments, 'Fidelity International's Proxy Voting Guidelines' (May 2019) www.fidelity.ca/cs/Satellite/doc/proxy_voting_guidelines_fil.pdf accessed 15 September 2020.

105 BlackRock, Inc 'Corporate governance and proxy voting guidelines for Canadian securities' (January 2020) www.blackrock.com/corporate/literature/fact-sheet/blk-responsible-investment-guidelines-canada.pdf accessed 15 September 2020.

106 GLC Asset Management, 'Proxy Voting Guidelines' (1 December 2018) www.glc-amgroup.com/content/dam/glc/documents/march-27/GLC%20Proxy%20Guidelines_EN.pdf accessed 15 September 2020.

107 Waste Connections, Inc., 'Schedule 14A Proxy Statement Pursuant to Section 14(a) of the Securities Exchange Act of 1934' 61–2 https://www.sec.gov/Archives/edgar/data/1318220/000130817919000120/lwcn2019_def14a.htm. accessed 30 August 2020 (Waste Connections Proxy Statement).

108 Ibid., 62.

109 Waste Connections, 'Form 8-K' (17 May 2019) http://app.quotemedia.com/data/downloadFiling?webmasterId=101533&ref=113053375&type=HTML&symbol=WCN&companyName=Waste+Connections+Inc.&formType=8-K&dateFiled=2019–05–17&cik=0001318220&CK=1318220 accessed 30 August 2020.

110 Another proposal that the Taskforce put forward for comments pertains to board diversity. Specifically, the Taskforce proposed amending securities legislation to require public companies listed on the TSX to set targets and provide data annually on the representation of women, black people, indigenous people and people of colour (BIPOC) on their boards and in executive positions. The Taskforce solicited comments for appropriate potential quotas, although it noted that one target it heard was 40 per cent women and 20 per cent BIPOC. It remains to be seen whether the Taskforce recommends quotas to the Ontario government and whether the Ontario government chooses to amend the Ontario Business Corporations Act to integrate diversity targets. See Ontario Modernization Taskforce (n. 49) 23.

111 BlackNorth, 'Canadian Council of Business Leaders Against Anti-Black Systemic Racism Announces Formation; Launch of BlackNorth Initiative' (10 June 2020) https://blacknorth.ca/canadian-council-of-business-leaders-against-anti-black-systemic-racism-announces-formation-launch-of-blacknorth-initiative/ accessed 1 July 2021; BlackNorth,

11.4.1.2 Environmental Matters

Institutional investors are also playing an active role with respect to environmental issues. Under Canadian securities law, public companies are required to disclosure *material* information relating to environmental matters. Information is considered material if a reasonable investor's decision on whether to purchase, hold or sell the securities of an issuer would be influenced or changed by that information's omission or misstatement.[112] Although it may appear that this standard requires companies to disclose a broad range of climate-related information, most companies have provided and continue to provide what some would argue is inadequate disclosure. In 2017, the Chartered Professional Accountants of Canada (CPA Canada), Canada's national accounting professional organization, released a study analyzing the nature and extent of the climate-related disclosures made by Canadian public companies in their securities filings.[113] It found that although 79 per cent of companies were making climate-related disclosures, those disclosures did not provide (1) sufficient context for users to understand the significance of existing and potential business, risk-management and financial implications of climate change; (2) specific disclosure of board or senior management oversight of climate-related issues; or (3) financial metrics or targets or strategies for dealing with climate change.[114]

In March 2017, shortly after the release of CPA Canada's report and the publication of standards by the Financial Stability Board's Task Force on Climate-Related Financial Disclosures, the CSA announced a multiphase climate change disclosure review project to examine the disclosure of risks and financial impacts associated with climate change.[115] In April 2018 and August 2019, the CSA released staff notices containing guidance on these disclosures, including how companies can approach preparing disclosure of material climate change-related risks, assess climate change-related risk and opportunities, as well as questions boards and management should consider in the climate change context.[116] Despite this additional guidance, some investors argued that the problem of inconsistent and inadequate climate change-related disclosure persisted. In January 2020, CPA Canada published a follow-up report which found that, although 98 per cent of companies provide some form of climate change-related disclosure, such disclosure still lacks the scale and quality needed to satisfy investor demands.[117]

Interestingly, this is where institutional investors have come to play an important role. In Canada, institutional investors are advocating for greater climate change-related disclosure by

'Canadian CEOs Commemorate Launch of the BlackNorth Initiative' (21 July 2020) https://blacknorth.ca/canadian-ceos-commemorate-launch-of-the-blacknorth-initiative/ accessed 1 July 2021.

112 CSA, 'CSA Staff Notice 51–333 Environmental Reporting Guidance October 27, 2010' (27 October 2010) 5 www.osc.gov.on.ca/documents/en/Securities-Category5/csa_20101027_51–333_environmental-reporting.pdf accessed 30 August 2020.

113 CPA Canada, 'State of Play: Study of Climate-Related Disclosures by Canadian Public Companies' (2017) 13 www.cpacanada.ca/en/business-and-accounting-resources/financial-and-non-financial-reporting/sustainability-environmental-and-social-reporting/publications/climate-related-disclosure-study accessed 30 August 2020.

114 Ibid., 2–3.

115 CSA, 'Canadian Securities Regulators Announce Climate Change Disclosure Review Project' (21 March 2017) www.securities-administrators.ca/aboutcsa.aspx?id=1567 accessed 30 August 2020.

116 CSA, 'CSA Staff Notice 51–354 Report on Climate change-related Disclosure Project' (5 April 2018) 5–6 www.osc.gov.on.ca/documents/en/Securities-Category5/csa_20180405_climate-change-related-disclosure-project.pdf accessed 30 August 2020; Canadian Securities Administrators, 'CSA Staff Notice 51–358 Reporting of Climate Change-related Risks' (1 August 2019) 10–13 www.osc.gov.on.ca/documents/en/Securities-Category5/csa_20190801_51–358_reporting-of-climate-change-related-risks.pdf accessed 15 July 2020.

117 CPA Canada, 'Summary Report: Study of Climate-related Disclosures by Canadian Public Companies (January 2020)' (2020) 2, 9, 11 www.cpacanada.ca/en/business-and-accounting-resources/financial-and-non-financial-reporting/mdanda-and-other-financial-reporting/publications/climate-related-disclosure-study-2019-summary accessed 30 August 2020.

publishing guidance on their environmental priorities and supporting shareholder proposals calling for greater environmental disclosure.

For example, the CPPIB has established a multifaceted approach to improving climate change-related disclosure. It not only engages directly with companies that are high emitters of greenhouse gases to help them to improve their emission and environmental strategy disclosures, but it also actively supports shareholder proposals on climate change through its proxy voting activities.[118] The CPPIB generally supports all shareholder proposals that (1) request the reasonable disclosure of climate change-related information, including information on the environmental impact of a company's operations and products, and initiatives to mitigate environmental impact; (2) request the adoption or review of policies or practices with respect to environmental factors likely to enhance long-term company performance and/or mitigate potential exposure to environmental impacts; and (3) improve practices or disclosure on governance, strategy, risk management, performance metrics and targets and opportunities related to climate change.[119] In 2019, the CPPIB supported nineteen climate change-related shareholder proposals.[120]

TD Asset Management (TD), one of Canada's largest investment management firms, takes a similar approach. It incorporates environmental factors into its research and investment decision process; directly engages with companies to understand the potential impact of environmental risks on their business and the processes put in place to manage those risks; and exercises its voting power to support environmental proposals and vote against compensation committee members who express a disconnection between CEO compensation and shareholder performance.[121] In 2018, TD supported 132 environmental and social proposals, voted against the election of 494 compensation committee members and engaged with 13 companies to promote sustainable practices and push for environmental disclosure.[122] Several other large Canadian institutional investors, including the British Columbia Investment Management Corporation (BCIMC),[123] RBC Asset Management,[124] BlackRock Canada[125] and Mackenzie Investments,[126] have adopted similar policies.

118 CPPIB, 'CPPIB's Approach to Climate Change' (2017) www.cppinvestments.com/public-media/headlines/2017/cppibs-approach-climate-change accessed 30 August 2020. See also CCPIB, 'Investing Responsibly for CPP Contributors and Beneficiaries' (2019) 38–41 https://cdn3.cppinvestments.com/wp-content/uploads/2020/04/CPPIB-2019-Report-on-Sustainable-Investing-Board-EN_6MB_version.pdf accessed 30 August 2020 (CPPIB 2019 SI Report).

119 CPPIB, 'Proxy Voting Principles and Guidelines' (13 February 2020) https://cdn3.cppinvestments.com/wp-content/uploads/2020/04/cpp-investments-proxy-voting-principles-guidelines-2020-ENv5.pdf accessed 30 August 2020.

120 CPPIB 2019 SI Report (n. 118) 41.

121 TD Asset Management, 'TD Asset Management and Sustainable Investing' 1–2 www.tdassetmanagement.com/document/PDF/news-insight/sustainable-investing-en.pdf accessed 30 August 2020 (TD Sustainable Investing). See also TD Asset Management, 'RI Transparency Report' www.tdassetmanagement.com/document/PDF/news-insight/2019-RI-transparency-report.pdf accessed 30 August 2020.

122 TD Sustainable Investing (n. 121) 2.

123 British Columbia Investment Management Corporation, 'BCI's Climate Action Plan and Approach to TCFD Recommendations' 8 www.bci.ca/wp-content/uploads/2019/06/BCIs-Climate-Action-Plan-and-Approach-to-the-TCFD-Recommendations.pdf accessed 30 August 2020.
British Columbia Investment Management Corporation, 'Proxy Voting Guidelines 2019 Ninth Edition' (2019) 23 www.bci.ca/approach/responsible-investing/proxy-voting-record/ accessed 30 August 2020.

124 RBC GAM, 'Our Approach to Responsible Investment' www.rbcgam.com/documents/en/articles/approach-to-responsible-investment.pdf accessed 15 September 2020.

125 BlackRock, Inc., 'Corporate governance and proxy voting guidelines for Canadian securities' (January 2020) www.blackrock.com/corporate/literature/fact-sheet/blk-responsible-investment-guidelines-canada.pdf accessed 15 September 2020.

126 Mackenzie Investments, 'Sustainable, Responsible and Impact Investing' www.mackenzieinvestments.com/mi/en/assets/documents/mutualfunds/fp-sri-solutions-en.pdf accessed 15 September 2020.

Canadian institutional investor engagement on the issues of board diversity and climate change-related disclosure illustrates the evolution of the role of institutional investors in Canada's capital markets and the ability of such investors to drive change when there are gaps between corporate and securities law and shareholder expectations.[127] Institutional investors are increasingly taking an active stance on ESG issues and are increasingly willing and able to initiate change on these issues by directly engaging with companies to develop appropriate systems, controls and policies and by exercising their substantial share voting power to express their views on company boards and management. Through their activism and engagement, institutional investors have proved effective at reforming Canadian corporate and securities legal standards.

11.4.2 *The Influence of Proxy Advisory Firms*

Another interesting feature of Canadian capital markets is the role of proxy advisory firms and the influence they have on shareholders and shareholder engagement. Proxy advisory firms analyze matters put forward for consideration at shareholder meetings and make voting recommendations to their clients, who are typically institutional investors. Notably, proxy advisory firms do not have a direct vested ownership interest in corporations; they represent the interests of shareholders in monitoring and promoting good governance in corporations.

Proxy advisory firms are a relatively recent development. As institutional investors came to own a growing percentage of Canadian public companies, proxy advisory firms emerged to solve the logistical problems created by such investors' duty to vote.[128] In any given proxy season, an institutional investor may have to deal with thousands of shareholder resolutions. It takes an enormous amount of effort to research and evaluate these resolutions and to assess the performance of all of the corporations in its portfolio to cast informed votes for director elections, and all in a brief period of time (84 per cent of TSX-listed companies have year ends on 31 December, and are therefore likely to hold their shareholder meetings between April and June).[129] Although institutional investors are larger than individual retail investors, there are limits on their resources and in-house capabilities. Furthermore, institutional investors may not have the incentive to devote considerable resources to corporate governance issues because any gains generated by their corporate governance efforts will be shared by all shareholders in the corporation concerned. An agency problem thus arises whereby one institutional investor bears all of the costs of involvement in the corporation's corporate governance, whilst other

[127] In response to COVID, the Canadian government announced a Large Employer Emergency Financing Facility, which would provide bridge financing for large Canadian employers (i.e. businesses with annual revenues in excess of $300 million) impacted by the pandemic. Interestingly, recipient companies were required to commit to publish annual climate-related disclosure reports consistent with the Financial Stability Board's Task Force on Climate-Related Financial Disclosures, including how their future operations would support environmental sustainability and national climate goals. See: Canada, 'Prime Minister announces additional support for businesses to help save Canadian jobs' (11 May 2020) https://pm.gc.ca/en/news/news-releases/2020/05/11/prime-minister-announces-additional-support-businesses-help-save accessed 1 July 2021; Innovation, Science and Economic Development Canada, 'Large Employer Emergency Financial Facility Factsheet' (6 October 2020) www.cdev.gc.ca/leeff-factsheet/ accessed 1 July 2021.

[128] Yvan Allaire, 'The Troubling Case of Proxy Advisors: Some Policy Recommendations' (2013) Institute for Governance of Private and Public Organizations 8 http://igopp.org/wp-content/uploads/2014/04/pp_troublingcase proxyadvisors-pp7_short_3_.pdf accessed 30 August 2020 (IGOPP Report); Bryce C. Tingle, 'The Agency Cost Case for Regulating Proxy Advisory Firms' (2016) 49 *University of British Columbia Law Review* 725, 737.

[129] IGOPP Report (n. 128) 8; Tingle (n. 128) 740–1.

shareholders benefit at no cost to themselves.[130] Also, some institutional investors may be incentivized to focus their limited resources on the short-term value-producing activities of investing and trading rather than focus on corporate governance issues that may lead to long-term value.[131] Proxy advisory firms emerged as a solution to this quandary.

The proxy advisory industry in Canada is dominated by two firms, ISS and Glass Lewis, both of which are headquartered in the United States.[132] Glass Lewis is also a wholly owned subsidiary of OTPP, one of Canada's largest professional pension funds.[133] These proxy advisory firms analyze matters put forward for a vote at shareholder meetings and advise investors on how they should vote on those matters.[134] They also offer automatic vote execution services and consulting advisory services on corporate governance matters.[135]

Proxy advisory firms can exert considerable influence on shareholders. Although there is no conclusive evidence of their direct influence – some studies of institutional investors in the United States estimate that a negative ISS recommendation can shift institutional investor votes by 13.6–20.6 per cent, whilst others estimate a 6–10 per cent shift[136] – these firms can certainly exert a significant indirect influence. In a letter to the CSA on the subject of proxy advisory firms, BlackRock, Inc., one of the world's largest global asset managers, advised that whilst it submits votes at approximately 15,000 shareholder meetings in 90 countries every year, the bulk of them in the second quarter of the year, including 650 shareholder meetings in Canada, it employs only 20 corporate governance professionals globally.[137] According to BlackRock, proxy advisory firms are an 'integral and necessary part of institutional investors' execution of voting rights'.[138] The company uses research and other data services from proxy advisory firms as input in making proxy voting decisions, and it also benefits from their operational and administrative support related to proxy voting.[139] In BlackRock's view, most, if not all, institutional investors use proxy advisory research to help to identify resolutions that require greater attention or more in-depth analysis.[140] BCIMC and Caisse de dépôt et placement du Québec, two large Canadian pension funds, have expressed similar views. Given its volume of voting, BCIMC 'makes uses of the research provided by proxy advisory firms',[141] and Caisse 'uses the services of proxy advisory firms

130 Tingle (n. 128) 738. Indeed, this agency problem led in part to the creation of the Canadian Coalition for Good Governance (CCGG), an organization that specifically represents the interests of institutional investors and promotes good governance practices in Canadian public companies, the regulatory environment and the efficiency and effectiveness of Canadian capital markets. See CCGG, 'Our Missions & Objectives' https://ccgg.ca/mission-and-objectives/ accessed 30 August 2020; Janet McFarland, 'Good Governance Group Set' *The Globe and Mail* (Toronto, 12 April 2003) www.theglobeandmail.com/report-on-business/good-governance-group-set/article25282302/ accessed 30 August 2020.

131 Tingle (n. 128) 738–9.

132 CSA, 'Consultation Paper 25-401: Potential Regulation of Proxy Advisory Firms' (2012) 3 www.osc.gov.on.ca/documents/en/Securities-Category2/csa_20120621_25-401_proxy-advisory-firms.pdf accessed 30 August 2020.

133 Ibid., 3.

134 Ibid., 2.

135 Ibid., 2.

136 Jennifer E. Bethel and Stuart L. Gillan, 'The Impact of the Institutional and Regulatory Environment on Shareholder Voting' (2002) 31 *Financial Management* 29, 46; Stephen Choi, Jill Fisch and Marcel Kahan, 'The Power of Proxy Advisory Firms: Myth or Reality?' (2010) 59 *Emory Law Journal* 869, 871.

137 BlackRock, 'Re: Canadian Securities Administrators Consultation Paper 25-401: Potential Regulation of Proxy Advisory Firms' (2012) 1–2 www.osc.gov.on.ca/documents/en/Securities-Category2-Comments/com_20120920_25-401_zivnuskar.pdf accessed 30 August 2020.

138 Ibid., 1.

139 Ibid., 6.

140 Ibid., 6.

141 British Columbia Investment Management Corporation, 'Re: Canadian Securities Administrators Proposed National Policy 25-201: Guidance for Proxy Advisory Firms' (2014) 2 www.osc.gov.on.ca/documents/en/Securities-Category2-Comments/com_20140722_25-201_thomsonb.pdf accessed 30 August 2020.

to inform its deliberations [when] it takes a stand on any resolution'.[142] It is clear then that proxy advisory firms exert considerable influence on institutional investors, many of whom are amongst the most powerful shareholders in Canadian public companies. As a consequence, these firms play an important role in Canada's capital markets.

As institutional investors began to encompass an increasing percentage of shares in public companies and proxy advisory firms grew, many concerns about the latter's operation arose. In January 2013, for example, the Institute for Governance of Public and Private Organizations (IGOPP) published a report in which it criticized proxy advisory firms for their lack of transparency, conflicts of interest and vested interests and called their quality into question.[143] Many of the concerns mentioned by the IGOPP have also been voiced by academics and market participants in Canada and the United States since the early 2000s.

In June 2012, the CSA published a consultation paper soliciting comments on how to address the concerns that had arisen about the services provided by proxy advisory firms and the potential impact of such firms on Canadian capital markets and to determine whether and, if so, how those concerns should be addressed by Canadian securities regulators.[144] Based on the comments it received, the CSA developed – and released in April 2015 – a national policy, NP 25–201, that sets out non-prescriptive guidance for proxy advisory firms on recommended practices in respect of conflicts of interest, transparency and accuracy.[145]

Under NP 25–201, proxy advisory firms are expected to take specific steps to identify, manage, mitigate and disclose conflicts of interest.[146] NP 25–201 defines 'conflicts of interests' quite broadly, stating that such conflicts arise when the interests of a proxy advisory firm are or can be perceived to be inconsistent with, or diverge from, those of a client or when there is a conflict between the interests of different groups of a proxy advisory firm's clients,[147] including situations in which (1) a proxy advisory firm provides voting recommendations to a client on the corporate governance matters of a corporation to which it also provides consulting services; (2) a client submits a shareholder proposal that will be voted on at a shareholders' meeting that could be the subject of a favourable vote recommendation by the proxy advisory firm; or (3) a proxy advisory firm is owned in whole or part by a client who invests in corporations in which the firm has provided voting recommendations.[148] Proxy advisory firms are expected to address conflicts of interest by implementing appropriate practices and disclose conflicts of interests to clients.[149] In addition, to address the issue of lack of transparency and the quality of their voting recommendations, proxy advisory firms are expected to ensure that voting recommendations are determined in a consistent manner, based on up-to-date publicly available information, using methodologies that reduce the risk of factual errors or inaccuracies, and to describe and disclose the sources of their information and methodologies used to arrive at voting recommendations.[150]

[142] Caisse de dépôt et placement du Québec, 'Subject: CSA public notice – Draft Notice 25–201 relating to Guidance for Proxy Advisory Firms' (2014) 2 www.osc.gov.on.ca/documents/en/Securities-Category2-Comments/com_20140710_25–201_depelteaug-en.pdf accessed 30 August 2020.

[143] IGOPP Report (n. 128) 5–6.

[144] CSA, 'Consultation Paper 25–401: Potential Regulation of Proxy Advisory Firms' (2012) 2 www.osc.gov.on.ca/documents/en/Securities-Category2/csa_20120621_25–401_proxy-advisory-firms.pdf accessed 30 August 2020.

[145] CSA, 'National Policy 25–201: Guidance for Proxy Advisory Firms' (2015) www.osc.gov.on.ca/documents/en/Securities-Category2/csa_20150430_25–201-proxy-advisory.pdf accessed 30 August 2020.

[146] Ibid., pt. 2.1(1).

[147] Ibid., pt. 2.2(2).

[148] Ibid., pt. 2.1(2).

[149] Ibid., pts. 2.1(3) and (6).

[150] Ibid., pts. 2.2(1)–(3) and 2.4(2).

In developing NP 25–201, the CSA attempted to strike a balance between addressing the concerns of Canadian capital market participants relating to conflicts of interest, transparency and accuracy and recognizing the important role that proxy advisory firms play in 'advancing good corporate governance by facilitating institutional investors' ability to exercise their voting rights at shareholder meetings'.[151] No review of NP 25–201 has thus far been conducted, and so it remains to be seen whether the policy meaningfully addresses the concerns surrounding proxy advisory firms. In the meantime, these firms remain important actors in Canada's capital markets and continue to exert considerable influence on shareholders.[152]

11.4.3 *The Impact of COVID-19 on Shareholder Engagement in Canada*

As the COVID-19 pandemic continues to affect the world with no definite end in sight, it is clear that it will in the long term fundamentally change the way in which corporations operate, as well as the global corporate governance landscape. In the immediate short term, COVID-19 has already altered Canadian corporate governance practices and means of shareholder engagement.

11.4.3.1 Virtual-Only Meetings in Canada

In 2016, Lululemon Athletica Inc., a Delaware-based corporation that is a reporting issuer in all Canadian provinces and territories, became the first large-cap public company to hold a virtual shareholder meeting in Canada.[153] Then, in July 2017, Concordia International Corp became the first public company established under Canadian corporate law to hold such a meeting in Canada.[154] Since then, only a handful of other Canadian corporations and US corporations operating as reporting issuers in Canada have held virtual shareholder meetings.

Under Canadian corporate law, a Canadian corporation is permitted to hold a virtual shareholder meeting as long as the corporation's by-laws allow for it and the virtual means used for the meeting permit all participants to adequately communicate with one another during the meeting.[155] Virtual shareholder meetings offer several potential benefits. They can increase shareholder participation by eliminating the physical barrier of travel, which is particularly important when shareholders are geographically dispersed. Virtual meetings can also result in greater shareholder input, as some shareholders may feel more comfortable asking questions in an online forum than in an in-person meeting.

Canadian corporations have generally been slow to adopt virtual shareholder meetings, particularly relative to their US counterparts for a variety of reasons. Perhaps the most important reason is the limited number of technology providers. At present, there are only two companies

[151] CSA, 'Canadian Securities Regulators Public For Comment Guidance for Proxy Advisory Firms' (24 April 2014) www.securities-administrators.ca/aboutcsa.aspx?id=1237&terms=national%20policy%2025–201 accessed 30 August 2020.

[152] In its consultation report, the Taskforce also included a recommendation related to proxy advisory firms, recognizing the important role these firms play in the proxy voting process and the concerns that public companies and other stakeholders have expressed about the influence of these firms, errors in their reports and conflicts of interests. The Taskforce proposed creating a securities regulatory framework for proxy advisory firms that will provide public companies with a right to 'rebut' proxy advisory reports at no cost and restrict proxy advisory firms from providing consulting services to companies in respect of which they provide voting recommendations. See Ontario Modernization Taskforce (n. 49) 24.

[153] Davies GI 2018 (n. 55) 29–30.

[154] Ibid.

[155] CBCA (n. 21) s. 132(5).

in Canada that offer the technology needed to facilitate virtual meetings: LUMI Global (since 2017) and Broadridge (since 2019).[156] Broadridge, one of the primary providers of online meeting technology and services in the United States, launched its virtual shareholder meeting platform in that country in 2009.[157] But it is only in the past three years since 2019 that Canadian public corporations have been able to seriously consider holding virtual meetings in Canada.

Canadian companies may also have been slow to adopt virtual shareholder meetings because of the lukewarm response of influential proxy advisory firms. For instance, Glass Lewis has stated that it may vote against the members of a corporation's governance committee if the corporation decides to hold a virtual shareholder meeting and fails to provide adequate disclosure assuring shareholders that they will be afforded the same rights and opportunities to participate as they would have at an in-person meeting.[158] ISS has not released any formal guidance on virtual meetings, but in 2017 released the results of its annual global benchmark voting policy survey, in which it surveyed institutional investors, corporations, consultants/advisors to corporations, corporate directions, academics, non-profit organizations and other governance stakeholders on the issue.[159]

Moreover, there may have been concerns amongst Canadian companies that virtual shareholder meetings could have a negative effect on shareholder engagement. Companies could, for example, mute discontented shareholders and prevent them from voicing their concerns or select and answer only favourable shareholder questions. Put differently, relative to in-person shareholder meetings, virtual meetings carry the risk of management exercising a disproportionate amount of power, a situation that some would argue might lead to the censorship of dissenting shareholder opinions. Another argument is that the absence of physical contact between a corporation's directors and officers and shareholders could have a negative impact on the quality of discussion and debate. Indeed, some critics have argued that a lack of 'facetime' can lessen a corporation's accountability and transparency to its shareholders.

11.4.3.2 The Impact of COVID-19

One of the many immediate impacts of COVID-19 has been the accelerated adoption of virtual annual general meetings. With physical and social distancing measures in place, many corporations have had to consider suitable alternatives to their scheduled in-person shareholder meetings, although whether the adoption of virtual meetings by Canadian public corporations will prove to be a short- or long-term phenomenon remains uncertain.

156 Davies Ward Phillips & Vineberg LLP, 'Let's Get Practical: Moving to Virtual AGMs in Response to COVID-19' www.dwpv.com/en/Insights/Publications/2020/COVID-19-Virtual-AGMs accessed 30 August 2020; Norton Rose Fulbright, 'Will the Coronavirus Spark a New Era of Virtual Shareholder Meetings in Canada?' www.nortonrosefulbright.com/en/knowledge/publications/45533ab4/will-the-coronavirus-spark-a-new-era-of-virtual-shareholder-meetings-in-canada accessed 15 July 2020.

157 Broadridge Financial Solutions, Inc, 'Virtual shareholder meetings 2019 facts and figures' (2019) 3 www.broadridge.com/_assets/pdf/broadridge-virtual-shareholder-meetings-2019-facts-and-figures.pdf accessed 30 August 2020.

158 Glass Lewis, '2019 Proxy Paper Guidelines An Overview of the Glass Lewis Approach to Proxy Advice Canada' (2019) 35 www.glasslewis.com/wp-content/uploads/2018/10/2019_GUIDELINES_Canada.pdf accessed 30 August 2020.

159 Institutional Shareholder Services Inc, 'ISS Announces Results of 2018 Benchmark Voting Policy Survey' (25 September 2017) www.issgovernance.com/iss-announces-results-2018-benchmark-voting-policy-survey/ accessed 30 August 2020. Whilst one in five surveyed investors would be comfortable with virtual-only shareholder meetings without reservation, 44 per cent would not support such meetings, and 32 per cent would support them only if they provided the same shareholder rights as a physical meeting.

On 20 March 2020, the CSA issued guidance for companies considering alternatives to traditional in-person shareholder meetings.[160] Companies that had already sent and filed proxy-related materials could change the date, time or location of those meetings owing to COVID-19 without updating the materials as long as they promptly issued a news release announcing the change and took all reasonable steps necessary to inform all parties involved in the proxy voting infrastructure of the change.[161] Companies that had not yet sent their proxy-related materials were encouraged to consider including a disclosure therein of the possibility of such a COVID-necessitated change.[162] Any company that decided to conduct a virtual shareholder meeting was expected to notify shareholders and other relevant market participants of the change in a clear and timely manner and to provide logistical details of the virtual meeting, including how shareholders could access, participate in and vote at the meeting.[163]

In addition, the federal government and a number of provinces announced temporary measures or amendments to ease annual meeting requirements.[164] On 26 March 2020, the federal government announced that it still expected corporations incorporated under the CBCA to comply with all statutory requirements for annual meetings – hold the meeting within fifteen months of the previous meeting and no more than six months after the last financial year end – but encouraged virtual meetings to the extent they were allowed by the corporation's by-laws, and it noted that federally incorporated corporations could seek relief from the courts to delay their annual meetings.[165] On 8 August 2020, the federal government then issued a new order retroactively amending the statutory requirements for annual meetings – meetings could now be held within twenty-one months of the previous meeting and no more than twelve months after the last financial year end or by 31 December – and continued to encourage the use of virtual meetings to the extent they are allowed.[166]

Moreover, on 23 March 2020, the TSX announced that it would be providing 'temporary blanket relief' to all issuers from a variety of stock exchange requirements, including the requirement for issuers to hold their annual general meetings within six months of their fiscal year end.[167] The TSX said it would permit issuers that were required to hold an annual shareholder meeting during 2020 to hold the meeting on any date up to and including 31 December 2020, regardless of their fiscal year end.[168] However, even if a corporation was exempt under the TSX rules, it may

160 CSA, 'Canadian Securities Regulators Provide Guidance On Conducting Annual General Meetings During COVID-19 Outbreak' (20 March 2020) www.securities-administrators.ca/aboutcsa.aspx?id=1879 accessed 30 August 2020.

161 Ibid.

162 Ibid.

163 Ibid.

164 For a summary of the temporary measures or amendments announced in other Canadian provinces, see McMillan, 'May 1 Update: COVID 19: Temporary Relief of Corporate Requirements for Shareholder and Director Meetings' www.mcmillan.ca/COVID-19-Temporary-Relief-of-Corporate-Requirements-for-Shareholder-and-Director-Meetings accessed 30 August 2020.

165 Neil Weiner, '2020 Annual Meetings – Notice from Corporations Canada' *Fasken* (30 March 2020) www.timelydisclosure.com/2020/03/30/2020-annual-meetings-notice-from-corporations-canada/?utm_source=Mondaq&utm_medium=syndication&utm_campaign=LinkedIn-integration accessed 30 August 2020.

166 Corporations Canada, 'New Order Extends Deadline for Federal businesses, Not-for-profits and Cooperatives during COVID-19' https://corporationscanada.ic.gc.ca/eic/site/cd-dgc.nsf/eng/cs08730.html accessed 30 August 2020; Corporations Canada, 'Annual Meetings of Federal Corporations during the COVID-19 Outbreak' https://corporationscanada.ic.gc.ca/eic/site/cd-dgc.nsf/eng/cs08611.html accessed 30 August 2020.

167 TSX, 'Staff Notice 2020-0002' (23 March 2020) https://decisia.lexum.com/tsx/sn/en/item/466093/index.do accessed 30 August 2020.

168 Ibid.

still have been required to hold its annual shareholder meeting six months after the end of the corporation's preceding year end pursuant to Canadian corporate law.[169]

Furthermore, proxy advisory firms ISS and Glass Lewis both indicated that they would be relaxing their proxy voting guidelines, with the former stating that it would be 'very reasonable' in expressing caution about virtual meetings.[170] Glass Lewis announced that for companies opting to hold a virtual shareholder meeting between 1 March and 30 June 2020 because of COVID-19, it would refrain from voting against members of the governance committee provided that the company disclosed its rationale for doing so and cited COVID-19.[171]

Although the pandemic has accelerated the adoption of virtual shareholder meetings across Canadian public companies and Canadian legislators appear to be amending Canadian corporate law statutes to permanently permit the virtual shareholder meetings going forward,[172] concerns with respect to shareholder engagement in a virtual setting may remain and it will be important for corporations to ensure that they engage meaningfully with their shareholders. Will shareholders be afforded an equal, if not greater, opportunity to participate in the meeting, ask questions and voice concerns, even if those questions are critical of the company, directors and/or management? Moreover, aside from the structure of virtual meetings, COVID-19 also raises concerns about the ability of shareholders to effectively exercise their voting rights. If a corporation relies on already filed proxy-related materials, shareholders may be unable to vote in an informed manner on shareholder proposals and director elections in the absence of real-time information on the corporation's performance, contingency plans and long-term strategy. A similar problem exists for corporations that have filed or plan to file proxy-related materials with a COVID-19-related disclosure. As the pandemic continues, companies are having to respond to a constantly evolving situation. Even if a company provides up-to-date information, that information may not necessarily be complete or accurate, and, as a result, shareholders' votes may not be responsive to the company's actual business situation. Even after the COVID-19 pandemic subsides, this problem may persist for several months, at which point the pandemic's impact on other governance issues will begin to crystallize.

11.5 CONCLUDING REMARKS

This chapter has examined the role of Canada's corporate governance landscape from the perspective of shareholders. It has considered the legal and market tools available to shareholders to protect their financial investments and advocate for change. The chapter has also critically analyzed the limitations and effectiveness of these tools, and examined the various actors who influence shareholders and can facilitate shareholder engagement.

Although shareholders are granted a preferential role in Canada's corporate governance regime, most of the legal tools available to them remains out of reach of ordinary retail investors for reasons of financial cost, time and expertise. Nevertheless, these legal tools have a disciplinary purpose and are crucial in providing an active check on directors and officers to ensure they are acting in the best interests of the corporation and all of its stakeholders. Market mechanisms, such as the ability of all shareholders to 'vote with their feet' and sell their shares, can supplement

169 CBCA (n. 21) s. 133(1)(b).

170 Kingsdale Advisors, 'Kingsdale Advisors' (2020) https://mailchi.mp/kingsdaleadvisors/hlibt2xqzu-1071635?e=5bbb8b827b accessed 30 August 2020.

171 Aaron Bertinetti, 'Immediate Glass Lewis Guidelines Update on Virtual-Only Meetings due to COVID-19 (Coronavirus)' Glass, Lewis & Co., LLC (19 March 2020) www.glasslewis.com/immediate-glass-lewis-guidelines-update-on-virtual-only-meetings-due-to-covid-19-coronavirus/ accessed 30 August 2020.

172 See n. 95.

these legal shareholder engagement tools, reduce financial and knowledge barriers for ordinary investors, and provide all shareholders with additional means of protecting their financial investments.

Against this backdrop, this chapter also explored three specific developments in Canadian capital markets: (1) the engagement of institutional shareholders on ESG issues; (2) the role of proxy advisory firms and the influence they have on shareholders in Canada; and (3) the immediate impact of COVID-19 on shareholder engagement in the country's public corporations.

Canadian capital markets have undergone significant change over the past few decades. As we have seen, institutional investors have grown to dominate the ownership of Canadian public companies, and proxy advisory firms have emerged and grown to exert a significant influence on shareholders. One notable effect of these two developments, as explored herein, has been to push to the fore important issues such as board gender diversity and ESG disclosure that go beyond the requirements in Canadian corporate and securities law. The chapter has also explored how COVID-19 has facilitated a move towards virtual shareholder meetings, a move Canadian corporations have been reluctant to make.

12

Shareholder Engagement in the United States

Vikramaditya S. Khanna

12.1 INTRODUCTION

Shareholder voting and engagement in the United States have changed dramatically over the last half century. As recently as the late 1970s and early 1980s, shareholder voting was a relatively quiet corporate governance topic. Yet, by the beginning of the millennium shareholder voting had become one of the most important corporate governance topics and has only continued to grow in significance. A key contributor to this shift has been the change in ownership structure of publicly traded firms in the USA. They have moved from being diffusely held to being held by an assortment of institutional investors, including activist hedge funds, 'passive' index funds, pension plans and others. Indeed, some might argue that the changes in ownership structure constitute the most consequential change in US corporate governance, with ramifications for nearly every area of corporate law. This chapter thus focuses on how shareholder voting and engagement operate in the USA and where the current horizons lie for voting and engagement.

I begin in Section 12.2 by describing one of the primary drivers of shareholder voting – the collective action problem – and how changes in ownership structure have turned voting and engagement on their heads. Section 12.3 continues with a broad overview of the 'rules of the road' for voting and engagement. This necessarily encompasses a somewhat eclectic mix of rules and practices, but also provides an overview of the terrain over which voting and engagement occur. This section also explores how the Delaware courts are policing attempts to manipulate voting. Section 12.4 examines recent developments in activism and the issues likely to arise in the next few years. Section 12.5 concludes.

12.2 COLLECTIVE ACTION IN THE USA OVER TIME

Most scholars exploring shareholder voting and engagement in the USA start with the fundamental issue of what incentives shareholders have for voting on issues and engaging with the firm.[1] Those incentives depend in large measure on the ownership structure of the firm.

A standard starting point is the diffusely held firm in which no one shareholder has a large stake.[2] The archetypical example is a firm that has, say, 50,000 shareholders, each with a $10 stake in the firm (and each with one share carrying one vote). In such a firm, the shareholders are usually expected to be rationally apathetic for the reason that their stake is so small that the costs

[1] See William T. Allen, Reinier H. Kraakman and Vikramaditya S. Khanna, *Commentaries and Cases on the Law of Business Organizations* (6th edn, Aspen Publishers 2021) ch. 6; John Armour et al., 'The Basic Governance Structure: The Interests of Shareholders as a Class' in Reinier Kraakman et al. (eds.), *The Anatomy of Corporate Law: A Comparative and Functional Approach* (3rd ed., OUP 2017).

[2] See Frank Easterbrook and Daniel Fischel, 'Voting in Corporate Law' (1983) 26 *The Journal of Law & Economics* 395.

of becoming informed and voting (or engaging) are likely to swamp any gains.[3] For instance, even if winning a vote would quadruple firm value (a highly unlikely occurrence), for the individual shareholder that would mean gaining only $30 (moving from $10 per share to $40). It seems unlikely that the costs she would bear – of becoming informed, seeking advice, lobbying and coordinating with others – would be less than $30.[4] But even this understates the problem because those costs would potentially be worth it only if the shareholder's efforts changed the outcome of the vote. If this is unlikely, then why expend the money and effort?[5] Taking these factors together, it seems much more likely that a shareholder motivated by economic returns is highly unlikely to become informed and vote and would rather sell her shares or 'free-ride' on the efforts of others.[6] This is the standard collective action problem and leads to the key decision-maker in such diffusely held firms being top management.[7]

Of course, as Black argues,[8] a different ownership structure would provide different incentives. For example, assume there are still 50,000 shareholders, but five of them own 10,000 shares each, with the remaining 49,995 owning one share each (hence, the top five own 50,000 out of 99,995 shares). Now, each of the five shareholders with 10,000 shares has $100,000 at stake in the firm (10,000 shares at $10 each). A quadrupling of firm value would mean that each one of the top-five shareholder's interest in the firm would be worth $400,000 (a gain of $300,000), and it would thus make sense to bear some costs to become informed and persuade others.[9] Moreover, because these large shareholders have so much at stake (collectively, the top five have more than 50 per cent of the voting shares), the likelihood of any one of them being the marginal vote is much higher than in the diffusely held firm with only small shareholders, thereby enhancing their incentives to be more active.[10] Further, although there may be some conflicts of interest between the top five and smaller shareholders (and even amongst the top five), the behaviour of the top five sends signals to other shareholders at fairly low cost, which might encourage some of them to vote with the larger shareholders.[11] Thus, a shift towards more concentrated ownership is likely to lead to more active shareholders – both the large shareholders and some of the smaller ones who may simply follow (or receive signals from) the larger ones. Voting and engagement then become substantially more important than in the archetypical diffusely held firm.

Finally, although firms with controllers do not face the kind of shareholder collective action problem noted above, that does not mean shareholder activism is absent in these firms.[12] However, it tends to be more focused on constraining the controller than management.

The changes in ownership structure provide a useful frame for understanding the changing contours of US regulation. For much of the twentieth century, commentators usually thought of US publicly traded firms as being diffusely held with primarily rationally apathetic

3 See Allen, Kraakman and Khanna (n. 1); Easterbrook and Fischel (n. 2).

4 Ibid.

5 Ibid.

6 Ibid.

7 Under the standard corporate form, the board and management are expected to run the business subject to shareholder oversight. However, if no shareholders can overcome the collective action problem, then de facto decision-making authority rests with the board or management, a situation that lays fertile ground for a party to raise enough capital to purchase the majority of shares in a firm and change the board, and perhaps make money from doing so. Many consider this possibility to have been a key driver of the takeovers boom in the 1980s. See Allen, Kraakman and Khanna (n. 1).

8 See Bernard Black, 'Agents Watching Agents: The Promise of Institutional Investor Voice' (1991) 39 *UCLA Law Review* 811.

9 Ibid.

10 Ibid.

11 Ibid.

12 See Allen, Kraakman and Khanna (n. 1).

shareholders.[13] That view, in turn, led to a focus on preventing misleading or incomplete disclosures. Proxy rules under section 14 of the Securities Exchange Act 1934 compelled substantial disclosure backed by anti-fraud penalties and restrictions on communications. Ostensibly, this was to protect the small shareholder, but it may have discouraged activism by making it fairly expensive to comply.[14]

Nonetheless, change was in the offing. In the late 1980s and into the 1990s, the USA saw a large rise in institutional investors owning shares in publicly traded firms.[15] Now they have come to dominate ownership in the vast majority of publicly traded US firms, with estimates indicating that 80 per cent of the stock in Russell 3000 firms is held by institutional investors with much of it managed by large asset managers (e.g. BlackRock, State Street) whose incentives are not simply identical to those of their clients.[16] Although there are a number of reasons for the rise of institutional investors, their increasing presence has led to substantial changes in voting.[17] To gain a better grasp of these changes, it is important to note that institutional owners are not monolithic. They differ along many lines, including whether they seek only to maximize returns or have a mix of end goals, whether they manage their assets in house or rely on asset managers, to what extent they are willing to take (or invest in entities that take) more influential stakes in a firm and so forth.[18] Thus, we might expect different incentives to arise from (1) passive index funds (which invest in a pre-existing stock index), (2) active mutual funds focused on socially responsible investments, (3) activist hedge funds (which take funds and invest them in a handful of firms in the hope of agitating for a governance change leading to improvements in firm value) and (4) pension plans, to name just a few.[19]

Indeed, the compensation of these funds is often very different. For instance, passive index funds charge a very small fee based on assets under management (AUM; perhaps 0.1 per cent); indeed, because they are investing in pre-existing indices, their primary source of competition is offering low fees.[20] Hedge funds, in contrast, pay their top managers a higher proportion of AUM (e.g., around 2 per cent) plus a hefty percentage (e.g., circa 20 per cent) of the increase in individual investee firm value.[21] Unsurprisingly then, hedge fund activists are more incentivized to push for governance changes that might improve an individual firm's value, whilst index funds are less inclined to engage in such activity and more likely to focus on matters affecting the entire

[13] The usual starting point for discussion is the seminal work of Adolf Berle and Gardner Means, *The Modern Corporation and Private Property* (Macmillan 1932), in which they discuss the rise of the managerial class in the 1930s. However, this description has been challenged by some commentators. See Clifford G. Holderness, 'The Myth of Diffuse Ownership in the United States' (2009) 22 *Review of Financial Studies* 1377.

[14] See John Pound, 'Proxy Voting and the SEC' (1991) 29 *Journal of Financial Economics* 241.

[15] Ibid.

[16] See Charles McGrath, '80% of Equity Market Cap Held by Institutions', *Pensions & Investments* (25 April 2017).

[17] See Allen, Kraakman and Khanna (n. 1).

[18] See Lucian A. Bebchuk, Alma Cohen and Scott Hirst, 'The Agency Problems of Institutional Investors' (2017) 31 *Journal of Economic Perspectives* 89; John C. Coates, 'The Future of Corporate Governance Part I: The Problem of Twelve' (20 September 2018) Harvard Public Law Working Paper No. 19–07; Marcel Kahan and Edward B. Rock, 'Index Funds and Corporate Governance: Let Shareholders Be Shareholders' (4 April 2019) NYU Law and Economics Research Paper No. 18–39.

[19] See Bebchuk, Cohen and Hirst (n. 18); Lucian A. Bebchuk and Scott Hirst, 'Index Funds and the Future of Corporate Governance: Theory, Evidence, and Policy' (2019) 119 *Columbia Law Review* 2029; Coates (n. 18); Marcel Kahan and Edward B. Rock, 'Hedge Funds in Corporate Governance and Corporate Control' (2007) 155 *University of Pennsylvania Law Review* 1021; Kahan and Rock (n. 18).

[20] See Bebchuk and Hirst (n. 19); Coates (n. 18); Kahan and Rock (n. 18).

[21] See Kahan and Rock (n. 19); Bebchuk, Cohen and Hirst (n. 18).

market (e.g. climate risk).[22] This is but one example of the differences amongst institutional investors, asset managers and other players in the modern governance ecosystem.

These differences suggest that coordinating shareholder votes within such a heterogeneous group of institutional investors and their asset managers requires effort. We thus need to introduce two additional players. The first is proxy advisory firms (PAFs) – such as Institutional Shareholder Services (ISS) and Glass Lewis – which provide voting recommendations to institutional clients who usually pay them a subscription fee to receive such recommendations.[23] Because many institutions value the expertise of PAFs and because a number of institutions have pre-committed to following their recommendations, these firms can swing around 6–10 per cent of the vote according to some estimates.[24] The second is proxy solicitors – such as D. F. King and Okapi Partners – who are specialists in bringing shareholder votes together. They understand the dynamics of the voting system, how to identify the actual parties entitled to a vote on a given matter and how to encourage them to vote.[25] Anyone familiar with voting generally knows how indispensable such players are, which is reflected in their impressive fees. For example, estimates suggest that some of the more hotly contested recent proxy battles have involved proxy fees (for both sides) in the range of US$20–30 million.[26]

The lengthy cast of characters who now populate shareholder voting in the USA has led to a somewhat different set of regulatory and jurisprudential concerns than the diffusely held model would suggest. Amongst others, concerns have arisen due to the likelihood of conflicts of interest amongst institutional investors (and with the firm) and even conflicts on the PAF side.[27] Some of these concerns manifested themselves in the recently adopted US Securities and Exchange Commission (SEC) rules on PAFs (discussed infra). Further, in addition to voting, there are parallel behind-the-scenes discussions to effectuate change and engagement efforts where both insurgents and firms often communicate with institutional investors on an ongoing basis and in advance of an activist intervention.[28]

The impact of these changes on governance has been substantial. In the last twenty or so years, we have witnessed a cascade of governance changes that have been spearheaded by shareholder activists, including majority independent boards, de-staggered boards, 'say on pay' votes, increased share buybacks to send cash to shareholders, proxy access, changes of business strategy on the ground and many others.[29] There has been considerable debate over whether these changes, and the associated activism, are value-enhancing. Scholarly views range across the spectrum, from those concerned about whether activists push firms to focus on the 'short run' (at

[22] See Kahan and Rock (n. 18); Coates (n. 18); C. Scott Hemphill and Marcel Kahan, 'The Strategies of Anticompetitive Common Ownership' (2020) 129 *Yale Law Journal* 1392.

[23] ISS and Glass Lewis are the primary providers of proxy voting advice to institutional shareholders and corporate governance advice to large firms. Their recommendations are sometimes outcome determinative even though they typically do not own shares in the firms at issue (although they are for-profit firms). See Latham and Watkins, 'Corporate Governance Commentary' (September 2011) 3. For further discussion of proxy advisory firms (PAFs), see Andrey Malenko and Nadya Malenko, 'Proxy Advisory Firms: The Economics of Selling Information to Voters' (2019) 74 *Journal of Finance* 2441.

[24] See Stephen J. Choi, Jill E. Fisch and Marcel Kahan, 'The Power of Proxy Advisors: Myth or Reality?' (2010) 59 *Emory Law Journal* 869.

[25] See Proxy Solicitors, 'The Activist Investor' www.theactivistinvestor.com/The_Activist_Investor/Proxy_Solicitors.html accessed 15 July 2020.

[26] See Mike Coronato, '2017 Proxy Fights: High Cost, Low Volume' *FactSet* (6 November 2017) https://insight.factset.com/2017-proxy-fights-high-cost-low-volume. accessed 15 July 2020.

[27] See SEC, 'Final Rule: Exemptions from the Proxy Rules for Proxy Voting Advice' (22 July 2020).

[28] See Kirkland & Ellis, 'Slides on Shareholder Activism' 2020 (on file with author).

[29] See Allen, Kraakman and Khanna (n. 1); Bebchuk and Hirst (n. 19).

the expense of long-run value) to those arguing that, on average, activist interventions enhance firm value over the longer run.[30]

The aforementioned changes may, however, just be the start. In the last few years, we have witnessed a series of new moves by shareholder activists, ranging from seeking board seats to blocking mergers and acquisitions (M&A) transactions. On the horizon are more proposals to bring about greater social responsibility and board accountability, as index funds and others push for more inclusive and longer-term visions of profitability and growth. Before exploring these recent developments, it may be useful to highlight some of the key 'rules of the road' for voting in the USA.

12.3 RULES OF THE ROAD

Because corporate law in the USA depends on the state of incorporation, I focus my commentary on the rules of the road in Delaware both because it is the dominant player in US state corporate law and because these rules are fairly similar across US jurisdictions.[31] I divide the discussion into broad structural features in Section 12.3.1 (e.g. votes per share, the issues on which shareholders vote, board structure and corporate purpose), with Section 12.3.2 addressing the operational rules for shareholder voting and Section 12.3.3 then rounding out the discussion by highlighting how Delaware regulates the buying of votes and other types of behaviour associated with voting that might be considered manipulative.

12.3.1 *Structural Features*

First, shares in the USA can carry virtually any number of votes, as detailed in the firm's corporate charter. The default is 'one share, one vote',[32] but it is not uncommon to see considerable variation.[33] Many technology firms have recently begun to provide supermajority voting shares to their founders and key employees (e.g. ten votes per share), enabling them to remain a controlling group even if the firm becomes publicly traded.[34] This is usually achieved

[30] See Lucian A. Bebchuk, 'The Myth that Insulating Boards Serves Long-Term Value' (2013) 113 *Columbia Law Review* 1637; Lucian A. Bebchuk, Alon Brav and Wei Jiang, 'The Long-Term Effects of Hedge Fund Activism' (2015) 115 *Columbia Law Review* 1085; Matthew Denes, Jonathan M. Karpoff and Victoria McWilliams, 'Thirty Years of Shareholder Activism: A Survey of Empirical Research' (2017) 44 *Journal of Corporate Finance* 405; K. J. Martijn Cremers et al., 'Hedge Fund Activism and Long-Term Firm Value' (28 May 2020) https://papers.ssrn.com/sol3/papers.cfm?abstract_id=2693231 (arguing that the gains are from hedge funds' superior trading skills not governance changes); Ed deHaan, David Larcker and Charles McClure, 'Long-term Economic Consequences of Hedge Fund Activist Interventions' (2019) 24 *Review of Accounting Studies* 536. A number of recent studies explore the spillover effects of hedge fund activism onto other firms (see Nickolay Gantchev, Oleg R. Gredil and Chotibhak Jotikasthira, 'Governance Under the Gun: Spillover Effects of Hedge Fund Activism' (2019) 23 *Review of Finance* 1031) and on social performance (see Mark R. DesJardine and Rodolphe Durand, 'Disentangling the Effects of Hedge Fund Activism on Firm Financial and Social Performance' (2020) 41 *Strategic Management Journal* 1054).

[31] See Allen, Kraakman and Khanna (n. 1).

[32] See DEL CODE ANN tit. 8, § 212.

[33] Ibid. See, generally, David F. Larcker and Brian Tayan, 'Loosey-Goosey Governance: Four Misunderstood Terms in Corporate Governance' Harvard Law School Forum on Corporate Governance (16 October 2019) https://corpgov.law.harvard.edu/2019/10/16/loosey-goosey-governance-four-misunderstood-terms-in-corporate-governance/ accessed 15 July 2020.

[34] See Cristopher C. McKinnon, 'Dual-Class Capital Structures: A Legal, Theoretical & Empirical Buy-Side Analysis' (2016) 5 *Michigan Business & Entrepreneurial Law Review* 81, 82; Wilson Sonsini Goodrich & Rosati, '2019 Technology and Life Sciences IPO Report' www.wsgr.com/en/insights/2019-technology-and-life-sciences-ipo-report.html. Further, there has been a resurgence of dual-class stock globally. See Hal S. Scott and John Gulliver, 'Reforming U.S. Capital Markets to Promote Economic Growth' (May 2020) Committee on Capital Markets Regulation (e.g. Sweden).

via multiple classes of stock (e.g. Class A stock has one vote per share and is bought by the general public, and Class B has ten votes per share and is retained by the founders).[35] The major trading venues (e.g. the New York Stock Exchange and NASDAQ) prevent firms from disparately reducing or restricting voting rights per share of common stock unless the firm is doing so in an initial public offering.[36] It then seems unsurprising, perhaps, that in 2016, only 9 per cent of the S&P 100 had dual-class structures.[37]

Other types of share voting structures are possible but seen only occasionally. Loyalty shares, for example, are rare, with a recent study finding only twelve US firms offer them.[38] Further, although some states, including Delaware, permit cumulative voting, it is not very common except in the states where it is required (such as California).[39] Zero-vote shares are also permissible in the USA,[40] although they are rarely seen outside of it.

Second, shareholders in the USA vote on a variety of issues. For some matters statutory law requires a favourable shareholder vote to proceed at all (e.g. mergers, reorganizations, director elections, waivers of certain fiduciary protections).[41] For other matters there may be no statutory requirement for a vote (e.g. conflicted transactions with directors or controlling shareholders), but a favourable vote by disinterested and informed shareholders can be very beneficial because it results in the matter receiving a more deferential standard of judicial review.[42] There are yet other matters where shareholders get the opportunity to vote, such as matters for which a vote is explicitly provided for in the firm's incorporation documents (e.g. the corporate charter and by-laws) or where matters may be put to shareholders for a vote under SEC rules (e.g. under the SEC's Rule 14a-8 'town meeting' provision).[43] There is thus quite a large range of decisions on which shareholders can exercise their franchise in the USA.

Boards in the USA are typically single-tier (i.e. one board elected by shareholders has oversight responsibility for the firm), as opposed to the two-tier boards seen in Germany and Austria, where there is a management board (which manages the firm) and a supervisory board comprising shareholder and labour representatives that oversees the management board.[44] In the USA, management is thought to be centralized in the board, and the board is the decision-making

[35] See McKinnon (n. 34); Wilson Sonsini Goodrich & Rosati (n. 34); Scott and Gulliver (n. 34).

[36] Ibid.

[37] See Lucian A. Bebchuck and Kobi Kastiel, 'The Untenable Case for Perpetual Dual Class Stock' (2017) 103 *Virginia Law Review* 585, 594. But note that there has been a resurgence of dual-class stock globally – see Scott and Gulliver (n. 34) - and for firms conducting IPOs in the US – see Cremers, K. J. Martijn and Lauterbach, Beni and Pajuste, Anete, The Life-Cycle of Dual Class Firm Valuation (September 30, 2020). European Corporate Governance Institute (ECGI) - Finance Working Paper No. 550/2018, Available at SSRN: https://ssrn.com/abstract=3062895; Aggarwal, Dhruv and Eldar, Ofer and Hochberg, Yael V. and Litov, Lubomir P., The Rise of Dual-Class Stock IPOs (November 23, 2021). Journal of Financial Economics (JFE), Vol. 144, No. 1, 2022, European Corporate Governance Institute – Finance Working Paper No. 806/2021, Available at SSRN: https://ssrn.com/abstract=3690670.

[38] David J. Berger, Steven Davidoff Solomon and Aaron J. Benjamin, 'Tenure Voting and the U.S. Public Company' (2017) 72 *Business Lawyer* 305.

[39] See DEL CODE ANN tit. 8, § 214.

[40] See Randall Chase, 'Ruling Allows Google to Issue "Class C" shares' *USA Today* (28 October 2013); Tom Hals, 'Google Settlement Clear Way for New Class C Stock' *Reuters* (17 June 2013).

[41] Allen, Kraakman and Khanna (n. 1).

[42] Ibid.

[43] Ibid.

[44] See Paul Davies and Klaus J. Hopt, 'Corporate Boards in Europe – Accountability and Convergence' (2013) 61 *American Journal of Comparative Law* 301; Jens Dammann and Horst Eidenmuller, 'Codetermination: A Poor Fit for U.S. Corporations' (1 April 2020) European Corporate Governance Institute Law Working Paper No. 509/2020, Oxford Legal Studies Research Paper No. 17/2020, Available at SSRN https://ssrn.com/abstract=3565955 accessed 15 July 2020.

organ of the firm in most circumstances.[45] It is only for items listed in the corporate charter and certain kinds of shareholder suits that the board's decision-making role is sometimes eclipsed.

The power of the board is expected to be utilized in the interests of the corporation, which is usually taken to mean that the board should act primarily for the welfare of shareholders.[46] The courts typically do not cabin board discretion on this issue, and allow board members to make reasonably informed unconflicted decisions that the board believes will inure to the benefit of shareholders at some point in time (e.g. the benefit does not have to be short-term value maximization in general).[47] Thus, when a board decides that it would benefit the firm and shareholders (perhaps in the long run) to engage in charitable activities using corporate resources (e.g. provide funding to an institution of higher education) or utilize resources for environmentally friendly purposes or boost employee morale, there is little judicial scrutiny of that decision if the board is reasonably informed, unconflicted and has acted in good faith to (ultimately) benefit the firm and shareholders.[48] Even if the decision is later thought to have been foolish or even completely wrong-headed, little liability risk attaches.[49]

Although the legal rule is fairly clear, business practice in the USA is moving towards a version of enlightened shareholder value or long-term sustainable value. That shift has many potential causes, but one of the most noticeable is the increasingly vocal support by asset managers for long-term sustainable value.[50] That, however, is a topic meriting a much more fulsome discussion than can be presented in this chapter.

Finally, the ownership structure of publicly traded US firms represents a variety of hues. There are controlled firms (some by individuals, some by families),[51] diffusely held firms and firms that do not have a controlling entity but have concentrated ownership, usually reflecting

45 See Allen, Kraakman and Khanna (n. 1) ch. 3.

46 Ibid., ch. 8.

47 See Lucian A. Bebchuk et al., 'The Illusory Promise of Stakeholder Governance' (2021) 106 *Cornell Law Review* 91; Jonathan R. Macey, 'The Central Role of Myth in Corporate Law' (25 May 2020) European Corporate Governance Institute Law Working Paper No. 519/2020, available at SSRN https://ssrn.com/abstract=3435676 accessed 15 July 2020; Leo Strine, 'Toward Fair and Sustainable Capitalism: A Comprehensive Proposal to Help American Workers, Restore Fair Gainsharing between Employees and Shareholders, and Increase American Competitiveness by Reorienting Our Corporate Governance System Toward Sustainable Long-Term Growth and Encouraging Investments in America's Future' (3 October 2019) University of Pennsylvania, Institute for Law & Econ Research Paper No. 19-39, Harvard John M. Olin Discussion Paper No. 1018, Available at SSRN https://ssrn.com/abstract=3461924 accessed 15 July 2020; Leo Strine, 'The Dangers of Denial: The Need for a Clear-Eyed Understanding of the Power and Accountability Structure Established by the Delaware General Corporation Law' (2015) 50 *Wake Forest Law Review* 761.

48 See Allen, Kraakman and Khanna (n. 1) ch. 8 (discussing *A.P. Smith* v. *Barlow*); Strine, 'The Dangers of Denial' (n. 47).

49 Further, it is noteworthy that in most jurisdictions that espouse a stakeholder view of the firm, it is still the shareholders who typically vote on directorial positions. See Dionysia Katelouzou and Konstantinos Sergakis, 'Shareholder Stewardship Enforcement' (30 March 2020), an edited version of which will be published as a chapter in Dionysia Katelouzou and Dan W. Puchniak (eds.), *Global Shareholder Stewardship: Complexities, Challenges and Possibilities* (Cambridge University Press forthcoming), European Corporate Governance Institute Law Working Paper No. 514/2020, available at SSRN https://ssrn.com/abstract=3564266 accessed 15 July 2020.

50 See Letter to CEOs from Larry Fink, founder, chairman and CEO of BlackRock, Inc. (17 January 2018) www.blackrock.com/corporate/investor-relations/larry-fink-ceo-letter accessed 15 July 2020; Attracta Mooney, 'How Asset Managers Turned into Business Agitators' *Financial Times* (23 December 2019) www.ft.com/content/f568ec48-1840-11ea-8d73-6303645ac406 accessed 15 July 202. See also Robert G. Eccles and Svetlana Klimenko, 'The Investor Revolution' *Harvard Business Review* (May–June 2019) https://hbr.org/2019/05/the-investor-revolution accessed 15 July 2020.

51 Control is usually maintained either by the controlling group owning a sheer majority of voting stock or via dual-class structures. See Lucian A. Bebchuk, Reinier H. Kraakman and George G. Triantis, 'Stock Pyramids, Cross-Ownership, and Dual Class Equity: The Mechanisms and Agency Costs of Separating Control from Cash-Flow Rights' in Randall K. Morck (ed.), *Concentrated Corporate Ownership* (University of Chicago Press 2000).

a combination of institutional investors. This last category has grown considerably in the last forty years, as noted earlier, with most estimates suggesting that, on average, 80 per cent of the stock in Russell 3000 firms is held by institutions, an increasingly large share of which is held by index funds that are typically passive.[52] The most common types of institutional investors are index funds, pension plans, mutual funds, hedge funds, private equity funds and a smattering of other sorts of institutions (e.g. foreign investors or Sovereign Wealth Funds). The incentives of these institutional investors are not fully aligned, and it is indeed likely that their interests veer off in different and sometimes conflicting directions, as noted earlier.

12.3.2 *Operational Details on Voting and Engagement in the USA*

The broad structural features noted above are complemented by a series of operational rules that create the legal scaffolding for shareholder voting and engagement in the USA. I begin here with rules pertaining to the calling of a meeting at which a vote will be held (Section 12.3.2.1), and then continue to those pertaining to shareholder proposals and information rights (Section 12.3.2.2).

12.3.2.1 Calling a Meeting for a Shareholder Vote

The most frequent venue for shareholder voting is the annual general meeting (AGM), which in Delaware is held at least once every thirteen months for the election of directors.[53] These elections usually involve one slate of directors proposed by management and, if there are challengers, then another slate proposed by them (I defer discussion of other kinds of slates until later).[54] Other matters may also be voted upon during the AGM, including executive compensation,[55] shareholder proposals[56] and any other proper business[57] (e.g. reincorporation in another state, mergers, the approval of conflicted transactions). Director elections take place by written ballot, although ballots can be submitted electronically.[58] Indeed, even the AGM can be held remotely if the firm's charter or by-laws do not prohibit it[59] and if the corporation takes reasonable steps to identify shareholders entitled to vote and gives each of them a reasonable opportunity to participate and vote.[60] There has been a near tripling of virtual or hybrid meetings amongst Russell 3000 firms since 2014,[61] albeit from a low base. Pressure from the COVID-19 pandemic may accelerate the move away from physical meetings. In 2020, there were 560 hybrid

52 See McGrath (n. 16).
53 See DEL CODE ANN tit. 8, § 211.
54 See Allen, Kraakman, and Khanna (n. 1).
55 See Holly M. Bauer, Bradd L. Williamson and Adam L. Kestenbaum, 'Compensation in the 2018 Proxy Season' Harvard Law School Forum on Corporate Governance (2 February 2018) https://corpgov.law.harvard.edu/2018/02/02/compensation-in-the-2018-proxy-season/ accessed 15 July 2020.
56 See 17 CFR § 240.14a–8 (2011).
57 Ibid.
58 See DEL CODE ANN tit. 8, § 211.
59 Ibid.; see also Steven M. Haas and Charles L. Brewer, 'A Practical Guide to Virtual-Only Shareholder Meetings' Harvard Law School Forum on Corporate Governance (17 November 2017) https://corpgov.law.harvard.edu/2017/11/17/a-practical-guide-to-virtual-only-shareholder-meetings/ accessed 15 July 2020.
60 See DEL CODE ANN tit. 8, § 211; see also Haas and Brewer (n. 59).
61 See Marie Clara Buellingen, 'Virtual Shareholder Meetings in the U.S.' Harvard Law School Forum on Corporate Governance (10 October 2019) https://corpgov.law.harvard.edu/2019/10/10/virtual-shareholder-meetings-in-the-u-s/ accessed 15 July 2020.

meetings, compared with 286 in 2019.[62] There are also new SEC guidelines on best practices.[63] The AGM date is usually stated in the charter or by-laws, and failing that can be set by the board.[64] Notice to shareholders is required and must be 'not less than 10 nor more than 60 days' before the date of the meeting.[65] However, the notice of an AGM does not need to include the purpose of the meeting.[66]

In terms of the voting process, there are four modes of voting in Delaware: (1) voting in person if physically present at the meeting, (2) proxy voting,[67] (3) remote voting (by phone) and (4) internet voting if provided by the firm.[68] A quorum is required before a vote can be accepted and is met, absent any provision in the charter or by-laws, when a majority of shareholders who are entitled to vote are present in person or via proxy at the AGM.[69] Moreover, the charter or by-laws cannot require a quorum of less than one-third of voting shareholders.[70]

Assuming that the quorum is met, the percentage of votes necessary for success depends on what the charter or by-laws say. They may contain supermajority voting requirements for certain issues or for many issues, but if they are silent on the matter, then the percentage required is a simple majority except for director elections where the default is a plurality of shareholders present (or via proxy) at the AGM.[71] Recent activism by shareholders has led some firms to change their charter or by-laws to require a simple majority rather than a plurality to elect the board.[72] In addition some matters require a majority of financially disinterested shareholders to approve the decision for it to receive a more deferential standard of judicial review (e.g. a majority of minority shareholders to approve a freeze-out merger).[73] It is noteworthy that shareholders can enter into agreements with one another that bind them to vote in particular ways on certain issues. Although not discussed in great depth in most casebooks, these agreements have become more common and are covering more things than they did in the past.[74]

62 See Rebecca Grapsas, Holly Gregory and John Kelsh, 'Annual Shareholders Meeting in the Time of COVID-19' Harvard Law School Forum on Corporate Governance (02 April 2020) https://corpgov.law.harvard.edu/2020/04/02/annual-shareholders-meeting-in-the-time-of-covid-19/ accessed 15 July 2020.

63 See, e.g., SEC, 'Staff Guidance for Conducting Shareholder Meetings in Light of COVID-19 Concerns' (23 May 2012) www.sec.gov/ocr/staff-guidance-conducting-annual-meetings-light-covid-19-concerns accessed 15 July 2020.

64 Ibid.

65 See DEL CODE ANN tit. 8, § 222.

66 Ibid. The notification of the meeting must be in the form of writing or electronic transmission.

67 Ibid.; see also DEL CODE ANN tit. 8, § 212.

68 See 'Spotlight on Proxy Matters –The Mechanics of Voting, U.S. Securities and Exchange Commission' (23 May 2012) www.sec.gov/spotlight/proxymatters/voting_mechanics.shtml accessed 15 July 2020.

69 See DEL CODE ANN tit. 8, § 216.

70 Ibid.

71 Ibid; see also *Berlin* v. *Emerald Partners*, 552 A.2d 482 (Del 1989); Kosmas Papadopoulos, 'An Overview of Vote Requirements at U.S. Meetings' Harvard Law School Forum on Corporate Governance (6 July 2019) https://corpgov.law.harvard.edu/2019/07/06/an-overview-of-vote-requirements-at-u-s-meetings/ accessed 15 July 2020. Note that a Delaware Court recently held that a by-law requiring a supermajority vote for removing a board member violated Delaware law. See *Frechter* v. *Zier*, C.A. No. 12038–VCG, 2017 WL 345142 (Del Ch 17 January 2017); DEL CODE ANN tit. 8, § 141(k).

72 See Allen, Kraakman and Khanna (n. 1).

73 See Robert B. Little, Steve J. Wright and Kiel Sauerman, 'Standards of Review Applicable to Board Decisions in Delaware M&A Transactions' Harvard Law School Forum on Corporate Governance (6 July 2019) https://corpgov.law.harvard.edu/2020/05/20/standards-of-review-applicable-to-board-decisions-in-delaware-ma-transactions/ accessed 15 July 2020.

74 See Gabriel V. Rauterberg, 'The Separation of Voting and Control: The Role of Contract in Corporate Governance' (28 June 2020) available at SSRN https://ssrn.com/abstract=3637204 or http://dx.doi.org/10.2139/ssrn.3637204 accessed 15 July 2020.

Shareholder voting can occur outside the AGM in Delaware via the calling of special meetings.[75] Special meetings can be called by the board (or someone in the corporation so authorized in the charter or by-laws)[76] or by insurgent shareholders (depending on the charter and by-laws), albeit usually with some restrictions. For example, only shareholders who own a threshold percentage of shares may be entitled to call a special meeting or there may be limits on when the meeting can occur.[77] According to a 2018 study, 36 per cent of S&P 500 companies prohibit shareholders from calling special meetings.[78] Most other requirements for a special meeting mirror those for an AGM except that the notice of a special meeting needs to include the purpose of the meeting.[79] Shareholder consents rather than an AGM can be used in some instances, and are used with some regularity in Delaware.[80]

12.3.2.2 Shareholder Proposals and Information Rights

Shareholders can influence the agenda of a general meeting (or special meeting) and challenge management in various ways. First, shareholders can simply not vote in favour of, or vote against, management's proposals. Because most issues on which shareholders vote (save perhaps director elections) require at least a majority vote and must meet basic quorum requirements, shareholders can scuttle management's plans by 'withholding' their vote.[81] Second, shareholders can challenge management's proposals by putting forward their own proposals, either in the form of a Rule 14a-8 proposal or as a full competing proposal. Initially, many institutional investors may have favoured a Rule 14a-8 proposal because it was considerably cheaper than a full competing proposal.[82] A Rule 14a-8 proposal typically takes the form of a few pages appended to management's proxy materials (which makes it low cost for the shareholder), whereas a full competing proposal requires shareholders to put forward the same kind of information as that found in management's proxy materials (i.e. it must meet Regulation 14A's disclosure requirements and other requirements), which is quite expensive owing to the costs of producing and then verifying the information to ensure that it does not violate the proxy rules.[83] Given that reimbursement for shareholder proxy expenses by the corporation tends to arise only when the shareholder proposal succeeds (an infrequent occurrence initially),[84] insurgent shareholders have often preferred the lower-cost Rule 14a-8 option to a full competing proposal.

However, there are conditions for using Rule 14a-8.[85] For example, there are minimum holding requirements for shareholders who wish to submit a proposal (with respect to the

75 See Sofie Cools, 'The Real Difference in Corporate Law between the United States and Continental Europe: Distribution of Powers' (2006) 30 *Delaware Journal Corporate Law* 697, 731.

76 See DEL CODE ANN tit. 8, § 211.

77 See, e.g., Meredith Foster, 'Special Meetings and Consent Solicitations: How the Written-Consent Right Uniquely Empowers Shareholders' (2019) 128 *Yale Law Journal* 1706, 1729, 1732.

78 Ibid., 1709.

79 See DEL CODE ANN tit. 8, § 222.

80 Ibid., § 211. The stockholder consent statute in Delaware provides that any action that may be taken at a meeting of shareholders (e.g., amendment of by-laws or removal of directors from office) may also be taken by the written concurrence of the holders of the number of voting shares required to approve that action at a meeting attended by all shareholders. See DGCL §228.

81 See Kirkland and Ellis (n. 28).

82 See Allen, Kraakman and Khanna (n. 1).

83 Ibid.

84 Ibid (discussing the *Rosenfeld* decision).

85 See 17 CFR § 240.14a–8 (2011).

amount held and the time for which it is held).[86] Further, Rule 14a-8 allows management to exclude a shareholder proposal on a number of grounds, such as a conflict with state or federal law, the inclusion of materially false or misleading statements, or that the proposal pertains to ordinary business matters or director elections.[87] Many of these grounds reflect deference to the notion that a core attribute of the modern corporate form is management being centralized in the board, and others to the notion that certain matters (e.g. director elections) warrant full competing proposals from all sides.[88]

If management decides to exclude a proposal on one of these grounds, that decision is often reviewed by the SEC, with the firm bearing the burden of showing that the exclusionary grounds are satisfied.[89] If the SEC agrees with management, it will usually issue a 'no action letter' stating that it will not take any enforcement action against management for the exclusion (the SEC is the only party that can bring an action). If it disagrees with management, it will not issue such a letter.[90] SEC no action letters do not carry precedential effect, but it seems clear that they carry some weight on at least a probabilistic level.[91] However, in spite of the large number of grounds for exclusion, the SEC has displayed a willingness to work with shareholders to bring together a proposal that satisfies Rule 14a-8 (e.g. encouraging the redrafting of the proposal to avoid the exclusionary grounds).[92] Further, even if a shareholder proposal is excluded under Rule 14a-8, that does not per se mean that shareholders cannot put it to other shareholders for a vote; it simply means that they will need to put the proposal forward in the much more expensive full competing proposal format.[93]

It should be noted, however, that Rule 14a-8 proposals must be phrased as recommendations to the board in deference to conceptions of centralized management.[94] Thus, a shareholder challenger who obtains greater than 50 per cent support from the shareholder body may still not technically have the power to implement the recommendation in question against the board's wishes. However, a proposal that receives this level of support may well prompt judicious directors to consider ways in which they could implement it. After all, directors come up for election every so often, and having an irate shareholder body is unlikely to bode well for their re-election chances or for perceptions of their value as directors.[95]

Over the years, shareholders have put forward many different kinds of proposals. Leading casebooks suggest that they can be divided into proposals related to corporate governance (e.g. being desirous of a majority independent board, removing a staggered board) and those designed

86 Ibid. Until late 2020, a shareholder was required to hold at least $2,000 in market value or 1 per cent of the firm for at least one year prior to the proposal's submission and through the meeting date. In late 2020, the SEC promulgated new rules (discussed *infra* Section 12.4.3) that are now themselves being revisited by the SEC. See Brian V. Breheny, Raquel Fox and Caroline S. Kim, *Chair Gensler's Insight on the SEC's New Regulatory Agenda*, Harvard Law School Forum on Corporate Governance, available at: https://corpgov.law.harvard.edu/2021/07/16/chair-genslers-insight-on-the-secs-new-regulatory-agenda/#more-138992 accessed 17 July 2021.

87 Ibid.

88 See John G. Matsusaka, Oguzhan Ozbas and Irene Yi, 'Can Shareholder Proposals Hurt Shareholders? Evidence from SEC No-Action Letter Decisions' (1 April 2019) USC CLASS Research Paper No. CLASS17-4, Marshall School of Business Working Paper No. 17-7, available at SSRN https://ssrn.com/abstract=2881408 accessed 15 July 2020.

89 See Allen, Kraakman and Khanna (n. 1).

90 Ibid.

91 Ibid.

92 See Kirkland and Ellis (n. 28).

93 See Allen, Kraakman and Khanna (n. 1).

94 Ibid.

95 Ibid.; see also Kirkland and Ellis (n. 28). In addition, as noted in *infra* Section 12.4.3, support for proposals can increase over the years so that even a proposal that fails to pass in one year may be proposed again in a later year with potentially greater success.

to encourage socially responsible policies (e.g. being desirous of a ban on certain kinds of discrimination).[96] On governance matters, the SEC has built up a base of no action letters that signal its thinking on these issues. On socially responsible issues, the picture is less clear. Early on, the SEC seemed to take a somewhat negative view of such proposals, but over the years it seems to have moved towards a 'case-by-case' approach, with well-advised proponents now having a better chance of getting a socially responsible proposal put before the shareholder body.[97]

Recent years have witnessed something of a decline in total shareholder proposals, with a recent study reporting around a 14 per cent reduction between 2017 and 2019.[98] The decline can be explained in part by shareholders using other methods to influence governance (e.g. engagement, public campaigns)[99] and the fact that some of the issues most amenable to Rule 14a-8 proposals have already been voted on at many firms (e.g. removing a staggered board).

Of course, to have a chance of succeeding in a shareholder proposal, shareholders need access to information about the firm (to produce information of relevance to the vote) and its owners (to be able to contact other shareholders). Under section 220 of the Delaware General Corporation Law, a shareholder needs to make a written request to access a firm's shareholder list and its books and records for a proper purpose.[100] The courts usually grant access to the shareholder list, along with relevant supporting documents, when a proper purpose is provided without inquiring too deeply into the reasons behind it.[101] Books and records requests, which are costlier to satisfy than a shareholder list request, appear to face somewhat more exacting 'proper purpose' screening, wherein the focus is on whether the requesting shareholder can marshal credible evidence of wrongdoing at the firm or demonstrate that she has a legitimate business reason for the request.[102] The granting of such requests tends to result in the provision of those books and records deemed 'necessary and essential' to the purpose cited.[103]

12.3.3 *Vote Buying*

In addition to specific rules governing the voting process, Delaware case law also provides a more broad-based regulation of vote buying and voting manipulation. Generally speaking,

96 See Allen, Kraakman and Khanna (n. 1).

97 Ibid. For a more detailed discussion, see Virginia E. Harper Ho, 'From Public Policy to Materiality: Non-Financial Reporting, Shareholder Engagement, & the Rule 14a-8 Ordinary Business Exception' (2019) 76 *Washington & Lee Law Review* 3.

98 See Matteo Tonello, 'Proxy Voting Analytics (2016–2019) and 2020 Season Preview' Harvard Law School Forum on Corporate Governance (6 January 2020) https://corpgov.law.harvard.edu/2020/01/06/proxy-voting-analytics-2016-2019-and-2020-season-preview/ accessed 15 July 2020.

99 Ibid.

100 See DEL CODE ANN tit. 8, § 220.

101 See Allen, Kraakman and Khanna (n. 1) ch. 6.6. The supporting documents should enable easier communication with the owners of the stock.

102 Ibid. The Delaware Chancery Court has rejected books and records requests when their sole purpose is a "fishing expedition" to run a proxy contest. See *High River Limited Partnership* v. *Occidental Petroleum Corporation*, 2019 WL 6040285 (Del Ch 14 November 2019).

103 See Gail Weinstein, Warren S. de Wied and Steven Epstein, 'Shareholder Activism and Proxy Contests as a "Proper Purpose" for Books and Records Demands' Harvard Law School Forum on Corporate Governance (22 December 2019) https://corpgov.law.harvard.edu/2019/12/22/shareholder-activism-and-proxy-contests-as-a-proper-purpose-for-books-and-records-demands/ accessed 15 July 2020. Delaware law does not really confer 'question' rights to shareholders, but if a remote AGM is held the firm must provide ways for shareholders to 'participate', which may encompass some ability to question. See Noam Noked, 'Online Shareholder Participation in Annual Meetings' Harvard Law School Forum on Corporate Governance (19 July 2012) https://corpgov.law.harvard.edu/2012/07/19/online-shareholder-participation-in-annual-meetings/ accessed 15 July 2020.

shareholders are permitted to come to agreements with other shareholders regarding how they will vote.[104] However, if management or the firm attempts to buy votes, a more exacting judicial scrutiny is typically triggered under the entire fairness standard of review (i.e. not the deferential business judgment standard).[105] This means that management or the board must show that purchasing the votes was fair along all dimensions. Failure to disclose the purchase of votes is often sufficient to show a lack of entire fairness.[106] The main concern with vote buying is that it seems to separate votes from ownership, thereby worsening agency problems. In other words, the person voting does not necessarily have a weighty economic interest in the firm.[107]

In *Schreiber* v. *Carney*, the board of Texas International (the target) had provided Jet Capital (a large, but non-controlling, shareholder) with a loan at below market rates of interest to induce it to vote in favour of an acquisition of the target.[108] The differential between the market rate of interest and that charged for the loan was the 'price' of the vote. The court explored the various rationales for prohibiting vote buying and found that they did not prohibit all vote buying, but were instead most concerned with vote buying pursued in ways intended to defraud or harm shareholders.[109] In the case in question, it appeared that the vote buying had been done to benefit shareholders (as indicated by the evidence provided by management), had been disclosed to them and had received nearly unanimous shareholder support.[110] Given the circumstances, the court held that the loan to Jet Capital had not run afoul of vote buying restrictions.

Issues related to vote buying have attracted greater attention of late, as institutional investors have begun to play a more prominent role. Two developments are worthy of note. First, institutions (and others) often not only acquire shares but also take positions in the derivatives markets that result in a net position that leaves the owner with diminished economic interests in the firm while still having a vote (or sometimes in a 'net short' position that gives the owner an incentive to vote against the firm's interests).[111] Such 'empty voting' has generated quite a bit of discussion, but only limited regulation.[112]

Second, the longstanding practice of lending stock (often to enable the 'shorting' of stock) has become more prominent as institutional investors have increased their holdings. Securities lending is the practice of the owner of stock 'lending' it to someone else for a short period of time.[113] The transaction usually involves selling the stock with the condition that it will be bought back and charging fees for such 'lending' of stock.[114] Many large institutions earn

104 See DEL CODE ANN tit. 8, § 218(c).

105 See, e.g., *Schreiber* v. *Carney*, 447 A. 2d 17 (Del Ch 1982); *Williams* v. *Ji*, C.A. No. 12729-VCMR (Del Ch 28 June 2017).

106 See *Schreiber* (n. 105).

107 See Easterbrook and Fischel (n. 2).

108 447 A. 2d 17 (Del Ch 1982).

109 Ibid.

110 Ibid.

111 See Henry T. C. Hu and Bernard S. Black, 'The New Vote Buying: Empty Voting and Hidden (Morphable) Ownership' (2006) 79 *Southern California Law Review* 811; Henry T. C. Hu and Bernard S. Black, 'Equity and Debt Decoupling and Empty Voting II: Importance and Extensions' (2008) 156 *University of Pennsylvania Law Review* 625.

112 Ibid. See also Bernard S. Sharfman, 'Mutual Fund Advisors' "Empty Voting" Raises New Governance Issues' Columbia Law School Blue Sky Blog (3 July 2017) https://clsbluesky.law.columbia.edu/2017/07/03/mutual-fund-advisors-empty-voting-raises-new-governance-issues/ accessed 15 July 2020; Jordan Barry, John William Hatfield and Scott Duke Kominers, 'On Derivatives Markets and Social Welfare: A Theory of Empty Voting and Hidden Ownership' (2013) 99 *Virginia Law Review* 1103.

113 See Reena Aggarwal, Pedro A. C. Saffi and Jason Sturgess, 'The Role of Institutional Investors in Voting: Evidence from the Securities Lending Market' (2015) 70 *Journal of Finance* 2309.

114 Ibid. It also usually involves the right to recall the shares should the original owner wish to have them back.

considerable revenues from this type of activity.[115] When it occurs around the time of a shareholder vote, however, there is a very real possibility that the person entitled to vote is not the owner but rather the entity that 'borrowed' the shares. That entity's economic interest in the firm is likely more fleeting than that of the owner, raising concerns similar to those over vote buying.[116] A recent example is the well-publicized GameStop proxy battle, where some institutions appeared to have 40 per cent of the company's shares, but carried only 5 per cent of the vote at the time of the vote.[117] Securities lending has been subject to considerable discussion, but to date little regulation in the USA.

Activities designed to manipulate voting are also regulated, typically through judicial oversight utilizing fiduciary duties and statutes. However, this is a vast subject area, and as such I do not discuss it in depth here except to note that opportunistic behaviour (e.g. shifting the voting date or venue at the last minute) and vote rigging are likely to be punished under fiduciary duty analysis.[118]

12.4 SHAREHOLDER VOTING AND ENGAGEMENT AT PRESENT: BEGINNING TO SOAR

Given the regulatory structure and ownership changes discussed in the last two sections, the chapter now turns to an examination of how shareholder voting and engagement have developed in recent years and the likely developments in the future. Section 12.4.1 examines the last decade of voting and engagement. Section 12.4.2 looks more closely at activism in the governance arena in the past few years, and Section 12.4.3 rounds out the discussion by examining developments in the environmental, social and governance (ESG) arena.

12.4.1 *Shareholder Voting and Engagement over the Last Ten Years*

Given the rise of shareholder activism, it is useful to get a sense of the issues that shareholders find useful to put forward as resolutions. One can divide shareholder proposals into those pertaining to (1) pure governance and compensation issues and those pertaining to (2) social responsibility issues (often called environmental, social and political (ESP) issues).[119] In the ESP arena, political resolutions (e.g. requesting the disclosure of corporate political spending) were the most common in the first half of 2019, with ninety-three such resolutions, followed by health and safety and animal rights resolutions, with eleven and eight, respectively.[120] In the same time frame, the most common governance proposal was to have an independent director as the board chair, and the most common compensation proposal was to try to connect compensation to sustainability (this might also be viewed as an ESP proposal).[121]

115 See 'iShares by BlackRock, Unlock the Potential of Your Portfolios: iShares Securities Lending' (2020) 3 www.ishares.com/us/literature/brochure/securities-lending-unlocking-portfolios-en-us.pdf accessed 15 July 2020.

116 See Risk Management Association, SEC 'Concept Release on the U.S. Proxy System, Submission to the Committee on Securities Lending' (2010) www.sec.gov/comments/s7-14-10/s71410-174.pdf accessed 15 July 2020.

117 See Dawn Lim, 'How Investing Giants Gave Away Voting Power Ahead of a Shareholder Dispute' *Wall Street Journal* (10 June 2020) www.wsj.com/articles/how-investing-giants-gave-away-voting-power-ahead-of-a-shareholder-fight-11591793863 accessed 15 July 2020.

118 See Allen, Kraakman and Khanna (n. 1) ch. 6.7.

119 See Marc Treviño, '2019 Proxy Season Review: Part 1 – Rule 14a-8 Shareholder Proposals' Harvard Law School Forum on Corporate Governance (16 July 2019) https://corpgov.law.harvard.edu/2019/07/26/2019-proxy-season-review-part-1-rule-14a-8-shareholder-proposals/ accessed 15 July 2020.

120 Ibid.

121 Ibid.

The success of shareholder proposals has been chequered, although there has been a rise in successful actions in recent years. The proposals that usually obtain the highest level of support are those (1) requiring a majority vote for directors (as opposed to the statutory default of a plurality), (2) adopting shareholder proxy access[122] and (3) de-staggering the firm's board.[123] Most ESP proposals fail, although average support for them at Russell 3000 firms in 2019 was 27.3 per cent, an increase from 19.5 per cent in 2014.[124] Further, from 2018 to the first half of 2019, only nineteen proposals in the ESP and compensation areas passed out of a total of 357 proposals.[125] Governance proposals were somewhat more successful, but the majority there too failed (in the same time frame 72 out of 429 passed).[126] In battles for board seats, activists are more likely to gain seats via compromise or settlement rather than by winning elections.[127] In 2019, about 91 per cent of board seats won by activists were the result of compromise – up from 72 per cent in 2014.[128] In spite of the greater attention devoted to shareholder proposals, there has been a recent decline in the number of such proposals, and of this decreasing number even fewer were voted on (suggesting more settlements or behind-the-scenes negotiations or engagement).[129] The incentives for settlement are strong given that management does not generally want a costly and disruptive proxy battle (and certainly would prefer not to lose one) and activists are often seeking influence, which can be obtained through settlement and perhaps at a lower cost than via a pitched proxy battle.

There is something of a schism in voter turnout between retail and non-retail shareholders. In the S&P 500, the percentage of shares that do not vote (when they are entitled to) is significant: 21.7 per cent of the shares in these firms did not vote in 2015, and the rate is rising.[130] Moreover, another recent study found voting by only 32 per cent of retail shareholders (who owned about 26 per cent of firms – an effective vote of about 9 per cent of all shareholders).[131] Non-retail shareholders voted at a much higher rate (circa 80 per cent).[132] Further, retail shareholders generally provide less support for shareholder proposals than other investors (albeit similar support for management proposals).[133]

Although shareholder voting has garnered much of the attention, it is quite clear that shareholder engagement has become very important too. Engagement is on the rise as more and more large investors prefer to act behind the scenes.[134] In addition, we are witnessing an

122 See Kosmas Papadopoulos, 'The Long View: The Role of Shareholder Proposals in Shaping U.S. Corporate Governance (2000–2018)' Harvard Law School Forum on Corporate Governance (6 February 2019) https://corpgov.law.harvard.edu/2019/02/06/the-long-view-the-role-of-shareholder-proposals-in-shaping-u-s-corporate-governance-2000-2018/ accessed 15 July 2020.

123 See Treviño (n. 119).

124 Ibid.

125 Ibid.

126 Ibid.

127 See Josh Black, John Reetun and Eleanor O'Donnell, 'The Activist Investing Annual Review 2020' Harvard Law School Forum on Corporate Governance (19 February 2020) https://corpgov.law.harvard.edu/2020/02/19/the-activist-investing-annual-review-2020/ accessed 15 July 2020.

128 Ibid.

129 See Treviño (n. 119). There are generally more proposals at larger firms. See Black, Reetun and O'Donnell (n. 127). See also Lucian A. Bebchuk et al., 'Dancing with Activists' (2002) 137 *Journal of Financial Economics* 1.

130 See Yaron Nili and Kobi Kastiel, 'In Search of the "Absent" Shareholders: A New Solution to Retail Investors' Apathy' (2017) 41 *Delaware Journal of Corporate Law* 51, 61.

131 See Alon Brav, Matthew D. Cain and Jonathon Zytnick, 'Retail Shareholder Participation in the Proxy Process: Monitoring, Engagement, and Voting' Harvard Law School Forum on Corporate Governance (19 November 2019) https://corpgov.law.harvard.edu/2019/11/19/retail-shareholder-participation/ accessed 15 July 2020.

132 Ibid.

133 Ibid.

134 Doron Levit, 'Soft Shareholder Activism' (2019) 32 *Review of Financial Studies* 2775.

increase in public campaigns (e.g. disclosing letters written to the firm, putting out press releases) and other pressure tactics (e.g. litigation on fiduciary duty breaches, securities law violations and books and records demands) to push management to move on shareholder resolutions.[135]

As this overview suggests, institutional investors have already had significant effects on corporate governance in the USA, but they are poised to enhance their impact even further. There are many examples of this, but for expositional brevity I will focus on two broad categories: first, the strategies and tactics adopted by activists on the traditional governance front and, second, the push to develop more shareholder proposals and initiatives targeted at enhancing ESG indicators.

12.4.2 *Activism 2020 and Beyond?*

In the last two to three years, shareholder activists have pursued a number of strategies as they interact with firms. These involve (1) 'withhold the vote' campaigns to partially change board membership (short of obtaining control themselves), to change policy, or to register discomfort with business decisions; (2) bringing short slate proxy contests, often with the goal of pushing the firm to sell itself; (3) initiating contests for control of the board; and (4) challenging M&A transactions. Similar tactics are commonly seen in all of these strategies, such as initial overtures made to the board or investor relations of the firm. These tactics may then be followed by public pressure, although that is usually more indicative of moving towards step (3) or (4). In any of these strategies, it is important for the activist to have a plan for approaching the proxy advisors, as many institutional investors have committed to voting in line with proxy advisors' recommendations. Correlatively, a firm's management needs to have some engagement with its larger shareholders to better appreciate their positions. This terrain may shift somewhat, as the SEC has just adopted new rules governing the recommendations provided by PAFs, which are discussed at the end of this section (although they are currently being revisited by the SEC).

12.4.2.1 Withhold the Vote

So-called 'withhold the vote' campaigns involve situations where management's board nominees are unopposed (perhaps because it is too expensive to field alternatives) and a shareholder activist (typically a hedge fund) lobbies to have shareholders 'withhold' their votes, which has the effect of being counted as 'no' votes on that nominee director or nominee slate of directors.[136] A large number of withheld votes can jeopardize a director's appointment, and it also sends a strong signal to the board that some investors consider there to be serious problems at the firm (and with the director in question).[137] These campaigns can be viewed as 'softer' or 'early warning' versions of full-blown proxy contests (where an alternate slate of board nominees is suggested). In that sense, they are a form of shareholder voting that appears to also serve an engagement function. These campaigns represent a sizeable portion of activist interventions and in the last few years have become perhaps the third most common form of intervention.[138]

[135] See Melissa Sawyer, Lauren S. Boehmke and Nathaniel R. Ludewig, 'Review and Analysis of 2018 U.S. Shareholder Activism' Harvard Law School Forum on Corporate Governance (19 April 2019) https://corpgov.law.harvard.edu/2019/04/05/review-and-analysis-of-2018-u-s-shareholder-activism/ accessed 15 July 2020.

[136] See Kirkland and Ellis (n. 28).

[137] Ibid.

[138] Ibid.

12.4.2.2 Short Slate Proxy Contest

A 'short slate' occurs when an activist shareholder does not wish to gain control of the board, but would prefer to have a minority of the board. If the activist succeeds, then the minority of the board comes from the short slate, with the remainder coming from management's slate but recommended by the activist.[139] One might ask why an activist would aim for a *minority* of the board, which does not provide control. Although it does not grant control, a minority can still obtain influence, access and information, which an activist might prefer to outright control. In a world where intermediate choices are more available, the short slate allows activists greater flexibility in choosing a strategy that permits greater influence than the withhold the vote strategy but less of a need to commit to running the firm than other strategies (i.e. running a full slate of alternate board nominees).[140] Moreover, PAFs such as ISS and Glass Lewis may prefer to lend support to a short slate than to a whole new board, as might some shareholders.[141]

It is important to distinguish a short slate from a universal proxy (which allows shareholders to mix and match director nominees as they prefer).[142] The SEC has recently voted to adopt final rules for universal proxies, which are scheduled to affect proxy contests from August 2022 onwards.[143] Another option is shareholder proxy access, which allows qualifying shareholders to directly nominate directors for inclusion on management's proxy card.[144] This strategy has advantages because shareholders do not need to make a full competing proposal. Some firms have – often as a result of shareholder activists – made changes to their by-laws or charter to allow for shareholder proxy access.[145]

Short slates, universal proxies and proxy access all target similar sorts of activist behaviour: suggesting board nominees short of controlling the board. They have different costs, and hence different signalling effects, but the overall picture is that activists wish to have greater influence at the firm than regular shareholders, albeit less than someone who has control. In recent years, a short slate has often been the first step in trying to get the board to initiate the process of selling itself to an acquirer (for a premium of course). Moreover, the short slate has become the most common outcome of activist intervention.[146]

12.4.2.3 Control Contest

Further along the continuum of activist involvement is when an activist attempts to gain control of the firm. Because the goal is control of the firm, a short slate is not terribly useful, and hence the activist must consider a full-on proxy contest or an acquisition. These types of interventions have been used increasingly in recent years, with financial studies finding such activist interventions, when they lead to an acquisition, are associated with an increase in firm value.[147] The

139 See Allen, Kraakman and Khanna (n. 1).

140 See Kirkland and Ellis (n. 28); see also Jeffrey N. Gordon, 'Proxy Contests in an Era of Increasing Shareholder Power: Forget Issuer Proxy Access and Focus on E-Proxy' (2008) 61 *Vanderbilt Law Review* 475.

141 See Kirkland and Ellis (n. 28).

142 See Allen, Kraakman and Khanna (n. 1).

143 See *SEC Adopts New Rules for Universal Proxy Cards in Contested Director Elections*, Press Release, U.S. Securities and Exchange Commission, November 17, 2021, available at: https://www.sec.gov/news/press-release/2021-235.

144 See Lucian A. Bebchuk, 'The Case for Shareholder Access to the Ballot' (2003) 59 *Business Lawyer* 43.

145 See Allen, Kraakman and Khanna (n. 1); Bebchuk and Hirst (n. 19).

146 See Kirkland and Ellis (n. 28).

147 See, e.g., Karpoff and McWilliams (n. 30); Robin Greenwood and Michael Schor, 'Investor Activism and Takeovers' (2009) 92 *Journal of Financial Economics* 362; Mike C. Burkart and Samuel Lee, 'Activism and Takeovers' (20 September 2019) Swedish House of Finance Research Paper No. 15-04, European Corporate Governance

usual tactics are 'soft touch' initial overtures followed by public statements and perhaps a public offer and public pressure on management to either relinquish control or sell the firm.

According to some law firms, this has now become the second most common outcome of activism.[148] Intriguingly, many hedge fund activists are closely connected to the 'takeover' artists of the 1980s, suggesting a return to some of the business strategies of those days adjusted for the market and institutional structures of the 2020s.

12.4.2.4 Targeting a Merger or Acquisition

Activist intervention in a merger or acquisition is one of the newer activist strategies. The typical scenario is a merger or acquisition that is already being negotiated or is soon to be voted upon, and the activist intervenes and threatens to block the deal or otherwise delay it.[149] In response, the acquirer offers a higher price to target shareholders or provides other concessions. Although not yet the most common strategy, it is garnering considerable attention (and resources).[150] The strategy relies on the activist's potential to hold up the merger or acquisition and to make returns (for presumably all target shareholders) in the process.[151] In the USA, the term 'bumpitrage' has been coined to describe a situation in which an activist intervenes in an ongoing merger not to provide a higher bid but rather to 'bump up' the price the initial acquirer is offering.[152] According to some reports, nearly 30 per cent of M&A activism in 2018 ended in a bumpitrage scenario.[153]

12.4.2.5 Newly Adopted SEC Rules on Proxy Advisory Firms

After considerable debate, the SEC adopted new rules on PAFs in the middle of 2020. These rules impose additional regulatory burdens and liability risks on PAFs such as ISS and Glass Lewis that require them to (1) disclose material conflicts of interest; (2) provide the subject firm with a chance to review and respond to the recommendation (before or simultaneously with the release of the recommendation) and inform investors of the firm's response (if the PAF knows there is one); and (3) provide a hyperlink to the firm's response or some other way of accessing it.[154] The rules also provide examples of when failures to disclose material information may trigger liability for misleading conduct in a proxy solicitation, such as failure to disclose the PAF's methodology, sources of information, conflicts of interest, and so forth.[155] The concern with conflicts of interest also suggests that PAF business practices that might lead one to question their independence may also need to be disclosed (e.g. selective consultation with certain clients). In addition, the SEC has provided supplemental advice to large institutions, such as asset managers, reminding them that they have a duty to consider the firm's response to PAF recommendations

Institute (ECGI) Finance Working Paper No. 543/2018, available at SSRN https://ssrn.com/abstract=2585836 accessed 15 July 2020.

148 See Kirkland and Ellis (n. 28).

149 Ibid.

150 Ibid.

151 Ibid.

152 Ibid.; see also Richard J. Grossman and Alexander J. Berg, 'Recent Trends in Shareholder Activism' Harvard Law School Forum on Corporate Governance (11 October 2019) https://corpgov.law.harvard.edu/2019/10/11/recent-trends-in-shareholder-activism/ accessed 15 July 2020.

153 See Kirkland and Ellis (n. 28).

154 See SEC, 'Final Rule: Exemptions from the Proxy Rules for Proxy Voting Advice' (22 July 2020).

155 See Rule 14a-2(b)(9).

before they vote.[156] These rules are expected to affect the behaviour of PAFs and the ability of institutional investors to rely on this source of proxy voting advice. However, as of June 2021 the SEC is reviewing these rules and has held off on enforcing them until the review is complete and perhaps longer.[157]

12.4.3 *ESP Activism*

Although many shareholder activists have pushed firms on traditional governance issues, we have witnessed a surge in ESP-related proposals over the last few years.[158] Indeed, ESP proposals often outnumber governance proposals.[159] The topics of the proposals range across a broad spectrum, including issues such as political spending, climate change, gender and race diversity, and workplace environment.[160] Although only a handful pass, they are achieving greater success than in the past. For example, in 2020, seven out of twenty-three ESP proposals passed (double the percentage that passed in 2019), including one on which Chevron shareholders voted to recommend enhanced disclosure of climate lobbying.[161] In addition, resolutions are sometimes withdrawn because of agreements between the combatants. The New York City Comptroller's Office withdrew its proposal to recommend adoption of the 'Rooney rule' (which targets improved boardroom and C-suite diversity) at thirteen of the seventeen firms at which it had been proposed because the firms agreed to it.[162] Indeed, many activist groups are relying on the shareholder proposal system to advance their causes.[163]

This seems an area of likely future growth both because of changing attitudes towards ESG and climate change and because the largest investors (index funds) have stated quite clearly that they want their investee firms to focus more on ESG issues and sustainability in the long term.[164] Having said that, some of the regulatory developments of the last few years suggest greater scrutiny of ESP proposals.

[156] See Supplement to Commission Guidance Regarding Proxy Voting Responsibilities of Investment Advisers www .sec.gov/rules/policy/2020/ia-5547.pdf accessed 15 July 2020.

[157] See Breheny et al. (n. 86).

[158] See, e.g., Scott Hirst, 'Social Responsibility Resolutions' (2018) 43 *Journal of Corporation Law* 217; Caleb Griffin, 'Environmental & Social Voting at Index Funds' (2020) 44 *The Delaware Journal of Corporate Law* 167.

[159] See 'Proxy Preview 2020' (19 March 2020); Hannah Orowitz and Brigid Rosati, 'An Early Look at the 2020 Proxy Season' Harvard Law School Forum on Corporate Governance (10 June 2020) https://corpgov.law.harvard.edu/2020/06/10/an-early-look-at-the-2020-proxy-season/#:~:text=With%20only%20one%20month%20remaining,impact%20on%20the%202020%20season accessed 15 July 2020.

[160] Ibid.

[161] Some governance proposals are actually tied to ESP issues, so this undercounts the prevalence of ESP proposals; see Orowitz and Rosati (n. 159).

[162] See Michael Garland, Jennifer Conovitz and Yumi Narita, 'NYC Comptroller's Boardroom Accountability 3.0 Results' Harvard Law School Forum on Corporate Governance (24 June 2020) https://corpgov.law.harvard.edu/2020/06/24/nyc-comptrollers-boardroom-accountability-3-0-results/ accessed 15 July 2020.

[163] See Paul Rissman and Andrew Behar, 'A Successful Season for SASB-Based Shareholder Resolutions' Harvard Law School Forum on Corporate Governance (12 June 2020) https://corpgov.law.harvard.edu/2020/06/12/a-successful-season-for-sasb-based-shareholder-resolutions/ accessed 15 July 2020. Activism is also going 'global'. See, e.g., Autorite des Marches Financiers (French Financial Market Authority), 'The AMF Proposes Several Targeted Measures Concerning Shareholder Activism' Press Release (28 April 2020); Marco Becht et al., 'Returns to Hedge Fund Activism: An International Study' (2017) 30 *Review of Financial Studies* 2933. A recent example is the success of Engine No. 1 in garnering three board seats at Exxon Mobil. See Matt Phillips, Exxon's Board Defeat Signals the Rise of Social-Good Activists, *New York Times*, 9 June 2021, available at: www.nytimes.com/2021/06/09/business/exxon-mobil-engine-no1-activist.html, accessed 17 July 2020.

[164] See, e.g., Michal Barzuza, Quinn Curtis and David H. Webber, 'Shareholder Value(s): Index Fund Activism and the New Millennial Corporate Governance' (2020) 93 *Southern California Law Review* 1243; Fink (n. 49).

The SEC has a somewhat chequered history concerning ESP proposals, starting with a case-by-case approach, moving to a general exclusion, and then shifting back to a case-by-case approach at the turn of the millennium.[165] Since then, the SEC has focused on whether an ESP proposal tends to 'micromanage' the firm, and if it does so then it will likely exclude it under Rule 14a-8.[166] In 2018, the SEC's Division of Corporate Finance issued an SEC Staff Legal Bulletin that, amongst other things, discussed micromanagement as a basis for exclusion.[167] The key considerations were whether the proposals tended to push specific timelines (e.g. comply by 2025) or methods of implementation (especially for complex matters). The SEC has also granted no-action letters in cases where firms seek to exclude proposals recommending compliance with parts of the Paris Climate Agreement on micromanagement grounds because the proposals appeared to push specific methods of implementation.[168] The focus on micromanagement continued in the 2019 proxy season. In 64 of the 105 ESP proposals challenged by firms, the issue of micromanagement was cited as the ground for exclusion.[169]

Another regulatory development occurred at the end of 2019 when the SEC proposed a series of changes to Rule 14a-8, which were then adopted in late 2020. The rules mandated significant changes, including, amongst others, (1) heightening the ownership requirements for a shareholder to utilize Rule 14a-8,[170] (2) increasing the threshold support requirements before a proposal can be resubmitted to shareholders if it fails to pass[171] and (3) adding a new provision permitting a firm to exclude a proposal if support for it has declined.[172] The last two changes are likely to affect ESP proposals, which usually fail their first few times (often with increasing support each time), but may then pass or lead to management compromising and making changes. Tightening the resubmission requirements makes this process more difficult to effectuate.[173] Unsurprisingly, the

165 See Allen, Kraakman and Khanna (n. 1); Harper Ho (n. 97).

166 Ibid.

167 See SEC Staff Legal Bulletin No 14J(CF) (23 October 2018) www.sec.gov/corpfin/staff-legal-bulletin-14j-shareholder-proposals accessed 15 July 2020.

168 See Richard Alsop and Yoon-Jee Kim, 'Shareholder Proposals 2019 – ESG No-Action Letter Trends and Strategies' Harvard Law School Forum on Corporate Governance (25 March 2020) https://corpgov.law.harvard.edu/2020/03/25/shareholder-proposals-2019-esg-no-action-letter-trends-and-strategies/ accessed 15 July 2020 (referring to no-action letter requests by, amongst others, ExxonMobil Corporation, The Goldman Sachs Group, Inc and Wells Fargo & Company). A proposal recommending that a firm issue a report describing whether and how it plans to align with the Paris Agreements survived an exclusion attempt perhaps because it did not recommend compliance with anything but seemed to request information (see the no-action letter request by Anadarko Petroleum).

169 Ibid. The SEC has recently issued another Staff Legal Bulletin that appears to signal a relaxing of the micromanagement standard for exclusion (i.e., making it less likely that micromanagement would be used so often as a reason to exclude). See SEC Staff Legal Bulletin No 14L(CF) (03 November 2021).

170 A shareholder would need to show that she had continuously held either '$2,000 of the company's securities entitled to vote on the proposal for at least three years' or '$15,000 of the company's securities entitled to vote on the proposal for at least two years' or '$25,000 of the company's securities entitled to vote on the proposal for at least one year'. See Procedural Requirements and Resubmission Thresholds under Exchange Act Rule 14a-8: SEC, Proposed Rule (5 November 2019). This would change the existing rule, which is continuously holding $2,000 of firm securities for at least one year.

171 See ibid., which changes the thresholds for resubmission from 3 per cent (for the first time a proposal is voted on), 6 per cent (for the second time) and 10 per cent (for the third time) to 5 per cent, 15 per cent and 25 per cent, respectively.

172 See ibid.

173 See, e.g., Ernie Barkett, 'Estimating the Impact, Council of Institutional Investors' (April 2020) www.cii.org/files/publications/misc/CII_14a-8_Issue_Brief%20_April_2020_FINAL.pdf accessed 15 July 2020; Mark Tulay, 'SEC Rule Change Will Hobble Investors' *Barron's* (24 April 2020) www.barrons.com/articles/sec-rule-changes-will-hobble-esg-investors-51587739256#:~:text=The%20proposed%20SEC%20rule%20changes,five%20years%20would%20be%20excluded accessed 15 July 2020 (noting that according to the Sustainable Investments Institute, the proposed rule would have led to the exclusion of about 30% of environmental and social proposals that went to a vote between 2010 and 2019).

new rules have generated heated debate and the SEC recently announced it would revisit them.[174] A wait and see attitude may thus be necessary.[175]

12.5 CONCLUDING REMARKS

Shareholder voting and engagement in the USA have undergone substantial changes over the last fifty years. They have moved from being relatively sleepy issues to issues that trigger insomnia in even the most hardened executives. The changes in the ownership structure of publicly traded firms in the USA have probably been the most important reason for the shift, but so too have been the rule changes that have facilitated greater shareholder activism among other things. This chapter explores these developments while also describing the rules of the road for shareholder voting in the USA by focusing on Delaware jurisprudence and changes in US federal securities regulations. It also examines recent developments in shareholder activism and engagement, potential areas of shareholder voting and engagement going forward, and recent legal changes that attempt to rein in activism to some extent. There are many moving parts in the shareholder voting apparatus in the USA, and where things settle will be a contested and likely uncertain matter. Perhaps the wisest counsel is to stay tuned.

174 See, e.g., Council of Institutional Investors, Comment Letter (30 January 2020) www.cii.org/files/issues_and_advocacy/correspondence/2020/20200130%20PAF%20comment%20letter%20FINAL.pdf accessed 15 July 2020; Business Roundtable Public Comments to SEC on Procedural Requirements and Resubmission Thresholds under Exchange Act Rule 14a-8 (3 February 2020) www.businessroundtable.org/business-roundtable-public-comments-to-sec-on-procedural-requirements-and-resubmission-thresholds-under-exchange-act-rule-14a-8 accessed 15 July 2020; SEC Commissioner Robert J. Jackson, Jr, 'Statement on Proposals to Restrict Shareholder Voting, U.S. Securities and Exchange Commission' (5 November 2019) www.sec.gov/news/public-statement/statement-jackson-2019-11-05-open-meeting accessed 15 July 2020. For the SEC's most recent steps see Breheny, Fox and Kim (n. 86).

175 At around the same time, the US Department of Labor proposed new rules that would appear to make it more difficult for retirement plans (a large source of institutional funds in the US stock market) to make investments on ESG considerations. See Proposed Rule by Employee Benefits Security Administration, Financial Factors in Selecting Plan Investments (30 June 2020) www.federalregister.gov/documents/2020/06/30/2020-13705/financial-factors-in-selecting-plan-investments accessed 15 July 2020. Although not directly related to ESP proposals, the proposed rules suggest a tightening attitude towards these factors. Specifically, the proposed rules prohibit a retirement plan from investing based on ESG factors unless the factor concerned independently influences economic interests or serves as a tiebreaker in the rare situation where the plan is considering two economically equivalent investments. Moreover, the plan would be required to document its reasons and justifications for taking the ESG factor into account. It also prohibits 401(k) retirement plans from providing an investment alternative with an ESG component, which would naturally restrict the availability of ESG options in these plans. Unsurprisingly, the proposal has generated quite a lot of heated debate. See, e.g., Robert G. Monks and Nell Minow, 'Comment Letter on DOL Proposed Rule on ESG Investments' Harvard Law School Forum on Corporate Governance (25 July 2020) https://corpgov.law.harvard.edu/2020/07/25/comment-letter-on-dol-proposed-rule-on-esg-investments/ accessed 30 July 2020.

PART III

Europe

13

Shareholder Democracy in Denmark: Contrasting Law on the Books and Law in Practice

Hanne S. Birkmose and Karsten Engsig Sørensen

13.1 INTRODUCTION

13.1.1 *Danish Company Law and the Governance Framework*

The main source for corporate statutory law in Denmark is the Companies Act (CA) (*selskabsloven*).[1] The CA regulates both public (*aktieselskaber*) and private (*anpartsselskaber*) limited companies. In 2018, 112,556 private limited companies were registered with the Danish Business Authority, whilst the equivalent number for public limited companies was 28,355. At the end of 2019, 132 companies were listed on the Copenhagen Stock Exchange, 126 of which were registered as Danish public limited companies.[2] In June 2019, the amended Shareholder Rights Directive (SRD II) was implemented in Danish law,[3] although a number of its provisions did not come into force until later[4] to give the parties affected more time to adjust to the new legal framework. The provisions in SRD II have been implemented as amendments to several existing acts. For instance, the provisions on the transparency of institutional investors and asset managers can be found in a number of different acts,[5] including the CA, the Financial Business Act and the Managers of Alternative Investment Funds Act,[6] whilst those on remuneration are only in the CA.

In addition to statutory law, the Danish corporate governance framework is set by the Danish Committee on Corporate Governance,[7] which has adopted a set of Recommendations on

[1] Lov 2009–06-12 nr 470 om aktie- og anpartsselskaber (selskabsloven) (Act no. 470 2009 on Public and Private Limited Companies (the Companies Act or CA)). For an English translation, see https://danishbusinessauthority.dk/sites/default/files/danish_companies_act.pdf accessed 26 June 2021 (please note that the translated version is not updated with the latest amendments).

[2] Data from Statistics Denmark www.statistikbanken.dk/statbank5a/default.asp?w=1536 and Nasdaq OMX Nordic www.nasdaqomxnordic.com/news/statistics accessed 26 June 2021.

[3] Act no. 369 of 9 April 2019.

[4] Including the provisions on the transparency of institutional investors and asset managers and those on remuneration. The former came into force for financial years beginning 1 January 2020. Consequently, the first reporting began in 2021. Compliance with the remuneration provisions applies to ordinary general meetings (as annual general meetings (AGM) are known in Denmark) called in the financial year commencing on 10 June 2019 and thereafter. Most AGMs are held in March and April, and hence for most companies the provisions have been in force for general meetings called since spring 2020. The provisions on the identification of shareholders and transmission of information did not come into force until 3 September 2020.

[5] SRD II, ch 1b also includes provisions on the transparency of proxy advisors, although these provisions are not considered in this chapter.

[6] Consolidating Act no. 763 of 23 July 2019 (originally Act no. 470 of 12 June 2009), Consolidating Act no. 937 of 6 September 2019 (originally Act no. 501 of 7 June 2001) and Consolidating Act no. 1047 of 14 October 2019 (originally Act no. 598 of 12 June 2013).

[7] The Committee serves as an independent body under the Danish Business Authority. Its members, who represent the business community are all appointed by the Danish Minister of Business based on nominations by the Committee. See the Committee's articles of association (AoA) published on the Committee's website https://corporategovernance

Corporate Governance.[8] The Recommendations are considered best practice guidelines for the management of listed companies, and their purpose is to ensure transparency to give investors and other stakeholders an opportunity to assess company performance.[9] Although the Recommendations are only recommendations, they are anchored in the Danish Financial Statements Act, which requires listed companies to submit a statement indicating which corporate governance code they apply and the extent to which they comply with it (the 'comply or explain' principle).[10] The Committee amended the Recommendations in 2020. This update was needed primarily because of the transposition of SRD II into Danish law and its influence on the overall corporate governance framework.[11]

The Recommendations on Corporate Governance are supplemented by a Stewardship Code aimed at increasing the transparency of how institutional investors choose to exercise stewardship activities and ultimately at promoting listed companies' long-term value creation.[12] The Stewardship Code is also applied on a 'comply or explain' basis, but contrary to the Recommendations, their application is purely voluntary.[13] Due to the adoption of SRD II in Danish law, the Committee on Corporate Governance agreed with the Minister for Industry, Business and Financial Affairs in January 2020 that the Stewardship Code would be phased out in 2020. However, at the time of writing the Committee has still not issued any statement withdrawing the Code, why the formal status of the Code is uncertain.

13.1.2 *The Organization of Management in Danish Companies*

Since the reformed CA entered into force in 2009, Danish limited companies have had a choice between different board models.[14] The traditional model, which is predominant in the Nordic countries, is for companies to have a board of directors and an executive board.[15] Even though the model has two tiers and the board of directors appoints the executive board, it does not resemble most other two-tier models in Europe[16] because the board of directors also has management duties. The board of directors in a public limited company is not strictly separated from executive management, as executive officers may also be members of the board of directors.

.dk/sites/default/files/vedtaegter_for_komitten_for_god_selskabsledelse_-_januar_2017.pdf accessed 26 June 2021 (in Danish only).

8 Committee on Corporate Governance, 'Recommendations on Corporate Governance' https://corporategovernance.dk/sites/default/files/media/anbefalinger_for_god_selskabsledelse_engelsk.pdf accessed 24 June 2021.

9 Ibid., 3.

10 Danish Financial Statements Act, s. 107b.

11 See Hanne S. Birkmose and Marina B. Madsen, 'The Danish Stewardship Code – The Past, the Present and the Future' in Dionysia Katelouzou and Dan W. Puchniak (eds.), *Global Shareholder Stewardship* (Cambridge University Press 2022); Nordic & European Company Law Working Paper No 20-01 https://papers.ssrn.com/sol3/papers.cfm?abstract_id=3533834 accessed 24 June 2021.

12 Stewardship Code 2016, 3.

13 However, the Danish Committee on Corporate Governance has published a list of signatories (*positivliste*), which is a list of institutional investors who have declared to the Committee that they intend to respond to the Danish Code; see Committee on Corporate Governance, 'List of Signatories', https://corporategovernance.dk/sites/default/files/191007_positivliste_aktivt_ejerskab_071019f25667161156671152.pdf accessed 26 June 2021. As of 7 October 2019, thirty-five Danish institutional investors had signed up for the Danish Code.

14 CA § 111.

15 See Jesper Lau Hansen, *Nordic Company Law* (DJØF Forlag 2003) 109 ff.; Paul Krüger Andersen and Evelyne J. B. Sørensen, *The Danish Companies Act* (DJØF Publishing 2012) 127 ff.; Per Lekvall (ed.), *The Nordic Governance Model* (SNS Förlag 2014) 52 ff.

16 Lekvall (n. 15) 59 ff. However, a somewhat similar structure can be found outside Europe, e.g. in Japan. See Hideki Kanda, 'Western versus Asian Laws on Corporate Governance' in Jeffrey N. Gordon and Wolf-Georg Ringe (eds.), *The Oxford Handbook of Corporate Law and Governance* (Oxford University Press 2018).

However, the majority of board members must not be executive officers of the company, and the chair of a public limited company has to be a non-executive officer.[17] The other two options established by the 2009 CA were a two-tier model with a supervisory board and an executive management board, which is modelled on the German two-tier structure, and a one-tier model with a board of directors modelled on the UK's one-tier structure. The latter, however, is available only to private limited companies. Despite the CA's flexibility regarding the choice of board model, the prevailing model is still the Nordic two-tier model,[18] and the following discussion assumes its application.

In the Nordic two-tier model, the divide between the duties of the board of directors and those of executive management is not clear-cut. The board is responsible for overall and strategic management and for ensuring the proper organization of the company's activities.[19] The executive board is in charge of day-to-day management and, in general, must follow the guidelines and directions issued by the board of directors.[20] As the board of directors is superior to the executive board, it can delegate more or less power to the executive management, and in any case is responsible for the supervision of management.[21]

Even though it is clear that the board of directors and the executive board play the key role in the management of a company, it is widely acknowledged that shareholders at a general meeting may give the board binding instructions, and therefore in principle are the superior management organ of the company.[22] It is usually held that the general meeting is omnipotent and can decide on any matter concerning the company where power is not granted to either the board of directors or executive management by law.

13.1.3 *Shareholder Decision-Making Rights*

The potential effect of shareholder engagement in Denmark is significant. In addition to the appointment and removal of members of the board of directors,[23] shareholders have exclusive rights to decide on a number of other issues, as seen above. Thus, Danish shareholder democracy grants shareholders extensive powers that enable them not only to monitor and control corporate governance arrangements, but also to shape the rules of corporate governance. However, as Section 13.3 will show, this potential effect does not seem to be transformed into actual power at the general meeting in practice.

The general meeting has a number of formal decision-making rights, such as the approval of changes to the company's articles of association (AoA), including decisions related to share capital,[24] mergers, divisions or the winding up of the company.[25] The general meeting is also

[17] CA § 111 (1)(1). Furthermore, for listed companies, the chair of the board of directors or supervisory board must not perform any duties for a limited company that are unrelated to his or her duties as chair; cf. CA § 114.

[18] As of January 2018, only twenty-one public limited companies (listed and non-listed) had applied the new supervisory board structure; see Lars Bunch and Søren Corfixsen Whitt, *Selskabsloven med kommentarer* (3rd ed., Karnov Group 2018) 503.

[19] CA § 115. See also Andersen and Sørensen (n. 15) 131 ff.; Hansen (n. 15) 150 ff.

[20] CA § 117. See also Andersen and Sørensen (n. 15) 136 ff.; Hansen (n. 15) 162 ff.

[21] CA § 115.

[22] See Hanne S. Birkmose and Therese Strand, 'Institutional Investors: Active Ownership through Nomination Committees' in Stephen Gates and Suzanne Young (eds.), *Institutional Investors' Power to Change Corporate Behavior: International Perspectives* (Emerald Group Publishing 2011) 206; Hansen (n. 15) 81 ff; Andersen and Sørensen (n. 15) 162.

[23] The general meeting may remove the board at any time and without reason; see CA §§ 120 and 121.

[24] Such as capital increases (CA § 154), decreases (CA § 186), acquisitions of own shares (CA § 198), financial assistance using the limited company's own funds (CA §§ 207 and 210 (2)) and dividends (CA §§ 180 and 182).

[25] CA §§ 217, 245 and 263.

tasked with electing the majority of the board of directors and the external auditor.[26] The AoA may provide public authorities or other parties with the right to appoint one or more members of the board of directors or the supervisory board.[27] The CA requires that the annual general meeting (AGM) approves annual reports and the appropriation of profit or loss recorded in the adopted annual report.[28] In addition, there is a range of resolutions that requires the acceptance of the general meeting according to the CA or a company's AoA.

Traditionally, board remuneration has been approved as an integrated part of the annual report,[29] although this is changing under SRD II. Starting with the first ordinary general meeting called in the financial year commencing on 10 June 2019 and thereafter, the boards of directors of listed companies have to develop a remuneration policy that must be approved by the AGM.[30] Any significant changes to that policy also have to be approved, and the policy must in any case be submitted to a new vote at the AGM every four years. The vote is binding, and the CA sets out a procedure for situations in which a suggested policy or substantial change does not gain approval at an AGM. Companies that have adopted a remuneration policy also have to submit an annual remuneration report for a vote at the AGM, although the vote is only advisory.[31] In the event that an AGM rejects a remuneration report, the company has to explain in the report submitted the following year what considerations have been made as a result of the previous year's vote. Furthermore, following the transposition of SRD II, listed companies have to disclose information on transactions with related parties, although the CA does not give shareholders a say on the approval of such transactions.[32]

The general meeting is often regarded as a closed forum wherein shareholders can discuss the affairs of the company.[33] However, the board of directors has to be present in order to answer shareholders' questions,[34] and the external auditor must also be present in listed companies.[35] Apart from these two stipulations, only shareholders may participate, and it is therefore necessary to determine the identity of shareholders at the time of the general meeting to establish who is entitled to exercise rights related to the general meeting.

For listed companies, article 7(2) of the Shareholder Rights Directive[36] stipulates that EU member states must provide shareholders with the right to participate in general meetings and to vote in respect of his or her shares, as determined according to the record date. In Denmark, the record date is one week prior to the general meeting.[37] Consequently, even though shares are freely transferable in the period surrounding the general meeting, it is the person registered on the record date who can exercise the rights attached to the shares even if those shares were sold after the record date but before the general meeting.

26 CA §§ 120 and 144.

27 There are no restrictions as to who may be granted this right, cf. CA §120 (2). According to the practice of the Business Authority, it may not be the company itself though.

28 CA § 88.

29 However, in listed companies it is has become normal to approve board salaries as a separate item on the agenda of the general meeting; see Section 13.3.1.2 of this chapter.

30 CA § 139.

31 CA § 139 b(4).

32 CA § 139 d.

33 CA § 78. The board of directors may decide that the general meeting is open to parties other than shareholders unless the AoA stipulate otherwise; cf. CA § 76 (4).

34 CA § 102. In practice, the general meeting is always opened by the board chair, who offers an account of the company's state of affairs.

35 CA § 103(4).

36 Directive 2007/36/EC on the exercise of certain rights of shareholders in listed companies. The directive was transposed into Danish law by Act no. 470 of 12 June 2009.

37 CA § 84.

Shareholders registered on the record date do not necessarily attend the general meeting. The record of shareholders is only a snapshot of the composition of shareholders on a specific date based on the entries in the share register. Therefore, a company's AoA may prescribe that in order to participate in a general meeting, a shareholder must register with the company no later than a specific date stated in the AoA. That date must not be earlier than three days prior to the meeting[38] to allow the company to know who will participate.

In general, the CA allows shareholders who are unable to attend a general meeting to exercise their rights through a proxy appointed by the shareholder concerned.[39] The proxy holder has to hold a written proxy, which is dated and signed by the shareholder.[40] A proxy can be indefinite, although the shareholder must be able to recall it at any time.[41] Proxies can be blank – that is, without any voting instructions – leaving the decision on how to vote to the proxy holder. Listed companies must make a proxy form available to all shareholders.[42] As the CA includes no special rules on proxies given to directors, it allows the board of directors to solicit proxies by naming a member of the board or the managing director as a proxy holder. This is a widely accepted practice, and the board often holds a majority of votes at the general meeting, rendering ballots unnecessary.[43]

Institutional investors often hold shares through nominee accounts. Consequently, it is the nominee who is registered by name in the share register of the company. However, current Danish practice assumes that the registration of a named nominee does not suffice in terms of the nominee being entitled to exercise the rights attached to shares with the exception of economic rights.[44] Thus, a nominee is not able to vote at general meetings unless the de facto shareholder has given notice of his or her acquisition of the shares to the company and established a good title to them and has provided the nominee with a valid proxy. This practice often results in a large number of voting instructions being dismissed for non-compliance.[45] Various solutions have been suggested,[46] but thus far Danish legislators have taken no steps to change the existing rules on proxies. However, whilst the implementation of SRD II will not address this shortcoming in the Danish governance framework, it may still improve de facto shareholders' position, as amendments to the CA will increase the possibility of listed companies communicating directly with de facto shareholders.[47]

Traditionally, a general meeting is held at a limited company's head office or at a location specified by its AoA, although it may also be held electronically in part or in full. This possibility dates back to 2003,[48] but prior to 2020 no Danish listed company to date has opted for a full

38 CA § 84(1).

39 It should be mentioned that since 2010, it has also been possible to vote by post. CA § 104(2) implements the Shareholder Rights Directive, art. 12. This option seems to play a very small role in Denmark.

40 CA § 80.

41 CA § 80(2).

42 CA § 80(5), implementing art. 17(2) of the transparency directive (Directive 2004/109/EC).

43 See VP Securities, 'AGM Analysis 2018' (June 2018). The report is no longer available at www.vp.dk, but is on file with the authors. A short resume of the report is available at www.vp.dk/News-and-Insights/News-List/2018/6/VP-Annual-General-Meeting-Analysis-Active-ownership-and-digitisation-set-the-scene, last accessed 29 June 2021.

44 Bunch and Corfixsen Whitt (n. 18) § 52.

45 See VP Securities, 'Memorandum: The Possibility of Simplifying the Proxy Voting Process in Denmark' 2 www.vp.dk/News-and-Insights/News-List/2018/2/Memorandum-The-possibility-of-simplifying-the-proxy-voting-process-in-Denmark.

46 See, for instance, the solution suggested by VP Securities (n. 45).

47 It has been suggested that the new obligation to give shareholders feedback that was introduced as a consequence of the revised Shareholder Rights Directive will make foreign investors more aware of the problem and may trigger the more careful collection of powers of attorney; see Søren W. Langer, 'Selskaber skal åbne for flere aktionærfuldmagter' (2020) Økonomisk Ugebrev Ledelse 3–4.

48 Act no. 303 of 30 April 2003 (om ændring af lov om aktieselskaber og lov om anpartsselskaber).

electronic general meeting.[49] A number of companies live stream their general meeting, but that does not qualify as an electronic meeting as it does not allow shareholders to exercise their rights at the meeting, for example vote on their shares. The extent of the practice of live streaming has not been documented. From a shareholder engagement perspective, the possibility of holding an electronic general meeting is important, as doing so could increase the number of attending shareholders.[50] If a general meeting is to take place electronically, the underlying system has to be set up in a manner that satisfies the CA's requirements for holding general meetings, which include securing shareholders' rights to attend, speak and vote at the general meeting. Moreover, the system must be able to reliably determine which shareholders attend the general meeting, as well as the capital and voting rights they represent, and the voting outcome (CA section 77(4)). Although we are still waiting for a breakthrough in electronic general meetings, digitalization has made its way into Danish general meetings in other ways. A growing number of companies are making use of electronic broadcasting, and the 2003 amendment to the former CA also made it possible to communicate electronically with shareholders. A resolution on electronic means of communication must be passed by the general meeting to enable the company and its shareholders to exchange documents electronically and communicate by email instead of sending and submitting documents in hard copy form.[51] The resolution must specify which notices and other documents are covered by the resolution, as well as how electronic modes of communication must or can be used. It seems that some companies do now allow electronic voting before the AGM.[52] The digital transformation has also affected the voting process in other ways, with some companies making use of electronic voting at their AGMs.[53]

13.1.4 *Ownership Structure*

In general, Nordic markets are characterized by a high degree of ownership concentration, and Denmark is no exception. In 2014, 57 per cent of all companies listed on the Nasdaq OMX Copenhagen had at least one shareholder controlling more than 20 per cent of capital, and 28 per cent had at least one shareholder controlling more than 50 per cent of capital.[54] By the end of 2019, these percentages had changed slightly to 60 per cent (for a +20 per cent threshold) and 24 per cent (for a +50 per cent threshold).[55]

It is very difficult to find data on the composition of shareholders in Danish listed companies. Companies are required to disclose information only on shareholders holding more than 5 per cent of either the share capital or votes.[56] However, as in many other European countries,

49 However, a mutual fund held a full electronic meeting in 2018. See VP Securities (n. 43). Amongst the AGM notices we have examined, we found no companies that have held a partly electronic AGM.

50 However, one of the arguments for not opting for a full electronic general meeting is that it may not suit retail investors. See VP Securities (n. 43).

51 CA § 92.

52 See, e.g., Schouw & Co A/S, a large cap company www.globenewswire.com/news-release/2020/03/16/2000841/0/en/Notice-of-the-Annual-General-Meeting-of-Aktieselskabet-Schouw-Co.html accessed 26 June 2021.

53 According to information kindly provided by VP Securities A/S and Computershare A/S, which to our knowledge are the only suppliers of electronic voting systems in Denmark, only seven large cap companies make use of electronic voting at their AGMs.

54 Lekvall (n. 15) 48 ff. The +20 per cent cut-off level was chosen for this study to make it comparable to earlier studies of the same kind; see Lekvall, 281. The threshold carries no legal importance but may have some practical significance.

55 Our own data collected from the Orbis database. In comparison, in 2013, 57 per cent of all companies listed on the Nasdaq OMX Copenhagen had at least one shareholder controlling more than 20 per cent of the company's votes, and 28 per cent had at least one shareholder controlling more than 50 per cent of the company's votes; see Lekvall (n. 15) 283.

56 CA § 55.

the observed trend is for retail investors to hold a declining number of shares, with foreign investors increasing their share of listed shares.[57] In recent years, foreign institutional investors in particular have increased their ownership. In 2018, foreign investors, presumably mainly institutional investors, held 54 per cent of the total capital listed.[58] Despite the internationalization and institutionalization of the capital market, majority shareholders are not found amongst institutional investors. Industrial foundations play an important role as majority owners in a number of the largest listed companies in Denmark, including A.P. Møller Mærsk, Carlsberg and Novozymes.[59] These companies often make use of a dual share class structure, where the shares with the strongest voting power are held by the foundation concerned and that share class is often not listed.[60] The importance of ownership by industrial foundations is reflected in the fact that, in 2011, some 68 per cent of the total market capitalization of the Nasdaq OMX Copenhagen was held by such foundations. From 1980 until 2011, the number of listed companies owned by industrial foundations held steady at around sixteen to twenty companies.[61] Today, the number of listed companies with an industrial foundation amongst their majority shareholders falls within the same range.[62] It should be noted, however, that ownership structures vary greatly amongst companies.[63]

13.2 LEGAL MEANS OF SHAREHOLDER ENGAGEMENT

13.2.1 *Shareholders' Right to Call a Meeting*

The general meeting is always called by the board of directors,[64] but shareholders have a right to have a meeting called.[65] In a private limited company, any shareholder may request that a general meeting be called, whilst in a public limited company, the right applies to shareholders who represent at least 5 per cent of capital,[66] although the company's AoA may extend the right to minorities with less than 5 per cent. Whenever a shareholder or group of shareholders requests that a general meeting be called, it is a requirement that it be called for 'the transaction of specific business'. Thus, whilst shareholders may request that a general meeting be called for any reason, the request must specify the topic to be discussed at the meeting. General meetings can be called as often as needed, but must be held at least annually. The AGM (termed the 'ordinary meeting' in Denmark, as opposed to 'extraordinary meetings', which refers to all other meetings) must take place in connection with the approval of the company's annual financial reports.

57 The percentage of share capital held by foreign investors more than doubled from 2006 to 2016. See Klaus Søgaard, Michael Brichmann and Louise Celia Korpela Martiny, *Generalforsamlinger i børsnoterede selskaber – Udvalgte emner og problemstillinger (del 2)* (Revision & Regnskabsvæsen 2017) 15 f. See also Jesper Lau Hansen and Carsten Lønfeldt, 'Corporate Governance in Denmark' in Per Lekvall (ed.), *The Nordic Corporate Governance Model* (SNS Förlag 2014) 117 ff.

58 See VP Securities (n. 43) 7. Regarding 2019, data from the Danish National Bank show that of the twenty-five largest listed companies (the so-called C25 index) were owned by foreign investors in November 2019; see www.nationalbanken.dk/da/statistik/find_statistik/Documents/V%C3%A6rdipapirstatistik/V%C3%A6rdipapirer%2020200107.pdf accessed 26 June 2021. The largest percentage of foreign ownership is found in large cap companies. See Søgaard, Brichmann and Korpela Martiny (n. 57) 15 ff.

59 Steen Thomsen, *The Danish Industrial Foundations* (DJØF Publishing 2017) 13.

60 Ibid., 19.

61 Ibid., 112 ff.

62 Our own data collected from the Orbis database.

63 See Søgaard, Brichmann and Korpela Martiny (n. 57) 15 ff.

64 CA § 93(1).

65 In addition, companies' accountant may also call a meeting; see CA § 89(1).

66 CA § 89.

At the AGM, shareholders must also pass a resolution on the appropriation of profit or loss recorded in the approved annual report, and on any other business to be transacted by the general meeting under the company's AoA.[67] As a rule, notice of general meetings must be given in accordance with the provisions of the AoA. In addition, such notice by a listed company must always be published on the company's website.

13.2.2 *Shareholder Proposal Right*

Shareholders are not only afforded the right to have a general meeting called to discuss specific issues; they also have a right to have proposals included on the agenda of both the AGM and extraordinary meetings.[68] This right applies to all shareholders, regardless of the size of their shareholding or the period for which they have held their shares. Such a proposal must be submitted to the company in writing, and, in public companies, it must be received by the company at least six weeks before the meeting is held. However, if a company receives a shareholder proposal after the deadline, it must be added to the meeting agenda if the board decides that the request has been made with sufficient time for the issues concerned to be put on the agenda. If the formal requirements are fulfilled, the board of directors, as a rule, must include the proposal on the agenda. The proposal right includes the right for a shareholder to propose the scrutiny of certain aspects of the company's activities by an independent expert. Such a proposal has to be adopted by a simple majority of votes.[69] This right seems hardly ever to be applied in practice though.

13.2.3 *Voting*

The CA does not require a certain quorum of shareholders to be present at the general meeting for it to be qualified to transact business. However, a company's AoA may include quorum requirements. Some companies' AoA also require certain types of resolutions to be approved by two subsequent general meetings if the specified majority is not present at the first meeting.[70] Most often, such a requirement applies only to proposals to amend the AoA. The aim is to ensure that a sufficient number of shareholders support the proposal.

Unless otherwise provided by the CA or the company's AoA, all business transacted at general meetings must be decided by a simple majority of votes.[71] However, any proposed resolution to amend the AoA must be passed by at least two-thirds of the votes cast, as well as by at least two-thirds of the share capital represented at the general meeting.[72] This requirement is strengthened

67 CA § 88(1).

68 CA § 90.

69 CA § 150(1). However, if the proposal is not adopted, but shareholders representing 25 per cent of share capital vote in favour of it, any shareholder may, no later than four weeks after the general meeting, request that scrutinizers be appointed by the bankruptcy court with jurisdiction over the place where the company's registered office is situated; see CA § 150(2).

70 This is the case, for instance, with the AoA of several companies, including Jyske Bank, art. 12 https://investor.jyskebank.com/wps/wcm/connect/jbc/ef6138fb-3cf7-41da-9d2b-ec96a02fb296/Articles+of+Association.pdf?MOD=AJPERES&CACHEID=ef6138fb-3cf7-41da-9d2b-ec96a02fb296 accessed 26 June 2021; Sydbank, art. 10 www.sydbank.com/wps/wcm/connect/sydbankcom/616c4ed3-c486-477d-8a41-f6e1ffb5735b/articles_of_association.pdf?MOD=AJPERES&CVID=mGrTonH accessed 26 June 2021; and Novo Nordisk, art. 9.3 www.novonordisk.com/content/dam/nncorp/global/en/about-us/pdfs/corporate-governance/articles-of-association-2021.pdf accessed 26 June 2021.

71 CA § 105.

72 CA § 106.

where a resolution to amend the AoA would increase shareholder obligations to the company. Such resolutions require the unanimous agreement of all shareholders.[73] Finally, the CA sets out a limited number of resolutions where proposed resolutions to amend the AoA must be passed by at least nine-tenths of the votes cast, as well as by at least nine-tenths of the share capital represented at the general meeting.[74]

The double-majority requirement is important for minority protection, particularly when a company has different share classes that grant shareholders different voting rights. As a general rule, all shares carry voting rights. However, the AoA may provide that certain shares carry no voting rights or that the voting power of certain shares differs from that of other shares.[75] Approximately 20 per cent of listed companies in Denmark have dual class shares,[76] but none of them has share classes that carry no votes. However, if a company does have non-voting shares, those shares carry only a right of representation if the AoA provide for it. The AoA must always specify the different characteristics and size of each share class. Finally, the AoA may also restrict shareholders' exercise of voting rights to a specific portion of votes (voting ceiling) or voting share capital (voting cap).[77]

As mentioned above, a company's AoA may require a higher quorum or higher majority than that required by the CA. Where AoA stipulate a quorum or higher majority requirement, it is not unusual for them to allow a decision to be adopted with a lower quorum or majority if the matter is referred to a general meeting a second time.[78]

13.2.4 *Questions and Information Request Rights*

According to § 102 of the CA, all shareholders have the right to ask questions at the general meeting to be answered by the board of directors. In listed companies, shareholders may ask questions in writing in the three-month period leading to the general meeting. Whilst all questions asked at a general meeting should be answered at the general meeting as far as possible, written questions submitted to listed companies in the designated period should be answered in writing, and both questions and answers should be presented to all shareholders at the general meeting. It is not always possible to answer questions asked at the general meeting owing to a lack of information, and, in that case, the board may answer them in writing within two weeks of the meeting being held. The answers should be made available to all shareholders.

All questions relating to the position of the company or any other companies that are part of the same group must be answered. However, an exception is made if answering a question would cause 'significant detriment' to the company, normally because doing so would affect the company's ability to compete.

73 CA § 107(1).

74 CA § 107(2). These resolutions include resolutions that weaken shareholder rights, such as shareholders' rights to receive dividends or the distribution of the company's assets, and resolutions that restrict the transferability of shares or increase existing restrictions.

75 CA § 46.

76 Our own data collected from companies' AoA. The number is slightly higher for small cap companies than for large cap and mid cap companies.

77 CA § 107(2)(4). Very few companies have a voting cap. Those that do are primarily banks (hand-collected data based on AoA).

78 CA § 105.

13.3 SHAREHOLDER ENGAGEMENT AND VOTING IN PRACTICE

13.3.1 *Voting in Practice*

13.3.1.1 Who Votes and How?

To cast votes at a general meeting, it is necessary to register before the meeting (see Section 13.1.3). A registration can be requested either electronically via a company's investor portal or by writing to the company. Most registrations take place electronically,[79] and it is common for electronic admission cards to be issued.[80]

In recent years, the amount of registered capital has been around 50 per cent of total capital.[81] Based on our examination of listed companies,[82] the number of registered votes represented varies. Listed companies are not required to publish such data,[83] but data from companies that do so give us an indication of attendance. Looking only at large cap companies, 53 per cent published data on the votes represented at general meetings in the period we examined, which corresponds to nineteen companies.[84] Figure 13.1 shows that the represented votes in most of the nineteen companies fell between 40 and 69 per cent (four companies in each range), with four companies having a very high percentage of votes represented (80–89 per cent), and, in one company, 99 per cent of the votes were represented.

On average, 62.9 per cent of the votes were represented at the AGMs of the large cap companies that published data on shareholder representation. The number of shares represented at AGMs has increased in recent years.[85] If we compare these companies with the mid cap and small cap companies that published data on representation, we see that the average was lower for the latter (55.3 and 55.1 per cent, respectively). The relative number of companies that published data in these two groups was smaller though, and the uncertainty of the result is therefore greater.

Looking at the data on extraordinary general meetings, the small number of such meetings held, and our limited access to data, makes the results even more uncertain. However, bearing that in mind, it seems that the percentage of represented votes was smaller than that at AGMs. Of

79 According to VP Securities, three out of four shareholders in the 66 companies examined register electronically. See VP Securities (n. 43) 4. VP Securities is one of two major issuer service companies on the Danish market. The other is Computershare.

80 Whilst electronic admission cards seem to be a success, it has been suggested that electronic registration has resulted in a decrease in the number of registrations. See VP Securities (n. 43).

81 See the figures presented in VP Securities (n. 43) and for the AGM held in 2019 VP Securities concluded that based on the sixty-six companies analyzed, an average of 54 per cent of the capital was registered, see the post 'The 2019 AGM Season' available at www.vp.dk/News-and-Insights/News-List/2019/6/The-2019-AGM-season_overall-trends, accessed 25 June 2021.

82 We have examined all 126 listed companies registered as Danish companies by examining the AGMs they held in the period from 26 May 2018 to 25 May 2019.

83 In Denmark, not all of the details on the votes taking place at general meetings are made public. However, the voting results are always published, and so should usually details including the number of votes exercised, the number of votes for and against the proposal concerned, and so on. See also art. 14 of the Shareholder Right Directive 2007/36/EC. Making use of the exception in CA § 101(6) implementing art. 14(1), second sentence, of the Directive, companies may, however, choose not to publish the details (but only the result of the vote) if no shareholder demands that they do so. According to the Danish Business Authority, shareholders should request the details at the meeting, as afterwards it will be too late. See Bunch and Corfixsen Whitt (n. 18) 455.

84 Based on hand-collected data from the thirty-six listed companies in the large cap segment that held their AGMs in the period from 26 May 2018 to 25 May 2019 and were registered as Danish companies.

85 A survey by Georgeson shows that the level increased from 53.8 per cent in 2015 to 67 per cent in 2019 for large cap companies. See Georgeson, '2019 Proxy Season Review Denmark'. On file with the authors. Owing to the use of share classes and shares with multiple voting rights, the represented capital may differ from the represented votes.

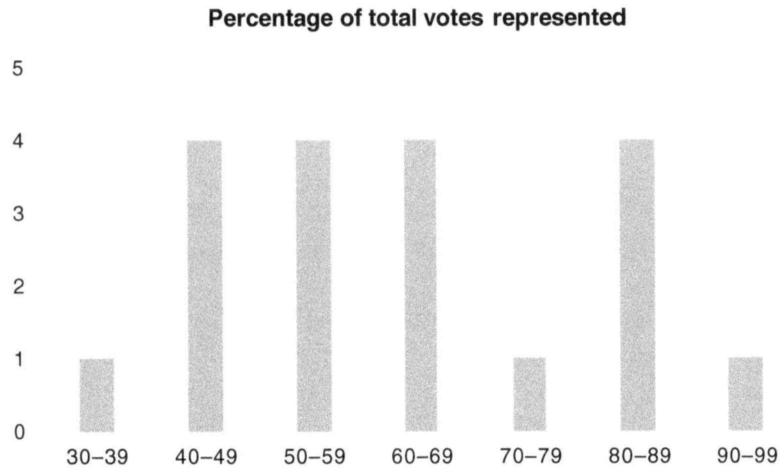

FIGURE 13.1 Votes represented at general meetings in large cap companies

the eight extraordinary general meetings held in large cap companies during the period examined,[86] data were published for only five, and three of the five were in the same company. The average votes represented was 51.7 per cent.

The minutes of general meetings do not report the identities of the shareholders represented at the meetings. We know that, on average, the majority of the capital in Danish listed companies is owned by foreign investors (see Section 1.4), but it seems that foreign investors are less likely than Danish investors to register. Surveys indicate that foreign investors represent around 40 per cent of represented capital.[87] In some companies, however, foreign investors have a majority of the represented *votes*. The number of companies in which foreign investors dominate is expected to increase, as the proportion of shares owned by foreign investors has increased in recent years, and fewer voting instructions by such investors are expected to be set aside in the future.[88]

As mentioned in Section 13.1.3, many shareholders are represented by proxies. Moreover, an increasing number of investors are voting in advance by casting their votes in writing in accordance with § 104(2) of the CA. Meeting minutes very seldom show how many votes are cast by proxy or in advance. However, surveys show that, in 2015, the percentage of investors represented by proxies was as high as 29 per cent.[89] It has also been reported that more than one-third of all voting instructions are normally rejected, primarily because of the shortcomings in complying with registration requirement described in Section 13.1.3.[90] Such rejections are often triggered by errors in the documentation.[91]

As noted in Section 13.1.3, none of Denmark's listed companies had before 2020 held an electronic general meeting, but a few are using electronic voting as a means of taking the vote

86 The period from 1 January–31 December 2019.

87 See the figures for 2018 and 2019 presented in VP Securities (nn. 43 and 81). According to VP Securities, the foreign investors in the sixty-six companies analyzed held, on average, 41 per cent of the total capital represented at the meetings held in 2019.

88 See the journal *Økonomisk Ugebrev Ledelse* (2016) issue no. 1, 1, 9–12.

89 Ibid. In 2015, the percentage of votes exercised in advance was around 7 per cent.

90 Ibid.; VP Securities (n. 43) 85.

91 See also Klaus Søgaard, Louise Celia Korpela-Andersen and Michael Brichmann, *Generalforsamlinger i børsnoterede selskaber – udvalgte emner og problemstillinger* (Revision & Regnskabsvæsen 2012) 56.

amongst those present at the general meeting. We have been informed that six of the twenty-five most traded companies (C25) used electronic voting during the 2019 AGM season.[92]

13.3.1.2 What Issues Are Voted on?

Danish law requires that two particular issues be addressed at a company's AGM: the approval of the annual report and the appropriation of profit or loss recorded in the adopted annual report.[93] In addition, there is a range of resolutions requiring the acceptance of the general meeting according to the CA or companies' AoA.

In addition to the two issues required by law, almost all of Denmark's thirty-six large cap companies had in the season examined (see footnote 83) placed the following issues on the agenda for their AGMs:

- election of some members of the board
- election of the accountant
- approval of board salaries and
- authorization for the board to acquire the company's own shares.

Further, more than one-third of the thirty-six large cap companies included the following issues:

- a decision to discharge the board and executive management from liability (called a 'decharge' in Danish)
- adoption of a remuneration policy and
- either a decrease of capital or an authorization for the board to conduct such a decrease.

All of the foregoing issues have been raised by the boards of these companies, and they cover most of the items on AGM agendas. The additional issues raised by boards that are the most common amongst large cap companies are resolutions

- authorizing the chair of the general meeting to register appointments and changes to the AoA agreed upon at the general meeting (twelve companies)
- related to the raising of capital, either by deciding on such a rise or authorizing the board to make such a decision at a later stage (eleven companies)
- eliminating the compulsory retirement age for board members (three companies)
- changing the company's language policy (three companies)
- changing the rules of representation (two companies)
- changing the rules on the conduct of general meetings (two companies)
- changing the company name (two companies) and
- authorizing the board to pay extraordinary dividends (two companies).

It is clear that the issues raised by the boards are most often included because the law requires them to be. However, there is nothing requiring a general meeting to decide on discharging a company's board and management from liability (decharge), and there was hitherto no requirement for a general meeting to decide on the company's remuneration policy.[94] It is not common to consult shareholders about issues relating to a company's strategy or specific

[92] This information was kindly provided by VP Securities and Computershare; see n. 53.

[93] See CA § 88.

[94] That changed with the transposition of SRD II. For all AGMs called from the financial year starting on 10 June 2019 and onwards, the general meeting has to approve the remuneration policy.

business decisions. When we look at the proposals forwarded by shareholders (see Section 13.3.2.3 below), however, the picture is quite different.

Proposals made by the board are normally accepted by the general meeting. In fact, in our examination of large cap companies, we found only one instance of a board proposal not being adopted out of a total of 237 board proposals.[95] In that instance, the board of Jyske Bank[96] had suggested the distribution of a dividend, and a shareholder proposed that no dividend be distributed, but that a buyback programme be initiated instead. Even though the board did not support the latter proposal (but neither did it argue against it), it was adopted. Not only are the proposals of boards normally adopted, but, when there is a vote, they are often adopted by a very high majority. A recent survey of large cap companies shows that of those that provide detailed voting results, four have had at least one management resolution receive more than 10 per cent shareholder opposition.[97] In total, eight resolutions have received more than 10 per cent shareholder opposition, equalling 1.21 per cent of resolutions. Five of the eight concerned remuneration. The meeting chair often abstains from voting, either because nobody requests a vote or because the chair concludes that a majority favours the proposal based on his or her knowledge of what the major shareholders want and the number of proxies the board holds. In none of the board elections or auditor elections conducted at the AGMs of the thirty-six large cap companies from 26 May 2018 to 25 May 2019 were there alternative candidates to the candidates proposed by the board. For this reason, no vote was taken. When summarizing the outcome of such votes, the votes represented at the meeting (whether or not by proxy) are included in the number of votes for the resolutions even though the vote was never taken.[98]

When we look at general meetings other than the AGM (i.e. extraordinary general meetings), we see a slightly different picture. In 2019, 23 such meetings were held in 18 of the 126 listed companies,[99] meaning that some companies have more than one. In many cases, additional meetings are held because the majority required by the AoA for the adoption of a proposal was not reached, or the required quorum was not present, at the AGM. Accordingly, some extraordinary general meetings address the same proposals that were voted on at a previous general meeting.

All twenty-three of the aforementioned extraordinary general meetings were called on the initiative of the board, and the board made the proposals put to the meetings. All of the proposals were accepted by a majority, although not always by a majority sufficiently large for the proposal to pass. Most of the issues considered were the same as those frequently seen in AGMs. Thus, in ten of the meetings, new board members were elected (again without any opposing candidates), and in fact six of the meetings were called solely for that purpose. Furthermore, in ten meetings, an increase or decrease in capital (or the authorization thereof) was on the agenda. Most of the other proposals concerned issues involving a change in the AoA or remuneration policy, along the lines of what we also see in AGMs. However, there were a few exceptions. In two cases,

95 Based on hand-collected data from the thirty-six listed companies in the large cap segment that held their AGMs between 26 May 2018 and 25 May 2019.

96 AGM held on 26 March 2019 www.jyskebank.dk/wps/wcm/connect/jfo/1a1f4782-8bfa-4edf-b570-7562afc88f84/Selskabsmeddelelse_Ordin%C3%A6r+generalforsamling+i+Jyske+Bank+2019_20190326_DK.pdf?MOD=AJPERES&CVID accessed 1 June 2020.

97 See Georgeson (n. 85).

98 This procedure appears from the statements with voting results published by the service providers. See, e.g., those for FLSmith A/S https://flsmidth-prod-cdn.azureedge.net/-/media/misc-files-excl-brochures/company-section/investor-relations/annual-general-meetings/2019/105-opgrelse-dk.pdf?rev=df1d2de0-f44f-4e7f-9613-96d5a5d5f644 accessed 26 June 2021 and Chr. Hansen A/S https://dk-investor.chr-hansen.com/da/generalforsamling accessed 26 June 2021.

99 We looked at the period from 1 January–31 December 2019.

shareholders were asked to accept the sale of a subsidiary[100] or the sale of substantial assets.[101] It should be noted that Danish law does not require shareholder approval for such transactions. Other noteworthy proposals involved a decision to enter into solvent liquidation[102] and a decision to distribute extraordinary dividends.[103] One proposal, put by the board, sought to reduce board members' remuneration for the remainder of 2019.[104]

13.3.2 *Shareholder Proposals and Proxy Fights*

We know from other studies (see Section 13.1.3 above) that proxies are frequently used in Denmark. However, the minutes of the general meeting seldom contain information on proxies, and we therefore do not know how proxies are used in various companies and whether proxy fights occur. Our impression – based on discussions with people who regularly frequent general meetings – is that proxy fights are unusual and that, if they do take place, they generally occur in takeover situations.

Shareholder proposals are quite common. Although we found no evidence of such proposals in the 24 extraordinary meetings held during the period examined, we identified them in the AGMs of 17 of the 126 companies considered. Although the total number of shareholder proposals was forty-seven, nineteen were proposed in one company (Danske Bank A/S). It is very unusual to see such a high number of shareholder proposals in a single company. In this case, the number stems from Danske Bank's widely publicized involvement in a money-laundering scandal in 2019. The 47 shareholder proposals should be considered in comparison with the 478 board-promoted proposals during the same period. Nevertheless, it still corresponds to approximately 10 per cent of all resolutions put forward at AGMs during the period being proposed by shareholders.

All forty-seven of the shareholder proposals presented in the period examined seem to have been suggested by individual shareholders or by the shareholder association called Kritiske Aktionærer; none was tabled by an institutional investor. Although the proposals addressed a wide variety of topics, the most popular topics were:

- issues related to corporate social responsibility (seven proposals)
- problems with money laundering and the consequences hereof (eight of the proposals in Danske Bank)
- a cap on management salaries (three proposals)
- lowering the prices of a company's products/services once a certain level of equity was reached (three proposals) and
- reducing the flight risks caused by birds (six different proposals addressing this issue were tabled by the same shareholder in Copenhagen Airport).

[100] See the decision taken at the meeting held on 26 February 2019 in Blue Vision www.blue-vision.dk/images/Artikler/GF/2019/selskabsmed3260220l9egfsalgportinho.pdf accessed 26 June 2021.

[101] See the decision taken at the meeting held on 4 June 2019 in Athena Investments https://newsclient.omxgroup.com/cdsPublic/viewDisclosure.action?disclosureId=892845&lang=en accessed 26 June 2021.

[102] Decided at the meeting held on 9 October 2019 in Scandinavian Private Equity https://newsclient.omxgroup.com/cdsPublic/viewDisclosure.action?disclosureId=906111&lang=da accessed 26 June 2021.

[103] Decided at the meeting held on 19 November 2019 in Athena Investments https://newsclient.omxgroup.com/cdsPublic/viewDisclosure.action?disclosureId=911892&lang=en accessed 26 June 2021.

[104] Decided at the meeting held on 25 September 2019 in Small Cap Denmark https://newsclient.omxgroup.com/cdsPublic/viewDisclosure.action?disclosureId=904546&lang=da accessed 26 June 2021.

The remaining proposals dealt with various aspects of corporate governance, often focusing on the board and general meetings. A few addressed more substantial issues. For example, one suggested that Danske Bank should be split up; one suggested that Skjern Bank should contemplate a merger and cut costs; and one suggested that Jyske Bank should not issue a dividend (but instead that its board should be encouraged to buy back shares). The latter proposal is interesting in that it was the only one adopted. All of the others were dismissed, either without any voting taking place or with an overwhelming majority, normally more than 95 per cent, in favour of dismissal.[105]

13.3.3 *Questions Asked by Shareholders and Addresses to Boards of Directors*

It is not unusual for shareholders to ask questions at general meetings. Based on what appears in the published minutes of ordinary general meetings in the 2018–19 period examined, 127 oral questions were asked in 27 of the 126 companies considered. In most cases, the questions were posed by associations representing shareholders[106] or by individuals. Questions posed by institutional investors were less common. It is not clear from the minutes how often written questions were asked in advance of general meetings, but it is our impression that this option was seldom used.

Shareholders also have a right to speak at a general meeting to address the board of directors. They most often do so to comment on the annual report or a statement made by the board on the company's activities during the past year. In the 2018–19 period we examined, we found that shareholders addressed the board of directors in the meetings of 27 companies, for a total of 144 addresses. Interestingly, we found such active shareholders in only a small number of companies. In the majority of companies considered, shareholders neither asked questions nor addressed the board. The total number of questions asked and addresses made by shareholders to boards of directors at AGMs in 2018–19 is reported in Table 13.1 below. The numbers in brackets indicate the number of companies in which the activity occurred. The percentage of companies indicates the occurrence within a given segment (large, mid or small cap).

13.4 COVID-19 AND THE 2020 AGM SEASON

In Denmark, the COVID-19 pandemic caused a general lockdown from mid-March 2020, which meant, inter alia, that the congregation of more than ten persons should be avoided, making it impossible for listed companies to hold normal general meetings.[107] This ban was later relaxed but were still in place during the months from April–June 2020 which is the most popular season for AGMs, as listed companies need to have their annual accounts approved to comply with the five-month deadline set in Financial Statements Act § 138.

The first government intervention to remedy the problem was Act no. 223 dated 17 March 2020,[108] according to which it was permissible for companies affected by the ban on

[105] The exception was a proposal by a shareholder in Glunz & Jensen Holding who suggested that the members of the board should be elected for one-year terms. Although the board of directors agreed with the proposal and it received a majority of votes (59.46 per cent), it did not receive the two-thirds majority needed for a change to the AoA www.glunz-jensen.com/investor/generalforsamling accessed 26 June 2021.

[106] The two dominating associations are the Danish Shareholders' Association (Dansk Aktionærforening) and an association calling itself Critical Shareholders (Kritiske Aktionærer).

[107] This was first put into Act no. 224 on 17 March 2020, which took effect on 18 March 2020.

[108] The official name of the act is Bekendtgørelse om fravigelse af privates pligter over for det offentlige på Erhvervsministeriets område i forbindelse med håndtering af Coronavirussygdom 2019 (COVID-19). The name in translation would be something like the Act on exemption of duties of private towards the public in areas governed by the Ministry of Business due to the handling of COVID-19.

TABLE 13.1 *Questions and addresses at AGMs 2018–19*

	Questions asked	Percentage of companies	Addresses to the board of directors	Percentage of companies
Large cap (36)	55 (11)	30.6%	96 (15)	41.7%
Mid cap (23)	35 (7)	30.4%	21 (5)	21.7%
Small cap (67)	37 (9)	13.4%	27 (7)	10.4%
In total	127 (27)	21.4%	144 (27)	21.4%

large congregations to submit their annual accounts eight weeks after the ban was lifted, and it thus became possible again to conduct a general meeting. Some conditions had to be fulfilled, namely, that the AGM had not already been held (i.e. before 16 March 2020) and annual accounts approved at the meeting, that there were more than ten shareholders in the company and that the company's AoA did not allow for a fully electronic meeting.

After this initial legislation, a more detailed regulation was adopted on 7 April 2020 as Act no. 393.[109] Listed companies whose financial year ended between 31 October 2019 and 30 April 2020 were allowed to hand in their annual accounts seven months after the financial year-end instead of the usual five months. However, they still needed to submit them no later than eight weeks after the ban on large congregations was overturned.[110] Act no. 393 also relaxed some of the usual requirements for general meetings. First, it allowed companies to ignore any date or time slot in their AoA for holding the AGM.[111] Second, it rendered the usual deadline applicable for submitting shareholder proposals for the AGM agenda, according to CA § 90(2) and (3), no longer applicable to listed companies if their boards are convinced that shareholders have sufficient time to submit any proposal they wish to make.[112] Third, it permitted boards to decide to hold a general meeting as a fully electronic meeting, without any physical presence required, even if their companies' AoA do not allow for it, as required by the CA.[113]

At the beginning of July 2020, we conducted a survey of forty[114] large cap companies to find out how they had modified their AGMs to cope with the situation. Three of them were not formed as Danish companies, and so we leave them out of our analysis here. Of the remaining thirty-seven companies, no fewer than twenty-six were affected by the lockdown, of which seven were able to conduct their 2020 AGM as usual (a result that bears witness to the very low AGM attendance in some companies). Of the nineteen remaining companies affected, only seven chose to postpone their AGM, and all but one had already held their AGM at the time of the survey. Seventeen companies chose to conduct a physical AGM, albeit with certain precautions in place. Most often, those precautions took the form

109 The name of the act is Bekendtgørelse om midlertidig fravigelse af virksomheders pligter på selskabs- og regnskabsområdet på Erhvervsstyrelsens område i forbindelse med covid-19 (translates as act concerned exemption of duties of enterprises in the area of company law and accounting law governed by the Business Authority as a consequences of COVID-19). Slightly different rules were adopted for financial institutions; see Act no. 396 from 8 April 2020.

110 From 8 June 2020 onwards, the ban was relaxed to 50 persons, and from 8 July 2020, to 100 persons. These relaxations were not likely to be sufficient to trigger the eight-week deadline, as most listed companies normally assemble more than these numbers at their AGMs.

111 See § 1(3) of Act no. 393 dated 7 April 2020. The same provision provides that any deadline provided in the articles for submitting annual accounts may be ignored.

112 See § 1(6) of Act no 393 dated 7 April 2020. According to § 1(3) of the same Act, any deadline for submitting shareholders proposals set out in the AoA can also be ignored.

113 Thus, according to CA § 77(2) a decision to have fully electronic general meetings must be implemented in the AoA.

114 An additional large cap company has been added compared to the survey made of the earlier AGM season.

of the board encouraging shareholders not to attend the meeting but instead vote in advance or give a proxy to the board. In some cases, it was explicitly announced in the AGM notice that no refreshments would be served, presumably to discourage attendance. Encouragements not to attend were almost always supplemented with the promise to web stream of the meeting. These precautions allowed the companies in question to conduct their AGMs without making use of the option to hold fully electronic meetings. However, one large cap company did choose to convert its AGM into a fully electronic meeting.[115] An amendment to the company's AoA was approved by that AGM, which will allow the company to hold fully electronic meetings in future. In another company, a shareholder put forward a similar proposal, but it was opposed by the board of directors and rejected by a 99.49 per cent majority vote. In principle, shareholders could have chosen to attend all of these companies' AGMs, as is their right, but the companies' encouragement to stay away – and the general encouragement of the Danish government to socially distance – allowed the meetings to be held despite the restrictions on large congregations.[116]

13.5 CONCLUDING REMARKS

Under Danish law, the general meeting is omnipotent, meaning that it can decide on most issues, including issues that deal with day-to-day management of the company. Thus, in theory, shareholders are in a position to ensure that the general meeting decides most issues of concern to them, and the rules on calling a general meeting or proposing topics for the meeting agenda are also rather generous to shareholders. In practice, however, shareholders rarely call a meeting. Although they occasionally propose issues for the meeting agenda, those proposals are almost always voted down by a very high majority. Therefore, the potential for shareholder democracy and activism is not being exploited by shareholders in Denmark.

Agenda items proposed by boards of directors are usually voted through by a very high majority.[117] Also, the directors proposed by boards for election or re-election, as well as the accountants they propose, are generally voted through, seemingly without any opposing candidates. Both phenomena indicate that boards of directors in Denmark clear important decisions with major shareholders before general meetings are held. We do not have empirical data to support this conclusion, but it is generally accepted. It seems that in normal circumstances, a board will propose agenda items only when the law requires it to do so (a rare exception in our data was a proposal to discharge the board and executive management from liability). We found only a few examples of boards requesting a general meeting to approve important strategic decisions. Again, we surmise that such issues are discussed with large shareholders in other fora, although we have no empirical data to support that conclusion.

We did find, however, that shareholders often ask questions and engage in debate at general meetings. We can therefore conclude that shareholder democracy and activism are present in Denmark, although they presumably take place to a large extent before general meetings are held.

[115] Moreover, we are also aware of two mid cap companies that have made use of this option.

[116] In most cases, it is not stated how the company will handle the situation if more than ten persons shows up. Only in one company, Unibrew A/S, was it announced that the consequence would be cancellation of the meeting.

[117] However, numbers from Georgeson show that a number of resolutions put forward by management have received a negative recommendation from Glass Lewis or Institutional Shareholder Services (ISS), with resolutions on remuneration receiving the most negative recommendations. Glass Lewis gave a negative recommendation in fourteen cases concerning the topic of remuneration in large cap companies in the 2019 AGM season (out of a total of sixteen negative recommendation). The comparable figure for ISS was six out of twelve. See Georgeson (n. 85) 18–19.

14

Shareholder Engagement and Voting in France

Christoph Van der Elst

14.1 INTRODUCTION

In the famous 'Law and Finance' studies of La Porta, Lopez-de-Silanes, Shleifer and Vishny (LLSV), France is cited as the representative example of a civil law country with weak investor and creditor protection rights.[1] It was listed amongst the countries with a concentrated ownership structure,[2] and pyramidal structures and other control enhancing mechanisms were also commonly found in France.[3] Whilst the LLSV studies have been criticized for underestimating the number of shareholder rights,[4] the French corporate landscape has changed dramatically since those studies were published. In particular, the French government took the lead in restructuring the French corporate governance landscape with the Act of 15 May 2001 on New Economic Regulations (*Loi NRE*), the Act of 26 July 2005 on Economic Confidence and Modernisation, the Act of 9 December 2016 on Say on Pay (*Loi Sapin II*) and the Act of 22 May 2019 on Transparency of Remuneration and Corporate Social Responsibility (*Loi Pacte*), to name but a few. Further, the network of companies (AFEP-MEDEF)[5] issuing regular updates of the corporate governance code, as well as the French regulator AMF[6] and the High Committee of Corporate Governance (HCGE),[7] have helped significantly to improve the French corporate governance setting.

Therefore, this chapter analyzes shareholder engagement and voting behaviour in a new era in which France has modernized its corporate governance system significantly since the publication of the LLSV studies. The internal structure of companies is sketched in Section 14.2.[8] France facilitates the establishment of public limited liability companies in

[1] Rafael La Porta et al., 'Law and Finance' (1998) 106(6) Journal of Political Economy 1113–55.

[2] Mara Faccio and Larry Lang, 'The Ultimate Ownership of Western European Corporations' (2002) 65 Journal of Financial Economics 365, 379. See also Section 14.3.1 of this chapter.

[3] ISS, Shearman and Sterling, and ECGI, *Report on the Proportionality Principle in the European Union* (Brussels 2007) 66–73.

[4] Sofie Cools, 'The Real Difference in Corporate Law between the United States and Continental Europe: Distribution of Powers' (2005) 30 Delaware Journal of Corporate Law 697–766.

[5] AFEP stands for the French Association of Private Enterprises, see www.afep.com accessed 15 July 2020, and MEDEF for Movement of the Enterprises of France, see www.medef.com accessed 15 July 2020. Both bodies defend the interests of companies and employers.

[6] AMF stands for Autorité des Marchés Financiers, the French equivalent of the US Securities and Exchange Commission (SEC). See www.amf-france.org accessed 15 July 2020.

[7] The High Committee of Corporate Governance discloses all its work on its website https://hcge.fr/ accessed 15 March 2021.

[8] After finalizing this chapter, French legislators changed the numbering of the articles in the Commercial Code for French listed companies (for the new numbering, see Ordonnance no. 2020–1142 du 16 septembre 2020 portant création, au sein du code de commerce, d'un chapitre relatif aux sociétés dont les titres sont admis aux négociations sur un marché réglementé ou sur un système multilatéral de négociation, *OJ* 17 September 2020).

accordance with their founders' demands. Once a certain structure has been selected, companies must comply with a large number of mandatory rules balancing stakeholders' interests. The second section thus briefly outlines board structures, the division of powers between the board of directors and shareholders, the role of the general meeting of shareholders and the ownership structure of companies. Section 14.3 then addresses the legal means of shareholder engagement and voting and the special measures introduced during the COVID-19 pandemic. Section 14.4 examines shareholder engagement in action. In this section, I provide insights on the development of shareholder participation in general meetings, as well as the voting weight of participating shareholders; the effects of the provision of double voting rights to loyal shareholders and the shift to remote voting during the COVID-19 era; the different voting modes that participating shareholders use; how shareholders vote on the voting items presented at ordinary general meetings and extraordinary general meetings; and the importance of shareholders' proposal and question rights and a number of other, some specifically French, engagement mechanisms. Section 14.5 concludes.

14.2 FRENCH CORPORATE LAW

14.2.1 *Board Structures*

French legislation provides a detailed framework for the organization of the boards of directors of public limited liability companies (*société anonyme*). In the nineteenth century, French companies had to have a one-tier board with shareholders as members, but in 1966 the French legislator offered them a choice between the two-tier and one-tier board structure.

In the one-tier board structure, the board of directors must comprise at least three members,[9] and the maximum number of directors is eighteen. All public limited liability companies must have a balanced gender representation, which, for listed companies and large non-listed companies, means that a maximum of 60 per cent of the board can be composed of one gender.[10] If the board of directors has nine or more members, the difference between the genders cannot be more than two directors.[11] Legal entities can be elected as board members if the entity identifies a permanent representative that has the same civil and criminal liability as the legal entity. The permanent representative must also comply with the rules on gender board composition.[12]

The general meeting of shareholders elects members of the board of directors for a maximum term of six years,[13] although the French Corporate Governance Code recommends a maximum term of four years.[14] Directors can be dismissed at any time for any or no reason.[15]

The board of directors must elect a chair from amongst its members. Until 2001, the board chair (*président*) combined this role with the role of CEO (*directeur-général*). The combination of the two roles was legal practice in France until that year. However, with the enactment of the *Loi relative aux Nouvelles Régulations Économiques* (the law pertaining to the new economic

[9] Article L 225–17 of the Commercial Code (hereafter CC).

[10] Article L 225–17 *juncto* L 225–18-1 CC. In smaller boards with four, six or eight members, it results in the requirement of a fully balanced composition.

[11] Ibid.

[12] Article L 225–20 CC.

[13] Article L 225–18 CC.

[14] Recommendation 14.1 of AFEP-MEDEF, *Corporate Governance Code of Listed Corporation* (Paris, January 2020) 11 https://afep.com/wp-content/uploads/2020/01/Afep_Medef-Code-revision-2020-EN-.pdf accessed 20 May 2020.

[15] Article L 225–18 CC.

regulations), boards of directors can choose between combining or separating the role of CEO and board chair.[16]

French public limited liability companies can also opt for a two-tier board structure with a supervisory board (*conseil de surveillance*) and a management board (*directoire*). The management board may comprise up to five members, or up to seven for listed companies.[17] The supervisory board elects the management board and its chair for a period of two to six years depending on the company's articles of association (AoA).[18] The general meeting of shareholders is empowered to dismiss members of the management board, although the AoA can also extend that power to the supervisory board as well.[19] Dismissal without good cause may give rise to damages. The supervisory board is elected by the general meeting of shareholders and must comply with a number of rules, which are similar to those for the one-tier board in terms of the number of members, gender diversity, age limitations and the like.[20] Membership of one board is incompatible with membership of the other within the same company.[21]

It should be noted that a limited number of companies are structured as partnerships limited by shares (*sociétés en commandite par actions* (SCA)), which have two classes of investors: one class resembling the shareholders of a public limited liability company, who cannot govern the company, and one class, *les commandités*, who have unlimited liability for the company's debts but can govern the company. This company type offers protection against a hostile takeover. There are two SCAs in France's major stock index, the CAC 40, the luxury brand Hermès International and the tyre company Michelin, both of which are organized with a management and a supervisory board.

Although less well-known than the German structure of labour representation, the French system also allows for employee-directors. The French system provides several complex mechanisms by which employees can or must be represented on the (supervisory) board of directors, which can be summarized as follows.

First, in accordance with the Labour Code, two – and sometimes four – employee representatives of the social and economic committee that mandatorily has to be established in companies with more than fifty employees have the right to participate in an advisory capacity in every (supervisory) board meeting.[22] Second, since 1986 French legislation has provided for an optional system of (supervisory) board representation by employees. In 2013, the optional system was made mandatory for certain types of companies, and its field of application was further expanded in 2019. Companies that employ more than 1,000 employees in France or more than 5,000 worldwide for two consecutive years must open their (supervisory) boards to one or two employee representatives who must be elected by an (extraordinary) general meeting.[23] Finally,[24] if employees hold more than 3 per cent of the capital of a listed French company or the company employs the numbers cited in the previous sentence, the general meeting of shareholders must elect one or more directors from amongst the company's employee-shareholders.[25] A similar requirement exists

16 According to article L 225–51-1 CC, it is an exclusive power of the board of directors to opt for this combination or separation of the two functions.
17 Article L 225–58 CC.
18 Article L 225–62 CC.
19 Article L 225–61 CC.
20 See articles L 225–69–L 225–73 CC.
21 Article L 225–74 CC.
22 Article L 2312–72 of the Labour Code.
23 Articles L 225–27-1 CC and L 225–79-2 CC.
24 Note that there are special employee representation requirements for privatized companies.
25 Article L 225–23 CC.

when employees indirectly control more than 3 per cent of the capital through a mutual fund of employees.[26]

French listed companies must also take into account the mandatory comply-or-explain corporate governance code.[27] The 2020 edition of the AFEP-MEDEF Corporate Governance Code for listed corporations recommends that at least one-third of the board of directors of a company with a controlling shareholder be independent directors, whilst companies with a widely held ownership structure should have boards with at least 50 per cent independent directors.[28]

These different models coexist in French businesses. According to data from the HCGE, the voluntary monitoring agency of corporate governance practices that was established in 2013, 56 per cent of CAC 40 companies and 44 per cent of the constituents of the larger SBF 120 index had a one-tier board structure with a *president-directeur-général* (PDG), that is, a CEO who combines that role with the position of board chair, in 2018. Twenty-eight per cent of companies in the CAC 40 and 39 per cent of those in the SBF 120 opted for a one-tier board with a separate role for the chair and CEO, whilst 11 per cent of the CAC 40 and 12 per cent of the SBF 120 chose the two-tier board model. Five per cent of companies in both indices were established as partnerships limited by shares.[29]

14.2.2 *Allocation of Powers*

The different board structures described above also have effects on the allocation of powers. The French legislator recently refined the general duties of the directors of one-tier boards. Whilst the board of directors previously had to determine the broad lines of the company's business activities and ensure their implementation, the *Loi Pacte* added, in article L 225–35 of the Commercial Code, that the setting of these lines and the implementation of decisions must take place in accordance with the company's social interest and take into account the social and environmental aspects of the company's activities.[30] This article makes it clear that the residual power belongs to the management board and that the board deals with all matters pertaining to the conduct of the company's business and decides all pertinent issues through its deliberations. The general meeting of shareholders, in contrast, has only those powers explicitly provided by law.

The Commercial Code also clarifies the functions of the board chair and CEO, which have been permitted to be separated since 2001. The chairperson of the board organizes and monitors the work of the board of directors and reports to the general meeting. He or she must make sure that the various bodies of the company can and do operate properly and ensure, in particular, that the directors are able to fulfil their duties.[31] The CEO has extensive powers under article L 225–56-I of the Commercial Code: he or she has the capacity to act on behalf of the company in all circumstances unless the law grants those powers to the board of directors or the general meeting of shareholders. The CEO represents the company in dealings with third parties. Any limitation of his or her powers, even if provided for in the company's AoA, is not effective with

26 Ibid.

27 European Directive 2006/46 introduced this mandatory comply-or-explain corporate governance system, which was transposed in French law by Law no. 2008–649 of 3 July 2008.

28 The Code refers to article L 233–3 CC.

29 HCGE, *Rapport du Haut Comité de gouvernement d'entreprise* (Paris, December 2019) 25.

30 Articles L 225–35 and L 225–64 CC.

31 Article L 225–51 CC.

respect to third parties. Accordingly, the CEO has a very strong position in the company, and, as a result, the board of directors plays more of a monitoring role.

In companies that have opted for the two-tier board structure, the division of powers between the management board and supervisory board resembles that between the CEO and board of directors in the one-tier structure, although there are a number of differences. Similar to the powers of the CEO, the management board has broad power to act on the company's behalf in all circumstances. However, that power was in 2019 complemented by the power to determine the broad lines of the company's business activities and to ensure that their implementation is in accordance with the company's social interest and takes the social and environmental aspects of the company's activities into account.[32] The latter power also belongs to the board in a one-tier board structure. The chair of the executive board represents the company in its dealings with third parties,[33] and the supervisory board's role is to 'permanently monitor the management board'.[34]

14.2.3 *Role and Position of Shareholders and the General Meeting of Shareholders*

As in many other countries, shareholders in French companies have only those powers that are conferred upon the general meeting of shareholders or upon individual shareholders with specific characteristics, such as the ownership of a specific number of shares, to call a meeting or ask questions outside the general meeting during the accounting period.[35] Nevertheless, the general meeting is vested with important rights: it is in charge of the election of the board of directors, a number of other recurrent corporate items and the 'fundamental decisions' of the corporation. The (limited) harmonization efforts of the European Union have resulted in some of these fundamental decisions being placed in the hands of shareholders. For example, mergers and divisions, as well as operations influencing the company's capital, must be approved by shareholders.[36]

The board of directors in a one-tier board structure and the management board in a two-tier structure must call a general meeting every year.[37] The annual general meeting votes on the company's annual accounts and, if applicable, on its consolidated accounts and the allocation of its financial results. This meeting also votes on the election, re-election and dismissal of board members, say-on-pay, related party transactions (RPTs), golden parachutes, and the appointment of statutory auditors. Further, it is also common practice for the board of directors to ask the meeting for authorization to trade in its own shares or buy back shares of the company. Some of these agenda items, for example say-on-pay and RPTs, can involve several rounds of voting. The practices for these items will be elaborated upon in the third section of the chapter.

It should be noted that some of these shareholder voting rights are specific to the French corporate environment. First, not only does the general meeting of shareholders have to vote on the company's annual accounts, but its consolidated accounts must also be voted on. Second, shareholders in French companies have for many years been afforded opportunities to voice their concerns regarding various types of RPTs. As of 22 May 1863, it was already prohibited by

[32] Article L 225–64 CC.
[33] Article L 225–66 CC.
[34] Article L 225–68 CC.
[35] See Section 14.3.3 below and article L 225–232 CC.
[36] Many of these rights for the general meeting of shareholders can be found in the first, second, third, sixth and other European company law directives. These directives have been codified in Directive (EU) 2017/1132 of the European Parliament and of the Council of 14 June 2017 relating to certain aspects of company law (2017) OJL 169/46.
[37] Article L 225–103 CC.

law for board members to have any interest in the operational activities of the company to avoid the risk of board members putting their personal interests above those of the company.[38] This prohibition has been amended numerous times in the years since, resulting in the current rule stipulating that any agreement between a company and its director, CEO, deputy CEO, or member of the management board or supervisory board or any shareholder owning more than 10 per cent of the voting rights (including, if the shareholder is itself a company, the controlling shareholder of that shareholder) must be submitted for pre-approval by the board of directors and approved by shareholders.[39] The rule has been further extended to agreements between the company and another business in which the CEO, deputy CEO or a director is the owner, an unlimited liable partner, a CEO, a director or member of the supervisory board or is in any other way involved in the management of that business.

Before its abolition by Ordonnance No 2019–1234 of 27 November 2019, the process for approving related-party agreements was also applicable to commitments made by a company or the controlled or controlling companies of that company for the benefit of the company's chairperson, CEO, deputy CEO or a member of the management board in relation to remuneration, indemnification or benefits due or likely to be due upon termination or defined retirement benefits.[40] The general meeting of shareholders must approve such commitments separately for each individual concerned. The transposition of the EU say-on-pay rules in the Shareholder Rights Directive (SRD) replaced this typical French requirement by an ex ante vote on remuneration policy. As this change in the law took effect after the 2019 general meeting season, the analysis in the next section is based on the results of the approvals of such transactions by shareholders.

The aforementioned related-party remuneration commitments, as well as the remuneration packages of top executives, were at the core of the French corporate governance debate of the last decade.[41] For many years, shareholders' only power with respect to director pay in France was their approval of total remuneration for the board of directors. In June 2013, the French Corporate Governance Code introduced a voluntary say-on-pay vote for shareholders, with shareholders voting separately on the remuneration packages of CEOs and other executive board members. If shareholders voted against the packages (identified as providing 'negative advice'), the board of directors had to, at one of its next meetings and after being advised by the remuneration committee, 'deliberate' on the implications of the shareholder vote. Although the enactment of the comply-or-explain principle in the French Corporate Governance Code avoided the introduction of a statutory say-on-pay requirement, that was not the case for long. In 2016, *Sapin Law II* introduced a binding say-on-pay vote for shareholders.[42] The Legislator intervened after generous remuneration packages at Renault, in which the French government holds a significant voting bloc, were disapproved by the company's shareholders but the board failed to take appropriate action. Subsequent to the new law, shareholders have to approve, at least yearly, the remuneration policy containing the principles and criteria for the determination and the distribution and allocation of fixed, variable and exceptional pay for the chair of the supervisory board, the CEO and the deputy CEO.[43] If the general meeting does not approve the

38 For a historical overview, see D. Schmidt, *Les conflits d'intérêts dans la société anonyme* (Joly 2004).

39 Article L 225–38 and following of the CC and article L 225–86 and following of the CC.

40 Former articles L 225–42-1 and L 225–90-1 CC.

41 See, for an overview, Randall Thomas and Christoph Van der Elst, 'Say on Pay around the World' (2015) 92 Washington University Law Review 680–8.

42 Law no. 2016–1691 of 9 December 2016 relating to transparency, the fight against corruption and the modernization of economic life.

43 Former article L 225–37-2 CC.

policy, the former policy must be used. The transposition of SRD II changed this requirement into a remuneration policy that is in line with the interest of the company, contributes to its sustainability and is part of its commercial strategy. It describes all the components of fixed and variable compensation and explains the decision process followed for its determination, review and implementation.[44]

In addition, *Loi Sapin II* also introduced a mandatory vote on the pay packages of the aforementioned corporate officers and board members. In the event that the general meeting of shareholders does not approve a pay package, only the fixed part of the remuneration can be paid; that is, the variable or exceptional part cannot be paid.[45] Furthermore, this mandatory rule was changed again when SRD II was transposed in 2019, although its main principle is maintained: variable or exceptional compensation can be paid only after the general meeting's approval of the compensation components for the persons concerned.[46]

Extraordinary general meetings must be held to change a company's AoA or its nationality by transferring its seat abroad if the receiving country concerned has entered into an agreement with France relating to the transfer and the maintenance of the company's legal personality.[47] It is also common practice[48] for extraordinary meetings to grant the board of directors the right to issue new shares or rights giving access to shares and other capital-related operations. More generally, operations concerning the company's capital require the approval of shareholders gathered in an extraordinary general meeting,[49] as do the dissolution of the company,[50] conversion of shares[51] and mergers and divisions.[52,53] Although operations pertaining to the capital of the company are often delegated to the board of directors, the authorization of the general meeting to do so can be provided for only a limited time. Hence, it is common for companies to combine the ordinary general meeting with a sequential extraordinary general meeting, during which authorization is granted to the board to perform the operation in question.

A feature specific to the French governance regime is that shareholders not only receive a significant amount of information from the board of directors in advance of the general meeting, but they also receive a substantial number of reports from external auditors, which are known as *commissaires aux comptes* in French. In addition to their report on the company's financial statements, external auditors also have to provide shareholders with, inter alia, their report on RPTs,[54] the remuneration of directors,[55] the provision of shares to employees,[56] the provision of options on shares for employees[57] and any reduction in capital.[58] Conversely, the company is

44 Article L 225-37-2 CC.

45 Former article L 225–100 CC.

46 By Ordonnance no. 2019–1234 of 27 November 2019 related to the remuneration of the corporate officers of listed companies.

47 Articles L 225–96 and L 225–97 CC.

48 See Section 14.3.

49 Article L 225–129 CC (capital increase) and articles L 225–198 and L 225–204 CC (capital decrease and redemption), including options on shares and allocating shares for employees without consideration; see articles L 225–177 and L 225–197-1 CC. However, the acquisition of own shares can be approved by the ordinary general meeting (article L 225–209 CC).

50 Article L 225–246 CC.

51 Article L 228–12 CC.

52 Article L 236–2 CC.

53 This list is not exhaustive.

54 Article L 225–40 CC.

55 Article L 225–115 CC.

56 Article L 225–197-1 CC.

57 Article L 225–177 CC.

58 Article L 223–34 CC.

required to feed the relevant information to their external auditors. When the chairperson of the management board addresses the written questions of shareholders (or associations of shareholders), he or she must also send the answers to the external auditors as well.[59]

14.2.4 *Ownership Structure of French Listed Companies*

Like many other continental European countries, France is generally known for its high ownership concentration, pyramidal structures and close relationships between the government and the shareholders and boards of large listed companies. The origins of these features lie in the privatization wave of the 1980s when so-called *noyaux durs*,[60] later identified as *groupements d'actionnaires stables*,[61] were formed and served as a protective wall against unrequested foreign interventions.[62]

Households and individuals significantly reduced their direct ownership of shares in French companies in the 1990s. In the 1980s, this class of owners held up to 40 per cent of all listed shares, but since the turn of the millennium their direct stake has stabilized at around 10 per cent of shares. This divestiture by households and individuals implies a shift from direct ownership to indirect ownership. The total indirect ownership of households through investment funds, life insurance companies and holding companies is still estimated at above 30 per cent.[63]

An opposite development took place with respect to the ownership of foreign investors. Until the early 1980s, foreign shareholders owned less than 10 per cent of the shares in listed French companies. Foreign investors discovered French companies in the mid-1980s, and since the turn of the millennium the rest of the world has owned roughly 40 per cent of the (value of) shares in them. Approximately one-third of all shares are owned by US (institutional) investors, and together with their UK counterparts they hold the majority of shares belonging to foreign shareholders.

A different trend can be distinguished for non-financial companies. The second largest class of shareholders in 1990, non-financial companies lost their importance around the turn of the millennium, but later regained it to own around 22 per cent of all shares in 2016. Significant increases and decreases can also be found in governmental ownership. It decreased in the first half of the 1990s, but then rose to more than 10 per cent in 2008. Since then, however, the French government has sold the major portion of its ownership stake.

Finally, the position of French financial institutions in the ownership of French listed companies is also significant, second only to foreign institutional investors. Since the mid-1990s, French banks, investment funds and insurance companies have owned over 20 per cent of French listed shares. More than half of this share belongs to investment funds.

The ownership structure reveals only limited information on the control of listed companies. For example, the government owned only 3.4 per cent of all shares in French listed companies in 2016, but it had absolute control over Electricité de France (EDF), with a stake of more than 85 per cent of the company's shares and votes.[64]

Further, the French system is also known for its double voting rights for loyal shareholders.[65] In 1903, France promulgated a law offering companies the right to issue multiple voting rights if

59 Article L 225–231 CC.
60 Which can be translated as 'stable relationships'.
61 Which can be translated as 'stable shareholder groups'.
62 ANSA, *Livre blanc de l'ANSA – Agissons d'urgence pour la croissance* (Paris 2016) 63.
63 Ibid., 11.
64 EDF, *Document de Référence* 2016, 516 www.edf.fr/groupe-edf/espaces-dedies/investisseurs-actionnaires/documents-de-reference accessed 10 June 2020.
65 Christoph Van der Elst, 'Do Loyalty Shares Affect the Engagement of Shareholders?' [2017] *International Journal for Financial Services* 33–7.

permitted by their AoA. In 1933, the law was then modified to allow only shares with double voting rights.[66] Article 175 of the 1966 Companies Code provides the right to grant double voting rights for named shares that have been registered for at least two years.[67] Sixty-eight per cent of SBF 250 companies provide long-term shareholders with double voting rights.[68] In 2014, the *Loi Florange* inversed the system of double voting rights. Whilst previously AoA had to provide for double voting rights for loyal long-term shareholders, now all named shares held for more than two years receive double voting rights unless the AoA explicitly stipulate otherwise.[69] The change increased the number of companies providing double voting rights: 69 per cent of SBF 120 companies versus 57 per cent before the *Loi Florange* was enacted.

Bloch and Kremp reported that in 1995 the capital stake of the largest shareholder in a CAC 40 company was, on average, 29.4 per cent of shares, after which the concentration dropped significantly.[70] According to research by Auvray, the average ownership block of the largest shareholder in CAC 40 companies decreased from 20 per cent in 2002 to 15 per cent in 2017, with the median block stabilizing at around 10 per cent.[71] The five largest shareholders held an average of 31 per cent of shares in 2002, decreasing to 28 per cent in 2017. These figures seem to indicate a relatively low ownership concentration in France compared with other continental European countries.[72] However, smaller listed French companies have much higher ownership concentrations. Bloch and Kemp found an average ownership block of more than 50 per cent in all French listed companies in 1995,[73] and, according to comparative analysis of more than 600 French listed companies in 1996, the largest shareholder in a French company controls, on average, 46.7 per cent of shares and 48.3 per cent of voting rights.[74] A study of almost 800 French companies conducted by Aminadav and Papaioannou at the end of 2012 confirmed the findings from the late 1990s: the mean ownership of the largest shareholder was 46.4 per cent, with a weighted mean of 39.4 per cent.[75] It thus follows that at least some of the largest companies in the CAC 40 have a dispersed ownership structure, which resulted in the modest average capital blocks found by Auvray.[76]

My own research of the capital and voting structure of CAC 40 companies in 2019 confirms these results.[77] Almost 70 per cent of these companies issued double voting right shares. As a result, the average voting bloc of the largest shareholders was 23.7 per cent of total votes, significantly higher than the average share block of 18.6 per cent of shares. In almost 20 per cent of the companies, the largest shareholder controlled more than 50 per cent of the voting rights, but in less than 10 per cent did that shareholder own more than 50 per cent of the shares. Conversely, in almost 40 per cent of

66 Christian Gaudin, *La bataille des centres de decision: promouvoir la souveraineté économique de la France a l'heure de la mondialisation (rapport)* (Sénat 22 February 2007) 253 www.senat.fr/rap/r06-347–1/r06-347–1.html accessed 20 June 2020.

67 Loi no. 66–537 du 24 juillet 1966 sur les sociétés commerciales.

68 Nicolas Chene, *Le droit de vote double en France* (Memoire de Recherche, HEC Paris 2008).

69 Article L 125–123 CC as amended by Loi no. 2014–384 du 29 mars 2014 visant à reconquérir l'économie réelle (law aimed at reclaiming the real economy).

70 Laurence Bloch and Elisabeth Kremp, 'Ownership and Voting Power in France' in Fabio Barca and Marco Becht (eds.), *The Control of Corporate Europe* (OUP 2001) 116.

71 Tristan Auvray, 'L'Évolution de l'Actionnariat en France: 1977–2017' (2018) 130 *Revue d'Economie Financière* 73–98.

72 For detailed comparative analysis, see Fabio Barca and Marco Becht, *The Control of Corporate Europe* (OUP 2001); Christoph van der Elst, *Aandeelhouderschap van beursgenoteerde vennootschappen* (Larcier 2001).

73 Laurence Bloch and Elisabeth Kremp, 'Ownership and Voting Power in France' in Fabio Barca and Marco Becht (eds.), *The Control of Corporate Europe* (OUP 2001) 116.

74 Mara Faccio and Larry Lang, 'The Ultimate Ownership of Western European Corporations' (2002) 65 Journal of Financial Economics 365, 392.

75 Gur Aminadav and Elias Papaioannou, 'Corporate Control around the World' (2020) 75 Journal of Finance 1191–246.

76 Auvray (n. 71) 73–98.

77 There are thirty-eight companies in this sample: STMicroelectronis and ArcelorMittal are excluded as they are Dutch and Luxemburg incorporated companies, respectively.

the companies no shareholder owned more than 10 per cent of the shares. The largest French companies present a mixed picture of companies with a large dispersed ownership structure and controlled companies, with the largest group comprising companies with one or more blockholders who have a major and sometimes decisive voice at the general meeting of shareholders. The controlling shareholders are mostly families, although one of the CAC 40 companies is a subsidiary of another listed company with a dispersed ownership structure, and, in another, the controlling shareholder is a vehicle of local financial institutions. The French state is the largest blockholder in five CAC 40 companies, with stakes ranging from 28 to 35 per cent of the voting rights.

14.3 LEGAL MEANS OF SHAREHOLDER ENGAGEMENT AND VOTING

France is well known for its codification process and codes of law. Many different ways by which shareholders can engage with companies and participate in the life of companies have also been codified in French law. This is the case for, inter alia, calling the meeting of shareholders, putting items on the agenda and raising questions.

14.3.1 *Calling a Meeting*

In normal circumstances, the (management) board calls the general meeting of shareholders.[78] However, the Commercial Code also empowers several other parties to call the meeting, including external auditors, the supervisory board, the employees' council and the liquidators of the company. In addition, shareholders were granted the right to call a meeting long before the first SRD offered that right to (larger) shareholders.[79] First, and in accordance with the European Takeover Directive, a majority shareholder can call the meeting after a takeover bid.[80] Second, shareholders holding more than 5 per cent of any class of shares can address the court for the appointment of a legal representative to call the general meeting of shareholders. Peculiar to French law is the right of the shareholder associations of listed companies to call a meeting (via a legal representative), a right they have enjoyed since 1994.[81] In this case, the association must represent shareholders owning at least 5 per cent of the voting rights attached to shares that have been registered for at least two years. Further, the association must have informed the company and the market regulator of the association's articles. The threshold of 5 per cent is gradually and step-by-step lowered with an increase in the company's capital to as low as 0.5 per cent if the company has capital exceeding €15 million.

Stock exchange-listed companies must inform shareholders of the general meeting with a notice published in the official *Bulletin des annonces légales obligatoires* at least thirty-five days before the meeting takes place.[82] The company must also inform them in detail of how they can participate in the meeting and provide them with all documents necessary to make an informed decision, as well as the informed judgement of the company's management and the progress of the company's business.[83] More precisely, the law requires disclosure of the procedure that shareholders must follow to vote, and to vote by proxy, mail or electronic means, how to send in draft resolutions and written questions, as well as the necessary accompanying documents, the deadlines for returning

78 Article L 225–103 CC.
79 Article 158 of former Law no. 66–537 of 24 July 1966.
80 France introduced this right for majority shareholders in 1989.
81 Articles L 225–103 and L 225–120 CC.
82 Article R 225–73 CC.
83 Article L 225–108 CC.

their vote by proxy or mail, the internet address where all information is stored, the exact record date, the draft resolutions of both management and shareholders and the place where all documents can be consulted and the date from which such consultation can take place.[84] Also, the content of those documents is prescribed in detail in the Commercial Code.[85]

The ordinary general meeting of French listed companies can validly take decisions only if at least 20 per cent of the shares are represented;[86] the threshold for extraordinary general meetings is 25 per cent.[87] Otherwise, the meeting must be adjourned. In a second call, the ordinary general meeting has no quorum limitations, but the threshold for the extraordinary general meeting is 20 per cent. Decisions taken at an ordinary general meeting require an absolute majority of the votes attached to the shares. Votes withheld or votes attached to shares that did not participate in the ballot are not considered to be votes. The latter rule was introduced by Law No. 2019–744 of 19 July 2019. Previously, all votes attending and all votes represented had to be taken into account in calculating the approval rate.

14.3.2 *Shareholder Proposals*

Shareholders can request to put an item on the meeting agenda. This right is reserved to shareholders owning more than 5 per cent of shares.[88] Similar to the right to call the general meeting, this threshold is gradually and step-by-step lowered with an increase in the company's capital to 0.5 per cent if the company has capital exceeding €15 million.[89] The company must be informed twenty-five days before the meeting of shareholder requests to include draft resolutions in the meeting agenda.[90] The shareholder concerned must send a registered letter with the request for acknowledgement by receipt or electronic telecommunication, along with a brief explanatory statement of the proposals concerned.[91]

14.3.3 *Shareholder Questions*

As soon as a general meeting has been called, every shareholder has a right to ask written questions, which the board of directors or management board must address during the meeting.[92] The questions should be addressed to the chairperson of the management board in the same way as a request to put an item on the meeting agenda.[93] They should arrive at the company's address four days before the meeting at the latest.[94] There is no limitation on the number of questions that a shareholder can raise, although it is assumed that the questions will relate to agenda items.[95] Questions can also be answered via the company's website. The French Commercial Code states that a written question is deemed to have been answered as soon as it appears on the company's website in a section devoted to questions and answers.[96]

84 Article R 225–73 CC.
85 Article R 225–73-1 and following CC.
86 Article L 225–98 CC.
87 Article L 225–96 CC.
88 Article L 225–105 CC.
89 Article R 225–71 CC.
90 Article R 225–73 CC.
91 Article R 225–71 CC.
92 Article L 225–108 CC.
93 Article R 225–84 CC.
94 Article R 225–84 CC.
95 Michel Germain and Veronique Magnier, *Les Sociétés commerciales* (Lextenso 2014) 914.
96 Article L 225–108 CC.

Furthermore, and this right goes beyond the questioning rights of shareholders in many other countries, one or more shareholders (or a shareholder association) representing at least 5 per cent of the company's capital have, twice a year, the right to pose questions in writing to the chairperson of the board of directors or the executive board on any fact likely to compromise the continuity of exploitation.[97] The chairperson has to address these questions in writing within one month,[98] and the response must also be communicated to the auditor, if any.

14.3.4 *COVID-19*

As in many other countries, the COVID-19 pandemic forced France to provide an alternative regime for organizing general meetings in spring of 2020. The French securities regulator first issued recommendations for the organization of meetings in early March 2020 when the lockdown of the country commenced.[99] The recommendations included the use of a paper voting form, a proxy voting form for the board chair or online voting via a secure voting platform, in France known as the VOTACCES platform. However, these measures were insufficient to address the French prohibition on large groups meeting in person. Hence, the government issued Ordonnance No. 2020–321 addressing the rules for convening the general meeting of shareholders and board meetings.[100] In short, the ordinance authorizes the board of directors, or by delegation the CEO, to organize the general meeting of shareholders without the attendance of shareholders, who can vote remotely by (1) making use of a voting paper form, (2) a proxy to the chair or (3) online via the VOTACCES platform, if the latter voting mode is provided for by the issuer's AoA and provided for by the issuer for the relevant meeting. In that case, all votes will be cast before the meeting takes place. Whilst this technique limits the use of the general meeting as a discussion platform and forces shareholders to make use of written questions to address the board of directors,[101] it allows the company to approve the financial statements and dividend payment. Decree No. 2020–418 further elaborates the various steps that the company must take in organizing the meeting.[102]

Another ordinance, Ordonnance No. 2020–318 of 25 March 2020, allows companies to postpone the approval of the financial statements until nine months after the close of the accounting period, and, consequently, the board can postpone the organization of the general meeting of shareholders for three months.[103] As we will see in the next section, many French companies have opted for the system of holding the general meeting behind closed doors and inviting shareholders to vote remotely instead of postponing the meeting.

97 Article L 225–232 CC.

98 Article R 164–164 CC.

99 AMF, *Communiqué de presse relatif aux assemblées générales de sociétés cotées* (6 March 2020) www.amf-france.org/fr/actualites-publications/communiques/communiques-de-lamf/communique-de-presse-relatif-aux-assemblees-generales-de-societes-cotees accessed 15 May 2020.

100 Ordonnance no. 2020–321 du 25 mars 2020 portant adaptation des règles de rgans et de rgansation des assemblées et rgans dirigeants des personnes morales et entités dépourvues de personnalité morale de droit privé en raison de l'épidémie de covid-19.

101 The ordinance does not as such waive the right of shareholders to ask questions during the general meeting, but holding a meeting behind closed doors results in the de facto waiving of that right.

102 Décret no. 2020–418 du 10 avril 2020 portant adaptation des règles de réunion et de délibération des assemblées et organes dirigeants des personnes morales et entités dépourvues de personnalité morale de droit privé en raison de l'épidémie de covid-19.

103 Ordonnance no. 2020–318 du 25 mars 2020 portant adaptation des règles relatives à l'établissement, l'arrêté, l'audit, la revue, l'approbation et la publication des comptes et des autres documents et informations que les personnes morales et entités dépourvues de personnalité morale de droit privé sont tenues de déposer ou publier dans le contexte de l'épidémie de covid-19.

14.4 SHAREHOLDER ENGAGEMENT AND VOTING IN PRACTICE

14.4.1 *Introduction, Data and Methodology*

In this section, hand-collected panel data from the websites of French listed large-cap SBF 120 companies are used to study the organization of ordinary and extraordinary general meetings (AGMs and EGMs). Further, a number of studies by Georgeson and the French securities regulator AMF are also taken into account. Depending on the type of engagement investigated, two partially overlapping groups of companies are included in the different samples. First, for the detailed assessment of the participation modes of shareholders in the AGMs of French companies, a selection of SBF 120 companies is used. More precisely, I include in my sample those companies that not only disclosed the voting turnouts and the results for each resolution but interpreted a requirement in the transposed French SRD I rule on the disclosure of voting results extensively[104] and disclosed, for the different voting modes, the number of participating shareholders and their shares and votes. Second, for the detailed assessment of voting results, use of the right to ask questions, shareholder proposals and other engagement opportunities, all or a sample of the French companies listed in the main stock index, CAC 40, are part of the analysis.

14.4.2 *Participation Rates in General Meetings of Shareholders*

Figure 14.1 illustrates the development of shareholder participation in the general meetings of large companies. The participation behaviour of shareholders in large French listed companies, the first proxy for measuring shareholder engagement, increased. For the largest companies, the CAC 40, the participation rate soared from around 60 per cent at the start of the decade[105] to 69 per cent in 2019. For the broader SBF 120 index, the rate increased from 66 per cent to 73 per cent over the same period. SBF 120 companies more frequently have blockholders in their shareholder base, and blockholders are generally more actively involved in the voting process.

I also investigated whether the increase could be the result of the *Loi Florange*. As a result of this law, which took effect in 2016, the default system moved from one share-one vote to double voting rights for loyal shareholders. However, it is unlikely that the law increased the willingness of shareholders to vote. Figure 14.1 also shows the evolution of shareholder participation in companies providing the system of double voting rights for loyal shareholders and those continuing to use the one share-one vote system before and after the law's enactment. It can be seen that the former observed a 2 to 4 per cent higher attendance rate than the latter.[106] In the group with double voting rights, the rate ranged from 69–72 per cent, with the highest attendance rates at the beginning and end of the decade. Attendance also grew in the one share-one vote group, ranging from 65–68 per cent. I further investigated the double voting right companies by deducting the evolution of the double voting rights shares from the difference between the number of attending shareholders

[104] Article R 225–106-1 CC: 'Companies whose shares are admitted to trading on a regulated market publish on the website referred to in article R 210–20, within fifteen days of the meeting, the results of the votes including at least: 1) the number of shareholders *present or represented* at the meeting; 2) the number of votes of the shareholders present or represented at the meeting; and 3) for each resolution, the total number of votes related to the number of shares and the proportion of the share capital they represent, the number and percentage of votes in favour of the resolution, the number and percentage of votes against the resolution, and abstentions' (author's translation, emphasis added).

[105] In the first decade of the millennium, participation rates were lower. See Christoph van der Elst, 'Aligning Shareholder Voting and Shareholder Engagement' in Abigail Levrau and Sandra Gobert (eds.), *Liber Amicorum Lutgart Van den Berghe* (Intersentia 2019) 55.

[106] In 2010, the difference was significantly higher. However, the number of observations for 2010 is low, which limits the reliability of the results.

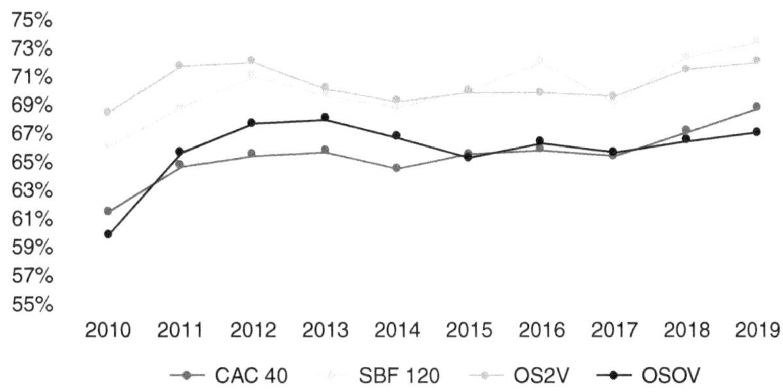

FIGURE 14.1 Evolution in the participation of shareholders (with or without double voting rights) in the AGMs of large listed companies (2010–19)
Note to figure: OS2 V = one share-two votes; OSOV = one share-one vote. Sources: Georgeson, *Georgeson's 2019 Proxy Season Review* (2019); Georgeson, *Georgeson's 2016 Proxy Season Review* (2016); Georgeson, *Georgeson's 2014 Proxy Season Review* (2014); author's own research.

and the total number of shares and voting rights: in the 2010–16 period, the mean percentage of double voting right shares was around 22–23 per cent of the shares, increasing to 24–26 per cent after 2016. The results also show that the overall participation of single voting right shares in companies with loyalty voting rights was significantly lower than that in one share-one vote companies. This lower attendance rate was compensated for by the very high participation levels of shares with double voting rights, as illustrated in Figure 14.1.

There were thirteen SBF 120 companies[107] that switched to double voting rights after implementation of the *Loi Florange*, either because a vote to remain a one share-one vote company was defeated or because the company did not table it as an agenda item at an AGM, which resulted in an automatic switch to the one share-two votes system. Overall, the participation of shares remained unchanged between 2015 and 2016, at 74 per cent in the year before and after the introduction of shares with double voting rights for loyal shareholders (see Table 14.1). Six companies experienced an increase in the participation of shares at their 2016 AGM, and six companies experienced a decrease. In two cases, the increase/decrease was significant. At Veolia, the participation rate soared with 7.5 per cent to 64 per cent. It was not only the holders of dual voting shares who increased their participation, but other shareholders too, which is exceptional. On the opposite site, Eiffage experienced a decrease of more than 8 per cent in the participation rate.[108] More generally, the introduction of double voting rights, which is aimed at engaging long-term shareholders, results in very high participation rates amongst the holders of such rights. The mean participation rate of these shareholders surpassed 90 per cent in the period considered, with almost half of the companies seeing nearly all – over 99 per cent – of them participating in the AGM. Hence, it seems that the *Loi Florange* achieved its goal.[109]

107 In 2016. In the meantime, some of the companies are no longer part of the current SBF 120 index. Renault also switched to double voting rights in 2016. However, its alliance with Nissan resulted in the suspension of a large number of the voting rights, which blurred the change in the results on participating shares and votes.

108 Eiffage's documentation does not disclose the total number of votes of the shares at the date of the meeting. I made use of the disclosure of the number of voting rights in the notification of the passing of a threshold of one of the shareholders close to the date of the meeting. Therefore, the participation rate of the number of votes in 2016 is an accurate estimation.

109 I also collected data for companies that already had double voting rights before the *Loi Florange*, and the results confirm the findings for the firms that moved to double voting rights after that law came into effect: the participation

However, a number of additional conditions for drawing that conclusion do not seem to have been satisfied. The first condition is that the use of double voting rights should positively affect the participation behaviour of shareholders. My initial (limited) analysis showed the introduction of loyalty shareholdings to affect voting engagement by 'single vote' shareholders. In all but one of the companies, the participation of single voting shares declined, and the decline was significant in a number of companies: the average attendance rate of single voting shares at the 2016 AGM topped 60 per cent, whilst the overall attendance in 2015, when all shares carried a single vote, was 74 per cent. The gain achieved by the provision of double voting rights to loyal shareholders resulted in an equally large decrease in the participation rates of shareholders holding single voting shares. Whilst nearly all of the shareholders who received double voting rights were provided with an additional incentive to participate, other shareholders, whether long-term shareholders whose shares had not been registered as named shares or short-term shareholders, could be, as their position worsened relative to the former, negatively affected by engagement behaviour. The second condition is that the *Loi Florange*, like the system that preceded it, requires shareholders to register their shares. As institutional investors generally endorse the one-share one-vote system,[110] they oppose the use of double voting rights. Accordingly, they do not register their shares, and consequently refrain from obtaining double voting rights.

TABLE 14.1 *Participation of shareholders in companies that switched to double voting rights after passage of the* Loi Florange

	AGM 2015[111]	AGM 2016[112]	AGM 2015/16	AGM 2016	AGM 2016	AGM 2016
Company	% participating shares	% participating shares	relative change in participating shares	% double voting rights	% double voting rights attending	% single voting shares attending
Orange	67.2%	67.7%	0.53%	14.9%	98.0%	62.4%
Vivendi	59.0%	59.4%	0.33%	4.0%	86.1%	58.3%
Veolia	56.2%	63.7%	7.48%	17.4%	85.0%	59.2%
Dassault Systèmes	88.1%	85.1%	−3.05%	77.9%	100.0%	32.8%
ADP	89.4%	88.7%	−0.66%	73.1%	99.9%	58.4%
Air France KLM	57.8%	56.1%	−1.72%	24.6%	72.3%	50.8%
Alstom	62.1%	66.8%	4.71%	2.4%	67.0%	66.8%
Bolloré	83.0%	85.2%	2.26%	64.0%	99.8%	59.2%
EDF	92.8%	92.7%	−0.15%	79.9%	99.5%	65.6%
Eiffaige	75.1%	66.5%	−8.69%	14.9%	97.4%	61.1%
Sopra Steria	79.7%	79.5%	−0.27%	29.5%	94.8%	73.1%
Havas	82.1%	82,6%	0.54%	31.9%	99.9%	74.5%
Mean	74.4%	74.5%	0.11%	36.2%	91.6%	60.2%

Source: author's own research based on disclosed company documents.

of the shares with double voting rights varied between 85 per cent and 90 per cent during the decade overall, and the average participation of the holders of other shares fluctuated between 57 per cent and 62 per cent.

110 For a discussion, see Council of Institutional Investors, *Dual-Class Stock* www.cii.org/dualclass_stock accessed 1 June 2020.

111 For Sopra Steria 2014.

112 For Sopra Steria 2015.

14.4.3 *Number of Participating Shareholders*

Many French companies also disclose the number of participating shareholders. In 2011, the average number of shareholders voting at the general meeting of large French companies was over 6,500 (Figure 14.2), although the number has declined over time. In 2019, the average number was 5,100 shareholders. The median number of participating shareholders also declined significantly, falling from 2,300 in 2011 to 1,600 in 2016 before rising again to more than 2,000 in 2019. Overall, the median remained relatively stable over the years, in contrast to the average, owing to a limited number of outliers. At Michelin, more than 30,000 shareholders participated in the general meetings held between 2011 and 2016, after which Total took over as the company with the most frequented meetings, with over 40,000 participants in 2017.[113] However, Michelin welcomed more than 27,000 shareholders in 2019. It is not uncommon for French companies to see the votes of more than 10,000 shareholders. Conversely, at some of the meetings of larger companies, only fifty shareholders participated. Notwithstanding the considerable number of shareholders participating in general meetings, a very large majority of (small) shareholders does not vote. For example, Total's 2019 meeting hosted 21,505 shareholders, of whom 2,081 attended in person, despite the company estimating its total number of shareholders to be 450,000.

14.4.4 *Shareholder Voting and Various Voting Modes*

Figure 14.3 divides participating shareholders into four classes according to their voting mode: shareholders who attend the general meeting in person, those represented by a third party, those providing a proxy (in the form of a power of attorney) to the chairperson and those sending their votes by mail (remote voting, which includes voting online).

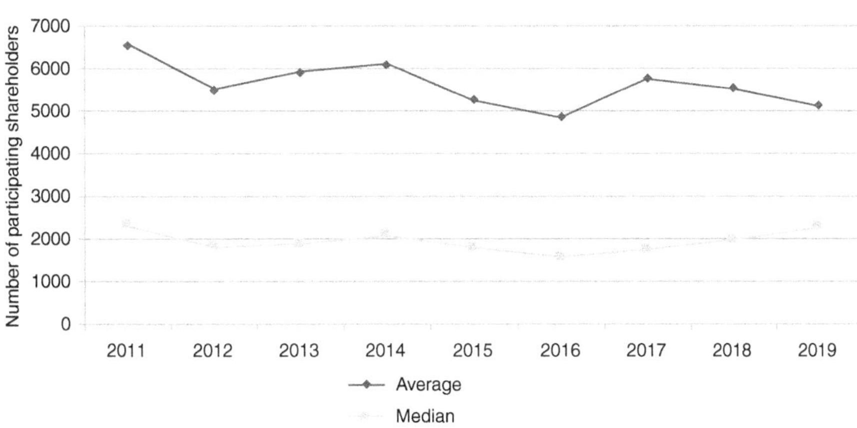

FIGURE 14.2 Evolution in the number of participating shareholders (all voting modes)
Source: author's own research based on disclosed company documents.

[113] The documents of Air Liquide, which are not in this sample, indicate that the number of participating shareholders passed the threshold of 100,000 shareholders.

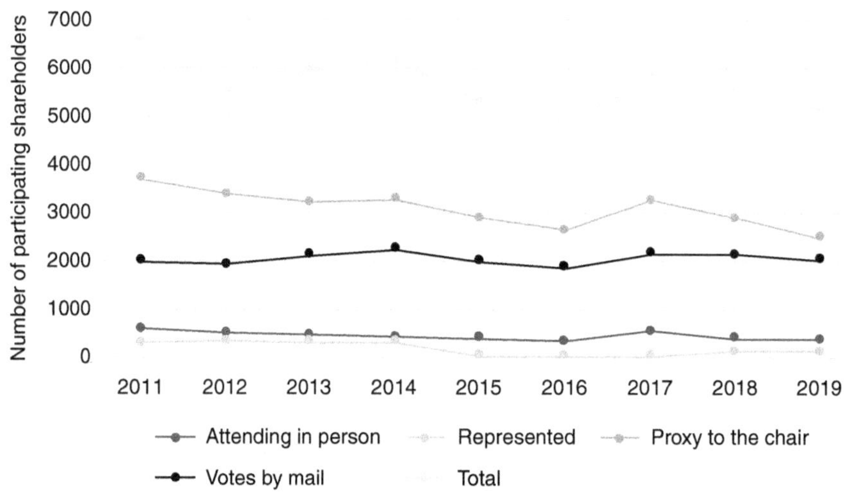

FIGURE 14.3 Evolution in the relative importance of the various voting modes
Source: author's own research based on disclosed company documents.

The first group is in steady decline. Whilst the relative percentage of these shareholders was close to 20 per cent in 2011 and 2012, in 2019 only seven per cent of attending shareholders were present *in personam*. In absolute numbers, the average number of attending shareholders dropped from 583 in 2011 to 388 in 2019.[114] During the research period, the median number of attending shareholders dropped from 350 to 173, with the latter figure representing a modest increase on the all-time low of 155 in 2018. An absolute low in the number of attending shareholders was found at the 2018 general meeting of Maison du Monde: two shareholders with a total number of 1,004 shares were present, representing just 0.003 per cent of all participating votes. Meetings with only ten to twenty shareholders attending in person are not uncommon.

Authorizing a proxy to participate in a general meeting on behalf of a shareholder is uncommon practice in France. Only 5 per cent of shareholders made use of a proxy at meetings in 2011, falling to less than 0.5 per cent in 2017, with a modest revival in 2019, when 2.2 per cent of shareholders used a proxy. During the first half of the decade, around 300 shareholders provided a proxy. In the second half, the number dropped to fewer than 30 in 2017 before increasing to around 140 in the last two years of the decade.

A far more common voting technique used by shareholders in French companies is to provide a power of attorney to the chairperson of the general meeting, who is commonly also the chairperson of the supervisory board. The average percentage of utilizers of this technique stabilized at around 30 per cent, with a low of 27 per cent in 2012 and a record high of almost 35 per cent in 2019. In absolute numbers, use of the technique experienced a steady decline: from 3,700 shareholders in 2011 to fewer than 2,700 in 2019.

The most common technique for participating in a general meeting of shareholders is to vote by mail (via the internet or post office). Since 2012, over 50 per cent of all shareholders have sent their votes to the company in advance of the general meeting. The percentage stabilized at

[114] The mean absolute numbers and mean relative numbers cannot directly be compared. A short example illustrates this. In two meetings of 100 and 1000 shareholders, the first is attended by 50 shareholders in person, and the second by 300 shareholders in person. In average numbers, the attendance in person is 32 per cent (350/1100), whilst the average attendance is 40 per cent ((50 per cent+30 per cent)/2).

around 58 per cent between 2016 and 2019. However, the higher average participation via a mail vote than by granting a proxy to the meeting chair is due to the absence of the latter option in a number of companies. In absolute numbers, more shareholders make use of the power of attorney mode. During the study period, only 1,850 to 2,200 shareholders, on average, voted by mail, with the median number remaining stable until 2017, when around 1,000 shareholders made use of this mechanism per year per company. By 2019, the median number of powers of attorney received by the chairperson exceeded 1,500. Figure 14.3 summarizes the development of the average number of shareholders making use of the various voting modes.

Figure 14.3 presents the results as if all shareholders owned an equal number of shares. Figure 14.4 weights the voting power of shareholders. It shows that two modes, as measured by voting turnout, are the most common: shareholders attending (and voting) in person and shareholders voting by mail. The two other modes, making use of a power of attorney for the chair of the general meeting or being represented at the meeting by a third party, are, when measured by the number of voting rights, little used.

First, remote voting has gained in importance over time. Forty-three per cent of all votes were voted through the channel of mail voting in 2011, rising to 57 per cent in 2018. However, the average of mail voting, which is almost equal to the median, does not highlight individual company differences. At the start of the research period, shareholders in some companies did not make use of voting by mail at all, whereas by the end of the period there were no companies without shareholders making use of this voting mode. Moreover, in 2019 one company in four received over 90 per cent of their votes by mail. Most of the companies with very low levels of voting by mail were companies with a (large) majority shareholder who attended the general meeting of shareholders *in personam*.

Second, the number of voting rights of shareholders attending the meeting in person has steadily declined. Accounting for more than 50 per cent of all voting rights participating in the meeting in 2011, the attending shareholders voted, on average, only 30 per cent of the participating votes in 2019, with the median percentage falling below the threshold of 20 per cent. The aforementioned controlled companies heavily influenced these levels, as all of these companies had attending shareholders voting up to 95 per cent of the participating voting rights.

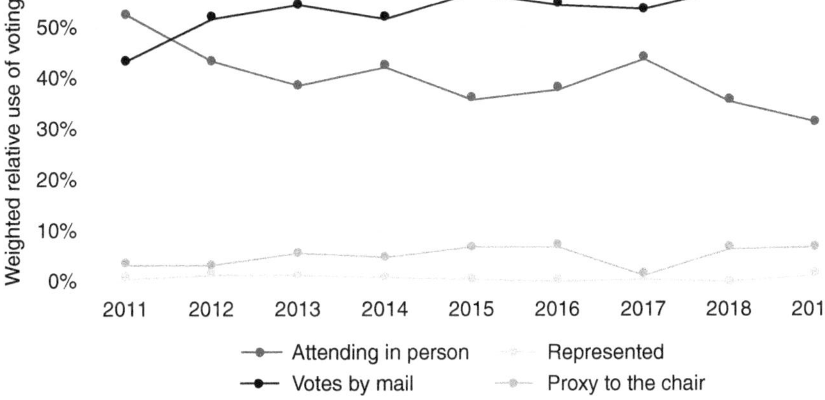

FIGURE 14.4 Relative weight of voting modes used by shareholders
Source: author's own research based on disclosed company documents.

The numbers show that the shareholders making use of a proxy to the meeting chair are commonly very small shareholders. With a median of 450 to 1,100 shareholders making use of this voting mechanism, the total voting turnout for the mode stands for 1.7–7.2 per cent of the participating votes in the meeting. In 2017, when approximately 3,300 shareholders provided a power of attorney to the meeting chair, their votes counted for 1.7 per cent of all votes. Proxies to other participants were negligible, with less than 2 per cent of the voting turnout flowing from this voting technique.

14.4.5 *COVID-19 and Shareholder Voting*

Like many other European countries, France has been severely hit by the COVID-19 pandemic, with the government locking down the country for many weeks during the period in which many general meetings would have taken place. As we saw in Section 14.4.3, the average number of shareholders attending meetings in person fluctuates between 400 and 600, but in individual cases can exceed 5,700. In light of the risk of participating shareholders infecting one another with the virus if they attend meetings in person, the government offered companies the option of either postponing the general meeting of shareholders or organizing the meeting behind closed doors without shareholders. At the time of writing, a majority of CAC 40 companies had organized their meetings behind closed doors. I collected data on twenty-six CAC 40 companies and found the average participation rate of shareholders to have been moderately higher in 2020 than in 2019: the average (median) in 2020 was 70.9 per cent (70.5 per cent) compared to 69.4 per cent (66.8 per cent) in 2019. Ten CAC 40 companies also disclosed the use of the different voting modes during the 2020 AGM. The results can be found in Table 14.2.

The 2019 meetings of the ten companies welcomed, on average, 631 shareholders in person, whilst another 330 shareholders were represented at the meeting by another person other than the chairperson. The bulk of these shareholders gave power of attorney to the meeting chair to vote their shares or sent in their votes by mail. Providing a proxy to the chair was used more often by small shareholders. The more than 3,600 shareholders making use of this mode represented only 2.3 per cent of the votes at the 2019 meetings.

As the meetings took place behind closed doors in 2020, no shareholders attended them in person. They opted either to send a proxy to the meeting chair or vote by mail, with both voting modes attracting more shareholders in 2020 than in 2019. Interestingly, although the COVID-19 pandemic reshuffled the voting modes, it does not appear to have had a negative effect on shareholders' willingness to cast votes, which increased by more than 6 per cent over the period.

TABLE 14.2 *Attendance and voting modes during the COVID-19 pandemic*

	Shareholders		Votes	
	2019	2020	2019	2020
Attending in person	631	0	19.38%	0%
Votes represented	330	0.8	0.06%	0.01%
Proxy to the chair	3,668	4,443	2.32%	7.38%
Votes by mail	3,134	4,036	78.24%	92.61%
Total	7,764	8,233	73.11%	72.60%
N	10	10	10	10

Source: author's own research based on disclosed company documents.

More precisely, the board chair received more than 20 per cent more proxies from shareholders in 2020 than in 2019 and represented more than half of the participating shareholders at the meeting. Also, this voting mode more than tripled in importance, representing more than 7 per cent of issued votes. However, it was not considered an option by larger shareholders. In only one company did the proxies to the chairperson matter, representing 44 per cent of participating votes. In six companies, the weight of such proxies declined in 2020 relative to 2019. The bulk of votes in all companies were sent in by mail, with all but one company in the sample receiving over 90 per cent of the votes by mail. In two companies, a handful of shareholders gave voting power to a person other than the chairperson.

14.4.6 *Voting Items*

In Section 14.3, I briefly sketched the various agenda items on which the shareholders of French companies vote. The items that ordinary general meetings vote on can be grouped into five categories: the approval of financial statements and the allocation of earnings; the election of boards of directors and auditors; agreements with boards, management and other related parties; the remuneration of management and the board, which has increased significantly as a voting item over the last decade; and a miscellaneous group of items that commonly includes the right to trade or buy back shares and the provision of powers to the management board for executing decisions. Overall, the number of voting items that shareholders have to approve is relatively high, with a mean of almost sixteen and a median of fifteen (see Table 14.3). Ordinary meetings are almost always combined with a subsequent extraordinary general meeting. The number of items that the latter has to approve is, on average, half that of the former, although some meetings have significantly more items put before them for approval (as the example of Orange will show). The large majority of these items relate to the company's capital. The board of directors invites shareholders to authorize it to issue shares and other capital-related securities, with or without pre-emptive rights, to be granted to employees, the board and executive officers or to defend the company in case of a hostile takeover bid. Each item requires a separate vote. Other items addressed by the extraordinary meeting of shareholders relate to the amendment of the company's AoA or to specific issues such as the company's transformation into a European company.

Table 14.4 provides an overview of the different voting items in each aforementioned category and the mean and median voting results for the 2019 AGMs of CAC 40 companies. The first category, items related to approval of the company's financial accounts and the allocation of profits, is almost always approved with supermajorities of more than 99 per cent. Opposition is exceptional. At Renault, 10 per cent of the votes were against the approval of the financial statement, but no information is available on the reasons for this high, albeit relative, level of opposition. It should be noted that French legislation requires shareholders to not only approve the financial statement of the parent company but also consolidated financial statements, a requirement that, as far as an approval

TABLE 14.3 *Number of voting items at 2019 AGMs and EGMs*

Voting items	AGM	EGM	*pertaining to capital-related operations*
Mean	15.7	7.7	7.2
Median	15	8	7

Source: own research based on disclosed company documents.

TABLE 14.4 *Voting results of agenda items at 2019 AGMs of CAC 40 companies*

	Mean	Median	N
Approval of parent company's financial statements	99.39%	99.76%	37
Approval of consolidated financial statements	99.29%	99.68%	37
Allocation of earnings	99.09%	99.75%	37
Election of directors	96.76%	98.95%	40
Re-election of directors	92.96%	96.26%	113
(Re)election of external auditors	95.70%	95.21%	13
Approval of related-party agreements	94.12%	99.51%	35
Approval of commitments	88.95%	94.85%	31
Approval of overall amount of annual directors' fees	97.37%	98.24%	9
Approval of compensation components of PDG (CEO and chair combined)	82.77%	87.61%	22
Approval of compensation components of chair	94.23%	99.23%	15
Approval of compensation components of CEO	87.40%	92.28%	18
Approval of compensation components of deputy CEO	86.27%	89.04%	23
Approval of compensation components of other executives	85.76%	78.78%	13
Approval of compensation policy for PDG (CEO and chair)	87.77%	90.40%	15
Approval of compensation policy for chair	95.67%	98.32%	13
Approval of compensation policy for CEO	88.39%	90.90%	16
Approval of compensation policy for deputy CEO	91.70%	92.10%	6
Approval of compensation policy for other executives	85.85%	86.44%	11
Authorization for the board to transact in shares/share buybacks	97.63%	99.01%	36
Formalities	99.47%	99.90%	33

Source: author's own research based on disclosed company documents.

mechanism for shareholders is an appropriate instrument, is to be considered more logical than the approval of the parent company's statutory statements.

The second category of voting items relates to the (re)election of directors and external auditors. These are the most common voting items, as each director must be elected with a separate vote, resulting in an average of four directors being (re)elected in each company. Directors standing for re-election experience, on average, more opposition than newly elected directors, as their track record in the company makes shareholders more critical. However, fierce opposition is exceptional: only two directors were not elected in 2019, but the proposal to elect them came from shareholders. Both of them would have been elected if the largest shareholder, with a voting bloc of more than 40 per cent, had not voted against them. One other director was re-elected thanks to the support of the majority shareholders alone: based on the voting results, the majority of the minority opposed his re-election. Opposition to the election of external auditors is modest, with more than 10 per cent opposing the election in one case.

It should come as no surprise that shareholder opposition to RPTs is relatively strong, especially when the transaction relates to commitments for directors and officers. In companies with widely dispersed ownership, in particular, it is not uncommon to find opposition rates of more than 30 per cent. However, in none of the companies examined was any RPT disapproved.

The highest levels of opposition are found for say-on-pay items. Remuneration policy and the remuneration packages of CEOs, whether or not they combine the position with that of chairperson of the board, faced opposition, on average, in the region of 15–20 per cent. Influential in the lower average for CEO remuneration packages (see the compensation components in Table 14.4) was the support of just 11 per cent of participating shareholders at Renault. This was an exceptional case, as the board of directors advised shareholders to vote against the package for Renault's CEO,[115] who was imprisoned in Japan in 2018 for tax fraud, resigned shortly after the general meeting and has since been replaced.[116]

Finally, shareholders generally do not object to the board of directors trading in the company's shares or buying back shares. French companies also ask for authorization to execute the decisions of the general meeting, although in my opinion this should be considered a superfluous voting item. If shareholders approve a particular voting item, then it is logical to assume that such approval includes the right and duty to execute the decision that has been taken.

As most companies combine their ordinary general meeting with a sequential extraordinary general meeting, Table 14.5 provides an overview of the typical agenda of the latter using Orange as an example. As we have already seen, almost all agenda items at an extraordinary general meeting relate to capital operations. In the case of Orange, all sixteen items relate to capital

TABLE 14.5 *Voting items at the extraordinary general meeting of Orange in 2019*

Voting item	Votes for	Accepted/ Failed
Delegation to issue shares in the company and complex securities, with shareholder preferential subscription rights (not to be used during a takeover offer)	99.01%	Accepted
Authorization to make use of the delegation of authority granted in the former resolution during a takeover offer	56.67%	Failed
Delegation to issue shares in the company and complex securities, without shareholder preferential subscription rights as part of a public offering (not to be used during a takeover offer)	86.28%	Accepted
Authorization to make use of the delegation of authority granted in the former resolution during a takeover offer	47.55%	Failed
Delegation to issue shares in the company and complex securities, without shareholder preferential subscription rights as part of an offer provided for in s II, art L 411–2 of the French Monetary and Financial Code (not to be used during a takeover offer period)	84.48%	Accepted
Authorization to make use of the delegation of authority granted in the former resolution during a takeover offer	47.12%	Failed
Authorization to increase the number of issuable securities, in the event of securities to be issued	63.31%	Failed
Delegation of authority to issue shares and complex securities, without shareholder preferential subscription rights, in the event of a public exchange offer initiated by the company (not to be used during a takeover offer period)	98.45%	Accepted
Authorization to make use of the delegation of authority granted in the former resolution during a takeover offer	58.46%	Failed
Delegation to issue shares and complex securities, without shareholder preferential subscription rights, as consideration for contributions in kind granted to the company and comprising equity securities or securities given access to capital (not to be used during a takeover offer period)	98.28%	Accepted
Authorization to make use of the delegation of powers granted in the former resolution during a takeover offer	58.42%	Failed

115 See Groupe Renault, *Notice of Meeting 12 June 2019*, 48 https://group.renault.com/wp-content/uploads/2019/05/renault-notice-of-meeting-2019.pdf accessed 15 June 2020.

116 See https://newmobility.news/2018/11/19/carlos-ghosn-arrested-in-japan-for-tax-fraud/ accessed 10 June 2020.

TABLE 14.5 *(continued)*

Voting item	Votes for	Accepted/ Failed
Overall limit on authorizations	88.21%	Accepted
Authorization to allocate the company's shares for free to corporate officers and certain Orange group employees	88.19%	Accepted
Delegation to issue shares or complex securities reserved for members of savings plans without shareholder preferential subscription rights	99.18%	Accepted
Delegation to increase the company's capital by the capitalization of reserves, profits or premiums	75.22%	Accepted
Authorization to reduce capital through the cancellation of shares	88.88%	Accepted

Source: author's own research based on disclosed company documents.

operations. Further, opposition can be significant. As these agenda items need a two-thirds majority of the votes, six items were defeated in 2019. Three types of items, in particular, often experience significant opposition: authorizations for granting (the option of) shares to employees and executives free of charge, offering the board of directors the right to issue shares and securities as an antitakeover device and, although it generally meets less opposition, issuing shares or securities without pre-emptive rights. At Orange, the defeated voting items related to the use of capital to combat a hostile takeover offer.

At one-third of the extraordinary meetings of CAC 40 companies in 2019, one or two voting items related to a change in the company's AoA. All such changes were approved. There were a few other items put before the extraordinary general meetings. For example, Unibail-Rodamco required approval to change its official name to Unibail-Rodamco-Westfield after its takeover of Westfield in 2018.

14.4.7 *Shareholder Proposals*

Shareholder proposals are an instrument of engagement familiar to French companies, although the limited evidence available shows that it is not as common an engagement practice as it is in the USA.[117] My investigation confirms this conclusion. In 2019, two companies were targeted with shareholder proposals. First, at Orange, the collective employee investment fund issued four different proposals: to distribute a smaller dividend, to change the bylaws against 'overboarding', to issue share capital in a restricted stock plan for employees and to amend the existing stock plan for employees. All four proposals were defeated with 86 per cent dissent, indicating that only a small group of shareholders supported the employee investment fund. Second, at the meeting of EssilorLuxottica, institutional investors led by Fidelity International and backed by, amongst others, the French activist Phitrust supported the election of two directors in an attempt to reduce the tensions (deblock the stalemate)[118] at board level that had come into existence following the merger of the French Essilor and Italian Luxottica. The

[117] Luc Renneboog and Peter Szilagyi, 'Shareholder Engagement at European General Meetings' in Marco Belcredi and Guido Ferrarini (eds.), *Boards and Shareholders in European Listed Companies* (Cambridge University Press 2013) 330.

[118] As reported by Bloomberg www.bloomberg.com/news/articles/2019–04-21/funds-seek-essilorluxottica-board-seats-amid-fight-for-control accessed 15 June 2020.

TABLE 14.6 *Voting recommendations 'against' CEO remuneration packages in 2019*

	50% highest approval rate	50% lowest approval rate
ISS	10.5%	61.1%
Glass Lewis	5.3%	44.4%

Source: based on Georgeson, *Georgeson's 2019 Proxy Season Review* (2019) 54–7.

board did not support the proposal. The two directors were backed by 44 and 34 per cent of shareholders, an insufficient percentage for election.

Proxy advisors are active in the French market, and their voting opinions seem to affect voting results. When the approval rates for CEOs' remuneration packages are ranked from the least to the most opposition, in the class of the highest degree of support for those packages, both ISS and Glass Lewis, the most prominent international proxy advisors, only seldom recommended a vote against (see Table 14.6). In the class of the lowest degree of opposition, ISS recommended a vote against in more than half of cases, and Glass Lewis in close to 45 per cent. In all cases, the level of opposition exceeded 15 per cent, although only one pay package (that of the former CEO of Renault) received a majority negative vote. Local proxy advisors such Proxinvest do not disclose such detailed information.

14.4.8 *Question Right*

Contrary to shareholder proposals, the right to ask questions at the general meeting and before it takes place is frequently, and often intensively, used, but only by certain types of shareholders. As the minutes of general meetings seldom record all of the questions that shareholders raise during the meeting, I investigated the written questions put to three CAC 40 companies, Total, Sanofi and Bouygues, from 2017 to 2020 to illustrate the importance and role of this engagement tool. The three companies belong to different industries and have different ownership structures. A summary of the findings is presented in Figure 14.5. Whilst the number of questions generally fluctuates, the organization of a closed meeting in 2020 had a dramatic impact on the number of written questions submitted: in all three companies, the number more than doubled, rising to 100 for Total. However, despite the participation of thousands of shareholders, the number raising questions ranged from only one to seven. These shareholders tend to be highly committed to the company, with some sending in questions year after year and sometimes asking similar or even identical questions. As noted, only some types of shareholders make use of this engagement tool. First, individual shareholders raised approximately half the questions from 2017–20, with many asking just one or two. In a number of cases, these shareholders had close connections with and/or were employees of the company. Second, the large majority of questions were raised by representative organizations such as the Association Initiative Pour un Actionnariat Citoyen or Forum d'Investissement Responsible, with similar questions often asked in different companies. The remaining questions came from other types of shareholders but only in one year, with one institutional investor raising questions in all three companies in 2018. Third, a large number of the questions raised concern environmental, social or governance issues (ESG), although their subject is often operational activities or financial issues. Finally, the companies' boards of directors sometimes made use of their right of confidentiality. The most notable examples were

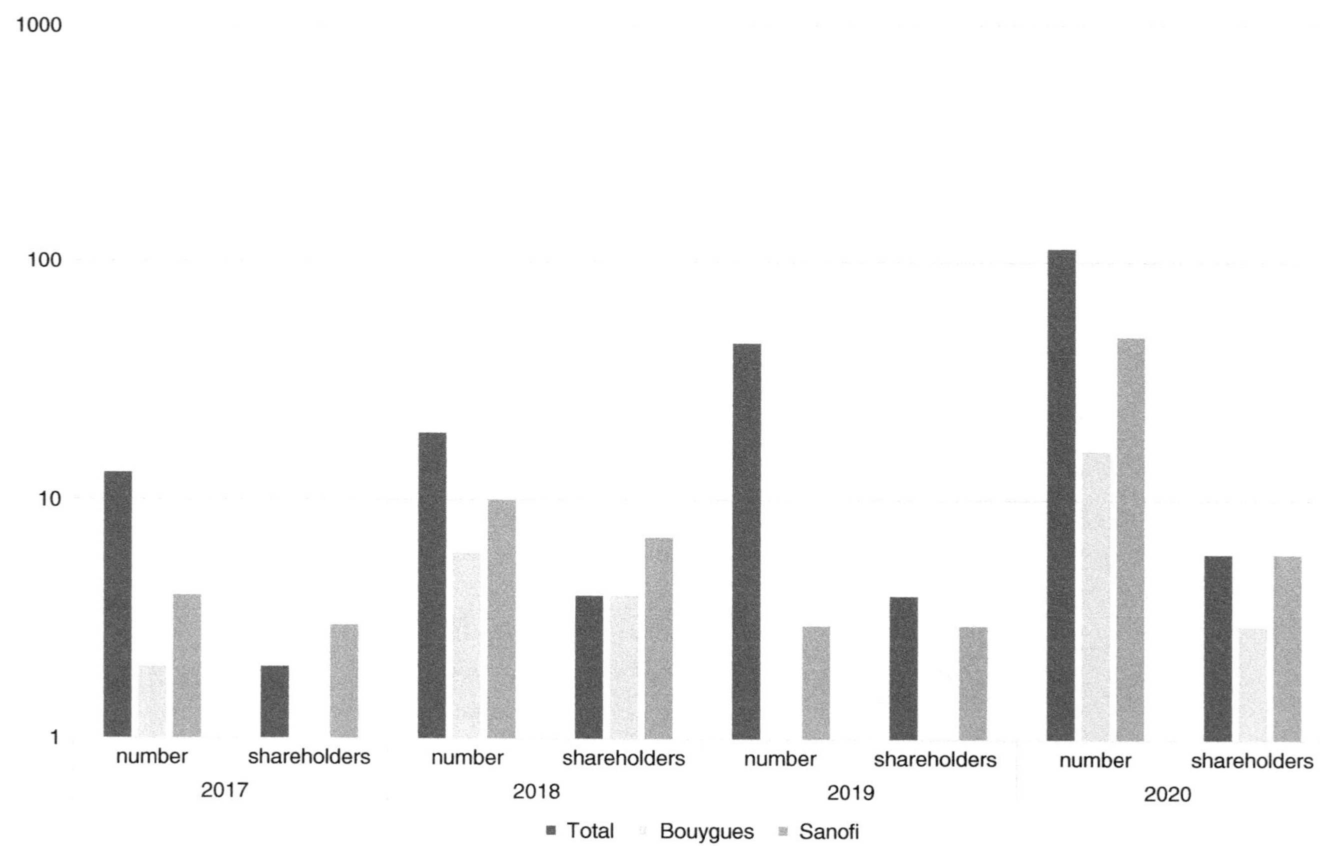

FIGURE 14.5 The use of shareholders' written question right
Source: author's own research based on disclosed company documents.

when a series of questions were raised by an attorney-at-law who represented a foreign company and when there was a question concerning a pending legal investigation.

14.4.9 *Engagement and Shareholder Activism*

Shareholder engagement is not limited to the participation of shareholders in the general meeting through voting, issuing proposals and asking questions. Many other types of engagement exist. In 2109, the French securities regulator AMF published a report on its study investigating the various mechanisms that French companies use to engage their shareholders.[119]

First, major shareholders and employee-shareholders are often present on companies' boards of directors. In 80 per cent of the French companies in the AMF study, there was an employee on the supervisory board of directors. Similarly, when there is a significant shareholder, the non-executive, non-independent directors, as well as some of the executive directors, commonly represent the major shareholders.

Second, it is common practice amongst French companies for their AoA to provide for the presence of advisory members on the board, often for the purpose of representing different groups of shareholders at the board level.[120] In approximately one in four companies, the board of directors is assisted by one or more *censeurs*, who often bring additional knowledge and useful skills to the board. However, not all shareholders, particularly institutional investors and proxy advisors, support the enlargement of boards with this type of advisor.[121]

Third, in the past few years more than 60 per cent of French companies have appointed a board director who is responsible for the establishment and development of relations with shareholders, in accordance with Principle 4.4 of the French Corporate Governance Code: 'Shareholder relations with the Board of Directors, particularly with regard to corporate governance aspects, may be entrusted to the Chairman of the Board of Directors or, if applicable, to the Lead Director. He or she shall report on this task to the Board of Directors'. AMF noted that companies with a dispersed ownership structure comply more often with this principle than companies with a controlling shareholder. The most common topic of dialogue is the 'G' component of ESG: governance.

Fourth, many French companies have established shareholder clubs called *club d'actionnaires*. Many of these clubs provide access to all shareholders, conditional upon their ownership of a (modest) number of shares. Shareholders need to register for the clubs, which regularly provide them with information on the development of the company and sometimes with other advantages. At Accor, every shareholder who owns more than fifty shares can become a club member and receive such perks as a reduction in hotel room rates and the option of staying

[119] AMF, *Rapport 2019 sur le gouvernement d'entreprise et la remuneration des dirigeants des sociétés cotées* (Paris, 3 December 2019) 38, n. 81.

[120] Germain and Magnier (n. 95) 483.

[121] The following is stated in Blackrock's 'Proxy Voting Guidelines for European, Middle Eastern, and African Securities' (January 2019): 'Censors: BlackRock recognises that there are circumstances under which companies might want to appoint censors and that censors are appointed for transitional/interim periods. However, we may vote against censor appointment if the appointment is not twined with sufficient levels of disclosure that would allow BlackRock to assess the reasons for the appointment, terms of the appointment, and any links that the censor might have with the company'.

longer in the room.[122] At LVMH's *club d'actionnaires*, shareholders receive discounted subscriptions on newspapers and magazines and are invited to exclusive premises of the company.[123]

As noted above, French companies have been familiar with shareholder engagement for many years.[124] In the past few years, French companies have also experienced US-style shareholder activism more frequently than their counterparts in many other European companies. According to Lazard, French and German companies are frequent targets of shareholder activism campaigns.[125] Activist Insight has confirmed the increase in such campaigns in France.[126] In a 2019 study for the French Parliament, Woerth and Dirx analyzed the different forms of shareholder activism that French companies have encountered over the years.[127] The trigger for activism can be a specific event[128] or a finding that the company is generating insufficient shareholder value. Recent developments prompted AMF to publish a report in which it makes a plea for a more level playing field for all parties.[129] In this respect, AMF recommends lowering the threshold for the notification of major holdings from 5 to 3 per cent, offering issuers the right to speak out during 'quiet periods'[130] when a public activist campaign is launched, broadening the scope for notification of short positions, repatriating loaned securities before the general meeting, and granting AMF more power to impose fines and provide a better definition of action in concert.

14.5 CONCLUDING REMARKS

France has modernized the framework for organizing the governance structure of companies significantly in the past few decades, in large part by modifying the corporate law sections of the Commercial Code. The French Commercial Code offers companies the option of a one-tier or two-tier board structure, and, in the case of the former structure, the option of combining the functions of the CEO and board chair or of separating those functions. Further, France has

122 For more information, see https://group.accor.com/fr-FR/investors/individual-shareholders/terms-and-conditions-of-accor-shareholders-club-membership accessed 15 June 2020.

123 For more information, see www.lvmh.com/investors/individual-shareholders/shareholders-club/ accessed 15 June2020.

124 In an old RiskMetrics report analyzing European general meetings in 2008, France took the lead in shareholder dissent in four out of six investigated agenda items (remuneration, share plans, nominations and article amendments). Out of 161 rejected or withdrawn proposals, 60 were recorded in French companies (RiskMetrics, *Voting Results in Europe* (2008)). According to ISS research, in a sample of seventeen European countries, more than half of the rejected proposals in 2010 and 2011 were found in France (ISS, *2011 Voting Results Report: Europe* (2011)).

125 Lazard, *2019 Review of Shareholder Activism* (January 2020). Also, 2020 was a year with significant shareholder activism in France, with board requests of Amber Capital at Lagardère and Teleios Capital Partners at Maisons du Monde (Activist Insight, *Shareholder Activism in Q1 2020* (April 2020) 10). The first activist lost the battle while Lagardère was allegedly breaching the law to shake off Amber Capital, whilst the second gained ground while using more private behind-the-scenes negotiations (Activist Insight, *Activist Insight Monthly: Activism in France* (June 2020) 7). For other cases, see AMF, *Rapport 2019 sur le gouvernement d'entreprise et la rémunération des dirigeants des sociétés cotées* (Paris, 3 December 2019) 25, n. 56.

126 Activist Insight, *Activist Insight Monthly: Activism in France* (June 2020) 6.

127 Eric Woerth and Benjamin Dirx, *Mission d'information sur l'activisme actionnarial* (Paris, 2 October 2019) www.assemblee-nationale.fr/dyn/15/dossiers/activisme_actionnarial_rap-info accessed 15 June 2020.

128 See AMF, *The Autorité des Marchés Financiers (AMF) has closed the investigation opened on 12 February 2016 into the financial information and market for the securities of CASINO and RALLYE as well as the behaviour of MUDDY WATERS CAPITAL* (17 December 2019) www.amf-france.org/en/news-publications/news-releases/amf-news-releases/autorite-des-marches-financiers-amf-has-closed-investigation-opened-12-february-2016-financial accessed 15 June 2020.

129 AMF, *Report by the AMF on Shareholder Activism* (April 2020) www.amf-france.org/sites/default/files/2020–04/report-by-the-autorite-des-marches-financiers-on-shareholder-activism_5.pdf accessed 15 June 2020.

130 The period before earnings are disclosed.

introduced a system of employee representation, as well as mandatory rules on gender diversity. Shareholders are empowered with approval rights on RPTs and on remuneration policies and packages, and there is an effective enforcement system in place. The regulatory system has also been modernized. The Corporate Governance Code is regularly updated and is monitored yearly. The French securities regulator is active, annually reviewing corporate governance practices and issuing recommendations for improving the corporate governance system and for balancing the interests of shareholders and investees.

Shareholder engagement in voting has increased significantly in the last decade, and COVID-19 does not seem to have affected voting engagement. There are some indications that shareholder questions during the general meeting have been replaced at least in part by higher numbers of written questions during the COVID-19 era. However, such questions cannot replace in-person debate, as some of the answers that boards of directors provide invite further questions, to say the least, but the mechanism provides no room for discussion. This development thus raises questions about the role and position of the general meeting of shareholders.

Finally, shareholder engagement involves more than just voting at the general meeting. Many French companies still make use of *censeurs*, persons who are elected in an advisory capacity to boards of directors and represent certain types of shareholders. In addition, increasing numbers of companies are also appointing a director with special responsibilities vis-à-vis shareholders. France has also experienced a growing level of activism in recent years. Every year, a number of companies are confronted with activist shareholders who want to effect changes in the strategy or governance of the company, albeit with varying degrees of success. The securities regulator has issued a number of recommendations for balancing the interests of companies and activist shareholders but it is not yet clear whether further legislative intervention will occur.

15

Shareholder Engagement in Germany

Florian Möslein and Christopher Rennig

15.1 INTRODUCTION

The German variety of capitalism has often been described as special and even bizarre.[1] This variety takes root in 'a corporatist system wherein key stakeholders – shareholders, workers, and the state – bargain for outcomes that maintain a balance between the profit motive of shareholders, labor interests, and broader social concerns'.[2] Within that system, however, shareholders have traditionally played only a minor role. For instance, a former German Federal Minister of Justice has prominently been quoted as stating that not too long ago, 'powerful directors selected their own controllers and refuge was sought in maximum and multiple voting rights and cross shareholdings ... In those days shareholders kept their distance, showed little interest, and some directors, in the harsh words of Carl Fürstenberg, ... were stupid and cheeky'.[3] Much has changed since then, of course. Shareholder activism has arrived in Germany, most visibly perhaps with the opposition of several hedge funds to the takeover of the London Stock Exchange by Deutsche Börse in 2005 and the subsequent ousting of its CEO, Werner Seifert, at the company's general meeting.[4] Various other activist campaigns have followed suit (and also happened before).[5] Directors are given plenty of legal advice on how to protect themselves against activist shareholders.[6] In brief, shareholder activism is now rightly

[1] In the latter sense, see Matt Phillips, 'Germany's Bizarre Version of Capitalism – Where Bosses and Workers Actually Cooperate – Is Winning' *Quartz* (9 August 2015) https://qz.com/452076/this-just-in-german-capitalism-has-won/ accessed 15 July 2020. More generally, see, e.g., Harald Bathelt and Meric S. Gertler, 'The German Variety of Capitalism: Forces and Dynamics of Evolutionary Change' (2005) 81 Economic Geography 1.

[2] Curtis J. Milhaupt and Katharina Pistor, *Law and Capitalism: What Corporate Crises Reveal about Legal Systems and Economic Development around the World* (University of Chicago Press 2008) 75.

[3] Jean J. du Plessis and Ingo Saenger, 'The General Meeting and the ManagementBoard as Company Organs' in Jean J. du Plessis et al. (eds.), *German Corporate Governance in International and European Context* (3rd ed., Springer Berlin Heidelberg 2017) 63, 68 (citing Brigitte Zypries).

[4] For a sketch of the incident, see Marco Becht et al., 'Returns to Hedge Fund Activism: An International Study' (2017) 30 The Review of Financial Studies 2933, 2941–4; cf. also Andreas Engert, 'Hedgefonds als aktivistische Aktionäre' (46/2006) Zeitschrift für Wirtschaftsrecht (ZIP) 2105; Andreas Engert, 'Shareholder Activism in Germany' (2019) FUELS Working Paper No. 33, 2 www.jura.fu-berlin.de/en/forschung/fuels/Research-Output/Working-Papers/FUELS_WP-Shareholder-activism-in-Germany-2019.pdf accessed 15 July 2020.

[5] For a report on the incidences, characteristics and outcomes of 253 activist events in Germany between 1999 and 2011, see C. Thamm and D. Shiereck, 'Shareholder Activism in Deutschland – Eine Bestandsaufnahme' (2014) 5 Corporate Finance 17, 21–7; see also H. Schaefer and C. Hertrich, 'Shareholder Activism in Germany: An Empirical Study' (2013) 12 IUP Journal of Corporate Governance 28.

[6] See, for instance, B. Graßl and T. Nikoleyczik, 'Shareholder Activism und Investor Activism' (3/2017) Die Aktiengesellschaft (AG) 49; M. Schiessl, 'Empfehlungen an Publikumsgesellschaften für den Umgang mit Hedgefonds' (15/2009) Zeitschrift für Wirtschaftsrecht (ZIP) 689; M. Schockenhoff, 'Vorstände im Visier aktivistischer Aktionäre' (38/2017) Zeitschrift für Wirtschaftsrecht (ZIP) 1785; Martin Schockenhof and Johannes Culmann, 'Shareholder Activism in Deutschland' (7/2015) Zeitschrift für Wirtschaftsrecht (ZIP) 297.

described as a 'firmly established part of the corporate governance landscape of German stock corporations'.[7]

Shareholder engagement may sound less controversial than shareholder activism, but, in fact, it serves as its very basis: if shareholders cannot engage in corporate decisions, they cannot play an active role in a stock corporation. Even if economic circumstances such as the structure of shareholdings have changed, the legal framework of shareholder engagement is still remarkably distinct under German law, although empirical data on shareholder engagement are scarce. Some of the peculiarities of that framework pose puzzles. For instance, Germany has been surprisingly reluctant to adopt a best practice code for the stewardship role of institutional investors and asset managers, unlike many other countries, most notably the UK.[8]

Yet shareholder engagement plays a central role in corporate governance. It is also the focal point of various regulatory initiatives, most notably the revised EU Shareholder Rights Directive[9] and its transposition in EU member states. Against this backdrop, this chapter analyses the engagement and voting behaviour of shareholders in Germany and their position in German corporate law. In Section 15.1, we introduce the German corporate law framework and describe the peculiarities of its two-tier board system and the role of shareholders. Section 15.2 then discusses the legal means of shareholder engagement in Germany in more detail. Whilst others distinguish three different forms of shareholder engagement (engagement in shareholder meetings, including voting and questions, engagement outside general meetings in a private setting and shareholder litigation), our focus is in accordance with that of the other chapters in this volume: shareholder engagement in shareholder meetings.[10] In Section 15.3, we draw on a set of empirical data to analyze the practice of shareholder engagement and voting in Germany. Section 15.4 provides concluding remarks.

15.1.1 *German Corporate Law*

Corporations exist in several legal forms in Germany, although we must first differentiate between the two basic forms: partnerships wherein the partners are personally liable (*Personengesellschaften*) and incorporated companies wherein liability is limited to the corporation's capital (*Kapitalgesellschaften*). In the following, the term 'corporation' is used only in reference to the latter form.

In the *Kapitalgesellschaften* category, German statutory law recognizes four types of corporations: the stock corporation (*Aktiengesellschaft* (AG)), the public partly limited partnership (*Kommanditgesellschaft auf Aktien* (KGaA)), the limited liability company (*Gesellschaft mit beschränkter Haftung* (GmbH)) and the entrepreneurial company (*Unternehmergesellschaft* (UG)). The latter is a trimmed-down version of the GmbH, to which the same rules apply in principle apart from the requirements regarding minimum share capital.[11] No other types of corporations exist under German law, as the corporation law defines the possible types of

7 Engert, 'Shareholder Activism' (n. 4) 3.

8 For details, see Wolf-Georg Ringe, 'Stewardship and Shareholder Engagement in Germany' (2020) European Corporate Governance Institute Law Working Paper No 501/2020 https://ssrn.com/abstract=3549829 accessed 15 July 2020 (arguing that the comparatively small size of the German fund industry relative to the economy leads to a reluctance in German politics to regulate institutional investors).

9 Directive EU 2017/828 amending Directive 2007/36/EC as regards the encouragement of long-term shareholder engagement, 2017 OJL 132/60.

10 Cf. in particular Anne Lafarre, 'Shareholder Engagement in the Netherlands', Chapter 19 of this Volume.

11 To fund a GmbH, the minimum share capital has to amount to 25.000€ (s. 5(1) GmbHG), whilst for the foundation of an UG a minimum share capital of 1€ would theoretically be sufficient.

corporations conclusively (the so-called *numerus clausus* of corporation types). In addition, corporations can be organized as *Societas Europaea* (SE) in accordance with European law.[12] An SE is akin to a supranational AG, as its capital is divided into shares (see article 1(3) of the SE Regulation). The similarity to an AG is illustrated by the fact that fundamental issues such as the formation or dissolution of the SE are governed by the law of the EU member state in which the SE has its registered office.[13]

The statutory law governing German corporations is not concentrated in a single legal act. Instead, there are specific accompanying acts for the various types of corporation: the AG and KGaA are governed by the German Stock Corporation Act (*Aktiengesetz* (AktG)), whilst the GmbH and UG (as a trimmed-down GmbH) are regulated by the German Limited Liability Companies Act (*GmbH-Gesetz* (GmbHG)). As corporations are seen as special forms of associations in the sense of the German Civil Code (*Bürgerliches Gesetzbuch* (BGB)) under German law, these rules governing the associations (sections 705 BGB et seq.) apply subsidiarily if a specific corporation act does not contain a provision for a given situation.

Some provisions of the AktG refer only to AGs listed on the stock exchange (listed AGs). According to section 3(2) AktG, companies listed on the stock exchange are companies whose shares of stock are admitted to trading on a market that is regulated and monitored by officially recognized bodies, that takes place on a regular basis and that is indirectly or directly accessible to the general public. One key difference between listed and non-listed AGs is the obligation of the former to publish annually an explanation of the extent to which the company complies with the recommendations of the German Corporate Governance Code (DCGK) pursuant to section 161(1)1. The DCGK was first introduced in 2002.[14] Since then, it has been revisited and adjusted approximately once a year. The last major reform, of 16 December 2019, forms the basis for declarations of compliance.[15] Section 161(1)1 AktG constitutes a comply-or-explain approach, whereby AGs are required to declare annually whether they have complied with the DCGK recommendations and, if they have not, provide reasons for their lack of compliance.

Regarding the possibility of being a shareholder of an AG, the AktG in principle differentiates between two types of stock in section 10(1). The standard type is registered shares of stock (*Namensaktien*). Only in specific cases (for instance if the AG is listed in the aforementioned sense), can an AG issue bearer shares (*Inhaberaktien*). Whilst the legal act of transfer between the two types differs, they are generally freely transferable. Restrictions can be placed only on the transferability of registered shares of stock and only if the corporation's by-laws pursuant to section 68(2) AktG contain a declaration to that effect (so-called *Vinkulierung*). The transferability of bearer shares cannot be restricted.

Statistics show that a total of 9,782 AGs and KGaAs were incorporated with a basic capital stock of €180,086 million as of March 2018.[16] On 1 July 2017, 458 incorporated AGs (and SEs) were listed.[17] Germany's thirty largest blue chip companies are listed in the DAX-30, membership of

[12] Council Regulation (EC) No. 2157/2001 of 8 October 2001 on the Statute for a European company (SE).

[13] Jürgen Oechsler and Elitza Mihaylova, in Wulf Goette and Mathias Habersack (eds.), *Münchener Kommentar zum Aktiengesetz* (5th ed., C.H. Beck 2021), art. 1 SE-regulation, para. 2.

[14] See the archive of the Deutscher Corperate Governance Kodex www.dcgk.de/de/kodex/archiv.html accessed 8 June 2020.

[15] A revised version of the DCGK was adopted by the competent government commission on 17 May 2022, but is not released in the Federal Gazette as of yet, available at: https://www.dcgk.de//files/dcgk/usercontent/de/download/kodex/220517_Deutscher_Corporate_Governance_Kodex_2022.pdf accessed 20 May 2022.

[16] Mathias Habersack, in Wulf Goette and Mathias Habersack (eds.), *Münchener Kommentar zum Aktiengesetz* (5th ed., C.H. Beck 2019) Introduction, para. 11.

[17] Walter Bayer and Thomas Hoffmann, 'Beherrschung und Unabhängigkeit in der deutschen Börsenlandschaft' (9/2018) Die Aktiengesellschaft R116.

which depends on the market capitalization of shares in free float.[18] The DAX-30 currently comprises eighteen AGs, seven SEs, four KGaAs and one PLC.[19] The following discussion concentrates on the legal provisions concerning AGs.

15.1.2 *Structure of the AG: Board and (Annual) General Meeting*

As seen in Figure 15.1., every AG is composed of three organs that are governed by the fourth part of the AktG: the general meeting (sections 118–49 AktG), the management board (sections 76–94 AktG) and the supervisory board (sections 95–116 AktG). German statutory law determines a dualistic board system comprising the management and supervisory boards.

15.1.2.1 Management Board

Whilst the management board can in theory have only one member, the average management board of a DAX-30 company consists of 6.2 members (as of March 2020), who are appointed through a resolution of the supervisory board for a maximum term of five years (section 84(1)1 AktG).[20] The passing of such a resolution requires a simple majority of votes, with a stricter provision in a company's by-laws requiring a qualified majority being invalid.[21]

The management board has responsibility for management of the company's affairs (section 76(1) AktG). In managing the company, the management board is independent in principle. An exception is possible if the by-laws of the corporation or supervisory board state that a certain type of business transaction may only be implemented with the supervisory board's consent (section 111(4)2 AktG). If such consent is not granted, then the management board can ask the general meeting for consent, which requires a three-quarters majority (section 111(4)3, 4 AktG). Other than in this exception, shareholders have no direct influence on the daily management of the company. In particular, the management board is not obliged to ask for the consent of the general meeting regarding important business decisions, and (major) shareholders are not authorized to give the board instructions.[22] Pursuant to section 78(1)1 AktG, the management board further represents the corporation both before and outside the court.

There has been intensive discussion amongst legal scholars on whether the management board should act predominantly in the interests of shareholders or stakeholders such as employees, customers or the general public. Dogmatically, the discussion hinges on the meaning of the term 'company interests'. It is now generally recognized that the interests of shareholders may have an influence on the business decisions of management, and they therefore constitute an element of the company's interests in the legal sense.[23] However, the precise balance between

18 Which is why Lufthansa AG was recently dropped from the DAX-30 owing to a loss in value in consequence of the COVID-19 pandemic, being replaced by Deutsche Wohnen SE. Data concerning Lufthansa are still used in this chapter.

19 The chemical company Linde is organized as a PLC because of the merger of Linde AG and US-based Praxair in 2018; see Linde, 'Business Combination Between Praxair and Linde AG Successfully Completed' (31 October 2018) www.linde.com/news-media/press-releases/2018/business-combination-between-praxair-and-linde-ag-successfully-completed accessed 26 July 2020. Starting in September 2021, the DAX will comprise of forty companies.

20 A re-appointment or extension of the term of office is possible, in each case for a maximum of five years.

21 Gerald Spindler, in Wulf Goette and Mathias Habersack (eds.), *Münchener Kommentar zum Aktiengesetz* (5th ed., C.H. Beck 2019) s. 84, para. 22.

22 BGH, AG 2008, 541 (542); Spindler, note 20, s. 76, para. 22.

23 OLG Frankfurt, 'Handeln des Vorstands auch gegen die Interessen des Hauptaktionärs' (42/2011) Zeitschrift für Wirtschaftsrecht (ZIP) 2006, 2010; Holger Fleischer, in Gerald Spindler and Eberhard Stilz (eds.), *Aktiengesetz* (4th ed., C.H. Beck 2019) s. 76, para. 36.

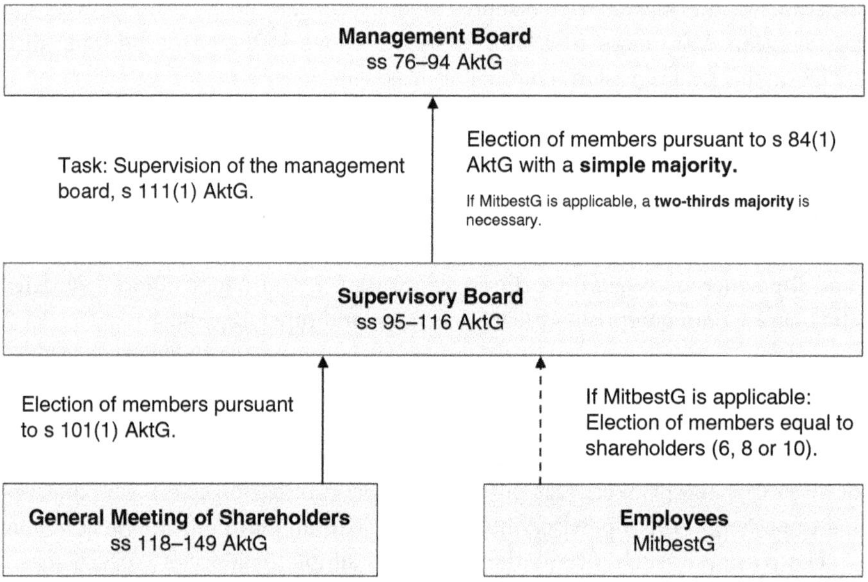

FIGURE 15.1 Organigram of an AG

the interests of shareholders and stakeholders remains unresolved. According to the prevailing opinion, it may in fact be impossible to make a general statement about that balance, as the company's interests have to be newly determined in each individual case.[24] There are voices supporting a so-called moderate or enlightened shareholder-value model, wherein there is a general prevalence of shareholder interests, but stakeholder interests – whilst diminished – are still an element that must be taken into account in the decision-making process. Such considerations are also influenced by the ongoing debate on corporate social responsibility.[25] In line with the EU's non-financial reporting directive (Directive 2014/95/EU), the German provisions primarily stipulate information obligations in non-financial disclosures, especially with regard to the environmental aspects of corporate activities.[26] Nevertheless, some authors fear that these information duties will also change management boards' discretion in substance, even if 'through the back door'.[27] In practice, the discussion mainly concerns theoretical issues, as differing views regularly come to similar legal conclusions.[28]

15.1.2.2 Supervisory Board

The supervisory board constitutes the connecting link between the management board and the general meeting: it elects the members of the management board and also supervises its activities (section 111(1) AktG). Supervisory board members are – in principle – appointed through

[24] See, for instance, Fleischer, note 22, s. 76, para. 44.

[25] See, for example, Florian Möslein and Karsten Engsig Sørensen, 'Nudging for Corporate Long-Termism and Sustainability? Regulatory Instruments from A Comparative and Functional Perspective' (2018) 24 Columbia Journal of European Law 391, 396.

[26] For details (and with an insightful comparison to US law), see Patrick A. Hell, *Offenlegungspflichten nichtfinanzieller Informationen* (Mohr Siebeck 2020).

[27] In this vein, see for instance Peter Hommelhoff, 'Aktuelle Impulse aus dem europäischen Unternehmensrecht: Eine Herausforderung für Deutschland' (34/2015) Neue Zeitschrift für Gesellschaftsrecht (NZG) 1329, 1330.

[28] Fleischer, note 22, s. 76, para. 44.

a resolution of the general meeting (section 101(1) AktG).[29] Passing a resolution of the general meeting requires a majority of the votes cast (simple majority) unless the law or company by-laws stipulate a greater majority ratio or impose further requirements (section 133(1) AktG). According to section 95 AktG, the supervisory board must have at least three members. However, if an AG has share capital in excess of €10 million, the supervisory board can have up to twenty-one members. The other tasks of the supervisory board include consultation of the management board as a preventive measure of supervision[30] and formulating the statement concerning DCGK adherence together with the management board pursuant to section 161(1)1 AktG.

For AGs or KGaAs that regularly have more than 2,000 employees, the legal requirements concerning the corporate structure and the composition of the supervisory board do not stem from the AktG alone; additional requirements arise out of the Employee Co-Determination Act (*Mitbestimmungsgesetz* (MitbestG)),[31] which aims to mitigate the heteronomy of employees by shareholders, as well as to promote the integration of employees inside the company.[32] A comparable legal act exists for SEs registered in Germany, that is, the *Societas Europeaea* Co-Determination Act (*SE-Beteiligungsgesetz* (SEBG)). Within the scope of MitbestG, companies are obliged to compose their supervisory board according to section 7 MitbestG, which stipulates that it must comprise members appointed by shareholders and an equal number of members appointed by employees.[33] Prospective members associated with shareholders are still elected by the general meeting in the aforementioned sense, whereas the process of appointing members associated with employees depends on the number of employees the company has (section 9 (1, 2) MitbestG).[34] In addition, the majority requirements for the election of management board members also differ, as the appointment of members to the organ that is in charge of the legal representation of the corporation (i.e. the management board; see above) requires a two-thirds majority instead of a simple majority according to section 31(2) MitbestG.[35]

15.1.2.3 General Meeting

The shareholders of an AG are organized in the general meeting, which is to be convened in the cases determined by law and by the AG's by-laws, as well as whenever the best interests of the AG so require (section 121(1) AktG). The meeting must take place at least once a year for the purpose

29 In certain cases, the by-laws of the corporation may establish a right of certain shareholders to delegate members to the supervisory board, s. 101 (2) AktG (so-called '*Entsendungsrecht*'). For instance, the state of Lower Saxony (*Niedersachsen*) holds the right to delegate two members to the supervisory board of Volkswagen AG, as long as it holds 15 per cent of the company's common shares; see Volkswagen, Aufsichtsrat www.volkswagenag.com/de/InvestorRelations/corporate-governance/AR.html accessed 14 March 2020.

30 BGHZ 114, 127 (130 f.); Mathias Habersack, in Wulf Goette and Mathias Habersack (eds.), *Münchener Kommentar zum Aktiengesetz* (5th ed., C.H. Beck 2019) s. 111, marginal no. 12.

31 Currently, twenty-nine of thirty DAX-30 corporations fall within the scope of the MitbestG or the *Societas Europeaea* Co-Determination Act (*SE-Beteiligungsgesetz* (SEBG)). Only Fresenius Medical Care AG & Co. KGaA does not operate within the scope of these legal acts.

32 BVerfGE 50, 350 (360) = NJW 1979, 705 (707); Mathias Habersack, in Habersack and Henssler (eds.), *Mitbestimmungsrecht* (4th ed., C.H. Beck 2018) Introduction, para. 4.

33 The exact number of members varies depending on the number of employees in the respective company. For instance, the supervisory board of companies with fewer than 10,000 employees has to consist of 6 members appointed by shareholders and 6 members appointed by employees (e.g. BASF). The number rises to 8 for companies with more than 10,000 and fewer than 20,000 employees (e.g. Merck) and to 10 for companies with more than 20,000 employees (e.g. Volkswagen, Daimler, BMW, Deutsche Bank).

34 In corporations that regularly have more than 8,000 employees, the supervisory board members of the employees are voted by delegates, s. 9 (1) MitbestG. In corporations that regularly have fewer than 8,000 employees, the supervisory board members of the employees are voted directly by the employees, s. 9 (2) MitbestG.

35 S. 31 (3, 4) MitbestG governs cases in which the required two-thirds majority is not reached.

of accepting the annual general account (sections 121, 175 AktG); this is called the annual general meeting (AGM).[36] The regular procedure for a general meeting will be discussed in further detail in Section 15.2.1 below.

15.1.3 *Decision-Making Rights of Shareholders*

Even without the analysis of empirical evidence, the combination of two legal factors concerning the structure of an AG already amounts to shareholders having limited ability to influence the daily management of the company. First, shareholders have practically no power regarding business decisions made by the company's management board, owing in large part to their lack of power to issue instructions. The weak position of shareholders in regard to daily management is manifested in section 119(2) AktG, according to which the general meeting is authorized to decide on management issues only if the management board explicitly demands such a decision. Second, because the management board members of companies that fall within the scope of MitbestG or SEBG have to be elected by the supervisory board with a two-thirds majority, it is virtually impossible for shareholders to install a shareholder-friendly management board member without the consent of several of the supervisory board members appointed by the company's employees.

Nevertheless, the AktG assigns certain items to general meeting decision-making. Some of those items are listed in section 119(1) AktG, whilst others result from other provisions of the AktG and other legal acts. In general, it is possible to assign additional voting items to the general meeting in a company's articles of association (AoA). However, this possibility is a very narrow one, as section 23(5) AktG declares that by-laws may deviate from the regulations of the AktG only where expressly permitted.[37] Additionally, if neither the law nor AoA state an explicit competence of the general meeting, it is ultimately undisputed by jurisprudence and scholars that the general meeting in certain cases has unwritten decision powers.[38]

In general, it is possible to differentiate between periodic and structural decisions, and moreover to define certain special cases. Section 119(1) nos. 1–4 AktG lists decisions that the general meeting has to take periodically. As set out above, the general meeting has competence to appoint members of the supervisory board (section 119(1) no 1 AktG). Yet this competence does not extend to members appointed by employees, according to MitbestG. Other decision rights in this category concern the appropriation of net income (section 119(1) no 2 AktG) and the compensation system for members of the management and supervisory boards (only for listed AGs, section 119(1) no. 3 AktG), as well as their discharge (section 119(1) no. 4 AktG). Outside section 119 AktG, there are no other provisions granting the general meeting the authority to make periodic decisions.

Structural decisions of the general meeting include the appointment of the auditor of the annual accounts (section 119(1) no. 5 AktG), amendments of the company's by-laws (section

[36] Other cases of determination by law are the convention of a general meeting in the case of a loss amounting to half of the share capital (s. 92 (1) AktG) and wherever stockholders, whose shares of stock, in the aggregate, are at least equivalent to one-twentieth of the share capital, demand that it be so convened (s. 122 AktG). Outside the AktG, banking supervisory law constitutes the duty to conduct a general meeting, e.g. s. 44 (5) of the German Banking Act (*Kreditwesengesetz* (KWG)).

[37] One of the few cases, for example, is the approval of the transfer of registered shares of stock by endorsement, s. 68(2)3 AktG, see Jochen Hoffmann, in Gerald Spindler and Eberhard Stilz (eds.), *Beck-Online Großkommentar zum AktG* (15 January 2020) s. 119, para. 63.

[38] See, for instance, Jens Koch, in Uwe Hüffer and Jens Koch (eds.), *Aktiengesetz* (15th ed., C.H. Beck 2021) s. 119, para. 16.

119(1) no. 6 AktG), measures pertaining to the procurement and reduction of capital (section 119(1) no. 7 AktG) and dissolution of the company (section 119(1) no. 8 AktG). The AktG also acknowledges several other decision rights of the general meeting in structural matters, for example the continuation of a dissolved company (section 274(1) AktG) or decisions concerning a squeeze-out (section 327a(1) AktG). Other important decision rights of the general meeting result from the Reorganisation Act (*Umwandlungsgesetz* (UmwG)), for instance, in cases of a merger (sections 65(1), 73 UmwG) or demerger (sections 125, 65(2) UmwG).

A special case of decision-making by the general meeting is the appointment of auditors, who audit actions taken and events occurring in the course of the company's formation or the management of its affairs (section 119(1) no. 7 AktG). Outside section 119 AktG, there are several other grounds for a decision by the general meeting,[39] for example the declaration of no-confidence in the management board (section 84(3)2 AktG) or the dismissal of a member of the supervisory board (section 103(1) AktG).

In addition to the foregoing competences explicitly granted by law, according to jurisprudence and the prevailing view of scholars and practitioners, the authority of the general meeting to take decisions is not limited to the possibilities afforded by written law. Since the famous *Holzmüller* decision of the Federal Court of Germany (*Bundesgerichtshof* (BGH)), it is widely recognized that the general meeting in some cases has decision-making power even in the absence of a corresponding competence in written law.[40] This becomes relevant, however, only if the law or the company's AoA do not stipulate an explicit competence of the general meeting or one of the boards. It applies to certain fundamental decisions that may interfere with the rights of membership and the financial interests of shareholders in such a way that the management board cannot reasonably assume that it is authorized to make the decisions instead of the shareholders themselves.[41] In the nearly forty years since the *Holzmüller* decision, jurisprudence has further developed the principles governing unwritten decision-making powers.[42] As a consequence, it is recognized that certain decisions reside with the general meeting even if written law does not explicitly say so. However, which instances constitute such an unwritten competence of the general meeting remain a matter of dispute, and jurisprudence tends to impose very strict requirements on such instances. They may include the spin-off of a company's business units, but in other cases it is necessary to differentiate on a case-by-case basis (e.g. an initial public offering or the disposal of a participation), with the exact demarcation lines still a subject of controversy amongst jurisprudence and scholars alike.[43]

39 For an exhaustive list of cases, see Dietmar Kubis, in Wulf Goette and Mathias Habersack (eds.), *Münchener Kommentar zum Aktiengesetz* (4th ed., C.H. Beck 2018) s. 119, para. 16.

40 BGH, NJW 1982, 1703. In the judgment, the BGH had to decide a situation in which the management body aimed to outsource the most profitable division of the corporation without consulting the general meeting.

41 BGH, NJW 1982, 1703 (1705). This conclusion is reasoned with a reduction of the management board's discretion to include the general meeting in the management of the corporation pursuant to s. 119(2) AktG.

42 Another significant decision regarding unwritten decision competences of the general meeting was the *Gelatine* decision of the BGH, in which the court confirmed and substantiated the principles laid out in the *Holzmüller* decision; see BGH, NJW 2004, 1860. In recent years, the BGH has had to decide about the right to participation of the general meeting regarding the delisting of a company. In the so-called *Frosta* decision, the court denied the shareholder the participation right in a departure from its earlier judicial practice; see BGH, NJW 2014, 146.

43 For detailed elaborations on possible case groups, see Dietmar Kubis, in Wulf Goette and Mathias Habersack (eds.), *Münchener Kommentar zum Aktiengesetz* (4th ed., C.H. Beck 2018) s. 119, para. 65.

15.1.4 *Ownership Structures and Control*

The ownership of DAX-30 corporations is generally widely dispersed. With only a few exceptions, the percentage of shares in free float is above 65 per cent. Table 15.1 shows the ownership structure of German DAX-30 corporations.

On average, 86.5 per cent of a DAX-30 corporation's shares were in free float from 2011 to 2019. There was little variation between these years, with the highest average (87.67 per cent in 2016) being only 2.29 per cent higher than the lowest average (85.38 per cent in 2016). Therefore, these data show a consistently high level of shares in free float. In 2019, one-third of DAX-30 corporations had 100 per cent of their shares in free float, whilst eighteen of them had a free float of at least 90 per cent. Only one DAX-30 company had a free float under 50 per cent (Covestro, with 43.33 per cent).

In terms of shareholder types, the major shareholders in DAX-30 companies are institutional investors, which in 2017 held 61.8 per cent (60.1 per cent in 2016) of all shares.[44] Private investors, in contrast, held only 17.2 per cent in that year (16.1 per cent in 2016), whilst strategic participations amounted to 18.4 per cent (20.8 per cent).[45] The remaining 2.6 per cent of shares were held by brokers and dealers. German public entities also hold a small number of shares in DAX-30 corporations. For instance, the federal government holds approximately 2.8 per cent of all DAX-30 shares, including shares in Deutsche Telekom and Commerzbank, and the state of Lower Saxony owns 11.8 per cent of the shares in Volkswagen.[46]

TABLE 15.1 *Free float data for German DAX-30 corporations in per cent*

Year	Mean	Standard deviation	Median	Minimum	Maximum
2011	86	17.59	94.9	43.94	100
2012	86	17.12	96.27	43.46	100
2013	87.4	16.72	98.45	43.93	100
2014	86.72	16.39	95.53	43.93	100
2015	85.40	19.28	95.4	30.86	100
2016	85.38	18.82	95.46	36	100
2017	86.93	16.63	95.33	43.33	100
2018	87.67	16.02	93.33	43.33	100
2019	87	15.93	92.1	43.33	100

Note to table: the data shown are retrieved from Thomson Reuters.

[44] Data retrieved from IHS Marktit/Deutscher Investor Relations Verband, 'Who Owns the German DAX? – The Ownership Structure of the German DAX 30' (3 June 2019) cdn.ihs.com/www/pdf/0519/DAX-Study-DIRK.pdf accessed 8 June 2020.

[45] Strategic participations includes anchor investors such as families, foundations, strategic participations of the German Federal Republic as well as foreign sovereign wealth funds; see Ipreo Ltd./Deutscher Investor Relations Verband, Investoren der Deutschland AG 5.0 (June 2018), 7 www.dirk.org/dirk_webseite/static/uploads/Investoren_der_Deutschland_AG_5-0_DAX-Studie-2018_Ipreo_DIRK.pdf accessed 27 July 2020.

[46] See Volkswagen, 'Aktionärsstruktur' www.volkswagenag.com/de/InvestorRelations/shares/shareholder-structure.html accessed 23 May 2020. On the historical and legal background of state participation in Volkswagen (and the respective ECJ judgement), see Florian Möslein, 'Compliance with ECJ Judgments vs. Compatibility with EU Law – Free Movement of Capital Issues Unresolved after the Second Ruling on the Volkswagen Law: Commission v Germany' (2015) 52 Common Market Law Review 801; on golden shares in general, see Stefan Grundmann and Florian Möslein, 'Golden Shares – State Control in Privatised Companies: Comparative Law, European Law and Policy Aspects' (2001–2) 4 European Banking and Financial Law Journal – EUREDIA 623.

In 2018, 15.3 per cent of shares in DAX-30 corporations were held by German investors, whilst North American investors held 34.6 per cent. Other European countries supply 44.8 per cent of shareholders.[47]

15.2 LEGAL MEANS OF SHAREHOLDER ENGAGEMENT AND VOTING

As noted, the decision-making rights of shareholder meetings are relatively limited under current German law. The German model is comparatively board-centric, and, in contrast to the early history of stock corporation law, it is widely agreed that the shareholder meeting no longer qualifies as the supreme organ (*oberstes Organ*).[48] Instead, the mutual relationship amongst the three company organs qualifies as a balance of power (*Machtbalance*), similar in some respects to the concepts of constitutional law.[49] Since the reform of 1937, both the management board and supervisory board enjoy inalienable decision rights, whereas the general meeting of shareholders is authorized to decide on management issues only if the management board explicitly demands such a decision (cf. section 119(2) AktG). In addition, economic factors such as dispersed ownership limit the factual influence of shareholders. Nonetheless, by electing the members of the supervisory board, the shareholder meeting has the means to influence the composition of the management board, at least indirectly (and where co-determination applies, at least in part). By this means, shareholders can influence corporate policy to at least some extent. Moreover, only the shareholder meeting has the competence to define (and amend) the object and purpose of the corporation.[50] Owing to these important powers, it is important to analyze the procedural framework of shareholder meetings and to discuss the rules for how shareholders can request meetings or submit proposals, ask questions and cast their votes.

15.2.1 *Shareholder Meetings (General Meetings)*

The forum for the exercise of shareholder rights is the general meeting: section 118(1) AktG provides that unless otherwise stipulated, shareholders shall exercise their rights in matters pertaining to the company at the general meeting. Until very recently, the principle of a meeting in person applied mandatorily, although the company's AoA may well allow (or authorize the board of directors to allow) shareholders to participate in the meeting electronically and to cast their votes in writing or electronically. According to the rules of general stock corporation law, however, presence at the meeting is still required: shareholders have the right to attend the meeting on site even if electronic participation is offered as an alternative. Recently however, the principle of in-person meetings was temporarily modified as a consequence of the COVID-19 pandemic. At the end of March 2020, the German government introduced an act aimed at mitigating the pandemic's impact (COVID-19 Mitigation Act),[51] which passed the German parliament (the *Bundestag*) as well as the Federal Council (the Bundesrat). It enables

[47] IHS Marktit/Deutscher Investor Relations Verband (n. 43). In the UK and Ireland, it is 20.4 per cent, in Scandinavian countries 6.3 per cent and in other European countries 18.8 per cent.

[48] See, for instance, Hugo Horrwitz, *Das Recht der Generalversammlungen der Aktiengesellschaften und Kommanditgesellschaften auf Aktien* (Vahlen 1913) 10; cf. also Wolf-Georg Rechenberg, *Die Hauptversammlung als oberstes Organ der Aktiengesellschaft* (Verlag Recht und Wirtschaft 1986).

[49] Koch, n. 37, s. 118, para. 4 and s. 119, para. 1.

[50] Similar Peter Mülbert, in Volker Butzke and Peter Mülbert (eds.), *Aktiengesetz – Großkommentar* (5th ed., C.H. Beck 2017) vol. 7/1, introduction to §§ 118–30 AktG, para. 43.

[51] Gesetz über Maßnahmen im Gesellschafts-, Genossenschafts-, Vereins-, Stiftungs- und Wohnungseigentumsrecht zur Bekämpfung der Auswirkungen der COVID-19-Pandemie vom 27. März 2020, BGBl. I S. 569, 570.

the management board of stock corporations to conduct shareholder meetings as 'virtual general meetings' if shareholders' only option is to participate by electronic means.[52] The physical presence of shareholders can therefore be excluded. Nonetheless, a physical meeting place at which members of the management board, amongst others, meet in person is still required.[53] The new rules apply for only a limited period since 2020, and hereinafter are addressed as a side note. After there was initial doubt concerning the legality of these provisions courts since have declared them to stand in harmony with superior law.[54] In April 2022, the German Federal Government has presented a draft law by which the possibility of holding a virtual general meeting is to be permanently inserted into the AktG.[55]

The general meeting must be convened. In principle, the management board is in charge of convening the meeting, and it decides by a simple majority (cf. section 121(2) AktG). The supervisory board is also entitled to convene the meeting, and, if required in the company's best interests, it is even obliged to do so (section 111(3) AktG). The supervisory board also decides by a simple majority. Under certain conditions, a minority of shareholders may also demand that a meeting be convened (section 122 AktG).[56] The meeting is convened by publication in the company gazette, that is, electronically in the company register via the so-called *eBundesanzeiger* (cf. section 121(4) AktG and section 8b HGB). Listed companies that do not exclusively issue registered shares and do not address their shareholders directly must make the content of the convening notice, along with further information, available on the company's website (section 124a AktG). The information must also be sent to the media for publication on the assumption that it will then be disseminated throughout the EU (section 121(4a) AktG). In accordance with the Shareholder Rights Directive, non-resident shareholders should be able to exercise their rights as easily as shareholders resident in the member state in which the company has its registered office. As a consequence, the courts also allow AoA to specify general meeting locales abroad.[57] To avoid abuses, however, the directive requires appropriate specifications oriented to shareholders' interest in participation, which binds the discretion of the person entitled to convene the meeting.[58]

The notice date must be at least thirty days before the meeting date (section 123 AktG),[59] although the COVID-19 Mitigation Act provides for a reduction of the notice period to twenty-one days. Moreover, an abbreviated fourteen-day period applies to general meetings in connection with takeover bids (section 16(5) *Wertpapiererwerbs- und Übernahmegesetz* (WpÜG)).[60] The notice convening the general meeting must state both the name and registered offices of the

[52] For detailed overviews, see inter alia Ulrich Noack and Dirk Zetzsche, 'Die virtuelle Hauptversammlung nach dem COVID-19-Pandemie-Gesetz 2020' (8/2020) Die Aktiengesellschaft (AG) 265; Eberhard Vetter and Jörgen Tielmann, 'Unternehmensrechtliche Gesetzesänderungen in Zeiten von Corona' (17/2020) Neue Juristische Wochenschrift (NJW) 1175.

[53] Nikolai Unmuth, 'Anwesenheitspflicht der Organmitglieder in der Hauptversammlung' (12/2020) Neue Zeitschrift für Gesellschaftsrecht (NZG) 448.

[54] Landgericht Köln, decision of 26 February 2021, Recht Digital (RDi), 306 with approving comment Christopher Rennig; Landgericht Frankfurt, verdict of 23 February 2021, Zeitschrift für Wirtschaftsrecht (ZIP), 1009.

[55] Available at https://www.bmj.de/SharedDocs/Gesetzgebungsverfahren/DE/Einfuehrung_virtueller_Hauptversammlungen_Aktiengesellschaften.html.) As of May 2022, the adoption of this (rather controversial) proposal is still pending.

[56] For details, see below Section 15.2.2.

[57] Bundesgerichtshof (BGH), Urt. v. 21.10.2014 – II ZR 330/13, 2015 Neue Juristische Wochenschrift (NJW) 336.

[58] More extensively, see Thomas Jansen, *Die Hauptversammlung im Ausland* (Peter Lang GmbH 2018); Hartwin Bungert and Benjamin Leyendecker-Langner, 'Hauptversammlung im Ausland' (6/2015) Betriebs-Berater (BB) 268.

[59] For a general overview on the various periods and dates in the rules on general meetings, see Tim Florstedt, 'Fristen und Termine im Recht der Hauptversammlung' (16/2010) Zeitschrift für Wirtschaftsrecht (ZIP) 761.

[60] On the details of these three different regimes (with a comparative table), see Ulrich Noack and Dirk Zetzsche, 'Die virtuelle Hauptversammlung nach dem COVID-19-Pandemie-Gesetz 2020' (8/2020) Die Aktiengesellschaft (AG) 265, 273.

stock corporation, as well as the time and place of the meeting (section 121(3) AktG). In the case of listed companies, the conditions on which participation in the general meeting and the exercise of voting rights depend must also be stated. Conversely, simplified conditions apply to companies with a limited number of shareholders (cf. section 121(4) AktG). The meeting agenda must be announced together with the notice convening the meeting. The agenda is important for two reasons: first, no resolutions can be passed on items that have not been duly announced, and, second, the agenda is decisive for shareholders' right to information (see Section 15.2.3 below).

The importance of depositary banks in Germany is reflected in section 125 AktG.[61] The rule provides that twenty-one days prior to the general meeting at the latest, the management board must notify the credit institutions and associations of stockholders that exercised voting rights on behalf of stockholders at the last general meeting, or demanded that such notice be given them, that the general meeting is being convened. According to section 128(1) AktG, depositary banks are required to transmit this information to shareholders without undue delay.

AGMs take place every year. At a minimum, they decide on the distribution of profits and the discharge of the management board and supervisory board.[62] In principle, AGMs need to be convened within the first eight months of the financial year (section 120(3) AktG). However, owing to the pandemic, the special rules of the COVID-19 Mitigation Act allow the management board, with the approval of the supervisory board, to convene the AGM after that period has elapsed. In any case, it must take place within the fiscal year.[63] Extraordinary general meetings, in contrast, need to be convened only if necessary, either if the best interests of the company so require (sections 121(1) and 111(3) AktG) or if a qualified minority of shareholders so requests (section 122(1) AktG; also see Section 15.2.2 below). Such special meetings are also required if half the share capital is lost (section 92(1) AktG).[64] A special form of such meetings is provided for in the event of a takeover bid, subject to modified rules on the notice period and place of the meeting (section 16 WpÜG).

15.2.2 *Shareholder Initiatives*

With respect to the holding of general meetings, shareholders can engage in two ways. The first way is to take the initiative to convene a general meeting. Shareholders whose shares of stock in the aggregate are equivalent to at least one-twentieth of share capital can request a meeting at any time.[65] These shareholders need to state the purpose of and reasons for their petition (section 122(1) AktG).[66]

[61] For details (but in various respects outdated) of the duties of banks in voting their client's stock, see Johannes Köndgen, 'Duties of Banks in Voting Their Clients' Stock' in T. Baums, R. M. Buxbaum, and K. J. Hopt (eds.), *Institutional Investors and Corporate Governance* (De Gruyter 1994) 531; more recently, Petri Mäntysaari, *Comparative Corporate Governance: Shareholders as a Rule-maker* (Springer Berlin Heidelberg 2005) 283.

[62] These powers of the general meeting are comparatively narrow relative to those of other counties such as France and China; cf. Mathias Siems, *Convergence in Shareholder Law* (Cambridge University Press 2007) 71, 155.

[63] See, for instance, Ulrich Noack and Dirk Zetzsche, 'Die virtuelle Hauptversammlung nach dem COVID-19-Pandemie-Gesetz 2020' (8/2020) Die Aktiengesellschaft (AG) 265, 274; Eberhard Vetter and Jörgen Tielmann, 'Unternehmensrechtliche Gesetzesänderungen in Zeiten von Corona' (17/2020) Neue Juristische Wochenschrift (NJW) 1175, 1175.

[64] See, for instance, in comparison with rules in other European jurisdictions, Björn Moßdorf, 'Spezielles Gesellschaftsrecht für börsennotierte Aktiengesellschaften in den EG-Mitgliedstaaten' in Horst Eidenmüller et al. (eds.), *Schriften zum Europäischen und Internationalen Privat-, Bank- und Wirtschaftsrecht* (De Gruyter 2010) 197.

[65] In more detail, Thomas Halberkamp and Olaf Gierke, 'Das Recht der Aktionäre auf Einberufung einer Hauptversammlung' (11/2004) Neue Zeitschrift für Gesellschaftsrecht (NZG) 494; Volker Heeg, 'Zum Verlangen einer Aktionärsminderheit auf Einberufung einer Hauptversammlung' (27/2012) Neue Zeitschrift für Gesellschaftsrecht (NZG) 1056.

[66] On the duties of the management board in the case of unlawful petitions, see Gerald Reger, 'Keine Pflicht des Vorstands zur Ablehnung rechtsmissbräuchlicher Einberufungsverlangen' (14/2013) Neue Zeitschrift für Gesellschaftsrecht (NZG) 536.

If the management board and supervisory board refuse to comply with their petition, they can force the convening of the meeting by appealing to the court of registration (section 122(3) AktG).[67] However, the petitioners need to submit proof that they have been holders of the shares of stock for at least ninety days prior to the date on which their demand was received and that they will continue to hold the shares until the management board takes a decision regarding their petition. This provision is mandatory for the protection of shareholders, but the company's AoA may change (not necessarily relax) these requirements in detail as long as they do not increase them. The practical significance of such shareholder initiatives has increased in recent years, albeit to a rather limited extent.[68] Although very few such initiatives have taken place in recent years,[69] the courts have had to deal with various issues related to them, thereby increasing their significance.[70] In substance, such initiatives generally relate to the discharge of the management board or the election of board members, but also to a broad range of other shareholder rights. The threshold required seems rather difficult to reach, however.

The second means of engagement available to shareholders is to propose items to be added to the meeting agenda.[71] The relevant provisions allow a qualified minority of shareholders to request that items for resolution at a general meeting (that is to be held anyway) be placed on the agenda and published accordingly (section 122(2) AktG). In addition to the threshold of one-twentieth of share capital, this right is also available to a minority of shareholders with a (calculated) nominal value of €500,000. Such shareholder proposals must be accompanied by either a statement of the grounds for adding the items or a draft resolution. The requests must be received by the company at least twenty-four days prior to the meeting (or thirty days prior in the case of listed companies). If the board does not comply with the request, the court may authorize the shareholders who have made the request to convene the AGM or to publish the item in question, and the court may also appoint the meeting chair. Similar to all other items on the agenda, these proposals must also be made public, according to the rules in sections 124 and 124a AktG. Similar to initiatives to convene a general meeting, the practical relevance of initiatives to add items to the agenda has risen in recent years, and, in comparison, is significantly higher.[72] Accordingly, the courts have also had to deal with a broader variety of issues related to the latter initiatives.[73] These initiatives often have little to do with the company's operational goals, relating instead to, say, environmental protection issues or a desire to promote the careers of women,[74] although debates surrounding the role of the

[67] König and Römer, 2003 Deutsches Steuerrecht (DStR) 219.

[68] Kubis, note 38, s. 122 AktG, para. 2.

[69] Walter Bayer and Thomas Hoffmann, 'Einberufung der Hauptversammlung auf Verlangen einer Minderheit' (3/2014) Die Aktiengesellschaft (AG) R 23, R 24 have identified twelve cases for the year 2013 in Germany, but this includes shareholder proposals to amend the agenda.

[70] See, for instance, Oberlandesgericht Düsseldorf, 'Keine Vorstandspflicht zur Ablehnung eines Einberufungsverlangens' (14/2013) Neue Zeitschrift für Gesellschaftsrecht (NZG) 546.

[71] In connection with the addition to the agenda, the AGM of FC Bayern Munich in particular has recently attracted attention in Germany, even though this was the meeting of the football club's association and not the annual general meeting of the stock corporation. The matter in question was the sponsorship of the club by companies with links to Qatar, therefore being connected to the aforementioned matters of Corporate Social Responsibility (CSR). However, the court, which was called upon by a member of the association, dismissed his complaint because the general meeting was not competent to deal with the matter, see Landgericht München I, Beschluss v. 19.11.2021 – 231 C 18299/21.

[72] Kubis, note 38, § 122 AktG, para. 2.

[73] See, for instance, OLG Köln, 'Gerichtliche Bestimmungen eines neutralen Versammlungsleiters' (28/2015) Neue Zeitschrift für Gesellschaftsrecht (NZG) 1118; OLG Karlsruhe, 'Zur Rechtsmissbräuchlichkeit des HV-Einberufungsverlangens eines Minderheitsaktionärs' (3/2015) Zeitschrift für Wirtschaftsrecht (ZIP) 125, 127; OLG Hamm, 'Beschränkung der Stimmrechtsausübung durch geschäftsmäßige Stimmrechtsvertreter' (8/2013) Neue Zeitschrift für Gesellschaftsrecht (NZG) 302.

[74] For some illustrative examples, cf. Hans-Joachim Mertens, 'Das Minderheitsrecht nach § 122 Abs. 2 AktG und seine Grenzen' (1997) Die Aktiengesellschaft (AG) 481.

supervisory board have also arisen in recent years,[75] and requests to discuss management measures are also occasionally made. Thanks to the increasing transparency of ownership structures, it has recently become possible for shareholders numbering far below the quorum to provide evidence of the prescribed minimum holding of nominal capital of €500,000 by contacting the holders of larger blocks of shares.[76] In addition, according to section 126 AktG, shareholders can file a counter motion against a proposal of the management board or supervisory board for a certain item on the agenda. Such a counter motion must be sent to a company address provided in the invitation to the general meeting at least two weeks before the date of the AGM. Also, according to section 127 AktG, the right to file a counter motion applies analogously to a nomination by a shareholder for the election of a member of the supervisory board or the appointment of an external auditor.[77]

15.2.3 *Shareholder Questions*

All shareholders enjoy a right to participate in the general meeting, regardless of whether they are entitled to vote. In addition, members of both the management board and supervisory board are entitled and even expected to participate (even if they do not own any shares; cf. section 118(3) AktG). According to general stock corporation law, a company's AoA can provide that supervisory board members are permitted to participate via video link. The articles may also permit the transmission of the entire meeting in sound and vision (cf. section 118(4) AktG).[78] However, remote viewing does not qualify as 'participation' in the meeting, although the articles may permit electronic voting or authorize the management board to permit it (section 118(2) AktG).[79] During the pandemic, the special rules of the COVID-19 Mitigation Act also allow the management board, with the approval of the supervisory board, to permit both the transmission of the entire meeting in sound and vision and electronic voting, even in the absence of respective provisions in the AoA. In addition, the same Act allows entirely virtual general meetings with no other option for shareholders to participate than by electronic means.[80] In that case, remote attendance qualifies as participation in the legal sense.

In the general meeting, any shareholder can request information on all company matters to the extent that such information is necessary for a proper assessment of the agenda item concerned (section 131(1) AktG).[81] This right of information is a means to enable the appropriate use of voting rights, but it also serves the purpose of incentives and control through information. Yet the scope of this right to information has long been a matter of controversy because practically all management issues can be relevant to, for example, the discharge of the management board. The courts usually refer to the 'point of view of an objectively thinking shareholder' (*Standpunkt eines objektiv denkenden*

75 Cf. Walter Bayer and Thomas Hoffmann, 'Einberufung der Hauptversammlung auf Verlangen einer Minderheit' (3/2014) Die Aktiengesellschaft (AG) R 23.

76 Kubis, note 38, § 122 AktG, para. 2.

77 See, from a comparative perspective, A. Lafarre, *The AGM in Europe: Theory and Practice of Shareholder Behaviour* (Emerald Publishing Limited 2017) 65.

78 In more detail, for instance, see Ulrich Noack, 'Briefwahl und Online-Teilnahme an der Hauptversammlung: der neue § 118 AktG' (49/2009) Wertapier-Mitteilungen (WM) 2289.

79 Cornelius Simons, 'Die Online-Abstimmung in der Hauptversammlung' (15/2017) Neue Zeitschrift für Gesellschaftsrecht (NZG) 567.

80 See already above, n. 50. On virtual shareholder meetings in general, see Walther Pielke, *Die virtuelle Hauptversammlung* (Nomos 2009); Axel M. Seeger, *Die Online-Hauptversammlung* (Deutscher Universitätsverlag 2002); *Dirk Zetzsche* (ed), *Die virtuelle Hauptversammlung* (Erich Schmidt 2002).

81 For details, see, for instance, Wolfgang Groß, 'Informations- und Auskunftsrecht des Aktionärs' (1997) Die Aktiengesellschaft (AG) 97; Jan Lieder, 'Auskunftsrecht und Auskunftserzwingung' (16/2014) Neue Zeitschrift für Gesellschaftsrecht (NZG) 601.

Aktionärs) as a benchmark.[82] The information must comply with the principles of conscientious and faithful accountability (section 131(2) AktG). In principle, it must therefore include all material facts. However, there is some information that may conflict with the company's legitimate interests in maintaining secrecy. The law therefore specifies the reasons that can be legitimately brought forward for refusing to supply information (section 131(3) AktG). The most important reason for refusal is that, according to reasonable commercial judgement, the information is likely to cause considerable harm to the company.[83] Although the management board decides on the refusal at its dutiful discretion, its decision is fully subject to judicial review. German courts have ruled that these restrictions on the right to information do not violate the provisions of the Shareholder Rights Directive (albeit without submitting the question to the European Court of Justice (ECJ)).[84] If information is wrongly refused or is incorrect or incomplete, there is a possibility of the resolutions adopted as a result being challenged (section 243(1) AktG), and the courts can rescind those resolutions on the ground of misinformation. To safeguard the principle of equal treatment of shareholders, information given to one shareholder outside the general meeting must also be provided to any other shareholder upon request at the general meeting (section 131(4) AktG). In this case, there is no right to refuse, and it is also irrelevant whether the information is necessary for the proper assessment of an item on the agenda.

In the case of electronic attendance or entirely virtual general meetings, as made possible by the COVID-19 Mitigation Act, the information rights of shareholders can be limited and reduced at the discretion of the management board within certain limits. By providing an option for the company to allow shareholders to 'exercise all or some of their rights in whole or in part by means of electronic communication', section 118(1) AktG does not mandate that the right to information be extended to online participants.[85] In fact, general company law is built on the principle of in-person meetings. The wording of the new provisions in the COVID-19 Mitigation Act also differentiates between the right to information, as provided for in section 131 AktG (and available only to shareholders present at general meetings), and a simple, less far-reaching 'right to ask questions', which is available to shareholders attending meetings online.[86] Moreover, the new rules provide the management board with far wider discretion on which questions to answer and how. They even allow the requirement that questions be submitted at least two days before the meeting. It is debatable, however, whether such limitations are legitimate if meetings are held entirely online or whether they unduly restrict shareholders' constitutional right to information.[87]

82 Bundesgerichtshof, 'Informationsrecht des Aktionärs bei Verschmelzung – Entlastung personengleicher Organmitglieder' (12/2005) Neue Juristische Wochenschrift (NJW) 828 Bundesgerichtshof, 'Kirch/Deutsche-Bank – Entlastungsbeschlüsse betreffend Vorstand und Aufsichtsrat nichtig' (9/2009) Neue Zeitschrift für Gesellschaftsrecht (NZG) 342 (para. 39).

83 See, for instance, Bundesgerichtshof, 'Anfechtung eines Hauptversammlungsbeschlusses wegen Auskunftsverweigerung' (16/1983) Neue Juristische Wochenschrift (NJW) 878; this limitation is constitutionally unobjectionable according to Bundesverfassungsgericht, 'Zulässige Auskunftsverweigerung des Vorstands einer AG in der Hauptversammlung – Stille Reserven' (2/2000) Neue Juristische Wochenschrift (NJW) 129.

84 Bundesgerichtshof, 'Anforderungen an das Auskunftsverweigerungsrecht der Gesellschaft – Porsche/VW-Beteiligungsaufbau' (11/2014) Neue Zeitschrift für Gesellschaftsrecht (NZG) 423 (Porsche/VW Beteiligungsaufbau). For details on the need to refer this question to the ECJ, see Christoph Teichmann, 'Fragerecht und Aktionärsrechterichtlinie' (11/2014) Neue Zeitschrift für Gesellschaftsrecht (NZG) 401.

85 Christian Kersting, 'Das Auskunftsrecht des Aktionärs bei elektronischer Teilnahme an der Hauptversammlung (§§ 118, 131 AktG)' (4/2010) Neue Zeitschrift für Gesellschaftsrecht (NZG) 130.

86 Cf. Ulrich Noack and Dirk Zetzsche, 'Die virtuelle Hauptversammlung nach dem COVID-19-Pandemie-Gesetz 2020' (8/2020) Die Aktiengesellschaft (AG) 265, 270 (claiming that this 'right to ask questions' is an aliud to section 131(1) AktG').

87 For further details, see references n. 61.

In corporate practice, the information rights of shareholders play a highly significant role that is quite distinct in international comparison.[88] In listed companies with dispersed ownership in particular, shareholders take intensive advantage of these rights. Accordingly, the average duration of AGMs in German is very long by international standards.[89] The relevance of these information rights is also reflected in a plethora of decisions by the courts, almost all of which deal with the scope of the information rights in question.[90] The reasons are manifold. Many shareholders use the meeting as a forum for presenting personal interests.[91] Moreover, the extension of information obligations required by capital market law is also creating demand for increasingly detailed information. From a legal point of view, the concentration of the right to information exclusively in the AGM is one of the causes of the numerous disputes. As a result, the management board often needs to decide within minutes on the legal justification for individual requests for information, and it is obvious that this leads to an increased error rate in legal assessments.[92] To minimize the potential for conflicts, a transparent information policy outside the general meeting is recommended, especially for annual reports.[93]

15.2.4 *Shareholder Voting*

Decision-making at the general meeting is based on shareholder resolutions. A quorum is not required by law but can be specified in AoA. Resolutions usually require a simple majority of the votes cast (section 133 AktG), although for certain fundamental decisions such as amendments to the AoA (section 179(2) AktG) or capital reductions (section 222(1) AktG), the law requires a qualified majority, usually three-quarters of the share capital represented.

In principle, each shareholder is entitled to vote at the AGM in proportion to his or her shareholding. The 'one-share-one-vote' principle therefore applies.[94] Voting rights cannot be made dependent on a certain minimum number of shares. Yet there are circumstances provided in the law where the voting right is excluded or suspended. On the one hand, the law permits a class of shares with preferential dividend rights but without voting rights (so-called *Vorzugsaktien*; cf. sections 11, 12(1) AktG).[95] On the other hand, shareholders are prohibited from voting if there is a risk of certain conflicts of interest, for example, if the resolution is intended to discharge the shareholder concerned or relieve him or her of liability (section 136 AktG).[96] In addition, voting rights from the company's own shares are suspended (section 71 AktG). Otherwise, voting rights are exercised according to capital amounts. In the case of shares with a nominal value, the voting right

88 In the same vein, see Mathias Siems, in Gerald Spindler and Eberhard Stilz (eds.), *Aktiengesetz* (4th ed., C.H. Beck 2019) § 131, para. 9 ('International ist die deutsche Situation . . . weitgehend singulär').

89 Siems, n. 85, § 131, para 6. For a comparative view, see also Mathias Siems and David Cabrelli (eds.), *Comparative Company Law: A Case-Based Approach* (2nd ed., Hart Publishing 2018) 339. The most recent DGCK even contains a recommendation that a standard general meeting should not last longer than four to six hours; see A.4 Deutscher Corporate Governance Kodex (DGCK).

90 Cf. Kubis, n. 38, § 131 AktG, para. 5.

91 For further details, see Klaus Trouet, 'Die Hauptversammlung – Organ der Aktiengesellschaft oder Forum der Aktionäre?' (20/1986) Neue Juristische Wochenschrift (NJW) 1302.

92 Siems, n. 85, § 131, para. 6. In this respect, the revised DCGK (see fn. 15) does not contain any changes, as it contains an identical reference in section A.7.

93 In this vein, see Kubis, n. 38, § 131 AktG, para. 5.

94 See, for instance, Wolfgang Zöllner and Ulrich Noack, 'Stimmrecht und Kapitalbeteiligung bei der Aktiengesellschaft' (1991) Die Aktiengesellschaft (AG) 117.

95 For empirical analysis on the historical roots and economic relevance, see Stefan Daske, *Vorzugsaktien in Deutschland* (Springer Gabler 2019). Cf. also T. Bezzenberger, *Vorzugsaktien ohne Stimmrecht* (C. Heymann 1991).

96 In more detail and in comparison with other European jurisdictions, see Nina Winkler, *Das Stimmrecht der Aktionäre in der Europäischen Union* (De Gruyter 2006) 26 and 78.

is based on the nominal value, and in the case of no-par value shares on their number. A restriction of voting rights by means of maximum voting rights can be provided for only in the AoA of non-listed companies (section 134(1) AktG).[97] Conversely, the granting of shares with multiple voting rights has been generally prohibited since 1998, even for unlisted companies (section 12(2) AktG). Some special features did, however, formerly apply for Volkswagen. These were enshrined in a special law but were declared largely inadmissible by the ECJ in 2007.[98]

15.3 SHAREHOLDER ENGAGEMENT AND VOTING IN PRACTICE

15.3.1 *Voting in Practice*

Regarding the casting of votes, the AktG does not contain mandatory provisions. Instead, according to section 134(4) AktG, the company's by-laws shall govern the form in which voting is exercised. In practice, however, by-laws most often merely contain the provision that the meeting chairperson is responsible for determining the voting form, with his or her decision being indisputable by the general meeting.[99] The chairperson is generally free to decide on the form as long as the voting result can be determined reliably and unequivocally.[100] Depending on the number of shareholders in attendance, it is acceptable to appoint an open (low number of attendees) or hidden (high number of attendees) form of vote casting. The open casting of votes includes such methods as a show of hands, standing up and vote by acclamation, whilst hidden voting is possible via written votes, voting cards or electronic votes.[101]

Although the casting of votes within the general meeting through an electronic voting system has always been legally permissible, since 2009 in certain cases shareholders have also been allowed to cast their votes without being physically present at the meeting. Pursuant to section 118-(1)2 AktG, a company's by-laws may provide, or may grant authority to the management board to provide, that shareholders may attend the general meeting without being physically present at the place at which it is being held and without an authorized representative and, furthermore, that they may exercise the entirety of their rights or individual rights, in full or in part, by means of electronic communication. As of June 2020, the by-laws of twenty-eight of the DAX-30 companies grant this authority to the management board. The by-laws of only Merck and Volkswagen do not contain a provision regarding the execution of rights by means of electronic communication. Nevertheless, the law still views the general meeting with shareholders physically present as the normal case, and the use of electronic participation possibilities in practice therefore remains underwhelming. In 2016 and 2017, there was not a single general meeting in which online

97 On the longstanding debate over the possibility of limiting voting rights, cf Michael Adams, 'Was spricht gegen eine unbehinderte Übertragbarkeit der in Unternehmen gebundenen Ressourcen durch ihre Eigentümer?' (1990) Die Aktiengesellschaft (AG) 63; Theodor Baums, 'Höchststimmrechte' (1990) Die Aktiengesellschaft (AG) 221; Uwe H. Schneider, ‚Gesetzliches Verbot für Stimmrechtsbeschränkungen bei der Aktiengesellschaft? Zugleich ein Beitrag zur statuarischen Konzerngründungsklausel bei der abhängigen Aktiengesellschaft' (1990) Die Aktiengesellschaft (AG) 56.

98 ECJ, decision of 27 October 2007, case C-112/05, EU:C:2007:623; for a comment on the decision see, for instance, n. 39 above; cf. also Sander, 'Case C-112/05, European Commission v. Federal Republic of Germany: The Volkswagen Case and Art 56 EC – A Proper Result, Yet Also A Missed Opportunity?' (2008) 14 Columbia Journal of European Law 359.

99 Koch, n. 37, § 134 AktG, para. 34; Micheal Arnold, in Wulf Goette and Mathias Habersack (eds.), *Münchener Kommentar zum Aktiengesetz* (4th ed., C.H. Beck 2018) § 134 AktG, para. 86.

100 Arnold, n. 96, § 134 AktG, para. 88.

101 Ibid., ; Oliver Rieckers, in Gerald Spindler and Eberhard Stilz (eds.), *Aktiengesetz* (4th ed., C.H. Beck 2019) § 134, para. 81.

participants had the same rights as the shareholders who were physically present.[102] In those two years, only ten DAX-30 companies live broadcast anything more than the opening address by the management board chair. In twenty-seven of thirty cases, however, it was possible for shareholders who were not physically present to vote digitally via an internet portal in 2017.[103] Owing to the COVID-19 Mitigation Act, virtual participation will necessarily gain in importance, at least for general meetings held while it is in effect. It remains to be seen whether this leads to DAX-30 companies making a virtue out of necessity in future.

Pursuant to section 134(3) AktG, the exercise of a voting right by an authorized representative is permitted. Since 2001, section 134(3)5 AktG requires companies that name representatives to exercise voting rights (e.g. executive employees, employees) to keep a verifiable record of the declaration of power. Consequently, the legitimacy of proxy voting is undisputed. However, as the AktG does not contain further legal provisions regarding the execution of voting rights through proxies, there is some dispute about the prerequisites for representation by the representatives of the company. According to the prevailing opinion in legal academia, section 134(3)5 AktG has to be interpreted in a way that it is necessary for the shareholder to instruct the proxy on each and every voting item.[104]

The turnout for AGMs is traditionally in the range of 50 per cent. Since the middle of the last decade there has been a slight uptick, with attendance in most years (except for 2013) being above 50 per cent, and even consistently surpassing 60 per cent. Although it may be premature to draw major conclusions, it is at least noteworthy that as of 8 June 2020 twelve DAX-30 corporations held virtual general meetings under the influence of the COVID-19 Mitigation Act, with the average turnout being 61.76 per cent.[105] It remains to be seen whether this is just a preliminary statistical anomaly or whether the conducting of virtual general meetings may lead to a lasting increase in shareholder turnout and, in consequence, shareholder engagement.

15.3.1.1 Voting Items

The typical agenda of the general meeting of a German stock corporation consists – mostly in this order – of the allocation of income and dividends (section 119(1) no. 2 AktG), the discharge of management and supervisory board members (section 119(1) no. 4 AktG), the ratification of auditors (section 119(1) no. 5 AktG) and the (re-)election of supervisory board members (section 119(1) no. 1 AktG). Other voting items are included only if necessary, for example the amendment of by-laws or capital measures.

To transpose article 9a of the Revised Shareholder Rights Directive (SRD II), German legislature inserted section 119(1) no. 3 AktG on 1 January 2020, according to which the general meeting of a listed company[106] is authorized in future to vote on the remuneration system for members of the management and supervisory boards. Pursuant to section 120a(1)1 AktG,

[102] See Matthias v. Holten and Tobias Bauerfeind, 'Die Online-Hauptversammlung in Deutschland und Europa' (20/2018) Die Aktiengesellschaft (AG) 729, 732.

[103] Ibid., 729, 733.

[104] Koch, n. 37, § 134, para. 26b; Arnold, n. 96, § 134 AktG, para. 42; Mario Hüther, 'Namensaktien, Internet und die Zukunft der Stimmrechtsvertretung' (02/2001) Die Aktiengesellschaft (AG) 68, 71; Ulrich Noack, 'Stimmrechtsvertretung in der Hauptversammlung nach NaStraG' (2/2001) Zeitschrift für Wirtschaftsrecht (ZIP) 57, 62.

[105] Allianz: 44.24 per cent, Bayer: 64.02 per cent, Beiersdorf: 76.18 per cent, BMW: 80.86 per cent, Deutsche Bank: 43.53 per cent, Deutsche Börse: 75.93 per cent, Heidelberg Cement: 72.31 per cent, Lufthansa: 32.82 per cent, Merck: 69.38 per cent, Munich Re: 44.6 per cent, SAP: 72.84 per cent.

[106] Schutzgemeinschaft der Kapitalanleger, SdK-Präsenzstatistik 2015 www.sdk.org/assets/Statistiken/HV-Praesenzen/praesenz-dax15.pdf accessed 8 June 2020.

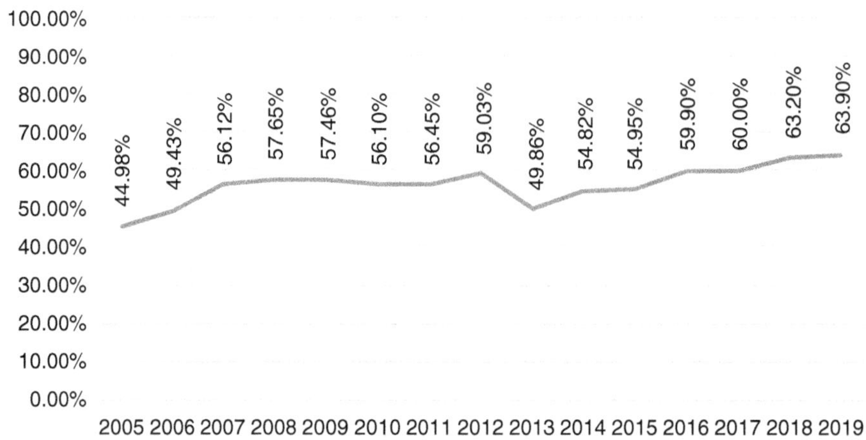

FIGURE 15.2 Turnout for general meetings of DAX-30 corporations
Note to figure: the data are retrieved from Schutzgemeinschaft der Kapitalanleger (2005–15)[107] and Georgeson (2016–19).[108]

a decision on the remuneration system for management board members has to take place at least every four years, as well as upon any major changes to that system. However, general meeting decisions do not have binding force on the supervisory board, even though SRD II provides the legal means for such an arrangement; German law still takes a 'say on pay' rather than 'decide on pay' approach.[109] In consequence, the decision ultimately has no legal effect; rather, its influence is restricted to a 'moral' effect on the supervisory board's execution of its tasks. Before the 2020 amendment, voting on remuneration systems by the general meeting was optional. Analysis of voting shows relatively high dissent rates. For example, the vote to approve the remuneration system for Lufthansa's management board members in 2019 generated an approval rate of only 57.4 per cent. The average approval rates in 2018 and 2019 were also relatively low at 75.2 per cent and 78.8 per cent, respectively. It remains to be seen whether such high dissent rates will continue now that every corporation's general meeting is entitled to vote on this matter.

In the general meetings of DAX-30 corporations, the approval rates are generally very high, as shown in Table 15.2.

The (re-)election of supervisory board members is normally no more than a technicality. Whilst there are a number of instances in which dissent rates have exceeded 10 per cent, they seldom exceed 20 per cent. From 2014 to 2019, there was no recorded failed (re-)election of a supervisory board member.

In a sample of 178 general meetings held from 2014 to 2019, only 3 voting items proposed by the management board were dismissed. In two of these instances, the general meeting dismissed the remuneration system for the management board (Merck in 2016, with a 54 per cent dissent rate, and Munich Re in 2016, with a 65.7 per cent dissent rate). However, as outlined above, the vote on remuneration systems by the general meeting was optional until 2020 and still has no binding

[107] Georgeson, '2019 Proxy Season Review' www.georgeson.com/uk/2019-season-review accessed 27 July 2020.

[108] The general meeting of an unlisted company does not have a comparable legal competence. However, companies' by-laws may provide the general meeting with the right to vote on the renumeration system; see Koch, n. 37, § 120a AktG, para. 1.

[109] Koch, n. 37, § 120a AktG, para. 1; extensively on this type of shareholder decisions, also from a comparative perspective: Sadik Capa, 'Konsultative Hauptversammlungsbeschlüsse im Aktienrecht aus rechtsvergleichender Sicht' (PhD dissertation, University of Marburg 2020).

TABLE 15.2 *Approval ratings (%) in general meetings of DAX-30 corporations*

Voting item	2014	2015	2016	2017	2018	2019
Election of supervisory board members, s 119(1) no 1 AktG	99.8	93	96.1	94.4	94.9	93.9
Appropriation of net income and dividends, s 119(1) no 2 AktG	99.3	99.4	99.1	98.4	98.6	98.7
Remuneration system of management board, s 119(1) no 3 AktG	/	95.9	93	82.8	75.2	78.8
Remuneration system of supervisory board, s 119(1) no 3 AktG	/	97.6	98.2	88.6	97.1	/
Discharge of management board members, s 119(1) no 4 AktG	100	97.8	98.8	98.3	97.3	96.4
Discharge of supervisory board members, s 119(1) no 4 AktG	99.8	96.5	96.9	95.4	96.4	94.9
Appointment of the auditor of annual accounts, s 119(1) no 5 AktG	99.2	98.3	96.7	97.1	97	96.7
Dissolution of the company, s 119(1) no 9 AktG	/	/	/	/	/	/

Note to table: the data are retrieved from Proxy Insight.

force.[110] In 2019, the AGM of Bayer dismissed the discharge of the management board for fiscal year 2018 with a 55.5 per cent dissent rate. The background to this unprecedented refusal to discharge was Bayer's recent acquisition of the controversial genetic engineering company Monsanto for a purchase price of US$66 billion and the subsequent loss in value of Bayer's stock.

Nonetheless, analysis of the data suggests that German shareholders are largely loyal to the corporation and, more importantly, to its boards. Such loyalty may best be illustrated by analysis of the voting practice of Volkswagen shareholders following the revelation of the so-called Dieselgate scandal[111]. Even though that scandal was uncovered in late 2015 and gained both national and worldwide prominence in 2016, all the while putting Volkswagen at risk of massive financial repercussions, the AGM in 2017 nevertheless discharged management and supervisory board members with an average approval rating of more than 99 per cent.[112] It remains to be seen whether the historic rejection by Bayer shareholders in 2019 and the inclusion of remunerations systems as a voting item mark watershed moments for more confrontational shareholder engagement in Germany. In this sense at least, shareholder turnout at general meetings and average dissent rates have exhibited a slight upward trend in recent years.

15.3.2 *Shareholder Questions and Proposals*

The right of every shareholder to be informed by the management board at the general meeting upon request is often made use of in practice, which leads to comparatively long general meetings in Germany and may discourage some shareholders from participating (although there are no empirical data, the most recent DCGK reminds meeting chairpersons that a normal general meeting should last no more than four to six hours; see suggestion A.4 DGCK),[113] ultimately weakening shareholder engagement. In addition, some shareholders use this right to exploit the general meeting as a forum to display improper personal interests.[114] The legal design of the

110 See Koch, n. 37, s. 120a, para. 2.

111 'Dieselgate scandal' means the intentional programming of turbocharged direct injection diesel engines by Volkswagen to detect laboratory emission testing and consequent adjustment of the emissions on the test station to meet legal requirements. The scandal began in September 2015 when the United States Environmental Protection Agency (EPA) issued a notice of violation of the Clean Air Act and concerned more than eleven million cars.

112 See Volkswagen, Abstimmungsergebnisse www.volkswagenag.com/presence/investorrelation/publications/shareholder-meetings/2017/voting-result/deutsch/VW_Internet_DE.pdf accessed 23 May 2020.

113 Siems, n. 85, § 131, para. 6.

114 Kubis, n. 38, § 131, para. 5.

shareholder question right in section 131 AktG further leads to the potential for legal errors, as the management board has to decide at the general meeting if it is required to answer particular shareholder questions.[115] In consequence, some efforts have been made to reform the shareholder question *de lege feranda*, for example make it optional in by-laws.[116]

Voting items proposed by shareholders are relatively rare. In the sample of 178 general meetings from 2014 to 2019, 40 shareholder proposals were voted on by the general meeting, not a single one of which received sufficient votes to pass. Shareholder proposals in Germany seem to be a sign of troubled times for the company. For example, during the Volkswagen AGM in 2016 – that is, at the time of Dieselgate – four shareholder proposals were voted on. Meanwhile, the AGMs of Deutsche Bank voted on twenty shareholder proposals from 2015 to 2019, most of them requesting special audits concerning irregularities in the company's management.

15.3.3 *Private Engagements*

Whilst it is widely known that institutional investors and other large shareholders are often given an opportunity to engage with corporate boards and company representatives during private meetings outside AGMs, it is difficult if not impossible to obtain empirical data on such behind-the-scenes engagement.[117] In this respect, one of the major shareholders in Lufthansa (Heinz Hermann Thiele) in June 2020 initially opposed federal government participation in the company in light of the ramifications of the COVID-19 pandemic. However, after negotiations with Lufthansa management and politicians, he ultimately approved it.[118]

Recently, however, there has been intense debate over whether any form of information privilege for specific shareholders outside the general meeting is permissible.[119] After all, the AktG provides for the principle of equal treatment in section 53a. This principle covers the entire relationship between the company and its shareholders, including equal treatment with regard to information.[120] As a consequence, no shareholder should have privileged access to information on the company. The idea is that no individual shareholder should gain an information advantage that can be exploited opportunistically to the detriment of other shareholders.[121] If for purposes of investor relations, however, a company provides individual shareholders with targeted information, the principle of equal treatment with regard to information gives rise to a conflict between the legitimate interests of the company on the one hand and the general interests of shareholders on the other. How to weigh these conflicting interests is still the subject of debate under German law.

[115] Siems, n. 85, § 131, para. 6; Kubis, n. 38, § 131, para. 5.

[116] See for instance Siems, n. 85, § 131, para. 11.

[117] Cf. however Sandra Tietz, Kerstin Hammann and Christian P. Hoffmann, 'Investoren und Aufsichtsrat im Dialog' (2019) 5 Der Aufsichtsrat 69.

[118] See Markus Fasse, 'Großaktionär Thiele will mehr Einfluss bei der Lufthansa' *Handelsblatt* (26 June 2020) www.handelsblatt.com/unternehmen/handel-konsumgueter/rettungspaket-grossaktionaer-thiele-will-mehr-einfluss-bei-der-lufthansa/25957522.html accessed 27 July 2020.

[119] See, for instance, Hans-Christoph Hirt, Klaus J. Hopt and Daniela Mattheus, 'Dialog zwischen dem Aufsichtsrat und Investoren' (2016) Die Aktiengesellschaft (AG) 725; Philipp Holle, 'Kommunikation des Aufsichtsrats mit Marktteilnehmern' (40/2019) Zeitschrift für Wirtschaftsrecht (ZIP) 1895; Pirmin Jonas Herz, 'Informationelle Selbstbehandlung und Informationsprivilegien im Aktienrecht' (8/2020) Neue Zeitschrift für Gesellschaftsrecht (NZG) 285.

[120] Extensively, Dirk Zetzsche, '§ 53a AktG als Informationsnorm?' (19/2019) Die Aktiengesellschaft (AG) 701; see also: Dirk Zetzsche, *Aktionärsinformation in der börsennotierten Gesellschaft* (Carl Heymanns Verlag 2006).

[121] In this sense, for instance, see Bundesgerichtshof, 'Kein Gleichbehandlungsanspruch auf pflichtwidriges Vorstandshandeln' (4/2008) Neue Zeitschrift für Gesellschaftsrecht (NZG) 149.

15.4 CONCLUDING REMARKS

To summarize, although shareholder engagement definitely plays an important role in Germany, there is significant room for improvement. In essence, there seem to be two factors constraining the engagement of shareholders. First, because of the current legal design of the AG structure, the general meeting of shareholders seems to have lost its historical position as the supreme organ of the corporation. Second, the restricted authority regarding management of the corporation, especially if it falls with the scope of MitbestG, gives employees a say in the company's affairs, and shareholder influence is correspondingly reduced. Both factors may also act as psychological deterrents, as shareholders may assume that their engagement will have no effect. In this respect, it seems unfortunate that the German legislature, while adding the vote on remuneration systems to the general meeting's competences, softened those decisions' binding force to a recommendation for the supervisory board. Ultimately, it seems that an opportunity was missed in this respect to strengthen the means of shareholder engagement in Germany. Nevertheless, by way of the general meeting shareholders still have significant competences through which they can influence the management of the company, at least indirectly.

Regardless of the legal framework, it seems questionable whether any additional competences would change shareholder engagement. From an empirical perspective, there seems to be little opposition to the activities of management boards. The empirical analysis of shareholder engagement in practice generally shows low dissent rates, especially concerning the discharge of board members. However, recent developments may indicate a paradigm shift in shareholder engagement in Germany. To begin with, Bayer shareholders in 2019 demonstrated that it is not only legally possible but actually practicable to sanction the management of a corporation at least retroactively by refusing to grant a discharge. Furthermore, even if voting on renumeration systems has no binding effect, the dissent rates hitherto have been relatively high, suggesting more confrontational shareholders. If such opposition is shown to have an effect on the management of corporations in future, more shareholders may be compelled to participate in the decision-making process. Finally, the COVID-19 pandemic forced German legislature to allow virtual general meetings under German corporate law at least temporarily. Early data suggest an increase in shareholder turnout. Politicians and academics will have to monitor this temporary legislative experiment very closely. It may ultimately show that the digitalization of the general meeting provides a unique opportunity to strengthen shareholder engagement in future. The 2020 as well as the 2021 seasons of general meetings promises to be the perfect test case for this hypothesis.

16

Shareholder Engagement and Voting in Greece

Vassilis Tountopoulos and Rigas Giovannopoulos

Greek law provides for a variety of forms for carrying on business. The main forms are: (1) companies (SA/AE (Société Anonyme), French and Greek acronyms respectively, ΕΠΕ (limited liability company), IKE (private company)) and (2) partnerships (OE (general partnership) and EE (limited partnership)).[1] There are also some specific company forms focusing on a specific sector such as shipping companies. The most important company form in the Greek legal order with regard to economic strength and social key role of the companies hosted thereunder is the Société Anonyme (SA/AE). Therefore, this study focuses on SAs, and more specifically on listed SAs.

16.1 THE STRUCTURE OF GREEK SAS

All SAs (whether listed or not) have basically the same structure. They have a General Meeting, a Board of Directors (BoD) and auditors[2] (collectively, the organs of the Société Anonyme). The interdependence between these organs, and the respective allocation of powers, will be discussed in Section 16.1.2.

16.1.1 *The Allocation of Corporate Decision-Making*

An SA is managed by a BoD, which, acting collectively, represents the company (a one-tier system)[3]. The BoD may assign the exercise of all or part of its rights, save those requiring collective action, to one or more of its members, acting jointly or severally, pursuant to a provision in the articles of association and the relevant decision of the BoD[4]. The BoD's rights may be delegated to one or more officials of the company or to any third party. Usually the delegation of powers is made to one member of the BoD.

The BoD of listed companies consists of executive,[5] non-executive[6] and independent non-executive[7] BoD members (three to fifteen members, either natural persons or even legal entities, if the articles of association provide accordingly).[8] Executive members have executive

[1] See generally on Greek Company Law Lambros E. Kotsiris and Evangeline L. Kotsiri, *Greek Law on Partnerships and Corporation* (5th ed., Sakkoulas 2018).

[2] Nikolaos Rokas, *Company Law* (9th ed., Sakkoulas 2019, in Greek) 243.

[3] Law 4548/2018 Greek Company Act (hereinafter GCA, art. 77(1)).

[4] GCA, art. 87.

[5] Law 4706/2020, art. 6.

[6] Law 4706/2020, art. 7.

[7] Law 4706/2020, art. 9.

[8] GCA, art. 77 (4), Law 4706/2020, art. 5 (1).

responsibilities for running the company's day-to-day business activities, while non-executive members are tasked with pursuing the company's general interests. More specifically, according to Article 7 of Law 4706/2020:

> The non-executive members of the Board of Directors including the independent non- executive members mainly have the following obligations: a) Monitor and review the strategy of the company and its implementation as well as the achievement of its goals, b) Ensure the effective supervision of the executive members including monitoring and examining their performance, c) Examine and express their opinion on the recommendation submitted by the executive members based on the existing information.

One-third of the BoD members of a listed company must be independent non-executive members and, in any case, no less than two.[9] Moreover, the BoD chairman must be a non-executive member of the BoD.[10] If the BoD fails to appoint a non-executive member as BoD chairman, it is compelled to appoint a non-executive member as BoD vice-chairman.[11]

The duties of directors are set out in Article 96 of Law 4548/2018 (the Greek Company Act, hereafter the GCA). According to this article, directors have to: (1) act in the company's best interests; (2) oversee the implementation of BoD and General Meeting resolutions; and (3) inform all other directors about the company's affairs.[12]

The notion of the 'company's interests' is interpreted narrowly. It comprises the interests of the company as a legal person and those of its shareholders.[13] The interests of other stakeholders are usually not taken into consideration. Nonetheless, the interests of other stakeholders and those of shareholders are usually interrelated and tend to converge in the long run.[14] Be that as it may, it has been hotly debated whether the interest of a group of companies can be recognized.[15]

Members of the BoD cannot act on behalf of the company in cases where a conflict of interest situation arises.[16] Moreover, with regard to related parties' transactions the law provides for special measures in order to safeguard the interests of the company, its creditors and its minority shareholders.[17]

All BoD members have supervisory duties on the overall operation of the BoD and of all business sections.[18] Such duties are not limited to implementing BoD decisions. Failure to monitor and control the activities of other Directors or employees of the company can establish personal liability for a Director.[19] Nonetheless, the extent of BoD members' liability is also related to the internal delegation of powers and duties within the company.

9 Law 4706/2020, art. 5(2).

10 Law 4706/2020, art. 8(1).

11 Law 4706/2020, art. 8(2).

12 GCA, art. 96(1).

13 Rokas (n. 2) 191.

14 Vassilios Tountopoulos in Evanghelos Perakis (ed.) *DikAE (=The SA' Law)*, vol. 10 (Special Issues: Corporate Governance (L. 3016/2002), Bonds and Claims' Securitization (L. 3156/2003))(2nd ed., Nomiki Bibliothiki 2005, in Greek); Art. 2 of Law 3016/2002, paras (18) and (19).

15 Vassilios Tountopoulos, 'National Report on Greece' in Rafael Mariano Manovil (ed.), *Groups of Companies* (Springer 2020) 569, 574.

16 GCA, art. 97(3).

17 GCA, art. 99.

18 Cf. Art. 96 (1) of GCA and explanatory report of the Law referring explicitly to the 'supervisory role' of all BoD members.

19 Athens Multi-Member First Instance Court 6042/2003, [2004] *Epitheōrēsē Emporikou Dikaiou [Commercial Law Review]* 69 (the ALA-LC transliteration standard dated July 2010 has been applied).

16.1.2 *Shareholder versus Board/Managerial Supremacy/Powers of the GM*

The General Meeting is the supreme organ of a Société Anonyme, and is tasked under the GCA with deciding on any matter related to the Company.[20]

The General Meeting alone is competent to decide on:[21] (1) any amendments to the articles of association (including resolutions to increase or decrease the share capital by a GM decision); (2) the election of the Board of Directors and the auditors;[22] (3) approval of overall management according to Article 108 GCA and the release from liability of the company's auditors; (4) approval and revision of the company's annual financial statements (whether separate or consolidated); (5) the appropriation of annual profits; (6) approval of the provision of remuneration or advance payments under Article 109 GCA; (7) approval of the remuneration policy under Article 110 GCA and the remuneration report under Article 112 GCA (for listed companies only); (8) the merger, split, transformation, revival, extension of duration or dissolution of the company; and (9) the appointment of liquidators.

Although not explicitly provided for in the law, the General Meeting also has to decide on all issues affecting the substance of the company, including the disposal of the company's core assets (implicit powers of the General Meeting).[23]

BoD members usually refer matters to the General Meeting for approval. The reason for this practice is that according to the GCA there is no liability for BoD members for any act or omission if they comply with a lawful resolution of the company's General Meeting.[24] Consequently, referring the matter to the General Meeting could limit the liability of BoD members.

However, the General Meeting cannot substitute the BoD when it comes to management of the company. The reason is twofold. First, the General Meeting is an internal organ without representative powers. Second, the law explicitly provides that the BoD manages the company.[25] Accordingly, the Athens Court of Appeal has ruled that the General Meeting cannot authorize specific persons to act on behalf of the company and substitute the BoD.[26]

16.1.3 *Ownership Structure*

Before addressing the issue of the ownership structure of Greek listed companies, it will be helpful to characterize the Greek capital market in terms of both the number of listed companies and their capitalization.

[20] GCA, art. 116.

[21] GCA, art. 117(1).

[22] The auditors in listed companies are proposed by the Auditing Committee according to art. 44(3)(f) of Law 4449/2017 (transposing art. 39(6)(f) Directive 2006/43/EC (SAD) as amended) but the election stays at the absolute discretions of the GM (Arts. 2(1)(A.1) and (3)(b) of the Law 4336/2015).

[23] See explanatory report on art. 117 of GCA. See also Corinth Single-Member First Instance Court 2263/2003, (2004) Hellenikē Dikaiosynē (Hellenic Justice) 722; Piraeus First Instance Court 5826/2006, (2007) Dikaio Epixeiriseōn & Etairiōn (Business & Company Law) 452 note Mantha Varela; Lia Athanassiou, *Shareholders and Corporate Supervision* (NB 2010, in Greek) 133; Rokas (n. 2) 246; Elisa Alexandridou, *Company Law* (3rd ed., NB 2019, in Greek) 339.

[24] Art. 102(4) of GCA, pursuant to which 'the members of the board of directors are not liable to the company in respect of acts or omissions that are based on a lawful decision of the general meeting'. The GM decides upon information provided by the BoD. There is no statistical data on the frequency of such decisions, but the application of the implied powers doctrine referred to in the previous footnote ensures that many of the major transactions are approved by the GM.

[25] Rokas (n. 2) 244.

[26] Athens Court of Appeal 4864/2000, [2003] Epitheōrēsē Emporikou Dikaiou 69.

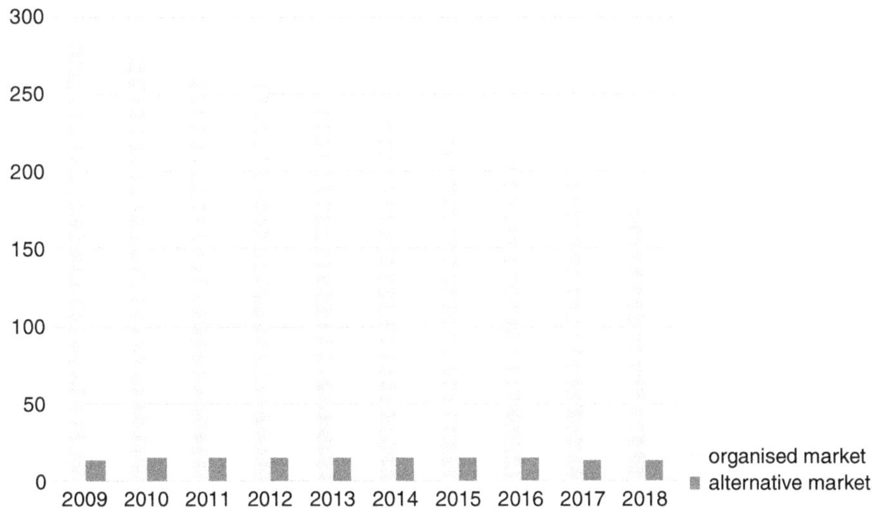

FIGURE 16.1 Number of Greek listed companies
Source: Athens Stock Exchange.

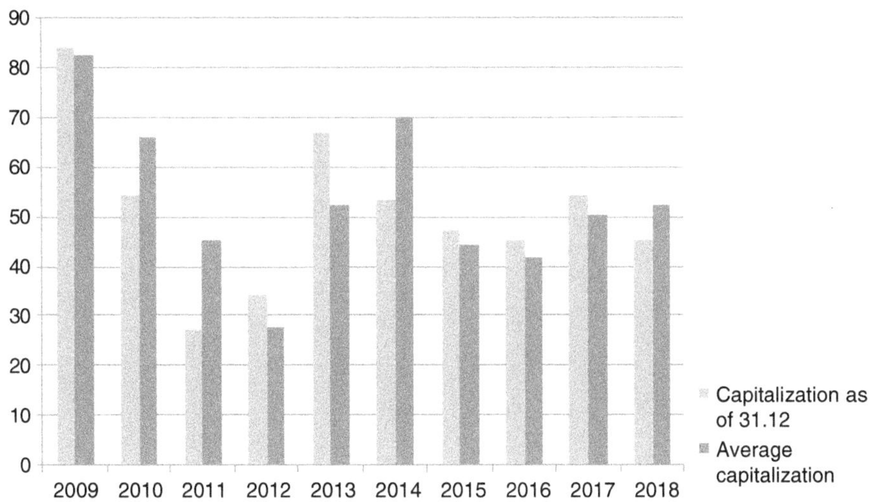

FIGURE 16.2 Capitalization of Greek listed companies (€ billions)
Source: Athens Stock Exchange; Y-axis: € billions.

Figures 16.1 and 16.2 make clear that the number of listed companies has declined over the last decade. Similarly, the capitalization of Greek companies decreased from €83.7 billion in 2009 to €45 billion in 2018. These trends are linked to the financial and debt crisis in Greece. However, the increase in capitalization in 2018 indicates that the Greek economy was recovering (prior to the outbreak of the COVID-19 pandemic).

Traditionally, the ownership structure of Greek listed companies has been highly concentrated.[27] The multiple recapitalizations of Greek banks in recent years has changed the paradigm in the

[27] See, indicatively, Themistokles Lazarides, Evaggelos Drimpetas and Dimitros Koufopoulos, 'Ownership Structure in Greece: Determinants and Implications on Corporate Governance' in Nicholas Tsounis (ed.), *International Conference on Applied Economics Proceedings* (2009) 379 http://i-coae.com/?cat=9 accessed 7 March 2022.

banking sector. Nowadays, banks in Greece have widely dispersed shareholdings. In the other sectors, however, concentration levels still remain high. Table 16.1 is enlightening in that respect.

The types of shareholders present in the listed companies also vary to a high degree. The different types of shareholders are described in Table 16.2.

It is clear from Table 16.2 that foreign investors hold the major stake in the Greek Exchange (63.26 per cent). Although, in specific cases, foreign investors act on behalf of national investors, the high percentage of foreign investors is a clear indication of the globalization of the Greek capital market.

TABLE 16.1 *Major shareholders in Greek listed companies as of 31 December 2018*

Number of Listed Companies %	Voting rights largest shareholder (%)
3.5%	0–25%
16.9%	26–50%
40.8%	51–75%
38.8%	76–100%

Source: Hellenic Capital Market Commission (hereinafter HCMC) Annual Report, 2018, 88.

TABLE 16.2 *Shareholders in Greek companies listed on the Athens Stock Exchange as of 31 December 2018*

	Accounts (Active)		Capitalization	
			Value	
	Number	Percentage %	Millions of Euro	Percentage %
I. Local Investors	580,129	98.20%	12,925.13	36.70%
- Private Investors	575,529	97.42%	6,146.65	17.45%
- Private financial companies	335	0.06%	2,131.22	6.05%
- Private not-for-profit institutions	551	0.09%	240.58	0.68%
- Non-financial companies	2,111	0.36%	2,920.93	8.29%
- Public Sector	109	0.02%	763.55	2.17%
- Others investors	1,493	0.25%	4.66	0.01%
- HFSF[28]	1	0.00%	717.55	2.04%
II. Foreign Investors	10,445	1.77%	22,276.54	63.26%
- Private Investors	7,115	1.20%	401.16	1.14%
- Private financial companies	2,571	0.44%	14,062.21	39.93%
- Private not-for-profit institutions	28	0.00%	42.63	0.12%
- Non financial companies	636	0.11%	6,949.16	19.73%
- Public Sector	79	0.01%	821.36	2.33%
- Others investors	16	0.00%	0.01	0.00%
III. Other Investors	198	0.03%	12.79	0.04%
Total I + II + III	590,772	100.00%	35,214.46	100.00%

Source: HCMC Annual Report, 2018, 48.

[28] The Hellenic Financial Stability Fund (HFSF) is a legal person tasked to contribute to the maintenance of the stability of the Greek banking system, in the public interest. The Fund acts in line with the relevant commitments of the Greek Republic under Law 4046/2012.

Globalization has also been driven by the privatization of formerly state-owned enterprises. The privatization of Hellenic Telecommunications Organisation, OTE (now owned by Deutsche Telekom), offers a good example.

The globalization of the Greek economy should not obscure the fact that a high number of listed companies are family owned (controlled).[29] We define family-owned companies as companies where two or more family members are involved and the majority of ownership or control lies within a family (classified under private investors). A family structure can positively influence the effectiveness of a small-/medium-sized company. Nonetheless, the family structure in a large public company with dispersed shares creates serious corporate governance concerns. The recent case of a listed family company which made false financial statements (also known as the 'Greek Parmalat case') typifies this problem.[30] The Greek legislator tried unsuccessfully to resolve this issue by introducing voting prohibitions for shareholders who were members of the BoD.[31]

Holding companies are common in the Greek capital market. Holdings can be listed or be used as a vehicle for the major shareholder (often families) to hold the shares of a listed company.

By comparison with other jurisdictions, the participation of employees in Greek listed companies is usually negligible. This is also the case for privatized (ex state-owned) companies. Furthermore, no successful cases are known of employee buyouts in Greece.[32]

16.1.4 *The Particularities of Greek Corporate Governance*

Corporate governance codes are usually issued by private organizations (associations and self-regulatory bodies), while the corporate governance framework is usually based on the 'comply or explain principle'. Under this principle, listed companies are not obliged to comply with the relevant corporate governance provisions, but they must explain their reasons for not doing so and inform market participants accordingly.

In Greece, corporate governance rules for listed companies are mandatory. The basic corporate governance rules are laid down in Law 4706/2020,[33] and listed companies are obliged to comply with them. A breach of the relevant provisions exposes them to sanctions imposed by the HCMC.[34] Of course, listed companies can adopt further corporate governance rules in accordance with international best practice, which go beyond the mandatory provisions.

Special governance rules also apply to state-owned companies. Although golden shares are not directly used as an instrument in the Greek legal framework,[35] many provisions recognize special rights and impose special obligations on state-owned companies. Employees in state-owned companies also enjoy special status. Furthermore, employees in state-owned companies are usually represented on the BoD (which rarely happens in the case of private and listed companies).

16.2 LEGAL FORMS OF SHAREHOLDER ENGAGEMENT AND VOTING

Until relatively recently, the law required a general meeting (GM) of shareholders to be a properly organized meeting of their representatives at a specific place at a specific time on

[29] See e.g. Cretafarm SA, Karelias SA and Athens Medical Center SA.

[30] See https://en.wikipedia.org/wiki/Folli_Follie accessed 7 March 2022.

[31] See analytically Vassilios Tountopoulos, 'Restrictions of Voting Rights in Company Law' (2019) Nomiko Bēma (Legal Tribune) 244 (in Greek).

[32] See analytically V. Tountopoulos, 'Employees Buyouts' in *Commemorative Volume for L. Georgakopoulos II* (Bank of Greece 2016) 1083 (in Greek).

[33] See a translation of Law 4706/2020 in English www.hcmc.gr/en_US/web/portal/iframework8 accessed 7 March 2022

[34] Law 4706/2020, art. 24.

[35] See e.g. the repealed art. 11 of Law 3631/2008.

the basis of a proper and timely invitation communicated to the shareholders by the BoD. Gradually, however, the Greek legislature has specified a variety of acceptable means of decision-making for shareholders falling within the scope of 'Annual GM Decisions', although a real calling or a real meeting of shareholders is not necessary any more. Nowadays, the GCA has enriched the procedural alternatives for shareholder decision-making to meet the requirements of SRD I[36] as amended by SRD II,[37] and to conform to modern international trends and practices.[38] Nevertheless, some of the alternatives to the traditional GM are reserved to non-listed companies. Listed companies or companies listed in Multilateral Trading Facilities, having voluntarily accepted in their Articles of Association the GM procedures of GCA provided for with regard to listed companies,[39] are excluded from all options of GM decision-making without any meeting of the shareholders, physical or virtual. Thus, alternative and mainly asynchronous, decision making procedures, without a GM calling or a GM place such as: (1) the signing[40] of minutes by all[41] shareholders or their representatives[42] and (2) the remote electronic voting on a draft forwarded by electronic means to all shareholders without a meeting having been called and is taking place at all[43] are reserved to non-listed companies.

This does not mean that listed companies are excluded from the use of electronic participation or remote voting methods, if the articles of association stipulate accordingly[44] or if any shareholder individually applies for a remote participation, if he resides in a different country than the place of the GM or if a serious ground arises (illness, disablility, pandemic).[44(a)] The GCA provides for two different options. The first one entails the real time distant participation of

36 Directive 2007/36/EC of the European Parliament and of the Council of 11 July 2007 on the exercise of certain rights of shareholders in listed companies [2007] OJ L184/17. See generally on the Implementation of SRD I in Greece and on Shareholders' rights (under former law): Report on Greece, in: TGS Baltic, 'Study on Minority Shareholders Protection' (Publications Office of the EU 2018) 260 https://op.europa.eu/el/publication-detail/-/publication/1893f7b8-93a4-11e8-8bc1-01aa75ed71a1/language-en accessed 11 April 2020; Marianna Rapti, 'Amendments of the Greek law on Sociétés Anonymes for the Implementation of Directive 2007/36 on the Exercise of Certain Rights of Shareholders in Listed Companies' [2012] ICCLR 24; Elisavet Tastsidou, 'The Effects of the Revision of the EC Shareholder Rights Directive, Proposed in April 2014, on Corporate Actions Processing in the Intermediated Chain' (2016) *Xrēmatopistōtiko Dikaio [Financial Law]* 215; Panagiotis Staikouras, 'Corporate Governance and Investor Protection in Greece: Regulatory and Supervisory Reform from a Law and Finance Perspective' (2008) EBOR 983; Alexandros Spyridonos, *Minority Rights in the Public Company* (2nd ed., NB 2016, in Greek) *passim*; Christina Tarnanidou, *Special Shareholders' Rights of Listed Companies* (Sakkoulas 2009, in Greek); Christina Tarnanidou, 'Reform of the Law on Listed Companies Following the Amendment of L 2190/1920 by virtue of L 3884/2010' (2010) Xrēmatopistōtiko Dikaio (Financial Law) 154 (in Greek). Cf. in a comparative approach: Andreas Cahn and David C. Donald, *Comparative Company Law* (Cambridge University Press 2010) 467; Carsten Gerner-Beuerle and Michael Schillig, *Comparative Company Law* (OUP 2019) 380.

37 Council Directive (EU) 2017/828 amending Directive 2007/36/EC as regards the encouragement of long-term shareholder engagement [2017] OJ L 132/1, arts. 3c and 8. GCA has implemented the SRD II within the time limit of art. 2 thereof.

38 See GCA, arts. 118, 120(2) and (3), 121(5), 125, 126, 135 and 136.

39 GCA, art. 119(5).

40 If the articles of associations stipulate respectively, hand signature could be substituted by the exchange of proper emails between the shareholders or by alternative electronic means; GCA, art. 136(2); Council Regulation (EU) 910/2014 on electronic identification and trust services for electronic transactions in the internal market and repealing Directive 1999/93/EC [2014] OJ L257/73, applies as well.

41 Without any exception. If a single signature or electronic declaration is missing, the 'decision' is qualified as nonexistent by the law itself (art. 140(2) of GCA).

42 See GCA, arts. 118 and 136.

43 GCA, arts. 118 and 135 (1)(a). Art. 135 (1)(b) GCA restricts further the scope of such decision taking procedures. These are an option only for issues other than those on the obligatory agenda of the so-called 'ordinary annual' GM of art. 119(1) of GCA (approval of the Company's annual Financial Statements and, where applicable, election of the auditors, etc.).

44 An exception has been introduced due to the COVID-19 pandemic, so that no proviso in the articles of association is necessary, if a serious ground can be established (art. 120(3) GCA as amended by Law 4712/2020).

44(a) Art. 125(3) GCA as amended by law 4712/2020

a shareholder or a shareholders' proxy in the GM procedure by audiovisual or electronic means that ensure his identification, participation, communication (either orally or in writing),[45] voting and voting registration.[46] The second option restricts the distant participation of shareholders exclusively to the voting procedure (remote voting). Such voting takes place prior to the start of the ordinary GM, and the votes are transmitted either in writing (postal voting) or by electronic means (electronic voting).[47] The options of Articles 125 and 126 GCA require, however, a specific meeting place, an obligation that differentiates them from the previously mentioned alternatives under (1), (2) and (3). Even if all shareholders make use of any of these options of Articles 125 or 126 GCA, the GM is not degraded to an alternative procedure without meeting.

Practically reserved to (non-listed) companies with a small number of shareholders and an interpersonal nexus between them is the alternative of a GM without calling a meeting, where all shareholders without exception are simultaneously present or duly represented at a meeting, and none of them objects to the meeting being held and decisions being taking on the basis of minutes prepared and approved in situ ('omnilateral GM without convocation').[48] All listed companies and many non-listed companies, either with a larger number of shareholders, or if the shareholders are not able to agree on any of the aforementioned alternatives, convene a GM in the overwhelming majority of cases, by a decision of the BoD,[49] drafting a specific notice calling the GM to meet (which includes the agenda) that has to be made public.[50]

Public companies are obliged to call the 'ordinary annual' GM once a year, within a specific period of time pursuant to Article 119(1) GCA (at least once in every corporate financial year and within a period of nine months and ten days from the end of that year). In all other cases, they have, generally, the option to call an extraordinary general meeting (EGM), whenever this is deemed appropriate or necessary by the BoD.[51] There are also cases where the calling of an EGM is obligatory.[52] If the BoD fails to call the GM, in violation of the GCA, it faces criminal sanctions (fines).[53]

16.2.1 *Calling A Meeting*

Pursuant to Article 121(1) and (2) GCA, the GM is usually called by the BoD or, in exceptional cases, by other officials, such as bankruptcy administrators, special administrators or special liquidators assuming their statutory authority directly from their role in restructuring and insolvency frameworks. Articles 121(3) and (4) and 122(1) to (3), in compliance with the requirements of Articles 5 and 3 SRD I, stipulate a minimum convening period of twenty-two days[54] furthermore they provide for publication of the notice and, where applicable, of all relevant

45 GCA does not clarify whether the communication has to be one or two way.

46 GCA, art. 125.

47 GCA, art. 126. The law does not elaborate on the eligible transmission methods of votes but require procedures and methods ensuring the authenticity and integrity of the vote and the security of the communication means provided.

48 See GCA, arts. 120(2) and 121(5).

49 GCA, art. 121(1). The decision on a GM calling cannot be delegated to substitute organs, such as the Directors. Under circumstances, the remainder of BoD members is able to convene a GM exclusively aiming practically at the election of the vacant members.

50 GCA, arts. 121, 122.

51 GCA, art. 119(2).

52 See e.g. the procedure to approve related parties dealings according to art. 100(3) of GCA or the call of GM in case the total shareholder's equity becomes lower than the share capital according to art. 119(4) of GCA.

53 GCA, art. 180(1).

54 The provision indicates the number of twenty days but the date of publication of the notice and the date of GM do not count.

information: (1) on the publicly and freely accessible website of the Greek Business Registry[55] and (2) with regard to listed companies, on the company's website as well.[56]

Minority shareholders individually or collectively representing 5 per cent[57] of the paid-up share capital, and the shareholder associations referred to in Article 144 GCA,[58] representing minority shareholders with the necessary number of shares, are also entitled to call a GM, but may not do so directly.[59] Initially, they have to ask the BoD to call the meeting, indicating in their application the items to be included in the relevant agenda for the GM. The BoD is obliged to comply with the request within twenty days from the request being sent to the Chairman of the BoD and to call the GM no later than forty-five days from the day of service.[60] If the BoD fails to call the GM within these time limits,[61] the requesting shareholders can initiate interim proceedings and enforce the calling of the meeting with the requested agenda at the expense of the company by court decision.[62] This decision must be properly published as a notice by the requesting shareholders themselves[63]. Rights to call the GM either directly[64] or indirectly (by means of a request to the BoD according to Article 121(2) GCA, providing for a procedure similar to that pursued by minority shareholders) are also granted to the company's appointed auditor(s).[65] The recently enacted Law 4640/2019[66] has granted a direct right to call a GM to the supervisory authority for the capital market and listed companies (the Hellenic Capital Market Commission, or HCMC) in respect solely of the companies that do not fall within the exception in paragraph 4 of that provision (entities supervised by the SSM or the Greek Central Bank ('Bank of Greece')).

55 See www.businessregistry.gr. accessed 7 March 2022.

56 Art. 122(2) of GCA allows the articles of association of a non-listed company to provide for additional means for the proper and timely notification of shareholders and imposes the burden of proof that such additional requirements have been met on the company.

57 Pursuant to Art. 141(13) of GCA the articles of association may decrease, but not for more than one half, the threshold required in order to exercise the minority rights provided for in art. 141 of GCA, which comprises all rights examined in this chapter. Qualified minorities-bearers of special minority rights are determined in Greek Law only on the basis of participation in registered share capital and not according to other alternative criteria, such as the financial value of their shares or the number of shareholders.

58 See under Section 16.3.5.

59 GCA, arts. 121(2) and 141(1).

60 Contrary to the right to postpone the taking of a resolution by the GM, where the shareholder is entitled to set a specific date in his request within a term of twenty days from the date of the postponement, minority shareholders are not entitled to request the call of a GM at a specific date. The BoD has the option to set the exact date of the GM within the term of forty-five days.

61 In case of listed companies, the BoD has to call a GM. In case of non-listed companies it has the alternative to make use of the option of remote voting without a meeting pursuant to art. 135 of GCA, unless the requesting shareholders have opted out of such an alternative.

62 GCA, art. 141(1). Although this court decision is issued following the procedure of interim measures (Greek Civil Procedure Code, GCPC, art. 682), which would render it non-appealable, it is deemed as a decision of the voluntary jurisdiction (GCPC, art. 739) and thus subject to review proceedings: cf. Greek Supreme Court 1200/2019, Nomos.

63 Nikolaos Rokas, 'The New Law on Sociétés Anonymes: A First Critical Approach' (2019) Nomiko Bēma 258 (in Greek); Theodoros Katsas, 'The Rights of Shareholders' Minority Pursuant to Law 4548/2018' (2019) Nomiko Bēma 217 (in Greek). Cf. under the former GCA: Pelayia Yesiou-Faltsi, 'Issues Arising of Article 39(1) CL 2190/1920, As Amended by the Article 47(2) Law 3604/2007 with Regard to the General Meeting Calling of a SA by Virtue of a Court Decision (Expertise)' (2011) Epharmoges Astikou Dikaiou kai Dikaiou Politikēs Dikonomias (Theory and Practice of Civil Law & Civil Procedure Law) 273 (in Greek); Evanghelos Perakis, 'Risk of Cancellation of the Minority Calling Right (Article 39(1) of CL 2190/1920)' (2010) Dikaio Epixeiriseōn & Etairiōn (Business & Company Law) 1133 (in Greek).

64 Art. 119(4) of GCA as amended by Law 4609/2019.

65 Art. 121(2) of GCA, art. 2 (1) (A.1) (4) (c) of the Law 4336/2015.

66 Art. 40(1).

There is no reliable statistical data on the frequency with which all aforementioned special procedures are used in Greek company practice. Court proceedings based on applications from minority shareholders calling meetings are relatively uncommon, judging by the court decisions published in the last decade.[67]

16.2.2 *Shareholder Proposals*

Even before the implementation of SRD I, Greek Law provided for the right of shareholders to ask the BoD to include additional items on the agenda of every GM, whether annual or extraordinary, that had been already called. The GCA[68] has retained the threshold of 5 per cent of the paid-up share capital, whereas the bearers of the proposal rights are not only qualified minorities but shareholder associations under Article 144 GCA as well. The law introduces a separate rule with regard to non-listed and listed companies. In the context of non-listed companies, the request must be communicated to the BoD seventeen[69] days before the GM, and the BoD must make the revised agenda public in the same way as the initial notice, nine[70] days before the GM. In the context of listed companies, the request to introduce additional items must be accompanied by a written justification or by a draft resolution to be approved by the GM and the revised agenda has to be made public just like the initial one, fifteen[71] days before the GM. If the BoD fails to comply with the shareholders' legitimate request, the requesting shareholders are entitled to postpone the GM for a subsequent date within a period of twenty days after the initial date and proceed individually to the necessary publications of the revised agenda (and of the written justification or the draft resolution, in the case of listed companies), at the company's expense.[72] There are no reliable statistical data on the frequency with which such procedures are used in Greek company practice.

In both cases the BoD members (natural persons),[73] who fail to comply with the shareholder's convocation and proposal rights could face a criminal fine of up to €15,000 following a complaint made by the requesting shareholder(s).[74]

16.2.3 *Modes of Participation and Voting*

The right to vote is recognized as the paramount right of a shareholder. Greek law, in accordance with SRD I, has introduced various provisions to facilitate the use of this right by shareholders in a way that guarantees participation and the equality of shareholders. As already mentioned above,

67 Greek Supreme Court 1200/2019 and 684/2013, Nomos; Rhodes Single-Member First Instance Court 422/2017, Nomos; Larissa Single-Member First Instance Court 194/2015, [2015] Xronika Idiōtikou Dikaiou (Private Law Chronicles) 299 (Note Ioannis Papadimopoulos, in Greek); Sparta Single-Member First Instance Court 10/2014, [2013] Episkopēsē Emporikou Dikaiou (Commercial Law Overview) 75; Athens Court of Appeal 1486/2011, [2011] Dikaio Epixeiriseōn & Etairiōn (Business & Company Law) 682 [2011] Epitheōrēsē Emporikou Dikaiou 603 [2011] Episkopēsē Emporikou Dikaiou 1078 (Note K. Pampoukis, in Greek); Thessaloniki Single-Member First Instance Court 4529/2011, [2011] Harmenopoulos 788 (Note Achilleas Bechlivanis, in Greek); Athens Single-Member First Instance Court 5570/2010, [2010] Dikaio Epixeiriseōn & Etairiōn 1185 [2011] Nomiko Bēma 36 (Note Spyros Alexandris, in Greek).

68 GCA, art. 141(2).

69 The provision indicates the number of fifteen days but the date of communication of the request and the date of GM do not count.

70 The provision indicates the number of seven days but the date of communication of the request and the date of GM do not count.

71 The provision indicates the number of thirteen days but the date of communication of the request and the date of GM do not count.

72 GCA, art. 141(2).

73 Legal persons face no penal liability according to Greek General Penal Law.

74 GCA, art. 180.

the GCA has introduced, under the aforementioned prerequisites. modern voting methods, such as distance voting (by audiovisual or electronic means) in the course of virtual, real-time, attendance at the GM or remote distance voting (postal or electronic) before the GM actually takes place.

Greek law is traditionally characterized by the one-share-one vote principle,[75] in respect of fully paid-up shares with equal nominal value. Statutory provisions restricting the voting rights of ordinary shares are deemed null and void.[76] It is also explicitly prohibited for a company to issue shares granting multiple voting rights.[77] Nonetheless, the GCA provides for the option of a company issuing preference shares with or without limited voting rights, pursuant to its articles of association.[78] Bearers of preference shares without voting rights have nevertheless a right to participate in the meeting, without affecting the quorum[79] or have exceptionally a voting right in case of approval of a resolution on capital increases or decreases or redemption of shares.[80] Finally, the right to vote may be temporarily limited under certain circumstances.[81]

In accordance with Article 10 SRD I, Greek Law provides for proxy voting (up to three proxies at every GM, with the exemption of multiple securities accounts) in the context of listed companies.[82] Restricting stipulations in the Articles of Association are not valid.[83] On the contrary, non-listed companies may stipulate limitations in their articles of association on the eligibility of specific proxies, without being entitled to entirely exclude proxy voting as such.[84] The identity of the proxy must be communicated to the company prior to the GM either in written form or by electronic means. Greek law has made use of several options under Article 10 SRD I. Proxy holders at the GMs of listed companies have to disclose, before the beginning of the meeting, certain specified facts which may be relevant for the shareholders in assessing any risk that the proxy holder might pursue any interest other than the interests of the shareholder, adopting the enumeration of conflict of interest cases which is set out in Article 10(3) SRD I.[85] Greek Law excludes the exercise of shareholder rights through proxy holders without specific voting instructions in a vote in respect of the approval of overall management of the company, when the proxy holder is a member of the BoD.[86] Furthermore, Greek Law has not made use of the option provided for in Article 10(3)(c) SRD I, not explicitly restricting the transfer of the proxy to another person and thus allowing transferability according to general principles of civil law, that allow a proxy to be given the right to grant a substitute power of attorney. Finally, it imposes a duty on proxy holders at the GMs of listed companies to keep a record of the voting instructions for a minimum period of one year from the effective GM date.[87]

The GCA explicitly prohibits specific voting methods (e.g. secret voting), and prescribes open voting procedures in specific cases[88] or upon a request of minority shareholders representing

75 GCA, art. 36(1).
76 Florina Multi-Member First Instance Court 9/2015, [2016] Xronika Idiōtikou Dikaiou 451.
77 GCA, art. 38(4).
78 Ibid.
79 GCA, art. 124(1).
80 GCA, arts. 25(3), 29(5), 32(5). Cf. articles 68(3), 74 and 81 of Council Directive (EU) 2017/1132 [2017] OJ L 169/46.
81 See, e.g. art. 100(5) of GCA (the shareholder concerned is under specific circumstances excluded from the voting with regard to the approval of his or his related parties' dealings with the company) or art. 124(8) of GCA (natural person who are both BoD members and shareholders of listed companies are under specific circumstances excluded from the voting rights with regard to the election of auditors).
82 GCA, art. 128(4).
83 GCA, art. 128(2).
84 GCA, art. 128(2).
85 GCA, art. 128(5).
86 GCA, art. 108(2).
87 GCA, art. 128(6).
88 See on obligatory open voting arts. 108(1) and 131(2) of GCA.

5 per cent of the paid-up share capital.[89] Normally, the matter is either determined in the articles of association or left to the discretion of the Chairman of the Meeting or of the Shareholders participating in a GM to apply a specific voting method. Slate voting is provided for as an option in the law itself with regard to the election of BoD members (proportional list voting).[90] Alternative voting methods are provided for in Article 101 of the Greek Bankruptcy Code in the case of distressed companies and for approval of restructuring measures in order to resolve any shareholders' hold out[91].

The quorum for an ordinary GM is 20 per cent of the paid-up share capital (ordinary quorum).[92] If such a quorum has not been attained at the initial meeting, Article 130(2) GCA provides for an iterate GM with no quorum threshold. Exceptionally, the so-called 'statutory GM', a GM called to pass a resolution on vital, exclusively enumerated items on the agenda (such as amendment of the company's objects, capital increase/decrease or dissolution), requires a quorum of 50 per cent[93] of the paid-up share capital at the initial meeting and of one-fifth (one-third in the case of non-listed companies) of the paid-up share capital at the iterate GM.[94] The articles of association may increase the quorum generally or for specific issues, whereas the increased quorum of an ordinary GM cannot exceed two-thirds of the paid-up share capital.[95]

An absolute majority (50 per cent +1) is the minimum majority threshold at an ordinary GM.[96] Blanks and abstentions are counted and treated as negative votes. At statutory GMs an increased majority of two-thirds of the votes represented at the Meeting is required.[97] Unlike its predecessor, the GCA allows the articles of association to increase the majority without limit (even unanimity is now acceptable).[98]

No general 'Majority of Minority rules' have been introduced in Greek law. Such rules apply exceptionally in specific cases. One such case is provided for in Article 105(1) GCA. This provision enables a qualified majority (the majority of minority shareholders), under certain circumstances, to ask the court to appoint a special representative in order to bring an action for corporate damages against BoD members. This is the only feasible protection measure, as minority shareholders are not entitled pursuant to Greek Law, to bring a derivative action.[99] An additional case that can be assigned to the 'Majority of Minority rule' is the case of approval of related party transactions by the GM pursuant to Article 100(3) et seq. GCA, if the related party concerned is a shareholder of the specific company. Insofar as the law prohibits this shareholder (as well as other shareholders related to him) from participating in voting on the approval of the

[89] GCA, art. 141(9).

[90] GCA, art. 80.

[91] Rigas Giovannopoulos, 'Bypass of Disagreements between Debtor, Creditors and Shareholders (Hold out) within the Scope of the Application and the Implementation of Rehabilitation Procedures' in Association of Greek Commercialists (ed.), *Recent Developments in Bankruptcy Law* (Nomiki Bibliothiki 2018, in Greek) 281; Georgios Psaroudakis, *Shareholders in Restructuring Proceedings* (Nomiki Bibliothiki 2020, in Greek).

[92] GCA, art. 130(1).

[93] Former company act provided for a quorum of two-thirds of the paid-up share capital for the statutory GM.

[94] GCA, arts. 130(3) and (4).

[95] GCA, art. 130(5).

[96] GCA, art. 132(1).

[97] GCA, art. 132(2).

[98] GCA, art. 132(3).

[99] Nikolaos Tellis, 'Internal Liability of S.A. Directors: Filing a Corporate Action. A First Approach under the New Corporate Law (Law 4548/2018)' (2019) Episkopēsē Emporikou Dikaiou 21, 38 (in Greek). See generally on corporate and derivative actions under Greek Law, Panagiotis Panagiotou, *The Corporate and Derivative Action against the Board of Directors in Public Companies by Shares* (Nomiki Bibliothiki 2016, in Greek); Panagiotis Panagiotou, 'The derivative action in Greek corporation law' (2017) The Company Lawyer 329; Achilleas Christodoulou, 'Remarks on Articles 103–105 of Law 4548/2018 Regarding the Filing of the Company's Action' (2018) Dikaio Epixeiriseōn & Etairiōn 1267, 1271 (in Greek); Georgios Zouridakis, *Shareholder Protection Reconsidered. Derivative Action in the UK, Germany and Greece* (Routledge 2020) 145.

transaction in question, even if he represents the majority of the GM votes, a situation similar to the 'Majority of Minority rule' could arise. The decision must be taken by the majority of the minority shareholders, unless a veto right has been exercised under Article 100(4)or (5) GCA.[100]

16.2.4 *Shareholder Questions*

Greek law elaborates on the shareholder's right to request information both as a minority right,[101] and as an individual right,[102] in compliance with Article 9 SRD I. Information related to a GM must be requested seven days[103] before the meeting, and the BoD must provide the requested information not on an individual basis but collectively during the GM. At the discretion of the BoD, and taking into account feasibility considerations, information can be provided either orally or in written format.[104] In the case of listed companies, the provision of information must take into account the need to ensure that investors are treated equally, as well as any insider dealing issues arising from the Market Abuse Regulation.[105]

GM-related information requested when exercising an individual right must be relevant to the agenda.[106] Information on renumeration of the BoD members and of directors can be requested only before an ordinary annual GM.[107] A broader information right, going beyond the scope of an ordinary annual GM, is attributed to minority shareholders individually or collectively holding 10 per cent of the paid-up share capital[108] or shareholder associations representing such shareholders, covering information about the course of company affairs and the company's financial situation. The BoD can decline to provide such information if it is already accessible on the company's website, or can do so generally, if it cites a 'sufficiently significant reason' which must be noted in the minutes. The GCA provides a legislative example of a significant reason: representation of the requesting shareholder on the Board of Directors, whose members have an individual information right irrespective of GM procedures.[109] It is almost unanimously accepted that the vague term 'sufficiently significant reason' covers conflicts of interest, where the interest of the requesting shareholders is outbalanced by the negative impact on material company interests of granting the requested information (once the facts of the specific case and the specific profile and structure of the company affected have been taken into account).[110]

100 Theodoros Katsas, 'Mechanisms of Corporate Law for Managing Conflicts of Interests' (2019) Dikaio Epixeiriseōn & Etairiōn 10, fn. 73 (in Greek) and under a comparative perspective: OECD, *Related Party Transactions and Minority Shareholder Rights* (OECD Publishing 2012), 14, 24, 32, 34, 103, 116 www.oecd.org/daf/ca/50089215.pdf accessed 11 April 2020.

101 GCA, arts. 141(6), 3rd sentence and (7).

102 GCA, art. 141(6), 1st sentence, (10) and (11).

103 The *relevant* provisions indicate the number of five days but the date of communication of the request and the date of GM do not count.

104 Athens Single-Member First Instance Court 463/2011, [2011] Xronika Idiōtikou Dikaiou 106 (Note Michail-Theodoros Marinos, in Greek); Michail-Theodoros Marinos, 'The Individual Information Right of the Shareholder' in Michail-Theodoros Marinos (ed.), *Queries on the New Law on Sociétés Anonymes* (Sakkoulas 2009, in Greek) 257, 289; Petros Drakopoulos in Evangelos Perakis (ed.), *DikAE*, vol. 2 (3rd ed., Nomiki Bibliothiki 2010), art. 39, para. 214 (in Greek).

105 Regulation (EU) No. 596/2014 of the European Parliament and of the Council of 16th April 2014 on market abuse (market abuse regulation) and repealing Directive 2003/6/EC of the European Parliament and of the Council and Commission Directives 2003/124/EC, 2003/125/EC and 2004/72/EC [2014] OJ L 173/1.

106 GCA, art. 141(6), 1st sentence.

107 GCA, art. 141(6), 3rd sentence.

108 GCA, art. 141(7).

109 GCA, art. 141(6).

110 Dodecanese Court of Appeal 49/2018, 146/2017, 96/2013, Nomos; Athens Multimember First Instance Court 2206/2017, [2017] Epitheōrēsē Emporikou Dikaiou 819.

The indicatively enumerated cases comprise information on commercially sensitive topics or ongoing negotiations or requests made in an abusive way with regard to the object, scope or timing of the request.[111] The validity of such reasons can be contested in court in different contexts: (1) either directly in a dispute aiming at enforcing the information right against the company (in which case the court will render a decision in interim proceedings after having weighed up the validity of the reasoning on which the BoD based its refusal to provide the requested information);[112] (2) in an incidental way in the context of annulment proceedings against GM resolutions, insofar as the GCA, adopting the provisions of the former GCA, stipulates that a resolution taken without the BoD having provided the requested information can be annulled by the court where a lawsuit is filed by the requesting shareholders, if they represent 5 per cent of the paid-up share capital;[113] or (3) also in an incidental way, in the context of criminal proceedings against the BoD members (natural persons individually or as representatives of legal persons-BoD members), upon a complaint from the requesting shareholders.[114]

Although not explicitly stipulated in the law, it is also generally acknowledged that a shareholder, who is represented at the GM, in the course of his right to address the meeting within a reasonable timeframe, has an individual right to pose clarifying questions to the BoD or to the auditors, if they are present at the GM,[115] without any procedural prerequisites. There are no explicit remedies and sanctions, if the persons questioned refuse to answer (properly) such questions or if the chairman of the GM dismisses such questions, using his authority to moderate the discussion during the GM.[116] On the contrary, Article 129(3) GCA provides that the breach of such formalities does not affect the validity of the GM resolution, unless other reasons for invalidity have arisen. Such a case could be established if the limitation of the right to pose questions could be classed as exclusion from the GM, which would under specific circumstances render the resolution voidable according to the second sentence of Article 137(1) GCA.

Finally, minority shareholders have, under certain circumstances, the right to request, via judicial proceedings, that the auditor carries out an audit on the company.[117] Shareholders are also entitled, even on an individual basis, to request documents in accordance with general civil law mechanisms such as Article 902 of the Greek Civil Code,[118] but are not entitled to request a rendering of account in accordance with the general rules.[119]

111 Christina Livada, in Georgios Sotiropoulos (ed.), *The Law of Société Anonyme* (Nomiki Bibliothiki 2020), art. 141, paras. 5, 7.

112 GCA, art. 141(8).

113 Arts. 137(2) and (3) of GCA. Cf. under the former GCA: Heraklion Multimember First Instance Court 178/2018, Nomos; Athens Multimember First Instance Court 2206/2017, [2017] Epitheōrēsē Emporikou Dikaiou 819; Athens Multimember First Instance Court 3810/2010, Nomos.

114 GCA, art. 180(3).

115 GCA, art. 127(1).

116 GCA, art. 129(2).

117 GCA, arts. 142 and 143.

118 Kos Single-Member First Instance Court 522/2015, Nomos; Piraeus Single-Member First Instance Court 1062/2009; Kavala Single-Member First Instance Court 738/2007, [2007] Episkopēsē Emporikou Dikaiou 935 (Note Konstantinos Pampoukis, in Greek); Sparta Single-Member First Instance Court 906/2005, [2006] Nomiko Bēma 441; Sparta Single-Member First Instance Court 1209/2005, Nomos; Athens Single-Member First Instance Court 12707/1999, [1999] Epitheōrēsē Emporikou Dikaiou 751; Athens Single-Member First Instance Court 22214/1999, [1999] Epitheōrēsē Emporikou Dikaiou 752 (Note Georgios Stefanakis, in Greek); Contra: Athens Court of Appeal 10090/1980, [1981] Harmenopoulos 479 (Note Vassilios Antonopoulos, in Greek).

119 Greek Civil Code, art. 303; Greek Civil Procedure Code, art. 473; Thessaloniki Court of Appeal 1048/2003, [2003] Episkopēsē Emporikou Dikaiou 1148 (Note Konstantinos Pampoukis, in Greek).

16.2.5 *Access to Shareholders' Register*

With effect from 1 January 2020, bearer shares are no longer allowed in Greece.[120] A Greek SA is obliged to issue only registered shares and keep a shareholders' register. The status of shareholder is attributed solely to the person entered in the shareholders' register[121] or, in the case of dematerialized shares, the person entered in the Central Depository or authenticated as the shareholder by the intermediaries.[122] Consequently, access to the shareholders' register is possible either through the company or the Central Depository. Nonetheless, registrations at the Central Depository are covered by professional secrecy. Therefore, the only option is access through the issuer.

Although in common law countries access to the shareholders' register kept by a company does not normally pose any problems, in continental legal orders access to shareholders' register may be restricted on data protection grounds (as, for example, in Article 67(6) of the German AktG).[123]

In Greece, the right of access to the shareholders' register was hotly debated until 2018. According to the prevailing view, special emphasis needed to be placed on the argument that shareholders have a vested right to know the names of other corporate members, particularly if the corporation has issued registered shares. Based on this argument, a Greek court ruled that a shareholder of a stock corporation has the right to be informed of the names of other shareholders entered in the shareholders' register.[124] Be that as it may, the new Company Act introduced a new provision with regard to access to the shareholders' register. According to Article 141(11) GCA, every shareholder has the right to ask for a copy of the shareholders' register if so provided in the articles of association and in accordance with the relevant data protection rules. The copy of the shareholders' register must contain information about: (1) the number of shareholders, (2) the address of shareholders and (3) the number of shares held by each shareholder. The company is not obliged to provide information about shareholders with shareholdings of less than 1 per cent of the share capital.[125]

[120] GCA, art. 184.

[121] GCA, art. 40(2).

[122] GCA, art. 40(6).

[123] See § 67(6) AktG: 'Der Aktionär kann von der Gesellschaft Auskunft über die zu seiner Person in das Aktienregister eingetragenen Daten verlangen. Bei nichtbörsennotierten Gesellschaften kann die Satzung Weiteres bestimmen. Die Gesellschaft darf die Registerdaten sowie die nach Absatz 4 Satz 2 und 3 mitgeteilten Daten für ihre Aufgaben im Verhältnis zu den Aktionären verwenden. Zur Werbung für das Unternehmen darf sie die Daten nur verwenden, soweit der Aktionär nicht widerspricht. Die Aktionäre sind in angemessener Weise über ihr Widerspruchsrecht zu informieren' ('The stockholder may demand that the company inform him about the data concerning his person that have been entered in the share register. In the case of companies not listed on the stock exchange, the by-laws may make further provisions. The company may use the data contained in the register as well as the data provided pursuant to subsection (4), second and third sentences, in order to fulfil the tasks incumbent on it in its relationship with the stockholders. It may use the data to advertise the enterprise only insofar as the stockholder does not object to this being done. The stockholders are to be appropriately informed on their right to lodge an objection')..

[124] Kavala Single-Member First Instance Court 738/2007, [2007] Episkopēsē Emporikou Dikaiou 943. See also Vassilios Antonopoulos, *The Law on Sociétés Anonymes and Limited Companies* (3rd ed., Sakkoulas 2009, in Greek) 278, fn. 25; Nikolaos. Vervessos in Evanghelos Perakis (ed.), *DikAE*, vol. 2A (2nd ed., NB 2003, in Greek), art. 8β, para. 53; Konstantinos Pampoukis, 'Share Subscriptions in Public Offerings' (1979) Harmenopoulos 836 (in Greek); Ioannis Varvitsiotis, *The Registered Share* (Sakkoulas 1961, in Greek) 43; Christos Chrysanthis in Vassilios Antonopoulos and Spilios Mouzoulas (eds.), *Sociétés Anonymes* vol. I (Sakkoulas 2013, in Greek) art. 8β, para. 31.

[125] GCA, art. 141(11).

16.3 SHAREHOLDER ENGAGEMENT AND VOTING IN PRACTICE

The collection of reliable statistical data on the specific voting methods and practices applied in Greek GM practice presents formidable difficulties.[126] The reason is that the minutes submitted to the registry by all companies,[127] as well as the announcements of GM resolutions for listed companies,[128] are in summary form only, and rarely contain detailed information on the way individual shareholders voted. Voting data are given in aggregated numbers referring to the total number of shares and/or voting rights represented at each GM, and the total numbers and percentages of positive and negative votes as well as void votes and abstentions. To the best of our knowledge, no institutions or public bodies monitor and systematically collect such data, and the companies concerned seldom publish the full text of their GM minutes. Finally, the printed and digital press only occasionally publish reports on GMs. They tend to confine their reports to GMs featuring shareholder disputes in listed companies (e.g. the Ellaktor GM), as such disputes are of compelling public interest. Our only reasonable course of action was to make random use of internet search engines in order to retrieve a tiny but representative set of listed companies which are members of the FTSE/Athens Large Cap (FTSE 25)[129] for a period of the last two years and to gather some characteristic examples of listed companies. 2019, in particular, was a particularly representative year, since all listed companies had the option to update their articles of association through a simplified procedure, to be implemented by 31 December 2019 at the latest, in order to comply with the new GCA,[130] and also had a duty to introduce new frameworks with regard to remuneration policy for the BoD.

16.3.1 *Voting in Practice*

As discussed above, Greek law allows three different voting modes: (1) voting in person, (2) proxy voting and (3) remote voting. The latter is possible either before or during a normal GM, if the articles of association provide for remote participation at a GM and the BoD opts for such an approach,[131] or in the course of a virtual-only GM[132] or a voting procedure of Article 135 GCA, whereas the last two alternatives are an option solely for non-listed companies. Most remote voting mechanisms are recent and companies (both listed and non-listed) have been extremely reluctant to make use of them (before COVID-19), partly because of an aversion towards technological innovations due to reasonable doubts about the reliability and safety of the communications, and partly because of unexplored issues concerning the impact of possible technical deficiencies on the validity of the resolutions affected. Moreover, major shareholders in family owned companies are not always in favour of shareholder engagement. One observation

126 Some statistical data appear in several publications with scarce information, if any, with regard to census and methodology: cf. Indicatively, Report Greece, The 2019 European AGM Season, (2019) Lighthouse, p 17 https://morrowsodali.com/uploads/insights/attachments/7af99e9ab81e4dabb28883b8f1735043.pdf accessed 11 April 2020, ISS 2018 European Voting Results Report, pp. 7 and 39 www.issgovernance.com/file/publications/2018_European_Voting_Results_Report.pdf accessed 11 April 2020; P. Hewitt, 'The Exercise of Shareholder Rights: Country Comparison of Turnout and Dissent' (OECD Corporate Governance Working Papers no. 3 (OECD 2011) www.oecd-ilibrary.org/docserver/5kg54d0l1lvfen.pdf?expires=1585733538&id=id&accname=guest&checksum=026B44108535862B6BFC0D5E42121174 accessed 11 April 2020.

127 See art. 134(1) in fine GCA.

128 GCA, art. 133(2).

129 With the exemption of companies having their registered seat abroad, such as Viohalko (Belgium).

130 GCA, art. 183.

131 GCA, arts. 126, 125.

132 GCA, art. 120(3).

that can be made is that proxy voting is the norm at all GMs of listed companies, in some cases, even with regard to shareholders present *in corpore*. Proxies are usually granted to lawyers, auditors and other professionals or BoD members. There is no real local market for stewardship services. Even foreign (institutional) investors resort to the services of banks/investment companies or local professionals, mainly lawyers. Absenteeism among small shareholders is a very common phenomenon, even among entities of public interest. This can be deduced from Table 16.3.

16.3.2 *Voting Items*

An ordinary AGM, held once a year, has to decide on the following items: (1) approval of the company's annual Financial Statements and, where applicable, the appropriation of profits, (2) election of the auditors,[133] where applicable and (3) approval of overall management.[134] Fairly common resolutions for listed and non-listed companies are those with respect to the approval of related party transactions,[135] the removal and/or election of BoD members (at least once every six years), amendments to the articles of association and capital increases (in order to finance various projects and investments) or, more seldom, decreases (mainly as a means of restructuring, combined with a subsequent capital increase).

Monitoring the agendas of the FTSE 25 listed companies over the last two years (2018 and 2019) provides the following picture:

(1) Agenda issues identified in all convocation notices of listed companies (mainly because obligatory at each annual GM):

  (a) Submission and approval of Annual Financial Statements and, respectively, of Annual Consolidated Financial Statements, where applicable, along with the Annual Report of the Board of Directors and the Auditors' Report and the corporate governance declaration.
  (b) Approval of profit appropriation, where applicable.

TABLE 16.3 *Number of shareholders participating in AGM*

	2017	2018	2019
Alpha Bank (1)	842	686	625
Athens Medical Center (2)	11	8	8
PPC (3)	179	181	142
Hellenic Petroleum	207	258	207
% of share capital presented			
Alpha Bank (1)	63.14%	58.93%	59.26%
Athens Medical Center (2)	78.09%	42.17%	79.01%
PPC (3)	81.74%	80.21%	76.02%
Hellenic Petroleum	85.28%	88.47%	86.49%

Source: company data.

133 GCA, art. 119(1).

134 See GCA, art. 108(1). The former GCA provided for a special resolution on the discharge of the BoD members. See on this issue art. 35 of former GCA.

135 This was formerly an issue of the exclusive GM authority pursuant to art. 23a of former GCA.

(c) Approval of overall management of the Company by the Board of Directors or formerly release of BoD from any liability during the respective financial year. Release of Auditors from any liability during the respective financial year.
(d) Election of Certified Public Accountants /Auditors for the respective financial year (regular and substitute) and approval of their remuneration.
(e) Appointment of members to the Audit Committee under Article 44 of Law 4449/2017 (cf. Article 39 of Directive 2006/43/EC as amended by Directive 2014/56/EU).
(f) Approval and/or Pre-approval of remuneration and compensation of members of the BoD.

Approval of related party transactions.

(g) In 2019 all listed companies included items with regard to: (aa) amendment of the articles of association to comply with the new GCA[136] and (bb) approval of the Company's Remuneration Policy in accordance with Article 110(2) GCA.

(2) Usual additional agenda issues:

(a) Election of BoD members. Appointment of the Board's Independent Members.
(b) Granting of exemption to the non-compete clause in accordance with Article 98(1) GCA.
(c) Approval of acquisition of own shares (own share buyback programmes).
(d) M&A or Splits
(e) Approval of capital increases/decreases and other capital-related measures (special reserves etc.).

16.3.3 *Controversial Resolutions*

To the best of our knowledge, no empirical data has been compiled on controversial resolutions at the General Meetings of Greek SAs. In any case, their highly concentrated ownership and low rates of attendance for minority shareholders do not allow much scope for controversial decisions. Nevertheless, we conducted a limited random check on the announcements of listed companies with regard to their ordinary General Meetings and the resolutions taken. According to this check, the election of certified public accountants-auditors seems to be the least controversial resolution, especially if the auditor is member of a well-known auditing firm. The most controversial resolution seems to be approval of the remuneration of BoD members. This is due to the fact that institutional investors prefer to abstain from voting rather than vote in favour of this item. Moreover, in case of disputes between shareholders, dissenting shareholders vote down almost all items on the agenda, especially (1) approval of the remuneration of BoD members, (2) the items relating to approval of the financial statements and (3) the approval of overall management.

16.3.4 *Shareholders' Proposals: Proxy Fights*

Shareholders' proposals do not often feature on the agenda of Greek General Meetings, mainly because of the inhibiting structure of Greek SAs. As mentioned above, the main characteristic of Greek SAs is highly concentrated ownership. BoD members are usually the controlling shareholders or persons elected by the controlling shareholders. The controlling shareholders can

[136] GCA, art. 183.

therefore always determine, either directly or indirectly, the items on the agenda and the voting results. Consequently, any proposals from minority shareholders have no chance if they are not in accordance with the interests of the main shareholders. In other words, the support of the controlling shareholders is a necessary prerequisite for the success of the shareholders' proposal. Moreover, it seems that controlling shareholders do not encourage shareholders' proposals. Quite the opposite is true. Since dialogue and democratization is not a usual phenomenon in Greek SAs, controlling shareholders tend to consider that proposals from other shareholders amount to a criticism of their management, and they therefore usually vote down any proposal from minority shareholders.

Nonetheless, both shareholders' rights, that is, (1) to add an item to the agenda and (2) to make shareholders' proposals, play a key role in the following cases:

(1) when the BoD has failed to include the relevant items in an already published agenda. Major shareholders can resolve the issue by requesting that new items be added to the agenda. Characteristic examples of items added to the agenda by major shareholders are the appointment of the audit committee and the appointment of new BoD members.
(2) when dissenting shareholders want to take over control of a company. In such a case the proposal is to remove the old BoD members and appoint new ones.
(3) when minority shareholders question the management of the company and want to ask for information about specific transactions which have either been concluded or are proposed.

As already mentioned above, proposals or items added by minority shareholders are usually voted down.

Nevertheless, proposals from the minority shareholders have occasionally been successful. The most famous example in Greece is the Ellaktor case.[137] Ellaktor is Greece's largest construction company. Two members of the BoD holding approximately 12 per cent of the share capital 'accused fellow directors of, in effect, running each of Ellaktor's divisions as their own personal kingdoms'.[138] Hence, the shareholders' proposal was to sideline the other executive members of the BoD who controlled approximately 25 per cent of the voting rights. The majority of shareholders voted in favour of this proposal. The positive outcome was due to the company's dispersed ownership as well as proper preparation of the shareholders' proposals. Of course, proper preparation also presupposes a proxy fight, that is, a fight to gather shareholder proxies to win a corporate vote. A necessary precondition for a proxy fight is access to the shareholders' register.[139]

16.3.5 *Other Forms of Shareholder Activism*

As mentioned in Section 16.2.2, the GCA has introduced shareholders' associations,[140] a legal transplant from French[141] and German Law.[142] More specifically, the GCA provides for the

137 www.ft.com/content/53c72d84-6e58-11e8-92d3-6c13e5c92914 accessed 11 April 2020.
138 See above n. 139.
139 See above under Section 16.2.5.
140 See GCA, art. 144. See also Evanghelos Perakis, *The New Law of Limited Companies* (6th ed., Nomiki Bibliothiki 2019, in Greek) 118; Anthoula Papadopoulou, 'Shareholders Rights and Minorities' in Association of Greek Commercialists (ed.), *The Reform of Company Law 2018–2019* (Nomiki Bibliothiki 2019, in Greek) 117; Katsas (n. 59); Livada (n. 107), art. 144 (in Greek).
141 Law of 23.6.1989 (Associations de défense d'actionnaires et d'investisseurs).
142 See § 127a AktG (Aktionärsforum) and German Decree on Shareholders' Associations (AktFoV).

option of shareholders to collectively exercise minority rights[143] (as far as they individually or collectively reach the respective threshold) by seeking recourse to the services of shareholders' associations. These can be constituted in the legal form of an 'association' under the Greek Civil Code by shareholders of one or more companies. Shareholders can acquire or abandon membership of shareholders' associations in accordance with the articles of association of those bodies. Nonetheless, the new provision remains simply law on the book, as the special presidential decree provided for in the second subparagraph of Article 144 GCA, which will set out special matters relating to the operation of such shareholders' associations, has not yet been issued. To the best of our knowledge, no such association has made a public presence so far.

With regard to alternative forms of shareholder engagement, there are usually no private meetings between minority shareholders and BoD members, company representatives or other company officials, other than some roadshows of major listed companies, mainly banks[144]. All listed companies have created special infrastructure for communicating with actual or potential investors, but no real board and shareholders engagement is being pursued. No practical examples or anecdotal evidence related to this type of engagement can be provided.

16.4 CONCLUDING REMARKS

Although there is no reliable statistical data on General Meetings of listed SAs,[145] it seems that shareholder activism and engagement in Greek listed SAs going beyond voting the shares is a quantitatively rare and qualitatively limited phenomenon. The few examples of shareholders' proposals described above are more a tool to (indirectly) acquire control of a listed company than an attempt to improve its internal organization and function. Significantly, the relevant proposals originate from major shareholders and not from minority shareholders or even portfolio investors. Hence, the limited level of shareholder engagement in Greek companies must rather be attributed to the structure of Greek companies, that is, the limited dispersion of shares and the high concentration of majority power even in listed companies.[146]

The Greek legislature seems to acknowledge the importance of shareholder activism and engagement. Therefore, the new GCA offers several modern institutional and technical tools in this direction. Moreover, the stabilization of the Greek economy and the development of the Greek capital market are expected to improve the investment environment and attract foreign investors familiar with shareholder activism and engagement, who may in turn demand, encourage and enhance corresponding initiatives by issuers. Nonetheless, as long as the concentration of majority power remains high in Greek companies, shareholder engagement and activism is expected to remain limited.

143 Art. 144(1), 2nd sentence of GCA explicitly excludes individual shareholders' rights from the authority of Shareholders' Associations.

144 Though recommended in the Greek Corporate Governance Code for Listed Companies dated October 2013. See www.athexgroup.gr/documents/10180/2227277/HCGC_EN_20131022.pdf/e8e7b6da-6dd0-4c30-90e9-79fe9ca8383d accessed 11 April 2020. See also Sections 8 and 9 of the Greek Corporate Governance Code for Listed Companies dated June 2021. See www.esed.org.gr/code-listed accessed 7 March 2022.

145 See above under Section 16.3.1.

146 Cf. in a comparative approach, Christoph van der Elst, 'Attendance of Shareholders and the Impact of Regulatory Corporate Governance Reforms' (2004) EBOR 471; Luc Renneboog and Peter Szilagyi, 'Shareholder Engagement at European General Meetings' in Massimo Belcredi and Guido Ferrarini (eds.), *Boards and Shareholders in European Listed Companies* (CUP 2013), 315 under 2.2; Anne Lafarre, *The AGM in Europe* (Bingley 2017).

17

Shareholder Engagement and Voting in Italy

Gaia Balp and Giovanni Strampelli

17.1 INTRODUCTION

The basic regulatory framework for shareholder voting and engagement in Italy is set out in the Civil Code (enacted by Royal Decree No. 262 of 16 March 1942), applicable to any corporation, and Legislative Decree No. 58 of 24 February 1998 (*Testo unico della finanza*, the Consolidated Law on Finance (CLF)), which lays down additional rules for publicly listed corporations. Regulations implementing the CLF are drawn by Consob, the Italian financial markets supervisory authority.[1] In addition, the Corporate Governance Code sponsored by Borsa Italiana, the Italian Stock Exchange, provides for non-binding best practice principles and recommendations applicable to publicly listed companies based on a comply-or-explain approach that is explicitly endorsed by law.[2] In effect, under article 123-bis(2)(a) CLF, publicly listed corporations are required, ahead of the annual general shareholder meeting, to publicly file a corporate governance report detailing, inter alia, their compliance with the Corporate Governance Code or, in the absence of compliance, their reasons for not adopting any of the Code's provisions. Based on their corporate governance reports, 94 per cent of the companies listed on the MTA (the leading regulated equity market managed by Borsa Italiana for mid- and large-sized companies)[3] on 31 December 2018 had adopted the then current version of the Corporate Governance Code.[4]

[1] See, most notably, Consob, 'Regulation Implementing Italian Legislative Decree No. 58 of 24 February 1998, Concerning the Discipline of Issuers' (adopted under Resolution No. 11971 of 14 May 1999 and subsequently amended) www.consob.it/web/consob-and-its-activities/laws-and-regulations accessed 26 March 2020 (Consob Regulation No. 11971). Additional rules and regulations relevant to corporate governance may also apply, depending on the industry the company belongs to. Most notably, banks and the parent companies of banking groups are subject to the set of rules set by Legislative Decree No. 385 of 1 September 1993 (the so-called Consolidated Law on Banking (*Testo unico bancario*)), as well as the Bank of Italy's implementing regulations laid out in Circular No. 285 of 17 December 2013 (*Disposizioni di vigilanza per le banche*), which was subsequently amended. Insurance companies are also subject to specific rules imposed on them by Legislative Decree No. 209 of 7 September 2005 (the so-called Private Insurance Code (*Codice delle assicurazioni private*)) and the implementing regulations set by Ivass, the supervisory authority.

[2] First released in 1999, the Corporate Governance Code has been updated several times. Most recently, it underwent a major review following the release of the UK Stewardship Code 2020. The January 2020 version of the Italian Corporate Governance Code took effect from January 2021. See Corporate Governance Committee, 'Corporate Governance Code' (2020) www.borsaitaliana.it/comitato-corporate-governance/codice/2020eng.en.pdf accessed 26 March 2020.

[3] Borsa Italiana currently manages three equity markets, with companies being listed on the Mercato Telematico Azionario (MTA) and Euronext Growth Milan, and financial vehicles on the Market for Investment Vehicles (MIV) and Partnership Equity Markets.

[4] See Assonime – Emittenti Titoli, 'Report on Corporate Governance in Italy: The Implementation of the Italian Corporate Governance Code' (2019) 4 www.assonime.it/_layouts/15/Assonime.CustomAction/GetPdfToUrl.aspx?PathPdf=http://www.assonime.it/attivita-editoriale/studi/Documents/nsexecutivesummary.pdf accessed 26 March 2020.

Eleven of the fourteen companies that had not adopted the Code referred to specific firm characteristics – particularly their small size and concentrated ownership – as an explanation for their determination not to adopt the Code.

Since the enactment of the Civil Code in 1942, the Italian corporate structure has traditionally been based on the two-board corporate governance system comprising a shareholder-elected board of directors,[5] which may delegate managing powers to an executive managing director or an executive committee,[6] and a board of statutory auditors (*collegio sindacale*). The board of directors thus includes executive and non-executive members elected for a term of up to three years.[7] The board of statutory auditors, whose members are also elected by shareholders, is in charge of overseeing compliance with the law and the adequacy of the company's organizational and accounting systems.[8]

The traditional two-board corporate governance system can be regarded as an endogenously developed legal rule, as it has some specific features that make it a unique such system at the European level. Nevertheless, in the sense that the non-executive members of the board of directors chiefly play a supervisory role, given that most management functions are delegated to executives, Italian listed companies feature a corporate structure that in fact owes most of its substantive inspiration to the Anglo-American one-tier board system rather than the German two-tier system. Indeed, the board of statutory auditors cannot be regarded as a functional equivalent to the German *Aufsichtsrat* because, unlike the latter, it lacks any power to interfere with the board of directors' decision-making, either strategic or managerial, let alone the power to appoint its members.

Following a wide-reaching company law reform enacted in 2003, a corporation may choose to adopt a one-tier or two-tier management and control system as an alternative to the traditional structure, which applies as a default rule unless there is an opt-out in the company's articles of association (AoA)[9] by an absolute majority shareholder resolution.[10] Under the one-tier structure, an oversight committee, whose members must be non-executive and independent, is appointed within the shareholder-elected board of directors.[11] Whilst it performs most of the functions of the board of statutory auditors, the oversight committee is not formally a separate corporate organ but rather a committee established by and within the board of directors.[12] Therefore, in the one-tier structure, the principle of separation between the corporate bodies that perform managerial and monitoring functions is abandoned.[13] Under the two-tier structure, a supervisory board is elected alongside the management board. The supervisory board is elected by shareholders, but is vested with the authority to elect the members of the management board.[14] The supervisory board is also granted the power to approve the company's financial statements, and, if the AoA so stipulate, it may also approve key transactions and strategic plans drafted by the management board.[15] These additional powers vested in the supervisory board

[5] See art. 2364 Civil Code.

[6] See art. 2381 Civil Code.

[7] See art. 2388 Civil Code.

[8] See arts. 2400, 2403 and 2403-bis Civil Code.

[9] See arts. 2380, 2409-octies and 2409-sexiesdecies Civil Code.

[10] See art. 2368 Civil Code.

[11] See arts. 2409-septiesdecies and 2409-opctiesdecies Civil Code.

[12] Filadelfio Mancuso, 'Article 2409-octiesdecies Civil Code' in Pietro Abbadessa and Giuseppe B. Portale (eds.) *Le società per azioni* (Giuffrè 2016) 1980.

[13] See Federico Ghezzi and Corrado Malberti, 'The Two-Tier Model and the One-Tier Model of Corporate Governance in the Italian Reform of Corporate Law' (2008) 5 *ECFR* 1, 23.

[14] See arts. 2409-novies and 2409-duodecies Civil Code.

[15] See art. 2409-terdecies Civil Code.

render the Italian two-tier system the nearest equivalent to the German model, although differences persist. In particular, under Italian law, all members of the supervisory board are elected by shareholders, as the Italian legislature does not require some board members to be appointed by workers or other stakeholders, as is the case in Germany.[16]

Despite the availability of alternative structures, more than fifteen years after reform the vast majority of Italian listed companies maintain the traditional corporate structure. At the end of 2018, Italian listed companies adopting the traditional structure comprising a board of directors and board of statutory auditors accounted for 92 per cent of market capitalization, with just four firms out of 231 adopting the one-tier or two-tier structure.[17] This chapter thus assumes that structure in its analysis.

The proposition that the board of directors is the key entity within the corporate structure does not mean that the shareholder meeting is irrelevant. That meeting actually plays a role in director accountability, as it holds the power, above all, to elect (and remove) members of the board of directors and approve any amendments to the company's AoA.[18] It should be further noted that within corporate ownership structures characterized by the principal-principal agency problem, as those of many Italian listed companies can be, shareholder monitoring becomes a matter of minority oversight and minority challenges to the authority of the board and controlling stockholders. Therefore, unsurprisingly, the evolutionary process that national corporate governance regulations underwent through the 1998 CLF and subsequent developments, including the transposition of the EU Shareholder Rights Directive and amended directive (SRD I and SRD II), was strongly shaped by the direct and indirect empowerment of minority shareholders, whether by enhancing their rights and prerogatives, facilitating their ability and willingness to exercise those rights and prerogatives, or strengthening oversight by the board of statutory auditors and additional gatekeepers.

A parallel force shaping corporate governance in Italy has been the development of financial intermediary regulation, starting with the reform enacted in 1974 (which established Consob as the national financial markets supervisory authority). Although the aim of such regulation is to ensure end-investor protection, it has in fact exerted an indirect influence on corporate governance. In a context increasingly characterized by intermediated investments, regulation has increasingly focused on institutional investors as owners and has enhanced their oversight role, particularly with respect to voting obligations. Regulatory action in this area is further supported by self-regulation. Following the adoption of a Stewardship Code by the European Fund and Asset Management Association (EFAMA) in 2011, Assogestioni, a non-profit association of Italian asset managers, adopted Stewardship Principles in 2013. The Italian Stewardship Principles were last revised in 2016.[19] In line with the EFAMA Code, as well as a growing number of similar stewardship initiatives, the Italian principles target collective investment management and portfolio management companies with the aim of 'promot[ing] discussion and cooperation between Investment Management Companies and [the] listed companies in which they invest',

16 Ghezzi and Malberti (n. 13) 10.

17 See Consob, 'Report on Corporate Governance of Italian Listed Companies 2019' (2020) 23 www.consob.it/web/consob-and-its-activities/report-on-corporate-governance accessed 26 March 2020. Interestingly, the one-tier structure is adopted by two major Italian banks (IntesaSanPaolo spa and UBI Banca spa). They seem to have chosen it because of the increased efficiency afforded in terms of intra-board information flow and because of Anglo-Saxon institutional investors' familiarity with the one-tier board system. See e.g. https://group.intesasanpaolo.com/en/governance accessed 15 July 2020.

18 See arts. 2364 and 2365 Civil Code (laying down the decision-making powers that rest with the shareholder meeting, either ordinary or extraordinary).

19 See Assogestioni, 'Italian Stewardship Principles for the Exercise of Administrative and Voting Rights in Listed Companies' (2016) https://ecgi.global/code/italian-stewardship-principles-2016 accessed 26 March 2020.

thereby exerting an indirect impact on both listed companies, 'which are called upon to promote dialogue with investors, asset managers and their respective advisors' and institutional investors 'that entrust the management of their assets to third parties, and are requested to share with their managers certain decisions on how to interact with the investee companies'.[20]

As will be shown, by leveraging stronger shareholder rights and shareholder-friendly regulatory measures, Assogestioni has greatly contributed to shaping the practice of institutional investor engagement in Italy. In particular, the enabling and coordinating role performed by the association underpins the rise of effective forms of collective engagement by mainstream, non-activist institutions, thereby providing an alternative to hedge fund-driven activist intervention, which has become quite popular in Italy despite the still predominant ownership concentration of publicly listed corporations.

Against this backdrop, the remainder of the chapter proceeds as follows. Section 17.2 briefly draws the ownership patterns in Italy. Section 17.3 illustrates the legal framework for shareholder voting and engagement. Whilst recognizing that not all of the many tools introduced by the Italian legislature have proved successful in driving increased institutional investor engagement, it shows that minority-empowering shareholder rights can contribute to creating an environment favourable to non-activist institutional investor active ownership. Section 17.4 follows up on the previous analysis by reporting evidence regarding the practice of shareholder voting and engagement in Italy. Section 17.5 offers concluding remarks.

17.2 THE RISE OF INSTITUTIONAL OWNERSHIP IN ITALY

As is well known, a key structural development in recent years has been the growth of institutional investors throughout the European Union, where corporate ownership and voting are increasingly institutionalized. Despite corporate ownership still being remarkably concentrated in the EU in general, over the last several years 'large companies in several continental European countries have experienced a significant drop in ownership concentration levels', with 'the ownership structure of the largest companies [becoming] more dispersed'.[21]

Within such an institutionalized corporate ownership and voting scenario, the Italian landscape is no exception, despite the concentrated corporate ownership of publicly listed corporations and the fact that Italy's stock market development still lags behind that of other European countries.[22] According to the OECD, '[t]he proportion of households' financial assets managed by institutional investors has been growing in recent years' in Italy.[23] If, in 2017, 'only one-third of Italian households' financial assets were managed by institutional investors compared to 40% in the Euro area and two-thirds in the United Kingdom', this is largely because the share of household financial assets held by pension funds is low compared with Italy's European peers.[24] Private pension plans are merely voluntary in Italy, and the public pension system thus predominates.

20 Ibid., 11.

21 Christoph Van der Elst, 'The Corporate Response to Shareholder Activism' (2014) 15 *ERA Forum* 229, 231.

22 See OECD, 'OECD Capital Market Review of Italy 2020: Creating Growth Opportunities for Italian Companies and Savers' (2020) OECD Capital Market Series, 17, 23 www.oecd.org/corporate/OECD-Capital-Market-Review-Italy.htm accessed 26 March 2020 (noting that '[d]uring the last ten years, on average less than four companies per year became listed on the regulated market of the Italian stock exchange and the Italian market capitalisation as per cent of GDP remains well below that of its European peers').

23 Ibid., 42.

24 Ibid.

As regards ownership structure, although the use of control-enhancing mechanisms has decreased significantly over the last twenty years,[25] the vast majority of Italian listed companies are still controlled. Consob found that, as of the end of 2018, 203 of the 231 companies listed on Borsa Italiana (accounting for 88 per cent of the total number of publicly listed corporations) were controlled companies, about 77 per cent of which were controlled by a single stockholder holding more than half of the share capital (123 companies) or a lower stake (57 firms).[26] Moreover, 23 companies were controlled by a shareholder coalition.[27] Consob also reported that the ultimate controlling agent was the family in 152 listed firms, accounting for 33 per cent of market capitalization; the state (and other local authorities) in 23 large companies (37.8 per cent of market capitalization); a financial entity in eleven cases (mainly small firms); and a mixed coalition of controlling agents in seven cases (e.g. companies controlled by both financial institutions and families).[28] Only twenty-eight were non-controlled companies, thirteen of which were widely held, that is, with a free float higher than 70 per cent of ordinary shares.[29]

In spite of the high number of controlled companies, free-float ratios for Italian listed companies are relatively high. As far as FTSE-MIB[30] companies are concerned, the free-float ratio is currently more than 60 per cent and has recorded an increase in the past few years. Hence, the free-float ratio in the Italian regulated market is in line with those of France, Germany and Spain.[31]

Despite the predominance of controlled companies, institutional investors are relevant shareholders in a not negligible number of Italian listed companies. As confirmed by the OECD, 'in Italy, institutional investors hold, on average, lower stakes in listed companies compared to the global average (41 per cent), but at similar levels with many European peers'.[32] In fact, as of the end of 2018, institutional investors hold stakes exceeding the 3 per cent threshold[33] – averaging 7.7 per cent – in sixty-two companies listed in Italy, accounting for 26 per cent of the market. Notably, Italian institutional investors are relevant shareholders[34] in only thirteen companies, with foreign institutional investors the relevant shareholders in fifty-one.[35]

In effect, domestic and foreign institutional ownership of publicly listed equities evolved along opposite lines over the last decade, with Italian institutions' holdings steadily decreasing since 2011, and non-resident institutions' holdings increasing and stabilizing from 2015 onwards.[36] National and foreign institutional share ownership also differ in respect of the size of investee companies and the industry they belong to. Italian institutions tend to more frequently take major stakes in

25 For example, in 2018, 12 per cent of MTA-listed issuers belonged to pyramidal or mixed business groups compared to 44 per cent in 1998. In addition, non-voting shares have also gradually decreased over time. See OECD (n .22).

26 There is no defined threshold for de facto control under Italian law; it depends on the circumstances, such as the turnout at shareholder meetings, and thus needs to be ascertained on a case-by-case basis.

27 Consob (n. 17) 13.

28 Ibid., 16.

29 Ibid., 15.

30 The FTSE MIB is the primary benchmark Index for the Italian equity markets. FTSE MIB stands for Financial Times Stock Exchange Milano Indice di Borsa.

31 OECD (n. 22) 92.

32 Ibid.

33 According to Legislative Decree No. 25 of 15 February 2016, 3 per cent of share capital is the threshold for initial ownership disclosure.

34 For the purposes of Consob's statistics, major institutional investors are defined as investment funds, banks and insurance companies subject to reporting obligations according to Consob rules and whose shareholdings are lower than 10 per cent. See Consob (n. 17) 18.

35 Ibid., 18.

36 See OECD (n. 22) 17.

TABLE 17.1 *Controlled companies publicly listed (end 2018, MTA Stock Exchange)*

	Controlled Companies						Non-Controlled Companies						Total	
	Majority Controlled[37]		*Weakly Controlled*[38]		*Controlled by a Shareholder Agreement*[39]		*Cooperative Companies*		*Widely Held*[40]		*Non-Widely Held*[41]			
	No	*% Market Cap.*[42]	No	*% Market Cap.*	No	*% Market Cap.*	No	*% Market Cap.*	No	*% Market Cap.*	No	*% Market Cap.*	No	*% Market Cap.*
1998	122	31.2	33	21.8	28	8.3	10	3.1	10	24.1	13	11.5	216	100.0
2010	128	20.6	53	43.0	51	12.4	8	3.4	11	20.3	19	0.3	270	100.0
2011	123	22.3	55	45.8	48	12.0	8	3.2	8	16.4	18	0.3	260	100.0
2012	125	22.8	49	44.0	42	10.1	8	3.2	10	19.2	17	0.7	251	100.0
2013	122	24.1	48	40.1	38	10.4	8	3.3	10	21.6	18	0.5	244	100.0
2014	116	25.0	51	36.8	32	9.6	8	4.0	13	24.0	18	0.5	238	100.0
2015	115	28.1	52	34.8	30	6.0	7	3.2	15	27.3	15	0.6	234	100.0
2016	116	27.2	53	43.6	29	6.5	4	1.3	14	20.6	14	0.7	230	100.0
2017	120	29.8	57	39.8	22	5.3	2	0.5	16	23.5	14	1.1	231	100.0
2018	123	29.7	57	42.3	23	5.3	2	0.5	13	20.5	13	1.6	231	100.0

Data: Consob, 2019 Report on Corporate Governance of Italian Listed Companies.

37 Companies not controlled by a shareholders' agreement where a single shareholder owns more than half of ordinary shares.
38 Companies neither controlled by a shareholders' agreement nor majority controlled that are included in one of the following categories: (1) a single shareholder holds at least 30 per cent of ordinary shares; (2) a single shareholder holds a stake (a) higher than 20 per cent of ordinary shares and (b) higher than half the sum of the ordinary shares held by all major shareholders.
39 Companies not controlled by a single shareholder that are controlled by either a shareholders' agreement regarding more than 20 per cent of ordinary shares or an unlisted company where a shareholders' agreement regarding the majority of the capital is in force.
40 Companies neither controlled by a single shareholder (majority controlled and weakly controlled) nor by a shareholders' agreement with a free float higher than 70 per cent of ordinary shares.
41 Non-controlled companies are not included in any of the previous models.
42 Market value of ordinary shares of companies in each group in percentage of the market capitalization of ordinary shares of all listed companies.

TABLE 17.2 *Free float (%) of FTSE-MIB companies*

Company	2015	2016	2017	2018	2019	*Mean*	*Median*
A2A	49.57	49.62	49.62	49.62	49.62	49.61	49.62
Amplifon	39.45	36.35	53.59	53.90	54.44	47.55	50.57
Assicurazioni Generali	92.27	92.35	93.29	90.12	90.14	91.63	91.95
Atlantia	53.58	53.44	56.02	56.02	56.09	55.03	55.52
Azimut Holding	100.00	100.00	83.49	84.97	77.53	89.20	87.09
Banco Bpm	97.11	97.11	100.00	100.00	100.00	98.84	99.42
Bper Banca	97.92	91.96	87.10	78.90	67.42	84.66	85.88
Buzzi Unicem	43.16	43.16	41.35	38.44	41.06	41.43	41.39
CNH Industrial NV	72.21	72.20	72.10	72.86	72.72	72.42	72.32
Davide Campari	48.92	48.94	48.60	48.33	48.39	48.64	48.62
DiaSorin	41.90	41.66	41.63	40.83	41.12	41.43	41.53
Enel	72.50	76.42	76.42	76.42	76.42	75.63	76.42
Eni	67.29	69.62	69.62	69.62	69.42	69.12	69.52
Exor NV	46.00	45.54	45.66	45.66	44.85	45.54	45.60
Ferrari NV	90.00	65.69	65.69	66.28	66.27	70.79	66.28
Fiat Chrysler NV	67.65	69.50	69.77	70.67	70.61	69.64	69.70
FinecoBank	34.37	64.48	64.57	64.53	99.99	65.59	64.55
Hera	52.14	51.95	59.57	61.10	65.14	57.98	58.77
Intesa Sanpaolo	83.78	87.76	92.17	92.91	95.62	90.45	91.31
Italgas	-	56.45	54.92	54.99	55.69	55.51	55.51
Juventus FC	40.00	36.23	36.23	36.20	51.40	40.01	38.12
Leonardo	67.54	67.34	69.61	69.63	69.64	68.75	69.18
Mediobanca	79.75	79.03	86.02	83.40	82.82	82.20	82.51
Moncler	52.47	62.89	67.62	66.81	75.43	65.04	65.93
Nexi	-	-	-	100.00	47.62	73.81	73.81
Pirelli & C	-	100.00	34.53	39.89	40.07	53.62	40.07
Poste Italiane	35.30	35.30	35.74	35.74	35.48	35.51	35.50
Prysmian	91.68	91.68	95.88	94.00	93.39	93.33	93.36
Recordati	44.40	47.76	47.99	46.87	47.34	46.87	47.10
Saipem	30.91	51.64	56.62	56.44	56.39	50.40	54.02
Salvatore Ferragamo	25.54	22.47	28.55	39.72	28.98	29.05	28.77
Snam	55.60	65.74	57.80	61.82	60.36	60.26	60.31
STMicroelectronics NV	71.45	71.62	72.04	72.09	71.87	71.81	71.84
Telecom Italia	66.65	74.16	75.80	71.06	64.71	70.48	70.77
Tenaris SA	39.43	39.45	39.47	39.47	39.47	39.46	39.47
Terna	68.15	70.04	70.01	70.05	70.05	69.66	70.02
UBI	97.72	90.73	89.10	89.06	89.04	91.13	89.92
UniCredit	87.09	91.04	97.51	95.61	95.61	93.37	94.49
Unipol Gruppo	56.01	54.37	57.39	57.72	57.78	56.66	57.02
UnipolSai	37.72	31.99	25.38	19.27	18.96	26.66	26.02
Mean	60.45	62.44	61.71	62.46	63.47		
Median	56.01	65.69	64.57	65.41	64.93		

Data: Eikon.

small-sized and industrial companies, whereas foreign institutions tend to target large firms and the financial industry, with 35 per cent of FTSE-MIB firms and 25 per cent of financial industry firms featuring major foreign holdings.[43]

[43] Consob (n. 17) 19–20.

TABLE 17.3 *Major institutional investors' shareholdings in Italian listed companies (end 2018, MTA stock exchange)*

	At Least One Institutional Investor			At Least One Italian Institutional Investor			At Least One Foreign Institutional Investor		
	No. of Co.s	*Weight*[44]	*Mean Shareholding*[45]	*No. of Co.s*	*Weight*	*Mean Shareholding*	*No. of Co.s*	*Weight*	*Mean Shareholding*
2010	78	28.9	8.0	47	17.4	6.8	39	14.4	7.7
2011	75	28.8	7.7	48	18.5	6.7	36	13.8	7.1
2012	67	26.7	8.5	39	15.5	7.0	38	15.1	7.9
2013	66	27.0	7.7	32	13.1	6.9	41	16.8	7.0
2014	74	31.1	7.7	27	11.3	7.6	55	23.1	6.6
2015	68	29.1	7.9	18	7.7	7.8	53	22.6	7.5
2016	61	26.4	7.5	14	6.1	6.9	50	21.6	7.2
2017	60	26.0	7.7	12	5.2	7.6	51	22.1	7.3
2018	62	26.8	7.6	13	5.6	6.9	51	22.1	7.5

Data: Consob, 2019 Report on Corporate Governance of Italian Listed Companies.

TABLE 17.4 *Major institutional investors' shareholdings in Italian listed companies by industry (end 2018, MTA stock exchange)*

	At Least One Institutional Investor			At Least One Italian Institutional Investor			At Least One Foreign Institutional Investor		
	No. of Co.s	*Weight*[46]	*Mean Shareholding*[47]	*No. of Co.s*	*Weight*	*Mean Shareholding*	*No. of Co.s*	*Weight*	*Mean Shareholding*
Financial	13	26.0	8.1	3	6.0	6.8	10	20.0	8.5
Industrial	31	24.8	8.0	5	4.0	6.3	27	21.6	87.0
Services	18	32.1	6.7	5	8.9	7.6	14	25.0	5.9
Total	62	26.8	7.6	13	5.6	6.9	51	22.1	7.5

Data: Consob, 2019 Report on Corporate Governance of Italian Listed Companies.

Such divergent evolutionary patterns for domestic and foreign institutional ownership can possibly be explained by the fact that the corporate ownership of publicly listed companies in the financial industry, the banking industry in particular, is radically different from that of industrial companies. At the end of 2014, only six listed banks were controlled companies, whereas the remaining twelve, accounting for 21 per cent of total market capitalization, were either widely held companies or cooperative companies, which typically feature one-member-one-vote voting structures.[48] In turn, dispersed bank ownership is largely a consequence of the privatization

44 The number of companies in each group as a percentage of the total number of companies.

45 Simple mean of shareholdings by institutional investors at all listed companies where at least one institutional investor of the relevant category is present.

46 The number of companies in each group as a percentage of the total number of companies.

47 Simple mean of shareholdings by institutional investors in all listed companies where at least one institutional investor of the relevant category is present.

48 See Angela Ciavarella et al., 'La corporate governance delle società quotate italiane. Focus sul settore bancario' ['Corporate Governance Trends in Italian Listed Banks'] (2016) 4 *Bancaria* 82.

TABLE 17.5 *AGM attendance at 100 largest Italian listed companies*

		Share Capital Attending (%)			
		Total	Institutional Investors	*Italian Institutional Investors*	*Foreign Institutional Investors*
2012	Mean	70.2	11.5	1.1	10.4
	Median	70.5	9.8	0.0	7.9
2013	Mean	70.3	13.0	0.9	12.1
	Median	71.6	10.7	0.0	9.8
2014	Mean	70.7	17.5	0.9	16.5
	Median	72.9	16.2	0.0	15.6
2015	Mean	71.1	18.1	0.9	17.3
	Median	74.5	17.8	0.1	15.9
2016	Mean	70.6	19.1	1.2	17.9
	Median	73.1	18.1	0.5	17.1
2017	Mean	71.3	19.4	1.2	18.3
	Median	72.0	18.2	0.5	16.2
2018	Mean	72.6	21.4	1.7	19.7
	Median	75.1	19.4	1.0	17.9
2019	Mean	72.0	20.6	1.8	18.7
	Median	74.6	18.4	0.9	16.6

Data: Consob, 2019 Report on Corporate Governance of Italian Listed Companies.

process the financial industry underwent in the 1990s, which triggered large-scale acquisitions and mergers.[49]

The increasing weight of institutional investors within the shareholder base of Italian listed companies has been accompanied by a tendency for investors to be more active owners. The 2018 annual general meeting (AGM) season recorded record highs in terms of the share capital represented at meetings (72.6 per cent on average) and participation by institutional investors (exceeding 21 per cent of the company's capital).[50] Over the 2012–18 period, the attendance rates for institutional investors grew significantly in terms of both the number of investors attending and the percentage of share capital they represented.[51] Significantly, foreign institutions have attended the meetings of all 100 of the largest Italian companies since 2015; in 2018, they cast, on average, around 19 per cent of the votes.[52]

Their prominence was even more notable in the 2020 proxy season, when institutional investors collectively held a majority of the votes cast at the general meetings of approximately one-third of the Italian listed companies included in the FTSE-MIB that held their shareholder meetings in the spring.[53] Altogether, as noted by Consob, 'larger institutional investors or those with a stronger stewardship vocation are increasingly active in direct communication with companies for a number of issues, including corporate governance. In addition, investors have shown increasing interest in issuers' approach to social and environmental issues'.[54]

49 Ibid., 84–5.

50 Consob (n. 17) 40–1.

51 Ibid.

52 Ibid., 39.

53 For the 2019 proxy season, see Antonella Olivieri, 'L'avanzata dei fondi: in Borsa comandano in una blue chip su tre' ['The Rise of Mutual Funds: They Control One Third of Blue Chips'] Il Sole24ore (Milano, 4 August 2019) 8.

54 See Consob, 'Report on Corporate Governance of Italian Listed Companies 2018' (2019) 5 www.consob.it/documents/46180/46181/ar2018.pdf/cdc8a77f-f096-4e92-af53-94305683aec9 accessed 26 March 2020.

TABLE 17.6 *Asset managers (% share capital attending, FTSE-MIB companies)*

Company	2019	2020
A2A	29.41	28.71
Amplifon	34.20	27.87
Atlantia	52.62	53.21
Azimut Holding	39.02	60.49
Banca Generali	35.96	36.62
Banco BPM	63.44	70.91
BPER	33.26	28.28
Buzzi Unicem ord.	25.64	27.60
Davide Campari	40.32	39.32
CNH	40.26	41.49
Enel	61.33	65.51
Eni	50.52	45.87
Exor	34.70	33.51
Ferrari	29.40	28.15
FinecoBank	56.24	99.58
Assicurazioni Generali	38.94	43.44
Hera	33.44	35.15
Intesa San Paolo	65.22	65.45
Italgas	42.57	41.14
Leonardo	53.04	51.59
Poste Italiane	18.50	17.84
Prysmian	83.41	88.13
Recordati	34.14	38.32
Saipem	37.20	31.60
Salvatore Ferragamo	14.57	20.22
Tim	35.16	39.81
Terna	54.16	53.83
UBI Banca	40.35	54.39
Unicredit	78.30	89.59
Unipol	26.83	32.79

Data: Studio legale Trevisan & Associati; Il Sole 24 Ore.

It is finally worth mentioning that the institutional investor base is quite composite, as it includes asset managers, banks and insurance companies, private equity and venture capital firms, as well as sovereign funds. Whilst 2018 saw an increase in the stakes held by private equity, venture capital and sovereign funds, especially foreign ones, asset managers, banks and insurance companies are predominant by far.[55]

17.3 THE LEGAL FRAMEWORK FOR SHAREHOLDER VOTING AND ENGAGEMENT

Alongside the surge in institutional ownership, regulatory factors have also contributed to the increase in (institutional) shareholder voting at Italian publicly listed companies. Over the last two decades, the legal framework for participating and voting in shareholder meetings has been gradually reshaped so as to craft an engagement-friendly regulatory environment. In point of

[55] Consob (n. 17) 13.

TABLE 17.7 *Stakes held by major institutional investors in Italian listed companies (MTA stock exchange)*

	Asset Managers		Banks & Insurance Companies		Private Equity, Venture Capital & Sovereign Funds		Total	
	No. of Stakes	*Mean Stake*	No. of Stakes	*Mean Stake*	No. of Stakes	*Mean Stake*	No. of Stakes	*Mean Stake*
2010	35	6.3	56	5.3	16	6.7	107	5.8
2011	29	5.9	55	5.3	18	6.5	102	5.7
2012	30	6.4	51	5.3	17	6.3	98	5.8
2013	33	6.3	41	5.4	12	6.5	86	5.9
2014	45	6.3	40	5.2	13	6.1	98	5.8
2015	55	6.1	24	5.1	13	6.1	92	5.8
2016	44	6.5	12	6.4	19	5.0	75	6.1
2017	46	6.0	11	6.8	19	6.1	76	6.1
2018	44	5.7	8	6.7	27	6.2	79	6.0

Data: Consob, 2019 Report on Corporate Governance of Italian Listed Companies.

fact, 'a number of self-enforcing rules (especially on voting) and a broader set of minority shareholder rights have made today's Italian legal environment no less friendly to activist investors than most other jurisdictions'.[56] Enhanced shareholder rights and asset managers' quasi-duty to vote as part of their fiduciary duties to end-investors can be regarded as parallel forces driving the increase in voting in spite of the weak incentive structure of non-activist, traditional institutions. In addition, the list of issues falling within the remit of the general meeting has broadened over time.[57] For example, defensive measures against hostile takeovers (unless the company has opted out of the so-called board neutrality rule) now need to be authorized by the shareholder meeting. Similarly, the requirement that any AoA amendments be approved by a supermajority of two-thirds of the share capital represented at the meeting is clearly aimed at incentivizing attendance by minority shareholders.

Soft regulation in the form of corporate governance and stewardship principles has also contributed to more active institutional ownership. In effect, provisions strengthening shareholder rights operate in conjunction with those set by stewardship and corporate governance codes that target institutional investors as shareholders to foster their constructive engagement with investee companies as part of their investment management activities.

17.3.1 *Asset Managers' Quasi-Duty to Vote and Institutions' Engagement Policy*

In analyzing the EU regulatory environment as a supportive factor for shareholder voting, one relevant issue to be considered is that, based on the framework for discretionary portfolio and collective investment management, intermediaries are entitled to vote the shares owned by the funds they manage. Because of this entitlement, UCITS[58] management companies (see article

[56] Massimo Belcredi and Luca Enriques, 'Institutional Investor Activism in a Context of Concentrated Ownership and High Private Benefits of Control: The Case of Italy' (2014) ECGI Working Paper Series in Law no. 225/2013, 7 http://ssrn.com/abstract=2325421 accessed 26 March 2020.

[57] Ibid., 7–8.

[58] UCITS stands for 'undertakings for collective investment in transferable securities'. UCITS compliant funds are invested in in transferable securities or in other liquid financial assets and can be marketed to retail investors.

21 of Directive 2010/43/EU) and alternative investment fund managers (see article 37 of Commission Delegated Regulation (EU) No. 231/2013) are required to establish a voting policy specifying *when and how* to exercise voting rights, whereas voting determinations are to be made to the exclusive benefit of the funds and the investors therein. Voting is thus conceived of as a duty that intermediaries owe to end-investors wherever – based on a cost-benefit analysis – it is in the best interests of the beneficial owners of the shares. The end-investor best-interest standard overarching the entire regulation of investment intermediaries does not in itself entail a duty to vote *every share*.[59] However, investment managers are clearly not allowed to simply remain passive and choose not to vote because, depending on the investment strategies adopted, voting passivity can be at odds with institutions' duty to manage investments in the best interest of their clients. EU regulation thus provides an incentive structure that 'rel[ies] on the presumption that shareholder voting preserves, or even increases, the long-term value of the investment', which eventually translates into an 'implicit duty to vote'.[60]

In keeping with the EU provisions, article 35-decies 1(e) CLF states that asset management companies 'must provide, in the investors' interests, for the exercise of the voting rights associated with the financial instruments of the collective investment schemes managed, unless required otherwise by law'. Despite the wording used within the legislation ('must provide'), the prevailing view is that article 35-decies CLF does not establish an obligation for asset management companies to exercise their voting rights in all circumstances.[61] In keeping with their general duty to 'operate diligently, correctly and with transparency in the best interests of the collective investment schemes managed, the relevant investors and the integrity of the market' – as set out in article 35-decies 1(a) CLF – asset management companies are expected to vote (only) when it is in the interest of the ultimate beneficiaries of the funds managed.[62]

In addition, article 124-quinquies CLF – implementing articles 3 g and 3 f SRD II – requires institutional investors and asset managers, if only based on a comply-or-explain approach, to adopt an engagement policy that, inter alia, illustrates how they exercise voting rights and other shareholder rights. Institutional investors and asset managers are further required to publicly disclose each year how their engagement policy has been implemented and provide a general description of their voting behaviour, an explanation of the most significant votes and the use they made of proxy advisory services. Although it remains questionable whether the newly added rules for institutional investors and asset managers (both Italian and foreign) will actually contribute to fostering greater investor engagement with investee companies, the requirement that information on their engagement and actual voting conduct, and the reasons therefore, be disseminated indirectly exerts pressure on the exercise of voting rights.

59 See recital no. 16 to Directive 2010/43/EU.

60 Christian Strenger and Dirk A. Zetzsche, 'Corporate Governance, Cross-Border Voting and the (Draft) Principles of the European Securities Law Legislation. Enhancing Investor Engagement Through Standardisation' (2013) 13 *JCLS* 511, 515–17. See also Marco Maugeri, 'Proxy advisors, esercizio del voto e doveri "fiduciari" del gestore' ['Proxy Advisors and Asset Managers' Voting and 'Fiduciary' Duties'] in R. D' Apice (ed.), *Profili evolutivi della disciplina sulla gestione collettiva del risparmio [The Evolution of the Regulatory Framework for Collective Investments]* (Il Mulino 2016) 667, 680–2.

61 Renzo Costi, 'Risparmio gestito e governo societario' ['Asset Management and Corporate Governance'] [1988] *Giurisprudenza commerciale* 322; Renzo Costi and Luca Enriques, 'Il mercato mobiliare' ['Financial Market'] in Gastone Cottino (ed.), *Trattato di diritto commercial*, vol. VIII (Cedam 2004) 420.

62 Mario Stella Richter Jr, 'L'esercizio del voto con gli strumenti finanziari gestiti' ['Asset Managers' Voting'] in Enrico Gabrielli and Raffaele Lener (eds.) *I contratti del mercato finanziario* (2nd ed., Utet 2010) 800.

17.3.2 *Participation in Shareholder Meetings: Information and Duty to Call*

The reform enacted in 2010 to transpose SRD I into Italian law[63] significantly contributed to the provision of better shareholder information and greater efficiency in the mechanics of shareholder meetings, thereby helping to alleviate the disincentives that institutional investors may previously have encountered in participating in such meetings.

A clear example of such pro-shareholder regulatory effort can be drawn from article 125-bis (4) CLF concerning the content of the notice calling shareholder meetings, which stipulates that said notice must include, amongst other items, 'a clear, precise description' of the procedures for attending and voting at the shareholder meeting and for exercising further shareholder rights. In particular, the notice is to provide information concerning the terms for exercising the right to raise questions prior to the meeting and the right to have additional items placed on the agenda or present further proposals on items already on the agenda.

Article 125-bis (4) CLF can actually be viewed as a summary of a wider set of provisions emphasizing the active role that investors are expected to play in respect of the shareholder meeting. First, acknowledging that being an active owner requires adequate and timely information, article 125-ter CLF requires that a report on each item on the agenda be made available by the board of directors by a specified deadline ahead of an upcoming shareholder meeting, thereby obliging institutions to organize and be prepared for making appropriate voting determinations and limiting the chilling effect associated with the delivery of relevant company information much too close to the date of the meeting to be useful. Prior to the introduction of the so-called record date system into national law to regulate attendance and voting in shareholder meetings,[64] the inadequate timing of information delivery was shown to adversely affect both meeting participation and voting.[65]

Second, a shareholder-friendly, efficiency-promoting intent clearly underpins article 127-ter (1) CLF, which grants any shareholder the right to submit questions on the items on the agenda prior to the shareholder meeting and to receive the relevant answers during the meeting 'at the latest'.

Finally, active ownership is further incentivized by the right granted to shareholders who hold a specified minimum shareholding threshold – and are thus usually institutional investors[66] – to directly activate the shareholder meeting. Shareholders holding – either individually or collectively – at least 5 per cent of the company's share capital have the right to call a general meeting.[67] In addition, those holding – either individually or collectively – at least 2.5 per cent of the share capital may ask for additional matters to be put on the meeting agenda and may table new proposed resolutions for a vote.[68] Making voting proposals can serve not only to oppose the board and controlling stockholders, but also to remedy the much criticized board-friendly practice of bundling together two or more – generally related – issues into the same agenda item in such a way as to prevent those issues being voted on separately. Bundling – most typically concerning the approval of financial statements and dividend distributions, the approval of a set of changes

63 SRD I was transposed in Italy by Legislative Decree No. 27/2010.

64 Regarding the record date system see Section 17.3.3.5.

65 See Fabio Bianconi, 'L'attivismo delle minoranze in Italia: un commento, in FTSE MIB Proxy Season 2010' ['Minority Shareholder Activism. FTSE MIB Proxy Season 2010'] (2011) 70–1 www.proxitalia.com/dld/files/Downloads/Pubblicazioni/FTSE%20MIB%202010%20-%20Georgeson.pdf accessed 26 March 2020.

66 Stella Richter (n. 62) 800.

67 See art. 2367 Civil Code.

68 See art. 126-bis CLF.

to the AoA or director elections and compensation – has been a particular target of proxy advisors in Italy for being contrary to best practice and inhibiting voting by proxy.

17.3.3 *Regulatory Incentives to Participate in the Shareholder Meeting*

Beyond enhancing shareholder information rights, both passive and active, and providing shareholders with the power to proactively initiate the calling of a shareholder meeting and make voting proposals, regulatory action taken ahead and in the wake of SRD I was also intended to provide a set of tools incentivizing active and long-term ownership. These tools range from additional voting rights or dividends, conceived of as a reward for shareholder loyalty, to multiple voting rights, through to simplified proxy voting and proxy solicitation, say-on-pay votes and the enhanced role to be played by shareholders in the context of related party transactions (RPTs). Whilst not all of these tools have proved successful in accomplishing the policy goal set and actually driving increased shareholder engagement with Italian investee companies, some indeed have, as is most notably the case for say-on-pay votes, alongside the record date regime concerning shareholder meeting attendance and the slate voting system concerning director elections.

17.3.3.1 Limited Relevance of Loyalty-Based Dividend and Vote Rewards to Institutional Shareholder Engagement

With the explicit aim of encouraging longer-term investments, two mechanisms were introduced in 2010 and 2014 to reward shareholder loyalty in terms of cash flow rights or control rights. First, article 127-quarter CLF allows for a dividend-increasing mechanism to be adopted in AoA by which 'each share held by the same shareholder for a continuous period of time indicated in the articles, in any case of no less than one year or the lesser period running between two consecutive payment dates of the annual dividend, shall assign the right to an increase of no more than 10 percent of the dividend distributed to the other shares'.

Significantly, additional dividends may not be granted to (de jure or de facto) controlling stockholders, whether individually or jointly in control, nor to any shareholder wielding a significant influence on the company or taking part in a shareholder agreement accounting for more than the shareholding thresholds relevant to the rules on the mandatory bid laid down in article 106 CLF. Therefore, quite evidently, the investor category targeted by the dividend-increasing incentive is mainstream institutional investors, who typically do not seek to gain control over the company, are unwilling to take part in shareholder agreements owing to the chilling effect associated with the rules on concerted action and the triggering of mandatory bids, and whose holdings usually do not allow them to individually exert any significant influence over the company. It is thus traditional institutions such as pension and mutual funds, whether actively managed or passive, that are candidates to possibly be rewarded for loyalty.

Second, article 127-quinquies CLF allows loyal shareholders – including those who exercise control or significant influence over the company – to enjoy additional, time-phased voting rights (up to two votes depending on the arrangements made in the AoA) for each share uninterruptedly held by them for no less than two years, with additional voting rights expiring upon the sale of the shares. Tenured voting may be adopted by any listed company as an incentivizing tool, provided, however, that no multiple voting structure is in place. Hence, additional voting rights and multiple voting may be only an alternative. Multiple voting structures – up to three votes per share – have been permitted under Italian law since 2014, when they were introduced with the aim of inducing family-owned firms (which are the core business organization in Italy) to list more shares on the stock market without necessarily losing control, thus rendering Italian companies less reliant on bank lending.[69] Shares with multiple voting rights can in fact be issued only by private companies; companies that issued such shares prior to listing are allowed to maintain them if they so choose, but are prohibited from issuing new ones and from adopting additional, time-phased voting rights. At the same time, eliminating the ban on multiple voting rights, which had characterized corporate voting in Italy since the enactment of the Civil Code in 1942, was also a reaction to the Chrysler-Fiat migration from Italy to the Netherlands.

Private ordering has exhibited little interest in dividend-increasing mechanisms, whether owing to the many practical problems associated with implementation of the relevant provisions or simply because the long-term financial incentive provided by heightened dividends arguably cannot outweigh the short-term opportunities associated with trading stocks.[70] Time-phased voting, in contrast, has proved more successful, with 61 of the 231 companies listed on the Italian exchange having adopted tenured voting.[71] However, given that time-phased voting requires the AoA to be amended, and that in order to enjoy the loyalty reward a shareholder is required to file a request with the company, the finding that adopters are almost exclusively family-owned controlled firms and that registrant shareholders are almost exclusively controllers, especially de jure controllers, is quite deceiving, if not unsurprising, from the standpoint of achievement of the policy goal to incentivize the long-term engagement of institutional shareholders.[72] The clear dominance of controlling shareholders in the ownership of companies adopting time-phased voting seems to contradict the reasoning according to which tenured voting encourages longer-term investments by investors other than controlling shareholders. In fact, the practice of time-phased voting in Italy suggests that the effectiveness of such a mechanism as a means for retaining shareholders over the long term or, at any rate, as a tool for encouraging institutional investor engagement with investee companies is questionable.[73] In a context of high levels of ownership concentration, tenured voting appears instead to further empower pre-existing long-term shareholders. In effect, because controllers do not reduce their stake despite enjoying additional voting rights, the overall net effect of time-phased voting is actually to allow those already in control to also gain control over extraordinary shareholder meetings, where a two-thirds majority of the share capital represented at the meeting is required for making any decision.[74] Similarly, the fundamental lack of institutional investors and asset managers amongst the beneficiaries of time-phased voting supports the view that such voting seems not, in and of itself, to subsidize institutional shareholder engagement.[75] Indeed, the two-year lock-up period poses a clear liquidity problem for institutional investors, particularly those adopting an active investing strategy that involves the ability to freely sell portfolio assets.

69 See OECD (n. 22) 34–5.

70 See, generally, Mario Stella Richter Jr, 'I Troppi Problemi del Dividendo Maggiorato' ['The too many problems of increased dividends'] (2011) I *Riv dir comm* 89.

71 See www.consob.it/web/area-pubblica/quotate/main/emittenti/societa_quotate/voto_maggiorato_plurimo_lnk.htm?nav=true accessed 15 July 2020.

72 See Chiara Mosca, 'Should Shareholders Be Rewarded for Loyalty? European Experiments on the Wedge Between Tenured Voting and Takeover Law' (2019) 8 *Michigan Business & Entrepreneurial Law Review* 245, 266–8.

73 See Christoph Van der Elst, 'Do Loyalty Shares Affect the Engagement of Shareholders: A Study of the French CAC-40 Companies' (2017) *International Journal for Financial Services* 33.

74 Mosca (n. 72) 271.

75 Ibid., 272.

17.3.3.2 Proxy and Remote Voting

As mentioned above, one aim of SRD I was to remove some of the procedural hurdles that have inhibited shareholder participation in shareholder meetings. Along the same lines, the Italian rules on proxy voting and proxy solicitation were simplified in 2010 to render them less restrictive than they previously were. Changes were also made to the rules on voting by correspondence and via electronic means.

Removing unnecessary restrictions on proxy voting is in fact a tool for facilitating shareholder participation, as are other tools that allow cost-effective participation at a distance and in absentia or voting in advance of a meeting, such as the electronic real-time transmission of meetings, real-time two-way communication enabling shareholders to address the meeting from a remote location, electronic voting and voting by correspondence. However, with respect to voting at a distance or in absentia, practical experience in Italy casts doubt on their efficacy for achieving the intended policy goal.

Under article 2370(4) Civil Code and article 127 CLF, voting at a distance is allowed both by correspondence and by remote means – a technique that, unlike voting by correspondence, also allows, at least theoretically, for direct and potentially interactive participation in the meeting. However, electronic and online voting are not mandatory under Italian law, and neither is voting by correspondence, and it is thus left to issuers to decide whether to adopt any of these enabling tools. Hence, despite the alternative-design approach adopted at the regulatory level, enhanced shareholder empowerment relies primarily on the arrangements made by individual companies. A shareholder wishing to vote her shares without appointing a proxy agent may or may not be able to do so remotely or in advance of the meeting, depending on whether her investee company offers her (one or more of) these tools. In fact, voting by correspondence is rare in Italy.[76] Similarly, Italian listed companies do not necessarily afford investors an opportunity to participate in a meeting and vote their shares at a distance via electronic means, possibly because of cost concerns about the relevant technology. At any rate, it is unclear whether institutional investors, at least larger institutions, who are willing to routinely employ proxy advisors to help them make voting determinations would really refrain from voting their shares simply because of the need, absent electronic voting, to appoint a local proxy agent.[77] Such a state of affairs helps to explain why appointing a proxy agent remains by far the voting tool most commonly employed by institutional shareholders. Voting by proxy is possible under Italian law in different ways, whether according to the regime established by article 2372 of the Civil Code or that provided for by articles 135-novies–135-undecies CLF for publicly listed corporations.

However, proxy fights based on the proxy solicitation regime set out in articles 136–138 CLF remain rare in the Italian context despite the changes made in 2010 to the relevant rules with the aim of removing the many substantive limitations that, alongside high costs, had prevented proxy solicitations from growing into a workable pathway for active share ownership. A shareholder looking to solicit proxies is no longer under an obligation to enlist an intermediary to carry out the process, as she was before the 2010 changes. In addition, a soliciting shareholder is no longer required to meet certain requirements in terms of minimum shareholding thresholds or to solicit

76 See Carlo Bellavite Pellegrini, 'Corporate Governance e assemblea delle società quotate in Italia: un'indagine empirica' ['An Empirical Inquiry into Corporate Governance and the Shareholders Meeting at Corporations Publicly Listed in Italy'] [2006] *Rivista delle società* 416.

77 See Marco Cian, 'Intervento e voto in assemblea: le nuove tecnologie come mezzo per promuovere l'attivismo degli investitori istituzionali?' ['Participating in the Shareholders Meeting and Voting: New Technologies As a Tool to Promote Institutional Investor Activism?'] in Marco Maugeri (ed.), *Governo delle società quotate e attivismo degli investitori istituzionali* [*Corporate governance and institutional investor activism*] (Giuffrè 2015) 104.

proxies from amongst her fellow shareholders. In its current version, article 136(1)(b) CLF allows a minimum of 200 shareholders to be addressed by the soliciting party, thereby allowing her to selectively address her fellow shareholders.[78] Alongside the possibility of disseminating proxy materials (a proxy statement and proxy form) via a website chosen by the soliciting party – which may be the issuer's site if the issuer so agrees[79] – these measures have helped to reduce the costs associated with the process that are to be borne by the soliciting party, thereby theoretically enabling a shareholder to strengthen her voting power more cost-effectively with respect to specific voting proposals by soliciting proxies from like-minded shareholders. Moreover, one-way proxies are no longer mandatory for soliciting shareholders. Allowing two-way proxies – which, importantly, are mandatory when the soliciting party is the issuer itself[80] – mitigates the chilling effect associated with one-way proxies for solicited shareholders actually wishing to vote by proxy but to do so in a way other than that proposed by the soliciting party. Lower costs and greater flexibility seem to have revitalized proxy solicitation as a lever for active share ownership, at least to some extent. Although proxy solicitation is still not commonplace in Italy, probably as a consequence of concentrated ownership, it has become less infrequent than in the past, at least in specific circumstances concerning the issuer.[81]

17.3.3.3 Say-on-Pay Votes on Remuneration Policy and Director Compensation Transparency

After introducing a precatory say-on-pay vote in respect of a company's remuneration policy in 2012, the current version of article 123-ter CLF – as amended by Legislative Decree No. 49 of 10 May 2019 implementing Article 9a SRD II – makes say-on-pay votes binding. A say-on-pay is to be granted at least every three years or when the board proposes any changes to the remuneration policy last approved by shareholders. Hence, companies 'shall only allocate fees in compliance with the remuneration policy most recently approved by the shareholders' (see article 123-ter (3-bis) CLF). As an explanation for rendering say-on-pay binding in nature, the draft explanatory report to Legislative Decree No. 49/2019 emphasizes the need to align the remuneration policy provisions of all listed companies with those already in force for banks and insurance companies, which provide for binding say-on-pay votes.[82] In addition, the scope of application of binding say-on-pay votes on remuneration policy was broadened to include compensation to members of the board of statutory auditors, alongside that regarding members of the board of directors, general managers and executives with strategic responsibilities (see article 123-ter (3)(a) CLF).

As a tool for enhanced director accountability, say-on-pay votes are clearly meant to strengthen institutional investor monitoring.[83] First, from the standpoint of shareholder oversight,

[78] Under art. 136 (1)(b) CLF, proxy solicitation is defined as 'a request to more than two hundred shareholders for proxy to be conferred in relation to specific voting proposals, or accompanied by recommendations, statements or other indications capable of influencing the vote'.

[79] See art. 136(3) of Consob Regulation no. 11971.

[80] See art. 138(2) of Consob Regulation no. 11971.

[81] One proxy fight that became famous for being 'Italy's fiercest proxy contest in decades' occurred in 2012 when a shareholder meeting was called by Salini at Impregilo to remove the Gavio group-dominated board; the context in which the case occurred was a peculiar one, as it was characterized by both hedge fund activism targeting Salini and an unstable ownership structure as a consequence of shareholder coalitions dominating the company with stakes less than 30 per cent of the share capital. See Belcredi and Enriques (n. 56) 26–7.

[82] See Draft Explanatory Report to Legislative Decree no. 49/2019 (in Italian only) (8 February 2019) 7 http://documenti.camera.it/apps/nuovosito/attigoverno/Schedalavori/getTesto.ashx?file=0071_F001.pdf&leg=XVIII#pagemode=none accessed 26 March 2020. See also Bank of Italy Circular no. 285/2013, pt I, title IV, ch. 2, s. II, para. 1 (providing that remuneration policies for corporate boards be approved by the shareholder meeting by a binding vote).

[83] See e.g. recital 10 to Recommendation 2009/385/EC.

significant levels of 'against' and withheld say-on-pay votes quite clearly indicate that (some portion of) shareholders have withdrawn their support from the board, and their dissent is made public. Second, say-on-pay votes can be regarded as functionally complementary to the right granted to shareholders under the slate voting system for director elections[84] to demand that at least one director be elected by minority shareholders. If one considers that minority-elected directors are very often elected to the remuneration committee within the board, the combined potential effect of say-on-pay votes and slate voting can be to provide minority shareholders with a form of intra-board monitoring over determinations concerning board compensation that may favour alignment with international best practices – first and foremost in regard to enhanced transparency – thereby further encouraging shareholder engagement. Interestingly, following the initial implementation of precatory say-on-pay, a positive correlation has been found to exist between the presence of minority-elected directors within remuneration committees and increased institutional investor participation in shareholder meetings.[85] Moreover, low-quality information in remuneration reports has been found to positively correlate with higher levels of dissenting and withheld say-on-pay votes, suggesting that shareholders do lever such votes as a tool for corporate stewardship.[86] The significance of say-on-pay votes for remuneration policy is, in fact, further heightened by the fact that the fees actually paid to directors, general managers, executives with strategic responsibilities and members of the board of statutory auditors during the financial year need to be submitted to a (non-binding) shareholder vote.[87] Moreover, the board of directors is also required to illustrate annually how the company has taken account of the vote cast the previous year on the fees paid.[88]

17.3.3.4 Related Party Transactions and Shareholder Oversight

Amongst the most significant rulings intended to reduce the principal-principal agency costs associated with controllers' potential for self-dealing is that on RPTs, which was first introduced in Italy in 2010, although it was slightly amended in 2019 in the process of transposing article 9(c) SRD II into national law. The general provisions on RPTs are set out in article 2391-bis of the Civil Code, which vests Consob with the authority to lay down rules aimed at ensuring that such transactions are transparent, are illustrated in the board's annual report on financial statements, and comply with procedural and substantive fairness requirements, and in article 154-ter (4) CLF, which requires the board's interim report on half-yearly financial statements to also include information on significant RPTs. Rules on the content of such information, as well as the substantive regulation of RPTs, were laid down by Consob in Regulation No. 17221 of 12 March 2010, which envisages safeguards aimed at protecting the company and its non-controlling shareholders against potential value diversion or misappropriation by controllers and further related parties, including detailed provisions involving independent directors in the decision-making process and, in some cases, empowering dissenting minorities to prevent the transaction from being entered into. Regulation No. 17221 is currently in the process of being updated

84 See Sections 17.3.4.1 and 17.4.1.
85 See Section 17.4.
86 See Massimo Belcredi and others, 'Proxy Advisor and Shareholders Engagement. Evidence from Italian Say-on-Pay' (2015) 20, 25–6 ssrn.com/abstractid=2616258 accessed 26 March 2020.
87 See art. 123-ter (6) CLF.
88 See art. 123-ter (4) (b-bis) CLF.

in accordance with SRD II,[89] although few changes are expected. The following paragraphs provide an overview of the general regime governing RPTs in Italy.

First, article 4 of Regulation No. 17221 requires that boards of directors adopt a specified internal procedure to ensure the transparency and substantial and procedural fairness of RPTs. Second, article 5 of the same regulation requires that material transactions be publicly disclosed by the company in accordance with article 114(5) CLF and article 17 of Regulation (EU) No. 596/2014. Third, according to article 8 of Regulation No. 17221, the board of directors may approve material RPTs (transactions 'of greater importance', as identified through a set of quantitative parameters) only if favourable advice has previously been provided by a committee of independent directors involved in the negotiations. However, company-specific related party procedures may stipulate that the board is permitted to approve such a transaction despite a negative opinion from the committee if, and only if, a shareholder meeting is convened and a majority of unrelated shareholders approve it (a so-called whitewash). Transactions 'of lesser importance', in contrast, may be approved by the board notwithstanding the negative opinion of the committee, which, in addition, is not required to lead the negotiations, and without recourse to shareholder meeting whitewash.[90] According to Annex 1 of Regulation No. 17221 (concerning definitions functional to the definitions of related parties and RPTs), an entity is a related party to a company if, inter alia, that entity 'controls the company, is controlled by [it], or is under common control'.[91]

Once again, the interaction between the Italian regimes for RPTs and for director elections through the mandatory slate voting system need to be considered in order to fully understand how such interaction can support active shareholder monitoring and stewardship. In effect, because ex ante independent scrutiny of RPTs is required to ensure that the transaction in question is fair to the company and all of its shareholders, the minority board representation ensured by slate voting can strengthen self-dealing oversight. At Italian listed companies, the presence of minority-elected directors appointed by institutional investors has had a positive impact on the adequacy of internal procedures for addressing RPTs.[92] In particular, 'the presence of at least one minority director is indeed associated with adoption of stricter internal codes, not only when minority directors are members of the committee of independent directors vetting internal codes, but also when they merely sit in the board'.[93] Indeed, the very reason that mandatory slate voting was originally adopted for listed company board elections in Italy was to secure minority board representation as a monitoring tool deployed by active shareholders, in keeping with the view that institutional investors should be encouraged to act as corporate stewards.[94] Further findings from Italy seem to support the hypothesis that non-executive minority directors reduce the principal-principal agency costs associated with potential self-dealing by controllers and positively affect firm value 'even in [the] presence of factors (uncertainty about future financial results and high information asymmetry) that might exacerbate the

89 See Consob, Regulation no. 17221/2010 concerning transactions with related parties, www.consob.it/web/consob-and-its-activities/laws-and-regulations/documenti/english/laws/reg17221e.htm?hkeywords=&docid=10&page=0&hits=21&nav=false accessed 26 March 2020.

90 See art. 7 of Consob Regulation no. 17221/2010.

91 See Annex 1 to Consob Regulation no. 17221/2010 (emphasis added).

92 See Marcello Bianchi and others, 'Regulation and Self-Regulation of Related Party Transactions in Italy – An Empirical Analysis' (2014) ECGI Finance Working Paper no. 415/2014, 25 https://papers.ssrn.com/sol3/papers.cfm?abstract_id=2383237 accessed 26 March 2020.

93 Ibid., 25.

94 See Giovanni Strampelli, 'How to Enhance Directors' Independence at Controlled Companies' (2018) 44 *J Corp L* 103, 135–6; Marco Ventoruzzo, 'Empowering Shareholders in Directors' Elections: A Revolution in the Making' (2011) 8 *ECFR* 105, 141.

risk of hold-up by minority shareholders'.[95] Thus, 'the benefits associated [with] the active monitoring role [of] independent minority directors outweigh the costs of potential frictions within the board'.[96]

17.3.3.5 Pivotal Impact of the Record Date System on Boosting Institutional Investor Voting

Although they do significantly empower minority shareholders, most of the regulatory measures illustrated above would still not have provided institutional investors with an incentive strong enough to subsidize increased participation in shareholder meetings had it not been for the mandatory adoption of the record date regime to regulate attendance and voting in such meetings. In point of fact, the blocking requirement imposed on shares for up to two days prior to a shareholder meeting, which was previously enshrined in article 2370 Civil Code, amounted to a significant economic impediment to institutional investor attendance because it seriously restricted the ability of investors to freely trade their shares for a not insignificant number of days ahead of the meeting.[97] Thus, the shift towards the mandatory record date system (see article 83-sexies CLF) has greatly mitigated the main economic disincentive associated with meeting participation and has proved crucial to boosting institutional investor voting, especially by foreign institutions.[98] Indeed, according to the record date system, the legitimate attendance of shareholder meetings and the exercise of voting rights are confirmed by a statement sent to the issuer by the custodian bank on behalf of the shareholders willing to participate in the meeting. That statement is communicated by the custodian bank seven market days prior to the meeting date. Therefore, as shareholders' entitlement to participate in the meeting is based on communications issued by the intermediary, shareholders are entitled to exercise their voting rights even if they sell their shares between the record date and meeting date.

As the available evidence quite clearly shows,[99] since the introduction of the record date regime in 2010, institutional investors' participation in shareholder meetings has virtually doubled at non-controlled Italian listed companies, and has increased remarkably even at de jure-controlled companies, even though in the latter control over voting outcomes is restricted to the controlling blockholders.[100]

17.3.4 *Shareholder Engagement*

As illustrated above,[101] various actions have been taken to support, facilitate and incentivize institutional investor participation and voting at shareholder meetings. However, there are other forms of engagement that usually take place outside the general meeting that remain substantially unregulated, despite their increasing relevance to engagement practice.[102]

95 Nicola Moscariello et al., 'Independent Minority Directors and Firm Value in a Principal-Principal Agency Setting: Evidence from Italy' (2019) 23 *Journal of Management and Governance* 18–19.

96 Ibid.

97 See B. Espen Eckbo and Giulia Paone, 'Reforming Share-Voting Systems: The Case of Italy' (2011) Tuck School of Business Working Paper no. 2011-93, 7–8 https://ssrn.com/abstract=1822287 accessed 26 March 2020.

98 Belcredi and Enriques (n. 56) 21.

99 See Section 17.2 of this chapter.

100 See Mario Notari, 'Diritti di voice degli azionisti e tutela delle minoranze' ['Shareholders' Voice and Minority Protection'] in F. Annunziata (ed.), *Il Testo Unico della Finanza. Un bilancio dopo 15 anni [Taking Stock of the Consolidated Law on Finance 15 Years After its Introduction]* (Egea 2015) 247, 256–7.

101 Sections 17.3.1–17.3.3.

102 See Joseph A. McCahery, Zacharias Sautner and Laura T. Starks, 'Behind the Scenes: The Corporate Governance Preferences of Institutional Investors' (2016) 71 *The Journal of Finance* 2905, 2911–16; Giovanni Strampelli,

Article 124-quinquies CLF (which almost literally transposes article 3 g(1)(a) SRD II) now requires – if only on a comply-or-explain basis – that institutional investors publish their engagement policy annually to illustrate, inter alia, the ways in which they 'monitor investee companies on important issues, including strategy, financial and non-financial results as well as risks, capital structure, social and environmental impact and corporate governance, interact with investee companies, . . . cooperate with other shareholders, and communicate with the relevant stakeholders of the investee companies'.

In line with the principles set by virtually any stewardship code, whether national or international, article 124-quinquies CLF makes it clear that engagement is more than just voting and includes – borrowing the words of the UK Stewardship Code – 'investment decision-making, monitoring assets and service providers, engaging with issuers and holding them to account on material issues, collaborating with others, and exercising rights and responsibilities'.[103]

Although much engagement takes place behind closed doors,[104] there are forms of public engagement that have proved quite effective in the Italian context. In particular, the Italian experience of director elections through the slate voting system suggests that coordinated engagement by institutional investors can have a positive impact on investee companies, especially with regard to corporate governance issues. Closely following EFAMA,[105] the Italian Stewardship Principles acknowledge that collective engagement 'may be the most effective method of engagement'.[106] Over the years, Assogestioni has been playing an increasingly active role in providing operational support to its affiliates,[107] thus developing a particular pathway for collective engagement and demonstrating that investor associations can play a proactive role within the stewardship framework, as they can catalyze investors' stewardship efforts by favouring the redistribution of engagement costs amongst the institutional investors carrying out engagement activities collectively. Moreover, collective (and individual) engagement may further be facilitated by the new rules on shareholder identification set out in article 83-duodecies CLF, as amended following SRD II.

17.3.4.1 Director (and Statutory Auditor) Elections through Slate Voting

As already mentioned, the most distinctive feature of the Italian corporate governance framework is the right to board representation that is granted to minority shareholders through the slate voting system (*voto di lista*), which is mandatory for corporate elections at all listed companies. Minority shareholders enjoy the right to elect at least one member of the board of directors and one member of the board of statutory auditors because, under slate voting, corporate boards are elected from competing slates of nominees, which are usually submitted by sponsoring shareholders. The majority of directors are elected from the slate receiving the largest number of votes at the shareholder meeting (the so-called majority slate), but at least one director must be

'Knocking at the Boardroom Door: A Transatlantic Overview of Director-Institutional Investor Engagement in Law and Practice' (2018) 12 *Virginia Law and Business Review* 187.

103 Financial Reporting Council, 'The UK Stewardship Code 2020' (October 2019) 7 www.frc.org.uk/getattachment/5aae591d-d9d3-4cf4-814a-d14e156a1d87/Stewardship-Code_Dec-19-Final.pdf accessed 26 March 2020.

104 See Strampelli (n. 94); Ventoruzzo (n. 94). See also Elroy Dimson, Oğuzhan Karakaş and Xi Li, 'Coordinated Engagements' (2019) 9 https://ssrn.com/id=3209072 accessed 26 March 2020.

105 See EFAMA, 'Stewardship Code. Principles for Asset Managers' Monitoring of, Voting in, Engagement with Investee Companies' (2018), Principle 4, www.efama.org/Publications/Public/Corporate_Governance/EFAMA%20Stewardship%20Code.pdf accessed 26 March 2020 (recommending that asset managers 'should consider acting with other investors, where appropriate'. Guidance to Principle 4 further emphasizes that shareholder collaboration may sometimes be 'the most effective manner in which to engage').

106 Assogestioni (n. 19) 17–18.

107 See, generally, Strampelli (n. 94) 134–5.

selected from the slate that obtains the largest number of votes after the majority slate (the so-called minority slate)[108] and that is not linked in any way, either directly or indirectly, to the majority slate.[109] In particular, under article 147-ter CLF, shareholders holding a minimum threshold of shares – set by Consob and currently varying between 0.5 and 4.5 per cent[110] – are entitled to present lists of candidates for election to the board of directors. The same applies to elections to the board of statutory auditors according to article 148 CLF, under which, moreover, the board chair must be selected from the statutory auditors elected from the minority slate. Mandatory slate voting was first introduced in 1998, although it was limited to statutory auditor board elections.[111] In 2005, in the wake of the Parmalat financial scandal,[112] slate voting was extended to board of director elections as well.[113]

Minority shareholders willing to submit a slate of director nominees and ready to bear the (non-negligible) costs associated are thus offered a way of gaining access to the boardroom and direct insight into the company's affairs. Arguably, cost considerations provide a partial explanation for the crucial role that Assogestioni – which represents most of the Italian and foreign asset managers operating in Italy – has played in the process of selecting director nominees and submitting minority slates since the introduction of slate voting. If one considers that, under the Italian Stewardship Principles, '[t]he presentation of candidates for election as independent minority members of boards of investee companies, also through the [Assogestioni's] Investment Managers' Committee, represents a continuous and constructive method of engaging with investee companies',[114] submitting slates of director nominees has indeed become an increasingly significant tool for exercising active investor ownership. Moreover, slate voting, combined with the proactive role played by Assogestioni as an enabling entity, has proved to be a fundamental lever by which to support (non-activist) institutional investors' collective action as a viable, cost-effective pathway for engaging investee companies.

Assogestioni does not promote shareholder collaboration loosely, but provides institutionalized support for collective engagement by leveraging the national regulatory framework for corporate elections at listed companies. Based on a formalized procedure, the Investment Managers' Committee is in charge of selecting candidates with the assistance of independent advisors appointed by the Assogestioni's Corporate Governance Committee. Independent advisors play a key role in the candidate selection process, as they are in charge of maintaining

108 See art. 147-ter (3) CLF (under which 'the member elected from the minority slate must satisfy the integrity, experience and independence requirements established pursuant to Articles 148(3) and 148(4). Failure to satisfy the requirements shall result in disqualification from the position'). See, generally, Gian Giacomo Peruzzo, Marta Roberti and Guido Ferrarini, 'Corporate Boards in Italy' in Paul Davies et al. (eds.), *Corporate Boards in Law and Practice* (OUP 2013) 367, 392–3.

109 Art. 144(6) of Consob Regulation no. 11971 clearly states that 'A shareholder may not submit or vote for more than one list, including through nominees or trust companies. Shareholders belonging to the same group and shareholders participating in a shareholder agreement involving the shares of the issuer may not submit or vote for more than one list, including through nominees or trust companies. A candidate may only be present in one list, under penalty of ineligibility'. See Belcredi and Enriques (n. 56) 8–9; Massimo Belcredi, Stefano Bozzi and Carmine Di Noia, 'Board Elections and Shareholder Activism: The Italian Experiment' in Massimo Belcredi and Guido Ferrarini (eds.), *Boards and Shareholders in European Listed Companies: Facts, Context and Post-Crisis Reforms* (OUP 2013) 378–83.

110 See art. 144-quater of Consob Regulation no. 11971. The minimum threshold set by Consob varies depending on the company's capitalization. Shareholders are not however prevented from setting a lower shareholding threshold in the company's articles of association.

111 See Belcredi, Bozzi and Di Noia (n. 109) 367.

112 For a comprehensive analysis of the Parmalat scandal see Guido Ferrarini and Paolo Giudici, 'Financial Scandals and the Role of Private Enforcement: The Parmalat Case' in John Armour and Joseph A. McCahery (eds.), *After Enron* (Hart Publishing, 2006), 159.

113 Ibid.

114 Assogestioni (n. 19) 17.

a database of possible candidates and submitting a shortlist of those who appear to best meet the requirements of each corporate office to the Investment Managers' Committee.[115] To prevent potential conflicts of interest and ensure the independence of candidates included in the minority slate, director nominees are selected by the Investment Managers' Committee from amongst those selected by independent advisors in keeping with the 'Principles for the Selection of Candidates for Corporate Bodies of Listed Companies' drawn up by the Assogestioni Corporate Governance Committee.[116]

Further still, candidates must have adequate professionalism, integrity and independence.[117] To avoid possible conflicts of interest, the legal representatives of investment management companies and – unless at least one year has elapsed since the relevant appointments were relinquished – anyone who has served in a senior management or executive role at an investment management company may not be selected as a candidate.[118] In addition, to ensure that candidates are independent vis-à-vis the company for which they are nominated, 'members of governing or supervisory bodies and senior managers of institutions and companies that have significant business ties with the company for which they are nominated may be selected as candidates provided that at least one year has elapsed since the end of these appointments'.[119]

If elected, candidates are required not to accept any senior management position or corporate appointment at the company or at any company belonging to the same corporate group for at least one year after the end of their term, unless they are nominated once again as candidates by the Investment Managers' Committee.[120]

Since its adoption, slate voting has been conceived of as a lever to secure minority board representation and subsidize active shareholder monitoring.[121] However, chiefly on account of the ownership structure of Italian listed companies, such a system for board elections sometimes leads to unexpected – and to some extent counterintuitive – situations. For example, at so-called de facto controlled companies, where controllers hold less than 50 per cent of the voting rights, institutional investors may collectively own the majority of votes or, at any rate, a proportion of votes larger than that of the controlling stockholders.[122] Hence, it is increasingly the case – especially at larger corporations where de facto controllers hold a relatively small stake – that the list submitted by institutional investors under the coordination of Assogestioni actually receives more votes than that submitted by the (de facto) controlling shareholders, and sometimes even an absolute majority of votes.[123] If one considers that, based on the engagement strategy adopted by Assogestioni, affiliated institutions present only shortlists of director nominees to avoid taking control of the company by electing the majority of the board,[124] if minority-submitted lists receive the majority of the votes cast, then a majority of shareholders ends up appointing

[115] Ibid., 25–6.

[116] Such a committee is composed of members of Assogestioni's board and representatives of member companies. See Assogestioni, 'Protocol of Duties and Responsibilities of the Corporate Governance Committee and the Investment Managers' Committee' (2017) 20–1 www.assogestioni.it/index.cfm/3,139,12309/protfunzccg_cge_dic_2017.pdf accessed 26 March 2020.

[117] Ibid., 26.

[118] Ibid., 28–9.

[119] Ibid., 27.

[120] Ibid., 28.

[121] See Strampelli (n. 94) 135–6.

[122] OECD, 'Capital Market Review of Italy 2018: Mapping Report' (2018) 53–4 www.oecd.org/corporate/OECD-Capital-Market-Review-Italy-Mapping-Report-2018.pdf accessed 26 March 2020.

[123] Mario Stella Richter Jr and Federico Ferdinandi, 'The Evolving Role of the Board: Board Nomination and the Management of Dissenting Opinions' (2018) 4 *Italian Law Journal* 611, 613.

[124] See Assogestioni (n. 116) 23.

a minority of the directors, whilst a minority (the de facto controlling shareholder) appoints the majority. Paradoxical as it may appear, such an outcome is in line with the approach to investor stewardship adopted by the Italian Stewardship Principles, according to which the appointment of some independent directors 'serve[s] [only] as a method of monitoring'.[125] Consistent with that approach, the engagement promoted by Assogestioni is aimed primarily at minimizing 'the agency costs arising from the presence of a controlling shareholder by sharing management decisions, and thus by exercising closer monitoring',[126] not – in contrast to the usual approach of hedge funds – at influencing firms' strategic and financial decision-making by replacing management.[127]

17.3.4.2 Shareholder Identification As a Tool for Collective Shareholder Initiatives

Article 83-duodecies CLF, last amended in 2019 to transpose SRD II, explicitly conceives of shareholder identification as a means by which to 'facilitate issuers' communication with shareholders as well as the exercise of shareholder rights, *including in a coordinated manner*'.[128]

Issuers are entitled to require intermediaries along the investment chain to identify shareholders (limited to those holding more than 0.5 per cent of voting rights), although the costs associated with the identification process are borne by the issuer (see article 83-duodecies (1)). Importantly, article 83-duodecies (3) CLF imposes an obligation on the company to initiate the identification process upon the request of minority shareholders, with the minimum threshold required for shareholders to make such a request being the same as that for submitting a slate of director nominees under article 147-ter CLF. Hence, the threshold that shareholders are required to meet to initiate the process varies from 0.5–4.5 per cent of share capital depending on the size of the company and its ownership structure. If the process is initiated upon shareholder request, the costs are shared between the issuer and the requesting shareholders based on criteria set by Consob to align shareholder requests with the aim of facilitating shareholder coordination.[129] In any case, data concerning shareholder identification are made available to shareholders 'on a commonly-used electronic storage device free of charge' (see article 83-duodecies (4) CLF), irrespective of whether the process was initiated by the issuers or shareholders.

It should be apparent that, alongside the rules on the top-down and bottom-up transmission of information relevant to the exercise of shareholder rights along the investment chain (see article 83-novies (1)(g-bis), article 82 (4-bis) CLF and implementing regulations), shareholder identification is intended to support the exercise of shareholder rights as a policy goal. Shareholder identification encourages engagement between a company's investor relations department and its shareholders, as it can improve communication with the shareholder base and allows the company to develop more targeted communication programmes. Further, the right granted to minority shareholders to activate the identification process promotes active shareholder

125 Assogestioni (n. 19) 16.

126 Matteo Erede, 'Governing Corporations with Concentrated Ownership Structure: An Empirical Analysis of Hedge Fund Activism in Italy and Germany, and its Evolution' (2013) 10 *ECFR* 328, 371.

127 Ibid., 370.

128 See art. 83-duodecies (1) CLF (emphasis added).

129 See art. 133-bis of Consob regulation no. 11971 (providing that cost allocation be regulated by each issuer in the articles of association; if the articles of association fail to do so, the costs of shareholder identification will be borne entirely by the issuer. However, if the shareholders make a request for shareholder identification in the six months following the end of the fiscal year, and in any case prior to the annual general meeting, and no identification request is made directly by the issuer in the same period of time, the company will fully incur the costs for disclosure of the shareholder identification data and the number of shares registered on the securities accounts).

ownership because it favours non-activist institutional investor collective action, whether through voting, convening a general meeting, putting a new item on a meeting's agenda, or asking questions or simply by facilitating the sharing of views on agenda items, corporate action and governance or gauging preferences (e.g. on an important and uncertain vote or challenging the board or controlling shareholders).

17.4 THE PRACTICE OF SHAREHOLDER VOTING AND ENGAGEMENT IN ITALY

This section briefly follows up on the foregoing analysis by reporting evidence on the practice of shareholder voting and engagement in Italy. We focus on say-on-pay and director elections through slate voting, as these tools have been proven to catalyze institutional investors' preferences in the Italian context.

17.4.1 *Say-on-Pay Votes*

Alongside enhanced attendance rates at shareholder meetings,[130] increased institutional investor engagement with companies publicly listed in Italy can be clearly inferred from data on say-on-pay votes since the initial application of article 123-ter (6) CLF in 2012, whose outcomes seem in line with those characterizing other EU member states: on the whole, 'for' votes prevail over 'against' and withheld votes, with most investors tending to side with directors.[131] Still, 'against' votes are all but irrelevant, particularly if ownership concentration is accounted for.[132]

With respect to the early application of say-on-pay, if major stakeholder votes are left aside, consensus on remuneration at larger issuers averaged 57 per cent in 2012 and 67 per cent in 2013. Interestingly, 'against' votes nonetheless accounted for more than 50 per cent in ten of the 32 FTSE-MIB companies in 2013, chiefly as a consequence of foreign institutional investor votes.[133] In fact, in the early years of say-on-pay's application, increased attendance by foreign institutions at shareholder meetings has been found to positively correlate with both the size of investee firms and higher rates of dissenting votes, with these institutions also seeming to drive the votes of domestic institutions.[134] Hence, institutional investor scrutiny appears to be stronger at larger firms.[135] The fact that dissent over remuneration policies is negatively correlated with ownership concentration, in turn, can generally be explained by the closer monitoring performed by controlling shareholders.[136] Majorities of against votes are found to occur in particular circumstances and within complex contexts, typically in situations in which the firm is facing financial distress, suits are brought against corporate directors or all directors resign in the context of a control contest.[137] The highest dissent rates are typically associated with unsatisfactory information in the remuneration policy proposed by the board, exceedingly generous compensation levels, especially in regard to CEO severance contracts, or performance-based vesting conditions in equity grants.[138]

130 See Section 17.2 of this chapter.

131 See Georgeson et al., 'FTSE MIB Proxy Season 2013' (2013) 34–41 https://archivioceradi.luiss.it/files/2011/10/FTSE-MIB-2013-Evoluzione-degli-assetti-proprietari-ed-attivismo-delle-minoranze.pdf accessed 26 March 2020.

132 See Belcredi and Enriques (n. 56) 18–19.

133 See Georgeson et al. (n. 131) 35.

134 See Belcredi and others (n. 86) 28–9 (according to whom non-national institutions perform a dissent-aggregation function vis-à-vis domestic investors).

135 Ibid., 25, 26, 28.

136 Ibid., 27–8.

137 Ibid., 22.

138 Ibid., 27.

TABLE 17.8 *Shareholders' say-on-pay at the 100 largest Italian listed companies*

		Institutional Investors			Other Shareholders		
		Share/ Total Capital	Share/ Capital Attending	Share/ Institutional Investors Votes	Share/ Total Capital	Share/ Capital Attending	Share/Other Shareholders Votes
2012	against	3.4%	5.2%	29.6%	0.6%	0.9%	1.1%
	abstention	0.3%	0.5%	2.6%	0.4%	0.5%	0.6%
2013	against	3.6%	5.3%	28.2%	0.1%	0.2%	0.2%
	abstention	0.2%	0.4%	1.4%	0.1%	0.1%	0.2%
2014	against	4.0%	5.8%	30.8%	0.6%	0.8%	1.4%
	abstention	0.2%	0.4%	1.4%	0.1%	0.1%	0.2%
2015	against	5.1%	7.2%	33.8%	0.2%	0.3%	0.4%
	abstention	0.5%	0.8%	2.6%	0.2%	0.3%	0.5%
2016	against	5.5%	7.8%	30.3%	0.3%	0.4%	0.5%
	abstention	0.6%	0.8%	3.1%	1.0%	1.2%	2.3%
2017	against	5.9%	8.2%	32.8%	0.1%	0.1%	0.2%
	abstention	0.3%	0.6%	1.6%	0.5%	0.7%	1.8%
2018	against	7.2%	9.8%	38.7%	0.0%	0.1%	1.1%
	abstention	0.5%	0.8%	2.3%	0.2%	0.4%	0.5%
2019	against	7.2%	10.1%	41.7%	0.0%	0.0%	0.1%
	abstention	0.5%	0.7%	2.2%	0.3%	0.4%	1.9%

Data: Consob, 2019 Report on Corporate Governance of Italian Listed Companies.

During the 2014–2019 period, against and withheld say-on-pay votes by institutional investors progressively – save for 2016 – increased to about 10 per cent of share capital and 42 per cent of the total number of shares held.[139]

The relative average say-on-pay consensus in Italy has been interpreted not as a measure of institutional investors' lack of awareness and conformity of opinion, but rather as a confirmation of the efficacy of say-on-pay as a lever by which to promote higher levels of transparency concerning remuneration policies, as well as a signal of enhanced transparency[140] achieved as a response to increased shareholder oversight.[141]

Interestingly, proxy advisors have been found to exert a remarkable impact on the outcome of say-on-pay proposals, with a strong correlation between negative proxy advisor recommendations and lower vote results[142]: in the 2019 proxy season, for instance, 'in the FTSE MIB, the five

[139] Consob (n. 17) 35.

[140] See Frontis Governance, 'Studio sulle remunerazioni 2012 nelle società quotate italiane. Abstract' ['A Study on 2012 Remunerations at Publicly Listed Companies in Italy'] 6 www.frontisgovernance.com/attachments/article/315/Studio%20Remunerazioni%202012%20-%20Abstract.pdf accessed 26 March 2020.

[141] See, for a similar view referring to the UK, Fabrizio Ferri and David A. Maber, 'Say on Pay Votes and CEO Compensation: Evidence from the UK' (2013) 17 *Review of Finance* 527, 530.

[142] Massimo Belcredi et al., 'Proxy Advisors and Shareholder Engagement. Evidence from Italian Say-on-Pay' Consob Working Papers No. 81 (2015) 30 www.consob.it/documents/46180/46181/wp81.pdf/2e3c4c91-4b20-4471-8f8a-7dc5ce90506f accessed 15 July 2020 (further illustrating that '[t]he influence of PA [proxy advisor] recommendations is . . . higher on non-blockholders (mostly internationally diversified pension and mutual funds), while institutional blockholders, having a stronger incentive to perform their own research, appear to be less sensitive to PA recommendations', and noting that 'the effect of PAs on institutional investors' voting in Italy is at least as strong as (and probably stronger than) that observed in the US', which is consistent with the weight of non-domestic institutions and with the features of listed companies in terms of small/medium cap firms on a comparative basis. More

remuneration reports with the lowest level of support all received a negative recommendation from the majority of the [most significant] proxy advisors'.[143] Indeed, at FTSE-MIB companies (those most covered by proxy advisors' voting recommendations), the rate of against say-on-pay votes is higher both overall and for institutional investors.

Furthermore, the previously non-binding nature of say-on-pay votes seems not to have reduced investors' oversight incentive. Rather, precatory say-on-pay, even if achieving well below a majority vote, seems to exert a disciplinary effect on the remuneration committees within boards of directors, given that shareholder resolutions adopted with relatively high numbers of dissenting and withheld votes signal a lack of trust in directors and expose the

TABLE 17.9 *Dissent votes (including abstentions) in percentage of total votes (including abstentions) at FTSE-MIB companies*

	Total Dissent (%)[144]		Institutional Investors: Dissent/ Total Votes (%)[145]		Institutional Investors: Dissent/Total Votes by Investor (%)[146]	
	Mean	Max	Mean	Max	Mean	Max
2015	9.4	38.1	9.0	38.1	25.8	83.1
2016	8.7	39.4	9.0	39.4	27.0	82.4
2017	11.5	43.7	11.3	39.6	32.4	96.3
2018	12.3	32.6	12.1	30.8	36.8	100.0
2019	13.4	56.2	12.0	32.4	36.5	96.5

Data: Consob, 2019 Report on Corporate Governance of Italian Listed Companies.

generally, the notion according to which proxy advisors wield influence on voting outcomes is widespread in Europe, and, in Italy as in other EU countries, the risks associated with institutions' overreliance on proxy advisors' recommendations are exacerbated by concerns about the industry, which can be summarized into three main and often mutually interacting categories: the fact that the market for proxy advisory services is largely uncompetitive, with the two leading firms virtually exclusively dominating the business and no other firm having a market share significant enough to be considered a serious competitor; conflict-of-interests issues; and shortfalls associated with the methodologies used for proxy analysis, as well as the fundamental lack of transparency surrounding conflicts of interests and the methodologies employed for proxy analysis. See, generally, EC, 'Green Paper – The EU Corporate Governance Framework' (2011), 14 (COM (2011) 164 final); ibid., 'Proposal for a Directive of the European Parliament and the Council amending Directive 2007/36/EC as regards the encouragement of long-term shareholder engagement and Directive 2013/34/EU as regards certain elements of the corporate governance statement' (2014), 3 (COM (2014) 0213 final, (2014) 0121 (COD)) 5; ESMA, 'Discussion Paper. An overview of the Proxy Advisory Industry. Considerations on Possible Policy Options' (2012), 17 and No. 66 (ESMA/2012/212); ibid., 'Final report. Feedback statement on the consultation regarding the role of the proxy advisory industry' (2013), 12 (ESMA 2013/84). See also Gaia Balp, 'Regulating Proxy Advisors through Transparency: Pros and Cons of the EU Approach' [2017] 14 ECFR 1–36. As regards the transposition of article 3j SRD II concerning proxy advisors' disclosures, legislation enacted in Italy (art. 124-octies CLF introduced by Legislative Decree No. 49 of 10 May 2019) features no remarkable deviation from the text of the directive. This copy-out approach to implementing SRD II was actually adopted by many other member states, which chose to not further detail, or add to, the relevant EU provisions.

143 Georgeson, 'Georgeson's 2019 Proxy Season Review' (2019) 97 www.georgeson.com/it/2019-season-review accessed 26 March 2020.

144 Dissenting votes (including abstentions) as a percentage of total votes.

145 Institutional investors' dissenting votes (including abstentions) as a percentage of total votes.

146 Institutional investors' dissenting votes (including abstentions) as a percentage of total votes by institutional investors.

board to adverse reputational effects.[147] Therefore, say-on-pay can also serve to support fruitful shareholder-director dialogue as a form of engagement, in quite the same way as so-called withhold – or vote-no – campaigns have been proven to do in the United States.[148] It remains to be seen whether, and if so how, the transition towards binding say-on-pay votes will change investor attitudes towards investee companies' compensation practices.[149] It should be noted that binding say-on-pay votes were already in place at publicly listed banks and insurance companies, where lower levels of dissent were observed as compared with those featured by other companies subject to non-binding say-on-pay. Such comparatively lower levels of dissent associated with binding say-on-pay have been regarded as indicative of more responsible shareholder voting.[150]

17.4.2 *Slate Voting*

Beyond say-on-pay, director elections have become the main target of institutional investors, both domestic and foreign, at Italian listed companies.[151] This is chiefly a consequence of the enactment of slate voting, on the one hand, and the record date regime for shareholder voting on the other. Crucially, director elections at publicly listed companies feature the substantive convergence of foreign and domestic institutional investor votes on the slates submitted by Italian asset managers through Assogestioni, with institutional investors' votes often coming quite close to the votes cast by the major stakeholders in the company.

Although slate voting was introduced earlier,[152] until 2010 institutional investors were able to appoint corporate board members in only a small group of listed companies,[153] and Italian institutions tended to concentrate their submission of director nominee slates on a limited number of major issuers featuring better relative performance and better corporate governance, as well as on longer-term investee companies. Since the introduction of the record date system in 2010,[154] however, there has been a significant rise in voting by institutional investors, with growing numbers of directors and statutory auditors being elected by such investors.[155] Moreover, several bylaws, especially at larger corporations, have made room for two or three minority-appointed directors, although the average is approximately two.[156] Currently, the boards of 100 – out of 232 – listed companies include at least one minority-appointed director.[157] Minority-appointed directors represent, on average, 17 per cent of the members of

147 See Guido Ferrarini, Niamh Moloney and Maria Cristina Ungureanu, 'Understanding Directors' Pay in Europe: A Comparative and Empirical Analysis' (2009) 17-18 EGCI Law Working Paper no. 126/2009, 14–15 https://papers.ssrn.com/sol3/papers.cfm?abstract_id=1418463 accessed 26 March 2020.

148 See Ferri and Maber (n. 141) 531.

149 Based on art. 7(2)(b) of Legislative Decree no. 49/2019 (transposing SRD II into national law), the updated version of art. 123-ter CLF, which includes binding say-on-pay on remuneration policies, was applicable from the 2020 proxy season.

150 See Belcredi and others (n. 86) 32.

151 See Massimo Belcredi and Guido Ferrarini, 'The European Corporate Governance Framework: Issues and Perspectives' (2013) 47 http://ssrn.com/abstract_id2264990 accessed 26 March 2020.

152 See Section 17.3.3.3 of this chapter.

153 Belcredi and Enriques (n. 56) 19–20.

154 See Section 17.3.3.5 of this chapter.

155 Belcredi and Enriques (n. 56) 21.

156 Piergaetano Marchetti, Gianfranco Siciliano and Marco Ventoruzzo, 'Disclosing Directors' (2018) ECGI Working Paper no. 420/2018) 7 https://ssrn.com/abstract=3264763 accessed 26 March 2020.

157 Assonime, 'La Corporate Governance in Italia: Autodisciplina, Remunerazioni e Comply-or-Explain' ['Corporate Governance in Italy: Soft Law, Remunerations and Comply-or-Explain'] (2019) 37 www.assonime.it/attivita-editoriale/studi/Pagine/note-e-studi-1-2019.aspx accessed 26 March 2020; Consob (n. 17) 17.

TABLE 17.10 *Director elections (FTSE-MIB, mid-cap and small-cap companies)*

	Slates Submitted (No)	Directors Elected (No)	Average Stake Held by Submitting Shareholders		Average 'For' Votes Received		Average Votes Received/Share Capital	
			Mean	Median	Mean	Median	Mean	Median
2015	18	29	2.79%	2.87%	25.87%	21.43%	17.73%	15.21%
2016	21	35	2.22%	1.77%	27.62%	21.76%	16.33%	15.07%
2017	23	50	2.13%	1.86%	33.85%	29.70%	23.29%	22.36%
2018	44	58	3.13%	2.60%	26.14%	23.08%	17.04%	15.73%
2019	30	45	3.05%	2.21%	29.92%	23.21%	21.58%	19.12%
2020	38	66	3.37%	2.81%	27.34%	21.70%	18.08%	17.00%
Total	174	283						

Source: Assogestioni – Comitato dei Gestori, Stagioni Assembleari 2015–2016–2017–2018–2019–2020.

the boards on which they are present.[158] The boards of statutory auditors at 112 listed companies include at least one minority-appointed member.[159]

As mentioned above, owing to the enabling role played by Assogestioni in the process of selecting director nominees, a significant proportion of minority-elected directors are chosen from the lists coordinated by the association. Since 2015, the slates submitted by Assogestioni have garnered the support of a wide range of Italian and foreign institutional investors, accounting, on average, for around 20 per cent of share capital. For example, in 2020, 76 slates of director nominees were submitted to the vote by minority institutions, appointing 101 candidates at 50 listed companies.[160] It should be noted that, although the shareholdings of the Italian institutional investors who formally submit the lists do not exceed, on average, 3.5 per cent of the votes cast, the lists promoted by Assogestioni are able to catalyze the votes of a sizeable number of Italian and foreign institutional investors, meaning that minority slates frequently end up receiving more than 30 per cent –and sometimes as much as 50 per cent – of the votes cast.[161] Given the decreasing weight of Italian mutual funds in the Italian stock market, the support of foreign institutional investors is proving to be essential.

17.5 CONCLUDING REMARKS

Despite the high levels of concentrated ownership of publicly listed companies in Italy, institutional investors have become prominent players on the Italian corporate governance scene. Various factors, both economic and regulatory, have contributed to bringing about such an outcome. First, corporate ownership and voting are increasingly institutionalized throughout the EU, and Italy is no exception. Second, corporate ownership of Italian listed companies has become increasingly international in recent decades. Third, in a context dominated by the principal-principal agency problem, regulatory action taken over time has been strongly focused on empowering minority shareholders, whether by

158 Consob (n. 17) 17.

159 Ibid.

160 Assogestioni, 'Stagione Assembleare 2020' ['2020 Proxy Season Review'] (2020) 10 www.comitatogestori.it/sites/comitatogestori.it/files/docs/report_stagione_assembleare_2020_10072020_0.pdf accessed 30 July 2020.

161 Assogestioni, 'Stagione Assembleare 2019' [2019 Proxy Season Review] (2019) 10 www.comitatogestori.it/sites/comitatogestori.it/files/docs/stagione-assembleare-2019.pdf accessed 26 March 2020.

TABLE 17.11 *Statutory auditor elections (FTSE-MIB, mid-cap and small-cap companies)*

	Slates Submitted (No)	Statutory Auditors Elected (No)	Average Stake Held by Submitting Shareholders		Average 'For' Votes Received		Average Votes Received/Share Capital	
			Mean	Median	Mean	Median	Mean	Median
2015	21	24	2.06%	3.50%	25.33%	15.71%	17.79%	11.44%
2016	23	24	1.97%	1.66%	21.44%	18.62%	15.14%	14.68%
2017	28	28	1.96%	1.57%	26.13%	18.68%	16.37%	14.30%
2018	39	41	3.07%	2.83%	21.37%	18.27%	15.62%	14.46%
2019	33	31	3.29%	2.65%	25.31%	21.38%	16.65%	14.99%
2020	38	35	3.08%	2.47%	19.05%	14.73%	13.75%	9.95%
Total	**182**	**183**						

Source: Assogestioni – Comitato dei Gestori, Stagioni Assembleari 2015–2016–2017–2018–2019–2020.

enhancing their rights or facilitating their ability and willingness to exercise those rights. Moreover, the regulation of intermediaries has focused on institutional investors and asset managers as owners and enhanced their oversight role, particularly with respect to voting obligations. Coupled with the support provided by self-regulation, particularly the Italian Stewardship Principles, these factors have driven institutional investors to become more active owners and more engaged stewards at Italian listed companies.

Say-on-pay votes, enhanced shareholder oversight of RPTs and slate voting for director elections, alongside the pivotal effect of the record date regime on boosting institutional participation in shareholders meetings, have proved particularly successful in boosting institutional investor engagement with Italian listed companies. These three mechanisms appear to exert complementary effects on shareholder engagement in Italy. First, say-on-pay is conducive to greater minority representation on boards of directors, thereby fostering institutional investor stewardship. In fact, the presence of minority-elected directors on a board's remuneration committee is positively correlated with greater institutional investor participation in shareholder meetings, and greater transparency concerning remuneration policies has frequently been the result of relatively high percentages of dissenting and withheld say-on-pay votes. Second, minority board representation secured through slate voting improves self-dealing oversight because the ex-ante independent scrutiny of RPTs is required. Moreover, at Italian listed companies, the presence of minority-elected directors has been shown to exert a positive impact on the adequacy of internal procedures for addressing such transactions.

Finally, the Italian experience of director elections through slate voting suggests that coordinated engagement by institutional investors can have a positive impact on investee companies. The Italian Stewardship Principles emphasize the importance of collective engagement, and Assogestioni has greatly contributed to developing a pathway towards collective engagement that leverages slate voting to catalyze investors' stewardship efforts. By redistributing engagement-associated costs amongst affiliated investors, Assogestioni promotes shareholder collaboration within a formalized framework for the selection of candidates and submission of shortlists of director nominees as a tool for shareholder monitoring. In fact, slate voting, subsidized by the proactive role played by Assogestioni as an enabling entity and combined with the incentivizing effect of the record date system, has become a fundamental lever by which to support collective action by mainstream institutional investors as a viable, cost-effective pathway for engaging and monitoring investee companies in Italy. An ever-growing number of directors and statutory auditors are now elected by institutional investors.

18

Shareholder Voting and Engagement in Norway

Berte-Elen Konow

18.1 GENERAL ACCOUNT OF NORWAY'S CORPORATE LAW AND CORPORATE GOVERNANCE

18.1.1 *Norwegian Company Law and Governance Framework at a Glance*

In Norway, there are two statutes covering companies with limited liability: the Norwegian Private Limited Liability Companies Act and the Norwegian Public Limited Liability Companies Act.[1] Both Acts date from 1997 and were drafted in parallel. Hence, the preparatory work for the two Acts can be found in the same documents.[2]

Before 1997, the limited liability companies were governed by the Limited Liability Companies Act from 1976. This Act was a result of Nordic legal cooperation. A report from 1970 written by experts in company law from all of the Nordic countries resulted in basically identical legislation regarding companies with limited liability in Denmark, Finland, Iceland, Norway and Sweden.[3] In Norway, the 1976 Act was amended in 1995 to comply with EU law, but in 1997 it was decided to have two separate Acts governing the two types of limited liability companies. At an early stage of the preparation of the 1997 Acts, there was cooperation between law preparation committees in Norway, Sweden, and Finland. As a result of the legislative cooperation between the Nordic countries over many years, it has become common to speak of a 'Nordic Corporate Governance Model'.[4]

The Acts have been amended several times since their enactment. Many of the changes have been made by reference to EU law in order to meet Norway's obligations under the EEA Agreement.[5] For example, the Shareholder Rights Directive II was implemented in Norwegian

[1] Act of 13 June 1997 No. 44: The Norwegian Private Limited Liability Companies Act and Act of 13 June 1997 No. 45: The Norwegian Public Limited Liability Companies Act 45. The Acts are translated into English by the law firm Schjødt AS, and Schjødt AS holds the copyright to the translations. Translations of the Public Limited Companies Act together with some other relevant Acts and regulation regarding stock exchange and trading in securities are available online, www.euronext.com/en/markets/oslo, accessed 15 July 2020.

[2] The most important preparatory works are NOU 1996:3 Ny aksjelovgivning and Ot.prp. nr. 23 (1996–1997) Om lov om aksjeselskaper (aksjeloven) og lov om allmennaksjeselskaper (allmennaksjeselskapsloven) and Innst. O. 80 (1996–1997), but Ot. prp. nr. 36 (1993–1994) and Innst. O. 45 (1994–1995) must also be mentioned in order to get the full picture of why Norway got two acts for limited liability companies. There are of course also preparatory works for later amendments of the acts.

[3] NUT 1970:1 Innstilling til lov om aksjeselskap.

[4] As for literature in English on similarities and differences between the legislative basis of corporate governance in the Nordic countries relevant for this Shareholder engagement and voting project, Per Lekvall (ed.), *The Nordic Corporate Governance Model* (SNS FÖRLAG 2014) can be mentioned.

[5] Agreement on the European Economic Area from May 1992 between EU and (now) Norway, Iceland and Lichtenstein including these EFTA states in the Internal Market. Entered into force 1 January 1994. EEA relevant EU acts are continuously incorporated into the EEA Agreement.

law in December 2019, requiring amendments not only to the ASA Act (Norwegian Public Limited Liability Companies Act), but also to several other relevant acts.[6] To date, only some of the provisions have entered into force, such as the provisions on the renumeration of directors.

Many of the provisions in the ASA Act and the AS Act are similar, and the structure of the two Acts are also basically the same. There are, however, some major differences. A Public Limited Liability Company is required to have a share capital of minimum NOK 1,000,000, whereas the minimum share capital for ordinary Private Limited Liability Companies is NOK 30,000.[7] Public Limited liability Companies must also meet stricter reporting requirements.

In addition to the Public Limited Liability Companies Act, listed companies must also act in compliance with several other statutes (with additional regulations), for example the Business Enterprise Registration Act, the Stock Exchange Act, the Securities Trading Act and the Accounting Act.[8] Listed companies must also comply with the Stock Exchange's Issuer Rules. In addition, Oslo Børs gives Notices and other documentation supplementing the Issuers Rule Books.[9] The Oslo Stock Exchange requires its listed companies to comply with the Norwegian Code of Practice for Corporate Governance.[10] The Norwegian Code of Practice for Corporate Governance applies the principle of 'comply or explain'. If companies deviate from any of the principles, they need to explain why and propose alternative solutions. The Accounting Act also requires companies to report on their corporate governance principles and practice.[11]

Due to the Covid-19 pandemic, a temporary Act was passed by the Norwegian parliament.[12] According to § 2–3 of this temporary Act, the board may decide that the AGM is to be held fully or partly on digital platforms. The board may also decide that shareholders can vote in advance, even if this possibility is not stated in the company's Articles of Association. The temporary Act was repealed 1 June 2021.[13] The provision in the ASA Act governing the conduct of ordinary general meetings, was amended in 2021 so that it now is possible to organize fully digitalized general meetings after the pandemic has recede.[14][15]

18.1.2 *Corporate Decision-Making, the Role of the Board and the Board Structure*

The main corporate bodies in the corporate decision-making processes are:

The general meeting, see ASA Act §§ 5–1 – 5–28
The company assembly, see ASA Act §§ 6–35 – 6–40
The board, see ASA Act §§ 6–1 – 6-11a

6 Directive EU 2017/828 implemented by LOV 2019–12-06–77. Preparatory works: Prop 135L (2018–2019).

7 According to the ASA Act § 3–1 (1) and the AS Act § 3–1 (1).

8 See Act 2003–12-19–120, Act 2007–06-29–74, Act 2007–06-29–75 and Act 1998–07-17–56.

9 Oslo Børs is part of Euronext. Rule Book I is a set of harmonized rules for companies listed at Euronext whereas Oslo Rule Book II – Issuers Rules governs the Stock market of Oslo Børs. See www.oslobors.no/ob_eng/Oslo-Boers/Regulations/The-Issuer-Rules accessed 15 July 2020.

10 The current Norwegian Code of Practice is from 2018, see https://nues.no/wp-content/uploads/2018/10/NUES_eng_web_okt2018_2.pdf accessed 15 July 2020. The Norwegian Code of Practice is issued by the Norwegian Corporate Governance Board (NCGB, or the Norwegian abbreviation NUES. See https://nues.no accessed 15 July 2020.

11 The Accounting Act § 3-3b.

12 LOV-2020–05-26–54 Temporary Act on exceptions from the requirements for physical attendance etc according to legislation for business enterprises. Preparatory work: Prop. 115 L (2019–2020).

13 LOV-2020–10-30–124.

14 § 5-8 of the ASA Act was amended by Lovvedtak 111 (2020-2021)

15 See Section 18.3.1.1 for further details on how voting is done prior to as well as under the intermediate Covid-19 Act.

The CEO, see ASA Act §§ 6–14 and 6–15.
The role of the CEO is explained in Section 18.1.3.

18.1.2.1 The General Meeting

The *general meeting* ranks at the top of the decision-making hierarchy of a limited liability company. The ASA Act § 5–1 (1) states that 'through the general meeting the shareholders exercise the supreme authority in the company'. This 'supreme authority' means that shareholders can instruct and control other corporate bodies, including the board of directors, reverse resolutions and decide on any company matters, provided that no third party right binds the company.[16]

All the shareholders have the right to attend the general assembly, either personally, digitally or by representation (proxy).[17] The annual general meeting (AGM) must be organized at least once a year and must take place within six months from the end of the financial year.

According to the ASA Act § 5–6 (2), the AGM must address and vote on:

(1) Approval of the annual financial statement and the annual report, including the distribution of dividends;
(2) Other issues that according to statutory provisions or the articles of association are to be governed by the general meeting.

In other words, it is up to the general meeting to treat and vote on the board's annual financial statement and report, as well as deciding on the distribution of dividends.[18] The ASA Act § 5–6 (3)–(5) expanded the list of issues to be treated and decided upon at the AGMs of listed companies. A statement of business management is one of these issues.[19]

As a general rule, members of the board are elected by the general meeting.[20] If the ASA company has a corporate assembly, it is the task of this assembly to elect both the chair of the board and board members.[21] For board members elected by employees, special provisions apply.[22]

The board of directors, the corporate assembly or the chairman of the corporate assembly may decide to call for an extraordinary general meeting (EGM). The board is obliged to call for an EGM if the auditor of the company's annual accounts so demands, or if shareholders representing at least 20 per cent of the shares so demand.[23]

18.1.2.2 The Corporate Assembly

A limited liability company with more than 200 employees must establish a *corporate assembly*.[24] However, it does not have to do so if the majority of the employees or the local unions

16 See the ASA Act § 6–33 regarding exceeding authority. See also Gudmund Knudsen and Harald Norvik, 'Corporate Governance in Norway' in Per Lekvall (ed.), *The Nordic Corporate Governance Model* (SNS FÖRLAG 2014) 211.

17 See the ASA Act § 5–8 a as amended in 2009 regarding electronic participation on general meetings. See also Section 18.3.1 on how voting is done in practice.

18 The ASA Act § 5–6 gives a list of matters that must be dealt with by the ordinary annual meeting of the general assembly. For the private limited liability companies, provisions covering the general assembly are also found in chapter 5 of the AS Act. For the AS, there is an option of a simpler procedure of the meeting which can be used if none of the shareholder objects, see the AS Act § 5–7. See also Section 18.3.1.2 on what issues are voted on at the AGM.

19 The ASA § 5–6 (5) referring to the Accounting Act § 3–3b.

20 The ASA Act § 6–3.

21 See the ASA Act § 6–37 (1).

22 The ASA Act § 6–4 or § 6–37 if there is a corporate assembly.

23 See the ASA Act § 5–7.

24 See the ASA Act § 6–35 and the AS Act § 6–35. Special provisions for companies that have a corporate assembly is given in the ASA Act §§ 6–35–6–40 and the AS Act § 6–35.

representing the majority of the employees agree that it need not.[25] In practice, many of the listed companies make use of this exception.[26] If a company chooses not to have a corporate assembly, the competences of the AGM, CEO and the board of directors are given by the ordinary provisions in the ASA or AS Acts.

The main tasks of the corporate assembly are to elect the chair and members of the board of directors, and to supervise the board's and CEO's administration of the company. The corporate assembly considers the annual report and financial statement and addresses a recommendation to the AGM on whether it should approve the board's draft annual financial statement and report. It also considers and gives a recommendation on proposals by the board of directors for the disposal of profit or coverage of losses. The corporate assembly can decide to give recommendations to the board of directors regarding any matter. The corporate assembly may also undertake inspections on its own or through a committee.[27] According to the ASA Act § 6–37 (4), the corporate assembly, at the proposal of the board of directors, decides in matters regarding

(1) investments that are substantial compared to the company's resources, and
(2) such efficiency measures or alteration of the operations as will entail a major change or reallocation of the labour force.

In companies without a corporate assembly, the board has the authority to take decisions regarding substantial investments or efficiency measures and matters of reorganization and major changes in the workforce.[28]

The corporate assembly must consist of a minimum of twelve members, but a higher number may be chosen if it is divisible by three. Within these limits, the AGM of the company decides the appropriate number of members of the corporate assembly. Two-thirds of the corporate assembly are elected by the AGM, and the remaining third is elected by and amongst the employees.[29]

18.1.2.3 The Board of Directors

Every limited liability company must have a board. For SMEs, those companies governed by the AS Act, the board may consist of only one member. For listed companies, the Public limited liability companies governed by the ASA Act, the minimum size of the board is three members. Companies with more than 200 employees and having a corporate assembly must have a board with a minimum of five board members.[30]

The board's members are elected by the AGM, or by the corporate assembly (in the case of companies which have one).[31] The ASA Act § 6–6 (1) generally requires members to be appointed for two years, but also states that the articles of association may set a shorter term or a longer term (provided that it does not exceed four years). In recent years, it has become more common for listed companies to elect board members for only one year. The same corporate

25 The ASA Act § 6–35 (2) on agreement of not having a corporate assembly.

26 See Knudsen and Norvik (n. 16) 219. See also Gudmund Knudsen and Erik Langseth, 'Norway' in Willem J. L. Calkoen (ed.), *The Corporate Governance Review* (10th ed., The Law Reviews 2020).

27 The tasks of the corporate assembly are governed by the ASA Act § 6–37.

28 This is explicitly stated in the ASA Act § 6–12 (5).

29 See Regulation regarding the employees' right to board representation and representation in corporate assemblies: FOR-2017–08-24–1277.

30 See the ASA Act § 6–1 as compared to the AS Act § 6–1 for the smaller businesses.

31 The ASA Act § 6–3 (the AGM electing board members) and § 6–37 (the corporate assembly electing board members).

body that elected the board member may, at any time and without needing to give a reason, decide to remove the board member. Board members who have been elected by the employees cannot, however, be removed by the AGM.[32]

According to the ASA Act § 6–11, at least half of the number of board members must be domiciled in Norway or in a Member State of the EEA Agreement. The ASA Act § 6-11a also put forth requirements of gender equality when it comes to the composition of the board.[33]

In addition to the requirements in the ASA Act regarding the composition of the board, the Norwegian Code of Practice for Corporate Governance provides further guidelines to ensure that 'the board can attend to the common interests of all shareholders and meets the company's need for expertise, capacity and diversity' and that the board 'operates independently of any special interests'.[34]

The main structure and the task of the board are basically the same for listed and unlisted companies.[35] The board's responsibility is both managerial and supervisory. The managerial responsibility is stated in the ASA Act § 6–12, and the supervisory responsibility is governed by the ASA Act § 6–13. The provisions on company management do not distinguish between executive and non-executive persons in the different positions. In practice, however, board members in Norwegian listed companies are non-executives. The ASA Act § 6–1 (3) explicitly states that the CEO may not be a member of the board. The Norwegian Code of Practice for Corporate Governance clearly advises that the board of directors should not include executive members. In general, Norwegian listed companies elect independent, non-executive board members.[36]

There has been some discussion in the legal literature on whether the board structure under the Nordic corporate governance model can be characterized as a single or dual board model, or if the Nordic countries can be said to have a third version. In Norway, following the 'Nordic board structure', the listed companies have one board. As explained above, the board has both supervisory and managerial powers. The board members are in practice non-executive, and it is regarded as a core value in Norway that board members are independent of the company. The day-to-day executive power lies with the CEO. In addition to its supervisory obligation, the board also has far-reaching managerial powers, as it appoints, but may also remove or instruct, the CEO. However, it is the shareholders, through decisions made at the general meeting, who have the supreme authority in the company. The distinct hierarchy between the general meeting, the board and the CEO and the division of powers between the company bodies are 'trademarks' of the Norwegian as well as the Nordic model.[37]

The board is first and foremost an agent of company interests. While the interest of the company will normally coincide with the interest of the shareholders, the main loyalty of the board members is directed towards the interest of the company.[38]

The company as such may hold a member of the board liable for any damage caused, intentionally or negligently, by a person acting in the capacity of a board member. Board members are, however, not only liable towards the company. Shareholders or 'others', may

[32] See Knudsen and Norvik (n. 16) 220. See also Knudsen and Norvik (n. 16) 221–2 on the use of nominee committees.

[33] See Section 18.1.5.

[34] See also Knudsen and Norvik (n. 16) 220. See Knudsen and Norvik (n. 16) 225–7 on requirements of the board members when it comes to independence. See also Knudsen and Langseth (n. 26).

[35] The company's management is governed by chapter 6 in both the ASA Act and the AS Act.

[36] See s. 8 of the NCCG and Knudsen and Norvik (n. 16) 227. See also Knudsen and Langseth (n. 26).

[37] See the explanation and comparison of the one-tire, the two-tire and the Nordic board structure given in Lekvall (ed.) (n. 4) 59–64.

[38] See ibid. 209, 225. See also Anne Kaurin, Janne Kaada Erichsen and Marius L. Andresen, 'Norway' in Holly J. Gregory (ed.), *Getting the Deal Through – Corporate Governance 2018* (Law Business Research Ltd 2018) www.kvale.no/gtdt-corporate-governance-2018/ accessed 15 July 2020.

also claim damages intentionally or negligently caused by a member of the board. This means that the board members must balance the different interests linked to the company in a prudent and proper manner. The liability of board members is several and not joint. Each individual board member may be responsible for their actions or lack of action.[39] The same liability as for board members lies with the CEO, a member of the corporate assembly, or even another shareholder, cf. ASA Act § 17–1 (1).

18.1.3 *Shareholder versus Board, Managerial Supremacy and Powers of the AGM*

The board is responsible for the management of the company. The board must also ensure a proper organization of the business of the company.[40] In addition, the board has a supervisory role as regards the daily management of the company.[41]

The ordinary daily management of the company's business is the responsibility of the general manager (CEO). The CEO must run the business in compliance with the guidelines and instructions issued by the board of directors.[42] The board is responsible for supervising how the day-to-day management is carried out, and for the development of the company's business in general. The allocation of the managerial power of the CEO in comparison to that of the board can only be understood by reading several of the provisions in Chapter 6 of the ASA Act in relation to each other.

It is up to the board to make basic strategic decisions. The board draws up plans and budgets for the company's business. The board also decides guidelines for the business. In companies where the employees are represented on the board, instructions must be issued which detail the board of directors' activities and procedure. The instructions must specify the matters to be dealt with by the board, and also the functions and duties of the CEO towards the board. The instructions must also contain rules for notices of meetings and proceedings at meetings.[43]

The board must keep itself informed of the company's financial position, and is obliged to ensure that the company's activities, accounts and capital management are subject to adequate control.[44] According to the ASA Act § 6–13 (3), the board has a supervisory authority towards the CEO to make sure that the CEO carries out the daily business in compliance with plans and budget made by the board and the board's instructions on management. The CEO is responsible for assuring that the company's accounts are in accordance with statutory provisions and regulations, and that the capital management is properly organized.[45]

The board may authorize the CEO to take decisions in concrete cases. The CEO can also make decisions on behalf of the company whenever the board's decision cannot be further delayed without major inconvenience to the company. In such cases, the board must be notified about the decision as soon as possible.[46]

[39] See the ASA Act § 17–1 and AS Act § 17–1 on liability. The provision includes a wide range of potential tortfeasors or claimants. But in this context, it is important to illustrate that the board member has an independent duty to take care of the company's interest.

[40] Duties of management of the company are governed by the ASA Act § 6–12 with a parallel provision for private limited liability companies in § 6–12 of the AS Act.

[41] The supervisory responsibility is stated in § 6–13 of the ASA Act with a similar provision in § 6–13 of the AS Act for the smaller companies.

[42] The ASA Act § 6–14 (1).

[43] See § 6–23 of the ASA Act.

[44] The ASA Act § 6–12 (3).

[45] See the ASA Act § 6–14 (4).

[46] The ASA Act § 6–14 (3)–(4).

Shareholders basically exercise their power through decisions made by the AGM.[47] Some issues can only be dealt with at an AGM.[48] For example, the ordinary general meeting must decide on approving the annual financial statement and annual report of the company. It is also up to the AGM to decide whether or not dividends should be paid to shareholders. The board provides a recommendation for an amount to be distributed in dividends, but it is the AGM that approves the payment. The AGM must also deal with any other matter that, according to legislation or according to the articles of association, belongs to the general meeting.[49]

Shareholders have the right to have matters considered at the AGM. The board must be notified of such matters prior to distributing the AGM call to the shareholders. If a shareholder wishes to bring up a matter at the AGM which is not included in the agenda, this will require the consent of all shareholders, including those who have not attended. In order to reach a decision in these cases, all the shareholders must attend the AGM and agree to decide on the matter.[50] It is, therefore, important that shareholders give notice to the board if they wish to add an additional item to the proposed agenda at the AGM so that other shareholders are informed and could prepare themselves.

The shareholders' interests are addressed indirectly in Norwegian company legislation through company organization, and through proposal rights and voting rights. The AGM is a meeting where every shareholder has a right to meet and vote. As previously mentioned, the AGM represents the highest authority of the company. The AGM elects the board members (except for those companies that have a company assembly). The chairman of the board, the CEO, and the chairman of the corporate assembly must attend the general assembly. The members of the board, the CEO and members of the corporate assembly are entitled to meet and to speak at the general assembly. Shareholders' powers by right to call general meetings, and to propose items for inclusion on the agenda are explained in more detail in Section 18.2.

18.1.4 *Ownership Structure in Norway: Facts and Figures*

According to Statistics Norway, there are 590,810 establishments registered in Norway, including all varieties of business entities. Only 845 of the companies have 250 or more employees.[51] 202 companies are listed on Oslo Stock Exchange, including 21 saving banks that have equity certificates instead of shares as their base capital.[52]

The spread in the ownership structure has varied over years, and it also differs between companies. Oslo Stock Exchange publishes an overview of the current shareholder structure in the listed companies on a monthly basis.[53] By the end of September 2020, the ownership structure showed this spread: 27.9 per cent owned by the government/municipalities, 0.87 per cent by private pension funds/life insurance, 7.54 per cent by mutual funds,

47 The ASA Act § 5–1 (1).

48 See Section 18.1.3.2 for an extended list of issues to be voted on at AGMs.

49 The ASA Act § 5–6 (2). A short description in English of the responsibility of the board and the main content of an ordinary general meeting can be found on the website of Altinn, the internet portal for digital dialogue between businesses, private individuals and public agencies in Norway, see www.altinn.no/en/start-and-run-business/running-business/running-a-private-limited-company/holding-of-a-general-meeting-in-a-private-limited-company/ accessed 15 July 2020.

50 The ASA Act § 5–14 (1) and comments to the provision in Ot.prp. nr. 23 (1996–1997).

51 See www.ssb.no/en/virksomheter-foretak-og-regnskap/statistikker/bedrifter accessed 15 July 2020. The numbers were updated 9 January 2020.

52 By 18 March 2021, the total number of securities being traded including the sub-markets Oslo Axess and Merkur Market is 262, see https://live.euronext.com/en/markets/oslo/equities/euronext/list accessed 15 July 2020.

53 See www.oslobors.no/ob_eng/Oslo-Boers/Statistics/Monthly-statistics accessed 15 July 2020.

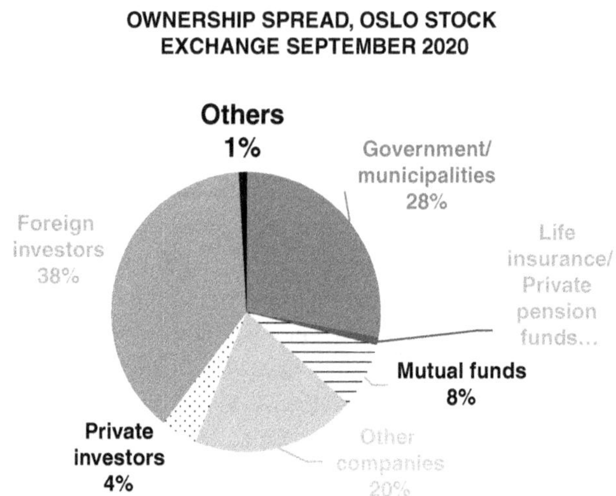

FIGURE 18.1 Ownership structure of Norwegian companies listed on the Oslo Stock Exchange
Source: Oslo Stock Exchange.

19.83 per cent by other companies, 4.36 per cent by private investors and 38.51 per cent by foreign investors.[54]

Statistics show that the number of foreign investors (investors domiciled outside Norway) has varied over the years, but now seems to have been stabilized at just below 40 per cent.[55] The category 'mutual funds' includes fund manager companies in the Norwegian fund and asset management industry.

According to statistics, 12.7 per cent of owners of limited liability companies (AS and ASAs) are private persons.[56] But as the statistics from Oslo Stock Exchange show, only approximately 4 per cent of the shares in the listed companies are owned by private persons. The numbers of private persons owning shares in listed companies has increased during recent years.[57]

The spread of shareholders differs between listed and unlisted companies. Private Limited Liability Companies are often owned by one person or are 'family companies'. Some of the larger AS companies have a wider spread of stockholders, much as do the ASAs.

Although the ASA Act is designed to apply also for companies with a wide spread of shareholders, many listed companies in Norway, as well as in other Nordic countries, have a dominant shareholder.[58] In 2014, 65 per cent of the companies had a shareholder controlling at least 20 per cent of the shares of the company and 23 per cent of the companies had a shareholder controlling more than 50 per cent.[59]

In Norway, the government plays an important role as investor – also dominant investor – in some of the biggest ASA companies in Norway. As the statistics from Oslo Stock Exchange show, governmental ownership accounts for approximately one-third of the shares, but this includes

54 See https://live.euronext.com/resources/statistics accessed 15 July 2020.

55 See www.oslobors.no/ob_eng/Oslo-Boers/Statistics/Annual-statistics accessed 15 July 2020.

56 See Statistics Norway www.ssb.no/virksomheter-foretak-og-regnskap/statistikker/aksjer accessed 15 July 2020.

57 Source: AksjeNorge, see https://aksjenorge.no/wp-content/uploads/2020/01/Statistikk-Årsrapport-2019.pdf accessed 15 July 2020.

58 The ASA Act does not give any preference when it comes to ownership structure, see Knudsen and Norvik (n. 16) 209.

59 Se Lekval (ed.) (n. 4) 24.

also shares owned by municipalities and shares held by the governmental pension fund. According to information supplied on the web page of the Norwegian government, the government has *direct ownership* in seventy-four Norwegian companies.[60] Nine of these companies are public limited liability companies listed on the Oslo Stock Exchange. The percentage of governmental shares in these companies varies from 67.0 per cent (Equinor ASA) to 12.1 per cent (Akastor ASA).

The government's shares in the nine listed companies are:

- Equinor ASA (Energy) 67.0 per cent
- Telenor ASA (telecommunication) 54.0 per cent
- Kongsberggruppen ASA (Technology) 50.0 per cent
- Yara International ASA (Fertilizer) 36.2 per cent
- Norsk Hydro ASA (Aluminium) 34.3 per cent
- DNB ASA (Bank) 34.0 per cent
- Eksportfinans ASA (Export Finance) 15.0 per cent
- Aker Solutions ASA (Energy) 12.2 per cent
- Akastor (Oil services investments) 12.1 per cent

Governmental ownership as shareholder in companies is practised when this is considered to be the best solution to protect the interests of the state. It is the government's policy that private ownership is the basic foundation and main principle for Norwegian industry. Governmental ownership may cause some unclear legal issues such as role overlap, financial liability or exercise of control over the firm's board or management.[61] The government has enunciated ten principles in a code of conduct for how to practice the ownership to create predictability for the company as well as for the capital market. These principles are available online.[62]

Even though the government may have a large ownership ratio, the state is not represented on the boards of companies in which it holds shares. This stands in contrast to those listed companies that have a private dominant owner. These companies will typically have an active owner who sits on the board and may often be its chairman. Even though the state is not represented on the board, it often plays a role in determining the composition of the board of directors.[63]

The government makes an annual report to the Storting (the Norwegian Parliament). The annual report includes information on the number of companies with governmental ownership, the main reason behind governmental ownership in the companies concerned and the objective of having an ownership position in each of the companies.[64]

60 See www.regjeringen.no/en/topics/business-and-industry/state-ownership/hva-staten-eier/id2604524/ accessed 15 July 2020.

61 Tore Bråthen, 'Legal Challenges of State Ownership' in Amir Sasson (ed.), *At the Forefront, Looking Ahead: Research-Based Answers to Contemporary Uncertainty of Management* (Open Access 2018) 119–33 www.idunn.no/doi/pdf/10.18261/9788215031583-2018. See also Jukka T. Mähönen, Beate Sjåfjell and Monica Mee, 'Stewardship Norwegian-Style: Fragmented and State-Dominated (But Not Without Potential?)' (25 June 2020). An edited version of the paper will be published as a chapter in Dionysia Katelouzou and Dan W. Puchniak (eds.), *Global Shareholder Stewardship: Complexities, Challenges and Possibilities* (Cambridge University Press, forthcoming) https://ssrn.com/abstract=3635359 or http://dx.doi.org/10.2139/ssrn.3635359 accessed 15 July 2020.

62 See www.regjeringen.no/en/topics/business-and-industry/state-ownership/statens-ti-prinsipper-for-god-eierstyring/id613433/ accessed 15 July 2020.

63 See Knudsen and Norvik (n. 16) 203, 222.

64 Melding til Stortinget 8 (2019–2020) Report to the Storting (white paper), 'The state's direct ownership of companies – Sustainable value creation'. Also available in English: www.regjeringen.no/contentassets/44ee372146f44a3eb70fc0872a5e395c/en-gb/pdfs/stm201920200008000engpdfs.pdf accessed 15 July 2020.

In addition to direct ownership in business entities, the Norwegian government is a major investor through the Norwegian Government Pension Fund. The Government Pension Fund includes two main divisions: The Government Pension Fund Global (the 'Oil Fund') and the Government Pension Fund Norway (Folketrygdfondet).

The Government Pension Fund Norway invests in the Norwegian and Nordic market. Of the capital, 85 per cent of the capital is invested in Norway, and 15 per cent in the other Nordic countries. The Government Pension Fund Global invests in foreign markets. In 2008, the Folketrygdfondet was transformed into a company by special statute governed by the Ministry of Finance. This marks a clear distinction between the capital (Government Pension Fund Norway) and the manager of the capital (Folketrygdfondet).[65] The Government Pension Fund Global (the Oil Fund) is governed by Norges Bank (the National Bank of Norway).[66]

The Government Pension Fund Norway (Folketrygdfondet) is an important investor in the Norwegian stock market. The mandate of this fund is to achieve the highest possible return after management costs over time, measured in NOK. It is also stated in the mandate that 'A good return in the long term is regarded as being dependent upon sustainable development in economic, environmental and social terms, as well as well-functioning, legitimate and effective markets'.[67] In the annual ownership report, the Folketrygdfondet gives further details on how the mandate is met and how the assets have been managed.

According to the 2020 annual report, the Folketrygdfondet's ownership share at Oslo Stock Exchange amounts to 5.7 per cent which makes it the biggest institutional investor. According to its mandate, the Folketrygdfondet can own maximum 15 per cent of the shares in a Norwegian listed company. The maximum limit for the other Nordic countries is 5 per cent. The Folketrygdfondet is amongst the three largest owners in fifty two of the listed companies in Norway. It is the largest shareholder in five of the listed companies, the second largest shareholder in a further thirty three and the six largest in a further thirteen listed companies.

18.1.5 *Other Country Specific Topics*

18.1.5.1 Employee Representation

There is a relatively long tradition in Norway of having employee representatives at the board of directors. When a company has more than thirty employees, a majority of the employees may demand to have board representation by one board member – that is if the company does not have a corporate assembly. For companies with more than fifty employees, a majority may demand the election of up to one-third of the board's membership, and at least two members of the board.[68] Companies with more than 200 employees ought, according to the ASA Act, to have a corporate assembly with employee representation in the corporate assembly. In practice, however, many of the larger companies make use of provisions giving room for exception from the obligation to have a corporate assembly. There are provisions in place ensuring board representation for employees in case the company does not have a corporate assembly.[69]

65 See www.folketrygdfondet.no/history/category406.html accessed 15 July 2020 on the history and development of The Government Pension Fund Norway (Folketrygdfondet).

66 See www.nbim.no accessed 15 July 2020. See Section 18.1.4 and Section 18.1.5.4 regarding The Government Pension Fund Global.

67 See www.folketrygdfondet.no/mission/category408.html accessed 15 July 2020.

68 See the ASA Act § 6–4 (1) and (2).

69 See the ASA Act § 6–4 (3) and § 6–35.

There is no specific legislation in Norway addressing employees' right to own shares in the company, but these questions may be dealt with in the individual employment agreements.

18.1.5.2 Transparency

Transparency is considered to be an important value in Norwegian society.[70] A *register for business entities* in Norway has been established, with mandatory provisions on information that must be given to this register.[71] Both private and public limited liability companies must have a list or a register of shareholders.[72] As a rule, the company's annual report and annual financial statement are public.[73] There are also mandatory provisions regarding information that must be distributed to shareholders before the AGM.[74]

18.1.5.3 Gender Equality

A notable difference between the ASA and the AS companies is that the ASAs are obliged to meet requirements for *gender equality* when it comes to board members. In 2003, a mandatory provision was introduced in the ASA Act § 6-11a stating that both genders must be represented on the board. The minimum number of individuals of each gender being represented varies according to total number of board members. For the larger companies with nine or more board members, the ASA Act states that each gender must have a board representation of at least 40 per cent. According to recent statistics, the rate of female board members in the Public Limited Liability Companies is currently 41.8 per cent.

There was considerable debate in Norway before the introduction of the mandatory provision on positive discrimination based on gender in ASA boards. Some of the opposing voices claimed that there were not enough qualified women to fill the positions in the ASA boards. A survey published in 2017 concluded that these concerns were exaggerated.[75]

There is no requirement for gender equality in the ordinary private limited companies. According to recent statistics, there is only 19 per cent female representation on the boards of these companies.

Norway is considered to be one of the world's leading exponents of gender equality.[76] Nevertheless, a statistical comparison of the number of men and women acting as CEOs in companies shows that it has quite a long way to go in order to reach gender equality. 83.4 per cent of the CEOs in private limited liability companies are men, and in the public limited liability companies the proportion of male CEOs is as high as 92.3 per cent.[77] As another example of gender bias in the financial sector, only 21 per cent of the value on the Oslo Stock Exchange is owned by women, while 79 per cent is owned by men.[78] The percentage of women investing through the Oslo Stock Exchange is, however, increasing.

70 That transparency is a core value in Nordic corporate governance is also underlined in Lekvall (ed.) (n. 4) 19.

71 See the Busines Enterprise Registration Act (Foretaksregisterlov, LOV-1985–06-21–78), § 3-1a listing which information it is mandatory to register in accordance with a Public Limited Liability Company (ASA company).

72 See the ASA Act § 4–4 and the AS Act § 4–5 (called a shareowner book).

73 See the Act related to annual accounts etc (Regnskapsloven LOV-1998–07-17–56) § 8–1.

74 See the ASA Act § 5–10 and further explanations in Section 18.2.4 below.

75 See Marianne Bertrand and others, 'Breaking the Glass Ceiling? The Effect of Board Quotas on Female Labor Market Outcomes in Norway' (2017) NBER Working Paper Series www.nber.org/papers/w20256 accessed 15 July 2020.

76 See the Global Gender Gap Report 2020 made by the World Economic Forum ranking Norway as number 2 behind Iceland www3.weforum.org/docs/WEF_GGGR_2020.pdf accessed 15 July 2020.

77 See www.ssb.no/en/virksomheter-foretak-og-regnskap/statistikker/styre accessed 15 July 2020.

78 See https://aksjenorge.no/wp-content/uploads/2020/01/Statistikk-Årsrapport-2019.pdf accessed 15 July 2020.

18.1.5.4 Norwegian Investments of Public Assets (the Oil Fund)

Although this report primarily considers shareholder engagement and voting in the reporter's own jurisdiction, a few comments will be made regarding the Norwegian Government Pension Fund Global, popularly known as 'The Oil Fund'.[79] This is one of the world's largest sovereign wealth funds, and it invests in stock exchange listed companies all over the world.

As explained in Section 18.1.4, the Government Pension Fund Norway (Folketrygdfondet) makes investments in the domestic market, while the Norwegian Government Pension Fund Global (the Oil Fund) invests in foreign stock markets. The Oil Fund is managed by the Norwegian National Bank, Norges Bank. The nickname 'Oil Fund' refers to the fact that the income of the Government Pension Fund Global consists of the net cash flow from petroleum activities transferred from the central government budget, net financial transactions relating to petroleum activities and the return on the Fund's investments.[80]

The Norwegian Oil Fund has made investments in seventy-three countries. As one of the largest investors in the world, the Oil Fund holds 1.5 per cent of the shares of all of the world's listed companies. There is transparency when it comes to information on ownerships, as a list of the more than 9,000 companies that the Oil Fund has invested in is available online.[81]

The purpose of the Oil Fund is to help to finance Norway's welfare services for future generations. The Fund is concerned with making responsible investments; the future value of the fund depends upon sustainable growth, well-functioning markets and value creation. Principles for sustainable investments as well as expectations of the companies in which the fund invests in are available online. The Government Pension Fund Global recognizes a set of international principles and standards from both the UN and the OECD, and also participates in the development of international standards for sustainable investments.

As mentioned above, the Oil Fund formulates expectations towards the companies it invests in. Expectation documents address issues such as children's rights, climate change, water management, human rights, tax and transparency, anti-corruption and ocean sustainability. The Fund generally engages in long-term ownership. Guidelines for the fund's voting and positions on governance issues are made public and are available online.[82] An investment in a company by the Oil Fund is widely seen as a vote of confidence in the company's management. It is stated in the voting guidelines that 'the starting point when deciding how to vote is to support the board'.[83] In the annual report for 2020, it is stated that the Government Pension Fund Global owns shares in 9123 companies worldwide. The Fund attended 11,871 general meetings. The Fund voted in line with the board's recommendation in 95.1 per cent of the cases, which was on a par with its voting record in 2019. The Fund has a significant record of supportive voting for shareholder proposals in sustainability issues. The Fund voted in favour of 35.1 per cent of shareholder resolutions in 2020, compared with 39.9 per cent in 2019 and 52.0 per cent in 2018.[84]

79 See www.nbim.no/en/ accessed 15 July 2020.

80 The Government Pension Fund Act § 4,(1), Act 21st of December 2005 no. 123.

81 The figures are taken from the web page of the Government Pension Fund Global www.nbim.no/en/ accessed 15 July 2020.

82 See www.nbim.no/en/the-fund/responsible-investment/principles/ accessed 15 July 2020.

83 Voting guidelines, see www.nbim.no/contentassets/3dbdc33d893f4e82b63198025c2dde99/global-voting-guidelines-2020.pdf accessed 15 July 2020.

84 Annual Report 2020 pp 71–2 and Annual Report 2019 pp 73–4, www.nbim.no/contentassets/fd871d2a4e2d4c1ab9d3d66c98fa6ba1/annual-report-2020_government-pension-fund-global_web.pdf. accessed 15 July 2020.

18.2 LEGAL MEANS OF SHAREHOLDER ENGAGEMENT

18.2.1 *Main Rules Regarding the Call for AGM and EGM, and Agenda Setting*

Ordinary general meetings (AGMs) are held on an annual basis. It is a requirement that the AGM is held within six months from the end of each financial year.[85]

The meeting is initiated by the board. Companies which have a corporate assembly may state in the articles of association that the AGM shall be called by the chairman of the corporate assembly.[86] If there is no such provision in the articles of association, the call for AGM will be made by the board.

The call must be sent in form of a written notice to all shareholders whose address is known.[87] According to the ASA Act § 1–6 (2), a digital solution may be in compliance with a requirement of a written notice. Public limited liability companies must maintain a register of shareholders.[88] Shares that are traded on the Oslo Stock Exchange are registered in the Securities Trading Register.[89] Due to these provisions, a company will reach out to its shareholders with the call for the AGM. A list of the company's shareholders, including the number of shares they hold, must be made available at the beginning of the AGM.

In its call for an AGM, the board will attach a proposal for the agenda.[90] The proposal of the agenda must specify the issues which will be addressed at the AGM. The board must prepare the proposal for the agenda in accordance with any statutory requirements and any requirements stated in the articles of association. Certain matters are required by law to be treated at the general assembly meeting, such as adoption of the annual financial statement, annual report and distribution of dividends. Any other matter which, pursuant to legislation or the articles of association, are up to the general meeting to decide on, must of course also be put on the agenda and treated at the AGM.[91]

Shareholders' right to put matters on the agenda for the general meeting will be elaborated upon in Section 18.2.3.

A Public Limited Liability Company must send a call for an AGM at the latest two weeks prior to the meeting, unless the articles of association require a longer period.[92] For Private Limited Liability Companies, such announcements must normally be made at least one week in advance of the AGM.[93]

There are some modifications to the main rule of two weeks for the ASA companies whose shares have been admitted for quotation on a regulated market and which are situated in, or engage in, activity in an EEA state. For these companies, the time limit for the AGM call is normally twenty-one days, and information and the form regarding the AGM must be made available to shareholders on the company's website. In addition to the requirements in the ASA Act § 5–10, the notice must be in compliance with EU law in order to meet Norway's commitment under the EEA Agreement.[94]

85 See § 5–6 (1) of the ASA Act and §§ 5–5 and 5–6 of the AS Act. The Private Limited Liability Companies have the possibility of having a simplified procedure for the general assembly meeting.

86 See § 5–9 (1) of both the ASA Act and the AS Act.

87 This requirement is stated in § 5–10 (1) of the ASA Act. The provision also expresses other requirements for the content of the call.

88 See the ASA Act § 4–4 (1). Private limited liability companies must have a 'shareholder book', see the AS Act § 4–5.

89 Act on Securities Trading 29th of June 2007 no. 75.

90 See the ASA Act § 5–10 (3).

91 See the ASA Act § 5–6.

92 See the ASA Act § 5–10 (2).

93 See the AS Act § 5–10 (2).

94 This is stated in the ASA Act § 5–11 b, a provision that was added to the act in 2009 along with regulation FOR-2009-07-06-983 regarding the implementation of Directive 2007/36/EC Art. 5 and Art. 14.

Extraordinary general meetings (EGMs) are held whenever the board of directors, corporate assembly or chairman of the corporate assembly decide that one is needed. The board has a duty to call an EGM whenever the auditor who audits the company's annual accounts or shareholders representing at least one twentieth of the share capital so demands in writing, in order to deal with a specific matter. The EGM is held within one month from the submission of the demand.[95]

Extraordinary general meetings are often called because decisions on the increase or decrease of company capital need to be taken urgently and cannot wait until the next AGM. Amendments of articles of association, questions of forced transfer of shares, or creating/reducing classes of shares may also be addressed at an extraordinary general meeting.[96]

18.2.2 *Shareholders' Right to Call a Meeting*

As explained in Section 18.2.1, the board is responsible for making the call for a shareholders' meeting. For those companies that have a corporate assembly, this responsibility lies with the chairman of the corporate assembly, if it is so empowered by the articles of association. The board of directors, the corporate assembly or the chairman of the corporate assembly can call an EGM.[97]

Should the board or the chairman of the corporate assembly fail to call for an AGM, shareholders and certain other parties may take action. According to § 5–9 (2) of the ASA Act, the District Court must call for an AGM immediately upon request from either a member of the board, a member of the corporate assembly, the general manager, the auditor who audits the company's annual accounts *or a shareholder*. In these rare cases, it is the District Court that makes the formal call, but it is done on the initiative of a shareholder.[98] The shareholder cannot, simply by virtue of being a shareholder, make a direct call towards the other shareholders for an AGM. As there is no ownership requirement, any shareholder may make a request for assistance from the District Court to make a call for an AGM if this has not been done by the board or chairman of the corporate assembly.

In the case of EGMs, however, there is an ownership requirement. Only shareholders representing at least *one-twentieth of the share capital* may demand an extraordinary meeting.[99] The demand must be made in writing, and it must state the matter(s) that the shareholder wishes to put on the agenda for the EGM. The board must ensure that the EGM is held within one month from the issue of the demand.[100]

The District Court may only take action respecting a call for a general meeting which 'is to be held by virtue of statute, the articles of association or a former resolution by the general meeting'. Only the AGM is obligatory. But since the ASA Act states that that an EGM must be held within a month from the demand, the District Court may be asked to call for an EGM if this has not

The Norwegian Code of Practice for Corporate Governance supplements the abovementioned obligations in the ASA Act (in particular in #6 on general meetings.)

95 See the ASA Act § 5–7 and the AS Act § 5–6 regarding the question of when an extraordinary general meeting is to be held.

96 See HR-2013–01454-U (Rt 2013, 1045).

97 The authority and duty to call a general meeting is stated in § 5–9 of the ASA Act, and the call for EGM is governed by § 5–7.

98 The competence lies with the District Court at the place where the head office is located according to the Register of Business Enterprises, see the Civil Procedure Act § 4–4 (3) (LOV-2005–06-17–90).

99 This is stated in the ASA Act § 5–7 (1). For private limited liability companies, the ownership requirement is one-tenth, see the AS Act § 5–6 (2).

100 See the ASA Act § 5–7 (2).

been done in compliance with the ASA Act § 5–7. There are no statistics available on how often shareholders take the initiative to call for an EGM, but this does not happen often in Norway.[101]

18.2.3 *Shareholder's Proposal Right*

A shareholder has the right to put matters on the agenda of the general meeting.[102] A proposal from the shareholder to put a matter on the agenda must be reported in writing to the board within seven days prior to the time limit for the notice to the general meeting, along with a proposal to a draft resolution or an explanation as to why the matter has been put on the agenda. In the event that the notice has already been distributed, a new notice shall be sent if the time limit has not already expired.

The right to put additional matters on the agenda may be exercised by any shareholder. There are no ownership requirements. From time to time, shareholder proposals are put on the agenda, but this does not happen very often in Norway.[103] Some companies are more prone to shareholder activism than others. Equinor ASA, which saw four shareholder proposals in 2019 and six in 2020 regarding environmental issues, is a good example of a company where shareholder activism is prominent.[104]

Matters that have not been reported to the shareholders in due time may not be decided at the meeting without the consent of all shareholders.[105] In theory, shareholders may try to raise a matter orally at the general assembly meeting; in practice, however, it is unlikely that the shareholders attending the meeting will unanimously agree to their doing so.

18.2.4 *Voting*

At the opening of the general meeting – before the first vote is organized – a list must be provided of the shareholders who are attending the meeting, either in person or by proxy. The list must show how many shares are represented as well as the number of votes represented by each. The list is important, as it provides confidence in the voting regime to both shareholders and other parties.[106]

Voting at the AGM is normally conducted on the principle of a *simple majority*. Since the decision on electing board members is made by a simple majority, majority shareholders will basically be in control of the board's management of the company.[107]

Exceptions to the simple majority norm may, however, be stated in other provisions of the ASA Act or in the articles of association. Provisions requiring a higher degree of majority are part of the legislative framework on protection of minority shareholders' right. In order to amend the articles of association, a qualified majority of two-thirds is needed (two-thirds of the votes as well as two-thirds of the share capital being represented at the AGM). Even a higher degree of majority may be decided in the articles of association. Some resolutions even require unanimity, for example that the legal relationship among formerly equivalent shares is altered.[108]

101 See Knudsen and Langseth (n. 26).

102 Shareholders right to put a matter on the agenda is stated in the ASA Act § 5–11 with a parallel provision in § 5–11 of the AS Act.

103 See Section 18.3.1.3 on shareholders proposals and proxy fights. Statistics covering 1 January 2017–26 June 2020 from Proxy Insight as well as own examinations of minutes from AGMs.

104 See for a comparative perspective, Chapter 22.

105 ASA Act § 5–14 (1).

106 The duty for the person opening the meeting to make a list of participants is expressed in the ASA Act § 5–13.

107 Cf. Knudsen and Norvik (n. 16) 240.

108 See the ASA Act § 5–7 (1) and (3). Provisions on majority requirements are found in §§ 5–17 – 5–21 of the ASA Act, § 5–17 on ordinary majority, § 5–18 on amendments of the articles of associations, § 5–19 on requirements for qualified majority and § 5–20 dealing with matters that require unanimity. See also Knudsen and Norvik (n. 16) 240.

In the event of a tie, the chairperson has the casting vote, regardless of whether he or she has voting rights.[109] The general meeting may elect a non-shareholder to chair the meeting. Therefore, a situation may occur where the chairperson holds a casting vote in spite of otherwise not having voting rights.[110]

The main rule when it comes to the weight of the shares in the voting process is the *One Share One Vote principle*. Each share carries one vote unless otherwise stated either statutorily or in the articles of association.[111]

The articles of association may, for example, state that shares of a particular class are not allowed to vote, or that votes in this class have a lower ratio of weight. The ASA Act gives considerable leeway for the articles of association to restrict the voting rights for particular shares. If the combined nominal value of shares in the company with such voting restrictions makes up more than half of the share capital of the company, the voting restrictions are only valid if approved by the Ministry of Trade, Industry and Fisheries.[112]

Even though is it allowed to have different share classes, this is not common practice for listed companies in Norway.[113] In 2019 one of the few companies that had two share classes decided to change this and the company currently has only one class of shares.[114]

18.2.5 *Questions and Information Requests*

Shareholders are entitled to certain information in order for them to be able to prepare for the AGM. The annual financial statement, the annual report, the auditor's report, the statement by the corporate assembly and the declaration of the board must be sent to every shareholder whose address is known at the latest one week prior to the AGM.[115]

In addition to the information that the board is obliged to send to shareholders before the AGM, a shareholder can also during the AGM demand further information that is available – information that may affect the consideration of the adoption of the company's annual report or financial statement or any other matter that has been submitted to the shareholders for decision.[116]

There is no court practice regarding the ASA Act § 5–15 on the management's disclosure duty.

18.3 SHAREHOLDER ENGAGEMENT AND VOTING IN PRACTICE

18.3.1 *Voting in Practice*

18.3.1.1 Who Votes and How?

Traditionally a shareholder would vote by attending in person at the general meeting. However, this principle has been gradually eroded in recent years.

General meetings have traditionally been carried out as physical meetings. In 2009 the ASA Act § 5–8 was amended to allow the possibility of electronic participation in a general meeting

109 ASA Act § 5–17 (1).
110 ASA Act § 5–12 (3).
111 See the ASA Act § 5–4 (1).
112 This is also stated in the ASA Act § 5–4 (1).
113 cf. Knudsen and Norvik (n. 16) 214–15.
114 Adevinta ASA, decision at an Extraordinary General Meeting held in October 2019.
115 According to the ASA Act § 5–6 (5).
116 See the ASA Act § 5–15.

(§ 5–8 a).[117] This provision states that: 'Unless the articles of association provide otherwise, the board of directors may decide that shareholders may participate in the general meeting by electronic means, including a right for shareholders to exercise his or her shareholder rights by electronic means'. The ASA Act does not prescribe any particular form for the shareholders to attend the general meeting, so different companies have chosen different approaches. But the companies must explain the chosen procedure to the shareholders in the call for the general meeting. The shareholders must receive instructions on how to attend digitally, how to vote in advance and how to make use of proxy. It is common practice for listed companies to prepare a form for the appointment of a proxy (with or without voting instructions).

A shareholder meeting can take the form of a hybrid meeting, where some shareholders attend in person and some digitally. There is no requirement in the ASA Act that a minimum number of shareholders or minimum representation of shareholder capital must attend in person. It may, however, be decided in the articles of association that only personal appearance is allowed. Instructions on how to participate and how to vote may be decided upon in more detail in the articles of association.

Until 2020, the opportunity given in the ASA Act for digital appearance at the general meeting was not much used.[118] This changed entirely in 2020, as a digital solution was offered by most of the twenty-five largest listed companies. This is of course due to the Covid-19 situation and the temporary Covid-19 Act.[119] The goal of this Act was to facilitate for board meetings, general meetings etc. to be held without physical appearance. In the calls made for the AGMs in 2020, the companies outlined how the shareholders would be able to attend digitally, how they could vote in advance (also often by digital solutions) and how to make use of proxy.

The experience during the Covid-19 pandemic by conduction general meetings as digital meetings was quite good. This resulted in an amendment of the ASA Act § 5-8, so that the board may now choose between conducting the AGM as a physical or a digital meeting. If a physical meeting is decided, this will, as before, take place in the municipality where the company has its registered business office.

The board must ensure that the general meeting can proceed in a safe and orderly manner, and that there are systems in place which ensure compliance with statutory provisions regarding general meetings. The system must ensure satisfactory control of participation and voting at the general meeting, and a secure method must be in place to authenticate the sender.[120]

The articles of association may also stipulate whether it is possible for a shareholder to vote prior to the general meeting. If so, the vote must be sent in writing, and it must also be sent within a particular time limit. The procedure on voting beforehand must include a secure method to authenticate the sender. § 5–8 b of the ASA Act explicitly states that the 'writing' requirement includes the use of electronic means.

Questions concerning the shareholder's appearance at the meeting or use of proxy is governed by § 5–2 of the ASA Act. The shareholder may choose either to appear at the general assembly in person or to be represented by proxy. The right to attendance may not be restricted by the articles of association.

The person authorized to serve under proxy must submit a written and dated document of proxy. If the proxy is presented by way of electronic transmission, there must be a secure method

117 The ASA Act § 5–8 a.

118 See Knudsen and Norvik (n. 16) 218.

119 Act-2020–05-26–54 was prolonged until 1 June 2021. The ASA Act § 5-8 was amended in May 2021 by Lovvedtak 111 (2020–1).

120 See the ASA Act § 5–8 a (2) and (3).

to authenticate the proxy. The authorization of the proxy is deemed valid only for the specific general meeting, unless otherwise clearly provided.

Under Norwegian law, the shareholder may choose to be assisted by an adviser, and the shareholder may also give *one* adviser the right to speak.[121]

A review of the minutes from the AGMs in 2019 and 2020 of the twenty-five largest ASA companies in Norway shows that on average 63.05 per cent of the share capital was present at the AGM in 2020 and 63.85 per cent in 2019 (including shareholders present by proxy).[122] A previous study of the attendance of shareholders of Norwegian companies showed that during the years 2009–13, on average 59 per cent of the shareholders attended the general assembly meeting.[123] There are big differences in the use of proxy in AGMs between companies, and also from one year to another for the same company. On average, 28.27 per cent of the share capital was represented by proxy in 2020, compared to 16.09 per cent in 2019. The use of proxy advisors has recently become more common, especially amongst institutional shareholders.[124]

There is a requirement in § 2–3 of the temporary Covid Act that the organization and handling of the meeting must be secure and reliable. The Norwegian word used in the provision is 'forsvarlig', and it is to be treated as a legal standard. It can be variously translated into English as 'justifiable', 'defensible', 'proper', 'sound', 'responsible', 'secure' or 'warrantable'. The Act does not prescribe a specific procedure, and it is up to the board to make sure that the general meeting and the voting is done in a secure and trustworthy manner.

Information about how to attend the meeting and how to vote digitally must be provided in the invitation to the AGM. The practical realization of this provision may differ, but Equinor's AGM held on 14 May 2020 will serve as an example here of how digital general assembly meetings and digital voting may proceed. In the invitation, the shareholders were encouraged to follow the AGM digitally (webcast). The invitation also contained information on how to access the meeting and how to vote. The shareholders were encouraged to vote beforehand. Another example is found in the notice for the AGM of DNB ASA (Norway's largest bank) to be held in a fully digitalized format on 30 June 2020. The invitation contains detailed descriptions on secure identification, how to vote and how to use proxy.

The effects of the Covid-19 pandemic can be seen in the way in which AGMs were held in 2020. In the notice for the 2020 AGM that companies sent to the shareholders, the need to keep the number of participants at a minimum was emphasized. The companies recommended that shareholders should vote in advance and/or use proxy. Different approaches were adopted as to how the AGM was carried out and how the voting was done. Minutes from the 2020 AGMs in the largest ASA companies in Norway show that only a few of the companies chose a fully digitalized AGM, including real time voting. Most of the companies adopted an approach whereby the shareholder could follow the AGM digitally, often via webcast, but the voting was done in advance with or without use of proxy. Some companies chose to have the AGM as a physical meeting, but in these cases also the shareholders were encouraged to vote in advance and/or use proxy in order to minimize the number of people meeting physically at the AGM.

121 The ASA Act § 5–2 (3).

122 For other data on attendance, see the comparative Chapter 22. As the composition of the sample is different, the average result between the two samples is different for 2019 and 2020.

123 See Øyvind Bøhren, Sebastian Christophersen and Simen Lerfaldet, 'The Effect of Shareholder Turnout on Voting Rights and Separation' (22 March 2020). https://ssrn.com/abstract=3555404 or http://dx.doi.org/10.2139/ssrn.3555404 accessed 15 July 2020. The article in the newspaper Dagens Næringsliv 11 April 2020 is also written by Sebastian Christophersen, Simen Lerfaldet and Øyvind Bøhren.

124 See Knudsen and Norvik (n. 16) 218–19.

18.3.1.2 What Issues Are Voted on?

As described in Section 18.2, some issues are subject to a mandatory vote at the general meeting. The main decisions that must be adopted by the general meeting are:

- approval of the annual accounts (ordinary majority);
- election of board members (ordinary majority);
- amendments of the articles of association (two-thirds of the votes as well as of share capital);
- election of auditor (ordinary majority);
- distribution of dividends (ordinary majority);
- approval of agreements between a company and related parties (ordinary majority);
- amendments of the share capital (minimum two-thirds);
- mergers and de-mergers (minimum two-thirds);
- dissolving the company (minimum two-thirds);
- other matters that, pursuant to the articles of association, shall be resolved by the general meeting.

Renumeration of the CEO is determined by the board. The AGM decides on the renumeration of the board members.

As far as the distribution of dividend is concerned, the general meeting (the shareholders) may decide to give a lower dividend than that proposed by the board in the agenda. However, the shareholders may not decide on a higher dividend.[125]

In addition to the matters that are required to be presented to the shareholders at the AGM, the board decides which issues to address.

18.3.1.3 Shareholder Proposals and Proxy Fights

Shareholders' proposals rarely appear in the AGMs of Norwegian listed companies.[126] They are not entirely unknown, however, and some companies receive such proposals more often than others. Equinor ASA had six shareholders proposals included in the 2020 AGM addressing questions regarding the company's core business of oil and gas production and the company's environmental responsibility. The proposals were turned down by an overwhelming majority of votes (95–99 per cent).

Matters that are put on the agenda by the board, and that must be dealt with at the AGM (e.g. the annual report and the annual financial statement) are generally passed with no or only very few votes against. For these matters, there might be comments from the shareholders, but rarely alternative proposals to be voted on.

In practice, it is not easy achieving a majority vote for a shareholder's proposal that goes against the suggestion from the board. In most cases, shareholder proposals are voted down. This does not, however, mean that the shareholder's proposal is without any effect. Depending on the discussions at the general meeting, how close the outcome of the voting turned out, and how the discussion was reported in the media, the board and management of the company might have been given important inputs for their own discussions on strategical or other decisions.

There are no statistics available on which issues are most often addressed in shareholder's proposals. Based upon cases reported in the Norwegian media, the annual report 2020 from the Government Pension Fund Norway and examination of minutes from general meetings from

[125] See the ASA Act § 8–2 (1).

[126] Statistics from Proxy Insight and review of minutes from the twenty-five largest ASA companies in Norway.

2019 and 2020, environmental and societal responsibility and alternative suggestions for board members are the issues most often raised by shareholders.[127]

Shareholders are entitled to vote by proxy, and the use of proxy advisors has increased in Norway over the last decade. Proxy fights by way of one group of shareholders actively trying to get control over how other shareholders votes by persuading them to give proxy, is not a big issue in Norway.[128] It is allowed to make such agreements between shareholders, but there is a limit of tolerance. According to § 5–21 of the ASA Act, a general meeting may not adopt any resolution which is suited to give certain shareholders or others an unreasonable benefit at the expense of other shareholders or the company. In addition to this provision, it is assumed that there exists an unwritten (non-statutory) principle of prohibition of abuse of shareholders' rights. The existence of a non-statutory principle of loyalty and that abuse of shareholders rights is not tolerated has been confirmed in recent Norwegian Supreme Court practice.[129]

18.3.2 *The Use of Private Engagement Techniques*

In this part, two different types of situations will be discussed: (1) communication between the company's leadership and shareholders, and (2) agreements between shareholders. When important decisions are to be made, or important votes to be cast at an AGM, the board may need to communicate with core investors/major shareholders of the company prior to the meeting. Sometimes a single shareholder or a group of shareholders would like to meet with the management or chair of the board. At other times, single shareholders or groups of shareholders make agreements in order to influence the decisions to be made by the board or the management of the company. Contact between shareholder(s) and the management is quite common in companies with a dominant owner, but this must be done without infringing upon other shareholders' right.[130]

Listed companies must comply with regulations pertaining to the company's duty to inform shareholders as well as others (creditors, possible new shareholders etc.). Important regulations include:

(1) Mandatory provisions regarding which information to distribute when, and that the information is made publicly available.[131]
(2) Any shareholder may, in connection to the annual general meeting, demand information about matters that may affect the consideration of how to vote at the AGM.[132]
(3) The main principle of equality between shareholders is important when the company management or chair of the board is communicating with shareholders.[133]

In addition to the statutory provisions regarding the company's duty to inform, the listed companies must comply with Oslo Stock Exchange's 'Norwegian Code of Practice for Corporate Governance'.[134] The Norwegian Code of Practice only very briefly touches upon

[127] See for further data, Chapter 22.
[128] See Knutsen and Langseth (n. 26) 12.
[129] HR-2020-1947-A. See also Filip Truyen, 'General Principles on the Abuse of Shareholder's Rights in Nordic Legislation' in Mette Neville and Karsten Engsig Sørensen (eds.), *Company Law and SMEs* (Thomson Reuters 2010) 171–90.
[130] See Knudsen and Norvik (n. 16) 212–14. See also Knutsen and Langseth (n. 26).
[131] Such as the ASA Act § 5–10 and § 5–11b. See also Knutsen and Langseth (n. 26).
[132] See the ASA Act § 5–15.
[133] The principle of equality is expressed in the ASA Act § 4–1.
[134] See https://nues.no/wp-content/uploads/2018/10/NUES_eng_web_okt2018_2.pdf accessed 15 July 2020. See also Section 18.1.1 on legislative framework.

information and communications to shareholders (#13). The Code recommends that the board establishes guidelines for the company's contact with shareholders outside the frame of the general meetings. The Code recognizes the need for shareholders to communicate with the company occasionally, or for the company to communicate with shareholders to increase the board's understanding of which matters are affecting the company. The Code does not give any details on how these guidelines should be drafted, but states that the guidelines should make clear the extent to which the board has delegated the task of communication to the chairman of the board, the chief executive or any other of the executive personnel.

The engagement or communication between the company and the shareholder must not infringe upon other shareholders' rights. The general anti-abuse provisions in the ASA Act § 5–21 and § 6–28 will apply.[135] These provisions prohibit the shareholders, the directors and the CEO from adopting any resolution that may provide certain shareholders or others with an unreasonable advantage at the expense of the other shareholders or the company itself. They also prohibit the board of directors and the CEO from effecting resolutions made by superior corporate bodies that would violate mandatory laws or the company's articles of association.

The anti-abuse provisions are limited in scope to 'unreasonable' abuse of majority power resulting in unequal treatment. This implies that unequal treatment per se is not prohibited, and that majority shareholders as well as the board and the CEO can pass resolutions that provide for de facto unequal treatment as long as there is a good and valid reason for passing such a resolution.[136] This also implies that there could be meetings between some shareholders and the company to discuss important issues, but that these kinds of engagements must not lead to unreasonable advantages on behalf of some shareholders in AGM voting at the expense of other shareholders or the company itself.

If a shareholder receives inside information – information which is likely to have a significant effect on the price of the shares – the shareholder is prohibited from trading in the shares.[137]

18.4 CONCLUDING REMARKS

In general, listed companies in Norway have a wider ownership dispersion than private limited liability companies, but dominant shareholder positions can often be found also in listed companies. The Norwegian Public Limited Liability Act has in practice functioned well to companies with a wide spread as well as companies with a greater concentration of ownership interests.

The Norwegian government plays an important role as an investor on the Oslo Stock Exchange. The government has direct ownership in 9 listed companies, but also acts as an important investor through The Government Pension Fund Norway (Folketrygdfondet), owning 5.7 per cent of the share market value of the Oslo Stock Exchange.

It is difficult to characterize the board structure under Norwegian company law as either a single board structure or a dual board structure. Limited liability companies only have one board, but the board structure of Norwegian companies shares characteristics of both the one-tier and the two-tier board system. The board is both managerial and supervisory. The board

[135] For listed companies, the anti-abuse provision in the Public Companies Act is supplemented by a provision on equal treatment in the Securities Trading Act and also a non-statutory principle of loyalty.

[136] See Knudsen and Langseth (n. 26).

[137] See the Security Trading Act § 3-3 cf. § 3-2 on what is regarded as inside information. See also Knudsen and Norvik (n. 16) 213–14.

members in the listed companies are independent of the company, and they are non-executive. The CEO of a listed company is not a member of the board.

There is a strong hierarchy and division of roles and responsibilities between the main corporate bodies. Shareholder meetings represent the supreme authority. Shareholder meetings decide on appointment of board members and can also remove them before end of the time they are appointed for. Board members act primarily in the interest of the company, but they can be held responsible towards the shareholders as well as other stakeholders.

The CEO is responsible towards the board. The CEO is hired by the board and can be either instructed or removed by the board. The CEO is not a member of the board, but regularly attends the board meetings to share information regarding the ongoing business or present background information on cases.

The principle of simple majority is the main rule for decisions made by the general meeting. Majority shareholders thus have great power over the company. Majority voting rules are, however, limited by several provisions designed to protect minority shareholders. In addition to statutory provisions on minority shareholder protection, there exist non-statutory principles of loyalty and fair play between shareholders. Abuse of power is not accepted from majority shareholders.

Gender equality must be observed in the composition of the board, to comply with mandatory provisions in the Public Limited Liability Act. For Private Limited Liability Companies, gender equality regarding board composition is not mandatory.

Employee representation on the board of directors has a relatively long tradition in Norwegian company law. Mandatory provisions exist both in the Public and the Private Limited Liability Act.

Transparency is a core value and is expected in all areas of company law; from the company towards the rest of the world, from the CEO towards the board and from the board towards the shareholders. There are several mandatory provisions to comply with in order to secure that shareholders and others are sufficiently informed.

General meetings are normally organized as physical meetings. Since 2009 digital solutions for attending shareholder meetings as well as voting digitally have been possible. There were few digital shareholder meetings before 2020. But in order to reduce the risk of Covid-19 transmission, the government urged companies to make use of digital solutions to organize general meetings as well as voting, and the relevant legislation has been amended in order to facilitate non-physical meetings. Examination of calls for and minutes from general meetings in 2020 show that Norwegian companies have complied with the government's request to find digital solutions.

Overall, except for some companies like Equinor where shareholders have made active use of their shareholder rights and issue shareholder proposals, the Norwegian AGM landscape is characterized by low levels of confrontation between shareholders and the board. The structure of company law with employee participation, the role of the general assembly and other mechanisms seems to satisfy most of the involved parties.

19

Shareholder Voting and Engagement in the Netherlands: The Dutch Institutional Approach

Anne Lafarre

19.1 INTRODUCTION

Shareholder engagement plays a central role in (Dutch) corporate governance and is the focal point of many (soft) regulatory initiatives. Shareholders can use their 'voice' to influence the way businesses are managed and reshape corporate policies.[1] The first Shareholder Rights Directive (SRD I) states that 'effective shareholder control is a prerequisite to sound corporate governance and should, therefore, be facilitated and encouraged'.[2] The Revised Shareholder Rights Directive (SRD II), which was incorporated into the Dutch legal framework at the end of 2019, places a large degree of emphasis on the role of institutional investor stewardship in listed companies.[3] Also the Dutch Stewardship Code, implemented in 2019 by Eumedion, puts large emphasis on institutional investors and their role in the Dutch corporate governance framework.[4] Institutional investors have a large impact on the Dutch corporate law landscape, as they own a vast majority of shares in most Dutch listed companies: previous research mentions that over 90 per cent of the shares of Dutch large cap companies (those companies that are part of the AEX-25) were owned by (foreign) institutional investors in 2014.[5] However, Dutch corporate law is characterized by a so-called *institutional approach*, in which shareholder interests do not take priority over the interests of other stakeholders, providing an important role for the corporate board (*institutionele visie*).[6] The 2016 Dutch Corporate Governance Code (DCGC) takes a clear stakeholder approach.[7] In addition, in Dutch

1 For instance, Stuart L. Gillan and Laura T. Starks, 'A Survey of Shareholder Activism: Motivation and Empirical Evidence' (1998) 2 *Contemporary Finance Digest* 10. Lately, particular focus is put on the role of shareholders in corporate sustainability. For instance, see Elroy Dimson, Oǧuzhan Karakaş and Xi Li, 'Active Ownership' (2015) 28 *Review of Financial Studies* 3225.

2 Directive 2007/36/EC of the European Parliament and of the Council of 11 July 2007 on the exercise of certain rights of shareholders in listed companies (2007) OJ L 184/17.

3 Directive (EU) 2017/828 of the European Parliament and of the Council of 17 May 2017 amending Directive 2007/36/EC as regards the encouragement of long-term shareholder engagement (2017) OJ L 132/60.

4 The Dutch Stewardship Code is available via www.eumedion.nl/en/public/knowledgenetwork/best-practices/2018-07-dutch-stewardship-code-final-version.pdf accessed July 2020. Eumedion is the Dutch Corporate Governance Forum that 'represents institutional investors' interests in the field of corporate governance and related sustainability performance' (Eumedion, 'Over Eumedion [About Eumedion]' www.eumedion.nl/en/abouteumedion accessed 13 July 2020.

5 See Rients Abma et al., *De algemene vergadering van Nederlandse beursvennootschappen, Recht en Praktijk Ondernemingsrecht* (Deventer: Kluwer 2017) 8. See for more information about the ownership structures of Dutch listed companies Section 19.2.4 of this chapter.

6 Also see Section 19.2.2 of this chapter.

7 For example, Principle 1.1 on long-term value creation states: 'The management board is responsible for the continuity of the company and its affiliated enterprise. The management board focuses on long-term value creation

case law it is emphasized that determining the strategy and policy of the (listed) company and its affiliated company is, in principle, the responsibility of the management board, under the supervision of the supervisory board.[8]

This research sheds fresh light on the engagement and voting behaviour of shareholders in the Netherlands and their position in Dutch corporate law. After an introduction to the Dutch corporate law framework and the role of the board and shareholders in Section 19.2, Section 19.3 discusses the legal means of shareholder engagement in the Netherlands. The commonly used definition of shareholder engagement – or shareholder activism – describes the attempts to 'change the status quo through "voice," without a change in control of the firm'.[9] Three forms of shareholder engagement can be distinguished in the Netherlands: (1) engagement in general meetings including voting and questions; (2) engagement outside general meetings in a private setting and (3) shareholder litigation.[10] In this contribution, I focus on shareholder engagement in general meetings in particular. In Section 19.4, drawing on a unique dataset on shareholder voting behaviour in Dutch general meetings, the practice of shareholder engagement and voting in the Netherlands is discussed. Section 19.5 provides some concluding remarks.

19.2 THE DUTCH NV

19.2.1 *An 'Institutional' Approach*

Dutch corporate statutory law is embedded in Book 2 of the Dutch Civil Code (DCC).The Dutch Civil Code recognizes two types of companies, the NV (*Naamloze Vennootschap*, or open or public corporation) and the BV (*Besloten Vennootschap*, or closed or private corporation). The shares of the NV may consist of registered or bearer shares and are generally freely transferable:[11] of course, the shares of a NV with its shares listed on the stock exchange have the highest liquidity. Data from Thomson Reuters shows that there are currently 172 listed NVs incorporated in the Netherlands, of which 145 also have their headquarters in the Netherlands.[12] This contribution focuses on the Dutch public company, the NV, and the listed NV in particular.

In addition to mandatory, statutory corporate law, the Dutch corporate governance system for listed companies is governed by the DCGC. The first DCGC was introduced in the aftermath of large-scale scandals like Enron, WorldCom and Ahold. However, after a few years, the short-termism of hedge funds and other activist investors became an important issue in the Dutch corporate governance debate. Accordingly, the DCGC was amended in 2008. Then, in December 2016 the DCGC was revised again to emphasize 'long-term value creation'.[13] Although the DCGC does not contain binding requirements per se, the 'comply or explain'

for the company and its affiliated enterprise, and takes into account the stakeholder interests that are relevant in this context. The supervisory board monitors the management board in this'.

8 The most recent cases are the AkzoNobel Case and the Boskalis/Fugro Case: Hof Amsterdam (OK) 29 May 2017, ECLI:NL:GHAMS:2017:1965 (*AkzoNobel*) r.o. 3.9; HR 20 April 2018, ECLI:NL:HR:2018:652 (*Boskalis/Fugro*) r.o. 3.3.6.

9 Gillan and Starks (n. 1).

10 For instance, shareholders that meet certain ownership thresholds have the right to inquiry (*enquêterecht*) and to request the launch of an investigation into the company's state of affairs and policy (art. 2:344 *et seq* DCC).

11 The articles of association (AoA) of an NV may contain limitations on the transferability of *registered* shares; bearer shares are by definition freely transferable.

12 Reference date for data collection: 24 June 2019.

13 The DCGC 2016 is applicable to the financial year starting on or after 1 January 2017.

principle is binding and embedded in the law: Dutch corporate law determines that a listed company must disclose, in their annual report, whether it complies with the DCGC's governance principles or explain why it deviates from its principles.[14]

Dutch scholars often suggest that the Dutch NV-framework, particularly for large Dutch companies, is characterised by an 'institutional' vision or approach (*institutionele visie*) that does not consider the company as a nexus of contracts, but an institution separate from its shareholders. This approach has clear links with the stakeholder model and puts emphasis on board autonomy. Board members have a duty to act in the best interest of the company and any affiliated enterprise.[15] In the *Cancun case*, the Dutch Supreme Court ruled that:

> [i]n the performance of their duties, directors must be guided by the interests of the company and its affiliated enterprise ... What that interest entails depends on the circumstances of the case. If an enterprise is associated with the company, the company's interest is generally determined primarily by promoting the continued success of this enterprise.[16]

There are different views on what the company's interest (*vennootschappelijk belang*) means. Dutch legal scholars generally distinguish three (interconnected) views, namely the (enlightened) shareholder interest view, the participants view (*participantenopvatting* or also called the *resultantenopvatting*), and the holistic view.[17] Proponents of the shareholder interest view consider the current and future shareholder interest in achieving long-term profits the company's interest, whereas with the participants view the interests of stakeholders are weighted as partial interests. In the latter view, the company's interest is considered the result of the weighting of these partial interests, in which the specific circumstances of the case play a large role.[18] Finally, shortly stated, the holistic view considers the interest of the company to be an independent interest. Despite these different views, there is a general consensus that the company's interest includes stakeholder interests, following from case law, parliamentary history and the DCGC.[19]

The Dutch institutional vision also implies that, in the Netherlands, the general meeting is not the highest power in the company, but instead shares its position with the corporate board. Board autonomy (*bestuursautonomie*) is widely established in seminal Dutch case law.[20] There are two recent cases that underline this division of powers between the corporate board and shareholders and board autonomy.[21] One involved the Dutch listed company AkzoNobel and hedge fund Elliott

14 Following art. 2:391(5) DCC and 5:86 Financial Supervision Act ('*Wft*').

15 Art. 2:129(5) DCC. Also see HR 4 April 2014, ECLI:NL:HR:2014:797 (*Cancun*).

16 HR 4 April 2014, ECLI:NL:HR:2014:797 (*Cancun*), r.o. 4.2.1. Translation by the author, original Dutch text: '[B]ij de vervulling van hun taak dienen de bestuurders zich naar het belang van de vennootschap en de met haar verbonden onderneming te richten ... Wat dat belang inhoudt, hangt af van de omstandigheden van het geval. Indien aan de vennootschap een onderneming is verbonden, wordt het vennootschapsbelang in de regel vooral bepaald door het bevorderen van het bestendige succes van deze onderneming'.

17 See Gerard van Solinge, 'Verschillende opvattingen over vennootschappelijk belang', in *Asser/Van Solinge & Nieuwe Weme 2-IIb Rechtspersonenrecht NV en BV – Corporate Governance* (Kluwer 2019) 126; Kid C. A. Schwarz, 'Oratie: De impact van het vennootschappelijk belang, deel 1' (2018) *Tijdschrift voor vennootschapsrecht, rechtspersonenrecht en ondernemingsbestuur* 4.

18 Dutch scholars have argued that the interest of the company would be either the common interest that results from weighting these stakeholder interests, or the most important interest. Note that if the shareholder interest is considered the most important interest, the participants view can be similar to the enlightened shareholder view. See van Solinge (n. 17).

19 The *AkzoNobel case* (n. 8) r.o. 3.9; Kamerstukken II 2018/19, 34491, nr. 9, p. 3. The DCGC 2016 takes a clear stakeholder view with its very first principle (n. 7).

20 Including HR 13 July 2007, ECLI:NL:HR:2007:BA7972, *NJ* 2007/434 (*ABN AMRO*), r.o. 4.3-4.5; HR 9 juli 2010, ECLI:NL:HR:2010:BM0976, *NJ* 2010/544 (*ASMI*), r.o. 4.4.1.

21 The *AkzoNobel case* and the *Boskalis/Fugro case*. See n. 8.

Management Corporation ('Elliott' hereafter). AkzoNobel received three unsolicited friendly offers from PPG in 2017, all of which the AkzoNobel board rejected, arguing, inter alia, that the offers did not reflect the value of the company and that PPG had not made any serious commitments to AkzoNobel's stakeholders. After the rejection of the second bid, Elliott issued a request to call an extraordinary general meeting to remove the chairman of AkzoNobel. Although the 10 per cent threshold required under Dutch law was met, the request was rejected by AkzoNobel.[22] Then, after the rejection of the third bid, Elliott launched an inquiry procedure (*enquêteprocedure*)[23] before the Dutch Enterprise Chamber[24] to investigate the decision-making concerning the rejection of PPG's offers. In the course of the procedure, Elliott filed for 'intermediate measures' (*onmiddellijke voorzieningen*), including the calling of a general meeting to vote on the ousting of AkzoNobel's chairman. The Enterprise Chamber rejected its request for these measures and held that there were no serious grounds to question the company's management.[25]

The other case concerned the shareholder proposal right in the Netherlands. Dutch listed company Fugro had several protective mechanisms installed, including one at the level of two Curaçao-based subsidiaries: Boskalis, the large shareholder of Fugro with a stake of about 28 per cent, objected particularly to this protection mechanism. Boskalis and Fugro agreed that the withdrawal of the protection mechanism is part of the board's authority, but Fugro refused the add the non-binding shareholder proposal of Boskalis on this matter on the general meeting's agenda. The Dutch Supreme Court, like the two lower courts, agreed with Fugro, first of all emphasizing that in principle, the management board is responsible for determining the policy and strategy of the company and its affiliated enterprise, under the supervision of the supervisory board. The management board is accountable for this policy to the general meeting, but is not obliged (except for deviating legal or contractual provisions) to involve the general meeting in advance in the decision-making or to consult the general meeting.[26] Hence, the Dutch shareholder proposal right[27] does not oblige the company to include a subject that is part of the management board's authority for a shareholder vote on the agenda of the general meeting, regardless of whether that vote has any formal effect or the way the proposal is formulated.[28] The Dutch Supreme Court concluded that this is also not against the SRD I.[29]

In the next two sections, the decision-making powers of the corporate board (Section 19.2.2) and the (annual) general meeting (or (A)GM) (Section 19.2.3) are delineated.

19.2.2 *The Dutch Corporate Board*

Listed NVs usually have a two-tier board structure with a management board and a supervisory board. In the Dutch listed company, the management board plays a central role: under the supervision of the supervisory board (or non-executive directors, see below in this section on the one-tier board), the management board independently determines the strategy and policies of

[22] Shareholders also need to have a 'reasonable interest' (in Dutch '*redelijk belang*') in order to request the convening of a general meeting ex art. 2:111(1) DCC. The supervisory board argued that this reasonable interest was lacking.

[23] See n. 10.

[24] The higher court in Amsterdam specialized in corporate law cases.

[25] *AkzoNobel case*, r.o. 3.25 and 3.28. See n. 8.

[26] *Boskalis/Fugro case*, r.o. 3.3.6. See n. 8.

[27] The Dutch shareholder proposal right is stipulated in article 2:114a DCC. See Section 19.2.2 of this chapter for more information.

[28] *Boskalis/Fugro*, r.o. 3.3.7. See n. 8.

[29] *Boskalis/Fugro*, r.o. 3.3.8. See n. 8.

the company.[30] The *Forumbank case* (1955) determined that the general meeting may not provide the management board with binding instructions with regard to the board's powers under the law and the company's articles of association (AoA).[31] The general meeting may not engage in the board's domain and, in principle, may not give instructions to the board, unless the right to do so is stipulated in the AoA and the instructions in question concern the general lines of a policy to be pursued.[32] As noted before, the board's autonomy (*bestuursautonomie*) in Dutch listed companies is widely established in Dutch case law.[33]

Until 2013, the two-tier board structure was mandatory for NVs classified as a 'large' company under the so-called *structuurregime*.[34] Under the *structuurregime,* the supervisory board has the authority to (re-)elect and dismiss members of the management board.[35] It also monitors and advises the management board and supervises the general course of the company's affairs.[36] The supervisory board is appointed by the general meeting[37] and has the legal duty to appoint and to remove members of the management board under the *structuurregime*.[38] The general meeting has the right to remove the board members appointed by the general meeting at any time and for any or no reason.[39] Article 2:140(2) DCC holds that also the supervisory board is required to act in the interest of the company and its enterprise,[40] and further stipulates that it is tasked with supervising the policy of the management board and the general course of affairs and assisting the management board with advice. These tasks are further outlined in the DCGC[41] and in some specific provisions of the DCC.

Subsequent to the Board and Governance Act (*Wet Bestuur en toezicht*),[42] Dutch companies may determine in their AoA whether they follow a one-tier or a two-tier board structure.[43] If a corporation chooses to adopt a one-tier board structure, Dutch law stipulates that several tasks (including monitoring executive directors, making nominations for the appointment of a director and determining the remuneration of executive directors) cannot be performed by executive directors.[44] These tasks, which are similar to the tasks of the supervisory board in a two-tier board structure, are thus necessarily performed by non-executive directors.

30 2:129 DCC. As regards board duties, art. 2:9 DCC stipulates the duty of care, which is directed towards the company. Art. 2:129(5) includes the duty of loyalty.

31 HR 21 January 1955, ECLI:NL:PHR:1955:AG2033, NJ 1959/43 m.nt. Hijmans van den Bergh (*Forumbank*).

32 Also see 2:129(4) DCC. See Abma et al. (n. 5) 5.

33 See n. 20.

34 A corporation is considered to be a 'large' corporation if it meets the size criteria that are stipulated in art. 2:153(2) DCC.

35 Art. 2:162 DCC. Not all listed companies need to mandatory follow the *structuurregime*. For instance, large corporations with mainly international activities are subject to a less strict version of this regime. Note that Dutch listed companies generally follow the *structuurregime* requirements, but many still allow shareholders to elect the management board members. Also see M. J. G. C. Raaijmakers, *Ondernemingsrecht*, Pitlo (2nd ed., Kluwer 2017) chapter 4.

36 Art. 2:140(2) DCC.

37 Arts. 2:142 and 2:144 DCC.

38 Art. 2:162 DCC. Also, since the Board and Governance Act, ex art. 2:164a DCC for the one-tier board system.

39 Following art. 2:134(1) DCC. However, it should be noted that all resolutions must be in accordance with the standard of reasonableness and fairness ex art. 2:15(1) DCC.

40 For more information see *Kamerstukken II* 1969/70, 10751, no. 3 (Memorie van Toelichting).

41 Including principle 1.5 of the DCGC.

42 Board and Governance Act. *Wet van 6 juni 2011 tot wijziging van boek 2 van het Burgerlijk Wetboek in verband met de aanpassing van regels over bestuur en toezicht in naamloze en besloten vennootschappen*, Staatsblad 2011, 265.

43 Art. 2:164a DCC.

44 Art. 2:129a(1) DCC.

19.2.3 *Shareholder Appointment and Decision-Making Rights*

Although the A general meeting shares its powers with the corporate board, it traditionally has an important position in the Dutch corporate law framework.[45] In particular, Dutch law allocates the residual power of decision-making to shareholders.[46] Article 2:107(1) DCC states that 'the general meeting, within the limits set by law and the AoA, has all powers that are not assigned to the board or to others'.[47] These powers also include the mandatory legal powers pertaining to supervision and decision-making assigned to the general meeting, which cannot be deviated from in the company's AoA.[48] In addition to the appointment and removal of board members, shareholders are granted several other statutory rights, which can be roughly categorized as information rights (including question rights) and decision-making rights. The right to request information is incorporated in article 2:107(2) DCC, which states that the management board and supervisory board must provide the general meeting with all requested information, unless such information would run contrary to a substantial company interest (see Section 19.2.4 of this chapter).

The general meeting has a large number of formal appointment and decision-making rights, including the adoption of the annual accounts,[49] the appointment of the external auditor[50] and the approval of mergers and takeovers.[51] Here, only the material (recurrent) decision-making rights are discussed. Shareholders have had a binding say on company's remuneration policy since 2004 (the Dutch say-on-pay). Article 2:135(1) DCC stipulates that the general meeting is the only corporate body that can adopt the company's remuneration policy and any amendments thereto.[52] In contrast to remuneration policy, the approval of compensation packages for individual board members can be delegated to another corporate body in the AoA,[53] which is usually the supervisory board.[54] In this case, article 2:135(5) DCC requires shareholder approval on pay schemes in the form of shares and options. The remuneration of the supervisory board also requires shareholder approval.[55]

On 2 April 2019, the Dutch House of Representatives passed a bill to implement the SRD II.[56] Article 9a(2) SRD II holds that where an approved remuneration policy exists and the general meeting does not approve a proposed new such policy, the company shall continue to remunerate its directors in accordance with the existing policy and submit a revised policy for approval at the next general meeting.[57] However, companies are allowed to temporarily derogate from the remuneration policy in exceptional circumstances to serve the long-term interests and

45 See e.g. Ageeth G. H. Klaassen, *Bevoegdheden van de algemene vergadering van aandeelhouders, Instituut voor Ondernemingsrecht no. 60* (Kluwer 2017) 15. The general meeting had a very important role in 1929, when the current corporate law framework of Dutch companies was introduced.

46 For more information on the residual power of decision-making and the right to residuarity, see John Armour and Michael J. Whincop, 'The Proprietary Foundations of Corporate Law' (2007) 27 *Journal of Legal Studies* 437.

47 Translation by the author.

48 See Raaijmakers (n. 35) 445.

49 Art. 2:101(3) DCC.

50 Art. 2:393(2) DCC. The general meeting provides the external auditor with the instruction to control the annual account.

51 Many of these decision-making rules stem from the European regulatory framework.

52 Derived from *Kamerstukken II* 2009/10, 31877, no. 5 (Nota naar aanleiding van het verslag) 25.

53 Art. 2:135(4) DCC.

54 Anne J. F. Lafarre and Christoph F. Van der Elst, 'Executive Pay and Say on Pay in the Netherlands' in Christoph F. van der Elst (ed.), *Executive Directors' Remuneration in Comparative Corporate Perspective* (Kluwer Law International 2015) 205–46.

55 Art. 2:145 DCC.

56 *Kamerstukken II* 2018/19, 35058, no. 2 (Voorstel van Wet). See also *Kamerstukken II* 2018/19, 35058, no. 3 (Memorie van Toelichting).

57 This requirement will be added in art. 2:135(9) DCC.

sustainability of the company as a whole or to assure its viability.[58] Although SRD II offers the possibility of an advisory shareholder vote on the remuneration policy ex article 9a(3), the Dutch legislature has confirmed that it will continue to be a binding vote under Dutch law.[59] In a letter to the Dutch House of Representatives, Eumedion successfully argued that the Dutch say-on-pay with respect to the remuneration policy should require a qualified majority vote of 75 per cent.[60] This qualified majority vote was adopted in the new article 2:135a(2) DCC that requires shareholder approval of companies' remuneration policy at least once every four years. Also, a yearly advisory vote on the remuneration report is now required,[61] which means that as of 2020, shareholders in the Netherlands have – in addition to the vote on remuneration policy they were granted in 2004 – an advisory say on the remuneration report.

With respect to decisions related to share capital that require shareholder approval in accordance with the Capital Directive,[62] the Netherlands closely follows that directive. Article 2:96(1) DCC holds that the general meeting may provide the board of directors with the authority to increase the company's share capital for up to five years. In practice, such authorization is often provided for a shorter period in listed companies and put on the general meeting's agenda every year. The cancellation of pre-emption rights is included in articles 2:96a(6) and (7) DCC. Although most resolutions require a simple majority,[63] the waiver of pre-emption rights requires a qualified majority of two-thirds of the votes *if* less than half of the issued capital is present at the AGM.[64]

In virtually all jurisdictions, shareholders have a say on any amendments to companies' AoA. However, whilst in many countries such amendments require a special majority, in the Netherlands an AoA amendment (*statutenwijziging*) does not require a qualified majority,[65] but the AoA may require a higher majority.[66] Another important voting item in the Netherlands is the discharge of directors (2:121 DCC). In some continental European jurisdictions, shareholders usually discharge directors for conduct in the past financial year. In the Netherlands, discharge can be understood as an act of the general meeting that bindingly declares that directors will not be held liable for conduct in the financial year for which they are being discharged. The decision to discharge, however, limits internal liability to conduct that was known upon the approval of the annual accounts.

The last important shareholder decision-making right discussed in this section pertains to so-called '107a decisions'.[67] Although determining the corporate strategy and policies is included in the task of the management board (see Section 19.2.1), the general meeting has an approval right in the case of a decision that involves a major change in the identity or character of the company

58 Art. 9a(4) SRD II. This provision will be implemented in art. 2:135a(3) and (4) DCC.

59 *Kamerstukken II* 2018/19, 35058, no, 3.

60 Eumedion, letter of 21 November 2018 to the *Vaste Commissie voor Justitie en Veiligheid*. www.eumedion.nl/nl/public/kennisbank/wet-en-regelgeving/2018/2018-11-commentaar-wetsvoorstel-implementatie-richtlijn-aandeelhoudersbetrokkenheid.pdf accessed 15 May 2019. Eumedion argued that Dutch shareholder dissent rates on remuneration matters with important Dutch companies were significantly larger in 2018 than in 2017.

61 Art. 2:135b DCC.

62 Directive 2012/30/EU, amended by Directive 2017/1132 of the European Parliament and of the Council of 14 June 2017 relating to certain aspects of company law [2017] OJL 169/46.

63 Art. 2:120 DCC.

64 Art. 2:96a(7) DCC.

65 Art. 2:121 *et seq*. DCC.

66 Refer to art. 2:120 DCC stating that all resolutions for which no greater majority is required either by law or by the AoA must be passed by an absolute majority (i.e., simple majority) of the votes cast.

67 Art. 2:107a DCC.

or enterprise.[68] Article 2:107a DCC also specifies three circumstances in which the AGM has to approve a board decision.[69] Approval by the general meeting requires a simple majority, although the company's AoA can require a qualified majority.

Decisions made by the general meeting can be annulled if there is a conflict with the standards of reasonableness and fairness.[70] However, seminal Dutch case law has confirmed that shareholders are permitted to primarily serve their individual interests in exercising their shareholder rights,[71] which is also explicitly stated in the DCGC:

> Shareholders can give priority to their own interests, as long as they act in keeping with the principles of reasonableness and fairness in relation to the company, its organs and their fellow shareholders. This includes the willingness to engage with the company and fellow shareholders. The greater the interest which the shareholder has in a company, the greater is his responsibility to the company, fellow shareholders and other stakeholders. Institutional investors are responsible to the ultimate beneficiary owners for the careful and transparent assessment of how to exercise their rights as shareholders of companies.[72]

To conclude, under Dutch law, despite the institutional vision and board autonomy, shareholders have many important control rights. However, shareholder control can be limited by oligarchic clauses that are used by many Dutch listed companies in practice.[73] These clauses may contain that the power of the general meeting with regard to, for example, the decision to amend the AoA, is limited and can only be exercised following a proposal by the management board and with approval the supervisory board: in these cases, shareholders thus only have ratification rights, and no initiation rights.[74] In contrast, shareholders in the Netherlands may dismiss the board members at all times and without reason, which indicates that oligarchic clauses with respect to these shareholder control rights are not allowed.

19.2.4 *Ownership Structures and Control*

The ownership structures of Dutch listed companies can differ substantially, but most large companies have a widely dispersed ownership structure. The average percentage of shares in free float for the 145 Dutch listed companies that also have their headquarters in the Netherlands is

68 For instance, see the *ABN AMRO case* (n. 20).

69 These include: (1) the transfer of the entire or substantially the entire enterprise to a third party; (2) entering into or terminating a long-term cooperation agreement with another company that is of major importance to the company; and (3) taking a participation in the capital of another company with a value of at least one-third of the (consolidated) balance sheet total (also including divestments).

70 Art. 2:15(1)(b) DCC jo art. 2:8 DCC.

71 HR 30 June 1944, ECLI:NL:HR:1944:BG9449 (*Wennex*). Also confirmed in HR 13 November 1959, ECLI:NL:PHR:1959:AG2043 (*Melchers*); HR 19 February 1960, ECLI:NL:PHR:1960:AG2044 (*Aurora*). Note that in the Dutch literature, authors have not yet reached full consensus as to the extent to which shareholders need to take into account the interests of others in their decisions.

72 DCGC 2016, 8.

73 See for the use of these oligarchic clauses by Dutch listed companies in practice: Bastiaan Kemp, Philippe Hezer and Sebastian Renshof, 'Limiting Shareholder Power in Dutch Listed Companies' (2020) Oxford Business Law Blog, www.law.ox.ac.uk/business-law-blog/blog/2020/05/limiting-shareholder-power-dutch-listed-companies accessed 15 July 2020. The authors argue that these oligarchic clauses contribute to balancing shareholder rights and stakeholder interests in the Dutch stakeholder-oriented model.

74 For the amendment to the AoA, one may find the explicit permission of an oligarchic clause in art. 2:121(2) DCC. In contrast, for a capital reduction, this possibility follows from the parliamentary history. See Asser/Maeijer, Van Solinge & Nieuwe Weme 2-II* 2009/181.

TABLE 19.1 *Free float data in % for Dutch large- and mid-cap companies (AEX-25 and AMX-25)*

Year	Mean	Standard deviation	Median	Minimum	Maximum
2009	85.0	17.6	90.6	44.5	100.0
2010	86.0	17.7	94.5	40.8	100.0
2011	84.7	18.3	94.3	39.7	100.0
2012	83.3	18.0	88.1	37.4	100.0
2013	83.5	19.6	89.0	34.3	100.0
2014	83.0	19.4	86.7	34.2	100.0
2015	81.1	21.5	86.6	20.7	100.0
2016	77.9	23.9	86.9	20.4	100.0
2017	80.2	21.9	91.8	21.1	100.0
2018	80.8	20.5	87.6	21.1	100.0
Total	82.3	20.1	89.6	20.4	100.0

Note to table: the data were retrieved from Thomson Reuters (December 2019).

around 66.9 per cent.[75] Table 19.1 shows the ownership structure of Dutch large-cap companies (AEX-25) and mid-cap companies (AMX-25).

It can be seen from Table 19.1 that the ownership structures of Dutch large-cap and mid-cap companies are generally widely dispersed. The companies with the highest ownership concentrations (less than 50 per cent of their shares in free float) in 2018 according to Thomson Reuters data were: Grandvision (21.1 per cent free float), OCI (39.3 per cent free float), Heineken (40.7 per cent free float), Adyen (46.2 per cent free float) and TomTom (48.7 per cent free float). Most Dutch large-cap companies have highly dispersed ownership structures: the average free float for those in the AEX-25 was 87 per cent across the 2009–18 period. Fifteen AEX-25 companies had a free float of more than 90 per cent in 2018. With respect to shareholder types, research by Abma and others shows that around 87 per cent of the shares in Dutch large-cap companies (part of the AEX-25) were owned by (mostly) foreign institutional investors in 2014; 6 per cent were owned by Dutch institutional investors, and another 6 per cent by Dutch non-financial companies. Only 1 per cent of the share capital was owned by Dutch retail shareholders.[76]

There is a particular large shareholder 'type' in Dutch listed companies: the trust office (in Dutch, *stichting administratiekantoor* or simply STAK). Dutch companies sometimes do not list (all of) their shares but issue non-voting depository receipts. The shares are issued to a trust office that is the legal owner of the voting rights, and holders of non-voting depository receipts receive financial rights and dividends. Voting rights are thus separated from capital rights. Pursuant to article 2:118a DCC, the holders of non-voting depository receipts may submit a request to receive proxies, except in takeover situations.[77] Depository receipt holders may also give binding instructions to the trust office.[78] Note that the DCGC supports depository receipts as

[75] Data retrieved from Thomson Reuters on 24 June 2019.

[76] Abma and others (n. 5) 8.

[77] In contrast, DCGC 2008 provides that the trust office shall issue proxies in all circumstances and without limitation to the holders of depository receipts who so request. The Dutch Code thus prohibits the use of depository receipts as an anti-takeover device (also see DCGC 2016, principle 4.4).

[78] The Transparency Directive (Directive 2004/109/EC) defines a shareholder as 'any natural person or legal entity governed by private or public law, who holds, directly or indirectly . . . depository receipts, in which case the holder of the depository receipt shall be considered as the shareholder of the underlying shares represented by the depository receipts', which means that holders of depository receipts must also disclose information about their major holdings. In this regard, readers may also refer to art. 5:33(1)(b) Wft, which states that depository receipts are defined as shares for the purpose of ch. 5.3 of the act (which includes disclosure requirements).

a solution to shareholder absenteeism in the general meeting, but prohibits their use as an anti-takeover device[79]: the trust office shall issue proxies in all circumstances and without limitations to the holders of depository receipts who so request.[80]

ING Group was a typical example of a Dutch listed company with depository receipts for virtually all of its shares. Until 2016, the trust office could exercise a large part of the voting rights in ING's general meeting (in 2016 it was 42.88 per cent). In 2016, the ING Group proposed to the general meeting that the company's AoA be amended, including the abolition of the depositary receipt structure via *Stichting Aandelen* (ING Trust Office). Following the amendments to the AoA, the depositary receipt structure was formally abolished on 26 July 2016. Every depository receipt holder became entitled to ordinary shares in ING in exchange for the depositary receipts previously held. Fugro, another Dutch listed company, in contrast, still had a depository receipt structure for all of its shares, at the time this research was conducted, meaning that only these non-voting depository receipts are listed and traded. Voting results show that the trust office represented 56.44 per cent of the shares voted in the company's 2019 AGM.

A majority of Dutch listed companies use (cumulative) preferred financing shares as a protection mechanism. Dutch companies use a so-called *Stichting Continuïteit* to which the board grants a call option for purchasing protective preferred shares. Such a friendly foundation can temporarily receive protective preferred shares in the event of a hostile takeover attempt or another event such that the stakes of the existing shareholders are diluted. Often these shares are not fully paid up.[81] Another protection mechanism used by Dutch listed companies is the issuance of shares with special control rights (so-called 'priority shares')[82] These shares are usually issued to a foundation or trust office.

19.3 LEGAL MEANS OF SHAREHOLDER ENGAGEMENT AND VOTING

19.3.1 *Calling a Meeting*

The general meeting is usually convened by the supervisory board and management board, although the authority to do so can also be granted to others in the company's AoA.[83] In that event, shareholders or other corporate actors granted this right must first ask the corporate board to convene a general meeting. Shareholders who are not granted this authority via the AoA are able to request the convening of a general meeting in court if they hold at least 10 per cent of the issued share capital.[84] Article 5 SRD I deals with the information that must be made available to shareholders prior to the general meetings,[85] and also stipulates that the minimum convening period is twenty-one days. In the Netherlands, since the implementation of SRD I, a minimum

79 DCGC 2016, principle 4.4.

80 Ibid.

81 Following art. 2:96a DCC shareholders have no pre-emption rights when these shares are issued. In addition, art. 2:80 DCC holds that only 25 per cent of the share price needs to be paid up.

82 Art. 2:92(3) DCC.

83 Art. 2:109 DCC.

84 See art. 2:110 et seq. DCC for the requirements. For instance, shareholders need to have a 'reasonable interest' (*redelijk belang*) in order to request the convening of a general meeting ex art. 2:111(1) DCC. Note that in the event that the management board or supervisory board remains in default as regards convening a general meeting, every shareholder has the right to obtain the authority of the temporary relief judge (*voorzieningenrechter*) to convene the meeting (ex art. 2:112 DCC).

85 Implemented in arts. 2:113 and 2:114 DCC.

call period of forty-two days has been applied to listed companies.[86] Article 7 SRD I introduced the record date, indicating that there should be no restrictions on the rights of shareholders between this record date and the date of the general meeting. The Dutch legislator finally chose the twenty-eighth day before the meeting as the registration date.[87]

19.3.2 *Shareholder Proposals*

Article 6 of SRD I affords shareholders the right to put items on the agenda of the general meeting (i.e. shareholder proposals). This individual shareholder right has been granted under article 2:114a DCC since 2004, but, in accordance with SRD I, the ground for refusal of an overriding interest was deleted from this article. The ownership requirement to add proposals to the general meeting agenda is a maximum 3 per cent of issued capital,[88] although companies may require a lower threshold in their AoA. Research by Abma and others showed for instance that Wolters Kluwer has lowered this threshold to 0.5 per cent.[89] Shareholders need to (electronically) send a reasoned request to the company no later than the sixtieth day before the general meeting concerned.[90] Shareholder proposals that are outside the decision-making powers of the general meeting cannot be put to a vote[91] but can be added to the agenda as a discussion item. However, as discussed in Section 19.2.1 of this chapter, the *Boskalis/Fugro case* shows that the board is not required to put such an item on the meeting's agenda.

19.3.3 *Modes of Participation and Voting*

Article 8(1) SRD I stipulates that shareholders must be able to exercise their rights electronically. Electronic participation may be made subject to requirements only if these are necessary to ensure the identification of shareholders and the security of electronic participation.[92] Electronic participation has been permitted in the Netherlands since 1 January 2007 pursuant to the *Wet elektronische communicatiemiddelen*, the only addition is that the conditions imposed on the use of particular electronic means of communication should be reasonable and necessary for the identification of the person entitled to attend the general meeting and the reliability and security of the communication.[93] The consensus view is that virtual-only meetings are not permitted in

86 Art. 2:115(2) DCC, with Amendment No. 16. The original legislative proposal contained a convocation period of thirty days.

87 The original bill to implement SRD I initially provided for a registration date on the twenty-first day before the general meeting. See the letter of 7 November 2009, *Kamerstukken II* 2009/10, 31058, no. 13, 4.

88 Before 1 July 2013, the legal requirement was 1 per cent. The Netherlands increased the threshold to 3 per cent owing to activist shareholder behavior such as seen in the *ABN Amro case* where the activist shareholder Children's Investment Fund Management (TCI) had acquired only 1 per cent of the share capital of *ABN Amro* and requested a split-up of the banking group.

89 Many Dutch companies have thresholds lower than 3 per cent because to increase the threshold, shareholder approval of an amendment to the AoA is needed, and shareholders have often voted against such amendments in the past. See Abma et al. (n. 5).

90 The AoA can provide for a shorter period. However, as Abma et al. (n. 5) indicate, the vast majority of Dutch listed companies do not deviate from this term in their AoA. Note that the minimum call period for the general meeting is forty-two days.

91 *Kamerstukken I* 2009/10, 31746, C, 6. Also see Abma et al. (n. 5).

92 Art. 8(2) SRD I.

93 Art. 2:117a DCC. In addition, following the implementation of SRD I it was added to art. 2:117b DCC that voting can also take place by means of a letter.

the Netherlands.[94] However, a hybrid meeting is allowed, and such a meeting was held for the first time by a Dutch listed company in 2019. During KPN's 2019 AGM, shareholders were – in addition to the physical general meeting – able to attend and vote in real time via the internet. Article 10 SRD I gives shareholders the right to appoint a natural or legal person as a proxy to participate in and vote at the general meeting in her name.

However, with the Covid-19 crisis, which has limited physical gatherings since March 2020, the Temporary Act Covid-19[95] came into force on 24 April 2020, allowing general meetings to take place entirely virtually from 16 March 2020 until 1 April 2022.[96] With this Temporary Act, a physical general meeting was still possible but was no longer mandatory for formal decision-making.[97] Companies can hold a virtual-only meeting under the following conditions: (1) shareholders who can access the meeting through electronic means of communication are identified; (2) shareholders can directly consult the treatises at the meeting by electronic means of communication (including, for instance, video or audio livestream); and (3) shareholders can exercise their voting rights via those electronic means during or in advance of the general meeting.[98] Whereas scholarship pays attention on the ability of shareholders to vote and participate online and in real time considering technological innovations,[99] the Temporary Act does not consider *voting as a necessary element* of a virtual-only meeting. Also using the right to speak and asking questions during the general meeting was not required per se:[100] shareholders, however, needed to be able to submit questions about agenda items in writing or electronically up to seventy-two hours before the general meeting.[101] These questions needed to be answered no later than at the general meeting (and could be bundled per theme) and answers should be posted on the company's website.

Finally, following SRD I, there are no restrictions on the possibility for persons to beappointed as proxies (other than legal capacity).[102] A resolution (for which the law and/or AoA do not require any qualified majority) is approved by *volstrekte meerderheid van de uitgebrachte stemmen* (absolute majority of the votes cast, which is a simple majority vote).[103] Dutch legal

94 Scholars often refer to art. 2:116 DCC, which seems to require a physical location for the AGM.

95 *Wet van 22 april 2020, houdende tijdelijke voorzieningen op het 23 errain van het Ministerie van Justitie en Veiligheid in verband met de uitbraak van COVID-19 (Tijdelijke wet COVID-19 Justitie en Veiligheid)*, Staatsblad 2020, 124 en inwerkingtredingsbesluit, Staatsblad 2020, 126 (Temporary Act Covid-19). *Kamerstukken II* 2019/20, 35434, no. 2.

96 The initial expiration date was 1 September 2020, which was increased to 1 April 2022 with the *Besluit van 26 januari 2022 tot wijziging van enkele vervaldata van wettelijke voorzieningen die zijn getroffen in verband met de uitbraak van COVID-19, Staatsblad* 2022, 42.

97 *Kamerstukken II* 2019/20, 35434, no. 3 (Memorie van Toelichting), 7.

98 Also see S. Rietveld and R. E. Stroeve, 'De Tijdelijke wet COVID-19 Justitie en Veiligheid' (2020) 3–4 *Maandblad voor Ondernemingsrecht* 88–107.

99 For instance, see Anne J. F. Lafarre and Christoph F. Van der Elst, 'Shareholder Voice in Complex Intermediated Proxy Systems: Blockchain Technology As a Solution?' (2021) 4(1) *The Stanford Journal of Blockchain Law and Policy* 29–52.

100 However, the board must ensure that during the meeting electronically or otherwise questions may be asked, except in the light of the circumstances cannot reasonably be required at that time. The chairman of the meeting can monitor the meeting order just like in a physical AGM, for example if it appears that too many questions are asked. See *Kamerstukken II* 2019/20, 35434, no. 3, 8–9 (Memorie van Toelichting).

101 If less than five days before the date of a physical AGM, the management board decides to convene the AGM virtually, shareholders can submit questions up to thirty-six hours before the meeting. Note that convening the virtual AGM is possible up to forty-eight hours before the meeting.

102 Following art. 11 of the SRD I, proxy holders can be appointed and notified by electronic means. These provisions have been implemented in art. 2:117(6) and art. 2:117a(5) DCC.

103 Art. 2:120 DCC.

scholarship agrees that a vote implies a declaration of intention, and hence, abstentions are generally not included in the number of votes cast.[104]

19.3.4 *Shareholder Questions*

Under Dutch law, individual shareholder's right to request information has been incorporated in article 2:107(2) DCC since 1971.[105] This provision states that the management board and supervisory board must provide the general meeting with all requested information unless such information would run contrary to a substantial company interest. According to the Dutch legislature, this article already included the right to ask questions as stipulated in article 9 SRD I, and hence no new provision was adopted.[106] Because the Dutch provision includes the phrase 'unless a substantial interest of the company opposes', this already entailed the second paragraph of article 9 SRD I as well. In a parliamentary document, the Dutch legislature provides an example of such a 'substantial interest' (*zwaarwichtig belang*): information that may harm the competitiveness of the company.[107] This example is in line with the 'business interests' mentioned in the SRD I.[108] It should be noted that the right to ask questions is also provided to proxy holders with written proxies (*bij een schriftelijke gevolmachtigde*).[109]

The first sentence of article 9(1) SRD I limits the scope of the questions that can be asked to items on the general meeting's agenda. In contrast, article 2:107(2) DCC does not limit that scope, and hence it may be reason to assume that individual shareholders have the right to request information about matters other than agenda items under Dutch law.[110] The general consensus is that shareholder questions are bounded by article 2:8 DCC, which stipulates that shareholders (and other corporate actors) should act in accordance with standards of reasonableness and fairness (*redelijkheid en billijkheid*). There are no legal provisions under Dutch law that explicitly allow the meeting chair to limit shareholders' question rights. The role of the chair is also not defined in the DCC. However, it is common practice for the AGM chair, in accordance with standards of reasonableness and fairness, to limit the amount of time shareholders speak during the meeting. In addition, article 2:117(1) DCC provides individual shareholders ('every shareholder') with the right to speak during general meetings. Shareholders may also put questions to the external auditor.[111]

104 In earlier days, scholars sometimes distinguished blanks from abstentions. A statutory provision stating that blanks be included with the amount of votes against was not inconceivable. See Schwarz, *GS Rechtspersonen*, art. 2:120 DCC. Nowadays many large listed companies have explicitly adopted in their AoA that these blanks not be included in the number of votes cast.

105 Although not explicitly stated in Dutch law, in line with SRD I, this right is an individual shareholder right. See the *ASMI* case. See n. 20.

106 *Kamerstukken II* 2008/09, 31 746, no. 3 (Memorie van Toelichting), 15. The parliamentary document refers to, inter alia, Asser-Maeijer 2-III, 2000, no. 256.

107 *Kamerstukken II* 2008/09, 31746, no. 3 (Memorie van Toelichting), 15.

108 Whether the term 'substantial interest' should be interpreted in a broad or narrow manner is not entirely clear. Dutch scholars generally argue that the refusal of an answer should only be exceptional.

109 Art. 2:117 DCC. This follows from SRD I: proxy holders enjoy the same rights as shareholders, such as the right to ask questions (discussed below) and engage in discussions (provision 10(1) of the directive).

110 In the *ASMI case*, the Dutch Supreme Court (*Hoge Raad*) ruled that this is indeed the case (*ro* 4.6): 'Iedere aandeelhouder heeft voorts ter vergadering zelfstandig het recht vragen te stellen – ongeacht of deze betrekking hebben op punten die op de agenda zijn vermeld'. Translation by the author: 'each individual shareholder also has the right to ask questions at the meeting regardless of whether these relate to items that are mentioned on the agenda'. See n. 20.

111 Art. 2:117(5) DCC holds that 'the auditor to whom the audit of the financial statements has been granted, as referred to in art 393, paragraph 1, is authorized to attend and to address the general meeting that decides on the adoption of the financial statements'. The DCGC states that the external auditor can be questioned by the general meeting about his statement on the fairness of the annual accounts (principle 4.1.9).

19.3.5 *An Overview*

Figure 19.1 summarizes the process flow of Dutch general meetings as discussed in the previous sections.

19.3.6 *Shareholder Stewardship*

Whilst the Dutch corporate law landscape was characterized by a number of landmark feuds between hedge funds and corporate board in the past,[112] today it is more common to observe increased engagement by institutional investors. Because the vast majority of shares in Dutch listed companies are owned by institutional investors, institutional shareholder stewardship can be considered important in the Netherlands.

SRD II puts a strong focus on institutional investors and asset managers and the disclosure of their engagement policy.[113] The voting behaviour of institutional investors and asset managers seems to be an important part of their engagement policy, particularly with respect to 'the most significant' votes[114] which are determined based on (1) the subject matter of the vote or (2) the size of the holding in the company.[115] SRD II mentions that investors should set their own criteria based on these two aspects and apply them consistently. In the parliamentary discussion pertaining to the implementation of this provision of SRD II under Dutch law[116] there was some discussion of what the 'most significant' votes entail. The Explanatory Memorandum explains that these votes at the very least pertain to matters receiving substantial media attention or that are considered to have been spearhead by an institutional investor or asset manager prior to the general meeting.[117]

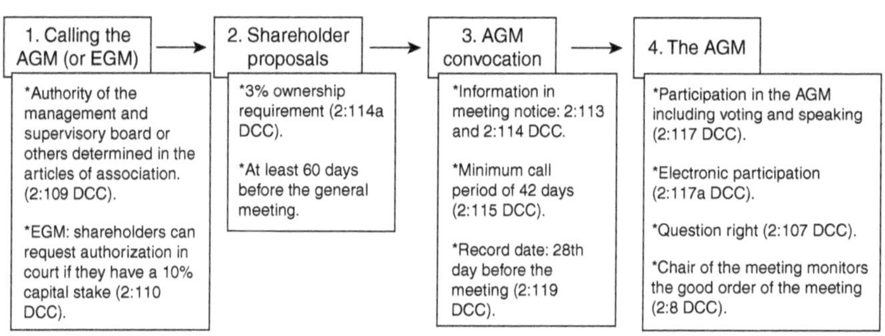

FIGURE 19.1 The Dutch AGM

[112] See for instance the *ABN AMRO* case, the *ASMI* case and the *AkzoNobel case*. See n. 20, 8.

[113] Preamble 14 explicitly links the greater involvement of these shareholders to environmental, social and governance factors. Also, in art. 3g, which refers to engagement policy, non-financial performance and risks are explicitly mentioned.

[114] Art. 3g(1)(b) SRD II.

[115] Art. 3g(1)(b) SRD II. Insignificant votes may include votes cast on purely procedural matters or votes cast in companies where the investor has a very minor stake compared to the investor's holdings in other investee companies. Art. 3g(1)(b) SRD II.

[116] In art. 5:87c(3) Wft.

[117] *Kamerstukken II* 2018/19, 35 058, no. 3, 34–5 (Explanatory Memorandum) https://zoek.officielebekendmakingen.nl/kst-35058-3.html accessed 31 October 2020. Note that insignificant votes are explained in the Explanatory Memorandum in the same way as in SRD II.

The Dutch Stewardship Code was launched by Eumedion in 2018 and entered into force in 2019. Unlike the DCGC, the Code has no statutory legal basis and does not explicitly use any comply-or-explain principle. However, because of the important role of the Eumedion in the Dutch corporate governance landscape and the significant institutional investor ownership, the Dutch Stewardship Code has significant practical implications. It contains eleven principles and, like in SRD II and the DCGC, many of these principles concern the disclosure of the engagement policy. However, the Dutch Stewardship Code also discusses, amongst other things, dialogue between institutional investors and their investees and other stakeholders and cooperation between institutional investors.[118]

19.4 SHAREHOLDER ENGAGEMENT AND VOTING IN PRACTICE

In this section, hand-collected data from the websites of the annual general meetings (AGMs) of Dutch listed large-cap companies are used to provide insights on the voting and engagement practices of shareholders in the Netherlands. [119] The voting information reported in documents disclosed by the companies on their websites is used for this purpose.[120] In addition, it is common practice amongst Dutch companies to disclose the transcripts of their general meetings on their corporate websites. In this way, companies comply with principle 4.1.10 DCGC, which holds that the report of the general meeting should be made available to the shareholders no later than three months after the end of the meeting.

A hand-collected dataset with voting information from 25 Dutch large-cap (AEX-25) companies for an 11-year period from 2010–20 was used,[121] constituting a relatively balanced panel dataset of 267 observations. For the 2010–15 period, data were available for all companies, whereas for 2016–18, data were available for twenty-four companies, for 2019 for twenty-three companies and for 2020 for twenty-two companies.[122] Most of the 245 meetings took place in April (154 meetings); 75 meetings took place in May, 14 in March and 2 in June.[123]

19.4.1 *Voting in Practice*

As stated in Section 19.3.3 of this chapter, electronic shareholder participation in general meetings is permitted in the Netherlands. As in many other countries, remote (electronic) voting prior to the general meeting has become an important voting mode for many shareholders. Dutch companies generally do not (fully) disclose the voting modes used. However,

118 In addition, it also provides further insights on what can be considered significant votes. These votes are linked to 'significant matters' in the Dutch Stewardship Code, which include the economic or strategic importance, whether the outcome of the vote is expected to be controversial, or whether the institutional investor disagrees with the voting advice of the corporate board. Note that Eumedion issues alerts to its members to indicate which voting items may be considered significant.

119 This research was finished in June 2020.

120 Art. 14 of the SRD I.

121 I retrieved this sample using the following requirements: (1) the company is part of the AEX-25 index for most years in the sample period (e.g., at least six years), and; (2) the company's registered office should be in the Netherlands guaranteeing the application of the Dutch rules. Hence, inter alia Shell and KLM-Air France are excluded from the dataset.

122 Royal Imtech went bankrupt in August 2015 and was thus no longer included in the sample from 2016. RELX (formerly Reed Elsevier) simplified its corporate structure in 2018 and merged RELX Plc and RELX NV, with RELX Plc becoming the sole parent company of the corporate group. During the course of 2019, Gemalto NV was acquired by the French company Thales Group.

123 A full list of the companies is available upon request from the author.

after the removal of depository receipts, the Dutch listed bank ING started to disclose the percentage of shareholders that used proxy voting prior to the meeting: 96.3 per cent in 2017, 99.3 per cent in 2018–19 and 100 per cent (rounded) in 2020. These figures may illustrate that remote voting has indeed become the main voting mode. Figure 19.2 shows the mean and median voter turnout rates for the AEX-25 companies. An increasing trend can be seen over time.

The average turnout rate for the entire sample was 65.8 per cent, with a standard deviation of 17.1 per cent. There was a decrease in voter turnout from 2019 (69.4 per cent) to 2020 (66.4 per cent) when the general meetings were conducted online. Although more research is recommended on the effects of virtual meetings, a paired t-test on the twenty-two observations available for both 2019 and 2020[124] shows that this difference of about 3 per cent is statistically significant at the 10 per cent level. The highest turnout rates were found for ING in the 2010–16 period (rounded to 100 per cent). ING issued depository receipts for almost all shares with voting rights in that period, and ING's trust office voted all shares for which depository receipt holders had not requested proxies (also see Section 19.4.1.1 below). As noted, in the 2016 AGM, ING proposed an amendment to its AoA to abolish the depository receipt structure. Hence, in the 2017 AGM, voter turnout was significantly reduced, falling to 60.7 per cent. The lowest turnout rates were found in 2014 and 2015 for Imtech and BAM Group, with 16.7 and 20.2 per cent, respectively. According to Eumedion, the low turnout rate at Imtech was probably the result of substantial short positions.[125]

19.4.1.1 Voting Items

The practical framework for shareholder decision-making rights in the Netherlands is now considered. The content of the general meeting's agenda is not harmonized at the European level, except for capital resolutions and merger approval (to some extent). It is important to note

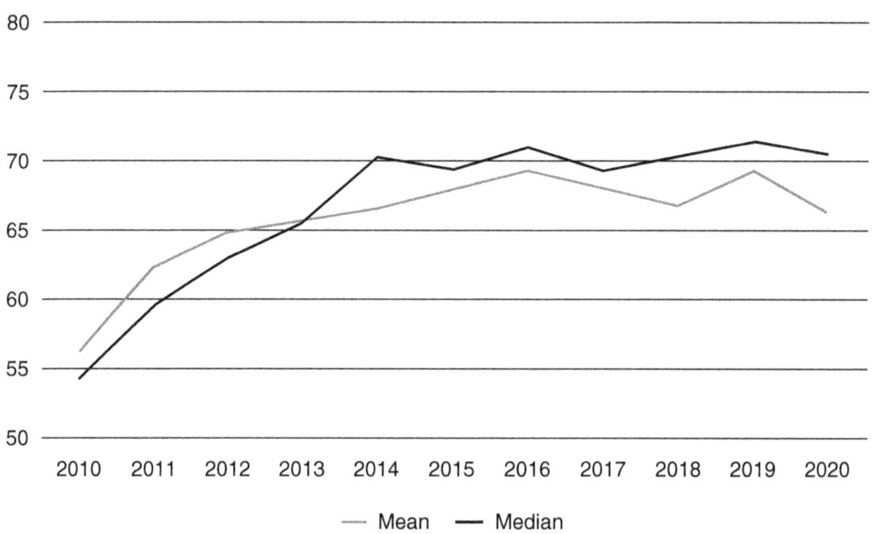

FIGURE 19.2 Turnout for Dutch AEX-25 companies (%)

124 See n. 122. Note that in the 2020 sample, Gemalto NV was no longer present, resulting in twenty-two observations for that year.

125 Eumedion, 'Evaluation 2014 AGM Season' (2014) 2.

that these decision-making rights are merely *approval rights*: in practice, shareholders usually decide whether to approve a resolution prepared by the corporate board.[126] This is not the case for shareholder proposals.

The average number of agenda items found in the sample was twelve, with a standard deviation of 3.8. The highest number of agenda items was found for the AGMs of RELX (formerly Reed Elsevier) and Unilever, with more than twenty voting items each. These two companies are listed and incorporated in the UK and follow the UK corporate governance code. Hence, all of their directors are re-elected every year. All of the voting items in the sample were management proposals: *no* shareholder proposals appeared on the agendas of the AGMs of AEX-25 companies in the 2010–20 period.[127]

Based on the legal analysis in Section 19.2.3 and data analysis, the following voting items categories are defined:

(1) *Financial accounts*: shareholders have the right to adopt the company's annual accounts (2:101(3) DCC).
(2) *Director (re-)elections*: depending on the board structure, shareholders appoint executive and non-executive directors or supervisory board members and, depending on the company's AoA, management board members as well.[128] Most Dutch listed companies voluntarily apply the *structuurregime* (2:132, 2:142, 2:144 and 2:162 DCC).
(3) *Discharge*: shareholders may discharge their directors (2:121 DCC).
(4) *Say-on-pay*: shareholders have a say on the company's remuneration policy, share and share option schemes, and supervisory board remuneration (2:135, 2:135a and 2:145 DCC). As of 2020, shareholders also have an advisory vote on the company's remuneration report, following the implementation of SRD II in article 2:135b DCC.
(5) *Capital resolutions*: shareholders *inter alia* need to approve the authority to increase share capital (2:96 DCC), waive pre-emption rights (2:96a DCC) and to allow the company to buy back shares (2:98(4) and 2:99(1) DCC).
(6) *Auditor appointment*: the AGM provides the external auditor with the instruction to control the annual account (2:393(2) DCC).[129]
(7) *Amendments to AoA*: the Dutch *statutenwijziging* requires shareholder approval (2:121 DCC).

In addition to annual account approval, in virtually all of the considered general meetings directors and supervisory board members were discharged. In 248 of the 267 AGMs, one or more board members were (re-)elected. Capital resolutions were also quite often on the agenda: shareholders were able to vote 232 times for the authorization to issue shares, 224 times for the waiver of pre-emption rights and 245 times for the company's acquisition of shares. Auditors were appointed 138 times, and say-on-pay-related resolutions appeared on the agenda 147 times. In contrast, AoA amendments appeared on the agenda only fifty-eight times.[130] Given the sample

[126] In the Netherlands, as per art. 2:133(1) DCC, the company's AoA may provide that the general meeting appoints directors based on nomination (*bindende voordracht*). Paragraph 2 of the article provides that the AGM may at any time overrule the binding effect of such nomination by means of a resolution passed with a two-thirds majority that represents more than half of the issued share capital.

[127] Proxy fights and proxy solicitation are also uncommon in the Netherlands. See Abma et al. (n. 5).

[128] See Section 19.2.2.

[129] Based on the Audit Directive. Directive 2014/56/EU of the European Parliament and of the Council of 16 April 2014 amending Directive 2006/43/EC on statutory audits of annual accounts and consolidated accounts (2014) OJL 158/19.

[130] In addition to these seven categories, the data suggest that although dividends do not require shareholder approval in the Netherlands, in practice companies usually put this agenda item to a vote (during 203 AGMs).

average of twelve voting items per AGM, these numbers indicate that the vast majority of the matters that shareholders decide on during Dutch general meetings probably fall in one of the aforementioned categories of recurrent voting items. During nine general meetings one or more voting items were withdrawn (see Table 19.2).

Dutch listed companies typically have a two-tier board structure, in which shareholders can either elect supervisory board members alone or both supervisory board members and management board members. Of the twenty-five listed companies in the sample, only Unilever and RELX have a one-tier board structure.[131] In these two companies, shareholders elect both non-executive and executive directors. Figure 19.3 shows the average number of board (re-)elections for each year in the study period. On average, one (supervisory) director was elected at every AGM and two (supervisory) directors were re-elected.

TABLE 19.2 *Voting items withdrawn*

Company	Year	Voting item	Reason?
Ahold	2015	Amend AoA to reduce the minimum number of members of the management board	According to the supervisory board, there was no longer a need for this voting item at the time of the vote.[132]
Boskalis	2013	Director re-election	Demise of the director.[133]
ING	2018	Remuneration policy	The public response to the remuneration policy amendments.
ING	2020	Dividend for 2019	Based on recommendation of the European Central Bank to not pay out dividends.[134]
Philips	2017	Remuneration supervisory board	Large shareholders did not support this proposal.
Philips	2020	Proposal to adopt dividend	Dividend proposal was amended and put on the agenda of a subsequent EGM.[135]
Wereldhave	2015	Remuneration policy	After publication of the agenda, several major shareholders scriticized the indicators chosen for the short-term and long-term variable remuneration.[136]
Wereldhave	2019	Excluding pre-emption rights	As another proposal on issuing shares was not approved, this proposal was not put to the vote.[137]
Wereldhave	2020	Dividend and reserves policy; Reappoint supervisory board member	The dividend proposal was cancelled to strengthen liquidity; the supervisory board size was reduced to three members to reduce costs.[138]

[131] These two companies are also incorporated and listed in the UK.
[132] Ahold Minutes 2015 AGM.
[133] Boskalis Voting Results 2013 AGM.
[134] ING Groep Minutes 2020 AGM.
[135] Philips Minutes 2020 AGM.
[136] Wereldhave Minutes 2015 AGM.
[137] Wereldhave Voting Results 2019 AGM.
[138] Wereldhave Minutes 2020 AGM.

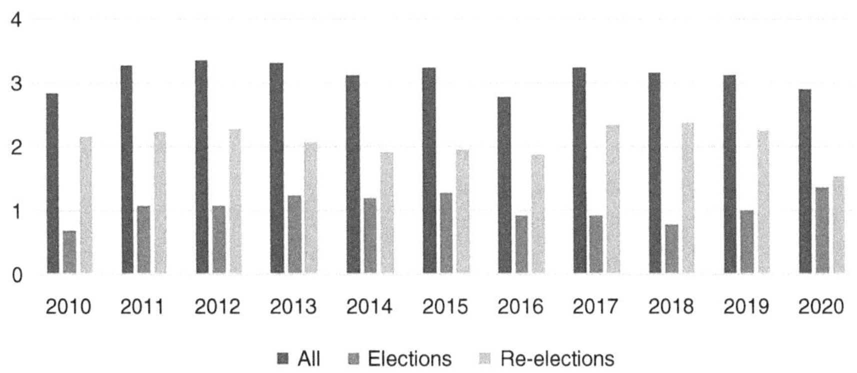

FIGURE 19.3 Average number of board (re-)elections in 2010–20

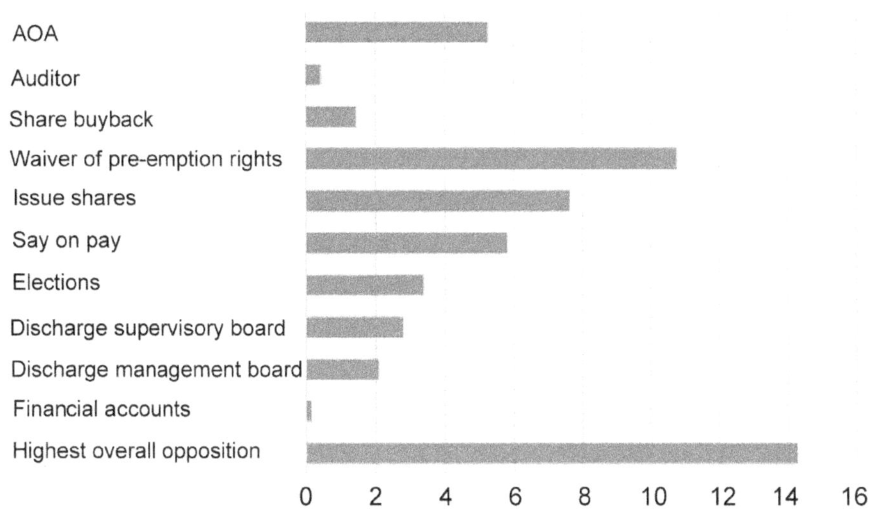

FIGURE 19.4 Highest dissent rates on average (%)[139]

Figure 19.4 shows the dissent rates for resolutions in the AEX-25 sample. It can be seen that the adoption of financial accounts is merely a formality, and thus receives very high approval rates. In contrast, capital-related resolutions, AoA amendments and say-on-pay resolutions often receive relatively high opposition rates. Several t-tests showed that most of the differences were statistically significant.

Not only was there a large difference between the approval rates for different voting items, as shown in Figure 19.4, but different companies also experienced different dissent rates. TNT[140] experienced the largest degree of shareholder opposition, with an average of about 30 per cent and a standard deviation of about 23 per cent at their AGMs in 2010–20. Other companies experiencing shareholder opposition rates of more than 20 per cent on average were SBM Offshore, Fugro and Wolters Kluwer. Amongst those experiencing relatively low opposition rates were Vopak (about 4 per cent on average), Royal Imtech (about 5 per cent) and Boskalis (6 per cent).

[139] In accordance with art. 2:120 DCC, these dissent rates are calculated as: votes against / (votes in favour + votes against).

[140] This company is now named PostNL.

Although the dissent rates can be higher for some voting items, including the cancellation of pre-emption rights and say-on-pay resolutions, resolutions are seldom dismissed in general meetings. In the sample of 267 AGMs, only twelve voting items were dismissed, as shown in Table 19.3.

For instance, as Table 19.3 shows, in the 2019 AGM, the discharge of supervisory board members and management board members at ING was not granted by shareholders. ING board members were criticized by shareholders for a money laundering affair that led to a fine of €775 million in 2018.[141] There was only one other general meeting in the sample in which shareholders did not approve the discharge of supervisory board members, with 60 per cent votes against: the 2011 TNT AGM was combined with an extraordinary general meeting (EGM) on the same day concerning the demerger of the company's express business.[142] In the minutes, it can be derived from the statement issued by the representative of several institutional investors that the disapproval of the board's discharge may be linked to the proposed demerger and related anti-takeover measures.[143]

During the 2010 TNT AGM, a proposal to maintain the Dutch *structuurregime* was defeated with more than 82 per cent of the vote. During the 2011 AGM of SBM Offshore, shareholders rejected a proposal containing '[a]mendments on profit and loss'. The proposal included an increase in the dividends for preference shares used as a protection device by the SBM Offshore trust office. Concerning the waiver of pre-emption rights, such resolutions passed at the AGMs of AkzoNobel, Koninklijke BAM, Fugro, KPN, SBM Offshore and Wolters Kluwer, with shareholder opposition ranging

TABLE 19.3 *Dismissed voting items (%)*

Resolution	Year	Dissent (%)	Voting item
BAM	2017	36.8	Cancel pre-emption rights
Gemalto	2013	55.5; 50.4	Cancel pre-emption rights; issue shares
ING Group	2019	62.7; 62.5	Discharge supervisory board; discharge management board
SBM Offshore	2011	83.4	Amend AoA
SBM Offshore	2020	30.0	Remuneration policy[144]
PostNL (TNT)	2010	82.4	Maintaining the *structuurregime*
PostNL (TNT)	2011	60.0	Discharge supervisory board
Wereldhave	2018	44.8	Cancel pre-emption rights
Wereldhave	2019	53.1	Issue shares
Wolters Kluwer	2020	47.9	Remuneration policy[145]

141 ING NV Minutes 2019 AGM, www.ing.com/Investor-relations/Shareholders-meeting/Annual-General-Meeting/Archive.htm accessed 31 October 2020.

142 After this EGM, TNT was renamed PostNL.

143 'Mrs. [X] (Robeco, APG, MnServices, Syntrus Achmea Vermogensbeheer, Pensioenfonds voor de Grafische Bedrijven) notes that TNT NV has included several protection arrangements for TNT Express NV in the split proposal ... The group of Dutch institutional investors on whose behalf it speaks is critical of the protection arrangements in the split proposal. The multitude of protection structures is not considered to be in the interest of long-term shareholders'. TNT Minutes 2011 AGM, 28. Translated by the author.

144 Following the implementation of SRD II in the Netherlands, the remuneration policy requires a 75 per cent majority vote ex art. 2:135a(2) DCC.

145 Ibid.

from 26.2 to 47.4 per cent. For this voting item, a qualified two-thirds majority is required only if less than 50 per cent of the capital is present during the meeting.[146] In contrast, the attendance rates at the 2017 AGM of Koninklijke Bam and the 2018 AGM of Wereldhave were not sufficiently high, with only 38.6 and 36.1 per cent, respectively. Therefore, their resolutions on the cancellation of pre-emption rights were not adopted, with dissent rates of 36.8 and 44.8 per cent, respectively.

19.4.1.2 Outsider Shareholder Opposition

The ownership structures of Dutch listed companies are generally widely dispersed, although some companies have more concentrated ownership structures. This can have a large impact on corporate governance, as the voting results in companies with large shareholders do not always reflect the discontent of outsider shareholders. For example, the Heineken family is the ultimate owner of Heineken, holding control of the company via a pyramid structure (holding 88.9 per cent of L'Arche Green, which holds a 52.6 per cent stake in Heineken Holding, which in turn holds a 50 per cent stake in Heineken, according to data from the annual reports for 2017–19). FEMSA is an allied shareholder of the Heineken family that holds an indirect stake of 8.63 per cent in Heineken. Hence, with the Heineken family and FEMSA together roughly holding 59 per cent of the shares in Heineken, and these insider shareholders exercising their voting rights, with a theoretical voter turnout of 100 per cent, opposition could never be higher than 41 per cent. In practice, however, turnout rates are generally much lower. From the data, it follows that the average turnout rate for Heineken is about 85 per cent. Hence, if *all* outsider shareholders opposed a particular resolution, the highest possible opposition rate would be 30.6 per cent.[147]

Other AEX-25 companies with controlling shareholders are TomTom, Boskalis and Vopak. For TomTom, each of the four founders possesses between 11.2 and 10.7 per cent of the shares, providing a total ownership stake of 44.1 per cent.[148] HAL Holding is the main shareholder in Boskalis, with a 40.3 per cent stake according to the company's 2018 annual report.[149] HAL Holding is also the main shareholder in Vopak, with a reported ownership stake of 48.15 per cent.[150]

Figure 19.5 shows the difference between the average overall opposition and outsider opposition rates[151] for these four concentrated ownership companies. The results are remarkable. The mean opposition rate is 49.2 per cent on average, for TomTom and 44.4 per cent on average, for Heineken.

During the 2011 AGM of Heineken, three say-on-pay proposals received opposition rates between 19.9 and 19.3 per cent. As the voting turnout at this meeting was 81.4 per cent, and

146 Hence, if this quorum of 50 per cent is met only a simple majority vote is required, which was indeed the case in these meetings.

147 Under the assumption that insider shareholders vote all of their shares.

148 Following the 2018 Annual Report of TomTom.

149 Following the 2018 Annual Report of Boskalis.

150 Following the 2018 Annual Report of Vopak.

151 Using the assumption that corporate insiders generally vote all of their shares in favour of a resolution prepared by the corporate board, outsider opposition is calculated in the following way, following Christoph F. Van der Elst and Anne J. F. Lafarre, 'Shareholder Voice on Executive Pay: A Decade of Dutch Say on Pay' (2017) 18(1) *European Business Organization Law Review* 51.

Step 1: % Shares represented by insider = (% Shares not in free float / % Turnout) * 100%

Step 2: % Outsider Opposition = % Opposition / (100% – % Voting rights represented by insider) * 100%.

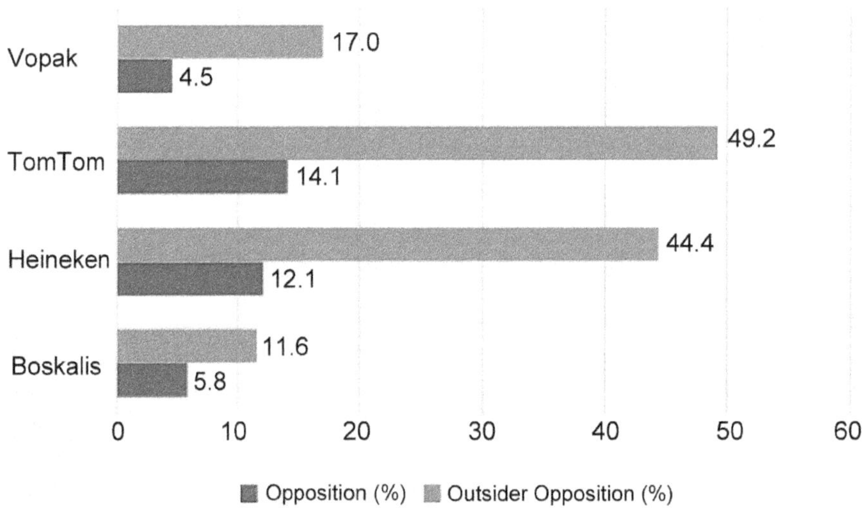

FIGURE 19.5 Opposition and outsider opposition (%)

the combined stake of the Heineken family and FEMSA was about 65 per cent, these insider shareholders represented about 80 per cent of the shares present at this general meeting. Hence, the opposition of outsider shareholders was almost unanimous. TomTom provides another notable example. During its 2018 AGM, the highest opposition rate, at 17.9 per cent, was against a say-on-pay resolution related to the stock option plans for employees and the management board. As the voter turnout was around 58.8 per cent and TomTom's founders represented about 44 per cent of the voting rights, outsider shareholder opposition was over 70 per cent. During thirteen AGMs – including the aforementioned examples – resolutions would have been defeated if outsider shareholders' votes had been decisive.

19.4.2 *Shareholder Questions*

In some jurisdictions, shareholder proposals are an often-used low-cost shareholder engagement tool. In the Netherlands, in contrast, there were zero shareholder proposals in the sample of 267 AGMs over the 11-year period.[152] The costs for submitting a shareholder proposal are generally high with an ownership requirement of 3 per cent in many companies. However, the general meeting transcripts show that Dutch shareholders often make use of another low-cost shareholder engagement tool: shareholder questions during general meetings. Research shows that the average number of questions posed in Dutch AGMs is thirty-nine, with approximately eight different shareholders asking questions.[153] A substantial portion of those questions are raised by large Dutch shareholder associations, which play an important role in advocating for collective

[152] Note that Shell is not included in the research sample as it is incorporated in the UK. Shell, often the target of environmentally engaged shareholders and other activists, experienced quit some shareholder proposals in the past few years according to the Proxy Insight database. A number of other Dutch listed -midcap companies have also received shareholder proposals in recent years.

[153] Anne J. F. Lafarre and Christoph F. Van der Elst, 'Corporate Sustainability and Shareholder Activism in the Netherlands' in Beate Sjåfjell and Christopher M. Bruner (eds.), *Cambridge Handbook of Corporate Law, Corporate Governance and Sustainability* (Cambridge University Press 2020).

shareholder interests in the Netherlands. The largest two are VEB (Association for Securities Holders) and VBDO (Shareholder Association for Sustainable Development).[154]

19.4.3 *Private Engagement*

Finally, it is well known that institutional investors and other large shareholders often have the opportunity to engage with corporate boards and company representatives during private meetings outside company AGMs. Some of the examples in Table 19.2 of withdrawn voting items show that such behind-the-scenes engagement indeed also takes place in the Netherlands and has an impact on AGM's agenda. Another case in point is the cancellation by Unilever of the agenda items that were put forward at the 2018 EGMs concerning the unification of the company's structure. The corporate board withdrew the restructuring proposal, arguing that it lacked support from a significant group of shareholders.[155] One of the larger shareholders in Unilever, Columbia Threadneedle, had announced its intention to vote against the proposal at an early stage. Other large shareholders, including Aviva and LGIM, later joined the opposition.[156]

19.5 CONCLUDING REMARKS

This chapter has provided legal and practical insights into the role of shareholders and Dutch general meetings. The Dutch (listed) NV is characterized by the institutional approach, where the general meeting has not the highest powers and the board's autonomy is widely established. Nonetheless, shareholder voting and engagement is an important aspect of Dutch corporate governance, marked by the large and systemic institutional ownership in many companies, but also by some companies with concentrated ownership structures. Practice suggests that say-on-pay proposals in particular are important channels to express shareholder discontent with corporate management. Although the Dutch corporate law framework for public companies assigns a pivotal role to the management board and allows for anti-takeover mechanisms and oligarchic clauses to limit shareholder powers, there seems to be an increasing focus on institutional investor engagement as a 'governance strategy'[157] to stimulate long-term value creation and sustainable companies. With the implementation of SRD II and the Dutch Stewardship Code, shareholders in the Netherlands, institutional investors in particular, have received more rights (including a qualified majority say on remuneration policy) and duties (including disclosures related to the engagement policy). Whether institutional investors will indeed actively stimulate long-term decision-making in companies and how the Dutch corporate law framework will evolve given the larger emphasis on corporate sustainability and responsibility, are interesting questions for further research.

154 VEB: www.veb.net; VBDO: www.vbdo.nl accessed 15 July 2020.

155 See the press release of 5 October 2018: 'We have had an extensive period of engagement with shareholders and have received widespread support for the principle behind simplification. However, we recognize that the proposal has not received support from a significant group of shareholders and therefore consider it appropriate to withdraw'. www.unilever.com/news/press-releases/2018/statement-from-the-board-of-unilever.html accessed 1 July 2020.

156 Some months later, it was announced that Unilever – under the leadership of its new CEO – would move in its entirely to the UK, thereby eliminating its dual structure.

157 John Armour, Henry Hansmann and Reinier Kraakman, 'Agency Problems and Legal Strategies' in Reinier Kraakman et al., *The Anatomy of Corporate Law: A Comparative and Functional Approach* (Oxford University Press 2017).

Although it cannot yet be said that the virtual meeting is here to stay in the Netherlands, as the Covid-19 legislation is only temporary,[158] even prior to the Covid-19 crisis, remote (electronic) voting has substantially increased voter turnout rates in Dutch general meetings. In the 2019 AGM season, for example, we saw a major Dutch listed company, KPN, holding a hybrid AGM where shareholders were able to attend and vote on resolutions in real time via the internet. The Covid-19 crisis may well open the door to further discussions on the modernisation of the traditional Dutch general meeting framework.[159]

158 See n. 95.

159 See inter alia David Yermack, 'Corporate Governance and Blockchains' (2017) 21(1) *Review of Finance* 7.

20

Shareholder Engagement and Voting in the United Kingdom

Suren Gomtsian

20.1 INTRODUCTION

Shareholder stewardship and participation in governance are amongst the cornerstones of an effectively functioning corporate governance system. Although the role of shareholders in corporate governance has long been recognized, most of the corporate governance initiatives in the early and mid-1990s predominantly targeted boards of directors and their structure, composition and procedures. That changed in the wake of the 2008 financial crisis, which was partially blamed on passive, unengaged shareholders.[1] Regulators around the world, and in the United Kingdom in particular, introduced new corporate governance reforms aimed at limiting excessive risk-taking by managers.[2] Essential amongst these reforms were efforts to empower shareholders and encourage them to engage more actively with companies.

The UK has traditionally been at the forefront of corporate governance innovations. The country took the lead again in 2010 by publishing the UK Stewardship Code, which offers a set of best practice recommendations for shareholders in publicly traded companies.[3] The primary intention of the Financial Reporting Council, the Code's author, was to strengthen shareholder engagement by institutional investors, who are the dominant shareholders in many large companies. The Stewardship Code has been updated twice since then, first in 2012[4] and then again in 2019.[5] The latest edition, the UK Stewardship Code 2020, was, at least in part, driven by the introduction of the Shareholder Rights Directive II (SRD II) in the European Union.[6] But the 2020 Code does more than just incorporate the requirements of SRD II. It substantially revises the structure and content of stewardship requirements by shifting the focus from developing and reporting on stewardship policies towards stronger emphasis on outcomes and specific stewardship actions taken by institutional investors and asset managers.[7]

[1] Brian R. Cheffins, 'The Stewardship Code's Achilles' Heel' (2010) 73 MLR 1004, 1009–10.

[2] Christopher M. Bruner, 'Corporate Governance Reform in a Time of Crisis' (2011) 36 The Journal of Corporation Law 309.

[3] Financial Reporting Council, The UK Stewardship Code (July 2010) www.frc.org.uk/getattachment/e223e152-5515-4cdc-a951-da33e093eb28/UK-Stewardship-Code-July-2010.pdf accessed 10 October 2019.

[4] Financial Reporting Council, The UK Stewardship Code 2012 (September 2012) www.frc.org.uk/getattachment/d67933f9-ca38-4233-b603-3d24b2f62c5f/UK-Stewardship-Code-(September-2012).pdf accessed 10 October 2019.

[5] Financial Reporting Council, The UK Stewardship Code 2020 (October 2019) www.frc.org.uk/getattachment/5aae591d-d9d3-4cf4-814a-d14e156a1d87/Stewardship-Code_Dec-19-Final-Corrected.pdf accessed 15 June 2020.

[6] Directive 2017/828/EU of the European Parliament and of the Council of 17 May 2017 amending Directive 2007/36/EC as regards the encouragement of long-term shareholder engagement [2017] OJL132/1 (SRD II).

[7] See Section 20.3.6 below.

According to prior common belief, institutional investors in the UK rarely participated in corporate governance and refrained from engaging actively with their portfolio companies.[8] Concerns and questions over institutional investor engagement continued after the introduction of the Stewardship Code.[9] It is only recently, however, that researchers have begun to explore the practice of shareholder engagement and voting behaviour amongst large institutional investors. The new evidence revealed by these researchers shows that large asset managers have been taking a more active approach to stewardship, although their engagement efforts generally focus on identifying and promoting best practice corporate governance standards and dealing with global threats such as climate change and calls for greater diversity.[10]

This chapter reports the state of the art and recent trends in shareholder engagement and voting in the UK. It begins with a brief overview of corporate governance in the UK by explaining the allocation of decision-making power between shareholders and directors and describing the ownership structure of large publicly traded companies. The next two sections then discuss legal means of shareholder engagement and explore engagement by large institutional investors through voting shares and private negotiations, respectively. The chapter concludes by highlighting the limits of shareholder engagement and the implications of those limits for regulators.

20.2 OVERVIEW OF CORPORATE LAW AND CORPORATE GOVERNANCE IN THE UNITED KINGDOM

20.2.1 *Allocation of Corporate Decision-Making*

The public limited company, which is the common business form of choice for publicly traded companies in the UK, has a centralized management structure separate from shareholders. UK company law requires that all public companies have a board of directors with at least two directors responsible for management.[11] Even in the absence of this prescriptive legal requirement, delegating management to a small number of professionals in public companies with hundreds of shareholders offers significant practical advantages in terms of quick decision-making, technical expertise and reducing the problems of collective action.[12] As with any delegation of power, however, centralized management raises concerns over potential opportunistic behaviour on the part of managers. UK company law uses several strategies to deal with this problem, including dividing the functions of shareholders and boards of directors. This section offers a brief overview of these strategies to demonstrate the importance of deciding on the allocation of corporate decision-making powers and the role of shareholder control and monitoring over certain key aspects of the company.

The separation of ownership and control, a common feature of listed companies in the UK, exposes shareholders to the risk that their goals for the company will diverge from the priorities of managers (termed the 'agency problem' in the literature).[13] Various legal and market forces aim

[8] Cheffins (n. 1) 1004–5.

[9] See e.g. Arad Reisberg, 'The UK Stewardship Code: On the Road to Nowhere?' (2015) 15 The Journal of Corporate Law Studies 217, 227–40 (arguing that structural problems in the Code undermine its goals); Alan Dignam, 'The Future of Shareholder Democracy in the Shadow of the Financial Crisis' (2013) 36 Seattle University Law Review 639, 682–8 (challenging the entire idea that stronger shareholder engagement can add value); Cheffins (n. 1) 1013 (arguing that key investors, particularly foreign investors, fall outside the Code's mandate).

[10] See Section 20.4.1 below.

[11] Companies Act 2006, s. 154(2).

[12] Paul Davies, *Introduction to Company Law* (2nd ed., OUP 2010) 12.

[13] Kathleen M. Eisenhardt, 'Agency Theory: An Assessment and Review' (1989) 14 The Academy of Management Review 57, 58.

to confine the agency problem. In particular, behavioural legal constraints imposed on managers restrict the (opportunistic) actions available to managers; outcome-based contracts and other market mechanisms align the interests of shareholders and managers; and information disclosure contributes to the better monitoring of managers by shareholders.[14]

Amongst the various forms of behavioural constraints, directors' duties of loyalty and care are arguably the most essential. These duties describe in abstract terms, which are further clarified in case law, what is expected of directors and what behaviour is not tolerated. The threat of liability for a failure to act in the interests of the company and its shareholders gives directors an incentive to act in those interests.[15] The directors of UK companies are expected to act in a way that they consider, in good faith, to be the most likely to promote the success of the company for the benefit of its shareholders as a whole.[16] In the decision-making process, directors also need to pay regard to the long-term consequences of their decisions and to the interests of various stakeholders, including different groups of shareholders.[17] There is considerable debate and disagreement in the literature regarding the implications of section 172 of the Companies Act 2006 for advancing the interests of stakeholders, but the mainstream interpretation gives priority to shareholders' interests.[18] The section's interpretation is likely to evolve over time along with changing societal attitudes in general, thereby strengthening the grounds for affording stronger weight to the interests of all stakeholders.

Various incentive structures are available, including executive remuneration contracts based on variable elements tied to company performance metrics. The idea is that such contracts give managers stronger incentives to act in line with the interests of the company and its shareholders.[19] Examples of other incentive structures are the market for corporate control and reputational effects. The early agency theory literature emphasized the disciplining role of hostile takeovers,[20] but the costliness of the takeover mechanism and its inherent conflicts have limited the role of takeovers in disciplining managers in practice.

For its part, information disclosure improves the ability of shareholders to monitor how directors and officers are exercising the powers delegated to them.[21] The central role in monitoring managers, however, is played by the company's board and its independent directors.[22] When boards are effective in performing their monitoring role in the interests of shareholders, companies are less dependent on behavioural constraints and outcome-based incentive schemes.[23] Not surprisingly, initial corporate governance measures focused almost exclusively on the structure, composition and practices of corporate boards.[24] UK companies

14 For an overview of various legal strategies for dealing with the agency problems of the corporate form, see Reiner Kraakman et al. (eds.), *The Anatomy of Corporate Law: A Comparative and Functional Approach* (3rd ed., OUP 2017), 31–9.

15 Robert H. Sitkoff, 'The Economic Structure of Fiduciary Law' (2011) 91 Boston University Law Review 1039, 1043.

16 Companies Act 2006 (c. 46), s. 172(1).

17 Ibid.

18 See e.g. Andrew Keay, 'Section 172(1) of the Companies Act 2006: An Interpretation and Assessment' (2007) 28 (4) Company Lawyer 106, 108 (arguing that directors are required to consider the interests of stakeholders other than shareholders as far as doing so offers benefits to shareholders).

19 Lucian Bebchuk and Jesse Fried, *Pay without Performance: The Unfulfilled Promise of Executive Compensation* (Harvard University Press 2004) 19–20; Michael C. Jensen and William Meckling, 'Theory of the Firm: Managerial Behavior, Agency Costs and Ownership Structure' (1976) 3 Journal of Financial Economics 305, 323.

20 Henry G. Manne, 'Mergers and the Market for Corporate Control' (1965) 73 The Journal of Political Economy 110, 112–13.

21 Kraakman and others (n. 14) 38.

22 Eisenhardt (n. 13) 65.

23 Ibid.

24 See e.g. Committee on the Financial Aspects of Corporate Governance, *Report of the Committee on the Financial Aspects of Corporate Governance*, para. 1.8 (1992) www.ecgi.org/codes/documents/cadbury.pdf accessed 29 October 2019 (stating that the Report's corporate governance proposals aim to strengthen boards and their

have unitary board structures that may combine both executive and non-executive directors. Although the functions of non-executive directors vary, they are primarily expected to take part in monitoring conflicts of interest involving executive directors and ensuring compliance with regulations.[25]

However effective the aforementioned solutions may be, they cannot eliminate the problem of opportunistic behaviour associated with the delegation of decision-making power altogether. There is therefore a small number of fundamental matters, including the appointment and removal of directors, for which shareholders retain decision-making rights.[26] Shareholder voting rights thus aim, first, to limit the effect of managerial opportunism on corporate decision-making in general by electing board members whom shareholders trust with the delegation of power and, second, to reduce the influence of directors and managers on fundamental decisions by reserving decision-making rights for shareholders alone.

Shareholder engagement can limit agency problems by ensuring that managers use their delegated power for proper purposes. There is generally strong demand for active shareholder engagement where corporate boards fail to perform their own monitoring tasks.[27] Yet the effectiveness of the division of corporate decision-making power between shareholders and managers obviously hinges upon the ability of the former to actively exercise their voting rights. Active engagement, while in the collective interest of shareholders, is not always guaranteed.

Shareholder apathy is especially severe in the context of companies with widespread ownership structures, where small individual shareholdings and the collective action problem do not justify the costs of informed voting.[28] The term 'absentee owners' has been used to describe dispersed individual minority shareholders with little ability to influence powerful company CEOs.[29] The evolving pattern of investing through intermediaries, however, has gradually changed corporate ownership structures in the UK. By the end of the 1980s, institutional investors, who combine the votes of thousands of individual shareholders, dominated the ownership structures of large companies,[30] giving rise to the hope that shareholders would finally step up their monitoring and stewardship efforts.[31] Positive expectations about the power of shareholders to restrain managerial discretion were revived again in the early 2000s following a number of high-profile campaigns by activist hedge funds targeting mostly US-based companies, as well as instances of shareholder activism in Europe.[32]

Nevertheless, the promise of active shareholder engagement remained largely unfulfilled. The 2008 financial crisis and recent corporate scandals suggest that shareholder apathy may contribute to increased risk-taking and director misconduct. The predominantly board-centric

effectiveness; the main proposals thus focus on the role of non-executive directors and board committees). The Report is better known as the Cadbury Report after the surname of the Committee's chairman.

25 Donald C. Clarke, 'Three Concepts of the Independent Director' (2007) 32 *Delaware Journal of Corporate Law* 73, 80–3. In some companies, non-executive directors are expected to be consultants on matters of their expertise. Ibid., 81.

26 Shareholders in UK companies are free to remove any director by a simple majority vote. Companies Act 2006, s. 168(1).

27 Stuart L. Gillan and Laura T. Starks, 'The Evolution of Shareholder Activism in the United States' (2007) 19 Journal of Applied Corporate Finance 55, 58.

28 Stephen M. Bainbridge, 'Director Primacy: The Means and Ends of Corporate Governance' (2003) 97 Northwestern University Law Review 547, 558; Bernard S. Black, 'Shareholder Passivity Reexamined' (1990) 89 Michigan Law Review 520, 576–8.

29 E. Merrick Dodd, Jr., 'For Whom Are Corporate Managers Trustees?' (1932) 45 Harvard Law Review 1145, 1153.

30 Black (n. 28) 567–8.

31 Paul L. Davies, 'Institutional Investors: A UK View' (1991) 57 Brooklyn Law Review 129, 131, 135.

32 Marcel Kahan and Edward B. Rock, 'Hedge Funds in Corporate Governance and Corporate Control' (2007) 155 *University of Pennsylvania Law Review* 1021, 1028, 1047.

focus of corporate governance measures has thus gradually shifted towards recognition of the importance of shareholder engagement. The UK was amongst the first countries to adopt a special Stewardship Code with the intention of strengthening shareholder engagement in corporate governance.[33] Accordingly, although shareholders vote on relatively few matters, shareholder engagement and voting have become pillars of corporate governance that can mitigate the agency problem.

20.2.2 *Powers of the Board of Directors and the General Meeting of Shareholders*

As discussed above, shareholders delegate all but the most fundamental decisions to a centralized board of directors. UK company law grants shareholders wide freedom in deciding how to divide powers between shareholders and the board.[34] The allocation of decision-making rights is defined primarily by the company's articles of association (AoA). Accordingly, the board's powers are derived not from statute but from the company's own AoA and can be as broad or narrow as the company's shareholders desire.[35]

Shareholders typically decide matters that are financially significant or may have a major impact on the company's business, involve a strong conflict of interest, or affect shareholders' rights.[36] Decision-making authority over certain key matters is granted to shareholders based on statutory provisions, and other shareholder rights may be included in the company's AoA. Shareholder powers derived from statute (statutory rights) include the right to (1) amend the AoA,[37] (2) alter (increase or reduce) the company's share capital,[38] (3) wind up the company,[39] (4) approve mergers and divisions,[40] (5) remove a director,[41] (6) appoint an auditor and fix the auditor's remuneration[42] and (7) vote on certain transactions involving directors, such as substantial property transactions between the company and its directors.[43] Shareholders in publicly traded companies also vote on the company's remuneration policy once every three years (a binding say-on-pay vote)[44] and have an annual non-binding vote on the remuneration report (advisory say-on-pay vote).[45] Advisory and binding say-on-pay votes were introduced in 2002[46] and 2013,[47] respectively, and initially applied solely to quoted companies, but were extended to all publicly traded companies in July 2019.[48]

33 See Financial Reporting Council (n. 3).
34 Davies (n. 12) 12.
35 Jennifer G. Hill, 'The Trajectory of American Corporate Governance: Shareholder Empowerment and Private Ordering Combat' [2019] *University of Illinois Law Review* 507, 553–4.
36 David Kershaw, *Company Law in Context* (2nd ed., OUP 2012), 190.
37 Companies Act 2006, s. 21(1).
38 Ibid., ss. 551 and 641(1). In private companies with one class of shares, the right to allot shares belongs to the board unless prohibited by the company's articles of association (AoA). Ibid., s. 550. In all other instances, the power to increase share capital by allotting new shares can be given to the board by the company's AoA. Ibid., s. 551(1).
39 Insolvency Act 1986, s. 84(1)(b).
40 Companies Act 2006, s. 907(1) (for mergers) and s. 922(1) (for divisions).
41 Ibid., s. 168(1).
42 Ibid., s. 489(4) (for appointment) and s. 492(1) (for fixing the auditor's remuneration).
43 Ibid., s. 190(1). A transaction is substantial if its value (1) exceeds 10 per cent of the company's asset value and is more than £5,000 or (2) exceeds £100,000. Ibid., s. 191(2).
44 Ibid., s. 439A(1).
45 Ibid., s. 439(1) and (5).
46 The Directors' Remuneration Report Regulations 2002 (No. 1986), s. 7 (amending the relevant provisions of the Companies Act 1985 to give shareholders a right to vote on directors' remuneration report).
47 Enterprise and Regulatory Reform Act 2013 (c. 24), s. 79(4) (introducing s. 439A in the Companies Act 2006).
48 The Companies (Directors' Remuneration Policy and Directors' Remuneration Report) Regulations 2019 (No. 970), ss. 19 and 20 (amending the relevant provisions of the Companies Act 2006 to extend say-on-pay votes to all publicly

In addition to these statutory rights, shareholders may also be granted other rights through the company's AoA. For example, publicly traded companies typically entitle shareholders to appoint directors[49] and approve dividend payments based on the board's recommendation.[50]

The board of directors is responsible for the executive management of the company, including its day-to-day management, and all residual powers not covered by the powers of the general meeting of shareholders. Therefore, board powers are largely dependent on the company's AoA. The breadth of board powers is also contingent on shareholders' right to intervene in board matters and give directions to the board. UK cases in the nineteenth century interpreted shareholders' right to decide on the allocation of powers to mean that directors were merely agents of shareholders.[51] Therefore, directors had to follow directions given by the majority of shareholders. This changed in 1906 when, in *Automatic Self-Cleansing Filer Syndicate Co Ltd* v. *Cuninghame*, the court held that where management powers are delegated to the board in AoA, directors are not compelled to obey a shareholder resolution.[52] Similarly, in *John Shaw & Sons (Salford), Ltd* v. *Shaw*, the court confirmed that if a company's articles grant the board the power to act, then the general meeting cannot interfere in the exercise of the board's power.[53]

Both cases recognized that a company's AoA create separate and independent spheres of authority for directors and shareholders.[54] Where the articles give power to the board, the board is immune from interference in decision-making by shareholders.[55] Shareholders can issue instructions only if the power to do so is granted to them by the company's articles. The model articles for both private and public companies include such a reserve power for shareholders. The model forms of AoA apply by default as internal governance documents for companies that, upon their formation, do not register their own tailored AoA.[56] Under the model articles for both types of companies, shareholders may, by special resolution, direct the directors to take, or refrain from taking, specified action on an ad hoc basis.[57] The requirement for a special resolution is that it be approved by three-quarters of the votes of shareholders participating in the vote.[58] Accordingly, as long as the board is acting within its powers, it can take action against the wishes of the majority of shareholders, which serves to strengthen the board's status as an independent corporate body.

20.2.3 *Ownership Structure*

Institutional investors have traditionally dominated the ownership structure of large publicly traded companies in the UK.[59] According to the latest data from the Office for National Statistics (see Figure 20.1), institutional investors owned 73.33 per cent of the shares of quoted UK

traded companies). Quoted companies are companies whose securities are traded on the London Stock Exchange's Main Market and thus represent a portion of publicly traded companies.

49 The Companies (Model Articles) Regulations 2008, Sch 3 (Model Articles for Public Companies), art. 20(a).

50 Ibid., s. 70(1) and (2).

51 Hill (n. 35) 554.

52 *Automatic Self-Cleansing Filer Syndicate Co Ltd* v. *Cuninghame* [1906] 2 Ch 34, 42.

53 *John Shaw & Sons (Salford), Ltd* v. *Shaw* [1935] 2 KB 113, 134.

54 Hill (n. 35) 554.

55 Ibid.

56 Companies Act 2006, s. 19; Companies (Model Articles) Regulations 2008, Explanatory Note.

57 Companies (Model Articles) Regulations 2008, sch 1 (Model Articles for Private Companies Limited by Shares), art. 4(1) (for private companies); sch. 3 (Model Articles for Public Companies), art. 4(1) (for public companies).

58 Companies Act 2006, s. 283(1), (4) and (5).

59 Brian R. Cheffins, *Corporate Ownership and Control: British Business Transformed* (OUP 2008) 344–6 (documenting the rise of institutional investors after the late 1960s).

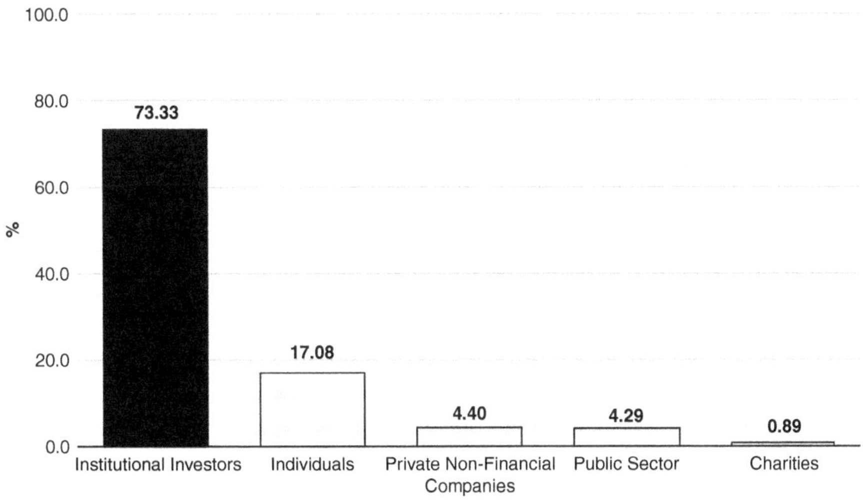

FIGURE 20.1 Beneficial owners of UK shares, 31 December 2018
Source: Own calculations based on data from the Office for National Statistics.
Note to figure: The Office for National Statistics breaks down beneficial owners into UK-domiciled and foreign owners; the category of foreign owners, in turn, includes different owners such as institutional investors, individuals, or states. The figure shows the combined beneficial shareholdings of each group of owners. For example, UK-domiciled company founders and retail investors owned 13.48 per cent of total shares in December 2018, with another 3.59 per cent owned by foreigners. The combined shareholdings of individuals thus stood at 17.08 per cent. Similarly, the UK government owned 0.92 per cent of shares in December 2018, but another 3.37 per cent of shares were controlled by foreign governments, putting the combined shareholdings of the public sector at 4.29 per cent. Institutional investors include different types of investment funds, pension funds, insurance companies and other financial organizations, whereas the public sector comprises central and local governments and public corporations.

companies in December 2018. British and North American institutional investors owned almost an equal portion of shares, with each controlling about 37.6 per cent of the total shareholdings of institutional investors, with the remaining quarter controlled by institutional investors from other countries. The combined shareholdings of UK-domiciled and all other individual investors, including company founders, totalled 17.08 per cent. The remainder of shares were owned by private non-financial companies (4.40 per cent), the UK government and foreign governments (4.29 per cent), and charities (0.89 per cent).

The leading position of institutional investors is a consequence of the global move away from direct ownership by individuals and households towards investments in the various financial products offered by banks, insurance companies and investment and pension funds.[60] The introduction of defined contribution pension plans, favourable tax treatment of pension savings and cheaper access to investment fund products have certainly contributed, to varying extents, to

[60] John Scott, *Capitalist Property and Financial Power: A Comparative Study of Britain, the United States and Japan* (Wheatsheaf 1986) 88; Gerald F. Davis, 'A New Finance Capitalism? Mutual Funds and Ownership Re-Concentration in the United States' (2008) 5 European Management Review 11, 15.

the ownership shift.[61] The recent spread of passive index tracking investment strategies has also allowed small investors to achieve diversification at low cost, a privilege previously available only to large investors.[62] These factors have not only contributed to the rise of institutional ownership at the expense of retail investors, but have also brought about changes in the composition of the largest institutional investors.

Insurance companies, which began to invest in corporate securities in the 1930s, dominated earlier lists of the largest British institutional investors,[63] with a significant portion of insurance company investments financed by pension savings contributed to insurance policies.[64] Ownership data collected by John Scott shows that almost half of the twenty largest British institutional investors in 1976 were insurance companies, although banks, both commercial and merchant,[65] also exerted significant influence over corporate decision-making.[66] Notably, the list of the largest shareholders in 1976 did not include a single foreign institutional investor. Foreign shareholders owned only 6 per cent of shares in British quoted companies in 1975, according to the Office for National Statistics.[67]

A wave of consolidation in the insurance and banking sectors helped banks and insurance companies to maintain strong positions in the league tables of the largest shareholders of companies in the UK in the 1990s and early 2000s.[68] However, the identities of the dominant shareholders in the ownership landscape have changed since the 2008 financial crisis. Figure 20.2 illustrates the evolution of the largest shareholders of the FTSE 100 companies since 2007. Three trends are notable. First, big investment fund managers have become a powerful force by filling the void left by banks and insurance firms, which scaled back after being hard hit by the crisis. For example, Barclays PLC, a British bank that was formerly amongst the top shareholders in many FTSE companies, sold its asset management subsidiary, including the iShares unit, which was at the time the leader in the business of passive exchange traded funds, to BlackRock, Inc, a US investment management firm.[69] The shareholdings of insurance companies had already started to decline, but that trend accelerated after 2008 when a number of large insurers, following a wave of mergers in the sector, spun off and sold their asset management arms.[70] Consequently, the holdings of banks and insurance companies have gradually declined in importance relative to the holdings of large fund families managed by independent asset managers. The growing role of large passive asset managers, primarily

61 Gile R. Downes, Jr, Ehud Houminer and R. Glenn Hubbard, *Institutional Investors and Corporate Behavior* (The AEI Press 1999), 1. See also Davies (n. 31) 131–3 (attributing the rise of institutional ownership in the UK to pension-driven investments).

62 Ronald J. Gilson and Jeffrey N. Gordon, 'The Agency Costs of Agency Capitalism: Activist Investors and the Revaluation of Governance Rights' (2013) 113 Columbia Law Review 863, 884–6 (explaining how households' desire to diversify risks led to investments through mutual funds).

63 Cheffins (n. 59) 345; Scott (n. 60) 88–9.

64 Davies (n. 31) 132–3.

65 The term 'merchant bank' was the common way of referring to a British investment bank.

66 Scott (n. 60) 100, 103.

67 Office for National Statistics, *Statistical Bulletin: Ownership of UK Quoted Shares: 2018* (14 January 2020) 7 www.ons.gov.uk/economy/investmentspensionsandtrusts/bulletins/ownershipofukquotedshares/2018#rest-of-the-world accessed 17 June 2020.

68 Cheffins (n. 59) 87–90.

69 Attracta Mooney and Peter Smith, 'Deal of the Decade: How BlackRock Buying BGI Changed the Industry' *Financial Times* (London, 6 May 2019) 6.

70 Office for National Statistics, *Statistical Bulletin: Ownership of UK Quoted Shares: 2018* (14 January 2020) 7 www.ons.gov.uk/economy/investmentspensionsandtrusts/bulletins/ownershipofukquotedshares/2018#insurance-companies accessed 18 June 2020.

FIGURE 20.2 Largest shareholders of FTSE 100 companies by average shareholding size
Source: Own calculations based on historical year-end ownership data from FAME (Bureau van Dijk).

the US giants BlackRock and Vanguard, has been a major driving force behind this change.[71]

Second, UK institutional investors have been losing ground among the largest shareholders. Whereas the two largest shareholders in 2007 had British origins, the top two shareholders both in 2016 and in 2019 were US fund families (see Figure 20.2). Third, the consolidation of shareholdings at the very top has increased over time. Although the combined average shareholdings of the top ten institutional investors remained largely unchanged (at 23.69 per cent in 2007 and 23.61 per cent in 2019), BlackRock had a clear leading position during the last decade with a shareholding about two times larger than the next largest investor (see Figure 20.2).

Today, the largest shareholders of publicly traded companies in the UK are all institutional investors dominated by independent asset management firms. Table 20.1a reports their average shareholdings on an equal and value-weighted (market capitalization adjusted) basis. BlackRock funds owned 5.74 per cent of the FTSE 100 companies, on average, at the end of 2019. BlackRock's market capitalization adjusted average shareholding in the FTSE 100 companies was even higher, at 6.40 per cent. The combined average shareholding of the twenty largest asset managers in the FTSE 100 firms, both on equal and value-weighted calculations, was just above 32 per cent.

[71] A recent study offers evidence linking the rise of index investing with the increased level of common ownership, a term often used to describe instances where one investor owns substantial shareholdings in many publicly traded companies. Importantly, the study refrains from making any causal claims. Erik P. Gilje, Todd A. Gormley and Doron Levit, 'Who's Paying Attention: Measuring Common Ownership and Its Impact on Managerial Incentives' (2020) 137 Journal of Financial Economics 152, 166–7.

TABLE 20.1A *Largest shareholders of FTSE 100 companies*

Panel A. Largest shareholders of FTSE 100 firms by shareholding size, December 2019					
		Average shareholding, %			
Fund group (asset manager)	Country code	Equal basis	Value-weighted	Max.	Firms with top owner
BlackRock	US	5.74	6.40	11.83	35
The Vanguard Group	US	3.01	3.27	5.09	0
Standard Life Aberdeen	GB	2.60	2.35	27.36	2
Capital Group Companies	US	2.49	3.28	12.26	6
Norway Government Pension Fund Global (NBIM)	NO	2.17	2.06	7.36	1
Legal & General Group	GB	1.93	2.01	3.82	0
State Street Corp (SSGA)	US	1.90	2.10	4.59	0
Invesco	US	1.41	1.16	11.17	1
Ameriprise Financial (Columbia Threadneedle Inv)	US	1.19	0.88	9.61	2
Schroders	GB	1.17	0.89	12.44	3
Fidelity*	US	1.15	1.04	10.98	0
Sun Life Financial (MFS Inv Mgmt)	CA	1.05	0.89	10.50	4
UBS Group	CH	1.03	1.08	9.56	0
M&G	GB	0.87	0.82	6.29	1
Affiliated Managers Group (Artemis Inv Mgmt)	US	0.82	0.71	5.22	0
Baillie Gifford & Co	GB	0.76	0.49	7.33	0
Fidelity International*	US	0.72	0.56	5.46	0
JPMorgan Chase & Co	US	0.69	0.74	4.99	0
Royal London Mutual Insurance Society	GB	0.68	0.66	2.34	0
Aviva	GB	0.68	0.68	6.96	1
Total		32.07	32.08		56

Table 20.1b shows how often the big asset managers were amongst the largest shareholders of the FTSE 100 firms. BlackRock and Vanguard were amongst the top ten shareholders in more than 90 per cent of the firms in 2019 (BlackRock's dominance was close to 100 per cent). Moreover, BlackRock was the largest shareholder in thirty-five companies, sometimes with shareholdings above 10 per cent. Other fund groups that appeared among the largest ten shareholders of more than half of the FTSE 100 firms included Norway's Government Pension Fund Global (NBIM), Legal & General Group, Standard Life Aberdeen, and State Street Corp. (SSGA). The top twenty institutional investors together were among the largest ten shareholders of the FTSE 100 firms in 61.3 per cent of cases; in 56 per cent of the firms, one of those fund groups was the largest shareholder.

The influence of institutional investors is even stronger in practice because not all shareholders vote their shares. Data on actual shareholder voting turnout, a measure showing the percentage of total outstanding shares voted during the general meetings of shareholders, show that the average attendance rate in UK companies has hovered just above 70 per cent in recent years.[72] In particular, the average voting turnout at FTSE 100 and FTSE 250 companies in 2018

[72] The shareholder attendance rate in UK companies, perhaps due to the growing dominance of institutional investors, has been increasing gradually in recent years. The average shareholder turnout for FTSE 100 companies, for

TABLE 20.1B *Number of FTSE 100 firms in which investor is among largest ten shareholders*

Panel B. Number of FTSE 100 firms in which investor is among largest 10 shareholders, over time					
Fund group (asset manager)	2007	2010	2013	2016	2019
BlackRock	13	92	98	95	97
The Vanguard Group	0	0	12	79	91
Norway Government Pension Fund Global (NBIM)	0	37	63	47	57
Legal & General Group	96	90	91	83	56
Standard Life Aberdeen**	29	21	14	28	55
State Street Corp (SSGA)	33	34	61	58	52
Capital Group Companies	27	35	42	38	40
Invesco	30	24	24	26	21
Ameriprise Financial (Columbia Threadneedle Inv)	20	14	17	23	19
Schroders	13	15	19	14	19
Fidelity*	33	48	37	20	17
Sun Life Financial (MFS Inv Mgmt)	1	7	14	16	15
Affiliated Managers Group (Artemis Inv Mgmt)	1	4	11	16	13
UBS Group	51	18	17	13	12
M&G***	49	36	18	9	11
Baillie Gifford & Co	10	11	14	10	11
Fidelity International*	11	3	1	4	11
Aviva	24	9	5	3	8
JPMorgan Chase & Co	16	8	10	5	7
Royal London Mutual Insurance Society	0	0	1	3	1
Total	457	506	569	590	613

Sources: FAME (Bureau van Dijk) for year-end ownership data; London Stock Exchange for market capitalization.
Note to table: The table shows the largest shareholders in the FTSE 100 firms by the average shareholding size in all firms and the number of times an investor appears amongst the largest ten shareholders. All of the largest shareholders are fund groups and their asset managers. An asset manager may control shareholdings through more than one investment fund affiliated with the manager. The table reports the combined results of all funds affiliated with an asset manager. It also reports the number of firms in which a fund group is the single largest shareholder and the fund group's maximum shareholding. Table 20.1a presents data on the largest shareholders in the FTSE 100 companies in December 2019; changes in the number of firms in which the top fund groups are among the largest ten shareholders over time are in Table 20.1b.

* Information on shareholdings controlled by Fidelity and Fidelity International are reported separately. Fidelity International, formerly Fidelity Worldwide Investment Ltd, was established in 1969 as a subsidiary of Fidelity to serve non-US markets. It was spun off in 1980 and currently is an independent asset manager controlled by its employees, although the founding family of Fidelity continues to own a substantial minority shareholding in Fidelity International.

** Aberdeen Asset Management and Standard Life Investments merged in 2017. The results reported before this date include information on the shareholdings controlled by Standard Life Investments only.

*** M&G, currently an independent fund group, was formerly part of Prudential PLC. The results before 2019 refer to data on shareholdings controlled by Prudential PLC.

stood at 75 per cent and 77 per cent, respectively.[73] This means that a shareholding of roughly 37–40 per cent may be sufficient to give its holder effective control over shareholder decision-making. Accordingly, a small number of large fund families controls the majority of votes at the annual meetings of FTSE companies.

example, increased from 67.9 per cent in 2010 to 71.1 per cent in 2014. Anne Lafarre, *The AGM in Europe: Theory and Practice of Shareholder Behavior* (Emerald Group Publishing 2017) 109.

73 KPMG, *Review of the 2018 AGM Season*, (September 2018) 3 assets.kpmg/content/dam/kpmg/uk/pdf/2018/09/review-of-the-2018-agm-season.pdf accessed 14 October 2019.

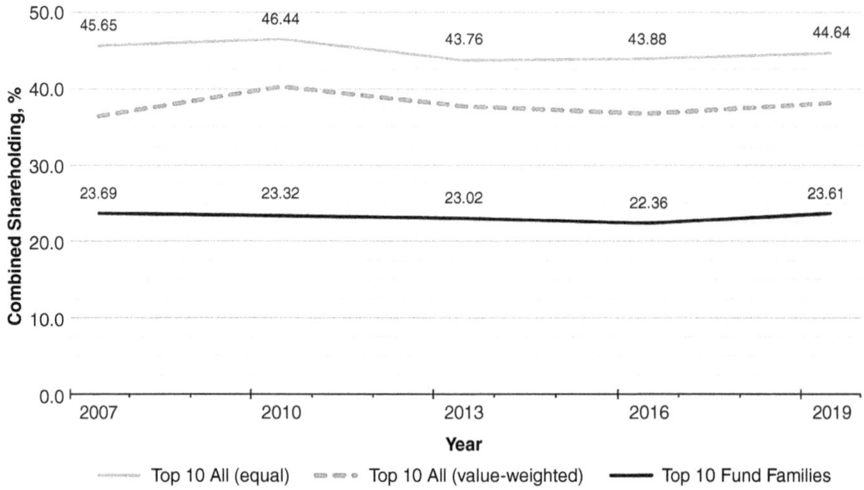

FIGURE 20.3 Ownership concentration by top ten shareholders, FTSE 100
Source: Own calculations based on historical year-end ownership data from FAME (Bureau van Dijk).

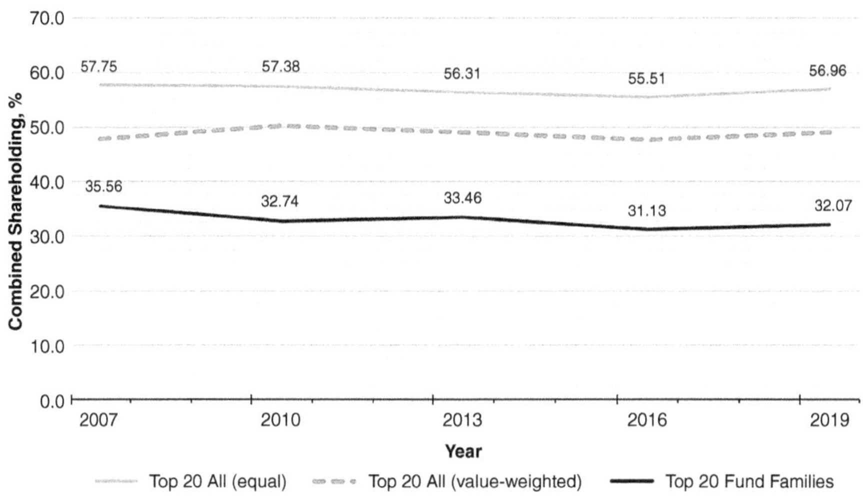

FIGURE 20.4 Ownership concentration by top twenty shareholders, FTSE 100
Source: Own calculations based on historical year-end ownership data from FAME (Bureau van Dijk).

The substantial influence of the largest fund families is not a recent phenomenon. Figures 20.3 and 20.4 show that the largest fund houses maintained a stable combined average shareholding in the FTSE 100 companies over time. Although the identities of the largest investors are subject to regular changes, the top ten and twenty investors have controlled around 23 per cent and 33 per cent of shares of the FTSE 100 firms since 2007, respectively. The combined shareholdings of the largest fund families represent substantial part of the ten and twenty largest all shareholders, especially when shareholdings are value weighted by the market capitalization of firms in the index.

20.3 LEGAL MEANS OF SHAREHOLDER ENGAGEMENT

20.3.1 *Shareholder Engagement Strategies*

The two traditional ways in which shareholders can engage with companies are to sell their shares or exercise their voice-based rights. 'Exit' by way of selling shares is considered a form of engagement because of its impact on share prices. When shareholders who are dissatisfied with a company's management sell their shares, they are punishing poor management by putting pressure on share prices. Similarly, good management is rewarded by an increase in share prices. The concentration of large shareholdings in the hands of a small number of asset managers has decreased the availability of exit as an engagement strategy. Larger shareholdings and the index investing strategies of large fund groups limit their ability to sell shares. When the possibility of an exit is reduced, shareholders increasingly rely on their voting power.[74]

The voice-based engagement strategies of shareholders involve reliance on voting rights to engage directly with management via private discussions behind the scenes, the use of shareholder proposal rights, or voting at shareholder meetings to support shareholder proposals or oppose management-sponsored governance initiatives. The main and most commonly used communication channel between managers and shareholders in publicly traded companies is voting at a general meeting of shareholders. Large institutional investors can also engage with companies informally through private meetings or phone calls, whereas retail investors can make use of their right to ask questions during annual shareholder meetings.

Recent studies have also identified a third and often neglected engagement strategy: the enforcement of shareholder rights via the courts.[75] Large institutional investors certainly have this strategy in their toolbox but are unlikely to rely on litigation often. With shareholdings in many publicly traded companies, institutional investors often lack sufficient resources to engage in time-consuming litigation, and can thus be expected to challenge companies in the courts only as a last resort in the most egregious of situations.

20.3.2 *Shareholders' Right to Call a Meeting*

As noted, the main engagement tool available to shareholders in publicly traded companies is the use of voting rights. Shareholders can communicate with management by supporting or voting against management-sponsored proposals, including the election of directors. Shareholders in publicly traded companies in the UK typically exercise their voting rights at the annual general meeting (AGM) of shareholders or, less often, at a special meeting, both called by directors.[76]

The minimum notice period for a general meeting is fourteen days for private companies[77] and twenty-one days for publicly traded companies.[78] However, publicly traded companies can call a meeting at shorter notice if all of the following conditions are met: (1) the meeting is not an AGM; (2) shareholders can vote electronically; and (3) shareholders voted in favour of calling

[74] Albert O. Hirschman, *Exit, Voice, and Loyalty: Responses to Decline in Firms, Organizations, and States* (Harvard University Press 1970) 34–6 ('[T]he role of voice would increase as the opportunities for exit decline, up to the point where, with exit wholly unavailable, voice must carry the entire burden of alerting management to its failings').

[75] Alexander I. Platt, 'Index Fund Enforcement' (2020) 53 UC Davis Law Review 1453, 1498–503; Sean J. Griffith and Dorothy S. Lund, 'A Mission Statement for Mutual Funds in Shareholder Litigation' (2020) 87 University of Chicago Law Review 1149, 1153–4.

[76] Suren Gomtsian, 'Voting Engagement by Large Institutional Investors' (2020) 45 The Journal of Corporation Law 659, 685.

[77] Companies Act 2006, s. 307(1).

[78] Ibid., s. 307A(1)(b).

a meeting at shorter notice at the preceding AGM or at a special meeting held after that meeting.[79] In practice, publicly traded companies commonly reserve a right to call a general meeting at notice of at least fourteen days in case they are a takeover target and shareholders move to adopt takeover defences to frustrate the bid.[80] The notice of a general meeting can be given in hard copy form, in electronic form or by means of a website.[81] In the latter case, the notice must be available on the website from the first notice date until at least the conclusion of the meeting.[82]

Shareholders may initiate a meeting themselves, although this rarely happens in publicly traded companies. Shareholders holding at least 5 per cent of the voting rights can request that directors call a general meeting of the company.[83] The request may also include the resolution sponsored by shareholders that will be voted upon at the meeting.[84] Directors must call the meeting within twenty-one days of the request date,[85] and the meeting must be held within twenty-eight days of the meeting notice date.[86] In the event that directors fail to call the meeting, shareholders can call it themselves at the company's expense.[87] Afterwards, the company is entitled to reimburse its expenses from the remuneration of the directors who failed to call the meeting at shareholders' request.[88]

20.3.3 *Shareholders' Proposal Right*

Shareholders in publicly traded companies may propose items for the agenda of AGMs, including proposing their own candidates for appointment as directors. However, shareholders' proposal right is subject to procedural hurdles requiring compliance with a minimum shareholding and advance notice requirements.[89] A proposal sponsor must own at least 5 per cent of the voting shares[90] or be a group of at least 100 shareholders each of whom owns no less than £100 worth of shares.[91] If one of these two requirements is met, the company must circulate shareholder-sponsored proposals amongst all shareholders in the same manner and at the same time as it gives notice of the annual meeting.[92] The question of who bears the costs of circulating shareholder proposals is defined based on the timing of the shareholder proposal request. If the company receives the request before the end of the financial year preceding the meeting, then the company bears the costs.[93] Otherwise, the shareholders advancing the proposal must cover the expenses.[94]

One of the distinguishing features of shareholder meetings in publicly traded companies in the UK is that management-sponsored proposals clearly dominate meeting agendas.[95] The number of shareholder-sponsored proposals voted on at the annual meetings of all FTSE 100

79 Ibid., ss. 307A(1)(a) and 307A(2)–(4).
80 Gomtsian (n. 76) 685.
81 Companies Act 2006, s. 308.
82 Ibid., s. 309(3).
83 Ibid., s. 303(2)(a).
84 Ibid., s. 303(4)(b).
85 Ibid., s. 304(1)(a).
86 Ibid., s. 304(1)(b).
87 Ibid., s. 305(1) and (6).
88 Ibid., s. 305(7).
89 Companies Act 2006, s. 338A(1).
90 Ibid., s. 338A(3)(a).
91 Ibid., s. 338A(3)(b).
92 Ibid., s. 340A(1)(a).
93 Ibid., s. 340B(1).
94 Ibid., s. 340B(2)(a).
95 Gomtsian (n. 76) 686.

companies each year typically does not exceed five.[96] By contrast, shareholders in US publicly traded companies voted on 788 shareholder-sponsored proposals during the 2018 proxy season alone, according to a report by the law firm Gibson, Dunn & Crutcher LLP.[97] The difference can be explained in part by the less demanding rules for submitting shareholder-sponsored proposals on social and environmental matters in the USA.[98]

In addition to the right to sponsor a proposal, shareholders may require a company to circulate amongst its shareholders a statement of no more than 1,000 words on any matter included in the shareholder meeting agenda.[99] Such a request can be made by shareholders owning at least 5 per cent of the voting shares[100] or by a group of at least 100 shareholders each of whom owns no less than £100 worth of shares.[101] The expenses will be covered by the company if the meeting to which the request relates is the AGM of a public company and the company receives the request before the end of the financial year preceding the meeting.[102]

20.3.4 *Voting, Majorities and Special Meetings*

Shareholders in private companies make decisions by either voting at a meeting or adopting written resolutions. Written resolutions can be adopted for all matters except resolutions to remove a director or auditor.[103] Public companies, by comparison, cannot use written resolutions and must hold a meeting for shareholder decision-making.[104] If at least two shareholders are attending the meeting, unless otherwise defined by the company's AoA, the meeting has a quorum.[105] Where shareholders vote on a written resolution or at a meeting by poll, every shareholder by default has one vote per share or per each £10 of stock.[106] By contrast, if shareholders vote at a meeting on a show of hands, then each shareholder has one vote.[107] Publicly traded companies typically vote by poll.[108] If a shareholder voting on a poll has more than one vote, he or she is free to use only some of the votes or to cast some of the votes differently.[109] Voting rules can easily be changed in AoA by creating, for example, shares with multiple voting rights or non-voting shares or by adopting cumulative voting.[110]

96 Ibid.

97 Gibson Dunn, *Shareholder Proposal Developments During the 2018 Proxy Season* (12 July 2018) www.gibsondunn.com/wp-content/uploads/2018/07/shareholder-proposal-developments-during-the-2018-proxy-season.pdf accessed 19 October 2019 (the sample covers all Russell 3000 companies; the '2018 proxy season' means the period between 1 October 2017 and 1 June 2018). See also Tatyana Shumsky, 'Investor Proposals Garner Support' *Wall Street Journal* (18 July 2018) B5B.

98 A shareholder who owns at least 1 per cent or US$2,000 worth of voting shares in a US corporation for at least a year is permitted to submit a shareholder proposal. Bonnie G. Buchanan, Jeffry M. Netter, Annette B. Poulsen and Tina Yang, 'Shareholder Proposal Rules and Practice: Evidence from a Comparison of the United States and United Kingdom' (2012) 49 American Business Law Journal 739, 754–5. Certain types of proposals, including matters relating to director elections or the company's ordinary business, are excluded from the easy access rules, which may explain the popularity of social and environmental proposals in US companies. Ibid., 770.

99 Companies Act 2006, s. 314(1).

100 Ibid., s. 314(2)(a).

101 Ibid., s. 314(2)(b).

102 Ibid., s. 316(1)

103 Ibid., s. 288(2). This exception is explained by the right of a director to protest against the removal and be heard at the meeting. Ibid., s. 169(2).

104 Ibid., ss. 281(2) and 288(1).

105 Ibid., s. 318(2).

106 Ibid., ss. 284(1)(a) and 284(3)(a).

107 Ibid., s. 284(2).

108 Brenda Hannigan, *Company Law* (5th ed., OUP 2018), 443.

109 Companies Act 2006, s. 322.

110 Ibid., ss. 284(4) and 630.

TABLE 20.2 *Types of resolutions and voting majorities*

Resolution type	Minimum votes needed to pass a decision	Freedom to amend the minimum voting threshold
Special resolutions	No less than 75% of the votes of shareholders voting on the resolution	No
Ordinary resolutions	Simple majority of the votes of shareholders voting on the resolution	No
Resolutions	Simple majority of the votes of shareholders voting on the resolution	Yes – higher majority or unanimous vote

Source: Companies Act 2006.

The Companies Act 2006 distinguishes amongst three types of resolutions, which vary based on the minimum threshold required to pass the resolution and the freedom afforded shareholders to alter that threshold. Certain matters, such as the removal of directors, require an ordinary resolution, which can be passed by a simple majority of shareholders voting on the resolution.[111] Other decisions, such as amendments to the company's AoA or a decision to wind up the company, require a special resolution that can be passed by no less than 75 per cent of the votes cast by shareholders voting on the resolution.[112] In these instances, shareholders cannot change the type of required resolution or the voting threshold. All other decisions can be passed by a resolution requiring a simple majority, and shareholders are free to increase, but not lower, the minimum voting threshold.[113] Table 20.2 provides a summary of the types of resolutions and minimum majority requirements.

A special (not annual) general meeting of shareholders may be called by directors at their own initiative or at the request of shareholders to deal with any matter that requires a shareholder vote and arises between two AGMs.[114] Special meetings generally involve such matters as the use of takeover defences, the approval of substantial conflicted transactions, mergers or divisions, or other matters subject to a shareholder vote. Most of the matters in publicly traded companies, however, are dealt with during annual meetings.[115] Public companies must hold an AGM within six months of the financial year end.[116]

20.3.5 *Information Disclosure and Question and Information Request Rights*

Information disclosure is one of the pillars of corporate governance that creates conditions for shareholders to effectively monitor managers.[117] Shareholder information rights include (1) the right to receive all information that companies disclose regularly under disclosure rules and (2) the right to request specific information from the company. Shareholders in all companies have information rights, but those rights are stronger in publicly traded companies because the law imposes additional disclosure requirements if a company's shares are traded publicly.

111 Ibid., s. 282(1) and (4).
112 Ibid., s. 283(1) and (5).
113 Ibid., s. 281(3).
114 Ibid., ss. 302 and 303(1).
115 See Gomtsian (n. 76).
116 Companies Act 2006, s. 336(1).
117 See nn. 21–5.

In addition to information rights, shareholders in publicly traded companies have a right to put questions to management during the company's shareholder meeting.

Company law in the UK, similar to that in other European countries, includes extensive requirements on the disclosure of company-related information. For example, whereas in many countries only publicly traded firms are required to disclose their financial results to the general public, in EU countries all incorporated business forms are obliged to disclose their accounting documents.[118] A UK company must keep (1) records about the company and (2) financial and accounting records. A portion of these records must be filed with Companies House on an annual basis, meaning that all interested persons, including shareholders, can access the information free of charge.

Information about a company must be filed with the company registrar in a document called a 'confirmation statement' (previously known as an annual return).[119] In particular, a company must annually update information on the address of its registered office, the address where its records are kept, the register of its directors and secretaries, the statement of capital and shareholder information, the SIC code and the register of people with significant control.[120]

Company directors or secretaries must within nine months of the end of the relevant accounting period file the annual accounts and auditor's report of the company with the company registrar.[121] For small companies, the filing requirement covers at a minimum the year-end balance sheet[122]; medium-sized and large companies, in addition to the balance sheet, must also file the profit and loss account and the auditor's report.[123]

In addition to public disclosures, companies must also disclose certain information to their shareholders directly. First, shareholders are entitled to notice of a company's general meetings with information on the meeting agenda.[124] Second, companies must prepare annual accounts that include the latest balance sheet and a profit and loss statement.[125] All companies, except those qualifying for the small company regime,[126] must also prepare a strategic report[127] and a directors' report.[128] Companies must send copies of all three documents to their shareholders[129] and publish annual accounts and reports on the company's website if the company is publicly traded.[130] Publicly traded companies must also prepare a remuneration report on an annual basis and submit it for an advisory shareholder vote.[131]

The information disclosure requirements imposed on companies are further supported by the right of shareholders to request relevant information. In particular, shareholders are entitled to demand, without charge, a copy of the company's last annual accounts, the directors'

118 Wolfgang Schön, 'Corporate Disclosure in a Competitive Environment – The Quest for a European Framework on Mandatory Disclosure' (2006) 6 Journal of Corporate Law Studies 259, 260.

119 Companies Act 2006, s. 853A.

120 The list of information required to be included in the confirmation statement is provided in s. 853B, with further clarifications in ss. 853C–853I of the Companies Act 2006.

121 Companies Act 2006, ss. 441 and 442(2).

122 Ibid., s. 444.

123 Ibid., ss. 445 and 446.

124 Ibid., ss. 310(1)(a) and 311(2).

125 Ibid., ss. 394 and 396(1).

126 A company qualifies as a small company if it meets two or more of the three following criteria during a financial year: (1) turnover of no more than £10.2 million; (2) balance sheet total of no more than £5.1 million; and (3) number of employees not exceeding fifty. Companies Act 2006, s. 382. Some companies, such as public companies, banks and insurance companies, cannot qualify as a small company regardless of size. Ibid., s. 384(1).

127 Companies Act 2006, s. 414A.

128 Ibid., s. 415.

129 Ibid., ss. 414D (for strategic reports), 419 (for directors' reports) and 423(1) (for annual accounts and reports).

130 Ibid., s. 430(1)(a).

131 Ibid., ss. 420(1) and 439.

remuneration report, the strategic report, the directors' report and the auditor's report on all of these documents.[132]

Shareholders in publicly traded companies are also entitled to ask questions at the company's general meeting.[133] The questions asked can pertain to any matter included in the meeting agenda.[134] The company must answer questions posed by shareholders at the general meeting with the exception of a limited number of circumstances, such as where the answer would involve the disclosure of confidential information, has already been supplied on the company's website in the form of an answer to a question or is undesirable in the interests of the company.[135]

20.3.6 *Voting and Engagement by Institutional Investors*

Given the dominant shareholdings of institutional investors in publicly traded British companies (see Figure 20.1 above), the effectiveness of shareholder control and monitoring depends to a large extent on the willingness of institutional investors to vote their shares and engage with corporate managers meaningfully. Generally, shareholders are free to vote their shares at their discretion, including by not attending company general meetings and not voting.[136] However, the growing influence of institutional investors has led to the realization that shareholder control and monitoring in publicly traded companies are matters too important to be left to the complete discretion of shareholders. As a result, we have witnessed significant attempts to improve the mechanisms of shareholder control and engagement, especially by institutional investors, over the last decade. Most of these attempts, with a few exceptions, including the introduction of statutory say-on-pay votes[137] and the implementation of EU shareholder rights directives,[138] have taken the form of soft law measures.

The Walker Report prepared in the aftermath of the 2008 financial crisis identified engagement by institutional investors as a key area in need of improvement and recommended the development of principles of best practice in stewardship by institutional investors and fund managers.[139] As a result, the Financial Reporting Council introduced the first Stewardship Code in July 2010 and updated the Code in September 2012.[140] The Stewardship Code 2012 defined stewardship by investors broadly as including not just voting, but also monitoring and engaging with companies.[141] Although falling short of imposing mandatory voting and engagement requirements,[142] the Code introduced principles of best practice stewardship aimed at enhancing the quality of engagement between institutional investors and companies. Key amongst these principles were recommendations for institutional investors to have stewardship[143] and

132 Ibid., ss. 431(1) and 432(1).

133 Ibid., s. 319A(1).

134 Ibid.

135 Ibid., s. 319A(2).

136 Certain narrow limits are imposed on the voting rights of controlling shareholders, who must exercise their voting power bona fide in the best interests of the company as a whole, particularly when voting for AoA amendments. *Allen* v. *Gold Reefs of West Africa Ltd* [1900] 1 Ch 656, 671; *Greenhalgh* v. *Arderne Cinemas Ltd* [1951] 1 Ch 286, 291.

137 See nn. 44–8.

138 See nn. 157–60.

139 David Walker, *A Review of Corporate Governance in UK Banks and Other Financial Industry Entities, Final Recommendations* (26 November 2009) 14–22 https://webarchive.nationalarchives.gov.uk/+/http:/www.hm-treasury.gov.uk/d/walker_review_261109.pdf accessed 18 June 2020.

140 See nn. 3–4.

141 Stewardship Code 2012 (n. 4) Preface.

142 For example, the Stewardship Code 2012 applied on a comply-or-explain basis. Stewardship Code 2012 (n. 4) Preface.

143 Stewardship Code 2012 (n. 4) Principle 1.

voting policies,[144] monitor portfolio companies,[145] vote all shares held and disclose their voting records,[146] and report periodically on their stewardship and voting activities.[147]

After the adoption of SRD II, the Stewardship Code required an update,[148] and the Financial Reporting Council used the opportunity for a major revision. The revised UK Stewardship Code 2020 was published in October 2019 and became effective in January 2020.[149] The Code's revision led to a substantial structural and content revision of the stewardship requirements by shifting the focus from developing policies and reporting on stewardship and voting activities towards stronger emphasis on specific stewardship actions that must be taken by investors and asset managers and on the outcomes of those actions.

The UK Stewardship Code 2020 recommends, for example, that institutional investors explain how they devote appropriate resources to stewardship activities,[150] consider the needs of their beneficiary investors and communicate their stewardship activities and outcomes to them,[151] and integrate stewardship in investment and exit decisions.[152] Similarly, the Code reformulated engagement requirements in terms of maintaining or enhancing the value of invested assets.[153] Institutional investors now need to explain how they select matters for engagement (e.g. based on the importance of the matter or the size of shareholdings), what methods of engagement they use, and how engagement differs based on the asset type or region of investment.[154] They are also expected to exercise their voting rights and disclose the proportion of shares voted, voting records and the reasons for major voting decisions, such as votes against management or shareholder-sponsored proposals or votes not in line with the investor's voting policy.[155] Where necessary, institutional investors are expected to collaborate with other investors and escalate activities to strengthen the effectiveness of stewardship.[156]

In addition to the UK Stewardship Code 2020, certain SRD II provisions implemented through regulatory requirements are mandatory for institutional investors. For example, insurance companies[157] and investment managers[158] are required to either (1) develop and publicly disclose an engagement policy and report annually on their implementation of that policy or (2) provide a reasoned explanation of why they have chosen not to comply with this requirement. The annual report must include a general description of voting behaviour, an explanation of the most significant votes and use of the services of proxy advisors.[159] Importantly, investors are not

144 Ibid., Principle 6.
145 Ibid., Principle 3.
146 Ibid., Principle 6. Importantly, the Code explained that institutional investors should not vote automatically to support management.
147 Ibid., Principle 7.
148 SRD II (n. 6).
149 UK Stewardship Code 2020 (n. 5).
150 Ibid., Principle 2. The appropriate resourcing of stewardship activities includes having special organizational structures for stewardship, qualified experts, and investing in research and analysis.
151 Ibid., Principle 6. Institutional investors should seek the views of their clients and align their own stewardship activities with the stewardship policies and preferences of their clients.
152 Ibid., Principle 7.
153 Ibid., Principle 9.
154 Ibid.
155 Ibid., Principle 12.
156 Ibid., Principles 10, 11.
157 FCA Handbook, Senior Management Arrangements, Systems and Controls Sourcebook (SYSC), s 3.4.4, SYSC 3/20 (June 2020), www.handbook.fca.org.uk/handbook/SYSC.pdf accessed 18 June 2020.
158 FCA Handbook, Conduct of Business Sourcebook (COBS), s. 2.2B.5, COBS 2/8-2/9 (June 2020) www.handbook.fca.org.uk/handbook/COBS.pdf accessed 18 June 2020.
159 FCA Handbook, SYSC (n. 157), s. 3.4.6(1) (for insurers); FCA Handbook, COBS (n. 158), s. 2.2B.7(1) (for investment managers).

required to disclose their full voting records.[160] These regulatory engagement requirements implement the minimum required by SRD II and clearly set engagement standards that are much less stringent than those included in the UK Stewardship Code 2020.

20.4 SHAREHOLDER ENGAGEMENT AND VOTING IN PRACTICE

20.4.1 *Voting in Practice*

Individuals directly controlled just over 17 per cent of the shares in quoted UK companies at the end of 2018, according to the latest data from the Office for National Statistics.[161] The shareholdings of company founders, directors, officers and retail investors are even lower in FTSE 100 companies.[162] The majority of shareholdings are controlled by institutional investors, but amongst many institutional investors there is a small group of large fund families that dominates the votes of the largest British publicly traded companies.[163] The voting practices of these investors are the focus of this section because of their growing influence over corporate managers.

Shareholders mostly vote on a standard set of proposals that can be grouped into several major categories. The largest category comprises proposals related to the election of new directors and re-election of incumbent directors. The next category includes various routine or business matters, such as the trivial acceptance of financial statements and statutory reports, approval of dividends, authorization of political donations, appointment of an auditor and authorization for the board to fix the auditor's remuneration, although proposals in this category may also include more important matters such amendments of the company's articles or changes in board structure. Two other large proposal categories include capitalization and compensation-related items. Capitalization proposals cover standard authorizations for share buy-backs and the issue of new equity, which companies vote on annually regardless of whether there is an actual intention to buy back or issue new shares. Compensation proposals pertain primarily to the ordinary approval of remuneration policies and remuneration reports, but may also include irregular matters such as the approval of incentive plans or making of one-time payments to specific directors. The next category is antitakeover proposals, which constitutes a distinct category of standard proposals voted on during the annual meetings of most publicly traded companies. These proposals allow the board to call a shareholder meeting at short notice – that is, two weeks – in the event that the company becomes a takeover target and intends to adopt takeover defences.[164] Most shareholders approach this category as a formality by approving the proposal concerned.

Two additional but relatively small categories of proposals deal with major events in the company's life – such as mergers, reorganizations and large asset sales or purchases – and with social, health and environmental topics. Proposals on mergers and reorganizations are often

[160] FCA Handbook, SYSC (n. 157), s. 3.4.6(2)(b) (for insurers); FCA Handbook, COBS (n. 158), s. 2.2B.7(2)(b) (for investment managers). Under the Companies Act 2006, the government has the power to require institutional investors to disclose the exercise of their voting rights, but it has opted not to require complete voting record disclosure, leaving the matter to self-regulation. Companies Act 2006, s. 1277(1).

[161] See Figure 20.1.

[162] Office for National Statistics, 'Statistical Bulletin: Ownership of UK Quoted Shares: 2018' (14 January 2020) www.ons.gov.uk/economy/investmentspensionsandtrusts/bulletins/ownershipofukquotedshares/2018#beneficial-owners accessed 19 June 2020.

[163] See Section 20.2.3.

[164] For an overview of regular and shorter notice periods, see nn. 77–80.

voted on during a special general meeting. Social and environmental proposals, although voted on at an AGM, as a rule, are sponsored by shareholders and are extremely rare. A recent study found only eight such proposals initiated by shareholders in FTSE 100 companies during the 2013–17 voting seasons.[165]

The largest fund groups have stepped up their engagement efforts in the past few years by opposing management-sponsored proposals more often. On average, less than 1.7 per cent of votes were cast against management recommendations in 2013, a percentage that rose to nearly 3 per cent during the voting seasons of 2016 and 2017.[166] Although that may appear to be a minor increase, given the routine or trivial nature of many of the proposals voted on, it is substantial. When routine proposals are excluded, the change in the rate of opposition to management on some types of proposals becomes more revealing. For example, votes against compensation proposals increased from 5.7 per cent in 2013 to more than 9.6 per cent in 2016.[167]

The increasing levels of shareholder engagement over time can, to a certain extent, be explained by the ongoing debates on the role of large institutional investors. If the dominant expectation of asset managers was previously to keep management costs to a minimum, today large asset managers are also expected to be responsible investors. Stewardship codes and broader discussion in the media have led to the development of a new societal norm over the past few years, which has in turn led to cultural changes in the asset management industry.

However, not all proposals attract the same degree of attention from large asset managers. These investors have shareholdings in hundreds of companies, and are thus too big to be active in all situations; they also face competitive pressure to reduce fund management costs. Large asset managers have responded by focusing their shareholder engagement efforts on corporate governance. As a result, certain types of proposals attract more attention than others, even though they may play a far less fundamental role in a company's management.

Amongst the various categories of proposals, director elections are the most important business-related matter on which shareholders vote regularly. It is through voting on director elections that shareholders can influence corporate decision-making. The procedure for director elections in publicly traded companies is highly uniform. Companies with a premium listing almost universally follow the UK Corporate Governance Code's requirement of annual re-election for the entire board of directors.[168] Director candidates are proposed by the board (or the board's nomination committee). Although shareholders may propose their own candidates subject to procedural hurdles, including compliance with minimum shareholding and advance notice requirements,[169] they rarely do so in practice.[170] Shareholders vote on each board candidate individually,[171] and a director must receive at least a simple majority vote to be appointed.[172]

As a rule, director elections are uncontested, and large institutional investors rarely vote against the candidates proposed by management.[173] The opposition rate of votes cast by large institutional investors on director election proposals increased only marginally from 2013 to 2017,

165 Gomtsian (n. 76) 685.

166 Ibid., 689.

167 Ibid., 690–1.

168 Financial Reporting Council, *The UK Corporate Governance Code* (July 2018) Principle 3, Provision 18 www.frc.org.uk/getattachment/88bd8c45-50ea-4841-95b0-d2f4f48069a2/2018-UK-Corporate-Governance-Code-FINAL.PDF accessed 17 September 2019.

169 Companies Act 2006, s. 338.

170 Analysis of all proposals voted on at the general meetings of FTSE 100 companies during the 2013–17 period identified only three instances of shareholders nominating their own candidate for an election. Gomtsian (n. 76) 685.

171 Companies Act 2006, s. 160(1).

172 Companies (Model Articles) Regulations 2008, sch. 3 (Model Articles for Public Companies), art. 20(a).

173 Gomtsian (n. 76) 696.

rising from 1.5 per cent to 2.3 per cent.[174] This increase is neither meaningful economically nor significant statistically, which suggests that most institutional investors consider director elections to be a business matter best left to management. The most likely trigger for intervention is the best practice governance standards that an investor follows not being met by the company. As a result, voting decisions are driven by standard corporate governance considerations, such as over-boarding, director independence, gender diversity or pay-related concerns. For example, an asset manager unhappy with a compensation proposal put to a vote may vote against all board candidates for the compensation committee or the committee's chair.[175] Similarly, a failure to meet recommended board diversity targets may lead to voting against all board candidates for the nomination committee or the committee's chair.[176]

The most controversial proposals, and hence those that receive the closest scrutiny and, as a result, the highest dissent rates, are management compensation proposals. On average, the largest institutional investors vote against management recommendations on compensation matters in almost 8 per cent of cases.[177] Interestingly, there are differences in the voting practices of UK- and US-domiciled investors on management compensation proposals. UK asset managers are three times more likely to vote against compensation proposals than their US peers.[178] The most likely explanation for the difference is that US shareholders are more accustomed to high executive pay, and will pay attention only in instances where pay is not aligned with performance. By contrast, high pay itself may provoke opposition amongst UK-based shareholders.[179]

20.4.2 *Private Engagement and Shareholder Activism*

Voting shares may well be the most commonly used communication channel between large institutional investors and corporate management, and is certainly the most easily observable engagement mechanism. Voting is not, however, the only engagement option available to investors. An alternative tool of engagement is for investors to use their shareholding as leverage in private informal discussions with company managers to influence their behaviour and/or collect information on the company.[180] Private engagement is often less confrontational and can contribute to building trust-based relationships between investors and managers over time.[181]

Engagement topics, resources and intensity vary across different types of large investors. Activist investors engage less frequently and more selectively, but their engagement efforts are more confrontational and intensive. The objectives of engagement by activists include having a say on operational matters, board changes, business strategy, and mergers and acquisitions (M&A). The dispersed ownership structures of UK publicly traded companies, strong shareholder rights and many similarities with the US make British companies convenient targets for activist shareholders. The UK has the highest number of activist campaigns in Europe (see Figure 20.5). Shareholder activists targeted forty-seven UK-based companies in 2018, accounting for 31.76 per cent of all activist

174 Ibid., 691.
175 Ibid., 696.
176 Ibid.
177 Ibid., 694.
178 Ibid., 699–700.
179 Ibid., 700.
180 Alan R. Palmiter, 'Mutual Fund Voting of Portfolio Shares: Why Not Disclose?' (2002) 23 Cardozo Law Review 1419, 1437–8.
181 Matthew J. Mallow and Jasmin Sethi, 'Engagement: The Missing Middle Approach in the Bebchuk-Strine Debate' (2016) 12 New York University Journal of Law & Business 385, 396.

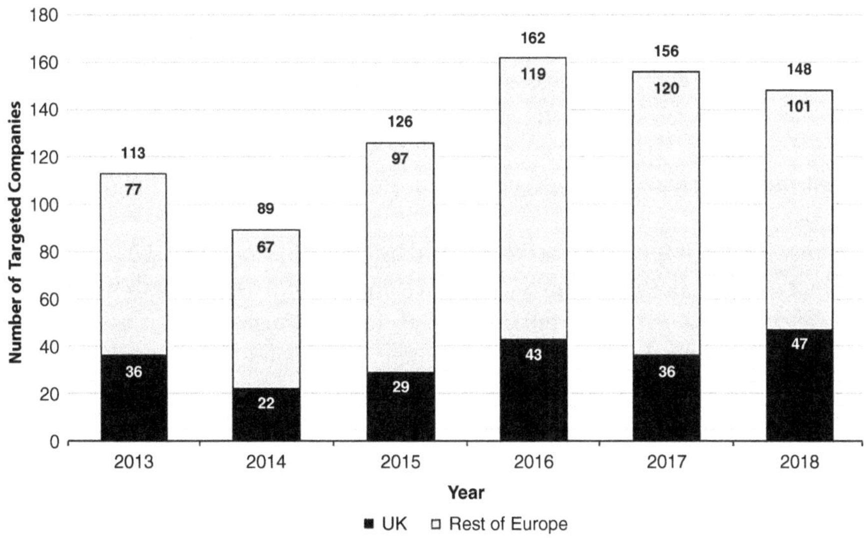

FIGURE 20.5 Companies targeted by activists in the UK
Source: Activist Insight.

demands in Europe and just over 5 per cent of activist targets worldwide. In total, 213 UK companies – almost 27 per cent of all European targets – received activist demands during the six-year period from 2013–18. The share of British companies targeted by activist shareholders has consistently stayed close to one-quarter of campaigns launched in Europe since 2013 (see Figure 20.5). Although activism is not the exclusive domain of hedge funds, repeat activists with a high degree of specialization are the most influential. The leading activist in the UK is Elliott Management Corp, an American activist hedge fund, which has been involved in a number of high-profile cases, including successful attempts to sell parts of the business of BHP Group PLC, a mining company.[182]

By contrast, large institutional investors engage more often on governance matters and prefer less confrontational means. The institutional environment in the UK creates favourable conditions for private engagement by institutional investors. A survey of the top officials of large British asset managers conducted in the early 1990s showed that, unlike institutional investors in the USA, British institutional investors often prefer to act behind closed doors instead of resorting to public activism.[183] The long tradition of strong investor associations[184] and a close-knit community of asset managers concentrated in a small area of the City of London and Edinburgh in Scotland[185] contribute to the effectiveness of private engagement, as institutional investors can leverage their influence by acting collectively. Furthermore, investors may prefer private engagement over

182 Eric Sylvers and Ben Dummett, 'US Activist Takes on Europe' *Wall Street Journal* (17–18 March 2018) B10.

183 Bernard S. Black and John C. Coffee, Jr, 'Hail Britannia?: Institutional Investor Behavior Under Limited Regulation' (1994) 92 Michigan Law Review 1997, 2033, 2054 (reporting that the prevailing view amongst institutional investors is that 'secrecy and trust are essential').

184 Historically, trade groups of institutional investors in the UK played a much bigger role than, for example, in the USA. Andrew F. Tuch, 'Proxy Advisor Influence in a Comparative Light' (2019) 99 Boston University Law Review 1459, 1481–9. See also Gomtsian (n. 76) 709–10.

185 Cheffins (n. 59) 372 (contrasting the UK's compact financial hubs with the fragmented financial centres in the USA).

selling shares not just because indexing strategies leave little scope for selling shares, but also because selling shares does not send a clear signal to the company about underlying problems.[186]

A more recent and comprehensive survey of investment managers from various countries offers evidence to suggest that private negotiations are indeed a common instrument used by institutional investors.[187] Of the 143 responses received from large institutional investors, 63 per cent indicated that they had engaged in direct discussions with management in the preceding five years.[188]

Private engagement is thus a common tool used by large investors in the UK. Unlike voting at a shareholder meeting, however, the results of such engagement are not easily observable. Apart from the surveys mentioned above, our knowledge of private engagement is based primarily on case studies and anecdotal evidence. Two prominent examples of comprehensive studies of private engagement by institutional investors are the studies analyzing engagement practices of Hermes UK Focus Fund, a special fund established in 1998 to actively engage with companies in the pension fund portfolios of British Telecommunications and the Post Office,[189] and of Aberdeen Standard Investments, one of the top UK-based asset managers.[190]

The Hermes study shows that the fund's engagement efforts during the study period clearly took a private rather than public form through numerous meetings or letter and phone contacts with top managers.[191] The fund also regularly contacted other large institutional shareholders to communicate its engagement objectives and gain support for its activities.[192] By contrast, interventions at public meetings were rare.[193] The Aberdeen study similarly illustrates the frequent use of private engagement. For example, during a typical year in the study period the asset manager was a shareholder in over 380 companies included in the FTSE All Share index; its governance and stewardship experts had 564 contacts with portfolio companies, of which the most frequent were face-to-face meetings; furthermore, internal analysts, most of whom were also fund managers, held 650 meetings with the top management of the portfolio companies.[194] The team engaged with every portfolio company at least once during the year.[195] Fund managers mostly engaged with companies on operational matters and M&A, whereas the dominant engagement focus of stewardship experts was governance matters, such as compensation, diversity and board independence.[196] Importantly, information was regularly exchanged between the groups, as stewardship experts, internal analysts and fund managers sit on the same floor and meet regularly, both formally and informally.[197]

186 Downes and others (n. 61) 31–2.

187 Joseph A. McCahery, Zacharias Sautner and Laura T. Starks, 'Behind the Scenes: The Corporate Governance Preferences of Institutional Investors' (2016) 71 The Journal of Finance 2905, 2906.

188 Ibid., 2911–12.

189 Marco Becht et al., 'Returns to Shareholder Activism: Evidence from a Clinical Study of the Hermes UK Focus Fund' (2009) 22 The Review of Financial Studies 3093, 3101–2. A large share of the pension savings' equity assets was invested in index tracking funds with the implication that possible gains from any engagement effort would flow to other free-riding investors as well. As a result, the trustees of the British Telecommunications Staff Superannuation Scheme created the Hermes UK Focus Fund to overweight the funds' position in underperforming companies that were selected for more intensive engagement, which would better justify the costs of engagement. Ibid., 3102.

190 Marco Becht, Julian Franks and Hannes F. Wagner, 'Corporate Governance Through Voice and Exit' (November 2019), ECGI Finance Working Paper No. 633/2019 https://ssrn.com/abstract=3456626 accessed 1 January 2020.

191 Becht et al. (n. 189) 3108.

192 Ibid.

193 Ibid.

194 Becht et al. (n. 190) 30.

195 Ibid., 11.

196 Ibid., 9, 10.

197 Ibid., 10.

Not only are private negotiations common, but they are also often successful in promoting changes in target companies, even though the institutional investors initiating negotiations rarely have majority votes. Consider again the case of the Hermes UK Focus Fund. In the aforementioned study, its most common engagement objectives were restructuring the business (thirty-eight cases) through the sale of noncore divisions or assets, and in more than half of those cases the objectives were met.[198] Other common engagement objectives involved opposing acquisitions or other capital expenditures and board changes, with success rates varying from 75–90 per cent.[199]

Other examples show how private engagement can complement or even replace shareholder voting. For instance, Unilever PLC, a British-Dutch consumer goods company, had to abandon the scheduled shareholder vote on consolidating its dual-listed corporate structure with single headquarters in Rotterdam after a significant revolt, first expressed privately and then made public, by large institutional shareholders.[200] The consolidation would have excluded Unilever from the FTSE indices, forcing some index tracking investors to sell their shareholdings at a time when the share price was low. Another example is the decision by Royal Dutch Shell PLC, a British-Dutch oil and gas company, to promise reductions in carbon emissions and link emission targets to executive pay, although a shareholder proposal with similar subject matter had been voted down earlier after a negative management recommendation.[201] Management had to change course under intensive behind-the-scenes shareholder pressure after the failed vote.[202] Therefore, voting outcomes alone may not fully reveal engagement efforts by shareholders.

These examples also demonstrate the differences in the engagement objectives of different institutional investors. The Hermes UK Focus Fund was established for a special purpose and resembles an activist shareholder, both by the small number of investments and demand topics, rather than a large asset manager with a diversified portfolio.[203] By contrast, Aberdeen Standard Investments has a much larger portfolio, with each governance expert engaging with more than twenty companies on average.[204] As a result, its engagement is more selective and is likelier to target companies that deviate from the best practices of corporate governance. Large fund families hold diversified portfolios, which necessarily changes the nature of their engagement efforts. Passive fund managers often point to their difference from activist hedge fund investors, as they prefer to work collaboratively behind the scenes instead of making public aggressive demands.[205] BlackRock, for example, describes itself as an 'engagement-first company' that meets with 1,500 companies a year to discuss company-related problems; only when engagement fails will it vote against a director or management.[206] BlackRock reported 1,603 engagements

198 Ibid., 3111.

199 Ibid.

200 Saabira Chaudhuri and Daphne Zhang, 'Unilever To Keep UK Base' *Wall Street Journal* (6 October 2018) B3; Leila Abboud and Attracta Mooney, 'Unilever Chief Blindsided by Investor Revolt' *Financial Times* (London, 6 October 2018) 17; Attracta Mooney, 'Adviser Calls on Investors to Veto Unilever Move' *Financial Times* (London, 4 October 2018) 20.

201 Sarah Kent, 'Shell Links Pay, Emissions' *Wall Street Journal* (4 December 2018) B2; Anjli Raval, Leslie Hook and Attracta Mooney, 'Shell Yields to Investors by Setting Target to Cut Its Carbon Footing' *Financial Times* (London, 3 December 2018) 1.

202 Kent (n. 201) B2 (reporting that the change in Royal Dutch Shell's position followed months of engagement with institutional investors); Raval, Hook and Mooney (n. 201) 1 (citing the CEO of Royal Dutch Shell who said that it was 'dialogue' with investors that had led to the 'evolution' in the company's position).

203 Becht et al. (n. 189) 3104 (reporting that the Hermes UK Focus Fund invested in a total of forty-one companies between 1 October 1998 and 31 December 2004).

204 Becht et al. (n. 190) 30.

205 Sarah Krouse, 'Index Funds Use Clout in Distinctive Ways' *Wall Street Journal* (22 January 2018) B10.

206 Justin Baer and Joann S. Lublin, 'State Street Falls Short in Bid for Women Directors' *Wall Street Journal* (27 July 2017) B10.

globally in 2017, whereas Vanguard and State Street Global Investors, the two other giant asset managers, had 954 and 676 engagements, respectively.[207]

The large number of annual engagements by large institutional investors, as opposed to the handful of interventions per year by specialized activist shareholders, has important implications. It is unrealistic to expect informed engagement with every portfolio company from large diversified fund families. A recent survey by Morningstar, an investment research company, suggests that engagement by passively managed fund managers occurs in situations where a company faces material risks or has a governance structure that deviates from commonly adopted governance practices.[208] Thus, similar to engagement through voting at a shareholder meeting, the private engagement efforts of large institutional investors are likely to focus on the promotion of the best standards of corporate governance or global challenges such as climate change and social matters.

In summary, large institutional investors are in a strong position to promote change through private shareholder engagement based on their large shareholdings in portfolio companies. However, the scarce information on private communications between institutional investors and their portfolio companies leaves many unanswered questions. Most of the existing studies rely on data from case studies and do not allow broad general conclusions to be drawn. It is nevertheless clear that institutional investors do engage with portfolio companies privately, although their engagement efforts vary widely. Private engagement remains an aspect of shareholder stewardship that requires greater scholarly attention and more studies based on comprehensive interviews with large institutional investors.

20.4.3 *The Role of Proxy Advisors*

One of the most hotly debated topics of recent years has been the role of proxy advisory firms in the process of shareholder voting. Proxy advisory firms collect information on all votes at publicly traded companies and use their corporate governance expertise to develop voting recommendations.[209] Economies of scale allow proxy advisors to supply their clients with information on voting at a lower cost than each client could obtain independently.[210] These recommendations can thus assist shareholders in casting their votes, especially when investors have highly diversified portfolios without sufficient resources to participate in the governance of their portfolio companies. Critics of the role of proxy advisors, however, point to their excessive influence over the outcomes of votes and the lack of oversight and accountability concerning their recommendations.[211] Although empirical evidence on the extent of the influence of proxy advisors remains inconclusive,[212] corporate advocacy groups in some countries have intensified

207 Krouse (n. 205) B10.

208 Hortense Bioy et al., 'Passive Fund Providers Take an Active Approach to Investment Stewardship' Morningstar Manager Research Paper (December 2017) 10 www.morningstar.com/content/dam/marketing/shared/pdfs/Research/Morningstar-Passive-Active-Stewardship.pdf accessed 15 July 2020.

209 Paul H. Edelman, Randall S. Thomas and Robert B. Thompson, 'Shareholder Voting in an Age of Intermediary Capitalism' (2014) 87 Southern California Law Review 1359, 1397.

210 Ibid.

211 See e.g. Daniel Thomas and Attracta Mooney, 'Proxy Advisers Under Attack in Battle for Influence' *Financial Times* (London, 27 August 2018) 17 (citing criticism of proxy advisors from influential corporate managers).

212 Empirical studies have found proxy advisor recommendations to exert a strong influence on shareholder votes, but a key challenge in these studies is identifying whether proxy advisor recommendations drive voting by shareholders or whether the voting preferences of large institutional investors influence proxy advisors' voting recommendations. Because proxy advisors interact constantly with their major clients, their voting recommendations may reflect both

their lobbying efforts to regulate proxy advisors in recent years.[213] But the UK discourse on proxy advisors has been much more muted than that in, for example, the USA.

Whilst it has been suggested that proxy advisors have weaker influence in the UK than in the USA, they still play a significant role.[214] The revised UK Stewardship Code 2020 includes recommendations for proxy advisers to disclose and explain how they address conflicts of interest.[215] This reform follows the introduction of similar rules in the EU. SRD II, which came into force on 10 June 2019, requires proxy advisors to adopt codes of conduct and disclose their actual or potential conflicts of interest.[216] Glass, Lewis & Co., the second largest proxy advisory firm, in an effort to ease regulatory and corporate pressure, went further by providing target companies with the right to submit a response to its recommendations that can be distributed amongst shareholders for a fee.[217]

In practice, although proxy advisors continue to play an important role, their influence seems to be on the wane, as some shareholders, especially large institutional investors, appear to be relying less on their recommendations in casting their votes than they previously did. The similarity between the votes cast by large asset managers and the recommendations of proxy advisors has been on the decrease in recent years during the shareholder meetings of FTSE 100 companies.[218] Indeed, many large asset managers claim that instead of simply delegating voting, they often rely on research conducted by their in-house investment stewardship teams,[219] although they use analysis by and the recommendations of proxy advisors as useful input in their decision-making.[220]

The extent to which large institutional investors influence, perhaps indirectly, the recommendations of proxy advisors is also unclear. As a result, proxy advisors may simply be aggregating the majority view or the views of the most influential shareholders in their voting recommendations.[221] As Professor Tuch explained, UK institutional investors, acting collectively through institutional investor trade groups, have traditionally wielded greater influence over the voting guidelines of proxy advisors than their US counterparts.[222] For example, until 2015, ISS, the largest proxy advisor, used the policy and voting guidelines of the Pension and Lifetime Savings Association (PLSA), a pension fund trade group, as their reference.[223] Since 2015, ISS's

their own independent assessments and the preferences of major institutional investors. James Cotter, Alan Palmiter and Randall Thomas, 'ISS Recommendations and Mutual Fund Voting on Proxy Proposals' (2010) 55 *Villanova Law Review* 1, 28, 56. But also see Cindy R. Alexander et al., 'Interim News and the Role of Proxy Voting Advice' (2010) 23 *The Review of Financial Studies* 4419, 4434–7 (finding that share prices respond to the direction of proxy advisor recommendations, which suggests that proxy advisors bring new information to the market rather than simply reflecting the consensus view amongst many large institutional investors).

213 Gabriel T. Rubin, 'Proxy Advisers Face an Oversight Push' *Wall Street Journal* (20 March 2019) B10 (reporting on lobbying and advertising campaigns against proxy advisors sponsored by corporate advocacy groups, such as the National Association of Manufacturers and the US Chamber of Commerce, and stock exchanges, such as Nasdaq and the New York Stock Exchange); Richard Henderson, 'Companies Call For Action on Proxy Advisers to Shareholders' *Fin Times* (London, 6 February 2019) 25 (the same).

214 Tuch (n. 184) 1479–81 (2019) (reporting industry perceptions of the influence of proxy advisors in the UK).

215 UK Stewardship Code (n. 5) Principles for Service Providers, Principle 3.

216 SRD II (n. 6) arts. 3j(1) and (2)(g).

217 Owen Walker, 'Glass Lewis Gives Groups a Right to Reply' *Financial Times* (London, 15 April 2019) 1, 2.

218 Gomtsian (n. 76) 696–7.

219 Bioy et al. (n. 208) 14 (reporting survey results indicating that asset managers use proxy advisory services for research or to identify important proposals, but do not follow their recommendations blindly); Giovanni Strampelli, 'Are Passive Index Funds Active Owners? Corporate Governance Consequences of Passive Investing' (2018) 55 San Diego Law Review 803, 821–2 (describing BlackRock's internal voting procedure).

220 Thomas and Mooney (n. 211) 17.

221 Cotter et al. (n. 212) 28, 56.

222 Tuch (n. 184) 1485.

223 Ibid.

voting guidelines for UK companies have generally been consistent with those of the PLSA and have also relied heavily on the guidelines of other trade groups.[224]

The situation may be very different amongst smaller diversified investors who lack the resources to vote in an informed manner in a large number of portfolio companies. Evidence from other countries supports this supposition, showing that many institutional investors vote along with ISS recommendations in 100 per cent or close to 100 per cent of cases.[225]

20.4.4 *Voting and Engagement during the COVID-19 Crisis*

Shareholder voting and engagement in UK companies have not been left untouched by the many disruptions of the COVID-19 crisis. The peak of the crisis came during a period when many publicly traded companies in the UK tended to organize their annual shareholder meetings, which meant that they had to quickly rethink their plans and either put in place contingency arrangements for holding the meetings or postpone them. The matter was further complicated by the unclear position of the UK Companies Act 2006 and the AoA of many companies on the permissibility of virtual only or hybrid shareholder meetings.

Shareholders in public companies, as explained above, can pass resolutions only at a meeting of shareholders, and the meeting has a quorum if at least two shareholders are in attendance.[226] It is not clear whether companies are permitted to dispense with meetings attended in person entirely and solely organize online meetings. Even if online only shareholder meetings are possible, they are not expressly stipulated in the model articles for public companies or in the articles of many publicly traded companies,[227] which has created uncertainty over the legality of online or hybrid annual shareholder meetings. To further complicate matters, companies were unable to hold in-person meetings after the UK government imposed a 'stay at home' requirement.

The government tried to ease matters by announcing plans to introduce temporary legislation allowing companies required by law to hold AGMs to postpone those meetings until the end of September 2020 or hold the meetings online.[228] Note that all public companies must hold an AGM within six months of the end of the company's financial year.[229] These temporary measures were to apply retrospectively from 26 March 2020.[230] In addition, on 27 March 2020, the Chartered Governance Institute (ICSA), an organization for governance professionals, published guidance for UK companies on how to conduct AGMs during the COVID-19

[224] Ibid.

[225] Cheng Shu, 'Proxy Advice Industry and Its Growing Influence' (May 2020) 16–17 https://ssrn.com/abstract=3614314 accessed 9 June 2020 (showing that investment fund asset size is negatively correlated with robo-voting with ISS); Timothy M. Doyle, *The Realities of Robo-Voting*, American Council for Capital Formation (ACCF) Report (November 2018) http://accfcorpgov.org/wp-content/uploads/ACCF-RoboVoting-Report_11_8_FINAL.pdf accessed 14 June 2019 (reporting that many asset managers vote consistently with ISS recommendations 99 per cent or even 100 per cent of the time). See also Palmiter (n. 180) 1438–9.

[226] See nn. 104–5.

[227] Companies (Model Articles) Regulations 2008, sch. 3, arts. 28–33.

[228] Department for Business, Energy and Industrial Strategy, Press Release: Regulations temporarily suspended to fast-track supplies of PPE to NHS staff and protect companies hit by COVID-19 (28 March 2020, updated 14 May 2020) www.gov.uk/government/news/regulations-temporarily-suspended-to-fast-track-supplies-of-ppe-to-nhs-staff-and-protect-companies-hit-by-covid-19 accessed 19 June 2020. See also Jim Pickard and Tabby Kinder, 'Insolvency Bill Introduced to Help Covid-Hit Business' *Financial Times* (London, 21 May 2020) 3.

[229] Companies Act 2006, s. 336(1).

[230] Department for Business, Energy and Industrial Strategy, *Press Release* (n. 228).

pandemic. The guidance was prepared in cooperation with four Magic Circle law firms and supported both by regulators and the trade bodies of company secretaries and general counsel, large investment managers, and quoted companies.[231] The guidance suggested that companies hold closed-door meetings and ensure quorum requirements by asking two director and/or employee shareholders to attend the meeting.[232] Shareholders, meanwhile, were encouraged to vote by proxy.[233]

In line with the ICSA guidance, most FTSE 100 companies that announced their meetings in April 2020 opted to hold the meetings behind closed doors with a minimum of participants.[234] A major concern for investors is that such meetings do not afford shareholders an opportunity to question directors and receive answers. Several companies, including HSBC PLC, allowed shareholders to submit written questions in advance of the meeting, which the company would answer 'where appropriate' by publishing responses on the company's website, and others held hybrid meetings allowing shareholders to join the meeting and post questions online.[235] In both situations, however, companies can avoid extensive shareholder scrutiny and questioning by setting maximum word count (character) limits on the length of questions or carefully selecting questions to be put to directors and managers. Many shareholders clearly do not consider remote shareholder meetings to be an effective alternative to physical meetings, as evidenced by the significant portion of votes cast against a management proposal at Standard Life Aberdeen PLC to allow the company to convene exclusively online shareholder meetings after the pandemic.[236]

The temporary nature of government-sponsored solutions and investor concerns about virtual annual meetings suggest that the in-person meeting norm is likely to return once life gets back to normal. Nevertheless, the COVID-19 crisis has prompted reflection on the role of annual shareholder meetings and the organization of those meetings in UK companies generally. Against the backdrop of falling attendance numbers, many critics of the current format consider virtual meetings to be the way forward. Such meetings allow organizational costs to be cut and the pre-screening of shareholder questions to remove those that are irrelevant.[237] For many shareholders and shareholder advocacy groups, however, in-person meetings in which shareholders can freely ask questions are an essential feature of shareholder democracy and management accountability.[238] Yet, there are questions about the effectiveness of the existing model in this camp too, especially about its efficacy as a forum for shareholder, and perhaps other stakeholder, voices.[239] The pandemic may accelerate the reform of shareholder meetings, but there is clearly a need for the careful design of minimum standards for online or hybrid meetings

231 The Chartered Governance Institute, *News Releases: Updated Guidance About AGMs and the Impact of Covid-19 Issued* (27 March 2020) www.icsa.org.uk/about-us/press-office/news-releases/updated-guidance-about-agms-and-the-impact-of-covid-19-issued accessed 19 June 2020.

232 The Chartered Governance Institute, 'AGMs and Impact of Covid-19: Supplement, Guidance Note' (March 2020) guidance 2 and 4 www.icsa.org.uk/assets/files/pdfs/guidance/agms-and-impact-of-covid-19-supplement-web.pdf accessed 19 June 2020.

233 Ibid., guidance 2.

234 Attracta Mooney, 'Investors Step Up Calls for "Virtual" Annual Meetings' *Financial Times* (London, 21 April 2020) 10.

235 Ibid.

236 Chris Flood, 'Standard Life Aberdeen Hit by Virtual AGM Backlash' *Financial Times* (London, 18 May 2020) 3.

237 Chris Flood and Attracta Mooney, 'Coronavirus Casts Doubt on Shape of Future AGMs' *Financial Times* (London, 15 June 2020) 6–7.

238 Ibid., 6.

239 Ibid.

to avoid situations in which a shift between meeting formats might limit opportunities for shareholder engagement.

COVID-19 disruptions have also affected shareholder engagement and activism. A number of activists suspended their campaigns to allow corporate managers to focus on urgent needs caused by the crisis. For example, Sherborne Investors, an activist hedge fund and the largest shareholder in Barclays PLC, with a 5.8 per cent stake, suspended its campaign to remove the bank's CEO in April 2020 with reference to the complexity of the management situation during the pandemic.[240] Several large institutional investors also admitted that their customary engagement efforts might deepen company problems by distracting corporate managers.[241] Engagement on many important topics risked being pushed to the sidelines, but anecdotal evidence suggests that institutional investors have not abandoned engagement entirely and will continue to press companies hard on matters high on their engagement agendas, such as executive pay, social issues and climate change.[242]

20.5 CONCLUDING REMARKS

Shareholder engagement and participation in corporate governance have been key corporate governance topics in the UK since the late 2000s. In an effort to improve corporate governance, the government has empowered shareholders through, for example, say-on-pay votes, and supported the promulgation of best practices of shareholder stewardship. In parallel, a small number of large fund groups has become an increasingly influential force by controlling a significant share of publicly traded companies. Their dominance has further increased the importance of shareholder engagement and put large institutional investors in the spotlight of media coverage and debates in regulatory and academic circles.

The growing shareholdings of large institutional investors have strengthened their influence over corporate boards, but they face a dilemma in using that influence. On the one hand, exercising voting rights actively risks inducing accusations of harming competition. That a single investor can be amongst the top shareholders in every listed company in a given sector leads to reasonable grounds for potential anti-competitive concerns. On the other hand, the passive exercise of voting rights raises legitimate concerns about large institutional investors being asleep at the wheel while businesses struggle with managerial misbehaviour, excessive risk-taking and a poor environmental and social record. These concerns are particularly strong for passively managed and exchange traded funds that track an index and have weak incentives to analyze every company individually.

The engagement practices of large institutional investors in the UK ease concerns about the anti-competitive effect of voting by investors with common ownership in many publicly traded companies. It is true that large institutional investors have intensified their use of voting rights by challenging management more often and have become less reliant on the recommendations of proxy advisory firms. Yet, their engagement efforts often concentrate on limited types of proposals, particularly proposals dealing with management compensation. Moreover, the primary targets of engagement are the promotion of best practice standards of corporate governance across portfolio companies and encouraging action to deal with global challenges.

240 Stephen Morris, 'Activist Suspends Drive to Oust Barclays Chief' *Financial Times* (London, 17 April 2020) 12.

241 Attracta Mooney, 'AGM Season Upended by Coronavirus Outbreak' *Financial Times* (London, 30 March 2020) 6, 7.

242 Attracta Mooney, 'Coronavirus Pandemic Forces Social Issues Up the Agenda' *Financial Times* (London, 4 May 2020) 6–7; Attracta Mooney, 'Shareholder Climate Rebellions Surge Despite Covid-19 Pandemic' *Financial Times* (London, 1 June 2020) 1, 2.

Accordingly, there are clear limits to the engagement efforts of large institutional investors. The narrow scope of strengthened engagement and concentration on proposals that can be easily shared amongst many companies is a natural response to the limited engagement resources available to large fund groups with diversified portfolios, which vote at hundreds, if not thousands, of shareholder meetings across borders every year. However, it leaves aside the business and operational monitoring of companies. Regulators need to recognize this limitation and remain realistic by not imposing impractical engagement expectations on large institutional investors.

PART IV

Comparative Perspectives

21

Shareholder Engagement and Corporate Voting in a Comparative Perspective

Anne Lafarre

21.1 INTRODUCTION

We have seen a presentation of shareholder voting and engagement rights and practices in a broad variety of jurisdictions in the previous chapters. In this context, based on the previous chapters and information collected from the authors, the present chapter summarizes and puts together the main findings from these jurisdiction analyses to describe the different legal means available for shareholders to engage with their companies by participating in the general meetings of shareholders. The chapter starts with a description of the ownership structures and corporate governance models across the different jurisdictions, and afterwards discusses the procedural and material shareholder voting and engagement tools.

21.2 OWNERSHIP STRUCTURES AND CORPORATE GOVERNANCE MODELS

Ownership patterns can vary greatly in different parts of the world. For instance, previous studies have shown that shareholdings in continental Europe and in Asia are more concentrated than in the Anglo-Saxon jurisdictions.[1] Also the types of shareholders are different: whereas in many jurisdictions institutional investors nowadays own a large part of the shares, government and family control seems still to be particularly present in civil law jurisdictions.[2] To put the findings in this Handbook in perspective, the ownership structures in the different jurisdictions were analyzed using 2019 data from Refinitiv Eikon and Factset. Table 21.1 below provides recent statistics on ownership patterns in the different jurisdictions. This table shows, in addition to the 50 per cent absolute control threshold, also the 30 per cent and 20 per cent control thresholds. We use this 20 per cent control threshold as it is commonly used in the Law and Finance literature.[3] The 30 per cent control threshold is the lowest full control threshold for the mandatory bid rule applying to member states of the European Union.[4]

Table 21.1 shows that the USA, Japan, UK and Canada are the jurisdictions with the highest dispersion in ownership structures. In contrast, Indonesia, Hong Kong, China and India are part

[1] Rafael La Porta, Florencio Lopez-De-Silanes and Andrei Shleifer, 'Corporate Ownership Around the World' (1999) 54 Journal of Finance 471.

[2] G. Aminadav and E. Papaioannou, 'Corporate Control Around the World' (2020) 75 Journal of Finance 1191; OECD, 'Owners of the Worlds Listed Companies' 2019, www.oecd.org/corporate/Owners-of-the-Worlds-Listed-Companies.htm accessed 15 July 2020.

[3] Including La Porta, Lopez-De-Silanes and Shleifer (n. 1).

[4] Article 5 of the Takeover Directive, Directive 2004/25/EC. Note that of the jurisdictions in this Handbook, France, Germany, Italy, the Netherlands and the UK use this threshold. See for more information Christophe Clerc and others, 'A Legal and Economic Assessment of European Takeover Regulation' (2012) CEPS 57 et seq. www.ceps.eu/ceps-publications/legal-and-economic-assessment-european-takeover-regulation/ accessed 15 July 2020.

TABLE 21.1 *Ownership concentration*

Jurisdiction	Total # Companies	c1 (%)	c2 (%)	c3 (%)	c4 (%)	c5 (%)	Free float (%)	# Top owner 50%	# Top owner 30%	# Top owner 20%
US	479	11.4	18.6	24.0	28.3	31.5	96.2	2 (0.4%)	10 (2.1%)	23 (4.8%)
Japan	225	11.8	17.4	21.5	24.9	27.2	86.6	7 (3.1%)	20 (8.9%)	28 (12.4%)
UK	85	12.0	17.5	21.7	25.1	27.7	90.9	5 (5.9%)	5 (5.9%)	11 (12.9%)
Canada	58	12.7	17.7	21.2	24.1	26.0	92.1	4 (6.9%)	6 (10.3%)	6 (10.3%)
Germany	29	14.1	18.0	20.9	23.2	25.0	85.5	1 (3.4%)	5 (17.2%)	8 (27.6%)
Australia	181	14.6	20.9	25.2	28.3	30.4	84.8	6 (3.3%)	20 (11.0%)	33 (18.2%)
Netherlands	20	16.0	20.9	23.8	26.1	28.1	82.6	3 (15.0%)	4 (20.0%)	4 (20.0%)
France	38	16.9	22.9	26.0	28.0	29.2	77.1	2 (5.3%)	7 (18.4%)	12 (31.6%)
Taiwan	94	17.5	24.7	29.3	32.3	34.4	68.4	3 (3.2%)	14 (14.9%)	27 (28.7%)
Denmark	20	20.6	25.8	29.2	31.6	33.3	79.5	3 (15.0%)	4 (20.0%)	7 (35.0%)
Average	-	**25.8**	**32.0**	**35.5**	**38.0**	**39.7**	**71.8**			
Italy	30	27.3	33.6	36.8	39.2	40.7	64.8	4 (13.3%)	11 (36.7%)	20 (66.7%)
South Korea	100	32.1	42.7	48.1	50.9	52.4	59.7	14 (14.0%)	47 (47.0%)	78 (78.0%)
Singapore	24	33.3	37.3	39.6	41.4	42.3	83.3	6 (25.0%)	11 (45.8%)	19 (79.2%)
Greece	22	36.1	46.2	49.6	51.4	52.6	58.0	6 (27.3%)	14 (63.6%)	19 (86.4%)
Norway	20	36.6	44.3	47.5	49.6	50.8	65.3	6 (30.0%)	11 (55.0%)	15 (75.0%)
India	50	38.3	46.2	50.2	52.8	54.4	52.9	39 (34.0%)	43 (54.0%)	43 (78.0%)
China	308	38.4	45.6	49.1	51.2	52.4	45.7	99 (32.1%)	187 (60.7%)	230 (74.7%)
Hong Kong	17	42.1	46.1	47.6	48.7	49.4	54.9	7 (41.2%)	11 (64.7%)	13 (76.5%)
Indonesia	45	57.6	61.8	63.7	65.2	66.3	35.8	39 (86.7%)	43 (95.6%)	43 (95.6%)

Note to Table 21.1. The table represents the ownership data from Refinitiv Eikon and FactSet for 2019 for the premium listed companies in the different jurisdictions. The following indices are used: ASX200 (Australia), TSX60 (Canada), CSI300 (China), Athex20 (Greece), HSI (Hong Kong), Nifty50 (India), LQ45 (Indonesia), Nikkei225 (Japan), STI (Singapore), KOSPI (largest 100 companies, South Korea), FTSE TWSE (Taiwan), FTSE100 (UK), S&P500 (US), DAX30 (Germany), CAC40 (France), AEX25 (the Netherlands), OMXC20 (Denmark), MIB30 (Italy), OBX (Norway). Only companies incorporated in a particular jurisdiction and doing most of their business there were taken into account. The Table represents the concentration ratios in % of the largest owner (c1), the two largest owners (c2), the three largest owners (c3), the four largest owners (c4), the five largest owners (c5) and the percentage of shares in free float in %. The table also reports the number (and %) of companies that has a (direct) top owner that owns more than 50, 30 and 20% of the share capital. For the sample average reported in the table, one average datapoint per jurisdiction is used.

of the jurisdictions with the highest ownership concentration. Yet, one should note that these numbers are not showing the complete picture: for instance, various authors described family control in Japanese firms using a relatively low ownership stake.[5] Table 21.2 below provides some additional insights on the type of largest shareholder present in the various jurisdictions.

Although one should note that also Table 21.2 is not able to provide the full picture as controlling minority structures like pyramid structures and dual-share classes and other types of control,[6] could not be fully identified in the financial datasets used, Table 21.2 shows some interesting differences between the jurisdictions. For instance, in China, the government is the largest owner in almost half of the listed companies in our sample: the same holds for Hong Kong

5 For instance, see Morten Bennedsen, Vikas Mehrotra, Jungwook Shim and Yupana Wiwattanakantang, 'Who is the Boss? Family Control without Ownership in Publicy-traded Japanese Firms', DBJ Discussion Paper Series no. 1903 (2019). These authors provide three case studies of Japanese companies, including Casio, Toyota Motor and Suzuki Motor, showing that family members hold top positions in these companies without significant ownership stakes.

6 For instance, Bennedsen, Mehrotra, Shim and Wiwattanakantang (n. 5).

TABLE 21.2 *Shareholder type of largest shareholder present*

Jurisdiction	Total # companies	# Fund	# Company	# Government	# Family/ Private	# Other
Australia	181	124 (68.5%)	22 (12.2%)	4 (2.2%)	30 (16.6%)	1 (0.6%)
Canada	58	50 (86.2%)	5 (8.6%)	1 (1.7%)	2 (3.4%)	0 (0%)
China	308	17 (5.5%)	52 (16.9%)	152 (49.4%)	87 (28.2%)	0 (0%)
Denmark	20	4 (20%)	3 (15%)	1 (5%)	5 (25%)	7 (35%)
France	38	12 (31.6%)	9 (23.7%)	8 (21.1%)	8 (21.1%)	1 (2.6%)
Germany	29	9 (31.0%)	7 (24.1%)	8 (27.6%)	4 (13.8%)	1 (3.4%)
Greece	22	1 (4.5%)	9 (40.9%)	6 (27.3%)	6 (27.3%)	0 (0%)
Hong Kong	17	2 (11.8%)	5 (29.4%)	4 (23.5%)	6 (35.3%)	0 (0%)
India	50	0 (0%)	30 (60%)	14 (28%)	6 (12%)	0 (0%)
Indonesia	45	0 (0%)	27 (60%)	12 (26.7%)	5 (11.1%)	1 (2.2%)
Italy	30	3 (10%)	11 (36.7%)	7 (23.3%)	7 (23.3%)	2 (6.7%)
Japan	225	160 (71.1%)	51 (22.7%)	6 (2.7%)	6 (2.7%)	2 (0.9%)
Norway	20	2 (10%)	3 (15%)	9 (45%)	4 (20%)	2 (10%)
Singapore	24	2 (8.3%)	7 (29.2%)	11 (45.8%)	4 (16.7%)	0 (0%)
South Korea	100	1 (1%)	58 (58%)	17 (17%)	23 (23%)	1 (1%)
Taiwan	94	13 (13.8%)	45 (47.9%)	4 (4.3%)	31 (33.0%)	0 (0%)
The Netherlands	20	10 (50%)	3 (15%)	1 (5%)	5 (25%)	1 (5%)
United Kingdom	85	66 (77.6%)	7 (8.2%)	7 (8.2%)	4 (4.7%)	1 (1.2%)
United States	479	448 (93.5%)	8 (1.7%)	1 (0.2%)	16 (3.3%)	6 (1.3%)

Note to Table 21.2. The table shows the number of companies with the largest shareholder of a particular type. The table represents the ownership data from Refinitiv Eikon and FactSet for 2019 the premium listed companies in the different jurisdictions. The following indices are used: ASX200 (Australia), TSX60 (Canada), CSI300 (China), Athex20 (Greece), HSI (Hong Kong), Nifty50 (India), LQ45 (Indonesia), Nikkei225 (Japan), STI (Singapore), KOSPI (largest 100 companies, South Korea), FTSE TWSE (Taiwan), FTSE100 (UK), S&P500 (US), DAX30 (Germany), CAC40 (France), AEX25 (the Netherlands), OMXC20 (Denmark), MIB30 (Italy), OBX (Norway). Only the companies incorporated in a particular jurisdiction and doing most of their business there were taken into account. The Table represents the frequency of the largest owner types (c1 in Table 21.1) per jurisdiction. The category 'Fund' contains all institutional investors and funds except for sovereign wealth funds (which are contained in the category 'Government'). The category 'Private/Family' represents all individual and family shareholders. The category 'Company' represents all shareholdings by companies (not being a family or individual owner). The category 'Other' contains all shareholders not included in any of the other categories.

and Norway. The data in the table also show that in some jurisdictions institutional investors as parts of the shareholder type category 'funds' are the largest shareholders present in the premium listed companies. Canada, the USA, the UK, Japan and the Netherlands are among these jurisdictions. The author of Chapter 6 already noted this substantial shift in ownership in Japanese companies, from 'stable shareholder' ownership that tend to support the incumbent management to more critical foreign institutional investors.[7] The author of Chapter 20 noted institutional ownership of 73.33 per cent of the shares of all listed UK companies in 2018.[8] Table 21.1 shows that ownership is generally more dispersed in these jurisdictions with more institutional ownership, however, it is also more systemic, usually covering a wide range of portfolio firms. Large institutional investors may use their ownership portfolio to decide on market wide corporate governance standards such as environmental, social and governance (ESG) standards and pay matters.[9] Given this large (potential) influence, in several jurisdictions, (soft) regulatory initiatives are used to encourage institutional investors to exercise their control rights and to disclose their engagement policies. For instance, the 2017 Revised European Shareholder Rights Directive (SRD II)[10] requires institutional investors and asset managers to disclose their engagement policies and explain how they are implemented on a comply-or-explain basis, including how they have voted their shares. In the USA, the Employee Retirement Income Security Act (1974) already required private pension fund to exercise proxy votes as part of their fiduciary duties.[11] In addition, we can find a broad variety of stewardship codes in the different jurisdictions. In Australia,[12] China,[13] Denmark,[14] Hong Kong,[15] India,[16] Italy,[17] Japan,[18] Taiwan,[19] the Netherlands,[20] the UK[21] and the USA,[22] a stewardship code is in place to steer institutional investor engagement. These codes are either based on a comply-or-explain principle laid down in a regulatory instrument, or are voluntary.[23] In the jurisdictions with large

7 See Chapter 6.

8 See Chapter 20.

9 See E. B. Rock and M. Kahan, 'Index Funds and Corporate Governance: Let Shareholders be Shareholders' (4 April 2019) NYU Law and Economics Research Paper No. 18–39.

10 Directive (EU) 2017/828 of the European Parliament and of the Council of 17 May 2017 amending Directive 2007/36/EC as regards the encouragement of long-term shareholder engagement [2017] OJ L132/60.

11 See www.sec.gov/comments/4–725/4725–4650533-176476.pdf accessed 15 March 2021. Note that also mutual funds are required to disclose their proxy voting policies in the USA. See SEC, Proxy Voting by Investment Advisers, Release No IA-2106, 68 FR 6585 (7 February 2003).

12 Available at https://acsi.org.au/wp-content/uploads/2020/01/AAOSC_-The_Code.pdf accessed 22 March 2021.

13 Available at www.csrc.gov.cn/pub/csrc_en/laws/rfdm/DepartmentRules/201804/P020180427400732459560.pdf accessed 22 March 2021.

14 Available at https://corporategovernance.dk/sites/default/files/180116_stewardship_code.pdf accessed 22 March 2021.

15 Available at www.sfc.hk/-/media/EN/files/ER/PDF/Principles-of-Responsible-Ownership_Eng.pdf accessed 22 March 2021.

16 Available at www.sebi.gov.in/legal/circulars/dec-2019/stewardship-code-for-all-mutual-funds-and-all-categories-of-aifs-in-relation-to-their-investment-in-listed-equities_45451.html accessed 22 March 2021.

17 Available at www.assogestioni.it/sites/default/files/docs/principi_ita_stewardship072019.pdf accessed 22 March 2021.

18 Available at www.fsa.go.jp/en/refer/councils/stewardship/20200324/01.pdf accessed 22 March 2021.

19 Available at https://cgc.twse.com.tw/static/stewardship_en.pdf accessed 22 March 2021.

20 Available at https://en.eumedion.nl/clientdata/217/media/clientimages/2018-07-dutch-stewardship-code-final-version.pdf?v=191126132016 accessed 22 March 2021.

21 Available at www.frc.org.uk/getattachment/5aae591d-d9d3-4cf4-814a-d14e156a1d87/Stewardship-Code_Final2.pdf accessed 22 March 2021.

22 Available at https://isgframework.org/wp-content/uploads/2020/07/ISG_Stewardship_Principles.pdf accessed 22 March 2021.

23 For instance, in the UK, the Stewardship Code has a mandatory element that is governed by the FRC, whereas in the Netherlands, Singapore, South Korea, the USA, Hong Kong and Japan, the code is voluntary, sometimes using a voluntary comply or explain-principle. Also see D. Katelouzou and K. Sergakis, 'Shareholder Stewardship Enforcement' (30 March 2020), Table 2. An edited version of this paper will be published as a chapter in

institutional ownership, including the UK, the USA and Canada, attention has been paid to proxy advisory firms, who supply their clients with information on voting at a large scale, thus offering this information at a relatively low cost. The authors of these jurisdictions pointed out the (potentially) large influence of these private parties on voting outcomes and the regulatory discourse in the three jurisdictions,[24] including the Canadian NP 25–201 initiative.[25]

Assisted by such stewardship codes and other regulatory initiatives, institutional investors can use their 'voice tools' to influence the way companies are managed and to reshape corporate policies. These voice tools do not only contain the formal shareholder rights related to general meetings, but also private engagements behind the scenes.[26] Changing the status quo in companies through voice, without a change in control, used to be termed 'shareholder activism',[27] although nowadays the actions of institutional investors are usually called 'engagement', which has a friendlier, more collaborative connotation and often a focus on ESG.[28] The Climate Action 100+ initiative, launched in December 2017 at the One Planet Summit in France, provides a good example of institutional investor engagement and coordination related to ESG: Climate Action 100+ engages with the largest listed energy companies around the world to reduce greenhouse gas emissions and has over 500 signatories, including some of the world's largest asset managers and asset owners.[29]

In the next sections of this chapter, we outline the different formal voice instruments shareholders have related to general meetings in the different jurisdictions, including the procedures for these meetings. This chapter provides a comparative perspective, highlighting the differences and similarities between various jurisdictions. Where possible, these differences are discussed in the light of the ownership structures, shareholder types and market developments.

21.3 PROCEDURES FOR GENERAL MEETINGS

General meetings provide an opportunity for shareholders to collectively discuss the affairs of the company and to exercise their (ultimate) control rights. For active minority shareholders, general meetings present the engagement occasion where they can, at the very least, communicate directly with the management and with fellow shareholders, and at best have their voice heard and concerns addressed. For institutional investors and large shareholders that have other informal engagement tools, general meetings are key too, for instance as an escalation strategy if friendly informal engagement is not leading to the desired result. In other words, general meetings are not always *just pro forma* occasions; they can be a primary avenue for shareholder engagement for many shareholders – and certainly shareholder voting. In recognition of this,

Dionysia Katelouzou and Dan W. Puchniak (eds.), *Global Shareholder Stewardship: Complexities, Challenges and Possibilities* (Cambridge University Press forthcoming).

24 See Chapters 11–12, 20.

25 See Chapter 11.

26 See for instance Joseph A. McCahery, Zacharias Sautner and Laura T. Starks, 'Behind the Scenes: The Corporate Governance Preferences of Institutional Investors' (2016) 71 The Journal of Finance 2905.

27 Stuart Gillan and Laura T. Starks, 'A Survey of Shareholder Activism: Motivation and Empirical Evidence' (1998) 2 Contemporary Finance Digest 10.

28 Research suggests that institutional investors have a larger focus on sustainability matters. For instance, see Oliver Hart and Luigi Zingales, 'Companies Should Maximize Shareholder Welfare Not Market Value' (2017) 2 Journal of Law, Finance, and Accounting 247; Patrick Bolton et al., 'Investor Ideology' (2020) 137 Journal of Financial Economics 320.

29 See for more information www.climateaction100.org/ accessed 22 March 2021.

most modern company laws, and all jurisdictions in this Handbook, require regular general meetings to be held for formal shareholder decision-making.

As we have seen in the various jurisdiction reports, all jurisdictions require companies to organize Annual General Meetings (AGMs). AGMs need to be held within a particular period after the closing of the financial year, for instance within six[30] or eight[31] months, whereas Extraordinary General Meetings (EGMs)[32] are usually convened in exceptional circumstances, for instance when the board needs shareholder approval for a particular important decision but cannot wait for this until the next AGM. Special rules have been adopted in response to the impact of the Covid-19 pandemic for the organisation of general meetings. For instance, in Germany the Covid-19 Mitigation Act allows the management board, with the approval of the supervisory board, to convene the AGM after the normally required period of eight months, so long as it is held within the same financial year. In the Netherlands, the normal period of six months has been extended for four months under the Temporary Act Covid-19. Despite this pandemic, no jurisdictions seem to have cancelled the convening of AGMs altogether. In contrast, Covid-19 has broken new ground by popularizing recourse to virtual-only meetings and hybrid-meetings, which will be discussed in Section 21.3.2.

The various jurisdictions surveyed in this Handbook vary in respect of their specific (shareholder participation) requirements for general meetings, particularly those concerning notice periods and record dates. The aim of the notice period is to ensure that shareholders are informed well in advance that a general meeting is to be held, so that they can arrange to participate or appoint a proxy if they wish to. Notice periods ranging between fourteen to forty-two days before the AGM are found across the jurisdictions in our Handbook. The shortest notice periods for AGMs are found in Japan[33] and Norway[34] where only two weeks' notice in advance of the general meeting is required. However, in Norway the articles of association may prescribe a longer period, and special rules apply to *allmennaksjeselskap* (ASA, public companies), which must give twenty-one days' notice.[35] In India, meeting notice of not less than twenty-one days is required, but this can be shortened if 95 per cent of the shareholders who are entitled to vote at the AGM consent either in writing or electronically.[36] In Europe, article 5 of the Shareholder Rights Directive (SRD I)[37] requires Member States to ensure that notice of the holding of the general meeting is issued at least twenty-one days before the meeting. Member States may reduce this period to fourteen days in the case of a general meeting (which is not an AGM) if the company makes voting by electronic means accessible to all shareholders: this possibility has been implemented by the UK.[38] In the UK, the notice period for AGMs is

30 Six months is the required period in many jurisdictions, including for instance Indonesia, Norway and the Netherlands.

31 In Germany, the AGM must be convened within the first eight months of the financial year (section 120(3) *Aktiengesetz*, 'AktG').

32 In most jurisdictions, these meetings are identified as extraordinary meetings or special meetings. In some jurisdictions (like France), these meetings are combined meetings. Exceptionally meetings are organized for a subgroup of shareholders or a class of shareholders or for the minority shareholders only.

33 Article 299(1) and (4), Japanese Companies Act (JCA).

34 Section 5-10(2) Norwegian Public Limited Liability Companies Act, regulating *allmennaksjeselskap* (ASA). See Chapter 18.

35 Special provisions are stated in sections 5–11b ASA.

36 Section 101 Indian Companies Act 2013 (ICA).

37 Directive 2007/36/EC of the European Parliament and of the Council on the exercise of certain rights of shareholders in listed companies, 2007 OJ L 157/87.

38 Section 307A(1)(a) and 307A(2)-(4) UK Companies Act 2006 (UK CA).

twenty-one days, whereas in France the notice period for all GMs is thirty-five days, and in the Netherlands as much as forty-two days. In Germany, notice must be given at least thirty days before the meeting,[39] but this period can be shortened to fourteen days in the case of general meetings held in connection with takeover bids.[40]

Due to the Covid-19 pandemic, some of the required notice periods have been temporarily changed to provide companies with more flexibility. In Germany, for example, the Covid-19 Mitigation Act provides for a reduction of the notice period from thirty to twenty-one days.

In addition to the notice period, the record date is also an important consideration for the participation by shareholders in general meetings. A record date acts as a cut-off point, by requiring shareholders to register for the general meeting by a certain date. In Europe, share blocking (the obligation to deposit shares for a few days before the general meeting to be able to vote) was banned with the implementation of the SRD I. Article 7 SRD I holds that the record date needs to be maximum thirty days before the meeting. Like those for the minimum notice period, the record date requirements also vary considerably across jurisdictions. In the UK, the record date is forty-eight hours before the general meeting, in France it is three business days, in Denmark it is one week and in the Netherlands it is twenty-eight days. There is also large variation outside Europe. For instance, in Australia the record date is forty-eight hours at most before the general meeting,[41] whereas in the USA (Delaware), it can be any date between ten and sixty days before the general meeting.[42]

A different approach can be found in Japan, where the record date is typically preset to coincide with the closing date of the business year (for many Japanese listed companies, this is March 31). As an effect, Japanese general meetings tend to cluster around the end of June.[43]

21.3.1 *Quorum Requirements and Calling a Meeting*

In all jurisdictions, the board has the authority to call a general meeting, whether an AGM or EGM. Most jurisdictions do not give the board a monopoly over calling an EGM. Most importantly from the viewpoint of active minority shareholders are the legal rules that vest the power of calling EGMs in the hands of shareholders. For instance, in Europe, Article 6 of SRD I states that if a Member State only allows shareholders to put items on the agenda of an AGM (and not an EGM), shareholders have the right to call (or can require the company to call) an EGM with an agenda which includes all the items requested by those shareholders. Similar rules can be found in other jurisdictions. For instance, in Australia, an EGM can be called by the company's directors or by the shareholders themselves, if they hold at least 5 per cent of the votes.[44] Alternatively, the shareholders may require the company's directors to call an EGM if shareholders holding at least 5 per cent of the votes in the meeting make a written request to the board of directors.[45]

In most of our jurisdictions the threshold for calling a meeting is between 3–10 per cent of total shareholdings, though there are several exceptions. In South Korea, the threshold is lower, requiring only 1.5 per cent of the issued and outstanding shares that are held for at least six months. In Taiwan, 3 per cent of the shares held consecutively over one year are needed to call

39 Section 123 AktG.
40 Section 16(5) *Wertpapiererwerbs- und Übernahmegesetz* (WpÜG).
41 Regulation 7.11.37. of the Corporations Regulations 2001. See Chapter 10.
42 Section 213 Delaware General Corporation Law (DGCL).
43 See Chapter 6.
44 Section 249F Australian Corporations Act (ACA).
45 Section 249D ACA.

a meeting, if the competent authorities give permission, and *to hold one's own* EGM requires 50 per cent of the total number of outstanding shares, which must have been held for at least three months. In the latter case, the shareholders do not have to ask the board of directors to facilitate the convening process or do not have to receive approval from competent authorities beforehand.[46] Also in Australia, shareholders can arrange a general meeting themselves: if the corporate board does not call the general meeting within twenty-one days after a request of the shareholders, shareholders with more than 50 per cent of the votes can themselves call and arrange the meeting.[47] Finally, in Delaware, shareholders are not offered the right to call an EGM. Companies can, however, provide this shareholder right in their corporate charter.

Table 21.3 below illustrates the various differences regarding the right of shareholders to call an EGM in the jurisdictions in this Handbook.

If a meeting is called, another important often used requirement for formal shareholder decision-making is a *quorum* of shareholders ('members') present. The quorum requirement can

TABLE 21.3 *Calling an EGM*

Jurisdiction	Minimum threshold for shareholders to call EGM	How specified, additional rules?
Australia	5%	Voting rights
Canada	5%	Voting shares
China	10%	Share capital
Denmark	5%[48]	Share capital
France	5%	Share capital
Germany	5%	Share capital
Greece	5%	Paid up share capital
Hong Kong	5%	Voting rights
India	10%	Share capital with voting rights
Indonesia	10%	Share capital with voting rights
Italy	5%[49]	Share capital
Japan	3%	Voting rights, at least 6 months[50]
Norway	5%	Share capital
South Korea	3%, 1.5%[51]	Issued and outstanding share capital, at least 6 months for listed companies
Singapore	10%	Voting rights
Taiwan	3%, 50% (self-organizing meeting)	Share capital, at least one year and approval of authorities, and at least 3 months for self-organizing the meeting
The Netherlands	10%	Share capital
United Kingdom	5%	Voting rights
United States	n.a.	n.a.

46 Article 173(1) Taiwanese Companies Act (TCA).
47 Article 249E ACA.
48 This is the case for a public limited company. In a private limited company, any shareholder may request the general meeting to be called regardless of the size of her stake.
49 Threshold at listed companies (a 10 per cent threshold is required for non-listed companies).
50 This only applies to 'public companies' in Japan.
51 The 1.5 per cent threshold applies to listed companies.

be a powerful engagement tool for minority shareholders, as evidenced by the experience of South Korea. The Korean quorum requirement is one-fourth of the shares for the appointment of directors, and one-third for extraordinary resolutions such as fundamental changes in corporate affairs. For decades, Korean companies were able to count on shares registered with the Korea Securities Depository to meet the quorum thresholds, but the 2017 reform banned this traditional practice. As a consequence, many Korean companies needed to reach out to minority shareholders to convince them to join the general meetings, fearing that without them they might not achieve the quorum necessary to take important corporate decisions.[52]

Quorum requirements are common but vary widely. Some jurisdictions require only two shareholders to be present to constitute a quorum (including Australia,[53] Hong Kong,[54] Singapore[55] and the UK[56]). Many other jurisdictions, however, use more extensive rules. In India, the quorum for general meetings is five shareholders who need to be *personally*[57] present for public companies which do not have more than 1,000 shareholders.[58] Furthermore, the mere presence of a quorum at the beginning of the general meeting is not sufficient in some jurisdictions: in India, general meetings must meet the quorum requirements throughout the decision-making process.[59]

In France, the commercial code requires a quorum of 25 per cent of the shares with voting rights on the first call of the EGM, and decisions require a two-thirds majority of the participating votes.[60] At a second meeting, at least 20 per cent of the shares with voting rights is required. Decisions in the ordinary meeting (AGM) require the presence of at least 20 per cent of the shares with voting rights at the first meeting the proposal is put to a vote. Note that in France, the EGM is used for special voting items, including any amendment to the articles of association:[61] these voting items thus follow the quorum requirements of an EGM. In Greece, the quorum for an AGM is 20 per cent of the paid-up share capital.[62] The second call does not require a quorum.[63] In contrast, general meetings with special resolutions, including the dissolution of the company or amending the company's objects, require a quorum of 50 per cent of the paid-up capital at first call and a 20 per cent quorum at the second call for listed companies.[64]

The 50 per cent quorum can also be found in Italy, South Korea[65] and Taiwan. In Italy, 50 per cent of the social capital excluding the shares without voting rights should be present at all general meetings for the first call. For the second call, Italian law differentiates between AGMs and EGMs. In the case of an AGM there is no quorum for the second call, whereas for the EGM there must be a quorum of 20 per cent for all later calls. In Taiwan, the Companies Act only allows resolutions to be adopted by shareholders representing more than half of the total number

52 See Song Jung-a, 'South Korean Groups Forced to Seek out Votes of Small Investors' *Financial Times* (21 March 2018).
53 Section 135 ACA.
54 Section 585, Hong Kong Companies Ordinance (HKCO).
55 Section 179 Singapore Companies Act (SCA).
56 At least two shareholders need to attend the meeting, unless otherwise defined by the company's articles of association, the meeting has a quorum, following section 318(2) UK CA.
57 This requires the physical presence of either the shareholder or the proxy holder.
58 In addition, if the number of shareholders is between 1,000 and 5,000, the quorum will be 15 shareholders personally present. If the number of shareholders is more than 5000, then 30 shareholders need to be personally present. See Chapter 4.
59 Secretarial Standards on General Meetings- SS-2 revised standards applicable from 1 October 2017. See Chapter 4.
60 Article L.225-96 of the French Commercial Code (FCC).
61 Article L.225-96 FCC.
62 The ordinary quorum ex article 130 Greece Companies Act (GCA).
63 Article 130(2) GCA.
64 Article 130(3)–(4) GCA. See Chapter 16 for further specifics.
65 Article 574 Korean Commercial Code (KCC).

of voting shares.[66] However, when the shareholder attendance is lower than 50 per cent of the voting shares, but the shareholders present represent at least one-third of the total number of issued shares, a tentative resolution may be passed by a majority of these shareholders.[67] Shareholders receive notice of such a tentative resolution, and another general meeting must be held within one month. If this resolution is again adopted by a majority of the shareholders representing at least one-third of the issued shares, the resolution is formally adopted.[68] Under US (Delaware) law, the default rule is that a quorum consists of a majority of the shares entitled to vote, present in person or represented by proxy; this threshold may be altered, albeit not lower than one-third of the shares entitled to vote at the meeting.[69]

Indonesia seems to have the most extensive quorum provisions.[70] Depending on the meeting's agenda, there are different quorum rules for the first, second and third call. In the first and second calls, different predefined quorums apply for different voting items. For the third call, however, the company must make a request to the Indonesia Financial Service Authority or *Otoritas Jasa Keuangan* (OJK): the OJK then determines the quorum that applies. These quorums range from 50 per cent for general agenda items to three-fourths of the shares for particular agenda items, for example those that change the corporate structure extensively (including a merger or a transfer of assets including more than 50 per cent of company's net worth). The second call quorum requirements range from one-third to two-thirds of the shares.

Finally, some jurisdictions seem to have no (mandatory) quorum rules at all in the statutory laws. These jurisdictions include China, Denmark, Germany, Japan and Norway. And in Canada, quorum requirements are addressed in the corporation's by-laws and the statutory law only provides for the default rule.[71] In the Netherlands, a quorum is required only for particular resolutions such as the waiver of pre-emption rights in a capital issuance: if the quorum of 50 per cent is not met, then the decision of the general meeting for a particular resolution can still be valid if a qualified majority threshold is met (which is two-thirds of the votes).[72]

21.3.2 *Electronic Means and Virtual Meetings*

The format in which general meetings are conducted, whether physically, electronically or in some combination of these modes, may have significant implications for shareholder voting and engagement. Advocates of fully electronic meetings (also called 'virtual-only meetings') argue that they can help to increase shareholder participation and cut costs for both companies and shareholders. Their opponents hold that the accountability of the corporate board can be diminished because of higher discretionary powers for board members, for instance to avoid

66 Article 174 Taiwanese Companies Act (TCA).

67 Article 175 TCA.

68 Article 175 TCA.

69 Section 216 DGCL.

70 See Chapter 4.

71 Section 139(1) of the Canadian Business Corporation Act (CBCA) requires 50 per cent of the shares entitled to vote at the opening of the meeting if the bylaws do not provide otherwise. Practice shows that companies generally opt for different quorums, and may require the attendance of some shareholders in person. For instance, Canadian Apartment Properties has set a quorum as 'at least two (2) individuals present online at the Meeting, each of whom is a holder of Trust Units or a proxyholder representing a holder of Trust Units, and who hold or represent by proxy not less than twenty-five percent (25%) of the total number of outstanding Trust Units' (Canadian Apartment Properties, *Notice of Annual and Special Meeting of Unitholders to be held June 1, 2020 and Management Information Circular*, 6), while in the bylaws of Enbridge it is stated 'at least three persons holding, or representing by proxy, at least 25% of the total number of issued and outstanding Enbridge shares' (Enbridge, *Notice of the 2020 Annual Meeting of Shareholders and Management Information Memorandum*, 4).

72 Article 2:96a(7) of the Dutch Civil Code (DCC).

uncomfortable questions from shareholders. These meetings may also limit the interaction with the management and increase information asymmetry.[73] In the past, particularly institutional investors, including the Council of Institutional Investors (CII) have been openly skeptical about these virtual-only meetings. Despite these possible drawbacks, already before the Covid-19 pandemic, the use of virtual-only meetings using the Broadridge virtual general meeting platform was steadily increasing in the USA, with 212 meetings in 2017 and 300 in 2019.[74]

Despite the technical possibilities to organize general meetings online, many jurisdictions still require some sort of physical format making virtual-only meetings unlawful, including for instance China,[75] Japan[76] and the Netherlands.[77] For instance, Chinese company law allows only for physical general meetings and virtual-only meetings are not permitted.[78] However, shareholder participation by internet or other electronic means has been strongly encouraged since 2004, and became mandatory in 2014.[79] Many other jurisdictions have allowed for the introduction of some electronic components during such a physical general meeting ('hybrid meetings') as well.[80] For instance, in the Netherlands, electronic participation and voting is allowed via the articles of associations.[81] This also holds for some Asian jurisdictions with a stronger focus on casting votes electronically.[82]

Jurisdictions where companies may organize 'virtual-only' meetings include Canada, Denmark, Norway, the UK and several states in the USA, including Delaware[83]. In the US state of Delaware, virtual-only meetings are more commonly used than in the other jurisdictions covered in this Handbook. The DGCL provides the board of directors with the discretionary power to hold virtual-only meetings and hybrid meetings, unless limited by the corporate charter or the bylaws.[84] In many other jurisdictions, provision for a virtual-only AGM must be specifically included in the articles of association. In Canada, although the Canadian Business Corporations Act recognizes the possibility of virtual-only meetings, they rarely occur in practice.[85] Like Delaware, Denmark also was an early adopter of the virtual-only meeting.[86]

There has been some discussion on whether the UK Companies Act and the articles of association (can) allow for virtual-only meetings in the UK, yet in practice it seems to be allowed: the UK company Jimmy Choo held its first virtual-only general meeting in 2016. Although Australia is not included in our list of jurisdictions that we consider to allow for a virtual-only general meeting, the pros and cons of virtual-only meetings have been vigorously debated in this

73 Elizabeth Boros, 'Corporate Governance in Cyberspace: Who Stands to Gain What from the Virtual Meeting?' (2003) 3 The Journal of Corporate Law Studies 149; Lisa A. Fonetenot, 'Public Company Virtual-Only Annual Meetings' (Winter 2017–18) 73 The Business Lawyer 35;

74 'Virtual shareholder meetings, 2019 facts and figures', Broadridge Financial Solutions, Inc. (2020).

75 Chapter 2.

76 See the references in Chapter 6.

77 Article 2:116 DCC.

78 Articles 20(1) and (2) of the Chinese GM Rules. See Chapter 2 for the origin of these GM Rules.

79 Article 20(2) of the Chinese GM Rules.

80 For instance, in Europe, Article 8 SRD I stipulates that Member States shall permit companies to use any or all of the following electronic forms of participation: (a) real-time transmission of the general meeting; (b) real-time two-way communication enabling shareholders to address the general meeting from a remote location; (c) a mechanism for casting votes, whether before or during the general meeting, without the need to appoint a proxy holder who is physically present at the meeting.

81 Articles 2:117a DCC and 2:117b DCC.

82 Note that, in addition, the SRD I also focuses on real-time transmission and real-time two-way communication (n.80).

83 Herrick k. Lidstone, 'Corporate Annual Meetings of Shareholders in the COVID-19 World' (2020) https://ssrn.com/abstract=3570989 accessed 15 July 2020

84 Section 211 of the DGCL.

85 See Chapter 11.

86 See Chapter 13.

jurisdiction.[87] In any case, Australian law covers hybrid meetings, allowing shareholders to choose between attending the meeting in person at a physical venue or attending the meeting online.[88]

Although in many jurisdictions some form of a hybrid meeting was already allowed, the remote 2020 AGM season during the Covid-19 pandemic required *ad hoc* measures on the part of many regulators. Most jurisdictions adopted these changes as a temporary measure.[89] In some jurisdictions, these measures allowed companies to organize (some sort of) hybrid general meeting, even if their articles of association did not allow for this: hence, discretionary powers were provided to the corporate board. For instance, in Germany, the temporary measures allowed the management board, with the approval of the supervisory board, to permit the transmission of the full AGM and electronic voting, irrespective of the provisions in the articles of association. Virtual-only meetings where shareholders had no choice but to participate by electronic means were allowed as well in Germany, so that remote attendance counted as participation in the meeting.[90] Similarly, in France, the corporate board was also empowered to organize an online meeting, regardless of the provisions in the articles of association.[91] Several jurisdictions also established (further) mandatory requirements for these online meetings. For instance, in Indonesia, the KSEI system was considered mandatory for these meetings,[92] and in the Netherlands, the shareholder question right became a mandatory condition for organizing an online meeting.[93] Many financial regulators issued guidelines for the online organization of general meetings in addition to the temporary legislative measures. In the USA additional guidelines were issued at the federal level.[94]

Some jurisdictions also addressed the AGM timing requirements, overriding the rules on the timing of the AGM contained in the articles of association. More specifically, as highlighted in the beginning of section 21.3, many jurisdictions allowed an extension to the period within which an AGM should be held. For instance, in Denmark[95] and Indonesia, there was an extension of two months, and in Italy and Singapore, the extension was sixty days. In contrast, in India, there was no formal extension, but companies were allowed to hold their AGM within nine months of the end of the financial year on 31 December 2019 in practice.[96]

87 See Chapter 10.

88 Section 249 S ACA. See Chapter 10.

89 Also see OECD, National Corporate Governance Related Initiatives During The Covid-19 Crisis (28 May 2020) www.oecd.org/corporate/National-corporate-governance-relatedinitiatives-during-the-covid-19-crisis.pdf accessed 15 July 2020.

90 See Chapter 15.

91 See Chapter 14.

92 OJK Letter Number S-92/D.04/2020 of 2020 on the Relaxation of Obligations for Submission of Reports and Implementation of General Meetings of Shareholders. See Chapter 5 also for more information about the KSEI system.

93 See Chapter 19.

94 SEC, 'Staff Guidance for Conducting Annual Meetings in the Light of COVID-19 Concerns' www.sec.gov/ocr/staff-guidance-conducting-annual-meetings-light-covid-19-concerns?auHash=zrsDVFen7QmUL6Xou7EIHYov4Y6IfrRTjW3KPSVukQs accessed 15 July 2020. This document notes that a corporation's ability to conduct a 'virtual' meeting is governed by the state law, where permitted, and the issuer's governing documents like the corporate charter.

95 This is the timing of submitting the annual accounts, which also allows for an extended period to hold the AGM. See Chapter 13.

96 See www.mca.gov.in/Ministry/pdf/Circular18_21042020.pdf accessed 15 July 2020.

21.4 RESOLUTIONS

As also described by the fifth fundamental characteristic of corporations in *The Anatomy of Corporate Law*, in virtually all jurisdictions, shareholders can vote on important matters in (annual) general meetings. As we have already observed, the jurisdictions covered in this Handbook are no exception to this rule. However, they differ greatly in their approach to stipulating which fundamental decisions require shareholder approval or advice and which do not.

The appropriate demarcation of powers between shareholders and the board has long been debated by policy makers, academics and other stakeholders, and this line varies considerably between jurisdictions. In nearly all jurisdictions, shareholders have appointment rights in one way or the other, and can vote on 'fundamental decisions', including end-game decisions like a merger, or when directors have conflicted interests.[97] In the next section, we further discuss how the appointments rights are shaped in the different jurisdictions and which fundamental decisions require shareholder approval. Particularly, we outline shareholder appointment rights (including the dismissal of directors) and shareholder decision-making rights including for instance amendments to the corporate charter, say-on-pay rights and major transactions.

21.4.1 *Appointment and Removal of Directors*

In all the jurisdictions covered in this Handbook, shareholders can appoint or remove the (supervisory) directors. Shareholder election of directors can be considered a fundamental shareholder right and a critical tool for ensuring greater director accountability and responsiveness to shareholders. When discussing appointment and removal rights, several factors need to be taken into account. First of all, there are different board structures, including the one-tier board structure, the two-tier board structure and some hybrid forms.[98] In the one-tier board, generally, all directors (executive and non-executive) are elected by the general meeting. The classical one-tier board structure can be found in Anglo-Saxon jurisdictions like the USA and the UK. In other jurisdictions workers are also represented on the one-tier board (for instance, France and Norway in larger companies). Under the classic two-tier board model, the supervisory board generally elects the management board members. This model can be found in Germany. Other jurisdictions vary this model or offer additional board structure options. For instance, Japanese law seems to provide three different options to listed companies for their board structure, including a board of statutory auditors which can be considered a horizontal two-tier board, a board with three committees that is comparable to the US-style one-tier board structure, and a board with an 'audit-plus committee', which can be seen as a one-tier board with lesser requirements.[99] In Italy, different one- and two-tier board structures are allowed, including a two-tier board model similar to the German type. In the Italian one-tier board, an oversight committee is appointed within the shareholder-elected board of directors, whose members must be non-executive and independent.[100] Hybrid board structures seem to occur in China, Taiwan and Norway. In Norway, for example, it seems that the general meeting elects the 'corporate assembly', which in turn elects the corporate board. However, many companies seem to deviate from this structure

97 Reinier H. Kraakman et al., *The Anatomy of Corporate Law* (Oxford University Press 2017) 57.

98 While the separation between the one-tier and two-tier board seems clear enough on paper, in practice, there is large functional convergence between the two board structures. See Paul L. Davies and Klaus J. Hopt, 'Corporate Boards in Europe – Accountability and Convergence' (2013) 61 The American Journal of Comparative Law 301.

99 See Chapter 6.

100 See Chapter 17.

in their articles of association and only have a corporate board.[101] Some jurisdictions allow companies to select their board structure: in France, for example, the default rule is the one-tier board and companies are allowed to deviate in their articles of association; while in the Netherlands, companies can choose between a one-tier and a two-tier board structure since 2013.

In Germany and some other jurisdictions that employ the two-tier board, there is labour representation, limiting shareholder appointment and removal rights. Yet, labour representation can also be found in one-tier board jurisdictions, as in France. Finally, some jurisdictions require qualified majorities for removing board members, as in Germany (shareholder representatives), Taiwan and South Korea. The different board structures and the appointment rights of shareholders are outlined in Table 21.4 below.

TABLE 21.4 *Shareholder appointment rights*

Country	Board structure?	Who appoints the management board or (executive) directors?	Stakeholder representation in statutory law?
Australia	One-tier	Shareholders	No
Canada	One-tier	Shareholders	No
China	Two-tier	Shareholders	Employee representation mandatory at the supervisory board; employee representation at the board of directors mandatory for the limited liability company set up by two or more state-owned entities
Denmark	Two-tier[102]	Shareholders	In companies with at least 35 employees, employees can elect at least two directors.[103] The AoA can allow for a number of members (less than the majority) to be appointed directly, by a shareholder or others.[104]
France	Optional[105]	Shareholders	Employee representation in larger companies[106]
Germany	Two-tier	Supervisory board	Employee representation up to half of the board members.
Greece	One-tier	Shareholders	Employee representation only in specific state-owned or controlled companies.
Hong Kong	One-tier	Shareholders	No
Indonesia	Two-tier	Shareholders	No

101 Two-thirds of the corporate assembly are elected by the general meeting, whereas one-third is elected by and amongst the employees. See Chapter 18.

102 Note that in Denmark, the board seems to have management duties as well, which deviates from the classical German two-tier board model.

103 Under Chapter 8 of the Danish Companies Act (DCA).

104 Section 120 Danish Companies Act. Note that, in a private limited liability company the entire board of directors can be appointed. In that case it has to be specified in the articles of association who has the right to appoint the board members. See Chapter 13.

105 Article L. 225 57 FCC. See Chapter 14.

106 Companies with 5,000 employees in France or 10,000 employees worldwide need to have one employee representative at the board level if there are up to eight board members, and two when there are more than eight board members. See Chapter 14.

TABLE 21.4 *(continued)*

Country	Board structure?	Who appoints the management board or (executive) directors?	Stakeholder representation in statutory law?
India	One-tier	Shareholders	No
Italy	Optional[107]	Shareholders or supervisory board[108]	No
Japan	Optional	Shareholders or Board of Directors[109]	No
Norway	Hybrid	Shareholders, with some exceptions[110]	Employee representation in companies with at least 30 employees.
South Korea	One-tier	Shareholders	No
Singapore	One-tier	Shareholders	No
Taiwan	Hybrid[111]	Shareholders	No
The Netherlands	Optional	Shareholders or supervisory board [112]	In companies that have work councils, work councils can nominate one-third of the board members.[113]
United Kingdom	One-tier	Shareholders[114]	No
United States	One-tier	Shareholders	No

The dismissal of board members is an important shareholder right as well. In most of the jurisdictions covered in this Handbook, shareholders can remove directors with a simple majority resolution, without cause and at any time. In Germany, South Korea, Taiwan and the USA, however, there are additional requirements for the removal of directors. For instance, in Germany, shareholders are only allowed to remove shareholder representatives in the supervisory board, and they need a 75 per cent majority.[115] In addition, also in South Korea

107 Article 2380 Italian Civil Code (ICC). See Chapter 17.

108 Shareholders appoint the board members in the traditional two-board structure (the Board of Directors and the Board of statutory auditors) and in the one-tier board structure. However, for the two-tier board structure that is similar to the German two-tier board model, the Board of Directors is elected by the supervisory board. See Chapter 17.

109 In case of companies with three committees (US-style one-tier board), the board of directors appoints executive directors.

110 Generally, it seems that shareholders appoint the board members. However, in companies that have a corporate assembly, this corporate assembly elects the board members. Note that two-thirds of the members of the corporate assembly are elected by the shareholders. See Chapter 18.

111 Taiwanese companies can be considered to have a 'Japanese style' hybrid two-tier board structure. See Chapter 9.

112 Under the Dutch *structuurregime*, the supervisory board has the authority to (re-)elect and dismiss members of the management board ex article 2:162 DCC. See Chapter 19.

113 Unless the supervisory board objects to the recommendation. This is called the *versterkt aanbevelingsrecht* of the works council. Following article 2:158(6) DCC.

114 Note that formally, UK law does not require that directors need to be appointed by shareholders. Shareholders have a right to remove directors (following section 168 UK CA), but the statute is silent on appointment rights. This means that it is possible for the board itself to appoint directors (if the board receives this power under the company's articles of association). According to the Model Articles, the right to appoint directors is given to shareholders. It is widespread practice that listed companies follow this rule in the Model Articles by giving shareholders a power to appoint directors in their articles of association. See Chapter 20.

115 See Chapter 15.

and Taiwan, we can find stricter voting rules for this shareholder right.[116] In Delaware, removal without cause can be restricted if a staggered board is in place.[117]

Whereas in the majority of the jurisdictions directors are elected by simple majority voting, there are important deviations. These include plurality voting in Delaware and Canada, cumulative voting in China and Taiwan, the Majority of Minority (MoM) Listing Rule for independent directors in the UK, and *Voto di Lista* in Italy. These special voting rules are discussed in Section 21.5 of this chapter. And, as the next chapter illustrates, both in Greece and Indonesia, shareholders (usually) elect all their board members in only one voting round (see Chapter 22).

In addition to the appointment of (supervisory) board members, in some jurisdictions, shareholders may also appoint the external auditor. For European Member States, this right can be traced back to the European level in the Audit Directive.[118] However, Member States may also allow for other 'systems or modalities for the appointment of the statutory auditor or audit firm'.[119] In the UK, shareholders also have the right to fix the remuneration of the auditors.[120] In other jurisdictions shareholders usually do not vote on auditor remuneration separately, but the vote to set the compensation of the auditor can be combined with the appointment of the external auditor, as in Singapore.[121]

21.4.2 *Changes in the Corporate Charter*

In all the jurisdictions covered in this Handbook, shareholders need to ratify amendments to the corporate charter (i.e. the articles of association or articles of incorporation). Amending the corporate charter is considered to be one of the most fundamental corporate decisions,[122] and therefore in many jurisdictions a qualified majority is required for such decisions. Particularly, charter amendment is an important way for minority shareholders to engage in the company with a view to blocking or removing governance arrangements that are perceived to harm shareholder welfare (such as a staggered board), or adopt governance initiatives enhancing shareholder value like proxy access. Charter amendments require a simple majority in only a few jurisdictions. In the Netherlands, a *statutenwijziging* requires a simple majority vote, but the articles of association may require a higher majority.[123] Also in Delaware, a simple majority vote is required (majority of the outstanding stock), and only the board can propose a charter amendment.[124]

116 In both jurisdictions, the removal of directors is a special resolution. As a result, in South Korea there is a qualified majority of two-thirds representing at least one third of the shares issued with voting rights and in Taiwan a quorum of half of the issued shares is required.

117 Section 141(k) DGCL.

118 Article 37(1) of the Audit Directive (2014/56/EU, which amended 2006/43/EC) states that '[a]ny contractual clause restricting the choice by the general meeting of shareholders or members of the audited entity pursuant to paragraph 1 to certain categories or lists of statutory auditors or audit firms as regards the appointment of a particular statutory auditor or audit firm to carry out the statutory audit of that entity shall be prohibited. Any such existing clauses shall be null and void'.

119 Article 37(2) Audit Directive.

120 Section 492 UK CA 2006.

121 Section 205 SCA.

122 Kraakman et al. (n. 97) 37 calls charter amendments amongst the 'most fundamental corporate decisions'.

123 Article 2:121 DCC. Article 2:120 DCC states that all resolutions for which no greater majority is required either by the law or by the articles of association must be passed by absolute majority (i.e., simple majority) of the votes cast.

124 Section 242 DGCL.

21.4.3 *Say-on-Pay*

Executive remuneration is a topic of corporate law that has been extensively debated. To strengthen executive compensation as a corporate governance mechanism and address excessive pay practices and agency problems resulting from these pay practices,[125] several jurisdictions have introduced regulatory reforms, including a shareholders' say-on-pay.[126] The first jurisdiction to introduce a non-binding shareholder vote on the remuneration report was the UK, in 2002.[127] Afterwards, the Netherlands introduced a binding shareholder vote on remuneration policy in 2004.[128] Like many other jurisdictions, the USA followed in 2010, providing shareholders with a non-binding or advisory say-on-pay vote.[129] With the adoption of the SRD II, and implementation of these provisions in the national laws of the EU's member states, shareholders in Europe also have both an ex ante say on the remuneration policy and ex post say on the remuneration report.[130]

Jurisdictions can generally be divided into two groups: one group which has at least some form of say-on-pay, and another group that generally has no say-on-pay in their (hard) legislative requirements. The latter group is substantially smaller. An overview of the findings is provided in Table 21.5 below. We first discuss the jurisdictions with (hardly any) (statutory) say-on-pay provisions. In Hong Kong, there is no statutory requirement for the directors' remuneration to be approved by the shareholders, however, the Hong Kong (HKEX) Listing Rules provide some form of say-on-pay: the Listing Rules require shareholder approval for certain types of directors' service contracts.[131] In Singapore, shareholder approval is only needed for directors' fees. Otherwise, executive pay is not subject to shareholder vote nor is its disclosure mandatory. In India, executive pay is generally not subject to a shareholder vote, with some exceptions. Specifically, executive pay cannot exceed 11 per cent of the net profits of the company in a financial year, otherwise shareholder approval is needed.[132] Also, with shareholder approval by a special resolution, the company can pay more than 5 per cent of the net profits to any one managing director or whole-time director or the manager.[133] At the moment of writing this chapter, Canada does not at present have a say-on-pay rule, but the Canadian legislature made amendments to the Canada Business Corporations Act (CBCA), providing inter alia for an annual say-on-pay for 'prescribed corporations'.[134]

We now consider jurisdictions that have some form of statutory say-on-pay rights. To structure this discussion, we divide the say-on-pay rules into different categories. First, we distinguish

[125] Lucian A. Bebchuk and Jesse M. Fried, *Pay Without Performance: The Unfulfilled Promise of Executive Compensation* (Harvard University Press 2004).

[126] Randall S. Thomas and Christoph Van der Elst, 'Say on Pay Around the World' (2015) 92 Washington University Law Review 653.

[127] For listed companies, section 439 UK CA.

[128] Article 2:135 DCC.

[129] Section 951 of the Dodd–Frank Act, Pub. L. No. 111-203, 124 Stat. 1899 (2010).

[130] Article 9a and 9b SRD II. For an analysis of the European say-on-pay rules in this Directive see C. Van der Elst and A. Lafarre, 'Article 9A and 9B: Say on Pay', in H. Birkmose and K Sergakis (eds.), *SRDII: A Commentary* (Edward Elgar 2021), 250–84; T. Dijkhuizen, 'Report from Europe: The Proposal for a Directive Amending the Shareholders Rights Directive' (2016) 12 *ECL* 45–50 and C. Van der Elst, 'Shareholders Holding the Reins on Remuneration: The European Say on Pay' (2017) 14 *European Company Law* 114–20.

[131] In addition, it seems that the Model Articles contain a provision stating that the remuneration of the directors needs to be determined by the general meeting, and some companies may thus provide a shareholders' vote to authorize the corporate board to set the compensation of the directors. See Chapter 3.

[132] The manner of calculation of net profits is provided by section 198 ICA.

[133] If there is more than one such person, total remuneration may be more than 10 per cent of the net profits for all concerned, subject to the cap of 11 per cent.

[134] See Chapter 11.

resolutions concerning the remuneration report (an ex post say-on-pay right). Other resolutions may include the approval of changes to the remuneration policy (an ex ante say-on-pay right), and approval of incentive schemes, share (option) grants and pay packages (usually ex ante rights).[135] Also, and this was already apparent in the examples at the beginning of this section, some forms of say-on-pay are *binding* and thus have legal consequences, whereas others are *non-binding* or *advisory*.

Since the implementation of the SRD II in the national laws of the member states of the European Union, all its jurisdictions have a shareholder say both on the remuneration report and on the remuneration policy. A vote on the renumeration policy can be binding or advisory, and must be conducted after every 'material change' and at least every four years.

Shareholders have a yearly advisory vote on the remuneration report. Some member states have adopted a *binding vote* on the remuneration policy. In the Netherlands, the Dutch legislature has confirmed that, with the implementation of the SRD II, the Netherlands would continue to have a binding vote for the remuneration policy under Dutch law.[136] Also in Italy,[137] France,[138] Denmark,[139] Greece,[140] Norway[141] and the UK,[142] it seems that a binding vote on the remuneration policy can be found. In Germany,[143] however, the say-on-pay vote related to the 'remuneration system' is not binding and therefore, the shareholder decision ultimately has no legal effect. Before the implementation of the SRD II in Germany, the non-binding approval of the remuneration system by the general meeting was optional.

Some European jurisdictions already included say-on-pay shareholder decision-making rights in their national laws before the implementation of the SRD II. We have already mentioned the Netherlands and the UK, but France also already facilitated a shareholder say-on-pay under the Sapin Law II. In 2016, this law introduced a French binding say-on-pay vote for the shareholders,[144] after generous remuneration packages at Renault. Sapin Law II holds that shareholders, at least every year, have to approve the remuneration policy that contains the principles and criteria for the determination, the distribution and allocation of fixed, variable and exceptional pay for the chairman of the (supervisory) board, the CEO and the deputy CEOs.[145] If the general meeting does not approve this policy, the former policy must be used. In addition, for these officers variable or exceptional compensation can only be paid after approval by the general meeting.[146]

In the USA, as we have seen before, shareholders have an *advisory vote* on executive compensation. Say-on-pay in the USA grew out of precatory shareholder-sponsored Rule 14a-8 resolutions that were uniformly opposed by management but received significant shareholder support.[147] In the wake of the financial crisis, say-on-pay was adopted at the federal level by the

135 We do not consider the fees for (non-)executive directors and supervisory board remuneration.

136 Kamerstukken II (2018-2019), 35058 nr.3.

137 Article 123-ter (3-bis) Consolidated Law on Finance (*Testo unico della finanza*, CLF). See Chapter 17.

138 Article L. 225-37-2 FCC.

139 Following section 139 DCA.

140 Article 110(2) GCA.

141 Section 6-16a ASA.

142 Section 439A(1) UK CA.

143 Pursuant to s. 120a (1) 1 AktG.

144 See Chapter 14.

145 Former article L. 225-37-2 FCC.

146 Former article L. 225-100 FCC. Since SRD II: By the Ordonnance n° 2019-1234 of 27 November 2019 related to the remuneration of the corporate officers of listed companies. See Chapter 14.

147 Thomas and Van der Elst (n. 126) 659.

Dodd-Frank Act.[148] With the introduction of this provision in the USA, say-on-pay votes are required for public companies with a 75 million USD or more public equity float. Only the pay packages of a company's executive officers named in the company's proxy compensation table are subjected to such an advisory shareholders' vote.[149] The say-on-pay vote needs to take place at least every three years, but shareholders also have a so-called advisory say-on-pay frequency vote, so that they can indicate how often they would like to have a say on these pay packages: every year, every second year or every third year.[150] The corporate board decides, based on this shareholder vote, how often shareholders can vote on these remuneration packages for a period of six year.

As in the USA and in many other jurisdictions, the Australian Two-Strikes rule was introduced to restrain executive compensation.[151] Before its introduction in 2011, shareholders already had an advisory say-on-pay as regards the remuneration report.[152] The Two-Strikes rule holds that when for two years in a row the remuneration report receives at least a 25 per cent dissent rate, shareholders vote during the later meeting in a spill resolution whether all directors would stand-up for re-election at a next meeting, which is called the spill meeting.[153] In the second AGM's meeting notice, the company must already include the potential for a spill resolution. If the spill resolution is approved (with a simple majority requirement of 50 per cent), an EGM needs to be held within ninety days to re-elect the board members (except for the managing director).[154]

China's Corporate Governance Code, which is commonly followed by Chinese listed companies, requires a shareholder approval right on executive pay packages in a binding vote.[155] This is also the case in Taiwan, as the remuneration of board members is determined ex ante by the general meeting, unless otherwise provided for by the articles of association.[156] In theory, the Taiwan say-on-pay is mandatory and the say-on-pay vote is binding, but in practice, it seems that this right is usually delegated to the board of directors. In Japan, all compensation paid to directors must be approved either in the articles of incorporation or by a resolution of the general meeting.[157] However, case law has limited the scope of this Japanese say-on-pay, such that these resolutions create only a ceiling on the maximum aggregate fixed compensation for the company's directors. The board may then divide this maximum aggregate compensation at its discretion. Since the articles of incorporation need to be approved by the shareholders, the

148 Section 951 of the Dodd–Frank Act, Pub L. No. 111-203, 124 Stat 1899 (2010).

149 SEC Final Rule, 17 C.F.R. section 240.14a-21(a). Thomas and Van der Elst (n. 126) 660.

150 Section 951 Dodd-Frank Act.

151 Executive Remuneration in Australia, IV. http://webarchive.nla.gov.au/gov/20091112003920/http://www.pc.gov.au/projects/inquiry/executive-remuneration/draft accessed 15 May 2019; R. Monem and C. Ng, 'Australia's "Two-Strikes" Rule and the Pay-Performance Link: Are Shareholders Judicious?' (2013) 9 *Journal of Contemporary Accounting & Economics* 237.

152 Corporate Law Economic Reform (Audit Reform & Corporate Disclosure) Act 2004 (CLERP 9), which became effective on 1 July 2004.

153 The Australian Two-Strikes Rule is contained in articles 250U–250Y ACA. The resolution to decide on the spill meeting is called the 'spill resolution' ex article 250V(1) ACA.

154 The EGM is called the 'spill meeting' in 250V(1)(a) ACA. Article 250V(1)(b) ACA requires that all directors must stand for re-election who: '(i) were directors of the company when the resolution to make the directors' report considered at the later AGM was passed; and (ii) are not a managing director of the company who may, in accordance with the listing rules for a prescribed financial market in whose official list the company is included, continue to hold office indefinitely without being re-elected to the office'. Note that article 250X ACA ensures that at least three directors remain after the spill meeting (including the managing director and the two board members that received the highest portion of the votes in favour).

155 In addition, article 38(2) PRC Company Law provides shareholders the right to approve the general remuneration. See Chapter 2 for more information about the Code of Corporate Governance of 2018.

156 Article 196 TCA.

157 Section 361 JCA.

effect of this rule is that the *aggregate director compensation* is subject to shareholder approval.[158] Similarly, in South Korea, the shareholders usually approve the maximum amount of compensation that can be granted to the directors..[159] In Indonesia, the remuneration of the members of the Board of Directors is determined by the AGM, but this can also be delegated to the Board of Commissioners.[160] In practice, the aggregate executive pay is usually determined by the AGM, and the individual pay is determined by the Board of Commissioners. It is also a common practice that the pay of the Board of Commissioners is determined by the AGM.[161]

Finally, most say-on-pay votes require simple majorities, with some exceptions. We have already considered the Australian Two-Strikes-Rule, which imposes some consequences when the remuneration report obtains a 25 per cent dissent rate for two years in a row. In addition, in the Netherlands, the approval of the remuneration policy now requires a 75 per cent majority vote: the Dutch implementation of the SRD II provides for a qualified majority requirement of 75 per cent for remuneration policy resolutions.[162]

These findings are summarized in Table 21.5 below.

TABLE 21.5 *Shareholder say-on-pay rights*

Jurisdiction	Is there a Say on Pay?	Vote on remuneration report?	Vote on remuneration policy?[163]	Vote on Remuneration (package)?	*Special remarks?
Australia	Yes	Yes, advisory*	No	Part of remuneration report	*Two-Strikes Rule
Canada	No*	No	No	No, frequently put to vote voluntarily	*But expected to be implemented
China	Yes*	No	No	Yes,* binding	* Following corporate governance code
Denmark	Yes	Yes, advisory	Yes, at least every 4 years, binding	Part of remuneration report	
France	Yes	Yes, binding	Yes, at least every year, binding	Yes, mandatory	
Germany	Yes	Yes, advisory	Yes, at least every 4 years, advisory*	Advisory as part of remuneration report	*Called 'remuneration system'
Greece	Yes	Yes, advisory	Yes, at least every 4 years, binding	previously yes, now part of remuneration report	
Hong Kong	No*	No	No	No	*But Listing Rules
India	Yes*	No	No	Yes, capped at 11% of net profits	*But under limited circumstances

158 See Chapter 6.

159 Article 388, KCC.

160 Section 96 Indonesian Company Law (ICL). In Indonesia, there are special rules for state-owned companies (SOEs) as Chapter 5 outlines.

161 Section 113 ICL. See Chapter 5.

162 In the new article 2:135a(2) DCC. See Chapter 19.

163 In many jurisdictions which have a shareholder vote on the remuneration policy, shareholder approval is also required when there is a material change to the remuneration policy.

TABLE 21.5 *(continued)*

Jurisdiction	Is there a Say on Pay?	Vote on remuneration report?	Vote on remuneration policy?	Vote on Remuneration (package)?	*Special remarks?
Indonesia	Yes	No	No	Yes, but usually aggregate*	*SOEs have different rules.
Italy	Yes	Yes, advisory	Yes, at least every 3 years, binding	Part of remuneration report	
Japan	Yes	No	No	Yes, aggregate, binding[164]	
Norway	Yes	Yes, advisory[165]	Yes, at least every 4 years, binding	No	
South Korea	Yes	No	No	Yes	
Singapore	No*	No	No	No	*Director fees only
Taiwan	Yes	No	No	Yes, aggregate, binding, but can be delegated.[166]	
The Netherlands	Yes	Yes, advisory	Yes, at least every 4 years, binding*	Yes, but can be delegated. Share (options) binding	*Qualified majority of 75%
United Kingdom	Yes	Yes, advisory	Yes, at least every 3 years, binding	Part of the remuneration report	
United States	Yes	No	No	Yes,* advisory	*Each 1–3 years

21.4.4 *Capital Resolutions*

In some jurisdictions, the corporate board needs to obtain shareholder approval for decisions related to share capital, including the issuance of new shares, or the cancellation of pre-emptive rights. This often has to do with the diluting effects of share issuances on shareholder ownership and changes in control after these transactions. Although this analysis is by no means complete, we generally find in the different jurisdictions that shareholder approval is necessary when a capital decision (e.g. the reduction of the share capital) either (1) requires an amendment to the articles of association, or (2) stems from an explicit shareholder right provided for in the law of a particular jurisdictions or in the articles of association. For instance, in Delaware, the authorized stock can only be increased through an amendment to the corporate charter.[167] A share issuance within the limits of the authorized stock, however, is generally part of the board's discretionary powers. The same rule is used in Japan: a shareholder vote is required only when the authorized capital needs to be changed so that shares can be issued. However, Japanese law requires shareholder approval when after the share issuance there is a large owner holding

[164] With a shareholders' vote or in the articles of association the maximum amount of aggregate remuneration is approved.

[165] Section 6-16b jo 5-6 ASA.

[166] In practice, shareholder approval pursuant to article 196 TCA is usually delegated to the board of directors.

[167] Sections 102(a) jo 242 DGCL.

the majority of the shares and at least 10 per cent of the incumbent shareholders oppose the issuance of shares.[168]

In Europe, by contrast, shareholders have several ratification rights as regards share capital. Article 68(1) and (2) of Directive 2017/1132 (which contains the rules of the Second Company Law Directive) state that:

> any increase in capital must be decided upon by the general meeting. ... Nevertheless, the statutes or instrument of incorporation or the general meeting, . . ., may authorise an increase in the subscribed capital up to a maximum. . . . The power of such body in this respect shall be for a maximum period of five years and may be renewed one or more times by the general meeting, each time for a period not exceeding five years.[169]

Hence, shareholders need to provide approval for a share issuance in Europe. However, they may also delegate this decision to the corporate board for a maximum period of five years. In practice, this delegation is not often provided for five years, as there is commonly a yearly shareholder vote on share issuances in European jurisdictions. In Germany, three types of share issuances are codified in its corporate law: there can be an increase in capital, a conditional capital increase that may be used only for the three purposes listed in section 192 AktG,[170] and a capital increase against contributions in cash or in-kind.[171]

Outside Europe, many jurisdictions provide shareholders with approval rights as regards share issuances, including Hong Kong and Singapore.[172] The same holds for China, where any change in share capital (both increase and reduction) requires shareholder approval.[173] In Indonesia, it seems that the corporate board needs shareholder approval for share issuances, and, if the ownership changes in such a way that a shareholder would own more than 5 per cent of the issued shares, the company also needs to submit a report to OKJ.[174] In Australia, the Listing Rules require shareholder approval when, in any twelve month-period, the company proposes to issue new capital amounting to more than 15 per cent of existing capital.[175]

In many jurisdictions shareholders also receive pre-emption or pre-emptive rights, which allow incumbent shareholders to purchase new shares pro rata before these shares are sold to new shareholders. Pre-emptive rights can be considered a minority shareholder protection mechanism: particularly, these rights prevent the invitation of new shareholders at a discount in the company at expense of the incumbent shareholders. Moreover, large shareholders cannot enhance their control cheaply if these rights are installed. In Europe, following the adoption of the Second Company Law Directive, all companies need to obtain shareholder approval to waive pre-emption rights (hence, an opt-out with a qualified majority shareholder vote, which is differently arranged in the various Member States). In the USA, Canada and Japan, shareholders of public companies only have pre-emption rights if these are included in a corporate charter. In

168 Section 206(2) JCA.

169 Directive (EU) 2017/1132 of the European Parliament and of the Council of 14 June 2017 relating to certain aspects of company law, OJ L 169, 30.6.2017.

170 Paragraph 192(2) AktG lists the following purposes: (1) to grant conversion rights or stock warrants to holders of convertible bonds or warrant bonds, (2) to prepare a merger of enterprises, iii) to grant rights to employees of the company to subscribe to new shares against the contribution of amounts due to such employees under a profit-sharing plan established by the company.

171 All these resolutions require a qualified majority, and since the authorized capital is stated in the corporate charter (the *Satzung*), these resolutions usually also require an amendment to the articles of association.

172 Rule 806 SGX listing rules. See Chapter 7.

173 Article 37(7) PRC Company Law. See Chapter 2.

174 See Chapter 5.

175 See further, ASX Listing Rules 7.1, 10.2, 11.1 and 11.2. Also see Chapter 10.

other jurisdictions too, including China, pre-emption rights are not provided to shareholders of public companies. In Delaware, the pre-emption right is only provided to a shareholder if such a right is expressly granted in the corporate charter.[176] In Hong Kong, it is clear that share issuances without pre-emption rights are allowed, but they also generate high shareholder dissent rates.[177] In India, by contrast, shareholders' pre-emption rights seem to be provided and protected.[178]

Repurchases of shares (or share buy-backs) are usually restricted by legal rules that safeguard the capital to protect creditors. Yet, in some jurisdictions, shareholder approval is also required for these transactions to restrict opportunistic behaviour of corporate insiders. Shareholder approval may also be needed for the cancellation of shares, although in some jurisdictions the board is empowered to cancel shares without further reference.[179] For instance, in Germany, the authority to cancel treasury shares is included in the authorisation to buy back own shares.[180] In India, a special resolution must be passed authorising the buy-back[181] and the sums involved should be less than 25 per cent of the aggregate of paid up and free reserves of the company.[182]

21.4.5 *Major Transactions and M&A*

In all the jurisdictions discussed in this Handbook, shareholders have some important control rights as regards fundamental changes that tend to reallocate control in the company. Because of their nature, these corporate decisions usually entail a high probability of opportunistic behavior by corporate insiders (managers, but also large shareholders) at the expense of (minority) shareholders. Fundamental changes include, for instance, amendments to the corporate charter or articles of association (see Section 21.4.2 of this chapter), and the various ways to transfer corporate assets to new control including the sale of all ('or substantially all') assets to another party and statutory mergers. In a sale of assets, the acquirer can buy specific assets and cherry-pick the most valuable ones. It is therefore necessary to determine when a purchase of assets is sufficiently substantial to constitute a fundamental change for which shareholder approval is needed. This allows for variations between jurisdictions, as in some jurisdictions the term 'major transaction' is addressed as a matter of law or jurisprudence, including for instance the well-known '*Holzmüller*' case in Germany.

Which major transactions require shareholder approval in the different jurisdictions? We offer some examples of these shareholder rights in this section. For instance, section 271 DGCL reflects our discussion: a shareholder vote is required before a company may transfer 'all or substantially all' of its assets. The term 'substantially all' has been addressed in case law using both quantitative and qualitative measures,[183] but it seems that no clear-cut norm has yet emerged.[184] Following the CBCA in Canada, 'a sale, lease or exchange of all or substantially

176 Section 102(b(3) DGCL.

177 See Chapter 3. The same seems to hold for Indonesia. See Chapter 5. See for a further practical analysis the next chapter in this Handbook.

178 See Chapter 4.

179 For instance, for the UK, see article 726 *et seq.* UK CA.

180 Section 71(8) AktG

181 No such requirement applies where the buy-back is less than 10 per cent of aggregate of paid up and free reserves of the company and it is authorized by the board of the company.

182 Section 68(2) ICA.

183 See *Gimbel* v. *Signal Companies* 316 A.2d 599 (1974).

184 The qualitative assessment of the court in Katz v. Bregman qualifying the transaction in this case as a 'radical departure' of its nature of business is highly debated, and it is generally considered that this case 'represents the outside boundary of this term' instead of a norm. See Andreas Cahn and David C. Donald, *Comparative Company*

all the property of a corporation other than in the ordinary course of business of the corporation' requires shareholder approval in a special resolution (two-thirds of the votes).[185] As with the courts in Delaware, Canadian courts seem to use both quantitative (in both jurisdictions, we can find an indication of 75 per cent of the assets for a substantial transaction)[186] and qualitative analyses.

In the UK, the 25 per cent threshold forms part of the detailed rules as outlined by the FCA in its Listing Rules. These rules require shareholder approval for transactions accounting for 25 per cent or more of the company's assets, profits, gross capital or the value of the ordinary shares for premium listings.[187] Other jurisdictions have also attempted to define the meaning of a major transaction. For instance, the HK Listing Rules outline in a very detailed manner that (minority) shareholder approval is required for transactions including major transactions,[188] very substantial disposals[189] and very substantial acquisitions,[190] for which (as in the UK) the 25 per cent rule is generally used. For all transactions, shareholders are excluded from voting if they have a material interest in the transaction,[191] making it a MoM-rule. In Singapore, a shareholder vote is required for the disposal of substantially all assets,[192] and the Listing Rules of the SGX provide further rules for listed companies including a threshold of 20 per cent.[193] China sets a substantially higher bar for major transactions requiring shareholder approval, namely 50 per cent (of audited total assets). In contrast, like in Delaware, the Australian Listing Rules do not provide an explicit threshold, but shareholders have approval rights when there is a sale of the main undertaking of the company or when the company makes a significant change to the nature or scale of its activities.[194]

Also in Germany, there is no clear-cut codified threshold for major transactions; moreover, in German statutory law there is no explicit shareholder approval right for major transactions. However, the 1982 landmark *Holzmüller* case determined that shareholder approval is needed when there is a major transaction.[195] Particularly, briefly stated, the judgment in the Holzmüller case went beyond the division of powers between shareholders and the corporate board in the *Aktiengesetz* to restore unbalances. In summary, the *Bundesgerichtshof* ruled that the transfer of an important part of the company to a subsidiary required shareholder approval because it

Law: Text and Cases on the Laws Governing Corporations in Germany, the UK and the USA (Cambridge University Press 2018) 802.

185 Section 189(3) CBCA. Also see Chapter 11.

186 The US Model Act explicitly states that a transaction with a value below 25 per cent of the balance sheet does not generally require shareholder approval. See section 12.02(a) Model Act. However, this does not mean that transactions of more than 25 per cent of the balance sheet assets by market value are always subject to shareholder approval, as this Model Act provision only codifies a rule of thumb as the lower threshold.

187 UK LR 10.2.2 jo LR 10.5.1 jo LR 10 Annex 1. See LR 10 Annex 1 for the different percentage ratios.

188 Hong Kong LR 14.06(3). Defined as 'a transaction or a series of transactions (aggregated under rules 14.22 and 14.23) by a listed issuer where any percentage ratio is 5% or more, but less than 25%'. These percentage ratios are outlined in section 14.07 and summarized in section 14.08.

189 Hong Kong LR 14.06(4). Defined as 'a disposal or a series of disposals (aggregated under rules 14.22 and 14.23) of assets (including deemed disposals referred to in rule 14.29) by a listed issuer where any percentage ratio is 75% or more'. These percentage ratios are outlined in section 14.07 and summarized in section 14.08.

190 Hong Kong LR 14.06(5). Defined as 'an acquisition or a series of acquisitions (aggregated under rules 14.22 and 14.23) of assets by a listed issuer where any percentage ratio is 100% or more'.

191 Note 2 to Hong Kong LR 14.33.

192 Section 160 SCA. See Chapter 7.

193 SGX Practice Note 10.1 Shareholder Approval for Major Transactions and Rule 1006 jo 1014 provide that a transaction is classified as a major transaction that requires shareholder approval if the relative figures (like the net asset value or net profits) cross the 20 per cent threshold.

194 See further, ASX Listing Rules 11.1 and 11.2 www.asx.com.au/regulation/rules/asx-listing-rules.htm accessed 31 July 2020. See Chapter 10.

195 25 February 1982 decision II ZR 174/80 (Holzmüller).

concerned the most valuable branch of the company and fundamentally changed the corporate structure.[196] The Holzmüller doctrine is extensively discussed by German scholars and further addressed by the German court in the *Gelatine* judgments.[197]

In the Netherlands, major transactions are codified as '107a decisions' that involve a major change in the identity or character of the company or enterprise and require shareholder approval: (1) the transfer of the entire or substantially the entire enterprise (*'vrijwel de gehele onderneming'*) to a third party; (2) entering into or terminating a long-term cooperation with another company that is of major importance to the company; (3) taking a participation in the capital of another company with a value of at least one third of the (consolidated) balance sheet total (also including divestments). Despite the codification of this major transaction rule, the notion transfer of *'vrijwel de gehele onderneming'* is extensively discussed by Dutch scholars.[198] Similarly, in India, shareholder approval via a special resolution is required for undertaking four major decisions.[199]

Some other jurisdictions do not offer any special shareholder approval rights on these major transactions. For instance, in France, it falls under the discretionary powers of the corporate board, as long as it does not concern a related-party transaction that requires shareholder approval (see Section 21.4.6 below), or is triggering a capital resolution (see Section 21.4.4). Finally, the authors of Chapter 13 found that shareholders were allowed to vote on a transaction of substantial assets in one of the companies they studied but noted that such a shareholder vote is not required under Danish law.

21.4.6 *Related-Party Transactions*

Related-party transactions are transactions between a company and its insiders (including managers, directors and controlling shareholders) that may create the opportunity to behave opportunistically at the expense of corporate outsiders, in particular minority shareholders. Hence, related-party transactions present a possible conflict of interest and thus are heavily regulated in many jurisdictions: in some jurisdictions, a shareholder approval mechanism is used for these transaction types to constrain opportunistic behaviour. Such a shareholder approval mechanism is usually constructed as MoM approval, excluding the corporate insiders from the decision-making, as outlined in Section 21.5.3 of this chapter.

The SRD II required European Member States to address these transactions in their laws. Article 9 c (1) SRD II requires Member States to define 'material' related-party transactions, taking into account the risks of these transactions for a company and its shareholders.[200] This

[196] In German: 'den wertvollsten Betriebszweig und änderte die Unternehmensstruktur von Grund auf'. *Bundesgerichtshof* 83, 122, 131–2, Holzmüller. In the Holzmüller case, the corporate management transferred about 80 per cent of its assets to a subsidiary.

[197] 26 April 2004 decision, II ZR 154/02, 26 April 2004 decision II ZR 155/02 (Gelatine).

[198] Including in the important ABN Amro case in which the Dutch Higher Court provided an explanation in line with the Dutch notion of board autonomy. See HR 13 July 2007, ECLI:NL:HR:2007:BA7972 (ABN AMRO). See Chapter 19.

[199] Section 180, Companies Act, 2013 ICA provides the following four situations: the power (1) to sell, lease or otherwise dispose of the whole or substantially the whole of the undertaking of the company; (2) to invest otherwise in trust securities the amount of compensation received by it as a result of any merger or amalgamation; (3) to borrow money, where the money to be borrowed, together with the money already borrowed by the company, will exceed the aggregate of its paid-up share capital, free reserves and securities premium, apart from temporary loans obtained from the company's bankers in the ordinary course of business; and (4) to remit, or give time for the repayment of, any debt due from a director.

[200] Article 9c SRD II. For an analysis of the related party transaction rules in this Directive see Marcello Bianchi and Mateja Milič, 'Article 9c: Transparency and Approval of Related Party Transactions' in H. Birkmose and K. Sergakis (eds.) *SRDII: A Commentary* (Edward Elgar 2021) 286–319.

provision also requires Member States to 'set one or more quantitative ratios based on the impact of the transaction on the financial position, revenues, assets, capitalization, including equity, or turnover of the company or take into account the nature of transaction and the position of the related party'. Hence, Member States can set the threshold for material related-party transactions that trigger the application of article 9 c SRD II in their national laws. These material transactions have to be disclosed before the transaction is concluded, and information must be provided on the nature of the relationship with the related party, the name of the related party, and the date and the value of the related-party transaction. Other information necessary for an assessment of whether or not the transaction is fair and reasonable from the perspective of the company and of the shareholders, including the minority shareholders, must also be provided. The SRD II also allows Member States to require a report that assesses 'whether or not the transaction is fair and reasonable from the perspective of the company and of the shareholders who are not a related party, including minority shareholders, and explaining the assumptions it is based upon together with the methods used'.[201] Although in the initial proposal of the EC the shareholder approval was the only available approval mechanism in article 9 c SRD II, the adopted provision in article 9 c stipulates that material related-party transactions are approved by the general meeting or by the administrative or supervisory body of the company in order to prevent opportunistic behaviour and protect the interests of the company and minority shareholders in particular. Member States may also provide a shareholder's vote on material transactions with related parties which have been approved by the administrative or supervisory body of the company. The related party cannot take part in the approval or voting process.[202] Article 9 c (6) SRD II stipulates some transactions that Member States may exclude from these related-party transaction approval requirements, including transactions regarding the remuneration of directors, or certain elements of the remuneration of directors, and transactions in corporate groups with wholly owned subsidiaries.

Since shareholder approval is not the only mechanism provided in the final version of article 9 c SRD II, the directive did not significantly change shareholder rights as regards related-party transactions. In France, any agreement between the company and the director, the CEO, the deputy CEO, a member of the management board, a member of the supervisory board or any shareholder who owns more than 10 per cent of the voting rights, including, if the shareholder is itself a company, the controlling shareholder of the shareholder, had already to be submitted to a pre-approval to the board of directors, and afterwards to an approval by the shareholders prior to SRD II.[203] If the transaction does not receive a simple majority of the disinterested shareholders, the conflicted party as well as the corporate board can be held liable for any of the consequences of the agreement, which are damaging to the company:[204] this mechanism provides an incentive for the corporate board to only approve related-party transactions that are also likely to obtain shareholder approval.

201 Article 9c (3) SRD II.

202 However, following article 9c (4) SRD, Member States may allow the shareholder who is a related party to take part in the vote provided that national law ensures appropriate safeguards which apply before or during the voting process to protect the interests of the company and of the shareholders who are not a related party, including minority shareholders, by preventing the related party from approving the transaction despite the opposing opinion of the majority of the shareholders who are not a related party or despite the opposing opinion of the majority of the independent directors.

203 Articles L. 225-38 and L. 225-86 FCC. In line with the European requirements, a shareholder being an interested party in the transaction cannot take part in the vote.

204 Article L.225-41 FCC. See Chapter 14.

The UK Listing Rules require shareholder approval (excluding the interested shareholder) of related-party transactions larger than a percentage ratio of 5 per cent for premium listings.[205] In contrast, Germany generally does not allow for a shareholder vote on related-party transactions, however, shareholder approval is required for transactions that require the supervisory board's consent but this consent is withhold.[206]

In Asia, several jurisdictions require shareholder approval for related-party transactions. Like the UK Listing Rules, Singapore uses a threshold of 5 per cent (of the issuer's latest audited consolidated net tangible assets) for shareholder approval. In Hong Kong, where also MoM approval is used for transactions with threshold of 5 per cent,[207] listed companies must set up an independent board committee to advise the shareholders on the related-party transaction based on the opinion of an independent financial adviser.[208]

Chinese general law requires shareholder approval of only one specific type of related-party transactions, namely the company's provision of a guarantee in favour of its shareholders.[209] The Chinese regulatory and listing rules further mandate in respect of listed companies shareholder approval of any related-party transactions breaching a prescribed size threshold.[210] Finally, in Indonesia, shareholder approval of disinterested shareholders seems to be required for particular related-party transactions that are deemed conflict of interest transactions.[211] For these transactions, in addition to a MoM vote, also special quorums are required (for the first and second call, more than 50 per cent of the voting rights of the independent shareholders, see Section 21.3.1 of this chapter on quorum requirements).

21.4.7 *Other Resolutions*

The subsections above outline the types of resolutions commonly seen in the jurisdictions featured in this Handbook. There are resolution types that are unique to individual jurisdictions, and they could offer additional avenues of engagement for (minority) shareholders investing in those jurisdictions. This subsection provides a non-exhaustive overview of these special resolution types.

Chinese general meetings have authority to transact a number of matters that are typically reserved for the board in other jurisdictions. Most notable is China's statutory requirement for shareholder approval of the company's 'business policies and investment plans'.[212] Managerial in nature, business- and investment-related proposals are the second most common type of resolution (after board elections) tabled before Chinese shareholders as the second chapter in this Handbook shows. Chinese statutory rules also require that shareholders approve the issuance of bonds,[213] as well as the provision of guarantee to the company's shareholders.[214]

[205] UK Listing Rules 11.1.7(3).

[206] Section 111(4) AktG.

[207] Or less than 25 per cent with a total consideration lower than HK$ 10,000,000, following Hong Kong LR 14A.76.

[208] Hong Kong LR 14A.39–14A.45.

[209] Article 16 PRC Company Law.

[210] More specifically, RMB 30 million (appropriately USD 4.5 million) or 5 per cent of the company's audited net asset value in the previous accounting period, whichever is higher. See section 10.2.5 Shanghai Stock Exchange Listing Rules.

[211] OJK defines conflict of interest as the difference between the economic interests of the public company and the personal economic interests of members of the board of directors, members of the board of commissioners, major shareholders, or controller that cause loss to the aforesaid public company. See Chapter 5.

[212] Article 37(1) PRC Company Law.

[213] Article 37(8) PRC Company Law.

[214] n. 212.

In some European Member States, shareholders are able to discharge their directors for misconduct in the past financial year. Generally speaking, discharge is an act of the general meeting, which declares that the shareholders will not have the intention to hold the directors liable for actions in a particular financial year. Discharge is binding in, for instance, the Netherlands[215] but in Germany it only constitutes an expression of trust.[216] In contrast, in France, discharge is not binding and is usually not even included in the general meeting's agenda. In the UK, discharge of directors is void.[217] UK law, however, allows that the general meeting ratifies the 'conduct by a director amounting to negligence, default, breach of duty or breach of trust in relation to the company':[218] this is, in contrast to the decision to discharge, a case-based ratification of the director's behaviour.

Two other UK-specific resolutions, namely political donations and expenditures, require a shareholder vote with only a simple majority required.[219] Management proposals regarding the notice period for general meetings on the agenda in the UK can also take the form of a special resolution.[220]

21.5 SPECIAL VOTING RULES AND DEVIATIONS FROM ONE-SHARE-ONE-VOTE

21.5.1 *Majority Rules*

In all the jurisdictions covered in this Handbook, there is a simple majority voting rule for general resolutions,[221] and there are some 'special' voting items that require a qualified majority in order to be approved by the general meeting. These higher thresholds make it easier for non-controlling shareholders to block a particular resolution they do not agree with, and thus can be considered a form of minority shareholder protection. Yet, such rules can also provide disproportional powers to some minority shareholders to strategically 'hold out' and thus can prevent efficient transactions from being approved. As this balancing act of minority shareholder protection and efficient corporate decision-making is carried out slightly differently in every jurisdiction, we can note not only differences in the voting thresholds that are used, but also which voting items are subject to these qualified majority rules. For instance, in Australia and in the Netherlands, a qualified majority is required for a say-on-pay related matter (the Two-Strikes rule in Australia, and the remuneration policy shareholder approval right in the Netherlands). Whereas Dutch law requires this qualified majority vote for the remuneration policy, it does not – like the CBCA in Canada, and also some transactions in India and Indonesia – require a qualified majority vote for major transactions. Interestingly, in Australia, we can find qualified

[215] Generally, directors cannot be held liable for conduct in the financial year they are discharged for by the AGM. The decision to discharge only limits internal liability for the conduct that was known upon approval of the annual accounts. See Chapter 19.

[216] Section 120(2) AktG states that ratification shall not constitute a waiver of claims for compensation of damage. Following Manifest (2008).

[217] Pursuant to section 232(1) UK CA: '[a]ny provision that purports to exempt a director of a company (to any extent) from any liability that would otherwise attach to him in connection with any negligence, default, breach of duty or breach of trust in relation to the company is void'.

[218] Section 239(1) UK CA.

[219] Section 366 UK CA.

[220] In accordance with section 307A UK, such a resolution can reduce the notice period to a minimum of fourteen days for the first general meeting after the annual general meeting at which the special resolution was passed (a special resolution with a 75 per cent majority).

[221] In all jurisdictions this is 50 per cent + 1 vote. However, in Japan the simple majority threshold can be lowered or increased following in the articles of association. For directors- and auditor-related voting items, the threshold cannot be lower than one-third of the votes. See Chapter 6.

majorities for 'ESG' (environmental, social and governance) resolutions as these are considered a constitutional amendment.[222] Yet even constitutional amendments (i.e., amendments to the articles of association or the corporate charter) do not require qualified majorities in all jurisdictions: as we have seen in Section 21.4.2 of this chapter, in the Netherlands and Delaware, these amendments (usually) require simple majorities. To conclude, although some resolutions like amendments to the articles of association or merger proposals require a qualified majority approval in most jurisdictions, for other resolutions there is far more variety. Since qualified majorities can also be determined at a company level in the articles of association, intra-jurisdictional variation also regularly occurs.

Table 21.6 provides a general overview of the qualified majority thresholds per jurisdiction, but note that the details may vary. Some jurisdictions base the calculation on the *votes* represented at the meeting, others focus on the *issued capital* represented by the attending shareholders (see for a further outline of these different calculation methods Chapter 22).

TABLE 21.6 *Qualified majority rules*

Jurisdiction	Qualified Majority Threshold (not less than)
Australia	75%
Canada	2/3 of the votes cast
China	2/3 votes present
Denmark	2/3 of the votes cast and 2/3 share capital represented[223]
France	2/3 of the votes cast
Germany	75% of the share capital represented
Greece	2/3 votes present and amendment to AoA
Hong Kong	75% of the votes cast
India	75%
Indonesia	2/3 to 3/4 of the votes cast
Italy	2/3 of the voting capital represented[224]
Japan	2/3 of the votes cast
Norway	2/3 of the votes present and share capital[225]
South Korea	2/3 votes present and 1/3 of the total number of issued and outstanding shares
Singapore	75% of the votes cast
Taiwan	2/3 of share capital represented (votes present for public companies[226]) and simple majority of the votes present
The Netherlands	2/3 of the votes cast[227] or 75%[228]
United Kingdom	75% of the votes cast
United States	Determined by corporate charter or by-laws.

222 See Chapter 10.

223 For some particular amendments to the articles of association a super majority of 90 per cent (thus, 90 per cent of the votes cast as well as 90 per cent of the share capital represented at the GM) is required.

224 This is the supermajority threshold that applies to listed companies' EGMs. See Chapter 17.

225 There is a qualified majority for amendments to the articles of association of two-thirds of the votes present as well as the share capital (section 5-18 ASA), but the articles of association may require a higher threshold. Section 5-19 ASA Act provides rules on qualified majority and section 5-20 ASA on the demand of unanimity. See Chapter 18.

226 In the case of public companies, there is an exception to this rule, requiring two-thirds of the votes present if there is a quorum of 50 per cent.

227 For special resolutions in the Netherlands, only a simple majority is required if a quorum of 50 per cent is met.

228 The 75 per cent relates to the remuneration policy. The Dutch law was amended with the implementation of the SRD II in 2019. See Chapter 19.

21.5.2 *Tenure Voting and Multiple Class Voting*

There exists a range of deviations from the one-share-one-vote rule in the different jurisdictions discussed in this Handbook. When combined with firm-specific share ownership structures and attributes (for instance, founder shareholders holding a minority stake), these deviations can play an important part in the dynamics of shareholder voting and engagement.

In many jurisdictions, there are multiple share classes allowed that lead to high and low voting shares. These high voting shares are also considered a controlling minority mechanism,[229] because cash flow and control rights differ, allowing shareholders to exercise more control with less equity. Although we were not able to take these fully into account in Table 21.1 and 21.2 in the beginning of this chapter, dual-class share structures exist in several jurisdictions, notably in the USA, where they have attracted both enthusiasm and opposition. Dual-class structures have also been adopted in recent years in a number of jurisdictions which have abandoned their traditional apathy to deviations from one-share-one-vote (OSOV). These include China, Hong Kong and Singapore, where the competition for listing of high-tech firms has driven recent legal and regulatory reforms in favour of the dual class structure.[230] In India, promoters or founders of tech companies are allowed to have 'superior rights shares' for limited purposes.[231]

Another important example of varied voting rights is tenure voting. For instance, in France and Italy, loyalty shares are adopted in the statutory laws. In 2014, the Florange Law inverted the French system of double voting rights: whereas before its implementation, the articles of association had to provide double voting rights for long-term shareholders, now all name shares of French listed companies which are held for more than two years receive double voting rights, unless the articles of association explicitly provide otherwise. In other words, the French system moved from an opt-in to an opt-out.[232] In Italy, a similar arrangement can be found,[233] but with an opt-in in the articles of association. This provision allows for tenured voting, which may be adopted by any listed company that does not have a multiple voting structure in place.

Non-voting shares are yet another example of an alternative voting system. In some jurisdictions (e.g. the USA), for public companies, non-voting shares are allowed to restrict the control of the outsider shareholders. In the Netherlands, control rights of outsider shareholders can, for instance, be limited using depository receipts. Using this construction, companies do not list all their shares, but issue (part of) their shares to a trust office which is the legal owner of the voting rights. Holders of non-voting depository receipts receive financial rights and dividends, but voting rights are thus separated from capital rights. The holders may submit a request to receive proxies, except in takeover situations, and may also give binding instructions to the trust office.[234]

The CBCA provides in a OSOV default rule in Canada, but the company's articles of association can deviate, and a significant number of companies make use of share classes.

[229] See Chapter 1.

[230] Perhaps the best example is the listing of Alibaba at the Hong Kong stock exchange in 2019. See for instance, Emma Dunkley, 'HKEX Admits Alibaba Forced it to Rethink Dual-Class Shares', *Financial Times*, 16 January 2018; Hudson Lockett, Mercedes Ruehl and Louise Lucas, 'Alibaba Listing Offers Hong Kong a Shot at the One That Got Away', *Financial Times*, 31 May 2019.

[231] See SEBI (Listing Obligations and Disclosure Requirements) Regulations, 2015 and SEBI (Issue of Capital and Disclosure Requirements) Regulations, 2018.

[232] Article L125-123 FCC as amended by Loi n° 2014-384 du 29 mars 2014 visant à reconquérir l'économie réelle, *JO* nr. 77, 1 April 2014.

[233] Article 127-quinquies CLF. See Chapter 17.

[234] Article 2:118a DCC.

Shares with ten voting rights seem to be the most common class, but fifty voting rights for a class of shares[235] and even one hundred to one are also found.[236]

21.5.3 *Special Voting Rules: Director Elections and RPTs*

Interestingly, most notable special voting rules discussed in this Handbook by the jurisdiction experts, including MoM rules, relate to either director elections or related-party transactions. These voting rules have generally been framed to empower minority shareholders and give them a stronger voice on matters that typically involve conflicts of interest.

In the UK, outsider shareholders vote separately on the election of independent directors in companies that have a controlling shareholder in the UK.[237] The threshold for control is set at 30 per cent and includes acting in concert.[238] In Italy, the so-called slate voting system (*Voto di Lista*), which is discussed in more detail in Chapter 17, allows minority shareholders who meet certain requirements to propose a slate of directors. Depending on the provision in the articles of association, the majority of the directors are selected from the slate that receives the highest number of votes, but one or two directors are selected from the so-called minority slate (i.e. the slate that received the highest number of votes after this majority slate). In the USA, in contrast, shareholder director nominations are generally considered hostile to the corporate board, and thus usually take the form of a proxy contest.[239] The author of Chapter 12 describes the latest trend of short slates, where the activist prefers to have a minority on the corporate board instead of board control.

A similarly spirited voting regime aimed at empowering minority shareholders is cumulative voting. This voting arrangement allows (minority) shareholders to place all of their accumulated votes on one (or more) of the multiple number of directors, so that their favoured candidate stands a much greater chance of being elected than under a simple majority voting regime. Cumulative voting is permissible in the USA (Delaware), though its actual use has been in decline. It is also popular in some Asian jurisdictions: China's general company law takes a permissive approach, allowing cumulative voting to be used in the election of board members.[240] Cumulative voting is mandatory for Chinese listed firms where a block holder owns 30 per cent of the company's outstanding shares, and it is optional for listed firms without such a 30 per cent block holder.[241] Taiwanese law makes cumulative voting mandatory for joint stock companies (i.e. public companies).[242]

Plurality voting is another area where shareholder empowerment has increased over the past years. Plurality voting can be considered board-centric and is the statutory default rule in Delaware. When an election is uncontested (i.e., the number of candidates equals the number of directors to be elected) any number of votes suffices to elect a nominee to a board seat.[243]

235 For instance, see the company Rogers Communications Inc.

236 For instance, see the company Teck Resources Limited.

237 In accordance with the UK Listing Rules, LR 9.2.2A jo 9.2.2E.

238 If the resolution is not approved, the company may propose a further resolution to elect or re-elect the proposed independent director which cannot be voted on until ninety days since the meeting have elapsed. It must be voted on within thirty days of this ninety-day wait period. This second resolution must be approved by the shareholders of the company ex LR 9.2.2F.

239 Also see Section 21.6 of this chapter on shareholder proposals.

240 Article 105 PRC Company Law.

241 Chao Xi and Yugang Chen, 'Does Cumulative Voting Matter? The Case of China: An Empirical Assessment' (2014) 15 European Business Organization Law Review 585.

242 Article 198 TCA. See Chapter 9.

243 Section 216(3) DGCL

Following institutional investors' discontentment as regards the reappointment of candidates for whom large numbers of votes had been withheld to protest their election,[244] most large US listed companies have nowadays opted out of this default rule in their corporate charters, switching to the simple majority voting standard.[245] In Canada, as in Delaware, the plurality voting system has long been used for director elections. Similarly, under this system, the candidate who receives the most votes is electedtes, and in uncontested elections, a single vote is sufficient[246] As in Delaware, this approach has been severely criticized. After the TSX rules for uncontested director elections were modified in 2014, the Canadian government introduced the new CBCA in 2018, which now requires all public companies to have a 'true' majority voting system for director elections.[247]

To conclude our discussion on special voting rules for director elections, we should mention the practice in Indonesia and (for a large number of companies in) Greece to have shareholders appoint all directors in a single voting round. Interestingly, Chapter 22 in this Handbook shows that in these two jurisdictions, the voting results for these *combined director elections* show significantly larger shareholder dissent, as any discontentment with the proposed board composition can only be signalled with a vote against all board members.[248]

Another area where special voting rules have flourished contains related-party transactions, as discussed in Section 21.4.6 of this chapter. There, a MoM voting arrangement excludes the related parties (typically corporate insiders) transacting with the company from casting a vote on the resolution in which they are interested. The rule in effect requires independent or disinterested shareholder approval of related party transactions that meet certain (size) thresholds. It is often seen in the listing rules (and sometimes in the statutory company laws) of the jurisdictions surveyed, including the UK, France, China, Hong Kong, Indonesia, India, Singapore, South Korea and Taiwan. Delaware law does not formally require MoM voting in respect of related-party transactions, but rather opts for a fairness test. However, a Delaware Chancery Court's ruling seems to have significantly increased the voluntary use of the MoM by US listed firms.[249]

21.6 SHAREHOLDER PROPOSALS

In nearly all the jurisdictions we discuss in this Handbook, shareholders have the right to put items on the agenda of the general meeting. Hence, in addition to ratification rights of important corporate decisions, in many jurisdictions, shareholders also have some initiation rights. However, the thresholds and additional requirements differ markedly between the jurisdictions. These requirements have an important bearing on minority shareholders' ability to propose corporate governance changes.

As illustrated in Section 21.6.1 of this chapter, shareholding thresholds for such proposals can be based on a percentage of the (paid-up) capital or voting rights, and/or a group of shareholders or a particular value in local currency. In addition to these ownership requirements, some jurisdictions also restrict the topics that can be the subject of shareholder proposals or the

[244] See Kraakman et al. (n. 97) 54 and the references therein.
[245] See Chapter 12.
[246] See Chapter 11.
[247] See the information and references in Chapter 11. Note that, although these rules have not yet come into force formally in Canada, the authors expect that 'both TSX and non-TSX listed companies will move to adopt a "true" majority voting system as a matter of best practice and to align their director election processes with the approved legislation'.
[248] Section 22.3.1 of Chapter 22.
[249] Re. MFW Shareholders Litigation No. 6566-CS, 2013 WL 2326879, at *1 (Del Ch 29 May 2013).

number of shareholder proposals that can be added to the agenda, usually with reference to the level of support those proposals received in previous general meetings. In some jurisdictions there is a cap on the number of proposals a shareholder can add to the agenda. In Japan, for example, the Companies Act was amended in 2019 to restrict each shareholder to no more than ten proposals per meeting, as a response to some abusive cases where a shareholder submitted more than fifty proposals, as explained in Chapter 6. In the USA, currently, each shareholder can only submit one proposal,[250] and there are resubmission thresholds of 3 per cent, 6 per cent and 10 per cent, depending on the number of times the proposals have been voted on before.[251] In some cases, the board has the right to exclude shareholder proposals, subject to administrative or judicial scrutiny (for instance, the non-action request process of the SEC in the United States, as explained below).

21.6.1 *Ownership Requirements*

In the European Union, shareholder proposals have been harmonized to a large extent. Article 6 SRD I allows shareholders to put items on the agenda of the general meeting (accompanied by a justification or a draft resolution) or to table draft resolutions. The minimum threshold that Member States may set for this right cannot exceed 5 per cent of the share capital. France, Greece,[252] Germany and the UK[253] have adopted this minimum threshold of 5 per cent. In Germany shareholders can also add a shareholder proposal when they have 500,000 euro in shares (nominal value).[254] In the UK too, a group of at least one hundred shareholders, each owning no less than £100 worth of shares, can put an item on the agenda. In France, depending on the capital of the company, the threshold falls gradually to 0.5 per cent.[255] Other Member States also use lower thresholds: for instance, in the Netherlands, the threshold is 3 per cent for public companies, while in Italy it is 2.5 per cent. In Denmark, there is no threshold, enabling any shareholder who wishes to add a shareholder proposal to the agenda: the same is true for Norway. In addition to the 5 per cent or 500,000 euros in nominal value of the shares in Germany for 'normal' shareholder proposals, any shareholder has the right to file a counter motion to a proposal of the management board and supervisory board.[256]

The threshold for shareholders to put an item on the meeting's agenda in Europe is generally higher than in the USA, as shareholders in the latter jurisdiction add a shareholder proposal to the proxy materials with only 1 per cent of the shares or $2,000 in market value at least one year before the proposal before January 2022. Amendments to Rule 14a-8 were announced in January 2020, adopted by the SEC at the end of September 2020, and will apply to shareholder proposals from January 2022.[257] The main amendments contain some higher ownership requirements, ranging

[250] The amendments to Rule 14a-8 would narrow the one-proposal limitation by prohibiting 'each person' to file more than one proposal, limiting shareholder representatives and proxy holders in submitting shareholder proposals. See for an overview of the amendments that apply from January 2022 onwards 'SEC Adopts Amendments to Modernize Shareholder Proposal Rule', www.sec.gov/news/press-release/2020-220 accessed 15 December 2020. Note that there is also a transition period.

[251] Rule 14a-8(i)(12). These thresholds would be amended to 5 per cent, 15 per cent and 25 per cent, respectively.

[252] 5 per cent of the paid up share capital.

[253] 5 per cent of the voting shares.

[254] Section 122 AktG.

[255] Article R. 225-71 FCC. The lowest threshold of 0.5 per cent of the shares is applicable when the capital exceeds EUR 15 million.

[256] Section 126 AktG. Note that the right to file a counter motion applies also to a supervisory board member or external auditor nomination ex section 127 AktG.

[257] See n. 250.

from $2,000–$25,000 of the company's shares linked to the holding time of the shares. Another amendment addresses shareholder proposals that are submitted more often to the general meeting. Particularly, Rule 14a-8 has been amended in such a way to provide that proposals must obtain a certain level of support before they can be resubmitted at the following year's general meeting. For instance, a proposal would need to be supported by at least 5 per cent of the voting shareholders in its first submission in order to be eligible for resubmission sometime in the following three years. Proposals that have been submitted two or three times during the previous five years must obtain 15 per cent and 25 per cent support, respectively, to qualify for resubmission within the following three years.

In Canada, similar thresholds apply: 1 per cent of voting shares or shares with a fair market value of at least $2,000 for a six-month period preceding the date on which the shareholder proposal is submitted. In the case of the nomination of directors, the threshold is increased to 5 per cent of the shares or class of shares entitled to vote.[258] In Australia, as in the UK, at least 100 shareholders who are entitled to vote (or shareholders with 5 per cent of the votes) at the general meeting can put forward a shareholder proposal.[259]

In the Asian jurisdictions covered in our Handbook, the thresholds range from 0.25 or 0.5 per cent in South Korea to 10 per cent in India. With this 10 per cent, India seems to provide the highest threshold for shareholder proposals of any of our jurisdictions discussed in this Handbook. In Taiwan and Japan, shareholders with 1 per cent[260] can add a shareholder proposal, whereas in Japan also shareholders with 300 voting rights held for over a six-months can also add a proposal. In China, the threshold is set at 3 per cent, and in Singapore, shareholders with 5 per cent of the total voting rights or a group of at least 100 shareholders holding shares on which there has been paid up an average sum per member of at least SGD 500 can put a proposal on the agenda. Finally, in Hong Kong, shareholders need 2.5 per cent of voting rights of total shares eligible to vote on that resolution or at least fifty shareholders entitled to vote on the proposed resolution to add an item to the agenda.[261]

Table 21.7 provides an overview of these thresholds and shows that there are various inter-jurisdictional differences. Chapter 22 shows the impact of these rules on the use of the shareholder proposal right. Due to the *Voto di Lista* mechanism for director elections in Italy, the use of shareholder proposals in Italy is more widespread than in the other European jurisdictions. Their use is also quite common in Germany and Denmark: it can be noted that in Denmark, the lowest threshold of only one share applies.[262]

21.6.2 *Additional Requirements*

The USA is probably the most well-known jurisdiction for shareholder proposals, though (as Chapter 22 shows) shareholder proposals are also common in Italy (*Voto di Lista*) and Germany (counter motions, see the previous section). The well-known Rule 14a-8 of the Exchange Act allows shareholders to make proposals, and these proposals must be sent out by the corporate management together with company's proxy materials. Following Rule

258 Section 137 (4) CBCA.
259 Section 249N(1) ACA.
260 In Taiwan, this is 1 per cent of the outstanding shares, whereas in Japan this is 1 per cent of the voting rights.
261 Section 615(2) HKCO.
262 Interestingly, whereas Denmark and Norway have comparable rules for shareholder proposals with the lowest thresholds in our sample of jurisdictions, shareholder proposals are less common in Norway. See Chapter 22.

TABLE 21.7 *Shareholder proposal thresholds*

Jurisdiction	Minimum threshold for shareholder proposal	Of what?
Australia	5% or at least 100 shareholders	Votes
Canada	1% or at least $2,000 in market value for more than 6 months; 5% for nomination directors	(eligible) voting shares
China	3%	Share capital
Denmark	*All shareholders*[263]	-
France	5%, according to the amount of capital lowered to 0.5%	Share capital
Germany	5% or 500,000 EUR nominal value shares (also: countermotions)	Share capital
Greece	5%	Paid up share capital
Hong Kong	2.5% or at least 50 shareholders entitled to vote on the proposed resolution.	voting rights of total shares eligible to vote on that resolution
India	10%	Share capital with voting rights
Indonesia	10%	5%
Italy	2.5% (also: *Voto di Lista*)[264]	share capital
Japan	1% or 300 voting rights for more than 6 months[265]	Voting rights
Norway	*All shareholders*[266]	-
South Korea	3%, at least six weeks prior to the date AGM, 1% or 0.5%[267]	issued and outstanding shares
Singapore	5% or at least 100 shareholders holding shares on which there has been paid up an average sum per member of at least SGD 500.	Voting rights
Taiwan	1%	Outstanding shares
The Netherlands	3%	Share capital
United Kingdom	5% or at least 100 shareholders with each owning no less than £100 worth shares.	Voting rights
United States	1% for at least one year or $2,000 in market value for at least one year[268]	Company's securities

14a-8, companies can file a no-action request at the SEC for shareholder proposals that fall within the thirteen grounds for exclusion. Such a no-action relief will be successful if the shareholder proposal fails to meet any of the (procedural and substantive) requirements of Rule 14a-8. Particularly, proposals related to the nomination of board candidates generally require an activist's own campaign instead of using the company's proxy materials. This is reflected in one of the refusal grounds: 'a specific individual in the company's proxy materials for election to the board of directors'.[269] Yet, despite failed efforts at the federal

263 This also holds true for non-voting shares, as all other shareholder rights (except for the actual voting process) are preserved in these shares: the status as shareholder provides the right to propose items for the agenda (and also to ask questions).

264 Note that this threshold only applies to listed companies: there is no right to submit shareholder proposals in non-listed companies provided. The threshold for submitting a slate of director nominees (*Voto di Lista*) varies between 0.5–4.5 per cent. See Chapter 17.

265 This requirement holds for public companies.

266 As in Denmark, any shareholder has the right to propose an issue to be voted on at the AGM. See Chapter 18.

267 For listed companies the thresholds are 1 per cent or 0.5 per cent (listed companies with equity capital valued at 100 billion won (₩) or more as at the end of the latest business year) of the issued and outstanding shares, not including non-voting shares. These stakes need to be held for at least six months.

268 New rules will apply from January 2022, ranging from $2,000 to $25,000. See n. 250.

269 Rule 14a-8(i)(8).

level,[270] proxy access has become more widely used due to the coordinated actions of institutional investors, allowing shareholders to use the management's proxy card.[271] Another of these grounds contains a proposal 'that deals with a matter relating to ordinary business operations'.[272] The SEC has recommended that shareholders should make use of advisory or precatory proposals: in contrast, micromanagement proposals are usually excluded.[273]

Part of the SEC amendments to Rule 14a-8 that will apply to shareholder proposals from January 2022 onwards, are similar to the current rules in Japan for shareholder proposals:[274] in Japan, shareholders are only able to submit proposals that did not fail in the last three years, where 'failure' is defined as receiving less than 10 per cent of the votes. And in Canada, a corporation can reject a shareholder proposal to be adopted in the proxy materials if the proposal does not relate in a significant way to the corporation's business or affairs, it is meant to enforce a personal claim or redress a personal grievance against the corporation or its directors, officers or shareholders, or it is substantially the same proposal that was submitted before and does not meet the minimum support requirements.[275]

In the USA, following SEC recommendations, shareholder proposals are often advisory or precatory. In Australia, by contrast, shareholder resolutions are generally considered binding decisions by their nature, and therefore advisory shareholder proposals are not allowed, unless permitted in the AoA.[276] Particularly, non-binding (ESG) shareholder proposals in Australia are considered to infringe the division of powers between the corporate board and the shareholders.[277] Hence, to make such proposals, shareholders first need to make an amendment to a company's constitution by way of a special resolution and then pass a non-binding resolution requiring some form of (ESG) disclosure or action by a company. This chapter has already shown many fundamental differences between jurisdictions, including this remarkable one: whereas in the USA we see many precatory ESG proposals over the past years, in Australia, an ESG-related proposal is considered to be a constitutional change resolution that requires a 75 per cent majority vote.

21.7 SHAREHOLDER QUESTIONS

As a final topic, in many jurisdictions covered in this Handbook, shareholders have the right to ask questions during the general meetings. This right can be a statutory right (for instance, in the European Member States), or a right acquired as a result of case law or common practice (for instance, Japan, and the USA). In many jurisdictions, the chair of the meeting can limit

[270] The 2010 Dodd-Frank Act granted the SEC power to make rules facilitating the inclusion of shareholder nominations in the corporate proxy materials. Using this power, the SEC adopted Rule 14a-11. This rule holds that a shareholder (or shareholders jointly) holding 3 per cent of the voting share capital for three years can include its own nominees with the company's proxy materials. However, in 2011, the DC Circuit ruled against this rule. *Business Roundtable* v. *Securities and Exchange Commission*, 647 Federal Reporter 3d 1144, at 1148.

[271] See Chapter 12.

[272] Rule 14a-8(i)(7).

[273] See for more information about the micromanagement no-action relief Staff Legal Bulletin No. 14K (CF) (SLB No. 14K). See also Chapter 12.

[274] See for the new rule www.sec.gov/rules/final/2020/34-89964.pdf accessed 22 March 2021.

[275] See Chapter 11 and section 137(5) CBCA.

[276] Section 250R ACA.

[277] See *ACCR* v. *CBA* [2015] FCA 785.

shareholder speaking time in the interests of good order. Yet directors generally have a duty to answer if the applicable requirements are met. As the right to ask questions is a statutory shareholder right in Europe, with a (minimum) harmonized framework, we further outline the European situation in this section.

The most detailed rules about the shareholder question right are laid down in the SRD I. The SRD I requires that 'every shareholder shall have the right to ask questions related to items on the agenda of the general meeting. The company shall answer the questions put to it by shareholders'.[278] If taken together with the preamble of the SRD I, this paragraph limits the right to ask questions to the items on the general meeting's agenda. Some Member States closely follow the text of the directive, whereas other jurisdictions, where the right to ask questions already existed in their national laws prior to the introduction of the SRD I (like France and the Netherlands) or it was already a common practice to ask questions, allow also for questions that are not (directly) related to the agenda of the general meeting. Member States can take measures, or can allow companies to take measures to ensure the identification of shareholders, the good order of general meetings and their preparation, and protection of confidentiality and companies' business interests.[279] Member States may also allow companies to provide a single overall answer to questions that have the same content, and they may consider that the question has been answered if the relevant information is available on the company's website in a 'question and answer' format. For instance, the UK closely follows these rules in the SRD I as regards the circumstances under which no answer need be given:[280]

> (a) if to do so would – (i) interfere unduly with the preparation for the meeting, or (ii) involve the disclosure of confidential information; (b) if the answer has already been given on a website in the form of an answer to a question; or (c) if it is undesirable in the interests of the company or the good order of the meeting that the question be answered.

In France, in addition to the shareholder question rights included in the SRD I, shareholders also have the right to submit written questions that are answered during the general meeting.[281]

21.8 CONCLUDING REMARKS

The chapter has summarized and compared the ownership structures, shareholder voting rights, and other voice tools particularly linked to the general meeting in the various jurisdictions. Table 21.8 provides an overview of the main findings. The darker the cells in Table 21.8, the stronger (minority) shareholder rights a particular jurisdiction has.[282]

We see some important similarities in terms of fundamental shareholder rights. In all jurisdictions covered in this Handbook, shareholders have appointment rights for board members, although these are sometimes shared with other stakeholders like employees. Where there is a (hybrid) two-tier board structure with more than one board, the management or executive directors are often elected by the supervisory board. The voting modes for director appointment rights also differ substantially. For instance, in Canada and the USA, plurality voting can still be practiced, whereas other jurisdictions allow for voting rules that empower minority shareholders,

[278] Article 9(1) SRD I.
[279] Article 9(2) SRD I.
[280] Section 319A UK CA.
[281] In accordance with article L.225-108(3) FCC. See Chapter 14 for more information about the French question right.
[282] The first column signals the ownership concentration.

including cumulative voting in China and Taiwan, and MoM voting for independent directors in the UK in companies with concentrated ownership. In Indonesia and Greece, we found combined director appointments in one voting round. Although the effect of the latter practice is less clear, such a voting rule may also empower shareholders, as boards may be more inclined to put forward candidates less likely to encounter dissent, as high shareholder discontentment with a candidate can impact all directors. In the next chapter in this Handbook, the effects of combined voting are further explored.

A substantial number of jurisdictions have companies with a fairly concentrated ownership structure. Yet, nearly all these jurisdictions offer important minority shareholder protection rights against possible opportunistic behaviour by corporate insiders, including MoM-approval for related-party transactions, special minority appointment rights, or low thresholds for submitting a shareholder proposal or calling a general meeting. Although we did not explicitly address this in this chapter, some authors in this Handbook offer insights derivative actions, which can be considered another form of minority shareholder protection. For instance, the author of Chapter 3 outlines that it can be an effective tool, despite its rare use.[283] The USA, which is the jurisdiction with the lowest ownership concentration in our study, has traditionally focused on strong and powerful boards and ex post shareholder litigation procedures (see Chapter 12). Delaware offers fewer statutory shareholder rights, at least by comparison with European jurisdictions, yet shareholder activism is fiercer than in other jurisdictions and private enforcement offers a strong minority protection tool. The rise of institutional ownership has led to some systemic changes in corporate governance, including the switch from plurality voting to simple majority voting and proxy access at the level of many large companies. At the moment, the SEC is considering adopting a universal proxy for contested director elections.[284] In contrast, the recent amendments to Rule 14a-8 that are effective from January 2022 onwards may constrain shareholder activism to some extent, but given the traditionally fierce use of shareholder proposals in the USA and increased openness to ESG proposals under recent SEC policy,[285] the impact may perhaps be limited. Particularly, as the UK author already noted, there are typically only five shareholder proposals at the general meetings of all FTSE 100 companies, in contrast to hundreds of shareholder proposals at all US listed companies.[286] Moreover, as Chapter 22 shows, there is not always a strong pattern between lower (or no) limitations to the shareholder proposal right and the use of these rights. In Norway, for example, any shareholder can put an item on the agenda, but the use of the shareholder proposal right is below average compared to the other jurisdictions in this Handbook.[287] This indicates that although the legal infrastructure is a very important factor for the practice of shareholder rights, cultural and political factors often play a major role, even in today's globalized markets.

Nevertheless, the globalization of capital markets and the systemic rise of institutional ownership is expected to provide more and more alignment on particular governance issues, including say-on-pay. This is particularly signalled in Table 21.8: taking into account that Canada's say-on-pay is about to be introduced, only Hong Kong and Singapore do not grant shareholders a (real) say on the executive pay. Two remarks can be made here. First of all, both jurisdictions grant MoM approval rights for related-party transactions, showing that shareholders

283 See Chapter 3 and the reference to the Passport case.

284 See www.sec.gov/news/press-release/2021-64 accessed 15 May 2021. Also see Chapter 12. Note that these rules were adopted by the SEC by the end of 2021.

285 See SEC Staff Legal Bulletin No. 14L (CF) of 3 November 2021.

286 See Chapter 20.

287 See Table 22.9 of Chapter 22.

TABLE 21.8 *Overview (darker cells show stronger (minority) shareholder rights)*

Jurisdiction	Ownership[288] concentration	Calling EGM[289]	Appointment rights[290]	MoM RPT[291]	Director elections[292]	Shareholder proposals[293]	Say on Pay[294]	# Voting items[295]
Australia						Supermajority non-binding proposals		
Canada					plurality		Forthcoming	
China								
Denmark								
France								
Germany						counter-motions		
Greece			Combined					
Hong Kong							Director service contracts	
India								
Indonesia			Combined					
Italy								
Japan								
Norway								
South Korea								
Singapore							Only director fees	
Taiwan								
The Netherlands								
United Kingdom								
United States				voluntary	plurality	Rule 14a-8 extra conditions		

288 Dark grey cell, c1 (Table 21.1) is 30 per cent or higher; light grey cell, c1 is between 20–30 per cent; white cell, c1 lower than 20 per cent.

289 Dark grey cell, threshold is 5 per cent or lower; light grey cell is higher than 5 per cent; white cell, no statutory right.

290 Dark grey cell, shareholders can elect all (supervisory and management) board members; light grey cell, employee representation present and other deviations possible, but shareholders usually have appointment rights for both board member types; white cell, supervisory board always appoints the management board and employee representation.

291 Dark grey cell, there is a MoM-rule for related-party transactions.

292 Dark grey cell, special minority rights for director elections (cumulative voting, slate voting, combined voting).

293 Dark grey cell, threshold is 1 per cent or lower (for some proposals); light grey cell, higher than 1 per cent but lower or equal to 5 per cent or and other options; white cell, only 5 per cent (no other capital thresholds) or higher.

294 Dark grey cell, some sort of say-on-pay; white cell, no say-on-pay or only non-executive fees/ certain types of directors' service contracts.

295 Dark grey cell, relatively many different shareholder voting resolutions (generally more than ten voting items, board elections counted as one resolution); light grey cell, medium number of voting resolutions (generally between five and ten voting items, board elections counted as one resolution); white cell, relatively few different shareholder voting resolutions (often five or less voting items, board elections counted as one resolution).

can already restrain opportunistic behaviour of corporate insiders in another way. Secondly, one may recognize that these jurisdictions have relatively concentrated ownership structures (Table 21.1) and a relatively low presence of institutional investors (Table 21.2) who have been among the largest advocates of say-on-pay. Moreover, Table 21.2 shows that the largest owners are often families (Hong Kong) or the government (Singapore), perhaps signalling that the complete ecosystem including cultural and political factors play a role in legal reform and convergence.

22

Shareholder Engagement and Corporate Voting in Action: The Comparative Perspective

Christoph Van der Elst

22.1 INTRODUCTION

The role of shareholders in corporate governance and law in the books has been discussed in the previous chapter. Shareholders can play many different roles. Unsatisfied shareholders leave the company and vote with their feet. Other shareholders make use of the different mechanisms offered by corporate law. Shareholders have different legal means for discussing corporate behaviour, ranging from voting for or against management proposals and raising questions at general meetings of shareholders, to requiring a shareholder proposal to be tabled on the agenda of the general meeting, and even launching a proxy contest or filing a court case. This list is not exhaustive, and the different chapters in this Handbook illustrate major differences in the rights of shareholders as well as in the way they use the available mechanisms. Not in all countries, shareholders can vote for the same topics. Generally, shareholders have a right to vote for their board members as well as for major transactions, but corporate laws differ substantially in the way they define a major transaction and specify the ways in which shareholders can elect these board members, and how frequently they may do so. Even if a major transaction requires a shareholder vote according to almost all the company laws in the world, many differences co-exist, as an empirical paper of Holderness illustrates.[1] In some jurisdictions, shareholders must approve all kinds of equity issuances, while other company laws allow shareholders to vote a mandate for the board for the issuance of shares for a limited amount or a limited period of time or a combination of both. In another group of jurisdictions, shareholders only have to vote for issuances that do not respect the pre-emptive rights for incumbent shareholders, like private placements. In some jurisdictions, boards can issue stock if authorized by the shareholders, and this can be provided without any limits on time or amount. Holderness cites Facebook as an example: in its IPO it issued 180 million shares without shareholder approval, as there were more than four billion shares authorized.

In this chapter, we describe, analyze and assess a number of the different means that shareholders of companies in the nineteen different jurisdictions covered in this Handbook make use of for reaching out to their investees and signalling their approval or discontentment. In the next section, we study the likelihood that shareholders participate in general meetings in the nineteen jurisdictions, and consider the methods they generally use to participate. In the third section, a comparative study is provided of the differences in agenda items as well as the vote outcomes of these agenda items. This part shows that companies in different jurisdictions have relatively few items in common, but the voting results are very similar for almost all agenda

[1] Clifford Holderness, 'Equity Issuances and Agency Costs: The Telling Story of Shareholder Approval Around the World' (2018) 129 Journal of Financial Economics 415.

items. The fourth section investigates the shareholders' use of tabling shareholder proposals at the general meeting and the way they use the question right mechanism. In Section 22.5, we compare the use of other forms of shareholder engagement in our sample of nineteen jurisdictions. Section 22.6 provides some concluding remarks.

22.2 VOTING MODES AND TURNOUT

22.2.1 *Presentation of Voting Turnout Data*

Voting is a convenient, low cost engagement activity of shareholders that serves as an important signal to the company. Therefore, we start with an analysis of the willingness of shareholders to participate in the annual general meeting of shareholders (AGM) by exercising their voting rights. Table 22.1 provides an overview of the participation of shareholders in the AGMs (no extraordinary meetings) from 2016 to 2020 of companies that belong to a major index in the nineteen jurisdictions. Comparisons based on this data should be made with due care, given our dependence on the resources from which the data are collected.

The data in Table 22.1 show unweighted means of the participation of shareholders of the included companies in each jurisdiction, measured in a number of different ways. In a number of jurisdictions, especially those that make use of a quorum like France, participation is calculated as the number of shares of participating shareholders as a fraction of the total number of issued shares. These numbers are commonly published in the meeting minutes of listed companies. The method is used to prove compliance with the quorum requirements. The

TABLE 22.1 *Evolution of shareholder participation turnout (2016–20)*

		2016	2017	2018	2019	2020
Australia	ASX 50	63.5%	64.5%	65.7%	66.3%	65.9%
Canada	TSX 60	72.5%	72.1%	70.9%	67.8%	68.4%
China	CSI 300	55.7%	56.0%	56.4%	57.8%	
Denmark	OMX C25	57.5%	57.8%	59.7%	62.1%	62.9%
France	CAC 40	65.8%	65.4%	67.1%	68.7%	70.1%
Germany	DAX 30	59.9%	60.0%	63.2%	63.9%	65.3%
Greece	Athex Large	71.0%	74.0%	71.5%	72.0%	69.6%
Hong Kong	Hang Seng (selection)	73.2%	72.9%	74.1%	75.8%	75.7%
India	Nifty 50		82.5%	83.5%	82.4%	82.2%
Indonesia	LQ45	81.7%	81.0%	82.7%	81.9%	81.3%
Italy	FTSE MIB	66.6%	66.3%	67.5%	69.0%	70.9%
Japan	TOPIX 30	78.8%	79.7%	79.7%	80.7%	80.8%
Netherlands	AEX 25	70.4%	72.1%	72.9%	73.4%	71.2%
Norway	OBX	59.3%	59.7%	59.8%	58.1%	58.9%
S. Korea	KOSPI (lim. selection)		81.1%	75.0%	77.7%	76.0%
Singapore	Straits Time	67.1%	64.4%	64.2%	66.2%	65.6%
Taiwan	TSX-FTSE 50	82.5%	84.3%	84.6%	83.8%	84.5%
UK	FTSE 100	72.9%	72.9%	74.3%	73.8%	74.9%
US	S&P 500 (selection)	87.2%	88.6%	88.1%	88.4%	87.4%

Source: own research (and calculations) of the minutes of the AGMs, notices, proxy documents and annual reports; Georgeson for Denmark, France, Germany, Italy and the Netherlands; Proxy Insight data for the USA; chapter author for Indonesia for 2017 to 2019 and own research for 2016 and 2020 (selection of LQ45 companies).

results for India, Indonesia, Taiwan, Germany, the UK, Italy, the Netherlands, Norway and Denmark were obtained in a similar manner.[2] The results for Australia, Mainland China, Singapore and Greece were obtained by calculating the number of attending votes as a proportion of the total number of votes attached to the issued shares. However, the meeting minutes do not always specify the exact number of issued shares with voting rights. In such cases, the total number of shares with voting rights was obtained from the annual report published before the general meeting or from the meeting notice or from a proxy statement to the meeting, and may therefore differ from the number of issued shares at the record date or date of the meeting.

Further, in some countries, the participation of shareholders is not calculated or provided as a percentage in the published records. For companies in those countries, the participation of shareholders is estimated as *the total number of votes cast by shareholders as expressed in the voting results as a proportion of the total votes of the issued shares*. When the minutes or voting records disclose not only the votes for and against but also the votes withheld or abstained, the latter are added in the nominator for calculating the participation. If the records do not disclose these votes, the combined highest number of votes for and against were used as the best proxy for defining the participation of shareholders. For instance, in Hong Kong, the published voting results do not provide information on the number of abstentions.[3] Conversely, companies in some countries only publish the votes for and the votes withheld. In Canada, most companies report the votes for and the votes withheld, which, taken together, are the nominator for calculating the attendance. A number of these Canadian companies have issued classes of shares with different voting rights. In such cases, the results reflect the total number of participating voting rights, taking into account the differences in voting rights in both nominator and denominator. In Japanese companies, it is common to obtain one voting right per share unit. A unit of shares combines a number of shares, often 100 shares. Therefore, the total number of voting rights is only a fraction of the total number of issued shares.

22.2.2 *Voter Turnout in Nineteen Jurisdictions*

The shareholder participating rates in Table 22.1 show significant differences between jurisdictions and lower intra-country differences over time. Shareholders of American companies show the greatest interest in voting: the average attendance is close to 90 per cent and has remained stable over time. Low participation rates are unknown in American shareholder meetings, with a standard deviation of less than 4 per cent and an absolute minimal participation in a meeting over the five years of 72 per cent. In Asian jurisdictions, including India, Indonesia and Taiwan, the average attendance rates range from 80 to 90 per cent, and have also remained stable over time. However, the differences between AGMs in these jurisdictions are much higher than in the USA, with standard deviations of approximately 8 per cent and minimum attendance rates between 50 and 60 per cent. Significantly lower attendance rates can be found in China, Norway, Germany and Denmark, although in the latter two jurisdictions the averages increased by more than 5 per cent between 2016 and 2020, the largest growth in any of the jurisdictions covered. This increase also conceals large differences between the jurisdictions. Standard deviations of more than fifteen per cent have been found for several years. In Norway, for example, the company NEL ASA experienced a dramatic decrease in the willingness of its

[2] The participation data for the European companies, with the exception of the Norwegian and Greek companies, were taken from the study of Georgeson, *Georgeson's 2020 AGM Season Review* (2020) 145.

[3] The listing rules of the Hong Kong stock exchange specifically provide for how to address abstentions (see Rule 13.40).

shareholders to participate in meetings. The participation rate dropped from 46 per cent in 2016 to 16 per cent in 2019, and to only 7 per cent in 2020. The largest shareholder, which was only a small shareholder in 2018 and was not present in the disclosed shareholder base before 2018, build up a 35 per cent voting stake at the start of 2020 to more than 43 per cent at the end of 2020.[4] Consequently, the finding shows that this shareholder did not participate (with its full stake) in the meeting. There may be idiosyncratic reasons for such a situation. Chinese companies also experience low participation rates, especially of minority shareholders. As large(st) shareholders, the government or governmental agencies often own a substantive voting stake and the remaining shares are generally widely distributed in the market. As a result, the position of institutional investors is weaker than in many other countries,[5] and the overall participation of minority shareholders is very low.[6] These (anecdotal) findings raise the question as to why the mean participating rate differs approximately by 30 per cent between the highest mean of the USA and the lowest mean of Norway and China. Why does the willingness of shareholders to attend meetings differ so markedly in the jurisdictions in this study? In the Law & Finance literature, it is argued that the legal origin, and in particular the common law versus civil law origin, affects different corporate governance issues. In particular, higher share ownership concentration levels are found in jurisdictions with weaker shareholder protection rights, especially civil law jurisdictions. Accumulating more shares offers the shareholders an adequate countervailing power for the absence of sufficient shareholder protection.[7] The dichotomy of the common legal system and the civil legal system as identified in the Law & Finance literature, was not found in our data on shareholder voting. Canada, Australia, the UK and other common law jurisdictions display participation rates that are in line with many civil law jurisdictions, while Indonesia (a civil law country) and Taiwan (whose legal system is based on German law) achieve shareholder attendance close to that of the United States. Our data do not reveal any causes for those differences and it is likely that different reasons coexist. Below, some of these reasons are outlined.

First, different shareholder classes seem to behave differently in their participation in meetings. Institutional shareholders show greater willingness to participate in meetings, partly because there are several mandatory voting requirements or fiduciary duties for these types of shareholders.[8] As a large majority of the shares of US companies belongs to institutional shareholders, the participation rates of US companies are high(er). Chinese institutional investors, by contrast, are not required to vote, and our data show that they commonly shy away from voting, resulting in lower participation rates. Second, very small shareholders lack incentives for any kind of active engagement in the company in which they invest, even for low-cost voting engagement. For instance, in the Australian financial institution Westpac Banking,

4 The ownership data are taken from the different annual reports of the company https://nelhydrogen.com/investor-relations/ accessed 15 July 2020.

5 See Adriana De La Cruz, Alejandra Medina and Yung Tang, *Owners of the World's Listed Companies* (OECD: Paris 2019), table 3.

6 Chao Xi, 'Shareholder Voting and Covid-19: the China Experience' (2021) 9 Chinese Journal of Comparative Law 125–56.

7 Rafael La Porta et al., 'Law and Finance' (1998) 106 Journal of Political Economy 1113–55; Rafael La Porta et al., 'Legal Determinants of External Finance' (1997) 52 Journal of Finance 1131–50. However these studies are also heavily criticized (see for example Sofie Cools, 'The Real Difference in Corporate Law between the United States and Continental Europe: Distribution of Powers' (2005) 30 Delaware Journal of Corporate Law 697), whilst other studies have shown that these differences, if any, diminished over time (Priya Lele and Mathias Siems, 'Shareholder Protection: a Leximetric Approach' (2007) 7 Journal of Corporate Law Studies 17; Dionysia Katelouzou and Mathias Siems, 'Disappearing Paradigms in Shareholder Protection: Leximetric Evidence for 30 Countries, 1990–2013' (2015) 15 Journal of Corporate Law Studies 127).

8 For a detailed analysis of the American situation, see Yaron Nili and Kobi Kastiel, 'In Search of "Absent" Shareholders: A New Solution to Retail Investors' Apathy' (2016) 41 Delaware Journal of Corporate Law 55, 61. Also see Chapter 21.

87 per cent of all shareholders hold fewer than 1,000 shares and only 10 shareholders own more than 100,000 shares, of the over 14 million issued shares in October 2020. The December 2020 AGM welcomed shareholders holding approximately 46 per cent of the shares, showing that a large share of the minority shareholders do not exercise their voting rights. At the Australian real estate company Vicinity Centres, 75 per cent of the shareholders held up to 10,000 shares, and 303 shareholders owned more than 100,000 shares of the 4.5 billion shares issued in 2020, and the AGM participation passed 80 per cent of all issued shares. Hence, holding more shares heightens willingness to participate, as this anecdotic finding shows.[9] According to a study of Lafarre, in most Western European countries small(er) shareholders vote less than half of their shares and according to a study of Xi, small shareholders in Chinese companies vote less than 10 per cent of their shares.[10] Conversely, large and controlling shareholders are seldom absent from GMs. Our Indian data show that the 'promotor' (founders) of the company always participates in the meeting. Further, shareholders' participation behaviour can also be negatively affected by the (changes in) the behaviour and stakes of the other (major) shareholdings. In France, a number of companies switched from the one-share-one-vote (OSOV) structure to a structure with double voting rights in 2016 (loyalty shares or tenure shares, see Chapter 21, Section 22.5.2). Consequently, the major shareholder, which is often the French State, gained double voting rights in 2016 and continued to participate in the AGMs with a significantly large voting block. However, these loyalty shares resulted in lower participation by other shareholders not holding tenure shares in a number of companies.[11] Hence, the potential gains of participation dropped as the likelihood that their voting behaviour could affect the outcome of the voting items decreased.

Another set of arguments that can help to explain various differences between the participation rates of shareholders relates to the role of the (A)GM. First, in some jurisdictions, the role of the general meeting is relatively modest. The statutory laws of many jurisdictions limit the power of the general meeting to well-defined items and allocate all residual powers to the board of directors. As a result, few items remain to be approved by the shareholders.[12] The common agenda of the meetings of US companies includes (1) the ratification of the approval of the external auditor, (2) the election of the board members and (3) a say-on-pay vote. At Japanese meetings, the approval of dividend distribution and the election of the (audit and supervisory) board members are common agenda items. Participating shareholders of French companies commonly, and on top of the aforementioned US agenda items, have to approve (either because this is required by law or as a matter of common practice) the financial statements, the consolidated financial statements, related party agreements, the remuneration report (and regularly the remuneration policy), the share buy back, and the authorization for executing all formalities. This means that there are often more than fifteen agenda items at French AGMs.[13] This shows a clear diversity in the importance and the role of the general meeting, and may affect the readiness of shareholders in voicing their shares.

The agenda topics not only diverge between jurisdictions but also between companies in a single jurisdiction, as items that the shareholders must approve, such as modifications to the articles of association, occur at different times. For instance, the analysis of the use of e-voting at

9 However, the difference in the denominator requires a more cautious interpretation.

10 Anne Lafarre, *The AGM in Europe* (Emerald Publishing 2017) 113; Xi (n. 6).

11 See Chapter 14.

12 In some countries, many discretionary powers are allocated in corporate documents, such as bylaws, charters and articles of association.

13 Chapter 14, Section 14.4.6.

ten Indian companies shows that shareholders of the Indian company TCS had to vote for three resolutions, while shareholders of another Indian firm, ITC, could (dis)approve twelve agenda items.[14] This issue of divergence is provoked even further in the organization of general meetings itself. While the legal system in some jurisdictions allows the general meeting to table special items like amendments to the articles of association or the corporate charter, other (statutory) laws request separate, special or extraordinary general meetings (EGMs) to deal with these items. For these meetings different rules apply, such as different quorum requirements.[15] Consequently, the composition of the agenda likely affects the shareholder's willingness to participate. The data in Table 22.1 focus on the AGMs and do not refer to the participation rates of EGMs or special meetings.[16]

A third set of reasons relates to the other functions of (A)GM, in addition to the decision-making function.[17] The general meeting serves as a platform for discussion with the board of directors and other shareholders and nearly always offers shareholders the opportunity to ask questions and comment on the directors, the forum function.[18] Next, the board of directors informs the shareholders on the financial results of the company, its ambitions for the future and (increasingly) on non-financial information and environmental, social and governance (ESG) related issues, the information function. These two other functions can affect the eagerness of, especially smaller, shareholders to attend and vote at the AGM. Yet, the latter function has lost much of its importance, as the information must be provided long before the meeting takes place, allowing shareholders to prepare in advance and largely preventing any abusive use of inside information. Moreover, (statutory and soft) corporate law and corporate governance offer other engagement tools to (small) shareholders and companies. For instance, it is common knowledge that companies connect with shareholders via roadshows, investor conferences, one-on-one meetings, and shareholder clubs, to name but a few. Shareholders as well as companies can prefer to express their views through these mechanisms instead of voicing their support or discontent, especially when companies promote the use of these other instruments as alternatives to discussion at the AGM. Section 22.4 provides more information about the use of different shareholder engagement tools in the various jurisdictions.

The ease with which shareholders voice their votes could also affect their willingness to do so. Many legal systems allow for remote voting or the use of proxies, offering shareholders the opportunity to conveniently participate in meetings taking place simultaneously, something which was not possible in 'the old days'. Many shareholders, especially institutional investors, nowadays make use of remote voting. For instance, data for France and India show that a large

14 Chapter 4. The participation of shareholders in the AGM of TCS was higher than in that of ITC. In both cases all agenda items were approved with very low opposition rates.

15 See Chapter 21, Section 21.3. There is not much information on the participation of shareholders in EGMs. According to the study of the Danish extraordinary meetings, the participating level is, if anything, lower during these meetings (Chapter 13, Section 13.3.1.1). This confirms the findings of an older study of Belgian ordinary and extraordinary meetings (Christoph Van der Elst, *Aandeelhouderschap van beursgenoteerde vennootschappen* (Larcier 2001) 218–19). These results come as a surprise, as the significance of the items addressed in these meetings, often changes of the articles of association, might have been expected to increase the willingness of the shareholders to vote.

16 Different kinds of special meetings exist. When the French company Alstom wanted to abolish its loyal double voting right system in 2020, it called a special meeting for shareholders that hold double voting rights. In 2018 Hellenic Petroleum called a special meeting exclusively for its minority shareholders, allowing them to elect two directors pursuant to its articles of association. In 2019 the German BMW held a separate meeting for its preferred shareholders before issuing non-voting preferred stock.

17 Anne Lafarre, *The AGM in Europe* (Emerald Publishing, 2017) 7.

18 See Section 22.4.

majority of the votes are remotely issued.[19] Similarly, electronic voting has been required for Chinese listed companies since 2014. It seems to have stimulated a steady, albeit modest, rise in shareholder turnout in the CSI-300 firms.[20]

In short, the divergence in participation rates of shareholders can be explained by a large number of reasons, related to the legal system, the company, shareholder types, common governance practices and the role and position of the general meeting itself. Finally, it should be noted that our data show that Covid-19 generally had no major effect on the willingness of shareholders to participate. Whilst hybrid meetings and virtual meetings quickly surged in importance, in half of the jurisdictions there was a slight increase in the mean participation rate in 2020, while in the other half there was a modest decrease.

22.3 VOTING ITEMS AND OUTCOMES

In this section we study how shareholders voted for the various (common) agenda items at AGMs. The first subsection addresses the election of the board of directors. Say-on-pay votes are studied in practice in the second subsection, as these voting items usually receive a lot of attention. Finally, subsection 22.3.3 provides a comparative numerical overview of the other common (and uncommon) voting items.

22.3.1 *The Corporate Board*

The board of directors is responsible for the business and the affairs of the company, and it should take care of the value creation of the company. As such, the board of directors, and its members, play a pivotal role in the company's operations, and its composition is considered a key element in corporate governance. The UK Corporate Governance Code 2018 starts by enunciating the following principle: 'a successful company is led by an effective and entrepreneurial board, whose role is to promote the long-term sustainable success of the company, generating value for shareholders and contributing to wider society'.[21] As Chapter 21 illustrates, the shareholders play an important role in the election and removal of directors. In all jurisdictions in our study, the (A)GM elects (part of) the (supervisory) board members. Therefore, we study how shareholders in the AGM vote for the directors in the different jurisdictions. The results are summarized in Table 22.3 below.

The methodology for calculating the (dis)approval rates for the election of directors is straightforward. The nominator contains all the votes of shares of participating shareholders that voted in favor of the election of the director(s). The denominator is either the total number of all votes of the shares of the participating shareholders or the total number of votes 'for' and the total number of votes 'against' the election. In some jurisdictions and companies the votes from abstaining shareholders are not considered as votes, and thus do not have to be taken into account in the calculation of the approval rate. In Hong Kong and Singapore, abstentions are not reported. The French legislature excluded abstentions from the calculation of majorities during our research period, in 2019.[22]

19 In France votes by mail represented on average almost 60 per cent of the participating votes, see Chapter 14, Section 14.4.4. In India, e-voting accounted for 85 to 94 per cent of all the votes cast between 2016 and 2019, see Chapter 4, Section 4.3.3.1.

20 See Chapter 2.

21 Financial Reporting Council, *The UK Corporate Governance Code* (Financial Reporting Council 2018) 4.

22 See article 16 of the Loi n° 2019–744 du 19 juillet 2019 de simplification, de clarification et d'actualisation du droit des sociétés, *Official Journal* nr. 167 of 20 July 2019.

In the USA and Canada, plurality voting for directors is often applied (see Chapters 11, 12 and 21). In uncontested elections, this means that a shareholder can either vote 'for' the director or withhold her vote, but is not permitted to vote against the nominee.[23] If one shareholder votes for the nominee, the candidate is elected. In these cases, the results for board elections are calculated as the votes for this director to the sum of the votes for and withheld, without taking into account broker non-votes.[24]

Currently, the plurality system thus still provokes different election outcomes than a majority vote (used in most other jurisdictions). According to the minutes of Netflix's 2020 AGM, one director was elected with 45.2 per cent of the votes in favour and 54.8 per cent of the votes withheld. As the nominees with the three highest affirmative votes were elected and only three directors were eligible, all three directors (including the director with a majority of the votes withheld) were elected. Further, 12.7 per cent were broker non-votes.[25] While more and more majority voting takes place in US companies,[26] the US majority voting system does not automatically result in an outcome similar to that seen in many other jurisdictions, namely that only nominees that are supported by a majority of the votes cast will become director. At Abiomed, a US company that applies the majority voting rule, one director received at the 2018 general meeting only 30.5 per cent 'for' votes of the participating shareholders (considered for the quorum which includes the broker non-votes), and only 25.8 per cent of the affirmative votes of the shareholders (indicating that 74.2 per cent of the votes were withheld). Consequently, the director 'must tender a conditional offer of resignation subject to acceptance or rejection by the Company's Board of Directors'.[27] As the director was listed as a board member in the 2018 annual report of the company, it appears that the board of Abiomed rejected the director's conditional offer of resignation, notwithstanding the majority votes against his re-election.

In Taiwan and Mainland China, cumulative voting is used in elections. The approval rates for director elections in systems that apply cumulative voting differ substantially from the systems that make use of majority voting. Consequently, those results are not presented in Table 22.3. Table 22.2a and Table 22.2b provide illustrations respectively of cumulative voting in Taiwan for the Taiwanese company Uni-President Enterprises Corporation, and of cumulative voting in China for the Chinese company Hubei Yangfan Holding in 2019. The cumulative number of shareholder votes is equal to the number of board positions multiplied by the votes that the shareholders hold. The directors are elected in a single voting round, resulting in an approval rate for the first director significantly exceeding 100 per cent, as both Tables illustrate. All the directors of the Taiwanese company were elected, but not all the directors of the Chinese company.

23 For the USA this is further specified in SEC rule 14a-4(b). For an overview of the different options that US companies can use, see Steven Stokdyk and Joel Trotter, 'Proxy Disclosure Recommendations' (2016) Harvard Law School Forum of Corporate Governance https://corpgov.law.harvard.edu/2016/03/14/proxy-disclosure-recommendations/ accessed 21 March 2021.

24 Most of the shares of US companies are held through brokers, and many of the investors do not instruct the brokers how to vote the shares. Previously, the brokers were voting these uninstructed voting rights. In 2012, the NYSE changed this system and for routine matters brokers' discretionary votes are no longer taken into account. Hirst showed that this regulatory move had an impact on the outcome of the votes (Scott Hirst, 'Frozen Charters' (2017) 34 Yale Journal on Regulation 91).

25 If 83 per cent of the latter broker non-votes would have voted for the director, he would have received the majority of the participating votes. The shares connected to the broker non-votes are taking into account for the quorum requirements.

26 Institutional investors' dissatisfaction about plurality voting and its outcomes has caused most large companies to opt out of this default voting rule in Delaware. See Stephen J. Choi et al., 'Does Majority Voting Improve Board Accountability?' (2016) 83 University of Chicago Law Review 1119–80.

27 Abiomed, *Form 8-K*, 8 August 2018, 2.

TABLE 22.2A *Election of board members at Uni-President Enterprises in 2019*

Director (anonymized)	number of votes	participating votes	approval	elected
Director 1	6,667,986,383	4,882,819,748	136.6%	Yes
Director 2	4,164,012,277	4,882,819,748	85.3%	Yes
Director 3	3,487,029,859	4,882,819,748	71.4%	Yes
Director 9	3,144,439,160	4,882,819,748	64.4%	Yes
Director 8	3,105,981,847	4,882,819,748	63.6%	Yes
Director 4	3,073,805,929	4,882,819,748	62.9%	Yes
Director 5	3,066,382,815	4,882,819,748	62.8%	Yes
Director 10	3,018,226,251	4,882,819,748	61.8%	Yes
Director 6	3,017,926,222	4,882,819,748	61.8%	Yes
Director 7	2,889,290,264	4,882,819,748	59.2%	Yes
Independent director 1	6,402,212,455	4,882,819,748	131.1%	Yes
Independent director 2	6,002,065,924	4,882,819,748	122.9%	Yes
Independent director 3	2,164,094,688	4,882,819,748	44.3%	Yes

Source: minutes of the meeting of 18 June 2019 of Uni-President Enterprises.

TABLE 22.2B *Election of board members at Hubei Yangfan Holding in January 2019*

Director (anonymized)	number of votes	participating votes	approval	elected
Director 1	137,546,512	119,992,832	114.6%	Yes
Director 2	137,275,315	119,992,832	114.4%	Yes
Director 3	12,116,893	119,992,832	10.1%	No
Director 4	10,449,790	119,992,832	8.7%	No
Director 5	21,001	119,992,832	0.02%	No
Director 6	84,457,981	119,992,832	70.3%	Yes
Director 7	0	119,992,832	0.0%	No
Director 8	84,457,980	119,992,832	70.3%	Yes
Independent director 1	106,094,279	119,992,832	88.4%	Yes
Independent director 2	105,918,282	119,992,832	88.3%	Yes
Independent director 3	11,956,490	119,992,832	10.0%	No
Independent director 4	1	119,992,832	0.0%	No
Independent director 5	128,486,970	119,992,832	107.1%	Yes
Independent director 6	0	119,992,832	0.0%	No

Source: minutes of the meeting of January 2019 of Hubei Yangfan Holding.

In Table 22.3, the election of two types of boards are distinguished for Japan and the Netherlands. Section 22.4.1 of Chapter 21 outlines that in the Netherlands, companies can select a one-tier or a two-tier board structure since 2012. However, the two-tier board is most commonly selected, allowing shareholders to often elect both the supervisory and the management board members.[28] In Japan, the executive board and the audit and supervisory board are elected by the shareholders.[29] Other jurisdictions have also adopted a two-tier board structure or hybrid structure, including Germany, Italy, Norway and Indonesia. However, in Germany, the supervisory board elects the management board, and therefore, only the election of the supervisory

[28] See Chapter 19, Section 19.1.2.
[29] See Chapter 6.

board members is included in Table 22.3. The common Italian board structure is a board of directors and a board of statutory auditors.[30] In Indonesia, both the members of the board of commissioners as well as the members of the board of directors are elected simultaneously in a single voting round. In Norway, in the default regime, the (A)GM elects a general assembly that in turn appoints the board of directors. However, many Norwegian companies have made special arrangements and opted for a one-tier board structure: the data in Table 22.3 below illustrate the election of the board members in the one-tier board structure.

In a number of jurisdictions, including Denmark, Norway, Germany and France, other stakeholders (in particular employees) have the right of representation on the (supervisory) board of directors. In Germany and Denmark, the (A)GM does not approve the election of the employee representatives, whereas the French general meeting approves the election of those representatives up to the number of representatives that the law prescribes. If more employee representatives are presented to the general meeting, there is majority support for only those employees necessary to meet the required number of members. As an illustration, during the AXA 2020 AGM, shareholders approved the election of one director representing the employees with over 98 per cent of the votes, and rejected the election of six other nominees representing the employees with rejection rates of 97 to 99.5 per cent of the votes. A similar result can be found for the employee-shareholders presenting two nominees to the board of Cap Gemini at the 2020 AGM. One nominee was elected with 99 per cent approval, while the other was rejected with 92 per cent of the votes. Obviously, these different approaches influence our reported voting results.

Exceptionally, other parties can also enjoy special representation rights. The Norwegian company Schibsted provides a special representation right for the major shareholder that directly appointed its representative in the board of directors.[31] According to the Articles of Association of the Greek company Eydap, controlled by the Greek state, the minority shareholders have the right to elect two board members in a special minority shareholders' meeting called by the Board of Directors.[32]

More generally, the Italian legislature has provided a specific minority protection mechanism via a system of slate voting (*Voto di Lista*, see Section 21.5.3 of Chapter 21). This rule holds that minority shareholders passing a certain threshold can provide a list of board nominees. At least one nominee will be selected from the list that received the second highest number of votes. The election of the board of directors of Unicredit at its 2018 AGM illustrates the functioning of this special voting mechanism in practice. In total, 15 board members were to be elected, and 2,200 shareholders holding 1.3 billion shares and votes supported the list with the board nominees, suggested by the departing board of directors. Yet, a group of institutional investors holding 1.6 per cent of the shares of the company presented a second list of director nominees, and 295 shareholders holding 100 million shares voted in favour of this second list of nominees.[33] As the articles of association of Unicredit provide that two minority shareholders directors will be part of the board, two nominees on the second list were considered elected next to the thirteen directors on the first list.[34]

30 See Chapter 17. The chapter provides insights into the election of members of the board of statutory auditors. However, the results are based on another method and cannot be compared with the other data in Table 22.3.

31 Article 8 of the articles of association of Schibsted.

32 See article 11 and 36 of Eydap's articles of association.

33 The institutional investors presenting the second list of board nominees held together only 36 million shares. Consequently, a large number of other shareholders supported the second list.

34 Data derived from the company documents of Unicredit (see www.unicreditgroup.eu/content/dam/unicreditgroup-eu/documents/en/governance/shareholders-meetings/archive/2018/agm-12-april-2018/List-no.-2–documentation.pdf accessed 15 March 2021).

The United Kingdom has introduced a majority of minority rule for the election of independent directors of controlled companies (UK FCA Handbook LR 9.2.2E, also see Section 21.5.3 of Chapter 21). The nominee must not only be approved by the majority of the votes of all participating shareholders, but also by a majority of the votes of the participating minority shareholders. The independent shareholders are those that are not the controlling shareholder, meaning 'any person who exercises or controls on their own or together with any person with whom they are acting in concert, 30% or more of the votes able to be cast on all or substantially all matters at general meetings of the company'. Only a handful companies in the FTSE-100 have a controlling shareholder. For those companies, unsurprisingly, the votes in favour of the independent shareholders are lower than the voting results including those of the controlling shareholder.[35] India has also recently introduced a similar system for the election of independent directors.[36] Note that, for comparative reasons, Table 22.3 only presents the overall shareholder approval rates, not those of the 'independent' shareholders only.

TABLE 22.3 *Average approval rates for board nominees*

	2016	2017	2018	2019	2020	all
Australia	97.2	97.0	96.7	95.4	95.9	96.4
Canada	97.2	97.3	97.5	97.2	97.0	97.2
China			cumulative voting (bifurcated)			
Denmark	100	99.8	100	100	100	99.9
France	95.7	94.6	93.7	94.8	90.9	94.0
Germany*	93.0	93.6	96.5	92.9	93.7	94.0
Greece	88.7	84.9	85.3	88.3	90.5	87.0
Hong Kong	99.4	94.4	94.6	94.2	93.3	94.1
India		95.6	94.9	94.3	96.2	95.2
Indonesia	85.3	89.4	90.8	90.8	90.3	89.9
Italy	92.0	94.5	95.1	91.5	97.1	94.0
Japan Board	96.6	96.1	96.3	96.0	96.2	96.2
Japan Audit&Sup.	94.5	94.1	95.7	96.5	96.0	95.5
Netherlands MB[37]	98.6	98.8	99.3	99.0	98.1	98.7
Netherlands SB[38]	99.0	96.2	96.4	98.2	96.6	97.1
Norway	99.8	98.7	97.8	97.2	95.1	97.2
Singapore	97.8	97.5	98.0	96.9	96.1	97.2
South Korea	97.2	98.4	95.7	92.7	96.0	95.3
Taiwan			cumulative voting			
UK	98.6	98.2	97.9	98.2	98.4	98.3
US	97.2	97.1	97.1	96.7	96.5	96.9

Source: hand-collected data for Greece, Hong Kong, India, Indonesia, Norway (2020), Singapore, China and South Korea, calculations based on the Proxy Insight database for Australia, Canada, Denmark, France, Germany, Italy, Japan, the Netherlands, Norway, UK and USA; *: the difference with the data provided in Chapter 15 is due to the continued update of the database Proxy Insight.

35 A good example is provided by Associated British Food, a company that has Wittington Investments Limited, itself controlled by a family foundation, as a controlling shareholder holding close to 60 per cent of the shares and voting rights. The company holds double voting rounds. During the general meeting of 2016 to 2020, twenty-three (re-)elections took place. The AGM approved all (re-)elections of the independent directors with an average affirmative vote of 98.4 per cent. The non-controlling shareholders approved all independent candidates with an average approval rate of 95.3 per cent.

36 See Chapter 4.

37 Management Board in a two-tier structure.

38 Supervisory Board in a two-tier structure.

The results in Table 22.3 show that in all but two jurisdictions the average approval rates for the members of the board of directors exceed 90 per cent. Only in Greece, with an average opposition rate of 13 per cent, and Indonesia, with an average of slightly over 10 per cent, did a significant proportion of shareholders raise concerns. A common feature of those two jurisdictions are the *combined director elections*: all Indonesian companies (re-)elect the directors and commissioners simultaneously in a single voting round. Any discontent with the proposed board composition can only be signalled with a vote against all members that stand for (re-)election, while in other jurisdictions shareholder opposition against the (re-)election of a director can be specifically addressed in a vote against her (re-)election. The Indonesian approach may negatively affect the average voting results for the election of directors. It is a regular practice in Greece for shareholders to (re-)elect directors in a single round. Eight general meetings of six Greek companies offered the (re-)elections of two to all directors as a single voting item which resulted in an average opposition of 11.2 per cent, negatively affecting the overall average of the (re-)election of board members in Greek companies. In Norway too it is a common practice to (re-)elect all directors with one vote. This happened in almost half of the meetings in 2020 of Norwegian companies and resulted in an average approval rate of 92.9 per cent, while individual (re-)elections received on average 95.6 per cent approval rates.

Conversely, Danish board members experience the least opposition. The overall average approval rates are close to 100 per cent, and more than 90 per cent of all the directors that were presented to the shareholders were unanimously (re-)elected. However, as in several other jurisdictions, Danish law does not consider an abstention to be a vote in law. This may explain these high approval rates, as many shareholders of Danish companies, in some cases up to 30 per cent of all the votes, abstained from voting. The mean approval rate would be around 97.5 per cent if abstentions were included in the denominator, closer to the average in many other jurisdictions.

In all other jurisdictions, the average approval rates of board nominees are both relatively fixed over time as well as stable between the jurisdictions. Opposition rates vary from less than 2 per cent in the UK to just over 6 per cent in France, Germany and Italy. Overall, it looks as if the candidates are screened appropriately before being presented to the shareholders.

However, the mean approval rates presented in Table 22.3 can hide significant individual differences. Table 22.4 below visualizes the dispersion of the director elections in the different jurisdictions, taking into account the frequencies of some 'standard' ranges of dissent rates, which best practice provisions recommend companies to respond to.[39] For comparative reasons, this table contains the ratios of the votes 'for' to the votes 'for', 'against' and 'abstain', with the exception of the data for Hong Kong and Singapore, where the number of abstentions is not disclosed.

Very few nominees received a majority of votes against, and in light of the inclusion of the abstentions in Table 22.4, the number of effectively 'rejected' board nominees is even lower (as many jurisdictions do not consider an abstention as a vote). In the sample of over 50,000 board elections, only 23 directors received a majority of dissenting votes. In most jurisdictions, candidates are always appointed and never rejected (at least not in the period 2016 to 2020, and for the companies in the sample).

Significant opposition is more common in a number of jurisdictions. In Greece and Indonesia, a large group of (supervisory) board nominees received a compelling number of

[39] See the 20 per cent threshold in Provision 4 of the Principles regarding board leadership and company purpose in the UK Corporate Governance Code (Financial Reporting Council, *The UK Corporate Governance Code* (Financial Reporting Council 2018), 5).

TABLE 22.4 *Dispersion of approval rates of board nominees (2016–20)*

	100%	90%–99%	80%–90%	50%–80%	<50%
Australia	0.0%	88.1%	7.2%	4.5%	0.2%
Canada	2.6%	90.3%	4.9%	2.2%	0.0%
Denmark	3.0%	89.6%	6.1%	0.9%	0.4%
France	0.1%	80.7%	14.1%	5.1%	0.0%
Germany	0.0%	79.2%	14.4%	6.4%	0.0%
Greece	2.1%	48.6%	19.4%	29.2%	0.7%
HK	0.4%	81.1%	9.1%	9.3%	0.0%
Indonesia	8.1%	54.6%	12.8%	24.4%	0.0%
Italy	1.6%	71.1%	19.8%	7.4%	0.0%
Japan	0.0%	90.4%	7.5%	2.1%	0.01%
Netherlands MB	1.0%	98.9%	0.0%	0.0%	0.0%
Netherlands SB	3.2%	86.2%	9.0%	1.6%	0.0%
Norway	18.2%	74.4%	5.8%	1.6%	0.0%
Singapore	0.8%	94.0%	3.3%	1.9%	0.0%
S-Korea	0.5%	85.1%	9.8%	4.2%	0.5%
UK	0.9%	94.9%	3.5%	0.6%	0.02%
US	0.2%	93.6%	3.9%	2.3%	0.06%
Total	0.8%	91.4%	5.3%	2.5%	0.04%

Source: hand-collected data for Greece, Indonesia, Norway (2020), Singapore and South Korea, calculations based on the Proxy Insight database for Australia, Canada, Denmark, France, Germany, Hong Kong, Italy, Japan, the Netherlands, Norway, UK and USA.

dissenting votes. The 'collective' election process in these jurisdictions can at least partially explain this high number of dissenting votes, although in Norway, where 'grouped' elections are also common practice, significant opposition is lower. As the first table in Chapter 21 shows, ownership concentration is significant in the former two jurisdictions, and many companies are majority controlled. As it is likely that the majority shareholder participated in the general meeting and supported the election of the nominees, minority shareholder opposition must have been fierce.

In other jurisdictions high levels of dissenting votes are more company or director specific. Many shareholders of the Canadian company Kirkland Lake Gold voted against the re-election of one of its directors, as the board member was considered to be 'overboarded' and some shareholders doubted his independence.[40] A more company-oriented argument for voting against the re-election of a board member is illustrated by the case of the Dutch company Corbion. When the remuneration committee approved a special transaction bonus for its CEO, dissatisfied shareholders voted against the re-election of one of the members of this committee.[41]

In France, Germany, Greece and Italy, modest opposition of 10 to 20 per cent of the votes against the (re-)election of directors is common. Our data does not provide any evidence as to why this modest opposition is part of the voting process in continental European jurisdictions. Directors are hardly ever considered as the best choice by all the shareholders. With the exception of Norway, where many directors are unanimously approved, directors tend to be

40 See for the voting rationale of NN North America Fund, one of the shareholders that voted against the re-election of the director https://viewpoint.glasslewis.net/webdisclosure/FundList.aspx?RestorePreviousState=false accessed 15 March 2021.

41 Christoph Van der Elst and Anne Lafarre, 'Shareholder Voice on Executive Pay: A Decade of Dutch Say on Pay' 2017 (18) European Business Organization Law Review 51, 77.

elected or re-elected by a very large majority of the shareholder community, but a number of small shareholders always oppose any and every nominee.

The election term seems to have no effect on the approval rates. In the US and the UK, it is a common practice to (re-)elect the members of the board at every general meeting. In many other jurisdictions (e.g. France), directors can serve for up to six years, but the latter term is uncommon in practice. Election for a term of three to four years election terms is normal in many other jurisdictions, but there are also many companies that deviate from these practices, depending on specific features, including for instance the types of directors that stand for (re-) election.

Finally, voting for the removal of an elected director is very rare. As there are no data of voting for the removal of the directors in our sample, it is understood that directors resign from office or the term ends, which is commonly implicitly approved with the election of a new board member.

22.3.2 *Executive Remuneration*

Since the publication of the first UK corporate governance code, the 1992 Cadbury Code, remuneration of directors and executive officers has become a key topic in debates on governance. Since executive pay, according to the managerial power theory,[42] also contributes to corporate governance problems, the focus of the debate has shifted to the involvement and role of the shareholders in establishing and approving the remuneration of the directors and executive officers.

In almost all jurisdictions, shareholders have obtained some kind of say-on-pay right, although, as can be seen in Table 22.5 below, the kind of say-on-pay right they enjoy can vary considerably.[43] As an exception, shareholders of Indian companies do not (regularly) vote on any item related to board and executive remuneration. In India, there are specific legal rules as to executive pay, which must not exceed 11 per cent of the net profits of the company in a financial - year.[44] Shareholders of French, Greek, Italian, Japanese, Norwegian, Dutch and UK companies regularly vote on four or five items related to executive or (supervisory) board pay. Shareholders of Australian and US companies regularly vote on an executive pay related instrument which is unique.[45]

Shareholders vote on any kind of equity-based compensation in many jurisdictions. In almost all jurisdictions, the board of directors must obtain shareholder approval for launching a stock compensation plan or any kind of equity-based plan for executive directors/officers. The requirement for obtaining shareholder approval generally follows from the general right of shareholders to vote on any amendment of the share capital, including an equity based (stock option) plan.

Voting items related to executive compensation plans regularly show significant shareholder opposition rates, as Table 22.5 shows. In Canada, Greece, Hong Kong, Indonesia, Taiwan and the Netherlands, the mean dissent exceeds 10 per cent. In China, by contrast, opposition to an equity plan is almost unknown, as evidenced by a mean approval rate of more than 99 per cent.

42 See, for an extensive discussion of the managerial power theory, Lucian Bebchuk and Jesse Fried, *Pay without Performance* (Harvard University Press 2004).

43 See for a comparative overview of the types of say-on-pay, the terms as well as the advisory or mandatory nature of the vote, Section 21.4.3 of Chapter 21.

44 Shareholders can approve a deviation, but in our sample of observations, this seldom happens. See Chapter 4.

45 See infra in this section 'say-on-frequency'.

Very occasionally, in France, Australia and Singapore, shareholder dissent has resulted in a rejection of the equity plan. But this has happened in less than 1 per cent of the voted plans.

The frequency of approving these equity plans differs between jurisdictions. In France, Italy, Canada, China and Australia, it is common practice for AGMs to approve almost yearly some kind of equity plan. In the UK, the USA, Singapore and the Netherlands this also regularly occurs, although not annually, in Greece, Hong Kong, Indonesia, Norway, South Korea and Taiwan it is occasionally a voting item, and particularly in Denmark and Germany, the approval of equity-based plans are rare decisions for shareholders.

Next, also the approval of the remuneration package is a common voting item for shareholders in most jurisdictions, including in some of those for which no directly related data are shown in Table 22.5, where the shareholders still indirectly have some say over the remuneration package of the (executive) directors. In the UK and Italy, the remuneration of the directors is part of the remuneration report, and the shareholders of companies in these jurisdictions yearly approve the remuneration report, which recently became a voting item in almost all EU jurisdictions with the introduction of SRD II (see Section 22.4.3 of Chapter 21).

The rate of shareholder dissent regarding remuneration packages also differs between jurisdictions. Votes 'against' are negligible in the Netherlands, Norway, Singapore and Hong Kong, while shareholders of French companies and to a lesser extent shareholders of US companies often oppose the remuneration package with 20 per cent of the votes and more. The explanation partly lies in the differences in the voting item submitted for approval, and in the differences in the number of topics related to remuneration that shareholders can approve. In EU Member States it is common for shareholders to vote both for the remuneration policy and for the remuneration report (including the remuneration package), capturing the dissenting voice of the shareholders. In the US, the shareholders have a regular advisory 'say-on-pay' vote on the compensation the company pays to its named executives. This vote addresses the high end packages of top executives of American companies, and is frequently fiercely contested when shareholders consider the compensation to be out of line with the performance of the company. The US advisory say-on-pay vote for the remuneration package of executives is accompanied with a right for the shareholders to vote on the recurring approval term. This so called 'say-on-frequency' gives shareholders the right to vote on this remuneration issue annually, biennially or triennially. In our sample of all S&P 500 companies, shareholders always approved the proposal of the board, with an overwhelming majority of 99.5 per cent of the votes or more.

As in the USA, the French data concern the CEO remuneration packages – and sometimes the pay packages of other executives. This voting item relates to one of the few instances in our French (and in fact all jurisdictions) sample, where the board of directors advised the shareholders' meeting to vote against a corporate agenda item. A meeting of Renault's shareholders in 2019 voted against the CEO remuneration package on the board's recommendation (separating the roles of chairman and CEO), by a majority of nearly 90 percent. At the other end of this spectrum, say-on-pay votes in Hong Kong receive on average more than 99.5 per cent shareholder approval. This vote relates to the remuneration that the members of the board of directors receive, a modest amount compared to the executive pay packages that shareholders approve in the USA. Also in Norway, the compensation relates to the members of the board of directors for their work as board members, and in the Netherlands the remuneration of the non-executive supervisory board members receives approval rates of more than 99 per cent. Consequently, in our opinion, a better comparison between the executive pay voting results in the US and the remuneration report voting results in the Netherlands containing the remuneration packages of the management board, since the transposition of SRD II, can be made: this latter Dutch voting item also experiences significant shareholder dissent, with a mean dissenting rate of more than 10 per cent.

As in the USA, shareholders of a large majority of the Canadian companies are commonly offered a say-on-pay vote on executive compensation, as disclosed in the management proxy circular. Notwithstanding the advisory nature of this shareholder vote, in close to 1 per cent of all voting items in the period of 2016 to 2020, the shareholders' dissent exceeded the shareholders' consent, resulting in an average approval rate lower than in most other sampled jurisdictions.

Say-on-pay items in a European context nowadays refers to the approval of the remuneration policy and the remuneration report (SRD II, see Section 21.4.3 of Chapter 21). By 2020, all European jurisdictions had transposed the provisions of SRD II into their national laws, and with the exception of Germany (where determining the top executive remuneration stayed an important duty for the supervisory board), all European jurisdictions have chosen to apply a binding vote on remuneration policy and an advisory vote for the remuneration report. Both agenda items regularly experience significant opposition by the shareholders, as the mean results in Table 22.6 illustrate. For Germany, two results have been reported for the remuneration policy: before the transposition of SRD II, the German legislator already made available a voluntary advisory vote of the *remuneration system* and most of the large companies invited their shareholders to give their opinions on this.[46] It resulted in a limited number of rejections at some of the largest German companies, including Munich Re and Deutsche Bank, signalling major discontentment of the shareholders with a number of remuneration packages, and bringing the average approval rate of this system to a low of 79 per cent. In 2020, shareholders of German companies started to approve the remuneration policies, and approval rates fell into line with those in the other European jurisdictions.

As in the European jurisdictions where the remuneration report is now part of the recurring (advisory) voting items, shareholders of Australian companies have a yearly vote on the remuneration report, according to 250 R Australian CA.[47] Although advisory in nature, this vote can have major consequences if the remuneration report of the company receives more than 25 per cent dissenting votes of shareholders twice in a row, resulting in a spill resolution which may eventually result in a spill meeting (see Section 21.4.3 of Chapter 21). The effects of the two strikes rule have been investigated in a number of studies. One such study found for the period between 2011–14, 369 strikes for all listed Australian companies, namely 7 per cent of all remuneration report resolutions.[48] Strikes were found to decrease comparatively from 2011 to 2014 (102 in 2011 compared to 70 in 2014).[49] The authors observed that sixty companies faced a second strike during the same period: fifty-one of these companies disclosed the voting results of the spill resolution, while another twelve merely reported that the spill resolution had been passed. In turn, nine companies conducted spill meetings to re-elect their directors. A significant change in the board's composition after the spill meeting was observed in only one company.[50]

46 See for more information Chapter 15.

47 Section 300A Australian CA contains a detailed framework of the content of the remuneration report.

48 Martin Bugeja et al., 'Life after a Shareholder Pay "Strike": Consequences for ASX-Listed Firms', CIFR Paper No. 130/2016 (28 November 2016).

49 Although qualitatively similar, the numbers reported in this study differ somewhat from the numbers reported by Reza Monem and Chew Ng, 'Australia's "Two-Strikes" Rule and the Pay-Performance Link: Are Shareholders Judicious?' (2013) 9 Journal of Contemporary Accounting & Economics 237. For instance, these authors report 104 firms that received a first strike in 2011.

50 Bugeja et al. (n. 48).

One can conclude on such findings that the rule has an ex ante disciplining effect in comparison to the ex post impact.[51] Our data in this study confirm the trend first identified by Bugeja et al. We found several spill resolutions between 2016 and 2020, but only one was supported by a majority of the shareholders. The average approval rate of the spill resolutions was just over 15 per cent.[52] This indicates that views on the desirability of the two-strikes rule are still far apart.[53]

Finally, in some jurisdictions, companies regularly provide the shareholders with the right to vote on director's bonuses. We found six jurisdictions in our sample where the bonus was a recurring topic at general meetings, although the number of companies where this agenda item was scheduled was modest in most jurisdictions. In some jurisdictions, the dissent of shareholders was significant, but a bonus plan was only rejected outright in one Italian company.

It should be noted that not all remuneration items are addressed in Table 22.5, and in some jurisdictions specific regimes exist. As an example we refer to the Greek practices prior to the transposition of SRD II, to approve the remuneration of the board of directors of the last accounting period as well as the approval of the advanced payment of the remuneration for the current accounting period during which the general meeting took place.

22.3.3 *Other Common Agenda Items*

In addition to electing directors and casting say-on-pay votes, in many jurisdictions shareholders can also regularly vote on many other agenda items. Table 22.6 presents an overview of these different agenda items that company laws of several to all jurisdictions consider as important collective shareholder rights. Columns two to four of Table 22.6 specify the voting items, which are generally presented to the shareholders at every general meeting, while columns five to seven show the voting items which require shareholder approval, but only when the company wants to take specific action or requires amendments, for example, to the articles of association or corporate charter. In the next tables, agenda items that are common in a few or only one jurisdiction are presented.

In most jurisdictions, shareholders approve – although in different ways – the financial statements. Exceptions to this are some major common law jurisdictions, including the USA, Canada and Australia. In a number of jurisdictions, the financial statements are not approved, but (as in the UK) there is a shareholder vote on the reception of the financial statements, and the board of directors approves the financial statements. The legal consequences of the vote for the financial statements is not developed in all statutory laws, but in some jurisdictions like Indonesia, the vote on the annual report is combined with the discharge of both the board of directors and the board of commissioners for their (monitoring) duties. In other jurisdictions, the discharge of the directors is tabled as a separate agenda item.[54] In the Netherlands, the adoption of the financial statements is a prerequisite for the approval of a distribution of the profit. The approval of the financial statement incorporates the determination that this distribution is

[51] 'Consistent with the view that the "two-strikes" rule serves as a governance mechanism imposed by shareholder votes, we find Australian firms respond to negative say-on-pay votes by curbing excessive CEO pay, reducing the growth rate of pay and changing the pay mix' (Bugeja et al. (n. 48) 36).

[52] The number of spill votes is modest, but the number of strike votes has soared during the past few years (see Chapter 10, Section 10.3.1.2) and Lighthouse, *2019 AGM Season* (MorrowSodali 2019) 6–7.

[53] Patrick Durkin, 'Mortgage Choice CEO Slams "Ridiculous" Proxy Firms Amid AGM Pay Protest' *Financial Review* (18 October 2016) www.afr.com/business/banking-and-finance/mortgage-choice-ceo-slams-ridiculous-proxy-firms-amid-agm-pay-protest-20161017-gs4101 accessed 12 May 2019.

[54] See infra in this Section and Table 22.7.

TABLE 22.5 *Say-on-pay votes*

	Remuneration policy	Remuneration report	Remuneration package	Equity Based Plan/ Stock Purchase Plans	Bonus	Other issues
Australia		92.4	94.4	93.5		95.3+ / 15.2++
Canada			92.6	88.3		
China			99.2	99.1		
Denmark	90.2	99.5	93.7			
France	88.8	96.0	88.5	94.8		
Germany			98.4			
Greece	91.3	92.2	95.9	86.0	93.8	
HK			99.5	81.9		
India						
Indonesia			97.6	86.7		
Italy	92.3	89.1		91.9	92.2	
Japan			96.2* /97.5**	95.0	96.3	
Norway	93.6	98.9	99.4	96.1		
Singapore			99.7	90.2		
S-Korea			95.8	96.3		
Taiwan				80.1	87.9	
The Netherlands	92.0	89.6	99.2	85.2		
UK	91.9	92.6		95.6	96.2	
US			91.1	93.2	97.2	99.5***

+ severance pay; ++ spill vote; *: audit&supervisory board; ** board of directors; ***say-on-pay frequency.
Source: hand-collected data for China, Greece, Hong Kong, India, Indonesia, Norway, Singapore, South Korea and Taiwan, calculations based on the Proxy Insight database for Australia, Canada, Denmark, France, Germany, Italy, Japan, the Netherlands, UK and USA.

allowed.[55] In all but one jurisdiction, the adoption or approval of the financial statements met no significant shareholder dissent. Only some small shareholders opposed the adoption or approval, and significant opposition is very rare, resulting in homogenous voting turnouts with standard deviations of less than 2 per cent. In Taiwan, however, many financial statements received moderate opposition of more than 10 per cent, with a standard deviation of 5 per cent. It is unclear why the shareholders of Taiwanese companies are more prone to dissent than their counterparts elsewhere.

Similar results can be found for the approval of profit distribution. The distribution of the profit requires shareholder approval in an even larger number of jurisdictions than the adoption of the financial statements. In Germany and Japan, the shareholders also approve the allocation of the profits. In South Korea, the Companies Act allocates the power for the distribution of the profits to the general meeting of shareholders, but the companies combine the approval of the dividend with the approval of the financial statements.

In all jurisdictions in our sample, the AGM approves the distribution of the profit as presented in the notice of the meeting. The board of directors provides a distribution proposal, which the AGM either approves or disapproves. If the proposal is rejected, the board of directors considers a new distribution proposal.

55 The distribution of the profit is only allowed if the equity of the company passes certain thresholds (article 105 Book 2, Dutch Civil Code).

TABLE 22.6 *Voting results of other common agenda items*

	approval/receiving financial statement	profit allocation/ dividend	auditor election	amendment Articles of Association	issuance shares	share repurchase
Australia			99.1	96.4	97.3	
Canada			98.3	96.6	97.1	
China	99.6	99.5		98.9	98.2	99.9
Denmark	99.9	99.9	99.9	99.9	93.8	98.8
France	99.3	99.2	96.3	96.2	91.6	97.6
Germany		98.6	97.1	98.2	89.7	93.2
Greece	98.8	99.4	95.1	96.8	96.9	97.0
Hong Kong	>99.9	>99.9	99.2	99.9	80.3	99.9
India	99.5	99.9	96.1	99.7	95.2	
Indonesia	99.8	99.7	96.9	85.1		
Italy	99.9	99.8		98.4	95.6	93.4
Japan		98.9		99.0	96.0	96.1
Netherlands	99.8	99.6	99.4	98.5	92.2	98.7
Norway	>99.9	>99.9	99.6	99.7	97.3	98.4
Singapore	99.8	99.9	99.1	98.3	92.6	95.5
S-Korea	94.4			98.6		
Taiwan	89.3	89.6		89.0	88.2	
UK	99.6	99.9	98.7	98.7	96.2	98.8
US			97.9	92.7		

Source: hand-collected data for China, Greece, Hong Kong, India, Indonesia, Norway, Singapore, South Korea and Taiwan, calculations based on the Proxy Insight database for Australia, Canada, Denmark, France, Germany, Italy, Japan, the Netherlands, UK and USA.

A third topic, included among the voting items for shareholders of Australian, Canadian and US companies, is the election of the external auditor (also see Section 21.4.1 of Chapter 21). In contrast, Taiwan, Japan, Italy and China have another governance model with a specific board or committee that takes responsibility for the audit and, as in Italy and Japan, includes one or more certified auditors. Under South Korean law, it is the audit committee or the auditor appointment committee that takes responsibility for the external audit(or) (election). While the overall voting results for these agenda items concerning the external auditor are similar to the approval rates for the financial statements and the profit allocations, some shareholders in a number of jurisdictions raise questions regarding the suitability of the auditor nominee, resulting in significant opposition. For instance, in Greece, almost 10 per cent of the auditor nominees receive 20 per cent dissenting votes, resulting in a very high standard deviation of nine per cent. These rates are significantly higher than in most other jurisdictions. In Australia, for example, no major opposition was found, with a standard deviation of auditor elections of only one per cent. Greece is also the only jurisdiction in our sample in which a company experienced a battle over the election of auditors. After a tender process in which eight audit firms participated, the board called the meeting to appoint one audit firm, according to the corporate documentation of this company. Nevertheless, the AGM was provided with a choice between two audit firms. The board's nominee received 48.8 per cent of the votes, while the other audit firm received 44.4 per cent of the votes. The nominee with the highest number of votes was retained. It seems that this incident had further repercussions, as the chairman suspended the first general meeting during the session and postponed it for two weeks.

The three topics discussed above are recurrent, and shareholders must often approve them annually. Other topics that require shareholder approval, but are not standard voting items, are the approval of changes to the Articles of Association (or corporate charter), the issuance of shares, and share buybacks. In most jurisdictions, amendments to the Articles of Association are subject to specific quorum and approval requirements (and must take place in special or extraordinary meetings).[56] Most of these amendments in our sample were approved with an overwhelming majority of the votes, and thus are similar to those of the aforementioned recurring agenda items as listed in Table 22.6, with three important exceptions outlined below.

First, in Indonesia and Taiwan, amendments to the Articles of Association are generally critically received by a significant number of shareholders, resulting in average opposition rates of more than 10 per cent. In Taiwan, we should recall that the abstentions are both added in the nominator and the denominator as votes: in a number of cases, the dissenting votes are insignificant, but a large number of shareholder votes were abstentions. In Indonesia, there was significant opposition of more than 20 per cent in almost half of the proposed changes to the Articles of Association. However, no proposals were rejected, as the controlling shareholders approved all these proposals. In general, information disclosure about the reasons for amending the articles of information is scarce, which can result in the high numbers of dissenting votes. For example, at the 2019 AGM of Ciputra Development, over 20 per cent of the shareholder votes were against the resolution 'to approve to change of Article 3 of the Articles of Association of the Company regarding the objective and purpose and business activities in order of adjustment to the Standard Classification of Indonesian Business Fields (KBLI) with regard to the application of Online Single Submission and Principal Identification Number for Conducting Business'.[57] There is no further information available as to why these amendments were tabled for approval and received such a large proportion of dissenting votes.

Second, dissent rates for the amendments of the articles of association vary considerably in different jurisdictions, and the dissenting rates differ substantially from those of the aforementioned recurring agenda items. In Canada, France, Indonesia and the US, the standard deviation of the average approval rates (85 to 96 per cent on average) is around 10 per cent or more. In the former three jurisdictions, several proposed amendments were rejected by a majority of the votes. One US company proposed to add a number of supermajority voting provisions in the corporate charter, and a Canadian company requested shareholder authorization in 2019 for organizing a general meeting in a virtual-only format (see for a discussion on virtual-only meetings in Section 21.3.2 of Chapter 21). Both agenda items were rejected with a majority of the votes. Yet, the latter majority dissent rate may still have resulted in the implementation of the virtual-only format, as the vote was only advisory.

Third, the number of changes to the articles of association differs significantly between the different jurisdictions. In France, the number of times at least one change has been proposed to the shareholders exceeds one per company per year,[58] while companies in Australia, Singapore, Norway and Hong Kong seldom ask their shareholders to approve a change in the Articles of Association.

Other recurring voting items (which are not necessarily on the agenda of each AGM) are the approval of the issuance of new shares and share repurchases. While the former capital adjustment item regularly meets fierce opposition by a large number of shareholders, share buy-backs

56 See Chapter 21, Section 21.3.1.

57 Ciputra Development, 'Announcement on Summary Minute of Annual General Meeting of Shareholder' (27 June 2019) 10.

58 The shareholders of French companies often have to approve several changes of the articles in a single meeting.

hardly ever receive a significant number of dissenting votes. The shareholders of a Hong Kong company found 'the general mandate to the Directors to allot, issue and deal with additional shares not exceeding (i) in the case of an allotment and issue of shares for cash, 5% of the aggregate nominal amount of the share capital of the Company in issue at the date of the resolution and (ii) in the case of an allotment and issue of shares for a consideration other than cash, 20% of the aggregate nominal amount of the share capital of the Company in issue at the date of the resolution (less any shares allotted and issued pursuant to (i) above' an inappropriate mandate, and voted it down with a 54 per cent majority.[59] As with changes in the Articles of Association, the frequency with which shareholders are able to vote on any kind of share issuances differs between jurisdictions. This is a standard item in the agenda of French, Dutch, Singaporean and UK companies, an infrequent item in Greece, Canada and Japan, and a very rare agenda item for US companies. The same holds for share repurchases: this is a common voting item in France and the UK, but a very exceptional item at Japanese AGMs. However, share repurchases (or share buy-backs) differ from share issuances in that the dissent of shareholders is generally low. Shareholders have never rejected any proposal for a share buy-back.

Besides recurring voting items, which are found in many jurisdictions, a number of voting items occur only in a limited number of jurisdictions. Table 22.7 lists those items that are regularly found in at least two jurisdictions, while Table 22.8 lists the voting items that are unique to a particular jurisdiction.

In Australia and Japan, companies regularly ask shareholders to approve anti-takeover mechanisms. Shareholders can be expected to oppose anti-takeover devices, as they often benefit from takeovers. An important reason for companies to request shareholder approval of an anti-takeover device – according to the notices to the meetings of the Japanese companies in our

TABLE 22.7 *Selection of multiple jurisdiction-specific items*

	takeover provision	discharge directors	discharge sup board members	audit committee	Related party agreement	approve M&A
Australia	99.3					
Japan	66.3					
Germany		97.8	96.6			
Netherlands		97.6	97.2			
Denmark		99.7				
Greece		97.9		93.8	91.1	
China					96.4	
France					94.4	
Singapore					97.8	99.0
UK						98.5
S-Korea				94.6		

Source: hand-collected data for China, Greece, Singapore and South Korea, calculations based on the Proxy Insight database for Australia, Denmark, France, Japan, Germany, the Netherlands and the UK.

[59] Such findings affect the mean results and can explain differences over time (see for example the results for these items in the period 2010–13 in Chapter 3, Section 3.3.1).

sample – can be found in the business continuity of the company. For example, in a description of one fiercely opposed anti-takeover device, it was stated:

> The purpose of the Plan is to prevent decisions on the Company's financial and business policies from being controlled by persons deemed inappropriate, to deter large-scale acquisitions that are detrimental to the corporate value of the Group and, in turn, the common interests of its shareholders, and on the occasion that the Company receives a large-scale acquisition proposal regarding the shares in the Company from an acquirer, to enable the Company's Board of Directors to present an alternative proposal to the shareholders or ensure necessary time and information for the shareholders to decide whether or not to accept the large-scale acquisition proposal, and to enable the Board of Directors to negotiate for the benefit of the shareholders.[60]

The corporate board can make use of the free allotment of subscription rights to dilute the acquired voting block of a raider. Unsurprisingly, these measures arouse significant shareholder dissent rates in Japanese companies, and the average approval rate of these agenda items is only 66 per cent. Further, all Japanese items related to anti-takeover measures met major opposition. With a standard deviation of less than 8 per cent and a minimum dissent rate of almost 20 per cent, all these proposals were firmly queried by the shareholders. At the same time, all agenda items concerning these anti-takeover instruments were approved.

Conversely, shareholders of Australian companies did not oppose the introduction of takeover instruments. On average, 99.3 per cent of all shareholders' votes were in favour of these types of provisions. The explanation probably lies in the different approach of the takeover provisions in Australian companies. These provisions often put the incumbent shareholders first, providing them a larger say in the transaction. For instance, one of the approved provisions reads:

> If rule ... is renewed and a proportional takeover bid is made for ..., the Directors will be required to convene a general meeting of shareholders to vote on a resolution to approve the proportional takeover bid. The resolution must be voted on at least 14 days before the last day of the takeover bid period. The bidder and any associates of the bidder will be excluded from voting. If the resolution is rejected by the shareholders, then the bid will be deemed to be withdrawn and registration of any transfer of shares resulting from the proportional takeover bid will be prohibited. Acceptances will be returned, and any contracts formed by acceptances will be rescinded. If the resolution is approved, transfers to the bidder of shares which have been accepted into the bid will be registered provided they comply with the other provisions of the Constitution. ... The proportional takeover provisions do not apply to full takeover bids.[61]

Next, four European jurisdictions include as a common shareholder voting item the discharge of the directors, often as a mandatory agenda item. The legal consequences of this voting item differ.[62] In all jurisdictions motions to discharge received a large majority of the votes, and were voted down only in exceptional circumstances, as happened once in the Netherlands and once in Germany. In the German case, the former CEO of the company was believed to be involved in insider trading. In the Dutch case, the company was fined for installing insufficient measures against money laundering. The shareholders held the management board responsible, and consequently declined to discharge the particular management board members.[63]

In two jurisdictions, Greece and South Korea, shareholders elect the members of the audit committee in addition to the board of directors. The shareholders always supported the

[60] Minebea Mitsui, 'Notice of the 71st Ordinary General Meeting of Shareholders' (6 June 2017) 20.
[61] South32 Limited, 'Notice of Annual General Meeting' (23 September 2020) 11.
[62] See Section 21.4.7 of Chapter 21.
[63] See for the discussion of this Dutch situation, Chapter 19.

nominees to the audit committee, although, as with the election of board members, some nominees received significant minority opposition.[64]

Other voting items that are regularly subject to shareholder approval are related-party transactions (RPT).[65] Although many jurisdictions permit shareholder votes on related-party transactions, they only appear as regular topics on general meeting agendas in China, France, Greece and Singapore. Singapore, for example, operates an ex ante approval system. The shareholders approve the transactions that the company will enter into during the current accounting period during which the AGM takes place, provided that these transactions take place on normal commercial terms and are in the interest of the company. This pre-approval vote results in less shareholder dissent for related-party transactions in Singaporean companies, compared to approval for transactions that are clearly identified and specified as they take place in the other jurisdictions.

As with other voting items, a large number of shareholders regularly oppose related-party transactions, but such transactions are rarely rejected. At one French company, the shareholders rejected a consultancy contract with a company of which the vice-chairman of the board was the only shareholder. Shareholders raised questions related to the compatibility of the services with the position of this non-executive vice-chairman. Nearly all related party transactions are approved with only modest dissent from shareholders.

In Mainland China, the UK and Singapore, shareholders regularly approve important acquisitions. There is evidence that this practice has beneficial results. A recent study of acquisitions in the USA and the UK (where larger transactions have to be approved by the shareholders)[66] demonstrates that acquirers of UK companies in larger transactions experienced a significant cumulative abnormal return, whereas their American counterparts (where no such vote exists) lost value. This suggests that shareholder voting can deter companies from making bad acquisitions.[67]

Table 22.8 provides a list of agenda items that are regularly found in the companies of a single jurisdiction in our study. In not less than eight of the jurisdictions in our sample, shareholders have a voting right that does not exist (or is very rarely tabled) in the other jurisdictions. In the UK, shareholders have several of these 'unique' shareholder voting rights, including the approval of political donations, granting the board of directors the right to call a meeting on short notice and, in addition to the election of the auditor, also approve the audit fee.[68] In many other jurisdictions, the audit fee is automatically approved when the shareholders appoint the external auditor, whereas some other jurisdictions delegate the remuneration of the auditor to the board of directors. These three UK-specific items are always approved in the general meeting of the UK companies in our sample, although curbing the time for studying the agenda items by calling a meeting on short notice generates more shareholder dissent. The audit fee never meets significant shareholder opposition.

China's corporate law requires shareholder approval of the company's 'business policies and investment plans'.[69] These plans are rarely disapproved, and significant opposition is scarce. France not only requests the shareholders to approve the financial statements of the (listed)

[64] At one AGM of a South Korean company two nominees were rejected, but the voting results were not disclosed.

[65] See for an extensive analysis of rules and frameworks of related party transaction, Luca Enriques and Tobias Tröger, *The Law and Finance of Related Party Transactions* (Cambridge University Press 2019). Also see Chapter 21, Section 21.4.6.

[66] See Section 21.4.5 of Chapter 21.

[67] Marco Becht, Andrea Polo and Stefano Rossi, 'Should Shareholders Have a Say on Acquisitions?' (2021) 33 The Bank of America Journal of Applied Corporate Finance 48.

[68] Also see Sections 21.4.1 and 21.4.6 of Chapter 21.

[69] See Chapter 2.

TABLE 22.8 *Selection of jurisdiction-specific items*

	approve business plan	consolidated accounts	affiliation agreement	allowing directors to take positions in other companies	release restrictions of competitive activities directors	nomination committee	political donations	authorize company to call AGM 14 days	auditor remuneration	eliminate/reduce supermajority vote requirement
China	96.4									
France		99.2								
Germany			99.9							
Greece				98.6						
Taiwan					81.4					
Norway						99.4*				
UK							97.8	93.6	99.4	
US										97.4

*Only data for 2020

Source: hand-collected data for China, Greece, Norway and Taiwan, calculations based on the Proxy Insight database for France, Germany, the UK and the USA.

parent company, but also requires the consolidated accounts to be submitted for shareholder approval. As it raises some legal questions on the consequences of a majority dissenting vote for these consolidated accounts (or of the disapproval of one or more company financial statements that are part of the group), practice shows that shareholder opposition for the consolidated statement is rarely a problem. In our sample, only one consolidated financial statement received more than 10 per cent votes against: the CEO of this car producer first turned the company into a profit-making business, but was later charged for misappropriation of assets, which could have caused the significant dissent in respect of the consolidated accounts.

Germany has developed group law and, consequently, the law provides in an elaborated framework of structuring the corporate relationships. One of these relationships, the *affiliation agreement*, needs shareholder approval.[70] None of these agreements that were covered in our sample received more than 1 per cent dissenting votes.

While in some jurisdictions 'external board membership' falls under the directors' (fiduciary) duties – and some jurisdictions, including Germany, even forbid board memberships in other companies[71] – Greece and Taiwan require the shareholders to vote whether their director can accept another directorship in other companies: both the shareholders of Greek companies and those of Taiwanese companies support the engagement in other boards or the development of competing activities, but, particularly in Taiwan, approval is far from unanimous. In a few cases, this release of restrictions was rejected.

In Greece and South Korea, the shareholders can voice their opinion on the composition of the audit committee, while shareholders of Norwegian companies can vote for the nominees of the nomination committee. This is due to the specificities of the Norwegian corporate governance system[72] where the default system is that shareholders vote for the corporate assembly that elects the board of directors. However, in the absence of a corporate assembly, shareholders vote for the nominees of the nomination committee. Most shareholders raised no concerns over the nominees for this committee.

Finally, and also due to the different governance structure, shareholders of many US companies have the opportunity to vote on the abolition or reduction of several supermajority requirements. As this tends to improve the position of the shareholders, opposition for this agenda item was unsurprisingly low, with an average approval rate of more than 97 per cent.

Although the previous tables provide important insights into the use of shareholder voting rights in practice, they do not provide an exhaustive overview of all the different items shareholders can vote on in all jurisdictions. In fact, there are many more company- and/or jurisdiction- specific issues, but those topics are less frequently tabled as agenda items.

22.4 SHAREHOLDER PROPOSALS AND QUESTIONS

In addition to shareholder voting at (A)GMs, shareholders can take additional actions during these meetings. They can launch shareholder proposals, ask questions during the meeting, and can start a discussion with the corporate board. All these actions are subject to certain requirements, as discussed in Chapter 21.[73] In this section we address the use of these rights in the different jurisdictions in practice.

70 See Chapter 15.

71 See §88 Aktiengezetz, but the supervisory board can provide in an exception and agree with the board membership in another company.

72 See Chapter 18.

73 See Section 21.6 of Chapter 21 on shareholder proposals, and Section 21.7 of Chapter 21 on shareholder questions.

22.4.1 *Shareholder Proposals*

Table 22.9 provides an overview of the use of shareholder proposals in the nineteen jurisdictions covered in this Handbook. The second and third columns address the frequency of the use of this shareholder engagement mechanism. Specifically, the second column shows a general appreciation of the occurrence of shareholder proposals. The third column quantifies this occurrence as the average number of shareholder proposals per company per year. The table shows that there are many and major differences between the various jurisdictions. For instance, in Italy, shareholders very often make use of their shareholder proposal rights. However, the overwhelming majority of all these proposals relate to the election of directors (following *Voto di Lista*, see Section 21.5.3, Chapter 21) or members of the board of *sindici* (statutory auditors), due to the specific right of minority shareholders to board representation.[74] In fact, shareholders of Italian companies very rarely table other agenda items.

In the USA, Canada, Denmark and Germany, the shareholders regularly submit shareholder proposals. Each company in these jurisdictions receives on average at least every two AGMs one shareholder proposal to be tabled. However, there exist significant differences between the USA and Canada on the one hand, and Germany and Denmark, on the other. As the final column in Table 22.9 illustrates, a large majority of all the companies in the USA and Canada had one or more shareholders that asked to table one or more proposals. This may highlight the shareholder proposal culture that has been developed in these jurisdictions. As shown in Chapters 11 and 12,[75] shareholders can relatively easily use their shareholder proposal right, given the capital thresholds shareholders face.[76] Conversely, in the USA and Canada, approval of a shareholder proposal does not necessarily bind the company, as in these jurisdictions shareholder proposals are often precatory. In Germany and Denmark, the shareholder proposals were concentrated in a small number of companies. In Denmark, one company accounted for over 80 per cent of all shareholder proposals. The use of shareholder proposals in Denmark and Germany can be attributed to some legal and company-related specificities. Due to a major money laundering scheme, a financial institution experienced major opposition and activism of the shareholders and the media.[77] In Germany, shareholders often make use of 'counter motions'.[78] A major German financial institution ran into financial difficulties, resulting in shareholders not only voting against the discharge of the directors, but also launching shareholder proposals to require investigations, dismissing some board members, and starting a vote of no-confidence. Furthermore, the threshold for issuing a counter motion is low. Any shareholder has the right to file such a motion, and almost two-thirds of German shareholder proposals take the form of such a counter motion.

In all other jurisdictions in our sample, shareholders' use of the proposal mechanism is considerably less common, and only a relatively small number of companies are confronted with these proposals. Further, in the group of jurisdictions where the proposals are less regularly found, it often happens that one particular company rouses many shareholders to take this shareholder action. This is the case in Japan, Greece, Taiwan and France, where between a third and a half of all shareholder proposals were (repeatedly) presented to the shareholders in one company.

74 See Chapter 17.
75 See Chapters 11 and 12.
76 Also Chapter 21, Section 21.6.
77 See Chapter 13.
78 See Chapter 15.

TABLE 22.9 *Shareholder proposals (2016–20)*

	occurrence	estimated comp./year	mean support	distribution support	majority support	companies involved
Australia	regular	0.11	15.6%	0.5%–99%	7.9%	15.0%
Canada	common	0.85	15.4%	0.3%–99.9%	6.6%	70.0%
China	very common	1.26	98.32%	39.0%–100%	99.7%	19.0%
Denmark	common	0.61	1.4%	0.05%–7.4%	0.0%	35.0%
France	regular	0.23	11.8%	1.3%–43.7%	0.0%	17.5%
Germany	common	0.63	10.3%	0%–46.4%	0.0%	30.0%
Greece	regular	0.11	49.3%	25.7%–73.6%	50.0%	11.8%
Hong Kong	very rare	0.006				
India	very rare	0.04	93.7%	71.2%–100%	100%	12.0%
Indonesia	very rare	0.05				8.9%
Italy	very common	1.70	67.9%	0–100%	66.9%	97.1%
Japan	regular	0.30	10.9%	0.2%–54.3%	0.6%	9.8%
Netherlands	very rare	0.05	7.3%	2.8%–14.4%	0.0%	8.0%
Norway	regular	0.14	0.6%	0.06%–3.1%	0.0%	8.0%
S. Korea	rare	0.08	37.6%	13.8%–98.3%	20.0%	6.0%
Singapore	very rare	0.00				
Taiwan	regular	0.21				16.0%
UK	very rare	0.05	25.7%	0.7%–99.2%	13.6%	9.0%
US	common	0.75	29.3%	0%–99.8%	9.6%	58.4%

Source: hand-collected data for China, Greece, Hong Kong, India, Indonesia, Norway, Singapore, South Korea and Taiwan, calculations based on the Proxy Insight database for Australia, Canada, Denmark, France, Germany, Italy, Japan, the Netherlands, UK and USA. China data is limited to 2019. The vast majority of shareholder proposals in China were initiated by controlling shareholders.

In India, Indonesia, Singapore and Hong Kong, hardly any shareholder proposals were reported.[79]

Support for shareholder proposals also varies widely. In Europe, the likelihood of a proposal being supported by the majority of the participating shareholders is very low. In all European jurisdictions with the exception of Italy (which applies a specific minority shareholder slate proposal right), all shareholder proposals have been defeated by a large majority. The results for Greece relate to a single company where two alternative nominees were presented for a board position and an audit committee membership, and should therefore be interpreted with caution.

In a second group of jurisdictions, a minority of the shareholder proposals were supported by a majority of the shareholders. This is the case in the common law jurisdictions of the UK, the USA, Australia and Canada. In Australia in particular, non-binding resolutions are not provided, and shareholders must work with constitutional amendments, for which a supermajority requirement of 75 per cent is necessary.[80] There are only five vote recordings for South Korea and one proposal was backed by the majority of the shareholders, too limited a number to draw general conclusions on how shareholder proposals are supported. Exceptionally, two shareholder proposals for changing the articles of association of a Japanese company received a small majority of the votes. As the proposals required a two-thirds majority, the proposals were rejected.

79 In a number of cases it is not clear whether a reported proposal is a shareholder proposal.

80 See Chapter 10, Section 10.3.1.3. Only half of the majority approved shareholder proposals in Table 22.9 passed the 75 per cent threshold.

Third, in India very few shareholder proposals are tabled. India has a very high shareholder threshold for the submission of a shareholder proposal, strongly limiting the number of shareholders that comply with the ownership requirements. As only large shareholders can submit a proposal, the few proposals (almost all of which relate to the nomination or dismissal of a board member) that are submitted are acknowledged by the board of directors and the controlling shareholders (identified as the promotors of the company). A similarly large number of approvals can be found in Italy. This is due to the specificities of slate voting whereby shareholders, including the major shareholders, table their list. Accordingly, majority approval of these lists is common. When only the list of the minority shareholders is withheld, approval rates of these 'shareholder proposals' have a mean around 30 per cent.[81]

Third, the topics raised in shareholder proposals also differ between jurisdictions. Italian and Indian shareholder proposals, as we have seen, mostly relate to board elections, while German proposals are commonly 'counter motions'. Table 22.10 summarizes the most important shareholder proposal classes and their relative weight in the total number of shareholder proposals. In many jurisdictions shareholder proposals are a rarely used shareholder engagement tool and consequently a ranking of topics of the proposals in these jurisdictions is rather redundant.

The results show that shareholder proposals focus on director elections in several jurisdictions, not only in Italy and India. In Canada, France, Greece, Indonesia, South Korea and Taiwan it is the most common reason for shareholders for starting this type of engagement. In Taiwan, South Korea, India and Greece (jurisdictions with few shareholder proposals) it is, in combination with the desire of the shareholders to strive for a more balanced board structure, the only reason for tabling a shareholder proposal. Also in Germany, although disguised in the form of a countermotion, the board composition, in particular that the participation of some board members should be reconsidered, is the most important concern of shareholders (measured via the relative number of shareholder proposals). In the other jurisdictions, board elections are also important, but shareholders also raise proposals that address other concerns. In the US, board elections account for less than 5 per cent of the proposals, by no means a negligible figure when taken in combination with concerns about the board structure. However, the governance structure of companies raises more shareholder concerns in the USA.

In many jurisdictions, shareholders are keen to take responsibility for environmental issues and make the company more responsive to environmental concerns. In Australia, Denmark, Japan, the UK, the Netherlands and Norway, environmental shareholder proposals are the most important class of proposals. In the latter two jurisdictions, although the number of proposals is limited, environmental issues are the only shareholder concern sufficiently weighty to justify launching a proposal. In some cases, shareholders recurrently request the company to take more responsibility for the environment. The shareholders of the Norwegian company Equinor ASA, whose general meetings accounted for most of the shareholder proposals initiated in Norway, voted in 2017 and 2018 on a proposal to refrain from drilling oil in the Barents Sea, and in 2019 and 2020 to phase out all exploration activities. A large majority of the shareholders rejected the proposals.

Many shareholders want to change the structure of a company and suggest – via a shareholder proposal – an amendment of the articles of association. This tactic is often over-ambitious, as an amendment of the articles of association requires in most jurisdictions a supermajority approval, a threshold which few proposals ever reach.

Finally, in some jurisdictions, the proposals are jurisdiction-specific, most likely due to the path dependent developments in corporate law and corporate governance. In the US, the most

[81] See, for more detailed information, Chapter 17, Section 17.4.2.

TABLE 22.10 *Overview of most common subjects of shareholder proposals and their relative frequency*

	Topic	number	Topic	number	Topic	number
Australia	environmental	34.2%	change articles	19.3%	director elections	14.9%
Canada	director elections	26.4%	remuneration	20.1%	board structure	14.6%
China	director election	31.7%	bond issuance	9.0%	private issuance	7.9%
Denmark	environmental	19.7%	remuneration	13.1%	AGM organization	13.1%
France	director elections	37.0%	board structure	21.7%	dividend	13.0%
Germany	counter motion	62.1%	special audit	16.8%	dismiss board member	9.5%
Greece	director election	77.8%	dismiss board member	22.2%		
Hong Kong	director election	100%				
India	director election	50.0%	dismiss board member	30.0%		
Indonesia	director election	63.6%	change articles	27.3%		
Italy	director election	55.0%	internal auditor election	38.6%		
Japan	environmental	23.2%	board structure	17.6%	director election	8.5%
Netherlands	environmental	66.7%				
Norway	environmental	66.7%	energy	11.1%		
S. Korea	director election	42.1%	audit com election	26.3%		
Singapore						
Taiwan	director election	71.2%	change articles	7.7%		
UK	environment	40.0%	change articles	15.0%		
US	shareholder rights	22.2%	political activities	15.6%	board structure	14.2%

Source: hand-collected data for China, Greece, Hong Kong, India, Indonesia, Norway, Singapore, South Korea and Taiwan, calculations based on the Proxy Insight database for Australia, Canada, Denmark, France, Germany, Italy, Japan, the Netherlands, UK and USA.

common shareholder proposals relate to the strengthening of the rights of shareholders (e.g. proxy access rights or the right to call a meeting with a lower ownership threshold), the latter being provided in many jurisdictions in their corporate laws. The 'political activities' relate to issuing a report on the political contributions and expenditures of American companies. This is much less of a concern of shareholders in most other jurisdictions, particularly where, as in the UK, the shareholders already have a say on political expenditure.

22.4.2 *Shareholder Questions*

Shareholders do not always make use of the mechanism of shareholder proposals to attempt to change corporate policy. Many shareholders adopt the cheap and simple approach of raising questions to the board, especially during the general meeting of shareholders. Whereas details of shareholder proposals are readily available, information on the type and quantity of shareholder questions is scarce. In many jurisdictions, like in the USA, the UK and Australia, only the voting results of the companies must be officially reported, and it is normal practice not to disclose details of this kind. In Norway, India, Japan and Germany there is no information on the shareholder engagement mechanism of questioning the board. However, it is clear from webcasts that shareholders of companies in these jurisdictions often do raise questions at the meeting. The US Berkshire Hathaway general meeting of 2020, which was broadcast online, showed that Warren Buffett, the company's legendary CEO and chairman of the board, received over 2500 remarks and questions as soon as he opened the 'virtual' floor for questions. A journalist made a short selection of these questions, which were addressed in a session that lasted more than two hours.[82]

An assessment of the documents of the general meetings of the companies in the other jurisdictions show different trends in the use of the question right. First, in some jurisdictions, the Q&A session is considered the most important part of the meeting, at least in terms of the amount of time spent on it. Especially in Italy and the Netherlands, but also in France and Denmark, a long list of questions is addressed during the meeting and many shareholders take the floor to challenge the board with their questions. It is not uncommon to find in the minutes of the meetings over 100 questions raised by shareholders, as occurred in the 2020 meeting of the French company Total.[83] A similar picture emerges from a number of Dutch meetings.[84] This trend has resulted in further coordination guidelines to structure the process of the meeting, including the limitation of the speaking time of the shareholders or the number of questions that each shareholder can raise or the eligibility requirements a shareholder must fulfil to be allowed to take the floor.[85] It is also common to find on the website of the company general Q&A lists which the companies can refer to for similar questions, as well as invitations to the shareholders to send the questions before the start of the meeting.

Second, while the question right provides a group of shareholders with an effective tool to approach their company's board of directors, not all shareholders make use of this instrument equally. According to the Danish study, the board of directors were required to address shareholder questions in only 13 per cent of the small companies and up to 30 per cent of the largest companies. Bearing in mind that not all companies report their Q&A sessions, it is clear that shareholders of a large majority of the companies do not make use of this shareholder right.

Third, there are different patterns in the way companies address and approach the questions. In some companies and jurisdictions, it is common to group the Q&A session into a single timeslot during which all the questions are addressed. Sometimes the Q&A session is organized before the voting takes place. This seems logical, as it provides the shareholders with the requested additional information before voting. This system is often found in France, Italy, the UK and the Netherlands. However, in the Berkshire Hathaway meeting of 2020, the Q&A session was organized after the voting, as the final part of the general meeting. A third approach can be found in jurisdictions like Indonesia and Singapore. The shareholders can ask questions before each agenda item goes to a vote.

82 See the broadcast of the meeting at https://finance.yahoo.com/news/berkshire-hathaway-annual-shareholder-meeting-2020-161426594.html accessed 22 March 2021 (the Q&A session starts at minute 2:45:10).

83 See Chapter 14.

84 See Chapter 19.

85 See for an example, the rules of UniCredit, 'One Bank, One Team, One UniCredit' www.unicreditgroup.eu/content/dam/unicreditgroup-eu/documents/en/governance/shareholders-meetings/meeting-regulations/Regulations%20Governing%20General%20Meetings.pdf accessed 22 March 2021.

Fourth, the process of organizing a Q&A round affects the behaviour of shareholders at the meeting. In Italy, France, Denmark, the Netherlands, the UK and probably other jurisdictions, the data and anecdotal evidence shows that shareholders not only limit their interventions to raising questions but also put forward comments, compliments or criticisms, or try to start a debate. The Danish report found in its assessment that in around 40 per cent of the largest companies, one or more shareholders had 'addressed' the board of directors.

Fifth, there seems to be no relationship between the number of questions and the results of the vote. During the meetings of the Indonesian companies, most of the questions were raised before voting on the financial statements of the company, and the approval rates for these reports were higher than those for most other agenda items for which no further questions were raised. This was in particular the case for the voting items regarding the election of the board of directors and the remuneration of the board.

Sixth, in a limited number of jurisdictions, the minutes of the meeting also provide information on the type of shareholders that make use of the question rights. According to the study of engagement in Denmark[86] and the Netherlands[87], questions are raised by individual shareholders and shareholder associations, as well as by lobby groups that strive to achieve particular ESG goals, as is often the case in France.[88] These European findings are comparable with the situation in Indonesia. Table 22.11 provides an overview of the type of shareholders who asked questions and the type of those questions raised during the 2018 meeting of PT Aneka Tambang Tbk. The Q&A report contains the questions of five shareholders, of which 4 related to the first agenda item and a fifth to the third item, the latter question not being related to the topic of the profit distribution. In the minutes of the meeting the company referred to seven shareholders that addressed the board regarding the first item but no shareholder raised a question related to the other agenda items. More importantly, the Q&A report shows that only individual shareholders, each owning a small voting block in the company that represented less than 0.6 per cent of all the attending votes, raised questions, and in one case the shareholder was represented by a proxy.

Finally, the topics that shareholders raise during the Q&A session also show a wide diversity. In Table 22.10, we have already seen how the questions in that particular company relate to the strategy and a number of operational issues, but other research[89] and minutes of the meeting show that a wide variety of questions are asked. Limited to the questions – next to the complaints, compliments and discourses – we distinguish two major sets of question types, which can be subdivided in several topics. First, similar to the questions that have been raised in PT Aneka Tambang Tbk, many questions relate to the different corporate specific and technical issues, and can be very precise.[90] The general meeting 2019 of the Singaporean Wilmar provides in an illustration. The minutes of the meeting record:

> Shareholder D referred to Note 17 (Investment in Joint Ventures) on page 143 of Wilmar's Annual Report 2018 ('AR 2018'). He noted that the Company's investment of 50% in FPW Singapore Holdings Pte. Ltd. ('FPW'), which owns Goodman Fielder ('GF'), stood at US$544 million as at end of FY2018. He also noted that Wilmar has announced its intention

86 Chapter 13.

87 Chapter 19.

88 Chapter 14.

89 Anne Lafarre and Christoph Van der Elst, 'Corporate Sustainability and Corporate Activism in the Netherlands' in Beate Sjåfjell and Christopher Bruner (eds.), *Corporate Law, Corporate Governance and Sustainability* (Cambridge University Press 2019) 260–75.

90 See also Chapter 5.

TABLE 22.11 *Overview of the shareholders and questions raised during the 2018 meeting of PT Aneka Tambang Tbk*

Type shareholder	Shares	Voting block in meeting	Question regarding	Type questions	Nr. of questions
X individual proxy of other individual Y	1066433	0.57392%	financial statement	financial	1
individual	15500	0.00834%	financial statement	strategy	3+1 reply
individual	300	0.00016%	financial statement	operational	1
individual	112500	0.06054%	financial statement	operational	1+1 reply
individual			dividend	operational	1

Source: company minutes.

> to acquire the remaining 50% in FPW from First Pacific Company Limited ('FP') in March 2019 for US$180 million. He asked the Chairman to explain the valuation of FPW which has dropped and how could the value of the FPW shares come down so much, when GF is profitable compared to previous year.

Next, a number of shareholders take the opportunity to raise very general questions, sometimes only loosely related to company's business affairs. During the M&S meeting of 2019, a shareholder said that her mother, who had ordered flowers from M&S to be sent to some relatives, discovered that they had instead received chocolates, wine and a plant. She asked how this had happened, and the chairman apologized.[91] It is not surprising that many such questions are replied to in very general terms, or are politely dismissed. One of the questions during the 2020 general meeting of Mediaset was whether the chairman believed in paradise, and what the trends would be in turnovers, divided by sector. The first question was not addressed, while the second was answered by referring to the next financial report.[92] M&S provides an overview of all shareholder questions since 2004.[93] The answer on the 2018 question what the results are of a private shareholder panel meeting reads:

> Our second private shareholder panel met with Steve Rowe and other members of the senior leadership team in June 2018 for a roundtable and store tour in Westfield in White City. The key themes discussed were clothing concerns, our customers, availability and the sparks programme. We have found the panel to be incredibly insightful and knowledgeable about M&S and have welcomed their views and challenges, which we are routinely considering and taking on board as part of our decision-making processes.

[91] See the broadcast of the meeting https://secure.ctn.co.uk/marksandspencer_sites/marks-and-spencer/agm/2019/home/ accessed 23 March 2021 (the Q&A of this shareholder and the board starts at 1:02:02).

[92] See Question 6 and 48 in the report Answers to Q&A Ex Art 127-Ter TUF https://corporate.mediaset.it/binary/documentRepository/46/23.06.2020%20-%20Answers%20to%20Q&A%20ex%20art.%20127-ter%20TUF.pdf accessed 22 March 2021.

[93] See https://corporate.marksandspencer.com/investors/shareholder-information/agm-information/agm-questions-and-answers accessed 23 March 2021.

22.5 OTHER FORMS OF SHAREHOLDER ENGAGEMENT

Shareholder engagement does not stop when participants leave a general meeting. Many shareholders make use of other mechanisms to engage with their investees, and companies reach out in different ways to their shareholders. As these mechanisms often take place, either in the 'shadow' of the legal engagement instruments which have been discussed in the previous sections, or embedded in a jurisdiction specific engagement framework, this section cannot, like the previous sections, summarize the findings in comparative tables.

In many jurisdictions, (larger) (institutional) shareholders engage with companies 'behind the scenes', 'less confrontational'. It is even reported in a number of jurisdictions that these investors prefer this mechanism to all other engagement instruments.[94] Evidence on the frequency and effects of this type of shareholder engagement is scarce and mostly anecdotal.[95] In the UK several studies have shown that this type of engagement is preferred by a large majority of the institutional investors, and several institutional investors hold a meeting with the management of the investees at least once a year.[96] While the level of success achieved by these private engagement to bring change in the investees is not available – not all private engagements seek to bring changes in the behaviour of the investees[97] – the outcome is often considered satisfactory. A UK study on engagements to discuss a different approach in the restructuring or acquisitions policy of the company has shown success rates of more than 50 per cent.[98] Some anecdotal evidence in other jurisdictions supports both the frequency of this engagement technique and its effectiveness. In the Netherlands a management proposal for a merger between the two parent companies of Unilever was withdrawn after consultation with a significant group of shareholders.[99] In Germany private negotiations with a major shareholder convinced the latter of the need for the federal government to intervene in Lufthansa.[100] The withdrawal of management proposals, more than likely due to private negotiations with major shareholders of the company, is noticed in several other Dutch general meetings.[101] In France private engagement is partially institutionalized as a desirable practice. France's corporate governance code recommends the appointment of a director responsible for shareholder relations, and shareholder clubs regularly meet with company management.[102]

Another mechanism that has gained importance in a number of jurisdictions over the last years is the involvement of proxy advisors.[103] These parties prepare voting policies in the pre-AGM season that can be commented on by the shareholders, analyze matters that are tabled at the meetings and advise the shareholders how to vote. There is significant evidence that their role should not be underestimated.[104]

There are also a number of jurisdiction specific instruments of shareholder engagement. One example is the slate voting system in Italy. This system encourages large shareholders to put

[94] See Chapter 20.
[95] See Chapters 2, 7 and 9.
[96] See Chapter 20, Section 20.4.2.
[97] In Japan, Nippon Life Insurance frequently organizes meetings with its investees to discuss a wide variety of issues (see Chapter 6, Section 6.4.2).
[98] See Chapter 20, Section 20.4.2.
[99] See Chapter 19, Section 19.3.2.
[100] See Chapter 15, Section 19.3.3.
[101] Christoph Van der Elst and Anne Lafarre, 'Shareholder Voice on Executive Pay: A Decade of Dutch Say on Pay' (2017) 18 European Business Organization Law Review 51.
[102] See Chapter 14, Section 14.4.9.
[103] And mentioned as part of the engagement tools in Canada, France and the UK.
[104] See Paul Calluzzo and Evan Dudley, 'The Real Effects of Proxy Advisors on the Firm' (2019) 48 Financial Management 917.

forward a list of candidates for the board of directors and the statutory auditors, and small shareholders also make active use of this instrument.[105] The US is not unfamiliar with the system, as there are practices of active shareholders providing a 'short slate' to gain a number of board seats.[106] The Indonesian system is familiar with 'circular resolutions' to take decisions and engage shareholders outside the formal approval system of the general meeting.[107]

In Asian jurisdictions in particular, shareholders rely on public monitoring. Although it is legitimate to ask whether public interventions can be considered as a form of shareholder engagement, these interventions are sometimes initiated by shareholders in Hong Kong, China and Singapore through requisition filings.[108]

Obviously, shareholders can move from engagement with companies to actively trying to change their company's and board's behaviour. This is shareholder activism, through activism campaigns and proxy contests. During the past decade, activism campaigns have gained ground all over the world. A limited number of activist funds are very active in launching campaigns. In 2020, Elliott Management launched almost 10 per cent of all campaigns worldwide.[109] These campaigns aim at gaining board seats, selling the company, divestitures or changing M&A deals, and (increasingly) pursuing ESG demands.[110]

A common technique for this type of shareholder behaviour is launching a proxy contest. A study of the American proxy fight market showed that of 350 proxy fights over the last years, 25 per cent were withdrawn, 42 per cent were voted and the remainder were settled. In approximately half of the cases that were voted, the proxy fight delivered a board seat for the activist. When it comes to a vote, techniques like vote buying and lending of stock are used to increase the likelihood of a majority support.[111] When the proxy contest was settled this ratio was much higher, so that over 80 per cent of the cases ended with a board seat for the activist.[112] In the USA and Canada this technique is particularly well established, but also other jurisdictions, such as China and Taiwan, are also familiar with proxy contests.[113]

22.6 CONCLUDING REMARKS

There is no doubt that many shareholders engage with their investees. However, this engagement comes in different shapes and forms. First, this chapter finds that not all shareholders engage with their companies. Notwithstanding the worldwide development towards facilitating remote voting at the general meetings of shareholders, lowering this engagement cost significantly, the absentee rate of shareholders is, calculated in percentages of shares or votes, between 10 and 45 per cent. In fact, only a small fraction of small shareholders actively engage with their investees.[114] Different types of shareholders participate in a different way. Larger shareholders, for several reasons, are more ready to participate in the general meeting than small shareholders,

105 See Chapter 17, Section 17.3.4.1.
106 See Chapter 12, Section 12.4.
107 See Chapter 5, Section 5.3.3.3.
108 See Chapter 7, Section 7.3.1.2, Chapter 3, Section 3.3.2.3.
109 See Lazard's Shareholder Advisory Group, '2020 Review of Shareholder Activism', 2 www.lazard.com/media/451536/lazards-2020-review-of-shareholder-activism-vf.pdf accessed 25 March 2021.
110 Ibid., 14–18.
111 See Chapter 12, Section 12.4.
112 Activist Insight, *Proxy Fights 2020* (Activist Insight Ltd 2020), 20.
113 See Chapter 2 and Chapter 9.
114 Tata Consultancy Services Limited offers a good example. During the AGMs of 2016 to 2020 the company registered between 588,000 and 910,000 shareholders at the record date. Between 404 and 1006 shareholders voted their shares, representing between 90.7 per cent and 92.7 per cent of the votes of the issued shares.

and institutional investors are more likely to participate than retail investors. The larger the number of (very) small shareholder and retail investors, the greater the number of shareholders that only vote with their feet. While this is not the only reason for the differences in participation levels across companies and across jurisdictions, it definitely is an explanatory variable.

In all jurisdictions, the shareholders have some say over the election of the board of directors. In the majority of jurisdictions the shareholders are the ultimate decision takers for the election of a (majority of) the directors. In some jurisdictions where a majority rule is not (necessarily) applied, the shareholders' vote signals to other corporate incumbents that action must be considered. Overall, a very large majority of the board nominees are elected in all jurisdictions. Overall, this finding seems to indicate that the selection process for board nominees is generally to be considered as adequate. Only in very exceptional cases will a board nominee experience majority dissent. There are indications that shareholders dislike a majority voting system for combined voting for more than one director. As board composition is a key feature of corporate governance and an important ESG-issue, individual director elections are recommendable.

Other common agenda items are few. Only amendments to the corporate constitution or articles of association need the approval of the shareholders in all jurisdictions. As the content of these articles differs according to national company law, the approval right can be different. For all other agenda items, there are jurisdictions where the shareholders have no say on this item. It is however common in most jurisdictions that the shareholders elect the external auditor, approve capital issuances, authorize the board to buy back the shares, approve the profit allocation and approve or confirm the reception of the financial statements. In the United States, famous for its shareholder activism, shareholders are only given a say on the election of the auditor. The rise of shareholder activism in the USA can be largely explained by the fact that shareholder engagement via the AGM is so limited.

Many jurisdictions offer shareholders unique voting items: the spill vote in Australia, the approval of affiliation agreements in Germany, the endorsement of political donations in the UK,[115] the abolition of supermajority voting requirements in the USA and the approval of a business plan in China. Some of these rights are derivatives of specificities of corporate law, as in Germany with group law, while others flow from national legislative consideration that the shareholders are the appropriate incumbent party to decide on the issue (as with political donations in the UK) or, from companies inviting shareholders to express their consent with a specific corporate decision (as with the abolition of the supermajority approval system in the USA). As with the more common agenda items of the AGM, these specific items are not lightly presented to the shareholders, and majority dissent for this specific item is an exception to the rule.

Most jurisdictions give shareholders a say-on-pay right. However, there are almost as many different systems of say-on-pay as there are jurisdictions in our analysis. Shareholders normally vote to approve the remuneration package and any equity plan. However, if the remuneration package concerns non-executive or independent directors, shareholder dissent is close to zero. If the remuneration package includes executive remuneration packages, a wide variety of shareholder voting outcomes can be noticed. Packages that are considered inappropriate experience significant and sometimes even majority dissenting votes. A similar result can be found for the equity plans, remuneration policies and reports.

115 Currently, shareholders of US companies are launching many shareholder proposals for obtaining more insights in the lobbying activities of their investees, see Rebecca Sherratt, 'Reaching a Boiling Point' (2021) 8 Proxy Insight 2, 3.

In a number of companies, shareholders go a step further and table shareholder proposals, especially in the field of ESG issues and board structures and director elections. There seems to be a relationship between ease of launching a shareholder proposal and the number of such proposals. However, the number of successful shareholder proposals is modest, unless the proposal is launched by the large shareholders (as in China) or by a minority shareholder in the context of specific rights granted by the legislator to these minority shareholders (as in Italy). The modest success rate of shareholder proposals questions the general alignment of shareholders with the management of the company or with the initiating shareholder.

An instrument that is important, particularly for small shareholders and shareholder associations, is the right to ask questions during the general meeting (or outside it, if the legislature permits, as in France). It provides equal treatment and equal distribution of information to all shareholders, which is not guaranteed when other shareholder engagement techniques are used, in particular in one-on-one meetings between a major (institutional) shareholder and company executive (board) members.

In short, this comparative report shows that shareholder engagement is here to stay, that the role of the general meeting of shareholders should not be underestimated, and that many shareholder engagement instruments serve their goals. Nevertheless, an appropriate balance between the position and powers of the shareholders and boards in many companies and the balance between the different shareholder engagement instruments has not yet been found. These pivotal issues offer plenty of scope for further research and analysis.

23

Shareholder Engagement and Voting

Where Does the Future Lie?

Chao Xi

The nineteen jurisdiction studies featured in this Handbook, together with the comparative perspectives offered in the preceding two chapters, represent our collective attempt to address some of the most pressing questions in the current debate on comparative corporate law and governance from the viewpoint of the position and role of shareholders. We hope our inquiries have yielded new insights into the central question posed in the Handbook: how shareholders make use of their voting rights and other engagement instruments within their own jurisdictions' legal, regulatory and broader institutional contexts. The Handbook has portrayed – and also offered an approach to interpreting – the richness and sophistication of the differences and convergences in voting and engagement law and practices in today's (globalized) capital markets. This concluding chapter builds on what the Handbook has so far achieved, and reflects upon more general questions. It also identifies some avenues for future research in this fast-growing field.

23.1 COMPARATIVE SHAREHOLDER VOTING AND ENGAGEMENT: A GENERIC CONCEPTUAL FRAMEWORK

Jurisdiction-specific and comparative analyses in the Handbook are organized by way of an analytical framework specifically designed for the present project, as set out in detail in Chapter 1. We attempt to further conceptualize that framework and hope that it can be adopted as a basis for future comparative research on shareholder voting and engagement. We visualize our conceptual framework in Figure 23.1.

At the centre of the conceptual framework, as illustrated in Figure 23.1, lies the body of shareholder voting laws, essentially a jurisdiction's web of laws, regulations and rules setting the parameters of shareholders' voting rights and the ways in which they can exercise these rights. Much of it is 'hard' in the sense that it consists of legal and regulatory rules that are binding. Yet some elements of it are necessarily 'soft', and are typically found in a jurisdiction's (voluntary) corporate governance or stewardship codes. This inner layer emphasizes the formal and instrumental aspects of shareholder voting and engagement, and has deservedly been the focus of traditional academic and professional discussion. In this regard, the Handbook advocates a holistic approach whereby a jurisdiction's voting laws must be understood against their broader legal backdrops, notably the demarcation of power between shareholders and management, the types of shareholders involved and the board characteristics. The Handbook shows that national differences and variations persist, reflecting deep-rooted political-economic, cultural and other

This research was supported by a General Research Fund (CUHK-14613616) from the Hong Kong SAR Research Grants Council.

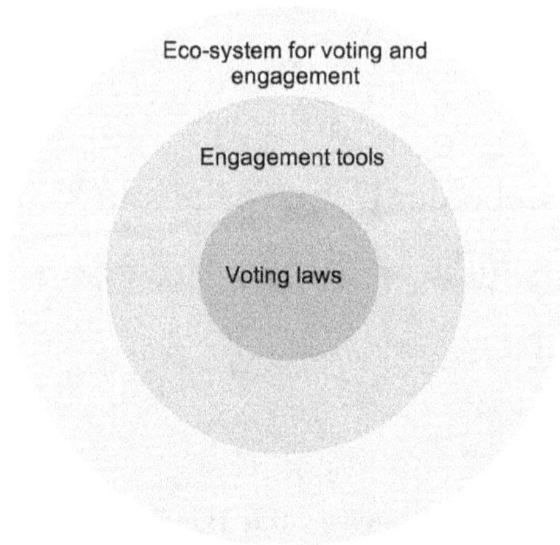

FIGURE 23.1 A generic conceptual framework for comparative shareholder voting and engagement

path-dependent conditionalities, which pertain to the outer layer of Figure 23.1. Some international convergence has started to emerge at this level, such as the adoption of say-on-pay rules in different jurisdictions in recent years, although this same trend also shows some diverging approaches to these say-on-pay rules. For instance, the Australian two-strikes rule and section 951 of the US Dodd Frank Act were both adopted to restrain executive pay, but they differ markedly with regard to their formal legal consequences. Yet, corporate governance movements that aim at empowering public shareholders and curbing managerial/controlling shareholder opportunistic behaviour have swept through global capital markets, forcing the gradual adoption of 'international best practice' – if not indigenous innovations (such as the Majority-of-Minority (MoM) rules seen in the UK Listing Rules for the election of independent directors in controlled companies, or the aforementioned two-strikes rule in Australia). Institutional investors have played an important role in these movements in various jurisdictions. For example, while plurality voting remains the default rule in Delaware and most other states in the United States, there has been a general shift toward simple majority voting for director elections, thanks to the influence of these institutional shareholders.[1]

The second layer of the generic framework relates to engagement tools that transcend the formal, if not mechanical, act of casting votes at the shareholders' meeting. These tools are wide-ranging, as the Handbook depicts, ranging from private, behind-the-scenes communications and negotiations with the corporate management/ controller[2] to the ability to table shareholder proposals for a vote,[3] from requisitioning information and questioning the management in a friendly manner[4] to the use of a naming and shaming tactic at the shareholders' meeting,[5] and from the initiation of a public campaign[6] to bringing a court fight or starting a class action.[7] These shareholder (engagement) tools are often intertwined – and can go hand in hand – with voting. (Activist) shareholders can use any mix or combination of them to engage with their investee companies at different levels to effect desired changes. In particular, as Chapter 22 in

[1] Stephen Choi et al., 'Does Majority Voting Improve Board Accountability?' (2016) 83 University of Chicago Law Review 1119.

[2] To name but a few, see Chapters 2 and 12.

[3] See e.g. Chapter 21.

[4] See e.g. Chapters 13, 14 and 19.

[5] See e.g. Chapters 2 and 12.

[6] See e.g. Chapter 2.

[7] See e.g. Chapters 3, 10 and 19.

this Handbook shows, voting against a management resolution is sometimes used as an escalation strategy, especially if friendly (behind-the-scenes) questioning has not led to the demanded result. Shareholder choices are usually framed by jurisdiction-specific substantive and procedural rules (including voting laws), firm attributes (such as a firm's ownership structure), as well as their own incentives, motives and the resources at their disposal. The globalization of capital markets has driven a cross-border migration of engagement tactics – in addition to voting laws – between jurisdictions, or as a JP Morgan report puts it, a 'rise of global activism'.[8] Inspired by practices seen elsewhere, activist investors in many jurisdictions featured in the Handbook have demonstrated their willingness to flex their muscles and deploy engagement tools, forcing a general rethink of traditional corporate governance practices.[9] Foreign institutional investors often serve as agents for change. Regulatory initiatives target these institutional investors, designating them as stewards for long-term value creation and sustainable corporate governance.

On a jurisdictional level, however, the popularity of a given voting strategy or engagement tool bears profoundly on the jurisdiction's broader ecosystem for voting and engagement (i.e. the outer ring of Figure 23.1). A jurisdiction's political economy settings perhaps stand out as the most prominent consideration. Of particular relevance are a jurisdiction's prevailing patterns of share ownership, the dynamics between different types of shareholders and corporate boards, the dynamics between shareholders and key stakeholders (such as employees or the government) and capital and financial market conditions. Also playing a crucial role is a jurisdiction's broader legal and justice system. For instance, the efficacy of US courts paved a clear path for shareholder litigation strategies. In Europe, however, the focus was often on ex ante shareholder control rights. Ultimately, voting rights and their enforcement hinge as much on the quality and effectiveness of the judiciary as they do on market-based 'private ordering'. Other path-dependent components of the ecosystem include social norms, traditions, ideological orthodoxies and sometimes political arrangements. Societal preferences for amicable or confrontational means of resolving discontents are often an important factor in voting and engagement strategies in a given jurisdiction. To put it in more vivid terms, in weighing their voting and engagement options, (activist) shareholders often find themselves wearing a jurisdictional straitjacket that limits their freedom of choices.

The three layers in Figure 23.1 are closely intertwined, and interact dynamically to shape the way in which laws and corporate practices of shareholder voting and engagement in a given jurisdiction have evolved. The Handbook highlights the tension between the globalization of capital markets and endogenous path-dependent institutions. The global rise of institutional investors, the diversified portfolio investment and index tracking strategies they commonly pursue and the generally lowered barriers to cross-border capital movements have combined to internationalize domestic capital markets.[10] The powerful forces of globalization place competitive pressures on domestic authorities to respond to the governance demands of foreign institutional investors and to adopt formal voting and engagement rules and standards commonly perceived as 'best practice' (i.e. the inner layer in Figure 23.1). Non-domestic institutional investors also help to bring voting and engagement practices in their home markets to foreign equity markets in which they invest, resulting in a proliferation and diffusion of engagement

[8] J.P. Morgan, 'Shareholder Activism in Asia: Confrontation Gaining Momentum' (May 2018).

[9] Lazard's Shareholder Advisory Group, '2020 Review of Shareholder Activism' www.lazard.com/media/451536/lazards-2020-review-of-shareholder-activism-vf.pdf. accessed 15 July 2020.

[10] A. De La Cruz, A. Medina and Y. Tang, 'Owners of the World's Listed Companies' (2019) OECD Capital Market Series www.oecd.org/corporate/Owners-of-the-Worlds-Listed-Companies.htm accessed 15 July 2020.

tools and tactics from one market to another[11] (i.e. the middle layer of Figure 23.1). At the same time, the persistence and resistance of pre-existing endogenous institutions, traditions and norms, whether social, economic, political, ideological or historical (i.e., the outer layer of Figure 23.1), should not be underestimated. They profoundly determine how a 'foreign' rule or tool of voting and engagement is perceived and received. Using a metaphor, the dynamic process of foreign plants (i.e. voting rule and practice) and domestic soil (endogenous conditionalities) creates a plant-soil feedback of shareholder voting and engagement.

The Handbook offers ample examples of these dynamics. In Japan, Indonesia and South Korea, the tradition of listed companies' annual general meetings clustering in a narrow time window in the year (in June) is widely perceived by institutional investors as imposing a severe constraint on their ability to vote and engage their investee companies. However, this practice has so far resisted pressure for change, and continues to be adopted.[12] In contrast, in the Netherlands, the institutional investor platform Eumedion played a large role in establishing a qualified majority voting rule of 75 per cent for the shareholder vote on remuneration policy, making the Dutch corporate boards more dependent on (international) institutional shareholders for their approval.

23.2 WHITHER THE SHAREHOLDERS' MEETING?

The enterprise of shareholder voting and engagement depends heavily on shareholders' meetings. In theory, the shareholders' meeting is a primary forum at which shareholders exercise their formal control rights. They can cast their votes at the meeting, elect directors and have their say on certain fundamental corporate matters (possibly the rules-of-the-game decisions).[13] They can engage with (or perhaps even confront) the management at the meeting, and influence each other, potentially exerting influence over how affairs of their invested companies are conducted. In a nutshell, the shareholders' meeting promises to be a hallmark of corporate democracy.[14]

The Handbook offers some evidence in support of this optimistic view of shareholder meetings. The shareholders' meeting has, at least formally, retained its relevance to corporate law and governance around the globe.[15] In all jurisdictions featured in the Handbook companies are required to hold an annual meeting once a year. They are also commonly allowed to hold extraordinary meetings, suggesting that shareholders' meetings are still considered to be a key feature of corporate law. In almost all jurisdictions (with the notable exception of the USA) shareholders holding certain minimum thresholds of share capital or voting rights are entitled to requisition a special meeting of shareholders to deliberate matters which concern the group of shareholders calling such a meeting. In addition, all jurisdictions allow for shareholders

[11] Peter Iliev et al., 'Shareholder Voting and Corporate Governance Around the World' (2015) 28 The Review of Financial Studies 2167.

[12] See e.g. Chapters 5, 6 and 8.

[13] Lucian Arye Bebchuk, 'The Case for Increasing Shareholder Power' (2005) 118 Harvard Law Review 833.

[14] Yaron Nili and Megan Wischmeier Shaner, 'Back to the Future? Reclaiming Shareholder Democracy through Virtual Annual Meetings' (August 2020) The University of Wisconsin Law School Legal Studies Research Paper Series Paper No. 1606, available at https://ssrn.com/abstract=3681578 accessed 15 July 2020. More generally, Paul Gompers, Joy Ishii and Andrew Metrick, 'Corporate Governance and Equity Prices' (2003) 118 Quarterly Journal of Economics 107. For a critique of the notion of corporate democracy, see e.g. Stephen Bainbridge, *The New Corporate Governance in Theory and Practice* (Oxford University Press, 2008). More fundamentally, it has been suggested that shareholder voting rights were historically part of consumer protection law, see Henry Hansmann and Mariana Pargendler , 'The Evolution of Shareholder Voting Rights: Separation of Ownership and Consumption' (2014) 123 Yale Law Journal 948.

[15] Chapter 21.

satisfying certain minimum share ownership requirements to make proposals to be tabled at the meeting (though jurisdictions differ greatly between themselves and over time, and also on how far this shareholder right is used in practice). The dynamic institution of shareholders' meeting seems to be well entrenched, so much so that its classical format – insofar as in its traditional, physical format is concerned – has become the central issue of a revived debate in the post-Covid-19 world.[16]

Lending some additional support to the optimistic view of the future of shareholder meetings – and more generally shareholder franchise – is shareholder participation in general meetings. Eleven out of the nineteen jurisdictions surveyed recorded voter turnout rates which comfortably exceeded 70 per cent in 2020. Even in jurisdictions with a lower rate of participation, there was a general trend towards greater shareholder attendance.[17] Prima facie, this can be seen as a rebuttal of a foundational premise of corporate law and governance scholarship: the rational passivity of shareholders.[18] The high participation ratios seen in our Handbook seem to suggest that shareholders discount the fact that most of the resolutions have perhaps been determined prior to the meeting, as these resolutions have the support of either the management or the controlling shareholder, or both. To account for this, the (soft) regulatory requirements for active ownership of institutional investors may have also stimulated this outcome.[19] In any case, shareholders seem to have defied the pessimistic view that it is only rational for shareholders holding a tiny fraction of the company's shares to be passive, if not absent from the meeting altogether.

Nevertheless, the Handbook cautions against over-optimism. For one thing, voter turnout is determined by jurisdiction-specific legal and regulatory environments, shareholder types and, more fundamentally, the role and functions of general meetings, as discussed at great length in Chapter 22, and thus requires a nuanced interpretation. Hence, enhanced shareholder rights – which would presumably increase the importance of the shareholder meeting – do not seem to be a reliable predictor of shareholder turnout. In Denmark and Norway, shareholders are supposedly empowered by their ability to initiate a shareholder proposal with only one share.[20] Yet the use of this shareholder proposal right is not as high as might perhaps be expected. If this one-share rule were transplanted to the United States, by contrast, the use of shareholder proposals by activist shareholders might very well increase to a dramatically high, and probably suboptimal, number.[21] The cultural dimension of the shareholder meeting (the outer layer of Figure 23.1) is another important consideration. Participation in general meetings may in some jurisdictions carry with it a significance and purpose other than just the exercise of shareholder rights. A case in point is Indonesia, a jurisdiction featured with concentrated share ownership, where general meetings constantly record attendance rates of over 80 per cent. When asked what motivated their participation in general meetings, 39.7 per cent of the respondents pointed to benefits such as souvenirs or goodie bags, while 29.7 per cent of the respondents looked forward to the post-meeting banquet.[22]

16 Miriam Schwartz-Ziv, 'How Shifting from In-Person to Virtual Shareholder Meetings Affects Shareholders' Voice' (August 2020), available at https://ssrn.com/abstract=3674998 accessed 15 June 2021.

17 Chapter 22.

18 Frank H. Easterbrook and Daniel R. Fischel, 'Voting in Corporate Law' (1984) 26 Journal of Law and Economics 395; Bernard S. Black, 'Shareholder Passivity Reexamined' (1990) 89 Michigan Law Review 520.

19 Shareholder attendance may have been stimulated by such inventive (soft) regulatory initiatives as the 20 per cent opposition rule in the UK Corporate Governance Code.

20 See e.g. Chapters 13 and 18.

21 Chapter 22.

22 Chapter 5.

Overall, this Handbook suggests that the global reality of the shareholders' meeting cannot be readily and categorically reduced to either one of the dichotomic stereotypes: the shareholders meeting as a *pro forma* or as an emanation of shareholder democracy. The modern shareholders' meeting will remain a rallying point in the shareholder engagement process, an important part of the escalation strategies of shareholders, and may perhaps be put to other innovative and creative uses by shareholders. The rise of institutional investors offers a real challenge for the management to confront.[23] Our Handbook also shows that today, there should be a *dynamic* approach to the shareholders' meeting, taking into account that there is more to it than only its static physical venue, as shareholders increasingly, when technically enabled, cast their votes remotely, prior to the meeting, or even participate electronically during hybrid meetings in many jurisdictions. Some jurisdictions (notably Canada, Denmark and Delaware) have allowed shareholders' meetings to be organized on a virtual-only basis, making the idea of a physical organization largely redundant. Our Handbook, to be sure, also points to the perhaps regrettable reality that the shareholder meeting can also be a mere legitimizer of managerial/controller overreach and opportunism and other sins.

So, whither the shareholders' meeting? It seems to be dependent critically, at least in the short term, on advances in meeting technologies, and on the results of worldwide experiments and experiences with the use of virtual-only and hybrid general meetings in response to the Covid-19 pandemic. In the longer term, it will depend on the institutional investor stewardship movement and, more generally, the (shifting) paradigm in the (re)allocation of corporate powers among managers, shareholders and stakeholders, and on the outcome of the ideological debate on the purpose of modern corporations.[24]

23.3 SHAREHOLDER VOICE AND ACTIVISM

The rising tide of shareholder activism around the globe has been greeted with much media fanfare.[25] Although this trend may temporarily have been checked by the global response to the Covid-19 pandemic,[26] a recent Ernst & Young report declares that '[s]hareholder activism has proved to be a permanent part of the global capital markets'.[27]

Our volume lends some support for the suggestion that shareholder activism and engagement are gaining a global presence. Most jurisdiction contributions to the Handbook report some forms of activism, often drawing upon anecdotes of activist investors, domestic or foreign, intervening – sometimes successfully – and seeking to change the direction of their investee companies, typically by electing representatives to the board or initiating a shareholder proposal.

23 A prime example of what can be done in this respect was an activist investor's successful campaign to win seats on the board of Exxon Mobil Corporation. Christopher M. Matthews, 'Activist Wins Exxon Board Seats After Questioning Oil Giant's Climate Strategy' *Wall Street Journal* (26 May 2021) www.wsj.com/articles/activist-wins-exxon-board-seats-after-questioning-oil-giants-climate-strategy-11622050087 accessed 10 June 2021.

24 Business Roundtable, Statement on the Purpose of a Corporation (2019). Cf.Lucian A. Bebchuk and Roberto Tallarita, 'The Illusory Promise of Stakeholder Governance' (2020) 106 Cornell Law Review 91.

25 Ajay Khorana and others, 'Rising Tide of Global Shareholder Activism' (Citi Global Perspectives & Solutions, November 2013) www.citivelocity.com/citigps/rising-tide-shareholder-activism/ accessed 15 July 2020; Ajay Khorana and others, 'Rising Tide of Global Shareholder Activism' (Citi Global Perspectives & Solutions, November 2013) www.citivelocity.com/citigps/rising-tide-shareholder-activism/ accessed 15 July 2020.

26 See e.g. Corrie Driebusch, 'Activists Lay Down Their Arms as Companies Cope With Coronavirus Spread' *Wall Street Journal* (29 March 2020) www.wsj.com/articles/activists-lay-down-their-arms-as-companies-cope-with-coronavirus-spread-11585474201 accessed 15 July 2020.

27 David A. Hunker, 'What Boards Need to Know About Shareholder Activism' (Ernst & Young LLP, 15 March 2021) www.ey.com/en_us/board-matters/what-boards-need-to-know-about-shareholder-activism accessed 15 May 2021.

In this light, it is fair to say that activism is expanding its bridgehead into some jurisdictions where it might least be expected to be welcome, particularly those with a concentrated share ownership, and a (cultural) tradition of and preference for reconciliation and comprise. Legal rules aimed at empowering minority shareholders (the majority of the minority rule, the say-on-pay rules, cumulative voting, slate voting and tenure voting,[28] to name just a few) seem to have played a part, emboldening minority shareholders to stand up against the powerful incumbents, sometimes successfully.

On closer scrutiny, however, the Handbook has some doubts as to how far-reaching and culture-changing shareholder activism can be in jurisdictions other than its place of origin, the United States.[29] Take shareholder proposals, for instance. This engagement tool, perhaps disappointingly, is rarely utilized in most common law jurisdictions featured in our Handbook, including Hong Kong, India, Singapore and the United Kingdom.[30] One may suggest that its under-utility has to do with the relatively demanding ownership thresholds in those jurisdictions. Yet in jurisdictions that lack meaningful ownership thresholds (such as Denmark and Norway) the use of shareholder proposals also remains low. To be sure, the Handbook's seemingly counterintuitive findings that shareholder proposals appear to be a common part of corporate life in China and Italy,[31] two civil law jurisdictions, might be cited as evidence for the ideological appeal of shareholder rights to initiate proposals, an icon in the shareholder franchise discourse. A glimpse at the Chinese shareholder proposals, however, shows that the overwhelming majority were proposed by controlling shareholders, rather than small investors, either individually or acting in concert, assembling a block that crosses the 3 per cent statutory threshold for proposal initiation under Chinese law.[32] In Italy, shareholder proposals are commonly used by minority shareholders because of the slate voting system for director elections. The perplexing picture of shareholder proposals seemingly proliferating outside the United States has been treated at length earlier in the Handbook.[33] It is worth highlighting here a fundamental need for nuance in interpreting its (limited) success in making inroads. Shareholder proposals are typically non-binding in the USA,[34] while they are binding in much of the rest of world.

Having said this, our Handbook also finds reasons for optimism. Overall, our jurisdiction reports and comparative analysis point to a worldwide 'awakening' of minority investors, in the sense that their voting behaviour appreciably deviates from the stereotype portrayed in the conventional literature of apathetic, passive or opportunistic providers of financial capital. Dissent votes are far from an anomaly in respect of, for instance, director elections and executive remuneration.[35] This matters, as recent evidence shows that dissent votes in even uncontested

28 See Chapter 21 for an overview.

29 Kosmas Papadopoulos, 'The Long View: The Role of Shareholder Proposals in Shaping U.S. Corporate Governance (2000–2018)' (2019) Harvard Law School Forum on Corporate Governance https://corpgov.law.harvard.edu/2019/02/06/the-long-view-the-role-of-shareholder-proposals-in-shaping-u-s-corporate-governance-2000-2018/ accessed 15 July 2020.

30 Chapter 22.

31 Ibid.

32 Chapter 2. It remains unclear why Chinese controlling shareholders, with the board at their direction, have any need at all to use shareholder proposals to advance their agenda.

33 Chapter 22.

34 Doron Levit and Nadya Malenko, 'Nonbinding Voting for Shareholder Proposals' (2011) 66 Journal of Finance 1579.

35 Chapter 22.

director elections are consequential,[36] and that say-on-pay votes rein in managerial greed and misappropriation and also improve firm performance.[37] Another important ground for optimism emerges from the Handbook's comparative analysis: minority shareholders seem to be casting votes in an intelligent and informed manner. The voting results regarding routine resolution types (such as financial accounts, dividends and auditor election) and those types more susceptible to conflicts of interest (such as say-on-pay and takeover amendments) show unmistakable differences in respect of their levels of shareholder dissent. While the former groups typically attract over 99 per cent shareholder support, the latter groups often generate shareholder disapproval at a level approaching the 10 per cent mark.[38] This implies that minority investors are strategically investing their time and resources on those aspects of the company's affairs that matter most to them. Depending on the jurisdictional context, these could be matters where their votes are pivotal and the magnitude of rents is sizable[39] or issues that are related to ESG and sustainability,[40] and say-on-pay.[41] In either case, these minority investors can scarcely be dismissed lightly as stereotypical 'free riders'.

To add another note of optimism, dissent votes, though significant, often understate the broader and deeper significance of shareholder voice. There can be private, behind-the-scenes, and thus usually less observable, negotiations and other engagement efforts which escape notice, an approach favoured by investors in some jurisdictions covered in our Handbook.[42] For instance, in the Netherlands, the influence of private engagements by institutional investors on corporate affairs surfaced with the cancelled agenda item to move the Anglo-Dutch company Unilever to the Netherlands.[43] Engagement priorities or concerns may have been taken directly to the management ahead of the general meeting, giving the board the opportunity to address them and try to resolve their differences with the dissenting shareholders. Votes cast against management proposals can thus be a public and visible manifestation of unsuccessful attempts to resolve matters in private.[44]

It is not the intention of our Handbook to give a normative, prescriptive verdict on shareholder voice and activism.[45] Greater accountability towards public investors does not mean that minority shareholders should be put in the driving seat. Nor does a constantly adversarial board-investor relationship necessarily best serve the interest of the company or (even) that of its public shareholders. On the other hand, shareholder voice and activism do seem to hold the promise of rebalancing the equilibrium between the board/controller and public shareholders – towards

36 Reena Aggarwal, Sandeep Dahiya and Nagpurnanand R. Prabhala, 'The Power of Shareholder Votes: Evidence from Uncontested Director Elections' (2019) 133 Journal of Financial Economics 134.

37 Ricardo Correa and Ugur Lel, 'Say on Pay Laws, Executive Compensation, Pay Slice, and Firm Valuation around the World' (2016) 122 Journal of Financial Economics 500; Jesse M. Fried, Ehud Kamar and Yishay Yafeh, 'The Effect of Minority Veto Rights on Controller Pay Tunneling' (2020) 138 Journal of Financial Economics 777.

38 Chapter 22.

39 Luigi Zingales, 'What Determines the Value of Corporate Votes' (1995) 110 The Quarterly Journal of Economics 1047. A prime example of these is the majority of minority votes on related-party transactions (see e.g. Chapter 2) and on the appointment of independent directors (see e.g. Chapters 4 and 22).

40 See e.g. Chapters 12 and 18.

41 See e.g. Chapter 10.

42 See e.g. Chapters 19 and 20.

43 Leila Abboud, Attracta Mooney and Arash Massoudi, 'Unilever Backs Down on Plan to Move Headquarters from UK' *Financial Times* (5 October 2018) www.ft.com/content/7c1cabf4-c864-11e8-ba8f-ee390057b8c9 accessed 15 July 2020.

44 See e.g. Chapters 2 and 7.

45 There is a voluminous literature on this topic. See e.g. Lucian A. Bebchuk, Alon Brav and Wei Jiang, 'Long-Term Effects of Hedge Fund Activism' (2015) 115 Columbia Law Review 1085; Leo E. Strine, 'Who Bleeds When the Wolves Bite? A Flesh-and-Blood Perspective on Hedge Fund Activism and Our Strange Corporate Governance System' (2017) 126 Yale Law Journal 1870.

a more accountable corporate sector. Our Handbook offers a footnote to this changing paradigm in the corporate landscape worldwide.

23.4 FUTURE DIRECTIONS OF SHAREHOLDER VOTING AND ENGAGEMENT RESEARCH

One of the greatest challenges facing any attempt to analyze shareholder voting and engagement is the availability of reliable, longitude, jurisdiction-specific data on shareholder voting around the world. The United States has good data, and so, to a lesser extent, do European countries. Elsewhere, however, the data is much patchier. Our Handbook represents a first step towards a global collaborative research network, collectively exploring the way forward in addressing the data challenges that academics, researchers, practitioners and policymakers commonly face. We demonstrate the great potential of a data-driven approach in yielding new jurisdictional, as well as international and comparative, insights, to supplement the more traditional, doctrinal and anecdotal approaches. To enable robust data-informed research and policymaking, a worldwide movement towards greater transparency of institutional investor voting behaviour is warranted. This can be achieved either by regulatory interventions (such as Regulation N-PX in the United States and SRD II in Europe), or by voluntary/soft industrial initiatives, or through a combination of both, depending on the jurisdiction-specific, path-dependent conditions.

Methodologically, our Handbook highlights the scope for developing a functional approach to comparative shareholder voting and engagement. Both the common analytical framework the Handbook's jurisdiction-based reports have built on and the more generic comparative framework the present chapter offers are exemplary of our endeavours on this front. Our overall approach, while functionalist in nature, also places great emphasis on the broader institutional environments in which voting and engagement are intrinsically embedded, by taking account of political, economic, social, cultural and historical factors. Our Handbook helps to demonstrate the considerable potential of what can be called an 'embedded' functionalist approach in extending the boundary of our knowledge of the ways in which shareholders make use of their voting rights and other engagement instruments.

Last but not least, our Handbook identifies an urgent need for research on comparative shareholder voting behaviour to proactively engage with a potentially fundamental paradigm shift. In the wake of the Global Financial Crisis and the Covid-19 pandemic, there have been important changes in voting and engagement practices, a global shift in ownership and control in the corporate sector (particularly public companies) and a rising tide of environment, social and governance (ESG) and sustainability concerns gaining ideological and policy prominence. The renewed ideological debates on the purpose of modern companies and, relatedly, on the (re)allocation of corporate power between shareholders and stakeholders, will have a fundamental impact on the way in which comparative voting and engagement are approached in the future.

Index

For EU product safety concerns, contact us at Calle de José Abascal, 56–1°, 28003 Madrid, Spain or eugpsr@cambridge.org.

www.ingramcontent.com/pod-product-compliance
Lightning Source LLC
LaVergne TN
LVHW060013210926
848481LV00013B/3699
* 9 7 8 1 1 0 8 8 2 3 7 0 8 *